Encyclopedia of
Cognitive Behavior Therapy

Encyclopedia of Cognitive Behavior Therapy

Arthur Freeman, *Editor-in-Chief*
St. Francis University
Fort Wayne, Indiana

Editors

Stephanie H. Felgoise
Philadelphia College of Osteopathic Medicine
Philadephia, Pennsylvania

Arthur M. Nezu
Drexel University
Philadelphia, Pennsylvania

Christine M. Nezu
Drexel University
Philadelphia, Pennsylvania

Mark A. Reinecke
Northwestern University
Chicago, Illinois

Library of Congress Cataloging-in-Publication Data

Encyclopedia of cognitive behavior therapy / [edited by] Arthur Freeman.
p. ; cm.
Includes bibliographical references and index.
ISBN 0-306-48580-X (alk. paper)
1. Cognitive therapy—Encyclopedias. I. Freeman, Arthur, 1942-
[DNLM: 1. Cognitive Therapy—Encyclopedias—English. WM 13 E553 2004]
RC489.C63E537 2004
616.89′142—dc22 2004051631

ISBN-10: 0-306-48580-X
ISBN-13: 978-306-48581-0

Printed on acid-free paper.

Printed in the United States of America. (NEW / EB)

9 8 7 6 5 4 3 2

springer.com

Foreword

I am honored and pleased to have been asked to write the foreword for this encyclopedic (literally) compendium of cognitive behavior therapy (CBT). Being there at the beginning, I have had the great opportunity and pleasure to see this broad-based field grow in many directions—both in terms of breadth and depth—over the past several decades. It becomes a difficult task to be able to be familiar, much less knowledgeable, with every therapeutic strategy that can be found under the umbrella of CBT. I believe that this team of editors, led by Art Freeman, has done that admirably.

The *Encyclopedia of Cognitive Behavior Therapy* represents a culmination of a revolution that changed the face of psychotherapy during the second half of the twentieth century. Starting with both the initial enthusiasm and excitement and also resistance of the psychological and psychiatric community for therapies that directly helped people to improve the way they behave and think, CBT has now emerged, at the beginning of the twenty-first century, as an expansive and diverse field. Had you asked me in 1979 what I would recommend as the goal of cognitive approaches to therapy, I would have stayed with the existing data and told you that we would treat depression. As our "appetite" grew, we experimented with the applications of cognitive therapy to anxiety disorders and later personality disorders. I was fortunate to have many of the authors represented in this encyclopedia as students, postdoctoral fellows, research associates, and colleagues, over the years. They have flourished, just as the field has grown and flourished by their efforts.

As an overall approach that emphasizes the scientific and clinical application of cognitive and behavioral sciences to understanding the human condition, as well as developing interventions that enhance life, CBT provides practical solutions to the broadest range of problems that people face everyday. Moreover, it embraces the responsibility to replicate its success in measurable ways in order to move the science forward. As a result, there are now empirically supported psychotherapy interventions for problems as diverse as mood disorders, substance abuse, social skills, violence and aggression, academic performance, sexual dysfunction, cognitive rehabilitation, health-related problems (e.g., eating disorders, coping with chronic illness), and stress management. As one looks over the Contents for this fine volume, it becomes evident that there are few areas of human functioning (or few areas of psychotherapeutic treatment) that have not been helped or enhanced with CBT interventions.

Due to the explosion in popularity and efficacy of interventions based on cognitive–behavioral principles, the field has become rich with handbooks devoted to a range of these specialized areas of assessment and treatment subsumed under its rubric. Many populations of individuals have been helped through these interventions, including children, adolescents, adults, and older adults. CBT procedures have been successfully applied to improve the lives of individuals, couples, groups, families, classrooms, organizations, as well as a variety of settings (e.g., homes, schools, clinics, hospitals, workplaces, correctional facilities, and rehabilitation centers).

There are a few books, however, that cover the full and broad scope of CBT. The present *Encyclopedia of Cognitive Behavior Therapy* was conceived to occupy this important place in the cognitive and behavioral literature. Tapping into the expertise and innovation of almost 200 authors, this volume captures the breadth of CBT and encompasses the interests of cognitive and behavioral therapists around the world. At the same time, streams of conceptual thought grounded in learning theories, cognitive information-processing and decision-making models, the science of emotions, developmental, biological, and evolutionary aspects of behavior are the principles that tie the extraordinary wealth of entries together.

This is the time to provide a collection of the rich contributions of CBT in one place and confront the challenge of how to move the field forward. This volume faces that challenge by providing clinicians with important sections that guide the synthesis of the impressive array of CBT techniques available into meaningful case formulations and treatment plans.

I am delighted to have been asked to contribute the foreword for this handbook. A collection of this magnitude can help to transform clinical practice and move CBT forward well into the new century.

Aaron T. Beck, M.D.

Preface

By definition, cognitive behavior therapy (CBT) is an active, directive, collaborative, structured, dynamic, problem-oriented, solution-focused, and psychoeducational model of treatment. From its earliest days, CBT has emphasized the importance of operational definitions as an essential ingredient in the therapeutic endeavor. The definitions were important to guide the therapy, enhance the collaboration, and stay problem-focused. After all, if the therapist and patient had not agreed on where they were going, had not agreed on the direction and focus of therapy, then it mattered little which road(s) they took. The working definitions of the patient's strengths, supports, and goals of therapy need to be explicated to give the therapy the needed structure. The *Oxford English Dictionary* defines an encyclopedia as a work "that aims at embracing all branches of learning; universal in knowledge, very full of information, comprehensive ... and alphabetical." Following our own focus, we tried to meet the dictionary definition of an encyclopedia, and decided that we needed to meet several criteria.

First, it was to be *comprehensive* and *inclusive*. We decided that we would try to cover as many of the major ideas, structures, and constructs that fell under the broad heading of CBT. We would scour the literature in an attempt to find just about every possible application and idea that had a relationship to CBT. When the relationship of the idea or construct was tangential to stricter CBT focus we had to then decide whether the omission of that topic would detract from the comprehensiveness of the volume. We worked to err more on the side of inclusion rather than exclusion.

Our second goal was to try to be *representative*. Given that there are many people who are working with, researching, and writing about a particular issue, we tried to be as even-handed as we could be and invite a broad range of individuals to participate in this project. We wanted to have a broad-based representation of individuals covering various theoretical and practice constituencies.

Third, we have endeavored to be as *enlightened* as we could be. Again, we chose to err on the side of a broad-based inclusion. Terms and issues that might be verboten to more strict adherents of one or another branch of CBT were included. We have chosen to not be parochially focused thereby limiting the areas to be discussed. Rather than try to limit CBT to the work of one theorist or one school, we have included contributors to CBT who may not typically be seen as "card-carrying" CBT persons.

Fourth, our collection of material was to be *multi-disciplinary*. We do not see CBT as the province of any one discipline, i.e., psychology, psychiatry, nursing, counseling, or social work. Our goal was to have representations by as many experts as we could gather without concern with their area of professional practice. We invited some individuals who are primarily therapists and others who are primarily clinical researchers and some who comfortably wear both hats.

Fifth, we would try to be *critical* and *selective/limiting* in our choice of contributors and contributions. There were in some cases individuals whom we had solicited to author a contribution but, for many reasons, were unable to participate. In other cases there were several persons who could equally represent a perspective and we had to make the incredibly difficult decision to have one person contribute the article rather than another. This selection was perhaps the most painful part of the process.

Our sixth goal was to make this encyclopedia an *educational* text that could be used as a reference for students, professionals, clinicians, or the lay public. We see this encyclopedia as a volume that will serve to share CBT with the broadest possible audience. We wanted the encyclopedia to be easily read, understandable, and available.

The seventh goal was one that was de facto in that the encyclopedia is by its very nature an *international* volume. We did not have to try to be international; it came about as we compiled the list of contributors, many from the United States, but many others from around the world.

Eighth, we determined that the volume would be *scholarly*. The contributors were asked to write at the highest level and to provide the broadest discussion of their area. This was perhaps the easiest part of the process. The contributing authors were able to walk the fine line between scholarly contributions and ease of reading and understandable text.

Our ninth focus was on CBT to be seen in its *historical* context. The field did not spring whole from the work of a particular person or group. Rather, CBT must be viewed in its historical context as a model that has evolved over the past fifty years and has strong roots in behavioral, psychodynamic, and person-centered approaches. Many of the contributions trace the historical and developmental experience of CBT. As with all histories, there may be disagreement as to who was there first and who were the upstarts merely claiming to be first. We have not tried to define CBT in this way. The historical references are to be read as the view of that contributor.

Tenth was to attempt to make the encyclopedia as *up-to-date* and *cutting edge* as editors can possibly make any volume. We asked the contributors to include the historical focus but also bring their area of concern into the twenty-first century.

Eleventh, we asked each contributor to discuss his or her view of the future of CBT in his or her area of interest and practice. This volume is not the last word in CBT. It is, at best, a summary of the progress of CBT over the last 50 years. We do not expect the final word on CBT to be written soon.

Goal twelve was to be *apologetic* for all that we had to leave out. Invariably there will be those who wonder why a particular idea, person, context, treatment, or research was not given as proper due and recognition by inclusion in this compendium. We must draw a line and call a halt to our collection activities so that this volume could be in the hands of you, the reader. We hope that you will let us know what we have omitted so that we can possibly include it in the next edition of this encyclopedia.

Finally, we know that we must be *grateful*. We are especially grateful to all of the contributors for their contributions. We are grateful to the editorial staff at Kluwer Academic Publishers who had the job of encouraging and challenging us to take on a job that was, at times, like herding cats. There were just so many things happening at once. We are especially grateful to Mariclaire Cloutier who initiated this volume. There are few editors with the patience, skill, and clear thinking of Sharon Panulla. Joe Zito helped to pull the diverse pieces together from the publisher's side. Herman Makler has been a joy to work with in moving this volume through the production process. We are immensely grateful for all of their work.

We are also grateful to all of the heroes, listed and unlisted, known and unknown who have contributed so much to the growth of CBT over the years as a treatment for a broad range of disorders. We are grateful for their contributions to the empirical base for CBT, we are grateful for the questions that they asked that then generated other ideas and possible solutions, and we are grateful to the many front-line therapists who have sought information about CBT so as to enhance their practices.

ARTHUR FREEMAN, STEPHANIE H. FELGOISE, ARTHUR M. NEZU, CHRISTINE M. NEZU, MARK A. REINECKE

A

Acceptance and Commitment Therapy

Steven C. Hayes and Heather Pierson

Keywords: acceptance, cognitive defusion, values, commitment, mindfulness, contextualism

PHILOSOPHICAL FOUNDATION: FUNCTIONAL CONTEXTUALISM

Acceptance and commitment therapy (ACT) is an experiential therapy that is based in clinical behavior analysis. Philosophically, ACT (as with clinical behavior analysis more generally) is based on the pragmatic world view of functional contextualism. In all forms of pragmatism, truth is measured by how well something works in the accomplishment of a particular goal. Functional contextualism (as compared to social constructionism or other forms of contextualistic thinking) seeks as its goal the prediction and influence of psychological events with precision, scope across phenomena, and depth across scientific domains and levels of analysis. Psychological events are treated as actions of the whole organism, interacting in and with a context. According to the contextual philosophy underlying ACT, the environment, behavior, history, and outcome of the behavior are all part of the context and need to be considered while proceeding through the therapy. The underlying philosophy especially can be seen in ACT's focus on the function of behavior, in its ontological approach to language (both of clients and of scientists), and in its holistic approach.

THEORETICAL FOUNDATION: RELATIONAL FRAME THEORY

Relational frame theory (RFT), a behavioral theory of language and cognition, is the theoretical foundation of ACT. ACT views language as the primary root of human suffering, particularly due to its creation of experiential avoidance and cognitive fusion. RFT offers an explanation of how this may happen and elucidates the processes by which ACT techniques work. RFT has a growing amount of empirical support, both its basic and applied aspects.

Framing events relationally has three features: mutual entailment, combinatorial entailment, and the transformation of function. Mutual entailment refers to the derived bidirectionality of stimulus relations. For example, if A is specified to be the same as B, it can be derived that B is the same as A. Combinatorial entailment refers to the ability to derive relations among two or more relations of this kind. For example, if A is smaller than B, and B is smaller than C, it can be derived that A is smaller than C and C is larger than A. Finally, functions can transform through relations of this kind. If in the previous example shock is paired with B, for example, a person may then respond more emotionally to C than to A. Entailment and transformation of functions are all regulated by context. A verbal event is any event that participates in a relational frame.

Relational frames explain the cognitive source of a great deal of human pain. For example, the bidirectionality of language means that a person's description of an aversive event may have some of the functions of that event. Thus, when a trauma survivor describes the traumatic event, through the transformation of function, the feelings that were present during the trauma may again be present during the description.

The root of several maladaptive behaviors according to an ACT model can be expressed with the acronym FEAR (fusion, evaluation, avoidance, reasons). Cognitive fusion refers to the domination of verbally derived behavioral functions over other, more directly acquired functions. People become fused with their verbal depictions, evaluations, and reasons. They no longer see them as their behavior, but as objective situations and thus, if they are aversive, as events to be avoided. For example, if a person is fused with the thought, "there is something deeply wrong with me," he or she will want to avoid situations that bring up that thought. Unfortunately, such experiential avoidance often paradoxically strengthens the avoided events because they strengthen the verbal/evaluative processes that give rise to such events. For example, a person avoiding the thought "there is something deeply wrong with me" strengthens the apparent literal truth of that thought since it confirms that something needs to change before one is acceptable—the very essence of the originating thought.

The source of cognitive fusion, and thus experiential avoidance, is thought to be the bidirectionality of verbal processes and their general utility in many domains. Because this process is thought to be under contextual control, the behavioral impact of thoughts and feelings is dependent on context. Therefore, ACT holds that thoughts and feelings are not mechanical causes of behavior, and that the impact of thoughts and feelings can be most readily influenced through a change in the context of verbal behavior. ACT has several techniques for doing so.

ACT COMPONENTS

ACT uses metaphors, logical paradox, and experiential exercises throughout its different components. The main reason for their use is that they are ways of undermining excessive literal language, basing action instead on experience.

The components in ACT are not a fixed or rigid set of techniques that occur in a definite order. In accordance with functional contextualism, they are a functional set of components that can be changed and rearranged to meet the client's needs. Nevertheless, what is present below is a typical sequence.

An ACT therapist first gathers information about all the different ways a client has tried to change his or her suffering and how these attempts have worked or not worked. The domination and workability of experiential avoidance is a primary focus. In this phase of treatment clients are asked to examine directly how successful their efforts to avoid have been, and if (as is most common) they have not been successful to consider the possibility that it is that agenda itself, not the technique or method, that might be the source of their difficulty.

What has not been working is gradually brought out: the deliberate control of private events. Many people struggle with their unwanted thoughts and feelings by trying to control them or get rid of them. In their experience, most clients have found that this ultimately leads to more unwanted thoughts and feelings. Conscious, deliberate control usually works when applied to the world outside the skin. When applied to private experiences, however, control usually works only temporarily. Exercises and metaphors are used as examples of how control does not work long term, of how language engrains unworkable control strategies.

Instead of avoidance, ACT clients are taught willingness and defusion as methods of coping with difficult psychological context. Willingness is the deliberate embrace of difficult thoughts, feelings, bodily sensations, and the like. Exposure exercises are used to contact troublesome private experiences. Cognitive defusion techniques are used to reduce the dominance of the literal meaning of thoughts and instead to experience them willingly as an ongoing process occurring in the present. In this phase, clients may be taught to watch their thoughts float by without trying to alter them; they may be asked to repeat thoughts until they lose all meaning; or they may be asked to think of thoughts as external objects and will be asked a variety of perceptual/sensory questions about them (e.g., What color are they?). Cognitive defusion undermines evaluation and teaches healthy distancing and nonjudgmental awareness. When this phase is successful the client will seem to notice reactions from the level of an observer and will take a more willing stance toward unwanted thoughts.

Much of the time people identify themselves by psychological content. They are the content of their thoughts. As cognitive content is defused, more emphasis is placed in ACT on self as context. The self as context is the observing self. It is the experience of an "I" that does not change or judge, but just experiences. Meditation and mindfulness exercises are used to help the client experience consciousness itself as the context for private experiences, not as the content of those experiences. Self as context work provides a safe psychological place from which acceptance, willingness, and defusion are possible.

When clients are no longer running from experience, direction in life is supplied by the client's values. Values are desired qualities of ongoing behavioral events that can only be instantiated, never obtained as an object. For example, a person who values being loving toward others can work to maintain those qualities in his or her human interactions, but this process will never be finished or obtained, as one might obtain a degree or buy a car. All ACT techniques are in the service of helping the client live life in accordance with his or her values. The exercises and metaphors in the values phase are geared toward helping clients identify what they want to stand for in their lives in a variety of domains (relationships, health, citizenship, and so on). Once values are identified, specific goals that fit with these values are identified along with behaviors that might produce these concrete goals. Finally the barriers to those actions are identified and dealt with through other ACT methods (e.g., defusion, acceptance, and willingness).

The final phase of ACT, the commitment phase, involves working with the client to apply what he or she has received in therapy to living life in accord with one's chosen values even if it involves experiencing psychological pain. This phase focuses on the client's willingness to experience whatever may come up and helps the client commit to acting in accordance with his or her values. Commitment is presented as an ongoing, never-ending process of valuing and recommitting. It assumes that the old change agenda has been abandoned, that some willingness has been contacted, and a valued life direction has been identified. The commitment stage looks the most like traditional behavior therapy, as the client passes through cycles of values, goals, actions, barriers, and dissolution of barriers. When this phase is completed, therapy is terminated. However, often with ACT, clients will come in for "tune-up" sessions after termination.

REVIEW OF RELEVANT LITERATURE

There is a growing amount of research that supports both ACT outcomes (see Hayes, Masuda, Bissett, Luoma, & Guerrero, 2004, for a review) and ACT processes. For example, controlled trials have shown ACT to be effective in several different areas including stress reduction (Bond & Bunce, 2000) and coping with psychotic symptoms (Bach & Hayes, 2002) among others. In addition to the efficacy research available, ACT has been shown to improve clinical outcomes in an effectiveness study (Strosahl et al., 1998).

COMPARISON TO TRADITIONAL CBT

ACT is part of the behavioral tradition and is similar in some ways to different forms of CBT. ACT shares the focus on cognition, emotion, and behavior. It incorporates traditional behavioral components like many forms of CBT. Some elements of acceptance and defusion can be found in mainstream CBT approaches, for example in Ellis's inclusion of acceptance of self or Beck's idea of distancing.

ACT differs from traditional CBT approaches in several ways as well. Perhaps the central theme of traditional CBT is the attempt to test and change the content of thought—an effort that ACT assiduously avoids. ACT relies on a functional contextual theory of cognition, and because of that emphasizes context over content. Its antimechanistic and explicitly contextualistic qualities differ from traditional CBT. Also, although some elements of acceptance and defusion are found in mainstream CBT, ACT dramatically increases the emphasis on these elements and disconnects them from their possible use as indirect change methods still focused on the content of private events. Finally, the strong emphasis on values and self-as-context is unlike traditional CBT.

FUTURE DIRECTIONS

At the present time there are 11 published randomized controlled trials of ACT, but there are many more outcome and process studies under way or under review which allow us to assess the future direction of ACT research. ACT seems to be a broadly applicable technology and future research seems likely to broaden the range of application even further. ACT is one of a family of new behavioral and cognitive therapies that are focusing on contextual change methods, including mindfulness, acceptance, and the like, and ACT studies are increasingly focused on the theoretical understanding of processes of this kind. More ACT research will be done in combination with other technologies, and more will be done to link ACT to RFT.

SUMMARY

ACT is a therapy that is based philosophically in clinical behavior analysis. Functional contextualism is the world view that underlies ACT. Theoretically ACT is based on RFT, which offers an account of how language creates pain and useless methods of dealing with it, and which suggests alternative contextual approaches to these domains. ACT uses metaphors, experiential exercises, and logical paradox to get around the literal content of language and to produce more contact with the ongoing flow of experience in the moment. The primary ACT components are challenging the control agenda, cognitive defusion, willingness, self as context, values, and commitment. ACT is part of the CBT tradition, although it has notable differences from traditional CBT. The main purpose of ACT is to relieve human suffering through helping clients live a vital, valued life.

REFERENCES

Bach, P., & Hayes, S. C. (2002). The use of acceptance and commitment therapy to prevent the rehospitalization of psychotic patients: A randomized controlled trial. *Journal of Consulting and Clinical Psychology, 70*, 1129–1139.

Bond, F. W., & Bunce, D. (2000). Mediators of change in emotion-focused and problem-focused worksite stress management interventions. *Journal of Occupational Health Psychology, 5*, 156–163.

Hayes, S. C., Masuda, A., Bissett, R., Luoma, J., & Guerrero, L. F. (2004). DBT, FAP, and ACT: How empirically oriented are the new behavior therapy technologies? *Behavior Therapy, 35*, 35–54.

Strosahl, K. D., Hayes, S. C., Bergan, J., & Romano, P. (1998). Assessing the field effectiveness of Acceptance and Commitment Therapy: An example of the manipulated training research method. *Behavior Therapy, 29*, 35–64.

GLOSSARY

Experiential avoidance: Any behavior that functions to avoid or escape from unwanted experiences despite psychological costs for doing so

Acceptance: An open and noncontrolling stance toward all experiences

Choice: A section among alternative that is not based on verbal formulations of pros and cons

Cognitive defusion: Reductions in the behavioral regulatory functions of verbal events, particularly thoughts, based on a reduction in the dominance of the literal content of those events as compared to the ongoing processes of formulating them

Values: Ways of living life that a person cares about deeply

Willingness: Openness to experiences that may be contacted in the process of living a valued life

Self as context: Also called the observer self; a psychological context from which thoughts, emotions, sensations, judgments, evaluations, and so on are observed as what they are and not what they say they are

RECOMMENDED READINGS

Hayes, S. C., Barnes-Holmes, D., & Roche, B. (2001). *Relational Frame Theory: A post-Skinnerian account of human language and cognition*. New York: Kluwer Academic/Plenum.

Hayes, S. C., Strosahl, K. D., & Wilson, K. G. (1999). *Acceptance and Commitment Therapy: An experiential approach to behavior change*. New York: Guilford Press.

Hayes, S. C., Wilson, K. W., Gifford, E. V., Follette, V. M., & Strosahl, K. (1996). Emotional avoidance and behavioral disorders: A functional dimensional approach to diagnosis and treatment. *Journal of Consulting and Clinical Psychology, 64*, 1152–1168.

Addictive Behavior–Nonsubstance Abuse

Frederick Rotgers and Ray W. Christner

Keywords: addiction, process addiction, gambling, sexual addiction, Internet addiction

When one thinks of addictive behavior, there is often reference to the use and/or abuse of chemical substances. However, in recent years theorists and clinicians have begun to include other excessive behaviors including eating, gambling, exercise, and sex under the umbrella of "addictions" (Greenfield, 1999; Koski-Jannes, 1999). Several researchers have classified problematic Internet use as an "addiction" (Bingham & Piotrowski, 1996; Young, Pistner, O'Mara, & Buchanan, 1999). Common to all the aforementioned behaviors are characteristics of preoccupation, impaired control, concealment of performing the behavior, and performance of the act despite being adverse to daily functioning (American Psychiatric Association, 2000; Greenfield, 1999; Ladouceur, Sylvain, Letarte, Giroux, & Jacques, 1998; Toneatto, 2002). The consequences of ongoing involvement in these behaviors include family discord, financial debt, employment loss, legal issues, and social difficulty.

Complicating the conceptualization and treatment of addictive behaviors is the incongruence in the terms and definitions of addictive behaviors. While the *Diagnostic and Statistical Manual of Mental Disorders—Fourth Edition—Text Revision* (DSM-IV-TR; American Psychiatric Association, 2000) classifies pathological gambling as a disorder of impulse control, some question whether it is best classified in this manner or as an addiction or obsession (Moreyra, Ibanez, Liebowitz, Saiz-Ruiz, & Blanco, 2002). This debate also extends to Internet use (Greenfield, 1999) and sexual behaviors (Harnell, 1995; Swisher, 1995). Further complicating the nosological picture is a failure among theorists to agree on what specific factors must be present in order to define an excessive behavior as "addiction" (e.g., cognitive distortions, behavioral reinforcement, physiological factors). Finally, there is great debate as to the appropriate treatments for these excessive behaviors (e.g., cognitive–behavioral, multimodal, self-help). We adopt the term "addictive behaviors" to summarize these nonsubstance use excessive behaviors (sex, gambling, Internet use, eating, exercise). We recognize that this is an arbitrary use of the term "addictive," and do so only for ease of communication.

To date, much of the understanding of addictive behaviors stems from research on pathological gambling.

Studies regarding other addictive behaviors are emerging, yet there continues to be much that is unknown. Research on cognitive and behavioral underpinnings and interventions with addictive behaviors is relatively young compared to other disorders (e.g., anxiety, depression).

THEORETICAL FOUNDATIONS

Although the impact addictive behavior has on one's daily functioning (e.g., family problems, employment difficulties) is often clear, there is less knowledge of the underlying processes contributing to the onset, maintenance, and relapse of these behaviors. The basic tenets of CBT suggest a relationship exists between cognitive, behavioral, and emotional factors in human functioning. The cognitive–behavioral conceptualization of addictive behaviors, therefore, focuses on the specific interaction between cognitive and behavioral processes resulting in maladaptive behavior. Subsequently, changing maladaptive or dysfunctional thought patterns will ultimately lead to behavioral change.

As mentioned earlier, much of the research with addictive behaviors concentrates on pathological gambling. Ladouceur and colleagues (1998) noted the importance of understanding the primary motivation to gamble—the acquisition of wealth. What differentiates "professional" from potentially addicted gamblers is the cognitive restriction that limits the amounts wagered. Nonprofessional gamblers who become "addicted" often lack this cognitive structure (among others). Thus, cognitive factors may explain the unrelenting play in the face of the odds, as the gamblers expect to win (e.g., "I will win this time"). Langer (1975) described this as the "illusion of control," in which the gambler thinks his or her probability of winning a "game of chance" is greater than that dictated by random chance. This is consistent with findings of Ladouceur and colleagues (Gaboury & Ladouceur, 1989; Ladouceur & Walker, 1996) who demonstrated cognitive biases and erroneous beliefs about gambling among problem gamblers. They found that problem gamblers engage in inaccurate verbalizations or thoughts (e.g., predicting outcomes, explaining losses, and attributing causal significance) during episodes of gambling, and the gamblers believe their "skill" or employment of various strategies and/or rituals improves the odds of winning.

Many studies highlight the importance of cognitive factors in the onset and maintenance of gambling behaviors. The cognitive perspective of gambling suggests that distorted cognitive factors (e.g., automatic thoughts, schemata, core beliefs) lead gamblers to maintain an inaccurate perception that they have a greater level of skill or control, which influences the gambling outcome. Blaszczynski and Silove (1995) indicated that gamblers also selectively recall wins over losses, they anticipate a win following a "near miss," or they await the end of the losing streak.

In addition to gambling, cognitive factors play a role in other addictive behaviors as well, although the research with other addictive behaviors is scant. Neidigh (1991) applied the relapse prevention model of Marlatt and Gordon (1985) to the treatment of sexual offenders/addicts. Consistent with the relapse prevention model, Neidigh (1991) noted that sex offenders often engage in distorted cognitions that place them in situations in which relapse is probable. Others have described the sex addict as having an "illusion of self-control" (Harnell, 1995). This illusion of self-control leads sex offenders/addicts to place themselves in high-risk situations. For instance, an individual with sexual impulses toward children may frequent a grocery store across from a school or playground. Cognitive distortion used by sex offenders/addicts may serve as a means to justify their sexual desires or behaviors (Neidigh, 1991). For instance, a child offender may make erroneous statements such as "she looked mature for her age" or "it's okay to have sex with her if she agrees."

Internet use is another addictive behavior in which cognitive explanations are useful. While there is still little research in this very new area, there is some consensus regarding the function of maladaptive cognitions in pathological Internet use (Davis, 2001; Hall & Parsons, 2001). The maladaptive cognitions exhibited by those involved in pathological Internet use can be broken down into thoughts of self and thoughts of the world (Davis, 2001). Specifically, these individuals hold cognitive distortions including self-doubt, negative self-appraisal, and a lack of self-efficacy. Thus, they may have the core belief that "I am a better person on the Internet than I am in reality." Thoughts about the world may be generalized and have an all-or-nothing quality. For example, one may believe, "I can only make friends on the Internet."

While researchers have categorized addictive behaviors into distinctly different problems—gambling, sex, and Internet—it is important to emphasize the complexity and interrelationship that may exist between them. With the increased amount of information available on the Internet, these specific addictive behaviors can occur in the confines of one's home. Technological advances provide access to gambling, shopping, pornography, and so on with a simple "click of a button." Because of this, Davis (2001) proposed *specific pathological Internet use* in which the individual's overuse of the Internet serves a specific purpose (e.g., pornography, gambling) rather than general Internet use. Some have suggested a possible evolution from online sexual behavior toward actual sexual contact (Greenfield, 1999). While these interactions are only now becoming more apparent, common to all addictive behaviors appears to be the vicious cycle of cognitive distortions or maladaptive thinking, which ultimately results in negative behaviors.

CBT TREATMENT STRATEGIES FOR ADDICTIVE BEHAVIORS

Individuals seeking treatment for addictive behaviors may experience serious financial, social, and interpersonal losses, as well as possible legal problems. There may be an initial motivation for these individuals to avoid engaging in the addictive behavior in order to prevent further psychosocial implications. Thus, the use of cognitive–behavioral treatment for addictive behaviors may play a more vital role in the long-term maintenance of behavioral change or in relapse prevention (Neidigh, 1991; Toneatto, 2002).

For example, Toneatto (2002) noted that if gamblers continue to believe in their abilities to predict outcomes or to control the situation, then they are more likely to relapse and reengage in excessive gambling once the difficulties leading them to treatment subside. Similarly, when working with sex offenders/addicts, it is necessary to become aware of cognitive distortions leading to them placing themselves in high-risk situations (Neidigh, 1991).

Strategies used for addictive behaviors vary depending on the case conceptualization of the client and the specific addiction presented. However, there are commonalities in the use of CBT across the treatment of addictive behaviors. Stress reduction techniques, social skills training, problem solving skills, and cognitive restructuring have been useful in the treatment of pathological Internet use (Bingham & Piotrowski, 1996; Davis, 2001; Hall & Parsons, 2001), sexual addictions (Neidigh, 1991), and pathological gambling (Sharpe & Tarrier, 1992; Sylvain, Ladouceur, & Boisvert, 1997).

EMPIRICAL SUPPORT OF CBT FOR ADDICTIVE BEHAVIORS

While clinicians are presently using CBT interventions for the treatment of addictive behaviors, few treatment programs exist and controlled studies are scarce. This is particularly true of sexual addictions and pathological Internet use, as no controlled studies were available as of this writing. Despite the lack of literature on a number of addictive behaviors, research on pathological gambling is emerging.

Sharpe and Tarrier (1992) offered a case study of a 23-year-old self-referred gambler. The treatment program focused on increasing awareness of the cognitive errors associated with gambling, teaching self-control, identifying replacement behaviors, and changing the relationships between cognitive distortions and physiological arousal and gambling. The investigators used relaxation training, imaginal and in vivo exposure, and cognitive restructuring as primary modalities. Following treatment the client showed a significant decrease in frequency and intensity of gambling impulses. With the exception of placing a single bet, the client did not gamble for 10 months. Additionally, the client reported a decrease in anxiety based on the Beck Anxiety Inventory.

In an experimental design, Bujold, Ladouceur, Sylvain, and Boisvert (1994) evaluated the effectiveness of a treatment program consisting of cognitive correction, problem solving training, social skills training, and relapse prevention with three male pathological gamblers. Individual intervention occurred once per week until the subjects maintained a high perception of control. Following treatment, the subjects terminated gambling behaviors, increased their perceptions of self-control, and reported ensuing problems as less severe. The subjects sustained the results at the 9-month follow-up.

Sylvain et al. (1997) assessed a treatment program consisting of the four components described above by Bujold et al. (1994)—cognitive correction, problem solving training, social skills training, and relapse prevention. The sample consisted of 29 individuals seeking help for gambling problems. The results demonstrated that CBT interventions significantly improve pathological gambling. Following treatment, 86% of the subjects no longer met the criteria for pathological gambling according to DSM-III-R. The investigators reported prolongation of the therapeutic gains at both 6- and 12-month follow-up.

Ladouceur et al. (1998) conducted a study evaluating the efficacy of cognitive interventions exclusively. The investigation involved the treatment of five pathological gamblers and used a single case experimental design across subjects. Cognitive intervention targeted the subjects' inaccurate perceptions of randomness and consisted of explaining the concept of randomness, offering an understanding of the illusion of control, increasing awareness of inaccurate perceptions, and correcting maladaptive verbalization and beliefs. Subsequent to the intervention, four of the participants lessened their urge to engage in gambling behavior and increased their perception of control, thus no longer meeting the DSM-IV criteria for pathological gambling. The subjects maintained these outcomes 6 months after treatment.

In a recent randomized controlled study, cognitive interventions targeting the erroneous perceptions of randomness reported by gamblers were evaluated (Ladouceur et al., 2001). The strategies involved cognitive correction (as described above in Ladouceur et al., 1998) and relapse prevention. Posttest outcomes indicated significant changes in the treatment group on measures of greater perception of control and increased self-efficacy. Additionally, 86% of the participants in the control group no longer met the criteria for pathological gambling. Participants retained improvement 6 and 12 months after treatment.

The studies reviewed demonstrate the growing empirical basis for the use of CBT with addictive behaviors, particularly gambling. While the use of CBT has been reported with sex addictions (Neidigh, 1991) and pathological Internet use (Davis, 2001; Hall & Parsons, 2001; Young et al., 1999), there is no empirical research demonstrating its efficacy and effectiveness with these populations. The nature of CBT lends itself well to the treatment of various addictive behaviors; however, there is a need for controlled studies to provide a firmer empirical base for its use with these disorders.

CRITICISMS OF CBT FOR ADDICTIVE BEHAVIOR

The use of CBT in the treatment of addictive behaviors is a recent phenomenon, and published critiques have not yet appeared. While the research in this area remains minimal, the use of CBT is promising and research outcomes largely favorable, especially with pathological gambling (Lopez Viets & Miller, 1997). There has been minimal research supporting the use of CBT with other addictive behaviors (e.g., sex addiction, Internet addiction).

In addition to the necessity for empirical treatment, there continues to be a need to better define and classify nonsubstance addictive behaviors, though this is not unique to CBT. The ongoing disagreement of whether these behaviors are best described as addictions, obsessive and compulsive behaviors, or impulse control disorder further clouds the conceptual picture. In order to develop and investigate effective and efficacious interventions for addictive behaviors, a consistent conceptual framework is essential.

FUTURE DIRECTIONS

A priority in the addiction field is the development of a conceptual structure in order to understand the processes of nonsubstance addictive behaviors. To facilitate progress in treatment and intervention, experts must reach consensus as to what these excessive and detrimental behaviors encompass. Current DSM-IV-TR (APA, 2000) nosology includes pathological gambling, although this and other nonsubstance addictive behaviors are not included in the same class of disorders (Substance-Related Disorders) as are substance use-related addictions. Achieving agreement on the description of addictive behaviors would allow for standard assessment criteria, the determination of similarities between various addictive behaviors, and perpetuate a consistent conceptualization to facilitate treatment. While recent studies are beginning to develop a knowledge base for gambling (e.g., Ladouceur et al., 1998; Toneatto, 2002) and Internet use (Davis, 2001; Greenfield, 1999), literature addressing the factors composing other addictive behaviors remains sparse.

There is also a dearth of investigative efforts into effective treatments for nonsubstance addictive behaviors. The current literature consists of a few controlled studies for gambling problems, but none addressing treatment of other nonsubstance addictive behaviors. Studies are needed to evaluate both the short- and long-term efficacy of treatments for addictive behaviors. The use of CBT with nonsubstance addictive behaviors is promising, though continued research efforts and efficacy studies are needed.

See also: Addictive behaviour—substance abuse, Relapse prevention

REFERENCES

American Psychiatric Association. (2000). *Diagnostic and statistical manual of mental disorders* (4th ed., text rev.). Washington, DC: Author.

Bingham, J. E., & Piotrowski, C. (1996). On-line sexual addiction: A contemporary enigma. *Psychological Reports, 79*, 257–258.

Blaszczynski, A., & Silove, D. (1995). Cognitive and behavioral therapies for pathological gambling. *Journal of Gambling Studies, 11*(2), 195–220.

Bujold, A., Ladouceur, R., Sylvain, C., & Boisvert, J.M. (1994). Treatment of pathological gamblers: An experimental study. *Journal of Behavioral Therapy and Experimental Psychiatry, 25*, 275–282.

Davis, R. A. (2001). A cognitive–behavioral model of pathological Internet use. *Computers in Human Behavior, 17*, 187–195.

Gaboury, A., & Ladouceur, R. (1989). Erroneous perceptions and gambling. *Journal of Social Behavior and Personality, 4*, 411–420.

Greenfield, D. N. (1999). Psychological characteristics of compulsive Internet use: A preliminary analysis. *CyberPsychology and Behavior, 2*(5), 403–412.

Hall, A. S., & Parsons, J. (2001). Internet addiction: College student case study using best practices in cognitive behavior therapy. *Journal of Mental Health Counseling, 23*(4), 312–327.

Harnell, W. (1995). Issues in the assessment and treatment of the sex addict/offender. *Sexual Addiction and Compulsivity, 2*(2), 89–95.

Koski-Jannes, A. (1999). Factors influencing recovery from different addictions. *Addictions Research, 7*(6), 469–492.

Ladouceur, R., Sylvain, C., Boutin, C., Lachance, S., Doucet, C., Leblond, J., & Jacques, C. (2001). Cognitive treatment of pathological gambling. *The Journal of Nervous and Mental Disease, 189*(11), 774–780.

Ladouceur, R., Sylvain, C., Letarte, H., Giroux, I., & Jacques, C. (1998). Cognitive treatment of pathological gamblers. *Behaviour Research and Therapy, 36*, 1111–1119.

Ladouceur, R., & Walker, M. (1996). A cognitive perspective on gambling. In P. M. Salkovskis (Ed.), *Trends in cognitive and behavioral therapies* (pp. 89–120). New York: Wiley.

Langer, E. J. (1975). The illusion of control. *Journal of Personality and Social Psychology, 32*, 311–321.

Lopez Viets, V. C., & Miller, W. R. (1997). Treatment approaches for pathological gamblers. *Clinical Psychology Review, 17*(7), 689–702.

Marlatt, G. A., & Gordon, J. R. (1985). *Relapse prevention: Maintenance strategies in the treatment of addictive behaviors*. New York: Guilford Press.

Moreya, P., Ibanez, A., Liebowitz, M. R., Saiz-Ruiz, J., & Blanco, C. (2002). Pathological gambling: Addiction or obsession? *Psychiatric Annals, 32*(3), 161–167.

Neidigh, L. (1991). Implications of a relapse prevention model for the treatment of sexual offenders. *Journal of Addictions and Offender Counseling, 11*(2), 42–50.

Sharpe, L., & Tarrier, N. (1992). A cognitive–behavioral treatment approach for problem gambling. *Journal of Cognitive Psychotherapy, 6*(3), 193–203.

Swisher, S. H. (1995). Therapeutic interventions recommended for treatment of sexual addiction/compulsivity. *Sexual Addiction and Compulsivity, 2*(1), 31–39.

Sylvain, C., Ladouceur, R., & Boisvert, J. M. (1997). Cognitive and behavioral treatment of pathological gambling: A controlled study. *Journal of Consulting and Clinical Psychology, 65*(5), 727–732.

Toneatto, T. (2002). Cognitive therapy for problem gambling. *Cognitive Therapy for Problem Gambling, 9*, 191–199.

Young, K., Pistner, M., O'Mara, J., & Buchanan, J. (1999). Cyber disorders: The mental health concern for the new millennium. *Cyber Psychology and Behavior, 2*(5), 475–479.

Addictive Behavior–Substance Abuse

Frederick Rotgers and Beth Arburn Davis

Keywords: alcoholism, drug abuse, drug addiction

Cognitive behavior therapy (CBT) in the treatment of substance abuse disorders (SUDs) has its roots in social learning theory and cognitive therapy and includes the groundbreaking work of Aaron Beck, Albert Ellis, and Albert Bandura. The work of these researchers is based on the notion that individuals' thoughts and feelings have a strong and directive impact on their behavior, and that much behavior is learned and can therefore be unlearned. Thoughts, feelings, and behaviors are amenable to adaptive modification via a collaborative alliance between patient and therapist, and the utilization of empirically supported techniques that developed from learning theory, behaviorism, and cognitive therapy.

THEORETICAL FOUNDATIONS AND CONCEPTS

CBT in the treatment of SUDs has drawn primarily from social learning theory and behaviorism, both of which provided complementary adjunctive theory to the later cognitive therapy (Carroll, 1999). For a comprehensive review of this topic, see Rotgers (1996). Early behaviorism in SUD treatment used classical conditioning to explain some of the reinforcing experiences of drug users such as cue exposure, but required the addition of the work of B. F. Skinner and operant conditioning to further the understanding. Later, social learning theory added to the awareness that substance users could be affected by the modeling of others both in maladaptive ways prior to treatment, and in treatment itself. It became clear that behavioral approaches and cognitive approaches to the treatment of these disorders were complementary.

As treatment has become more empirically based and sophisticated, it is understood that just as one does not expect a single antibiotic to be effective for every infection in every patient, it is unrealistic to think that only one type of treatment will be effective for everyone who suffers from SUDs. More and more, cognitive behavior therapies, the 12-step programs, and, more recently, pharmacological treatments are being used jointly to better meet the needs of the individual (Beck, Wright, Newman, & Liese, 1993). While widely used in the treatment of other disorders (most notably depression, but also numerous other Axis I disorders), CBT is not yet widely used for substance disorders—except in relapse prevention—although this is changing.

The goal of CBT in the treatment of SUDs is to help patients identify maladaptive thoughts, feelings, and behaviors that maintain or exacerbate their substance use, and to increase coping skills with regard to substance use and life problems in general. The method has several basics: collaboration between patient and therapist throughout treatment, agenda setting, homework assignments, and Socratic questioning. The latter is often referred to as "guided discovery" and

> is a powerful technique to use while discussing the various agenda items. [The] therapist asks questions in such a way as to help patients to examine their thinking, to reflect on erroneous conclusions, and, at times, to come up with better solutions to problems. This often leads to the patient's questioning, and thereby gaining greater objectivity from, their own thoughts, motives, and behaviors. Also, Socratic questioning establishes a nonjudgmental atmosphere and thus facilitates collaboration between patients and therapists. This can help patients come to their own conclusions about the seriousness of their drug abuse problem. (Beck et al., 1993)

In a National Institute on Drug Abuse (NIDA) treatment manual on the use of CBT in the treatment of cocaine addiction, Carroll (1998) states that there are two main components of CBT in the treatment of substance use: functional analysis and skills training. Functional analysis identifies "the patient's feelings, and circumstances before and after the cocaine use. Early in treatment, the functional analysis plays a critical role in helping the therapist assess the determinants, or high-risk situations, that are likely to lead to cocaine use and provides insights into some reasons why the individual may be using cocaine." Skills training "can be thought of as a highly individualized training program that helps cocaine abusers unlearn old habits ... and learn or relearn healthier skills and habits."

CBT TECHNIQUE

CBT, whether for SUDs or other disorders, is usually short-term (8 to 20 sessions, though it may be longer) and structured. Given that therapy time is limited, structure is critical to make certain that important topics are covered, and to model the idea that for patients who are suffering from disorders that often produce chaos, structure is positive, reassuring, and can help them meet their goals. Beck et al. (1993) state that structure is important for four reasons: (1) There is usually a large amount of material to cover and limited time to do so; (2) structuring helps maintain focus on what topics are most important to cover; (3) structure sets a "working atmosphere"; and (4) structure helps limit "therapy drift," in which continuity from session to session can be lost.

The structure of a session may differ somewhat from therapist to therapist, but generally, there are seven elements (Beck et al., 1993): setting the agenda, doing a check on the patient's current mood state, recalling what was covered in the last session ("session bridging"), discussing the day's agenda items (which probably will include reviewing the homework assignment from the previous session), periodic summaries by the therapist of what has been discussed (which fosters the therapeutic alliance), assigning new homework, and feedback about the therapy session. Underscoring all parts of the session is the use of Socratic questioning.

Carroll (1998) identified five critical tasks in CBT for cocaine addiction which can be generalized to treatment of other SUDs as well: fostering the motivation for abstinence, teaching coping skills, changing reinforcement contingencies, fostering the management of painful feelings, and improving the social support system and social skills. Specific interventions include functional analyses, recognizing and coping with cravings, understanding and managing thoughts about the substance use, problem solving, identifying and modifying maladaptive thoughts with regard to substance use, identifying high-risk situations and developing ways to avoid or cope with them, encouragement, reviewing newly learned skills and practicing them in the session.

These interventions are similar to those in the treatment of alcohol dependence (Longabaugh & Morgenstern, 1999). Identified as "cognitive behavioral coping skills training" (CBST), the treatment is "aimed at improving the patients' cognitive and behavioral skills for changing their drinking behavior. This type of treatment is considered to be broad spectrum in that it focuses not only on the patient's problem drinking, but "addressed other life areas that often are functioning related to drinking and relapse. For example, if anger can provoke a patient to drink, the focus of CBST will be on those circumstances that arouse anger in the patient, the thought and behavioral processes that occur between the onset of the anger and the patient's drinking, and on the events occurring after the patient drinks."

There are also several CBT manuals available that detail the delivery of CBT treatment in group format. Most prominent among these are the coping skills manual developed by Monti and colleagues (Monti, Kadden, Rohsenow, Cooney, & Abrams, 2002), and a manual based on Prochaska and DiClemente's (Prochaska, DiClemente, & Norcross, 1992) stages of change (Velasquez, Maurer, Crouch, & DiClemente, 2001).

CBT IN THE TREATMENT SPECTRUM

Though one of the most widely researched treatments for numerous Axis II and other Axis I disorders, CBT is not currently the most widely used in the treatment of SUDs, particularly alcohol. Fuller and Hiller-Sturmhofel (1999) reported that the 12-step programs, such as Alcoholics Anonymous, are most commonly used to treat alcoholism, with CBT a distant second, and pharmacological treatments such as disulfiram (Antabuse), acamprosate (Campral), and naltrexone (Revia) an even more distant third. In the field of substance abuse treatment, CBT is more commonly used in relapse prevention, and in academic and VA hospitals (Longabaugh & Morgenstern, 1999).

RESEARCH ON CBT

Cognitive behavior therapies are among the most empirically supported of psychotherapies. Research is ongoing in the use of CBT in numerous disorders including substance use (Carroll, 1999). In a review of research into cognitive behavior therapies as stand-alone treatments for alcohol abuse, Longabaugh and Morgenstern (1999) found that CBST "delivered as a stand-alone treatment does not differ in effectiveness from these other treatment approaches." This also was true when CBST was used for aftercare; however, patients who received CBST as part of a comprehensive program were "likely to have better drinking-related outcomes than patients" who did not receive CBST. They conclude that

"CBST is but one theoretically coherent treatment that can improve the outcome of alcohol-dependent patients" and may still be "possibly superior to other approaches under certain circumstances" such as certain treatment phases, in high-risk situations, or with certain patients.

In another extensive meta-analytic review of effective treatments for alcohol problems, Miller and colleagues (Miller, Wilbourne, & Hettema, 2003) found that 2 of the 10 treatment approaches with the greatest research support for their efficacy were ones that are part of CBT: behavioral self-control training and behavioral contracting. Cognitive therapy as a stand-alone treatment was 13th in the strength of evidence for its efficacy on their list of 48 well-researched treatment approaches.

In the treatment of cocaine use disorders, "behavioral and cognitive behavioral approaches have received the most empirical validation" and have been useful in relapse prevention (Van Horn & Frank, 1998). Studies of the use of cognitive behavior treatments for other SUDs such as marijuana are few, though encouraging. Copeland et al. (2001) reported that cognitive behavioral interventions "were clearly effective" for cannabis use disorders.

CRITICISMS OF CBT

Among the more common general criticisms of CBT are that it is formulaic and manualized, and that it "overemphasizes conscious controlled processing" (Clark, 1995).

Criticisms specific to the field of SUD treatment include the difficulty identifying what factors in CBT are useful in the treatment of SUDs, whether CBT must be modified for use in the treatment of specific SUDs, and what type(s) of individuals seeking substance abuse treatment may benefit from CBT versus other treatments (Fuller & Hiller-Sturmhofel, 1999).

FUTURE DIRECTIONS

The best estimates available at this writing suggest that in 1998 the combined cost to the U.S. economy of alcohol and drug abuse totals more than $325 billion. This includes the costs of substance abuse treatment and prevention, as well as lost job productivity, unemployment, crime, and social welfare costs. This represents an increase of nearly 50% from the total in 1992 (Harwood, 2000; Office of National Drug Control Policy, 2001). Given this trend, it is clear that SUD treatment will become even more important, making it imperative to identify critical factors in treatment and in patients.

Future directions for CBT include increasing the number of efficacy studies in the field of SUD treatment, broadening its focus, and examining how CBT can be used to potentiate or complement other treatments (Longabaugh & Morgenstern, 1999). Van Horn and Frank (1998) suggest that, at least in the area of cocaine addiction treatment, there should be greater efforts to "bridge the gap" between clinicians and researchers "both to evaluate existing programs and to disseminate new approaches." Carroll (1999) concluded that cognitive behavioral therapies are "well-defined approaches [that] should be a part of any clinician's repertoire."

See also: Addictive behavior—nonsubstance abuse, Couples therapy—substance abuse, Motivational interviewing, Relapse prevention

REFERENCES

Beck, A. T., Wright, F. D., Newman, C. F., & Liese, B. S. (1993). *Cognitive therapy of substance abuse*. New York: Guilford Press.

Carroll, K. M. (1998). *Therapy manuals for drug addiction manual 1: A cognitive–behavioral approach: treating cocaine addiction* (NIH Publication No. 98-4308). Rockville, MD: National Institute on Drug Abuse.

Carroll, K. M. (1999). Behavioral and cognitive behavioral treatments. In B. McCrady & E. Epstein (Eds.), *Addictions, a comprehensive guidebook* (pp. 250–257). New York: Oxford University Press.

Clark, D. A. (1995). Perceived limitations of standard cognitive therapy: A consideration of efforts to revise Beck's theory and therapy. *Journal of Cognitive Psychology: An International Quarterly, 9*(3), 153–172.

Copeland, J., Swift, W., Roffman, R., & Stephens, R. (2001). A randomized controlled trial of brief cognitive–behavioral interventions for cannabis use disorder. *Journal of Substance Abuse Treatment, 21*(2), 55–64.

Fuller, R. K., & Hiller-Sturmhofel, S. (1999). Alcoholism treatment in the United States: An overview. *Alcohol Research and Health, 23*(2), 69–77.

Harwood, H. (2000). Updating estimates of the economic costs of alcohol abuse in the United States: Estimates, update methods, and data. (Report prepared by The Lewin Group for the National Institute on Alcohol Abuse and Alcoholism). Rockville, MD: National Institute on Alcohol Abuse and Alcoholism.

Longabaugh, R., & Morgenstern, J. (1999). Cognitive–behavioral coping-skills therapy for alcohol dependence: Current status and future directions. *Alcohol Research and Health, 23*(2), 78–85.

Monti, P. M., Kadden, R. M., Rohsenow, D. J., Cooney, N. L., & Abrams, D. B. (2002). *Treating alcohol dependence: A coping skills training guide* (2nd ed.) New York: Guilford Press.

Office of National Drug Control Policy (2001). *The economic costs of drug abuse in the United States, 1992–1998* (Publication No. NCJ-190636). Washington, DC: Executive Office of the President.

Prochaska, J. O., DiClemente, C. C., & Norcross, J. C. (1992). In search of how people change: Applications to addictive behavior. *American Psychologist, 47*, 1102–1114.

Rotgers, F. (1996). Behavioral theory of substance abuse treatment: Bringing science to bear on practice. In F. Rotgers, D. Keller, & J. Morgenstern (Eds.), *Treating substance abusers: Theory and technique* (pp. 174–201). New York: Guilford Press.

Van Horn, D. H. A., & Frank, A. F. (1998). Psychotherapy for cocaine addiction. *Psychology of Addictive Behaviors, 12*(1), 47–61.

Velasquez, M. M., Maurer, G. G., Crouch, C., & DiClemente, C. C. (2001). *Group treatment for substance abuse: A stages-of-change therapy manual*. New York: Guilford Press.

Adolescent Aggression and Anger Management

Eva L. Feindler

Keywords: anger, anger management, adolescents

In response to the oft-presented problems of angry outbursts and aggressive behavior in children and adolescents, anger management interventions have been developed over the past 15 years by clinicians and educators. Unhappy with traditional behavior modification approaches, which handle these problems via contingency management and punishment strategies, some looked toward the cognitive behavioral self-control approach and developed a skills training program to help youth manage their anger experience and use more effective conflict resolution skills.

Across a variety of treatment settings, youth presenting with conduct and oppositional defiant disorders have patterns of irritability, anger outbursts, and aggressive behavior that result in poor conflict resolution, poor interpersonal skills, and a host of compliance problems. Although behavior modification strategies have been successfully implemented to provide contingencies that reduce occurrences of aggressive behavior especially in a controlled setting, these approaches were somewhat limited. Often when the youth returned to the natural environment or was beyond the control of these contingencies, aggressive behavior and conflict escalation would return. These behaviors would occur outside of the purview of adults, making it difficult to implement either punishment or response cost strategies, usually part of a more comprehensive behavior management program. Problems with maintenance and generalization of behavior change indicated that self-control skills of aggression management were not being learned, nor were youth gaining skills in appropriate conflict resolution.

Struggling with both clinical and safety issues for those who work with aggressive youth, Feindler and her colleagues developed an approach to treatment that would focus on the emotional arousal often preceding an aggressive outburst. Based on Novaco's (1979) early work with adults, anger management technology focuses on teaching skills of arousal reduction with direct emphasis on the physiological and cognitive components of anger. Hypothetically, aggressive behavior is elicited by an aversive "trigger" stimulus which is followed by both physiological arousal and distorted cognitive responses that result in the emotional experience of anger. Children and adolescents who have impulsive, aggressive behaviors in their repertoire often react toward the trigger and fail to solve the interpersonal conflict in an appropriate fashion. Much of the research by both Dodge (Crick & Dodge, 1994) and Lochman (Lochman & Dodge, 1994), who have studied the cognitive reactions of aggressive children, concludes that aggressive cognitions, in particular hostile attributions and negative outcome expectancies, influence the occurrence of behavioral responses to interpersonal situations. Aggressive youth seem to lack a prosocial reasoning process and instead engage in distorted thinking that intensifies their perceptions of injustice, fuels their rage, and justifies their use of aggression.

Further, these same youth, perhaps due to early family experiences or to an innate physiological dyssynchrony, suffer from emotion dysregulation (Keenan, 2000) and poor understanding of emotional states. They seem unable to cope with even mild levels of the affective experience of anger in a constructive way. The irritability or annoyance that results from goal blocking or mild interpersonal conflict often gives way to intensified anger and explosive rage. Before the work of Novaco (1979), little was understood about the components of the anger reaction that may be the precursor to the acting out behavior of children and adolescents without the capacity to either verbalize their experience or manage their internal arousal so as to prevent an aggressive episode.

ANGER MANAGEMENT INTERVENTIONS

In order to prevent an aggressive reaction to a triggering stimulus, it is necessary for youths to manage their anger arousal and process the interpersonal exchange such that a more prosocial response is exhibited. The anger management treatment protocols focus on the three hypothesized components of the anger experience: physiological responses, cognitive processes, and behavioral responses (Novaco, 1979). If anger reactions are comprised of heightened physiological arousal, cognitive distortions, impulsive thoughts, and aggressive responding, then the intervention must focus on helping young people develop self-control skills in each of these areas.

For the physiological aspect, anger management first directs the client to identify the experience of anger, to label the various intensities of the emotion, and to recognize the early warning signs such as a flushed feeling or quickened heart rate. The experience of anger is validated as a normal and frequently occurring emotion that has an intensity range under the youth's control. Further, clients are asked to identify and track common triggers of their anger by using a self-monitoring assessment called the Hassle Log (Feindler & Ecton, 1986). Charting daily occurrences of anger (whether handled well or not) helps the youth to recognize idiosyncratic patterns of anger loss and control, and to increase awareness of external triggers and internal physiological and cognitive reactions. Finally, several arousal management skills such as deep breathing, imagery, and relaxation are taught to help youths reduce the accumulated physical tension and to increase the probability that they will think through the interpersonal event in a more rational fashion.

The cognitive component of anger management targets both cognitive deficiencies and distortions that are characteristic of those with an aggressive and impulsive response to perceived provocation. Specific cognitive problem-solving skills seem to be missing for aggressive youth. They generate few possible solutions to interpersonal problems and seem unable to generate future consequences for their aggressive behavior. Further, their assumptions, expectancies, beliefs, and attributions are distorted in distinct ways that actually increase their anger experience. In particular, aggressive youth perceive triggering stimuli to be intentional and unjust acts on the part of others which are direct insults and are meant to be hostile. Their belief is that an aggressive counteraction is the best in terms of outcome, of ego protection, and of power in the eyes of others. They expect themselves and believe that others expect them to behave aggressively, but then they do not take responsibility for their actions. In fact, they blame others for their own misbehavior. These cognitive distortions combine to confirm that aggression is the only way to resolve a conflict and is therefore completely justified.

Cognitive restructuring strategies are used to help youth identify their distorted thinking styles and to encourage them to substitute a series of self-instructions that will guide them through effective problem solving. Strategies that assist in examining the irrationality and narrow focus of their cognitions help them to develop alternative causal attributions and a nonaggressive perspective. Youth are encouraged to engage in self-coaching of attributions that protect their sense of self, but also lead them to deescalate conflict and create "mental distances" from the trigger. This type of cognitive work seems to be the most difficult for aggressive and impulsive youth, but it is probably the most critical element of the anger management intervention. Altering those internal processes will help the youth to better manage their anger experience, rethink their optional responses to provocation, and select a more prosocial behavioral response.

The final component of the anger reaction is the behavioral one. Both verbal and nonverbal aggression as well as withdrawal patterns are the most typical responses to interpersonal conflicts and perceived provocation. However, once the youth have achieved competence at managing both their physiological arousal and their cognitive process, they will still need to respond to the situation and achieve some level of social competence. What is needed then is training in problem solving, assertiveness, and communication skills related to effective conflict resolution. Certainly, the probability that these skills will be implemented is enhanced when the accompanying emotional arousal is managed effectively. Otherwise, the intense anger often experienced by those with patterns of aggressive responding will disrupt or perhaps prevent the execution of more prosocial skills.

In sum, an effective anger management intervention targets each of the hypothesized anger reaction components (physiological, cognitive, and behavioral) and remediates the most characteristic skills deficiencies and cognitive distortions. Although research has yet to evaluate the "best" sequence, it seems that the arousal management and cognitive restructuring aspects should precede the behavioral skills training. But taken all together, the youth will have increased self-control skills as well as more effective interpersonal problem-solving skills.

TRAINING STRATEGIES AND PROGRAM CHARACTERISTICS

The anger control program originally described in Feindler and Ecton (1986) used a variety of training methods to reach the content objectives described above. The majority of anger management skills were modeled and rehearsed during extensive role-playing using scenarios generated from completed Hassle Logs. The role-plays should be arranged for the youth in such a fashion that graduated exposure to greater levels of provocation and conflict can be matched to better skill attainment. Each treatment session included a variety of graded homework assignments designed to have the clients practice newly acquired skills and to foster generalization to the natural environment. Many of the cognitive restructuring strategies have been transformed into games that participants in group treatment seem quite receptive to. Clients are able to learn aspects of problem solving, to develop alternative perspectives, and to generate nonhostile attributions in response to hypothetical conflict situations. Role-play with coaching then helps the youth to practice these improved cognitive responses to problem situations in which they themselves are provoked. Repeated practice once the "package" of skills has been taught seems necessary not only to reinforce the newly acquired responses but also to help the clients make the social judgments required to match their response to the perceived trigger to maximize positive outcome.

Although a number of anger management programs have been published in a curriculum format (Feindler & Ecton, 1986; Feindler & Scalley, 1998), there are several variables to consider which may require individualization of the program. Chronological age as well as cognitive level of the client group may determine the emphasis and the content of the cognitive interventions. Younger children and perhaps clients with developmental delays may struggle with the cognitive restructuring strategies and may need greater emphasis on the behavioral skills training. The setting for the anger management program will determine whether group or individual treatment is implemented as well as determine the length of sessions, the number of sessions, and the composition of the group. Clinicians in mental health settings have different choices and different constraints than those working in residential or educational settings. Personnel who will implement the program will also differ depending on the setting, thus bringing differing expertise and orientations to the intervention. Finally, in some settings, anger management may serve as an adjunct clinical intervention to other therapies received by clients, while for some, it serves as the sole training program for the learning of anger management and aggression control. In some settings, family members may be involved, but for most youth, the treatment is deemed solely for them.

Although consideration of all of these program variables as well as the variety of treatment strategies may seem confusing, it certainly highlights the tremendous flexibility found in the anger management technology. Developed in response to critical clinical needs and sustained across 15 years, anger management interventions have evolved and extended to a variety of populations of youth in a variety of settings. A review of published studies in the area of anger management underscores not just the utility of the approach but also the effectiveness in terms of aggression reduction in youth typically resistant to more traditional forms of therapy (Feindler & Baker, 2001). A recent meta-analysis of cognitive–behavioral interventions for child and adult anger (Beck & Fernandez, 1998) resulted in moderate treatment gains compared to control groups in 50 nomothetic studies.

DIRECTIONS FOR ANGER MANAGEMENT INTERVENTIONS WITH YOUTH

There is a general consensus that angry youth have parents who lack effective parenting skills and who evidence similar patterns of impulsive and aggressive responses to perceived provocations. Often there is an early use of extensive physical punishment and many aggressive youth have been victims of their parents' rage reactions. These youth develop in a home environment void of models of prosocial coping and with limited understanding of and communication about emotional expression. Their parents fail to use consistent and contingent reinforcement and the functional nature of escalating aggression sets in motion a process of coercive interaction between family members. Both parents and youth clearly need to learn more prosocial conflict negotiation responses as well as better emotional control. Integration of anger management skills either with traditional parent training approaches or with strategic family therapy intervention seems a necessary extension and a way to prevent the occurrence of family violence.

Future clinical research might focus on component analyses to determine which of the treatment components included in anger management are most effective for which children and which adolescents. Since the primary treatment component appears to be the cognitive strategies designed to reconfigure the biased information processing, developmental levels must be considered. For youth who have not yet reached the meta-cognitive level, perhaps anger management should emphasize problem-solving skills and alternative behavioral responses to triggering events. Perhaps youth who are more cognitively sophisticated need a greater emphasis on reattribution training and the identification of anger-engendering cognitive schemas. Matching the anger management skills to the cognitive level of the youth would certainly enhance the treatment outcome. Additional research might also focus on group versus individual versus family treatment approaches to the dissemination of an anger management program.

Lastly, there are many youth who approach anger management treatment with a good deal of resistance. Patterns of aggressive outbursts often result in a mandate for anger treatment, yet cognitive schemas characteristic of angry youth seem antagonistic to treatment. Youth may believe that anger is appropriate and quite justified. They feel low personal responsibility, blame others, and feel self-righteous in their expression of anger. These beliefs may in fact impede their readiness or responsivity to treatment. Future research may need to look at methods for increasing treatment responsivity and building a working alliance between the angry youth and the treatment provider. Few youth with anger problems will seek treatment voluntarily. But for the anger management approach described in this article to be effective, youth have to be willing to learn and apply a more reasonable and prosocial way to processing interpersonal conflict.

See also: Anger control problems, Anger management therapy with adolescents, Anger—adult

REFERENCES

Beck, R., & Fernandez, E. (1998). Cognitive–behavioral therapy in the treatment of anger. *Cognitive Therapy and Research*, *22*, 63–74.

Crick, N. R., & Dodge, D. A. (1994). A review and reformulation of social information-processing mechanisms in children's social adjustment. *Psychological Bulletin*, *115*, 74–101.

Feindler, E. L., & Ecton, R. (1986). *Adolescent anger control: Cognitive–behavioral techniques*. New York: Pergamon Press.

Feindler, E. L., & Scalley, M. (1998). Adolescent anger-management groups for violence reduction. In T. Ollendick & K. Storber (Eds.), *Group interventions in the school and community* (pp. 100–118). Needham Heights, UK: Allyn & Bacon.

Kassinove, H. (Ed.). (1995). *Anger disorders: Definition, diagnosis, and treatment*. London: Taylor & Francis.

Keenan, K. (2000). Emotion dysregulation as a risk factor for child psychopathology. *Clinical Psychology: Science and Practice*, *7*, 418–434.

Lochman, J. E., & Dodge, K. A. (1994). Social–cognitive processes of severely violent, moderately aggressive, and non-aggressive boys. *Journal of Child Clinical Psychology*, *62*, 366–374.

Novaco, R. W. (1979). The cognitive regulation of anger and stress. In P. Kendall & S. Hollon (Eds.), *Cognitive–behavioral interventions: Theory, research and procedures*. New York: Academic Press.

RECOMMENDED READINGS

Deffenbacher, J. L. (1999). Cognitive–behavioral conceptualization and treatment of anger. *JCLP/In Session: Psychotherapy in Practice*, *55*(3), 295–309.

Dodge, K. A. (1993). Social–cognitive mechanism in the development of conduct disorder and aggression. *Annual Review of Psychology*, *44*, 559–584.

Feindler, E. L. (1995). An ideal treatment package for children and adolescents with anger disorders. In H. Kassinove (Ed.), *Anger disorders: Definition, diagnosis, and treatment*. London: Taylor & Francis.

Feindler, E. L., & Baker, K. (2001). Current issues in anger management interventions with youth. In A. P. Goldstein, R. Nensen, B. Daleflod, & M. Kalt (Eds.), *New perspectives on aggression replacement training: Practice, research and application*. London: Wiley.

Aggressive and Antisocial Behavior in Youth

Pier J. M. Prins and Teun G. van Manen

Keywords: cognition, aggression, conduct problems, children, youth

Aggressive and antisocial behaviors in children and adolescents represent a major public health problem. Prevalence rates range from 2 to 16%. Children with high levels of aggressive behavior comprise a heterogeneous group covering a variety of rule violations and hostile acts, ranging in intensity from swearing to criminal assault. Moreover, they experience psychopathology and impairment in multiple areas. Various terms have been used to describe this group of youths. The DSM-IV, for example, distinguishes between the diagnostic categories of Conduct Disorder (CD) and Oppositional Defiant Disorder (ODD), the former referring to a pattern of behaviors that violate the rights of others, while the latter refers to a pattern of negativistic, hostile, defiant behaviors toward authority figures. Other distinctions are made based on the topography of the aggressive behavior, such as overt and covert aggression, or based on the age of onset such as childhood onset and adolescent onset conduct disorder. Another important distinction is made between an instrumental, proactive form of aggression and a hostile, reactive form of aggression (Dodge, Lochman, Harnish, Bates, & Pettit, 1997). The terms *aggressive behavior* and *conduct problems* will be used interchangeably throughout this article.

COGNITIVE–BEHAVIORAL ASSUMPTIONS AND AGGRESSION

The cognitive–behavioral framework assumes that aggression is not merely triggered by environmental events, but rather through the way in which these events are perceived and processed by the individual. This processing refers to the child's appraisal of the situation, anticipated reactions of others, and self-statements in response to particular events. A variety of cognitive and attributional processes have been found in aggressive youths. Deficits and distortions in cognitive problem-solving skills, attributions of hostile intent to others, and resentment and suspiciousness illustrate a few cognitive features associated with conduct problems. Individuals who engage in aggressive behaviors show distortions and deficiencies in various cognitive processes. These deficiencies are not merely reflections of intellectual functioning. A variety of cognitive processes have been studied such as generating alternative solutions to interpersonal problems (e.g., different ways of handling social situations); identifying the means to obtain particular ends (e.g., making friends) or consequences of one's actions (e.g., what could happen after a particular behavior); making attributions to others of the motivation of their actions; perceiving how others feel; and expectations of the effects of one's own actions and others. Deficits and distortions among these processes relate to teacher ratings of disruptive behavior, peer evaluations, and direct assessment of overt behavior (Kazdin, 1997).

Attribution of intent to others represents a salient cognitive disposition critically important to understanding aggressive behavior. Aggressive youths tend to attribute hostile intent to others, especially in social situations where the cues of actual intent are ambiguous. Some researchers relate the attributional bias to particular physiological processes, while others assume that the hostile attributional bias may be caused by the intense anger experienced by some aggressive individuals (see Lochman, Whidby, & Fitzgerald, 2000). Next to this attributional bias, aggressive children are characterized by cognitive deficits such as heightened sensitivity to hostile cues and by positive expectancies for aggressive behavior. Further, they have been found to value dominance and revenge over cooperation and affiliation, prefer aggressive solutions, have a restrictive repertoire of problem-solving strategies, and prefer action over thought and reflection (Durlak, Rubin, & Kahng, 2001).

A major model emphasizing the cognitive problems demonstrated by children with aggressive problems is the social information processing model developed by Crick and Dodge (1994). Briefly, this model identifies problems that aggressive children have in accurately judging social situations, selecting a strategy to deal with potential conflicts or challenges and then implementing and evaluating that strategy. The model postulates that socially competent behavior is dependent on (a) accurate encoding of social cues and interpretation of others' intent, (b) generation and selection of appropriate responses, and (c) skillful enactment of the chosen course of behavior.

Problems at one or more points in the information processing model may characterize aggressive youths. For example, reactively aggressive and proactively aggressive types of antisocial youth not only differ in developmental histories but also in social information processing patterns. Reactively aggressive youth tend to display poorer scores on measures of social cognition at early stages of cue-oriented processing (e.g., encoding and interpretation of social situations), whereas the proactively aggressive youth tend to demonstrate deficits at later stages of outcome-oriented processing (e.g., evaluation of selected response strategy) (Dodge et al., 1997).

TREATMENT PROCEDURES AND FORMATS

Child-based CBT interventions have been increasingly used to try to decrease children's aggressive, antisocial behavior and assume that children engage in aggressive behavior as a result of (a) learned cognitive distortions, such as biased attention to aggressive cues and the attribution of hostile intent to the action of others; (b) cognitive deficiencies, such as poor problem-solving and verbal mediation skills; and (c) a related tendency to respond impulsively to both external and internal stimuli, which has also been described as an inability to regulate emotion and behavior (Lochman et al., 2000). Accordingly, the child-focused CBT approach to treating child conduct problems targets the disturbed cognitive processes and behavioral deficits thought to produce aggressive and disruptive behaviors. They help the child identify stimuli that typically precede aggressive and antisocial behaviors and perceive ambiguous social situations in a nonhostile manner, challenge cognitive distortions, generate more assertive (versus aggressive) responses to possible social problems and develop more effective problem-solving skills, and tolerate feelings of anger and frustration without responding impulsively or aggressively (Nock, 2003).

Several CBT approaches have been developed to address these goals, such as problem-solving skills training, anger-coping training, assertiveness training, and rational–emotive therapy (Brestan & Eyberg, 1998). These CBT procedures use techniques such as cognitive restructuring and social skills training to remediate the cognitive and behavioral deficits of the aggressive youths. Several of these programs also place a great deal of emphasis on teaching youths how to solve problems rationally and respond nonaggressively when youths are actually aroused and angry.

Most of the treatment approaches occur within a short-term model of 10–15 weekly, hour-long sessions. No systematic reports on continued care studies are yet available. The format in which treatment is delivered is individual or group. Group format has been favored over individual treatments because of time and cost advantages. There are several advantages to the use of group therapy. Peer and group reinforcement are frequently more effective with children than reinforcement provided in a dyadic context, or by adults. This may be especially true for children with disruptive behavior disorders, who are relatively resistant to social reinforcement. Additionally, the group context provides in vivo opportunities for interpersonal learning and development of social skills (Lochman et al., 2000).

Two Examples

Problem Solving Skills Training (PSST) consists of developing interpersonal cognitive problem-solving skills. Although many variations of PSST have been applied to conduct-problem children, several characteristics are usually shared. First, the emphasis is on how children approach situations, i.e., the thought processes in which the child engages to guide responses to interpersonal situations. The children are taught to engage in a step-by-step approach to solve interpersonal problems. They make statements to themselves that direct attention to certain aspects of the problem or tasks that lead to effective solutions. Second, behaviors that are selected (solutions) to the interpersonal situations are important as well. Prosocial behaviors are fostered (through modeling and direct reinforcement) as part of the problem-solving process. Third, treatment utilizes structured tasks involving games, academic activities, and stories. Over the course of treatment, the cognitive problem-solving skills are increasingly applied to real-life situations. Fourth, therapists usually play an active role in treatment. They model the cognitive processes by making verbal self-statements, apply the sequence of statements to particular problems, and provide cues to prompt use of the skills. Finally, treatment usually combines several different procedures, including modeling and practice, role-playing, and reinforcement and mild punishment (loss of points or tokens). These are deployed in systematic ways to develop increasingly complex response repertoires of the child (Kazdin, 1997).

The Anger Coping Program addresses both cognitive and affective processes and is designed to remediate skills deficits in conflictual situations involving affective arousal. Specific goals are to increase children's awareness of internal cognitive, affective, and physiological phenomena related to anger arousal; enhance self-reflection and self-management skills; facilitate alternative, consequential, and means-end thinking in approaching social problems; and increase children's behavioral repertoire when faced with social conflict. To do so, sessions are organized around teaching specific social–cognitive skills. The major components of the program consist of self-management/monitoring skills, perspective-taking skills, and social problem-solving skills (Lochman et al., 2000).

EFFICACY OF COGNITIVE–BEHAVIORAL THERAPY WITH AGGRESSIVE YOUTH

Meta-analytic reviews have yielded medium to large effect sizes (ESs = 0.47 to 0.90) for this treatment approach for child conduct problems. Five child-centered CBT treatments have been identified that met the criteria for probably efficacious status including anger-control training, anger-coping training, assertiveness training, problem-solving skills training, and rational–emotive therapy. These treatments await systematic replication by a second research team before advancing to well-established status (Bennett & Gibbons, 2000; Brestan & Eyberg, 1998).

CBT treatment packages have proven more efficacious than credible comparison groups, and children receiving CBT are more likely to be in the normal range of functioning after treatment than children in comparison conditions, but, it is notable that many children receiving CBT fail to reach such levels of improved functioning. Furthermore, most studies have relied exclusively on parent and teacher report of child functioning and have not employed observational or performance-based measures in the laboratory, or more socially valid measures of functioning, such as records of actual offending from school or police sources. Thus, the actual impact of such interventions on subsequent child functioning has not been sufficiently established (Kazdin, 1997; Nock, 2003). Further, it is unknown at this point in time which of the many components involved in CBT treatment packages for child conduct problems is necessary and sufficient for therapeutic change (Nock, 2003).

Several studies have demonstrated the improved efficacy associated with combining CBT with parent management training (PMT) approaches. Children who participated in child-based CBT and whose parents participated in PMT had greater decreases in antisocial behavior than children assigned to a problem-solving-only or to a parent-training-only condition (Bennett & Gibbons, 2000).

The efficacy of CBT interventions may vary depending on factors such as the specific components addressed (presence or absence of self-monitoring), number of therapy sessions, and child age. Children of older age (11–13 years), for example, and with greater cognitive ability have been shown to benefit more from CBT than younger (5–7 years), less cognitively developed children. In addition, a greater degree of dysfunction present in the child (e.g., higher number of conduct disorder symptoms), in the parent (higher parenting stress and depression scores, or adverse child rearing practices), and in the family (more dysfunctional family environment) have all been associated with a poorer response to treatment (Nock, 2003).

In the meta-analyses of Bennett & Gibbons, none of the studies included examined the subtype of children's aggressive behavior. Given the greater peer problems, inadequate attention to relevant social cues, and more aggressive problemsolving of children who exhibit reactive (versus proactive) aggression, it is possible that child-based CBT interventions such as social problemsolving and anger control training may be most effective for children who exhibit high rates of reactive aggression.

In summary, cognitive–behavioral interventions for antisocial youth represent a promising approach by effectively addressing the youth's cognitive and social problems and by reducing conduct problem behaviors and building prosocial skills (Burke, Loeber, & Birmaher, 2002). However, the evidence has not been entirely supportive. Although child-focused CBT appears to foster some change in the problems of these youth, such short-term, child-focused interventions do not appear to be the ideal solution. Only parent-focused interventions have thus far met criteria for well-established status. By only focusing on the child, CBT may lack sufficient attention to the familial variables that have been implicated in the development and maintenance of antisocial behavior in children. Adopting a broader-based treatment strategy—integrating social–cognitive training interventions within a family or societal framework—may result in greater generalization or maintenance of treatment effects.

FUTURE DIRECTIONS

It thus appears that child-based CBT interventions can be an effective part of a multimodal treatment for children, particularly older children, who exhibit high levels of aggressive behavior. Future research will be concerned with the following four issues. First, although many studies have shown that conduct-disordered youths experience various cognitive distortions and deficiencies, the specificity of these cognitive deficits among diagnostic groups and youths of different ages (do cognitive distortions characterize youths with conduct problems rather than adjustment problems more generally?) needs to be established, as well as whether some of the cognitive processes are more central than others, and how these processes unfold developmentally (Kazdin, 1997). Second, intervention studies will have to be conducted with samples that are more similar to clinically referred subjects, that is, with high levels of comorbidity and living in disturbed families. Treatment trials will have to be extended to the clinical setting (real-world tests). Third, further work is needed to evaluate factors (child, family, and parent characteristics) that contribute to responsiveness to treatment, such as age, comorbidity, families with high levels of impairment, and lower reading achievement. Finally, more research will target the question of mechanisms of change in CBT for aggressive youths. Several studies have demonstrated that CBT affects the proposed mechanisms of change in the hypothesized directions (e.g., increases in problem-solving skills and self-control, and decreases in cognitive distortions and hostile attributions) and that changes in these proposed mediators are correlated with child behavior change at posttreatment. However, no studies have demonstrated that changes in the proposed mechanisms temporally precede the changes in therapeutic outcome and that changes in the proposed mechanisms account for the effect of treatment condition on therapeutic outcome. Until these criteria are met, researchers cannot be sure the therapeutic change associated with CBT for child conduct problem is the result of cognitive and behavioral changes in the child, rather than some other, related factor. Knowledge about why and how CBT with aggressive youths works eventually will serve as a basis for maximizing its efficacy in clinical practice (Weersing & Weisz, 2002).

See also: Anger management therapy with adolescents, Disruptive anger, Treatment of children

REFERENCES

Bennett, D. S., & Gibbons, T. A. (2000). Efficacy of child cognitive–behavioral interventions for antisocial behavior: A meta-analysis. *Child and Family Behavior Therapy, 22*, 1–27.

Brestan, E. V., & Eyberg, S. M. (1998). Effective psychosocial treatments of conduct-disordered children and adolescents: 29 years, 82 studies, and 5,272 kids. *Journal of Clinical Child Psychology, 27*, 180–189.

Burke, J. D., Loeber, R., & Birmaher, B. (2002). Oppositional defiant disorder and conduct disorder: A review of the past 10 years, part II. *Journal of the American Academy of Child and Adolescent Psychiatry, 41*, 1275–1293.

Crick, N. R., & Dodge, K. A. (1994). A review and reformulation of social information-processing mechanisms in children's social adjustment. *Psychological Bulletin, 115*, 74–101.

Dodge, K. A., Lochman, J. E., Harnish, J. D., Bates, J. E., & Pettit, G. S. (1997). Reactive and proactive aggression in school children and psychiatrically impaired chronically assaultive youth. *Journal of Abnormal Psychology, 106*, 37–51.

Durlak, J. A., Rubin, L. A., & Kahng, R. D. (2001). Cognitive behavioural therapy for children and adolescents with externalising problems. *Journal of Cognitive Psychotherapy: An International Quarterly, 15*, 183–194.

Kazdin, A. E. (1997). Practitioner review: Psychosocial treatments for conduct disorder in children. *Journal of Child Psychology and Psychiatry, 38*, 161–178.

Lochman, J. E., Whidby, J. M., & Fitzgerald, D. P. (2000). Cognitive–behavioral assessment and treatment with aggressive children. In P.C. Kendall (Ed.), *Child & adolescent therapy: Cognitive–behavioral procedures* (2nd ed., pp. 31–88). New York: Guilford Press.

Nock, M. K. (2003). Progress review of the psychosocial treatment of child conduct problems. *Clinical Psychology: Science and Practice, 10*, 1–28.

Weersing, V. R., & Weisz, J. R. (2002). Mechanisms of action in youth psychotherapy. *Journal of Child Psychology and Psychiatry, 43*, 3–29.

Aging and Dementia

Steven H. Zarit

Keywords: dementia, Alzheimer's disease, caregiving, stress, family support

There is no more feared or devastating disorder in late life than dementia. The dementia syndrome involves progressive deterioration of cognitive and functional abilities, leaving people unable to care for themselves and needing around-the-clock supervision and care. Alzheimer's disease is the most prevalent cause, accounting for between 50 and 70% cases (Mendez & Cummings, 2003).

Given the extensive cognitive deficits associated with dementia, opportunities for psychological and medical intervention with people suffering from the disorder are limited. A more usual and effective strategy is working with family and other caregivers to assist them in managing patients with dementia and help them deal with the associated stress. We will examine both direct patient interventions as well as strategies for treating caregivers.

INTERVENTIONS WITH PATIENTS WITH DEMENTIA

Medications are now available for Alzheimer's disease and other dementias that sometimes slow the progression of symptoms, but do not reverse the overall course of the disorder (Mendez & Cummings, 2003). Psychological interventions have focused on the early stages of the illness when people still have an awareness of their problems, and can actively participate in treatment. Early stage support groups for patients and their families have been very popular and can now be found in many communities (e.g., Yale, 1989, 1999). Examples of counseling with the person with dementia or with the person and his/her caregiver have also been reported (Zarit & Zarit, 1998). Many different treatment strategies have been described, including improving communication between the person with the illness and his/her spouse or other family caregiver, learning strategies for managing memory loss, exploring how to talk about the disease with family and friends, finding ways for the person with dementia to continue to feel useful, experiencing grief and loss, learning about the disease and treatment options, and planning for the care that will be needed in the future (Clare, 2002; Feinberg & Whitlatch, 2001; Kuhn, 1998; Moniz-Cook, Agar, Gibson, Win, & Wang, 1998; Whitlatch, 2001; Yale, 1989, 1999). Clare observes that interventions need to strike a balance between encouraging the person and family to fight the disease and finding ways to come to terms with it and the limitations it imposes. Preliminary findings from an evaluation of a structured 10-week group program suggest that people with the disease and their accompanying family member report a high level of satisfaction and experienced some benefit (Zarit, Femia, Watson, Rice-Oschger, & Kakos, 2004).

As dementia progresses, patients lose awareness of their situation and usually cannot participate actively in treatment or decisions about their care. There is some evidence that behavioral management strategies as well as environmental modifications are effective in reducing problem behaviors and improving well-being (e.g., Whall & Kolanowski, in press; Zimmerman & Sloane, 1999). Teri and colleagues (Teri, Lodsgon, Uomoto, & McCurry, 1997) found that training family caregivers to implement pleasant activities led to reductions in depressive symptoms among patients as well as the caregivers.

INTERVENTIONS WITH FAMILY CAREGIVERS

A variety of interventions with family caregivers have been developed to relieve stress and improve management of dementia-related problems. From a theoretical perspective, negative outcomes of caregiving such as depression and poor health are the result of primary stressors that are associated with primary care, secondary stressors that represent the spillover of care tasks into other areas of the person's life, as well as resources that limit or buffer the effects of stressors (Aneshensel, Pearlin, Mullan, Zarit, & Whitlatch, 1995). Among the resources that affect the impact of stressors on outcomes are how caregivers appraise stressors, how they cope with or manage stressors, and how much help or support they receive. In varying degrees, many different treatments have been developed that target these resources. Protocols involving 6 to 10 sessions with the primary caregiver and one or more meetings with other family members have been found to be particularly effective in relieving care-related stress (Marriott, Donaldson, Terrier, & Burns, 2000; Mittelman et al., 1995; Whitlatch, Zarit, & von Eye, 1991). Use of supportive services such as adult day care may also lessen caregiver burden and depression (Zarit, Stephens, Townsend, & Greene, 1998).

Treatment builds resources through the use of three strategies: helping caregivers examine the attributions they make about why patients behave the way they do, training caregivers to use behavioral management approaches, and helping caregivers identify sources of assistance and support (Zarit & Zarit, 1998). CBT is a critical component of these strategies.

The starting point in treatment often involves examination of caregivers' beliefs and knowledge about their relative's illness and the attributions they make about causes of behavior problems. Many caregivers believe that dementia-related behaviors such as asking the same question over and over again or claiming that personal items have been stolen are under the patient's control. They confront patients with the "facts" of the situation and expect that patients should be able to correct their cognitive errors, for example, recognizing that they had already asked the same question. The clinician identifies what types of these cognitive errors are troubling to caregivers and the beliefs associated with them. Providing information about the effects of dementia on the brain or on memory and discussing why patients might engage in these behaviors can help caregivers to change their attributions. Once caregivers view these problems as part of the disease, rather than as intentional or under the patient's control, they become open to responding in a different way. Responses that can be helpful for these kinds of problems include distraction or developing an intervention based on identifying the patient's underlying feelings.

For example, a person who asks to see her deceased mother might be feeling lonely or in need of reassurance. Providing comfort or talking with her about her mother will be more effective than telling her that her mother is dead, which will only increase her anxiety. The patient's cognitive errors are part of the disease and cannot usually be corrected, but the feelings that are associated with their beliefs can be addressed.

Other types of behavior problems that are common in dementia require a more focused approach. Problems such as restless or disruptive behavior or wandering off can be very troubling to caregivers. Use of a systematic behavioral problem-solving approach has proven effective with these kinds of problems (Teri et al., 1997; Zarit & Zarit, 1998). Problem solving begins with assessment. Caregiver and clinician first decide which problems are the most troubling or stressful. Caregivers may appraise behaviors in very different ways, so that a problem that is very stressful for one caregiver might be perceived as only a minor irritant by another. Once one or more specific behaviors are targeted, the caregiver will monitor their occurrence for several days, identifying the frequency with which the problems occur, when they occur during the course of the day, and antecedents and consequences of specific episodes. Working with the counselor or therapist, they then brainstorm to identify possible solutions. Solutions frequently involve preventing the antecedent event. As an example, a period of inactivity or napping may be the trigger for restlessness in the afternoon. Increasing the patient's activity during that period of the day could head off restlessness. Once caregivers identify possible solutions, they select one, rehearse carrying it out, and then implement and evaluate its use. Cognitive issues may arise at every step of this process. Caregivers may believe that nothing will make a difference, or that they will only make things worse by making a change in how they are handling a problem. They also may not be able to choose between alternative approaches. The therapist can engage them in examining their beliefs and developing alternatives that can lead to their taking new steps to manage problem behaviors.

The third strategy, increasing support, involves identifying assistance or emotional support the caregiver could potentially receive from family and friends, as well as from formal services. Often, support is available, but caregivers hold beliefs that block them from utilizing it. Many caregivers believe they ought to be able to do everything themselves, or that their relative will not accept help. Therapists can work with caregivers to identify their need to have an occasional break from providing care, and what types of potential sources of care might be available from their informal and formal network. They can also help caregivers to identify and generate alternatives to beliefs that prevent them from seeking out care. For example, caregivers often believe that a formal service such as adult day care will not be able to manage their relative, or that their relative will be unwilling to stay at the program. One alternative perspective is to suggest that the day care program is experienced in and able to manage these sorts of problems.

Besides these basic strategies, therapists will often explore a variety of other issues related to the caregiving situation. Foremost among these are questions about if and when to place the person with dementia in an institution. Caregivers have often received all kinds of advice on placement from family, friends, and their doctors. We stress that it is important for caregivers to decide about placement in a way that is consistent with their own values, and to make the decision to place when they are ready, not when other people think it is time. If they want to continue providing care at home, we will work with them to make it more manageable. If they want to place, we will help them in the search for a good setting for their relative. It is critical, however, to give caregivers the opportunity to talk about placement in a nonjudgmental way.

The decision is very difficult for many people and may require considerable discussion. A frequent issue is that caregivers had made a promise in the past never to place their relative. We will encourage them to consider an alternative perspective, that when their relative asked them to make that promise, he/she did not envision needing this type of intensive care. Often that approach helps caregivers to move on.

Physicians and mental health professionals often believe that they must rush caregivers to make the decision to place a relative, so that the stress on them does not become overwhelming. Placement, however, only shifts, but does not alleviate the burdens caregivers are experiencing (Zarit & Whitlatch, 1992). Although home care is often very stressful, caregivers will experience a different set of problems after placement, such as trying to get nursing home staff to provide more personalized care for their relative. Caregivers who are more prepared to make the decision may do better than someone who is rushed into placement. It is also important to continue to provide support for caregivers after placement, since they may now be feeling guilty, depressed, or, in the case of spouse caregivers, uncertain of their role with respect to the patient and to friends and family.

SUMMARY

Dementia is characterized by progressive deterioration of cognitive and functional abilities, leaving people unable to care for themselves. The burden of care typically falls on family members, who may experience high levels of stress trying to meet the demands of care that are placed on them. Interventions made directly with patients in the early stages of the illness appear promising. As the disease progresses, the goal of treatment is relieving stress on family caregivers. Cognitive–behavioral strategies play an important part in helping caregivers manage stressors more effectively, and in examining their role and involvement in providing care.

See also: Depression and personality disorders—older adults, Family caregivers

REFERENCES

Clare, L. (2002). We'll fight it as long as we can: Coping with the onset of Alzheimer's disease. *Aging and Mental Health, 6*, 139–148.

Feinberg, L. F., & Whitlatch, C. J. (2001). Are cognitively impaired adults able to state consistent choices? *The Gerontologist, 41*, 374–382.

Kuhn, D. R. (1998). Caring for relatives with early stage Alzheimer's disease: An exploratory study. *American Journal of Alzheimer's Disease, 13*, 189–196.

Marriott, A., Donaldson, C., Terrier, N., & Burns, A. (2000). Effectiveness of cognitive–behavioural family intervention in reducing the burden of care in carers of patients with Alzheimer's disease. *British Journal of Psychiatry, 176*, 557–562.

Mendez, M. F., & Cummings, J. L. (2003). *Dementia: A clinical approach* (3rd ed.). Woburn, MA: Butterworth–Heinemann.

Mittelman, M. S., Ferris, S. H., Shulman, E., Steinberg, G., Ambinder, A., Mackel, J., & Cohen, J. (1995). A comprehensive support program: Effect on depression in spouse-caregivers of AD patients. *The Gerontologist, 35*, 792–802.

Moniz-Cook, E., Agar, S., Gibson, G., Win, T., & Wang, M. (1998). A preliminary study of the effects of early intervention with people with dementia and their families in a memory clinic. *Aging and Mental Health, 2*, 199–211.

Teri, L., Logsdon, R. G., Uomoto, J., & McCurry, S. M. (1997). Behavioral treatment of depression in dementia patients: A controlled clinical trial. *Journals of Gerontology Series B: Psychological Sciences and Social Sciences, 52B*, P159–P166.

Whall, A. L., & Kolanowski, A. M. (2004). The need-driven dementia-compromised behavior (NDB) model: A framework for understanding the behavioural symptoms of dementia. *Aging and Mental Health, 8*(2), 106–108.

Whitlatch, C. J. (2001). Including the person with dementia in family caregiving research and practice. *Aging and Mental Health, 5*, Supplement, 72–74.

Yale, R. (1989). Support groups for newly-diagnosed Alzheimer's clients. *Clinical Gerontologist, 8*, 86–89.

Yale, R. (1999). Support groups and other services for individuals with early-stage Alzheimer's disease. *Generations, 23*(Fall), 57–61.

Zarit, S. H., Stephens, M. A. P., Townsend, A., & Greene, R. (1998). Stress reduction for family caregivers: Effects of day care use. *Journal of Gerontology: Social Sciences, 53B*, S267–S277.

Zarit, S. H., Femia, E. F., Watson, J., Rice-Oeschger, L. & Kakos, B. (2004). Memory club: A group intervention for people with early-stage dementia and their care partners. *The Gerontologist, 44*(2), 262–270.

Zarit, S. H., & Whitlatch, C. (1992). Institutional placement: Phases of the transition. *The Gerontologist, 32*, 665–672.

Zarit, S. H., & Zarit, J. M. (1998). *Mental disorders in older adults: Fundamentals of assessment and treatment*. New York: Guilford Press.

Zimmerman, S. I., & Sloane, P. D. (1999). Optimum residential care for people with dementia. *Generations, 23*(3), 62–68.

Anger—Adult

Christine Bowman Edmondson and Daniel Joseph Cahill

Keywords: anger disorders, anger attacks, irritable depression, intermittent explosive disorder

COGNITIVE-BEHAVIORAL TREATMENT FOR ANGER

This article describes cognitive–behavioral therapy interventions for anger in adult outpatient populations. Thus, it will not address interventions for reducing anger identified as being for children or adolescents. Readers interested in cognitive–behavioral interventions for oppositional defiant disorder, conduct disorder, or personality disorders are referred to the relevant articles in the present volume.

This article may have some relevance for populations that include individuals with personality disorders, perpetrators of domestic violence, and prisoners insofar as individuals from these populations have difficulties with anger. However, it should not be assumed that all individuals in these populations have difficulties with anger. Therefore, this article mainly focuses on populations in which the cognitive, behavioral, physiological, and experiential aspects of anger are problematic rather than on populations in which there are anger outbursts that are the manifestation of more generalized difficulties with cognitive and behavioral functioning. To facilitate the identification of individuals for which these interventions are appropriate, there is a section describing various types of anger disorders prior to the description of cognitive–behavioral interventions for anger.

ANGER DISORDERS

Anger is a common focus of treatment in a variety of health and mental health treatment settings. An "anger disorder" can be described as a symptom pattern consisting of the presence of anger attacks and/or irritability without the presence of another mood or anxiety disorder. An "anger attack" has been described by researchers (Fava & Rosenbaum, 1999) as sudden episodes of anger characterized by intense physiological reactions that are inappropriate to the situation and uncharacteristic of the person undergoing the attack. "Irritable depression" is a syndrome characterized by the presence of an irritable mood for 5 days or longer in conjunction with a decreased interest in regular activities and a number of the cognitive and vegetative symptoms of depression (WHO, 2002).

Intermittent Explosive Disorder (IED) is often cited as a possible *Diagnostic and Statistical Manual of Mental Disorders* (DSM; American Psychiatric Association, 1994) diagnostic category for individuals with anger problems. However, IED criteria are delineated on the basis of its being an impulse control disorder rather than an emotional disorder. The WorlOverview, analysis, and evaluationcollect epidemiological data on IED and another anger-related disorder referred to as "irritable depression." This research is an important step in operationally defining anger disorders in the DSM.

Other anger disorders have been proposed by Eckhardt and Deffenbacher (1995): General Anger Disorder (GAngD) and Specific Anger Disorder–Driving Situations. GAngD is characterized by experiencing anger daily or being in a chronically angry mood. In addition, people with GAngD are likely to be verbally aggressive and/or destroy objects. Eckhardt and Deffenbacher (1995) proposed that GangD has two subtypes: with physical aggression and without physical aggression. They emphasized that while people with GAngD without aggression may engage in aggression on occasion, it does not have the severity (i.e., sarcasm, loud arguments, and/or physical aggression) or frequency to meet the criteria of GAngD with aggression.

Eckhardt and Deffenbacher (1995) also suggested that there were "Specific Anger Disorders," in which anger is confined to a circumscribed set of situations. Deffenbacher, Filetti, Lynch, Dahlen, and Oetting (2002) described the characteristics of high-anger drivers, which could be described as having "Specific Anger Disorder–Driving Situations." Their research suggested that high-anger drivers are at risk of injury and death resulting from aggressive behavior associated with anger while driving. They also provide data on the efficacy of relaxation interventions for high-anger drivers.

Currently, there are no published studies that investigate the efficacy of cognitive–behavioral treatment for IED or irritable depression. Instead, studies of treatment for syndromes associated with these disorders (i.e., anger attacks) use primarily psychopharmacological interventions (Fava & Rosenbaum, 1999). It is likely that cognitive–behavioral therapy in combination with psychopharmacological interventions would maximize treatment efficacy for these disorders. Thus, cognitive–behavioral therapies that are developed for these disorders should include components that explore the use of medication and enhance compliance with medication regimens. There is a body of literature that provides empirical support for cognitive and behavioral therapies for anger defined in a manner that is similar to GAngD (Deffenbacher, Oetting, & DiGiuseppe, 2002).

Although IED, irritable depression, GAngD, and specific anger disorder–driving anger disorders are promising operational definitions of anger disorders, anger problems, such as irritable mood (i.e., frequent and intense anger) and anger outbursts, can still be identified as targets of change in cognitive and behavioral therapy. Irritable mood and/or anger outbursts co-occur with important psychiatric syndromes such as depression (Haaga, 1999), posttraumatic stress disorder (Novaco & Chemtob, 1998), and substance abuse (Awalt, Reilly, & Shopshire, 1997). The type of anger problem that is the focus of treatment (i.e., an anger disorder versus irritable mood versus anger outbursts) and the comorbidity of anger problems and other psychiatric syndromes all need to be considered when using cognitive–behavioral therapy interventions to address anger problems.

Cognitive–behavioral interventions for anger are generally effective across different populations; however, research is lacking that addresses issues of relative efficacy, causal mechanisms of treatment, and the specificity of treatment for different types of populations (Deffenbacher, Oetting, & DiGiuseppe, 2002). It is likely that more advances in the cognitive–behavioral treatment of anger will occur when commonly accepted definitions of anger disorders are used to identify participants for treatment outcome studies. Also, the definition and delineation of anger disorders would facilitate the understanding of the cognitive and behavioral processes that contribute to irritable mood and/or anger outbursts that are associated with clinically significant distress and interference with social and occupational functioning.

COGNITIVE–BEHAVIORAL THERAPY INTERVENTIONS FOR ANGER PROBLEMS

Deffenbacher (1999) suggests that the first goal of treatment should be to establish good rapport. Good rapport provides a foundation of trust that is essential for the success of treatment. In addition, Deffenbacher describes why it is important to build a common understanding of the presenting problem and to reach agreement as to what the goals of therapy should be for angry clients. Basic counseling skills such as empathy and positive regard are important for building this rapport. In addition, self-monitoring can be useful in negotiating shared expectations for the therapy process and goals. Self-monitoring can also be a part of a "safety plan" or no-violence contract. Self-monitoring encourages clients to take an active role in their change process. It enhances self-awareness of the intensity of irritable moods and anger, which is important in avoiding aggressive behavior. It also provides the therapist with relevant examples to use when highlighting important issues that form the basis of negotiating a shared understanding of the problem and an agreement for treatment procedures and goals. Self-monitoring is often used in conjunction with techniques such as relaxation training, cognitive restructuring, problem solving, and social skills training in order to track progress in using new skills outside of therapy sessions.

Relaxation training teaches clients to monitor levels of arousal and to use a variety of methods for lowering arousal in order to increase their ability to cope physiologically or emotionally during anger-provoking situations (Deffenbacher, 1999). Two useful interventions are autogenic relaxation training and progressive muscle relaxation. Autogenic relaxation training is useful when a quick and easy method for achieving relaxation is needed. However, progressive muscle relation may be more helpful when clients are not aware of their general level of physiological arousal and cues for anger outbursts. Relaxation training is a basic component of the stress inoculation protocols that have demonstrated therapeutic efficacy for anger problems.

Cognitive restructuring is a method of identifying maladaptive thoughts, beliefs, or attributions that lead to anger outbursts and learning appropriate responses. It is important to help angry clients accept the rationale for changing their thoughts (i.e., that thoughts influence feelings and the problematic behaviors associated with them) and to convince angry clients that they have a choice in how they decide to interpret anger-provoking situations. Once the client accepts this rationale, techniques of rational emotive behavior therapy or cognitive therapy can be used to restructure problematic thinking. The inductive nature of cognitive therapy techniques may be more acceptable to some types of angry clients and may be a better technique if an angry individual is struggling with the rationale for cognitive restructuring.

Some angry clients may benefit from imaginal methods for cognitive restructuring more so than the verbal methods that comprise cognitive therapy and rational emotive behavior therapy. Deffenbacher (1999) describes how imagining a visual image of an anger-provoking agent literally as a "jackass" could be effective in humorously restructuring an angry person's beliefs about another person who may be the source of ongoing anger provocations.

Although self-instructions and affirmations of coping skills are not techniques of cognitive restructuring, they are important aspects of self-talk that should be increased as problematic cognitions are decreased as a result of cognitive restructuring. They are also important components of stress inoculation and problem-solving interventions for anger.

The efficacy of problem solving training has also been evaluated in angry individuals. The structured nature of this intervention is helpful in encouraging angry clients to stop and think about their response options before responding to anger provocation. Angry clients could particularly benefit from systematically determining whether it is best to respond to their emotional reaction to a provocation versus the situation that caused the provocation to occur. Then, the discipline of systematically brainstorming response options and evaluating them will be most likely to encourage the selection of the most effective and appropriate response.

Social skills training has also received empirical support for the treatment of anger problems. In these studies, the social skills training tends to focus on global social skills such as listening, assertive self-expression, and negotiating resolutions to conflicts. However, angry individuals may also benefit from modifying microbehavioral aspects of their social interactions such as facial expressions, vocal intonation, voice volume, body postures, and gestures. Other interventions designed to enhance social functioning may also be needed for angry clients to repair the damage their anger has done to their social functioning.

INNOVATIONS AND FUTURE DIRECTIONS

Exposure Techniques for Anger Problems

Exposure techniques have been applied to the reduction of anger. Imaginal exposure techniques may be more amenable to practice settings than in vivo exposure techniques. Imaginal exposure involves the construction of anger-inducing scenarios in order to inoculate against real-life situations. Grodnitzky and Tafrate (2000) provide a description of clinical procedures utilizing imaginal exposure to reduce anger in adults.

Research on Cognitive and Behavioral Processes in Irritable Mood and Anger Attacks

It is important to conduct research designed to identify the differential cognitive and behavioral deficits associated with irritable moods and anger attacks. Research on cognitive– behavioral therapeutic efficacy has outpaced efforts in this realm. The benefits of identifying cognitive and behavioral processes unique to different anxiety disorders have resulted in significant advances in their treatment of these disorders. Similar advances could be experienced in the realm of anger disorders.

Innovations in Cognitive–Behavioral Therapy of Anger Disorders

Practitioners and researchers interested in treatment innovations could contribute to advances in cognitive–behavioral therapy for anger disorders by further developing exposure techniques for anger problems. In addition, cognitive restructuring for anger problems would be enhanced by innovations that use symbolic methods such as visual imagery and metaphors to assist with the restructuring of irrational beliefs or dysfunctional schemas associated with anger. Social skills interventions would benefit from the development of more systematic approaches to modulating nonverbal and paralinguistic behaviors in individuals with anger problems.

Finally, advances in cognitive neuroscience are contributing to the development of a better understanding of the role of biological factors in a variety of behavioral disorders, including anger problems. These advances neither mandate the use of pharmacological interventions nor preclude the use of cognitive–behavioral therapy. However, they do indicate that some people with anger problems may benefit from pharmacological interventions. Cognitive–behavioral therapists have developed treatment protocols that are designed to facilitate compliance with pharmacological intervention and/or the termination of pharmacological intervention in mood disorders and anxiety disorders. Cognitive–behavioral therapists interested in anger disorders would do well to also innovate in this area.

See also: Adolescent aggression and anger management, Anger control problems, Anger management therapy with adolescents, Disruptive anger

REFERENCES

American Psychiatric Association. (1994). *Diagnostic and statistical manual of mental disorders* (4th ed.). Washington, DC: Author.

Awalt, R. M., Reilly, P. M., & Shopshire, M. S. (1997). The angry patient: An intervention for managing anger in substance abuse treatment. *Journal of Psychoactive Drugs, 29*, 353–358.

Deffenbacher, J. L. (1999). Cognitive–behavioral conceptualization and treatment of anger. *Journal of Clinical Psychology, 55*, 295–309.

Deffenbacher, J. L., Filetti, L. B., Lynch, R. S., Dahlen, E. R., & Oetting, E. R. (2002). Cognitive–behavioral treatment of high anger drivers. *Behaviour Research and Therapy, 40*, 895–910.

Deffenbacher, J. L., Oetting, E. R., & DiGiuseppe, R. A. (2002). Principles of empirically supported interventions applied to anger management. *Counseling Psychologist, 30*, 262–280.

Eckhardt, C. I., & Deffenbacher, J. L. (1995). Diagnosis of anger disorders. In H. Kassinove (Ed.), *Anger disorders* (pp. 27–47). Bristol, PA: Taylor & Francis.

Fava, M., & Rosenbaum, J. F. (1999). Anger attacks in patients with depression. *Journal of Clinical Psychiatry, 60*, 21–24.

Grodnitzky, G. R., & Tafrate, R. C. (2000). Imaginal exposure for anger reduction in adult outpatients: A pilot study. *Journal of Behaviour Therapy and Experimental Psychiatry, 31*, 259–279.

Haaga, D. A. (1999). Treating options for depression and anger. *Cognitive and Behavioral Practice, 6*, 289–292.

Novaco, R. W., & Chemtob, C. M. (1998). Anger and trauma: Conceptualization, assessment and treatment. In V. M. Follette & J. I. Ruzek (Eds.), *Cognitive–behavioral therapies for trauma*. New York: Guilford Press.

World Health Organization. (2002). *Composite International Diagnostic Interview reference and training manual*. Geneva: Author.

RECOMMENDED READINGS

Cognitive Behavioral Case Conference section of *Cognitive and Behavioral Practice, 6*, 271–292.

Deffenbacher, J. L. (1999). Cognitive–behavioral conceptualization and treatment of anger. *Journal of Clinical Psychology, 55*, 295–309.

Anger Control Problems

Donald Meichenbaum

Keywords: anger, exposure-based therapies, self-instructional training, self-monitoring procedures, stress inoculation training

Anger-control problems are an often-overlooked disorder and they have received limited attention in the treatment literature. An examination of the American Psychiatric Association DSM-IV reveals nine diagnostic categories for Anxiety Disorders and ten diagnostic categories of Depressive Disorders, but only three diagnostic categories for anger-related problems, namely, Intermittent Explosive Disorders, and two Adjustment Disorders with Conduct-Disorder features. The dearth of research on anger is further highlighted by DiGiuseppe and Tafrate (2001) who noted that for every article on anger over the past 15 years, there are ten articles in the area of depression and seven articles in the area of anxiety. The absence of research activity on anger is somewhat surprising given that anger-related behaviors are one of the most common psychiatric symptoms that cut across some 19 different psychiatric conditions. Anger, hostility, and accompanying violence are often comorbid with other disorders. For example, veterans with PTSD have been found to be at increased risk for domestic abuse with as many as one-third of combat veterans with PTSD having assaulted their partners in the past year. Vietnam veterans with PTSD are six times more likely to abuse drugs compared to Vietnam veterans without PTSD, with anger being a significant relapse cue for substance abuse. PTSD, substance abuse, mood disorders, anger, and accompanying hostility and aggression go hand in hand and provide clinicians with major challenges.

Besides the challenge of comorbidity, Novaco (1996) has highlighted several additional challenges to the treatment of patients with anger and aggressive behaviors. These challenges include:

1. Angry patients may become angry during therapy and direct their aggression toward their therapist.

2. Angry patients need to be continually reassessed for the risk of violence toward themselves and toward others (according to the Tarasoff decision).
3. Angry patients are often resistant to treatment, highly impatient, easily frustrated, and unrealistic in their treatment goals and, moreover, are often noncompliant with treatment.

As DiGiuseppe and Tafrate (2001) observe, "angry clients do *not* come for therapy; they come for supervision" on how to fix people in their lives (bosses, co-workers, partners, children) whom they have failed to change or they come to vent on how unfairly and disrespectfully they have been treated.

Finally, the need for effective treatment approaches for aggressive behavior has been underscored by Slep and O'Leary (2001) who reported that in the United States each year 1.6 million women are severely assaulted by their partners and over 900,000 children are maltreated. In 6% of all U.S. households, partner and child physical abuse co-occur in families. The need is urgent and the question is: what do therapists have to offer to effectively treat individuals with angry and aggressive behaviors?

COGNITIVE–BEHAVIORAL TREATMENT (CBT)

Five meta-analytic reviews of anger treatment have appeared that have examined the relative efficacy of CBT with adults, adolescents, and children (Beck & Fernandez, 1998; Bowman-Edmondson & Cohen-Conger, 1996; DiGiuseppe & Tafrate, 2001; Sukhodolsky & Kassinove, 1997). The populations treated included college students selected for high anger, aggressive drivers, angry outpatients, batterers, prison inmates, students with learning disabilities, individuals with developmental delays, and people with medical problems such as hypertension and Type A personalities. The results of the meta-analyses indicate that "the anger treatments seem to work equally for all age groups and all types of populations and are equally effective for men and women.... The average effect sizes across all outcome measures ranged from .67 to .99, with a mean of .70" (DiGiuseppe & Tafrate, 2001, p. 263).

The results of these meta-analyses revealed that CBT for anger reduction was moderately successful. Patients in CBT were better off than 76% of control untreated patients, and 83% of the CBT patients improved in comparison to their pretest scores. This level of improvement was maintained at a follow-up period that ranged from 2 to 64 weeks.

While these initial results are encouraging, the effect sizes for CBT of anxiety disorders have been found to be around 1.00 and for depression it has reached 2.00. Meichenbaum (2001) has reviewed the intervention literature on spouse abusers and provides a cautionary note that 25% to 50% of men who batter who attend treatment programs repeat their violence during the period from 6 months to 2 years following treatment. While a review of the literature on intimate partner violence is beyond the scope of this brief article, there is increasing evidence that further development of effective treatments for aggressive behavior is required. The research by Holtzworth-Munroe (2000) is most promising, as she has identified different patterns of aggressive behavior (family-only versus generalized aggression versus aggression that accompanies comorbid disorders). Given the complexity and altered developmental patterns of aggressive behaviors (childhood onset versus adolescent onset) and the important role of gender differences, differential treatments of angry and aggressive behaviors are indicated (Reid, Patterson, & Snyder, 2002). Even with these caveats in mind, the initial results of cognitive–behavioral interventions with angry and aggressive individuals are encouraging.

THE NATURE OF COGNITIVE–BEHAVIORAL INTERVENTIONS

A number of varied interventions have been employed with individuals with anger-control problems including relaxation-based interventions, systematic desensitization, behavioral skills training, adjudicated psychoeducational counseling programs, rational–emotive behavioral therapy, and cognitive–behavioral programs, such as self-instructional training, stress inoculation training, problem-solving interventions, and exposure-based procedures. The CBT interventions are usually short-term (8 to 22 sessions) and may be conducted on an individual and/or group basis. The average length of treatment in various outcome studies was 12 sessions. The research indicates that on average individual treatment is more effective than group treatment. But this conclusion should be treated as preliminary given the limited number of such comparative outcome studies. A major finding of the meta-analyses was that programs that used standardized treatment manuals and that conducted treatment fidelity checks were the most effective. To quote DiGiuseppe and Tafrate (2001),

> Practitioners working with aggressive clients should choose structured interventions, delivered in an individualized format and employ safeguards to ensure that the treatment is delivered in a manner consistent with the manuals. (p. 264)

With this proviso in mind, the remainder of this article provides an outline of the content of the multicomponent cognitive–behavioral interventions with patients with anger-control problems. For more detailed accounts see Meichenbaum (2001) and the Recommended Readings.

Stress inoculation training (SIT) (Meichenbaum, 1985, 2001; Novaco, 1975) has provided the major conceptual and procedural framework for the cognitive–behavioral interventions of anger control. SIT is a broad-based multicomponent training that is arranged in flexible interlocking phases. The three phases are

- A conceptual educational phase
- A skills acquisition and consolidation phase
- An application (graduated exposure and practice) phase

SIT provides a set of procedural guidelines to be individually tailored to the needs of each patient. The treatment goal of SIT is to bolster the patients' coping repertoires and their confidence in being able to apply their coping skills in a flexible effective fashion. A central concept underlying SIT is that of "inoculation" and like the medical metaphor, the treatment involves exposing the patient to graduated doses of stressors that challenge, but do *not* overwhelm coping resources. The patient is taught a variety of cognitive modification, arousal reduction, acceptance, and behavior skills which are then applied to perceived provocations (stressor exposure) in a graduated hierarchical fashion. Such provocations may be simulated in the therapy settings by means of imagination and role-playing. The patients and therapist collaborate in establishing treatment goals and in formulating a hierarchy of anger incidents that can be used for training purposes. Table 1 provides an outline of the content of the respective treatment phases.

One goal of SIT is to teach patients with anger control to learn to ask themselves:

> "How can I *not* get angry in the first place?"
>
> "If I do get angry, how can I keep the anger at moderate levels of intensity?"
>
> "What did I want that I was *not* getting?"
>
> "What was I getting that I did *not* want?"
>
> "Was there some way I could have gotten what I wanted, or avoided what I did not want, without becoming angry?"

Table 1. Stress Inoculation Training for Individuals with Anger-Control Problems and Aggressive Behaviors

Phase I—Conceptual education phase

- Establish a therapeutic alliance with the patient.
- Conduct assessment and provide feedback.
- Educate the patient about the components and functions of anger and their relationships to stress, substance use, and aggression. Include a consideration of both the negative and positive aspects of anger and how to identify and differentiate various emotions.
- Teach patients to self-monitor—use Anger Logs to identify triggers, early warning signs, and develop a hierarchy of anger scenes based on self-monitoring.
- Engage the patient in collaborative goals-setting and enhance the patient's motivation to engage in treatment. (May involve significant others in treatment.)

Phase II—Skills acquisition and consolidation phase

- Collaborate with the patient to develop an action plan.
- Teach the patient self-control procedures such as emotion regulation, relaxation procedures, guided imagery, acceptance skills.
- Teach the patient cognitive modification and cognitive restructuring procedures such as self-instructional training and problem-solving skills (e.g., attentional refocusing skills, modifying expectations and appraisals).
- Teach the patients and have them practice conflict resolution and assertiveness skills.
- Have the patient consider anger and aggression in family of origin and developmentally with peers. Adopt a life-span perspective and have the patient consider what "lingers" from those experiences that impacts on present behavior. Consider what are the pros and cons of using angry and aggressive behaviors.
- Teach the patient how to engineer (select, create, and change) a social environment so that it supports nonaggressive behaviors.

Phase III—Application phase

- Have the patient practice coping skills while in the therapy session (imaginal and behavioral rehearsal).
- Have the patient perform graduated in vivo experiments to practice skills, namely,
  How to experience anger without reflexively acting out
  How to tolerate anger without immediate retaliation
  How to learn not to be afraid of angry feelings
- Ensure that the patient "takes credit" for change. The therapist should engage the patient in self-attribution activities.
- Include relapse prevention activities in the treatment process.
- Build-in the involvement of significant others and booster sessions.
- Do *not* "train and hope" for improvement; build into therapy the technology of generalization (as described by Meichenbaum, 2001).

In this manner, patients can learn how to:

1. "Deautomatize" the usual manner in which they respond to perceived provocations by developing cognitive, emotion-regulation, and behavioral skills.
2. Control anger by developing more appropriate interpersonal coping techniques.
3. Select, change, and create social environments that support assertive, but not aggressive, interpersonal repertoires.

There is much promise that effective interventions can be developed to prevent such violence. To learn more about empirically based treatment approaches that have been applied effectively along the entire life span, the interested reader can go to the following websites: *www.colorado.edu/cspv/blueprints* and *www.melissainstitute.org.*

See also: Adolescent aggression and anger management, Aggressive and antisocial behavior in youth, Anger—adult, Anger management therapy with adolescents, Disruptive anger

REFERENCES

Beck, R., & Fernandez, E. (1998). Cognitive–behavioral therapy in the treatment of anger: A meta-analysis. *Cognitive Therapy and Research, 22*, 63–75.

Bowman-Edmondson, C. B., & Cohen-Conger, J. C. (1996). A review of treatment efficacy for individuals with anger problems: Conceptual, assessment and methodological issues. *Clinical Psychological Review, 16*, 251–275.

Chemtob, C. M., Novaco, R. W., Hamada, R. S., & Gross, D. M. (1997). Cognitive–behavioral treatment for severe anger in post-traumatic stress disorder. *Journal of Consulting and Clinical Psychology, 65*, 184–189.

DiGiuseppe, R., & Tafrate, R. C. (2001). A comprehensive treatment model of anger disorders. *Psychotherapy: Theory, Research, Practice and Training, 36*, 262–271.

Gerlock, A. S. (1996). An anger management intervention model for veterans with PTSD. *NC-PTSD Clinical Quarterly, 6*, 61–64.

Holtzworth-Munroe, A. (2000). A typology of men who are violent toward their female partners: Making sense of the heterogeneity of husband violence. *Current Directions in Psychological Science, 9*, 160–170.

Meichenbaum, D. (1985). *Stress inoculation training: A practitioner's guidebook*. New York: Pergamon Press.

Meichenbaum, D. (2001). *Treatment of individuals with anger-control problems and aggressive behaviors: A clinical handbook*. Clearwater, FL: Institute Press.

Novaco, R. W. (1975). *Anger control: The development and evaluation of experimental treatment*. Lexington, MA: D. C. Heath.

Novaco, R. W. (1996). Anger treatment and its special challenges. *NC-PTSD Clinical Quarterly, 6*, 56–60

Reid, J. B., Patterson, G. R., & Snyder, J. (2002). *Antisocial behavior in children and adolescents*. Washington, DC: American Psychological Association.

Slep, A. M., & O'Leary, S. G. (2001). Examining partner and child abuse: Are we ready for a more integrated approach to family violence? *Clinical Child and Family Psychology Review, 4*, 87–107.

Sukhodolsky, D. G., & Kassinove, H. (1997). *Cognitive behavioral therapies for anger and aggression in youth: A meta-analytic review*. Poster presented at the 105th annual convention of the American Psychological Association, Chicago.

RECOMMENDED READINGS

Deffenbacher, J. L., & McKay, M. (2000). *Overcoming situational and general anger: Therapist protocol*. Oakland, CA: New Harbinger Publications.

Kassinove, H., & Tafrate, R. (2003). *Practitioner's guidebook to anger management*. Atascadero, CA: Impact Publishers.

Meichenbaum, D. (2001). *Treatment of individuals with anger-control problems and aggressive behaviors: A clinical handbook*. Clearwater, FL: Institute Press.

Anger Management Therapy with Adolescents

W. Rodney Hammond and Jennifer M. Wyatt

Keywords: anger management, anger control, adolescence, aggression, violence

Anger-control problems in adolescence are characterized by intense emotional reactions that, combined with cognitive distortions, high impulsivity, poor social skills, and a history of experience with aggression, often culminate in verbally or physically aggressive outbursts (Nelson & Finch, 2000). Poor anger management not only contributes to the likelihood of aggressive behavior, but also puts adolescents at increased risk for problems in school (e.g., failing classes, being expelled, or dropping out) and in the community (e.g., contact with juvenile or adult courts, and incarceration). In and of itself, anger generally does not necessitate treatment. The acting-out episodes are usually what draw the attention of parents and teachers, prompting a referral for some form of anger management therapy.

Characteristics of some adolescents and their environments make them more likely to experience intense anger, more likely to attend to anger feelings and cognitions, and more likely to act out as a result of anger (Feindler & Scalley, 1998). External risk factors include a history of witnessing or being victimized by aggression and a social environment that reinforces aggression, both of which imbue the adolescent with a schema of aggression as a viable and effective problem-solving technique. Internal risk factors include increased physiological reactivity, hostile attributional biases (the tendency to assume that others' behavior is driven by hostile intent), poor impulse control, and a lack of prosocial skills.

In order to be effective, treatment for anger-control problems needs to address all of these components in a manner palatable to adolescents. Feindler and Ecton (1986) published the first cognitive–behavioral approach to anger management with this population, which was an extension of Novaco's (1975) stress inoculation approach to anger management with adults. They argued that, given the normal developmental changes that occur during adolescence (including rejection of authoritarian rules and desire for increased autonomy), behavior modification programs that rely on external reinforcement would likely be met with resistance. A cognitive–behavioral approach to anger management, with a focus on reasoned decision-making over one's own behavior, would therefore be better suited to adolescents. In addition, the increased capacity for analytical thought and improved perspective-taking ability of adolescents would enable them to benefit from the cognitive skills acquisition components. As is common among cognitive–behavioral therapies, CBT for anger management with adolescents is composed of four modules: an educational phase, two skills acquisition phases, and a skills generalization phase. The educational phase includes instruction in identifying and understanding one's own anger patterns, with particular attention to how they follow an antecedent–behavior–consequence progression. For example, if an adolescent with anger management difficulties is falsely accused of stealing a classmate's lunch money (the antecedent), he may react with verbal and/or physical aggression (the behavior), and then be suspended for the aggression (the consequence). In such a situation, this adolescent is likely to blame the accuser for his suspension. By understanding these patterns, however, the emphasis can be shifted to how the adolescent's behavior is responsible for the consequence he received. During this phase, the therapist also focuses on fostering a therapeutic relationship with the client (by conveying the message that the therapist and client are united against the adolescent's maladaptive anger) and on providing the knowledge base necessary for the next component, which targets the cognitive aspects of anger.

The cognitive skills acquisition phase concentrates on teaching adolescents how to recognize and neutralize anger-escalating thoughts. Adolescents first learn how to identify their own anger "triggers" and how to change their cognitive appraisal of such situations, so that their emotional responses are less intense. Significant group time is devoted to the cognitive distortions frequently engaged in by adolescents with anger-control problems. Common distortions include feelings of being unfairly judged, a perceived lack of respect, and ignoring or misinterpreting social cues (Feindler, 1990; Yung & Hammond, 1998). For example, adolescents who have anger-control and aggression problems tend to assume that others' behavior is not only purposeful, but also malevolent, which further increases the likelihood that the adolescent will respond aggressively. Specific attention is paid to helping adolescents understand how their interpretation of others' intent fuels their own anger responses. Within this phase, adolescents are instructed on how to consider alternative nonhostile explanations for others' behavior, and shown how those alternative explanations help defuse their own anger. This phase also includes instruction on how the adolescents can use self-talk to reframe a situation to inhibit an aggressive impulse and to reinforce themselves for choosing not to act aggressively.

The third phase provides adolescents with behavioral skills to avert the progression from anger to aggression. One goal of this phase is to encourage adolescents to counteract the physiological symptoms of anger by teaching relaxation techniques that decrease the adolescent's general tendency to become angry (e.g., deep muscle relaxation, meditation) and techniques that decrease the level of situation-specific anger (e.g., deep breathing, backward counting). The physiological symptoms generally take the form of signals from the cardiovascular, endocrine, and/or neuromuscular systems, and often serve to facilitate aggressive actions (Feindler, 1990). By reducing or removing the potency of the autonomic response, the adolescent is able to make more reasoned decisions in difficult situations. The previously learned aggressive reactions to anger-provoking situations can then be replaced with more appropriate problem-solving responses, which are modeled for and practiced by the adolescents during treatment. The final component of this phase teaches prosocial skills that can be used to avert anger-produced aggressive situations. Some of the skills include those focused on proactively avoiding becoming enmeshed in a power struggle, such as how to make requests and state opinions assertively, but not aggressively. Other skills target behavioral responses that can deescalate a tense situation once it has begun, such as humor.

The ultimate goal of anger management therapy is to provide adolescents with the tools and capabilities to control their anger outside the therapeutic environment, the final phase programs for the generalization of learned techniques. Activities include behavioral rehearsal and role-play situations, and opportunities for adolescents to practice the new skills in their usual environment via homework assignments. These activities are a vital part of the program, for while adolescents' behavior may change during treatment, the adolescents' social environments may not (Nelson &

Finch, 2000). Providing them with the skills to manage naturally occurring situations also increases the likelihood that treatment gains will be maintained over time.

The early evaluations of adolescent anger management programs were reviewed by Feindler (1990), who concluded that group CBT had shown evidence of positive effects on problem-solving abilities, self-reported anger, behavior in role-playing situations, and external consequences for aggression. A later review (Feindler & Scalley, 1998) summarized the results of a dozen group treatment violence reduction programs that included anger management components. Significant effects were documented with youth in psychiatric facilities, detention centers, and residential treatment centers, as well as with at-risk youth in school settings. Beck and Fernandez (1998) conducted a meta-analysis of evaluations of CBT for anger management in adults, adolescents, and children. Effect sizes were computed for outcome measures of self-reported anger and behavioral ratings of anger or aggression, and an overall weighted mean effect size of .70 emerged. Of the 50 evaluations synthesized in their meta-analysis, 15 were specific to adolescents (including study samples of at-risk, clinical, and incarcerated youth). Reanalysis of their tabular data for those studies targeting only adolescents resulted in a weighted mean effect size of .65 (with a range of .22 to 1.20), providing further evidence for the effectiveness of this type of therapy with adolescents.

Recent developments in the use of CBT for anger management with adolescents have examined the generalizability of such programs beyond the samples and program formats with which they were originally tested. For example, Stern (1999) found that enhancing a family conflict-resolution treatment with a cognitive–behavioral anger management treatment resulted in more positive outcomes for adolescents and for their parents. Other researchers have investigated the utility of anger management techniques with nonclinical populations. The Responding in Peaceful and Positive Ways (RIPP) program incorporated cognitive–behavioral techniques for anger management into a broader school-based violence prevention program, and has shown positive effects on school disciplinary actions (Farrell, Meyer, & White, 2001). The Positive Adolescent Choices Training (PACT) program, designed to be a culturally sensitive approach to violence prevention with African American youth, has shown significant effects on a variety of variables related to physical aggression in school and violent and nonviolent criminal activity in the community (Yung & Hammond, 1998). Bosworth and colleagues (Bosworth, Espelage, DuBay, Daytner, & Karageorge, 2000) investigated an innovative delivery method of a standardized curriculum of violence prevention that included anger management components. A preliminary evaluation of their program, which is administered to individual students via computer, revealed significant effects on mediating variables such as attitudes and behavioral intentions. Although the original intent of CBT for anger management was for treatment of adolescents with diagnosed disorders, the results from these three programs suggest that anger management programs can be successfully integrated into primary and secondary prevention programs as well.

Cognitive–behavioral programs for adolescent anger management have been evaluated with different populations and by different investigators; however, some limitations still exist in the literature. The majority of the programs with published evaluations were conducted in a group format, so less is known about the effectiveness of these methods in individual therapy. In addition, little is known about which components or combination of components are necessary to produce reliable behavioral change. Existing programs have varied in their specific activities, but until controlled dismantling studies have been conducted, CBT for anger management with adolescents should still be used as a treatment package.

Aside from the limitations of the research, there is still ample evidence to support the use of cognitive–behavioral anger management programs. Future researchers should shift the field's focus to fine-tuning the model in order to promote optimal effectiveness. Investigations into the characteristics of adolescents who are most likely to benefit from anger management programs could provide clinicians with better information on which to base treatment and referral decisions, and could provide researchers with better information about variables that mediate and moderate the relation between anger and aggression. Greater attention to the generalization of learned skills would increase the likelihood that behavioral improvements would be sustained. Future research should also continue to explore the neurological causes and correlates of anger in adolescents, and if that knowledge can be used to improve CBT programs. Finally, evaluations should begin to include cost analyses, to determine how treatment dollars and hours can best be spent.

In summary, the cognitive–behavioral model posits that anger is activated, protracted, and intensified by the adolescents' thoughts and interpretations of others' behavior, which can lead to an aggressive outburst (Novaco, 1975). Aggressive behavior strengthens this link by inhibiting cognitive controls over behavior, maintaining heightened physiological arousal, and inviting aggressive responses from others. Cognitive–behavioral therapy for anger management with adolescents, therefore, focuses first on the cognitive distortions in order to break the cycle. Next, treatment includes behavioral skills such as relaxation, assertiveness, and problem solving, to help the adolescent prevent or diminish the experience of anger and subsequent aggressive responses. Treatment must also include activities to prepare adolescents for anger-provoking situations in their everyday environment. Research with group treatment models has provided evidence for positive effects on cognitive, affective, and behavioral measures. In addition, anger management components have been successfully integrated into other treatment and prevention programs. Future research can advance science and practice by seeking ways to improve the effectiveness of CBT for anger management with adolescents.

See also: Adolescent aggression and anger management, Anger—adult, Anger control problems

REFERENCES

Beck, R., & Fernandez, E. (1998). Cognitive–behavioral therapy in the treatment of anger: A meta-analysis. *Cognitive Therapy and Research, 22*, 63–74.

Bosworth, K., Espelage, D., DuBay, T., Daytner, G., & Karageorge, K. (2000). Preliminary evaluation of a multimedia violence prevention program for adolescents. *American Journal of Health Behavior, 24*, 268–280.

Farrell, A. D., Meyer, A. L., & White, K. S. (2001). Evaluation of Responding in Peaceful and Positive Ways (RIPP): A school-based prevention program for reducing violence among urban adolescents. *Journal of Clinical Child Psychology, 30*, 451–463.

Feindler, E. L. (1990). Adolescent anger control: Review and critique. In M. Hersen, R. M. Eisler, & P. M. Miller (Eds.), *Progress in behavior modification, Vol. 26* (pp. 11–59). Newbury Park, CA: Sage.

Feindler, E. L., & Ecton, R. B. (1986). *Adolescent anger control: Cognitive–behavioral techniques*. Elmsford, NY: Pergamon Press.

Feindler, E. L., & Scalley, M. (1998). Adolescent anger-management groups for violence reduction. In K. C. Stoiber & T. R. Kratochwill (Eds.), *Handbook of group interventions for children and families* (pp. 100–119). Needham Heights, MA: Allyn & Bacon.

Nelson, W. M., III, & Finch, A. J., Jr. (2000). Managing anger in youth: A cognitive–behavioral approach. In P. C. Kendall (Ed.), *Child and adolescent therapy: Cognitive–behavioral procedures* (2nd ed., pp. 129–170). New York: Guilford Press.

Novaco, R. W. (1975). *Anger control: The development and evaluation of an experimental treatment*. Lexington, MA: Lexington Books.

Stern, S. B. (1999). Anger management in parent–adolescent conflict. *American Journal of Family Therapy, 27*, 181–193.

Yung, B. R., & Hammond, W. R. (1998). Breaking the cycle: A culturally sensitive violence prevention program for African-American children and adolescents. In J. R. Lutzker (Ed.), *Handbook of child abuse research and treatment* (pp. 319–340). New York: Plenum Press.

RECOMMENDED READINGS

Dodge, K. A., & Schwartz, D. (1997). Social information processing mechanisms in aggressive behavior. In D. M. Stoff, J. Breiling, & J. D. Maser (Eds.), *Handbook of antisocial behavior* (pp. 171–180). New York: Wiley.

Furlong, M. J., & Smith, D. C. (Eds.). (1994). *Anger, hostility, and aggression: Assessment, prevention, and intervention strategies for youth*. Brandon, VT: Clinical Psychology Publishing.

Goldstein, A. P., & Glick, B. (1987). *Aggression Replacement Training: A comprehensive intervention for aggressive youth*. Champaign, IL: Research Press.

Anorexia Nervosa

Diane L. Spangler and Heather D. Hoyal

Keywords: anorexia nervosa, cognitive behavioral therapy

Cognitive–behavioral therapy (CBT) for anorexia nervosa (AN) is similar to that for bulimia nervosa, but, much less has been written regarding the cognitive–behavioral approach to AN. Treatment development and evaluation for AN has been slower than that for other eating disorders likely due to the ego-syntonic and intractable nature of AN. Current CBT treatments for AN draw on a cognitive–behavioral model of the precipitation and maintenance of the disorder, and are practiced with particular emphasis on the motivation and physical health of the client.

COGNITIVE-BEHAVIORAL MODEL OF ANOREXIA PRECIPITATION AND MAINTENANCE

Vitousek and Ewald (1993) proposed a cognitive–behavioral model that highlights common pathways in the precipitation and maintenance of AN. According to the theory, a confluence of individual variables (e.g., perfectionism, low self-esteem, compliance, preference for simplicity), sociocultural variables (i.e., an environment that equates thinness with beauty and worth), and personal stressors (e.g., loss, failure, onset of puberty or young adulthood) combine to create dysfunctional beliefs regarding weight and shape that center around the theme that thinness and weight control are key to solving life's problems and achieving success. Consequent to such beliefs, behaviors designed to control weight and shape ensue, such as dieting, excessive exercise, or purging. Restrictive eating is maintained through both positive reinforcement resulting from attention from others and a personal sense of achievement, superiority, or self-mastery, and through negative reinforcement resulting from the avoidance of intense anxiety associated with real or potential weight gain. In addition, schema-confirming processes such as selective attention and confirmatory bias along with the cognitive deficits resulting from starvation itself maintain the disorder.

Recently, Fairburn, Shafran, and Cooper (1999) suggested additional ways in which AN is maintained that highlight the issue of control. They propose that the need for and perceived attainment of control across three feedback-driven domains may be sufficient to maintain AN. These feedback domains are: (1) control over eating which becomes a convenient and tangible index of self-control and thus self-worth, (2) hunger due to dietary restriction, which is viewed as a threat to self-control thus increasing attempts to control, and (3) weight loss, which becomes a separate index of self-control and self-worth especially in cultures where thinness is highly valued and equated with self-control.

ANOREXIA TREATMENT

Vitousek (formerly Bemis) has been the most prominent theorist with respect to cognitive–behavioral treatment for AN. In her treatment model, motivation becomes a focal point in therapy as most AN clients do not seek help voluntarily. Motivational and empathetic interventions are interwoven throughout treatment, which is designed to eliminate self-starvation, reduce dysfunctional attitudes regarding weight, shape, and worth, increase personal efficacy, and prevent relapse. Because of the significant resistance to change in persons with AN and the intermittent need for hospitalization, CBT for AN usually lasts from 1 to 2 years and is divided into four stages (Garner, Vitousek, & Pike, 1997).

Stage 1

The foci of Stage 1 include the establishment of a strong alliance and the enhancement of client motivation for change. This stage is considered foundational since AN clients often enter therapy only under duress. Therapists attempt to establish an alliance and motivation through thought and feeling empathy, collaboration, respect for the client's individuality, and appreciation of the ego-syntonic nature of thinness and self-control (Vitousek, Watson, & Wilson, 1998). This includes (but is not limited to) cataloging how weight control strategies fulfill important functions for clients as well as hinder others, and the consideration of thinness as a life goal relative to other life goals. Client attempts to manipulate or resist treatment are viewed as attempts to maintain their preexisting thinness- and control-related values and schemata.

In concert with appreciation of the client's ego-syntonic view of AN, motivation is enhanced through psychoeducation regarding metabolism, nutrition, body weight, and the effects of dietary restriction. This information is used to illustrate how the symptoms of AN may be responsible for more of the client's distress than she had previously thought, to highlight the dangers of AN, or to depathologize some client behaviors by reframing them as natural responses to starvation.

Stage 2

The primary goal of Stage 2 is the normalization of eating pattern and body weight. Once a collaborative relationship and adequate motivation have been established, the therapist educates the client about a healthy body mass index and instructs the client to record her weight weekly. In addition, the client is instructed in self-monitoring and is given daily food records on which to log everything eaten or purged, laxatives taken, as well as thoughts and feelings elicited by these behaviors. Steady increases in the type, amount, and frequency of food eaten are then undertaken. Daily calorie intake guidelines (no lower than 1500 calories/day) and weekly weight gain goals (typically 1–2 pounds/week) are set and worked toward until the client reaches a weight at which menses resumes and dieting is not needed to maintain the weight. Some methods used for eating pattern modification include well-planned exposure to forbidden food types and amounts, delaying purging behaviors, distraction from disturbing thoughts while eating, and engagement in pleasant activities following eating. Treatment proceeds on an outpatient basis as long as a minimal weight threshold is maintained, and regular medical checkups are attended. When hospitalization is considered, a client may be given the opportunity to obtain a specific weight-gain goal in order to avoid hospitalization, but if she persists at a dangerously low weight, she is referred for inpatient treatment.

Stage 3

The focus of Stage 3 is the identification, evaluation, and modification of beliefs about weight, food, and self. Many of these beliefs emerge during the weight change interventions in Stage 2. The therapist's position is one of curiosity about the client's assumptions and predictions about weight gain and idiosyncratic "rule violations." New behaviors are presented as experiments, the purpose of which is to test the client's negative predictions. Other methods for modifying beliefs are cost–benefit analysis, decatastrophizing, decentering, and Socratic questioning of the client's assumptions. Through the use of a downward arrow, the client's core beliefs about the self can be more fully explicated. Particular attention is paid to the client's personal values. Clients often view their AN symptoms as the embodiment of these values. However, inconsistencies usually exist between personal values and the consequences and outcomes of AN. These inconsistencies between client values, life goals, and AN consequences are underscored while alternative more functional strategies for life goal attainment are explored (Vitousek et al., 1998).

Stage 4

The primary goals of Stage 4 are preparing the client for termination and preventing relapse. During Stage 4, the course of therapy is summarized and clients are encouraged to review improvement in functioning as well as areas of continued vulnerability and to discuss the methods that have been most personally helpful. In addition, a plan is generated for combating returning symptoms. This plan is tailored to target specific trouble spots the client may have encountered during treatment. Clients are encouraged to reframe a relapse as a "slip" and to immediately renew commitment to recovery and return to regular eating (Vitousek, 1996). In addition, critical points at which a return to treatment would be indicated are discussed.

With regard to these stages of treatment, it is important to note that recovery from AN has been described as occurring in a spiral pattern with recurrent gains and setbacks. Therefore, the four stages are often not discrete across time. Motivational issues, in particular, must often be revisited. For these reasons, persistence, patience, and imperturbability (mostly on the part of the therapist) are considered key to successful outcomes.

EMPIRICAL STATUS OF CBT FOR ANOREXIA NERVOSA

Empirical investigations of the efficacy of CBT for AN are just beginning to appear in the literature. Currently, only two controlled trials of CBT for AN have been published. Serfaty, Turkington, Heap, Ledsham, and Jolley (1999) randomized 35 persons with AN to either CBT or nutritional counseling. After 6 months of treatment, dropout rates were 8% for CBT and 100% for nutritional counseling. Those receiving CBT showed significant increases in body mass index, and significant decreases in eating disorder symptomatology and depression. Of those who completed CBT, 70% no longer met diagnostic criteria for AN. Adding to these findings, Vitousek (2002) described an unpublished study comparing CBT to nutritional counseling with medical management in the treatment of AN. Similar to Serfaty et al. (1999), fewer patients in the CBT condition dropped out (27% versus 53%) and more met criteria for "good" outcome at the end of treatment (44% versus 6%).

In contrast, Channon, De Silva, Hemsely, and Perkins (1989) reported no overall advantage of CBT over behavior therapy or treatment as usual. However, the Channon et al. study suffered from a low sample size of only eight patients per treatment condition resulting in very low power to detect treatment differences as well as problems with randomization and CBT treatment fidelity (see Vitousek, 1996). Despite the low number of subjects in the Channon et al. study, some isolated and somewhat inconsistent group differences emerged at various follow-up assessments. Overall, those in the CBT condition attended a greater number of sessions and were less likely to drop out of treatment. Those in the CBT condition also showed significantly higher gains in psychosexual and interpersonal functioning at the 6-month follow-up although all treatments showed similar gains in body weight.

Across all three of these studies of individual, outpatient CBT for AN, CBT produced significantly greater retention of patients as well as significant advantages on some outcome variables. The finding of higher retention rates for CBT compared to other forms of treatment is noteworthy given the low motivation for and resistance to any form of treatment that is typical of persons with AN. Although preliminary, these studies support the potential and continued investigation of CBT for AN.

One recent study examined the efficacy of CBT delivered in a 10-week group format using a pre–post design (Leung, Waller, & Thomas, 1999). No significant changes in eating disorder symptoms were observed during the 10-week group treatment. However, the *exclusive* use of group approaches to the treatment of AN has been specifically discouraged by those who have developed CBT protocols for AN, as have short-term treatment protocols (e.g., Vitousek, 2002). Thus, the finding of limited symptom change over 10 weeks of group treatment is not particularly surprising. Furthermore, given the specific recommendation against group-delivered CBT for persons with AN, it may be the case that findings from studies of group CBT for AN do not generalize well to outcome for CBT delivered in a one-on-one, individualized format.

FUTURE DIRECTIONS IN CBT FOR ANOREXIA NERVOSA

Treatment Evaluation

Evaluation of the efficacy of CBT for AN is in the beginning stages. As noted above, few comparative trials of CBT for AN have been conducted. Evaluating short- and long-term response rates via additional controlled studies is the first priority for future CBT studies of AN. The execution of such studies will be hampered by several methodological challenges. The reluctance of persons with AN to engage in treatment at all, let alone in research protocols, is a formidable challenge. Indeed, *all* existing studies of CBT for AN suffer from low numbers of subjects and hence low power, with some studies being more extreme than others. Obtaining large enough sample sizes to ensure adequate power to detect treatment effects is paramount. Based on the recovery rate found in their study, Serfaty et al. (1999) estimated that a minimum of 136 persons with AN would be required if equally divided into two treatment comparison groups. The development of adequate and safe control conditions presents another challenge. Use of wait-list controls has been criticized as unsafe due to the physical health risks of AN. The few existing controlled studies of CBT efficacy had large dropout rates in the control conditions attesting to the difficulty of establishing a credible control condition. At present, there are few outcome studies examining any type of treatment for AN, and no recognized treatment of choice. In addition, AN patients frequently require full or partial hospitalization while undergoing psychotherapy, which can confound findings of potential psychotherapy effects.

If, despite these methodological challenges, significant therapeutic outcome for CBT for AN is demonstrated and replicated, then greater attention to the mechanisms of action would be warranted. Initial studies suggest that CBT has greater retention rates than other forms of treatment; thus, one avenue for mechanism research would be to investigate how CBT increases motivation for treatment and treatment compliance. Those techniques used to purportedly establish and enhance AN client motivation and engagement in CBT would arguably be one of the most important mechanisms to study given the reluctance for treatment typical of AN. Other mechanisms of interest include examining the extent to which behavioral interventions increase food consumption and body mass index, and the extent to which cognitive interventions decrease dysfunctional beliefs and desire for control.

Treatment Development

Any modifications or additions to the initial CBT protocol for AN would ideally build on outcome and process study findings. Given the lack of such studies, significant modifications to the existing CBT protocol are likely premature at this point. However, some suggestions for plausible improvements to the existing protocol include the incorporation of motivational interviewing techniques, the incorporation of greater focus on early maladaptive schemas, and the incorporation of acceptance-based interventions.

See also: Body dysmorphia 1, Body dysmorphia 2, Bulimia nervosa, Dialectical behavior therapy for eating disorders

REFERENCES

Channon, S., De Silva, P., Hemsely, D., & Perkins, R. (1989). A controlled trial of cognitive–behavioural and behavioural treatment of anorexia nervosa. *Behavior Research and Therapy, 27*, 529–535.

Fairburn, C. G., Shafran, R., & Cooper, Z. (1999). A cognitive behavioural theory of anorexia nervosa. *Behaviour Research and Therapy, 37*, 1–13.

Garner, D. M., & Bemis, K. (1982). A cognitive–behavioral approach to anorexia nervosa. *Cognitive Therapy and Research, 6*, 123–150.

Garner, D. M., Vitousek, K., & Pike, K. M. (1997). Cognitive–behavioral therapy for anorexia nervosa. In D. M. Garner & P. E.Garfinkel (Eds.), *Handbook of treatment for eating disorders* (2nd ed., pp. 94–144). New York: Guilford Press.

Leung, N., Waller, G., & Thomas, G. (1999). Group cognitive–behavioural therapy for anorexia nervosa: A case for treatment? *European Eating Disorders Review, 7*, 351–361.

Serfaty, M., Turkington, D., Heap, M., Ledsham, L., & Jolley, E. (1999). Cognitive therapy versus dietary counselling in the outpatient treatment of anorexia nervosa: Effects of the treatment phase. *European Eating Disorders Review, 7*, 334–350.

Vitousek, K. (1996). The current status of cognitive–behavioral models of anorexia and bulimia nervosa. In P. M. Salkovskis (Ed.), *Frontiers of cognitive therapy* (pp. 383–418). New York: Guilford Press.

Vitousek, K. (2002). Cognitive–behavioral therapy for anorexia nervosa. In C. G. Fairburn & K. D. Brownell (Eds.), *Eating disorders and obesity* (pp. 308–313). New York: Guilford Press.

Vitousek, K., & Ewald, L. S. (1993). Self-representation in eating disorders: A cognitive perspective. In Z. Segal & S. Blau (Eds.), *The self in emotional distress: Cognitive and psychodynamic perspectives* (pp. 221–257). New York: Guilford Press.

Vitousek, K., Watson, S., & Wilson, G. T. (1998). Enhancing motivation for change in treatment-resistant eating disorders. *Clinical Psychology Review, 18*, 391–420.

Anxiety—Adult

Elizabeth A. Meadows and Jennifer Butcher

Keywords: anxiety, exposure, cognitive challenging, psychoeducation, relaxation

Anxiety is among the first emotions humans experience, and it is a familiar experience for most people. Anxiety developed to aid the body in reacting quickly to perceived danger, and humans likely would not have survived without it. The critical physical mechanism of anxiety is the fight-or-flight response, autonomic arousal that prepares the body to confront or flee from danger. This arousal leads to the physical feelings familiar to most people including racing heart, rapid breathing, and sweating.

Anxiety is useful because it helps people perform at their peak level. Research has consistently shown that people perform better when they experience some anxiety rather than none at all. It also allows people to make quick decisions regarding potentially dangerous situations. For example, it may keep someone from walking into a dark alley late at night, or jump quickly out of the way of a car.

However, just as a lack of anxiety can lead to poor performance, an excess of anxiety can also inhibit people from functioning at a high level. When anxiety becomes extreme or a chronic part of people's lives, it has transitioned from a useful indicator of danger into a maladaptive reaction.

An example of this transformation would occur if a person feared not only dark alleys at night but also safe shopping malls on Saturday afternoons.

The Anxiety Disorders category of the *Diagnostic and Statistical Manual of Mental Disorders, Fourth Edition–Text Revision* (DSM-IV-TR) includes a number of separate disorders. These disorders share the common feature of excessive or irrational anxiety, and they differ as to what prompts the anxiety, or how one reacts to it. For example, Panic Disorder is characterized by panic attacks, sudden rushes of intense fear and physical sensations, that seem to come from out of the blue. Panic Disorder is often accompanied by Agoraphobia, avoidance of situations related to those out-of-the-blue panic attacks. Someone who has panic attacks or strong anxiety in response to a specific situation, however, would be diagnosed with Specific Phobia (e.g., a fear of heights, or of dogs); if the fear was of social interactions, of negative evaluation by others, the diagnosis would be Social Phobia. Other anxiety disorders include Generalized Anxiety Disorder, excessive and uncontrollable worrying; Obsessive–Compulsive Disorder, intrusive repetitive thoughts or images and engaging in specific behaviors to neutralize those thoughts (e.g., repetitive handwashing to reduce thoughts of being contaminated); Post-Traumatic Stress Disorder (PTSD), symptoms such as reexperiencing and avoidance that stem from a traumatic event and have persisted for at least a month; and Acute Stress Disorder, symptoms such as emotional numbing that arise shortly following a traumatic event.

Because everyone experiences some anxiety, and because some anxiety is normal, not all experiences of anxiety are classified as anxiety disorders. However, when the anxiety becomes highly distressing and/or interferes with one's functioning, therapy may be needed to reduce these feelings.

COGNITIVE-BEHAVIORAL THERAPY FOR ANXIETY DISORDERS

Cognitive–behavioral therapy is the most empirically supported psychosocial treatment for anxiety disorders. The cognitive–behavioral understanding of anxiety disorders is largely based on learning theory. Mowrer's two-factor theory suggests that anxiety disorders are created initially via classical conditioning, and then maintained via operant conditioning. According to this theory, anxiety develops when a neutral stimulus becomes paired with an aversive response. For example, someone who was bitten by a spider begins to pair the concept of "spider" with anxious feelings through classical conditioning. The person then realizes that he or she feels better by avoiding spiders, and the drop in anxiety that follows that avoidance acts as a negative reinforcer, increasing the likelihood that the person will continue to avoid spiders in the future.

Cognitive factors can also play a large role in the development and maintenance of anxiety disorders, because in addition to learned associations, anxiety can also result from people's perceptions of a given situation. For example, while one person bitten by a spider may begin to think of all spiders as dangerous, another might instead note that the bite was annoying, but not particularly dangerous, because the spider wasn't poisonous. The first person might then be expected to develop a spider phobia, due in part to the perception that the spider bite was dangerous, while the second person develops no such disorder.

Cognitive–behavioral treatments for anxiety disorders generally directly target the hypothesized causal and especially maintaining factors. Treatment usually focuses on physiological, behavioral, and cognitive responses of anxiety. There are a number of manualized treatment packages that have been developed to target specific anxiety disorders, and these have generally been shown to be quite effective in reducing or eliminating the symptoms of the targeted disorder. The treatments vary somewhat depending on the anxiety disorder, but most share many common features including the use of exposure, cognitive challenging, relaxation, and psychoeducation.

EXPOSURE

Exposure is generally considered the treatment of choice for anxiety disorders, and is a major component of most empirically supported anxiety treatments. It involves confronting anxiety-provoking stimuli in a controlled way until anxiety is reduced, to end the tendency to avoid anxious feelings or stimuli. In addition, exposure helps clients realize that their anxiety will eventually decrease even without avoidance and that their unrealistic, negative beliefs are not true. Treatment is generally based on a hierarchy of anxiety-provoking situations, and can either be done gradually, where less distressing situations are mastered before moving on to harder ones, or through flooding, where the person is immediately confronted with the most anxiety-producing stimuli.

Three main types of exposure are generally used for the treatment of anxiety. The first is imaginal exposure. In imaginal exposure, clients imagine themselves in fear-producing situations. Imaginal exposure is used most often in situations such as PTSD where the anxiety-producing situation cannot be reproduced and when it is the memories of the event that are frightening to the person. Imaginal exposure can also be used in the treatment of other disorders as an early hierarchy item, and it can help to familiarize people with the process of exposure.

The second type is *in vivo* exposure, which refers to real-life exposure. This is where the person confronts the anxiety-producing stimuli explicitly either in the therapy session or during exposure exercises outside of treatment. Examples may include treatment for a Specific Phobia to dogs where a dog is brought into treatment, or having a person with Social Phobia call someone from his/her class.

The third type is interoceptive exposure, which is designed to lessen fears of bodily sensations by systematically and repeatedly inducing them, such as by spinning in a chair to induce dizziness. It is often used to treat Panic Disorder because in this disorder it is one's own physical sensations that are feared.

For some anxiety disorders, exposure is combined with various forms of response prevention in order to break the association between feelings of anxiety and a learned response. For example, many people with anxiety learn to associate certain behaviors, places, or people with safety. Some people with Agoraphobia feel less anxious going far from home if they have a cell phone with them to call for help; exposure in this case would involve not leaving home, but doing so without the cell phone. Distraction is another response to anxiety that is prevented in exposure therapy; instead, clients are instructed to fully experience the feelings of anxiety that are produced during the exposure exercises. Finally, a more formal type of response prevention is used in treating Obsessive–Compulsive Disorder, in which compulsions that serve to reduce anxiety are part of the disorder. In this treatment, prolonged exposure to the obsessions (e.g., by touching something one fears is contaminated) is combined with response prevention in which the compulsion is prohibited (e.g., no handwashing).

COGNITIVE CHALLENGING

Cognitive challenging is another useful treatment for anxiety disorders. Cognitive challenging is based on the assumption that thoughts play a powerful role in producing and maintaining anxiety, as in the spider bite example discussed earlier. The theory behind cognitive challenging suggests that people develop automatic thoughts that are often inaccurate. These thoughts are called automatic because people are usually unaware of them. A common automatic thought may be "If I have a panic attack in the store, I will pass out and no one will help me." During cognitive challenging, clients are taught to recognize automatic thoughts, test their accuracy, and challenge thoughts that are inaccurate or unhelpful.

Using the example above, cognitive challenging would be done by first identifying the specific automatic thoughts, which in this case include (1) having a panic attack in the store, (2) passing out, and (3) not being helped. These thoughts are then examined for their accuracy. In examining the likelihood of having a panic attack, questions such as "How often have you been to the store before? How many of those times have you panicked? How many have you not panicked?" might reveal that in fact the likelihood of panicking in the store is quite high, and thus that that thought is not particularly inaccurate. In examining the likelihood of passing out, questions such as "Have you ever passed out from a panic attack?" may show that passing out isn't nearly as likely as the client is assuming. Finally, questions such as "Would you help someone?" or "Have you ever seen someone who needed help ignored?" may suggest that the probability of being left alone passed out on the floor is really quite low. Thus, while it may be likely that the client will have a panic attack, the feared consequences of that attack aren't nearly as likely as the automatic thoughts suggested. In addition, clients are taught to evaluate whether their feared consequences would really be so bad. For example, in this case, the consequences may be that the client would get bruises from falling, or be embarrassed by passing out in public, but that both of these are manageable and tolerable situations with no lasting harm.

Automatic thoughts may fall into two general categories, maladaptive thoughts and irrational thinking. Maladaptive thoughts are those that seem logical; however, focusing on them increases anxiety and supports irrational thoughts. Common categories of maladaptive thoughts in anxiety include cognitive avoidance and rumination. Cognitive avoidance is too little focus on anxiety-producing thoughts. These thoughts are avoided at all costs, to the extent that the client may not perceive the source of anxiety. Rumination is in some ways the opposite of cognitive avoidance: repetitive, intrusive anxious thoughts that do not help decrease anxiety. Rumination is commonly seen in clients with Generalized Anxiety Disorder, who may, for example, spend all day worrying about paying bills without actually putting a check in the mail. Cognitive avoidance and rumination are not mutually exclusive, and people with anxiety often alternate between the two.

A second category of automatic thoughts is irrational thinking. For example, someone with PTSD might think, "I was assaulted in a parking lot; therefore, parking lots are dangerous," an example of overgeneralizing. Catastrophizing, a common type of irrational thinking in anxiety, is the tendency to think that something is intolerable or unbearable. Using the panic attack example from earlier, the thought that passing out would be a horrible thing is an example of catastrophizing; it might not be pleasant, but it's not as awful a possibility as the person initially assumed. Two other common types of irrational thoughts are mind reading, when someone infers what another person is thinking, often assuming something negative while ignoring other possibilities, and emotional reasoning, when people make inferences about something based on their feelings, such as "Because I am scared driving over this bridge, the bridge must be dangerous." In all of these cases, the key to change is in realizing that thoughts and feelings are not facts, and need not be acted on as if they were. By identifying the specific thoughts, and evaluating their accuracy and utility, people can begin to challenge irrational or unhelpful thoughts, leading to less anxiety.

METHODS OF PHYSICAL CONTROL

Another common method used in CBT for anxiety is physical relaxation, which can be especially useful because of the large physical component of anxiety, and because relaxation methods are often fairly easy to learn and use. Breathing retraining is one such method. People often begin hyperventilating when they become anxious. This irregular breathing leads to decreases in the amount of carbon dioxide in the person's body, which leads to symptoms such as breathlessness and dizziness. Breathing retraining teaches clients to take long, slow diaphragmatic breaths in order to combat the symptoms associated with hyperventilation. Clients generally learn to slow their breathing by pacing it to a count by the therapist, who slowly counts out the time to inhale and the time to exhale. Breathing retraining can often be learned effectively in an initial treatment session, providing not only a tool to be practiced for times of higher anxiety, but also giving the client a feeling of immediate control.

Another method of physical control is progressive muscle relaxation (PMR). Anxiety evolved to prepare the body to complete some action, so when anxiety occurs, the body becomes alert. However, when people feel continuous anxiety, their bodies continuously remain at a high level of alertness. As a result of this alertness, the muscles of the body remain tense, which can lead to muscle aches and soreness as the body tires. PMR teaches clients to recognize when their muscles are tense and to consciously relax them. In PMR, clients systematically tense and relax the various muscles in their bodies, often doing so in increasing groupings over time (so that, for example, initially each muscle is tensed separately, and later, four or eight muscles at a time are tensed). This technique is often used for Generalized Anxiety Disorder because muscle tension is one of its prominent symptoms, but it can be useful for other anxiety disorders as well.

PSYCHOEDUCATION

Psychoeducation is a critical part of cognitive–behavioral treatment for anxiety. Simply helping clients understand why they are experiencing symptoms and that others have them as well can make the symptoms less frightening. Psychoeducation also provides a rationale for treatment.

Psychoeducation typically involves defining anxiety according to three components: thoughts, behavior, and physical. This makes the problem seem less overwhelming and helps organize treatment by focusing on each of these components. The nature and reason for anxiety is often discussed in psychoeducation, so that clients understand the universality of the emotion, and its importance as a survival mechanism. Finally, psychoeducation helps clients realize that their symptoms are not insurmountable and that therapy involves treatment methods that make rational sense.

FUTURE DIRECTIONS

Cognitive–behavioral treatments for anxiety disorders have been empirically supported as effective in reducing anxiety symptoms. While these treatments have generally been targeted to specific disorders, a more recent trend has been to focus on commonalities among anxiety disorders, so that treatments can address these commonalities across diagnoses rather than using a different treatment package for each disorder. Clinical researchers have also been making strides in expanding the CBT packages that are available to additional populations, such as tailoring them to children, or to people with multiple diagnoses (such as those with both anxiety and substance abuse problems), and in disseminating these treatments to a broader range of clinicians.

See also: Anxiety/anger management training (AMT), Anxiety—Children, Anxiety in Children—FRIENDS program, Exposure therapy, Generalized anxiety disorder, Social anxiety disorder 1, Social anxiety disorder 2

RECOMMENDED READINGS

Antony, M. M., Orsillo, S. M., & Roemer, L. (2001). *Practitioner's guide to empirically based measures of anxiety*. New York: Kluwer Academic/Plenum.

Barlow, D. H. (2004). *Anxiety and its disorders* (2nd ed.). New York: Guilford Press.

Morris, T. L. & March, J. S. (2004). *Anxiety disorders in children and adolescents* (2nd ed.). New York: Guilford Press.

Anxiety/Anger Management Training (AMT)

Richard M. Suinn and Jerry L. Deffenbacher

Keywords: anxiety, anger management

Both anxiety and anger conditions can impair performance, influence health, or lead to psychological disorders. High anxiety affects academic work, mathematics learning, test taking, public speaking, and sport performance. Anxiety can be an obstacle to psychotherapy and increases vulnerability to physical illness.

Uncontrolled anger can have negative outcomes such as loss of employment, or family disruption. Anger can precipitate risk-taking/impulsive behaviors leading to self-injurious behaviors, property damage, and school or workplace violence. Finally, anger increases a person's vulnerability to physical illness. Although there is no current formal diagnostic category for anger, dysfunctional anger is associated with intermittent explosive disorder, posttraumatic stress disorder (PTSD), depression, impulse control disorders, and a number of personality disorders.

Anxiety/Anger Management Training (AMT) is a brief, structured intervention that is a proven intervention for both anxiety and anger and related conditions.

THE ANXIETY/ANGER MANAGEMENT TRAINING PROGRAM

In the early 1970s, Anxiety Management Training was developed as a behavioral alternative for treatment of Generalized Anxiety Disorder (GAD). Over the years, research documented its efficacy for GAD, phobic disorders, PTSD, and other conditions with anxiety as a primary factor, such as tension headaches, essential hypertension, dysmenorrhea, test or mathematics anxiety, and athletic or artistic performance. In 1986, the basic AMT approach was used for anger management. Since then, numerous studies have confirmed the appropriateness of AMT for anger. Hence, AMT can be viewed as a cognitive–behavioral intervention for either anxiety or anger management.

AMT is based on the learning principle that conceptualizes anxiety as a drive state such that individuals can learn behaviors that eliminate the drive. In essence, anxiety is viewed as having stimulus properties to which new behaviors can be linked, such as coping responses. AMT is founded on the view that clients can be taught: first, to identify their personal signs—physical, emotional, cognitive, behavioral—that signal the onset of anxiety or anger and then, to react to these signs using coping cognitive–behavioral responses that remove the emotionality.

The use of AMT for either anxiety or anger states recognizes that these emotional states have much in common. Both involve levels of arousal. Clients can be taught to recognize signs of arousal and use them to cue coping skills. Control of each involves a type of impulse control. AMT aims at gaining control by deactivating the arousal, whether anxiety arousal or anger arousal.

It is noteworthy that where anxiety has no specific focus, then the diagnosis of GAD is appropriate. However, anxiety can be directly linked to specific stimulus precipitants, such as in phobic disorders. Similarly, anger can be unfocused, in which case the individual is unpredictable about when the anger is precipitated. However, for some, the anger is specifically prompted such as in child abuse or angry drivers. AMT results are not dependent on the specificity of precipitants; hence, this intervention is appropriate for focused or unfocused arousal states.

DESCRIPTION OF AMT

AMT is a six- to eight-session structured exposure–relaxation procedure. AMT aims at self-regulation through gradually requiring the client to assume more and more responsibility for deactivating the arousal. Core characteristics include guided imagery, anxiety or anger arousal, use of relaxation and cognitive techniques for emotional deactivation or prevention, and transfer of such coping to the external environment. Self-monitoring and homework are also included.

Guided imagery is used to precipitate anxiety or anger arousal during sessions, in order for the client to practice use of coping responses to eliminate the arousal, i.e., to deactivate the arousal. Clients are not required to identify the causes or stimuli that precipitate the anxiety or anger. For example, a client suffering from GAD need only recall clearly an event such as, "The last time I became extremely anxious involved a discussion with my spouse which ended in our arguing. We were talking about ___, and I was saying ___. At this point I was overwhelmed by feelings that got in my way. … "

Later, clients also are taught to become aware of their initial arousal and to identify the early warning signals that anxiety or anger is developing. As the sessions proceed, the coping is activated to these early signals, as a means of controlling the anxiety or anger before the emotion builds to an uncontrollable level, i.e., in effect a prevention step (Deffenbacher, Filetti, Lynch, Dahler & Oetting, 2002; Deffenbacher & Stark, 1992). Such early signs might be physiological, emotional, behavioral, or cognitive and these signs are used to prompt the deactivation through relaxation responses.

Termination attends to steps to maintain the emotional control and to prevent relapse. For some clients, gaining control over the emotional arousal is sufficient to resolve dysfunctional consequences and allows them to access and deploy other social, interpersonal, and problem-solving skills so that no further intervention is necessary. For others, additional interventions are needed (see section on integration of AMT with other interventions).

OUTCOME RESEARCH: EVIDENCE OF AMT AS AN EMPIRICALLY SUPPORTED INTERVENTION

The efficacy of AMT with a variety of disorders and problems has received considerable research support (see Suinn, 1990, and Suinn & Deffenbacher, 1988, for review).

AMT was developed to address general anxiety and stress. AMT effectively lowers high-anxiety conditions such as high trait anxiety, GAD, PTSD, panic disorder, high levels of generalized tension and stress, and multiple sources of stress. For example, AMT reduced anxiety and use of anxiety medication in patients with GAD; lowered anxiety, avoidance, and intrusions of trauma memories in veterans suffering from PTSD; and reduced general anxiety and anger in schizophrenic outpatients while improving these patients' overall psychiatric status. Thus, AMT appears applicable and effective with highly anxious, stressed populations including those with severe pathology.

AMT also successfully reduces phobias and situational anxieties such as test, math, and public speaking anxieties. For example, AMT lowered mathematics anxiety and improved math performance in math-anxious university students. AMT is also effective with other performance anxieties (e.g., music or athletic performance), even when the level of anxiety is not sufficient to warrant a diagnosable social phobia. Moreover, AMT lowered anxiety and indecision in vocationally undecided college students. Together, such research shows AMT is effective with situational anxieties and performance problems.

AMT is also of value with patients suffering from physical diseases associated with stress. For example, AMT lowered anxiety and stress in generally anxious and stressed medical outpatients and was of help to patients with conditions such as diabetes, Type A behavior, essential hypertension, painful menstruation, and other gynecological conditions. AMT also has potential for training preventive coping skills. For example, AMT can be valuable in teaching relaxation coping skills to deal with distressing, uncomfortable, or painful medical procedures.

AMT is effective with other high-arousal emotional states. For example, AMT effectively lowered both general anger and specific sources of anger such as anger while driving. In applying AMT to other dysfunctional emotions, procedures remain essentially the same, except that emotion-relevant (e.g., anger) scenes rather than anxiety or stress scenes are employed to arouse emotion and train the application of relaxation coping skills.

Throughout outcome research, AMT was significantly more effective than no treatment, simple relaxation, and placebo control conditions. AMT effects have been maintained or slightly increased over short- and long-term follow-ups. When nontargeted measures (e.g., other sources of anxiety, anger, and depression) were included, AMT demonstrated generalization effects, i.e., AMT not only reduced problems that were the focus of treatment, but showed transfer effects to other problems as well. AMT was also generally as effective as other active treatments. For example, AMT was as effective as other relaxation interventions such as relaxation and self-control, self-control desensitization, and systematic desensitization, and, in some cases, led to greater generalization to nontargeted problems. AMT was equivalent in effectiveness to stress inoculation training, cognitive restructuring, cognitive therapy, cognitive relaxation, and social skill interventions, and AMT may be more effective than psychodynamic therapy. In summary, AMT is an empirically supported intervention for various anxiety and stress conditions, stress-related medical conditions, and other emotions such as anger. It leads to meaningful, maintained change in targeted problems, shows transfer effects in many cases, and is as effective as other interventions.

MODIFICATION, INTEGRATION, AND LIMITATIONS OF AMT

AMT may be conducted with individuals or in small groups. Group AMT requires several adaptations. (1) Groups are generally limited to 6 to 10 members since some research suggests a small group format may be more effective than large groups. (2) The number of sessions should be increased by two or three sessions to accommodate the slower members. (3) Sessions should be lengthened by approximately 30 minutes to allow time to attend to individual issues of all participants. This helps build a positive working alliance and helps clients feel individual issues are receiving attention. If sessions cannot be lengthened, an additional session or two may be needed to handle individual issues over time. (4) Groups can be composed of individuals with similar problems or can be quite heterogeneous, reflecting a wide variety of concerns. Therapists accommodate patient differences by having clients specify different scene content and having scenes labeled Scene 1 and 2. The therapist triggers off different scenes by instructing clients generally with some instruction such as to visualize their "first stress scene." Clients, therefore, can visualize quite different scenes of approximately the same arousal intensity. (5) Homework to develop relaxation and anxiety scenes is important in individual AMT, but even more important in group AMT, if time is to be used efficiently. Clients develop detailed scenes between sessions so that they can be quickly shaped up and so that the group is not slowed down by the need to develop scenes during the sessions. In summary, with a few modifications, AMT can be delivered efficiently in small groups, and although there are no studies comparing the relative effectiveness of group versus individual AMT, a considerable literature shows that group AMT is very effective.

AMT is easily integrated into a comprehensive, multicomponent treatment plan. For example, AMT might be mixed with sexual therapy for an anxious, timid, avoidant person experiencing a sexual dysfunction. Increasing control over anxiety and tension might assist the individual in talking more comfortably about sexual issues, approaching sexual encounters, and engaging in sex therapy homework. AMT might be integrated with cognitive therapy methods for a combined relaxation–cognitive coping skill intervention. In this format, both relaxation and cognitive strategies are rehearsed during the arousal induction/reduction procedures. Such cognitive–relaxation approach can broaden the applicability of AMT to persons who may be more responsive to cognitive strategies, but where purely cognitive restructuring methods have not helped. AMT can be integrated with behavioral rehearsal activities such that clients not only lower anxiety, but also visually rehearse appropriate behavior (e.g., assertiveness for a timid client). AMT can also be integrated with other nonbehavioral interventions (e.g., medications, career counseling, and psychodynamic therapy). For example, the combination of AMT and career counseling was most effective for anxious, vocationally indecisive individuals. Further, AMT was employed as an adjunct to ongoing psychodynamic psychotherapy for outpatient schizophrenics. Those receiving AMT lowered their anxiety and anger, but also were better able to use psychodynamic therapy. In another study, patients with GAD lowered general anxiety and voluntarily sought further psychotherapy for other personal and emotional concerns, suggesting AMT facilitated further psychotherapeutic involvement. In summary, AMT with its focus on arousal reduction can be easily integrated with a wide variety of interventions.

Although AMT is applicable with a wide range of clients and problems, some cautions are in order. (1) AMT has a self-control rationale, i.e., clients learn to employ relaxation skills for active anxiety/stress control. Some clients may not enter treatment with self-control expectancies consistent with the model and may resist learning anxiety self-management skills. (2) Another potential difficulty can be with patients initially too fearful at experiencing anxiety or anger arousal in the session, despite the therapist's assurance that the emotions will remain under control. Alternative interventions (e.g., systematic desensitization) might be chosen with a movement toward AMT procedures and rationale as client self-efficacy improved. (3) Clients must agree that AMT is an appropriate approach to the presenting problem. Without agreement on therapeutic approaches, the working alliance is likely to be breached and therapeutic impasses to ensue. For example, if clients were committed to a drug or spiritual intervention for anxiety reduction, or to a psychodynamic/humanistic therapy, then AMT would not fit their conceptualization of appropriate treatment, and AMT could be rejected. (4) Clients must have the cognitive and motivational capacities to follow through on the procedures of AMT. For example, they must be able to visualize images, become aroused, and follow instruction in relaxation methods. Without these basic characteristics, AMT is likely to fail. Sometimes, such difficulties can be circumvented. For example, if the client has difficulty visualizing, then an in vivo approach to anxiety induction might be employed. (5) Relaxation training sometimes induces rather than reduces anxiety (i.e., relaxation-induced anxiety). This can usually be resolved by changing to an alternative relaxation training procedure, repeating relaxation training in small steps, and/or counterdemand instructions and expectancies. If relaxation-induced anxiety cannot be reduced, an alternative intervention should be developed. (6) Religious and cultural factors must be taken into account. For example, some religious groups consider AMT a meditative procedure, which is counter to the person's belief system. Either AMT must be recast in a culturally congruent manner or an alternative culturally appropriate intervention should be sought. (7) Although AMT has been successfully adapted to angry middle school youth and elderly anxious patients, empirical support for AMT is limited primarily to young and middle-aged, white non-Hispanic adults. With these cautions, AMT should be considered an effective, empirically supported intervention for many anxiety, stress, and arousal states.

FUTURE DIRECTIONS

AMT has shown considerable clinical flexibility and adaptability. Future research and application should continue to map applicability to other arousal-related conditions such as shame, guilt, or dysthymia, or impulse control issues such as hyperactivity. The effectiveness of AMT alone and/or in combination with other psychological and medical interventions should be evaluated. The value of AMT as a preventive coping skill either with children or with at-risk populations such as individuals undergoing elective surgery, extensive dental procedures, or serving as caregivers for difficult populations should be explored. AMT also awaits culturally sensitive adaptations to and empirical validation in diverse populations.

See also: Anxiety—adult, Anxiety—children, Anxiety in children—FRIENDS program, Exposure therapy, Generalized anxiety disorder, Social anxiety disorder 1, Social anxiety disorder 2

REFERENCES

Cragan, M. K., & Deffenbacher, J. L. (1984). Anxiety management training and relaxation as self-control in the treatment of generalized anxiety in medical outpatients. *Journal of Counseling Psychology, 31*, 123–131.

Deffenbacher, J. L., Filetti, L. B., Lynch, R. S., Dahlen, E. R., & Oetting, E. R. (2002). Cognitive–behavioral treatment of high anger drivers. *Behaviour Research and Therapy, 40*, 895–910.

Deffenbacher, J. L., & Stark, R. S. (1992). Relaxation and cognitive-relaxation treatments of general anger. *Journal of Counseling Psychology, 39*, 158–167.

Suinn, R. M. (1990). *Anxiety management training: A behavior therapy*. New York: Plenum Press.

Suinn, R. M., & Deffenbacher, J. L. (1988). Anxiety management training. *The Counseling Psychologist, 16*, 31–49.

Anxiety—Children

Thomas H. Ollendick and Laura D. Seligman

Keywords: behavior therapy, children and adolescents, cognitive behavior therapy, developmental issues, evidence-based practice

The anxiety disorders describe a broad spectrum of syndromes ranging from very circumscribed anxiety to pervasive, sometimes "free-floating" anxiety or worry. With the 1994 edition of the *Diagnostic and Statistical Manual of Mental Disorders* and the 1992 rendition of the *International Statistical Classification of Diseases and Related Health Problems*, the symptoms of young persons (as well as adults) can now be categorized with eight major but separate diagnostic syndromes associated with anxiety: panic disorder with agoraphobia, panic disorder without agoraphobia, agoraphobia without history of panic, specific phobia, social phobia, obsessive–compulsive disorder, posttraumatic stress disorder, and generalized anxiety disorder. Additionally, the DSM-IV and ICD-10 specify one anxiety diagnosis specific to childhood, separation anxiety disorder. Earlier versions of the DSM included two additional anxiety diagnoses specific to childhood, namely, avoidant disorder and overanxious disorder. In the most recent revision, however, avoidant disorder and overanxious disorder have been subsumed under the categories of social phobia and generalized anxiety disorder, respectively.

Although diagnostic systems such as the DSM and ICD describe anxiety as falling into several distinct syndromes or categories, there is also a rich body of literature examining anxiety at the symptom level. Rather than defining categorical distinctions, this view embraces a dimensional approach, examining the number of anxiety symptoms experienced by children and adolescents and the frequency or severity of such symptoms. This tradition is perhaps best exemplified in the work of Achenbach and his colleagues and the development of such instruments as the Child Behavior Checklist, Teacher Report Form, and Youth Self-Report (Achenbach, 1991). Suffice it to indicate here that the dimensional approach oftentimes detects subsyndromal levels of anxiety in addition to the presence of clinical syndromes. Along with diagnostic status, it is frequently used as an outcome measure when evaluating treatment efficacy.

As is evident from the above discussion, a broad range of topics is subsumed under the heading of anxiety disorders in childhood. We have chosen to delimit our review of cognitive behavior therapy (CBT) and its efficacy to the perspective that examines anxiety as a syndrome or disorder and, more specifically, to the examination of separation anxiety disorder, generalized anxiety/overanxious disorder, and social phobia. Due to space constraints the current brief commentary cannot address the remainder of the anxiety disorders in sufficient depth; moreover, several recent books provide excellent resources for the interested reader on the treatment of these and other anxiety disorders of childhood (see Ollendick & March, 2003).

Before proceeding to treatment outcome, it should be mentioned that the anxiety disorders are the most commonly occurring disorders of childhood and adolescence (with estimates ranging from 15% to 20%) and that the comorbidity of anxiety disorders with one another and with other disorders is frequent. Most anxiety disorders are comorbid with at least one other anxiety disorder and many are comorbid with an affective disorder (e.g., major depression, dysthymia). In fact, considering lifetime diagnoses, researchers have found co-occurring anxiety disorders to be the rule in childhood (approximately 75%) and unipolar depression to be the most common comorbid diagnosis (approximately 65%) in adolescence. Furthermore, although anxiety and disruptive behavior are often thought to represent polar opposites, comorbidity of anxiety and the disruptive behavior disorders is not uncommon. Estimates of the comorbidity of disruptive disorders and anxiety disorders in children and adolescents are as high as 25% to 33%. Thus, when treating children with anxiety disorders, it is important to keep in mind that these other disorders will also need to be addressed in many of these youngsters.

COGNITIVE BEHAVIOR THERAPY

The major factors distinguishing CBT for children from other psychosocial interventions for youth are their focus on maladaptive learning histories and erroneous or overly rigid thought patterns as the cause for the development and maintenance of psychological symptoms and disorders. As such, CBT for children is focused on the here and now rather than oriented toward uncovering historical antecedents of maladaptive behavior or thought patterns. Treatment goals are clearly determined and parents and youth seeking treatment are asked to consider the types of changes they are hoping to see as a result of treatment. Progress is monitored throughout treatment using objective indicators of change, such as monitoring forms and rating devices. CBT for children also emphasizes a skills building approach, and thus is often action-oriented, directive, and frequently educative in nature. For this reason, CBT typically includes a homework component in which the skills learned in treatment are practiced outside the therapy room. Moreover, given its focus on the context of the behavior, treatments for children often incorporate skills components for parents, teachers, and sometimes even siblings or peers. Because the focus is on teaching the child and his or her family and teachers the skills necessary to effectively cope with or eliminate the child's symptoms of anxiety, the child and significant others become direct agents of change. In effect, they function as "co-therapists" and control of treatment is frequently "transferred" to them. In brief, CBT is designed to be time-limited and relatively short-term, rarely extending beyond 6 months of active treatment. In addition to the active treatment phase, CBT for anxious children may incorporate spaced-out "booster sessions" that extend over a longer period of time (i.e., another 4 to 6 months) to ensure maintenance and durability of change.

Surprisingly, no randomized, controlled between-group design outcome studies examining the efficacy of CBT with children evincing anxiety disorders, other than simple or specific phobias, existed until recently. However, several controlled single-case design studies provided preliminary support for the likely efficacy of behavioral and cognitive–behavioral procedures with overanxious, separation anxious, and socially phobic children (see Ollendick & March, 2003). These early studies provided the foundation for the between-group design studies that followed in evaluating the efficacy of CBT.

Cognitive–behavioral treatment for anxiety disorders in children, as pioneered by Philip Kendall and his colleagues (1992), serves as a prototype of these newer interventions. It is focused on both cognitive and behavioral components. Cognitive strategies are used to assist the child to recognize anxious cognition, to use awareness of such cognition as a cue for managing anxiety, and to help them cope more effectively in anxiety-provoking situations. In addition, behavioral strategies such as modeling, in vivo exposure to the anxiety cues, role-play, relaxation training, and reinforced practice are used. A workbook is typically provided to the parents and the child and weekly monitoring of gains is pursued. Thus, the cognitive–behavioral procedures are broad in scope and incorporate many of the elements of treatments used historically with phobic children.

In the first manualized between-group study, Kendall and his colleagues compared the outcome of a 16-session CBT treatment to a wait-list control condition. Children and their families were treated individually. Forty-seven 9- to 13-year-olds were assigned randomly to treatment or wait-list conditions. All of the children met diagnostic criteria for overanxious disorder, separation anxiety disorder, or social phobia and over half of them were comorbid with at least one other psychiatric disorder or an affective disorder. Treated children improved on a number of dimensions; perhaps the most dramatic difference was the percentage of children not meeting criteria for an anxiety disorder at the end of treatment—64% of treated cases versus 5% of the wait-list children. At follow-up 1 and 3 years later, and then again 7 years later, improvements were maintained and, in fact, were enhanced. Kendall and colleagues have reaffirmed the efficacy of this procedure with 94 children (aged 9–13) randomly assigned to cognitive–behavioral and wait-list control conditions. Seventy-one percent of the treated children did not meet diagnostic criteria at the end of treatment compared to 5% of those in the wait-list condition. Recently, they have obtained similar findings using a group treatment format. In addition, other researchers in the United States, as well as Australia, the Netherlands, and the United Kingdom, have replicated these findings using interventions either based on this intervention or very similar to it. Treatments have been delivered in both group and individual formats and the number of sessions has ranged from 10 to 18. Similar findings to those obtained by Kendall and colleagues have been noted in these programs.

As one example, subsequent to Kendall's first randomized clinical trial, his CBT approach was evaluated independently by a different investigatory team in Australia headed by Paula Barrett, Mark Dadds, and Ron Rapee. Children (aged 7 to 14) were assigned randomly to one of three groups: individual CBT, individual CBT plus Family Anxiety Management, and a wait-list control.

The cognitive–behavioral treatment was intended to be a replication of that used by Kendall (although it was shortened to 12 sessions). At the end of treatment, 57% of the anxious children receiving individual CBT were diagnosis free, compared to 26% of the wait-list children; at 6-month follow-up 71% of the treated children were diagnosis free (wait-list children were treated in the interim). In this study, as noted above, a CBT plus Family Anxiety Management component was also examined. In this condition, the children were treated individually *and* the parents were trained in how to reward courageous behavior and how to extinguish reports of excessive anxiety in their children. More specifically, parents were trained in reinforcement strategies including verbal praise, privileges, and tangible rewards to be made contingent on facing up to feared situations. Planned ignoring was used as a method for dealing with excessive complaining and anxious behaviors; that is, the parents were trained to listen and respond empathetically to the children's complaints the first time they occurred but then to withdraw attention if the complaints persisted. In this treatment condition, 84% of the children were diagnosis free immediately following treatment, a rate that persisted at 6-month follow-up. Thus, this treatment was superior to cognitive–behavioral treatment directed toward the child alone (57% diagnosis free) and the wait-list control condition (26% diagnosis free). Even better results were obtained at 3- and 6-year follow-up: nearly 90% of the children in the combined treatment condition were diagnosis free compared to about 80% in the individual CBT condition. Thus, it appears to be a very promising treatment package.

In summary, cognitive–behavioral and behavioral treatments have been shown to be quite effective with anxiety disorders in children. It should be noted that these treatments have been used primarily with anxious children between 7 and 14 years of age and, as with other problem areas and disorders, additional research is required to determine whether these treatments will be effective with adolescents.

DIRECTIONS FOR THE FUTURE OF CBT WITH ANXIOUS CHILDREN

One challenge currently facing CBT practitioners and researchers is how to more fully integrate developmental theory with cognitive–behavioral theory. As noted above, Kendall's CBT protocol appears to be particularly effective with children but its applicability, suitability, and efficacy with adolescents remain to be determined. What changes will need to be made in order to establish its efficacy with adolescents? And with preschool children? Similarly, it remains to be seen to what extent individual and family characteristics such as gender, race, ethnicity, socioeconomic status, and religion necessitate modification in CBT for children. As one brief example, Kendall's CBT protocol was found to be less effective with boys than girls in the Australian study mentioned above. Moreover, the intervention has rarely been used with minority children and thus its efficacy with these youngsters is untested. As research continues to establish the effectiveness of a growing number of CBTs for children, additional efficacy studies as well as studies examining moderators of treatment outcome (i.e., the conditions under which it is effective) will need to be conducted.

Understanding why CBT for children works and whether the mechanisms are the same for children, adolescents, and adults will also be an important challenge to meet in the future. Studies need to test mediational models as well as break down current CBT treatment packages to isolate the necessary and sufficient components. Recently, we have questioned the extent to which cognitive change occurs in CBT with anxious children and whether the acquisition of coping strategies is critical to its efficacy (Prins & Ollendick, 2003). Lastly, as we find more effective treatments, we must focus our energies on whether these same types of interventions or modified forms of CBT can be effective in preventing as well as ameliorating psychological disorders and symptoms in youth. CBT is an effective intervention with anxious children; however, much more remains to be done before we can rest on our laurels.

See also: Anxiety—adult, Anxiety in children—FRIENDS program, Children—behavior therapy

REFERENCES

Achenbach, T. M. (1991). *Integrative guide for the 1991 CBCL/4–18, YSR, and TRF profiles*. Burlington: University of Vermont.

Kendall, P. C., Chansky, T. E., Kane, M. T., Kim, R. S., Kortlander, E., Ronan, K. R., Sessa, F. M., & Siqueland, L. (1992). *Anxiety disorders in youth: Cognitive–behavioral interventions*. Needham Heights, MA: Allyn & Bacon.

Ollendick, T. H., & March, J. S. (Eds.). (2003). *Phobic and anxiety disorders in children and adolescents: A clinician's guide to effective psychosocial and pharmacological interventions*. New York: Oxford University Press.

Prins, P. J. M., & Ollendick, T. H. (2003). Cognitive change and enhanced coping: Missing mediational links in cognitive behavior therapy with anxiety-disordered children. *Clinical Child and Family Psychology Review, 6*, 87–105.

Anxiety in Children—FRIENDS Program

Paula M. Barrett and Robi Sonderegger

Keywords: anxiety, children, family, treatment, FRIENDS

Of all the problems experienced during childhood, anxiety is the most common. Maladaptive coping-response behaviors to anxiety can adversely impact school performance, social competence, interpersonal relationships, and the way children think about themselves. Left untreated, anxiety can have long-term implications for adult functioning. As such, it is essential to equip children with skills to manage angst and help prevent future emotional distress. Clinical research endeavors have identified both cognitive and behavioral techniques to be effective in targeting childhood anxiety problems. When confronted with feared stimuli, the use of competence-mediating self-statements serves to inhibit dysfunctional reactions (e.g., self-doubting and negativistic self-talk). At a behavioral level, in vivo and imaginal exposure (desensitization through systematic confrontation of anxiety-provoking stimuli), muscular relaxation, and contingency management (operant reinforcement of nonfearful behaviors) serve to extinguish fearful behaviors. Over the past decade, these applicable techniques have been combined in the development of individual, child-group, and family cognitive–behavioral therapy (CBT) programs.

PHILOSOPHY

Of all clinical initiatives, CBT programs feature the greatest empirical support. Considering anxiety as a multidimensional construct, CBT programs focus on the physiological, cognitive, and learning processes that are believed to interact in the development, maintenance, and experience of anxiety. Children are taught to be aware of somatic cues when they are feeling anxious, and learn relaxation techniques so as to eliminate tension, remain calm, and think clearly. Children are also taught to recognize negative self-talk and challenge unhelpful thoughts in positive ways. Because anxious children often exhibit perfectionist standards and unrealistic self-evaluations, children are taught to concentrate on the positive aspects of anxiety-provoking situations, to which they respond well. As detailed in Barrett and Shortt (in press), both self-confidence and esteem are gained when opportunities to reward and positively reinforce partial success are made available in step-problem-solving and graded exposure strategies which confront fearful stimuli.

PIONEERS

Kendall (1994) conducted the first randomized clinical trial evaluating the efficacy of CBT for childhood anxiety, comparing diagnostic change among 47 clinically anxious children (aged 9 to 13). Children participated in either a structured 16-session individual cognitive–behavioral treatment (ICBT) program or waitlist condition. Through comprehensive multimethod assessment, Kendall demonstrated that CBT was effective in reducing primary anxiety diagnoses among children from pre- to postintervention. Treatment gains were maintained across 1- and 3.35-year follow-up (Kendall & Southam-Gerow, 1996). Kendall's pioneering work has since been expanded on, with studies also evaluating the efficacy of CBT for children in group and family settings. Structured child-focused CBT programs have also emerged such as the *Coping Cat* (Kendall, 1990), *Coping Koala* (Barrett, 1995), and *FRIENDS* (Barrett, Lowry-Webster, & Turner, 2000a, b) programs, which promote important personal development skills such as building self-esteem, problem solving, and self-expression of ideas and beliefs.

CONTEMPORARY VIEWS OF CBT WITH CHILDREN

CBT for anxious children focuses on dysfunctional cognitions (misperceptions of environmental threats and/or one's ability to cope) and how these affect the child's subsequent emotions and behavior. ICBT aims to help children develop new skills to cope with their specific circumstances, facilitates new experiences to test dysfunctional as well as adaptive beliefs, and assists in the processing of such experiences. Modeling and direct reinforcement are used to facilitate the child's learning of new approach behaviors, and cognitive strategies address processes such as information processing style, attributions, and self-talk. Although ICBT has been found effective in helping children to build emotional resilience, children also learn by observing and helping others. As such, group-based CBT (GCBT) programs have been developed based on peer and experiential learning models. Learning in a group context provides a safe and familiar environment in which participants can gain peer support, work in partnership, and practice newly learned skills in fun ways.

In addition to a child's social network, the family is considered to be a favorable environment for effecting change in the child's dysfunctional cognition. Therefore, CBT-based family anxiety management (FAM) training programs have also been developed to incorporate family-directed problem-solving strategies. In addition to helping parents recognize and effectively manage their own emotional distress, and identify behaviors that may advance or sustain their child's anxiety, parents are taught to utilize their own strengths as care-providers by assisting their children to practice newly developed coping skills, facilitate new experiences for children to test dysfunctional beliefs, and provide positive reinforcement. While parents typically participate in FAM training as a supplement to their child's ICBT or GCBT involvement, FAM can also be conducted without child participation (parents only) or with the family unit as a whole (parents and children participating as a collaborative "team").

CONTEMPORARY CONTRIBUTORS

The FRIENDS program (Barrett, Lowry-Webster VI and Turner, 2000a, b) is an internationally recognized CBT program for anxious and depressed youth that has received much acclaim in recent years. Originating with the development of the *Group Coping Koala Workbook* (Barrett, 1995), an Australian adaptation of Kendall's *Coping Cat Workbook* (Kendall, 1990), parallel FRIENDS workbooks for children (aged 7–11) and adolescents (aged 12–16) have been developed through extensive research and clinical validation over the past decade. Set apart from other structured programs, FRIENDS also features a FAM parenting component. Although primarily developed as a GCBT program for implementation by mental health professionals, FRIENDS can also be utilized as ICBT with select clients. In addition, teachers, counselors, or youth workers who have undergone accredited training can implement FRIENDS in classroom settings as a universal preventive intervention.

FRIENDS has a reputation as the only clinically validated early intervention program for anxiety and depression in Australia, and has been distributed nationally under the Mental Health Strategy (satisfying federal guidelines for evidence-based research). Its strong evidence base has encouraged international demand, with the program now being used, validated, and translated in different languages around the world. While culturally sensitive supplements to FRIENDS have also been developed (Barrett, Sonderegger, & Sonderegger, 2001b), recent studies (e.g., Barrett, Moore, & Sonderegger, 2000; Barrett, Sonderegger, & Sonderegger, 2001a; Barrett, Sonderegger, & Xenos, in press) have shown FRIENDS in its current format to also be effective in reducing anxiety and stress among culturally diverse migrants and refugee youth. For more information on FRIENDS, see www.friendsinfo.net.

EMPIRICAL BASIS FOR CBT WITH CHILDREN

Although high parental control, parental anxiety, and parental reinforcement of avoidant coping strategies have been associated with children's anxiety symptoms (Shortt, Barrett, Dadds, & Fox, 2001), parents can also be a valuable resource in bringing about positive change in their children. Howard and Kendall (1996) were the first to evaluate the effectiveness of ICBT plus parent involvement using a multiple baseline design. Six clinically anxious children (aged 9–13) and their families participated in treatment that was initiated following baseline assessment periods of 2, 4, or 6 weeks (during which time diagnostic criteria was maintained). Four of six clients experienced treatment gains from pre- to posttreatment as indicated by self-, parent, and teacher reports, and diagnostic ratings by clinicians who were blind to participants' treatment status. The remaining two clients also showed treatment gains on most measures, and for five of the six participants, improvements were generally maintained at 4-month follow-up.

Barrett, Dadds, and Rapee (1996) conducted the first randomized, controlled trial of ICBT and FAM interventions. Seventy-nine children (aged 7–14) diagnosed with Separation-Anxiety (SAD), Overanxious (OAD), or Social Phobia (SP) Disorders were randomly allocated to ICBT or ICBT + FAM interventions, or a wait-list condition. At posttreatment 57.1% of children who participated in ICBT no longer met diagnostic criteria for an anxiety disorder, compared with 84% in the ICBT + FAM condition. In contrast to a 12-week wait-list condition (26% diagnosis free [DF] at postassessment), both treatment conditions were found to be superior. ICBT treatment gains continued to improve at 6-month follow-up (71.4% DF) whereas ICBT + FAM treatment gains were maintained (84% DF). At 1-year follow-up, ICBT treatment gains were maintained (70.3% DF) whereas ICBT + FAM treatment gains continued to improve (95.6% DF). While these findings may illustrate the general benefits of incorporating FAM into existing interventions for childhood anxiety, it should be noted that younger children and females responded significantly better to the ICBT + FAM condition than others.

Flannery-Schroeder and Kendall (2000) conducted randomized ICBT and GCBT clinical trials for 37 children (aged 8–14) diagnosed with Generalized Anxiety (GAD), SAD, and SP Disorders. Seventy-three percent of children who participated in the ICBT were DF at posttreatment compared with 50% of children who participated in the GCBT trial. In contrast to a 9-week wait-list condition (8% DF at postassessment), both treatment conditions were found to be superior, and treatment gains were maintained at 3-month follow-up. Using a child population with the same clinical pathologies, Shortt, Barrett, and Fox (2001) conducted the first randomized clinical trial evaluating the efficacy of the FRIENDS program. Seventy-one children (aged 6–10) participated in FRIENDS (GCBT + FAM) and wait-list conditions. It was found that 69% of children who participated in

FRIENDS were DF at posttreatment compared with 6% in the wait-list condition. These treatment gains were maintained at 1-year follow-up (68% DF). To gauge the effectiveness of FRIENDS as a universal intervention for the prevention of anxiety, the program was also administered to primary-school children considered to be "at risk" for anxiety problems (i.e., scoring above the Spence Children's Anxiety Scale clinical cutoff). Lowry-Webster, Barrett, and Dadds (2001) recruited 594 children aged 10–13 to participate in teacher-led FRIENDS GCBT and FAM ($n = 432$) and wait-list ($n = 162$) conditions. Regardless of risk status, children (and their parents) who participated in FRIENDS reported fewer anxiety symptoms at postintervention than children in the wait-list condition. Children deemed to be at high risk also reported significant improvements in depression ratings. Compared to 31.2% of wait-list participants, 85% of FRIENDS participants maintained intervention gains at 12-month follow-up (Lowry-Webster & Barrett, in press). Similar FRIENDS prevention effects have subsequently been found for high school students at 12-month postintervention (Barrett, Johnson, & Turner, in press).

Barrett and Turner (2001) further allocated 489 participants (aged 10–12) at random to a psychologist-led intervention, teacher-led intervention, or normal-class control condition. Using self-report measures, all participants regardless of intervention condition showed markedly fewer anxiety symptoms from pre- to postassessment compared with control participants who reported no change. This finding suggests that the administration of FRIENDS is both generalizable and sustainable within school-based settings for the early intervention and prevention of anxiety in children.

CRITICISMS OF CBT WITH CHILDREN

Despite the apparent effectiveness of combining education and graded exposure themes into one treatment package, it remains unclear which aspects of CBT are most active, and to what extent other factors (e.g., family dynamics, child demographics, order of treatment components) may influence treatment outcomes. With the exception of trials that have utilized structured manualized interventions, determining the efficacy of relative CBT components is difficult as the arrangement and emphasis on cognitive and behavioral strategies in published trials may vary. Moreover, for the majority of ICBT + FAM trials, it remains unclear as to what constitutes parent involvement. Coupled with contrasting results, it is difficult to determine whether particular treatment formats (e.g., ICBT, GCBT, FAM) and format combinations may be superior to others. Before clinicians can confidently select appropriate individual, group, family, or combined CBT interventions for specific childhood anxiety problems, much work is required to identify which therapeutic features are most effective in bringing about sustainable change for specific client populations.

FUTURE DIRECTIONS FOR CBT

Integration

The combination of cognitive and behavioral strategies has consistently been shown effective in treating childhood anxiety. Yet some CBT approaches have been paired with superior and more sustainable change than others. In recognizing the social elements that influence children's behavior (e.g., relationships with family members, peers, teachers), the efficacy of GCBT and FAM has received considerable attention in recent years. Because sociocultural support styles and family dynamics differ between cultural groups, the efficacy of these intervention formats requires closer scrutiny. It may be argued that diverse types of family closeness (i.e., closeness–caregiving and closeness–intrusiveness; Green & Werner, 1996) can dramatically impact therapeutic outcomes. Whereas caregiving serves to support child development, intrusiveness is characteristic of psychological coercive control and may even promote specific fears (Elbedour, Shulman, & Kedem, 1997). As multicultural populations continue to diversify Western nations, programs that expand ICBT to incorporate experiential peer learning and family-directed problem-solving strategies need to determine to what extent contextual influences maintain or change childhood functioning.

Research and Theory Development

Researchers are challenged to identify the active components of CBT in the treatment of childhood anxiety, and better understand the diverse roles of culture, socialization, and family contexts. To date, research trials have not adequately described the cognitive–behavioral content in child-focused and FAM sessions. So as to determine best practice, randomized controlled trials comparing the emphasis and order of CBT components need to be conducted in different intervention formats and among diverse cultural groups. Additional research into the trajectory of clinical anxiety, sociocultural support styles, and the dynamics of family structure may also lend insight to what role peers and parents should play in treatment, and contribute immensely to understanding the developmental pathways of childhood anxiety. In order to effectively reduce the incidence of anxiety problems among children and subsequently young people, it is fundamental that preventive interventions be further developed and validated. In this regard, annexing anxiety concerns among children early will inhibit the development of maladaptive coping-response behaviors and consequently the maintenance and escalation of anxiety symptoms.

See also: Anxiety—adult, Anxiety—children, Children—behavior therapy

REFERENCES

Barrett, P. M. (1995). *Group coping koala workbook*. Unpublished manuscript, School of Applied Psychology, Griffith University, Australia.

Barrett, P. M., Dadds, M. R., & Rapee, R. M. (1996). Family treatment of childhood anxiety: A controlled trial. *Journal of Consulting and Clinical Psychology*, *64*, 333–342.

Barrett, P. M., Johnson, S., & Turner, C. (2004). Developmental differences in universal preventive intervention for child anxiety. *Clinical Child Psychology and Psychiatry*.

Barrett, P. M., Lowry-Webster, H., & Turner, C. (2000a). *FRIENDS program for children: Group leaders manual*. Brisbane: Australian Academic Press.

Barrett, P. M., Lowry-Webster, H., & Turner, C. (2000b). *FRIENDS program for youth: Group leaders manual*. Brisbane: Australian Academic Press.

Barrett, P. M., Moore, A. F., & Sonderegger, R. (2000). An anxiety prevention program for young former-Yugoslavian refugees in Australia: A pilot study. *Behaviour Change*, *17*, 124–133.

Barrett, P. M., & Shortt, A. L. (2004). Parental involvement in the treatment of anxious children. In A. E. Kazdin & J. R. Weisz (Eds.), *Evidence-based psychotherapies for children and adolescents*.

Barrett, P. M., Sonderegger, R., & Sonderegger, N. L. (2001a). Evaluation of an anxiety prevention and positive-coping program (FRIENDS) for children and adolescents of non-English speaking background. *Behaviour Change*, *18*, 78–91.

Barrett, P. M., Sonderegger, R., & Sonderegger, N. L. (2001b). *Universal supplement to FRIENDS for children: Group leaders manual for participants from non-English speaking backgrounds*. Copyright © Griffith University and the State of Queensland through the Queensland Transcultural Mental Health Centre (QTCMH), Division of Mental Health.

Barrett, P. M., Sonderegger, R., & Xenos, S. (2004). Using FRIENDS to combat anxiety and adjustment problems among young migrants to Australia: A national trial. *Clinical Child Psychology and Psychiatry*.

Barrett, P. M., & Turner, C. M. (2001). Prevention of anxiety symptoms in primary school children: Preliminary results from a universal school-based trial. *British Journal of Clinical Psychology*, *40*, 399–410.

Elbedour, S., Shulman, S., & Kedem, P. (1997). Children's fears: Cultural and developmental perspectives. *Behaviour Research and Theory*, *35*, 491–496.

Flannery-Schroeder, E., & Kendall, P. C. (2000). Group and individual cognitive–behavioral treatments for youth with anxiety disorders: A randomized clinical trial. *Cognitive Therapy and Research*, *24*, 251–278.

Green, R. J., & Werner, P. D. (1996). Intrusiveness and closeness-caregiving: Rethinking the concept of family "enmeshment." *Family Processes*, *35*, 115–136.

Howard, B. L., and Kendall, P. C. (1996). Cognitive–behavioral family therapy for anxiety-disordered children: A multiple-baseline evaluation. *Cognitive Therapy and Research*, *20*, 423–443.

Kendall, P. C. (1990). *The coping cat workbook*. Ardmore, PA: Workbook Publishing.

Kendall, P. C. (1994). Treating anxiety disorders in children: Results of a randomized clinical trial. *Journal of Consulting and Clinical Psychology*, *62*, 100–110.

Kendall, P. C., & Southam-Gerow, M. A. (1996). Long term follow-up of a cognitive–behavioural therapy for anxious youth. *Journal of Consulting and Clinical Psychology*, *64*, 724–730.

Lowry-Webster, H. M., & Barrett, P. M. (2004). A universal prevention trial of anxiety and depression during childhood: Results at one year follow-up. *Behaviour Change*.

Shortt, A. L., Barrett, P. M., Dadds, M. R., & Fox, T. L. (2001). The influence of family and experimental context on cognition in anxious children. *Journal of Abnormal Child Psychology*, *29*, 585–596.

Shortt, A., Barrett, P. M., & Fox, T. (2001). Evaluating the FRIENDS program: A cognitive–behavioural group treatment of childhood anxiety disorders: An evaluation of the FRIENDS program. *Journal of Clinical Child Psychology*, *30*, 525–535.

Silverman, W. K., Kurtines, W. M., Ginsburg, G. S., Weems, C. F., Rabian, B., & Serafini, L. T. (1999). Contingency management, self-control, and education support in the treatment of childhood phobic disorders: A randomized clinical trial. *Journal of Consulting and Clinical Psychology*, *67*, 675–687.

RECOMMENDED READINGS

Barrett, P. M., Dadds, M. R., & Rapee, R. M. (1996). Family treatment of childhood anxiety: A controlled trial. *Journal of Consulting and Clinical Psychology*, *64*, 333–342.

Barrett, P. M., Sonderegger, R., & Xenos, S. (2004). Using FRIENDS to combat anxiety and adjustment problems among young migrants to Australia: A national trial. *Clinical Child Psychology and Psychiatry*.

Kendall, P. C. (1994). Treating anxiety disorders in children: Results of a randomized clinical trial. *Journal of Consulting and Clinical Psychology*, *62*, 100–110.

Applied Behavior Analysis

John W. Jacobson

Keywords: applied behavior analysis, operant process

Applied behavior analysis (ABA) and cognitive behavior therapy (CBT) represent two distinctive orientations to the improvement of human functioning that share certain elements of a common intellectual heritage, but also have disparate conceptual features that reflect the sequence of their inceptions as guiding orientations for therapists. ABA, in the guise of operant psychology, behavior management, or behavior modification, emerged as a guiding orientation at an earlier point than CBT, and hence developments in CBT have incorporated aspects of ABA, but have also entailed embracing other developments in mainstream aspects of clinical psychology, which emphasize cognitive processes, the relation of cognitions to affect, developmental psychopathology, and social psychological and cognitive and developmental constructs. From this standpoint, ABA may be viewed as a relatively noneclectic orientation, whereas CBT can be considered more eclectic in its origins and directly incorporating treatment evaluation and research findings in general, abnormal, and clinical psychology. ABA as a field is not isolated from developments within psychology more generally, but rather than incorporating procedures and treatments within its model and applications directly, it has broadened its focus over several decades to address similar concerns, and this has been reflected in the emergence of some treatment procedures targeted to typical child and adult clinical populations.

CBT is founded on the general model of psychological function and practice that distinguishes affect, behavior, and cognition as cardinal factors that differ in the applicability of various intervention strategies, whereas ABA is founded on a model that emphasizes that feeling, behaving, and thinking are classes of behavior that are similarly susceptible to alteration through application of the same or similar procedures. Moreover, CBT emerged as a therapeutic orientation focused on intervention with verbal, communicative children and adults, and ABA emerged as an orientation focused on intervention with less communicative children and adults, often with developmental delays or disabilities that affected cognitive functioning, and these considerations have also affected the form and extent of incorporation of various psychological and behavioral science constructs within the work of practitioners in ABA or CBT.

ABA organizes its interventions based on principles of operant processes, whereas CBT interventions are founded on a combination of operant and respondent processes and other orientations including information processing and cognitive models. Correspondingly, the principal theorist whose work underpins ABA is B. F. Skinner (1938, 1957). With respect to both theory and its application to clinical and educational settings, many behavior analysts and psychologists have made crucial contributions to ABA practice, including Ayllon, Azrin, Baer, Ferster, Keller, Lindsley, Risley, Sidman, and Wolf. Highly influential predecessors whose work formed the zeitgeist in which critical developments in operant psychology occurred included Pavlov, Thorndike, and Watson. The status of theoretical development and diversification by subarea of practice in ABA reflects in part that its leading theorist, Skinner, lived until 1990, and thus the influence of his work on theoretical and practical developments is still pervasive and pronounced. In addition to influences stemming from the work of those already mentioned, CBT has drawn heavily on, or bases specific models of intervention on, the work of Bandura, Beck, Ellis, Eysenck, Lazarus (Arnold and Richard), Meichenbaum, Patterson, and Wolpe, among many other recent and contemporary scientist-practitioners. Development and diversification of CBT models, rather than consolidation of a unitary model, continues apace, and reflects the fact that most prominent contributors to its focus continue their work through the present.

CHARACTERIZATION OF APPLIED BEHAVIOR ANALYSIS

The foundation of contemporary ABA is the three-term contingency, or functional relation, exemplified by the expression A–B–C, where A stands for "antecedent," B for "behavior," and C for "consequence." In a specific instance or intervention, A, B, and C may represent a discrete and particular antecedent, behavior, and consequence, or may represent classes of antecedents, behaviors, and consequences. In addition to the extant or baseline functional relation, other factors are stipulated in contemporary ABA models to be especially salient, including learning history (both in terms of skills salient to the particular relation, and other skill development), physiological factors affecting learning, performance, or baseline rates of behaviors (e.g., behavioral phenotypes), and social or cultural factors impinging on the relation. Behaviors may be altered through modification of antecedents (referred to as stimulus control) or consequences (referred to as consequence manipulation).

Contemporary antecedent models encompass concepts such as occasion-setting stimuli or establishing operations that entail events that alter later functional relations (and which can be relatively distal, rather than proximal or contiguous with the occurrence of a behavior of interest; see Michael, 1993). Intervention based on consequence manipulation entails provision of reinforcing (accelerative) or punishing (decelerative) events contingent on criteria for performance, and contingent alteration of schedules of reinforcement (with relevance to shaping a behavior, or duration and spread of a behavior across time and settings). In more recent years there has been an increased research and practitioner emphasis on stimulus control as a first-stage intervention model, but complex interventions including alteration of distal and proximal antecedents as well as the manipulation of multiple consequences.

Over the past 20 years, ABA has been variously and negatively characterized as an orientation that oversimplifies complex issues, is unconcerned or cannot address cognitive phenomena, ignores genetic influences, discounts or cannot account for complex behavior including language, does not address concerns regarding such phenomena as creativity or intrinsic motivation, relies entirely on animal models or analogues of human problems, or is incompatible with helping models of professions, mechanistic, or positivistic (see Wyatt, n.d.). These criticisms are essentially overgeneralizations, coarsely inaccurate, and belied by actual practice both in behavior analytic research and in ABA. Several contemporary developments in ABA are largely compatible with concerns of CBT practitioners, and conducive to adoption within CBT frameworks, albeit based on operant models (e.g., Moore, n.d.).

These developments include phenomena within the realm of verbal behavior (language) and complex verbal processes and functions. More specifically, phenomena of growing interest in research and application relevant to ABA include stimulus equivalence, rule-governed behavior, imitation, behavioral momentum, relational frames, interaction between operant and classical conditioning, and functional clinical assessment (Hawkins & Forsyth, 1997; Plaud & Vogeltanz, 1997). These developments are all relevant to treatment priorities within CBT, including the inception and maintenance of rule-governed behavior (e.g., in CBT terms, cognition–behavior and cognition–affect relations).

DISTINCTIVE BUT CONVERGING FEATURES OF ABA AND CBT

While there are important, if possibly irreconcilable, differences between the models underpinning ABA and CBT, there are some aspects of both theoretical focus and practical application that converge. Some of these aspects reflect common features of interventions, rather than conceptual features. First, ABA can and does encompass thinking, feeling, and behaving (as forms of behavior subject to experimental and applied analysis), whereas CBT encompasses cognition, affect, and behavior. Moreover, ABA and CBT both recognize the salience of operant processes in behavior change, and maintenance and generalization of change. ABA and CBT both focus on classes of behavior as the target of intervention (i.e., skills as utilized differentially consistent with environmental demands), but define them differently (e.g., ABA as functional classes reflecting shared motivational influences, CBT in culturally typical terms reflecting psychological constructs). ABA and CBT also both focus on alteration of environmental factors, in the former approach through alteration of factors that precede the problematic behavior, and of consequences, in the latter approach through resolution of stressors (e.g., active coping). ABA and CBT both share a primary goal of substantial change in human functioning through intervention.

ABA and CBT both utilize individual and group treatment research designs, although the former substantially emphasizes individual designs and the latter typically utilizes group designs (and possibly individual designs are underutilized in CBT research and group designs are underutilized in ABA research). In intervention, ABA and CBT both seek to achieve normal range functioning with respect to therapeutic targets as a short- to intermediate-term therapeutic outcome (i.e., a time-limited focus rather than an extended course, although either model can encompass extended clinical service). ABA and CBT both utilize frequently repeated measures to assess outcome of intervention, and where feasible and appropriate, utilize self-reports as components of both preintervention assessment and intervention monitoring methods.

Both ABA and CBT place emphasis, as appropriate, on increased self-determination by clientele, in the former approach through self-management, in the latter through increased self-direction and coping skills (and in some instances, while teaching methods may differ, the skills taught or practiced may be indistinguishable). Relatedly, ABA and CBT both focus on problem-solving skills as a component of intervention when applicable (e.g., social problem solving in CBT; decision-making or choice-making and preference assessment in ABA).

Procedurally, ABA and CBT both focus on classes of behavior as the target of intervention (i.e., skills as utilized differentially consistent with environmental demands), but may define them differently. Both models also focus on alteration of environmental factors, in the former approach through alteration of factors that precede the problematic behavior, and of consequences, in the latter approach through resolution of stressors. ABA and CBT both utilize observational learning and modeling as procedures to alter problem behavior and build skills. Finally, ABA and CBT both typically include interventions implemented outside of a professional office (e.g., interventions in multiple typical settings, homework assignments, in vivo extensions).

DISTINCTIVE BUT DIFFERING FEATURES OF ABA AND CBT

Despite the commonalities noted, there are many distinctive features of ABA and CBT that differ significantly. These differences reflect discrepancies in theoretical orientation, from which procedural differences also derive. A key difference is that ABA focuses on the functional relation of stimulus–response–consequence as the fundamental causal process underpinning human functioning, whereas CBT focuses on cognitive components or systems as a particularly important causal aspect of human functioning, such as cognition–behavior and cognition–affect relations. In turn, ABA focuses on environmental events as the primary causal factor affecting human functioning, and CBT focuses on cognitive processes, or a combination of cognition, affect, and behavior, as primary causal factors of varying salience depending on the condition or problem in human functioning. As a corollary, ABA focuses on observable behavior that is readily accessible (that is overt) as its dependent variable and defines treatment goals with respect to overt behavior change. In contrast, CBT includes observation of behavior that is either readily accessible or not so readily accessed as dependent variable (i.e., covert behavior) and defines treatment goals with respect to cognitive or affective change, as well as behavior change.

In ABA, limited distinctions are typically drawn among (operant) factors inducing changes in cognitive, affective, and behavioral domains of human functioning, although in recent years some variation in conceptualization of cognitive (i.e., verbal behavior) domain has emerged. In CBT, varying distinctions are drawn among (operant, respondent, observational learning) factors inducing changes in the three stipulated domains of human functioning. These distinctions between the two orientations are very pronounced and theory-driven, and constitute the critical differences that are largely irreconcilable. From these core distinctions, and the developmental course of theoretical and practical developments, other features derive.

Whereas ABA uses frequency, duration, intensity, or rate change metrics as primary expression of behavior change, CBT uses these measures as well as scales completed by therapists or systematic self-reports as primary expressions of behavior change. Whereas ABA has a primary or exclusive focus on specific maladaptive or problem behaviors, and organization of treatment literature in these terms, as well as de novo or restorative skill building, CBT shares a focus on specific maladaptive or problem behaviors, as well as on syndromes and conditions, and organization of treatment literature in these terms, as well as de novo or restorative skill building. ABA is primarily implemented as service delivery through consultation and training by the behavior analyst, with implementation by others (which may be seen as less compatible with private practice settings), while CBT is primarily implemented by the cognitive behavior therapist, as individual or group therapy (which may be seen as more compatible with private practice). In ABA, the primary focus of research and practice is on intervention with individuals with cognitive disabilities and individual and group educational applications, but in CBT the primary focus of research and practice is on intervention with individuals with psychopathology (i.e., entire range of maladaptive conditions or reactions) with normal range or superior cognitive functioning, and secondarily on group (preventive) educational applications. Correspondingly, while practitioners of ABA principally include psychologists, special educators, and general educators, practitioners of CBT include psychologists, psychiatrists, and members of other helping professions who provide individual therapeutic services. Many ABA practitioners view behavior analysis as a field separate from psychology and other disciplines, whereas CBT practitioners likely tend to designate their discipline as the one in which they received graduate training (e.g., psychology, social work).

A final and core distinction reflecting both theory and practice is that ABA uses technical and specific terms that are discrepant from culturally typical meanings, to refer to everyday behavioral processes (e.g., technical versus culturally typical meaning of "punishment"), while CBT uses technical and specific terms that are largely consistent with culturally typical meanings, to refer to everyday behavioral processes. The use of culturally atypical terms within ABA possibly hinders adoption of research findings by non-behavior analytic practitioners and educators, whereas, while the specific parameters of terms may not be fully recognized by nonbehavioral practitioners, the use of more culturally typical terms within CBT models may expedite adoption of related therapeutic practices.

A PARTIAL RECONCILIATION OF ABA AND CBT

Although ABA and CBT are not readily reconciled on theoretical grounds, pragmatic research on verbal and rule-governed behavior has begun to result in interventions (Hayes & Hayes, 1992; Kohlenberg, Kanter, Bolling, Parker, & Tsai, 2002) that are procedurally relevant to CBT models of intervention. Other developments, such as research on behavioral momentum, have implications for enhancing durability of treatment effects. Although models of verbal behavior and related phenomena on which ABA research is based are discrepant from those typical of how language is treated within CBT perspectives, in time this may prove to enhance, rather than vitiate, the range of contributions ABA research may make to CBT techniques.

See also: Behavioral assessment

REFERENCES

Hawkins, R. P., & Forsyth, J. P. (1997). The behavior analytic perspective: Its nature, prospects, and limitations for behavior therapy. *Journal of Behavior Therapy and Experimental Psychiatry, 28*, 7–16.

Hayes, S. C., & Hayes, L. J. (1992). Verbal relations and the evolution of behavior analysis. *American Psychologist, 47*, 1383–1395.

Kohlenberg, R. H., Kanter, J. W., Bolling, M. Y., Parker, C., & Tsai, M. (2002). Enhancing cognitive therapy for depression with functional analytic psychotherapy: Treatment guidelines and empirical findings. *Cognitive and Behavioral Practice, 9*, 213–229.

Michael, J. L. (1993). *Concepts and principles of behavior analysis.* Kalamazoo, MI: Association for Behavior Analysis.

Moore, J. (n.d.). *Explanation and description in traditional neobehaviorism, cognitive psychology, and behavior analysis.*

Milwaukee: Department of Psychology, University of Wisconsin–Milwaukee. Accessed via the Internet at ftp://ftp.csd.uwm.edu/pub/Psychology/BehaviorAnalysis/conceptual-analysis/papers-moore/ on June 18, 2003.

Plaud, J. J., & Vogeltanz, N. D. (1997). Back to the future: The continued relevance of behavior theory to modern behavior therapy. *Behavior Therapy, 28*, 403–414.

Skinner, B. F. (1938/1999). *The behavior of organisms: An experimental analysis*. Morgantown, WV: B. F. Skinner Foundation.

Skinner, B. F. (1957/2002). *Verbal behavior*. Morgantown, WV: B. F. Skinner Foundation.

Wyatt, J. (undated). *Clarifying some common misrepresentations of behavior analysis: A collaborative project sponsored by the BALANCE SIG of the Association for Behavior Analysis-International*. Accessed via the Internet at http://www2. carthage.edu/ departments/teachba/ on July 6, 2003.

Asperger's Disorder

Tony Attwood

Keywords: Asperger's syndrome, autism, pervasive developmental disorder

Asperger's disorder was originally described in 1944 by the Austrian pediatrician Hans Asperger. The disorder has more recently been classified as a Pervasive Developmental Disorder. It is a neurodevelopmental disorder generally considered to be on the autism spectrum. Individuals with this developmental disorder have an intellectual capacity within the normal range but a distinct profile of abilities that have been apparent since early childhood. The profile of abilities includes the following characteristics:

- A qualitative impairment in social interaction, for example:
  Failure to develop friendships that are appropriate to the child's developmental level
  Impaired use of nonverbal behaviors such as eye gaze, facial expression, and body language to regulate a social interaction
  Lack of social and emotional reciprocity and empathy
  Impaired ability to identify social cues and conventions
- Qualitative impairment in subtle communication skills, for example:
  Fluent speech but difficulties with conversation skills and a tendency to be pedantic, have an unusual prosody, and to make literal interpretations
- Restrictive interests, for example:
  The development of special interests that are unusual in their intensity and focus
  Preference for routine and consistency

The disorder can also include motor clumsiness and oversensitivity to auditory and tactile experiences. There can also be problems with organizational and time management skills.

The exact prevalence rates for the general population have yet to determined, but research suggests that it may be as common as 1 in 259. The etiology is probably due to factors that affect brain development and is not due to emotional deprivation or other psychogenic causes (Attwood, 1998).

When one considers the diagnostic criteria for Asperger's disorder and the effects of the disorder on the person's adaptive functioning in a social context, one would expect such individuals to be vulnerable to the development of secondary mood disorders. The current research indicates that around 65% of adolescent patients with Asperger's disorder have an affective disorder that includes anxiety disorders and depression (Attwood, 2002). There is also evidence to suggest an association with delusional disorders, paranoia, and conduct disorders. We know that comorbid affective disorders in adolescents with Asperger's disorder are the rule rather than the exception but why should this population be more prone to affective disorders?

Research has been conducted on the family histories of children with autism and Asperger's disorder and identified a higher than expected incidence of mood disorders. However, when one also considers their difficulties with regard to social reasoning, empathy, verbal communication, profile of executive skills, and sensory perception, they are clearly prone to considerable stress as a result of their attempts at social inclusion. Thus, there may be constitutional and circumstantial factors that explain the higher incidence of secondary affective disorders.

The theoretical models of autism developed within cognitive psychology and research in neuropsychologv also provide some explanation as to why such individuals are prone to secondary mood disorders. The extensive research on Theory of Mind skills confirms that individuals with Asperger's disorder have considerable difficulty identifying and conceptualizing the thoughts and feelings of other people and themselves (Baron-Cohen, Tager-Flusberg, & Cohen, 1993). Research on executive function in subjects with Asperger's disorder suggests characteristics of being disinhibited and impulsive with a relative lack of insight that affects general functioning (Russel, 1997). Impaired executive function can also affect the cognitive control of emotions. Clinical experience indicates there is a tendency on the part of these individuals to react to emotional cues without cognitive reflection. Research with subjects with autism using new neuroimaging technology has also identified structural and functional abnormalities of the amygdala, which is known to regulate a range of emotions including anger, fear, and sadness. Thus, we also have neuroanatomical evidence that suggests there will be problems with the perception and regulation of the emotions.

ASSESSMENT

There are several self-rating scales that have been designed for children and adults with specific mood disorders that can be administered to clients with Asperger's disorder. However, there are specific modifications that can be used with this clinical group, as they may be better able to accurately quantify their response using a numerical or pictorial representation of the gradation in experience and expression of mood. Examples include an emotion thermometer, bar graphs, or a "volume" scale. These analogue measures are used to establish a baseline assessment as well as in the affective education component.

The assessment includes the construction of a list of behavioral indicators of mood changes. The indicators can include changes in the characteristics associated with Asperger's disorder such as an increase in time spent in solitude or engaged in their special interest, rigidity or incoherence in their thought processes, or behavior intended to impose control in their daily lives and over others. This is in addition to conventional indicators such as panic attacks, feelings of low self-worth, or episodes of anger. It is essential to collect information from a wide variety of sources as children and adults with Asperger's disorder can display quite different characteristics according to their circumstances. For example, there may be little evidence of a mood disorder at school but clear evidence of the mood disorder at home.

The clinician will also need to assess their coping mechanisms and vocabulary of emotional expression. While there are no standardized tests to measure such abilities, some characteristics have been identified by clinical experience. For example, discussions with parents can indicate that the child displays affection, but the depth and range of emotional expression is usually limited and immature relative to what might be expected of a child their chronological age. Their reaction to pleasure and pain can also be atypical, with idiosyncratic mannerisms that express feelings of excitement, such as hand flapping, or a stoic response to pain and punishments. Examples of characteristics that parents may be concerned about are a lack of apparent gratitude or remorse and paradoxical and atypical responses to particular situations. For example, the child may giggle when expected to show remorse and be remarkably quick in resolving grief. They may also misinterpret gestures of affection such as a hug with the comment that the "squeeze" was perceived as uncomfortable and not comforting. Their emotional reactions can also be delayed perhaps with an expression of anger some days or weeks after the event.

AFFECTIVE EDUCATION

Affective education is an essential component of CBT for those with Asperger's disorder. The main goal is to learn why we have emotions, their use and misuse, and the identification of different levels of expression. A basic principle is to explore one emotion at a time as a theme for a project.

The affective education stage includes the therapist describing and the client discovering the salient cues that indicate a particular level of emotional expression in the facial expression, tone of voice, body language, and context. Once the key elements that indicate a particular emotion have been identified, it is important to use an instrument to measure the degree of intensity. The therapist can construct a model "thermometer," "gauge," or "volume control" and use a range of activities to define the level of expression. Clinical experience has indicated that some clients with Asperger's disorder can use extreme statements such as "I am going to kill myself" to express a level of emotion that would be more moderately expressed by another more "normal" client. During a program of affective education the therapist often has to increase the client's vocabulary of emotional expression to ensure precision and accuracy.

The education program includes activities to detect specific degrees of emotion in others but also detecting and identifying emotions in oneself. This can be done by using internal physiological cues, cognitive cues, and behavior. Technology can be used to identify internal cues in the form of biofeedback instruments such as EMG and GSR machines with auditory or visual feedback.

COGNITIVE RESTRUCTURING

People with Asperger's disorder can make false assumptions of their circumstances and the intentions of others. They have a tendency to make a literal interpretation of stimuli so that a casual comment may be taken out of context or be taken to a literal extreme. For example, common statements such as "I'm over my head" when referring to work may be seen as the person being swamped by papers to the height of his head.

In explaining a new perspective or to correct errors or assumptions, "Comic Strip Conversations" can help the client determine the thoughts, beliefs, knowledge, and intentions of the participants in a given situation (Gray, 1998). This technique involves drawing an event or sequence of events in story board form with stick figures to represent each participant and speech and thought bubbles to represent their words and thoughts. The client and therapist use an assortment of fibro-tipped colored pens, with each color representing an emotion (red = anger, blue = calm). As they write in the speech or thought bubbles, their choice of color indicates their perception of the emotion conveyed or intended.

Cognitive restructuring also includes activities that are designed to improve the client's range of emotional repair mechanisms. The author has extended the use of metaphor to design programs that include the concept of an emotional toolbox to "fix the feeling." Clients know that a toolbox usually includes a variety of tools to repair a machine and discussion and activities are employed to identify different types of tools for specific problems associated with emotions.

SELF-REFLECTION

In conventional CBT programs, the client is encouraged to self-reflect to improve insight into his or her thoughts and feelings, thereby ideally promoting a realistic and positive self-image as well as enhancing the ability to self-talk for greater self-control. However, the concept of self-awareness may be different for individuals with Asperger's disorder. There may be a qualitative impairment in the ability to engage in introspection. Research evidence, autobiographies, and clinical experience have confirmed that some clients with Asperger's disorder and high-functioning autism can lack an "inner voice" and think in pictures rather than in words. They also have difficulty translating their visual thoughts into words.

In keeping with the client's style, treatment modifications include a greater use of visual materials and resources such as drawings, role-play, and metaphor and less reliance on spoken responses. It is interesting that many clients find it easier to develop and explain their thoughts and emotions using other expressive media, such as typed communication in the form of an e-mail or diary, music, art, or a pictorial dictionary of feelings.

The therapy includes programs to adjust the clients' self-image to be an accurate reflection of their abilities and the neurological origins of their disorder. Some time needs to be devoted to explaining the nature of Asperger's disorder and how the characteristics account for their differences from others. The author recommends that as soon as the child or adult is told the diagnosis of Asperger's disorder, the clinician needs to carefully and authoritatively explain the nature of the disorder to his or her family but the child must also receive a personal explanation. This is to reduce the likelihood of their developing inappropriate or more maladaptive compensatory mechanisms to their recognition of being different, and to address their concern as to why they have to see psychologists and psychiatrists.

Once clients have improved their cognitive strategies to understand and manage their moods at an intellectual level, it would be necessary to start practicing the strategies in a graduated sequence of assignments. After practice during the therapy session, the client has a project to apply the new knowledge and abilities in real-life situations. The therapist will obviously need to communicate and coordinate with those who will be supporting the client in real-life circumstances. After each practical experience the therapist and client consider the degree of success using activities such as Comic Strip Conversations to debrief the client and to reinforce his or her achievements such as by a "boasting book" or certificate of achievement. It will also help to have a training manual for the client that includes suggestions and explanations. The manual becomes a resource for the client during the therapy but is easily accessible information when the therapy program is complete. One of the issues during the practice will be generalization. People with Asperger's disorder tend to be quite rigid in terms of recognizing when new strategies are applicable in a situation that does not obviously resemble the practice sessions with the psychologist. It will be necessary to ensure that strategies are used in a wide range of circumstances, and no assumptions be made that once an appropriate emotion management strategy has proved successful, it will continue to be used in all settings, and will continue to be successful.

Finally, our scientific knowledge in the area of psychological therapies and Asperger's disorder is remarkably limited. We have case studies, but at present no systematic and rigorous independent research studies that examine whether CBT is an effective treatment with this clinical population (Hare & Paine, 1997). This is despite the known high incidence of mood disorders, especially among adolescents with Asperger's disorder. As a matter of expediency, a clinician may decide to conduct a course of CBT on the basis of the known effectiveness of this form of psychological treatment in the general population. However, we have yet to establish whether it is universally appropriate and to confirm the modifications to accommodate the unusual characteristics and profile of abilities associated with Asperger's disorder.

See also: Autism spectrum disorders

REFERENCES

Attwood, T. (1998). *Asperger's syndrome: A guide for parents and professionals.* London: Jessica Kingsley Publications.

Attwood, T. (2002). Frameworks for behavioural interventions. *Child Adolescent Psychiatric Clinics of North America, 12*, 1–22.

Baron-Cohen, S., Tager-Flusberg, H., & Cohen D. J. (1993). *Understanding other minds: Perspectives from autism.* Oxford: Oxford Medical Publications.

Gray, C. (1998). Social stories and comic strip conversations with students with Asperger's syndrome and high functioning autism. In H. Schopher, G. B. Mesihov, & L. J. Kuuice (Eds.), *Asperger syndrome or high functioning autism*? New York: Plenum Press.

Hare, D. J., & Paine, C. (1997). Developing cognitive behavioural treatments for people with Asperger's syndrome. *Clinical Psychology Forum, 110*, 5–8.

Russel, J. (Ed.). (1997). *Autism as an executive disorder.* Oxford: Oxford Medical Publications.

Attention-Deficit/Hyperactivity Disorder (ADHD)—Adult

J. Russell Ramsay and Anthony L. Rostain

Keywords: adults, psychosocial, combined treatment, case conceptualization

Attention-deficit/hyperactivity disorder (ADHD) is the most prevalent behavioral disorder of childhood, with an estimated 4% of the school-age population affected. Recent prospective longitudinal research has shown that upward of 50–70% of children with ADHD will continue to experience clinically significant symptoms into adulthood (Barkley, 1998). Increasingly, these adults are seeking treatment for this complex neuropsychiatric disorder.

Whereas pharmacotherapy has been a mainstay of treatment for ADHD patients of all ages, the development of effective psychosocial treatments has lagged sorely behind, particularly for adult patients. As recently as 1997, data on psychosocial treatments for adults with ADHD could be summarized as being "entirely anecdotal" (American Academy of Child and Adolescent Psychiatry, 1997). Recently, a few studies of psychosocial approaches for adults with ADHD have appeared in the research literature, with cognitive behavior therapy (CBT) offering some of the more promising results.

The goal of this article is to provide a brief description of the emerging CBT approach for treating adult patients with ADHD. To do so, we will provide a description of the CBT model of adult ADHD, the elements of this treatment approach, and a review of preliminary studies showing the effectiveness of CBT for this clinical population.

DESCRIPTION OF CBT MODEL FOR ADHD IN ADULTS

The core symptoms of ADHD are developmentally inappropriate levels of impulsivity, inattention, and/or hyperactivity that have been present since childhood. To make the diagnosis in adulthood requires clear evidence that these symptoms have caused enduring difficulties throughout the individual's development, although there can be great variability in the intensity of symptoms and in the settings in which they occur. Finally, it must be determined that the symptoms are not better accounted for by another psychiatric or medical condition.

The scientific consensus is that ADHD is a developmental disorder with genetic and neurobiological underpinnings. Heritability ratios derived from research of the children with ADHD and their parents and from twin studies of ADHD probands are virtually equivalent to those derived in studies of height among first-degree family members, with an average of 80% of the variance being explained by genetics and only a trifle attributed to shared environmental factors (e.g., parenting). The core symptoms of ADHD reflect a neuropsychological profile of impaired executive functioning (associated with the prefrontal cortex) that significantly affects an individual's reciprocal interactions with the environment. In particular, impaired inhibition, planning, working memory, and cognitive processing speed appear to subserve the impulsivity and inattentiveness seen in these patients (Barkley, 1997; Faraone & Biederman, 1998).

From a CBT standpoint, then, these executive function deficits associated with ADHD exquisitely influence core beliefs by affecting the ongoing experiences from which individuals compose personal meaning. Considering the cumulative effects of the many problems associated with ADHD on one's adaptive functioning and ongoing sense of self, the adult with ADHD likely presents for assessment and treatment with a history of problems that may have been encoded in the form of maladaptive beliefs (e.g., "I'm a failure"; "I'm incompetent"). Consequently, the symptoms of ADHD and the reactivation of maladaptive beliefs (and concomitant emotions) routinely disrupt the individual's life, further eroding what is often an already fragile sense of self-efficacy and further impairing the effective execution of cognitive problem solving.

CBT offers a therapeutic approach that acknowledges the supreme difficulties associated with ADHD as well as the need to develop effective coping skills. It illuminates the explicit and implicit beliefs that arise from the experience of living with ADHD and offers a framework that integrates the biological and neuropsychological dimensions of the disorder. The next section outlines the core elements of this therapeutic approach.

ELEMENTS OF CBT FOR ADULT ADHD

The elements of CBT that follow will be familiar to any clinician well-versed in the model. What differentiates CBT from being merely a collection of techniques is that, done rightly, it endeavors to enlighten the unique experience of a patient and to help her/him explore possibilities for making desired changes. What follows represents a cross-sectional summary of ongoing efforts to modify CBT to the clinical needs of adults with ADHD (see McDermott, 2000; Ramsay & Rostain, in press).

Diagnosis/Education

Receiving the diagnosis of ADHD is often a liberating experience and offers the first cognitive reframe of a patient's chronic difficulties. To this point, most patients have viewed their difficulties as confirming their maladaptive core beliefs (e.g., "I'm lazy"). Many patients have communicated a sense of relief at finally having a coherent (and nonjudgmental) explanation of their difficulties, hearing that they are not alone in their struggles, and that there is indeed hope for change.

True to the CBT model, patients often have diverse personal notions of their difficulties and the steps they are willing to take in treatment. Some patients respond to the diagnosis with eagerness to explore new coping strategies and openness to making significant changes in their environments. Other patients, however, may be more suspect about the diagnosis and their abilities to change what seem to be uncontrollable cognitive and behavioral impulses. Spending time addressing these issues and matching CBT to the patient's therapeutic pace helps to increase treatment compliance and effectiveness.

The next step is providing psychoeducation about ADHD to the patient to demystify misconceptions about treatment and to shed light on the nature of this syndrome. To encourage further self-awareness we often encourage the patient to augment treatment with personal research, such as reading about adult ADHD or exploring reputable online resources. We caution that while these resources can be very helpful, they will not be as personalized to the patient's unique circumstances as would psychosocial treatment. We also encourage that patients share their impressions of these resources in treatment so that any potential misunderstandings or distortions can be addressed.

Therapeutic Alliance

The therapeutic relationship provides a safe place for the adult with ADHD to explore the nature of his/her difficulties, to develop new coping skills, and to discuss the range of emotions involved in this personal undertaking. Rather than being a blank slate, the therapist actively inquires about the patient's experience, keeps sessions focused, and helps the patient find a balance between accepting the reality of ADHD and making behavioral changes to minimize its negative impact.

A common therapeutic issue is managing what would typically be deemed "therapy-interfering" behaviors. Tardiness to sessions or failure to complete therapeutic homework, traditionally thought to be signs of hostility or resistance, are better understood as manifestations of the executive functioning deficits associated with ADHD. Framing them as opportunities to understand the effects of ADHD and to develop commensurate coping strategies gently addresses both the core symptoms of ADHD and the emotional frustration engendered by these sorts of recurring difficulties in a constructive, nonshaming way.

If patients have been prescribed a medication for their core symptoms, therapy can provide a regular opportunity to monitor both the patient's response and her/his attitudes that might interfere with compliance. Regular consultation between the therapist and prescribing physician, with the patient's expressed consent and input, helps to coordinate treatment.

Case Conceptualization

The neurobiological and cognitive–emotional elements of the experiences of adults with ADHD are unavoidably intertwined. An ongoing case conceptualization allows the clinician and patient to understand how these various factors coalesce to influence that patient's automatic reactions. It also provides a therapeutic touchstone for assessing efforts to modify these reactions and to develop alternative options, particularly for maladaptive core beliefs and self-defeating compensatory strategies.

The most common core beliefs encountered in adults with ADHD cluster around notions of *failure* ("I've not fulfilled my potential"), *defectiveness* ("I'm inadequate"), *social undesirability/exclusion* ("I'm different and no one understands me"), and *incompetence* ("I cannot handle life"). These beliefs often stem from actual life circumstances and seem to "make perfect sense" based on the patient's described experience (e.g., "I frequently failed exams and classes and often had to attend summer school"). However, reexamining these events, simultaneously affirming the patient's affective experience and reexamining the accounts based on a retrospective understanding of ADHD, often opens up novel and/or expanded interpretations (e.g., "I did better when I had a teacher who answered my questions without making me feel that I was stupid").

The most compelling experience that prompts patients to reconsider their beliefs seems to come when they alter their default compensatory strategies that have maintained the maladaptive core beliefs. Of the many compensatory strategies associated with ADHD, *anticipatory avoidance* is the most ubiquitous. This is sometimes referred to as the "excessive procrastination technique" based on the patient's wish that the task will just "go away." This strategy involves putting off a necessary task because the patient anticipates that it will be unpleasant, the benefit for doing the task is too vague or distant in time, and/or the patient assumes his/her performance will ultimately be inadequate. The immediate relief gained whenever the task is avoided, often with the aid of a permission-giving cognition (e.g., "I'll do it later when I'm more up to it"), negatively reinforces avoidance as a default behavior and leads to an accumulation of disappointments. Behavioral experiments permitting the patient to stay on-task for a minimal time (even during a therapy session) provide immediate and positive (or at least less negative than predicted) emotional experiences associated with proactive behaviors.

Ultimately, the case conceptualization for the adult patient with ADHD aids her/him in making informed decisions. No treatment can guarantee that patients will be unaffected by ADHD. It is a neurodevelopmental disorder that requires ongoing coping in order to transcend the core symptoms. CBT helps patients to face challenging life decisions by considering all options without falling into impulsive avoidance patterns. Further, CBT aims to foster resilience, maintaining a focus on important overarching goals in one's life, even in the face of apparent setbacks and delays.

The next section will review preliminary clinical research on the effectiveness of this therapeutic approach.

EMPIRICAL EVIDENCE FOR CBT FOR ADHD

Overall, the empirical literature on psychosocial treatments for adults with ADHD is sparse. CBT approaches have offered some encouraging preliminary results. Wilens et al. (1999) performed a chart review of 26 adults seeking treatment for ADHD. Clinical data were collected at baseline, at the point of medication stabilization, and at the end of CBT (introduced after medication stabilization). The findings indicated that CBT was associated with patient improvements on a measure of depression, on clinician ratings of anxiety and improvements on ADHD symptoms, and on a rating of overall functioning, both when comparing the overall effects of the combination of CBT and meds, and when assessing the effects of CBT after medication stabilization.

Rostain and Ramsay (2003) conducted a prospective pilot study of a treatment approach combining pharmacotherapy and CBT for 45 adults diagnosed with ADHD. Clinical data were gathered at initial assessment and at the end of approximately 16 sessions of CBT. The results indicated that the combined treatment was associated with statistically significant improvements on measures of depression, anxiety, hopelessness, ADHD symptoms, and clinician ratings of ADHD symptoms and overall functioning. A drawback of both studies is that it is difficult to tease apart the relative contributions of CBT and pharmacotherapy. However, anecdotal reports from patients indicate that CBT offers a valuable psychosocial component in their efforts to manage ADHD.

SUMMARY

ADHD is a neurodevelopmental disorder that does not automatically remit during childhood or adolescence, but instead leads to long-standing functional difficulties for a significant portion of those affected. While studies of psychosocial treatments for adults with ADHD have only recently appeared, CBT stands as a strong candidate for being able to effectively address the varied needs of this clinical population.

See also: Attention-deficit/hyperactivity disorder (ADHD)—child, Case formulation

REFERENCES

American Academy of Child & Adolescent Psychiatry. (1997). Practice parameters for the assessment and treatment of children, adolescents, and adults with attention-deficit/hyperactivity disorder. *Journal of the American Academy of Child and Adolescent Psychiatry, 36*(10, Suppl.), 85S–121S.

Barkley, R. A. (1997). *ADHD and the nature of self-control*. New York: Guilford Press.

Barkley, R. A. (Ed.) (1998). *Attention-deficit hyperactivity disorder: A handbook for diagnosis and treatment* (2nd ed.). New York: Guilford Press.

Faraone, S. V., & Biederman, J. (1998). Neurobiology of attention-deficit hyperactivity disorder. *Biological Psychiatry, 44*, 951–958.

McDermott, S. P. (2000). Cognitive therapy for adults with attention-deficit/hyperactivity disorder. In T. E. Brown (Ed.), *Attention deficit disorders and comorbidities in children, adolescents, and adults* (pp. 569–606). Washington, DC: American Psychiatric Press.

Ramsay, J. R., & Rostain, A. L. (in press). A cognitive therapy approach for adult attention-deficit/hyperactivity disorder. *Journal of Cognitive Psychotherapy: An International Quarterly*.

Rostain, A. L., & Ramsay, J. R. (2003). *Results of a pilot study of a combined treatment for adult attention-deficit/hyperactivity disorder*. Manuscript in preparation.

Wilens, T. E., McDermott, S. P., Biderman, J., Abrantes, A., Hahesy, A., & Spencer, T. (1999). Cognitive therapy in the treatment of adults with ADHD: A systematic chart review of 26 cases. *Journal of Cognitive Psychotherapy: An International Quarterly, 13*(3), 215–226.

Attention-Deficit/Hyperactivity Disorder—Child

Ricardo Eiraldi and Kimberly Villarin

Attention-deficit/hyperactivity disorder (ADHD) is a neurodevelopmental disorder characterized by behavior disinhibition, overactivity, and difficulty sustaining attention. It affects 3 to 7% of school-age children in the United States. Prevalence estimates in other industrialized and Third World countries indicate that ADHD affects children of all races, cultures, and socioeconomic status. The gender ratio in the United States is 3:1 male to female, with a larger ratio in clinical samples and a smaller ratio in community samples. Behaviors related to ADHD account for 33 to 50% of all referrals to psychiatric clinics in this country. Up to 70% of children with ADHD continue to meet diagnostic criteria into adolescence, and at least 50% meet diagnostic criteria into young adulthood. Core deficits in ADHD include deficient impulse control, poor affect regulation, difficulty sustaining attention, and hyperactivity. The *Diagnostic and Statistical Manual of Mental Disorders, Fourth Edition* (DSM-IV), distinguishes three subtypes, ADHD Predominantly Inattentive, ADHD Hyperactive-Impulsive, and ADHD Combined. In order to meet diagnostic criteria, symptoms of ADHD must be present across at least two settings and cause clinically significant impairment in social, academic, or occupational functioning. Children with ADHD are, in most cases, chronic underachievers at school, tend to have difficulty reading social cues, have social skills deficits, and often experience social isolation and bullying. The most pervasive and severe adolescent and adult outcomes of ADHD occur in children who have comorbid conduct disorder (CD) and/or mood disorders. The presence of comorbidity in children with ADHD appears to have a direct impact on treatment outcome. In the Multimodal Treatment Study of Children with ADHD (MTA), to date the largest, most comprehensive treatment study of ADHD in children, psychostimulant medication was found to be the single most effective treatment. The combination of behavior modification strategies and psychostimulant medication was the more effective treatment modality for children with ADHD and comorbid anxiety disorders and for those characterized as low socioeconomic status (SES). In the great majority of studies, including the MTA study, only children with ADHD Combined Subtype have been studied. Boys are greatly overrepresented in these studies and little is known about differences in treatment outcome for girls, ethnic/racial minorities, or children of low SES.

HISTORICAL PERSPECTIVE

Cognitive–behavioral interventions (CBI) specifically developed for impulsive and inattentive children have been widely used for over 30 years. In 1971, Meichenbaum and Goodman conducted the first study to test the effectiveness of cognitive training (CT), specifically, self-directed speech, in improving sustained attention and behavioral inhibition in impulsive children. Other studies have also assessed the effectiveness of cognitive modeling, attribution retraining, stress inoculation, self-monitoring, and interpersonal problem solving in treating children with symptoms of ADHD. The basic aim of those interventions was to target self-control, sustained attention, and reflective problem-solving deficits (Braswell, 1998). In those studies, it was expected that by learning the CT strategies, children would internalize self-control and problem-solving steps and apply those skills across situations. The results of earlier studies in this area were very encouraging and some were independently replicated. However, as the most influential meta-analytic study in this area showed, strategies using CBI were effective with mildly behaviorally disordered children, but they were not effective with children who met full diagnostic criteria for ADHD (Abikoff, 1991). Treatments using self-instruction training, cognitive modeling, self-monitoring, self-reinforcement, and cognitive and interpersonal problem solving for treating children with ADHD, generally have not shown significant effects on children's cognitive and behavioral functioning or academic performance when those treatments were used in isolation or in combination with psychostimulant medication (Abikoff, 1991). A notable exception cited in this meta-analysis was the use of self-reinforcement procedures for improving math productivity in children with ADHD. Self-reinforcement, which has been found to increase children's motivation and persistence, led to a significant increase in math productivity and a reduction in careless errors (Abikoff, 1991). Despite the rather discouraging track record of CBI for treating core symptoms of ADHD, the popularity of this type of treatment has not diminished and new applications are being developed.

INDIVIDUAL INTERVENTIONS

Two of the most widely used CBIs are self-instruction training and self-management. The main goal of self-instruction training is to teach children to utilize self-directed speech to guide their own behavior with the assumption that this will lead to improved self-control. Russell Barkley and others have observed that children with ADHD exhibit a developmental lag in developing verbal working memory, also known as internalization of speech. The progressive shift from public to private speech in children has been found to influence motor behavior and inhibitory control. According to Barkley, self-directed speech provides a means for description and reflection by which the child covertly labels, describes, and verbally contemplates the nature of an event or situation before responding to that event. Shapiro and Cole (1994) summarized the self-instruction training process in the following manner.

First, the instructor models self-speech out loud and engages in a task while the child listens and observes. Second, the instructor models self-speech out loud while the child concurrently engages in the activity. Next, the instructor observes and prompts the child when needed while the student uses self-speech out loud and engages in an activity. Then, the instructor observes and eventually discontinues prompting while the child whispers self-speech and engages in a task. The instructor then observes while the child engages in the task silently. From then on, the child is instructed to use private self-directed speech only. Shapiro and Cole (1994) note that children may have difficulty generalizing the behavior outside of the training situation. Repeated practice, especially across a variety of settings, helps to improve generalization. It is also important to consider whether or not the child is motivated, as this will be the deciding factor in the acceptability of this type of intervention. Finally, the instructor must also consider whether the child is more focused on the self-speech procedure than the activity in which he or she is to be engaged. Ervin, Bankert, and DuPaul (1996) found that self-instruction training can be effective with children with ADHD if used with concurrent behavioral components (i.e., contingencies of reinforcement).

Another popular set of strategies for helping children develop self-control is self-management. Self-management is often divided into self-evaluation and self-reinforcement. The original impetus behind these strategies was to develop a set of strategies that could allow teachers to shift the responsibility for monitoring children's behavior to the children themselves (Shapiro & Cole, 1994). In a typical procedure, the teacher identifies one or two behaviors the child needs to improve in class. For example, a third-grade teacher identifies "staying in my seat" and "finishing my work" as target behaviors for the intervention. The teacher then creates the criteria for rating the target behaviors. The teacher may create a Likert-type scale ranging from 1 to 4: 1, very low effort; 2, not enough effort; 3, sufficient effort; and 4, very good effort. The teacher trains the child in completing the ratings using specific examples to explain what each of the levels in the scale represents. The child is then instructed to monitor his or her behavior carefully and try to guess what score the teacher is going to give. The goal of the procedure is to enable the child to approximate and eventually match the ratings of an objective rater. Both the teacher and the child complete a rating at the end of each class period and then compare the results. If the child's ratings are within one point of the teacher's ratings, the child is awarded points. If the child's ratings match the teacher's ratings exactly, the child is awarded bonus points. Of crucial importance in these procedures is developing a reinforcement system that is initially managed by the teacher and then management is slowly transferred to the child. The teacher and the child develop a menu of reinforcements containing privileges or other rewards to be given at school or at home. Once the child consistently matches the teacher's ratings, the teacher's participation in the rating and reinforcement is slowly faded out until the child does both without assistance. Self-management is a popular intervention for addressing classroom disruption and off-task behavior in students with ADHD, especially those in middle school and later grades. Self-management has been found to be effective with students with ADHD, although training must occur at the point of performance in order to ensure maintenance across settings (Shapiro & Cole, 1994).

COMPREHENSIVE INTERVENTIONS

A number of cognitive–behavioral researchers have developed comprehensive interventions for children and adolescents with ADHD, which include individual skills training, family therapy, and school interventions. To our knowledge, none of these comprehensive intervention packages have been compared in their totality vis-à-vis stimulant medications, contingency management, or as an adjunct intervention to the established treatments. Building on the successes and failures of the first generation of CBI for ADHD, Lauren Braswell and Michael Bloomquist (1991) developed one of the most comprehensive treatment packages for children and adolescents with ADHD. This treatment package, *Cognitive–Behavioral Therapy with ADHD Children: Child, Family and School Interventions*, was developed based on an ecological– developmental model of cognitive–behavioral therapy to improve children's self-control. In contrast to previous treatment packages where most of the interventions focused on the child, Braswell and Bloomquist emphasized the role of parents and teachers in teaching, modeling, and monitoring strategies for enhancing self-control. According to Braswell and Bloomquist, just as children have cognitive and behavioral deficits that need to be addressed through skills training, so do parents and families. The primary aim of the treatment is to teach children self-control strategies using problem-solving and self-instruction training. These training strategies are employed in dealing with impersonal problems (e.g., academic work or poor effort) and/or interpersonal problems (e.g., interaction difficulties with peers and family members). Children and adolescents also receive social skills training, anger management training, and strategies for improving academic work. To modify parents' thoughts and attitudes, educational and cognitive restructuring are employed. Parents are taught effective behavior management skills and strategies for reinforcing what the children learn in individual and group sessions.

Families receive communication skills training, and anger and conflict management training. Finally, Braswell and Bloomquist (1991) offer a model for cognitive–behavioral school consultation and instructions for school-based interventions. The treatment manual is intended for children who have ADHD with and without conduct disorder. The manual contains separate child, parent-family, and school components. *Cognitive–Behavioral Therapy with ADHD Children: Child, Family, and School Interventions* (Braswell & Bloomquist, 1991) probably represents the most ambitious effort thus far to apply cognitive–behavioral methods and strategies to children with ADHD and their families. Even though many of the treatment components in this package have been found to be effective in treating a number of behavioral and emotional disorders in children, their effectiveness has not yet been assessed in children with ADHD.

Recent large, long-term, multisite studies indicate that a significant proportion of children with ADHD must be treated using a combination of several treatment modalities including medication and behavioral (contingent management) strategies. Despite the success of stimulant medication and contingency management for treating symptoms of ADHD and mild forms of the most common comorbidities, studies have shown that children with ADHD typically do not generalize skills learned across situations and that treatment gains decrease rapidly after treatment is terminated. Further, the chronic nature of this disorder makes it very difficult for patients and those involved in managing the interventions to coordinate the various treatments and maintain treatment fidelity. Although CBI has proven ineffective for treating clinical levels of inattention, hyperactivity, or impulsivity, it may be effective for treating common comorbidities such as internalizing disorders and thus serve as an effective adjunct treatment. Because CBI places great emphasis on enabling the child to develop self-control and problem-solving skills, it may prove to be effective in supporting generalization and maintenance of treatment gains. The next generation of multimodal treatment studies for ADHD should test the effectiveness of CBI as facilitators and boosters for proven effective treatments. For example, parents could be taught problem-solving steps that they can use to modify contingency management strategies between office visits or after treatment has been terminated. Cognitive restructuring and the scientific method of systematic evidence gathering and hypothesis testing can be taught to parents who hold negative biases or irrational beliefs about medication as a treatment for ADHD. Goal setting and self-management strategies could be used with adolescents who have difficulty managing their medication.

For the past three decades, CBI for ADHD has seen an initial period of theory development, application, and empirical effort, a longer period of critical evaluation followed by strong skepticism, and a more recent period of renewed interest. There is some indication that CBI for ADHD could serve an important role as an adjunct treatment to psychostimulant medication and behavioral contingency management. Future research should investigate what specific components of CBI should be used with specific children to supplement their established treatments.

See also: Attention-deficit/hyperactivity disorder (ADHD)—adult, Parents of children with ADHD

REFERENCES

Abikoff, H. (1991). Cognitive training in ADHD children: Less to it than meets the eye. *Journal of Learning Disabilities, 24*, 205–209.

Braswell, L. (1998). Cognitive behavioral approaches as adjunctive treatments for ADHD children and their families. In S. Goldstein and M. Goldstein (Eds.), *Managing Attention Deficit Hyperactivity Disorder in Children* (2nd Ed.) (pp. 533–544). New York: Wiley.

Braswell, L., & Bloomquist, M. (1991). *Cognitive–behavioral therapy with ADHD children: Child, family, and school interventions*. New York: Guilford Press.

Ervin, R. A., Bankert, C. L., & DuPaul, J. (1996). Treatment of attention-deficit/hyperactivity disorder. In M. A. Reineke, F. M. Dattilio, & A. Freeman (Eds.), *Cognitive therapy with children and adolescents: A casebook for clinical practice*. New York: Guilford Press.

Meichenbaum, D.H., & Goodman, J. (1971). Training impulsive children to talk to themselves. *Journal of Abnormal Psychology, 77*, 115–126.

Shapiro, E. S., & Cole, C. L. (1994). *Behavior change in the classroom: Self-management interventions*. New York: Guilford Press.

Autism Spectrum Disorders

Raymond G. Romanczyk and Jennifer M. Gillis

Keywords: autism, autism spectrum disorder, fears/phobias, Asperger's disorder, social skills anxiety

Currently, there are five different disorders under the category of Pervasive Developmental Disorders (PDD) in the DSM-IV-TR (APA, 2000). The term Autism Spectrum

Disorders (ASD) is commonly used in place of PDD, particularly by the lay public. The most prevalent diagnoses in this category—Autistic Disorder, Asperger's Disorder, and Pervasive Developmental Disorder-Not Otherwise Specified (PDD-NOS)—are the three most commonly associated with ASD. These developmental disorders have profound effects on specific areas of development. The three share substantial deficits in social development and restricted or stereotyped patterns of activities, interests, and behaviors. Unlike Asperger's Disorder, language development in individuals with autism and PDD-NOS is typically significantly delayed or absent. While specific prevalence rates are controversial (estimates of 2–6 per 1000 for ASD), the relative current prevalence rates can be ordered from most frequent to least frequent: PDD-NOS, autism, and Asperger's Disorder.

Autism, Asperger's Disorder, and PDD-NOS are heterogeneous disorders. Diagnostic criteria encompass a wide range of specific symptoms, which can vary substantially in their expression from individual to individual. Comorbidity is also an important factor with respect to heterogeneity as autism can occur with other disorders or conditions such as fragile X disorder, Anxiety Disorder, mental retardation, or epilepsy. While many hypotheses exist as to etiology, the cause (s) remains unknown. It is clear that these disorders have a neurobiological basis. However, the specific mechanisms and links between pathophysiology and behavior remain unidentified. These disorders are most likely present at birth, but may not manifest for several years. There is currently no physical or medical test for these disorders.

COMPLEX CLINICAL PRESENTING PROBLEMS

With regard to cognitive characteristics, individuals with autism, Asperger's Disorder, and PDD-NOS vary widely in terms of deficits, delays, and advanced skills. Some of these cognitive deficits include difficulty with categorical thinking, emotion recognition, rule-governed behavior, perspective taking, logical reasoning, executive functioning, and abstract and symbolic representations. Individuals with Asperger's Disorder often demonstrate minimal impairment compared to individuals with autism and PDD-NOS. As an example of a specific deficit, in the context of categorical thinking, the category of chair would include lawn chair, recliner, rocking chair, table chair, and so on; an individual with autism or PDD-NOS may have difficulty with placing these types of chairs under this one category. Rather, the individual might use each type of chair as its own category. Individuals with autism, Asperger's Disorder, or PDD-NOS may also have difficulty with rule-governed behavior either in comprehending the rule or in responding to nested rules. An individual with autism or PDD-NOS may take longer to comprehend a general rule than a specific rule. An example of a common rule-governed behavior is that children are told to look both ways before crossing a street. A child with autism or PDD-NOS may only understand this rule to apply to the specific street at which the rule was taught and not apply the rule to other streets, roads, pathways, and the like. Further, difficulty is often encountered with teaching a broad rule, for example, examining the environment for possible dangerous situations. The impairment in rule-governed behavior for individuals with Asperger's Disorder can be more subtle and is sometimes referred to as demonstrating a significant lack of common sense.

Individuals with autism, Asperger's Disorder, and PDD-NOS have significant difficulty in perspective taking, which makes traditional role-playing, modeling, and cognitive interventions problematic. Thus, modification of CBT procedures is necessary in order to address this fundamental deficit. It is important to note that this deficit is not a distortion (e.g., paranoia) but rather is the impairment in the ability to understand and recognize consequences and actions from another person's point of view (e.g., egocentrism). For individuals with autism and PDD-NOS, because of their typically significant language delays/deficits, modification of CBT procedures along this dimension must also be made.

OUTCOMES

Cognitive–behavioral therapy has not yet had a major influence in the treatment of individuals with ASD, as individuals with these disorders may have limited or impaired cognitive and language abilities. Applied behavior analysis (ABA) is a complex intervention process demonstrated to be effective in the treatment of ASD. It involves many similar components of CBT, and focuses strongly on experiential learning. ABA includes the comprehensive use of principles of learning in order to develop or enhance skills of individuals with and without disabilities. In ABA, interventions are designed, implemented, and evaluated in a systematic fashion. The individual's behavior and the environment are observed and measured to detect progress, impediments to progress, and other variables influencing behavior, thus making it conceptually similar to CBT.

Emerging CBT interventions for individuals with ASD, with influence from the ABA methodology, include the application of relaxation techniques and systematic desensitization procedures for individuals with fears and phobias. Since many individuals with ASD have impaired cognitive and communication abilities, these procedures are adjusted to the individual's specific limitations in understanding the language component of the intervention(s). Some of the symptoms that are impediments to CBT and therefore require adjustment are:

- Poor eye contact
- Poor reciprocal social interactions
- Poor social communication skills
- Poor recognition and expression of emotions
- Slow acquisition of new skills
- Poor generalization of skills
- Poor attention and motivation
- Poor behavioral flexibility
- Poor impulse control
- Intense behavioral outbursts in the absence of typical antecedents.

The initial assessment phase for CBT usually consists of interview, self-report, surveys, or questionnaires assessing current psychological functioning. These types of assessments can also be used with individuals with ASD, with certain modifications; for instance, pictures of faces displaying different emotions to assist the individual in correctly identifying his or her own emotions. Behavioral symptoms of individuals with ASD can also be measured (e.g., frequency, intensity) and monitored throughout a CBT intervention to indicate progress. Behaviors such as withdrawal, poor eye contact, and lack of reciprocal interaction are often clinically relevant and important variables.

Another component common to CBT is teaching clients to recognize their feelings and learn how their feelings and thoughts influence behavior. Teaching individuals with ASD the behavioral, cognitive, and physiological symptoms associated with different emotions is often an extreme challenge. Significant time may be devoted over numerous sessions to impact this limitation. Although it may seem contraindicated, group therapy may be effective as it allows for the use of peer modeling in order to teach imitation skills, appropriate use of language (communication), and social interactions. Even individuals with significant impairments in cognition and communication or language skills may benefit from group therapy. However, one-to-one therapy will typically also be needed to make interactions more discrete and sequential, in order to improve recognition and modeling. These sessions may include role-playing and using scripts to teach appropriate interaction skills that will be required in a group setting, which in turn will maximize generalization of these skills outside of the therapeutic context. It is often necessary to create multiple situations and create lists of choices as to what are appropriate and inappropriate ways of dealing with different situations, as self-generation of such options is typically highly impaired.

Social skills impairment in individuals with ASD can often impede developing friendships, holding conversations, and participating in employment, to name a few. For some individuals with ASD, such impact on social interaction with the resulting social isolation may lead to depression. Depending on the individual's chronological age and functioning level, different goals for therapy are addressed. For example, for children with ASD the social skills of being a good sport and learning how to appropriately handle losing may be taught, along with other social skills including teaching eye contact, inviting a friend to the movies, and even telephone conversational skills. For very young children with ASD, the simple task of sharing may be the focus.

Difficulty with language and communication abilities may also be a focus of CBT for individuals with ASD. Individuals with ASD tend to have difficulty with abstract concepts. For example, teaching humor or use of slang can be challenging as they involve the often subtle use of language and abstract concepts and relationships. Such seemingly simple skills as use of humor and slang can be essential in establishing and maintaining appropriate peer interactions.

Some individuals with ASD have difficulty with transitions or changes in routine. CBT procedures that focus on self-monitoring and anxiety reduction, as well as problem solving, can help with providing the skills to prepare for such change (expected or not) in their daily schedule.

Individuals with ASD have difficulty with self-perception and self-esteem. Self-talk strategies may help individuals with ASD improve in both areas. When using self-talk strategies for individuals with ASD, it may be necessary to have a more overt system for self-prompting than is usually the case, such as using a visual system. Thus, the extent to which each of these CBT interventions may be used will depend on the level of functioning of the individual with ASD and his or her particular pattern of symptom expression.

Homework is necessary in order to focus on practicing skills learned in therapy. This is all the more true for individuals with ASD who often display poor maintenance and generalization of skills. Usually skill practice for homework assignments will require a parent or other adult who can serve as an in vivo coach. It may be important to have a parent or peer education component to teach them how to participate as "co-therapists." Consistently practicing the skills learned in therapy is a critical component for individuals with ASD.

FUTURE DIRECTIONS

The discussion up to this point has focused on the clinical modification of CBT interventions for individuals with ASD. Specific outcome research for such modification is lacking, although there are encouraging case reports of success.

Perhaps the most neglected but potentially useful CBT intervention procedures involve the use of relaxation techniques in concert with cognitive structuring. It is not uncommon that the comorbidity of ASD and Anxiety Disorder is not detected/addressed, given the extreme behavior outbursts and the relative social isolation presumed to be simply a characteristic of ASD. Since social situations may increase the level of anxiety in general for individuals with ASD, this is particularly problematic because a primary goal of therapy is often to improve social interaction. The use of relaxation and/or diaphragmatic breathing in combination with CBT has proven useful for individuals with anxiety and related disorders. Application to individuals with ASD would appear to be a promising direction (Luscre & Center, 1996). However, systematic controlled outcome research for CBT with individuals with ASD is currently lacking, but there is increasing interest and activity in the clinical application of CBT.

See also: Anxiety—adult, Asperger's disorder, Social skills training

REFERENCES

American Psychiatric Association. (2000). *Diagnostic and statistical manual of mental disorders* (4th ed., text rev.). Washington, DC: Author.

Luscre, D. M., & Center, D. B. (1996). Procedure for reducing dental fear in children with autism. *Journal of Autism and Developmental Disorders, 26*, 547–556.

RECOMMENDED READINGS

Cautela, J. R., & Groden, J. (1978). *Relaxation: A comprehensive manual for adults, children, and children with special needs*. Champaign, IL: Research Press.

Groden, G., & Baron, M. G. (Eds.) (1991). *Autism: Strategies for change: A comprehensive approach to the education and treatment of children with autism and related disorders*. New York: Gardner Press.

Lesniak-Karpiak, K., Mazzocco, M. M. M., & Ross, J. L. (2003). Behavioral assessment of social anxiety in females with Turner or fragile X syndrome. *Journal of Autism and Developmental Disorders, 33*, 55–67.

Love, S. R., Matson, J. L., & West, D. (1990). Mothers as effective therapists for autistic children's phobias. *Journal of Applied Behavioral Analysis, 23*, 379–385.

Palkowitz, R., & Wisenfeld, A. R. (1980). Differential autonomic responses of autistic and normal children. *Journal of Autism and Developmental Disorders, 10*, 347–360.

Romanczyk, R. G., & Matthews, A. L. (1998). Physiological state as antecedent: Utilization in functional analysis. In J. K. Luiselli & M. J. Cameron (Eds.), *Antecedent control: Innovative approaches to behavioral support*. Baltimore: Brookes.

Steen, B. E., & Zuriff, G. E. (1977). The use of relaxation in the treatment of self-injurious behavior. *Journal of Behavior Therapy and Experimental Psychiatry, 8*, 447–448.

B

Behavioral Assessment

Robert A. DiTomasso and Robert Gilman

Keywords: functional analysis, behavior analysis, cognitive behavioral case conceptualization, case formulation, behavioral observation

Behavioral assessment is a specific empirically based assessment paradigm which evolved from the field of behavior therapy. Traditional assessment approaches, based on the trait model, lacked utility for behavioral clinicians and researchers who stressed the critical importance of directly observable phenomena and the verifiability of observations. According to Bellack and Hersen (1998), behavioral assessment, then, is an empirically driven, multimethod, multimodal, and multi-informant process that involves the carefully specified measurement of observable behavior and associated temporally related causal variables. Behavioral assessment is, therefore, a systematic approach designed to facilitate the understanding of behavior and its reliable and valid measurement for clinical and research purposes. Ultimately, the purpose of this process is to provide a sound basis for clinical decision making and the development of effective behavior change strategies (Haynes, Leisen, & Blaine, 1997; Haynes & Williams, 2003). Behavioral assessment procedures rely on minimally inferential tools that are applied in a repeated measurement format over a period of time for a given behavior of interest. These measurements target problem behaviors and associated antecedent and consequential social, physical, and environmental factors as they relate to the development and maintenance of problem behavior.

Behavioral assessment provides data about what a person does, the circumstances under which the behavior reliably occurs, how often the behavior occurs, whether a behavior should be increased or decreased, how long it lasts, and the consequences of the behavior, that is, its impact regarding what is obtained, escaped, or avoided as a result (Bellack & Hersen, 1998). These data provide a basis for conducting a functional analysis of behavior or behavior analysis specifying critical variables to consider in the development of treatment interventions.

DEVELOPMENT OF PARADIGM

The behavioral assessment model developed out of the growing dissatisfaction with traditional assessment approaches. These traditional approaches were based on a trait model of personality. Inferred enduring characteristics of individuals were used to explain and predict the behavior of individuals across different contexts and situations. Behaviorists viewed personality as the sum total of an individual's habit repertoire and behavior (Wolpe, 1973). As a result, traditional approaches simply could not provide the behavioral clinician with the data that were needed to develop a conceptualization of a patient's problem, let alone a behavioral intervention. The popularity of behavior therapy called for an assessment approach that made similar assumptions about human behavior. The behavioral assessment model shares the underlying assumptions of the behavioral approach. First, learning, a relatively permanent change in behavior that occurs as a result of the experience of the individual, is viewed as a primary mechanism for the development of maladaptive behavior. Principles of learning could be used to explain the onset, development, and maintenance of maladaptive responding. Second, this approach emphasizes the observable and focuses on the here and now. Third, the behavior, as opposed to some assumed underlying cause, is the problem to be targeted, Fourth, principles of learning could, then, be used to help clients learn more adaptive responses that are incompatible with maladaptive responses. The behavioral approach to assessment, therefore, encompassed these assumptions which led to the development of methods for actively gathering empirical information about maladaptive problems causing impairment. This information could then be used to inform a learning-based conceptualization of the client's problem.

Traditional assessment approaches relied heavily on inference, too subjective a process for most behaviorists. Behaviorists placed a premium on observation, not inference. The subjective nature of inference made it susceptible to bias in the interpretation of behavior. Behavioral clinicians sought an approach that provided an actual sample of the individual's behavior in the contexts of interest.

In the traditional model, the problematic behavior of an individual was viewed as a symptom of some underlying nonobservable cause. Failure to understand and treat the underlying cause was viewed as a sure means of promoting treatment failure and consequent symptom substitution. In the behavioral assessment model, the behavior is the problem to be treated by unlearning it and relearning more adaptive responses.

CRITICAL CHARACTERISTICS OF BEHAVIORAL ASSESSMENT

Empirical Basis

Behavioral assessment is empirically based, meaning that it is capable of being verified by direct observation. The criterion behavior of interest and the test situation are one and the same. Therefore, generalizing from the behavioral assessment data to the actual life situation of the client is usually not an issue. Obtaining an adequate sample of the situations in which the criterion behavior is likely to occur is, however, essential in providing a thorough understanding of the behavior in question. Therefore, scheduling and collecting observations across a variety of relevant situations is most beneficial. Limiting observations to a small number of situations may prevent a thorough understanding of the target behavior, especially if these situations preclude the emission of the target response (DiTomasso & Colameco, 1982). For some problems, setting the occasion for the response to occur may be necessary. Otherwise, waiting for situations to occur that include occasions for the response may be too time-consuming and impractical.

Multiple Methods

In behavioral assessment there is reliance on multiple methods, which are selected and based on the nature of the problem to be studied. The characteristics of the target behavior or problem measured, such as frequency, intensity, latency, duration, or a combination of such, depend on the nature of the problem. In some instances, multiple facets of the problem behavior may require observation. The intent is for the method to yield the maximum amount of relevant and usable information for the least amount of effort and cost. Behavioral assessment tools are tailor-fitted and designed to yield the most important information. Behavioral clinicians do not employ a measure of some underlying trait on which to infer behavior. Rather, the behavioral observations are directly obtained in the natural environment where the behavior is occurring, either directly observed by another or self-monitored by the patient. Even in situations where observable behavior is coded in some fashion, the reliance on inference is minimal.

Explicitly Defining the Target Behavior

The quality of the information obtained from behavioral assessment depends on explicitly defining the target behavior or complaint in question. Carefully and precisely delineating and operationalizing the critical components of the target behavior allows for clear discrimination of the occurrence and nonoccurrence of the behavior under observation (DiTomasso & Colameco, 1982). Clear specification of the target behavior allows for more precise measurement of the phenomena and ensures that when the behavior in question occurs, it is detected and recorded by the observer. It also serves to differentiate instances of the target behavior from other behaviors that could otherwise be confused with the target behavior. Over the years as the field has evolved, there has been a noticeably increasing trend to rely, or perhaps overrely, on self-report measures as opposed to observational methods (Taylor, 1999). One example of a self-report approach is behavior rating scales, which rely on a thorough representative sampling of the universe of behaviors that define a construct.

Multimodal Focus

Behavioral assessment is also multimodal and focuses on more than one aspect of the client. In this sense, behavioral clinicians are most often interested in more than just the behavior of the client. Behavior is therefore more broadly defined and may include cognitive, emotional, and physiological parameters. By engaging the client to become a direct observer and recorder of his/her own private events, the assessment helps to make in a sense the unobservable more observable.

Multiple Informants

This assessment approach may incorporate observational information from more than one source. Possible informants include the client as well as those who share the client's environment including family members, teachers, peers, psychiatric technicians, nurses, and the like. Reliance on other observers helps to provide a fuller understanding of the target behavior from different perspectives. All observers, however, employ behavioral assessment tools designed to provide useful information for the clinician and are asked to provide carefully collected observations. The use of observers necessitates that they are trained in the methods that are being employed. Training must ensure that the observers know how to use the tools correctly and complete them within the parameters that are likely to increase their utility. For example, when making observations, the data are recorded at the time of the occurrence and not completed at a later time when memory decay may threaten the validity of the information.

As far as observation is concerned, more is better. Other informants may shed light on some aspect of the problem behavior about which the client does not have access or awareness. An important by-product of this process is that it may ultimately help those in the client's environment learn how their own behavior may be intimately tied into maintaining the problem behavior of the client. These observational data may also serve to provide social validation about the change in a client's behavior, an important yardstick for determining the clinical significance of any change.

Identifying Antecedent Conditions

The identification of antecedent conditions is valuable in delineating specific circumstances and situations under which the target problem manifests itself. The problem behavior may be more likely to occur under one set of conditions than another. In this sense these situations may represent high-risk situations and associated cues to which the client and clinician need to be alerted. If the target problem is found to differentially occur across situations, the exploration of differences across these situations may provide helpful information about subtle precipitating factors.

Identifying Time-Associated Causal Variables

In understanding and predicting behavior, behavioral assessment considers time-associated causal variables. A complete picture of a problematic behavior involves considerably more than the mere observation of the behavior itself. Since the information derived from behavioral assessment is used to select, design, and implement interventions, information about the frequency of a problem behavior provides only part of the picture. Behavioral assessment data often include the circumstances under which a behavior is likely to occur; the target behavior itself; associated thoughts, images, and feelings; and the consequences in the client's environment that may serve to reinforce and maintain the problem. The determination of factors serving to reinforce and maintain problematic behavior is crucial. By observing the impact a problem has on the client's environment, it is possible to identify possible gains mediated through the role of positive reinforcement. It is also possible to determine how the problem may serve to prevent the client from contact with an anticipated aversive stimulus (avoidance) or remove the client from an aversive situation (escape).

Repeated Measurements Over Time

Behavioral assessment measures are usually collected across a variety of situations over time. Data are collected during baseline, treatment, and follow-up. Assessment is therefore not a one-shot deal. Rather, the clinician obtains a series of integrated snapshots of the targets by sampling across a variety of relevant contexts. The synthesis of this information provides a comprehensive view of the target problem yielding clinically useful information. Baseline information provides a measure of the severity of the problem, useful information for performing a functional analysis, and a criterion against which to measure treatment efficacy. Ongoing data obtained during treatment further inform the case conceptualization, either supporting the selection of treatment or necessitating a reanalysis of the problem and selection of another treatment. Data obtained during the treatment phase should confirm improvement of the problem. Otherwise, the treatment plan has been misinformed assuming the correct implementation of the treatment has occurred. Follow-up data provide a measure of the stability of the behavior change, identify possible relapse, and the degree to which alternative ways of responding have been learned.

Scheduling of Observations

In the assessment of targets, continuous observation would be costly in terms of time and effort and most assuredly impractical. To provide valuable information, behavioral assessments must be collected under circumstances that ensure adequate representation of the target problem. Therefore, decisions about when to collect observations involve selection and planning of observations during samples of time and events that are most likely to be representative of the problem. Otherwise, a biased and inaccurate view of the problem may be obtained.

Reliability of Observations Collected

When using an observer to collect information, an important question centers around the reliability of the information gathered. The key issue has to do with interobserver agreement, that is, the extent to which the observations are replicable by an independent observer. Although less frequently addressed, the reliability of self-monitored information is just as important. In either case, the use of an independent observer, when relevant, can add much to the confidence one places in the information obtained. Considering the extent to which two observers agree regarding, for example, the frequency and duration of a target behavior, lends credibility to the observational process and the information itself. The use of an independent observer with self-monitored information necessitates that the behavior being self-monitored be observable and open to public scrutiny (e.g., having a spouse monitor the amount of time it takes for an insomniac to fall asleep).

Reactivity Issues

The mere fact of knowing one is being observed or that one is observing oneself may produce reactive effects. Reactive effects occur when the knowledge of observation changes the phenomenon being observed. In short, the observations obtained when one is aware of the observation will not necessarily generalize to situations when observations are made without this awareness of the client. From a clinical standpoint, reactive effects appear to occur in a direction that is congruent with treatment effects and although transient in nature, may be initially confused with treatment effects.

Unobtrusive and Random Reliability Checks

Reliability between observers may be expected to be higher when observers, even self-observers, are aware that reliability will be checked. In this sense, the reliability of observations obtained when the observers are aware may not generalize to situations when they are aware they are not being checked. A possible solution to this problem is to make the observers aware that reliability will be checked, but not let them know when the checking is actually occurring (DiTomasso & Colameco, 1982).

METHODOLOGY OF BEHAVIORAL ASSESSMENT

There are many possible behavioral assessment tools available for use. The exact nature of these tools depends on the specific types of target problems being assessed. Methods of behavioral assessment include direct observation by another or self-observation in vivo, in vitro, or during performance on an analogue measure. Regardless of the specific tool selected or designed, a commonality across all tools is the monitoring of important and relevant aspects of the target response. For example, a behavioral assessment tool for monitoring panic attacks might include the day, situation, symptoms, thoughts, anxiety levels, the time the panic attack began, time ended, and behaviors. A mood diary might include the situation, feeling, rating of feelings, automatic thought, belief rating, specific type of cognitive distortion, rational thought, rerating of negative automatic thought, and rerating of feelings. A tool for monitoring tantrums might include the day, frequency of tantrums, duration of each tantrum, situations precipitating tantrums, and the behaviors of significant others in response to the tantrums. A food diary may include the foods, amounts of food, calories consumed at each meal, eating situations, thoughts, and associated feelings preceding eating. A headache chart may include the day, time of onset of headache, specific symptoms, duration of headache, pain intensity rating, and behavior of the client. A smoking chart may include the situations in which smoking occurs, the number of cigarettes smoked, relevant thoughts, and feelings.

USE OF BEHAVIORAL ASSESSMENT IN CASE CONCEPTUALIZATION

To develop accurate assessment plans, case conceptualizations, and, ultimately, effective treatment plans, cognitive–behavioral therapists must carefully assess the features, context, and manner in which a client's cognitive–behavioral difficulties develop (Thorpe & Olson, 1997). Both Persons (1989) and, more recently, Needleman (1999) offer clinically useful models. The case conceptualization, a template for understanding clients, accurately accounts for the client's past behaviors, explains the client's present behaviors, and predicts the client's future behavior (Needleman, 1999). A number of terms, synonymous with case conceptualization, describe the process for identifying antecedent variables for problematic behavior including functional analysis, behavior analysis, and functional assessment (Cone, 1997). Whatever term one chooses to use, the formulation is directly linked to behavioral assessment. As a higher-order process, case conceptualization firmly rests on the careful collection, evaluation, and interpretation of valid and reliable behavioral assessment data. The quality of behavioral assessment data directly affects the quality of the formulation. A poorly conceived and implemented behavioral assessment plan could misinform the conceptualization process and ultimately undermine treatment.

Behavioral assessment data, then, fuel the case conceptualization process by providing clinically relevant information that helps clients understand their problems more fully from a learning-based perspective. These data are integrated and synthesized with other relevant information about the client and form a solid foundation for the selection of specific treatment protocols. Finally, this information is helpful in predicting barriers to treatment.

USE OF BEHAVIORAL ASSESSMENT IN TREATMENT PLANNING AND IMPLEMENTATION

Treatment planning and implementation are critical to successful cognitive–behavioral therapy. Both are linked to the therapist's ability to generate clinical hypotheses and develop, refine, and tailor treatment to the client's needs. Behavioral assessment helps the clinician formulate case-specific treatment plans (Needleman, 1999; Persons, 1989) that are of direct relevance to the client's treatment.

Behavioral assessment enables the clinician to reduce target problems into observable and measurable units. It also informs the treatment process in an ongoing manner. For example, baseline data provide the clinician with important information about the state of the client's problem before an intervention has been made. During the course of treatment the clinician expects that if treatment is appropriately attending to the critical aspects of the problem, change will occur in the desired direction.

BEHAVIORAL ASSESSMENT IN CLINICAL RESEARCH

Behavioral assessment serves an important function in clinical research. It is used to substantiate the effects of treatments by providing evidence of change in the targets of treatment. Over the past many years it has been and continues to be an integral part of single-subject experimental methodology.

FUTURE DIRECTIONS IN BEHAVIORAL ASSESSMENT

Behavioral assessment is an integral and critical component of cognitive–behavioral approaches to assessment, case formulation, treatment planning, clinical outcome evaluation, and research. It lies at the very heart and soul of the cognitive–behavioral empirically supported model of treatment. As the field of cognitive–behavioral therapy continues to evolve and expand in the future, behavioral assessment is likely to remain a central and indispensable element of this important model.

See also: Applied behavior analysis

REFERENCES

Bellack, A. S., & Hersen, M. (1998). *Behavioral assessment: A practical guide*. Needham Heights, MA: Allyn & Bacon.

Cone, J. D. (1997). Issues in functional analysis in behavioral assessment. *Behavior Research and Therapy, 35*, 259–279.

DiTomasso, R. A., & Colameco, S. (1982). Patient self-monitoring of behavior. *Journal of Family Practice, 15*(1), 79–83.

Haynes, S. N., Leisen, M.B., & Blaine, D.D. (1997). Design of individualized behavioral treatment programs using functional analytical clinical case models. *Psychological Assessment, 9*(4), 334.

Haynes, S. N., & Williams, A. E. (2003). Case formulation and the design of behavioral treatment programs: Matching treatment mechanisms to causal variables for behavior problems. *European Journal of Psychological Assessment, 19*(3), 164.

Needleman, L. D. (1999). *Cognitive case conceptualization: A guidebook for practitioners*. Mahwah, NJ: Erlbaum.

Persons, J. B. (1989). *Cognitive therapy in practice: A case formulation approach*. New York: Norton.

Taylor, S. (1999). Behavioral assessment: Review and prospect. *Behavior Research and Therapy, 37*(5), 475–482.

Thorpe, G. L., & Olson, S. L. (1997). *Behavior therapy: Concepts, procedures, and applications*. Needham Heights, MA: Allyn & Bacon.

Wolpe, J. (1973). *The practice of behavior therapy*. New York: Pergamon Press.

Behavioral Neuropsychology

*Arthur MacNeill Horton, Jr.**

Keywords: neuropsychology, rehabilitation, behavioral treatment, brain damage, brain injury

The theoretical and scientific knowledge required for the specialty of behavioral neuropsychology concerns brain–behavior relationships and includes considerable portions of the human neurosciences and theories of hemispheric specialization (Kolb & Whishaw, 1996); in addition, knowledge of psychometrics and measurement theory is important (Reynolds, 1981). In pursuit of conceptual clarity, the following brief definitions are provided. The terms to be discussed have been used in idiosyncratic fashion by numerous authors. This practice has undoubtedly diminished the conceptual clarity of the issues. To date, satisfactory methods of correcting this situation have not been developed.

*Dr. Horton's contribution is based in part on his chapter in the *Neuropsychology Handbook* (Horton, 1997).

NEUROPSYCHOLOGY DEFINED

While different authors have advanced multiple definitions of neuropsychology, in the context of this contribution the following definition was selected: "Neuropsychology is the scientific study of brain–behavior relationships" (Meier, 1974). Some limitations of this definition will be briefly mentioned. The definition ignores distinctions among the many fields of neuropsychology that have developed over the years (Davison, 1974; Horton, Wedding, & Phay, 1981). In order to provide further clarification, the following will offer a brief definition of behavioral neuropsychology.

Behavioral neuropsychology is the most recent addition to the principal subfields of neuropsychology. Horton (1979) has offered the following definition of behavioral neuropsychology:

> Essentially, behavioral neuropsychology may be defined as the application of behavior therapy techniques to problems of organically impaired individuals while using a neuropsychological assessment and intervention perspective. This treatment philosophy assumes that inclusion of data from neuropsychological assessment strategies would be helpful in the formulation of hypotheses regarding antecedent conditions (external or internal) for observed phenomena of psychopathology. (p. 20)

This new area of research and clinical interest combines elements of both clinical neuropsychology and behavior therapy. Despite a focus on applied aspects of neuropsychology, behavioral neuropsychology may be easily discriminated from related subfields of neuropsychology by its reliance on behavior therapy/applied behavior analysis research for its treatment/intervention techniques. The major emphasis of behavioral neuropsychology is on the problems of management, retraining, and rehabilitation (Horton, 1994). In contrast, the related areas of clinical neuropsychology and behavioral neurology are more associated with the problems of clinical diagnosis. Furthermore, it should be clear that experimental neuropsychology can be easily separated from clinical neuropsychology, behavioral neurology, and behavioral neuropsychology by the primary research aims of the former and the more clinical aims of the latter (Horton & Wedding, 1984).

Essentially, the biological problem that behavioral neuropsychology addresses is that of impaired brain functioning due to cerebral dysfunction. The distinctive knowledge and skills that define the specialty which reflect the problem are knowledge of functional neuroanatomy, clinical neurology and neurosurgery, behavioral neurology, neuropathology, and psychopharmacology. The essential understanding is how the brain functions and how the functioning of the brain on multiple levels is related to behavioral functioning at various levels. The problem of impaired neuropsychological functioning can be seen in a number of varied settings with respect to physical and organizational aspects. Impaired functioning may be relatively obvious in terms of a stroke victim or relatively subtle in terms of a child with attention deficit disorder syndrome. The range of settings in which disordered brain functioning may cause behavioral disturbances can encompass a private practice setting, an educational setting, an industrial or occupational setting, a substance abuse treatment facility, a rehabilitation setting a neurology or psychiatry ward in a major teaching hospital or in a community hospital. In all of these settings, or impaired brain functioning may cause disturbances that are responsible for specific problems in terms of adapting to the behavioral demands of the setting. The sorts of problems that the biological insult causes may be related to cognitive skills, sensory–perceptual abilities, motor skills, or emotional/personality functioning. This may have psychological ramifications with respect to the person's adequacy or inability to self-manage his or her own behavior or may have social complications with respect to the person's ability to interact with others to maintain a productive lifestyle. The person may be unable to contribute through vocational activities to the welfare of society and also be limited in assuming mature roles in relationships and family activities such as parenting. The problem in terms of psychological or social aspects to a degree is related to the fit of the person in the special circumstances in which he or she finds him- or herself.

Examinations of major currents in behavioral therapy can help delineate the scope of behavioral neuropsychology. Behavior therapy can be seen as having developed three salient subareas: behavior, cognitive, and affective. Due to the work of Watson (1913), Skinner (1938), and others several decades ago, behavior therapy is premised on the principle that behavior is a function of environmental consequences and utilizes positive and negative reinforcement as major concepts.

The affective trend in behavior therapy owes much to the early work of Joseph Wolpe, M.D. (1958), the South African psychiatrist who is credited with the establishment of clinical behavior therapy. His techniques of systematic desensitization and assertiveness training have, in large part, sparked the clinical behavior therapy movement.

In contrast, the cognitive–behavioral trend postulates that inferred variables, such as thoughts and images, should be seen as legitimate concepts in the functional analysis of human behavior (Mahoney, 1974). The cognitive trend in behavior therapy has been a subject of controversy (Beck & Mahoney, 1979; Ellis, 1979; Lazarus, 1979; Wolpe, 1978). More recent contributions such as this volume demonstrate the current wide acceptance of cognitive–behavioral therapy and its preeminence in the human services and mental health fields.

HISTORICAL DEVELOPMENTS

One of the first to suggest that behavioral neuropsychological knowledge would be helpful in understanding childhood learning disorders was William Gaddes (1968). Many have advocated such a position (Hynd & Obrzut, 1981; Rourke, 1975); indeed, some have gone so far as to suggest that the interface of education and behavioral neuropsychology has been so productive that a subdiscipline has evolved. Various terms advocated to describe this new subdiscipline have included *school neuropsychology* (Hynd & Obrzut, 1981), *developmental neuropsychology* (van der Vlugt, 1979), and *educational neuropsychology* (Gaddes, 1981). Factors that have contributed to the current enthusiasm regarding the educational relevance of neuropsychological data include the wealth of reliable clinical findings correlating localized brain lesions and academic performance.

Of even more immediate value to the notion of promoting an interface between education and behavioral neuropsychology has been research demonstrating the value of neuropsychological data in treatment planning for educational deficiencies. Perhaps some of the most interesting results were obtained by Hartlage (1975). In this early study, first-graders were placed in reading programs based on neuropsychological assessment data. The experimental group was 1.5 standard deviations above the control group in reading after 1 year. Similar results have been obtained by others (Kaufman & Kaufman, 1983). It should be noted that these studies utilized a strengths approach to treatment planning (Reynolds, 1981). Expectations are that a strengths approach will be of great value and that more effective use of cognitive–behavioral therapy can be made with this approach (Horton, Wedding, & Phay, 1981). As noted by others (Satz & Fletcher, 1981), the therapeutic role of the behavioral neuropsychologist is emerging. A major and salient trend in human neuropsychology is the move away from the classic diagnostic role toward that of intervention/therapy (Diller & Gordon, 1981; Horton & Miller, 1984; Horton & Wedding, 1984). One strong trend in the therapy of the brain-impaired is the use of behavior modification with the brain-injured (Horton, 1979; Horton & Wedding, 1984). Research documents excellent results (Horton, 1997; Horton & Miller, 1984; Horton & Wedding, 1984).

See also: Developmental disabilities in community settings, Rehabilitation psychology

REFERENCES

Beck, A., & Mahoney, M. J. (1979). Schools of thought. *American Psychologist, 34*, 93–98.

Davison, L. A. (1974). Introduction. In R. M. Reitan & L. A. Davison (Eds.), *Clinical neuropsychology: Current status and applications.* New York: Wiley.

Diller, L., & Gordon, W. A. (1981). Interventions for cognitive deficits in brain injured adults. *Journal of Consulting and Clinical Psychology, 49*, 822–834.

Ellis, A. (1979). On Joseph Wolpe's espousal of cognitive–behavior therapy. *American Psychologist, 34*, 98–99.

Gaddes, W. H. (1968). A neuropsychological approach to learning disorders. *Journal of Learning Disabilities, 1*, 523–534.

Gaddes, W. H. (1981). An examination of the validity of neuropsychological knowledge in educational diagnosis and remediation. In G. W. Hynd & J. E. Obrzut (Eds.), *Neuropsychological assessment and the school-aged child: Issues and procedures* (pp. 27–84). New York: Grune & Stratton.

Hartlage, L. C. (1975). Neuropsychological approaches to predicting outcome of remedial education strategies for learning disabled children. *Pediatric Psychology, 23*, 8.

Heaton, R. K., & Pendleton, M. G. (1981). Use of neuropsychological tests to predict adult patient's everyday functioning. *Journal of Consulting and Clinical Psychology, 49*, 807–821.

Horton, A. M., Jr. (1979). Behavioral neuropsychology: Rationale and presence. *Clinical Neuropsychology, 1*, 20–23.

Horton, A. M., Jr. (1994). *Behavioral interventions with brain-injured children.* New York: Plenum Press.

Horton, A. M., Jr. (1997). Behavioral neuropsychology: Problems and prospects. In A. M. Horton, Jr., D. Wedding, & J. S. Webster (Eds.), *Neuropsychology handbook* (2nd ed., Vol. 2, pp. 73–98). New York: Springer.

Horton, A. M., Jr., & Miller, W. G. (1984). Brain damage and rehabilitation. In C. J. Golden (Ed.), *Current topics in rehabilitation psychology* (pp. 77–105). New York: Grune & Stratton.

Horton, A. M., Jr., & Wedding, D. (1984). *Clinical and behavioral neuropsychology.* New York: Praeger Press.

Horton, A. M., Jr., Wedding, D., & Phay, A. (1981). Current perspective on assessment of a therapy for brain-damaged individuals. In C. J. Golden, S. E. Alcaparras, F. Strider, & B. Graber (Eds.), *Applied technique in behavioral medicine* (pp. 59–85). New York: Grune & Stratton.

Hynd, G. W., & Obrzut, J. E. (1981). School neuropsychology. *Journal of School Psychology, 19*, 45–60.

Kaufman, A. S., & Kaufman, N. L. (1983). *Kaufman Assessment Battery for Children.* Circle Pines, MN: American Guidance Services.

Kolb, B., & Whishaw, I. Q. (1996). *Fundamentals of human neuropsychology* (4th ed.). New York: W. H. Freeman.

Lazarus, A. A. (1979). A matter of emphasis. *American Psychologist, 34*, 100.

Mahoney, M. J. (1974). *Cognition and behavior modification.* Cambridge, MA: Ballinger.

Meier, M. J. (1974). Some challenges for clinical neuropsychology. In R. M. Reitan & L. A. Davison (Eds.), *Clinical neuropsychology: Current status and application* (pp. 289–323). New York: Wiley.

Reynolds, C. R. (1981). Neuropsychological assessment and the habilitation of learning: Consideration in the search for the aptitude treatment interaction. *School Psychology Review, 10*, 342–349.

Rourke, B. P. (1975). Brain–behavior relationships in children with learning disabilities: A research program. *American Psychologist, 30*, 911–920.

Satz, P., & Fletcher, J. M. (1981). Emergent trends in neuropsychology: An overview. *Journal of Consulting and Clinical Psychology, 49*, 851–865.

Skinner, B. F. (1938). *The behavior of organisms.* New York: Appleton–Century–Crofts.

van der Vlugt, H. (1979). Aspects of normal and abnormal neuropsychological development. In M. S. Gazzaniga (Ed.), *Handbook of behavioral neurobiology* (Vol. 2, pp. 754–781). New York: Plenum Press.

Watson, J. B. (1913). Psychology as the behaviorist views it. *Psychological Review, 20*, 158–177.
Wolpe, J. (1958). *Psychotherapy by reciprocal inhibition*. Stanford, CA: Stanford University Press.
Wolpe, J. (1978). Cognition and causation in human behavior and its therapy. *American Psychologist, 33*, 437–446.

Behavior Therapy

L. Michael Ascher and Christina Esposito

Keywords: behavior therapy, behavioral treatment

The tenets of behavioral therapy are anchored in J. B. Watson's view of psychology (1913, 1924). It was his position that for psychology to advance it had to renounce the procedures and goals of many of his contemporaries in the field; these included the use of nonreproducible, subjective methods, such as introspection, to study "faculties of the mind." By restricting the subject matter of psychology to observable behavior, Watson held that behaviorism—his perspective of psychology—was amenable to the methods of scientific study. As such, psychological findings could be objective and reproducible and psychology could approach the status of biology and chemistry as a respected discipline for the study of a significant aspect of nature.

Watson was greatly impressed by the then recent findings of Ivan Pavlov (and his unsung assistant, Isabel Wringing) in the area of conditioning (Watson, 1916). In applying the methodology of science to behavior, Watson chose the empirical investigation of the environment considered by him to be the most important area of observable phenomena that affected behavior. He thus took the radical position of placing environmental influences, especially viewed from the perspective of classical conditioning, as the principal source of influence, while relegating those phenomena formerly held to be primary factors in the formation of behavior (e.g., thoughts, genetics, instincts), to inconsequential collateral roles.

If one assumes that behaviorism forms the foundation of behavior therapy—and this is not a universally accepted assumption—then its definition follows logically. Behavior therapy applies the scientific method to the amelioration of clinically significant behavioral problems. As science seeks relationships among observable sets of observables, behavior therapy primarily seeks relationships between behavior and the environment. It is this resolute reliance on empirical investigation of therapeutic methods and treatment outcomes that serves to differentiate behavior therapy from all other approaches to psychotherapy.

Watson (Watson & Rayner, 1920) demonstrated the basic tenets of his position by employing the principles of classical conditioning to establish a phobia to an albino rat—a phobia that was demonstrated not to preexist—in "little Albert," a preverbal child. Further verification of the role of learning in the phobia came from the generalization of Albert's conditioned emotional response to other white, furry objects. Watson intended to show that this phobia, like other conditioned responses, could be extinguished, but the child was removed from his care before this last phase could be conducted.

In 1924, Mary Cover Jones, one of Watson's graduate students, was able to complete this last stage with a young boy who demonstrated a phobia of unknown origin for rabbits. After observing children playing with rabbits, "little Peter" was gradually exposed to a rabbit using a rudimentary form of systematic desensitization. The counterconditioning agent was eating ice cream. In the study, Jones successfully extinguished the conditioned emotional response elicited by the rabbit.

The significance of these studies for behaviorism comes from the hypothesis that they supported, suggesting that emotional responses developed as the result of individuals' experience with their environment; and that this relationship could be understood from the perspective of Pavlov's model of classical conditioning. In the case of "little Albert," anxiety was conditioned to a stimulus complex with which it had not, prior to the study, been associated. In addition, Watson and Rayner (1920) demonstrated that the new emotional response followed classical conditioning phenomena reported by Pavlov (1941). And Jones (1924) provided evidence suggesting that a phobic response of unknown origin could be extinguished in the same manner as that of a conditioned emotional response.

Between Watson's studies in the 1920s and the middle to late 1950s, aside from the vast volume of work accomplished in the area of human and animal learning, little of great significance occurred that was specifically relevant to behavior therapy. However, there was some isolated writing that could be classified under the rubric of behavior therapy, and that did contribute to its later development. For example, Knight Dunlap (1928) received a good deal of attention after publishing several books that focused on his work with negative practice. Although criteria for classifying procedures as behavioral or nonbehavioral vary, it seems justified to consider negative practice—because of the ease with which it can be operationalized, tested experimentally, employed in a clinical setting, and placed within a general learning theory context—one of the earliest behavioral additions to the repertoire of the psychotherapist.

Other notable bridges between Watson and modern behavior therapy were contributed by Dollard and Miller (1950) and Salter (1949, 1952), among others. These psychologists presented early attempts to apply learning concepts to the amelioration of clinical difficulties. While Dollard and Miller were interested in adapting psychoanalytic components to learning-based explanations, Salter (1949) was a belligerent critic of psychoanalysis. He eschewed the accepted basis of psychotherapy and chose instead to develop an approach to behavior modification with classical conditioning as the foundation (1952).

In 1953, B. F. Skinner and Ogden Lindsley (Lindsley, Skinner, & Solomon, 1953) demonstrated the use of operant principles in an operant context with hospitalized schizophrenics. These authors were the first to use the term *behavior therapy* in association with the application of learning concepts to the modification of clinically significant behavioral problems.

Joseph Wolpe (1958) introduced the first systematic use of classical conditioning concepts to the amelioration of anxiety associated with phobic and other neurotic behavior. Although he credited much of the development of his position to the work of Pavlov and Hull, Guthrie's (1935) principles, particularly regarding the extinction of previously reinforced responses, formed the basis of counterconditioning, a central component of systematic desensitization.

Of primary importance for Wolpe (1958) was that all aspects of behavior therapy should have an empirical foundation. Thus, the technique with which he is most closely associated, systematic desensitization, was developed from experiments that he conducted in modifying experimental neurosis in cats. After delivering a number of painful shocks to cats in a test cage, Wolpe explored a variety of ways of reducing the high level of anxiety that these cats associated with that cage. The most consistently successful procedure formed the basis of the reciprocal inhibition component of Wolpe's model of systematic desensitization. This involved feeding the cats in cages that varied along a gradient of similarity to the test cage. The pleasurable component of eating was considered by Wolpe to have a reciprocally inhibiting relationship with anxiety. That is, at low levels of anxiety this positive experience would inhibit the anxiety and a new, more adaptive response would be associated with the cues that elicited anxiety and avoidance; whereas at high levels of anxiety, fear inhibited eating. Feeding began in the cage that was least similar to the original test cage and was transferred from cage to cage along the gradient of similarity until the cat was able to eat in the cage in which it was initially shocked. While this method was similar to a procedure that Mary Cover Jones (1924) found to be effective in the amelioration of the rabbit phobia of "little Peter," Wolpe's approach was more practical for application to a wide variety of outpatient clinical settings with many different phobic complaints.

These studies formed the basis of Wolpe's contention that the effective component of systematic desensitization was counterconditioning through the reciprocal inhibition of anxiety. In transferring his method to the clinic, he modified a procedure developed by Jacobson (1938) to reduce the physical tension that he hypothesized to form the foundation of anxiety. Labeled *deep muscle relaxation* by Wolpe, it functioned as the reciprocal inhibitor for most of his phobic cases. Another accommodation for adult phobics was a shift from the presentation of the actual graded phobic stimuli to the development of a hierarchical presentation of the phobic stimuli in imagination.

Although Wolpe's model for the effectiveness of systematic desensitization has been questioned, along with the exact nature of the components of the technique (e.g., Kazdin & Wilcoxon, 1976), the procedure as described by Wolpe and its modern variants have been demonstrated to be effective with many phobias. In addition, Wolpe emphasized the role of exposure to the anxiety-provoking stimulus as a major factor in neutralizing phobias. And, although he believed that this exposure should be of a gradual nature in order to avoid reconditioning anxiety, this general concept of exposure is central to most of the procedures that are associated with behavior therapy today.

A procedure that Wolpe found to be a useful supplement to systematic desensitization was assertive training (most closely associated with Salter [1949] at the time). Because it became a popular technique both within and outside of a behavioral orientation, numerous variations were developed. All had a common goal, the reduction of anxiety associated with interpersonal interactions. Thus, Wolpe is credited with establishing the utility of the technique of systematic desensitization though his more important contribution was the promotion of behavior therapy as an empirical psychotherapeutic approach. In fact, he tended to diminish in importance the role of the therapeutic procedures in behavior therapy in favor of his overarching theoretical position emphasizing scientific methodology and learning theory-based explanation.

A significant addition to the behavioral catalog was a set of procedures, developed by Joseph Cautela (Cautela & Kearney, 1986), that he labeled *covert conditioning*. He based these techniques on Skinner's position that thoughts were private events that were subject to the same learning principles as were external stimuli and responses. Cautela described practical methods for applying learning principles to imaginal stimuli and responses for the purpose of ameliorating clinically significant difficulties. Perhaps the most important of the covert conditioning techniques is covert sensitization (Cautela, 1967). This procedure pairs the imaginal representation of a maladaptive approach response, such as sexually offensive behavior, with the imaginal depiction of an event that is extremely aversive to the client. The goal is to assist individuals to remove from their behavioral repertoires responses that, although pleasant, reduce their quality of life by causing harm to themselves and/or to others. Covert sensitization represents a significant contribution to behavior therapy since it is the sole generally acceptable aversive method available to behavior therapists.

While all approaches to psychotherapy address clients' cognitions, covert conditioning is classified as a behavioral procedure rather than as a "cognitive–behavioral" procedure. This is due to Cautela's insistence that covert conditioning methods are based on principles of learning that are used to explain the dynamics of private events in a manner parallel to their use with publicly observable stimuli and responses. In contrast, cognitive behavior therapy suggests that cognitions represent a unique set of behaviors, when compared with observable events, and therefore require a different set of principles for understanding and addressing them.

The task that behaviorism has set for behavior therapy is quite difficult. The demand is to treat clinical problems while remaining strictly with observable phenomena. It is largely for this reason that some who are generally behaviorally oriented have found a pragmatic solution in the principles and techniques offered by cognitive–behavior therapy. Throughout its history, there have been, and remain, many controversies in behavior therapy; among these are its name and who was the first to use it, the extent to which behavior therapy is related to behaviorism and to learning theory in general, what constitutes a behavioral procedure, and what the role of cognitive factors should be in behavior therapy. In this brief definition our endeavor was to present a reasonable position on several important areas in the discipline.

REFERENCES

Cautela, J. R. (1967). Covert sensitization. *Psychological Reports, 20*, 459–468.

Cautela, J. R., & Kearney, A. J. (1986). *The covert conditioning handbook*. New York: Springer.

Dollard, J., & Miller, N. E. (1950). *Personality and psychotherapy*. New York: McGraw–Hill.

Dunlap, K. (1928). A revision of the fundamental law of habit formation. *Science, 67*, 360–362.

Guthrie, E. R. (1935). *The psychology of learning*. New York: Harper & Row.

Jacobson, E. (1938). *Progressive relaxation*. Chicago: University of Chicago Press.

Jones, M. C. (1924). A laboratory study of fear: The case of Peter. *Pedagogical Seminar, 31*, 308–315.

Kazdin, A. E., & Wilcoxon, L. A. (1976). Systematic desensitization and nonspecific treatment effects: A methodological evaluation. *Psychological Bulletin, 23*, 729.

Pavlov, I. P. (1941). *Lectures on conditioned reflexes*. New York: International Universities Press.

Salter, A. (1949). *Conditioned reflex therapy*. New York: Creative Age.

Salter, A. (1952). *The case against psychoanalysis*. New York: Holt, Rinehart & Winston.

Watson, J. B. (1913). Psychology as the behaviorist views it. *Psychological Review, 20*, 158–177.

Watson, J. B. (1916). The place of the conditioned reflex in psychology. *Psychological Review, 23*, 89–116

Watson, J. B. (1924). *Behaviorism*. New York: Peoples' Institute Publishing Co.

Watson, J. B., & Rayner, R. (1920). Conditioned emotional reaction. *Journal of Experimental Psychology, 3*, 1–14.

Wolpe, J. (1958). *Psychotherapy by reciprocal inhibition*. Stanford, CA: Stanford University Press.

Biofeedback

Deidre Donaldson and Dennis Russo

Keywords: behavioral medicine, biofeedback, EEG or electroencephalogram, EMG or electromyogram

Biofeedback is the process of providing an individual with physiological data of which he or she might be otherwise unaware. A key assumption is that by providing "feedback" to the individual about physiological responses ("bio"), it is possible for the individual to learn to become aware of and exert direct control over the physiology, the focus in clinical settings being to improve health outcomes.

Although the theoretical underpinnings of biofeedback (primarily physiological and learning) have existed since the turn of the century, biofeedback emerged as a clinical intervention in the late 1960s. The application of biofeedback to clinical problems evolved from laboratory research on operant control of the autonomic nervous system in animal models. Interest in biofeedback as a clinical application coincided with popular interest in altered states of consciousness and activities focused on reducing autonomic arousal (Roberts, 1985). This combination of scientific and popular interest in biofeedback and related applications fueled its popularity and generated widespread application throughout the 1970s and 1980s. Simultaneous advances in the technology used to measure the physiology, specifically electronics and computers, have further perpetuated this trend.

One of the central uses of biofeedback from a cognitive–behavioral point of view is to promote the acquisition of self-control training or self-regulation skills. For example, in behavioral medicine, the use of biofeedback assists the clinician in monitoring and guiding treatment involving relaxation training. As the client demonstrates control over the physiology, positive reinforcement may be provided. Thus, biofeedback is not a treatment modality per se but an adjunct to assist in the process of treatment. The field of cognitive–behavior therapy includes biofeedback as just one of many options in its armamentarium of biobehavioral treatment components. The feedback loop created by biofeedback has been theorized to result in cognitive change (for example, improved self-efficacy) that may also be important in the treatment process. This requires thorough knowledge of cognitive–behavior therapy in addition to specialized training in biofeedback. The American Association for Applied Physiology and Biofeedback is devoted to promoting the use of biofeedback and offers professional trainings. Board certification in biofeedback is also available through the Biofeedback Certification Institute of America (BCIA).

Biofeedback technology requires at least one sensor to obtain physiological information, a repository for this information, and a method of translating or feeding this information back to the patient. This is most commonly done through the use of a computer. Sensors are connected to the patient to monitor the indices of interest. These sensors connect the patient to the computer and special software reads the data and translates it to the monitor, allowing the information to be communicated to the patient in visual or graphical form. This is referred to as "computer-assisted biofeedback." Advances in computer technology have improved patient access to biofeedback as a clinical modality and further perpetuated its widespread application. Improvements in computer software have made biofeedback more user friendly and broadened its appeal to the general population. Patients now ask for biofeedback because of its technological appeal without any further knowledge of how it works.

CONTEMPORARY USES OF BIOFEEDBACK

Modes of Intervention

Biofeedback encompasses any physiological process that can be measured. The most common modes used in contemporary clinical practice assess autonomic nervous system functioning and are summarized in the following table:

Mode	Abbreviation	Application: Primary	Application: Secondary
Electromyogram	EMG	Tension headache	Stress
		Incontinence	Chronic pain
Thermal	Temp	Migraine	Relaxation training
		Raynaud's syndrome	
Electroencephalogram	EEG	Seizure disorder	ADHD symptoms
Galvanic skin response	GSR	Anxiety	Asthma

Electromyogram biofeedback involves sensors that measure skeletal muscle tension, particularly in the frontalis (forehead), masseter (jaw), and trapezius (upper back). Increased electrical firings indicate increased tension (Basmajian, 1989). The goal of EMG biofeedback is to learn to be aware of the cues of muscle tension, avoid escalating tension, and deescalate or reverse tension through the use of certain skills (e.g., progressive muscle relaxation). Thermal biofeedback assesses changes in skin temperature, which indicate changes in blood flow as well as the autonomic nervous system more generally as constriction is related to stress activation. EEG biofeedback measures electrical action of the cortex and translates it into frequencies and amplitudes yielding different types of brain waves (Basmajian, 1989). Changes in brain waves provide information about arousal level and attentiveness. Other commonly used modes include heart rate, blood pressure, and respirations (PNG or pneumogram). Many of these modes are also used in combination with one another.

Biofeedback is presently applied either as a means of directly addressing specific physical symptoms (primary intervention), or as an adjunct to teaching self-control skills to enhance coping with a variety of physical and emotional problems (secondary intervention). A good example of the former is migraine headaches. Thermal biofeedback, in which the peripheral temperature is the focus, has long been used to control blood flow, which has been implicated in this condition. Studies have shown that the ability to produce vasodilation is related to alleviation of migraine symptoms. An example of the latter is the use of EMG biofeedback to teach effective progressive muscle relaxation, which can be used to alleviate pain symptoms. These two modes are often used simultaneously.

Session Structure

The typical biofeedback treatment regimen mimics that of cognitive–behavioral treatment. If biofeedback is being used for a medical condition, treatment starts once a thorough medical evaluation has been conducted. The first session includes assessment of the presenting problem, including all symptom parameters, relevant psychological history, functional analysis, and initial baseline assessment of the physiology. Treatment duration is often 8–12 sessions lasting an hour each. However, this may be shorter or longer depending on the condition, treatment motivation and adherence, treatment attendance, and so on.

Treatment sessions include review of the session agenda, review of previous week and homework/monitoring, baseline reassessment, skill review or introduction, skill practice, and homework/monitoring assignment. In this case, skill practice would include practicing control over the physiological target(s) toward a desired goal. Portable biofeedback systems have made it easier to practice such skills at home and even in school (e.g., Osterhaus et al., 1993). Treatment success is ideally defined by the person's ability to attain desired goals while fading the use of the biofeedback equipment and generalizing this progress.

Biofeedback with Children and Adolescents

The use of biofeedback with children and adolescents is increasing. However, the number of clinicians appropriately qualified to provide biofeedback treatment in general remains quite limited, and even fewer have been trained to do so with children and adolescents. Biofeedback with children and adolescents has been used to address physical symptoms and enhance skills training, similar to that with adults.

Clinical anecdotal reports suggest that children are excellent candidates for biofeedback (Culbert, Kajander, & Reaney, 1996). Clinicians using biofeedback with children typically report that they are less skeptical than adults about treatment and have more flexible behavior patterns that are amenable to change. Compared to adults, they learn skills quickly and tend to be more susceptible to relaxation, which can be an added benefit. They also respond eagerly to praise and positive reinforcement. In addition, there are now several biofeedback software programs available that are particularly appealing to young clients, most of which present physiological data in the format of computer games (e.g., reducing muscle tension allows cars to go around a race track). Applications exist for different age categories. Most children enjoy computer games and technology, which not only help hold their interest but increase their interest and motivation in treatment.

As with any clinical intervention, special considerations around biofeedback with children can enhance its acceptability, appropriateness, and success. Biofeedback is appropriate for use across the developmental spectrum from the time an individual is considered able to develop self-modulation skills (early school age, or approximately 5 or 6 years old) throughout adulthood. The structure of treatment and sessions with children is similar to that with adults. In addition to using biofeedback within a cognitive–behavioral approach, family members are included in consultation around treatment components and education.

In general, as children develop, they form an increased capacity to direct and maintain attention, understand complex instruction, and maintain interest in having control over their bodies. They also possess greater knowledge and understanding about the world around them which assists in educating them about the body. Treatment should be modified to address these changing abilities. Generally speaking, treatment sessions may need to be altered in length, educational information must be tailored in complexity, and the mode of presentation should vary in intensity and format. Additionally, it may be more appropriate to focus goals on relative improvement targets rather than absolutes (Culbert et al., 1996). The selection of biofeedback modality can also vary depending on ease. For example, EMG biofeedback seems to be easier and thus might be chosen more frequently over other modes with younger clients. Allowing them to be creative in the treatment process also assists with motivation and skill generalization.

EMPIRICAL SUPPORT FOR BIOFEEDBACK

Scientific investigation of biofeedback has lagged behind its clinical application. This is true with both adult and child populations. Although a lot of literature on the topic has been published, empirical support for biofeedback has not clearly supported its widespread use.

Research during the late 1970s and 1980s focused on the use of biofeedback with adult populations for a variety of disorders. This literature base has been criticized for lack of scientific rigor. From the empirical studies that have been conducted with adults, biofeedback appears to be most useful in combination with other forms of biobehavioral interventions, most notably relaxation training. Specifically, support exists for the use of EMG biofeedback for tension headaches in combination with relaxation training. And, thermal biofeedback in combination with relaxation training appears to be effective in treating migraine headaches (Holroyd & Penzien, 1994).

Empirical studies of biofeedback with pediatric populations became more prevalent during the past decade. Similar to adults, empirical research with children and adolescents supports the use of biofeedback as part of a package of cognitive–behavioral treatment. Biofeedback-assisted relaxation training has been found to be efficacious in treating recurrent headache, particularly thermal biofeedback (Fentress, Masek, Mehegan, & Benson, 1986; Holden, Deichmann, & Levy, 1999). EMG biofeedback has also shown efficacy in treating emotion-induced asthma (McQuaid & Nassau, 1999). EMG biofeedback in combination with medical intervention has merit in treating functional encopresis (McGrath, Mellon, & Murphy, 2000), as does the related procedure of the bell and pad in treating nocturnal enuresis.

There is increasing evidence that children and adolescents do respond better than adults to biofeedback, at least in the area of headache management. Recent research on biofeedback has continued to empirically evaluate the efficacy of biofeedback treatment for other disorders (e.g., EEG biofeedback for ADHD) as well as compare the efficacy of different modes of biofeedback and potential mediators or mechanisms by which biofeedback may exert its effects (Hermann & Blanchard, 2002).

CRITICISMS OF BIOFEEDBACK

The most significant criticism of biofeedback involves the limited amount of empirical data supporting its widespread clinical application. In some cases, the application of biofeedback to certain clinical problems has progressed with even limited theoretical rationale, let alone empirical support.

Biofeedback by definition can involve a variety of physiological indicators, making its application highly variable. Thus, regardless of empirical findings, treatment using biofeedback is not well standardized. In some settings, biofeedback is equated with relaxation treatment and/or variations occur in the specificity and sophistication of the physiological data provided to the individual (e.g., using computerized versus noncomputerized information; real-time versus lag-time data).

A related problem is that biofeedback is used by clinicians with varying training backgrounds. There is board certification available but it is not required in order to practice. This problem is exacerbated by the limited number of trained professionals available. Also, those referring are not often knowledgeable about the appropriate uses of biofeedback or the benefits of the approach in the face of lagging empirical studies. It is not uncommon for referrals to request biofeedback either for problems for which it has limited support, or to address biobehavioral problems when other primary problems exist (e.g., mood disorders). The technological appeal of biofeedback tends to perpetuate referral in the absence of understanding. This highlights the need for more trained clinicians and for those clinicians to appropriately screen referrals, while continuing to educate referral sources and the general public.

FUTURE DIRECTIONS

The use of biofeedback in clinical settings has increased dramatically over the past three decades. At the same time, however, research regarding the underlying mechanisms and effectiveness of this approach lags behind its application. Moreover, results regarding its effectiveness have historically been inconsistent at best, depending on the type of biofeedback examined and the area to which it is applied.

It is important that scientist-practitioners continue to empirically examine the utility of biofeedback. This includes not only determining whether it is indeed effective for the myriad of applications for which it has been proposed, but also examining models that forward our understanding of how it works across different applications. It is proposed that different mechanisms may be operating depending on whether biofeedback is used as a primary or secondary intervention. Thus, models for understanding the mechanisms by which it exerts its effects may need to be altered accordingly. Training programs play a critical role in not only continuing to investigate the empirical merits of biofeedback, but also in training clinicians to provide biofeedback to persons across the developmental spectrum.

At the same time, there are areas where biofeedback has been shown to be a promising intervention within the context of a broader cognitive–behavioral treatment approach. As clinicians continue to use biofeedback it is important to stay abreast of the empirical findings and integrate them into clinical practice. Education of clients as well as referral sources will assist in ensuring biofeedback is applied in a helpful manner in the context of cognitive–behavioral treatment with patients who can most benefit.

See also: Clinical health psychology

REFERENCES

Basmajian, J. (1989). *Biofeedback: Principles and practice for clinicians*. Baltimore: Williams & Wilkins.

Culbert, T. P., Kajander, R. L., & Reaney, J. B. (1996). *Journal of Developmental and Behavioral Pediatrics, 17*, 342–350.

Fentress, D. W., Masek, B. J., Mehegan, J. E., & Benson, H. (1986). Biofeedback and relaxation-response training in the treatment of pediatric migraine. *Developmental Medicine and Child Neurology, 28*(2), 139–146.

Hermann, C., & Blanchard, E. B. (2002). Biofeedback in the treatment of headache and other childhood pain. *Applied Psychophysiology and Biofeedback, 27*(2), 143–162.

Holden, E. W., Deichmann, M. M., & Levy, J. D. (1999). Empirically supported treatments in pediatric psychology: Recurrent pediatric headache. *Journal of Pediatric Psychology, 24*(2), 91–109.

Holroyd, K. A., & Penzien, D. B. (1994). Psychosocial interventions in the management of recurrent headache disorders. I. Overview and effectiveness. *Behavioral Medicine, 20*(2), 53–63.

McGrath, M. L., Mellon, M. W., & Murphy, L. (2000). Empirically supported treatments in pediatric psychology: Constipation and encopresis. *Journal of Pediatric Psychology, 25*(4), 225–254.

McQuaid, E. L., & Nassau, J. H. (1999). Empirically supported treatments of disease-related symptoms in pediatric psychology: Asthma, diabetes, and cancer. *Journal of Pediatric Psychology, 24*(4), 305–328.

Osterhaus, S. O. L., Passchier, J., van der Helm-Hylkema, H., de Jong, K. T., Orlebeke, J. F., de Grauw, A. J. C., & Dekker, P. H. (1993). Effects of behavioral psychophysiological treatment of schoolchildren with migraine in a nonclinical setting: Predictors and process variables. *Journal of Pediatric Psychology, 18*(6), 697–715.

Roberts, A.H. (1985). Biofeedback: Research, training, and clinical roles. *American Psychologist, 40*(8), 938–941.

RECOMMENDED READING

Davis, M., Eshelman, E. R., & McKay, M. (1995). *The relaxation and stress reduction workbook* (pp. 117–125). Oakland, CA: New Harbinger.

Biopsychosocial Treatment of Pain

Barbara A. Golden and L. Stuart Barbera, Jr.

Keywords: pain, chronic pain, stress

> *But that I can save him from days of torture,*
> *That is what I feel is my great and ever new privilege.*
> *Pain is a more terrible lord of mankind than even death itself.*
>
> —Dr. Albert Schweitzer

Pain is a universal stress encounter. Despite advances in the understanding of the physiological process, pain continues to be a source of distress for patients, caregivers, and physicians. Chronic pain, that is, "pain which persists a month beyond the usual course of the acute disease or reasonable time for an injury to heal or that is associated with chronic pathological process that causes continuous pain or pain that recurs at intervals for months or years" (Bonica, 1990, p. 19), is considered to be an illness itself, which generally does not remit. Patients with chronic pain experience physical, psychological, and social factors as sources of distress. The biomedical model, which dates back to the ancient Greeks, views pain as an objective biological event and fails to address the roles of psychological and psychosocial variables in health and disease.

The contemporary biopsychosocial model includes complete understanding of pain with no single factor in isolation. Biological (physical), psychological (emotional, cognitive, and behavioral), and social (interactions with others) factors must be incorporated for assessment, diagnosis, and treatment. All of us may experience similar pain sensations, that is, the mental awareness of an unpleasant stimulus associated with an injury or illness. However, each of us manifests a very different pain experience, that is, the total subjective experience of pain associated with injury or illness.

The gate control theory (GCT) changed the way in which the pain experience is understood (Melzack & Wall, 1965). The pain experience is affected by three systems: the sensory–discriminative dimension, in which pain is sensed and perceived; the cognitive–evaluative dimension involving the primary cognitive constructs with which pain is evaluated, and its implications judged; and the motivational–affective dimension or the motivational forces that affect the patient's emotional reactions (Melzack, 1996). The GCT suggests that the central nervous system acts as a physiologic basis for the role of psychological factors in the pain experience. Within the spinal cord, sensory input is modified by neural mechanisms of the dorsal horn; this region acts as a hypothetical gate that inhibits or facilitates transmission of nerve impulses from peripheral sites to the brain. This process inhibits nociceptive signals, closes the gate, and decreases pain; alternatively, it facilitates transmission, opens the gate, and increases pain. This complex integration, orchestrated by the reciprocal interaction of cognitive, emotional, and physical factors, shapes the way that individuals perceive and respond to pain.

Patients with chronic pain often experience a wide range of distressing emotions including anger, anxiety, depression, and pain-related fears (Eccleston, 2001). These fears may be a result of social learning, respondent learning, operant learning, dysfunctional cognitions, and schema. As a result of social learning, pain behaviors may be acquired through observational learning and modeling processes. If, as a child, the adult patient may have observed a parent who had poor coping abilities for pain management, the pain-related behaviors might increase. As a result of respondent conditioning, a patient may have experienced pain through physical therapy and consequently the anticipation of suffering may be sufficient to establish a long-term avoidance of future physical therapy. Operant learning has been applied to overt expressions of pain behavior. This model suggests that avoidant behaviors and fears arise and are maintained as a result of environmental consequences. For example, if overt pain behavior results in being excused from household responsibilities and increased attention from a family member, the pain behavior is likely to be maintained. Avoidant behaviors and unrealistic fears can lead to a cascade of negative outcomes, including erosion of self-efficacy, restriction in patient's activity functioning, exacerbation of negative emotions such as anxiety and depression, and poor treatment compliance.

The cognitive–behavioral (CB) model has become the commonly accepted conceptualization of pain, and cognitive–behavioral therapy is recognized as an empirically supported treatment for chronic pain (Eccleston, 2001; McCracken & Turk, 2002; Morley, Eccleston, & Williams, 1999; Turk & Okifuji, 1999). According to the CB model, individuals actively process sensory information. This processing is based on past experiences, filtered through preexisting knowledge, and organized representations of this knowledge result in an idiosyncratic response rather than an objective response. Since information processing is not static, attention is given to the ongoing reciprocal relationships among physical, cognitive, affective, social, and behavioral factors, which ultimately influence the patient's pain experience.

There are five basic assumptions of the CB model of pain (Turk & Okifuji, 1999). The first assumption is that individuals actively process information; they do not passively react to the environment. Together, cognitions, schema, and previous learning all shape the perception of pain. For example, when patients receive the diagnosis of fibromyalgia or other pain-related syndromes they may perceive themselves as defective (self), their interactions with their healthcare providers as futile (world), and their prognosis as daunting (future) (Eimer & Freeman, 1998).

The second assumption is that thoughts (i.e., appraisals, beliefs, expectations) will have an influence on affect and behavior and influence one another in a reciprocal manner. For example, a chronic pain patient who perceives the duration, intensity, and frequency of the pain as unremitting, may feel helpless about the pain experience, have an automatic thought such as "I am helpless to control my pain," and may be noncompliant with treatment.

The third assumption is that behavior is reciprocally determined by the individual and the environment. For example, patients who receive positive reinforcement from others (i.e., family members, healthcare providers, or support groups) may experience an improvement in their overall level of functioning and self-efficacy as well as a decrease in emotional distress and suffering.

The fourth assumption is that patients are capable of learning more adaptive ways of thinking, feeling, and behaving. Providing patients with a variety of skills (i.e., cognitive restructuring, problem-solving skills, activity pacing, role-playing) can assist them in leading fuller lives with less distress and pain.

The last assumption is that patients should be integrally involved in treatment of their maladaptive behaviors, cognitions, and feelings. Patients in chronic pain should see themselves as active agents of change. Patients are integral members of the treatment team. By assuming an appropriate measure of responsibility for treatment, patients collaborate with the entire interdisciplinary treatment team in an effort to achieve their treatment goals.

Cognitive–behavioral therapy (CBT) is based on the assumption that patients will enter treatment with the belief that their pain problem is unmanageable, and this belief becomes the target for change. Patients have generally been to several physicians and have become frustrated and demoralized in the process of searching for successful pain management. Since "cognitive therapy [is] aimed at reducing pathogenic negative thinking [it] is a natural remedy for alleviating psychological and emotional distress associated with persistent pain and chronic pain syndromes" (Eimer & Freeman, 1998, p. 154). Other goals of CBT include changing patients' view that pain is unmanageable, educating patients about pain, teaching patients ways in which they can identify and restructure maladaptive cognitions and behaviors associated with pain, enhancing the self-efficacy of patients, and assisting patients in generalizing and maintaining treatment outcomes.

Turk and Rudy (1994) outlined seven objectives of CBT for chronic pain. The first, and perhaps most important, objective is to assist patients in conceptualizing their situation so that problems are perceived as manageable. This cognitive shift can provide patients with a sense of hope that their situation can improve and that their suffering can be reduced. Second, patients should understand that they will be taught how to manage their problems more effectively. Third, patients will develop a belief that through their active involvement in treatment they are able to manage their pain more effectively. The fourth objective is to teach patients how to self-monitor so that they can accurately observe and restructure their cognitions, feelings, and behaviors more effectively. The fifth objective includes teaching patients a variety of skills that they can use to solve problems. The sixth objective involves helping patients recognize and take ownership for the positive accomplishments that they achieve. The final objective is to teach patients how to anticipate difficulties and to develop strategies to overcome these obstacles if and when they occur.

Cognitive restructuring is one of the cardinal features of CBT treatment of chronic pain. As such, the clinician works with patients to change perceptions, behaviors, beliefs, and emotional reactions to their pain experiences so that their cognitions are accurate and adaptive. Feldman, Phillips, and Aronoff (1999) identified several common cognitive beliefs that patients develop regarding pain. These maladaptive beliefs are associated with: (a) control (i.e., there is nothing I can do about my pain), (b) disability (i.e., I am unable to do anything worthwhile because of my pain), (c) harm (i.e., if I engage in chores I will be in much worse pain), (d) emotion (i.e., my pain is always the same regardless of what I do), (e) medication (i.e., I will always need medication to manage my pain), (f) solicitude (i.e., my family should take better care of me because of my pain), and

(g) medical care (i.e., when I find the right doctor he/she will be able to get rid of my pain). In addition, there are many common cognitive distortions that pain patients experience such as all-or-nothing thinking, disqualifying the positive, selective abstraction, should statements, low frustration tolerance, perfectionism, pain-based emotional reasoning, mind reading and personalization, negative prediction, catastrophizing, and overgeneralization. These distortions further complicate treatment, drain coping resources, erode self-efficacy, and exacerbate distress (Eimer & Freeman, 1998).

There are several intervention strategies and techniques that are commonly utilized when working with chronic pain patients. These include socializing patients to the CB conceptualization of pain and approach to treatment. Introducing patients to the CBT model provides a context in which patients begin to see that problems are manageable, and that through collaboration with the interdisciplinary treatment team, some degree of control over circumstances can be achieved and, therefore, change is possible. Patients are also taught a variety of skills that facilitate adaptive thoughts, feelings, and behaviors relative to the pain. For example, patients are taught how to identify and restructure maladaptive thoughts by means of cognitive restructuring. Patients also are taught problem-solving skills, family interventions, and communication skills training. Respectively, these skills assist patients in meeting challenges more effectively and in communicating with others (family members, healthcare providers) and advocating more effectively. Likewise, patients also learn self-regulatory techniques such as various relaxation training interventions (diaphragmatic breathing), meditation, imagery, and distraction to relieve their pain (McCracken & Turk, 2002).

Providing patients with skills needed to negotiate the inevitable obstacles is critical to maintaining treatment gains. As treatment concludes, it is important for patients to review what skills they have learned, to identify possible setbacks and problems that may arise, and to consider how they can respond adaptively to these challenges. Incorporating this aspect into treatment can equip patients with the expectation and knowledge about ways to respond to future challenges more successfully.

CB interventions with chronic pain patients will continue to evolve as the science of pain management matures. Several points deserve particular attention. First, while there is a body of literature evaluating CBT interventions with various populations, future research should continue to address members of society who are marginalized such as children, adolescents, the elderly, people with disabilities, people with HIV-AIDS, and ethnic minorities patients. Second, a significant challenge for clinicians and researchers alike will be to provide culturally sensitive interventions while tailoring them to the specific needs of patients. Third, a CBT model should continue to emphasize and integrate a biopsychosocial perspective when conceptualizing, researching, and treating patients. Finally, refinements in psychological assessment measures will need to keep pace with technological advances so that these new developments can provide a more accurate complete assessment and treatment of pain.

See also: Chronic pain, Clinical health psychology

REFERENCES

Bonica, J. J. (1990). Definitions and taxonomy of pain. In J. J. Bonica (Ed.), *The management of pain* (pp. 18–27). Philadelphia: Lea & Febringer.

Eccleston, C. (2001). Role of psychology in pain management. *British Journal of Anaesthesia, 87*(1), 144–152.

Eimer, B. N., & Freeman, A. (1998). *Pain management psychotherapy: A practical guide*. New York: Wiley.

Feldman, J. B., Phillips, L. M., & Aronoff, G. M. (1999). Cognitive systems approach to treating pain patients and their families. In G. M. Aronoff (Ed.), *Evaluation and treatment of chronic pain* (3rd ed., pp. 313–322). Baltimore: Williams & Wilkins.

McCracken, L. M., & Turk, D. C. (2002). Behavioral and cognitive–behavioral treatment for chronic pain: Outcome, predictors of outcome, and treatment processes. *Spine, 27*(22), 2564–2573.

Melzack, R. (1996). Gate control theory: On the evolution of pain concepts. *Pain Forum, 5*(2), 128–138.

Melzack, R., & Wall, P. (1965). Pain mechanisms: A new theory. *Science, 50*, 155–161.

Morley, S., Eccleston, C., & Williams, A. (1999). A systematic review and meta-analysis of randomized controlled trials of cognitive behaviour therapy and behaviour therapy for chronic pain in adults, excluding headache. *Pain, 80*, 1–13.

Turk, D. C., & Okifuji, A. (1999). A cognitive–behavioral approach to pain management. In P. D. Wall & R. Melzack (Eds.), *Textbook of pain* (4th ed., pp. 1431–1444). London: Churchill Livingstone.

Turk, D. C., & Rudy, T. E. (1994). A cognitive–behavioral perspective on chronic pain: Beyond the scalpel and syringe. In C. D. Tollison, J. R. Satterhwaite, & J. W. Tollison (Eds.), *The handbook of pain management* (2nd ed., pp. 136–151). Baltimore: Williams & Wilkins.

Bipolar Disorder

Cory F. Newman

Keywords: bipolar, cognitive, prodromal, adherence, family

Bipolar disorder, known colloquially as "manic-depression," is a heterogeneous affective disorder, apparently related to unipolar depression, but also involving varying degrees of euphoria, impulsivity, irritability, hyperactivity, agitation, and (sometimes) psychotic ideation. Less prevalent than unipolar depression, it strikes 0.8–1.6% of the adult population. Less is known about the incidence in childhood and adolescence, as the field is still trying to disentangle and otherwise understand the relationship between early onset bipolar disorder and childhood disorders such as conduct disorder (CD) and attention-deficit/hyperactivity disorder (ADHD). Bipolar illness appears to be represented equivalently between the genders, and across ethnic groups (Bauer & McBride, 1996).

Symptom episodes involving depression and hypomania or mania often occur in cycles, thus causing serious, repeated psychological and general health problems for the sufferer. As the natural course of bipolar disorder often involves relapses, ongoing active treatment is necessary, preferably starting early in the course of the illness. When treatment is delayed, interrupted, or neglected, persons with bipolar disorder often experience a deteriorating course of their illness (Goldberg & Harrow, 1999). This involves shorter interepisode normality, greater duration of symptom episodes, and perhaps increased vulnerability to the triggering of mood swings with little environmental or biological provocation—a hypothesized phenomenon known as the "kindling effect" (Post & Weiss, 1989). At least half of all patients actively treated for bipolar illness do not respond quickly, or relapse after an initial, promising response. Thus, there is a pressing need to improve pharmacotherapeutic and psychotherapeutic interventions for this serious disorder.

Bipolar disorder is comprised of a number of subtypes, depending on the particular admixture of depression, hypomania, mania, and mixed episodes, as well as the duration and course of the symptom episodes (e.g., rapid-cycling). For example, a person diagnosed as "Bipolar II" does not have a history of full-blown mania, but rather has experienced at least one major depressive episode, and at least one hypomanic episode. Hypomania involves similar symptoms as mania—euphoria and irritability, decreased desire for sleep, racing thoughts and pressured speech, excessive goal-directed activities, increased distractibility, pursuit of high stimulation, decreased social judgment, and so on—but with lesser intensity and duration, and no sign of psychotic ideation. Those patients who have had full-blown manic episodes are designated as "Bipolar I," representing the individuals who are most at risk for serious interruptions in life functioning, damaged relationships, multiple losses, demoralization, and even suicide. For example, the conservative estimate of the proportion of patients with bipolar disorder who will ultimately die by suicide is 15% (Simpson & Jamison, 1999), a figure that takes into account those who are treated as well as those who are not. This ultimate hazard is worsened if the patients experienced *mixed episodes*, in which they have rapidly changing moods within the context of an overarching manic, impulsive, agitated presentation, and/or if they abuse psychoactive substances such as alcohol, cocaine, heroin, and others.

Prior to the development of mood stabilizers such as lithium, the standard treatments for bipolar disorder often involved the use of neuroleptics, electroconvulsive therapy, and institutionalization. As these approaches were largely ineffective, many individuals with bipolar disorder simply avoided treatment if they could, and their conditions deteriorated. The advent of lithium and its successors (e.g., Depakote, anticonvulsants, atypical antipsychotics) represented a significant improvement in the treatment of bipolar disorder, but there was still the problem of inconsistent medication adherence, toxicity, and symptom breakthrough. Thus, psychosocial treatment approaches came to the fore as a way to supplement the overall treatment of bipolar disorder. This makes intuitive sense—if we view bipolar disorder from a "diathesis–stress" model, medications are aimed at the biochemical diathesis, and the psychosocial interventions target the patients' "stress." For example, cognitive therapy (e.g., Newman, Leahy, Beck, Reilly-Harrington, & Gyulai, 2001) helps individuals with bipolar disorder to define and solve their problems more effectively, reframe life situations in a more constructive and less catastrophic way, improve self-efficacy so as to combat helplessness and hopelessness (and thus reduce the risk of suicide), and learn reliable self-instructional methods to moderate extreme moods and hyperarousal. Additionally, cognitive therapy has been shown to improve medication adherence, as the bipolar sufferers' misconceptions about their pharmacotherapy are addressed empathically, rationally, and with the aim of solving the problem (e.g., Lam et al., 2000; Scott, Garland, & Moorhead, 2001).

Another promising psychosocial model is focused family therapy (FFT; Miklowitz & Goldstein, 1997), an approach that reduces bipolar patients' stress by improving maladaptive family interactions that are associated with bipolar disorder. By working in session to reduce the frequency, intensity, and duration of hostile, accusatory, coercive communications between bipolar patients (many of whom feel overcontrolled, distrusted, and disrespected by their families) and their family members (many of whom feel frightened, frustrated, and depleted in the face of the chaotic life of their family member with bipolar disorder), practitioners of FFT can improve the quality of life of all parties in the family. Goals include improving intrafamilial empathy, cooperation, and problem-solving, and decreasing conflicts, blaming, shaming, and related forms of acting out. Presumably, bipolar patients' participation in pharmacotherapy is enhanced when adherence is no longer perceived as central to the power struggle within the family.

Another psychosocial model combines the tenets of interpersonal therapy (IPT) with a methodology to regulate the biopsychosocial rhythms of the bipolar patients—interpersonal, social-rhythm therapy (IP-SRT; Frank et al., 1994). As individuals with bipolar disorder are very sensitive to changes in their sleep–wake cycle (e.g., with the risk of mania increasing with disruptions in normal sleep), IP-SRT addresses the patient's world of relationships. The chief hypothesis is that by improving the stability of the personal life of the individual with bipolar disorder, there will be less of the sort of conflict and turmoil that will increase stress, cause loss of sleep, and exacerbate impulsivity. Thus, the bipolar patient will be more apt to maintain mood states within normal limits, provided that medication adherence is optimal.

TREATMENT

As depressive symptoms play a significant role in the course of bipolar illness, much attention is paid to patients' negative views of themselves, their lives, and their futures. Although it is important for patients to acknowledge that they have bipolar disorder and to engage in the proper treatment, it is not helpful if they make dire assumptions about their condition that make them feel helpless and hopeless. Thus, it is important to teach patients the basic cognitive therapy skills of recognizing their automatic thoughts and related beliefs, and rationally responding so as to reduce subjective stress, maintain a constructive outlook, and stay focused on goals in a productive manner. It is critical that individuals with bipolar disorder learn to utilize such skills in the face of their suicidal ideation and feelings, as well as when they maintain a sense of shame and stigma. For example, a patient who views himself as synonymous with his bipolar illness, and thus declares himself to be "fatally flawed," would be taught in cognitive therapy to assess and define his personal identity with as many variables as possible, taking into account his strengths, accomplishments, hopes, goals, and other personal resources. Thus, the individual who declares himself to be a "doomed misfit with manic-depression" would work to redefine himself perhaps as a "politically moderate, outdoors-loving, dog-owning, chess-playing, somewhat cynical, jazz-loving, loyal friend who is getting treatment for bipolar disorder." He would then strive to live his life in a way that better reflected these multiple facets of his persona, all the while receiving proper treatment in a consistent way.

MODIFYING HYPERPOSITIVE THINKING

The skills of rational responding also can be used to assess and modify hyperpositive thinking—the sort of thinking that can induce persons to act impulsively and recklessly. Patients are taught to spot the early warning signs of such hypomanic and manic symptoms—or "prodromes"—and to take a series of steps to mute the full expression of the symptom episodes while adjustments in pharmacotherapy are sought. Techniques include: (1) choosing trusted personal advisors with whom to consult about ambitious, goal-directed ideas, (2) waiting at least 48 hours (including at least one full night of sleep) before making big decisions and acting on them, (3) moderating activities so that there is time for the proper amounts of food, sleep, and taking care of basic responsibilities, and (4) implementing the principles of effective problem solving in a systematic, methodical fashion. Cognitive therapy employs homework assignments in which the patients can test and practice these all-important techniques and skills.

MODERATING AFFECT

As extreme mood swings are characteristic and problematic aspects of bipolar disorder, cognitive therapists help their patients to take measures to moderate their emotionality. For example, the patients schedule their live's activities so that they are taking care of their chief responsibilities (balanced with family time, and rest and relaxation), but not to the extent that they are working frenetically or excessively. Similarly, patients are taught to reduce excessive arousal via the techniques of relaxation and breathing control. Self-instructional statements can be used to remind individuals with bipolar disorder to refrain from acting on bursts of anger and ardor, and instead to monitor the intensity and longevity of these moods prior to taking any action. The therapist must be sensitive to the patients' difficulties in managing their moods, acknowledging that high affect (and its concomitant urges to express them publicly) is quite a challenge to contain. Further, some patients believe that their manic episodes are glorious experiences, and/or that these represent their times of greatest creative output. Therapists must be respectful of such views, all the while focusing on the down side of the equation (e.g., depressive crashes, impulsive harm done to one's life, suicidality), as well as being willing to assist the patients in their "grief work" for the loss of their manic highs through treatment.

COMPLEMENTARITY WITH OTHER TREATMENT APPROACHES

Cognitive therapy synergizes with other treatment approaches such as pharmacotherapy and family therapy. Above and beyond the ubiquitous phenomenon of medication side effects, some patients have more individualized complaints about their pharmacotherapy as a result of maladaptive beliefs that—left unchecked—could needlessly interfere with a vital part of their treatment. Cognitive therapists assess and address patients' negative views about taking medications, including the following examples:

- Medication will take away all my creativity.
- Medication will change my personality and I'll lose my identity.
- If my meds are changed, it means that my therapist doesn't know what she's doing.
- If I feel better, it means that I no longer have to take my medications.
- I can maintain my privacy better if I stop taking my medications.

In cognitive therapy, patients are helped to find the flaws in the above arguments, and to look for evidence in support of alternative views that support ongoing pharmacotherapy. In the end, the goal is to facilitate the patients' "making peace" with the need to take medications for their bipolar illness, and to find the appropriate medications that will do the best job with the fewest side effects.

Similarly, cognitive therapy has a great deal to offer in working with individuals with bipolar disorder and their families. As in the case of schizophrenics and their families, bipolar patients and their families often experience harmful interactional cycles of mutual criticism, control issues, and general conflict—a concept broadly known in the literature as high "expressed emotion" (EE). High EE in the families of persons with bipolar disorder has been associated with a more problematic course of the illness. Thus, it is often beneficial for such families to attend therapy sessions in which they can learn more effective communication skills, as well as become more aware of their propensity for making excessively negative interpretations of each other's behaviors. Cognitive therapists endeavor to understand the unique history and interactional patterns of each family so as to provide accurate empathy and to develop a solid case formulation. Therapists model the process of trying to be compassionate in describing the problematic behaviors of the patients and their families, giving each person the benefit of the doubt that they are not deliberately trying to make things worse, and initiating the process of constructive problem solving. In order to help the patients and their families acquire such skills, cognitive therapists actively use such techniques as reframing, role-playing, and the assignment of homework for the family.

EMPIRICAL FINDINGS

A number of studies suggest that significant life events, such as those bringing hardship or major life changes, are linked to an increased onset of affective episodes in bipolar disorder. Additionally, the bipolar patients' cognitive styles play an important interactional role, thus supporting the contention that a cognitive case conceptualization is important even in the treatment of a disorder that seems to be so frequently driven by biological factors. In general, bipolar patients who demonstrate maladaptive thinking styles are more apt to develop affective symptoms, including both depressive and manic episodes. Specifically, there is some evidence that perfectionistic beliefs, poor autobiographical recall, excessive goal-directedness, and high degrees of both sociotropic and autonomy-related beliefs represent vulnerability factors that need to be addressed in cognitive therapy for bipolar disorder (see Newman et al., 2001, for an overview).

Recently, a number of randomized, controlled trials have shown the promise that cognitive therapy holds for improving the overall treatment package for bipolar disorder. For example, Perry, Tarrier, Morriss, McCarthy, and Limb (1999) used a brief trial of 12 sessions of cognitive therapy with a large sample of individuals with bipolar disorder, mainly focusing on teaching them how to spot and manage prodromal signs of symptom episodes. The result was that patients achieved longer periods of wellness between episodes, and shorter hospital stays. In a similar project, Lam et al. (2000) offered 20 sessions of cognitive therapy to those patients who had been refractory to pharmacotherapy alone. Compared to the group receiving treatment as usual (TAU), the cognitive therapy participants had fewer symptoms, better coping skills in response to early warning signs of impending depression or mania, less hopelessness, and better adherence to medication. In another study, Scott et al. (2001) showed that the addition of cognitive therapy relative to TAU reduced the patients' medication nonadherence rates from 48% to 21%, and 29 of the 33 patients completed the cognitive therapy program, an extraordinary figure. Replications and extensions of these studies are being conducted, using both individual and group treatment formats. Currently under way in North America is a major, long-term, 20-site effectiveness study called the Systematic Treatment Enhancement Program for Bipolar Disorder (STEP-BD). The application of cognitive therapy for bipolar disorder is a most promising development, and will become more so as the field learns more about the specific interactions between cognitive styles, major life events, medication adherence, and family factors.

See also: Depression—adult, Mood disorders—bipolar disorder

REFERENCES

Bauer, M., & McBride, L. (1996). *Structured group psychotherapy for bipolar disorder: The life goals program.* New York: Springer.

Frank, E., Kupfer, D. J., Ehlers, C. L., Monk, T. H., Comes, C., Carter, S., & Frankel, D. (1994). Interpersonal and social rhythm therapy for bipolar disorder: Integrating interpersonal and behavioural approaches. *Behaviour Therapy, 17*, 143–149.

Goldberg, J. F., & Harrow, M. (1999). Poor-outcome bipolar disorders. In J. F. Goldberg & M. Harrow (Eds.), *Bipolar disorders: Clinical course and outcome* (pp. 1–19). Washington, DC: American Psychiatric Press.

Jamison, K. R. (1995). *An unquiet mind: A memoir of moods and madness*. New York: Knopf.

Lam, D. H., Bright, J., Jones, S., Hayward, P., Schuck, N., Chisholm, D., & Sham, P. (2000). Cognitive therapy for bipolar disorder—A pilot study of relapse prevention. *Cognitive Therapy and Research, 24*, 503–520.

Miklowitz, D. J., & Goldstein, M. J. (1997). *Bipolar disorder: A family-focused treatment approach*. New York: Guilford Press.

Newman, C. F., Leahy, R. L., Beck, A. T., Reilly-Harrington, N. A., & Gyulai, L. (2001). *Bipolar disorder: A cognitive therapy approach*. Washington, DC: American Psychological Association.

Perry, A., Tarrier, N., Morriss, R., McCarthy, E., & Limb, K. (1999). Randomised controlled trial of efficacy of teaching patients with bipolar disorder to identify early symptoms of relapse and obtain treatment. *British Medical Journal, 318*, 139–153.

Post, R. M., & Weiss, S. R. (1989). Sensitization, kindling, and anticonvulsants in mania. *Journal of Clinical Psychiatry, 50*(Suppl.), 23–30.

Scott, J., Garland, A., & Moorhead, S. (2001). A randomised controlled trial of cognitive therapy for bipolar disorders. *Psychological Medicine, 31*(3), 459–467.

Simpson, S. G., & Jamison, K. R. (1999). The risk of suicide in patients with bipolar disorders. *Journal of Clinical Psychiatry, 60*(Suppl. 2), 53–56.

Body Dysmorphia 1

Melanie L. O'Neill and Maureen L. Whittal

Keywords: body dysmorphia, body dysmorphic disorder, obsessive–compulsive disorder, exposure and response prevention

Body Dysmorphic Disorder (BDD) is a fixation or preoccupation with an imagined defect in appearance or, if a physical defect or anomaly is present, the individual's concern is clearly excessive (APA, 2000). Although prevalence rates remain largely unknown, APA (2000) suggests that BDD may range from under 5% to a high of 15% in medical/cosmetic settings. Individuals with BDD can focus on flaws of the head and face such as hair thinning, acne, asymmetry, excessive hairiness, or the shape and size of body parts including the eyes, mouth, head, buttocks, legs, or genitals. The concern may be limited to one or many areas and can range from extremely specific to vague and diffuse (APA, 2000).

Individuals with BDD frequently engage in repetitive behaviors such as excessive grooming, exercise or dieting, and reassurance seeking and present with avoidance behaviors such as wearing hats all day long or being around mirrors and fluorescent lighting. They are exceptionally distressed by their symptoms, describe their fixations as "devastating," and often have poor insight. Work and social functioning can suffer enormously due to the time and energy consumed by the preoccupation. Severe BDD can lead to suicidal ideation and attempts, repeated medical and dermatological surgeries, and, in some cases, even self-surgery (APA, 2000).

ASSESSMENT AND DIFFERENTIAL DIAGNOSIS

Asking specific BDD diagnostic questions is crucial to a complete assessment. The diagnosis is frequently missed because clients tend to be reluctant to spontaneously disclose their symptoms (Castle & Phillips, 2002). Common assessment instruments include semistructured clinical interviews such as the Body Dysmorphic Disorder Examination (BDDE; Rosen & Reiter, 1996), the structured clinical interview for DSM-IV disorders with a BDD module (First, Spitzer, Gibbon, & Williams, 1996), and the Yale–Brown Obsessive Compulsive Scale modified for assessing BDD (BDD-YBOCS; Phillips et al., 1997).

BDD is regularly associated with comorbid or secondary disorders, including major depression (approximately 60–80%), social phobia (lifetime rate of 38%), substance use disorder (lifetime rate of 36%), and obsessive–compulsive disorder (lifetime rate of 30%) (Phillips & Diaz, 1997). Individuals with BDD may hold their preoccupations with a delusional intensity, which would warrant the added diagnosis of delusional disorder, somatic type (APA, 2000). However, recent theory suggests that adding the delusional diagnosis has little value and contradicts current etiopathology and treatment response indications (Castle & Phillips, 2002).

REVIEW OF RECENT PSYCHOSOCIAL RANDOMIZED CONTROLLED TRIALS FOR BDD

Few randomized controlled treatment studies have been conducted. Four trials of CBT for BDD indicated significant levels of symptom reduction (e.g., improved or very much improved) often leading to loss of diagnosis (Butters & Cash, 1987; Rosen, Reiter, & Orosan, 1995; Rosen, Saltzberg, & Srebnik, 1989; Veale et al., 1996). The effect sizes for individual treatment ranged from 1.34 to 2.65 and from 1.62 to 2.26 for group treatment. Gains made throughout treatment are typically maintained at 6-month and 1-year follow-ups.

THERAPY FOR BDD

Treatment Guidelines

BDD treatment can be offered on an individual or small group basis. Treatment is typically delivered between 8 and 12 weeks, with the session length ranging from 60 to 120 minutes. Treatment can also be delivered more intensively with daily ERP sessions between 4 and 6 weeks. Rosen et al. (1995) believe there may be additional effects with group treatment including normalizing, direct and indirect encouragement, and the provision of impartial feedback about perceived bodily flaws by fellow group members.

Introduction to BDD

The first component of treatment involves an introduction to the nature of BDD and factors that contribute to the development and maintenance of the disorder. Veale et al. (1996) collaboratively consider the possible impact of biological predispositions, early childhood experiences, and cultural factors. Most clients can connect a number of factors contributing to the development and maintenance of the disorder. A visual depiction of a BDD model, such as the one described by Veale (2002), can be enormously helpful for clients in thoroughly understanding their disorder.

Therapists can also highlight the impact of cognitions and behavior on emotion and the role of avoidance in the maintenance of the symptoms and the disorder (Wilhelm, Otto, Lohr, & Deckersbach, 1999). For example, a woman who is concerned about her long disjointed nose begins avoid dating and developing friendships, thus preventing herself from gathering disconfirming evidence. She may also be experiencing intrusive self-defeating thoughts such as "I look like Pinocchio," which can alter one's mood and create feelings of depression and disgust. Those feelings may lead to her engaging in depressed behaviors such as isolating herself from friends and loved ones. Selective attention and recall also plays a role in the maintenance of BDD symptoms. Individuals with BDD selectively focus on their distorted internal body image, assuming their image is an accurate depiction, and conclude that others see this too (Veale, 2002). For example, the woman concerned about her long bumpy noise may only be seeing and remembering women with small straight noses.

A thorough presentation of each treatment component along with a collaborative discussion of the rationale should be provided. Presenting this information early (preferably in the first treatment session) aids understanding and processing of new information and will likely engage and motivate clients. Clients may be cautious and hesitant of exposure-based treatments because of the anxiety evoked and their typically lengthy avoidance history. Thoroughly and repeatedly discussing the rationale for ERP along with an emphasis on the gradual graded nature of exposure may help ease anticipatory anxiety and reduce treatment dropouts.

Self-Monitoring

Self-monitoring begins in the early stages of treatment and can be incredibly helpful in facilitating a number of objectives. Clients can be encouraged to use a daily body image diary for recording relevant items. For example, Rosen et al. (1995) recorded situations, body image thoughts or beliefs, and the impact of these thoughts on mood and behaviors. The diary allows clients to increase their awareness of BDD-related behaviors and thoughts and facilitates an understanding of the link between body image thoughts and the impact on emotions and behavior. The diary can also highlight any particular triggers or precipitants that initiate or aggravate BDD symptoms. In addition, the diary documents gains made throughout treatment, which is encouraging and reinforcing for clients (Veale, 2002). The self-monitoring also sets the stage to begin cognitive restructuring with the more damaging thoughts and BDD-related beliefs.

Targeting Appraisals and Beliefs

Cognitive restructuring is designed to correct irrational, self-depreciating, or maladaptive cognitions and beliefs. Clients are taught to identify dysfunctional BDD thoughts and to record alternative thoughts, evidence, and rational responses in their diaries. Veale (2002) suggests that cognitive restructuring is most helpful when working with beliefs about being defective and the role that appearance plays in identity rather than attempting to restructure beliefs like "I am excessively hairy." Rosen et al. (1995) state that some body dissatisfaction is normative and may be challenging to eliminate completely, even with individuals not exhibiting BDD concerns.

Clients may discount or distort information not consistent with their BDD-related belief systems and referential thinking can play a significant role in the clinical picture (Castle & Phillips, 2002). Clients often disregard positive feedback about their appearance and magnify neutral or negative comments. Therapists can encourage clients to record positive, negative, and neutral comments (both solicited and unsolicited) made about their general physical appearance and their particular BDD preoccupation. Behavioral experiments can also be helpful in testing assumptions about appearance and identity. Therapists and clients can collaboratively design experiments such as soliciting feedback from cosmetic staff in department stores about the client's long crooked nose or asking close family members about their most engaging personality and physical traits.

An important aspect of targeting appraisals and personal meaning is helping the client construct an alternative model or story for consideration. Veale (2002) suggests the two models include the client's standard assumption, which typically involves being ugly or defective, with the alternative story, which suggests that excessive preoccupation with appearance makes that fixation the most identifiable aspect of self. The models are described as "What you see is what you get" versus "What you see is what you have constructed." This alternate model is most helpful when presented in earlier sessions so clients are able to evaluate both models throughout the course of treatment.

Exposure Hierarchy and Response Prevention

A hierarchy of graded imaginal and in vivo exposures is collaboratively constructed in the early stages of treatment. For clients with BDD concerns, exposure therapy is helpful in decreasing self-consciousness and body-related anxiety and minimizing the avoidance of feared body image situations (Rosen et al., 1995). Hierarchy items can be adjusted by modifying situations with respect to familiarity of people, physical proximity to others, and type of social interaction (Rosen et al., 1995).

Exposure is initially therapist-assisted during sessions with more hierarchy items being completed as homework as the client progresses through treatment. Standard assignments include exposure to mirrors, extended social interactions with strangers or co-workers, and exercises designed to accentuate the perceived flaw such as wearing little or no makeup and avoiding hats or other camouflaging clothing. For clients with minimal or no flaws, McKay et al. (1997) used imaginal exposure to have clients exaggerate their perceived defect into a severe deformity and picture the negative reaction of family and friends.

Response prevention is helpful in decreasing undesirable BDD-related behaviors such as mirror checking, skin picking, or reassurance seeking (e.g., Are you sure my head isn't misshapen?). Veale (2002) suggests creating a compulsive behaviors hierarchy, particularly for one of the more common difficulties, mirror gazing. Therapists should be alert to both overt (e.g., a quick mirror or reflection check) and covert (e.g., mental reassurances) BDD-related behaviors for targets of response prevention. There may also be subtle BDD safety behaviors to target and eliminate during exposures, such as turning one's head away.

Relapse Prevention

The final aspect of BDD treatment is relapse prevention. Clients can list all of the interventions they learned and discoveries about their beliefs and assumptions. The therapist and client can collaboratively identify any gains made throughout treatment, the interventions that facilitated those gains, and discuss areas that continue to need attention. Clients should predict any potential stressors and future difficulties that might arise and have contingency plans and coping strategies in place. For example, a variety of stressful "red-flag" situations (e.g., rejection, changing jobs) that can increase the client's vulnerability to BDD symptoms should be identified. Therapists may want to consider offering brief booster or telephone sessions into the follow-up care plan for the year following treatment.

SUMMARY

Despite earlier understandings of the disorder, BDD is treatable and responsive to CBT-based interventions. Most sufferers achieve significant symptom reduction, with many individuals losing the diagnosis altogether. Further gains in the field will depend on training treatment providers, which will increase accessibility to CBT.

See also: Anorexia nervosa, Body dysmorphia 2, Bulimia nervosa, Exposure therapy, Severe OCD

REFERENCES

American Psychiatric Association. (2000). *Diagnostic and statistical manual of mental disorders* (4th ed., text rev.). Washington, DC: Author.

Butters, J. W., & Cash, T. F. (1987). Cognitive–behavioral treatment of women's body-image dissatisfaction. *Journal of Consulting and Clinical Psychology, 55*, 889–897.

Castle, D. J., & Phillips, K. A. (2002). *Disorders of body image*. Petersfield, England: Wrightson Biomedical.

First, M. B., Spitzer, R. L., Gibbon, M., & Williams, J. B. W. (1996). *Structured Clinical Interview for DSM-IV Axis I Disorders-Patient Edition* (SCID-I/P, Version 2.0, 4/97 revision). Unpublished, Biometrics Research Department, New York State Psychiatric Institute.

McKay, D., Todaro, J., Neziroglue, F., Campisi, T., Moritz, E. K., & Yaryura-Tobias, J. A. (1997). Body dysmorphic disorder: A preliminary evaluation of treatment and maintenance using exposure with response prevention. *Behaviour Research and Therapy, 35*, 67–70.

Phillips, K. A., & Diaz, S. F. (1997). Gender differences in body dysmorphic disorder. *Journal of Nervous Mental Disease, 185*, 570–577.

Phillips, K. A., Hollander, E., Rasmussen, S. A., Aronowitz, B. R., DeCaria, C., & Goodman, W. K. (1997). A severity rating scale for body dysmorphic disorder: Development, reliability, and validity of a modified version of the Yale–Brown Obsessive Compulsive Scale. *Psychopharmacology Bulletin, 33*, 17–22.

Rosen, J. C., & Reiter, J. (1996). Development of the body dysmorphic disorder examination. *Behaviour Research and Therapy, 34*, 755–766.

Rosen, J. C., Reiter, J., & Orosan, P. (1995). Cognitive–behavioral therapy for body dysmorphic disorder. *Journal of Consulting and Clinical Psychology, 63*, 263–269.

Rosen, J. C., Saltzberg, E., & Srebnik, D. (1989). Cognitive behavior therapy for negative body image. *Behavior Therapy, 20*, 393–404.

Veale, D. (2002). Cognitive behaviour therapy for body dysmorphic disorder. In D. J. Castle & K. A. Phillips (Eds.), *Disorders of body image* (pp. 121–138). Petersfield, England: Wrightson Biomedical.

Veale, D., Gournay, K., Dryden, W., Boocock, A., Shah, F., Willson, R., & Walburn, J. (1996). Body dysmorphic disorder: A cognitive behavioral model and pilot randomized controlled trial. *Behaviour Therapy and Research, 34*, 717–729.

Wilhelm, S., Otto, M. W., Lohr, B., & Deckersbach, T. (1999). Cognitive behavior group therapy for body dysmorphic disorder: A case series. *Behaviour Therapy and Research, 37*, 71–75.

Body Dysmorphia 2

David Veale

Keywords: body dysmorphic disorder

Body Dysmorphic Disorder (BDD) is characterized by a preoccupation with an "imagined" defect in one's appearance or, in the case of a slight physical anomaly, then the person's concern is markedly excessive (American Psychiatric Association, 1994). The most common preoccupations are with the nose, skin, or hair and other features on the face; however, any part of the body may be involved and the preoccupation is frequently focused on several body parts simultaneously. Complaints typically involve perceived or slight flaws on the face, asymmetrical or disproportionate body features, thinning hair, acne, wrinkles, scars, vascular markings, pallor, or ruddiness of complexion.

BDD is a hidden disorder, with many patients not seeking help or not realizing there is any help for their condition. When patients do seek help, they are more likely to consult a dermatologist or cosmetic surgeon than a mental health professional (Phillips et al., 2000; Sarwer, Wadden, Pertschuk, & Whitaker, 1998). When BDD patients seek help from mental health practitioners, they are often too ashamed to reveal their main problem and present with symptoms of depression, substance abuse, or social phobia unless they are specifically questioned about symptoms of BDD. Patients may be secretive because the condition is trivialized and they think they will be viewed as vain or narcissistic. The key criterion in the diagnosis of BDD is the *preoccupation* with imagined or minor defects, which should last at least an hour a day (Phillips, 1996). The diagnostic criteria from DSM-IV also state that if a minor physical anomaly is present, then the sufferer's concern must manifestly be excessive. Note that it is possible to find minor physical anomalies on anyone you care to examine if you (a) look closely and for long enough and (b) raise your aesthetic standards. There is evidence that BDD sufferers typically engage in both of these behaviors, and so the condition begins to become more understandable. Patients are frequently unemployed or disadvantaged at work, housebound, or socially isolated, and at higher risk of suicide, self-harm, or DIY cosmetic surgery. There is frequent comorbidity with depression, social phobia, obsessive–compulsive disorder, or a personality disorder (Veale, Boocock et al., 1996). Not surprisingly, BDD patients can be difficult to engage and treat.

EVIDENCE FOR COGNITIVE BEHAVIOR THERAPY

Preliminary evidence for the efficacy of cognitive behavior therapy (CBT) in BDD comes from two randomized controlled trials (RCT) (Rosen, Reiter, & Orosan, 1995; Veale, Gournay et al., 1996). There are also several case series of behavioral and cognitive therapy (Geremia & Neziroglu, 2001; Gomez Perez, Marks, & Gutierrez Fisac, 1994; Marks & Mishan, 1988; Neziroglu & Yaryura Tobias, 1993; Wilhelm, Otto, Lohr, & Deckersbach, 1999). In the first RCT, Rosen et al. (1995) randomly allocated 54 patients diagnosed as having BDD to either group CBT or a waiting list. After treatment, 82% (22 out of 27 subjects) of the CBT group were clinically improved and no longer met the criteria for BDD compared to 7% (2 out of 27 subjects) in the waiting list group. The subjects were, however, different from those described at other centers; for example, they were all female, 38% were preoccupied by their weight and shape alone, and they tended to be much less socially avoidant and handicapped than BDD patients generally. Veale et al. (1996b) randomly allocated 19 patients with BDD to either CBT over 12 weeks or a waiting list and found a 50% reduction in the treated group on the main outcome measure for BDD and no change in the waiting list group. The main weaknesses of this study were the preponderance of female subjects (90%); the lack of a nonspecific treatment condition; the absence of any follow-up or measurement of the conviction of belief on a standardized scale. Much therefore remains to be done in developing the effectiveness of CBT for BDD and to demonstrate that CBT is superior to any nonspecific therapy (for example, anxiety management) or an alternative such as interpersonal psychotherapy. As yet, there is no evidence for the use of CBT in children and adolescents with BDD.

ASSESSMENT

A detailed and accurate cognitive–behavioral assessment is an essential precursor to making a formulation and helping the patient to engage in therapy. Patients are often dissatisfied with multiple areas of their body. A patient can be asked to complete a checklist of different parts of the body and to say exactly what they believe is defective about each part, how they think it needs to be altered, and the degree of distress that it causes. A patient's beliefs about his or her appearance are likely to be based on spontaneous images (Osman et al., 2004). Compared to healthy controls, BDD patients are more likely to rate the images as significantly more negative, recurrent, and vivid. Images of the "defect" also took up a greater proportion of the whole image in BDD patients and was viewed from an observer perspective (similar to social phobia). Images are used by patients as evidence as to how they appear to others. They are associated with early memories such as being teased and bullied at school or self-consciousness about changes in appearance during adolescence or after cosmetic surgery.

BELIEFS ABOUT APPEARANCE

The next step is to assess what the patient's assumptions are about the "defects" or the image they experience. What personal meaning does it have for him? What effect does his failure to achieve the aesthetic standard he demands have on his life? Patients may have difficulty in articulating the meaning but a "downward arrow technique" can usually identify such assumptions. After eliciting the most dominant emotion associated with thinking about the defect, the therapist inquires about what is the most shameful (or other emotion) aspect of the defect. For example, the patient might believe that having a defective nose will mean that he will end up alone and unloved. For another person, the meaning of flaws in his facial skin is the feeling of disgust at being dirty and the consequent fear of humiliation. It is important to identify such assumptions as they, rather than the immediate beliefs about the defect, are a focus of cognitive therapy and behavioral experiments. Some patients may have many unconditional beliefs and a very global low self-esteem that require a more detailed assessment. Assessing cognitions also involves determining the values of the individual and the degree to which they have become identified with the self. In BDD, appearance is almost always the dominant and idealized value and the means of defining the self. Other important values in some BDD patients may include perfectionism, symmetry, and social acceptance which may take the form of certain rules, for example, "I have to be perfect." BDD patients implicitly view themselves as an aesthetic object. This refers to the extreme self-consciousness and negative evaluation by self and others.

SAFETY BEHAVIORS

The aim of safety behaviors in BDD is usually to alter or camouflage their appearance. Patients are especially secretive about symptoms such as mirror gazing, which is at the core of BDD (Veale & Riley, 2001). The main motivation for mirror gazing appears to be the hope each time that they would look different; the desire to know exactly how they look; a desire to camouflage themselves; and a belief that they would feel worse if they resist gazing. BDD patients are more likely to focus their attention on an internal impression or feeling (rather than their reflection in the mirror) and on specific parts of their appearance. They may perform "mental cosmetic surgery" to change their body image and to practice different faces to pull in the mirror. A detailed assessment is required of exactly what the patient does in front of a mirror and his motivation, as this will be used in therapy and the construction of behavioral experiments to test out beliefs. Other reflective surfaces such as the backs of CDs or shop windowpanes may also be used as substitute mirrors though they are liable to distort further body image. Patients may also check their appearance by measuring their perceived defect, by feeling the contours of the skin with their fingers, or by repeatedly taking photos of or videotaping themselves. Other repetitive behaviors include asking others to verify the existence of the defect or whether they are suitably camouflaged; making comparisons of their appearance with others or with old photos of self; excessive grooming of hair; excessive cleansing of the skin; excessive use of makeup, facial peelers or saunas, and facial exercises to improve muscle tone; beauty treatments (for example, collagen injections for the lips); cosmetic surgery or dermatological treatments. There may also be impulsive behaviors such as skin picking, which produce a very brief sense of satisfaction or pleasure (similar to trichotillomania) followed by a sense of despair and anger.

SOCIAL AVOIDANCE AND ANXIETY

Beliefs about being defective and the importance of appearance to the self will drive varying degrees of social anxiety and avoidance. Thus, depending on the nature of their beliefs, patients will tend to avoid a range of public or social situations or intimate relationships because of the fear of negative evaluation of the imagined defects. Many patients endure social situations only if they use camouflage (for example, excessive makeup) and various safety behaviors. These are often idiosyncratic and depend on the perceived defect and cultural norms. Behaviors such as avoidance of eye contact or using long hair or excessive makeup for camouflage are obvious but others are subtler and are more difficult to detect unless the patient is asked or observed as to how they behave in social situations. For example, a BDD patient preoccupied by his nose avoided showing his profile in social situations and only stood face on to an individual. A patient preoccupied by "blemishes" under her eye wore a pair of glasses to hide the skin under her eyes. Safety behaviors contribute to the inability to disconfirm beliefs and further self-monitoring in mirrors to determine whether the camouflage is "working." The self-focused attention will increase awareness of interoceptive information such as imagery and anxiety. This is taken as evidence of a failure to achieve an aesthetic standard and activates assumptions about the likelihood of rejection or humiliation.

SUITABILITY FOR THERAPY

The very nature of BDD means that a therapist will disagree with a patient's description of the problem in terms of the exact beliefs about appearance. However, both patient and therapist can usually agree on a description of the problem as a preoccupation with their appearance leading to various self-defeating behaviors. It may be possible to agree initially on goals such as stopping specific behaviors like skin picking or to enter public situations that were previously avoided. Here the implicit message is to help the patient function and lead a fuller life despite their appearance and aesthetic standards. At this stage, patients often have covert goals of wanting to remain excessively camouflaged in public or of changing their appearance. It is preferable to ask patients not to plan cosmetic surgery or dermatological treatment during therapy and to reconsider their desire for surgery after they have recovered from BDD (or at least finished therapy). In patients who are unable to engage in therapy, it is best to put the goals to one side and to concentrate on engaging the patient in a cognitive model. Detailed goals can be negotiated later. Not all patients want "therapy." It is very important to determine the agenda of patients and whether they have made the appointment voluntarily or whether they have been coerced to see you by their relative or sent to you by a surgeon. Some are too suicidal or lacking in motivation. Some may accept the offer of medication and this may act as a holding operation while the therapist tries to engage the patient in a psychological treatment.

ENGAGEMENT

Therapeutic engagement is helped by the credibility of a clinician who has treated other patients and can talk about the disorder knowledgeably. It is important to validate the patient's beliefs and not discount or trivialize them. The clinician should search for and reflect on the evidence collected by the patient for his or her beliefs (rather than seek evidence against the belief he or she are defective) and the factors that have the contributed to the development of those beliefs. Patients have typically had the experience of teasing about their appearance during childhood or adolescence. The aim of therapy is then to normalize their experience and help them to understand what the problem is and to update their "ghosts from the past." Therapists should avoid repeatedly reassuring patients that they look "all right" as it does not fit with their experience and they have heard it many times. Patients may be referred by a psychoeducational book about BDD which is written for sufferers (Phillips, 1996) or to meet other sufferers in a patient support group or national charity of users with Obsessive–Compulsive Disorder (which usually has a BDD section). Patients are often extremely relieved and surprised to talk to other BDD patients. Patients assume a model of "What You See Is What You Get" in front of a mirror. An alternative model of "What You See Is What You Feel" is presented because of selective attention to specific aspects of their appearance and their body image. Body image will depend more on their mood, early memories, the meaning that they attach to their appearance, and the expectations that they bring to a mirror. This leads to a description of a cognitive–behavioral model for BDD (Veale, 2004) and how a person with BDD becomes excessively aware of his or her body image by giving examples of selective attention in everyday life. Motivational interviewing can be used to focus on the consequences of patients' preoccupation with an emphasis on occupational and social handicap. The therapist would ask the patient to suspend judgment and to test the alternative cognitive– behavioral model for the period of therapy. If the patient is open to accepting the possibility that they are basing judgments on their body image, are unusually aware of their appearance, and set high standards, this might lead to a discussion of the prejudice model of information processing (Padesky, 1993).

Another method of engagement in CBT is similar to that described for hypochondriasis (Clark et al., 1998). A patient is presented with two alternative theories to test out in therapy. Theory "A" (that the patient has been following) is that he is defective and ugly and he has tried very hard to camouflage or change his appearance. Theory "B" to be tested during therapy is that the problem is of excessive worrying about his body image and making his appearance the most important aspect of his identity. Furthermore, the various safety behaviors used to camouflage or alter his appearance make the worrying about his body image worse. Patients should have an individual formulation based on the model, which emphasizes the cognitive processes and behaviors that maintain the disorder. Once a patient is engaged in therapy and willing to test out alternatives, the therapist can choose from a variety of strategies. These include (a) cognitive restructuring and behavioral experiments to test out assumptions, (b) motivational interviewing and reverse role-play for the rigid values, (c) behavioral experiments or exposure to social situations without safety behaviors, (d) dropping of safety behaviors such as mirror gazing, and (e) self-monitoring with a tally counter and habit reversal for impulsive behaviors such as skin picking.

Sometimes patients are impossible to engage in either CBT or pharmacotherapy and have to go through a long career of unnecessary surgery, beauty therapies, dermatological treatment, or suicide attempts before seeking help from a mental health professional. Patients should be advised that there are always cosmetic surgeons, dermatologists, and beauty therapists willing to treat them and that BDD patients report marked dissatisfaction with cosmetic surgery or dermatological treatments. Alternatively, even if the patient is somewhat satisfied, the preoccupation moves to a different area of the body so that the handicap remains the same (Phillips, Grant, Siniscalchi, & Albertini, 2001; Veale, 2000).

See also: Anorexia nervosa, Body dysmorphia 1, Bulimia nervosa, Exposure therapy, Severe OCD

REFERENCES

Thirty-three cases of body dysmorphic disorder in children and adolescents. *Journal of the American Academy of Child & Adolescent Psychiatry, 38*, 453–459.

American Psychiatric Association. (1994). *Diagnostic and statistical manual of mental disorders* (4th ed.). Washington, DC: Author.

Clark, D. M., Salkovskis, P. M., Hackmann, A., Wells, A., Fennel, M., Ludgate, J. et al. (1998). Two psychological treatments for hypochondriasis. A randomised controlled trial. *British Journal of Psychiatry, 173*, 218–225.

Geremia, G., & Neziroglu, F. (2001). Cognitive therapy in the treatment of body dysmorphic disorder. *Clinical Psychology and Psychotherapy, 8*, 243–251.

Gomez Perez, J. C., Marks, I. M., & Gutierrez Fisac, J. L. (1994). Dysmorphophobia: Clinical features and outcome with behavior therapy. *European Psychiatry, 9*, 229–235.

Neziroglu, F., & Yaryura Tobias, J. A. (1993). Exposure, response prevention, and cognitive therapy in the treatment of body dysmorphic disorder. *Behavior Therapy, 24*, 431–438.

Osman, S., Cooper, M., Hackman, M., & Vegle, D. (2004). Spontaneously occuring images and early memories in persons with body dysmorphic disorder. *Body Image, 1*, 113–125.

Padesky, C. A. (1993). Schema as self-prejudice. *International Cognitive Therapy Newsletter, 5/6*, 16–17.

Phillips, K. (1996). *The broken mirror—Understanding and treating body dysmorphic disorder*. New York: Oxford University Press.

Phillips, K. A., Dufresne, R. G., Jr., Wilkel, C. S. et al. (2000). Rate of body dysmorphic disorder in dermatology patients. *Journal of the American Academy of Dermatology, 42*, 436–444.

Phillips, K. A., Grant, J., Siniscalchi, J., & Albertini, R. S. (2001). Surgical and non psychiatric medical treatment of patients with body dysmorphic disorder. *Psychosomatics, 42*, 504–510.

Rosen, J. C., Reiter, J., & Orosan, P. (1995). Cognitive–behavioral body image therapy for body dysmorphic disorder [published erratum appears in *Journal of Consulting and Clinical Psychology, 63*(3), 437]. *Journal of Consulting and Clinical Psychology, 63*, 263–269.

Sarwer, D. B., Wadden, T. A., Pertschuk, M. J., & Whitaker, L. A. (1998). Body image dissatisfaction and body dysmorphic disorder in 100 cosmetic surgery patients. *Plastic & Reconstructive Surgery, 101*, 1644–1649.

Veale, D. (2004). Advances in a cognitive behavioral model of body dysmorphic disorder. *Body Image, 1*, 113–125.

Veale, D., Boocock, A., Gournay, K., Dryden, W., Shah, F., Willson, R. et al. (1996). Body dysmorphic disorder. A survey of fifty cases. *British Journal of Psychiatry, 169*, 196–201.

Veale, D., Gournay, K., Dryden, W., Boocock, A., Shah, F., Willson, R. et al. (1996). Body dysmorphic disorder: A cognitive behavioural model and pilot randomised controlled trial. *Behaviour Research and Therapy, 34*, 717–729.

Veale, D., & Riley, S. (2001). Mirror, mirror on the wall, who is the ugliest of them all? The psychopathogy of mirror gazing in body dysmorphic disorder. *Behaviour Research and Therapy, 39*, 1381–1393.

Wilhelm, S., Otto, M. W., Lohr, B., & Deckersbach, T. (1999). Cognitive behavior group therapy for body dysmorphic disorder: A case series. *Behaviour Research and Therapy, 37*, 71–75.

Bulimia Nervosa

Diane L. Spangler

Keywords: bulimia nervosa, eating disorders

Cognitive–behavioral therapy (CBT) for bulimia nervosa (BN) is part of a group of therapies that grew out of the initial work of Beck and colleagues which described a cognitive–behavioral treatment for depression. Current CBT interventions for BN are based on a cognitive–behavioral model of the precipitation and maintenance of BN, and attempt to systematically target the primary factors identified in that model.

COGNITIVE-BEHAVIORAL MODEL OF BULIMIA NERVOSA PRECIPITATION AND MAINTENANCE

Cognitive–behavioral conceptualizations of BN precipitation and maintenance are based on schema theory and on dietary restraint theory. According to the theory, dysfunctional beliefs about bodily appearance influence attention to and interpretation of everyday stimuli resulting in overvaluation and manipulation of body weight and shape. BN-related dysfunctional beliefs occur in several domains, including (a) body weight expectation, (b) meaning of body weight and shape, and (c) food and eating pattern. In particular, persons with BN often hold unrealistic expectations for how low their own body weight should be, and believe that acquiring a specific (usually thin) body appearance will result in a host of desired consequences (e.g., increased interpersonal popularity and prowess, increased self-esteem, decreased negative emotion). Thus, obtaining the "ideal" body is viewed as a principal strategy for achieving idiosyncratically defined positive life outcomes and coping with or solving life problems. Dietary restriction is employed in an attempt to conform the body to "ideal" specifications. Dietary restriction typically includes restricting how often food is eaten, how much food is eaten, and what types of foods are eaten. This restrictive eating pattern results in both physiological and psychological deprivation, which increases susceptibility to binge eating. Purging follows binge eating as an attempt to compensate for the calories consumed during binge eating and to reduce anxiety about predicted weight gain. Feelings of lack of control, failure, and anger for breaking self-imposed dietary rules often follow the binge–purge episode, which reinforces the desire to gain control, esteem, and approval via attaining the idealized body. Lastly, a rededication to dietary restriction follows the binge–purge episode in an attempt to regain a sense of self-control and self-esteem, and as a behavioral recommitment to dysfunctional beliefs about the "necessity" of an ideal body. This cycle of restriction–deprivation–bingeing–purging– negative self-view repeats itself indefinitely resulting in the development of BN.[1]

COGNITIVE–BEHAVIORAL MODEL OF BULIMIA NERVOSA TREATMENT

CBT for BN was originally developed by Fairburn (1981), and has continued to evolve (see Cooper, Todd, & Wells, 2000; Fairburn, Marcus, & Wilson, 1993). Reduced to its essence, CBT for BN seeks to eliminate excessive dietary restriction and dysfunctional beliefs about the self, body, and food, and to enhance cognitive flexibility, problem-solving, and relapse prevention skills. To achieve these ends, treatment is divided into three phases.

[1] The current description focuses on purported proximal precipitating and maintenance factors in BN. Some cognitive–behavioral theorists also discuss more distal etiologic factors that are thought to influence the development of dysfunctional body-related beliefs such as thin-ideal media, parental body dissatisfaction, and peer group. Thus, the cognitive–behavioral model can be viewed as being consistent with empirical literature documenting such variables as risk factors for BN.

Phase 1

Phase 1 focuses on reducing excessive dietary restriction. During this phase, clients monitor their eating pattern and food intake on a daily basis in order to identify the ways in which they typically restrict and to identify any additional triggers for binge eating or purging. Clients are then helped to regularize their eating pattern by developing regimented times for eating and by identifying activities that are incompatible with binge eating or purging to use at times when they feel the urge to engage in either of these behaviors. Clients are also educated about: (a) the ineffectiveness of vomiting and laxative use in expelling calories and controlling weight, (b) the effects of dietary restriction on increased binge eating and on metabolism, and (c) healthy body mass index for their body. Clients are encouraged to weigh themselves once a week to test (unfounded) predictions that altering their restrictive eating pattern will result in weight gain. Exposure-based interventions are also used during Phase 1 in the form of gradually incorporating moderate amounts of feared or avoided foods into the client's meals. Although eating behaviors are the primary focus of Phase 1, cognitive interventions that seek to identify and alter automatic thoughts which either hinder regular eating (e.g., negative predictions regarding change) or encourage binge eating or purging (e.g., permissive thoughts) are also routinely utilized during Phase 1.

Phase 2

Phase 2 primarily targets dysfunctional thoughts and beliefs about the self and the meaning of the body. Clients are encouraged to explicate their own definition of an ideal body, their view of their departure from this ideal, and their predictions about the consequences of obtaining this ideal. Body exposure is also used both to identify dysfunctional beliefs about current bodily appearance and to habituate to current body appearance. Although initial CBT protocols for BN emphasized the use of evidence-based interventions to counteract dysfunctional thoughts and beliefs about the body and self, more recent protocols incorporate a much wider range of standard CBT restructuring techniques such as cost–benefit analysis, core belief worksheets, downward arrow, and behavioral experiments (see Cooper et al., 2000). A second focus of Phase 2 is training in problem-solving skills. The rationale for problem-solving training derives from the assumption that persons with BN either believe that obtaining their ideal body will solve life problems, or else use binge eating and purging to cope with stressful situations and negative mood. Since such beliefs and behaviors are evaluated and often refuted during Phase 2, problem-solving training is offered as a replacement strategy for addressing life problems. Other skills such as emotion regulation skills may also be taught and applied during Phase 2 on an as needed basis.

Phase 3

The main goal of Phase 3 is relapse prevention. During this phase, progress is reviewed as are the methods used to reduce and eliminate primary symptoms. Clients are encouraged to differentiate between a lapse (i.e., normal overeating) and a relapse (i.e., return of BN symptoms). Clients create a relapse plan or list of things to do if they believe BN symptoms are returning. The relapse plan is individualized for each client based on his or her primary difficulties and triggers, and on the interventions that were most useful during treatment. Phase 3 concludes with an exploration of thoughts and feelings about treatment termination.

EMPIRICAL STATUS OF THERAPY FOR BULIMIA NERVOSA

The efficacy of CBT for BN has been evaluated in nearly 30 controlled studies. The percentage reduction in binge eating and purging across all clients receiving CBT is typically 80% or more compared to virtually 0% reduction in wait-list controls. Approximately 50% of those treated with CBT report complete cessation of all binge eating and purging at treatment termination. Large effect sizes for CBT are found for both behavioral symptoms (e.g., binge frequency = 1.28) and cognitive symptoms (e.g., eating attitudes = 1.35) (Whittal, Agras, & Gould, 1999; see also Lewandowski, Gebing, Anthony, & O'Brien, 1997). Furthermore, symptom reduction and cessation are fairly well-maintained across time with the majority of clients retaining therapeutic changes 1 year after treatment. The study with the longest follow-up period found that two-thirds of clients treated with CBT had no eating disorder at a 5-year posttreatment assessment (Fairburn et al., 1995). Furthermore, CBT has effects on the associated features of BN. In addition to reduction in binge eating and purging, those treated with CBT show decreases in dietary restraint, depression, and shape-weight concerns as well as increases in social functioning and self-esteem.

In comparison to alternative forms of treatment for BN, CBT has superior response rates. CBT has most often been compared to antidepressant medication in the treatment of BN. In a meta-analysis including 9 double-blind, placebo-controlled medication trials and 26 randomized CBT trials, CBT was found to be significantly more effective than medication in reducing binge eating, purging, depression, and weight-shape concerns (Whittal et al., 1999). In comparison to alternative psychotherapies, CBT has been found to have significantly higher response rates than supportive psychotherapy, behavior therapy, psychodynamic therapy, stress management, and nutritional counseling. The one exception to this pattern of findings concerns interpersonal psychotherapy (IPT): CBT and IPT show similar long-term outcomes. However, in comparison to IPT, CBT is significantly more fast-acting and has significantly higher acute response rates (Agras, Walsh, Fairburn, Wilson, & Kraemer, 2000). The rapid response to CBT for BN has now been documented in several studies which report that approximately 60–70% of the reduction in binge eating and purging occurs within the first 6 sessions of CBT. For all of these reasons, CBT is identified as the treatment of choice for BN in each of the recent meta-analyses of BN treatment.

FUTURE DIRECTIONS IN CBT FOR BULIMIA NERVOSA

Although CBT is currently the most effective form of treatment for BN with most clients exhibiting significant reductions in BN symptoms following treatment, only roughly 50% of clients treated with CBT are *completely* free of BN symptoms in the long term. Given this rate of full response, the need to improve the efficacy of CBT for BN is clear especially since administering an alternative therapy to those who do not initially respond to CBT for BN has, in most instances, not resulted in treatment gains. Mechanism of action research is a primary avenue for understanding how CBT for BN works and thereby providing direction into how to enhance CBT's efficacy (Spangler, 2002). Statements of hypothesized mechanisms of action in CBT for BN are available (Spangler, Baldwin, & Agras, 2004; Wilson, 1999; Wilson & Fairburn, 1993), but studies of the mechanisms of action in CBT for BN are still in their infancy. Of the few mechanism studies conducted, those examining the role of the therapeutic alliance find that it is not associated with changes in BN symptoms (Spangler et al., 2004; Wilson, Fairburn, Agras, Walsh, & Kraemer, 2002). Spangler et al. (2004) found that therapist behavioral interventions were the interventions most associated with BN symptom change, whereas therapist relational interventions were most associated with client motivation for change (but not actual symptom change). Continued research on the mechanisms of action in CBT is needed.

Other theorists have suggested that an expansion of the scope of CBT for BN may enhance its efficacy. Additional treatment foci that have been suggested include incorporating a component that is focused on interpersonal schemas, incorporating a well-defined component on body image exposure, or incorporating a component that directly addresses client negative affect. Indeed, several studies have documented that clients with high levels of negative affect respond less well to CBT for BN than clients with lower levels of negative affect. Including additional components in CBT for BN may, however, be premature until the mechanisms by which the current form of CBT has its effects have been more clearly elucidated. Additionally, effectiveness studies of the current (as well as any modified) form of CBT for BN are needed to determine response rates to CBT in typical practice (rather than research) settings.

Alternative forms of delivery of CBT for BN are also of interest. Few therapists are well trained in CBT for BN, making the accessibility of the treatment problematic. In an effort to increase CBT availability, some have proposed a stepped care model of delivery. This model proposes beginning BN clients at a level of care that requires the lowest amount of provider resources (such as use of self-help manuals with occasional therapist phone contact) and then adding more "steps" of care as symptom severity or nonresponse to "lower" steps of treatment warrant. Initial studies of the use of CBT self-help materials for BN clients are promising (Carter, 2002). However, how, when, and for whom self-help materials are best integrated with current CBT treatment for BN remain to be determined. Other forms of delivery in need of further examination include group treatment and shortened forms of CBT for BN.

See also: Anorexia nervosa, Body dysmorphia 1, Body dysmorphia 2, Dialectical behavior therapy for eating disorders

REFERENCES

Agras, W. S., Walsh, B. T., Fairburn, C. G., Wilson, G. T., & Kraemer, H. C. (2000). A multicenter comparison of cognitive–behavioral therapy and interpersonal psychotherapy for bulimia nervosa. *Archives of General Psychiatry, 57*, 459–466.

Carter, J. C. (2002). Self-help books in the treatment of eating disorders. In C. G. Fairburn & K. D. Brownell (Eds.), *Eating disorders and obesity* (2nd ed., pp. 358–361). New York: Guilford Press.

Cooper, M., Todd, G., & Wells, A. (2000). *Bulimia nervosa: A cognitive therapy programme for clients*. London: Kingsley Publishers.

Fairburn, C. G. (1981). A cognitive–behavioral approach to the management of bulimia. *Psychology and Medicine, 11*, 707–711.

Fairburn, C. G., Marcus, M. D., & Wilson, G. T. (1993). Cognitive–behavioral therapy for binge eating and bulimia nervosa: A comprehensive treatment manual. In C. G. Fairburn & G. T. Wilson (Eds.), *Binge eating: Nature, assessment and treatment* (pp. 361–404). New York: Guilford Press.

Fairburn, C. G., Norman, P. A., Welch, S. L., O'Connor, M. E., Doll, H. A., & Peveler, R. C. (1995). A prospective study of outcome in bulimia nervosa and the long-term effects of three psychological treatments. *Archives of General Psychiatry, 52*, 304–312.

Lewandowski, L. M., Gebing, T. A., Anthony, J. L., & O'Brien, W. H. (1997). Meta-analysis of cognitive–behavioral treatment studies for bulimia. *Clinical Psychology Review, 17*, 703–718.

Spangler, D. L. (2002). How does cognitive–behavioral therapy work? Using structural equation modeling to pinpoint mechanisms and mediators of change. In T. Scrimali & L. Grimaldi (Eds.), *Cognitive psychotherapy Toward a new millenium: scientific foundations and clinical practice* (pp. 161–164). New York: Kluwer Academic/Plenum Publishers.

Spangler, D. L., Baldwin, S. A., & Agras, W. S. (in press). An examination of the mechanisms of action in cognitive behavioral therapy for bulimia nervosa. *Behavior Therapy*.

Whittal, M. L., Agras, W. S., & Gould, R. (1999). Bulimia nervosa: A meta-analysis of psychosocial and pharmacological treatments. *Behavior Therapy, 30*, 117–135.

Wilson, G. T. (1999). Treatment of bulimia nervosa: The next decade. *European Eating Disorders Review, 7*, 77–83.

Wilson, G. T., & Fairburn, C. F. (1993). Cognitive treatments for eating disorders. *Journal of Consulting and Clinical Psychology, 61*, 261–269.

Wilson, G. T., Fairburn, C. G., Agras, W. S., Walsh, B. T., & Kraemer, H. (2002). Cognitive behavior therapy for bulimia nervosa: Time course and mechanisms of change. *Journal of Consulting and Clinical Psychology, 70*, 267–274.

C

Cancer

Arthur M. Nezu and Christine Maguth Nezu

Keywords: cancer, psychosocial oncology, problem-solving therapy

During the past several decades, considerable medical progress has been made in treating cancer. Many forms are curable and there is a sustained decline in the overall death rate from this set of diseases when assessing the impact on the total population. Because of improvements in medical science, more people are living with cancer than ever before. However, psychosocial and emotional needs are frequently overlooked by the traditional health care team, and despite improved medical prognoses, cancer patients often continue to experience significant emotional distress. For example, compared to the general population, cancer patients experience a fourfold increase in the rate of depression. Other significant psychological problems include pain, anxiety, suicide, delirium, body image difficulties, and sexual dysfunctions. Various psychological and physical symptoms frequently occur as a function of the cancer treatment itself (e.g., fear, nausea). Even for people who historically have coped well with major negative life events, cancer and its treatment greatly increase the stressful nature of even routine daily tasks (Nezu, Nezu, Felgoise, & Zwick, 2003).

In response to these significant negative consequences, a variety of psychosocial interventions, including various cognitive–behavioral therapy (CBT) approaches, have been applied to address both specific negative symptoms (e.g., anticipatory nausea, pain) as well as overall psychological distress and quality of life.

CBT FOR ANTICIPATORY NAUSEA

Clinically, negative side effects of both emetogenic chemotherapy and radiotherapy, common forms of medical treatment for cancer, include anticipatory nausea and vomiting. From a respondent conditioning conceptualization, this occurs when previously neutral stimuli (e.g., colors and sounds associated with the treatment room) acquire nausea-eliciting properties due to repeated association with chemotherapy treatments and its negative aftereffects. Investigations conducted in the early 1980s (e.g., Burish & Lyles, 1981) found progressive muscle relaxation, combined with guided imagery, to be effective in reducing anticipatory nausea and vomiting among samples of patients already experiencing such symptoms. Systematic desensitization has also been found to be an effective intervention for these problems. Moreover, conducting CBT *prior* to receiving chemotherapy has been found to *prevent* anticipatory nausea and vomiting, as well as fostering improved posttreatment emotional well-being.

CBT FOR PAIN

CBT strategies that have been posited as potentially effective approaches for the reduction of cancer-related pain include relaxation training, guided imagery and distraction, and cognitive coping and restructuring. Although there have only been a few empirical investigations evaluating such hypotheses, more recent research is underscoring the promise of such interventions. For example, Liossi and Hatira (1999) recently compared the effects of hypnosis and CBT as pain management interventions for pediatric cancer patients undergoing bone marrow aspirations. Their results indicated that both treatment protocols, as compared to a no-treatment control condition, were effective in reducing pain and pain-related anxiety.

CBT FOR EMOTIONAL DISTRESS

CBT approaches are increasingly being evaluated as a means to decrease psychological distress symptoms (e.g., depression, anxiety) among cancer patients, as well as to improve their overall quality of life. This trend began with a landmark study conducted by Worden and Weisman (1984) in which they found an intervention package that included training in problem-solving and relaxation skills to promote effective coping and adaptation among newly diagnosed cancer patients. Behavioral stress management strategies, such as progressive muscle relaxation and guided imagery, have also been found to be effective in reducing symptoms of emotional distress among cancer patients.

In general, with regard to enhancing cancer patients' emotional well-being, the trend has been to evaluate the efficacy of multicomponent protocols that include a variety of CBT strategies. For example, Telch and Telch (1986) found a group-administered multicomponent CBT coping skills training protocol, composed of relaxation and stress management, assertive communication, cognitive restructuring and problem solving, management of emotions, and planning pleasant activities, to be superior to a supportive group therapy condition. A landmark multicomponent CBT-based investigation was conducted by Fawzy and his colleagues (Fawzy et al., 1990) and included patients who were newly diagnosed with malignant melanoma. The 6-week CBT intervention was comprised of four components—health education, stress management, problem-solving training, and group support. At the end of the 6 weeks, patients receiving the structured intervention began showing reductions in psychological distress as compared to "medical treatment as usual" control patients. However, 6 months posttreatment, such group differences became very pronounced.

More recently, Nezu, Nezu, Felgoise, McClure, and Houts (in press) published a study which found that: (a) problem-solving therapy by itself was a robust treatment approach in decreasing psychological distress and improving the quality of life of adult cancer patients, and (b) including a patient-identified significant other (e.g., spouse, adult son or daughter) in treatment who served as a "problem-solving" coach significantly enhanced positive treatment effects as evidenced at 6-month and 1-year follow-up evaluations.

Despite the literature documenting the efficacy of psychosocial interventions for cancer patients, a major obstacle to the potential utilization of such protocols is accessibility. In response to such barriers, various programs using the telephone as a communication tool have been developed in order to provide health education, referral information, counseling, and group support. With regard to CBT interventions, for example, Allen et al. (2002) recently evaluated the effects of a combined face-to-face and telephone problem-solving-based intervention. In general, their results provide support for the efficacy of such an approach in reducing cancer-related difficulties for young breast cancer patients.

EFFECTS OF CBT INTERVENTIONS ON HEALTH OUTCOME

The above brief review underscores the efficacy of CBT for cancer patients with regard to reducing specific psychological (e.g., depression, anxiety) and physical (e.g., anticipatory nausea and vomiting, pain) cancer-related symptoms, as well as improving their overall adjustment and emotional well-being. However, the question remains as to whether such psychosocial-based therapies have any impact on actual health outcome. In other words, do they affect the course or prognosis of the disease itself? Possible routes of impact of such interventions on the health of cancer patients include (a) improving patient self-care (e.g., reducing behavioral risk factors), (b) increasing patients' compliance with medical treatment, and (c) influencing disease resistance regarding certain biological pathways, such as the immune system.

To date, few studies, regardless of the theoretical orientation on which the psychosocial intervention is based, have addressed this question directly. One example involves the investigation conducted by Fawzy and his colleagues (1993) with malignant melanoma patients noted previously. Although this study was not originally designed to specifically assess differences in survival rates as a function of differing treatment conditions, this research team did find 6 years later that the CBT group experienced longer survival as compared to control participants, as well as a trend for a longer period to recurrence for the treated patients.

In addition to the increased longevity associated with their CBT intervention, Fawzy et al. (1993) provide some evidence indicating that the possible mechanism of action for this improved health might involve the immune system. More specifically, in their study, at the end of the 6-week intervention, those patients receiving the CBT protocol evidenced significant increases in the percentage of large granular lymphocytes. Six months posttreatment, this increase in granular lymphocytes continued with increases in natural killer cells also being evident. Although research investigating the link between immunologic parameters and psychosocial variables in cancer patients is in its nascent stage, and therefore can only be viewed as suggestive in nature at this time, such a framework provides for an exciting area for future research and a possible means of explaining one pathway between behavioral factors and cancer-related health outcome.

PREVENTION ISSUES

All of the above interventions are geared to impact on health and mental health parameters *after* a person is diagnosed with cancer. However, treatment strategies can also affect behavioral risk factors, thus attempting to *prevent* cancer to some extent. Some of the most important cancer-related behavioral risk factors include smoking, alcohol, diet, and sun exposure. Reviews of the relevant CBT treatment literature bases concerning the first three areas are included in other sections of this encyclopedia and therefore will not be repeated here. With regard to sun exposure, some interventions have led to increased knowledge of skin cancer and awareness of protective measures; however, programs have had only limited success with increasing preventive behaviors in at-risk groups.

Prevention strategies are also important for individuals considered at high risk due to genetic and familial factors. For example, a positive family history of breast cancer is an important risk factor for breast cancer in women. As such, first-degree relatives of women with breast cancer may also be at risk for psychological distress. With this in mind, Schwartz et al. (1998) evaluated a brief problem-solving-based intervention as a means to reduce distress among women with a first-degree relative recently diagnosed with breast cancer. Results indicated that for participants who regularly practiced the problem-solving techniques, their cancer-specific distress was significantly reduced as compared to control participants and those treatment participants only infrequently using the problem-solving skills.

SUMMARY

Overall, research has amply demonstrated that a variety of cognitive–behavioral interventions are effective in reducing specific cancer-related physical (e.g., pain, nausea, and vomiting) and emotional (e.g., depression, anxiety) symptoms, as well as enhancing the overall quality of life of cancer patients. More recently, using the telephone to increase accessibility to such programs has also begun to show promise. In addition to improving cancer patients' emotional well-being, data exist suggesting that psychosocial interventions can also lead to improved survival by affecting the course of the cancer itself. One biological pathway that has been identified as a potential mechanism by which this can occur is the immune system. However, the literature providing evidence to support a link between behavioral variables and health outcome as mediated by the immune system is only in its infancy with regard to cancer. Therefore, substantial additional research is necessary before the nature of these relationships can be clearly elucidated.

Psychosocial interventions have also been developed for at-risk groups (e.g., first-degree relative of a woman with breast cancer) or people engaging in risky cancer-engendering behaviors (e.g., excessive sun exposure) as a means of reducing risk and preventing cancer.

See also: Caregivers of medically ill persons, Clinical health psychology, Problem solving therapy—general

REFERENCES

Allen, S. M., Shah, A. C., Nezu, A. M., Nezu, C. M., Ciambrone, D., Hogan, J., & Mor, V. (2002). A problem-solving approach to stress reduction among younger women with breast carcinoma: A randomized controlled trial. *Cancer, 94*, 3089–3100.

Burish, T. G., & Lyles, J. N. (1981). Effectiveness of relaxation training in reducing adverse reactions to cancer chemotherapy. *Journal of Behavioral Medicine, 4*, 65–78.

Fawzy, F. I., Cousins, N., Fawzy, N. W., Kemeny, M. E., Elashoff, R., & Morton, D. (1990). A structured psychiatric intervention for cancer patients: I. Changes over time in methods of coping and affective disturbance. *Archives of General Psychiatry, 47*, 720–725.

Fawzy, F. I., Fawzy, N. W., Hyun, C. S., Guthrie, D., Fahey, J. L., & Morton, D. L. (1993). Malignant melanoma: Effects of an early structured psychiatric intervention, coping and affective state on recurrence and survival 6 years later. *Archives of General Psychiatry, 50*, 681–689.

Liossi, C., & Hatira, P. (1999). Clinical hypnosis versus cognitive behavioral training for pain management with pediatric cancer patients undergoing bone marrow aspirations. *International Journal of Clinical and Experimental Hypnosis, 47*, 104–116.

Nezu, A. M., Nezu, C. M., Felgoise, S. H., McClure, K. S., & Houts, P. S. (2003). Project Genesis: Assessing the efficacy of problem-solving therapy for distressed adult cancer patients. *Journal of Consulting and Clinical Psychology, 71*, 1036–1048.

Nezu, A. M., Nezu, C. M., Felgoise, S. H., & Zwick, M. L. (2003). Psychosocial oncology. In A. M. Nezu, C. M. Nezu, & P. A. Geller (Eds.), *Health psychology* (pp. 267–292). New York: Wiley.

Schwartz, M. D., Lerman, C., Audrian, J., Cella, D., Garber, J., Rimer, B., Lin, T., Stefanek, M., & Vogel, V. (1998). The impact of a brief problem-solving training intervention for relatives of recently diagnosed breast cancer patients. *Annals of Behavioral Medicine, 20*, 7–12.

Telch, C. F., & Telch, M. J. (1986). Group coping skills instruction and supportive group therapy for cancer patients: A comparison of strategies. *Journal of Consulting and Clinical Psychology, 54*, 802–808.

Worden, J. W., &Weisman, A. D. (1984). Preventive psychosocial intervention with newly diagnosed cancer patients. *General Hospital Psychiatry*, *6*, 243–249.

RECOMMENDED READINGS

Baum, A., & Andersen, B. L. (Eds.) (2001). *Psychosocial interventions for cancer*. Washington, DC: American Psychological Association.

Jacobsen, P. B., & Hann, D. M. (1998). Cognitive–behavioral interventions. In J. C. Holland (Ed.), *Psycho-oncology* (pp. 717–729). New York: Oxford University Press.

Nezu, A. M., Lombardo, E., & Nezu, C. M. (in press). Cancer. In A. R. Kuczmierczyk & A. Nikcevic (Eds.), *A clinician's guide to behavioral medicine: A case formulation approach*. London: Brunner-Routledge.

Nezu, A. M., Nezu, C. M., Friedman, S. H., Faddis, S., & Houts, P. S. (1998). *Helping cancer patients cope: A problem-solving approach*. Washington, DC: American Psychological Association.

Caregivers of Medically Ill Persons

Stephanie H. Felgoise and Krista Olex

Keywords: medical illness, caregivers, chronic illness

Changes in the philosophy underlying the provision of health care and medical technology have extended the lives of patients with chronic illnesses and have resulted in increased numbers of patients requiring in-home medical care. Often, the responsibility of providing such care lies with family members, also termed *caregivers*. *Informal* or *lay caregivers* is operationally defined as those unpaid carers who provide physical, practical, and emotional care and support for a loved one with a chronic or terminal illness (Harding & Higginson, 2003). Duties that had previously been the responsibility of formally trained health care professionals are now performed by lay caregivers, essentially rendering them members of the patient's health care treatment team. Fairly recent estimates have indicated there are over 52 million lay caregivers in the United States (Health and Human Services, 1998). As such, caregivers have and will continue to become a more prominent population seeking services by cognitive and behavioral clinicians.

OVERVIEW OF THE CAREGIVING LITERATURE

Historically, the study of caregiving has developed within the context of caring for persons with schizophrenia or dementia. Thus, until the rise in focus on clinical health psychology and behavioral medicine, little attention had been given to caregivers of medically ill persons, or differences between various caregiving populations. More recently, variables affecting the well-being of caregivers of patients with medical illnesses such as cancer, HIV/AIDS, traumatic brain injury, spinal cord injury, and ALS have been examined independently and in comparison to other caregiver groups. Although limited, research findings suggest that the experiences of individuals caring for family members with different medical and care needs may differ significantly. Differences may occur due to patients' rate of disease progression, functional abilities, or palliative care requirements, for example. Also, caregiver variables such as age, coping abilities, relationship variables, and other factors may differ based on the demographics of persons likely to contract specific diseases, or the age at which persons do so. Lastly, differences are likely to be significant between caregivers of chronically ill versus terminally ill care recipients in stressors, adjustment, and coping. However, few studies actually make such direct comparisons. The literature offers much regarding caregiver needs assessments, but generally lacks empirically tested interventions to match these reported needs. Given this limitation in the literature, several global statements can be made about caregiving and interventions to aid individuals in this role.

Across groups, it is accepted that most caregivers face multiple challenges and stressors, and therefore, many often experience feelings of depression, anxiety, powerlessness, role strain, guilt, and grief (Ruppert, 1996). Caregivers struggle with juggling multiple roles (family, work, household) with their caregiving responsibilities and often do so without adequate support. The psychological distress that results when caregiving responsibilities exceed caregivers' available resources has been defined throughout the literature as "caregiver burden."

Caregiver stress, distress, and burden have negative implications for individual caregivers' health, and also for the psychological and physical health and well-being of the care recipients. Research has shown that caregiving stressors can indirectly compromise caregivers' immune functioning, and also care recipients may receive inadequate or suboptimal care when caregivers are burdened or coping with stressors poorly. Consequently, understanding the stressors and psychological aspects of providing care to loved ones is important for caregivers and patients alike.

Research has also found that some caregivers report increased meaning and satisfaction through this role. For instance, couples may develop more emotional connection, intimacy, and trust, and reevaluation of existential issues and spirituality may result in positive emotional well-being. Individuals experiencing these feelings may be less in need of therapeutic intervention, but they too may benefit from learning ways to enhance adaptive skills that may serve to improve their overall quality of life in the face of new challenges.

Given the inconclusive nature of the caregiving literature, application of cognitive–behavioral theory to working with caregivers dictates the use of multidimensional, biopsychosocial assessments and interventions to devise services based on individual or population needs. Specific attention to cultural, spiritual, and religious beliefs, values, and practices regarding illness, loss, family, and life meaning is critical.

OVERVIEW OF INTERVENTION APPLICATIONS

Although relatively recent within the past 15 to 20 years and few in number, cognitive–behavioral interventions have been developed specific to various caregiving populations (e.g., caregivers of patients with cancer, traumatic brain injuries, spinal cord injuries, dementia, HIV/AIDS) to help individuals adjust to the caregiving and personal challenges that often arise. The literature suggests caregivers benefit from individual, group, couples, and family interventions, or a combination of treatment modalities. Decisions regarding types of interventions to offer may depend on several factors: the relationship of the caregiver to the patient, accessibility of services, longevity of the caregiving role, type of patient illness, individual needs and characteristics (i.e., coping skills, supports) of caregivers and care recipients. Anecdotally, the biggest obstacle to participation in available clinical services seems to be related to limited time for self or coverage for caring for the patient. Given the unique difficulties caregivers have in arranging time to participate in office or hospital-based treatments, researchers are investigating the feasibility and benefits of nontraditional delivery of services (i.e., computer, telephone, home- or community-based programs).

General behavioral target areas common to most caregiving populations include increasing coping skills, problem-solving skills, time management, prosocial and health behaviors, relaxation, assertiveness, and communication skills. Cognitive targets may focus on decreasing maladaptive thoughts and beliefs in connection with feelings of depression, anxiety, or guilt, and increasing positive coping and self-efficacy or self-affirming statements. Services may be structured as therapy, support, psychoeducation, respite, self-enhancement, or a combination of these approaches. Interventions may focus on interpersonal (social isolation, competing work, family, and recreational demands) or intrapersonal (finances, emotional and physical well-being, changes in identity or future goals and expectations) variables, preexisting stressors or problems further complicated by the caregiving role, symptom management, and grief and loss issues. Contrary to many theorists' and researchers' hypotheses, qualitative research reveals that more often caregivers' distress is reportedly due to interpersonal and familial stressors, rather than disease-related or instrumental care activities (Elliott & Rivera, 2003) for some populations. Cognitive–behavioral interventions for decreasing psychological distress and improving quality of life and general well-being are described below.

COGNITIVE–BEHAVIORAL INTERVENTIONS

Cognitive–behavioral interventions have been used with caregivers to improve time management, coping, problem-solving skills, assertiveness, relaxation, positive experiences, and self-care, and to decrease distorted thought processes regarding the caregiving experience. Regardless of the specific technique or modality utilized, the fundamental goal of these interventions is to decrease distress and to improve the caregiver's ability to cope with the multifaceted caregiving challenges and role changes, improve their sense of control, and overall quality of life. Many of these interventions can be offered in individual, group, or family modalities, and with or without the care recipient present, depending on the nature of individual concerns.

Problem-Solving Training for Caregivers

The construct of social problem-solving has long been of interest to researchers and clinicians, but has only been specifically applied to the caregiver population within the past decade. Problem-solving has been integral to the application of cognitive–behavioral interventions to the caregiver population (Toseland, Blanchard, & McCallion, 1995) and many of the problem-solving-based interventions (i.e., Houts, Nezu, Nezu, & Bucher, 1996; Kurylo, Elliott, & Schewchuk, 2001) are adaptations of Nezu and D'Zurilla's (1989) and Nezu, Nezu, Friedman, Houts, and Faddis's (1998) problem-solving therapy for social competence and distressed cancer patients, respectively. Social problem-solving therapy has been extensively researched in whole and in parts, according to basic science and clinical principles, as a theoretical model for understanding stress and distress, as a clinical therapeutic intervention for many populations, and in various adaptations (see D'Zurilla & Nezu, 1999, for review).

The work of Nezu and D'Zurilla challenged the view that problem-solving represents a form of problem-focused, as opposed to emotion-focused, coping. Whereas problem-focused coping refers to attempts to change the problematic situation in some way, emotion-focused coping refers to attempts to manage the emotional distress that results from the problem (Lazarus & Folkman, 1984). According to Nezu and D'Zurilla, social problem solving can include both problem-focused and emotion-focused goals. Thus, problem-solving coping represents a set of strategies that can help individuals change the nature of problematic situations, one's reactions to them, and often both.

Problem-solving interventions incorporate principles of cognitive restructuring (challenging maladaptive thoughts and irrational beliefs, strategies to increase self-efficacy), techniques to counter maladaptive behavioral response styles (avoidance, impulsiveness, carelessness), and specific skill instruction to increase positive, systematic, and rational thinking. Social problem-solving skills, according to D'Zurilla, Nezu, and colleagues, include problem orientation variables and rational problem-solving skills. Problem orientation variables describe a cognitive mind-set of how individuals view problems in daily living, and their perceived ability to solve them. With respect to caregiving, problem orientation refers to the caregiver's view of the role of caregiving, as well as the caregiver's expectations for meeting the demands of the role. For example, a caregiver may view the role as being a burden, while another may view the role as representing a challenge. These differences with respect to problem orientation have implications for the outcome of the problem-solving process, with a negative problem orientation (e.g., "this is a burden") contributing to negative outcomes. The second process is problem-solving proper, which refers to the actual process of devising a solution to the problem through rational and systematic means. Four skills comprise this portion of the problem-solving process: problem definition and formulation, generation of alternatives, decision making, and solution implementation and verification, and specific subsets of skills and techniques are taught within each of these components.

Although the therapeutic social problem-solving model is structured, it is also flexible so as to be tailored to individual learning styles, with emphasis on specific target problems, and can be applied as psychoeducational training for prevention or intervention, or in conjunction with other therapeutic strategies. Thus, its practical focus and flexibility makes this packaged intervention particularly well-suited to many caregivers, who face daily problems and challenges allowing for varying degrees of control. Houts et al. (1996) modified the problem-solving therapy intervention, for example, to develop the Prepared Family Caregiver conceptual model for caregivers of persons with cancer. This derivation uses the acronym "COPE" to emphasize creativity, optimism, planning, and expert information, within the context of social problem solving and by use of these skills. Similarly, Kurylo et al. (2001) developed Project FOCUS to emphasize that "If you know the *F*acts and are *O*ptimistic and *C*reative, you can *U*nderstand the problem better and *S*olve it effectively." These models particularly attend to the uncertainty often experienced by caregivers of medical patients, and to using problem-solving strategies to decrease this uncertainty and related distress, increase acquisition of resources and support, and positive interactions with medical staff.

Toseland and colleagues' (1995) intervention for caregivers of cancer patients represents the integration of problem-solving skills training with other cognitive–behavioral intervention strategies. Their intervention protocol, known as "Coping with Cancer," is a six-session program combining supportive therapy, coping skills training, and problem-solving training. The problem-solving component involves training the caregivers in the use of the steps of the problem-solving process, much like those described by Nezu and D'Zurilla (1989). Within the context of a supportive therapeutic relationship, an oncology social worker helped caregivers take necessary steps to develop and implement potential solutions to three problems identified by each caregiver as being the most distressing or pressing. Adaptive coping responses to those problems were also discussed and reinforced when utilized. In sum, treatment plans consisted of the following goals: reappraisal of problem situations, increasing the use of formal and informal supports, and changing coping responses. Caregivers in the control condition did not receive this problem-solving intervention, but were free to seek other forms of individual and group interventions (e.g., marriage counseling and support groups) offered by the oncology center. Outcome measures of caregivers' coping skills, burden levels, marital satisfaction, social supports, and emotional disturbances were administered both prior to and after implementation of the intervention. Despite caveats concerning the small sample size of distressed caregivers used in data analysis, results of the study indicated that the intervention was effective in alleviating the distress experienced by this subset of participating caregivers. Those who were identified as being moderately burdened demonstrated significant improvement in their ability to cope with problems following the intervention. Further, those who were identified as being moderately distressed in terms of their marital adjustment demonstrated significant improvements in physical, role, and social functioning following the intervention. No such improvement was noted in their control group counterparts.

Cognitive Restructuring

Negative or maladaptive thoughts can be generated by caregivers in response to the challenges and stressors they face, thereby contributing to negative affective and emotional states. For example, in a qualitative study investigating the psychological effects of lay caregiving in a sample of 68 caregivers, Ruppert (1996) noted that guilt was a common emotion experienced and expressed by the caregivers in her sample. Ruppert cited examples of thoughts beginning with phrases such as "I should have … ," "Why didn't I … ," or "If only I had … " as being commonly expressed by these caregivers. Ruppert also noted that the caregivers made these statements despite being responsible, conscientious, and fully involved in the care of their loved ones. The cognitions that underlie feelings of guilt are particularly amenable to cognitive restructuring. Other maladaptive cognitions expressed by caregivers may contribute to feelings of hopelessness, powerlessness, and depression. Thus, cognitive restructuring techniques can be an integral component of the cognitive–behavioral approach to the treatment of caregiver distress.

Systematic Desensitization and Relaxation Training

Systematic desensitization and relaxation training can be used with caregivers to decrease emotional and physical symptoms of stress, and can be especially important for caregivers who are unable to leave the environment of their caregiving role to engage in other stress reduction activities. Cary and Dua (1999) utilized relaxation training, systematic desensitization, and other cognitive–behavioral procedures with a sample of caregivers of patients with intellectual or physical disabilities. Two intervention groups and one wait-list control group, each consisting of 12 caregivers, were formed. Participants in the self-instructional training group were instructed in the use of visualization and imagery techniques. Subsequently, self-instructional training occurred, which consisted of asking participants to imagine a stressful situation and then to repeat a series of positive self-statements. This procedure was repeated for five situations identified by the participants to be highly stressful. Caregivers in the systematic desensitization group were initially instructed in the use of progressive muscle relaxation. Once this technique had been learned, a standard systematic desensitization procedure was used to help caregivers reduce their anxiety related to problematic situations they encountered. Results of the study supported the efficacy of systematic desensitization and self-instructional techniques in reducing the perceived stress of caregivers. Compared to participants in the wait-list control condition, those in the two treatment conditions demonstrated a significant reduction in perceived stress.

SUMMARY AND CONCLUSION

The stressors and demands associated with providing care to a loved one with a debilitating or terminal illness have been well-documented throughout the literature. There is no question that the role of caregiver is one that can be extremely challenging and can contribute to considerable psychological distress on the part of the caregiver. Given that there are over 52 million lay caregivers in the United States (Health and Human Services, 1998), and that depression, anxiety, powerlessness, role strain, guilt, and grief are common feelings experienced by caregivers, the need for intervention is clear. While supportive and educational group interventions have long been utilized with this population, caregivers are likely to have needs that are not sufficiently addressed by these types of interventions alone. Thus, the need for more active, directive, goal-driven interventions has been recognized. As discussed in this article, cognitive–behavioral interventions have been increasingly used with the caregiver population to improve coping and problem-solving skills, promote relaxation, enhance self-efficacy and quality of life, and decrease distorted thought processes regarding the caregiving experience. While the systematic investigation of the efficacy of these interventions represents a relatively recent undertaking, early evidence certainly supports the application of cognitive–behavioral therapy to the caregiver population.

FUTURE DIRECTIONS

Given the current status of the literature, a possible future direction for research could be guided by acknowledgment of the heterogeneity of caregiving experiences. As opposed to directing efforts toward discovering features of caregiving that are common to all diseases and illnesses and developing generalized, global interventions, it may be more beneficial to develop an understanding of illness-specific caregiving stressors and demands. Clinicians and researchers are challenged to develop new ways to apply cognitive and behavioral interventions and prevention services to populations who are not usual consumers of psychological services, or who may not have the time or ability to attend traditional outpatient treatments.

See also: Clinical health psychology

REFERENCES

Bucher, J. A., Houts, P. S., Nezu, C. M., & Nezu, A. M. (1999). Improving problem-solving skills of family caregivers through group education. *Journal of Psychosocial Oncology, 16*(3/4), 73–84.

Cary, M., & Dua, J. (1999). Cognitive–behavioral and systematic desensitization procedures in reducing stress and anger in caregivers for the disabled. *International Journal of Stress Management, 6*(2), 75–87.

Elliott, T., & Rivera, P. (2003). Spinal cord injury. In A. Nezu, C. Nezu, & P. Geller (Eds.), *Comprehensive handbook of psychology: Vol. 9. Health psychology* (pp. 415–435). New York: Wiley.

Harding, R., & Higginson, I. J. (2003). What is the best way to help caregivers in cancer and palliative care: A systematic literature review of interventions and their effectiveness. *Palliative Medicine, 17*, 63–74.

Health and Human Services (1998, June). *Informal caregiving: Compassion in action*. Washington, DC: Author.

Houts, P. S., Nezu, A. M., Nezu, C. M., & Bucher, J. A. (1996). The prepared family caregiver: A problem-solving approach to family caregiver education. *Patient Education and Counseling, 27*, 63–73.

Kurylo, M., Elliott, T., & Schewchuk, R. (2001). FOCUS on the family caregiver: A problem-solving training intervention. *Journal of Counseling and Development, 79*, 275–281.

Lazarus, R. S., & Folkman, S. (1984). *Stress, appraisal, and coping*. New York: Springer.

Nezu, A. M., & D'Zurilla, T. J. (1989). Social problem-solving and negative affective states. In P. C. Kendall & D. Watson (Eds.), *Anxiety and depression: Distinctive and overlapping features* (pp. 285–315). New York: Academic Press.

Nezu, A. M., Nezu, C. M., Friedman, S. H., Houts, P. S., & Faddis, S. (1998). *Helping cancer patients cope: A problem-solving approach*. Washington, DC: American Psychological Association.

Ruppert, R. A. (1996). Psychological aspects of lay caregiving. *Rehabilitation Nursing, 21*(6), 315–320.

Toseland, R. W., Blanchard, C. G., & McCallion, P. (1995). A problem solving intervention for caregivers of cancer patients. *Social Science and Medicine, 40*(4), 517–528.

RECOMMENDED READINGS

D'Zunilla, T. J., & Nezv, An (1999). *Problem solving therapy: A social competence approach to clinical intervention* (2nd ed.). New York: Springer.

Elliott, T. R., & Rivera, P. (2003). The experience of families and their carers in health care. In S. Llewelyn & P. Kennedy (Eds)., *Handbook of clinical health psychology* (pp. 61–77). New York: Wiley.

Nezu, A. M., Nezu, C. M., Friedman, S. H., Houts, P. S., & Faddis, S. (1998). *Helping cancer patients cope: A problem-solving approach*. Washington, DC: American Psychological Association.

Case Formulation

Lawrence D. Needleman

Keywords: case formulation, cognitive case formulation, cognitive case

Cognitive case formulation (CCF) is the process of developing an explicit, individualized, and parsimonious understanding of the factors that caused and currently maintain a client's psychological problems. The formulation is an integration of relevant disorder-specific cognitive models (e.g., Beck, Rush, Shaw, & Emery, 1979; Beck et al., 1990); thorough, empirically validated or theoretically derived assessment methods; collaboration with clients; and clinical judgment.

Cognitive–behavioral therapy (CBT)—unlike some other theoretical perspectives—is predicated on the notion that targeted interventions are largely responsible for therapeutic improvement. As a result, CCFs play an important role in CBT, because CCFs help therapists select appropriate interventions.

INTERACTING ELEMENTS OF CCF

The cognitive therapy literature recommends including the following elements in CCFs (Needleman, 1999; Persons, 1989):

- *Problem list*
- *Stressors* that precipitated the client's chief complaint
- *Diagnoses*
- *Core beliefs* or schemas—longstanding, deeply held, emotionally laden beliefs about self, others, and the world that have a profound influence on behavior (e.g., "I'm a loser"; "People are only out for themselves")
- *Other salient beliefs* (e.g., conditional assumptions—"If I work extremely hard at all times, I might not fail"; implicit rules—"One should never show their weaknesses"; beliefs about therapy—"Therapists manipulate people for their own self-serving ends")
- *Cognitive processes*—rumination, avoidance, cognitive distortions, and explanatory style
- *Compensatory strategies*—internal or external coping responses performed to manage distress, challenging circumstances or to achieve life goals. They can be adaptive or maladaptive depending on the context and flexibility of use. Some examples of common maladaptive compensatory strategies include experiential avoidance, social withdrawal, maintaining a facade, self-sacrifice, addictions, and workaholism
- *Current, problematic, cognitive–emotional–behavioral responses* to triggering situations. For example, a client's girlfriend was 30 minutes late coming home. This triggered the automatic thought, "Something terrible happened to her," intense anxiety, and frantic search efforts
- *Clients' strengths*—examples include the ability to form healthy relationships, discipline, self-efficacy, social support, and work skills
- *Learning history* that contributed to the client's vulnerability to specific stressors (e.g., parent's death in early childhood resulting in intense distress when confronted with interpersonal loss)
- *Maintaining mechanisms*

Because cognitive therapy theorists consider identifying and targeting maintaining mechanisms crucial to successful therapy, they are important components of the CCF (e.g., Needleman, 2003). Some of the most common examples include: (a) schema-consistent appraisal of situations, (b) skills deficits, (c) high levels of distress, which interfere with effective problem solving, (d) reinforcing and punishing consequences of behavior, (e) valuing short-term over long-term consequences, (f) avoidance, which prevents both disproving maladaptive beliefs and desensitizing to triggering situations, (g) self-handicapping strategies that bolster one's self-concept, (h) self-fulfilling expectations, (i) anxiety about change, (j) feelings of hopelessness, and (k) acquiescing to or overcompensating for core beliefs.

BENEFITS OF CCF

CCF proponents suggest that CCFs confer a variety of benefits. First, formulations can help therapists select effective interventions and tailor interventions to client needs. Second, CCFs might increase clients' optimism for therapeutic improvement. For example, by illustrating that clients' problems are related to a small number of underlying themes, formulations might foster clients' hope. CCFs also can increase clients' confidence in their therapists by demonstrating therapists' sophisticated understanding of clients' problems and by helping therapists to provide clients with convincing rationales for interventions.

A third way CCFs might be beneficial is by helping therapists predict and circumvent difficulties that arise in therapy. For example, the formulation can increase therapists' awareness of potentially derailing beliefs, attitudes, or behavioral patterns (i.e., perfectionism, mistrust, rebelliousness, avoidance) early in therapy and address these issues, or CCFs can help therapists appropriately modify treatment if clients are not improving (Needleman, in press).

THE CCF PROCESS

The cognitive therapy literature provides several guidelines for the CCF process (Needleman, 1999; Persons, 1989). These guidelines suggest that therapists should base CCFs on empirically validated and theoretically derived assessment methods. In addition, the CCFs should result from collaboration between therapist and client; the therapist should elicit the client's feedback about each element of the individualized formulation. CCFs should be parsimonious, including the fewest underlying beliefs and mechanisms that can comprehensively explain clients' behavior and problems. The guidelines also suggest that the formulation is a working model and an ongoing process throughout the course of therapy. CCFs consist of interrelated, testable hypotheses.

In addition to the overall formulation, therapists should continually *microconceptualize*, that is, attempt to remain mindfully attuned to clients' moment-by-moment experiences. Microconceptualizations, while informed by the overall formulation, can help therapists refine their overall understanding of clients' experiences (Needleman, in press). (In addition, therapists' ongoing awareness allows them to work with clients' relevant experiences in the present.)

According to the cognitive therapy literature, therapists should neither hold on to their CCFs too rigidly nor should they modify the CCFs too easily (i.e., without sufficient justification). To decrease the likelihood of confirmatory bias, therapists should search for evidence that refutes their model and honestly consider alternate hypotheses to explain clients' behaviors. Also, the formulation process is bidirectional. Observation and assessment data lead to hypothesized mechanisms. These hypotheses can help therapists generate predictions about clients' in-therapy, extra-therapy, and questionnaire response behaviors that, in turn, guide further assessment.

RESEARCH ON CCF

The CCF process is the product of empirically based and theoretically driven assessment, the cognitive model, and clinical judgment. Therefore, the reliability and validity of formulations depend on no less than the reliability and validity of the CBT assessment methods used, the quality of clinical judgment, and the validity of the cognitive model itself. These are enormous topics, which cannot be covered in depth here. This review is limited to studies addressing the reliability of CCF and studies that compared individualized CBT based on CCFs with standardized CBT.

Reliability

Developing methods for reliably generating formulations is important for advancing knowledge of CCF and presumably increasing the efficacy of cognitive therapy. Persons and Bertagnolli (1999) investigated whether clinicians could correctly identify depressed clients' overt problems and their underlying core beliefs. During CCF workshops, 47 clinicians were trained in developing CCFs. After brief training, workshop participants reviewed audiotapes and written transcripts of initial interviews of three depressed female outpatients. Workshop participants were asked to identify clients' core beliefs and overt problems. To assist participants in identifying overt problems, participants were provided with a specific list of problem domains. Similarly, to help participants identify core beliefs, they were given lists of adjectives for describing clients' views of self, others, and the world. Workshop participants identified 67% of patients' overt problems. Regarding core belief ratings, individual clinicians showed poor interrater agreement, with coefficients averaging 0.37. When core belief ratings were averaged over five clinicians, interrater reliability coefficients improved to 0.72.

Muran, Segal, and Samstag (1994) developed an idiographic interview-based measure of self-schemas—a crucial CCF component—using self-scenarios. Each self-scenario consisted of four components reflecting schema structure: a triggering situation and cognitive, affective, and behavioral responses. Schema components from each client's own self-scenarios and components from other clients' self-scenarios were presented in random order to the client, his or her therapist, and a third-party observer for ratings of clinical relevance. Reliability coefficients were excellent. When averaged across clients on each separate component, coefficients ranged from 0.90 (SD ± 0.05) to 0.93 (SD ± 0.04). In addition to showing excellent reliability, this research suggested that self-scenarios are clinically relevant, have predictive validity, and are sensitive to change in therapy. Thus, self-scenarios are a promising methodology for assessing self-schemas.

An alternative method for identifying elements of the CCF is to use questionnaires or structured clinical interviews having good psychometric properties. For example, the Dysfunctional Attitude Scale (Weissman & Beck, 1978) identifies core beliefs in depression and has good psychometrics.

Individualized versus Standardized CBT

Within the field of CBT, there is a debate about whether individualized CBT with CCF versus standardized CBT is more effective. Traditionally, CBT has been individualized and included functional assessments that—regardless of diagnosis—identified the mechanisms that maintained clients' problems and targeted these mechanisms.

However, over the last two decades, CBT researchers have developed many treatment manuals with proven effectiveness for use with particular psychiatric diagnoses. When clinicians use these manuals for clients having the relevant diagnoses, clients receive all the treatment components included in the manual. That is, interventions are based primarily on diagnoses, not on functional assessments of the clients' problems. A question becomes which is more effective—standardized or individualized treatment?

In many common clinical situations, individualized CBT based on a formulation is essential. Treating clients who have comorbidity is one such situation. The literature does not have guidelines regarding which of the possible treatment manuals to use for clients with comorbid conditions or how to select the most salient treatment components for these clients. Another common clinical situation where individualized CBT is essential is for clients having psychological problems for which no empirically validated treatment manual yet exists. A third situation occurs when therapy is not working. When clients are not improving, therapists should refer to their formulation to determine what factors are preventing their clients from benefiting from treatment.

For clients having a circumscribed problem for which an empirically validated treatment manual exists, the question of individualized versus standard CBT is less clear. Outcome studies have yielded inconsistent results. For example, most studies of phobias have found that standardized CBT is as effective or more effective than individualized CBT. Schulte, Kuenzel, Pepping, and Schulte-Bahrenberg (1992) randomly assigned 120 clients having different kinds of phobias to one of three treatment groups: (a) a standardized treatment group in which clients received *in vivo* exposure and cognitive restructuring, (b) an individualized treatment group in which therapists had free reign to use any CBT methods they deemed appropriate based on a functional assessment, and (c) a yoked control group (in this group, each client was randomly matched with a client from the individualized treatment group and received identical treatment to that client). Contrary to expectations, the standardized group proved to be most effective.

In explaining their findings, Schulte et al. (1992) suggested that perhaps the standardized treatments are more effective than individualized CBT for phobias because individuals with phobias are homogeneous with respect to maintaining mechanisms. Therefore, they are likely to respond well to treatment that targets those mechanisms. In contrast, many other disorders are less homogeneous. For similar reasons, many CBT theorists have argued that—unlike the prevailing diagnostic system—diagnostic categories should be based on underlying maintaining mechanisms as opposed to clustering symptoms.

Unlike studies of phobias, most studies comparing individualized to standardized CBT for clients having major depression found that individualized treatment improved outcome. For example, McKnight, Nelson, Hayes, and Jarrett (1984), using an elegant treatment design, compared the effectiveness of interventions that matched depressed clients' specific skills deficits with interventions that were mismatched. Based on pretreatment assessments, the depressed clients in the study had (a) social skills deficits, (b) cognitive deficits (i.e., irrational cognitions), or (c) both types of deficits. All clients received four sessions of social skills training and four sessions of cognitive restructuring. Following interventions that matched depressed clients' deficits, clients improved significantly more in terms of both depression and the relevant deficit than when receiving mismatched interventions (e.g., when receiving social skills training, those with social skills deficits improved more on both depression and social skills than during the cognitive restructuring intervention). These findings suggest that individualized CBT for depressed clients can improve outcome.

In the debate between individualized and standardized treatment, another perspective is that the difference between standardized and individualized treatment appears to be a false dichotomy. To optimize psychotherapy effectiveness, many leading CBT researchers recommend that clinicians individualize interventions from treatment manuals for each client [see Special Series Going Beyond the Manual: Insights from Experienced Clinicians, *Cognitive and Behavioral Practice*, *10*(1), 2003]. This represents a middle ground between following treatment manuals in a lockstep fashion and completely individualizing treatment.

Such an approach may confer the advantages of both individualized and standardized approaches. On the one hand, by using CCF, therapists could select the most salient treatment components from relevant treatment manuals and spare clients from unnecessary treatment components. When implementing interventions, therapists could be sensitive to clients' needs, as well as creative and flexible.

On the other hand, from the standardized perspective, therapists could limit their choices of interventions primarily to those that are components of relevant treatment manuals. Because these interventions are ones that are included in empirically validated treatment approaches, using these interventions with relevant client populations might lead to higher success rates than if therapists were choosing from the universe of possible interventions.

EXAMPLE OF A CCF

Figure 1 is a CCF diagram for a complex client having several comorbid conditions. She had anorexia (without body image disturbance) that—according to the formulation—was secondary to obsessive–compulsive disorder and panic disorder. Her major depressive disorder was conceptualized as being the result of loss of reinforcement

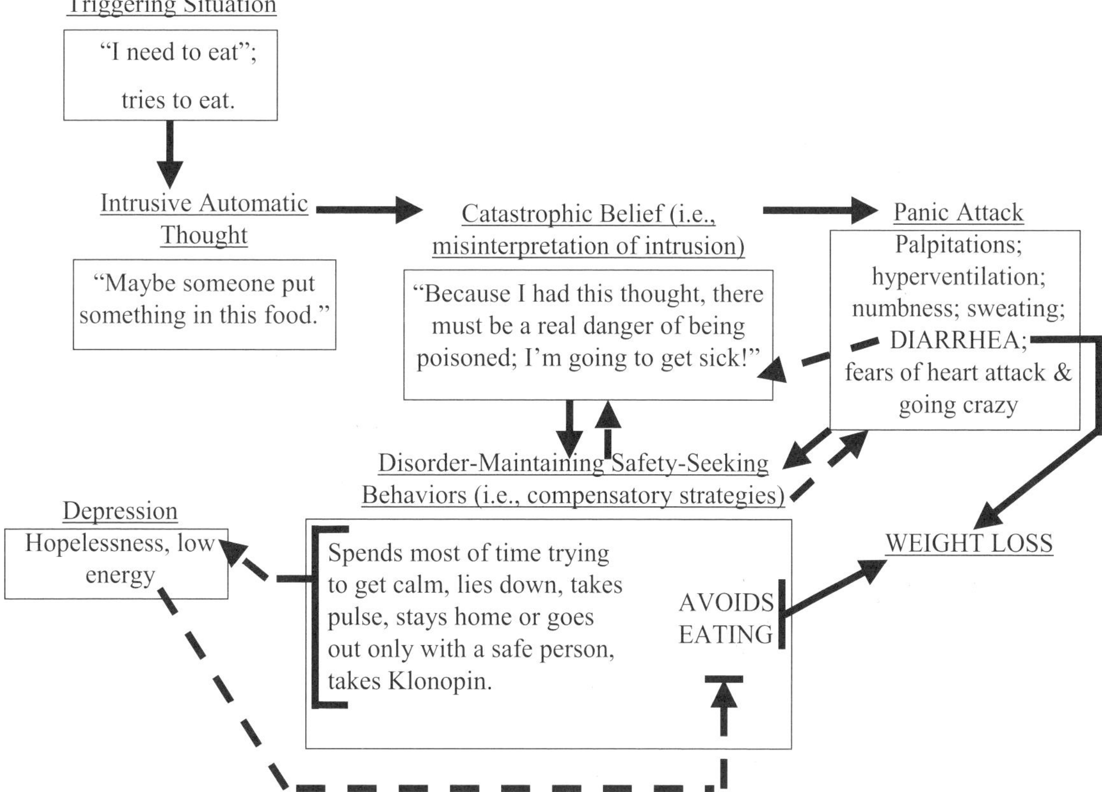

Figure 1. Cognitive case formulation for a patient with co-morbid anorexia, panic, OCD, and severe major depressive disorder. (From Needleman, L. (in press). Case conceptualization in predicting and responding to difficulties in cognitive therapy. In R. Leathy (Ed.), *Overcoming resistance in cognitive therapy*. New York: Guilford Press.)

(as well as direct effects of starvation). Although this was a complicated case, a graphically depicted CCF made selection of interventions fairly straightforward. To facilitate the client's weight gain early in therapy, interventions targeted panic attacks, the belief that someone was attempting to poison her, and food-related anxiety cues. After a year in CBT, the client made marked progress. She was out of medical danger and her psychosocial adjustment had improved markedly.

See also: Applied behavior analysis, Behavioral assessment

REFERENCES

Beck, A. T., Freeman, A., & Associates. (1990). *Cognitive therapy of personality disorders*. New York: Guilford Press.

Beck, A. T., Rush, A. J., Shaw, B. F., & Emery, O. (1979). *Cognitive therapy of depression*. New York: Guilford Press.

McKnight, D. L., Nelson, R. O., Hayes, S. C., & Jarrett, R. B. (1984). Importance of treating individually assessed response classes in the amelioration of depression. *Behavior Therapy*, *15*, 315–335.

Muran, J. C., Segal, Z. V., & Samstag, L. W. (1994). Self-scenarios as a repeated measures outcome measurement or self-schemas in short-term cognitive therapy. *Behavior Therapy*, *25*, 255–274.

Needleman, L. (1999). *Cognitive case conceptualization: Guidebook for practitioners*. Mahwah, NJ: Erlbaum.

Needleman, L. (2003). Case conceptualization in predicting and responding to therapeutic difficulties. In R. Leahy (Ed.), *Overcoming resistance in cognitive therapy*. New York: Guilford Press.

Persons, J. B. (1989). *Cognitive therapy in practice*: A *case formulation approach*. New York: Norton.

Persons, J. B., & Bertagnolli, A. (1999). Interrater reliability of cognitive–behavioral case formulations of depression: A replication. *Cognitive Therapy and Research*, *23*, 271–283.

Schulte, D., Kuenzel, R., Pepping, G., & Schulte-Bahrenberg, T. (1992). Tailor-made versus standardized therapy of phobic patients. *Advances in Behaviour Research and Therapy*, *14*, 67–92.

Weissman, A., & Beck, A. T. (1978). *Development and utilization of the Dysfunctional Attitude Scale*. Presented at the annual meeting of the Association for the Advancement of Behavior Therapy, Chicago.

Child Abuse

Esther Deblinger and Melissa K. Runyon

Keywords: child sexual abuse, child physical abuse, posttraumatic stress disorder, parenting, cognitive–behavioral therapy

Child maltreatment is a highly prevalent public health problem that results in short- and long-term emotional and behavioral consequences for children and their families. Based on recent statistics reported by the U.S. Department of Health and Human Services (USDHHS), 879,000 substantiated cases were reported to child protective service agencies across 50 states in 2000 (USDHHS, 2002) with 10% (88,000) of these cases being related to child sexual abuse (CSA) and 19% (167,000) being related to child physical abuse (CPA).

These alarming statistics are most likely an underestimate given that these numbers are based on narrow definitions of abuse and only on those children who are abused by a caretaker. Other surveys, such as the National Incidence Study-3 (NIS-3; Sedlak & Broadhurst, 1996), have categorized CSA more broadly as the exploitation, involvement, or exposure of children, to age-inappropriate sexual behavior by older or "more powerful" peers or adults, for purposes of sexual gratification. CPA has also been more broadly defined as physical punishment administered by caregivers if either the Harm (sustained injury) or Endangerment standard (at-risk for injury) were met as a result of being hit by a hand or object, kicked, thrown, shaken, burned, stabbed, or choked. Indeed, studies utilizing these broader definitions have yielded higher rates of child sexual and physical abuse (see Finkelhor, 1994; Finkelhor & Dziuba-Leatherman, 1994). For example, the NIS-3 study reported incidence rates of 9 and 4.4 per 1000 children for CPA and CSA, respectively (Sedlak & Broadhurst, 1996).

Although CSA occurs in all educational, socioeconomic, racial, and ethnic groups (Wyatt & Peters, 1986), there are factors associated with an increased risk for experiencing such abuse. Based on reported prevalence and incidence rates, females are at greater risk than males to experience CSA, particularly in cases of intrafamilial abuse. Regardless of the child's gender, CSA has been associated with living with a surrogate parent, experiencing significant family conflict (Finkelhor, 1993) or exhibiting behavioral or developmental disabilities (Sullivan & Knutson, 2000).

Multiple factors have been identified in the literature as being associated with an increased risk for a CPA (see Black, Heyman, & Smith-Slep, 2001). For example, anecdotal reports and statistics based on reports to child protective services perpetuate the myth that a young, single woman with a low socioeconomic status from an ethnic minority population may be at greater risk for engaging in CPA. To the contrary, research involving nationally representative samples have not demonstrated significant relationships between severe child–parent physical abuse and age of perpetrator, marital status, parent gender, or socioeconomic status (Chaffin, Kelleher, & Hollenberg, 1996). Investigations examining the relationship between CPA and ethnic group have yielded variable results (see Black et al., 2001). This variability is most likely related to professionals being more likely to report child abuse and child protective service workers being more likely to investigate cases involving lower-income minority groups. Parental depression has been identified as the strongest risk factor (Chaffin et al., 1996) and parental abuse history was also associated with perpetrating CPA (see Black et al., 2001).

Empirical and clinical studies have documented a wide range of emotional, behavioral, and interpersonal difficulties, ranging from mild to severe, that are exhibited by children who have experienced CPA and/or CSA. The impact on children can be similar regardless of the type of abuse suffered. Child victims commonly report emotional responses such as anger, hostility, guilt, shame, anxiety, and depression (e.g., Kendall-Tacket, Williams, & Finkelhor, 1993; Pelcovitz et al., 1994). Posttraumatic stress disorder (PTSD) has also been documented among children who have suffered abuse (Ackerman, Newton, McPherson, Jones, & Dykman, 1998; Pelcovitz et al., 1994).

Children who have suffered CPA and/or CSA may exhibit immediate and long-term behavioral responses that increase their risk for victimizing others or being revictimized themselves. For example, children who experience CPA frequently display aggressive behavior, poor social problem-solving skills and communication skills, as well as lower levels of empathy and sensitivity toward others (e.g., Dodge, Bates, & Pettit, 1990; Salzinger, Feldman, Hammer, & Rosario, 1993). In fact, children who suffer CPA are more likely than their nonabused peers to alienate themselves from other children (Salzinger et al., 1993) by responding in a retaliatory manner during their interactions with peers which they tend to interpret as hostile (Dodge, Pettit, & Bates, 1994). These negative behaviors may escalate across the life span resulting in a chronic pattern of negative relationships with others. For instance, a history of CPA has been associated with criminal behavior in adolescents (Herrenkohl, Egolf, & Herrenkohl, 1997) and adults (Widom, 1989), abusive or coercive behaviors in dating relationships (Wolfe, Wekerle, Reitzel-Jaffe, & Lefebvre, 1998). During adulthood, children who suffered CPA are at increased risk of being battered by a partner (see Kaner, Bulik, & Sullivan, 1993) and abusing their own children (Crouch, Milner, & Thomsen, 2001).

While children who have suffered CSA are less likely to engage in physically aggressive behaviors, inappropriate sexualized behavior has been reported in the literature for child victims of all ages (Beitchman et al., 1992) and may be directed toward other children and adults alike. It is notable that a majority of child victims do not develop a longstanding pattern of offending behaviors that persist into adulthood. However, research has provided evidence suggesting that CSA increases one's risk for suffering sexual dysfunctions, substance abuse difficulties, suicidal behaviors as well as revictimization experiences in adulthood (Arata, 2000; Dube et al., 2001). These studies suggest that child abuse not only has an immediate negative psychological impact on children, but may lead to psychosocial difficulties that persist into adulthood and potentially impact the victims' adult relationships, as well as the next generation of children.

A number of protective factors have been identified that may buffer children from the negative effects of child abuse and may explain the variability in symptom development in child victims. Numerous investigations, for example, have documented the powerful influence of the reactions and adjustment of parents on children's outcomes following abuse (Cohen & Mannarino, 1996a; Deblinger, Steer, & Lippmann, 1999; Kelly, Faust, Runyon, & Kenny, 2002). With respect to child-specific traits, a number of studies have demonstrated that negative general and abuse-specific attributions are related to anxious and depressive symptoms in children who have suffered CPA or CSA (Brown & Kolko, 1999; Cohen & Mannarino, 1996a; Runyon & Kenny, 2002). These studies support the notion that children's perceptions about the abuse, themselves, others, and the world mediate the development of postabuse symptomatology.

Given the evidence that the above parental and cognitive factors may importantly influence outcomes for children who have suffered abuse, cognitive–behavioral therapy (CBT) seems well suited for the treatment of this population. First, CBT interventions can be applied to children as well as their parents. This is important, because as noted above, enhanced parental responses and support appear to facilitate a child's recovery and thus reduce his/her risk of suffering ongoing difficulties. In addition, CBT's focus on targeting and correcting dysfunctional thoughts and beliefs may help to alter the problematic attributions that often lead to more negative outcomes.

It should also be noted that CBT is applicable to a wide array of symptom difficulties which is crucial given the significant and highly diverse psychosocial reactions presented by survivors of childhood abuse. In fact, CBT is intended to be individually tailored to suit the specific therapeutic needs of each child and family. In addition, the collaborative nature of the therapist–client relationship in the context of CBT may be particularly beneficial when working with this population of parents and children. The cognitive–behavioral therapist listens and educates, sharing specific rationales underlying cognitive–behavioral interventions and encouraging collaboration in the implementation of treatment. This type of empathic and empowering therapist–client relationship in and of itself may be healing and restorative for children and parents who may feel out of control and who may have limited influence over child protection and legal decisions that are being made on their behalf.

It is also noteworthy that cognitive–behavioral interventions, perhaps, because of their active and structured nature, have been found to be appealing to and effective with diverse minority populations (Paniagua, 1994). This is critically important because, as noted earlier, child abuse impacts children from all ethnic, religious, and socioeconomic backgrounds.

Finally, recent research suggests that child abuse may not only lead to severe and sometimes chronic psychosocial difficulties, but the aftereffects may also lead to changes in brain functioning and development (DeBellis et al., 1999). Thus, not only is it important for children who are suffering abuse to be identified and protected, it is also critical for them to receive demonstrably effective interventions as early as possible in their development.

Recent reviews of the treatment outcome literature in the area of CSA find that cognitive–behavioral models have the strongest empirical support for the effective treatment of PTSD and related difficulties in this population (Cohen, Berliner, & March, 2000; Saunders, Berliner, & Hanson, 2003). One such model manualized by Deblinger and Heflin (1996) conceptualizes the development, maintenance, and treatment of psychological difficulties of children who have suffered sexual abuse by integrating learning theory, particularly the influence of conditioning, modeling, and contingencies in the environment, with the importance of cognitive, affective, and physiological influences. This CBT model incorporates specific interventions that are designed to target the psychosocial processes that may be responsible for the maintenance and exacerbation of abuse-related difficulties long after the abuse has ended. These interventions include: education about sexual abuse and healthy sexuality, coping skills training, gradual exposure and processing of traumatic memories and reminders, body safety skills training, and parenting skills training. The treatment approach involves the participation of the child and nonoffending parent in individual therapy sessions that ultimately build toward joint parent–child sessions as well as family sessions when appropriate.

A series of randomized controlled trials have documented the efficacy of abuse-focused CBT approaches utilized with children who have suffered sexual abuse. These studies have established the superior effectiveness of CBT interventions, as compared to the passage of time, nondirective supportive therapy, and standard community care, in terms of treating children's PTSD symptoms, depression, social competence, abuse-related fear, general behavior problems as well as age-inappropriate sexual behaviors (Cohen & Mannarino, 1996b, 1998; Deblinger, Lippmann, & Steer, 1996; King et al., 2000). In addition, recent findings have demonstrated that children's significant improvements in response to CBT interventions have been maintained over a 2-year follow-up period (Deblinger et al., 1999). Abuse-focused CBT delivered in group format has also been found to be more efficacious than educational support groups with respect to the amelioration of parental abuse-specific distress and the learning and retention of body safety skills in very young survivors of sexual abuse (Deblinger, Stauffer, & Steer, 2001). Finally, a recently completed two-site treatment outcome investigation, involving a large and diverse sample of children who suffered sexual abuse as well as other traumas, replicated the findings of earlier studies further documenting the superior benefits of abuse-focused CBT as compared to a client-centered treatment approach for both the children and their nonoffending parents (Cohen, Deblinger, Mannarino, & Steer, 2003). These studies have not only established the direct benefits of CBT interventions with children who have suffered sexual abuse, but the findings have highlighted the value of involving the nonoffending parent in the child's treatment in terms of both alleviating parental distress and enhancing children's outcomes.

The empirical literature is more limited in terms of the treatment of children who have suffered physical abuse. However, there have been a significant number of studies that have examined the treatment of punitive parents. These studies have demonstrated the efficacy of a variety of CBT interventions with this population of parents, including child management skills training, stress management skills training, as well as a combination of these interventions (see Runyon, Deblinger, Ryan, & Kolar, in press). The research on interventions for parents seems to reflect the practice in the field which often focuses on the parents' difficulties with much less attention given to the psychosocial needs of children who have suffered physical abuse. Although a few studies have examined the treatment of children who have suffered CPA, most of these investigations were not randomized controlled trials and/or did not focus on children with documented histories of CPA (Oates & Bross, 1995). In fact, there appears to be only one randomized controlled trial in which therapies designed for at-risk or physically abusive parents as well as their children were examined. The findings of this study demonstrated that as compared to those receiving standard community care, families assigned to CBT or family therapy demonstrated greater improvements on measures of child externalizing behavior problems, parental distress, abuse risk, family conflict and cohesion as well as children's levels of anxiety and depression. CBT, however, was more effective than the other two conditions for reducing parental anger and the use of physical punishment (Kolko, 1996). Since this study, there has been increased emphasis on the integration of the treatment of parents and children in families in which physical abuse has taken place (Runyon et al., in press). Runyon et al. (in press) describe a CBT treatment protocol for children and families at risk for physical abuse that incorporates elements from empirically supported CBT models for sexually abused children (Deblinger & Heflin, 1996), as well as from CBT models designed for families in which physical abuse (Donohue, Miller, Van Hasselt, & Hersen, 1998; Kolko, 1996; Kolko & Swenson, 2002) or domestic violence (Runyon, Basilio, Van Hasselt, & Hersen, 1998) occurs. Although the proposed model in its entirety has not been evaluated with children and families at risk for CPA, the individual CBT components have been effective in addressing many of the psychological and behavioral difficulties exhibited by physically abused children and their parents (see Runyon et al., 2004).

In sum, although researchers examining alternative treatments have established the value of cognitive–behavioral interventions particularly for children who have suffered sexual abuse, there remain many questions to be answered. The field would greatly benefit from further research examining the impact and treatment of the aftereffects of all forms of family violence. Moreover, it will be important to establish the transportability of proven CBT interventions for this population to community settings including urban, suburban, and rural environments. In addition, specific information identifying "active ingredients," optimal "dosage," preferred and/or more efficacious formats (i.e., individual, group, or family), as well as differential treatment responses as a function of developmental stage, coping style, and other child, family, and cultural characteristics would greatly enhance our ability to individually tailor treatment and optimize outcomes for all children and their families.

See also: Children—behavior therapy, PTSD—childhood, Sex offending, Treatment of children

REFERENCES

Ackerman, P. T., Newton, J. E. O., McPherson, W. B., Jones, J. G., & Dykman, R. A. (1998). Prevalence of posttraumatic stress disorder and other psychiatric diagnoses in three groups of abused children (sexual, physical, and both). *Child Abuse and Neglect, 22*, 759–774.

Arata, C. M. (2000). From child victim to adult victim: A model for predicting sexual revictimization. *Child Maltreatment, 5*, 28–38.

Beitchman, J. H., Zucker, K. J., Hood, J. E., daCosta, G. A., Akman, D., & Cassavia, E. (1992). A review of the long-term effects of child sexual abuse. *Child Abuse and Neglect, 16*, 101–118.

Black, D. A., Heyman, R. E., & Smith-Slep, A. M. (2001). Risk factors for child physical abuse. *Aggression and Violent Behavior, 6*, 121–188.

Brown, E. J., & Kolko, D. J. (1999). Child victims' attributions about being physically abused: An examination of factors associated with symptom severity. *Journal of Abnormal Child Psychology, 27*, 311–322.

Chaffin, M., Kelleher, K., & Hollenberg, J. (1996). Onset of physical abuse and neglect: Psychiatric, substance abuse, and social risk factors from prospective community data. *Child Abuse and Neglect, 20*, 191–203.

Cohen, J. A., Berliner, L., & March, J. S. (2000). Treatment of children and adolescents. In E. B. Foa, T. M. Keane, & M. J. Friedman (Eds.), *Effective treatments for PTSD* (pp. 106–138). New York: Guilford Press.

Cohen, J. A., Deblinger, E., Mannarino, A. P., & Steer, R. (2003). *A multisite, randomized controlled trial for sexually abused children with PTSD symptoms*. Manuscript submitted for publication.

Cohen, J. A., & Mannarino, A. P. (1996a). Factors that mediate treatment outcome in sexually abused preschool children. *Journal of the American Academy of Child and Adolescent Psychiatry, 35*, 1402–1410.

Cohen, J. A., & Mannarino, A. P. (1996b). A treatment outcome study for sexually abused preschool children: Initial findings. *Journal of the American Academy of Child and Adolescent Psychiatry, 35*, 42–50.

Cohen, J. A., & Mannarino, A. P. (1998). Interventions for sexually abused children: Initial treatment outcome findings. *Child Maltreatment, 3*, 17–26.

Crouch, J. L., Milner, J. S., & Thomsen, C. (2001). Childhood physical abuse, early social support, and risk for maltreatment: Current social support as a mediator of risk for child physical abuse. *Child Abuse and Neglect, 25*, 93–107.

DeBellis, M. D., Baum, A., Birmaher, B., Keshavan, M. S., Eccard, C. H., Boring, A. M. et al. (1999). Developmental traumatology part I: Biological stress systems. *Biological Psychiatry, 45*, 1259–1270.

Deblinger, E., & Heflin, A. (1996). *Treating sexually abused children and their nonoffending parents: A cognitive–behavioral approach*. Thousand Oaks, CA: Sage.

Deblinger, E., Lippmann, J., & Steer, R. (1996). Sexually abused children suffering posttraumatic stress symptoms: Initial treatment outcome findings. *Child Maltreatment, 1*, 310–321.

Deblinger, E., Stauffer, L. B., & Steer, R. (2001). Comparative efficacies of supportive and cognitive–behavioral group therapies for young children who have been sexually abused and their non-offending mothers. *Child Maltreatment, 6*, 332–343.

Deblinger, E., Steer, R. A., & Lippmann, J. (1999). Two-year follow-up study of cognitive behavioral therapy for sexually abused children suffering post-traumatic-stress symptoms. *Child Abuse and Neglect, 23*, 1371–1378.

Dodge, K. A., Bates, J. E., & Pettit, G. S. (1990). Mechanisms in the cycle of violence. *Science, 250*, 1678–1683.

Dodge, K. A., Pettit, G. S., & Bates, J. E. (1994). Effects of physical maltreatment on the development of peer relations. *Development and Psychopathology, 6*, 43–55.

Donohue, B., Miller, E. R., Van Hasselt, V. B., & Hersen, M. (1998). An ecobehavioral approach to child maltreatment. In V. B. Van Hasselt & M. Hersen (Eds.), *Handbook of psychological treatment protocols for children and adolescents* (pp. 279–358). Mahwah, NJ: Erlbaum.

Dube, S. R., Anda, R. F., Felitti, V. J., Chapman, D. P., Williamson, D. F., & Giles, W. H. (2001). Childhood abuse, household dysfunction, and the risk of attempted suicide throughout the span: Findings from the adverse childhood experiences study. *Journal of the American Medical Association, 286*, 3089–3096.

Finkelhor, D. (1993). Epidemiological factors in the clinical identification of child sexual abuse. *Child Abuse and Neglect, 17*, 67–70.

Finkelhor, D. (1994). Current information on the scope and nature of child sexual abuse. *The Future of Children, 4*, 31–53.

Finkelhor, D., & Dziuba-Leatherman, J. (1994). Children as victims of violence: A national survey. *Pediatrics, 94*, 413–420.

Herrenkohl, R. C., Egolf, B. P., & Herrenkohl, E. C. (1997). Preschool antecedents of adolescent assaultive behavior: A longitudinal study. *American Journal of Orthopsychiatry, 67*, 422–432.

Kaner, A., Bulik, C. M., & Sullivan, P. F. (1993). Abuse in adult relationships of bulimic women. *Journal of Interpersonal Violence, 8*, 52–63.

Kelly, D., Faust, J., Runyon, M. K., & Kenny, M. C. (2002). Behavior problems in sexually abused children of depressed and non-depressed mothers. *Journal of Family Violence, 17*, 107–116.

Kendall-Tackett, K. A., Williams, L. M., & Finkelhor, D. (1993). Impact of sexual abuse on children: A review and synthesis of recent empirical studies. *Psychological Bulletin, 113*, 164–180.

King, N. J., Tonge, B. J., Mullen, P., Myerson, N., Heyne, D., Rollings, S. et al. (2000). Treating sexually abused children with post-traumatic stress symptoms: A randomized trial. *Journal of the American Academy of Child and Adolescent Psychiatry, 39*, 1347–1355.

Kolko, D. J. (1996). Individual cognitive–behavioral treatment and family therapy for physically abused children and their offending parents: A comparison of clinical outcomes. *Child Maltreatment, 1*, 322–342.

Kolko, D. J., & Swenson, C. (2002). *Assessing and treating physically abused children and their families: A cognitive–behavioral approach*. Thousand Oaks, CA: Sage.

Oates, R. K., & Bross, D. C. (1995). What have we learned about treating child physical abuse? A literature review of the last decade. *Child Abuse and Neglect, 19*, 463–473.

Paniagua, F. A. (1994). *Assessing and treating culturally diverse clients: A practical guide*. Thousand Oaks, CA: Sage.

Pelcovitz, D., Kaplan, S., Goldenberg, B., Mandel, F., Lehane, J., & Guarrera, J. (1994). Post-traumatic stress disorder in physically abused adolescents. *Journal of the American Academy of Child and Adolescent Psychiatry, 33*, 305–312.

Runyon, M. K., Basilio, I., Van Hasselt, V. B., & Hersen, M. (1998). Child witnesses of interparental violence: Child and family treatment. In V. B. Van Hasselt & M. Hersen (Eds.), *Handbook of psychological treatment protocols for children and adolescents* (pp. 203–278). Mahwah, NJ: Erlbaum.

Runyon, M. K., Deblinger, E., Ryan, E., & Kolar, R. (2004). An overreview of child physical abuse: Developing an integrated parent–child approach. *Trauma, Violence, and Abuse: A Review Journal, 5*, 65–85.

Runyon, M. K., & Kenny, M. (2002). Relationship of attributional style, depression, and post-trauma distress among children who suffered physical or sexual abuse. *Child Maltreatment, 7*, 254–264.

Salzinger, S., Feldman, R. S., Hammer, M., & Rosario, M. (1993). The effects of physical abuse on children's social relationships. *Child Development, 64*, 169–187.

Saunders, B. E., Berliner, L., & Hanson, R. F. (Eds.). (2003). *Child physical and sexual abuse: Guidelines for treatment* (Final Report: January 15, 2003). Charleston, SC: National Crime Victims Research and Treatment Center.

Sedlak, A. J., & Broadhurst, D. D. (1996). *Executive summary of the Third National Incidence Study of Child Abuse and Neglect*. U.S. Department of Health and Human Services, Administration for Children and Families, National Center on Child Abuse and Neglect, Washington, DC: U.S. Government Printing Office.

Sullivan, P. M., & Knutson, J. F. (2000). Maltreatment and disabilities: A population-based epidemiological study. *Child Abuse and Neglect, 24*, 1257–1273.

U.S. Department of Health and Human Services. (2002). *National Center on Child Abuse and Neglect, Child Maltreatment, 2000: Reports from the States for the National Child Abuse and Neglect Data Systems*. Washington, DC: U.S. Government Printing Office.

Widom, C. S. (1989). Child abuse, neglect, and violent criminal behavior. *Criminology, 27*, 251–271.

Wolfe, D. A., Wekerle, C., Reitzel-Jaffe, D., & Lefebvre, L. (1998). Factors associated with abusive relationships among maltreated and nonmaltreated youth. *Development and Psychopathology, 10*, 61–85.

Wyatt, G. E., & Peters, S. D. (1986). Methodological considerations in research on the prevalence of child sexual abuse. *Child Abuse and Neglect, 10*, 241–251.

RECOMMENDED READINGS

Deblinger, E., & Heflin, A. (1996). *Treating sexually abused children and their non-offending parents: A cognitive–behavioral approach*. Thousand Oaks, CA: Sage.

Kolko, D. J., & Swenson, C. (2002). *Assessing and treating physically abused children and their families: A cognitive–behavioral approach*. Thousand Oaks, CA: Sage.

Runyon, M. K., Deblinger, E., Ryan, E., & Kolar, R. (in press). Cognitive–behavioral treatment of child physical abuse: Developing an integrated parent–child approach. *Trauma, Violence, and Abuse: A Review Journal*.

Children—Behavior Therapy

Laura D. Seligman and Thomas H. Ollendick

Keywords: behavior therapy, children and adolescents, cognitive behavior therapy, developmental issues, evidence-based practice

The roots of cognitive behavior therapy (CBT) for children are inextricably intertwined with the roots of CBT more broadly. Like CBT with adults, CBT for children grew out of two schools of thought—both embedded in experimental psychology; namely, learning theory and cognitive psychology.

First proposed by John Watson in the 1920s, the focus of learning theory and early behaviorism was on overt or observable behaviors rather than inferred processes thought to regulate those behaviors (e.g., ego defenses) that had been the focus of treatments for children in vogue at that time. Although Watson is considered the father of behaviorism, it was one of his students, Mary Cover Jones, who was among the first to apply behavioral principles to the treatment of children. Specifically, Cover Jones used modeling and exposure procedures to treat a child's fear of rabbits. Early behavioral applications for children were later expanded to treatments for disorders such as enuresis, stuttering, and other habit problems.

Behavioral therapies for youth are based on the premise that children learn maladaptive behaviors in the same way they learn adaptive behaviors. More specifically, learning occurs because behavior results in a reward or punishment (operant or instrumental conditioning) or because of associations between stimuli (classical conditioning). Whereas behavioral theory was considered quite controversial at first, growing discontent with psychoanalysis and humanistic or Rogerian therapy, the prevailing therapies, led to some degree of acceptance by the early 1960s and certainly in the 1970s. However, around this time, behavioral theory itself underwent change in that cognition and its role in both producing and maintaining behaviors was recognized. This evolution occurred for several reasons. First, Albert Bandura developed a social learning theory, an expansion of behavioral theory that suggested that people could learn behavior through indirect experiences (vicarious conditioning) as well as direct ones (direct conditioning). In other words, a child could learn a new behavior or might be more or less likely to exhibit a behavior after observing someone else (i.e., a model) exhibit the behavior and witness the consequences of that behavior. Bandura's social learning theory integrated cognitive constructs, such as expectations and intentions, with behavioral theory and observable behaviors. Additionally, around this same time, Aaron "Tim" Beck and Albert Ellis began developing cognitive therapies that focused not on external stimuli but on the individual's perceptions, thoughts, and beliefs about those stimuli. Although somewhat controversial even to this day, these therapies were soon integrated with behavioral therapies to form cognitive–behavior therapy. Several early studies documented the utility of these principles with children and Donald Meichenbaum was among the first to incorporate them in his pioneering book published in 1977, *Cognitive–Behavior Modification*. Subsequently, Thomas Ollendick and Jerome Cerny explicated these principles more broadly in their book, *Clinical Behavior Therapy with Children*, published in 1981 and, more recently, Philip Kendall has expanded and promulgated these principles, particularly so in his edited book, *Child and Adolescent Therapy*, published in 2000.

BASIC TENETS AND PHILOSOPHY

The major factors distinguishing CBT for children from other psychosocial interventions for youth are their focus on maladaptive learning histories and erroneous or overly rigid thought patterns as the cause for the development and maintenance of psychological symptoms and disorders. However, several other central tenets differentiate CBT from other treatments for children.

Not surprisingly, given CBT's foundations in experimental psychology, CBT has at its core a commitment to the scientific process. In practical terms this implies that testable hypotheses derived from cognitive–behavioral theory are subjected to rigorous study. This is most amply demonstrated today by the endorsement of many cognitive–behavioral psychologists for the empirically supported treatments movement. Undoubtedly, the scientific standards applied in the development of CBTs for children contribute to the overwhelming representation of CBTs for children on the list of empirically supported treatments (see below).

Additionally, CBT for children is focused on the here and now rather than oriented toward uncovering historical antecedents of maladaptive behavior or thought patterns. Treatment goals are often operationalized and parents and youth seeking treatment are asked to consider the types of changes they are hoping to see result from treatment. Progress is monitored throughout treatment using objective indicators of change, such as monitoring forms and rating devices.

CBT for children emphasizes a skills building approach; as a result, it is often action-oriented, directive, and frequently educative in nature. Also for this reason, CBT typically includes a homework component in which the skills learned in treatment are practiced outside the therapy room. Moreover, given the focus of behavioral theory on the context of the behavior, treatments for children often incorporate skills components for parents, teachers, and sometimes even siblings or peers. Because the focus is on teaching the child and his or her family and teachers the skills necessary to effectively cope with or eliminate the child's symptoms, the child and significant others become direct agents of change. In effect, they function as "co-therapists." Therefore, CBT is designed to be time-limited and relatively short term, rarely extending beyond 6 months of active treatment. More recently, however, some CBTs for children have started to incorporate spaced-out "booster sessions" that extend over a longer period of time to ensure maintenance and durability of change.

EMPIRICAL SUPPORT FOR CBTs FOR CHILDREN

Relative to other treatment approaches, CBT for children has received strong empirical support. Today CBTs are applied to a wide range of childhood problems and disorders including anxiety and phobic disorders, depressive disorders, aggressive and disruptive behavior problems, substance abuse and eating disorders, as well as pediatric or medical concerns (e.g., coping with painful medical procedures, enuresis, and irritable bowel syndrome). Although reviews clearly highlight the need to develop more and better empirically supported treatments for youth, CBTs for children and adolescents stand out in that they have led the way in doing so. For example, a recent review of the empirically supported treatment literature finds support for CBTs in the treatment of anxiety disorders and phobic disorders, conduct disorder/oppositional defiant disorder, chronic pain, depression, distress due to medical procedures, and recurrent abdominal pain (Chambless & Ollendick, 2001). In addition, behavior therapy or components of behavior therapy were found to be effective in the treatment of attention-deficit/hyperactivity disorder, encopresis, enuresis, obesity, obsessive–compulsive disorder, recurrent headache, and the undesirable behaviors (e.g., self-injury) associated with pervasive developmental disorders. A growing body of research is addressing the mechanisms of change in these therapies as well as questions about the applicability of these treatments to a variety of clinical settings and populations (i.e., the moderators of change).

ISSUES SPECIFIC TO CBT WITH CHILDREN

As noted above, CBT requires that participants are active both in session and outside of session. Among the activities typically required is the completion of between-session homework assignments. Oftentimes homework assignments require the child and/or parent to engage in or focus on some unpleasant activities or thoughts. For example, a child who is afraid of dogs might be required to prac tice approaching a small dog or he/she might be asked to monitor the thoughts he/she has when seeing a dog during the walk to school. Although active engagement in the therapy process and particularly completion of homework assignments may also be an issue for adults, it can be especially problematic for children. Because children are typically referred to treatment by parents, teachers, or physicians and are rarely self-referred, motivation for treatment may be an issue that needs to be addressed early in treatment. Developmental issues may also become important in increasing motivation and compliance in that young children may find the link between CBT and symptom improvement difficult to understand or the cognitive tasks required in some treatments may be difficult for a young child to undertake. For this reason, CBT for children and adolescents is often slightly different, in terms of both the specific tasks and rationale given.

The degree of parental participation in CBT may also vary as a function of the child's developmental level. Although parental participation is typically involved in CBT for younger children, less parental participation is routinely solicited with adolescents. Of course, parental involvement may also vary as a result of the specific disorder or problem behavior being treated. For example, although parents often play an adjunctive or "assistive" role in treatments for internalizing disorders, most research suggests that parent training, rather than individual treatment focused on work with the child, is the most effective treatment for some externalizing disorders. The role of the parents in CBT for children is different from that expected in more traditional therapies for children and, as such, parents may come to CBT expecting to have little or no involvement with the treatment process. Since it is rarely the case that parents are not involved at all in their child's treatment, orientation to this aspect of the CBT treatment model is very important to ensure that all involved parties are working collaboratively.

To a certain degree these statements can also be applied to the involvement of other significant people and systems in the child's life—such as teachers and other school personnel, siblings, peers, and, in the case of interventions for medically related disorders, medical personnel. In fact, some CBTs may focus almost exclusively on changing the child's environment, requiring significant behavioral changes on the part of the individuals who interact with the child on a daily basis. Therefore, CBT therapists often function as consultant to the individuals within the systems targeted for change. Similarly, CBT is increasingly being applied in community-type interventions for children (e.g., school interventions to decrease violence).

DIRECTIONS FOR THE FUTURE OF CBT WITH CHILDREN

Although some CBTs are already modified depending on the developmental level of the child being treated, one challenge currently facing CBT practitioners and researchers is how to more fully integrate developmental theory with cognitive–behavioral theory. Similarly, it remains to be seen to what extent individual and family characteristics such as race, ethnicity, socioeconomic status, and religion demand modification in CBTs for children. As research continues to establish the effectiveness of a growing number of CBTs for children, additional efficacy studies as well as studies examining moderators of effectiveness will need to be conducted.

Understanding why CBT for children works and whether the mechanisms are the same for adults and children will also be an important challenge to meet with studies testing mediational models as well as studies that break down current CBT treatment packages to isolate the necessary and sufficient components. Lastly, as we find more effective treatments, we must focus our energies on whether these same types of interventions or modified forms of CBT can be effective in preventing as well as ameliorating psychological disorders and symptoms in youth.

See also: Aggressive and antisocial behavior in youth, Anxiety—children, Play therapy, Social cognition in children and youth, Suicide—child and adolescent, Treatment of children

REFERENCES

Chambless, D. L., & Ollendick, T. H. (2001). Empirically supported psychosocial interventions: Controversies and evidence. *Annual Review of Psychology, 52*, 685–716.
Kendall, P. C. (Ed.). (2000). *Child and adolescent therapy* (2nd ed.). New York: Guilford Press.
Meichenbaum, D. H. (1977). *Cognitive–behavior modification*. New York: Plenum Press.
Ollendick, T. H., & Cerny, J. A. (1981). *Clinical behavior therapy with children*. New York: Plenum Press.

Chronic Pain

Carrie Winterowd, Aaron Beck, and Dan Gruener

Keywords: pain, chronic pain

Everyone has been in pain at some point in his or her life. However, unrelieved chronic pain is perhaps one of the most challenging problems faced by health care consumers as well as practitioners and providers. It is estimated that 75–80 million people in the United States suffer from some sort of chronic pain, at an annual cost of $65–70 billion (Tollison, 1993). There are a number of personal, social, and environmental consequences of having unrelieved, chronic pain (see Gatchel & Turk, 1999) that may be very difficult for clients to deal with including physical suffering, emotional distress, negative thoughts, behavioral problems (e.g., inactivity, seeking attention), and psychosocial stress (e.g., life role changes, relationship issues, legal problems). Given these experiences, psychological interventions are important for clients who have chronic pain.

TREATING PAIN: MOVEMENT FROM BEHAVIORAL TO COGNITIVE–BEHAVIORAL THERAPY TREATMENT

Behavioral therapy approaches with the chronic pain population were introduced in the late 1960s and early 1970s. Fordyce (1976) was one of the pioneers who applied operant conditioning with chronic pain clients and their families. Many behavioral therapy programs for pain management combine behavioral techniques in treating pain, for example, classical and operant conditioning, relaxation training, biofeedback, communication training, and problem solving.

Cognitive–behavioral approaches with chronic pain clients were introduced in the 1980s, with continued refinements over the past two decades. Turner (1982) and Turk, Meichenbaum, and Genest (1983) were among the first pain researchers to apply cognitive–behavioral principles with the chronic pain population. More recently, Beck's cognitive therapy approach with chronic pain clients has been presented (Winterowd, Beck, & Gruener, 2003).

Beliefs and attitudes are very important in managing physical illnesses and conditions such as chronic pain. Chronic pain clients tend to have specific thoughts and beliefs about their pain as well as the impact of pain on their lives. For example, they might be distressed about their ability to be engaged in activities, their relationships with others, their work and family roles, and their sense of identity, given their chronic pain condition. It is not uncommon for these thoughts and beliefs to have negative, unrealistic, and potentially catastrophic qualities. For example, a chronic pain client might think, "The pain has taken my life. I can't get beyond this pain. God must be punishing me for my sins." Catastrophizing thoughts about pain have been associated with pain, psychological distress, and perceived disability (see reviews by Boothby, Thorn, Stroud, & Jensen, 1999; Sullivan et al., 2001).

How people act or behave can also influence their physical health. Chronic pain clients may behave or act in specific ways when they are in pain, for example, wincing, lying down, complaining, and taking pain medication, otherwise known as "pain behaviors" (Fordyce, 1976). Chronic pain and the physical limitations related to it can lead to a number of potentially troublesome behaviors, including inactivity, social withdrawal and isolation, overeating, complaining, and frequent office visits to physicians.

Cognitive–behavioral therapy (CBT) addresses these aspects of pain management: the importance of realistic, healthy beliefs, attitudes, and behaviors in reducing the emotional and physical suffering associated with pain. Clients learn to view pain as a dynamic, multifaceted experience involving sensory perceptions, thinking patterns, affective responses, and behaviors, given their environmental contexts (e.g., level of support and cultural/societal attitudes toward pain).

Therapy is geared toward identifying any emotional, cognitive, behavioral, physiological, and/or environmental (e.g., family, social, cultural, and societal) difficulties that might be influencing clients' experience of pain. Although it is rare for clients to become pain free, CBT teaches clients how to cope with their pain and enhance their functioning in

Note. Significant portions of this manuscript have been excerpted from Winterowd, C., Beck, A., & Gruener, D. (in press). *Cognitive therapy with chronic pain patients*. New York: Springer.

various life roles. Below are some of the components of most CBTs with chronic pain clients.

PAIN ASSESSMENT

Therapists typically conduct a thorough intake interview prior to the start of therapy, to obtain a clear picture of the client's presenting problems and history, including a thorough assessment of his or her pain (including its location, duration, intensity, frequency, fluctuations, the client's descriptions of it, "triggers" and "alleviators" [what makes the pain worse or better], the client's emotions, thoughts, and behaviors when in pain, personal coping efforts, the associated physical limitations and other consequences of pain [e.g., role limitations, financial and/or legal difficulties], other psychosocial stressors that affect pain [e.g., personality, relationship issues, environment], medical/health care history including how the pain condition developed, types of treatments received for pain, pain medications prescribed). Questionnaires can be administered to assess clients' pain experiences (e.g., Behavioral Assessment of Pain), personality styles (see Gatchel & Weisberg, 2000), mood states (e.g., BDI-II, BAI, BHS, Pain Anxiety Symptom Scale), cognitions (e.g., Survey of Pain Attitudes), and behaviors (e.g., Coping Strategies Questionnaire, Illness Behavior Inventory, observations). See Turk and Melzack (2001) for a detailed account of pain assessment measures and procedures available.

Pain levels are also assessed at the beginning of each therapy session (i.e., "How would you rate your pain since our last session on a scale from 0 to 10, with 0 being no pain at all and 10 being the worst possible pain?").

COGNITIVE CONCEPTUALIZATION OF PAIN

Throughout the course of therapy, the client's presenting problems are conceptualized from a cognitive–behavioral framework.

Cognitive-behavioral Model of Pain

Negative, unrealistic thoughts, images, and beliefs about pain and other life events can have a significant and negative impact on the experience of pain sensations, moods, behavior (e.g., isolation, disturbed sleep), and other adverse physiological sensations. How people act or behave can also influence their moods, thoughts, and physical health. In fact, pain includes not only physiological sensations, but also our emotions, behaviors, and thoughts; all of these experiences are interrelated. Pain also includes the personal, social, and environmental influences or stressors in our lives, including our individual characteristics, our personality styles, physical limitations, relationships with others, medical care, and life roles, as well as aspects of our physical environment (e.g., weather and climate).

Cognitive Quad

People can have negative, unrealistic thoughts and beliefs about their pain (e.g., "My pain is untreatable," "I shouldn't have pain all of the time"), themselves (e.g., "I am powerless," "I am vulnerable," "I shouldn't be so needy"), their personal world (including their relationships with others and life roles; "My doctors don't care about my pain," "People will criticize me"), and their future (e.g., "I am doomed to be pain-ridden") given their chronic pain condition.

Pain–Distress Cycle

Our negative, unrealistic thoughts about pain and other life events can have a significant and negative impact on how we perceive pain sensations, how we feel emotionally, and what we do when we are in pain. When we think negatively, we are more likely to feel emotionally distressed, which can result in (1) muscle tension, making the pain even worse, and (2) a hyperaroused state in the nervous system (e.g., sympathetic), activating more pain messages in our body (e.g., peripheral and central nervous system), leading to more pain. When we think negatively, we are also more likely to engage in self-defeating behaviors, such as inactivity, social isolation, or overreliance on pain medication, which can affect the pain.

THERAPY

Therapy sessions focus on helping the client learn (1) cognitive restructuring skills (i.e., identifying, evaluating, and modifying negative automatic thoughts and beliefs) related to pain and emotional distress, (2) relaxation techniques (i.e., deep abdominal breathing, progressive muscle relaxation, hypnosis, and/or biofeedback) and other behavioral strategies (e.g., pain and activity monitoring, distraction, assertiveness training), and (3) problem-solving skills to cope with pain and other psychosocial stressors. The course of CBT typically starts with a focus on pain management and then moves to other concerns or issues (assuming pain management is the primary goal of therapy). The primary target for change is clients' negative, unrealistic cognitions about pain, the consequences of having pain, and other life stresses. Therapists also help clients identify behaviors that exacerbate pain and stress and teach clients new coping strategies as well as adaptive, healthy behaviors.

Behavioral Interventions

Behavioral approaches to pain management refer to skills such as relaxation training, pain monitoring, activity scheduling and monitoring, distraction techniques, assertiveness training, and problem solving. To provide some immediate relief from pain, the client can be taught a series of relaxation techniques early in therapy, including deep breathing, progressive muscle relaxation (tensing and relaxing different muscle groups in the body), guided imagery (e.g., imagining a safe place, a place that is free from pain and stress; beach or nature scenes), hypnosis (e.g., imagining relaxation moving into different parts of the body), and/or biofeedback.

The purpose of pain monitoring is to see how the client's pain varies over time and by activity. The client learns how to track pain, so that he or she becomes more aware of how often the pain occurs, what his or her experience of pain is like, and factors that may affect it both positively and negatively. Clients' participation and involvement in daily activities can have a direct bearing on their pain and their moods. The purpose of activity monitoring is to assess how active the individual client is and to assess his or her level of mastery (e.g., sense of accomplishment) or pleasure when participating in activities. Activity scheduling may be recommended if the client is too active or underactive.

Distraction techniques help clients shift their focus of attention away from their pain and other bodily sensations, which is usually a temporary solution to pain management. Clients can learn to distract themselves from their pain by turning their attention and focus toward their environment, for example, describing their surroundings or engaging in pleasurable activities (e.g., watching their favorite TV show, talking with a friend).

Sometime, during the course of therapy, clients learn assertiveness training skills. Learning how to communicate openly and directly without offending others is a very important skill for this client population given the number of health care professionals involved in their care. In addition, other people may not understand how clients experience pain and how it affects them. Therefore, communicating these experiences to others helps chronic pain clients feel more supported and understood than before.

Problem-solving strategies are typically used when a client's thoughts or beliefs about his or her pain or other life events are indeed true, or when the client is ready to take some behavioral action in resolving a problem. Clients learn how to identify key problems, brainstorm possible solutions, select a solution, implement it, and evaluate its effectiveness in resolving the problem.

Cognitive Interventions

Therapists help clients identify, evaluate, and modify automatic thoughts, images, and beliefs about pain.

Restructuring Automatic Thoughts about Pain

Negative automatic thoughts often accompany fluctuations in pain intensity and moods. However, these thoughts are not always in our immediate awareness. A variety of events or experiences can "trigger" negative self-talk or imagery, for example, the onset of pain, elevations in pain levels, negative mood states, lack of a clear-cut diagnosis, lack of social support, and financial problems, to name a few. Once these situations are identified, therapists can explore how clients are feeling at the time—both physiologically (e.g., pain intensity and location) and emotionally—followed by an exploration of their thoughts. The experienced cognitive–behavioral therapist will use a variety of questions to identify and evaluate negative automatic thoughts about pain with clients (i.e., guided discovery). Automatic thought records are used to identify, evaluate, and modify negative thoughts about pain. The client is asked to identify his or her hottest negative thought about pain from journal entries, viewing it as a hypothesis or hunch instead of a fact, and begin to evaluate it.

Clients learn that there are identifiable types of errors in thinking (i.e., cognitive distortions) that negatively impact their pain and moods. For example, clients may focus exclusively on the negative aspects of pain, how horrible it is, and how it prevents them from doing the things they want to do in their lives. They may blame themselves for their pain condition or feel punished for having pain.

To further evaluate the accuracy and usefulness of negative automatic thoughts about pain, the client learns to explore evidence for and against these thoughts. As part of the evaluation process, the client may be asked to imagine the worst, best, and most realistic scenarios assuming the negative thoughts are true, to assess the helpfulness of these thoughts by using the advantages/disadvantages analyses, and to identify what he or she would tell a friend who had the same thought. Alternative thoughts are developed in session based on this review of the evidence.

Once clients have developed their skills in using the automatic thought record, they can be asked to conduct behavioral experiments to test the validity and helpfulness of their negative thoughts about pain.

Imagery Work

Chronic pain clients can have very vivid, catastrophic images about their pain and its consequences. There are four general types of images clients have: (1) images of the pain itself, (2) images of oneself in pain, (3) images of how people will interact with or relate to them given their pain, and (4)images of the future with pain (Winterowd et al., in press). Once images are identified, the goal is to teach clients how to respond to them. Clients learn to take charge of their image by stopping them, redirecting them, or changing or responding to images in some way. For example, the client could be asked to put images to his or her pain experience and is asked to change the image in some way as though he or she were the director of that image.

Restructuring Core Beliefs about Pain

Once clients have mastered how to deal with automatic thoughts (i.e., self-talk and imagery), they can work on their core beliefs about their pain. Clients learn that automatic thoughts, or thought and images about pain and life events at a particular moment (e.g., "This pain is too much to bear"), are related to deeper underlying beliefs, known as intermediate (i.e., rules: "There should be a cure for my pain"; attitudes: "It's horrible that the doctors can't find a cure for my pain"; assumptions: "If I have pain, then I will be doomed to a life of despair and suffering") and core beliefs (i.e., basic beliefs people have about their pain, themselves, their world, and their future; "I am helpless," "I am pain-ridden"). These underlying beliefs may have developed in childhood or later in life when they developed their chronic pain condition and/or experienced significant traumas.

Pain beliefs often center on themes of loss (e.g., "I can't do things the way I used to"), danger (e.g., "The pain never ends"), or entitlement ("My doctors are supposed to find a cure"). Core beliefs about self, world, and future are typically related to themes of helplessness, inadequacy, dysfunction, disconnection, and social worthlessness (Winterowd et al., in press).

The client is asked for historical information about how these core beliefs developed as well as their function and purpose. The core belief worksheet (Beck, 1995) can be introduced to explore historical evidence for and against a core belief that is troubling the client. The therapist and client review this evidence, identify possible errors or distortions, and consider other information that they had not considered before. Reframes (alternative explanations) are developed in response to the evidence that the core belief is true. Rational–emotive role-plays might be incorporated to help the client explore the core belief further as well as identify alternative core beliefs. The same core belief may be further modified using imagery (e.g., go back to memories of the past that "support" the core belief).

LAST SESSION AND BOOSTER SESSIONS

At the end of therapy, the therapist and client review what has been learned over the course of therapy and what the client needs to continue to work on after therapy is over (i.e., self-help plan). Follow-up booster sessions are scheduled in 1 to 3 months to see how the client is coping with his or her pain and current life events.

REVIEW OF THE RESEARCH LITERATURE ON CBT AND CHRONIC PAIN

There is firm evidence in the research literature that both cognitive–behavioral and behavioral treatments are superior to no-treatment control conditions on a variety of outcomes (e.g., reducing pain levels, use of pain medications, negative thoughts, extent of physical disability as well as enhancing pain control, psychological adjustment, physical functioning and health status and psychosocial functioning) and these effects are maintained at follow-up for a variety of chronic pain clients (see meta-analysis studies by Morley, Eccleston, & Williams, 1999, and van Tulder et al., 2000). In addition, multidisciplinary pain treatment programs that incorporated CBT and behavioral therapy approaches were significantly more successful than unimodal treatment or no-treatment controls (see meta-analysis studies by Cutler et al., 1994, and Flor, Fydrich, & Turk, 1992).

Overall, it appears that the cognitive–behavioral approach has a positive additive effect to active treatments (e.g., medications, physical therapy, and medical treatments) for chronic pain clients (in treating pain, cognitive appraisals, and pain behavior problems; see meta-analysis study by Morley et al., 1999). However, for chronic low back pain clients, this did not appear to be the case (see meta-analysis by van Tulder et al., 2000).

CRITICISMS OF CBT WITH CHRONIC PAIN CLIENTS

In summary, CBT has strong empirical support as an effective treatment for chronic pain clients. More research is needed to explore whether cognitive therapy or behavior therapy is superior with chronic pain clients in general and for what types of problems or outcomes. In addition, the benefits of adding CBT to active treatments for chronic pain clients, especially low back pain clients, demand further exploration.

Some of the criticisms of the research on CBT or behavioral therapy with chronic pain clients include the intraparticipant variability in chronic pain conditions, small sample sizes, attrition, the short-term nature of the therapy (see Keefe & Van Horn, 1993; Parker, Iverson, Smarr, & Stucky-Ropp, 1993), and the use of primarily Caucasian samples in these studies. In addition, CBT methods vary considerably from study to study (i.e., lack of uniformity in therapy protocols; different models and techniques emphasized). Therefore, what is meant by CBT may be unique to each study and may not represent a coherent theoretical model of treatment. Clients' adherence to treatment is an important consideration when conducting these types of studies because it can influence outcomes. A better understanding of which interventions are most effective for which types of clients with chronic pain may provide researchers and clinicians with more answers about what really works in CBT with this population.

FUTURE DIRECTIONS

Future directions in CBT with chronic pain clients could include the incorporation of additional approaches to the current theoretical model, for example, the stages of motivation to change model (motivational interviewing), acceptance-based interventions (see McCracken & Turk, 2002), schema therapy, and multicultural counseling interventions. More attention will be given the therapist factors (e.g., individual characteristics [age, gender, race], personality, commitment, optimism, and flexibility) that interact with client factors (e.g., individual characteristics, personality, motivation to change, acceptance of their chronic pain condition) in promoting positive changes for chronic pain clients. More research will explore the effectiveness of CBT with chronic pain clients in other settings besides multidisciplinary pain treatment centers, and with more diverse groups of chronic pain clients. The wave of the future will be therapists providing cognitive–behavioral pain management services in primary care, specialist, and private practice settings. Future directions in practice will focus more on (1) the training of physicians and other health care professionals in CBT principles to promote better relationships with their clients and to enhance referral relationships with these professionals, and (2) outreach programming on pain prevention and pain management to people at the local, state, national, and international levels.

RECOMMENDED READINGS/ADDITIONAL SOURCES

There are resources for readers who are interested in cognitive–behavioral and behavioral therapy applications with chronic pain populations (e.g., Blanchard & Andrasik, 1985; Jamison, 1996; Winterowd, Beck, & Gruener, in press), as well as self-help books for chronic pain clients (e.g., Catalano & Hardin, 1996; Caudill, 2002; Jamison, 1996). There are also a number of professional organizations committed to the topic of chronic pain and pain treatments, such as the American Pain Society and the International Association for the Study of Pain.

See also: Biopsychosocial treatment of pain

REFERENCES

Beck, J. (1995). *Cognitive therapy: Basics and beyond*. New York: Guilford Press.

Blanchard, E., & Andrasik, F. (1985). *Management of chronic headaches: A psychological approach*. New York: Pergamon Press.

Bonica, J. (1953). *The management of pain*. Philadelphia: Lea & Febiger.

Boothby, J., Thorn, B., Stroud, M., & Jensen, M. (1999). Coping with pain. In R. Gatchel & D. Turk (Eds.), *Psychosocial factors in pain: Critical perspectives* (pp. 343–359). New York: Guilford Press.

Catalano, E., & Hardin, K. (1996). *The chronic pain control workbook* (2nd ed.). Oakland, CA: New Harbinger Publications.

Caudill, M. (2002). *Managing pain before it manages you* (rev. ed.). New York: Guilford Press.

Cutler, R., Fishbain, D., Rosomoff, H., Abdel-Moty, E., Khalil, T., & Rosomoff, R. (1994). Does nonsurgical pain center treatment of chronic pain return patients to work? A review and meta-analysis of the literature. *Spine, 19*, 643–652.

Flor, H., Fydrich, T., & Turk, D. (1992). Efficacy of multidisciplinary pain treatment centers: A meta-analytic review. *Pain, 49*, 221–230.

Fordyce, W. (1976). *Behavioral methods for chronic pain and illness*. St. Louis: Mosby.

Gatchel, R., & Turk, D. (Eds.). (1999). *Psychosocial factors in pain: Critical perspectives*. New York: Guilford Press.

Gatchel, R., & Weisberg, J. (2000). *Personality characteristics of patients with pain*. Washington, DC: American Psychological Association.

Jamison, R. (1996a). *Learning to master your chronic pain*. Sarasota, FL: Professional Resource Press.

Jamison, R. (1996b). *Mastering chronic pain: A professional's guide to behavioral treatment*. Sarasota, FL: Professional Resource Press.

Keefe, F., & Van Horn, Y. (1993). Cognitive–behavioral treatment of rheumatoid arthritis pain. *Arthritis Care and Management, 6*, 213–222.

McCracken, L., & Turk, D. (2002). Behavioral and cognitive–behavioral treatment for chronic pain: Outcome, predictors of outcome, and treatment process. *Spine, 27*, 2564–2573.

Morley, S., Eccleston, C., & Williams, A. (1999). Systematic review and meta-analysis of randomized controlled trials of cognitive behaviour therapy and behaviour therapy for chronic pain in adults, excluding headache. *Pain, 80*, 1–13.

Parker, J., Iverson, G., Smarr, K., & Stucky-Ropp, R. (1993). Cognitive–behavioral approaches to pain management in rheumatoid arthritis. *Arthritis Care and Research, 6*, 207–212.

Sullivan, M., Thorn, B., Haythornwaite, J., Keefe, F., Martin, M., Bradley, L. et al. (2001). Theoretical perspectives on the relation between catastrophizing and pain. *Clinical Journal of Pain, 17*, 52–64.

Tollison, C. (1993). The magnitude of the pain problem: The problem in perspective. In R. Weiner (Ed.), *Innovations in pain management: A practical guide for clinicians* (Vol. 1, pp. 3–9). Orlando: Paul M. Deutsch Press.

Turk, D., & Gatchel, R. (Eds.). (2002). *Psychological approaches to pain management: A practitioner's handbook* (2nd ed.). New York: Guilford Press.

Turk, D., Meichenbaum, D., & Genest, M. (1983). *Pain and behavioral medicine: A cognitive–behavioral perspective*. New York: Guilford Press.

Turk, D., & Melzack, R. (2001). *Handbook of pain assessment* (2nd ed.). New York: Guilford Press.

Turner, J. (1982). Comparison of group progressive-relaxation training and cognitive–behavioral group therapy for chronic low back pain. *Journal of Consulting and Clinical Psychology, 50*, 757–765.

van Tulder, M., Ostelo, R., Vlaeyen, J., Linton, S., Morley, S., & Assendelft, W. (2000). Behavioral treatment for chronic low back pain. *Spine, 26*, 270–281.

Winterowd, C., Beck, A., & Gruener, D. (2003). *Cognitive therapy with chronic pain clients*. New York: Springer.

Clinical Health Psychology

Barbara A. Golden and Stephanie H. Felgoise

Keywords: clinical health psychology, illness, behavioral medicine, health

Cognitive–behavioral theories and principles offer a natural fit for the practice of psychology as it interfaces with medicine. Cognitive–behavioral therapy (CBT) is widely accepted as the therapeutic modality of choice for working with medical patients for promotion of health and well-being, prevention, assessment, and treatment of illness. This article aims to provide an introduction to clinical health psychology and the practice of CBT within this field, including training requirements, problems addressed by the clinical health psychologist, the biopsychosocial model of illness, assessment and interventions, and empirical support for the use of CBT in the medical setting.

DEFINITIONS

"Clinical health psychology" is the discipline of psychology that, perhaps, best represents psychologists' contributions to the field of behavioral medicine. The American Psychological Association formally recognized the specialty of clinical health psychology within the practice of professional psychology by recording the following definition in 1997:

> Clinical Health Psychology applies scientific knowledge of the interrelationships among behavioral, emotional, cognitive, social and biological components in health and disease to the promotion and maintenance of health; the prevention, treatment and rehabilitation of illness and disability; and the improvement of the health care system. The distinct focus of Clinical Health Psychology is on physical health problems. The specialty is dedicated to the development of knowledge regarding the interface between behavior and health, and to the delivery of high quality services based on that knowledge to individuals, families and health care systems.

Theoretically, clinical health psychologists could ascribe to any theoretical orientation; however, cognitive–behavioral theories, principles, and therapy-outcome research have been most represented in the behavioral medicine literature when prescriptive interventions have been offered. The clinical applications in this article are limited to CBT and clinical health psychology.

In addition to its roots in psychology, clinical health psychology has its place among other social sciences.

> Biological, cognitive, affective, social and psychological bases of health and disease are bodies of knowledge that, when integrated with the knowledge of biological, cognitive–affective, social and psychological bases of behavior, constitute the distinctive knowledge base of Clinical Health Psychology. This includes a broad understanding of biology, pharmacology, anatomy, human physiology and pathophysiology, and psychoneuroimmunology. Clinical health psychologists also have knowledge of how learning, memory, perception, cognition, and motivation influence health behaviors, are affected by physical illness/injury/disability, and can affect response to illness/injury/disability. Knowledge of the impact of social support, culture, physician–patient relationships, health policy and the organization of health care delivery systems on health and help-seeking is also fundamental as is knowledge of diversity and minority health issues, individual differences in coping, emotional and behavioral risk factors for disease/injury/disability human development issues in health and illness, and the impact of psychopathology on disease, injury, disability and treatment. (APA, 1997)

TRAINING REQUIREMENTS FOR CLINICAL HEALTH PSYCHOLOGISTS

When working with physicians, it is important to recognize and practice within our boundaries of competence. Psychology has largely relied on self-regulation for determining competency, ethical practice, and qualifications for working with special populations (Belar et al., 2001). As such, there are few guidelines or enforced credentialing options to ensure appropriate training for psychologists who wish to specialize in this field. The American Board of Professional Psychology offers certification in Clinical Health Psychology, although there is a small subset of psychologists who have sought this certification in comparison to the numbers of psychologists practicing in this area. Therefore, clinical psychologists are encouraged to self-evaluate their knowledge, training, and experience commensurate with best practice recommendations for clinical health psychology, as established by leading experts in the field (Belar et al., 2001). Specifically, individuals should determine if they are knowledgeable and experienced in the following aspects of health, disease, and behavior, when considering working with particular patient populations: biological bases; cognitive–affective bases; social bases; developmental and individual bases; interactions among biological, cognitive–affective, social bases, and developmental bases of health, disease, and behavior, and their interactions with the environment; empirically supported clinical assessment and treatment relating to the specified problems; roles and functions of other health professionals who will be working with patients on health, illness, and behavioral matters; sociopolitical features of the health care system; health policy issues; distinctive legal, ethical, and professional issues relating to health, the particular disease(s), and behavior (Belar et al., 2001). The need for this extensive self-evaluation becomes evident in review of the scope of practice for clinical health psychologists, including assessment and treatment.

PRACTICE OF CLINICAL HEALTH PSYCHOLOGY

The clinical health psychologist may be called on to deal with many problems in research and practice: psychological factors secondary to a disease/illness or injury, somatic presentations of a psychological problem, psychophysiological disorders, psychological and behavioral aspects of medical procedures, behavioral risk factors for disease/illness/injury.

Growing attention has been paid to the influence of health behaviors, which may prevent or exacerbate chronic illness. Advances in the physiology of stress and its role in the development of physical disorders combined with behavioral change have influenced our management of chronic illness. Research demonstrating the preoperative psychological state (anxiety, depression, coping styles) influencing the postoperative outcomes of surgery encouraged the use of brief, structured psychosocial interventions for surgery patients. All of this evidence points to the imperative need to assess and treat patients with medical illness from a biopsychosocial perspective.

BIOPSYCHOSOCIAL MODEL

The biopsychosocial model of health and illness reflects a mind–body relationship that has reemerged in the last 25 years as a more integrated approach. The biomedical model has been criticized due to its simplicity and reduction of all medical conditions to single etiology. It fails to accommodate the increasing role of psychological and social factors as major sources of morbidity and mortality. Engel (1977) suggested that a biopsychosocial view is more appropriate. The biopsychosocial model suggests:

- All illness affects people on multiple levels (biological, emotional, cognitive, interpersonal, and environmental).
- These different levels interact with each other to produce a clinical outcome.
- Multiple factors influence reporting of symptoms (e.g., health beliefs, access to health care, reactions of physicians/family).
- Somatic expressions of psychological distress are normal.

ASSESSMENT AND TREATMENT

Assessment

An effective intervention for a patient must begin with a biopsychosocial assessment, and is recommended to be multimodal and multimethod in format. Belar and Deardorff (1995) propose targets of assessment by four domains of information (biological, affective, cognitive, and behavioral) and four units of assessment (patient, family, health care system, and sociocultural context). This model for clinical services has been combined with a model related to psychological services in health care developed by the APA Workgroup on the Expanding Role of Psychology in Healthcare (1998) to provide a range of clinical services on several different levels with a wide range of health problems.

The clinical health psychologist should try to understand the patient's current status, change since onset of the illness, and patient's history. The assessment should include identification of problem areas and also consider assets and resources of the patient and the environment. This same model can be used in consideration of behavior change for improvement of quality of life, prevention of illness, and promotion of well-being.

Basic demographics of the patient and the patient's illness or condition should be the first point of information. The physiological symptoms, risk factors, history and prognosis, and treatment procedures are evaluated in consideration of *biological targets*. The patient's *affective targets* include assessment of the patient's current mood, and information about the patient's feelings about the illness, treatment, health care, and support network among other information. The influence of the patient's *cognitive* functioning including general intelligence, knowledge, attitudes, perceived threat, and control of the illness are a critical part of the assessment. Evaluation of health beliefs, religious values and spirituality, and cultural norms is critical for optimal patient care.

Assessment of *behavioral targets* such as the patient's functional abilities, self-care, and occupational and recreational functioning are critical to the comprehensive evaluation. Attention to other behavioral targets is warranted regarding the patient's current and past health habits and health care utilization, compliance behaviors, and potential behavioral obstacles to successful treatment.

Often overlooked in the traditional medical assessments, the clinical health psychologist should assess the environment of the patient: family, health care system, and sociocultural environment. For example, what are the family economic resources, how does the family feel about the patient's illness, what are the perceptions and/or attitudes of the family, and has the family made any changes in their behavior as a result of the illness?

Evaluation of the patient's environment necessitates the following inquiries. What are the patient's relationships with the health care team? The setting of the health care provider and the interventions being considered should be examined and explained. How do members of the team feel about the patient and the patient's illness? Do the health care providers have an understanding and experience in the treatment of the illness? Do the behaviors of the health care system encourage easy access? In addition, sociocultural variables that may affect treatment and care include the work schedule flexibility, and social and financial resources.

Treatment and Intervention

Clinical health psychologists have a full range of therapeutic interventions available, but the medical setting can be challenging. The range of medical and psychological problems seen in health care requires training as a generalist with the ability to investigate and problem-solve in an interdisciplinary nature. Psychologists use individual therapy as a common intervention, but in addition, family therapy, group therapy, and interventions for the health care team are often used in the medical setting. All interventions should follow the biopsychosocial targets of the concerns reviewed during the assessment. The use of CBT is widespread in health care settings including strategies to reduce the risk of developing an illness, improving illness outcomes, and improving quality of life and the emotional health of patients.

Behavioral interventions to modify risk factors such as smoking, obesity, and risky sexual behaviors are recommended as good practice in medical settings. Variables such as personality, stress, negative emotions, and impaired social systems are important factors to consider with the risk of developing an illness. CBT has shown improvement for physical inactivity (Dubbert, 2002), smoking cessation (Compas, Haaga, Keefe, Leitenberg, & Williams, 1998), and HIV risk behaviors (Kelly & Kalichman, 2002; NIH, 1997).

Improving illness outcomes includes targeting behaviors and psychosocial variables that improve adherence to medical interventions, helping patients to adopt lifestyles to medical regimens, reduction of stress, and enhancement of social support. Research supports a multicomponent CBT intervention for coronary heart disease with reduction of recurrent cardiac events compared with usual care (Ornish et al., 1998). Cognitive–behavioral stress management (CBSM) including illness education, relaxation, cognitive restructuring, and provision of social support offers promising results. Brief CBT has been effective in the reduction of depression for patients in medical settings (Coyne, Thompson, Klinkman, & Nease, 2002; Lustman, Griffith, Kissel, & Clouse, 1998).

Increasing functioning and improving overall quality of life includes improvement of emotional, social, occupational, and financial wellness of patients and families. CBT has been used to manage symptoms; for example, the reduction of pain and nausea in cancer patients (Compas et al., 1998), the treatment of migraine and tension headaches (Holroyd, 2002), and multicomponent CBT (i.e., relaxation, cognitive restructuring, coping skills training, and goal setting) are effective for improving pain, physical activity, and psychological distress for patients with arthritis (Compas et al., 1998; Keefe et al., 2002). CBSM seems to enhance emotional functioning, coping abilities, and/or quality of life for patients with HIV and the effects of depression were mediated by increased cognitive coping and social support in a sample of HIV-positive gay men (Lutgendorf et al., 1998). Problem-solving therapy has also been empirically shown to improve quality of life, reduce distress, increase sense of control (Nezu, Nezu, Felgoise, & McClure, 2003), and decrease caregiver burden (Elliott & Rivera, 2003) for a variety of medical populations (see D'Zurilla & Nezu, 1999, for a review).

FUTURE DIRECTIONS

Given that CBT originated within the unitary discipline of psychology, criticisms regarding practice and theory suggest psychologists have much work yet to be done to help bridge the gaps between this discipline and others. Future directions for the field of clinical health psychology include increasing other health professionals' awareness of the need to address psychological factors associated with chronic illnesses, continuing research in areas of prevention, consultation, behavioral modification, and clinical treatment, and expanding patient-, setting-, and community-focused multidisciplinary research and practice. Lastly, with continuing change and rising costs in the health care system, clinical health psychologists are challenged to further support and defend the cost-effectiveness of empirically supported psychological treatment for medical illnesses, enhancement of emotional well-being, and improved quality of life.

See also: Caregivers of medically ill persons, Medically unexplained symptoms, Somatization, Terminal illness

REFERENCES

American Psychological Association. (1997). *Archival Description of Clinical Health Psychology as a Specialty in Professional Psychology*. Minutes of the Council of Representatives Meeting, August 1997. Washington, DC: Author.

American Psychological Association. (1998). *Report of the Workgroup on the Expanding Role of Psychology in Healthcare*. Washington, DC: Author.

Belar, C. D., & Deardorff, W. W. (1995). *Clinical health psychology in medical settings: A practitioner's guidebook*. Washington, DC: American Psychological Association.

Belar, C. D., Brown, R. A., Hersch, L. E., Hornyak, L. M., Rozensky, R. H., Sheridan, E. P., Brown, R. T., & Reed, G. W. (2001). Self-assessment in clinical health psychology: A model for ethical expansion of practice. *Professional Psychology: Research and Practice, 32*(2), 135–141.

Compas, B. E., Haaga, D. A., Keefe, F. J., Leitenberg, H., & Williams, D. A. (1998). Sampling of empirically supported psychological treatments from health psychology: Smoking, chronic pain, cancer, and bulimia nervosa. *Journal of Consulting and Clinical Psychology, 66*, 89–112.

Coyne, J. C., Thompson, R., Klinkman, M. S., & Nease, D. E., Jr. (2002). Emotional disorders in primary care. *Journal of Consulting and Clinical Psychology, 70*, 798–809.

Dubbert, P. M. (2002). Physical activity and exercise: Recent advances and current challenges. *Journal of Consulting and Clinical Psychology, 70*, 526–536.

D'Zurilla, T. J., & Nezu, A. M. (1999). *Problem-solving therapy: A social competence model*. New York: Springer.

Elliott, T. R., & Rivera, P. (2003). The experience of families and their carers in health care. In S. Llewelyn & P. Kennedy (Eds.), *Handbook of clinical health psychology* (pp. 61–80). New York: Wiley.

Engel, G. L. (1977). The need for a new medical model: A challenge for biomedicine. *Science, 196*, 129–136.

Holroyd, K. A. (2002). Assessment and psychological management of recurrent headache disorders. *Journal of Consulting and Clinical Psychology, 70*, 656–677.

Keefe, F. J., Smith, S.J., Buffington, A. L., Gibson, J., Studts, J. L., & Caldwell, D. S. (2002). Recent advances and future directions in the biopsychosocial assessment and treatment of arthritis. *Journal of Consulting and Clinical Psychology, 70*, 640–655.

Kelly, J. A., & Kalichman, S. C. (2002). Behavioral research with HIV/AIDS primary and secondary prevention: Recent advances and future directions. *Journal of Consulting and Clinical Psychology, 70*, 626–639.

Lustman, P. J., Griffith, L. S., Kissel, S. S., & Clouse, R. E. (1998). Cognitive behavioral therapy for depression in type 2 diabetes mellitus: A randomized, controlled trial. *Annals of Internal Medicine, 129*, 613–621.

Lutgendorf, S. K., Antoni, M. H., Ironson, G., Starr, K., Costello, N., Zuckerman, M., Klimas, N., Fletcher, M.A., & Schneiderman, N. (1998). Changes in cognitive coping skills and social support during cognitive behavioral stress management intervention and distress outcomes in somatic HIV seropositive gay men. *Psychosomatic Medicine, 60*, 204–214.

National Institutes of Health. (1997). *NIH consensus statement: Interventions to prevent HIV risk behaviors*. Bethesda, MD: U.S. Public Health Service.

Nezu, A. M., Nezu, C. M., Felgoise, S. H., & McClure, K. (2003). Problem-solving therapy for cancer patients. *Journal of Consulting and Clinical Psychology, 71*, 1036–1048.

Ornish, D., Scherwitz, L. W., Billings, J. H., Brown, S. E., Gould, K. L., & Merritt, T. A. (1998). Intensive lifestyle changes for reversal of coronary heart disease. *Journal of the American Medical Association, 280*, 2001–2007.

Cognitive Distortions

Carrie L. Yurica and Robert A. DiTomasso

Keywords: cognitive distortions, cognitive errors, cognitive biases, cognitive processing, distorted thinking, thinking errors, cognitive schemata, heuristic thinking, cognitive processing errors

HISTORY AND OVERVIEW OF COGNITIVE DISTORTIONS

Cognitive distortions were originally defined by Beck (1967) as the result of processing information in ways that predictably resulted in identifiable errors in thinking. In his work with depressed patients, Beck defined six systematic errors in thinking: arbitrary inference; selective abstraction; overgeneralization; magnification and minimization; personalization; and absolutistic, dichotomous thinking. Years later, Burns (1980) renamed and extended Beck's cognitive distortions to ten types: all-or-nothing thinking; overgeneralization; mental filter; discounting the positive; jumping to conclusions; magnification; emotional reasoning; should statements; labeling; and personalization and blame. Additional cognitive distortions, defined by Freeman and

DeWolf (1992) and Freeman and Oster (1999), include: externalization of self-worth; comparison; and perfectionism. Most recently, Gilson and Freeman (1999) identified eight other types of cognitive distortions in the form of fallacies: fallacies of change; worrying; fairness; ignoring; being right; attachment; control; and heaven's reward.

The conceptual framework of cognitive therapy is structured on the notion that an individual's subjective assessment of early life experience shapes and maintains fundamental beliefs (schemas) about self (Beck, 1970, 1976). In support of, or in defense against, early schemas, secondary beliefs develop and function as rules or assumptions about the self and the world. These beliefs define personal worth, are associated with emotions, and develop further into learned, habitual ways of thinking (Beck, Rush, Shaw, & Emery, 1979; Ellis & Grieger, 1986). Habitual ways of thinking function to support core beliefs and assumptions by generalizing, deleting, and/or distorting internal and external stimuli, thus creating cognitive distortions. Cognitions and, specifically, cognitive distortions have been identified as playing an important role in the maintenance of emotional disorders.

Researchers have developed various information processing models in an attempt to understand the processing of cognitive information. Kendall (1992) proposed a cognitive taxonomy model with a description of the relevant aspects of cognition involved in the creation of cognitive distortions. Kendall's taxonomy includes the following features: cognitive content; cognitive process; cognitive products; and cognitive structures. These features form the overall cognitive structure that serves to filter certain cognitive processes. Cognitive distortions reside within the domain of cognitive processes.

Within the realm of cognitive processes, Kendall made distinctions between processing deficiencies and processing distortions. Deficient processing occurs when a lack of cognitive activity results in an unwanted consequence. Distorted processing occurs when an active thinking process filters through some faulty reasoning process resulting in an unwanted consequence. The difference is failure to think versus a pattern of thinking in a distorted manner (Kendall, 1985, 1992).

Finally, Kendall (1992) also suggested that more accurate perceptions of the world do not necessarily lead to more successful mental health or behavioral adjustment. Cognitive distortions skewed in an overly positive direction tend to be functional, and benefit the individual in maintaining positive mental health (although a "too positive" view might be interpreted as narcissism).

The opposite may also occur. In studies of depressed and nondepressed students, Alloy et al. (1999) reported that depressed subjects were more accurate in their perceptions and judgments as compared to nondepressed subjects, a phenomenon called "depressive realism." Subsequent research was less endorsing of this phenomenon, and researchers have concluded the process of distortion is more complex than merely perception (Ingram, Miranda, & Segal, 1998).

Within the fields of cognitive and social psychology, other information processing systems have been developed that suggest theories for the formation of cognitive distortions (e.g., Berry & Broadbent, 1984; Hasher & Zacks, 1979; Nisbett & Wilson, 1977; Schneider & Shiffrin, 1977). In addition, developmental psychologists have suggested thinking or distorting processes may develop from learned behavior, while evolutionary psychologists (Gilbert, 1998) have suggested the development of an evolutionary information processing system over time that has led to a "better safe than sorry" processing approach.

TYPES OF COGNITIVE DISTORTIONS

Axis I Disorders

Cognitive distortions were originally identified in patients with depression. Since then, clinicians have expanded their identification and treatment of cognitive distortions to many other disorders (DiTomasso, Martin, & Kovnat, 2000; Freeman, Pretzer, Fleming, & Simon, 1990, 2004; Freeman & Fusco, 2000; Wells, 1997). Further, cognitive distortions have been found to play a role in sexual dysfunction (Leiblum & Rosen, 2000), eating disorders (Shafran, Teachman, Kerry, & Rachman, 1999), sex offender behavior (McGrath, Cann, & Konopasky, 1998), and gambling addictions (Delfabbro & Winefield, 2000; Fisher, Beech, & Browne, 1999). In addition to the identification of cognitive distortions in Axis I disorders, distortions appear to play an important role in Axis II disorders.

Axis II Disorders

Cognitive distortions have been identified in patients diagnosed with personality disorders. Freeman et al. (1990, 2004) have identified dichotomous thinking as a primary distortion in patients with Dependent Personality Disorder. Layden et al. (1993) have identified several cognitive distortions used by patients with Borderline Personality Disorder. Similarly, use of cognitive distortions by patients with Histrionic Personality Disorder (dichotomous thinking, jumping to conclusions, and emotional reasoning), Narcissistic Personality Disorder (magnification of self, selective abstraction, minimization of others), and Obsessive–Compulsive Personality Disorder (magnification, "should" statements, perfectionism, and dichotomous thinking) have been documented in the clinical literature (Beck, Freeman, et al., 1990; Beck, Freeman, Davis, et al., 2004).

DEFINITIONS OF COGNITIVE DISTORTIONS

Typical distortions include:

Arbitrary Inference/Jumping to Conclusions. The process of drawing a negative conclusion, in the absence of specific evidence to support that conclusion (Beck et al., 1979; Burns, 1980, 1989, 1999). *Example*: "I'm really going to blow it. What if I flunk?" (Burns, 1989).

Catastrophizing. The process of evaluating, whereby one believes the worst possible outcome will or did occur (Beck et al., 1979; Burns, 1980, 1989, 1999). *Example*: "I better not try because I might fail, and that would be awful" (Freeman & Lurie, 1994).

Comparison. The tendency to compare oneself whereby the outcome typically results in the conclusion that one is inferior or worse off than others (Freeman & DeWolf, 1992; Freeman & Oster, 1999). *Example*: " I wish I were as comfortable with women as my brother is" (Freeman & DeWolf, 1992).

Dichotomous/Black-and-White Thinking. The tendency to view all experiences as fitting into one of two categories (e.g., positive or negative; good or bad) without the ability to place oneself, others, and experiences along a continuum (Beck et al., 1979; Burns, 1980, 1989, 1999; Freeman & DeWolf, 1992). *Example*: "I've blown my diet completely" (Burns, 1989).

Disqualifying the Positive. The process of rejecting or discounting positive experiences, traits, or attributes (Burns, 1980, 1989, 1999). *Example*: "This success experience was only a fluke" (Freeman & Lurie, 1994).

Emotional Reasoning. The predominant use of an emotional state to form conclusions about oneself, others, or situations (Beck et al., 1979; Burns, 1980, 1989, 1999; Freeman & Oster, 1999). *Example*: "I feel terrified about going on airplanes. It must be very dangerous to fly" (Burns, 1989).

Externalization of Self-Worth. The development and maintenance of self-worth based almost exclusively on how the external world views one (Freeman & DeWolf, 1992; Freeman & Oster, 1999). *Example*: "My worth is dependent on what others think of me" (Freeman & Lurie, 1994).

Fortunetelling. The process of foretelling or predicting the negative outcome of a future event or events and believing this prediction is absolutely true for oneself (Burns, 1980, 1989, 1999). *Example*: "I'll never, ever feel better" (Burns, 1989).

Labeling. Labeling oneself using derogatory names (Burns, 1980, 1989, 1999; Freeman & DeWolf, 1992). *Example*: "I'm a loser" (Burns, 1989).

Magnification. The tendency to exaggerate or magnify either the positive or negative importance or consequence of some personal trait, event, or circumstance (Burns, 1980, 1989, 1999). *Example*: "I have the tendency to exaggerate the importance of minor events" (Yurica & DiTomasso, 2001).

Mind Reading. One's arbitrary conclusion that someone is reacting negatively, or thinking negatively toward him/her, without specific evidence to support that conclusion (Burns, 1980, 1989, 1999). *Example*: "I just know that he/she disapproves" (Freeman & Lurie, 1994).

Minimization. The process of minimizing or discounting the importance of some event, trait, or circumstance (Burns, 1980, 1989, 1999). *Example*: "I underestimate the seriousness of situations" (Yurica & DiTomasso, 2001).

Overgeneralization. The process of formulating rules or conclusions on the basis of limited experience and applying these rules across broad and unrelated situations (Beck et al., 1979; Burns, 1980, 1989, 1999). *Example*: "It doesn't matter what my choices are, they always fall flat" (Freeman & Lurie, 1994).

Perfectionism. A constant striving to live up to some internal or external representation of perfection without examining the evidence for the reasonableness of these perfect standards, often in an attempt to avoid a subjective experience of failure (Freeman & DeWolf, 1992; Freeman & Oster, 1999). *Example*: "Doing a merely adequate job is akin to being a failure" (Freeman & Lurie, 1994).

Personalization. The process of assuming personal causality for situations, events, and reactions of others when there is no evidence supporting that conclusion (Beck et al., 1979; Burns, 1980, 1989, 1999; Freeman & DeWolf, 1992). *Example*: "That comment wasn't just random, it must have been directed toward me" (Freeman & Lurie, 1994).

Selective Abstraction. The process of exclusively focusing on one negative aspect or detail of a situation, magnifying the importance of that detail, thereby casting the whole situation in a negative context (Beck et al., 1979; Burns, 1980, 1989, 1999). *Example*: "I must focus on the negative details while I ignore and filter out all the positive aspects of a situation" (Freeman & Lurie, 1994).

"Should" Statements. A pattern of internal expectations or demands on oneself, without examination of the reasonableness of these expectations in the context of one's life, abilities, and other resources (Burns, 1980, 1989, 1999; Freeman & DeWolf, 1992). *Example*: "I shouldn't have made so many mistakes" (Burns, 1989).

ASSESSMENT IN CLINICAL PRACTICE

Cognitive–behavioral clinicians commonly use self-report measures such as a thought record (e.g., Thought

Record, Persons, Davidson, & Tompkins, 2001; Daily Record of Dysfunctional Thoughts, Beck et al., 1979) to identify automatic thoughts, underlying schema, and cognitive distortions.

Successful use of the thought record depends on a number of factors: the clinician's willingness to use this tool; the clinician's knowledge about how to use this tool to help the patient identify cognitive distortions; the ability of the patient to consciously access and write down his/her automatic thoughts; the ability of the patient to see this as a valuable tool; and the willingness of the patient to use the thought record outside of session. Persons and colleagues (2001) identified other drawbacks to this tool such as: difficulty in eliciting automatic thoughts from patients; reluctance by patients to use the thought record in session; beliefs by patients that it is not helpful; and noncompliance with homework assignments to complete thought records. Despite these limitations in clinical practice, results from randomized clinical trials have demonstrated support for the value of the thought record in the treatment of depressed patients as a tool for identifying and changing dysfunctional thinking (Craighead, Craighead, & Ilardi, 1998; DeRubeis & Crits-Christoph, 1997).

REVIEW OF AVAILABLE MEASURES OF COGNITIVE DISTORTIONS

A review of available measures of cognitive distortions reveals five clinical instruments designed to measure the general construct of cognitive distortion within the cognitive therapy literature: the Dysfunctional Attitude Scale (DAS, Weissman, 1979; Weissman & Beck, 1978), Cognitive Error Questionnaire (CEQ, Lefebvre, 1981), Automatic Thoughts Questionnaire (ATQ, Hollan & Kendall, 1980), Cognitive Distortion Scale (CDS, Briere, 2000), and Inventory of Cognitive Distortions (ICD, Yurica & DiTomasso, 2001).

USE OF COGNITIVE DISTORTION INSTRUMENTS IN CLINICAL RESEARCH

Cognitive distortion instruments have been used in research around the world. The DAS-A is the most widely used instrument in research studies around the world and measures the dysfunctional attitudes of depressives (Chen et al., 1998; Leyland & Teasdale, 1996; Marton & Kutcher, 1995; Oei-Tan & Yeoh, 1999; Ohrt & Thorell, 1999; Otto, Favia, Penava, & Bless, 1997; Wertheim & Poulakis, 1992; Zaretsky, Fava, Davidson, & Pava, 1997). The DAS-A has been translated into several languages, including a Swedish version (Ohrt & Thorell, 1999) and a Chinese version (Chen et al., 1998).

The ATQ has been used in conjunction with the DAS (Weissman, 1979) in other countries to measure cognitive distortions in panic disorder (Ohrt, Sjodin, & Thorell, 1999) and the difference in cognitive–behavioral therapy for medicated and nonmedicated groups (Oei-Tan & Yeoh, 1999). Further, the ATQ was extended beyond adult populations to assess depressive cognitions in children (Kazdin, 1990).

Research findings indicate the CEQ distinguished between depressed and nondepressed older adults (Scogin, Hamblin, & Beutler, 1986), and depressed and nondepressed pain patients (Smith, O'Keeffe, & Christensen, 1994). In an effort to examine the role of depression in rheumatoid arthritis patients, Smith, Peck, Milano, and Ward (1988) adapted the CEQ to include symptomatology for rheumatoid arthritis. The internal consistency of the modified CEQ was high (Cronbach's alphas = .92 and .90 for RA and general scales, respectively).

USE OF COGNITIVE DISTORTION INSTRUMENTS IN CLINICAL TREATMENT

The use of cognitive distortion instruments in clinical settings could serve a number of functions: (1) provide an efficacious method for identifying patients' major forms of distorted thinking, (2) identify patients' use of particular types of distortions for particular diagnoses, (3) provide an educational tool geared toward improving patients' metacognitive skills, (4) help understand the role cognitive distortions play in maintaining dysfunctional cognitive, emotional, and behavioral patterns, and (5) provide the clinician with a clinical tool for use as pre-, post-, and interval test to track changes in patients' distorted thinking patterns.

FUTURE DIRECTIONS IN COGNITIVE DISTORTION ASSESSMENT

Assessment of cognitive distortions will undoubtedly continue into the future in an effort to more accurately qualify and quantify specific cognitive distortions. Continued assessment of this cognitive construct is important for several reasons. First, cognitive distortion assessment is necessary for case conceptualization, treatment planning, and implementation of treatment techniques and patient involvement. Second, additional clinical information is needed concerning the interactions of various cognitive processes. Third, assessment and subsequent treatment of cognitive distortions will likely lead to symptom relief in immediate and longer-term time frames. Fourth, assessment may provide insight into disorder-specific cognitive constructs. Finally, research-based measures of cognitive distortions can provide the field with more effective tools to measure the cognitive construct of cognitive distortions.

REFERENCES

Alloy, L. B., Abramson, L. Y., & Francis, E. L. (1999) Do negative cognitive styles confer vulnerability to depression? *Current Directions in Psychological Science, 8*, 128–132.

Beck, A. T. (1970). Cognitive therapy: Nature and relation to behavior therapy. *Behavior Therapy, 1*, 184–200.

Beck, A. T. (1976). *Cognitive therapy and emotional disorders*. New York: International Universities Press.

Beck, A. T., Freeman, A., & Associates. (1990). *Cognitive therapy of personality disorders*. New York: Guilford Press.

Beck, A. T., Freeman, A., Davis, D., & Associates. (2004). *Cognitive therapy of personality disorders*. New York: Guilford Press.

Beck, A. T., Rush, A. J., Shaw, B. F., & Emery, G. (1979). *Cognitive therapy of depression*. New York: Guilford Press.

Berry, D. C., & Broadbent, D. E. (1984). On the relationship between task performance and associated verbalized knowledge. *Quarterly Journal of Experimental Psychology: Human Experimental Psychology, 36A*, 209–231.

Brewin, C. R. (1996). Theoretical foundations of cognitive–behavior therapy for anxiety and depression. *Annual Review of Psychology, 47*, 33–57.

Briere, J. (2000). *Cognitive Distortion Scales professional manual*. Odessa, FL: Psychological Assessment Resources.

Burns, D. (1980). *Feeling good*. New York: Morrow.

Burns, D. (1989). *The feeling good handbook*. New York: Morrow.

Burns, D. (1998). Why are depression and anxiety correlated? A test of tripartite model. *Journal of Consulting and Clinical Psychology, 66*, 461–473.

Burns, D. (1999). *The feeling good handbook* (2nd. ed.). New York: HarperCollins.

Chen, Y., Xu, J., Yan, S., Xian, Y., Li, Y., Chang, X., Llang, G. T., & Ma, Z. (1998). A preliminary study of the Dysfunctional Attitude Scale. *China: Chinese Mental Health, 12*, 265–267.

Delfabbro, P. H., & Winefield, A. H. (2000). Predictors of irrational thinking in regular slot machine gamblers. *The Journal of Psychology, 134*, 117–128.

DiTomasso, R. A., Martin, D. M., & Kovnat, K. D. (2000). Medical patients in crisis. In F. M. Dattilio & A. Freeman (Eds.), *Cognitive–behavioral strategies in crisis intervention* (pp. 1–23), New York: Guilford Press.

Dobson, K. S., & Breiter, H. J. (1982). Cognitive assessment of depression: Reliability and validity of three measures. *Journal of Abnormal Psychology, 92*, 107–109.

Ellis, A., & Grieger, R. M. (Eds.). (1986). *Handbook of rational emotive therapy*. New York: Springer.

Fisher, D., Beech, A., & Browne, K. (1999). Comparison of sex offenders to nonoffenders on a selected psychological measures. *International Journal of Offender Therapy and Comparative Criminology, 43*, 473–491.

Freeman, A., & DeWolf, R. (1990). *Woulda, coulda, shoulda*. New York: Morrow.

Freeman, A., & DeWolf, R. (1992). *The 10 dumbest mistakes smart people make and how to avoid them*. New York: HarperCollins.

Freeman, A., & Fusco, G. (2000). Treating high arousal: Differentiating between patients in crisis and crisis prone patients. In F. M. Dattilio & A. Freeman (Eds.), *Cognitive behavioral strategies in crisis intervention*. New York: Guilford Press.

Freeman, A., & Lurie, M. (1994). Depression: A cognitive therapy approach—a viewer's manual. New York: Newbridge Professional Programs.

Freeman, A., & Oster, C. (1999). Cognitive behavior therapy. In M. Hersen & A. S. Bellack (Eds.), *Handbook of comparative interventions for adult disorders* (2nd ed., pp. 108–138). New York: Wiley.

Freeman, A., Pretzer, J. C., Fleming, B., & Simon, K. (1990). *Clinical applications of cognitive therapy*. New York: Plenum Press.

Hasher, L., & Zacks, R. T. (1979). Automatic processing of fundamental information. The case of frequency of occurrence. *American Psychologist, 29*, 1372–1388.

Hollan, S. D., & Kendall, P. C. (1980). Cognitive self-statements in depression: Development of an automatic thoughts questionnaire. *Cognitive Therapy and Research, 4*, 383–395.

Ingram, R. E., Miranda, J., & Segal, Z. V. (1998). *Cognitive vulnerability to depression*. New York: Guilford Press.

Kazdin, A. E. (1990). Evaluation of the Automatic Thoughts Questionnaire negative cognitive processes and depression among children. *Psychological Assessment: A Journal of Consulting and Clinical Psychology, 2*, 73–79.

Kendall, P. C. (1992). Healthy thinking. *Behavior Therapy, 23*, 1–11.

Kessler, R. C., McGonagle, K. A., Zhoa, S., Nelson, C. B., Hughes, M., Eshleman, S. et al. (1994). Lifetime and 12-month prevalence of DSM-III psychiatric disorders in the United States. Results from the National Comorbidity Survey. *Archives of General Psychiatry, 51*, 8–19.

Lefebvre, M. F. (1981). Cognitive distortion and cognitive errors in depressed psychiatric and low back pain patients. *Journal of Consulting and Clinical Psychology, 49*, 517–525.

Leiblum, S. R., & Rosen, R. C. (Eds.). (2000). *Principles and practice of sex therapy* (3rd ed.). New York: Guilford Press.

Leyland, S., & Teasdale, J. D. (1996). Depressive thinking: Changes in schematic mental models of self and world. *Psychological Medicine, 2*, 1043–1051.

McGrath, M., Cann, S., & Konopasky, R. (1998). New measures of defensiveness, empathy, and cognitive distortions for sexual offenders against children. *Sexual Abuse: Journal of Research and Treatment, 10*, 25–36.

Marton, P., & Kutcher, S. (1995). The prevalence of cognitive distortion in depressed adolescents. *Journal of Psychiatry & Neuroscience, 20*, 33–38.

Mineka, S., Watson, D., & Clark, L. A. (1998). Comorbidity of anxiety and unipolar mood disorders. *Annual Review of Psychology, 49*, 377–412.

Nisbett, R., & Wilson, T. (1977). The halo effect. Evidence for unconscious alteration of judgements. *Journal of Personality and Social Psychology, 35*, 250–256.

Oei-Tan, P. S., & Yeoh, A. (1999). Pre-existing antidepressant medication and outcome of group cognitive–behavioral therapy. *Australian and New Zealand Journal of Psychiatry, 33*, 70–76.

Ohrt, T., & Thorell, L. H. (1999). Ratings of cognitive distortion in major depression: Changes during treatment and prediction outcome. *Nordic Journal of Psychiatry, 21*, 239–244.

Otto, M. W., Fava, M., Penava, S. J., Bless, E. et al. (1997). Life event, mood, and cognitive predictors of perceived stress before and after treatment for major depression. *Cognitive Therapy and Research, 21*, 409–420.

Persons, J. B., Davidson, J., & Tompkins, M. A. (2001). *Essential components of cognitive behavioral therapy for depression*. Washington, D.C: American Psychological Association.

Scogin, F., Hamblin, D., & Beutler, L. (1986). Validity of the Cognitive Error Questionnaire with depressed and nondepressed older adults. *Psychological Reports, 59*(1), 267–272.

Schneider, W., & Shiffrin, R. (1977). Controlled and automatic human information processing: Detection, search, and attention. *Psychological Review, 84*, 1–66.

Shafran, R., Teachman, B. A., Kerry, S., & Rachman, S. (1999). A cognitive distortion associated with eating disorders: Thought-shape fusion. *British Journal of Clinical Psychology, 38*, 167–179.

Smith, T. W., Christensen, A. J., Peck, J. R., & Ward, J. R. (1994). Cognitive distortion, helplessness, and depressed mood in rheumatoid arthritis: A four year longitudinal analysis. *Health Psychology, 13*, 213–217.

Weissman, A. N. (1979). The Dysfunctional Attitude Scale validation study. *Dissertation Abstracts, 40*(3-B), 1389–1390.

Weissman, A. N., & Beck, A. T. (1978). *Development and validation of the Dysfunctional Attitude Scale: A preliminary investigation.* Paper presented at the meeting of the American Educational Research Association, Toronto.

Wertheim, E. H., & Poulakis, Z. (1992). The relationship among the General Attitude Scale, other dysfunctional cognition measures, and depressive or bulimic tendencies. *Journal of Rational Emotive and Cognitive Behavior Therapy, 10*, 219–233.

Yurica, C. L. (2002). *Inventory of Cognitive Distortions: Development and validation of a psychometric test for the measurement of cognitive distortions.* Unpublished doctoral dissertation, Philadelphia College of Osteopathic Medicine.

Yurica, C. L., & DiTomasso, R. (2001). Inventory of Cognitive Distortions (ICD). In *Inventory of Cognitive Distortions: Development and validation of a psychometric test for the measurement of cognitive distortions.* Unpublished doctoral dissertation, Philadelphia College of Osteopathic Medicine.

Zaretsky, A. E., Fava, M., Davidson, K. G., & Pava, J. D. (1997). Are dependency and self criticism risk factors for major depressive disorders? *Canadian Journal of Psychiatry, 42*, 291–297.

Cognitive Vulnerability

John H. Riskind and David Black

Keywords: cognitive vulnerability, cognitive bias, beliefs, cognitive structures

Cognitive vulnerabilities are faulty beliefs, cognitive biases, or structures that are hypothesized to set the stage for later psychological problems when they arise. They are in place long before the earliest signs or symptoms of disorder first appear. These vulnerabilities are typically purported to create specific liabilities to particular psychological disorder after individuals encounter stressful events, and to maintain the problems after their onset. Only by addressing these vulnerabilities can long-term therapeutic improvements be maintained, and the risk of recurrences or relapse be reduced. Before further reviewing the roles of cognitive vulnerability concepts in cognitive-behavior therapy (CBT), it is necessary first to briefly describe several components of the CBT model as a whole.

According to CBT, each disorder is associated with particular cognitive content (e.g., Beck, 1976). To illustrate with specific examples, the particular cognitive content of anxiety is associated with an overarching theme of vulnerability to the threat of future harm, whereas the particular cognitive content of depression is associated with the theme of past "loss." Each disorder's particular cognitive content is elaborated in the typical "automatic," stream-of-consciousness images and thoughts, as well as in the underlying cognitive schemas used as frameworks for selecting, processing, coding, and interpreting relevant information. Individuals who are prone to disorders have typically developed maladaptive schemas that cause their ongoing thought processes to be distorted and subsequent actions to be dysfunctional. Maladaptive schemas distort information processing and generate cognitive biases (e.g., biased memory and attention for certain stimuli at the expense of others).

The cognitive model of psychopathology in CBT conceptualizes each distinct syndrome or form of psychological problem in terms of its particular cognitive content. This concept, known as the "cognitive content specificity" hypothesis, helps to account for the differences between each particular syndrome or disorder. The particular ideational themes, automatic thoughts, schematic biases, and so on, in each disorder, provide a way of sensibly understanding the links between the phenomenology and symptoms in each disorder and its cognitive underpinnings.

A corollary of the cognitive model of psychopathology in CBT is that each specific disorder is associated with particular cognitive vulnerabilities. These are hypothesized to be characterized in content-specific schemas, including sets of disorder-relevant maladaptive beliefs, which represent maladaptive generalizations extracted from previous experience. Past developmental experiences (e.g., early emotional abuse) or negative life events (e.g., severe personal illness) lead individuals to develop maladaptive concepts, attitudes, beliefs, or mental rules, for interpreting experiences relevant to their problems. For example, highly depression-prone individuals have often learned to construe personal mistakes as failures and indicators of irreversible personal defects. Cognitive vulnerabilities are hypothesized to increase the probability that the individuals will develop future disorders when exposed to future stressful events (e.g., future mistakes or failures may lead to depression). The term *cognitive vulnerability* refers to those cognitive characteristics of people (such as maladaptive beliefs, attributional patterns, thought processes, schemas) that increase the likelihood they will develop future disorders or problems.

In the clinical setting, identifying the cognitive vulnerabilities, or mechanisms for the psychological problems, is part of a clinical practitioner's cognitive case conceptualization in CBT, and often anchored in the careful identification of specific, recurring themes in the patient's images and ideation. The practitioner can also identify these cognitive vulnerabilities by using measures of dysfunctional attitudes, attributional patterns, or other possible cognitive vulnerability mechanisms. Addressing the automatic thoughts and images in therapy sessions helps the patient to attain *immediate* symptomatic relief. To produce *durable improvement*, the practitioner needs to identify and modify the cognitive vulnerabilities (schemas, cognitive biases, beliefs) that put the patient at risk for the psychological problem.

CONTEMPORARY VIEWS OF COGNITIVE VULNERABILITIES

Today, most investigators recognize that most individuals who are exposed to precipitating stressful events do not develop clinically significant psychological disorders. Moreover, the specific disorder that emerges for different individuals is not determined just by the stressful event alone (i.e., precipitating stresses do not just occur in conjunction with any one clinical disorder), and is hypothesized to depend on their particular cognitive vulnerabilities (Riskind & Alloy, in press). In CBT, cognitive vulnerabilities are hypothesized to help account for not only *who* is vulnerable to developing disorders (e. g., individuals with a particular cognitive style) and *when* (e.g., after a stress), but to *which* disorders they are vulnerable (e.g., depression, anxiety disorder, eating disorder).

In cognitive theory, cognitive vulnerability factors are considered potential antecedent causes (*distal* causes) that operate toward the beginning of the temporal sequence, distant in time from the first occurrence (or reoccurrence) of the disorder (Abramson, Metalsky, & Alloy, 1989; Alloy, Abramson, Raniere, & Dyller, 1999). *Proximal* cognitions (such as specific thoughts or images) are typically produced when people interpret the meaning of stressful events in terms of their cognitive vulnerabilities (e.g., maladaptive beliefs). Proximal cognitive and emotional responses may lead to compensatory or defensive behaviors (such as physical avoidance, worry, or thought suppression) that in turn can reciprocally reinforce or support the continuation of maladaptive beliefs or other cognitive vulnerabilities.

METHODOLOGICAL CONSIDERATIONS IN COGNITIVE VULNERABILITY THEORY AND RESEARCH

Several methodological considerations are critical when evaluating theory and research on cognitive vulnerabilities (Alloy et al., 1999). Research on cognitive vulnerability factors requires the use of prospective, longitudinal designs in which cognitively vulnerable individuals without symptoms are followed over time. Only such longitudinal designs provide convincing evidence that a hypothesized vulnerability factor temporally precedes the initial onset of a disorder, or that it precedes future episodes or relapses of the disorder. Such designs also permit the researcher to test whether the hypothesized vulnerability factor is more than just a transient state-manifestation or consequence of the changing symptoms of the disorder.

In a perfect test of a hypothesized cognitive vulnerability factor, a full experimental design would be used in which participants are assigned on a purely random basis to different experimental conditions of manipulated cognitive vulnerability (e.g., high versus low) and level of stress (high versus low). For example, some people would be experimentally induced to have a cognitive vulnerability to depression, and then months or years later would be experimentally exposed to a precipitating stressful event. As such experimental manipulation studies are normally almost impossible as well as unethical to implement when studying cognitive vulnerability, researchers almost inevitably rely on other research designs, including prospective, analogue, and cross-sectional correlational research designs (Alloy et al., 1999).

Despite containing some elements of experimental control (i.e., there is at least one experimental manipulation), quasi-experimental designs are not true experiments because they do not assign participants on a random basis to one of the key independent variables (i.e., the "quasi-experimental variable"). For example, individuals are not randomly assigned to high-risk (cognitively vulnerable) and low-risk (nonvulnerable) groups but are "self-selected" to the groups. Because these cognitive vulnerability groups can differ on more than the selected characteristic, one may also be inadvertently selecting individuals for neuroticism, gender, or other psychopathology that is correlated with the particular cognitive vulnerability.

Analogue studies (which can use laboratory animals or nonclinical human participants as proxies for actual clinical patients) can sometimes have value for testing parts of cognitive vulnerability theories. For example, experimental manipulations in animal analogue studies have been used to test potential causal variables featured in the learned helplessness model of depression in humans.

Cross-sectional (case control) studies can be seen as preliminary tests or sources of hypotheses of potential vulnerability factors, but cannot rule out the possibility that scores on vulnerability measures are simply correlates, or consequences of the disorder, rather than antecedents or prior vulnerabilities to the disorder (Lewinsohn, Steinmetz, Larson, & Franklin, 1981).

In retrospective studies, participants who currently suffer from an episode or symptoms of a disorder are asked to recall information about their cognitive vulnerabilities (or past stresses) before their first episodes. The major scientific shortcoming of such designs is that a participant's recall can be influenced by forgetting, cognitive biases, or even the disorder itself. For example, depressed individuals who are asked to recall past life experiences might exhibit biased recall of stressful events or past dysfunctional attitudes as a consequence of their current depressive moods.

Overall, prospective or longitudinal designs provide the best way to test the merits of hypothesized cognitive vulnerability factors, and the most preferred of these designs is the behavioral high-risk design. In this kind of design, the researcher selects participants who are presently nondisordered because they possess behavioral (or cognitive) characteristics hypothesized to make them vulnerable to developing a particular disorder in the future. The researcher then follows these "high-risk" participants prospectively, along with a comparison group of individuals who score low on the hypothesized risk factor. Behavioral high-risk designs allow one to establish the precedence and stability of the hypothesized cognitive vulnerability factor in individuals who do not presently possess the disorder of interest.

On the basis of these features, prospective designs can help to establish both the vulnerability factor's temporal precedence and independence from symptoms (Alloy et al., 1999). An additional reason to prefer prospective studies is that "high-risk" participants have not yet ever experienced the clinical disorder. Although other kinds of research designs are not as convincing, they can provide supplemental evidence for purported cognitive vulnerabilities (Riskind & Alloy, in press).

CONTEMPORARY CONTRIBUTORS AND EMPIRICAL RESEARCH ON COGNITIVE VULNERABILITY

Two current researchers, Lauren Alloy and Lyn Abramson, have played a major role in spearheading the use of behavioral high-risk designs of cognitive vulnerability. Their Temple–Wisconsin Cognitive Vulnerability to Depression (CVD) Project is more advanced in testing prospective designs than any comparable program of vulnerability research in other disorders, and is an exemplary program of cognitive vulnerability research. In the case of other disorders (e.g., anxiety, eating disorders), research has moved more slowly—but is speeding up.

The Temple–Wisconsin CVD Project (Alloy et al., 1999, 2003) has provided strong evidence for cognitive vulnerability models. The prospective findings from the CVD Project are particularly exciting as they seem to be the first and most clear-cut demonstration that cognitive vulnerabilities (negative cognitive styles) put people at higher risk for full clinically significant depressive disorders as well as suicidality. The CVD Project has tested both Beck's cognitive model, which hypothesizes that dysfunctional attitudes create a susceptibility to later depression, and the hopelessness model of depression (Abramson et al., 1989), which proposes that individuals who attribute negative life events in terms of internal, stable, and global causes are at more risk for depression. Results from the first $2\frac{1}{2}$ years of follow-up in the CVD Project indicate that these negative cognitive styles predict prospectively both first onsets and recurrences of depressive disorders (Alloy et al., 1999, 2003), controlling for initial levels of depression at the start of the prospective study. Notably, the effect of cognitive vulnerability to depression in conferring higher vulnerability to later psychological problems was limited to depression, and no differences were found in the likelihood of first onsets of anxiety or other psychiatric disorders. The findings of the CVD project provide especially strong support for the general concept of cognitive vulnerability because the project used a rigorous prospective research design that controls for prior history of depression.

Given this evidence for cognitive vulnerability to depression, it is important to study cognitive vulnerability to anxiety and other disorders. There has been some research on anxiety sensitivity (the belief that symptoms of anxiety themselves have threatening physical and social consequences). Some longitudinal studies have provided evidence that anxiety sensitivity may be a vulnerability factor in panic disorder (see Schmidt & Woolaway-Bickel, in press, for a review).

Similarly, research has found that cognitive vulnerability (a negative cognitive style) called "looming vulnerability" (Riskind, Williams, Gessner, Chrosniak, & Cortina, 2000) functions as a danger schema for the processing of threat information, and increases the probability that individuals will develop future anxiety and worry symptoms, but not depression. The concept of looming vulnerability refers to an anxiety-provoking cognitive style characterized by a pattern of generating and maintaining images and mental scenarios of rapidly unfolding and intensifying danger.

Recent cognitive vulnerability research has examined developmental antecedents as well as information-processing correlates and personality correlates of hypothesized cognitive vulnerability factors (Alloy & Abramson, 1999). Consistent with hypotheses generated by cognitive theory, there is evidence that cognitive vulnerabilities are associated with particular patterns of developmental antecedents (e.g., parenting, attachment) and information-processing (e.g., memory) biases associated with disorders such as depression (Ingram & Ritter, 2000) and anxiety (Riskind et al., 2000).

Consistent with cognitive theory, some important findings on cognitive vulnerability to depression indicate that such vulnerabilities are modified by CBT but not by pharmacological intervention. In contrast, scores for automatic thoughts are likely to abate with depression without reference to whether depression is treated by CBT or pharmacology (Hollon, 2003). Similar studies are needed of the effects of CBT on cognitive vulnerabilities for other psychological problems.

CRITICISMS OF COGNITIVE VULNERABILITY RESEARCH

Cognitive vulnerability research can be considered to play an important role in providing empirical support of the theoretical underpinnings of CBT, but it is important for cognitive vulnerability researchers to show the relevance of their research to cognitive assessment and treatment outcome evaluation in clinical practice. Demonstrating that CBT decreases patients' scores on cognitive vulnerabilities to depression, and that posttreatment on cognitive vulnerabilities are predictive of risk of relapse can go far in this direction. A past criticism of studies testing the cognitive vulnerability hypothesis is that the findings may be supportive of the alternative hypothesis that negative cognitive styles are a consequence or "scar" left by the past episodes of psychological problems rather than the hypothesis that negative cognitive styles provide vulnerability to depression. This criticism is now addressed by the CVD project and other prospective studies.

Another criticism of cognitive vulnerability research is that most of the work has concentrated on depression. As noted, cognitive vulnerability research on factors involved in risk of future anxiety, eating disorders, or schizophrenia is in need of further development, particularly in terms of high-risk, behavioral designs.

BENEFITS OF KNOWLEDGE OF COGNITIVE VULNERABILITY

General knowledge of cognitive vulnerability research has practical benefits for the clinical practitioner. The legitimacy of cognitive therapy is supported by empirical evidence, not just on treatment outcome, but on the background principles and assumptions of a cognitive perspective to psychological problems. Cognitive vulnerability research comprises an important component of this basic scientific evidence. A second benefit is that cognitive vulnerability research offers the future hope for more efficacious treatments. Such research offers the promise to clinical practitioners of better identifying specific mechanisms that help to maintain psychological problems and create a susceptibility for first and repeated episodes of disorders. This can lead to more refined treatment strategies in the future. Finally, knowledge of cognitive vulnerability research provides the practitioner with direction for understanding lack of progress in treatment, or of subsequent relapse, even though the practitioner has addressed automatic thoughts. Unless the underlying mechanisms are altered (e.g., the depressive attributional style or dysfunctional attitudes, the anxiety sensitivity), patients' disturbing ideation is likely to persist or recur in the face of future precipitating stress.

See also: Cognitive vulnerability to depression

REFERENCES

Abramson, L. Y., Metalsky, G. I., & Alloy, L. B. (1989). Hopelessness depression: A theory-based subtype of depression. *Psychological Review, 96*, 358–372.

Alloy, L. B., & Abramson, L. Y. (1999). The Temple–Wisconsin Cognitive Vulnerability to Depression (CVD) project: Conceptual background, design and methods. *Journal of Cognitive Psychotherapy, 13*, 227–262.

Alloy, L. B., Abramson, L. Y., Raniere, D., & Dyller, I. (1999). Research methods in adult psychopathology. In P. C. Kendall, J. N. Butcher, & G. N. Holmbeck (Eds.), *Handbook of research methods in clinical psychology*, (2nd ed., pp. 466–498). New York: Wiley.

Alloy, L. B., Abramson, L. Y., Whitehouse, W. G., Hogan, M. E., Panzarella, C., & Rose, D. T. (2003). *Prospective incidence of first onsets and recurrences of depression in individuals at high and low cognitive risk for depression*. Manuscript under editorial review.

Beck, A. T. (1976). *Cognitive therapy and the emotional disorders*. New York: International Universities Press.

Hollon, S. D. (2003). Does cognitive therapy have an enduring effect? *Cognitive Therapy and Research*, 27, 71–75.

Ingram, R. E., & Ritter, J. (2000). Vulnerability to depression: Cognitive reactivity and parental bonding in high-risk individuals. *Journal of Abnormal Psychology, 109*, 588–596.

Riskind, J. H., & Alloy, L. B. (in press). Cognitive vulnerability to emotional disorders: Theory, design, and methods. In L. B. Alloy & J. H. Riskind (Eds.), *Cognitive vulnerability to emotional disorders*. Hillsdale, NJ: Erlbaum.

Riskind, J. H., Williams, N. L., Gessner, T., Chrosniak, L. D., & Cortina, J. (2000). The looming maladaptive style: Anxiety, danger, and schematic processing. *Journal of Personality and Social Psychology, 79*, 837–852.

Schmidt, N. B., & Woolaway-Bickel, K. (in press). Cognitive vulnerability to panic disorder. In L. B. Alloy & J. H. Riskind (Eds.), *Cognitive vulnerability to emotional disorders*. Hillsdale, NJ: Erlbaum.

RECOMMENDED READINGS

Alloy, L. B., Abramson, L. Y., Whitehouse, W. G., Hogan, M. E., Tashman, N. A., Steinberg, D. L., Rose, D. T., & Donovan, P. (1999). Depressogenic cognitive styles: Predictive validity, information processing and personality characteristics, and developmental origins. *Behaviour Research and Therapy, 37*, 503–531.

Alloy, L. B., & Riskind, J. H. (Eds.). (in press). *Cognitive vulnerability to emotional disorders*. Hillsdale, NJ: Erlbaum.

Ingram, R. E., Miranda, J., & Segal, Z. V. (1998). *Cognitive vulnerability to depression*, New York: Guilford Press.

Cognitive Vulnerability to Depression

Lauren B. Alloy and Lyn Y. Abramson

Keywords: depression, vulnerability, negative cognitive styles, hopelessness

DEFINITIONS

Dysfunctional attitudes—A set of attitudes characterized by the belief that one's happiness and self-worth depend on being perfect or on others' approval

Hopelessness—The expectation that desired outcomes will not occur or that negative outcomes will occur combined with the expectation that there is nothing one can do to change this situation

Inferential feedback—Communications from other people regarding the causes and consequences of stressful events in a person's life

Negative inferential style—A tendency to attribute negative life events to stable (persisting over time) and global (widespread) causes, to catastrophize about the consequences of negative life events, and to infer that the occurrence of a negative event means that one is flawed or worthless

Negative self-schemata—Organized memorial representations of prior knowledge about the self that guide the perception, interpretation, and memory of information relevant to the self

Rumination—An emotion-regulation strategy involving perseverative self-focus that is recursive and persistent

Stress-reactive rumination—The tendency to ruminate in response to stressful life events

Vulnerability—A predisposition to an illness or disorder

COGNITIVE VULNERABILITY-STRESS THEORIES OF DEPRESSION

Two women are fired from their jobs at the same firm. One becomes seriously depressed; the other one suffers only mild discouragement. Why are some people vulnerable to depression whereas others never seem to become depressed? From the cognitive perspective, the way people typically interpret or understand events in their lives, or their cognitive styles, importantly affects whether or not they become depressed. Two major cognitive theories of depression, the hopelessness theory (Abramson, Metalsky, & Alloy, 1989) and Beck's (1987) theory, are vulnerability–stress models, in which variability in people's susceptibility to depression following stressful life events is understood in terms of differences in cognitive styles that affect how those events are interpreted.

According to the hopelessness theory (Abramson et al., 1989), people who exhibit a negative inferential style, characterized by a tendency to attribute negative life events to stable (persisting over time) and global (widespread) causes ("it will last forever and affect everything I do"), to catastrophize about the consequences of negative life events, and to infer that the occurrence of a negative event means that they are flawed or worthless, are vulnerable to depression when they experience stressful events. Individuals who exhibit such an inferential style should be more likely than those who do not to make negative inferences regarding the causes, consequences, and self-implications of any stressful event they encounter, thereby increasing the likelihood that they will develop hopelessness, the proximal cause of episodes of depression—particularly the subtype of "hopelessness depression."

Similarly, in Beck's (1987) theory, negative self-schemata revolving around themes of inadequacy, worthlessness, and loss are hypothesized to contribute vulnerability to depression. These negative self-schemata are often represented as a set of dysfunctional attitudes in which one's happiness and self-worth depend on being perfect ("If I fail partly, it is as bad as being a complete failure") or on others' approval ("I am nothing if a person I love doesn't love me"). When they experience negative events, people who hold such dysfunctional attitudes are hypothesized to develop negatively biased perceptions of their self, personal world, and future (hopelessness), which then lead to depression.

NEGATIVE COGNITIVE STYLES AS VULNERABILITIES FOR DEPRESSION

Do negative cognitive styles actually increase people's vulnerability to depression? Recent prospective studies have obtained considerable support for the cognitive vulnerability hypothesis (see Alloy et al., 1999). In the Temple–Wisconsin Cognitive Vulnerability to Depression (CVD) Project (Alloy et al., 1999), nondepressed college freshmen, with no other mental disorders, were selected to be at hypothesized high risk (HR) or low risk (LR) for depression based on the presence versus absence of negative cognitive styles. These cognitively HR and LR freshmen were followed every 6 weeks for $2\frac{1}{2}$ years and then every 4 months for an additional 3 years with self-report and structured interview assessments of stressful life events, cognitions, and psychopathology.

More than half of the CVD Project sample had no prior history of clinical depression. Among these participants, the HR freshmen were more likely than the LR freshmen to develop a first onset of major depression, minor depression, and hopelessness depression during the first $2\frac{1}{2}$ years of follow-up and these risk group differences were maintained even when initial depressive symptoms were controlled (Alloy et al., 1999). What about those participants who, though nondepressed at the outset of the study, did have a prior history of clinical depression? This subsample allows a test of whether the cognitive vulnerability hypothesis holds for recurrences of depression, which is important given that depression usually is a recurrent disorder. Among participants with past depression, HR freshmen were more likely than LR freshmen to develop recurrences of major, minor, and hopelessness depression, and these differences were also maintained when initial depressive symptoms were controlled (Alloy et al., 1999). Thus, negative cognitive styles provided risk for both first onsets and recurrences of clinically significant depression, suggesting that similar processes may, at least in part, underlie the first and subsequent episodes of depression.

Among the entire CVD Project sample, HR participants were also more likely than LR participants to develop suicidality, ranging from suicidal thinking to actual suicide attempts, during the follow-up, even when prior history of suicidality and other risk factors for suicidality were controlled (Abramson et al., 1998). Moreover, the association between cognitive vulnerability and the prospective development of suicidality was completely mediated by hopelessness. That is, only those participants who became hopeless about their futures developed suicidality during the follow-up period.

According to the cognitive theories of depression, people with negative cognitive styles are vulnerable to depression in part because they perceive and recall information about stressful events that has negative implications for themselves. Thus, we (see Alloy et al., 1999) examined whether our nondepressed HR participants did, in fact, process information about themselves more negatively than LR participants, based on a Self-Referent Information Processing (SRIP) Task Battery administered at the outset of the CVD Project. Consistent with prediction, we found that relative to LR participants, HR participants showed greater endorsement, faster processing, and better recall of negative depression-relevant stimuli involving themes of incompetence, worthlessness, and low motivation. They were also less likely to process positive depression-relevant stimuli than were LR participants. Similar negative biases in information processing about the self have been obtained among nondepressed individuals who have recovered from a past depression when their cognitive vulnerability is activated by a negative mood state. These findings are significant because they indicate that negatively biased information processing previously shown to be characteristic of depressed individuals also occurs among cognitively vulnerable nondepressed individuals. Moreover, such negatively biased information processing also predicted onsets of major, minor, and hopelessness depressive episodes during the $2\frac{1}{2}$-year follow-up of the CVD Project in combination with cognitive HR status.

Robinson and Alloy (2003) hypothesized that individuals who exhibit negative cognitive styles and who also tend to ruminate about these negative cognitions in response to the occurrence of stressful life events ("stress-reactive rumination") may be especially vulnerable to depression. Rumination is an emotion-regulation strategy involving perseverative self-focus that is recursive and persistent. Robinson and Alloy (2003) reasoned that negative cognitive styles provide the negative content, but that this negative content is more likely to lead to depression when it is "on one's mind" and recursively rehearsed than when it is not. Consistent with this hypothesis, they found that negative cognitive styles and stress-reactive rumination measured at Time 1 of the CVD Project did indeed interact to predict onsets of major depression and hopelessness depression during the $2\frac{1}{2}$-year follow-up period. HR participants who were also high in stress-reactive rumination were more likely to develop major and hopelessness depression episodes than HR participants who did not tend to ruminate or LR participants regardless of their levels of stress-reactive rumination.

The CVD Project results are important because they provide the first and clearest demonstration that negative cognitive styles, information processing, and rumination, or for that matter, any psychological vulnerability factor, confer vulnerability to full-blown, clinically significant depressive episodes. This is noteworthy because a criticism of the cognitive theories of depression is that they apply only to mild depression. In the case of the participants with no prior history of depression, these findings provide especially strong support for the cognitive vulnerability hypothesis because they are based on a truly prospective test, uncontaminated by prior history of depression.

DEVELOPMENTAL ORIGINS OF COGNITIVE VULNERABILITY TO DEPRESSION

If negative cognitive styles do confer vulnerability to depression, then it is important to understand how these styles develop. In the CVD Project, we also studied HR and LR participants' parents as well as the participants' early developmental experiences (Alloy et al., 2003). Our findings suggest several potential antecedents of negative cognitive styles. Mothers of HR participants had greater histories of depression than mothers of LR participants. This could occur due to shared genetic risk for depression or to learning of negative cognitive styles from parents. Children's cognitive styles may develop in part through modeling of their parents' cognitive styles or through parental inferential feedback regarding the causes and consequences of negative events in the child's life. In the CVD Project, mothers of HR individuals had more dysfunctional attitudes, but not more negative inferential styles, than mothers of LR individuals, even after controlling for the mothers' levels of depressive symptoms. Fathers' cognitive styles did not differ for HR and LR participants (Alloy et al., 2003). Similarly, other studies have obtained only limited support for the modeling hypothesis (see Alloy et al., 2003, for a review).

In contrast, studies have provided more consistent support for the hypothesis that negative inferential feedback from parents and others may contribute to children's development of negative cognitive styles (Alloy et al., 2003). For example, in the CVD Project, according to both participants' and parents' reports, mothers and fathers of HR individuals provided more negative attributional (stable, global) and consequence feedback for negative events in their child's life than did the parents of LR individuals. Moreover, parents' inferential feedback predicted their child's likelihood of developing a depressive episode during the 2.5-year follow-up, mediated in part by the child's cognitive risk status (Alloy et al., 2003).

In addition to parental inferential feedback, negative parenting practices may also contribute to the development of cognitive vulnerability to depression. In particular, a parenting style involving lack of emotional warmth and negative psychological control (criticism, intrusiveness, and guilt-induction), has been most consistently implicated in the association between children's risk for depression and parent–child relations (see Alloy et al., 2003, for a review). In the CVD Project, negative cognitive styles (HR status) were associated with low emotional warmth from participants' fathers, whereas a tendency to ruminate was associated with high negative psychological control from both parents (Alloy et al., 2003). Low emotional warmth from fathers and high psychological control from both parents predicted prospective onsets of depression among the participants, mediated, at least in part, by participants' negative cognitive styles. Thus, both low emotional warmth and overcontrolling parenting may be related to offspring's cognitive vulnerability to depression, through the alternative mechanisms of negative cognitive styles and ruminative styles, respectively.

Rose and Abramson (1992) argued that a history of maltreatment, particularly emotional abuse, may also contribute to cognitive vulnerability because in emotional abuse, the abuser by definition supplies negative cognitions to the victim (e.g., "You're so stupid; you'll never amount to anything"). Consistent with this formulation, in the CVD Project, HR participants reported a greater history of emotional (but not physical or sexual) abuse than LR participants (Alloy et al., 2003). This was true for emotional maltreatment by nonrelatives (peers, boyfriends/girlfriends) as well as for emotional abuse by parents. Moreover, a history of childhood emotional abuse predicted onsets of major and hopelessness depression episodes during follow-up, mediated by participants' negative cognitive styles and ruminative styles (see Alloy et al., 2003). To provide initial support for a potentially causal role of emotional maltreatment in the development of negative cognitive styles, we (see Alloy et al., 2003) examined the role of emotional maltreatment in predicting change in attributional style over a 6-month period in children. Emotional maltreatment occurring during the 6-month follow-up, as well as in the 6 months prior to Time 1, predicted change in children's attributional styles over the follow-up. The more emotional abuse a child experienced, the more negative his or her attributional style became. These findings suggest that emotional maltreatment may be predictive of and, at least, show temporal precedence with respect to the development of some negative cognitive styles. Thus, emotional criticism and rejection from significant others, such as parents, teachers, and peers, may provide a psychological environment that promotes the development of depressogenic cognitive styles whether it is expressed indirectly through provision of negative inferential feedback or lack of affection or directly through explicitly abusive language (Alloy et al., 2003).

COGNITIVE VULNERABILITY IN CONTEXT

What has the work on cognitive vulnerability to depression taught us? That negative cognitive styles confer increased risk for clinically significant depressive disorders not only provides the first demonstration of a psychological vulnerability to depression, but suggests that purely biological approaches to understanding depression are likely to fall short. Indeed, our recent research indicates that even bipolar spectrum mood disorders (manic-depression, cyclothymia), which have traditionally been viewed as almost entirely genetic in origin, may also be influenced by cognitive styles for interpreting life events. Both hypomanic/manic and depressive symptoms among bipolar individuals were predicted prospectively by individuals' cognitive styles and information processing in interaction with the occurrence of intervening life events (Reilly-Harrington, Alloy, Fresco, & Whitehouse, 1999).

More broadly, the work on cognitive vulnerability to depression suggests that the content of one's thinking may profoundly affect one's health. The notion that mental contents influence physical health has been highly controversial and the present findings add to the growing body of research indicating that pessimistic versus optimistic thinking predicts, and possibly contributes to, poor health.

FUTURE DIRECTIONS

A limitation of the CVD Project and a key issue for the cognitive theories of depression in general is the need to demonstrate that negative cognitive styles not only predict depression prospectively, but also contribute causally to their onset. Such a demonstration would require, in addition, that manipulations of cognitive vulnerability lead to corresponding changes in the likelihood of depression onset. Consistent with a potential causal role for cognitive vulnerability to depression, DeRubeis and Hollon (1995) reported that decreases in depressed patients' negative cognitive styles following cognitive therapy for depression predicted corresponding reductions in relapse of depression. Specifically, depressed patients successfully treated with cognitive therapy were less likely to suffer relapses of depression, and the reduced relapse rate was mediated by the therapy's effect on decreasing patients' stable and global styles for inferring causes of negative events. Similarly, Gillham, Reivich, Jaycox, and Seligman (1995) delivered a 12-week cognitive therapy-based preventive intervention to school children that was designed to teach the children to adopt more adaptive beliefs about themselves and to replace negative explanations for their successes and failures with more optimistic ones. At a 1-year follow-up, only about 7% of the children in the prevention group reported high levels of depressive symptoms compared to nearly 30% of the control group. Inasmuch as disagreement exists about whether cognitive therapy works by remediating negative cognitive styles or by providing compensatory skills for overriding the effects of such styles (DeRubeis & Hollon, 1995), future studies must find a way to directly manipulate cognitive styles in order to more clearly test the causal role of these styles for depression onset.

In addition, the developmentally relevant findings from the CVD Project are mostly retrospective. Thus, they may be seen as providing a conceptual and empirical basis for further investigations of the development of cognitive vulnerability to depression. Future studies, particularly prospective studies beginning earlier in childhood, should devote considerable attention to the role of negative parenting practices and inferential feedback, as well as emotional abuse from parents and peers, as important contributors to the development of cognitive vulnerability to depression and to depression itself.

See also: Cognitive vulnerability

REFERENCES

Abramson, L. Y., Alloy, L. B., Hogan, M. E., Whitehouse, W. G., Cornette, M., Akhavan, S., & Chiara, A. (1998). Suicidality and cognitive vulnerability to depression among college students: A prospective study. *Journal of Adolescence, 21*, 157–171.

Abramson, L. Y., Metalsky, G. I., & Alloy, L. B. (1989). Hopelessness depression: A theory-based subtype of depression. *Psychological Review, 96*, 358–372.

Alloy, L. B., Abramson, L. Y., Gibb, B. E., Crossfield, A. G., Pieracci, A. M., Spasojevic, J., & Steinberg, J. (2003). *Developmental antecedents of cognitive vulnerability to depression: Review of findings from the Cognitive Vulnerability to Depression (CVD) Project.* Manuscript under editorial review.

Alloy, L. B., Abramson, L. Y., Whitehouse, W. G., Hogan, M. E., Tashman, N. A., Steinberg, D. L., Rose, D. T., & Donovan, P. (1999). Depressogenic cognitive styles: Predictive validity, information processing and personality characteristics, and developmental origins. *Behaviour Research and Therapy, 37*, 503–531.

Beck, A. T. (1987). Cognitive models of depression. *Journal of Cognitive Psychotherapy: An International Quarterly, 1*, 5–37.

DeRubeis, R. J., & Hollon, S. D. (1995). Explanatory style in the treatment of depression. In G. M. Buchanan & M. E. P. Seligman (Eds.), *Explanatory style* (pp. 99–111). Hillsdale, NJ: Erlbaum.

Gillham, J. E., Reivich, K. J., Jaycox, L. H., & Seligman, M. E. P. (1995). Prevention of depressive symptoms in school-children: Two-year follow-up. *Psychological Science, 6*, 343–351.

Reilly-Harrington, N. A., Alloy, L. B., Fresco, D. M., & Whitehouse, W. G. (1999). Cognitive styles and life events interact to predict bipolar and unipolar symptomatology. *Journal of Abnormal Psychology, 108*, 567–578.

Robinson, M. S., & Alloy, L. B. (2003). Negative cognitive styles and stress-reactive rumination interact to predict depression: A prospective study. *Cognitive Therapy and Research, 27*, 275–291.

Rose, D. T., & Abramson, L. Y. (1992). Developmental predictors of depressive cognitive style: Research and theory. In D. Cicchetti & S. L. Toth (Eds.), *Rochester symposium on developmental psychopathology* (Vol. 4, pp. 323–349). Hillsdale, NJ: Erlbaum.

RECOMMENDED READINGS

Abramson, L. Y., Alloy, L. B., Hankin, B. L., Haeffel, G. J., MacCoon, D. G., & Gibb, B. E. (2002). Cognitive vulnerability–stress models of depression in a self-regulatory and psychobiological context. In I. H. Gotlib & C. L. Hammen (Eds.), *Handbook of depression* (3rd ed., pp. 268–294). New York: Guilford Press.

Alloy, L. B., Abramson, L. Y., Whitehouse, W. G., Hogan, M. E., Tashman, N. A., Steinberg, D. L., Rose, D. T., & Donovan, P. (1999). Depressogenic cognitive styles: Predictive validity, information processing and personality characteristics, and developmental origins. *Behaviour Research and Therapy, 37*, 503–531.

Ingram, R. E., Miranda, J., & Segal, Z. V. (1998). *Cognitive vulnerability to depression.* New York: Guilford Press.

Computer Programs for Cognitive–Behavior Therapy

Jesse H. Wright and D. Kristen Small

Keywords: computers, computer-based therapy, treatment for depression

The first computer programs for cognitive–behavior therapy (CBT) were developed in the 1980s by teams of investigators in the United Kingdom (Carr, Ghosh, & Marks, 1988; Ghosh, Marks, & Carr, 1984) and the United States (Selmi, Klein, Greist, & Harris, 1982; Selmi, Klein, Greist, Sorrell, & Erdman, 1990). Using the computer technology of the time, these researchers produced programs that relied on written text, checklists, and multiple-choice questions for communication with the patient. More recently developed computer tools for CBT have incorporated multimedia, virtual reality, hand-held devices, or other methods to rapidly engage the user and stimulate learning (Newman, Kenardy, Herman, & Taylor, 1997; Rothbaum et al., 1995; Rothbaum, Hodges, Ready, Graap, & Alarcon, 2001; Wright & Wright, 1997; Wright et al., 2002). Computer programs have been tested and found to be useful for a variety of Axis I disorders including depression, simple phobia, agoraphobia, and PTSD (Ghosh et al., 1984; Gruber, Moran, Roth, & Taylor, 2001; Proudfoot et al., 2003; Rothbaum et al., 1995, 2001.

Some of the potential advantages of using computer programs as a component of psychotherapy are that they may provide innovative and effective learning experiences, reduce the cost of treatment, increase access to CBT, and help therapists and patients reach treatment goals more rapidly or efficiently (Greist, 1998; Marks, Shaw, & Parkin, 1998; Wright & Wright, 1997). Because computers have the ability to store and analyze large amounts of data, give systematic feedback, and measure progress, they may extend the ability of the clinician to monitor and direct the course of therapy. In addition, computer programs have the capacity to immerse the patient in learning situations that could not be easily re-created in standard, clinician-administered therapy. For example, virtual reality can be used to effectively mimic the cues of feared situations, while multimedia programs can use emotionally charged video and audio to stimulate patient cognitions.

Computer tools for psychotherapy also have significant liabilities in comparison to human therapists. Early in the history of computer-assisted therapy, there were attempts to develop programs that conducted interviews using typical therapist–patient dialogue (often termed "natural language") (Colby, Watt, & Gilbert, 1966; Weizenbaum, 1966). However, these efforts were fraught with problems such as miscommunications and negative reactions of patients (O'Dell & Dickson, 1984). Thus, developers of computer programs for CBT have steered away from "natural language" programming. Instead of trying to replicate therapist–patient communication, authors of CBT programs have focused on using the unique strengths of computers to provide psychoeducation, involve patients in self-directed exposure, promote cognitive restructuring, and encourage use of other CBT methods.

CBT computer programs are typically designed by highly experienced cognitive–behavior therapists and contain the core methods of empirically studied treatments. They provide supportive feedback to users, reinforce self-monitoring, and assign homework. However, they cannot be programmed (at least with current technology and resources) to have the wisdom, flexibility, creativity, and empathy of human therapists (Nadelson, 1987; Wright & Wright, 1997). Most programs are designed to deliver specific elements of CBT for a targeted disorder or symptom (e.g., exposure therapy for phobia, cognitive and behavioral interventions for depression) and thus are not able to perform full diagnostic assessments, evaluate suicide risk, or deliver treatment for a wide range of problems. Because of these limitations, clinical applications of computer-assisted CBT typically include assessment, monitoring, and direction from a clinician.

All computer programs developed to date for CBT have been designed to reduce therapist contact to some degree. In some applications, the clinician's involvement has been limited to an initial assessment and minimal monitoring of a computer-based therapy intervention (Ghosh et al., 1984; Kenwright, Liness, & Marks, 2001; Selmi et al., 1990). However, many investigators have had more modest goals of lowering the requirement for therapist time. For example, Newman et al. (1997) used a hand-held computer program to substantially reduce the number of clinicians required for treatment of panic disorder. Some computer programs have been produced in "Professional" and "Consumer" editions (Colby & Colby, 1990; Wright, Wright, & Beck, 2003). The professional edition is intended for use in clinical settings under the supervision of a therapist; the consumer version may be recommended for home use, much like self-help books are commonly used as adjuncts to CBT. The consumer versions are clearly labeled as products that are not to be used as a substitute for professional diagnosis and treatment.

The author may receive a portion of profits from sales of *Good Days Ahead*, a computer program described in this article. A portion of profits from sales of *Good Days Ahead* is donated to the Foundation for Cognitive Therapy and Research and the Norton Foundation.

Research studies on computer-assisted CBT have found that computer programs are well accepted by patients and are usually efficacious in treating symptoms (Greist, 1998; Marks et al., 1998; Wright & Wright, 1997; Wright et al., 2002). Investigations reviewed below are limited to those that involved the use of a computer to deliver a significant element of CBT for depression, anxiety disorders, and eating disorders. Programs developed for habit control and sex counseling are not included because they were not designed to augment or provide psychotherapy. Also, interactive voice response (IVR) systems are not discussed. These interventions use an automated, computer-controlled telephone system, in addition to manuals and videotapes, to provide treatment (Griest et al., 2002; Osgood-Hynes et al., 1998). But, they do not utilize a computer interface to communicate with patients.

An early prototype for computerized exposure therapy for snake phobia was reported in 1970 by Lang, Melhamed, and Hart; but the first controlled trial of computer program designed for a wide range of phobias did not appear until over a decade later (Ghosh et al., 1984). This software was based on the book *Living with Fear* (Marks, 1978). A text-only format was used to provide psychoeducation on exposure therapy, generate a problem list text, and encourage users to become involved in self-directed exposure. Two studies with different versions of this software found that computerized therapy was equivalent to standard clinician-administered exposure therapy (Carr et al., 1988; Ghosh et al., 1984).

Another early computer program for CBT was found to be effective in the treatment of depression (Selmi et al., 1982, 1990). This program included questionnaires, case illustrations, and multiple-choice questions to convey the basics of CBT. Because it was produced for the DOS operating system and relies completely on text for communication with patients, it is not being used in contemporary clinical practice. In a study with mildly to moderately depressed patients, computer-assisted therapy with the Selmi et al. (1990) software was observed to be equal to standard CBT and superior to a wait-list control condition.

The only investigation of computer-assisted therapy for depression or anxiety disorders that did not show positive results was reported by Bowers et al. (1993) who tested the usefulness of *Overcoming Depression* (Colby & Colby, 1990; Colby, 1995) with depressed inpatients. The *Overcoming Depression* software has a few components that introduce cognitive and behavioral concepts; but unlike more fully developed programs for CBT (e.g., Proudfoot et al., 2003; Selmi et al., 1982, 1990; Wright, Salmon, Wright, & Beck, 1995; Wright et al., 2002, 2003), this program does not present comprehensive or detailed cognitive–behavioral interventions. Also, *Overcoming Depression* is the only currently available software that includes a "natural language" module. This part of the program appeared to confuse depressed inpatients in a controlled study (Bowers et al., 1993; Stuart & LaRue, 1996). In the investigation by Bowers et al. (1993), computer-assisted treatment did not significantly improve outcome in hospitalized patients who were receiving other treatments including medications and milieu therapy.

More recently developed multimedia programs for computer-assisted therapy have fared much better in randomized, controlled trials. For example, Wright et al. (1995, 2001, 2002) have reported on the development and testing of software that uses multimedia and a variety of interactive exercises to assist clinicians in treatment with CBT. This computer program (*Good Days Ahead*), like other newer multimedia software produced by Proudfoot et al. (*Beating the Blues*, 2003), is primarily targeted at depression, but also covers core CBT methods that may be helpful to patients with anxiety symptoms.

Studies with the Wright et al. program found high levels of user satisfaction with the software, efficacy that was equal to standard CBT, and robust effects in improving measures of automatic thoughts and dysfunctional attitudes (Wright et al., 2001, 2002). In an investigation of medication-free patients with major depressive disorder, both computer-assisted CBT and standard CBT were superior to a wait list control group in relieving symptoms of depression, even though therapist contact was substantially reduced in the computer-assisted therapy condition. *Good Days Ahead* was originally produced in laser disk format but is now available on DVD-ROM.

Proudfoot et al. (2003) have reported that another multimedia program (*Beating the Blues*) was effective in the treatment of a group of primary care patients with depression, anxiety, or mixed depression and anxiety. Subjects in this study were randomly assigned to receive treatment as usual (TAU) from their primary care practitioner or TAU plus *Beating the Blues*. Patients who used the multimedia software had significantly better outcomes than those who received standard treatment alone. *Beating the Blues* was developed and tested in the United Kingdom. It includes video illustrations of fictional characters, voice-overs, animations, and interactive exercises that teach CBT skills.

Virtual reality programs have been developed for height phobia (Rothbaum et al., 1995), fear of flying (Muehlberger, Herrmann, Wiedemann, Ellgring, & Pauli, 2001; Rothbaum et al., 2000), claustrophobia (Botella, Villa, Banos, Perpina, & Garcia-Palacios, 2000; Wiederhold & Wiederhold, 2000), social phobia (North, North, & Coble, 1998; Petraub, Slater, & Barker, 2001; Wiederhold & Wiederhold, 2000), spider phobia (Carlin, Hoffman, & Weghorst, 1997), agoraphobia (Wiederhold & Wiederhold,

2000), PTSD (Rothbaum et al., 2001), and body image problems in persons with binge eating disorder (Riva, Bacchetta, Baruffi, & Molinari, 2002). Applications of virtual reality technology focus on producing computer-generated simulations of feared objects, situations, or images that can be used for exposure-based interventions. Three-dimensional computer graphics, head sets, speakers, body tracking instruments, and other sensory input devices are used to immerse patients in realistic scenes such as glass-enclosed elevators.

In a preliminary study, Rothbaum et al. (1995) observed that virtual reality exposure therapy (VR) for height phobia was more effective than a wait-list control condition. This research group also has reported that VR was equal to standard exposure therapy and superior to a wait list in helping persons with fear of flying (Rothbaum et al., 2000). Another VR application was evaluated in a small controlled study that compared a multidimensional treatment approach (including a virtual reality component) with group CBT for binge eating disorder (Riva et al., 2002). Subjects in this investigation also received dietary counseling and physical exercise. There were no significant differences found between the groups in reducing binge eating behavior, but patients treated with VR had significantly greater improvement in measures of body satisfaction and self-efficacy (Riva et al., 2002).

Hand-held computers have provided another format for using computer technology to assist therapists and patients. Newman et al. (1997) developed a method of using palmtop computers to shorten CBT for panic disorder by giving computer-based instructions on self-monitoring, exposure and response prevention, breathing training, and positive self-statements. In a study with 20 patients, both computer-assisted CBT (4 sessions with a clinician plus hand-held computer program) and standard CBT (12 sessions with a clinician) were found to be effective. Standard CBT was superior to computer-assisted CBT on some measures at the end of treatment, but both forms of therapy were equally effective at the follow-up assessment.

Gruber et al. (2001) have reported similar findings in a study of a hand-held computer program for social phobia. Their computer program was designed to assist in group cognitive therapy by reinforcing the material taught in group sessions, giving prompts to confront fears, involving users in exercises to modify automatic thoughts, and providing progress reports. In a study comparing standard group CBT and computer-assisted CBT (with reduced therapist contact), there were advantages on some measures for standard therapy at the end of treatment; but at the follow-up assessment, no differences were found between the treatments (Gruber et al., 2001).

Another investigation of computer-assisted CBT tested the usefulness of *Fear Fighter*, an updated version of a text-based program for phobias (Ghosh et al., 1984; Marks, 1978). The software has been upgraded to include graphic illustrations and voiceovers, but does not include all features of fully developed multimedia programs (e.g., Proudfoot et al., 2003; Wright et al., 1995, 2002). A preliminary, uncontrolled study found that computer-assisted therapy with *Fear Fighter* reduced symptoms of agoraphobia as effectively as standard clinician-administered CBT (Kenwright et al., 2001).

Research on computer-assisted CBT has demonstrated that computer technology has the potential to increase the efficiency of treatment, decrease cost, and improve access to empirically tested interventions. However, there have been a limited number of well-controlled investigations, and most studies have utilized a small number of subjects. Larger controlled studies and replications in multiple settings are clearly needed. Broader availability of highly refined programs with demonstrated efficacy, greater use of computers throughout society, and pressures to develop cost-effective treatments could lead to the future growth of computer-assisted psychotherapy.

See also: Computers and technology

REFERENCES

Botella, C., Villa, H., Banos, R., Perpina, C., & Garcia-Palacios, A. (2000). The treatment of claustrophobia with virtual reality: Changes in other phobic behaviors not specifically treated. *CyberPsychology and Behavior, 2*, 135–141.

Bowers, W., Stuart, S., MacFarlane, R., & Gorman, L. (1993). Use of computer-administered cognitive-behavior therapy with depressed inpatients. *Depression, 1*, 294–299.

Carlin, A. S., Hoffman, H. G., & Weghorst, S. (1997). Virtual reality and tactile augmentation in the treatment of spider phobia: A case report. *Behaviour Research and Therapy, 35*, 153–158.

Carr, A. C., Ghosh, A., & Marks, I. M., (1988). Computer-supervised exposure treatment for phobias. *Canada Journal of Psychiatry, 33*, 112–117.

Colby, K. M. (1995). A computer program using cognitive therapy to treat depressed patients. *Psychiatric Services, 46*, 1223–1225.

Colby, K. M., & Colby, P. M. (1990). *Overcoming depression*. Malibu: Malibu Artificial Intelligence Works.

Colby, K. M., Watt, J. B., & Gilbert, J. P. (1966). A computer method of psychotherapy: Preliminary communication. *Journal of Nervous and Mental Disease, 142*, 148–152.

Ghosh, A., Marks, I. M., & Carr, A. C. (1984). Controlled study of self-exposure treatment for phobics: preliminary communication. *The Royal Society of Medicine, 77*, 483–487.

Griest, J. H. (1998). Computer interviews for depression management. *Journal of Clinical Psychiatry, 59*(Suppl. 16), 20–42.

Greist, J. H., Marks, I. M., Baer, L., Kobak, K. A., Wenzel, K. W., Hirsch, M. J., Mantle, J. M., & Clary, C.M. (2002). Behavior therapy for obsessive–compulsive disorder guided by a computer or by a clinician compared with relaxation as a control. *Journal of Clinical Psychiatry, 63*(2), 138–145.

Gruber, K., Moran, P. J., Roth, W. T., & Taylor, C. B. (2001). Computer-assisted cognitive behavioral group therapy for social phobia. *Behavior Therapy, 32*, 155–165.

Kenwright, M., Liness, S., & Marks, I. (2001). Reducing demands on clinicians time by offering computer-aided self help for phobia/panic: Feasibility study. *British Journal of Psychiatry, 179*, 456–459.

Marks, I., Shaw, S., & Parkin, R. (1998). Computer-aided treatments of mental health problems. *Clinical Psychology: Science and Practice, 5*(2), 151–170.

Muehlberger, A., Herrmann, M. J., Wiedemann, G., Ellgring, H., & Pauli, P. (2001). Repeated exposure of flight phobics to flights in virtual reality. *Behaviour Research and Therapy, 39*, 1033–1050.

Nadelson, T. (1987). The inhuman computer/the too-human psychotherapist. *American Journal of Psychotherapy, 41*, 489–498.

Newman, M. G., Kenardy, J., Herman, S., & Taylor, C. B. (1997). Comparison of palmtop-computer assisted brief cognitive–behavioral treatment to cognitive–behavioral treatment for panic disorder. *Journal of Consulting and Clinical Psychology, 65*, 178–183.

North, M. M., North, S. M., & Coble, J. R. (1998). Virtual reality therapy: An effective treatment for phobias. In G. Riva, B. K. Wiederhold, & E. Molinari (Eds.), *Virtual environments in clinical psychology and neuroscience: Methods and techniques in advanced patient–therapist interaction* (pp. 112–119). Amsterdam: IOS Press.

O'Dell, J. W., & Dickson, J. (1984). Eliza as a "therapeutic tool." *Computerized Psychotherapy, 40*, 942–945.

Osgood-Hynes, D. J., Greist, J. H., Marks, I. M., Baer, L., Heneman, S. W., Wenzel, K. W., Manzo, P. A., Parkin, J. R., Spierings, C.J., Dottl, S. L., Vitse, H. M. (1998). Self-administered psychotherapy for depression using a telephone-accessed computer system plus booklets: An open U.S.–U.K. study. *Journal of Clinical Psychiatry, 59*(7), 358–365.

Petraub, D. P., Slater, M., & Barker, C. (2001). An experiment of public speaking anxiety in response to three different types of virtual audience. *Presence: Teleoperators and Virtual Environments, 11*, 68–78.

Proudfoot, J., Goldberg, D., Mann, A., Everitt, B., Marks, I., & Gray, J. (2003). Computerised, interactive, multimedia cognitive behavioural therapy reduces anxiety and depression in general practice: A randomised controlled trial. *Psychological Medicine, 33*, 217–227.

Riva, G., Bacchetta, M., Baruffi, M., & Molinari, E. (2002). Virtual-reality-based multidimensional therapy for the treatment of body image disturbances in binge eating disorders: A preliminary controlled study. *IEEE Transactions on Information Technology in Biomedicine, 6*(3), 224–234.

Rothbaum, B. O., Hodges, L. F., Kooper, R., Opdyke, D., Williford, J. S., & North, M. (1995). Effectiveness of computer-generated (virtual reality) graded exposure in the treatment of acrophobia. *American Journal of Psychiatry, 152*, 626–628.

Rothbaum, B. O., Hodges, L. F., Ready, D., Graap, K., & Alarcon, R. D. (2001). Virtual reality exposure therapy for Vietnam veterans with posttraumatic stress disorder. *Journal of Clinical Psychiatry, 62*, 617–622.

Rothbaum, B. O., Hodges, L., Smith, S., Lee, J. H., and Price, L. (2000). A controlled study of virtual reality exposure therapy for the fear of flying. *Journal of Consulting and Clinical Psychology, 60*, 1020–1026.

Selmi, P. M., Klein, M. H., Greist, J. H., & Harris, W. G. (1982). An investigation of computer-assisted cognitive–behavior therapy in the treatment of depression. *Behavior Research Methods and Instruments, 14*, 181–185.

Selmi, P. M., Klein, M. H., Greist, J. H., Sorrell, S. P., & Erdman, H. P. (1990). Computer-administered cognitive-behavioral therapy for depression. *American Journal of Psychiatry, 147*, 51–56.

Stuart, S., & LaRue, S. (1996). Computerized cognitive therapy: The interface between man and machine. *Journal of Cognitive Psychotherapy, 10*, 181–191.

Weizenbaum, J. (1996). Computational linguistics. *Communications of the ACM, 9*, 36–45.

Wiederhold, B. K., & Wiederhold, M. D. (2000). Lessons learned from 600 virtual reality sessions. *CyberPsychology and Behavior, 3*, 393–400.

Wilson, P. H., Goldin, J. C., & Charbonneau-Powis, M. (1983). Comparative efficacy of behavioral and cognitive treatments of depression. *Cognitive Therapy and Research, 7*(2), 111–124.

Wright, J. H., Salmon, P., Wright, A. S., & Beck, A. T. (1995). *Cognitive therapy: A multimedia learning program*. Louisville, KY: Mindstreet.

Wright, J. H., & Wright, A. (1997). Computer assisted psychotherapy. *Journal of Psychotherapy Practice and Research, 6*, 315–329.

Wright, J. H., Wright, A. S., Basco, M. R., Albano, A. M., Raffield, T., Goldsmith, J., & Steiner, P. (2001, July). *Controlled trial of computer-assisted cognitive therapy for depression*. World Congress of Cognitive Therapy, Vancouver, Canada.

Wright, J. H., Wright, A. S., & Beck, A. T. (2003). *Good Days Ahead: The multimedia program for cognitive therapy*. Louisville, KY: Mindstreet.

Wright, J. H., Wright, A. S., Salmon, P., Beck, A. T., Kuykendall, J., Goldsmith, J., Zickel, M. B. (2002). Development and initial testing of a multimedia program for computer-assisted cognitive therapy. *American Journal of Psychotherapy, 56*(1), 76–86.

Computers and Technology

Bruce M. Gale

Keywords: computers, technology, virtual reality, teletherapy, distance learning

Evolutionary rather than revolutionary, use of technology has built on existing theories supporting cognitive–behavioral assessment and treatment. Just as radiologists and surgeons found that new technology tools led to more efficacious and novel treatments in their fields, mental health professionals have been discovering innovative assessment and intervention techniques. By the late 1990s, many of the barriers preventing widespread use of technology in clinical applications had largely disappeared. This led to the expansion and "trickle down" effect where technology tools were no longer the domain of well-funded laboratories at major universities, but could now be found on portable systems used by clinicians in small clinic and private practice settings. Equipment and software that was unheard of in 1985, and that cost \$50,000 in 1995, could now be purchased for under \$5000.

Some of the earliest mainstream applications using technology included the use of biofeedback. Colors and sounds from computers changed, signaling to clients that their minds and bodies had become fully relaxed. As part of client psychoeducation, practitioners often explained how the systems operated and that the equipment could not harm them. This appeared to allay fears for most clients and this treatment approach has continued through to the present. Other early uses of computers involved collecting data on client progress, evaluating outcomes, and using games to motivate children. However, for most clinicians, this was more of a conceptual rather than practical application of technology. Word processors, computerized billing, and scoring tests comprised the most common applications of computer technology until the early 1990s.

Since then, the scope of technology applications has increased at an exponential rate. Many devices currently in use are more advanced than those described in science fiction novels from earlier decades. Even biofeedback has become more sophisticated due to the increased types of biometric monitoring available, level of interactivity between user and computer, and use of wireless sensors. These changes provide for more precise measurements, a greater sense of involvement, and increased comfort.

Technology began to emerge as a mainstream concept for conducting assessments and providing treatment as a result of the confluence of several related events: (1) expansion of the Internet for public use in the early 1990s; (2) availability of increasingly powerful yet affordable computers with user-friendly GUIs (graphical user interfaces); (3) public acceptance of email as a viable form of communication; and (4) hardware and software advances in digital video, graphics, and computer animation.

ASSESSMENT

Assessment techniques have benefited considerably from advances in technology. Many advantages using computerized interviewing have been reported. These include increased consistency in the interview process by asking the same set of questions in the same manner with standardized follow-up queries. This has the added benefit of freeing the therapist from having to conduct lengthy, monotonous interviews to engage in more rewarding therapeutic activities. Clients have reported preferring computer-based interviews, since it gives them more time to think about their responses to questions (Newman, Consol, & Taylor, 1997). For those with reading or visual deficits, interactive voice response (IVR) systems allow clients to listen to questions and speak their response or press a number on a telephone keypad. Because IVR or computer-administered surveys can be programmed to include branching, meaning that specific answers lead to more detailed questioning while skipping less relevant areas, clinicians can design surveys to pinpoint specific clinical concerns without presenting clients with a seemingly endless array of questions.

The revelation that successful cognitive therapy produces neurochemical changes in the brains of successfully treated individuals diagnosed with Obsessive–Compulsive Disorder is consistent with changes reported through medication use (Schwartz, 1996). This served as a significant validation for the cognitive therapy field. As costs further reduce, it may become more commonplace for clinicians to conduct pre- and postassessments that include a greater emphasis on biometric measures. This is consistent with the ongoing trend to employ treatments based on empirical support.

More recently, information collected by computer has been mated with sophisticated brain imaging systems. These scans can effectively map which sections of the brain are being used while the individual is engaged in a variety of daily tasks, providing for far more detailed analysis of behavioral and emotional responses. Researchers are currently attempting to combine the use of functional magnetic resonance imaging (fMRI), positron emission tomography (PET), or magnetoencephalography (MEG) with more complex neurobehavioral tasks to simulate real-life, everyday experiences. By choosing common everyday tasks, brain activity can be correlated with eye movements, attention, decision-making latency, and the effects of stimulus complexity, duration, and factors affecting fatigue, anxiety, or depression. Researchers can determine not only what cognitive or behavioral changes have occurred, but actually measure a variety of biometric indicators. This has opened the door for assessing the efficacy of a variety of treatments, regardless of whether they involve cognitive–behavioral, psychopharmacological, or other treatments for dysfunctions.

TREATMENT

One of the most important advances has been in the area of virtual reality (VR), which involves real-time computer graphics, tracking devices, and other sensory input devices to immerse participants in a computer-generated virtual environment. Early research using VR focused on treating fear of heights (Rothbaum et al., 1995); however, this has expanded broadly to other anxiety problems such as panic disorder, claustrophobia, spider phobia, flying phobia, social shyness, and posttraumatic stress disorder.

Clinicians have also found VR to be a useful adjunctive tool to help patients tolerate extraordinarily painful treatments by distracting them from perceiving pain and permitting treatment to occur for longer time periods, e.g., skin grafts for burn victims and changing dressings for leg ulcers. Other uses of computers and technology have facilitated patients tolerating less painful, but highly anxiety-provoking treatments, such as chemotherapy. Compared to control groups, patients who have used these technology-based interventions report feeling less anticipatory anxiety when facing such difficult treatments, have less recollection of the painful or lengthy treatment, and feel more relief once the treatment is over.

Psychoeducation, an important element of cognitive–behavioral therapy, has been similarly enhanced using technology. Demonstration projects have been successfully implemented to train astronauts to consult on-board computer systems for extended-mission space flights to receive cognitive–behavioral treatment for depression, social isolation, and other related effects of space flight or extended time on the international space station (Owens, 2002). Police and the armed forces have successfully created simulated environments to train officers and military personnel to assess and improve judgment, reaction time, and to tolerate the effects of harsh conditions.

Technology in clinical treatment addresses some of the common dilemmas in more traditional therapy settings. Having individuals practice successful strategies while spending time in troublesome environments can be expensive or nearly impossible to arrange. Incorporating content-oriented or multimedia practice exercises between sessions permits clinicians to more closely monitor client follow-through and independent problem-solving outside the therapy environment.

Data and client progress can easily and confidentially be made available to the clinician through survey software and online data recording methods. This can create a more seamless link between practice during and outside the traditional therapy environment. Clients can seek additional support through Internet discussion boards and chat rooms, sharing experiences with other affected persons. During therapy sessions, clinicians have made greater use of computers. Some simply use a word processor to create customized scenarios or practice assignments with clients, while others employ video or computerized assessment techniques.

Distance learning, telemedicine, and teletherapy have made treatment more available to more individuals with no reported reduction in treatment effectiveness. Clients participate while in front of a computer or television with a camera facing them and usually can interact with the presenter. In a study of clients who were successfully treated for obesity using videoconferencing and compared with an identical face-to-face group, the majority of participants felt they had been just as successful as they would have been if they had been in the more traditional face-to-face group (Harvey-Berino, 1998). They reported following the class leader and lessons via videoconferencing without difficulty. The biggest current problem appeared to be that only half of them felt they could communicate effectively via videoconferencing, suggesting that passive participation (one-way communication) was easier than active participation (two-way communication). It is likely that future cognitive therapists will use more suitable techniques to enhance participants' sense of realism and interactivity via videoconferencing.

In a variation merging teletherapy and VR, clients were able to rehearse strategies and hold conversations with avatars or "virtual humans," i.e., animated characters that can appear to talk and interact. Combined with artificial intelligence, it is possible to produce avatars with distinct personalities that can respond to the client through biometric monitoring or recognition of word patterns. This represents a higher-tech variation on an earlier computer approach developed in the 1960s, "ELIZA." This computer program provided a sample of person-centered therapy and was based on statements typed in by the user (Weizenbaum, 1966).

OUTCOME VALIDATION

Because so much of the technology still remains new, and to many, an unproven area, researchers worldwide have embarked on a peer-review method for researching effectiveness. Even the most useful, established applications seemed at first to be little more than novel high-tech variations on more traditional approaches. Now as some technologies have matured, researchers are more closely examining their cost-effectiveness, level of public acceptance, and ways they can provide treatment that would simply not be possible otherwise. In looking at the durability of technology-based behavioral interventions, initial findings have supported the long-term efficacy of self-help, computer-based treatment (Gilroy, Kirkby, Daniels, Menzies, & Montgomery, 2003). A 6-month follow-up on binge eating disorders comparing a multifactorial treatment, which included VR, to traditional cognitive therapy found that a significantly higher number of patients (77% versus 56%) had quit bingeing after 6 months, with better scores on psychometric measures and body image scores (Riva, Bacchetta, Cesa, Conti, & Molinari, 2003).

Such outcome data do not come easily or inexpensively, but are critical to helping the public understand what works and what is little more than slick packaging. Many resources on the Internet promote technologies that have little empirical data to support their efficacy. Clinicians have an obligation to learn which treatments have been subjected to study and which are more likely to be unfounded advertisements. The latter may not only fail to help clients, but may dissuade them from seeking more effective treatment.

The ethical principles ensuring that the public continues to receive useful and safe therapy through technology are continuing to evolve. It is clear that, as technology continues to become more interactive and realistic, clinicians will continue to find useful means for incorporating cognitive approaches into the therapy process.

"As with any new technology or methodology, there is always a period of conflict and debate as the technology is tested, assessed, and, if found to be valuable, integrated into the mainstream" (Romanczyk, 1986, p. 114). Although this statement was written in the mid-1980s, the controversy continues. Most clinicians were not trained in the use of computers to deliver clinical treatment. Some view it as an intrusion on face-to-face therapy, while others wholeheartedly embrace as yet unproven methodologies. For the public, these can be confusing times. Useful web sites that are listed on the Internet may no longer exist. It can be difficult to tell whether information comes from objective sources or is little more than the well-written personal opinions of individuals.

FUTURE DIRECTIONS

Several areas of key research still need to be identified before the more cutting-edge forms of technology gain acceptance (Kaltenthaler et al., 2002). These include: (1) comparison studies to determine the level of therapist involvement required when using computer-based cognitive therapy programs; (2) direct comparison with other adjunctive approaches, such as a bibliotherapy; (3) the types of patients most likely to benefit from computerized approaches; (4) more comprehensive measures of the cost-benefit ratio compared to more traditional cognitive–behavioral approaches; and (5) how to best standardize the use of existing technological adjuncts that have proven effective.

Still in its infancy, the use of computers and technology appears destined to expand into areas that can only be envisioned once new technology becomes available. What is clear, however, is that the use of technology has provided for new ways of understanding human behavior. Practitioners have at their disposal a variety of tools that can now be considered part of mainstream cognitive therapy assessment and treatment.

See also: Computer programs for cognitive–behavior therapy

REFERENCES

Gilroy, L. J., Kirkby, K. C., Daniels, B. A., Menzies, R. G., & Montgomery, I. M. (2003). Long-term follow-up of computer-aided vicarious exposure versus live graded exposure in the treatment of spider phobia. *Behavior Therapy, 34*, 65–76.

Harvey-Berino, J. (1998). Changing health behavior via telecommunications technology: Using interactive television to test obesity. *Behavior Therapy, 29*, 505–519.

Kaltenthaler, E., Shackley, P., Stevens, K., Beverley, C., Parry, G., & Chilcott, J. (2002). A systematic review and economic evaluation of computerized cognitive behaviour therapy for depression and anxiety. *Health Technology Assessment, 6*, 1–112.

Newman, M. G., Consol, A., & Taylor, C. B. (1997). Computers in assessment and cognitive behavioral treatment of clinical disorders: Anxiety as a case in point. *Behavior Therapy, 28*, 211–235.

Owens, L. (2002). A computer-based, self-help system for the space age. National Space Biomedical Research Institute. News release, June 26, 2002.

Riva, G., Bacchetta, M., Cesa, G., Conti, S., & Molinari, E. (2003). Six-month follow-up of in-patient experiential cognitive therapy for binge eating disorders. *CyberPsychology and Behavior, 6*, 251–258.

Romanczyk, R. (1986). *Clinical utilization of microcomputer technology.* (p. 114). New York: Pergamon Press.

Rothbaum, B., Hodges, L., Kooper, R., Opdyke, D., Willliford, J. S., & North, M. (1995). Virtual reality graded exposure in the treatment of acrophobia: A case report. *Behavior Therapy, 29*, 505–519.

Schwartz, J. M. (1996). *Brain lock: Free yourself from obsessive–compulsive behavior*. New York: HarperCollins.

Weizenbaum, J. (1966). ELIZA—A computer program for the study of natural language communication between man and machine. *Communications of the ACM, 9*, 36–45.

Couple and Family Therapy

Frank M. Dattilio

Keywords: cognitive, behavioral, couples, family, schema

While Albert Ellis has written that he adapted his model of rational emotive therapy (RET) to work with couples as early as the late 1950s, little has appeared in the professional literature on cognitive–behavioral marital and family therapy prior to the 1980s. Principles of behavior modification were initially applied to interactional patterns of family members only subsequent to their successful application to couples in distress. This work with couples was followed by several single case studies involving the use of family interventions in treating children's behavior. For the first time, behaviorists recognized family members as having a highly influential effect on the child's natural environment and were integrated into the treatment process.

Several years later, a more refined and comprehensive style of intervention with the family unit was described in detail by Patterson, McNeal, Hawkins and Phelps (1967). Since that time, the professional literature has addressed applications of behavioral therapy to family systems, with a strong emphasis on contingency contracting and negotiation strategies as well as environmental reprogramming

(Patterson et al., 1967). Its reported applications remain oriented toward families with children who are diagnosed with specific behavioral problems (Dattilio, 1998a).

The cognitive approach or cognitive component to behavioral marital and family therapy subsequently received attention as providing a supplement to behavioral-oriented couples and family therapy. In addition to the work of Ellis, an important study by Margolin and Weiss (1978), which suggested the effectiveness of a cognitive component to behavioral marital therapy, sparked further investigation of the use of cognitive techniques with dysfunctional couples (Dattilio & Padesky, 1990; Epstein & Baucom, 2002). Only a few studies have actually examined the impact of adding cognitive restructuring interventions to behavioral protocols, typically by substituting some sessions of cognitive interventions for behaviorally oriented sessions in order to maintain equality across the treatments that were compared (Dattilio & Epstein, 2003). The results suggest that the combination of cognitive and behavioral interventions was equally effective as the behavioral conditions, although cognitively focused interventions tend to produce more cognitive change, while behavioral interventions modify behavioral interactions (Baucom, Shoham, Mueser, Daiuto, & Stickle, 1998).

THEORY DEVELOPMENT

The rational–emotive behavioral approach (REBT) to couple and family therapy places emphasis on each individual's perception and interpretation of the events that occur in the family environment. The theory assumes that "family members largely create their own world by the phenomenological view they take of what happens to them." The therapy focuses on how particular problems of the family members affect their well-being as a unit. During the process of therapy, family members are treated as individuals, each of whom subscribes to his or her own particular set of beliefs and expectations. The role of the couple and family therapist is to help members make the connection that illogical beliefs and distortions serve as the foundation for their emotional distress. The cognitive–behavioral approach, while much like REBT, assumes a different posture by focusing in greater depth on family interaction patterns and underlying dynamics.

Consistent and compatible with systems theory, the cognitive–behavioral model of couples and families includes the premise that members of a family simultaneously influence and are influenced by each other. Consequently, a behavior of one family member leads to behaviors, cognitions, and emotions in other members, which, in turn, elicit cognitions, behaviors, and emotions in response in the former member. As this cycle continues, the volatility of the family dynamics escalates, rendering family members vulnerable to a negative spiral of conflict. As the number of family members involved increases, so does the complexity of the dynamics, adding more fuel to the escalation process.

Cognitive therapy places a heavy emphasis on schema or what has otherwise been defined as core beliefs. It was not until much later in his career that Beck applied his theories of schema to couples in his book, *Love Is Never Enough* (Beck, 1988). Many of the concepts in this book sparked my enthusiasm to apply these concepts to my work with families. As this concept is applied to family treatment, the therapeutic intervention is based on the assumptions with which family members interpret and evaluate one another and the emotions and behaviors that are generated in response to these cognitions (Dattilio, 2001). While cognitive–behavioral theory does not suggest that cognitive processes cause all family behavior, it does stress that cognitive appraisal plays a significant part in the interrelationships existing among events, cognitions, emotions, and behaviors. With the cognitive component of CBT, restructuring distorted beliefs has a pivotal impact on changing dysfunctional behaviors and vice versa.

EMPIRICAL BASIS OF CBT WITH COUPLES AND FAMILIES

As stated earlier, early studies in behavior therapy with couples and families set the pace for more contemporary research. The use of social exchange theory and operant learning strategies to facilitate more satisfying interaction among distressed couples subsequently surfaced in the professional literature. Later, Patterson et al. (1967) applied operant conditioning and contingency contracting procedures to develop parents' abilities to control behaviorally regressive children. It was subsequently that behaviorally oriented therapists added communication and problem-solving skills training components to their interventions with couples and families. Research studies confirm the premise of social exchange theory, indicating that members of distressed couples exchange more displeasing and less pleasing behaviors than members of nondistressed relationships and the behavioral interventions (see Epstein & Baucom, 2002, for a more extensive review).

It was not until the late 1970s that cognitions were introduced as an auxiliary component of treatment with behavioral paradigms in couple and family therapy (Margolin & Weiss, 1978). During the 1980s and 1990s, cognitive factors became an increasing focus in the couples research and therapy literature, and cognitions were addressed in a more direct and systematic way than in the other theoretical approaches to family therapy (Dattilio, 1998; Dattilio & Padesky, 1990).

Similarly, behavioral approaches to family therapy were broadened to include members' cognitions about one another. Ellis was also one of the pioneers in introducing a cognitive approach to family therapy. A more progressive expression of literature on cognitive–behavior family therapy expanded rapidly throughout the 1980s and 1990s (Dattilio, 1998).

Epstein (2001) has produced an excellent overview of the empirical status of CBT with couples. More recently, Dattilio and Epstein (2003) published an overview of both couples and family therapy with additional emphasis on family schema.

Unfortunately, the area of CBT in couples has substantially more quantitative studies than family therapy (Baucom et al., 1998; Dattilio & Epstein, 2003; Epstein, 2001). The most recent of the family therapy studies include addressing the treatment of schizophrenia in the early 1980s as well as those studies conducted by Barrowclough and Tarrier (1992).

CRITICISMS OF CBT WITH COUPLES AND FAMILIES

The vast majority of criticisms concerning CBT come predominantly from the field of marriage and family therapy. CBT was, and in some cases still is, perceived by the other modalities as lacking depth in dealing with the underlying dynamics of family dysfunction. Moreover, CBFT is often regarded as being useful only with cases involving children who have behavioral disorders or family problems, especially when parenting issues are the focus of treatment. CBT tends to be viewed by some mental health professionals as rigid, mechanistic, and too wooden in its approach. It is also the erroneous impression of others that CBT tends to downplay affect and may be very insensitive to cultural issues in couples and family therapy. One of the other criticisms is that the more direct treatment posture of CBT has been viewed as being intrusive. For example, many of the proponents of system theory tend to view the therapist as a reflective instrument of change as opposed to maintaining a more direct style as with CBT. This regard is surprising, however, particularly in light of the amount of empirical evidence that the field of CBT maintains in general.

It is hypothesized that much of the criticism of CBT stems from a lack of knowledge and understanding of what is entailed in the treatment process. It is anticipated that perhaps with an increased understanding and more balanced perspective of the approach, many of the existing criticisms may dissipate with time.

DIRECTIONS FOR CBT IN THE FUTURE

The future of CBT with couples and families appears to be very promising. The integration of CBT with other modalities of couples and family therapy is on the rise. It was actually highlighted in a recent edited text by Dattilio (1998a), in which CBT was proposed as having strong, integrative potential with many of the 16 different modalities of couples and family therapy featured in the text. CBT techniques and strategies are very versatile in dealing with contemporary issues of couples and families.

Theoretically, because most approaches to couples and family therapy involve human intellectual communication, the majority of therapies may be said to be "cognitive," or at least maintain a cognitive component. For similar reasons, most therapies can be considered behavioral as well because communication and interaction exchange is often behavioral, and all behaviors are communicative. Because the human condition also involves emotions, most psychotherapies address emotion to a significant degree. Consequently, any particular therapy can be viewed through a variety of lenses—as cognitive, behavioral, emotional, and so on. Cognitive–behavior therapies have even gone a step further and suggested that behaviors, cognitions, emotions, physiological, and interpersonal components are integrated, so that if any one element changes during the course of therapy, it has a chain reaction on the others. It appears that most modalities of psychotherapy are moving toward an integrative perspective. This clearly includes the cognitive–behavioral approaches, particularly with couples and families. Also, the application of CBT with couples and families of varying cultures is imperative in order to better understand the cultural strengths and limitations of CBT in this domain.

FUTURE RESEARCH

Future research in couples and family therapy clearly needs to focus on examining the application of CBT that has been so successful with individuals. Certainly, more long-term outcome studies need to be conducted along with studies comparing CBT with other approaches to couples and family therapy. It would also be interesting to examine the various characteristics of family members and determine what might constitute differential responses to treatment as well as optimal sequences of behavior and the restructuring of schemas. It would also be helpful for comparative studies to be conducted in order to isolate the specific characteristics that make CBT effective, and also discover which components are most advantageous for integrative purpose with other modalities.

See also: Couples therapy, Couples therapy—substance abuse

REFERENCES

Barrowclough, C., & Tarrier, N. (1992). *Families of schizophrenic patients: Cognitive–behavioral interventions*. London: Chapman & Hall.

Baucom, D. H., Shoham, V., Mueser, K. T., Daiuto, A. D., & Stickle, T. R. (1998). Empirically supported couples and family therapy for adult problems. *Journal of Consulting and Clinical Psychology, 66*, 53–88.

Beck, A. T. (1988). *Love is never enough*. New York: Harper & Row.

Dattilio, F. M. (Ed.). (1998a). *Case studies in couple and family therapy: Systemic and cognitive perspectives*. New York: Guilford Press.

Dattilio, F. M. (1998b). Finding the fit between cognitive–behavioral and family therapy. *The Family Therapy Networker, 22*(4), 63–73.

Dattilio, F. M. (2001). Cognitive–behavioral family therapy: Contemporary myths and misconceptions. *Contemporary Family Therapy, 23*(1), 3–18.

Dattilio, F. M., & Epstein, N. B. (2003). Cognitive–behavioral couple and family therapy. In G. Weeks, T. Sexton, & M. Robbins (Eds.), *Handbook of family therapy: Theory research and practice* (pp. 147–173). New York: Routledge.

Dattilio, F. M., & Padesky, C. A. (1990). *Cognitive therapy with couples*. Sarasota, FL: Professional Resource Exchange.

Epstein, N. B. (2001). Cognitive–behavioral therapy with couples: Empirical status. *Journal of Cognitive Psychotherapy, 15*(2), 299–310.

Epstein, N. B., & Baucom, D. H. (2002). *Enhanced cognitive–behavioral therapy for couples: A contextual approach*. New York: Guilford Press.

Margolin, G., & Weiss, R. L. (1978). Comparative evaluation of therapeutic components associated with behavioral marital treatments. *Journal of Consulting and Clinical Psychology, 46*, 1476–1486.

Patterson, G. R., McNeal, S., Hawkins, N., & Phelps, R. (1967). Reprogramming the social environment. *Journal of Child Psychology and Psychiatry, 8*, 181–195.

Couples Therapy

Brian Baucom

Keywords: couples, relationship therapy, behavioral couples therapy

Cognitive–behavioral couples therapy (CBCT) has been evolving since the late 1960s when the first study of a behaviorally based treatment for couples was published. The first behavioral treatments for couples attempted to increase the frequency of discrete, desired behaviors by using direct reinforcement by partners. Since that time, CBCT has been refined as couples researchers have developed a better understanding of the ways that couples function and a more detailed picture of frequent sources of distress. CBCT continues to evolve with recent interventions focusing on broadening the scope of case formulations to include emotions, broad patterns and core themes, and environmental influences on couples' relationships as well as incorporating a new class of therapeutic strategies based on the idea that emotional acceptance on the part of both spouses is highly beneficial to healthy relationship functioning.

Early behavioral couples interventions drew heavily on reinforcement theory as well as social exchange theory. Reinforcement theory suggests that frequent, positive interactions between partners serve as reinforcers that maintain satisfying relationships and that a lack of such reinforcers is a hallmark of troubled relationships. Social exchange theory suggests that individuals compare the ratio of benefits and costs of their current relationship with the potential benefits and costs of alternative relationships to determine if they want to stay in their current relationship. Based on these understandings of relationship functioning, the primary task of early behavioral couples therapy (BCT) was to change the ratio of positive to negative behaviors in an effort to maximize the benefits of the relationship for each spouse. Direct efforts at changing the ratio of positive to negative behaviors is known as the strategy of behavior exchange. Stuart (1969) applied this notion in the first BCT by having spouses make a list of desired partner behaviors and agree on a corresponding list of reinforcement behaviors.

Therapists soon realized that negotiation was necessary if any controversial behaviors were to be a part of the exchange and began to encourage couples to negotiate and to make contracts for change with each other. Two different forms of contracting were used: contingency contracting and good faith contracts. In contingency contracting, partners listed the changes they desired and then negotiated with their spouses to arrive at an agreement for the desired behavioral change. The agreement specified a contingent relationship between each spouse's desired behaviors. If one partner did not keep his or her part of the agreement, then the other partner may refuse to comply with his or her part. For example, suppose the husband agreed to get home from work at a given time and the wife agreed to go for a walk each night. If the husband was able to get home at the scheduled time that night, then the wife was obligated to go for a walk. Additionally, if the wife went on a walk one night, then the husband was obligated to get home from work the next day by the specified time. If either spouse did not fulfill his or her end of the bargain, then the other was freed from their responsibility under the agreement until the original offending spouse behaved in accordance with the contract. In good faith contracts, on the other hand, each spouse agreed to change his or her specified behaviors independent of the other partner's behaviors. Two contracts were made, one for the husband and one for the wife. Reinforcing behaviors were also a component of good faith contracts. There was a reward behavior built in to the good faith contract that was intended to reinforce successful behavioral change, but the reward was not the behavior under negotiation. In our example above, the husband might get 15 minutes alone with his newspaper if he came home on time while the wife might get a special night out with her friends once she had done five walks with her husband. The major difference between the two types of contracts is that in good faith contracts, each partner is responsible for changing his or her behavior regardless of how his or her partner behaves.

As is implied by the use of reinforcement in both contingency contracting and good faith contracting, BCT views individual partner's behaviors not as existing in a vacuum but rather as being inextricably intertwined, with each partner's behaviors simultaneously affecting and being altered by the other spouse's behaviors. BCT considers the antecedents of behaviors and the consequences of behaviors, in addition to the behaviors themselves, as a very important part of understanding the way that spouses behave. From a BCT perspective, it would be impossible to create maximally effective behavioral change without understanding what precedes the behavior and what happens after it is exhibited. However, often the important antecedents and consequences for each spouse's behavior are the other partner's behaviors, so BCT views partners as operating within a reciprocal, causal, behavioral exchange system.

In addition to focusing on behavior exchange, BCT also places a heavy emphasis on teaching couples the skills they need to communicate effectively. The importance of effective communication skills was first emphasized by Liberman in the early 1970s. Employing observational learning concepts from social learning theory, Liberman (1970) used role rehearsal and the modeling of alternative communication patterns in his work with distressed couples. Early observational studies showed the importance of communication patterns in finding frequent, highly negative interaction patterns that distinguished distressed couples from satisfied couples (Gottman, Markman, & Notarius, 1977). Coercion emerged as a pattern of interaction that is frequent in distressed relationships and particularly destructive to marital satisfaction.

Coercion is the use of aversive techniques, such as nagging or yelling, by one spouse to get the other partner to make a change in behavior. In a typical coercive interaction, both partners are reinforced for their behavior. The coercer is reinforced by getting what he or she wants and the coerced partner is reinforced since he or she is no longer subject to the abrasive interaction. There are aspects of coercion that make it highly resistant to efforts to change. In coercion, individuals are reinforced in an intermittent fashion. Because the coercer is only sometimes able to achieve the desired behavioral change, persistence on the part of the coercer is rewarded. Additionally, the abrasive techniques used by coercers often increase in intensity as the coerced partner develops a tolerance to the abrasion over time. These aspects of coercion can result in abrasive behavior occurring at a higher intensity and lasting for a longer period of time the more a couple engages in it.

One very common example of coercion is the demand/withdraw pattern. It occurs when one spouse actively pursues the other for change while the other partner simultaneous backs away from the pursuer. Typically wives are in the demanding role while husbands are in the withdrawing role (Christensen & Heavey, 1990). As in coercion, the demander typically increases the intensity and duration of his or her requests in an attempt to get the withdrawer to give in and change. The withdrawer may respond to increases in the intensity and duration of demanding behaviors by going to greater lengths to withdraw from the demander. As a result, spouses can become polarized with each partner becoming more extreme in their behaviors in an attempt to create or to resist change. However, partners persist in their roles because each gets occasionally reinforced for their efforts in that the withdrawer may sometimes escape from demands and the demander may sometimes get a response.

BCT assumes that couples engage in negative interaction patterns, such as coercion and its example demand/withdraw, because they lack the necessary communication skills to effectively ask for change. Based on this assumption, it is possible to improve the communication of couples by teaching them the skills that they lack. BCT uses didactic instruction, modeling, and monitored rehearsal to teach communication skills that are assumed to be adaptive for all couples. Both speaking and listening skills are taught. Speaker skills include paraphrasing, asking open-ended questions, behavioral pinpointing, speaking subjectively (for example, using words that convey feelings), speaking about the partner and the relationship, and using tact and timing. Skills for the listener include demonstrating acceptance, adopting the speaker's perspective, and responding empathically and respectfully (Epstein & Baucom, 2002).

Studies demonstrated the effectiveness of both behavioral exchange and communication skills training. In an important early study, couples were randomly assigned to one of three treatment conditions: behavior exchange, communication skills training, or both behavior exchange and communication skills training. Results showed that although all three conditions led to greater satisfaction in spouses, the combination of behavioral exchange and communication skills training worked better than either alone (Jacobson, 1984). Researchers thought that these results suggested that the improvement in reported satisfaction was being driven by improvements in communication skills. This interpretation may have been in error. For many of the couples who were able to learn and effectively engage in the communication skills taught in therapy, the improvements in communication skills were not statistically related to increases in marital satisfaction (Iverson & Baucom, 1990). Results from other studies also made BCT researchers question some of their assumptions about the mechanisms of change in BCT. When BCT was compared to nonbehaviorally oriented couples therapies, results indicated that nonbehaviorally oriented couples therapies were often as efficacious as BCT (Baucom, Shoham, Mueser, Daiuto, & Stickle, 1998), even though they did not focus on training communication skills. Additionally, researchers were able to identify five couple characteristics that predicted the effectiveness of BCT: younger age, more commitment to the relationship, more emotional engagement in the relationship, less traditional roles in the relationship, and a shared sense of what the relationship would ideally look like. BCT researchers interpreted these results to mean that there was something missing from the strategies and techniques that they were currently using.

Some researchers responded to these findings by giving increasing attention to the cognitive factors that contribute to marital distress. These researchers went on to found the field of cognitive–behavioral couples therapy (CBCT). CBCT views marital distress as resulting not simply from a lack of positive reinforcers and a lack of communication skills but rather as the result of inappropriate information processing stemming from extreme or distorted interpretations of relationship events and/or unreasonable expectations of how a relationship should work. A major goal of the CBCT therapist is to help spouses become aware of their information processing errors and extreme standards, assuming that once partners are aware of their information processing errors and extreme relationship standards, positive changes in behaviors will result (Epstein & Baucom, 2002).

Numerous studies provided empirical support for CBCT, with findings indicating that CBCT successfully improved the level of relationship satisfaction for many couples (Baucom et al., 1998). However, the existence of a number of notable limitations in the early versions of CBCT caused researchers and clinicians to continue the evolution of CBCT. First, CBCT largely ignored broader patterns and core themes of couples' relationships, instead opting to focus on discrete and specific behaviors. Second, there was a major focus in CBCT on creating deliberate change. Third, CBCT largely ignored the contribution of environmental factors to relationship distress. Fourth, an overwhelming focus of CBCT was on reducing the negative behaviors while much less attention was given to increasing the positive behaviors.

Recent revisions of CBCT have incorporated additional theoretical approaches to treating couples in attempting to address the shortcomings listed above. Epstein and Baucom's (2002) Enhanced Cognitive Behavioral Couples Therapy (ECBCT) utilizes a systems perspective in combining elements from CBCT, emotionally focused couples therapy, and insight-oriented couples therapy in providing a much broader perspective on relationship functioning by considering not only cognitions and discrete behaviors but also including broader patterns and core themes, the developmental stage of the relationship, the role of the environment, and the role of the individual in his or her adaptation to the model of couple functioning. In ECBCT, the developmental stage of a relationship contributes both protective factors and stressors to the relationship. For example, older couples are often more financially solvent but are also less able to accommodate change into their relationship. Similarly, the environment can contribute both positively and negatively to a relationship by providing coping resources as well as additional stressors. For example, living in a certain area may allow a couple to be closer to their families but it may also be in a place where there are not many job opportunities for one of the spouses. Greater attention is also given to the role of the individual in ECBCT. ECBCT is concerned not only with the role that individual factors, such as motives, personality, and individual psychopathology, play in relationship functioning, but also with helping the individual to achieve self-actualization by using the relationship as a vehicle for growth. ECBCT also considers it important not only to reduce the frequency of negative behaviors and cognitions but also to increase the frequency of positive behaviors and cognitions. In terms of actual intervention techniques, ECBCT maintains the original focus on cognitive restructuring and behavioral change from earlier versions of CBCT but does so using the broader systems perspective described above. Due to the recentness of the development of ECBCT, there is currently no empirical evidence available for the effectiveness of ECBCT.

Halford, Sanders, and Behren's (1994) Self-Regulation Couples Therapy (SRCT) attempts to empower spouses by teaching them to identify problems and to create change within themselves in order to enhance their satisfaction with their relationship. The explicit behavior exchange strategies of traditional CBCT are not a major focus of SRCT. Rather, spouses learn to change themselves instead of relying on a therapist to initiate change. The major role of the SRCT therapist is to help spouses determine what it is that they want to change and to teach spouses ways of handling the problems once they are identified. There are three major ways that SRCT encourages couples to deal with problems: finding a new way to communicate the problem to the spouse, altering personal responses to the problematic behaviors so that it is less personally distressing, and trying to satisfy unmet needs in a new way. Additionally, much less time is spent on communication skills training in SRCT than is spent in traditional CBCT. Instead, SRCT therapists guide spouses in identifying strengths and weaknesses in their communication skills and in setting personal goals for change.

Preliminary evaluations of SRCT suggest that it is a promising alternative to traditional CBCT. In a study comparing the effectiveness of SRCT to that of CBCT, the two therapies were found to produce similar levels of improvement in couple functioning. It is important to note that couples receiving SRCT in this study received an average of 3 sessions while couples receiving CBCT received an average of 15 sessions (Halford, Osgarby, & Kelly, 1996). Though more evaluation of SRCT is needed, it appears that it creates comparable levels of change in relationship functioning to CBCT and may do so in many fewer sessions.

Jacobson and Christensen (1996) incorporate the idea of emotional acceptance as a major tenant of Integrative Behavioral Couples Therapy (IBCT). They see an increased ability to accommodate or willingness to change as the common thread that runs through the five factors that determined better successful response to BCT: younger age, greater commitment to the relationship, more emotional engagement, more successfully egalitarian, and similar ideas of ideal relationship. In BCT, there was no method for helping couples learn a greater willingness to change if that was not already part of their relationship. Additionally, IBCT presumes that the changes needed to address some problems are at best extremely difficult and at worst simply impossible. IBCT suggests instead that it is possible to use the idea of acceptance to alter what was once a source of distress into a vehicle for increased intimacy and closeness, even if some of the desired changes never take place.

IBCT retains the behavioral exchange strategies and communication skills training from earlier versions of CBCT but also uses an entirely new class of techniques intended to enhance intimacy and relationship functioning through the use of acceptance. Acceptance can be used to enhance intimacy through empathic joining around a problem and unified detachment. Empathic joining around a problem counteracts blame by encouraging empathy and compassion through reformulating a problem such that both spouses are able to experience a previously frustrating problem as understandable and to help them communicate that understanding to one another. Unified detachment encourages couples to step back from their problems and to view the problem as an "it" by engaging in a detailed description of the problematic sequence. This process allows couples to become aware of their problematic patterns and themes while also providing an opportunity for insight into how problematic interactions are interrelated. IBCT also seeks to build tolerance by pointing out the positive features of negative behavior, role-playing negative behavior in the therapy session, faking negative behavior at home, and encouraging greater self-care. Some of these strategies for promoting acceptance are similar to the strategies of emotionally focused and strategic family therapies.

In an initial study comparing IBCT to BCT (Jacobson, Christensen, Prince, Cordova, & Eldridge, 2000) and in an ongoing clinical trial (Christensen et al., 2004), IBCT appears to result in as much positive relationship change as BCT does, though there are some important differences to note in how the change appears to occur (Christensen et al., 2004). The change in satisfaction by BCT couples was rapid early on in therapy and then plateaued, while the change in IBCT couples was slower but steady throughout the course of treatment. Early follow-up results suggest that IBCT couples showed greater continuing improvement than BCT couples.

As is indicated by the underlying theories and assumptions of IBCT, SRCT, and ECBCT, cognitive–behavioral couples therapy is headed toward an integrative approach where additionally complex formulations are used to understand why particular behaviors are occurring and what their impact on a relationship is. CBCT's original focus on altering cognitive experience and on creating behavior exchange has broadened to include a focus on emotion. Efforts are also being made to make CBCT therapies more effective for a wider spectrum of couples in fewer numbers of sessions. Finally, researchers and theorists are attempting to increase the duration of the impact of CBCT. Through continued evolution, CBCT may be able to produce longer-lasting change for a wider spectrum of couples with a greater diversity of problems.

See also: Couple and family therapy, Couples therapy—substance abuse

REFERENCES

Baucom, D., Shoham, V., Mueser, K., Daiuto, A., & Stickle, T. (1998). Empirically supported couples and family therapies for adult problems. *Journal of Consulting and Clinical Psychology, 66*, 53–88.

Christensen, A., Atkins, D., Berns, S., Wheeler, J., Baucom, D. H., & Simpson, L. (2004). Traditional versus integrative behavioral couple therapy for significantly and chronically distressed married couples. *Journal of Consulting and Clinical Psychology, 72*, 176–191.

Christensen, A., & Heavey, C. (1990). Gender and social structure in the demand/withdraw pattern of marital interaction. *Journal of Personality and Social Psychology, 59*, 73–81.

Epstein, N., & Baucom, D. (2002). *Enhanced cognitive–behavioral therapy for couples: A contextual approach*. Washington, DC: American Psychological Association.

Gottman, J., Markman, H., & Notarius, C. (1977). The topography of marital conflict: A sequential analysis of verbal and nonverbal behavior. *Journal of Marriage and the Family, 39*, 461–477.

Halford, K., Osgarby, S., & Kelly, A. (1996). Brief behavioral couples therapy: A preliminary evaluation. *Behavioural and Cognitive Psychotherapy, 25*, 263–273.

Halford, K., Sanders, M., & Behren, J. (1994). Self-regulation in behavioral couples therapy. *Behavior Therapy, 25*, 431–452.

Iverson, A., & Baucom, D. (1990). Behavioral marital therapy outcomes: Alternative interpretations of the data. *Behavior Therapy, 21*, 129–138.

Jacobson, N. (1984). A component analysis of behavioral marital therapy: The relative effectiveness of behavior exchange and problem solving training. *Journal of Consulting and Clinical Psychology, 52*, 295–305.

Jacobson, N., & Christensen, A. (1996). *Integrative couple therapy: Promoting acceptance and change*. New York: Norton.

Jacobson, N. S., Christensen, A., Prince, S. E., Cordova, J., & Eldridge, K. (2000). Integrative Behavioral Couple Therapy: An acceptance-based, promising new treatment for couple discord. *Journal of Consulting and Clinical Psychology, 68*(2), 351–355.

Liberman, R. (1970). Behavioral approaches to family and couples therapy. *American Journal of Orthopsychiatry, 40*, 106–118.

Stuart, R. (1969). Operant-interpersonal treatment for marital discord. *Journal of Consulting and Clinical Psychology, 33*, 675–682.

Couples Therapy—Substance Abuse*

Timothy J. O'Farrell and William Fals-Stewart

Keywords: alcoholism, drug abuse, couples therapy, behavioral contracts, communication skills training

Although alcoholism and drug abuse have been historically viewed as individual problems best treated on an individual basis, there has been a growing recognition over the last three decades that couple and family relationship factors often play a crucial role in the maintenance of substance misuse. The relationship between substance abuse and couple relationship problems is not unidirectional, with one consistently causing the other, but rather each can serve as a precursor to the other, creating a vicious cycle from which couples that include a partner who abuses drugs or alcohol often have difficulty escaping.

Viewed from a couple perspective, there are several antecedent conditions and reinforcing consequences of substance use. Poor communication and problem-solving, arguing, financial stressors, and nagging are common antecedents to substance use and abuse. When a non-substance-abusing spouse engages in caretaking behaviors during or after episodes of drinking or drug taking, this can inadvertently reinforce continued substance-using behavior. Often spouses ignore rather than reinforce abstinence because they are understandably resentful over past transgressions and skeptical of short-lived changes.

A number of early pioneers (Nathan Azrin in 1973 and Allan Hedberg in 1974) studied behavioral couples therapy (BCT) that combined a behavioral contract to reward abstinence and communication and problem-solving training to reduce relationship problems among male alcoholic patients and their wives. A second wave of researchers (Timothy O'Farrell in 1985 and Barbara McCrady in 1986) provided initial, well-controlled studies of BCT with alcoholism. More recently in 1996, William Fals-Stewart published the first study of BCT with primary drug abuse patients.

TREATMENT METHODS

The purpose of BCT is to build support for abstinence and to improve relationship functioning among married or cohabiting individuals seeking help for alcoholism or drug abuse. The BCT intervention for substance abuse is founded on two fundamental assumptions. First, family members, specifically spouses or other intimate partners, can reward abstinence. Second, reduction of relationship distress and conflict reduces a very significant set of powerful antecedents to substance use and relapse, thereby leading to improved substance use outcomes. See O'Farrell (1993) for more details.

Building Support for Abstinence with the Recovery Contract

The therapist, with extensive input from the partners, develops and has the partners enter into a daily Recovery Contract (also referred to as a Sobriety Contract). As part of the contract, partners agree to engage in a daily Sobriety Trust Discussion, in which the substance-abusing partner states his or her intent not to drink or use drugs that day (in the tradition of one day at a time from Alcoholics Anonymous). In turn, the nonsubstance-abusing partner verbally expresses positive support for the patient's efforts to remain sober. For substance-abusing patients who are medically cleared and willing, daily ingestion of medications designed to support abstinence (e.g., naltrexone, disulfiram), witnessed and verbally reinforced by the nonsubstance-abusing partner, is often a component of and occurs during the daily Sobriety Trust Discussion. The nonsubstance-abusing partner records the performance of the Sobriety Trust Discussion (and consumption of medication, if applicable) on a daily calendar provided by the therapist. As part of the Recovery Contract, both partners agree not to discuss past drinking or drug use or fears of future substance use when at home (i.e., between scheduled BCT sessions). This agreement reduces the likelihood of substance-related

* Preparation of this article was supported by grants to the first author from the National Institute on Alcohol Abuse and Alcoholism (K02AA0234) and to the second author from the National Institute on Drug Abuse (R01DA14402)), and by the Department of Veterans Affairs.

conflicts that can trigger relapses. Partners are asked to reserve such discussions for the BCT sessions, which can then be monitored and, if needed, mediated by the therapist. Many contracts also include specific provisions for partners' regular attendance at self-help meetings (e.g., Alcoholics Anonymous meetings, Al-Anon), which are also marked on the provided calendar during the course of treatment.

At the start of each BCT session, the therapist reviews the calendar to ascertain overall compliance with different components of the contract. The calendar provides an ongoing record of progress that is rewarded verbally by the therapist at each session. It also provides a visual (and temporal) record of problems with adherence that can be addressed each week. When possible, the partners perform behaviors that are aspects of their Recovery Contract (e.g., Sobriety Trust Discussion, consumption of abstinence-supporting medication) in each scheduled BCT session to highlight its importance and to allow the therapist to observe the behaviors of the partners, providing corrective feedback as needed.

Improving Couple Relationship Functioning

Through the use of standard couple-based behavioral assignments, BCT also seeks to increase positive feelings, shared activities, and constructive communication; these relationship factors are viewed as conducive to sobriety. *Catch Your Partner Doing Something Nice* has each of the partners notice and acknowledge one pleasing behavior performed by their mate each day. In the *Caring Day* assignment, each partner plans ahead to surprise his or her significant other with a day when he or she does some special things to show their caring. Planning and engaging in mutually agreed-upon *Shared Rewarding Activities* is important because many substance abusers' families have ceased engaging in shared pleasing activities; participating in such activities has been associated with positive recovery outcomes. Each activity must involve both partners, either as a couple only or with their children or other adults—and can be performed at or away from home. Teaching *Communication Skills* (e.g., paraphrasing, empathizing, validating) can help the substance-abusing patient and his or her partner better address stressors in their relationship and in their lives as they arise, which also is viewed as reducing the risk of relapse.

Relapse Prevention and Maintenance

Relapse prevention planning occurs in the final stages of BCT. At the end of weekly BCT sessions, each couple completes a *Continuing Recovery Plan*. This written plan provides an overview of the couple's ongoing post-BCT activities to promote stable sobriety (e.g., continuation of a daily Sobriety Trust Discussion, attending self-help support meetings). It also has contingency plans if relapses occur (e.g., recontacting the therapist, reengaging in self-help support meetings, contacting a sponsor).

EMPIRICAL BASIS FOR BCT

Meta-analytic reviews of randomized studies show more abstinence with family-involved treatment than with individual treatment in drug abuse (Stanton & Shadish, 1997) and in alcoholism (O'Farrell & Fals-Stewart, 2001). Overall the effect size favoring family-involved treatments over individual-based treatments was classified as a medium-size effect. BCT is the family therapy method with the strongest research support for its effectiveness in substance abuse (Epstein & McCrady, 1998). *Research shows that BCT produces greater abstinence and better relationship functioning than typical individual-based treatment and reduces social costs, domestic violence, and emotional problems of the couple's children.* Details of the following studies are provided elsewhere (O'Farrell & Fals-Stewart, 2000, 2002, 2003).

Primary Clinical Outcomes: Abstinence and Relationship Functioning

A series of 14 studies have compared substance abuse and relationship outcomes for substance-abusing patients treated with BCT or individual counseling. Outcomes have been measured at 6-month follow-up in earlier studies and at 12–24 months posttreatment in more recent studies. The studies show a fairly consistent pattern of more abstinence and fewer substance-related problems, happier relationships, and lower risk of couple separation and divorce for substance-abusing patients who receive BCT than for patients who receive only more typical individual-based treatment. These results come from studies with mostly male alcoholic and drug-abusing patients and one study with female drug-abusing patients.

Social Cost Outcomes and Benefit-to-Cost Ratio

Three BCT studies (two in alcoholism and one in drug abuse) have examined social costs for substance abuse-related health care, criminal justice system use for substance-related crimes, and income from illegal sources and public assistance. The average social costs per case decreased substantially in the 1–2 years after as compared to the year before BCT, with cost savings averaging \$5000–\$6500 per case. Reduced social costs after BCT saved more than 5 times the cost of delivering BCT, producing a benefit-to-cost ratio greater than 5 : 1. Thus, for every dollar spent in delivering BCT, \$5.00 in social costs is saved. In addition,

BCT was more cost-effective when compared with individual treatment for drug abuse and when compared with interactional couples therapy for alcoholism.

Domestic Violence Outcomes

Two studies with male alcoholics found nearly identical results, indicating that male-to-female violence was significantly reduced in the first and second year after BCT and that it was nearly eliminated with abstinence. For example, in the year before BCT, 60% of alcoholic patients had been violent toward their female partner, five times the comparison sample rate of 12%. In the year after BCT, violence decreased significantly to 24% of the alcoholic sample but remained higher than the comparison group. Among remitted alcoholics after BCT, violence prevalence of 12% was identical to the comparison sample and less than half the rate among relapsed patients (30%).

Two studies showed that BCT reduced partner violence and couple conflicts better than individual treatment. Among male drug-abusing patients, the number reporting violence in the year after treatment was significantly lower for BCT than for individual treatment. Among male alcoholic patients, those who participated in BCT reported less frequent use of maladaptive responses to conflict (e.g., yelling, name-calling, threatening to hit, hitting) during treatment than those who received individual treatment.

Impact of BCT on the Children of Couples Undergoing BCT

Two studies (one in alcoholism, one in drug abuse) examined whether BCT for a substance-abusing parent also has beneficial effects for the children in the family. Results were the same for children of male alcoholic and male drug-abusing fathers. BCT improved children's functioning in the year after the parents' treatment more than did individual-based treatment or couple psychoeducation. Only BCT showed reduction in the number of children with clinically significant impairment.

Integrating BCT with Recovery-Related Medication

BCT has been used to increase compliance with a recovery-related medication. Among male opioid patients taking naltrexone, BCT patients, compared with their individually treated counterparts, had better naltrexone compliance, greater abstinence, and fewer substance-related problems. Among HIV-positive drug abusers in an outpatient drug abuse treatment program, BCT produced better compliance with HIV medications than did treatment as usual. BCT also has improved compliance with pharmacotherapy in studies of disulfiram for alcoholic patients and in an ongoing pilot study of naltrexone with alcoholics.

BCT with Family Members Other Than Spouses

Most BCT studies have examined traditional couples. However, some recent studies have expanded BCT to include family members other than spouses. These studies have targeted increased medication compliance as just described. For example, in the study of BCT and naltrexone with opioid patients, family members taking part were spouses (66%), parents (25%), and siblings (9%). In the study of BCT and HIV medications among HIV-positive drug abusers, significant others who took part were: a parent or sibling (67%), a homosexual (12%) or heterosexual (9%) partner, or a roommate (12%).

CONTRAINDICATIONS FOR BCT

A few contraindications for BCT should be considered. The first is current psychosis for either the alcoholic patient or the family member. The second is an acute risk of severe family violence with a potential for serious injury or death. Cases with less severe forms of family violence can be treated successfully in BCT. In such cases, conflict containment is an explicit goal of the therapy from the outset, and you will need to take specific steps to avoid violence (for more details see O'Farrell & Murphy, 2002). Third, couples for which there is a court-issued restraining order for the spouses not to have contact with each other should not be seen together in therapy until the restraining order is lifted or modified to allow contact in counseling. Finally, if the spouse also has a current alcohol or drug problem, BCT may not be effective. In the past, we have often taken the stance that if both members of a couple have a substance use problem, then we will not treat them together unless one member of the couple has been abstinent for at least 90 days. However, in a recent project we successfully treated over 20 couples where both the male and female partner had a current alcoholism problem. If both members of the couple want to stop drinking or if this mutual decision to change can be reached in the first few sessions, then BCT may be workable.

FUTURE DIRECTIONS FOR BCT

In terms of future directions, we do need more research on BCT, to replicate and extend the most recent advances, especially for women patients and broader family constellations. Research on BCT for couples in which both the male and female member have a current substance use problem is particularly needed because prior BCT studies have not addressed this difficult clinical challenge. Finally, we need technology transfer so that patients and their families can benefit from what we have already learned about BCT for alcoholism and drug abuse.

See also: Addictive behavior—substance abuse, Couple and family therapy, Relapse prevention

REFERENCES

Epstein, E. E., & McCrady, B. S. (1998). Behavioral couples treatment of alcohol and drug use disorders: Current status and innovations. *Clinical Psychology Review*, *18*, 689–711.

O'Farrell, T. J. (Ed.). (1993). *Treating alcohol problems: Marital and family interventions*. New York: Guilford Press.

O'Farrell, T. J., & Fals-Stewart, W. (2000). Behavioral couples therapy for alcoholism and drug abuse. *Journal of Substance Abuse Treatment*, *18*, 51–54.

O'Farrell, T. J., & Fals-Stewart, W. (2001). Family-involved alcoholism treatment: An update. In M. Galanter (Ed.), *Recent developments in alcoholism: Vol. 15. Services research in the era of managed care* (pp. 329–356). New York: Plenum Press.

O'Farrell, T. J., & Fals-Stewart, W. (2002). Behavioral couple and family therapy with substance abusing patients. *Current Psychiatry Reports*, *4*, 371–376.

O'Farrell, T. J., & Fals-Stewart, W. (2003). Marital and family therapy. In R. Hester & W. R. Miller (Eds.), *Handbook of alcoholism treatment approaches* (3rd ed., pp. 188–212). Needham Heights, MA: Allyn & Bacon.

O'Farrell, T. J., & Murphy, C. M. (2002). Behavioral couples therapy for alcoholism and drug abuse: Encountering the problem of domestic violence. In C. Wekerle & A. M. Wall (Eds.), *The violence and addiction equation: Theoretical and clinical issues in substance abuse and relationship violence* (pp. 293–303). New York: Brunner-Routledge.

Stanton, M. D., & Shadish, W. R. (1997). Outcome, attrition, and family-couple treatment for drug abuse: A meta-analysis and review of the controlled, comparative studies. *Psychological Bulletin*, *122*, 170–191.

Crisis Intervention

Gina M. Fusco

Keywords: crisis, crisis intervention, trauma, psychological distress

The world's recent traumatic events have introduced the term *crisis* not only to working clinicians but also to the mass public. Crisis conjures not only images related to individuals experiencing psychological distress, but also images related to the broadly based and broad impact of the traumatic events of September 11th, war, and terrorism. Society has become more knowledgeable about trauma, stress reactions, and crisis intervention. As a means of responding to the many varying types of crises that occur, specific therapeutic approaches to manage crisis and stress are a necessary and integral aspect of general psychotherapy practice.

Slaiku (1990) presents a comprehensive definition of crisis that outlines key areas of potential intervention. Slaiku writes that crisis is "a temporary state of upset and disorganization, characterized chiefly by an individual's inability to cope with a particular situation using customary methods of problem-solving, and by the potential for a radically positive or negative outcome" (p. 15). Following Freeman and Dattilio's (2000) conceptualization of Slaiku's definition, areas of intervention can be clearly defined by focusing on these specific areas. First, crisis is a *temporary* or transient state. However, for some individuals, managing "brushfires" or being crisis-prone (Freeman & Fusco, 2000) is a way of life. A second aspect of the definition refers to the patient responding to a crisis with *upset*. Upset can be broadened to include anxiety and depressive reactions, or the more severe forms of disorganization, such as a brief reactive psychosis. Disorganization can refer to cognitive, behavioral, or emotional realms. Individuals approach problems in consistent and predictable patterns. During a crisis, an individual's *inability to cope* refers to the failure of one's usual coping repertoire to manage the situation. Their homeostasis has been disrupted, which may cause usual *problem-solving skills* to be compromised. Difficulty processing potential options does not occur as readily, and cognitive rigidity prevents alternative strategies of coping and managing with the crisis. Finally, crisis situations can create the potential for *radical positive or negative outcomes*. Negative losses associated with crisis are substantial and include threats of loss of life, loved ones, property, and health. Psychologically, in the face of crisis, one may experience a loss of self-esteem, self-efficacy, or deference to others. Although crisis is more often associated with negative outcomes, positive outcomes can also occur. Positive outcomes can result from an individual learning to approach problems in a new and different way, discovering new support systems both internally and externally, learning about one's unique strengths, and perhaps experiencing new existential challenges. The clinician, aware of this very fundamental aspect of a crisis situation, can foster a patient's positive experience by acknowledging the depth and potential for a positive outcome. By providing a safe, holding environment, the individual can explore and emotionally process the crisis in a supportive, empathic way.

Freeman and Fusco (2000) differentiate between two types patients who experience crisis. The first type are patients who have experienced a traumatic life circumstance or a man-made or natural disaster. The second type is the patient for whom awakening to everyday life is fraught with the potential for crisis, or the crisis-prone patient. Basic coping strategies are compromised as a result of longstanding personality patterns. As conceptualized by Millon and Davis (2000), one's personality represents the immune system to manage life's stressors. If one has experienced ongoing upset, trauma, or turmoil, basic coping strategies are not formed as an intrinsic aspect of the personality. The long-term result is that one becomes prone to experiencing crises and lacks problem-solving skills. Both patient types can benefit from crisis intervention strategies based on a cognitive–behavioral approach.

DIAGNOSTIC CONSIDERATIONS

Comprehensive evaluation of a patient in crisis includes considering diagnoses commensurate with acute stress reactions and posttraumatic stress diagnoses. The DMS-IV-TR (APA, 2000) identifies several diagnoses that include as a criterion exposure to a stressor. These include adjustment disorders, acute stress disorder (ASD), posttraumatic stress disorder (PTSD), and brief reactive psychosis. Meeting the criteria for any of these disorders requires the clinician to consider ongoing treatment. Adjustment disorders present the least impairment along the continuum and include varying types of reactions (with depression, anxiety, mixed disturbance, and so on). ASD requires the patient to have experienced, witnessed, or confronted an intense stressor that involved actual or threatened death or serious injury, or even a threat of the physical integrity of the self or others. Additionally, three main clusters of symptoms must be present. These include the reexperiencing of the event (e.g., dreams, flashbacks), avoidance (e.g., things associated with the trauma, "psychic numbing"), and hyperarousal (e.g., hypervigilance, anxiety symptoms). ASD differs from PTSD in terms of time, onset, and duration of symptoms. The DSM-IV-TR (APA, 2000) defines that ASD symptoms occur within 2 days of the stressor but no longer than 4 weeks. If symptoms persist beyond 4 weeks, the diagnosis of PTSD should be considered. Interventions need to assist the patient to manage the reexperiencing of the event (coping with flashbacks, grounding), avoidance (graded exposure, exposure techniques), and hypervigilance (anxiety-reduction techniques, relaxation).

CRISIS INTERVENTION

Crisis intervention treatment involves identifying relevant automatic thoughts and discerning and manifesting relative schemas. This assists the therapist in examining the advantages and disadvantages to maintaining schemas, and introduces ways to dispute/alter held schemas (through assimilation and accommodation). Overall the immediate goals of cognitive–behavioral therapy (CBT) with individuals in crisis include evaluation and assessment of the immediacy of the crisis situation, assessment of the individual's coping repertoire to deal with the crisis (defined by their relevant cognitive processes), and the generation of options of thought, perception, and behavior (includes problem-solving skills). Specifically, the following details the Five Steps of Crisis Intervention with CBT (Freeman & Dattilio, 1990).

I. Development of Relationship with the Patient and a Building of Rapport

Setting of agenda includes introductions, and defining what overall goals are in the initial assessment, and the possibility of including family members if necessary. The structure of agenda setting is essential in crisis work. Rather than having the therapy session meander, the therapist must work with the patient to set an agenda for the session, help to focus the therapy work, and make better use of time, energy, and available skills.

Utilize nonjudgmental attitude throughout, and express empathy through active listening and empathic reframing.

Use of metaphors conveys understanding and helps to build rapport (black holes, swallowed up, towel wringing, telescope filter).

Mirror language, voice, and body communications to assist in building rapport.

Maintain good eye contact with the patient.

Monitor reactions to include not conveying surprise, or disgust.

Remain consistent with style (voice inflections, rate of speech).

Setting limits establishes and models structure.

Weave history taking while remaining in the present.

II. Initial Evaluation of Severity of Crisis Situation

During this phase of intervention, specific evaluation strategies must not only determine the overall conceptualization of the crisis, but also evaluate the safety risk of the patient and others. The reader is referred to Reinecke (2000) for comprehensive evaluation strategies for high-risk patients.

Assessing Risk to Self and Others. The assessment of risk to self and others is a complicated, necessary, and often difficult evaluation process. The therapist directly elicits information from the patient to assist in defining the overall level of treatment intervention that will ensure the safety and physical integrity of the patient and others. Suicidal and homicidal behavior, threats, or ideation that is undiminished will require a change in treatment plan to include the potential for hospitalization, family sessions, psychiatric consultation, emergency services intervention, and commitment (Freeman & Fusco, 2004). Key to successful evaluation of a suicidal or homicidal patient is the understanding that these thoughts can exist at many different levels.

Thoughts: Refers to individuals experiencing fleeting thoughts of suicide or homicide. These are relatively harmless and do not include any intent.

Ideation: Refers to actual *ideas* about harming oneself or others. They are more formed ideas rather than fleeting thoughts. How frequent are the thoughts? How intense?

Cognitive urge: Indicates that the patient is experiencing thoughts to continue the process of planning or moving forward in momentum to harm themselves or others. Thoughts such as "how should I go about figuring out how to do this?" may occur.

Plan: Has the patient established a plan as to how they may harm themselves or someone else? What are the specifics involved with the plan? Does it involve others? Does the patient have access to the plan? If the patient has identified a plan, it is essential to determine and assess the actual lethality of the plan (Roberts, 1994). Brent (1987) demonstrated a strong relationship between the medical lethality of the plan chosen and suicide intent. Roberts (1994) writes that in general those plans considered to be more lethal include concrete, specific, and dangerous methods. Additionally, the author states that "suicidal plans generally reveal the relative risk in that the degree of intent is typically related to the lethality of the potential method (e.g., using a gun or hanging implies higher intent whereas overdosing or cutting implies lower intent" (Roberts, 1994, p. 70). This, however, is not a blanket statement, as all suicidal plans have the potential to be lethal and should be considered as such.

Behavioral urge: Behavioral urges occur when the patient actually moves from the cognitive realm into the actual behavioral realm. The person may begin procuring items to complete their plan. A behavioral urge may include the patient holding and considering their means to complete their plan (e.g., picking up a bottle of pills and considering their effects).

Intent: Refers to whether one has the actual intention to die or harm others. Have they identified that they actually intend to die or kill someone else? Is the patient experiencing thoughts of hopelessness, a key predictor of suicide? (Beck & Weishaar, 1986).

Attempt/gesture: Has the patient made an attempt to kill themselves or someone else? What was the result of the attempt? What are the patient's thoughts concerning surviving the attempt? Gestures can be construed either an episode of self-injury, or a "practice" run to plan a larger attempt.

Second attempt: Patients who have made a prior attempt are more likely to make a second attempt (Reinecke, 2000).

Impulsivity: At any point along the continuum, if the patient has a history of impulsivity, which may or may not include substance abuse, the patient may immediately progress to actually making an attempt. By its nature, impulsivity increases the risk one may commit an act of harm. Create an impulse management program to attempt to decrease impulsivity.

Risk factors: Several risk factors exist that may increase the likelihood of harm and include social, psychiatric, demographic, and psychological factors (see Reinecke, 2000). Assist the patient in identifying the specific problem he or she is having. This is achieved by providing a structured and reframed synopsis of dilemma(s). As a result of being in crisis, confusion and disorganization often render patients unable to actually define their problem. Assist the patient to focus on the specific areas that create problems as opposed to attempting to deal with the actual symptoms created by the distress of the crisis (anxiety and depression). A directive approach identifying specific problems creates fundamental components of the treatment plan by outlining and identifying options. An actual problem list may help with this.

III. Help the Patient Assess and Mobilize His or Her Strengths and Resources

Perception of Risk and Resources. To assist in identifying the patient's automatic thoughts and underlying schema related to the crises he or she is experiencing, and the available resources to cope with the crisis, it is helpful to conceptualize the crisis as a ratio. A crisis results when one's perception of the risk is more powerful or threatening than the perception of his or her resources. By challenging cognitive distortions that may overestimate the risk and underestimate their resources, the patient's perception of the crisis may then become less overwhelming and manageable.

Identify support networks: friends, family, church, EAP, employees, support groups, 12-step groups, sponsors, hotlines.

Bring support network into sessions. If possible and if the patient agrees (if emergency, no waiver needed), bring a support network into the initial evaluation to activate or challenge held beliefs. For example, if the patient's schema includes themes that he or she is incapable of handling a crisis, a family member may assist in challenging this belief.

Assist patients to identify their own internal resources and strengths which they may be overlooking. The patient may readily identify held beliefs (I can't do anything right, no one loves me, or there's no hope). These beliefs offer data and information as to areas to challenge, dispute, or modify.

Call on previous challenges. Patients largely have been able to overcome stresses and challenges throughout their lives. Disputing evidence that enforces the belief that they can manage stress could include reminding the patient they conquered any one of life's challenges; maintained employment, completed a course, took care of children, were able to get themselves dressed or care for their home.

Imagine role model managing problem. Ask the patient to imagine how someone they respect and admire would handle the crisis.

IV. Therapist and Patient Must Work Together to Develop a Positive Plan of Action

This includes the therapist and patient working collaboratively and problem-solving.

Elicit commitment from patient to the plan of action. A plan of action can be written and given to the patient. Simple and clear steps to assist in managing the crisis are integral to successful use of the plan.

Bring supports in to provide backup and motivation to completion of plan. Supports may also be necessary for the plan to work.

Advocate for patient. This may include helping the patient secure ongoing outpatient treatment appointments, securing needed community resources, or assisting in meeting the patient's most basic of needs (e.g., housing, medical care, involving police).

Pros and cons. Problem-solving requires that the patient consider the pros and cons of crisis management and attempts new and different behaviors. Identifying current coping strategies should be followed by suggestions for alternative type strategies and the pros and cons of adapting to new options. What are the patient's automatic thoughts to each suggestion? What are the impediments?

Use of imagery. Ask patients to imagine completing their goals, overcoming the crisis, or seeing themselves attempting and completing stepwise tasks.

Be very concrete and specific in identifying the plan ahead and the related goals. The more specific, the more the patient can gain feedback that he or she actually accomplishing something.

V. Test Ideas and New Behaviors

Testing to determine whether the plan is working allows for adjustments to be made to the plan. Encouraging the patient to challenge held beliefs about the crisis and the means of coping with the crisis will require ongoing evaluation to ensure the most effective of interventions are being utilized.

Evaluate strategies. What strategies have been identified? Is the patient comfortable in using these strategies? Are they feeling competent? Are they feeling overwhelmed with the strategy chosen?

Redefine mechanisms if they are not appropriate. It is imperative that the expectations of patient and therapist be appropriate and realistic.

Continue to elicit feedback from the patient and his or her supports to assist in better definition of goals.

Elicit feedback from supports to help patient gather evidence that he or she is succeeding in their goals.

COGNITIVE DISTORTIONS AND TREATMENT INTERVENTIONS

Several cognitive and behavioral techniques can be used by the therapist to help to question both the distortions and the schema that underlie them. These techniques can be taught to patients to help them respond in more functional ways.

The goals in using behavioral techniques within the context of CBT are manifold. The first goal is to utilize direct behavioral strategies and techniques to test dysfunctional thoughts and behaviors. A second use of behavioral techniques is to practice new behaviors as homework. Certain behaviors can be practiced in the office, and then practiced at home. Homework can range from behaving and acting differently, practicing active listening, being verbally or physically affectionate, or doing things in a new way. Activity scheduling is especially useful for patients who have experienced a crisis and are feeling overwhelmed, the activity schedule can be used to plan more effective time use. Time can be allotted for both caring for oneself and completing necessary tasks.

Graded tasks assignments (GTA) involve a shaping procedure of small sequential steps that lead to the desired goal. By setting out a task and then arranging the necessary steps in a hierarchy, patients can be helped to make reasonable progress with a minimum of stress. As patients attempt each step, the therapist can be available for support and guidance. As the patient's coping skills may be compromised by the very crisis itself, small incremental goals will seem less overwhelming.

Relaxation training. The anxious patient can profit from relaxation training inasmuch as the anxiety response and the quieting relaxation response are mutually exclusive. The relaxation training can be taught in the office and then practiced by the patient for homework. Relaxation training can be particularly helpful in reducing the symptoms associated with hyperarousal.

Homework

Therapy, of necessity, needs to take place beyond the confines of the consulting room. Homework for the crisis patient may be limited to seeking follow-up outpatient therapy, or seeking needed services (housing and the like). For patients who may remain in brief psychotherapy after a crisis, it is important for the patient to understand that extension of the therapy work to the nontherapy hours allows for a greater therapeutic focus. The homework can be either cognitive or behavioral. It might involve having the patient complete an activity schedule (an excellent homework for the first session), complete several DTRs, or try new behaviors. The homework needs to evolve from the session material. The more meaningful and collaborative the homework, the greater is the likelihood of patient compliance with the therapeutic regimen.

SUMMARY

Imperative to crisis intervention is a thorough and complete evaluation, assessment, and triage of the patient. Throughout crisis intervention, challenging dysfunctional beliefs through a myriad of techniques creates options, alternatives, and ultimately fosters hope for the patient. The method of these challenges is an opportunity for the therapist to utilize creativity and apply the patient's strengths to the task set forth. By recognizing the potential for radical positive or negative outcomes to a crisis, the therapist can provide the necessary safety and impetus for patients to take control, adapt, and move forward in their lives.

REFERENCES

American Psychiatric Association. (2000). *Diagnostic and statistical manual of mental disorders* (4th ed., text rev.). Washington, DC: Author.

Beck, A., & Weishaar, M. (1986). *Cognitive therapy*. Philadelphia: Center for Cognitive Therapy.

Brent, D. (1987). Correlates of the medical lethality of suicide attempts in children and adolescents. *Journal of the American Academy of Child and Adolescent Psychiatry, 26*, 87–91.

Freeman, A., & Dattilio, F. (2000). Introduction. In F. Dattilio & A. Freeman (Eds.), *Cognitive–behavioral strategies in crisis intervention* (2nd ed., pp. 1–23). New York: Guilford Press.

Freeman, A., & Fusco, G. (2000). Treating high-arousal patients: Differentiating patients in crisis and crisis-prone patients. In F. Dattilio & A. Freeman (Eds.), *Cognitive–behavioral strategies in crisis intervention* (2nd ed., pp. 27–58). New York: Guilford Press.

Freeman, A., & Fusco, G. (2004). *Borderline personality disorder: A therapist's guide to taking control*. New York: Norton.

Millon, T., & Davis, R. (2000). *Personality disorders in modern life*. New York: Wiley.

Reinecke, M. (2000). Suicide and depression. In F. Dattilio & A. Freeman (Eds.), *Cognitive–behavioral strategies in crisis intervention* (2nd ed., pp. 84–125). New York: Guilford Press.

Roberts, A. (1994). *Crisis intervention handbook*. New York: Oxford University Press.

Slaiku, K. A. (1990). *Crisis intervention* (2nd ed.). Needham Heights, MA: Allyn & Bacon.

D

Depression–Adult

Mark J. Williams and Robin B. Jarrett

Keywords: depression, treatment, bipolar disorder, chronic depression, childhood depression

Cognitive–behavior therapy (CBT) is a general term for psychosocial interventions designed to change responding and to improve symptoms and quality of life. Historically, the distinctions among cognitive behavior *therapies* for depression concern what type of responding (*cognition* or *behavior*) is targeted to change mood. Behavioral conceptualizations emphasize changing mood by first altering overt behavior, or its environmental context, while cognitive conceptualizations assume that in order to change mood or emotion, one must change associated (antecedent or consequent) cognition. As the field of CBT for mood and other disorders has evolved, these theories have *merged* with less time devoted to discriminating cognition from behavior. Both approaches focus on stabilizing, increasing, or decreasing the *targets* patient and therapist predict will reduce current depressive symptoms, as well as reduce vulnerability for future depression. Gathering data is standard within CBT. Interventions are evaluated not only in randomized clinical trials but also within single case studies to evaluate the extent to which CBT *works* for a given patient. There is more than one type of CBT and more than one type of depression. Some of the best known and studied are described below.

UNIPOLAR DEPRESSION

Adult Cognitive Therapy (CT)

Cognitive Therapy for Depression (Beck, Rush, Shaw, & Emery, 1979) is an active, structured, time-limited, problem-oriented therapy to reduce depressive symptoms by altering negative views of self, world, and future (the *cognitive triad*). Early sessions focus on educating patients about depression and the cognitive model as well as identifying and testing negative automatic thoughts (i.e., thoughts correlated with negative mood). Thoughts are then evaluated through cognitive (logical analysis) and behavioral (hypothesis testing) tasks. Collaboratively, the patient and therapist determine whether the evidence supports the negative thoughts. Patients learn to identify logical errors in their thinking and consider alternative views. Effective treatment of major depressive disorder may include acute, and when necessary, continuation, and maintenance phase therapies as discussed below.

The primary goals of acute-phase CT (A-CT) are to reduce or eliminate depressive symptoms and acquire skills that facilitate remission. Researchers have consistently found A-CT to be more effective than minimal treatment control conditions and as effective as pharmacotherapy and other depression-specific psychotherapies in treating adult outpatients with mild to moderate depression (Depression Guideline Panel, 1993; Wampold, Minami, Baskin, & Callen, 2002). Although less studied, CT shows promise when adapted for use in primary (Schulberg, Katon, Simon, & Rush, 1998), inpatient (Stuart, Wright, Thase, & Beck, 1997), and group settings (DeRubeis & Crits-Christoph, 1998).

The effectiveness of A-CT for outpatient adults with severe major depressive disorder (Hamilton Rating Scale for

Depression [HRSD] > 19) is a point of contention in the treatment community. Based on the controversial findings from the first placebo-controlled trial (Elkin et al., 1989, 1995), the Depression Guideline Panel (1993) recommended pharmacotherapy as the preferred treatment for severe depression. In contrast, previous controlled trials (DeRubeis, Gelfand, Tang, & Simons, 1999) and a recently completed placebo-controlled trial (DeRubeis, Hollon, Amsterdam, & Shelton, 2001) have shown no advantage for pharmacotherapy over CT in the treatment of severely depressed adults. These results, particularly if replicated, suggest that A-CT may be a viable treatment option for severely depressed adults. Moreover, A-CT appears to have an enduring preventive effect after it is discontinued that is not shared with pharmacotherapy. In promising studies, patients who responded to A-CT were about half as likely to relapse as those receiving pharmacotherapy without a continuation-phase antidepressant (Blackburn, Eunson, & Bishop, 1986; Evans et al., 1992; Simons, Murphy, Levine, & Wetzel, 1986).

Eighty percent of depressive episodes are recurrent and the risk of future recurrences appears to increase following each episode (Keller & Boland, 1998) without continuation and/or maintenance-phase treatments (Angst, 1986; Frank et al., 1990). The aims of continuation-phase treatment are to promote remission (a sustained reduction in symptoms) and to reduce relapse (a continuation of the presenting episode) following acute-phase treatment. While pharmacotherapy has traditionally been the standard continuation-phase treatment (APA, 2000), recent studies have evaluated the efficacy of continuation-phase CT (C-CT) following either acute-phase pharmacotherapy or A-CT. Results are encouraging, suggesting that CT targeting residual symptoms during the continuation phase of treatment reduces the risk of relapse and perhaps recurrence in depressed adult outpatients (Fava, Rafanelli, Grandi, Conti, & Belluardo, 1998; Jarrett et al., 2001; Paykel et al., 1999).

Maintenance-phase treatment is provided after recovery (the end of the depressive episode) to prevent recurrence (a new depressive episode) and to maintain treatment gains. Although little studied, early data suggest that maintenance-phase CT is no less effective than maintenance-phase pharmacotherapy (the current standard of treatment; Blackburn & Moore, 1997). It may also be an effective adjunct to antidepressant medication for patients who experience a loss of clinical effectiveness during long-term maintenance pharmacotherapy (Fava, Ruini, Rafanelli, & Grandi, 2002).

Adult Behavior Therapy (BT)

Behavior therapists attempt to elevate mood by improving target response(s) or by changing the low rate of response contingent reinforcement resulting from inadequate reinforcers, or skills deficits (Bandura, 1977; Ferster, 1973). Examples of behavioral techniques include activity scheduling, behavioral marital therapy, self-control techniques, social skills training, and stress management techniques (see Lewinsohn, Gotlib, & Hautzinger, 1998, for overview of behavioral techniques). The treatment manual entitled *The Coping with Depression Course* outlines strategies often used in BT with depressed adults and adolescents (Lewinsohn, Antonuccio, Breckenridge, & Teri, 1984).

Studies have generally found that BT and CT do not differ in their effects in the treatment of depression (see reviews by Jarrett & Rush, 1994; Rush & Thase, 1999). A component analysis showed that the treatment gains achieved by the behavioral activation component of CT do not differ from approaches that also target cognition (Jacobson et al., 1996). If subsequent studies support this finding, and behavioral activation is found to be as effective as CT and pharmacotherapy in treating major depressive disorder and preventing relapse, this would be significant, as behavioral activation may be easier to disseminate and implement than classic CT.

CHRONIC DEPRESSION

When depression lasts 2 years or more, it is considered chronic. The Cognitive Behavior Analysis System of Psychotherapy (CBASP) is tailored for adults with chronic depression. In CBASP, patients learn how their cognitive and behavioral patterns produce and maintain interpersonal problems and experiment with new interpersonal behaviors, and note the associated consequences of the new strategies (McCullough, 2000). *Treatment for Chronic Depression: Cognitive Behavioral Analysis System of Psychotherapy* (McCullough, 2000) is the recognized treatment manual.

In a large multisite study, the combination of CBASP and nefazodone produced significantly higher remission rates and therapeutic response (73%) compared to either treatment alone (48%) in the treatment of chronic depression (Keller et al., 2000). These encouraging results have renewed interest in combined treatments for depression.

BIPOLAR DISORDER (BD)

Historically, BD has been treated with pharmacotherapy, with less focus on psychosocial factors. However, the high incidence of recurrence, the persistence of residual symptoms while patients are on mood-stabilizing medications (Gitlin, Swendsen, Heller, & Hammen, 1995), and poor medication compliance (Colom et al., 2000) have promoted research on the psychosocial as well as the somatic factors in treating BD. CBT treatment manuals for BD include: *Structured Group Psychotherapy for Bipolar Disorder: The Life Goals Program* (Bauer & McBride, 1996) and *Cognitive–Behavioral Therapy for Bipolar Disorder* (Basco & Rush, 1996).

Among the few controlled studies evaluating the effectiveness of CBT as an adjunct to pharmacotherapy for patients with BD, preliminary results are encouraging (see review by Scott, 2001). The largest controlled study of CBT to date (Lam et al., 2003) found that a sample of patients with bipolar illness who received mood-stabilizing medication plus CBT had significantly fewer relapses, days in bipolar episodes, hospital admissions, and higher social functioning compared to controls who receiving pharmacotherapy and usual care. In addition, CBT participants reported less fluctuation in manic symptoms and better ability to cope with prodromal symptoms than controls. These findings supported earlier hypotheses that CBT is an effective adjunct to pharmacotherapy in treating patients suffering from bipolar illness.

CHILD AND ADOLESCENT THERAPY

Research on treatment of child and adolescent depression is increasing. Curry (2001) reviewed the six controlled CBT studies with children (<12 years old), employing highly structured cognitive or behavioral interventions in a school-based setting, and found five of the six studies supported the efficacy of acute-phase CBT relative to control or alternative treatment conditions in reducing depressive symptoms, with no difference between behavioral and cognitive treatment approaches (studies are cited in Curry, 2001).

There is emerging evidence supporting the efficacy of acute-phase CBT in treating adolescent depression. Curry (2001) reviewed nine adolescent studies and found CBT to be effective in reducing depressive symptoms and promoting remission in seven studies. CBT was found to be more effective than wait listing controls in four studies, more effective than supportive therapy in two studies, and more effective than family and relaxation therapy (studies are cited in Curry, 2001). Furthermore, CBT led to a more rapid reduction in depressive symptoms than alternative treatments (Brent et al., 1997).

Further research is necessary to determine whether the prophylactic effects of adolescent A-CT following discontinuation are comparable to adult findings, as well as the indications, optimal frequency, and duration for continuation therapy with adolescents (Curry, 2001). In addition, large multisite clinical trials are under way comparing the incremental benefits of combined CBT and pharmacotherapy versus monotherapy (Treatment of Adolescent Depression Study [TADS]; Treatment of SSRI-Resistant Depression in Adolescents [TORDIA]) in the treatment of adolescent depression. Finally, a promising 15-session CT prevention program was shown to reduce the risk of depression in the offspring of parents with a history of depression as evidenced by a significantly lower incidence of depression at 15-month follow-up compared to usual care (Clarke et al., 2001). These results have important treatment ramifications for adolescent patients.

FUTURE DIRECTIONS

Priorities for future research include conducting rigorous clinical trials with sufficiently large sample sizes to: replicate promising findings, resolve areas of controversy, and test innovations in CBT. Representative sampling, including the understudied, will increase the external validity of future findings.

Preventive strategies for first onset, relapse, and recurrence will remain important priorities for researchers, as well as the development of flexible psychosocial treatment algorithms that match the course of the illness, the treatment setting, and the target group. Several large NIMH-funded studies are currently under way which may significantly affect treatment standards for depressed adults (i.e., The Sequenced Treatment Alternatives to Relieve Depression [STAR*D]) and patients with bipolar disorder (i.e., Treatment Enhancement Program for Bipolar Disorder [STEP-BD]). It is most important to isolate the curative components of CBT that promote change and to identify the specific brain–behavior relationships.

Challenges include increasing the application of CBT across diverse patient groups and treatment settings and increasing public awareness of the effective boundaries of the intervention. Public health issues include how best to train and maintain competent clinicians, design cost-effective treatment delivery systems, and educate consumers about the benefits of CBT versus other treatment alternatives. Exploiting emerging new technologies (e.g., software for personal computers, the Internet, and *telemedicine*) could be instrumental in the need to disseminate both efficacy data and effective practices in CBT.

See also: Bipolar disorder, Cognitive vulnerability to depression, Depression and personality disorders—older adults, Depression—general, Depression—youth, Mood disorders—bipolar disorder, Problem solving—depression

REFERENCES

American Psychiatric Association. (2000). Practice guidelines for the treatment of patients with major depressive disorder (revision). *American Journal of Psychiatry, 159*, 1–50.

Angst, J. (1986). The course of affective disorders. *Psychopathology, 19*(Suppl. 2), 47–52.

Bandura, A. (1977). *Social learning theory*. Englewood Cliffs, NJ: Prentice-Hall.

Basco, M. R., & Rush, A. J. (1996). *Cognitive–behavioral therapy for bipolar disorder*. New York: Guilford Press.

Bauer, M. S., & McBride, L. (2003). *Structured group psychotherapy for bipolar disorder; The Life Goals Program* (2nd ed.). New York: Springer.

Beck, A. T., Rush, A. J., Shaw, B. F., & Emery, G. (1979). *Cognitive therapy for depression*. New York: Guilford Press.

Blackburn, I. M., Eunson, K. M., & Bishop, S. (1986). A two-year naturalistic follow-up of depressed patients treated with cognitive therapy, pharmacotherapy and a combination of both. *Journal of Affective Disorders, 10*, 67–75.

Blackburn, I. M., & Moore, R. G. (1997). Controlled acute and follow-up trial of cognitive therapy and pharmacotherapy in out-patients with recurrent depression. *British Journal of Psychiatry, 171*, 328–334.

Brent, D. A., Holder, D., Kolko, D., Birmaher, B., Baugher, M., Roth, C. et al. (1997). A clinical psychotherapy trial for adolescent depression comparing cognitive, family, and supportive therapy. *Archives of General Psychiatry, 54*, 877–885.

Clarke, G. N., Hornbrook, M., Lynch, F., Polen, M., Gale, J., Beardslee, W. et al. (2001). A randomized trial of a group cognitive intervention for preventing depression in adolescent offspring of depressed parents. *Archives of General Psychiatry, 58*, 1127–1134.

Colom, F., Vieta, E., Martinez-Aran, A., Reinares, M., Benabarre, A., & Gasto, C. (2000). Clinical factors associated with treatment noncompliance in euthymic bipolar patients. *Journal of Clinical Psychiatry, 61*, 549–555.

Curry, J. F. (2001). Specific psychotherapies for childhood and adolescent depression. *Biological Psychiatry, 49*, 1091–1100.

Depression Guideline Panel. (1993). *Depression in primary care: Vol.2. Treatment of major depression* (Publication No. 93-0551). U.S. Department of Health and Human Services, Agency for Health Care Policy and Research. Washington, D.C.

DeRubeis, R. J., & Crits-Christoph, P. (1998). Empirically supported individual and group psychological treatments for adult mental disorders. *Journal of Consulting and Clinical Psychology, 66*, 37–52.

DeRubeis, R. J., Gelfand, L. A., Tang, T. Z., & Simons, A. D. (1999). Medications versus cognitive behavior therapy for severely depressed outpatients: Meta-analysis of four randomized comparisons. *American Journal of Psychiatry, 156*, 1007–1013.

DeRubeis, R. J., Hollon, S. D., Amsterdam, J., & Shelton, R. C. (2001, July). *Cognitive therapy versus medications in the treatment of severely depressed outpatients: Acute response*. Paper presented at the World Congress of Behavioral and Cognitive Behavior Therapy, Vancouver, Canada.

Elkin, I., Gibbons, R. D., Shea, M. T., Sotsky, S. M., Watkins, J. T., Pilkonis, P. A. et al. (1995). Initial severity and differential treatment outcome in the National Institute of Mental Health Treatment of Depression Collaborative Research Program. *Journal of Consulting and Clinical Psychology, 63*, 841–847.

Elkin, I., Shea, M. T., Watkins, J. T., Imber, S. D., Sotsky, S. M., Collins, J. F. et al. (1989). National Institute of Mental Health Treatment of Depression Collaborative Research Program. General effectiveness of treatments. *Archives of General Psychiatry, 46*, 971–982.

Evans, M. D., Hollon, S. D., DeRubeis, R. J., Piasecki, J. M., Grove, W. M., Garvey, M. J. et al. (1992). Differential relapse following cognitive therapy and pharmacotherapy for depression. *Archives of General Psychiatry, 49*, 802–808.

Fava, G. A., Rafanelli, C., Grandi, S., Conti, S., & Belluardo, P. (1998). Prevention of recurrent depression with cognitive behavioral therapy: Preliminary findings. *Archives of General Psychiatry, 55*, 816–820.

Fava, G. A., Ruini, C., Rafanelli, C., & Grandi, S. (2002). Cognitive behavior approach to loss of clinical effect during long-term antidepressant treatment: A pilot study. *American Journal of Psychiatry, 159*, 2094–2095.

Ferster, C. B. (1973). A functional analysis of depression. *American Psychologist, 28*, 857–870.

Frank, E., Kupfer, D. J., Perel, J. M., Cornes, C., Jarrett, D. B., Mallinger, A. G. et al. (1990). Three-year outcomes for maintenance therapies in recurrent depression. *Archives of General Psychiatry, 47*, 1093–1099.

Gitlin, M. J., Swendsen, J., Heller, T. L., & Hammen, C. (1995). Relapse and impairment in bipolar disorder. *American Journal of Psychiatry, 152*, 1635–1640.

Jacobson, N. S., Dobson, K. S., Truax, P. A., Addis, M. E., Koerner, K., Gollan, J. K. et al. (1996). A component analysis of cognitive–behavioral treatment for depression. *Journal of Consulting and Clinical Psychology, 64*, 295–304.

Jarrett, R. B., Kraft, D., Doyle, J., Foster, B. M., Eaves, G. G., & Silver, P. C. (2001). Preventing recurrent depression using cognitive therapy with and without a continuation phase: A randomized clinical trial. *Archives of General Psychiatry, 58*, 381–388.

Jarrett, R. B., & Rush, A. J. (1994). Short-term psychotherapy of depressive disorders: Current status and future direction. *Psychiatry, 56*, 115–132.

Keller, M. B., & Boland, R. J. (1998). Implications of failing to achieve successful long-term maintenance treatment of recurrent unipolar major depression. *Biological Psychiatry, 44*, 348–360.

Keller, M. B., McCullough, J. P., Klein, D. N., Arnow, B., Dunner, D. L., Gelenberg, A. J. et al. (2000). A comparison of nefazodone, the cognitive behavioral-analysis system of psychotherapy, and their combination for the treatment of chronic depression. *New England Journal of Medicine, 342*, 1462–1470.

Lam, D. H., Watkins, E. R., Hayward, P., Bright, J., Wright, K., Kerr, N. et al. (2003). A randomized controlled study of cognitive therapy for relapse prevention for bipolar affective disorder: Outcome of the first year. *Archives of General Psychiatry, 60*, 145–152.

Lewinsohn, P. M., Antonuccio, D. O., Breckenridge, J. S., & Teri, L. (1984). *The coping with depression course*. Eugene, OR: Castalia Publishing.

Lewinsohn, P. M., Gotlib, I. H., & Hautzinger, M. (1998). Behavioral treatment of unipolar depression. In V. E. Cabello (Ed.), *International handbook of cognitive and behavioral treatments for psychological disorders* (pp. 441–488). New York: Pergamon Press.

McCullough, J. P. (2000). *Treatment for chronic depression: Cognitive behavioral analysis system of psychotherapy (CBASP)*. New York: Guilford Press.

Paykel, E. S., Scott, J., Teasdale, J. D., Johnson, A. L., Garland, A., Moore, R. et al. (1999). Prevention of relapse in residual depression by cognitive therapy. *Archives of General Psychiatry, 56*, 829–835.

Rush, A. J., & Thase, M. E. (1999). Psychotherapies for depressive disorders: A review. In M. Maj & N. Sartorius (Eds.), *Depressive disorders (WPA Series in Evidence and Experience in Psychiatry)* (pp. 161–206). New York: Wiley.

Schulberg, H. C., Katon, W., Simon, G. E., & Rush, A. J. (1998). Treating major depression in primary care practice: An update of the Agency for Health Care Policy and Research Practice Guidelines. *Archives of General Psychiatry, 55*, 1121–1127.

Scott, J. (2001). Cognitive therapy as an adjunct to medication in bipolar disorder. *British Journal of Psychiatry, 178*, S164–S168.

Simons, A. D., Murphy, G. E., Levine, J. L., & Wetzel, R. D. (1986). Cognitive therapy and pharmacotherapy for depression. Sustained improvement over one year. *Archives of General Psychiatry, 43*, 43–48.

Stuart, S., Wright, J. H., Thase, M. E., & Beck, A. T. (1997). Cognitive therapy with inpatients. *General Hospital. Psychiatry, 19*, 42–50.

Wampold, B. E., Minami, T., Baskin, T. W., & Callen, T. S. (2002). A meta-(re)analysis of the effects of cognitive therapy versus "other therapies" for depression. *Journal of Affective Disorders, 68*, 159–165.

RECOMMENDED READINGS

Beck, A. T., Rush, A. J., Shaw, B. F., & Emery, G. (1979). *Cognitive therapy of depression*. New York: Guilford Press.

Padesky, C., & Greenberger, O. (1995). *Clinicians guide to mind over mood*. New York: Guilford Press.

Search *Cochrane Database of Systematic Reviews* under the keyword *depression*.

Depression and Personality Disorders—Older Adults

Steven R. Thorp and Thomas R. Lynch

Keywords: aging, depression, DBT, personality disorders

Older adults represent the most rapidly growing age group in the United States, and in recent decades there has been increasing attention paid to mental health issues in this population. In the past, psychotherapeutic interventions have been discouraged for older adults or it had been assumed that older adults would derive sufficient benefits from unmodified interventions designed for their younger counterparts. In this article, we report the rates of depression and personality disorders among older adults and we describe how cognitive–behavioral therapy (CBT) has been utilized to address these significant late-life problems. We review some of the major empirical literature, suggest areas of special consideration in assessment and treatment, and identify future directions for practice and research.

PREVALENCE AND CORRELATES OF DEPRESSION AND PERSONALITY DISORDERS IN LATE LIFE

Geriatric depression is a widespread problem with serious adverse consequences. Depression in late life is underdiagnosed, but epidemiological studies have found that clinically significant depression impacts up to 15% of older adults living in the community and a much higher percentage of patients who are chronically ill or who are treated in hospitals and nursing homes (Reynolds & Kupfer, 1999; Thompson, 1996). Depressive symptoms in late life are associated with increased risk of death from suicide (older adults have the highest suicide rate of any age group) and medical illness in addition to higher levels of functional impairment and health services utilization (Lynch, Morse, Mendelson, & Robins, 2003; Reynolds & Kupfer, 1999).

The vast majority of treatment outcome studies for mental health problems have focused on pharmacotherapy, but medication treatment in the elderly is complicated by sensitivity to side effects, potential for harmful interactions with other medications, and comorbid medical and neurological disorders (Hollon, Thase, & Markowitz, 2002; Thompson, 1996). Psychosocial interventions, such as CBT, may thus be particularly appropriate for older adults. The American Psychiatric Association (APA, 2000) guidelines for treating major depressive disorder suggest that CBT is warranted if patients prefer not to take medications or if they experience significant psychosocial stressors, interpersonal difficulties, or comorbid Axis II disorders.

Although clinical lore may suggest that personality disorders "fade away" in late life, geriatric depression is often accompanied by Axis II disorders. Structured clinical interviews suggest that the prevalence of personality disorders for community-dwelling older adults is about 13%, with higher rates for outpatients and rates of up to 63% of older inpatients (Seidlitz, 2001). Older patients with major depressive disorder have higher rates of personality disorders than those with other Axis I disorders or with no Axis I diagnoses (Bizzini, 1998; Seidlitz, 2001).

There is mounting evidence that older adult patients with personality disorders have poor response to mental health interventions (Morse & Lynch, 2000). For example, Thompson, Gallagher, and Czirr (1988) analyzed the impact of personality disorders on psychotherapy treatments for depression. Although the study relied primarily on retrospective patient reports to generate Axis II diagnoses, it offered compelling data about personality disorders in late life. One-third of the participants could be diagnosed with at least one personality disorder irrespective of Axis I diagnoses, yet over two-thirds met criteria for personality disorders at the point when they sought help for their depression. Patients with personality disorders, independent of their level of depression, were less likely to benefit from short-term psychotherapy. Four times as many patients without a personality disorder had successful responses to treatment than failed responses.

EMPIRICAL STATUS OF CBT FOR OLDER ADULTS WITH DEPRESSION AND PERSONALITY DISORDERS

The efficacy of CBT for younger adults has a growing base of evidence. CBT has generally yielded effect sizes as large or larger than treatment with antidepressant medications or other forms of psychotherapy in the treatment of depression, and it may be more effective than other treatments for depressed individuals with personality disorders (APA, 2000). Presumably because of the emphasis on patient skill acquisition in CBT, patients are less likely to relapse after treatment to remission if they have been treated with CBT than if they have been treated to remission with medication, and there are even indications that CBT may help to prevent the recurrence of depression (Hollon et al., 2002).

Historically, there has been pessimism about the utility of psychotherapy with older adults. Sigmund Freud, for example, argued that older adults were overly rigid and would not be able to make the changes necessary for psychotherapy to work (Bizzini, 1998). Many of the early stage theorists did not consider old age a time of change or growth. In the twenty-first century, many mental health professionals and nonprofessionals remain doubtful that older adults can learn the concepts presented in psychotherapy. These views are changing, however, partly because of positive results from rigorous psychotherapy studies on geriatric populations during the past two decades. CBT has now been studied for treating late-life depression by a number of different investigators using diagnostic interviews, treatment manuals, supervision of therapists, and control conditions (Areán & Cook, 2002).

The majority of the studies of psychotherapy for older adults have focused on treating depression. Randomized controlled trials (RCTs) for this population suggest that CBT appears to be superior to usual care and no treatment for major depressive disorder and depressive symptoms, with persistence in treatment gains for up to 3 years following acute treatment (Areán & Cook, 2002). CBT appears to work at least as well as other psychotherapies for treating major depression in older adults (Hollon et al., 2002; Thompson, 1996). Despite data from younger adult samples that suggest that pharmacotherapy augmented with psychotherapy can effectively treat depression (APA, 2000; Reynolds & Kupfer, 1999), there are few studies comparing CBT to medications in older adults.

Two studies have indicated that CBT augmented with an antidepressant is more efficacious than the medication alone for treating depressive symptoms in late life (see review by Areán & Cook, 2002). In addition, one study of chronically depressed older adults found that patients on antidepressants who participated in a CBT skills training group (i.e., dialectical behavior therapy [DBT]) were significantly more likely to be in remission at a 6-month follow-up compared to those in medication treatment alone (Lynch et al., 2003).

There is a paucity of studies on personality disorders in older adults in general, and there are no published RCTs that have specifically targeted the treatment of late-life personality disorders. Much of the research has been limited because studies lack (1) clear descriptions of treatments, (2) considerations of comorbid Axis I disorders, (3) standardized assessment instruments, and (4) treatment adherence and competence ratings of therapists (Morse & Lynch, 2000). Fortunately, increasing awareness of late-life personality disorders is generating more rigorous research (Bizzini, 1998; Lynch et al., 2003; Morse & Lynch, 2000; Seidlitz, 2001).

THE PRACTICE OF CBT FOR OLDER ADULTS WITH DEPRESSION AND PERSONALITY DISORDERS

There are several assessment and treatment issues to consider when working with older adults who have depression and personality disorders. Accurate diagnostic assessment is important for communication among clinicians and patients, for selecting treatments, for monitoring change over time, and for evaluating outcomes. Assessors should avoid questions that involve slang or jargon, and should be aware of potential sensitivities to sexual content. Patient questionnaires should be printed in large and bold fonts to facilitate reading. When working with older adults, it is important to consider how social desirability of responses and cohort differences may affect the expression of mental health symptoms. Older adults may be hesitant to "air dirty laundry" about themselves or their families. Older adults, compared to their younger counterparts, may be more likely to report problems with appetite, sleep, or cognitive problems than subjective problems with mood (APA, 2000; Reynolds & Kupfer, 1999). Whenever possible, it is worthwhile to include family members, friends, or other caregivers in the assessment process to augment patient reports, interviews, and direct observation.

It is imperative to evaluate cognitive status, comorbid physical and mental health problems, medication adherence, substance use and abuse, risk of suicide, social support, mobility, and self-care (e.g., grooming, shopping, cooking, medication management). Each of these areas can dramatically impact treatment outcomes and how treatment is implemented. During the assessment process it is important to bear in mind that some dementias, anxiety disorders, Parkinson's disease, and substance abuse problems may resemble depressive disorders. It is also important to consider how age of onset and course of disorders may impact treatment.

CBT highlights the importance of the relationship between the therapist and patient and the value of specific, measurable goals. Sessions typically begin with the collaborative development of an agenda, and treatment typically combines (1) psychoeducation about psychiatric problems; (2) methods of managing cognitive distortions, behavioral deficits and excesses, and problematic physical environments;

and (3) structured skills training for social functioning, problem-solving, and communication. Relevant homework assignments are used to monitor and modify thoughts, emotions, and behaviors.

Thompson (1996) provides an excellent description of CBT adapted for late-life depression. The cognitive and sensory deficits associated with aging can be managed by presenting material in a loud, distinct voice or clear written format. It may be useful to present new material slowly and to alternate verbal reviews by the therapist and patient to consolidate learning. Sessions can be audio- or videotaped for later review by patients as well. Therapists can use role-play exercises, metaphors, visual representations of concepts, and video presentations in addition to modeling effective behaviors. Older patients who are excessively talkative or tangential may need to be educated about the importance of structure and focus in the therapy. Thompson (1996) and others have suggested that additional sessions or more schema-focused CBT may be required for older adults with personality disorders.

THE CHALLENGES FOR CBT IN OLDER ADULTS

CBT does not work for all patients, and more research is needed to determine why some patients fail to respond to treatment. The effectiveness of CBT is dependent on attendance and adherence to in-session and extra-session exercises designed to challenge previous learning. This may be challenging for older people who have cognitive impairment, low levels of commitment to treatment, or trouble managing their time. Patients who desire less structure, a more historical focus (e.g., frequent discussions of childhood events), or discussions of hidden or unconscious motivations may be unsatisfied and perhaps less responsive to CBT. The response to CBT may be slower than to pharmacotherapy or other somatic treatments (e.g., electroconvulsive therapy), and this potential delay must be considered when there are concerns about imminent risks.

FUTURE DIRECTIONS FOR PRACTICE AND RESEARCH

Late-life depression and personality disorders are relatively young areas of treatment research. There are several new CBT-based approaches that hold promise for acute treatment or relapse prevention, and myriad opportunities for innovative studies. Lynch and colleagues (Lynch et al., 2003; Morse & Lynch, 2000) have successfully adapted DBT for older adults with depression, and this approach is now being tested in an RCT for older adults with comorbid depression and personality disorders. DBT adapted for older adults combines the change-based strategies (e.g., modification of distorted thoughts, problem-solving, behavioral activation) emphasized in traditional CBT with more acceptance-based strategies (e.g., mindfulness, validation). In our experience, a more acceptance-based approach is especially useful for maximizing patient comfort early in the process of therapy (i.e., during initial assessment and psychoeducation). Other approaches that are gaining scientific support also utilize mindfulness exercises and emphasize the process of thinking rather than the content of thoughts (see Bizzini, 1998; Hollon et al., 2002).

Social support can have a strong impact on the occurrence, severity, and duration of psychopathology, and friends and family should be involved in treatment if possible. This may simply involve obtaining information about patients from loved ones or educating those loved ones about depression and personality disorders. However, there is also evidence that couple and family therapy can be used to treat patients' mental health problems in addition to ameliorating relationship problems (APA, 2000; Hollon et al., 2002).

Although CBT interventions are often efficacious, we know little about which components of treatment are responsible for improvements and little about the mechanisms of change. Research on CBT with older adults would benefit from outcome measures that evaluate processes of change, cost-effectiveness, and quality-of-life/functioning issues (e.g., living conditions, health care management, work activities, interpersonal relationships) as well as the standard measures of psychopathology. More research is also needed on how age-related changes in memory and information processing affect treatment response.

Much of the research on late-life mental health problems has presumed traditional office treatment by specialists (e.g., weekly 1-hour office visits to a psychologist or psychiatrist). Many older adults do not access mental health treatment in this manner, and there is a need for more studies that demonstrate effectiveness in nontraditional settings such as patients' homes, primary care outpatient services, and long-term-care facilities. There is also a need for studies that use less restrictive inclusion and exclusion criteria and more diverse samples based on race and ethnicity, location (e.g., urban and rural), and income (Areán & Cook, 2002).

Little is known about how patient factors (such as expectations and commitment to treatment) impact treatment response, and we could learn a great deal by determining why some older patients respond to treatments while others do not. Therapist factors such as level of training, allegiance to CBT or other therapies, and specific skill repertoires may similarly influence treatment outcome. There is some evidence to suggest the utility of matching certain types of clients to particular therapists or methods of treatment (APA, 2000; Areán & Cook, 2002). It is also important to determine the effects of CBT at different phases of treatment. For example, in addition to acute treatment studies (e.g., 12–20 weeks to reduce the impact of existing problems), prevention studies could reduce vulnerabilities for future problems. More longitudinal studies would help to determine how CBT affects depression and personality features in the years following acute care.

The widespread clinical practice of combining medications with psychotherapy and the potential for complications due to pharmacotherapy in older adults suggest a need for more research in this area. There are few data to guide combination treatment, including who will benefit most and how treatments should be sequenced. More research is also needed to determine if CBT can improve medication adherence and health care management in older adults.

We could take advantage of existing resources and new technologies to facilitate access to treatment for older adults. There are many exciting treatment formats to explore through rigorous research, including interventions conducted over the telephone or via books (i.e., bibliotherapy), the Internet, or DVD-ROM. The latter three methods have the advantages of consistency of presentation (which is ideal for reducing presentation variance in research) and ease of review for patients.

Finally, it is important to rectify the underdiagnosis and undertreatment of geriatric depression and personality disorders. Mental health professionals could use existing marketing techniques to increase professional and public awareness of these problems and appropriate treatments while reducing the stigma associated with mental disorders. Better patient access and continued research on CBT can go far to prevent or reduce the suffering of many older adults.

See also: Aging and dementia, Depression—adult, Depression—general, Family caregivers

REFERENCES

American Psychiatric Association. (2000). Practice guidelines for the treatment of patients with major depressive disorder (revision). *American Journal of Psychiatry, 157*(Suppl. 4), 1–45.

Areán, P. A., & Cook, B. L. (2002). Psychotherapy and combined psychotherapy/pharmacotherapy for late-life depression. *Biological Psychiatry, 52*, 293–303.

Bizzini, L. (1998). Cognitive psychotherapy in the treatment of personality disorders in the elderly. In C. Perris & P. D. McGorry (Eds.), *Cognitive psychotherapy of psychotic and personality disorders: Handbook of theory and practice* (pp. 397–419). New York: Wiley.

Hollon, S. D., Thase, M. E., & Markowitz, J. C. (2002). Treatment and prevention of depression. *Psychological Science in the Public Interest, 3*, 39–77.

Lynch, T. R., Morse, J. Q., Mendelson, T., & Robins, C. J. (2003). Dialectical behavior therapy for depressed older adults. *American Journal of Geriatric Psychiatry, 11*, 33–45.

Morse, J. Q., & Lynch, T. R. (2000). Personality disorders in late life. *Current Psychiatry Reports, 2*, 24–31.

Reynolds, C. F., & Kupfer, D. J. (1999). Depression and aging: A look to the future. *Psychiatric Services, 50*, 1167–1172.

Seidlitz, L. (2001). Personality factors in mental disorders in later life. *American Journal of Geriatric Psychiatry, 9*, 8–21.

Thompson, L. W. (1996). Cognitive–behavioral therapy and treatment for late-life depression. *Journal of Clinical Psychiatry, 57*(Suppl. 5), 29–37.

Thompson, L. W., Gallagher, D., & Czirr, R. (1988). Personality disorder and outcome in the treatment of late-life depression. *Journal of Geriatric Psychiatry, 21*, 133–146.

Depression—General

Daniel R. Strunk and Robert J. DeRubeis

Keywords: cognitive therapy, depression, Aaron T. Beck, pharmacotherapy, dissemination

A basic supposition in cognitive models of depression is that depression is characterized by systematic negative biases in thinking. Depressed people harbor negative beliefs about themselves, the world, and their futures (Beck, 1967). For example, a depressed person may believe "I am a terrible person," "people think I have nothing to offer," or "there's no point in trying." Negative biases are also manifested through errors in logic. Overgeneralization, drawing a global conclusion from a single fact, is one such error. A depressed woman might exhibit overgeneralization by concluding that she will never get a job after not being offered a job following one interview. Aaron Beck has argued that the wide variety of specific errors and biases that characterize depressed people's thinking accounts for their other symptoms of depression (Beck, 1967).

Cognitive therapy (CT) involves an effort to correct patients' biased thinking patterns, which, in turn, is thought to help them to overcome their depressive symptoms. Although several cognitive–behavioral psychotherapies for depression exist, researchers have focused primarily on Beck's CT (Beck, Rush, Shaw, & Emery, 1979). Beck's CT is a short-term, structured, manualized therapy. As in other psychotherapies, CT therapists strive to form a good collaborative working relationship with their patients. However, in contrast to some psychotherapies, CT also involves specific techniques. These CT techniques fall into three classes. Behavioral techniques are used to facilitate patients' engaging in activities that give them a sense of pleasure or mastery, as well as to test beliefs (e.g., "I can't even get out of bed in the morning"). Cognitive techniques are used to encourage patients to treat their cognitions as hypotheses and subject them to careful scrutiny. A depressed man might learn to challenge the thought "I have nothing to offer" by considering specific, relevant evidence. Perhaps, on reflection, he would identify some of his virtues. Finally, typically in the later stages of therapy, patients are encouraged to recognize and modify patterns of negatively distorting thinking (i.e., schemas). Through the application of these techniques, patients are expected to experience less severe depressive symptomatology and learn to use the techniques taught in therapy in their daily lives.

While Beck's CT has received the most research attention, other approaches have also been influential. One such approach is the "hopelessness/helplessness" model of depression. Seligman's original "learned helplessness" model was based on the observation that dogs given inescapable shock over repeated trials did not attempt later to escape shock, even when escape was possible. This phenomenon of "learned helplessness" has served as a model of depression in humans. The model was later revised to better account for cognitive processes believed to underlie the onset of depression. According to this revised model, depressed people have learned to explain events in a negatively biased manner. People with a vulnerability to depression tend to attribute events to permanent, universal, and internal factors. Although not widely used in psychotherapy, this model of depression has been utilized in developing programs to prevent depression.

The Cognitive Behavioral Analysis System of Psychotherapy (CBASP) is a relatively new therapy designed by James McCullough for chronic forms of depression. It utilizes many of the cognitive and behavioral techniques used in CT. However, unlike the CT model of depression, the CBASP model of depression posits that depressed patients think preoperationally and that a major contributor to patients' depression is that they cause stress in their own lives. Specific CBASP techniques have been developed to deal with these problems. Although developed recently, CBASP has been tested in a large randomized controlled trial of chronically depressed patients. The main findings were that CBASP and pharmacotherapy were equivalently effective in the short run (12 weeks), and the combination of CBASP and pharmacotherapy was substantially (and significantly) more effective than either treatment alone.

EVIDENCE OF EFFICACY

The strongest evidence for the efficacy of Beck's CT has come from randomized clinical trials comparing CT to pharmacotherapy. In four major studies, investigators failed to find a significant advantage for pharmacotherapy (for a recent review, see Strunk & DeRubeis, 2001). Averaging across these four studies, the pre- to posttreatment effect size (as measured by Cohen's d) for those who completed CT was 2.9 on the Beck Depression Inventory (BDI) and 3.0 on the 17-item Hamilton Rating Scale for Depression (HRSD). Averaging across studies, 66% of completers meet BDI recovery criteria (i.e., BDI $\leq$ 9). For the three studies for which HRSD recovery rates were reported, 53% of completers meet recovery criteria (HRSD $\leq$ 6). Thus, CT patients experienced a large change in depressive symptoms, and a substantial portion of CT patients reached a priori recovery criteria. Another study, which focused on recurrent depression, also found no difference in effectiveness between CT and pharmacotherapy.

Recently, there has been controversy over whether CT is appropriate as a first-line treatment for severe depression. The Treatment of Depression Collaborative Research Program (TDCRP) failed to find significant differences between CT and pharmacotherapy across the whole sample. However, subsequent analyses showed that pharmacotherapy was superior to CT among more severely depressed patients (Elkin et al., 1995). In fact, this finding has been the basis of treatment guidelines recommending pharmacotherapy for severely depressed people. However, in a meta-analysis of four randomized controlled trials including the TDCRP study, DeRubeis, Gelfand, Tang, and Simons (1999) found a nonsignificant advantage for CT over pharmacotherapy. Therefore, available data suggest CT is as effective as pharmacotherapy regardless of initial severity of symptoms.

Whether CT outperforms control conditions has received less attention. In the TDCRP, CT failed to outperform a pill-placebo condition (Elkin et al., 1995). However, problems in the way in which CT was conducted may have contributed to this result (Jacobson & Hollon, 1996). A study of atypical depression has since found CT to be superior to pill-placebo (and not different from pharmacotherapy).

Few studies have examined CT in comparison to other psychotherapies. In a small study, group CT outperformed a behavior modification group, a nondirective control group, and a wait-list control group. In contrast, the TDCRP failed to find differences between CT and interpersonal therapy, either at the end of treatment or at a 1-year follow-up. Similarly, Jacobson and his colleagues found that CT was not significantly different than behavior therapy at the end of treatment or at 1- and 2-year follow-ups (Gortner, Gollan, Dobson, & Jacobson, 1998; Jacobson et al., 1996). More research is needed in this area.

LONG-TERM EFFECTS OF COGNITIVE THERAPY

Naturalistic follow-ups of responders in clinical trials have yielded evidence suggesting that CT has a prophylactic effect relative to short-term pharmacotherapy. Several studies have found a significantly lower rate of relapse for CT compared to pharmacotherapy 1 or 2 years after the termination of treatment (Strunk & DeRubeis, 2001). Only the TDCRP study failed to find this result. Due to their remarkable 90% follow-up rate, Gortner et al. (1998) were able to provide valuable data on how the 58% of their CT patients who responded to treatment fared following treatment. One year after treatment, 19% of CT responders had relapsed. Two years after treatment, 46% had relapsed. Thus, 27% of patients assigned to the CT condition recovered and remained well for 2 years. Taken together, these findings suggest that despite producing long-term recovery only in a minority of patients, CT appears to have a prophylactic effect relative to short-term pharmacotherapy.

HOW COGNITIVE THERAPY WORKS

Having established that CT has beneficial and relatively long-lasting effects, researchers have sought to address how CT achieves its effects. Such efforts provide an important test of the validity of the cognitive theory of depression and may provide useful information for refining CT. Some researchers have argued that factors not specific to CT (most notably the therapeutic alliance) are responsible for effects in all forms of therapy. Beck's theory clearly states that while a good working relationship is a necessary condition, specific interventions largely drive symptom change in CT. Consistent with Beck's theory, DeRubeis and his colleagues have found that use of specific cognitive techniques predicts subsequent symptom change (Feeley, DeRubeis, & Gelfand, 1999). Similarly, sessions immediately prior to sudden gains (i.e., session-to-session intervals in which patients' symptoms improved substantially) were found to include more discussion of changes in cognitions than control sessions (Tang & DeRubeis, 1999). Another important component of the theory of how CT achieves its effects has to do with what patients learn in CT. In one study, patients who complied more with their CT homework were found to have better outcomes. Patients who learned not to think in an absolutist, dichotomous style have been found to be at lower risk for relapse following treatment (Teasdale et al., 2001).

CRITICISMS

Perhaps the most serious criticism of CT is that the form and quality of CT may not be widely available. Aside from training centers and the research centers in which clinical trials have been conducted, it may be difficult for patients to find high-quality CT. Indeed, some researchers have argued that not only are CT providers not currently widely available, but that it may prove too difficult to disseminate CT widely. Recall that Jacobson et al. (1996) and Gortner et al. (1998) found that a behavioral activation treatment performed as well as CT. These researchers have argued that the relative ease with which therapists can learn behavioral activation may make it a superior treatment. Little is known about the dissemination of CT: either the extent to which CT can be transported to new clinics or what methods are best for attempting to disseminate the treatment. One recent, preliminary study found that the effects of CT in a community mental health center were similar to the effects reported in clinical trials (Merrill, Tolbert, & Wade, 2003). However, more research on this topic is needed.

Several other areas will also be important to address. How long do CT's prophylactic effects last? What can comprehensive cost–benefit analyses reveal about CT compared to other treatments? Can CT be modified to increase the response rate? Can any strategies enhance CT's promising prophylactic effects?

SUMMARY

Several cognitive models and therapies have been developed. Beck's CT has received more research attention than any other psychotherapy for depression. Available evidence suggests that CT is as effective as alternative treatments, including pharmacotherapy. Moreover, short-term CT appears to have a prophylactic effect relative to short-term pharmacotherapy. CT appears to achieve its effects through the use of specific cognitive techniques and teaching patients to change their thinking styles. Research is now needed to ensure that, if feasible, CT is disseminated widely to clinics so that it is readily available to the patients who would benefit from it.

See also: Bipolar disorder, Cognitive vulnerability to depression, Depression—adult, Depression and personality disorders—older adults, Depression—youth, Problem solving—depression

REFERENCES

Beck, A. T. (1967). *Depression: Causes and treatment*. Philadelphia: University of Pennsylvania.

Beck, A. T., Rush, A. J., Shaw, B. F., & Emery, G. (1979). *Cognitive therapy of depression*. New York: Guilford Press.

DeRubeis, R. J., Gelfand, L. A., Tang, T. Z., & Simons, A. D. (1999). Medications versus cognitive behavior therapy for severely depressed outpatients: Meta-analysis of four randomized comparisons. *American Journal of Psychiatry, 156*, 1007–1013.

Elkin, I., Gibbons, R. D., Shea, M. T., Sotsky, S. M., Watkins, J. T., Pilkonis, P. A., & Hedeker, D. (1995). Initial severity and differential treatment outcome in the National Institute of Mental Health Treatment of Depression Collaborative Research Program. *Journal of Consulting & Clinical Psychology, 63*, 841–847.

Feeley, M., DeRubeis, R. J., & Gelfand, L. A. (1999). The temporal relation of adherence and alliance to symptom change in cognitive therapy for depression. *Journal of Consulting & Clinical Psychology, 67*, 578–582.

Gortner, E. T., Gollan, J. K., Dobson, K. S., & Jacobson, N. S. (1998). Cognitive–behavioral treatment for depression: Relapse prevention. *Journal of Consulting & Clinical Psychology, 66*, 377–384.

Jacobson, N. S., Dobson, K. S., Truax, P. A., Addis, M. E., Koerner, K., Gollan, J. K., Gortner, E., & Prince, S. E. (1996). A component analysis of cognitive–behavioral treatment for depression. *Journal of Consulting & Clinical Psychology, 64*, 295–304.

Jacobson, N. S., & Hollon, S. D. (1996). Cognitive-behavior therapy versus pharmacotherapy: Now that the Jury's returned its verdict, it's time to present the rest of the evidence. *Journal of Consulting & Clinical Psychology, 64*, 74–80.

Merrill, K. A., Tolbert, V. E., & Wade, W. A. (2003). Effectiveness of cognitive therapy for depression in a community mental health center: A benchmarking study. *Journal of Consulting & Clinical Psychology, 71*, 404–409.

Strunk, D. R., & DeRubeis, R. J. (2001). Cognitive therapy of depression: A review of its efficacy. *Journal of Cognitive Psychotherapy: An International Quarterly, 15*, 289–297.

Tang, T. Z., & DeRubeis, R. J. (1999). Sudden gains and critical sessions in cognitive–behavioral therapy for depression. *Journal of Consulting & Clinical Psychology, 67*, 894–904.

Teasdale, J. D., Scott, J., Moore, R. G., Hayhurst, H., Pope, M., & Paykel, E. S. (2001). How does cognitive therapy prevent relapse in residual depression? Evidence from a controlled trial. *Journal of Consulting & Clinical Psychology, 69*, 347–357.

Depression—Youth

Elizabeth A. Gosch and Aaron Pollock

Keywords: depression, children, parenting, treatment, self-control

A number of cognitive and behavioral models of depression have influenced treatment approaches with children. Most notably, Beck's model of depression emphasizes that maladaptive schemas cause negative distortions in perceiving and processing information that lead to depressive symptoms. Negative cognitions about the self, world, and future (the cognitive triad) characterize and maintain depressive symptoms. Also influential, the learned helplessness/ hopelessness model (Abramson, Metalksy, & Alloy, 1989) posits that individuals who attribute the cause of negative events to internal, stable, and global causes while attributing the cause of positive events to external, unstable, and specific causes are at risk for depression. Thus, cognitive interventions are frequently geared toward helping children modify maladaptive cognitive processes (self-talk, beliefs, attributions) through affective education, collaborative empiricism, behavioral experiments, cognitive restructuring activities, and self-instruction training. Behavioral models for treating depression in children tend to focus on operant principles. Lewinsohn (1974) associates depression with low levels of positive reinforcement, particularly social reinforcement, due to problems in available reinforcement systems and deficits in social skills. Behavioral interventions designed to increase the child's access to positive reinforcement and decrease depressive symptoms include activity scheduling, pleasant events monitoring, selective reinforcement, and skills training (e.g., social, problem solving, and relaxation skills). Self-control models incorporate behavioral and cognitive components by focusing on overly high expectations, selective attention to negative events, and rates of positive self-reinforcement/punishment.

PHILOSOPHY

CBT for childhood depression is based on a multiple pathway model that views depression as resulting from the reciprocal influence of cognitive, behavioral, contextual/interpersonal, and biological factors. The treatment package for childhood depression is often multidimensional, targeting depressive symptoms and other problems often accompanying depression (e.g., familial conflict, interpersonal skill deficits, oppositional behavior). The child's social context (family, school, and peers) is often a focus of treatment. Children are seen as experiencing depressive symptoms due to the stress of negative events or a lack of positive events in their lives, the effects of which are mediated by cognitive factors. Consideration of a child's cognitive developmental level is crucial in designing interventions. Younger children or children with less developed intellectual abilities may not be able to utilize complex cognitive interventions but require behavioral or contextual (e.g., parenting) interventions to evince change in cognitions and depressive symptoms.

CBT for children with depression focuses on identifying and challenging unrealistic beliefs that exacerbate depressive feelings and associated problem behaviors (Friedberg, Crosby, Friedberg, Rutter, & Knight, 2000). Identifying and modifying inaccurate beliefs is accomplished through collaborative experimentation between patient and therapist. The therapist works as consultant; a person with ideas worth trying out and a sounding board for ideas that do not work, diagnostician; making meaningful decisions about treatment based on data and knowledge of psychopathology; and educator, assisting in finding the most effective ways to learn to control behavior and increase cognitive and emotional skills (Kendall, 1993). In the context of a caring, therapeutic relationship, the therapist seeks to nonreinforce depressive affect and behavior while increasing reinforcement for positive, active behaviors. Sessions are generally guided by an agenda and/or goal setting, client feedback is seen as an integral part of the CBT session, and homework is assigned by the therapist to instill a practical and experiential focus to the goals of therapy (Friedberg et al., 2000).

CONTEMPORARY TREATMENT PRACTICES

Cognitive–behavioral treatments typically begin with a focus on behavioral components. If necessary, therapists first manage suicidal symptoms. They also seek to increase the child's experience of positive reinforcement through their relationship with the child, activity scheduling and pleasant-events monitoring. The therapist provides positive incentives for the child to engage in adaptive activities, social interaction, and mastery experiences. Therapists may seek to decrease the child's reinforcement for depressive symptoms (e.g., ignore non-life-threatening depressive behaviors such as whining). Therapists also increase the child's use of self-reinforcement (e.g., pleasurable activities or self-praise) for engaging in adaptive behavior. If skill deficits exist, the therapist teaches skills (e.g., social skills, problem solving) that will help the child receive more positive reinforcement from the environment. Social skills training approaches have frequently been implemented in a group where children are taught to engage in eye contact, smile, play games, plan social activities, and make age-appropriate conversation. Children are also encouraged to decrease socially inappropriate behaviors (e.g., temper tantrums). The therapist uses instruction, modeling, role-play, shaping, practice, and feedback to help children learn new skills. Homework or take-home projects help the child generalize therapeutic benefits. For example, children may be asked to engage in pleasurable activities or to log and dispute their self-talk when feeling sad.

Cognitive therapy components aim to change the child's maladaptive beliefs, images, thoughts, and self-talk which influence their behavior and perceptions. The therapist often does so through eliciting what the child is thinking when experiencing negative mood states or during upsetting events. The child engages in affect education exercises (practice recognizing and differentiating feelings) and learns about the cognitive model in which thoughts impact feelings and behavior. The therapist helps the child identify maladaptive or distorted thinking and engage in cognitive restructuring activities. These activities include identifying the type of distortion being exhibited (e.g., overgeneralization, mind reading), weighing the evidence for and against the thought or belief, testing the belief through behavioral experiments, and substituting more realistic interpretations. To help children interact more effectively with their environment, they are taught problem-solving skills (orientation, problem definition, generation of alternatives, evaluation of alternatives, selection of alternatives, and evaluation of outcome). Younger or cognitively delayed children may not be able to engage in complex cognitive evaluation exercises and may only change cognitions through direct experiences that contradict their beliefs or the use of self-instruction/self-statements.

Given that a major source of reinforcement for children is their interpersonal environment, particularly the family, the therapist seeks to ameliorate negative or coercive interaction patterns in the family that interfere with the child receiving positive reinforcement and promote negative cognitive patterns in the child. For example, studies have established that children who are depressed often have parents suffering from depression. Parents who are depressed may neglect their children, model depressed affect, or be excessively critical. Children, in turn, may suffer from the lack of positive reinforcement and learn depressive beliefs from their experiences with their parents. Recent treatment studies have begun to include parents by providing education about depression and interventions to change parenting practices that may exacerbate depressive symptoms. Children may also experience rejection from peers and school personnel that exacerbates depression. In this case, social skills training and interventions to address the peer or school environment are required.

EMPIRICAL BASIS

Only a few empirical studies for childhood depression exist before 1990, in part due to the lack of recognition for depression as a clinical disorder in children before that time. These landmark studies incorporated treatment components that remain a cornerstone of treatment for childhood depression. Butler, Miezitis, Friedman, and Cole (1980) treated fifth and sixth graders with depressive symptoms in either role-play, cognitive restructuring, attention placebo, or control groups that met weekly for 10 weeks. The cognitive restructuring condition but not the attention placebo group was associated with significant improvement from pre- to posttreatment; however, no comparisons between treatment conditions were conducted. Stark, Reynolds, and Kaslow (1987) randomly assigned a sample of 29 elementary school children who scored 13 or higher on the Children's Depression Inventory (CDI) to either self-control, behavioral problem solving, or a wait-list control group. The self-control condition emphasized attribution training, self-monitoring, self-evaluating, and self-reward. The behavioral condition emphasized pleasant activity scheduling, self-monitoring, sensitivity training, problem solving, and social skills. After 12 treatment sessions spanning 5 weeks, results showed significant reductions in depressive symptoms for participants in both treatment groups. In 1990, Liddle and Spence (as cited in Curry, 2001) compared a primarily behavioral social competence training group with an attention group and a no-treatment group and found no differences among the three conditions; however, the sample consisted of only 31 children in grades 3 to 6. Also in 1990, Kahn, Kehle, Jenson, and Clark (as cited in Curry, 2001) compared CBT to relaxation, self-modeling, and a wait-list for 68 middle school students twice a week for 6 to 8 weeks. All treatment conditions led to significantly more symptom reduction than the wait-list but no differences were found between the results for the treatment conditions.

Trends in recent studies include the incorporation of control enhancement, family, and prevention interventions. For example, Weisz and colleagues demonstrated a relationship between perceived control and childhood depression (Weisz, Thurber, Sweeney, Proffitt, & LaGagnoux, 1997). They implemented an effective 8-session primary and secondary control enhancement program (PASCET) with 500 elementary school children from grades 3 to 6 identified with depressive symptomatology. Their program involved training children to apply primary control (enhancing reward by making objective conditions conform to the child's wishes) to modifiable conditions and applying secondary control (enhancing reward by adjusting one's beliefs or understanding in response to objective conditions) to conditions that could not be altered.

Asarnow, Scott, and Mintz (2002) designed an efficacious beyond that combined CBT and family education intervention to address data suggesting that family factors can predict outcomes and treatment response in depressed children. They selected 23 fourth-through sixth-grade-children to participate in the "Stress Busters" afterschool program twice a week for 5 weeks. "Stress Busters" included family education to enhance generalization of CBT technique to the real world and promote family support; the creation of a video viewed by parents that exhibited the children practicing newly learned CBT skills; and utilized generic as well as depression-focused CBT techniques. Sessions included activities such as games, homework, and role-playing designed to assist children in building problem-solving skills, goal-setting skills, social skills, relaxation techniques, as well as learning to effectively respond to positive or negative emotional spirals.

The Penn Resiliency Program (PRP) (Freres, Gillham, Reivich, & Shatte, 2002) aimed at preventing depression in children before it occurred. Children (aged 10–13) at risk for future depression learned CBT techniques and coping skills so that they could more effectively handle negative life events and increase their global sense of mastery and competence. Results indicate that depressive symptoms have been significantly reduced in many trials using this program regardless of the differing cultural and socioeconomic backgrounds of the participants (Freres et al., 2002).

Recent studies have also shown the longitudinal effectiveness of CBT. For example, in a study that included 54 children and adolescents aged 5 to 17 with depression or significant depressive symptoms, Vostanis, Feehan, and Grattan (1998) showed a significant difference between a CBT group and a nonfocused treatment group in remission of depressive symptoms over a 2-year follow-up. Such findings show the promise of CBT to remit symptoms over a brief time and to help curtail them over the long term.

A number of treatment studies with depressed adolescents exist and have informed treatment approaches with children (e.g., Lewinsohn's Coping with Depression Course). However, it is unknown whether the treatment effects seen with adolescents generalize to children. Currently, the Treatment for Adolescents with Depression Study (TADS) Team (2003) at Duke University Medical Center has begun to look at the effectiveness of brief CBT interventions for depression in adolescents in combination with and versus mood-stabilizing medication. The TADS study will help clinicians better understand the best treatment combination for adolescents with depression and as a result may impact the way childhood depression is treated.

CRITICISMS

Due to the structured, didactic, and directive nature of CBT, some therapists may argue that CBT is not appropriate for use with children. They point out that CBT techniques may exceed children's developmental capabilities, direct challenges of a child's beliefs may be off-putting to the child, the CBT approach neglects children's affect, and children may find the work dull (Friedberg et al., 2000). Friedberg's group recommend presenting CBT concepts in simple terms and in the context of negative feelings experienced by the child to avoid these roadblocks. Furthermore, games and play can be used as nonthreatening means to present the CBT approach and assist the child in viewing beliefs that may be confirmed or discounted through behavioral experimentation (Friedberg et al., 2000).

Although CBT for childhood depression appears promising, few empirical studies of effectiveness and mechanisms of effect have been conducted. Research to date has yielded modest results with CBT and supportive therapy conditions demonstrating similar levels of improvement following treatment. Furthermore, most studies have been conducted with small sample sizes of mild to moderately depressed children as opposed to clinical cases. Also, CBT treatment packages make it difficult to identify the mechanisms responsible for treatment gains. There are no guidelines to date on how a child's developmental cognitive level impacts on the implementation of CBT or which treatment components may be better suited to particular types of cases.

FUTURE DIRECTIONS

It is crucial that multisite, randomized clinical outcome studies be conducted with a sufficient sample of clinical cases with long-term follow-up to establish the relative effectiveness of CBT compared to other treatment approaches. Pharmacological, group, individual, family, and combined treatments must be compared for effectiveness. There is also a need for studies to address mechanisms of change in treatment. Ideally, these studies will assess a variety of mediator mechanisms (e.g., problem-solving skills) and outcomes beyond depressive symptoms. To guide interventions, more research must be conducted to further our understanding of the etiology, risk factors, and associated features of depression in children. Although some important research has addressed the impact of a depressed caretaker (particularly mothers) on children, greater understanding of the role the familial context plays in childhood depression is warranted. Given that the rates of depression increase dramatically in adolescence with evidence supporting a chronic course to the disorder, it is important to study the impact of prevention programs in childhood.

SUMMARY

Although many studies document an association between childhood depression and various cognitive distortions, further work is necessary to better understand the nature of the relationship between cognitive processes and depression in children. For example, it appears that while cognitions moderate the relationship between stressful life events and depression in adults, they act as mediators in children. Also, gender differences in treatment effects suggest the need for the development of gender-specific intervention models. As families have come to be considered important avenues for intervention, models that specify the relationship between family variables and childhood depression are receiving greater attention. Finally, there is movement in the field toward incorporating developmental models of affect regulation (e.g., Garber's information processing model), attachment, and cognitive change into CBT intervention approaches.

See also: Children—behavior therapy, Treatment of children

REFERENCES

Abramson, L. Y., Metalksy, G. I., & Alloy, L. B. (1989). Hopelessness depression: A theory-based subtype of depression. *Psychological Review, 96*, 358–372.

Asarnow, J. R., Scott, C. V., & Mintz, J. (2002). A combined cognitive–behavioral family education intervention for depression in children: A treatment development study. *Cognitive Therapy and Research, 26*, 221–229.

Butler, L., Miezitis, S., Friedman, R., & Cole, E. (1980). The effect of two school-based intervention programs on depressive symptoms I preadolescents. *American Educational Research Journal, 17*, 111–119.

Curry, J. F. (2001). Specific psychotherapies for childhood and adolescent depression. *Biological Psychiatry, 49*, 1091–1100.

Freres, D. R., Gillham, J. E., Reivich, K., & Shatte, A. J. (2002). Preventing depressive symptoms in middle school students: The Penn Resiliency Program. *International Journal of Emergency Mental Health, 4*, 31–40.

Friedberg, R. D., Crosby, L. E., Friedberg, B. A., Rutter, J. G., & Knight, R. (2000). Making cognitive behavioral therapy user-friendly to children. *Cognitive and Behavioral Practice, 6*, 189–200.

Kendall, P. C. (1993). Cognitive–behavioral therapies with youth: Guiding theory, current status, and emerging developments. *Journal of Consulting and Clinical Psychology, 61*, 235–247.

Lewinsohn, P. M. (1974). A behavioral approach to depression. In R. J. Friedman & M. M. Katz (Eds.), *The psychology of depression: Contemporary theory and research* (pp. 157–184). Washington, DC: Winston-Wiley.

Stark, K. D., Reynolds, W. M., & Kaslow, N. (1987). A comparison of the relative efficacy of self-control therapy and a behavioral problem-solving therapy for depression in children. *Journal of Abnormal Child Psychology, 15*, 91–113.

Treatment for Adolescents with Depression Study Team. (2003). Treatment for Adolescents with Depression Study (TADS): Rationale, design, and methods. *Journal of the American Academy of Child and Adolescent Psychiatry, 42*, 531–542.

Vostanis, P., Feehan, C., & Grattan, E. (1998). Two-year outcome of children treated for depression. *European Child and Adolescent Psychiatry, 7*, 12–18.

Weisz, J. R., Thurber, C. A., Sweeney, L., Proffitt, V. D., & LeGagnoux, G. L. (1997). Brief treatment of mild to moderate child depression using primary and secondary control enhancement training. *Journal of Consulting and Clinical Psychology, 65*, 703–707.

Developmental Disabilities in Community Settings

Michael R. Petronko and Russell J. Kormann

Keywords: developmental disabilities, mental retardation, community inclusion, behavior management, social problem solving

Forty years ago, prior to several daring investigative exposés depicting the deplorable conditions in which those with developmental disabilities (DD) lived in institutions such as Willowbrook and Pennhurst, this article would not have been written. Individuals with DD, and certainly almost all with challenging behaviors, lived in institutions. The deinstitutionalization movement that followed produced community visibility, and with it, the professional community as well as the public at large could no longer remain blithely unaware of the mental health challenges faced by this group.

In spite of the right-to-treatment movement associated with deinstitutionalization in the 1960s, which resulted from the above scandals, few therapeutic breakthroughs were forthcoming outside of improved pharmacological interventions. It is interesting to note that President John F. Kennedy's administration was the first to recognize the plight of persons with mental retardation for which he appointed the first Presidential Commission on Mental Retardation, which has met annually since. It is also noteworthy that his administration was responsible for developing the community mental health centers act. Of most significance, however, is the fact that while both initiatives were individually distinguished social milestones, neither the twain would meet. No provisions were made in the latter to accommodate the former. Therefore, treatment advances made possible by the adoption of CBT into the Community Mental Health Center/Managed Care movement supported by the Zeitgeist of evidence-based treatments were not considered systemically applicable for persons with DD. Instead, schedules of reinforcement, behavior control techniques, and contingency management dominated the research and clinical landscape for these individuals, in addition to the widespread use of antipsychotics. It is fair to say that persons with DD had been viewed as responders or Middleville serfs, lacking free will, self-awareness, and therefore much in need of our pity, care, and benevolence, but more importantly, our control. How then would one consider attempting CBT, when *feeble-minded, idiocy*, and *mentally retarded* were/are terms used synonymously with this group? This article looks at factors effecting the application of CBT endemic to the community at large. Specifically, CBT utilization requires us to look outside of the proverbial CBT box and address: the environment (professional reticence to consider using CBT with the DD), the larger system (public policy), and finally parent/caregiver (alternatives to infantalization).

ATTRIBUTIONAL BIASES (THE PROFESSIONAL)

Few other clinical populations have suffered the myriad of attributional biases as has the DD population. Reiss, Levitan, and Szyko (1982) perhaps best described this phenomenon in their work on diagnostic overshadowing. This suggests that when professionals encounter the potent label of mental retardation (MR), it essentially disguises or masks any other potential comorbid condition from being considered. It is as if the DD individual were essentially immune from other conditions so long as the DD label exists. Thus, depression and anxiety, found to be more frequently displayed in this group, are more likely to be viewed as behavioral sequelae to the MR, not as discrete conditions.

If psychiatric disorders have not been acknowledged, especially in a population not expected to experience any, as has been the case with the developmentally disabled, then mental health treatment need not be considered. From an economic standpoint, it is too convenient for financially strapped state/federal systems to collude with this myth and save money.

Even when a mental health issue has been accurately identified, there is a prevailing attitude that people with MR/DD cannot benefit from CBT or from psychotherapy in general because they do not have the verbal or cognitive skills necessary to participate. Whitman (1990) was one of the first to recognize that there were CBT alternatives to strict "S-R" contingency management intervention models for the DD, advocating instead for social learning theory approaches. Likewise, Nezu, Nezu, and Gill-Weiss (1992) outlined the unique challenges associated with using cognitively based strategies with this group, and provided viable remedies to produce efficacious CBT treatment. Attributional biases are maintained by the treating community, not the individuals in need of treatment. Therefore, any potential CBT intervention must begin with programs directed at attitude change on a systemswide level targeting professionals, as well as the larger community.

THE SPECTRUM OF DEVELOPMENTAL DISABILITIES (THE SYSTEM)

With the enlightenment provided by Reiss et al. (1982), dual diagnoses began to be recognized within the DD population and with this recognition, not surprisingly, was found a full spectrum of mental health challenges. A virtual replica of conditions was found not to be indistinguishable from this group's intellectually "normal" counterparts, including PTSD, OCD, depression, and all the anxiety disorders. Notice that these conditions were not created by the process of deinstitutionalization (or at least not solely) as iatrogenic effects, but were now recognized because of the visibility afforded by community inclusion. The system must not only recognize that the population of DD individuals have anxiety disorders, and that CBT can be a treatment of choice, but also not infantilize the individual, by disallowing their responsibility for engaging in aberrant behavior and/or his or her responsibility for maintaining treatment. For example, while in a residential setting, sexual assault might be viewed, if acknowledged at all, as a behavior problem (men and women who have been raped in residential settings are rarely treated for PTSD). In the community, it is rape, and punishable by law. The person with DD as the perpetrator or the assaulted or both is/are victims and deserve state-of-the art treatments (CBT). To the degree that the community perceives persons with DD as children, regardless of their chronological age, sexual deviations will never be considered, for the prevailing view is more likely to see them as asexual (Thompson & Bryson, 2001).

Offenders with DD face the same assessment and treatment obstacles in the legal system as do dually diagnosed individuals in free society. Previous approaches predominantly employed aversive approaches to reduce behavior, whereas more recent work encourages the learning of new skills. CBT work is being done with this population, largely incorporating anger management programs within broader interventions that include lifestyle changes, prevention and management of future offenses, and collaboration with caregivers. Treatment needs to be of sufficient duration to reduce recidivism.

Anger management, a key element of work with offenders, is also commonly and more widely used to address aggression in persons with DD not currently implicated in criminal behavior. Novaco, Ramm, and Black (2000) differentiate between anger management and anger treatment. Anger management, often delivered in group formats, is a structured psychoeducational approach that is less intensive than anger treatment. Anger treatment involves individualized analysis of anger experience, and endeavors to minimize anger via the restructuring of cognitions, and the development of self-monitoring and self-regulation skills. Graded exposure to provocation is conducted as a key component of stress inoculation training. Likewise, the work in the offenders project (Nezu, Nezu, & Dudeck, 1998) utilizes CBT procedures with the DD. However, their project acknowledges that community placement necessarily brings troublesome behaviors (iatrogenic effects), such as sexual offenses. With these troublesome behaviors, the best of treatments available should be brought to bear on them—hence CBT!

GETTING OUT OF THE CBT BOX: WHO IS (ARE) THE CLIENT(S)?

While it is true that some individuals with DD can participate in CBT, many cannot. Moreover, it is clear that many people with DD are supported by and work with parents and staff members who are both intimately involved in the display of their behaviors as well as are affected by their outcome. These individuals simultaneously function as loving family members; motivated care providers, informal clinicians, and case managers attempting to navigate a service delivery system that is foreign to them. They are also the major sources of referrals (few individuals with DD are self-referred). Most of the CBT literature, therefore, speaks to the importance of staff and parent consultation and identifies it as an integral component of the treatment regimen (Benson, 1992).

The use of family members or staff of the referred individual as the consumers of CBT and ultimately as the agent of change describes a different "point of entry" than that which is typically discussed in the CBT literature. While it is clear that parents and staff play a role that is critical in not only the referred individual's daily well-being, but in their therapeutic success, developing a treatment plan that utilizes staff and parents as the agents of change requires a shift in clinical focus (Petronko, Harris, & Kormann, 1994). That is, obstacles, which prevent them from competently serving as change agents, become viable targets of intervention along with the behavior of the DD person. Moreover, several challenges face treatment models that utilize direct service individuals (i.e., staff, teachers, or parents) as change agents. First, the stress associated with providing services to individuals with DD and psychiatric/behavioral challenges is well documented. The literature is replete with discussions of the burden of ongoing crisis management, burnout, and turnover (Petronko et al., 1994). Second, low pay, long hours, inadequate training, and the potential for personal injury are all obstacles that the disability community must overcome in its attempt to provide effective and consistent behavioral support to individuals with dual diagnoses. Third, attributional biases, such as those outlined by "diagnostic overshadowing" (Reiss et al., 1982), present clinicians with yet another challenge that must be addressed. Parents' and staff members' belief systems that individuals with DD are inherently dangerous, unable to change or that their developmental disability "overshadows" and therefore defines any behavioral or psychiatric manifestation rendering them "unavailable" to therapeutic intervention, severely interfere with their ability to participate in effective treatment models. Consultation models designed to assist family members and staff in serving individuals with DD, therefore, must possess aspects of CBT that can address the misattributions, dysfunctional thought processes, and ineffective problem-solving skills which are common to caregivers struggling with dually diagnosed family members or consumers (Nezu et al., 1992; Petronko et al., 1994). A CBT model that promotes self-efficacy through the development of management skills and an intervention plan specifically tailored to the needs of the individual, caregiver(s) environment, and system would engender a sense of control in not only the caregiver, but also in the identified consumer (Kormann & Petronko, 2002; Petronko et al., 1994). CBT assessment strategies must be robust enough to highlight the contribution of each of these areas as they impact on the target behavior in question. Subsequent treatment must therefore address more than the individual with a disability.

MULTIPLE MODEL APPROACHES TO INTEGRATING CBT AND COMMUNITY INCLUSION PROJECT: NATURAL SETTING THERAPEUTIC MANAGEMENT (NSTM)

Project NSTM is one of a few CBT treatment programs which incorporates the principles outlined above. NSTM is a behavioral consultation and training program designed to enrich the therapeutic capacity of a referred person's natural environment by increasing the behavioral competence of the caretakers, environment (which includes the other indigenous people as well as the physical environment), and system in which all operate in that setting (Petronko, Anesko, Nezu, & Pos, 1988; Petronko et al., 1994). Competence is achieved by mastering the precepts of 11 interactive models, which collectively represent the NSTM multiple-model system. All program activities take place in the referred individual's natural environment, which is behaviorally scrutinized and subsequently transformed into a therapeutic milieu. This milieu, the behavior of the person with developmental disability, the individual(s) responsible for managing the program, and the sociopolitical system in which all of the above exist, collectively represent the four discrete areas within which a complete NSTM assessment is conducted. It is not assumed that the problem exists within the individual, as might be implied by using a strict ABA approach. Rather it is assumed that the problem reflects contributions from each of the four areas. CBT interventions which become generated by the NSTM four-factor assessment protocol therefore employ strategies, not techniques. The interventions by necessity are robust by virtue of incorporating each of the four factors in their focus. Transfer of ownership to these multiple consumers represents the ultimate goal, thus providing for maintenance of change across time and settings and generalization.

FUTURE DIRECTIONS AND RESEARCH

The mental health plight of persons with developmental disabilities has improved immeasurably over the last decade, but it has only begun to be considered within the CBT community. A strong advocacy position therefore must be assumed by all of us before this untenable situation improves. Research in overcoming attributional biases in both the professional and lay community is an essential precursor. Further research into evaluating the four-factor assessment model proposed by Petronko et al. (1994) as it attempts to highlight the various foci of intervention also needs to be done.

See also: Mental retardation—adult, Problem solving—depression

REFERENCES

Benson, B. A. (1992). *Teaching anger management to persons with mental retardation*. Chicago: IDS, Inc.

Kormann, R. J., & Petronko, M. R. (2002). Crisis and revolution in developmental disabilities: The dilemma of community based services. *The Behavior Analyst Today, 3*, 434–442.

Nezu, C. M., Nezu, A. M., & Dudeck, J. (1998). A cognitive–behavioral model of assessment and treatment for intellectually disabled sexual offenders. *Cognitive and Behavioral Practice, 5*, 25–64.

Nezu, C. M., Nezu, A. M., & Gill-Weiss, M. J. (1992). *Psychopathology in persons with mental retardation: Clinical guidelines for assessment and treatment*. Champaign, IL: Research Press.

Novaco, R. W., Ramm, M., & Black, L. (2000). Anger treatment with offenders. In C. R. Hollin (Ed.), *Handbook of offender assessment and treatment*. New York: Wiley.

Petronko, M. R., Anesko, K. M., Nezu, A., & Pos, A. (1988). Natural setting therapeutic management (NSTM): Training in the natural environment. In J. M. Levy, P. H. Levy, & B. Nivin (Eds.), *Strengthening families* (pp.185–193). New York: Young Adult Institute Press.

Petronko, M. R., Harris, S. L., & Kormann, R. J. (1994). Community-based training approaches for people with mental retardation and mental illness. *Journal of Consulting and Clinical Psychology, 62*, 49–54.

Reiss, S., Levitan, G., & Szyko, J. (1982). Emotional disturbance and mental retardation: Diagnostic overshadowing. *American Journal on Mental Deficiency, 86*, 567–574.

Thompson, S. A., & Bryson, M. (2001). Prospects for identity formation for lesbian, gay, or bisexual persons with developmental disabilities. *International Journal of Development and Education, 48*, 53–65.

Whitman, T. L. (1990). Self-regulation and mental retardation. *American Journal on Mental Retardation, 94*, 347–363.

Dialectical Behavior Therapy for Eating Disorders

Marsha M. Linehan and Eunice Y. Chen

Keywords: dialectical behavior therapy, DBT, bulimia nervosa, anorexia nervosa, eating disorders not otherwise specified, binge eating disorder, borderline personality disorder

Dialectical Behavior Therapy (DBT) is a multimodal cognitive–behavioral treatment originally developed to treat chronically suicidal individuals meeting borderline personality disorder (BPD) criteria. DBT is informed by Eastern mindfulness practices and behavior therapy, and is conducted within the frame of a dialectical epistemology. The underlying dialectic involves acceptance of clients in their current distress, yet aiding clients with skills to alter their dysfunctional behavioral patterns. The behavior change strategies it employs include methodical and iterative behavioral analyses of dysfunctional chains of behavior, the use of commitment strategies to engage clients in treatment, didactic strategies, exposure-based strategies to block avoidance and repetitive behaviors and reduce maladaptive emotions, contingency management to reduce, suppress, or prevent disordered responses and to strengthen skillful responses and cognitive modification strategies. Acceptance procedures consist of mindfulness (learning to observe, describe, and participate in the moment, without judgment, effectively and one-mindfully) and a variety of validation and stylistic strategies. It has been developed for various subgroups of BPD clients (e.g., highly suicidal or substance-dependent BPD) and more recently for BPD clients with eating disorders (ED) or clients with only ED diagnoses.

The reasons for developing DBT for ED are: (1) current treatments for binge eating disorder (BED) and bulimia nervosa (BN) are effective for only 50% of clients and even less for chronic anorexia (AN), (2) BPD and parasuicidal behavior is common among ED clients with suicide being a leading cause of death in AN, (3) ED involve emotion regulation difficulties and skills deficits despite clients' "apparent competence" in other areas of their lives, (4) ED are often stigmatized as trivial problems despite high death rates in AN and significant impairment of functioning in other ED, and (5) ED, especially AN, differ from other mental illnesses in the significant degree of ambivalence about symptoms and treatment.

BRIEF DEFINITION OF BULIMIA NERVOSA, ANOREXIA NERVOSA, EATING DISORDERS NOT OTHERWISE SPECIFIED, AND BINGE EATING DISORDER

An ED, as defined by current clinical classification systems, the *Diagnostic and Statistical Manual of Mental Disorders–Fourth Edition* (DSM-IV, APA, 1994) and *International Classification of Disorders-10* (ICD-10 WHO, 1992), involves extreme forms of eating behavior accompanied by an extreme dependence on weight and shape as a means of self-evaluation. This leads to a significant impairment of health and psychosocial functioning and significant mortality in AN. ED diagnoses are classified into AN and BN, and for those who meet neither criteria, "eating disorders not otherwise specified" (ED-NOS; DSM-IV) or "atypical eating disorders" (ICD-10). The ED-NOS criteria include those meeting the BED research criteria (DSM-IV). AN is marked by amenorrhea and low weight (body mass index [BMI] < 17.5 or a body weight 85% of expected) due to dieting, vomiting, overexercise, and the abuse of laxatives, diuretics, or diet pills. BN is marked by a preoccupation with thinness despite being a healthy weight together with bingeing on objectively large amounts of food followed by inappropriate compensation (e.g., dieting, vomiting, overexercise, laxative, diuretic, or diet pill abuse). BED involves binge eating in the absence of compensatory behaviors and is highly comorbid with obesity (BMI > 30), with about a third of obese clients meeting criteria for BED. BED is the most frequently occurring ED followed by BN and then AN.

DBT MODEL OF EATING DISORDERS

DBT for ED is based on a broadly defined affect regulation model of eating disorders. The basic premise of the theory is that disordered eating serves to regulate intolerable affective states in individuals with few or no other adaptive strategies for regulating affect. Bingeing or bulimic behavior is explained as a result of trying to escape or block primary or secondary aversive emotions that may be triggered by thoughts regarding food, body image, perfectionism, the self, or interpersonal situations. Bingeing functions to quickly narrow attention and cognitive focus from these thoughts and to provide immediate escape from physiological responses and feelings. Over time, bingeing, as an escape behavior, becomes reinforced, especially if there are no more adaptive emotion regulation skills present. Eventually bingeing becomes an overlearned dysfunctional response to dysregulated emotions. The longer-term effects of bingeing or bulimic behaviors are secondary emotions such as feeling ashamed that can also promote the eating disordered behavior.

DBT argues that the extreme weight loss seen in AN is an escape from tolerating primary or secondary affect in the absence of other more adaptive emotion regulation skills. These emotions may be generated by cues such as developmental challenges, perfectionist standards, low self-esteem, situations involving perceived loss of control (e.g., eating, interpersonal or familial situations), or an extreme desire to be thin. These cues may be multiple and may vary from individual to individual.

Previous treatments for eating disorders have focused on various factors maintaining ED symptoms including: the violation of dietary restraint (cognitive–behavioral therapy for BN) or interpersonal problems (interpersonal psychotherapy for BN), or maturational difficulties (Crisp's psychobiological theory of AN), or a combination of clinical perfectionism, low self-esteem, mood intolerance, and interpersonal difficulties (transdiagnostic theory of ED). Parsimoniously, DBT theory suggests that the processes purported to maintain disordered eating (distorted body image, interpersonal difficulties, poor self-efficacy for meeting pubertal demands, perfectionist standards, and pervasive low self-esteem) are mediated by the effects of emotional responses and the inability of the individual to prevent, tolerate, or modulate these emotional responses. So, for instance, DBT postulates that it may be the secondary emotion of shame that is the important mediator in the relationship between self-critical thoughts and binge eating. Empirical research on the precursors of ED will be important in generating hypotheses about (1) specific emotions, (2) their degree of intensity, and (3) the kinds of emotional contexts related to the maintenance of particular ED (e.g., fear of "growing up" in AN, extreme shame in the obese client with BED with chronic and pervasive low self-esteem). Until this research is done, DBT emphasizes the necessity of evaluating the specific pattern of emotions, their precipitants, and their contextual associations, and the individual's skill level. DBT targets disordered eating behaviors directly and as emotions are generated by efforts to regulate eating, treatment targets the increase of distress tolerance and emotion regulation. Emotion regulation from this point of view includes both the reduction of emotional vulnerability and the increase of emotion modulation.

DBT FOR ED: TARGETS

There are four treatment stages matching four levels of severity, each with a hierarchy of treatment targets. Stage I focuses on increasing behavioral control of clients meeting ED and BPD criteria who engage in parasuicidal behaviors or clients whose ED behavior puts them at imminent high risk of death or self-injury. The hierarchy of treatment targets is: (1) life-threatening behaviors (e.g., starvation, ipecac abuse, or fluid restriction in AN clients with an extremely low BMI, vomiting despite risk of heart attack, and bingeing and purging in diabetic clients who risk inducing diabetic shock), (2) therapy-interfering behaviors (e.g., AN clients falling below an agreed outpatient weight range or refusing to discuss their restriction in therapy), (3) eating disorders (e.g., bingeing, restriction, laxative, diuretic, and diet pill abuse), (4) problems interfering with quality of life (e.g., unemployment), (5) increasing skills to facilitate a life worth living, and (6) other individual goals. An example of Stage I treatment is described in an uncontrolled DBT trial with ED clients meeting BPD criteria (Leicester General Hospital, UK; Palmer et al., 2003). Stage II involves exposure to avoided emotions associated with "quiet desperation" as a way of preventing a recurrence of life-threatening behavior. Otherwise the majority of clients with ED who do not have complex out-of-control behaviors fall into Stage III, where ED behavior interferes with quality of life. Stanford University was the first to develop and evaluate Stage III DBT and their hierarchy involves stopping: (1) therapy-interfering behavior, (2) binge eating, and decreasing: (3) mindless eating, (4) cravings, urges, and preoccupation with food, (5) capitulating, and (6) apparently irrelevant behaviors (e.g., weighing). Weight loss is not a goal of treatment. Stage IV treatment for recovered ED clients would involve focusing on developing relationships, careers, and hobbies.

DBT FOR ED: THERAPIST STRATEGIES

This section will describe dialectical, core (change and validation), communication, and case management strategies that have been or are being developed for ED (e.g., McCabe, La Via, & Marcus, in press). See the manual for protocols for crises management, suicidal behaviors, and relationship problems.

Dialectical Strategies

The dialectical philosophy that informs treatment views the aim of DBT as replacing extreme and rigid response patterns with more synthesized and balanced ways of thinking and doing, using dialectical strategies (e.g., metaphor, paradox, cognitive restructuring). One exemplar of this application of dialectical philosophy, borrowed from DBT for substance abuse, is in the concept of "dialectical abstinence," which synthesizes the goal or thesis of treatment as binge abstinence with the antithesis: acceptance and preparation for the possibility of lapses. Other areas where synthesis is important are: encouraging a more moderate standard of achievement than extreme perfectionist standards; challenging the illusion of control motivating overeating; and accepting the changes a client is currently making but also encouraging further change. This latter dialectic is important in targeting clients' ambivalence about treatment and the frustration and hopelessness that therapists and family may experience.

Change Strategies

In Stage III DBT, at each session, a diary card modified for ED is reviewed (including ratings of urges to binge, binge eating, mindless eating, apparently irrelevant behavior [e.g., easy access to binge foods], goal capitulation, food cravings, food preoccupation, and weekly weight). The client reports on the key link in the chain analysis (a description of the problem, its antecedents, its consequences, and its context) that led to the bingeing, or otherwise, a lower-ranked target for behavioral change, and what skills the client has used or will use in the future (solution analysis). The therapist establishes reasons for skills failure, reinforces approximations of skills, and ensures broad skills use rather than overreliance on one skill.

As ambivalence is a major barrier to success in ED treatment, commitment strategies (e.g., highlighting the freedom to make the choice of continuing treatment in the absence of alternatives, given their health, or analysis of pros and cons of behavior) are used throughout. In the initial session, the devil's advocate strategy is used to elicit reasons for bingeing abstinence from clients if they wish to have a life worth living.

The use of didactic strategies is typical of the Stanford program which is based on teaching three skills modules (Mindfulness, Emotion Regulation, and Distress Tolerance) and the Leicester General Hospital program which adds an "Eatingness" module that includes didactics about the invalidating cultural and nutritional environment, weight regulation, and the effects of starvation.

Exposure and response prevention in the context of "opposite action" (where urges to engage in dysfunctional behavior are overcome by doing the action opposite to the urge) are important in targeting urges to avoid (difficult foods, eating situations or body image situations, negative moods, interpersonal situations, maturational situations) and urges to engage in repetitive acts (e.g., body checking). In these situations, clients are asked to construct a hierarchy of avoided situations and exposed to these with plans to prevent the old dysfunctional response and to engage in new adaptive behaviors. The aim would also be to generalize new adaptive responses to other situations and contexts.

Other change strategies important in the treatment of ED include contingency management using the therapeutic relationship (e.g., by making outpatient DBT contingent on the client observing weight limits) and cognitive modification strategies to reappraise weight and shape concerns, the self, interpersonal relationships, and perfectionist beliefs.

Acceptance

In DBT for ED, every change strategy is paired with an acceptance-based validation strategy. Validation involves responding in a genuine way to the client's thoughts and feelings as understandable given his or her current situation, learning history, beliefs, and in terms of the model of ED behavior. It does not involve validating the invalid. Thus, if a client comments that he feels fat but is in the normal weight range, then it is important to validate the feelings of fatness as a habitual thinking pattern that occurs after eating a meal, although commenting that it is a thought, not a feeling, and that there is no evidence for this thought being true, given his weight.

Communication Strategies

Standard DBT communication strategies for building a collaborative relationship (e.g., warmth) and to shift the client's attention from dysfunctional interactions or behaviors (irreverence) are also used in DBT for ED.

Case Management Strategies

The consultation-to-the-therapist strategy, which involves the use of the consultation team of therapists, is important as: (1) ED often involve intense feelings on the therapist's part and (2) it may draw on the expertise of differently trained professionals (e.g., medical doctors, nutritionists), vital in the treatment of chronic ED (e.g., AN). Finally, other case management strategies are important for ED clients in coaching them to manage an often extensive health provider network and to build a sense of control and self-efficacy and thus to meet maturational and interpersonal goals.

Treatment Structure

Stage I DBT for ED with BPD (e.g., Leicester General Hospital) includes weekly: individual psychotherapy (1 hour), skills group (2 hours), consultation team for therapists (2 hours), and out-of-session phone consultation, and ancillary treatments (e.g., pharmacotherapy). Individual psychotherapy involves focusing on the highest behavior according to the treatment hierarchy. Skills group involves four modules: mindfulness, interpersonal effectiveness, emotion regulation, and distress tolerance. The Leicester General Hospital trial included these modules and an Eatingness module (five to six sessions). This involves didactics as described but also application of mindfulness to eating (e.g., mindfully planning, regular eating), problem-solving and distress tolerance skills for urges to binge and purge, and radical acceptance of body image. Stanford's Stage III DBT program involves three skills modules delivered in groups (BED) or individually (BN) (20 sessions).

RESEARCH ON DBT FOR ED

One uncontrolled trial and two randomized controlled trials have been conducted on Stanford's adaptation of DBT for Stage III clients. In a randomized controlled trial that compared DBT to wait-list control in obese BED women, there were no differences between treatments in dropouts. Those in DBT compared to controls reported significantly greater abstinence from bingeing (89% versus 12.5%) and significantly improved body image, eating concerns, and reduced urge to eat when angry. At 3-month follow-up, 67% of 18 in DBT were abstinent and at 6-month follow-up, 56% of 18 were abstinent. These results for DBT were consistent with those of the smaller uncontrolled trial of DBT.

Another randomized controlled trial compared individual DBT for BN clients with a wait-list control. DBT was well accepted and there was a median purge reduction of 98% and an abstinence rate of 28.6%, which was similar to findings in a large multisite CBT for BN trial at posttreatment. DBT appeared to improve urges to eat in response to negative emotions.

Finally, in an uncontrolled trial of DBT (6 to 18 months) for clients with ED and BPD (Leicester General Hospital), clients (3/7) who had inpatient stays before the program, had no hospital days 12 months after DBT. There was a decrease in self-harm episodes 18 months after DBT in the clients (4/5) who self-harmed before the program. No other standardized outcome measures were used although ED symptoms improved in all and notable psychosocial changes (e.g., employment progress) at posttreatment were described. While the results of this trial are anecdotal, they are suggestive.

RESEARCH DIRECTIONS

The promising results from the Stanford trials using DBT for ED and the preliminary findings of Leicester General Hospital suggest that further treatment development work and clinical trials are warranted for DBT for ED and for DBT for ED and BPD. The current absence of empirical work examining DBT for clients meeting AN and BPD is also notable.

See also: Anorexia nervosa, Bulimia nervosa

REFERENCES/RECOMMENDED READINGS

DBT for ED and BPD

Palmer, R. L., Birchall, H., Damani, S., Gatward, N., McGrain, L., & Parker, L. (2003). A dialectical behavior therapy program for people with an eating disorder and borderline personality disorder description and outcome. *International Journal of Eating Disorders, 33*, 281–286.

DBT and BED and BN

Safer, D. L., Lively, T. I., Telch, C. F., & Agras, W. S. (2002). Predictors of relapse following successful dialectical behavior therapy for binge eating disorder. *International Journal of Eating Disorders, 32*, 155–163.

Safer, D. L., Telch, C. F., & Agras, W. S. (2001). Dialectical behavior therapy for bulimia nervosa. *American Journal of Psychiatry, 158*, 632–634.

Safer, D. L., Telch, C. F., & Agras, W. S. (2001). Dialectical behavior therapy adapted for bulimia: A case report. *International Journal of Eating Disorders, 30*, 101–106.

Telch, C. F., Agras, W. S., & Linehan, M. M. (2000). Group dialectical behavior therapy for binge-eating disorder: A preliminary, uncontrolled trial. *Behavior Therapy, 31*, 569–582.

Telch, C. F., Agras, W. S., & Linehan, M. M. (2001). Dialectical behavior therapy for binge eating disorder. *Journal of Consulting and Clinical Psychology, 69*, 1061–1065.

Wiser, S., & Telch, C. F. (1999). Dialectical behavior therapy for binge-eating disorder. *Journal of Clinical Psychology, 55*, 755–768.

Descriptions of DBT, AN, and ED

McCabe, E. B., La Via, M. C., & Marcus, M. D. (in press). Dialectical behavior therapy for eating disorders. In J. K. Thompson (Ed.), *Handbook of eating disorders and obesity*. New York: Wiley.

McCabe, E. B., & Marcus, M. D. (2002). Question: Is dialectical behavior therapy useful in the management of anorexia nervosa? *Eating Disorders: The Journal of Treatment and Prevention, 10*(4), 335–337.

Disruptive Anger

Howard Kassinove and Raymond Chip Tafrate

Keywords: anger, aggression, hostility, experiences, expressions, outcomes

Anger is a basic human emotion (Plutchik, 1980, 2000). When it is mild, infrequent, and fleeting, it can be helpful as an alerting stimulus or a motivating force. In contrast, when it is strong, frequent, and enduring, anger is highly disruptive to effective functioning. Practitioners certainly know that strong anger is a major presenting and continuing problem in child, adolescent, and adult cases. Yet, much more of our research and clinical efforts have been devoted to the treatment of anxiety and depression; anger has been relatively ignored. This is surprising since effective treatments for anger reduction do exist. In fact, meta-analytic reviews of treatment outcome studies indicate a moderate to large magnitude of improvement across a variety of subject samples (Beck & Fernandez, 1998; Bowman-Edmondson & Cohen-Conger, 1996; DiGiuseppe & Tafrate, 2003; Sukhodolsky, Kassinove, & Gorman, in press; Tafrate, 1995).

Anger is defined as a negative psychobiological state, of varying intensity and duration, which is reported by verbal labels such as "annoyed," "pissed-off," "angry," and "furious." Angry states are associated with cognitive distortions and unrealistic evaluations of the triggering stimulus, moderate to high autonomic reactivity, private experiences that often include fantasies of revenge, and public expressive behaviors that may include yelling, gesturing, and profanity. Whether or not public behavioral expressions of anger actually emerge will vary, based on the individual patients' social learning history and the contingencies of the present environment.

Although anxiety and depression are also negative, anger is an energizing emotion that typically elicits retaliatory fantasies and behaviors. In contrast, anxiety typically elicits avoidance behaviors. Depression is not at all energizing. When anger occurs with significant frequency, across a variety of situations, it is conceptualized as a personality trait. Although traits are interesting and important for theory building, practitioners can only work with the individual anger episodes of their patients in order to understand their response patterns and reduce the likelihood of anger responses in the future.

Anger is different from hostility, which is defined as a set of attitudes that may lead to anger, and from aggression, which is defined as overt motor behavior with the intent to harm others. Recognizing the confusion that has existed, Spielberger (1988) called anger, hostility, and aggression the "AHA" trio to highlight the fact that they are different phenomena. He also noted that anger can be conceptualized as a trait or a state, both of which are measured by his State–Trait Anger Expression Inventory (STAXI-2; Spielberger, 1999). Persons high on trait anger are more likely to experience states of anger in a variety of situations and in response to varying stimuli. Although interesting, traits are hypothetical entities inferred from states. Thus, practitioners focus on the individual anger episodes of their patients in order to understand their response patterns and reduce the likelihood of anger in the future.

THE ANGER EPISODE MODEL

Kassinove and Tafrate (2002) developed a five-stage anger episode model to guide treatment (Figure 1). They recommend that the model be used as a reference point for joint practitioner–patient understanding of anger as well as an idiographic assessment strategy. Elements of the model have been validated by Kassinove, Sukhodolsky, Tsytsarev, and Solovyova (1997) and Tafrate, Kassinove, and Dundin (2002).

Triggers. Each episode begins with a triggering event. These triggers are usually unwanted behaviors of persons who are well-known or loved and are most likely to occur at home in the afternoon or evening hours. By objective standards, the triggers are usually negative and may consist of insults, neglect by loved ones, unfair treatment, and the like. Some triggers, however, are objectively neutral or may even be positive, as when unwanted compliments are repeatedly received from disliked persons. If fact, almost any stimulus can be a trigger for anger.

Appraisals. Aversive triggers lead to a general state of arousal (Berkowitz, 1990, 1993). In order for the arousal to then emerge as "anger," the triggers must be appraised or interpreted in specific ways. Tafrate, Kassinove, and Dundin (in press), using a community sample, found that adults high on the trait of anger endorsed a greater number of dysfunctional cognitions than did low-trait-anger adults and were particularly prone to believe that the triggering events for their anger were "awful" (as opposed to simply very bad) and "intolerable" (as opposed to difficult to manage), to engage in distortions, and to believe they were bad people (see Beck, 1999; Ellis, 1994). In addition, the angry person may believe that he or she does not have the skill to deal with the instigator. This conclusion, of course, may or may not correspond to reality.

The *combination* of triggers and appraisals leads to anger as a specific emotional response. The internal, private part of the response is the anger experience. The external, public part of the response represents the expression of anger.

Experiences. Private experiences may consist of thoughts about the importance of retaliation, images of harming others, or physiological arousal unseen by others. Adults high on the trait of anger seem to experience anger episodes of greater intensity and longer duration than do low-trait-anger adults. The most common physical sensations associated with anger are muscle tension, rapid heart rate, headache, and upset stomach.

Expressions. Study of the expressive behaviors associated with anger leads to some surprising conclusions. For example, aggression is *not* commonly reported by nonspecific samples of angry adults. The most common expressive pattern is verbal and consists of shouting, demanding, use of sarcasm, and profanity. Physical aggression is typically reported to occur only about 10% of the time. However, aggression is more common among high-trait-anger adults and is likely to be more prominent in selected samples (e.g.,

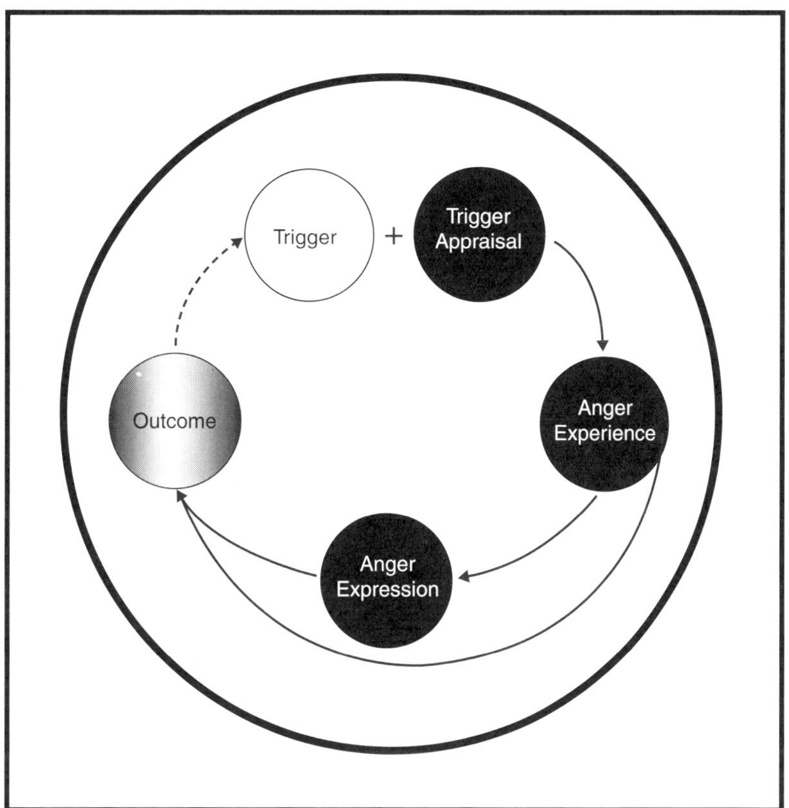

Figure 1. The anger episode model.

clients in criminal justice settings, schools for disturbed children). Differences in expressive patterns between men and women are minor.

Outcomes. Anger becomes a clinical problem when the outcomes are more negative than positive. Outcomes can be interpersonal, emotional, cognitive, and medical. At the interpersonal level, relationships are likely to be weakened following an anger episode as less time is spent with the person viewed as the instigator Also, angry people are avoided by others. This leads to additional problems such as job dissatisfaction, greater likelihood of disagreements at work, and more conflict with friends and romantic partners. Anger is also likely to be followed by other negative emotions such as continued irritation, sadness-depression, disgust, concern, and guilt. These are especially likely to emerge for persons high in trait anger. It is also important to note that some positive feelings may also emerge including a feeling of relief and satisfaction. Some people do report that their anger serves them well. Nevertheless, for high-trait-anger adults, short- and long-term outcomes of anger are twice as likely to be negative rather than positive.

Cognitively, anger is associated with rumination about the trigger. This rumination is likely to increase the intensity and duration of the episode, and sets the stage for additional anger as a negative distorting filter likely to be applied to further actions by the trigger. Angry adults who are high on trait anger also report more mental health problems such as depression, anxiety, panic attacks, substance use, and marital problems, all of which have strong cognitive elements.

The medical problems associated with anger are particularly problematic since they often are not linked to anger episodes by patients. Outcomes linked to a stimulus are likely to be those that are close in time. Thus, patients are most likely to see the interpersonal costs of anger. In contrast, many medical anger outcomes are like those associated with cigarette smoking—they do not appear for years. Nevertheless, the data show that longer term, persistent anger is associated with hypertension, stroke, myocardial infarction, and cancer. For example, Williams and her associates (2000) completed a large-scale prospective study of the relationship of trait anger to cardiovascular heart disease (CHD). Middle-aged men and women (n = 12,986), initially free of coronary disease, were followed for a mean of 53 months. Results indicated that among adults with normal blood pressure, the risk of coronary events increased directly with increasing levels of trait anger. High-anger adults were 2.6

times more likely to have a cardiac event than low-anger adults. The risk posed by high trait anger was found to be independent of other established biological risk factors. These and other data strongly suggest the importance of treating high-trait-anger persons.

TREATMENT

CBT treatment for anger (Kassinove & Tafrate, 2002) consists of four stages: (1) preparing the patient for intervention, (2) working toward anger reduction through behavior change, (3) reducing anger by developing acceptance skills, and (4) preparing the patient for relapse.

Preparation. Angry patients are often resistant to treatment. As compared to anxious or depressed patients, who often seek help on their own, angry patients are typically referred by others. Moreover, when they do come for treatment, it is often the trigger (e.g., their husband, wife, child, employer, or employee) that they want to change—not themselves. Thus, angry patients must often be prepared to accept treatment. This process begins by assessing motivation for change (which is typically low) and by developing a strong therapeutic alliance. Trust will be enhanced by agreeing on the goals and methods to be used. In addition, it is important to develop and increase awareness of the short- and long-term consequences associated with individual episodes of anger. These preparations for the main CBT intervention strategies, noted below, will increase the likelihood of success.

Behavior Change. Five CBT procedures can be used for the treatment of anger. As a short-term solution, *avoidance* and *escape* are useful. Avoidance from aversive stimuli (such as a verbally combative colleague) or escape (as when one leaves an unpleasant meeting) prevent escalations and allow for a time delay for cognitive reevaluation of the problem situation. Since anger is associated with discomforting physical sensations, deep *muscle relaxation*, or a variant, helps change response patterns to aversive stimuli and increases a sense of control. In addition, it gives patients a sense of confidence in their therapist. Muscle relaxation remains one of the most powerful techniques for CBT practitioners (Deffenbacher et al., 1996). Sometimes, skill training is important. Anger can be reduced if the patient has a true sense of competence (such as a typist, computer repair person, chef) in areas of importance. Of course, conflicts emerge for everyone. Thus, anger management includes the development of social problem-solving skills and assertive verbal behaviors. Finally, imaginal and in vivo exposure sessions help patients become desensitized to the aversive triggers in their lives.

Acceptance. Even in the best of cases, with a skilled practitioner and a motivated patient, many anger triggers will continue. Some triggers will be novel, as when "sweet" children enter adolescence and become noncompliant and moody. Others will be repeated triggers, as when a boss continues to make unrealistic demands, even after assertive discussions. Thus, anger management also consists of learning to see the world realistically and developing a flexible philosophy. Often, for example, patients overgeneralize with statements such as "My child never listens" or "My husband is a total slob." It is always useful to help them see that it is more realistic to talk about the specific behaviors of their child or spouse rather than exaggerated and unrealistic statements that contain words such as "always" or "is" (see Beck, 1999; Korzybzi, 1933). It is also useful to teach patients that their anger is increased when they appraise realistically bad triggers as "awful" or "horrible" and when they believe they "can't stand" what has happened. Verbal discrimination training, with the goal of semantic precision (e.g., "that was very unpleasant and I am finding it difficult to cope with it"), is likely to reduce the frequency, intensity, and duration of anger episodes (Tafrate & Kassinove, 1998). Finally, patients can be taught to forgive and let go of the negative feeling associated with the anger trigger. This does not mean they are to forget about it, nor to accept it. Rather, they are to remember what was done by their family member, friend, or stranger and to work to reduce the likelihood that it will occur again. However, they are taught that recall of past problems is best done with mild arousal rather than in anger or rage.

Relapse Prevention. Seasoned practitioners know well about relapse. A large number of patients with all sorts of presenting problems return to treatment after a period of time. This is not unusual and represents either some kind of spontaneous response to old stimuli or is a response to a new situation that was previously not dealt with. It is useful to prepare patients, and plan, for this likelihood as treatment reaches the final stages. When done as part of the basic anger management program, it is less likely to cause patient distress.

SUMMARY

Anger is a basic and common emotion. It begins with a triggering event that is appraised in a manner that turns general arousal into anger. The private anger experience consists of thoughts and fantasies, often of revenge, and physiological reactions. The public expression most often consists of verbal responses such as yelling, insulting, and profane exclamations. Anger is associated with many negative short- and long-term outcomes including interpersonal maladjustment and medical problems. Angry people are often avoided by others, resulting in isolation and occupational difficulties. A good anger management program consists of preparation, teaching strategies for change and acceptance, and preparing for relapse. One useful adjunct to the methods presented above is for practitioners to reflect on their personal anger experiences and to share some examples with patients as to how these have been handled constructively. In some ways, practitioners and patients are "in the same boat." Anger is universal and we all develop personal methods that work for us.

See also: Adolescent aggression and anger management, Anger—adult, Anger control problems, Anger management therapy with adolescents

REFERENCES

Beck, A. T. (1999). *Prisoners of hate: The cognitive basis of anger, hostility, and violence*. New York: HarperCollins.

Beck, R., & Fernandez, E. (1998). Cognitive behavioral therapy in the treatment of anger: A meta-analysis. *Cognitive Therapy and Research, 22*, 63–75.

Berkowitz, L. (1990). On the formation and regulation of anger and aggression: A cognitive–neoassociationistic analysis. *American Psychologist, 45*, 494–503.

Berkowitz, L. (1993). *Aggression: Its causes, consequences, and control*. New York: McGraw-Hill.

Bowman-Edmondson, C. B., & Cohen-Conger, J. C. (1996). A review of treatment efficacy for individuals with anger problems: Conceptual, assessment, and methodological issues. *Clinical Psychology Review, 16*, 251–275.

Deffenbacher, J. L., Oetting, E. R., Huff, M. E., Cornell, G. R. et al. (1996). Evaluation of two cognitive–behavioral approaches to general anger reduction. *Cognitive Therapy and Research, 20*, 551–573.

DiGiuseppe, R., & Tafrate, R. (2003). Anger treatment for adults: A meta-analytic review. *Clinical Psychology: Science and Practice, 10*, 70–84.

Ellis, A. E. (1994). *Reason and emotion in psychotherapy: Revised and updated*. New York: Carol Publishing.

Kassinove, H., & Sukhodolsky, D. G. (1995). Anger disorders: Basic science and practice issues. In H. Kassinove (Ed.), *Anger disorders: Assessment, diagnosis, and treatment* (pp. 1–26). Washington, DC: Taylor & Francis.

Kassinove, H., Sukhodolsky, D. G., Tsytsarev, S. V., & Solovyova, S. (1997). Self-reported constructions of anger episodes in Russia and America. *Journal of Social Behavior and Personality, 12*, 301–324.

Kassinove, H., & Tafrate, R. C. (2002). *Anger management: The complete practitioner's manual for the treatment of anger*. Atascadero, CA: Impact Publishers.

Korzybzi, A. (1933). *Science and sanity: An introduction to non-Aristotelean systems and general semantics*. Lakeville, CT: The Institute of General Semantics.

Plutchik, R. (1980). A general psychoevolutionary theory of emotion. In R. Plutchik & H. Kellerman (Eds.), *Emotion: Theory, research, and experience: Vol. 1. Theories of emotion* (pp. 3–31). New York: Academic Press.

Plutchik, R. (2000). *Emotions in the practice of psychotherapy*. Washington, DC: APA Books.

Spielberger, C. D. (1988). *Professional manual for the State–Trait Anger Expression Inventory*. Odessa, FL: Psychological Assessment Resources.

Spielberger, C. D. (1999). *Manual for the State–Trait Anger Expression Inventory—2*. Odessa, FL: Psychological Assessment Resources.

Sukhodolsky, D. G., Kassinove, H., & Gorman, B. S. (in press). Cognitive behavioral therapy for anger in children and adolescents: A meta-analysis. *Aggression and Violent Behavior*.

Tafrate, R. (1995). Evaluation of treatment strategies for adult anger disorders. In H. Kassinove (Ed.), *Anger disorders: Definition, diagnosis, and treatment*. Washington, DC: Taylor & Francis.

Tafrate, R., & Kassinove, H. (1998). Anger control in men: Barb exposure with rational, irrational, and irrelevant self-statements. *Journal of Cognitive Psychotherapy, 12*, 187–211.

Tafrate, R., Kassinove, H., & Dundin, L. (2002). Anger episodes in high and low trait anger community adults. *Journal of Clinical Psychology, 58*, 1573–1590.

Williams, J. E., Paton, C. C., Siegler, I. C., Eigenbrod, M. L., Nieto, F. J., & Tyroler, H. A. (2000). Anger proneness predicts coronary heart disease risk. Prospective analysis from the Atherosclerosis Risk in Communities (ARIC) Study. *Circulation, 102*, 2034–2039.

Dreams

Arthur Freeman and Beverly White

Keywords: dreams, images, dream images, imagery

When one thinks of dreams as part of the raw material for psychotherapy, one immediately thinks of Freud and his "royal road to the unconscious." Dreams have traditionally been an important part of psychotherapeutic treatment since the days of the early pioneers in the development of psychotherapy. Freud, Adler, Jung, and others, despite major disagreements on the foci or overall goals of treatment, all agreed on the importance, if not the primacy, of the dream as one of the most essential psychotherapeutic tools. Freud's notion was that through an understanding of the dream theme, content, images, and subsequent associations, the analyst could understand the workings of the patient's unconscious. Conflicts as yet unspoken or dynamics not fully understood (by patient or analyst) could be clarified through the interpretation to the patient of the symbols of the dreams. For Jung, the dream symbol was important, as it reflected not only the personal unconscious of the individual but also the collective unconscious of the group.

The dream became the way of fulfilling desires that could not otherwise be fulfilled during the waking life for any of a number of reasons. The effect of the dream could have an impact and manifestation into the waking state that might affect one's mood (feeling down), one's behavior (wakefulness), one's pleasure (arousal and sexual release), or one's cognition (being scared).

For Adler, however, the patient's dream life corresponded directly and entirely to the dreamer's world picture or lifestyle. The dream state, according to Adler, was part of a continuum of consciousness that allowed for problem solving when the demands of reality were far less pressing. Ideally, this would allow for the possibility of more creative problem solving without the constraint of reality. Adler (1927) states: "The purpose of dreams must be in the feelings they arouse. The dream is only the means, the instrument to stir up feelings" (p. 127).

Whether the dreams are upsetting and frustrating, or gratifying and pleasurable, patients may bring their dreams to the therapy work. As any practicing clinician will affirm, dreams are commonly mentioned or referred to in therapy. This can present a dilemma for any therapist who has limited training in the use of dreams as grist for the therapeutic mill.

Dreams have not been a part of CBT, because cognitive therapists generally come from a more behavioral tradition and orientation. Their clinical training might have had little or no reading, training, or supervision in the use of dreams in the therapeutic encounter. There have been few resources that have offered guidelines for using dreams. There has been no manual developed for CBT dream work. As another source of data, the dream can become a valuable tool in the overall CBT armamentarium, and a fruitful area for exploration (Mahoney, 1974).

CONSCIOUSNESS AND AWARENESS OF DREAM THEMES

From the classical psychoanalytic perspective, two types of dream content were identified, manifest content and latent content. The manifest content was the way the dream appeared to the dreamer (a much more direct and conscious focus), while the latent content reflected the unconscious conflicts. It is necessary to view dreams as reflecting the cognitions and affective responses of waking experience and of the patient's life in general rather than as mysterious reflections of so-called "deeper" issues.

Dreams and CBT

The first CBT outline for dream work was formulated by Beck (1971). Beck regarded dreams as a snapshot or sort of biopsy of the patient's psychological process and processing style. The patient's dreams were seen to be idiosyncratic and dramatic expressions of the patient's view of self, the world, and the future. Given that the dream material reflected the cognitive triad, it would follow that the dream would also embody the patient's cognitive distortions in those three broad areas. Beck (1967) pointed out that concentrating on the manifest content (the aware and easily described aspect of dreams) is far more satisfactory than attempting to infer underlying processes which may be vague or unreachable. Since the manifest content is readily available to the dreamer and can be reported to the therapist, it is available for immediate use in the therapy session. Utilizing material that is readily available, the patient can obtain a sense of mastery and self-knowledge without depending on the therapist to interpret the symbolism of the dream. Beck states, "If the patient has a dream in which he perceives other people as frustrating him, it would be more economical to simply consider this conception of people as being frustrating rather than to read into the dream an underlying 'masochistic wish'" (p. 180). Further, Beck found that "dream themes are relevant to observable patterns of behavior" (p. 181), and that "dreams were analogous to the kind of suffering the depressed patient experienced in his waking life" (p. 208). These findings are in full accord with Adler's contention that the dream themes are directly relevant to the patient's waking life and identified behavioral experience.

Dreams are the product of the dreamer's internal world, but maintain an essential continuity with the waking thought process. In studying typical dreams of psychiatric patients, Ward, Beck, and Roscoe (1961) and Beck and Ward (1961) found dream themes characteristic of the particular disorder manifest in the patient's waking experience. Beck (1967) states: "In the course of the psychotherapy of patients with neurotic-depressive reactions, it was noted that there was a high incidence of dreams with unpleasant content" (p. 170). As treatment progresses, and the individual is better able to meet and overcome the day-to-day problems of life, the dream content will change to reflect the waking changes. Beck had suggested in 1971 that the dominant cognitive patterns (or schemata) of waking life not only structure the content of waking ideational experiences but also have the capacity to exert varying degrees of influence on dreams. As a result, he suggested, dream reports in clinical contexts might function as a kind of "biopsy" of the client's dysfunctional schemata. Doweiko (2004) and Freeman and White (2004), working in the Beckian tradition, suggest that the themes of a client's manifest dream content often reflect the client's waking cognitive distortions. The dreams, they argue, are amenable to the same cognitive restructuring and "reality" testing procedures that may be applied to the client's nondream realm of automatic thoughts and beliefs.

Freeman (1981) and Freeman and Boyll (1992) addressed the use of dreams and attendant imagery integrating both Beckian and Adlerian perspectives. Doweiko (1982, 2004), using a rational emotive (RET) approach, suggested that the therapy could help the patient to directly challenge depressive cognitions reflected in the dream. This would have the effect that the depression would not be so powerfully reinforced. Doyle (1984) tested whether dreamers could learn to control their dream content through several skills training sessions using cognitive restructuring, self-instruction techniques, and maintenance of a dream log in which they recorded their dreams on a daily basis. She found that the group trained in the restructuring strategies was able to control the dream content in a pleasurable direction. Rosner (1997) suggests that the Constructivist approach of helping patients to understand the reality that they construct is applicable to the dream phenomenon and would be a useful approach to cognitive therapy work with dreams. Perris (1998) described the use of dreams in the cognitive therapy of chronic psychiatric patients. She found that using dream work was well accepted by the patients and easily integrated into the broader treatment that examined the patient's automatic thoughts and schemas. More recently, Rosner, Lyddon, and Freeman (2003) have compiled the first collection of CBT-oriented dream work.

The volume includes an overview of the intellectual and social history behind the development of Beck's dream theory and behind his decision to stop pursuing dream research in the early 1970s (Rosner, 2003). From a narrative–constructivist perspective, Goncalves and Barbosa (2004) describe a cognitive, narrative approach to dream work designed to (a) expand the client's sensorial, emotional, and cognitive experience and (b) allow for the emergence of a coherent and meaningful dream narrative organized around a central or root metaphor. Once the metaphor is constructed, the client is encouraged to project an alternative and potentially more viable dream metaphor.

Leijssen (2004) brings the focusing technique of Gendlin (1996) to cognitive therapy by suggesting that the lived and "felt sense" of cognitions in dreams can enrich and deepen therapeutic work. Leijssen's five steps of entering, elaborating on, and challenging dream images introduce the experience of the body, as it tells and inhabits dreams, as an additional source of information in testing hypotheses. In a similar vein, Hill and Rochlen's (2004) cognitive–experiential model of dream work underscores an active and creative role for clients as they explore their dreams, achieve insights into the meaning of their dreams, and take action by making changes in their dreams (and in their lives), and then use this new meaning to guide future decisions and actions.

An example of a marker of movement or improvement in therapy might be the patient who previously had dreams of helplessness or failure and now begin to have dreams that reflect his or her coping, mastery, and success.

WORKING WITH DREAMS

The cognitive view of dreams is that the dream material is idiosyncratic to the dreamer. It is essential that the therapist avoid the pitfall of universal dream symbols, e.g., a certain symbol always has the same meaning. The therapist must work to understand the dream content and the broader dream themes in the context of the patient's life, experience, and base of knowledge. Since the dream is not fettered by the constraints of the waking state, e.g., attending to necessary or vital circumstances such as watching the road while driving, the dreamer is freer to express a broad range of ideas, utilize magical thinking, and be as creative and unreal as possible. Some dreams may goad the person into action, and may presage activities. In keeping all possible avenues opened for data collection in the therapy, the dream can add immeasurably to the therapy work. It should be stressed that not all patients will come in reporting their dreams. The therapist need not suggest or require that the patient record and report his or her dreams, but should be prepared to deal with them when offered.

Recording and Reporting Dreams

Two reporting techniques are used, the Dream Log (DL) and the Dream Analysis Record (DAR), an adaptation of the Dysfunctional Thought Record (DTR). Both are done as homework, though the DAR can be used in the office as part of the session. For the dream log, patients keep a small notebook near their beds so that they can record dreams, dream fragments, and images. They are also asked to record affective responses and physiological responses. For the latter issues, they are also asked to use scaling to identify their level of response on a 0–10 scale, e.g., "woke up scared—8." Or, "the dream was sad—4."

The DAR asks the patient to enter the date of the dream in column 1. In column 2 they enter the highlights of the dream. In column 3 they give their affective reactions, and rate the degree of their reaction. In column 4 they include any thoughts that were associated with the dream image. In column 5 they enter the restructuring of the image. In column 6 the patient gives a reassessment of the degree of emotion associated with the dream image.

Guidelines for Using Dreams

The following guidelines can assist the clinician in utilizing dreams within the context of CBT.

1. The dream needs to be understood in thematic rather than symbolic terms. The particular images and ideas scale the level of emotion.
2. The thematic content of the dream is idiosyncratic to the dreamer and must be viewed within the context of the dreamer's life.
3. The specific language and imagery of the dream are important to the meaning.
4. The affective responses to the dreams can be seen as similar to the dreamer's affective responses in waking situations.
5. The particular length of the dream is of lesser import than the content.
6. The dream is a product of, and the responsibility of, the dreamer.
7. Dream content and images are amenable to the same cognitive restructuring as are any automatic thoughts.
8. Dreams can be used when the patient appears "stuck" in therapy.
9. The dream material and images will reflect the patient's schema.
10. Dreams need to be dealt with as part of the session agenda setting.
11. Encourage a system and regimen for the collection and logging of the dream material.
12. Help the patient develop skill at restructuring negative or maladaptive dream images into more functional and adaptive images.
13. Use the collection and analysis of the dream content as a standard homework task.
14. The dream images can be used, as appropriate, as a shorthand in the therapy.
15. Have the patient try to capsulize and to draw a "moral" from the dream.

Dreams and Related Imagery

Using dreams in therapy requires the use of the associated imagery. The dream restructuring process is, by definition, an exercise in imagery. Since few patients can describe symptoms without describing accompanying images, the image is a ready and accessible entry point for cognitive intervention. Images may be visual, auditory, gustatory, or olfactory. They may utilize an economy of words, but they provide a directness of meaning and a vivid affective experience for the patient. The affect-laden image can often penetrate the depression and isolation of the lonely patient just as the calming image can reduce the arousal of the anxious patient.

The image-maker does not always have to be the patient, since the therapist can suggest images and imagining techniques to effectively break through a number of symptoms. Images can be made more powerful and evocative through the inclusion of multisensory elements. Beck, Laude, and Bohnert (1974) observed that with the onset or exacerbation of anxiety, many patients have thoughts or visual fantasies revolving around the theme of danger. The anxiety, they conclude, was a direct result of the visualization of the danger-laden image. Their observations have direct implications for the treatment of anxiety.

The imaging can become part of the homework assignment arrived at between the patient and the therapist. The patient can be asked to develop a number of images that help focus on the particular symptoms currently being addressed in treatment. The therapist can, of course, utilize imagery and imaginal restructuring as a major tool for both dream-related images and waking images (Edwards, 1989). Krakow's (2004) imagery rehearsal therapy (IRT) has been developed with groups of survivors of sexual abuse suffering from posttraumatic stress disorder (PTSD) to reduce the number, intensity, and intrusiveness of nightmares. Repeated rehearsals of alternate imagery offer the patients a feeling of mastery over the intrusive and noxious stimuli and help them sleep through the night. Improved sleep, Krakow suggests, is then instrumental in reducing other symptoms of PTSD.

SUMMARY

While dreams have historically been an important part of the psychotherapeutic process, the therapist trained in CBT is frequently not trained or prepared to work with dreams. The cognitive model sees the dreamer as idiosyncratic and the dream as a dramatization of the patient's view of self, world, and future, subject to the same cognitive distortions as the waking state.

The cognitive therapist can enrich his or her armamentarium by including dreams and imagery as part of the psychotherapeutic collaborative process. They offer an opportunity for the patient to understand his or her cognitions as played out on the stage of the imagination and to challenge or dispute those depressogenic or anxiogenic thoughts, with a resultant positive affect shift.

The dream would not then necessarily be the royal road to the unconscious. It is far more a commonly traveled route toward the individual's conscious personal interpretations of that most human of experiences, the dream.

REFERENCES

Adler, A. (1927). *The practice and theory of individual psychology.* New York: Harcourt, Brace & Co.

Beck, A. T. (1967). *Depression: Clinical, experimental, and theoretical aspects.* New York: Harper & Row. (Republished as Beck, A.T.

(1972). *Depression: Causes and treatment*. Philadelphia: University of Pennsylvania Press.)

Beck, A. T. (1971). Cognition, affect and psychopathology. *Archives of General Psychiatry, 24*, 495–500.

Beck, A. T., Laude, R., & Bohnert, M. (1974). Ideational components of anxiety neurosis. *Archives of General Psychiatry, 31*, 319–325.

Beck, A. T., Rush, A. J., Shaw, B. F., & Emery, G. (1979). *Cognitive therapy of depression*. New York: Guilford Press.

Beck, A. T., & Ward, C. H. (1961). Dreams of depressed patients: Characteristic themes in manifest content. *Archives of General Psychiatry, 5*, 462–467.

Doweiko, H. E. (1982). Neurobiology and dream theory: A rapprochement model. *Individual Psychology: The Journal of Adlerian Theory, Research, and Practice, 38*(1), 55–61.

Doweiko, H. E. (2004). Dreams as an unappreciated avenue for cognitive–behavioral therapists. In R. I. Rosner, W. J. Lyddon, & A. Freeman (Eds.), *Cognitive therapy and dreams*. New York: Springer.

Doyle, M. C. (1984). Enhancing dream pleasure with the Senoi strategy. *Journal of Clinical Psychology, 40*(2), 467–474.

Freeman, A. (1981). The use of dreams and imagery in cognitive therapy. In G. Emery, S. Hollon, & R. Bedrosian (Eds.), *New directions in cognitive therapy*. New York: Guilford Press.

Freeman, A., & Boyll, S. (1992). The use of dreams and the dream metaphor in cognitive behavior therapy. *Psychotherapy in Private Practice, 10*(1–2), 173–192.

Freeman, A., & White, B. (2004). Dreams and the dream image. In R. I. Rosner, W. J. Lyddon, & A. Freeman (Eds.), *Cognitive therapy and dreams*. New York: Springer.

Gendlin, E. T. (1996). *Focusing-oriented psychotherapy: A manual of the experiential method*. New York: Guilford Press.

Goncalves, O. F., & Barbosa, J. G. (2004). From reactive to proactive dreaming. In R. I. Rosner, W. J. Lyddon, & A. Freeman (Eds.), *Cognitive therapy and dreams*. New York: Springer.

Hill, C. E., & Rochlen, A. B. (2004). To dream, perchance to sleep: Awakening the potential of dream work in cognitive therapy. In R. I. Rosner, W. J. Lyddon, & A. Freeman (Eds.), *Cognitive therapy and dreams*. New York: Springer.

Krakow, B. (2003). Imagery rehearsal therapy for chronic posttraumatic nightmares: A mind's eye view. In R. I. Rosner, W. J. Lyddon, & A. Freeman (Eds.), *Cognitive therapy and dreams* (pp. 89–112). New York: Springer.

Leijssen, M. (2004). Focusing-oriented dream work. In R. I. Rosner, W. J. Lyddon, & A. Freeman (Eds.), *Cognitive therapy and dreams*. New York: Springer.

Mahoney, M. J. (1974). *Cognitive behavior therapy*. Cambridge, MA: Ballinger.

Perris, H. (1998). Less common therapeutic strategies and techniques in the cognitive psychotherapy of severely disturbed patients. In C. Perris and P. D. McGorry (Eds.), *Cognitive psychotherapy of psychotic and personality disorders*. New York: Wiley.

Rosner, R. I. (1997). Cognitive therapy, constructivism, and dreams: A critical review. *Journal of Constructivist Psychology, 10*(3), 249–273.

Rosner, R. I. (2003). Aaron T. Beck's dream theory in context: An introduction to his 1971 article on cognitive patterns in dreams and day dreams. In R.I. Rosner, W. J. Lyddon, & A. Freeman (Eds.), *Cognitive therapy and dreams* (pp. 9–26). New York: Springer.

Rosner, R. I., Lyddon, W. J., & Freeman, A. (Eds.).(2004). *Cognitive therapy and dreams*. New York: Springer.

Ward, C. H., Beck, A. T., & Roscoe, E. (1961). Typical dreams: Incidence among psychiatric patients. *Archives of General Psychiatry, 5*, 606–615.

Dual Diagnosis

Michael Petronko and Doreen M. DiDomenico

Keywords: developmental disabilities, mental retardation, dual diagnosis, anger management, social skills training

There is a widely held, albeit elitist, opinion among mental health professionals that cognitively based treatments cannot be applied to cognitively challenged individuals. Indeed, save for rare exceptions, one will not find mention of this population in any evidence-based CBT treatment manual or text on empirically validated treatments. It is a bias that unfortunately judges the book by its proverbial cover. This article seeks to change this travesty, both because of the overwhelming needs of this population for treatment and the concomitant potential success of a CBT approach.

PREVALENCE OF DUAL DIAGNOSIS

Mental health professionals have long been aware of the concept of "dual diagnosis" as it applies to the comorbidity of mental illness and substance abuse. The application of the concept to the existence of psychiatric disorders in persons with developmental disabilities only dates back to the midtwentieth century, and still remains largely unrecognized by the mental health community. Current research suggests that psychiatric disorders are at least three to four times more prevalent among people with MR/DD than among the general population. Such a high prevalence statistic is not surprising on consideration of the physical, psychological, and social vulnerabilities of persons with DD. Many individuals with mental handicaps are now facing new tensions as they assimilate to life in the community while the national deinstitutionalization movement continues to press forward.

OBSTACLES TO ASSESSMENT AND TREATMENT

Attitudinal Biases

Several explanations may account for professionals' lack of familiarity with this population of the "other" dually diagnosed. The most basic misconception underlying this unawareness is that people with MR are immune to mental illness. A seminal body of research on attitudinal biases originated in the early 1980s with the concept of diagnostic overshadowing (Reiss, Levitan, & Szyszko, 1982). Diagnostic overshadowing conjectures that psychiatric symptoms are not independently identified as mental health problems, but are instead attributed to the condition of mental retardation.

A historical review of psychotherapy effectiveness research from the 1950s through the 1970s revealed an overall level of ineffectiveness, which was attributed to the failure of therapeutic techniques. Interestingly, however, research conducted during the same time on persons with MR attributed psychotherapy ineffectiveness to the character and limitations of this disabled population.

Practical Factors

Another professional issue, more realistic in nature than prejudiced, is that practitioners are not trained in the unique manifestation of symptoms and treatment modifications for this specific subset of patients. For those who operate from a scientist-practitioner model, the scarcity of research on which to take direction adds to the mystification of clinicians.

A myriad of other practical factors complicate the competent execution of assessment and treatment with dually diagnosed individuals. The pursuit of diagnostic evaluation reveals that standard classification systems are not tested on people with intellectual disabilities, whose psychiatric symptoms may manifest differently and/or not conform to the range of symptoms necessary to yield a diagnostic label. The mental status examination is rarely a reliable endeavor when the person with MR/DD is the sole reporter. Developmentally disabled individuals may exhibit response biases of acquiescence, suggestibility, and confabulation when being interviewed. A comprehensive evaluation relies on the reports of care providers who are subjective in their view of the referred patient, and cannot reliably report on unobservable psychic phenomena (e.g., hallucinations).

Some practical issues that interfere with the treatment of dually diagnosed individuals involve their care providers to a great extent. If a person with MR/DD does not self-refer, which is typically the case, assessment and treatment rely on the identification of a problem and the pursuit of services by others closely involved with the individual. Often, another person must agree to bring the person to treatment sessions and reliably and consistently assist with CBT homework.

CBT APPLICATIONS: CONSIDERATIONS FOR THE DUALLY DIAGNOSED PATIENT

Optimal Patient Characteristics

There are, without a doubt, certain characteristics that render some individuals with MR/DD as more suitable candidates for CBT than others. It has been recommended that assessment should be done in the following areas before embarking on CBT: communication skills, cognitive aptitude (e.g., understanding of concepts of gradation), capacity to identify emotions, and capacity to understand the CBT model (Hatton, 2002). With regard to this last requisite, research has been conducted on whether persons with MR could distinguish an activating event, its meaning, the emotional and behavioral consequences, and especially the concept that beliefs may mediate these reactions (Dagnan, Chadwick, & Proudlove, 2000). Researchers found a higher success rate of individuals with MR/DD correctly linking situations to emotions than identifying the potential mediating cognitions.

Informed Consent

According to U.S. legal criteria, the general requirements for informed consent for treatment include knowledge, capacity, and voluntariness. These decisions must be made free from coercion. The AAMR Expert Consensus Guidelines on the treatment of psychiatric and behavioral problems in MR/DD (2000) additionally emphasize the considerations of the involvement of families/guardians in a collaborative decision-making team, the provision of information to the individual in a form he or she can understand, and the view of informed consent as an ongoing process (as opposed to a discrete event).

There are several challenges faced by treatment providers in acquiring informed consent from persons with MR/DD. Possible deficits in comprehension, memory and verbal expression, problem-solving difficulties, concreteness, and problems processing complex sequences of information challenge the requirements of knowledge and capacity. Tendencies toward acquiescence, and limited experience with decision making challenge the requirement of voluntariness.

Several studies have investigated the ability of individuals with MR/DD to provide informed consent and found that approximately two-thirds of their subjects with MR/DD were able to consent to at least one form of proposed treatment.

Motivation and Active Participation

The provision of informed consent to treatment typically implies one's motivation to participate in the treatment and achieve the desired results. However, given the fallibility of achieving consent from individuals with DD that is fully informed and/or fully voluntary, the assumed motivation for treatment also comes into question. Exacerbating this issue further is the fact that more often than not, dually diagnosed individuals do not self-refer, i.e., they are typically brought to treatment by care providers or court mandate and often do not even acknowledge their current condition as problematic in any way. Nezu, Nezu, and Gill-Weiss (1992) identify such motivational issues as examples of initiation difficulties in that their presence may obstruct the conduct of assessment and treatment in these individuals.

In contrast to other modes of clinical intervention, cognitive–behavioral therapy requires active participation on the part of the "patient," to the extent that many conceptualize CBT patients as becoming their own therapists/trainers through the use of many self-directed treatment techniques.

Compounding the motivation issue further is the fact that many cognitive–behavioral treatment approaches require exposing the individual to the source of his or her distress in order to desensitize negative emotion and practice coping skills. Without the overriding intrinsic motivation to overcome the presenting emotional challenge, an individual with MR is likely to resist treatment techniques that exacerbate distress in the moment.

Motivation is often enhanced in treatment with developmentally disabled individuals via the use of contingent reinforcement for all phases of assessment and treatment, from session attendance and participation to practicing coping skills and other therapeutic "homework."

Choice of Treatment Techniques

Nezu et al. (1992) list the following special considerations for using CBT strategies with clients with MR: incorporate strategies for maintaining attention to optimize social learning; make use of modeling, especially peer models; acknowledge the need for repetition and extended time for learning to occur with the need for later booster sessions to promote generalization; use concrete examples from a variety of situations; and utilize contingent positive reinforcement to strengthen the practice and retention of newly learned skills.

The use of technology may facilitate treatment with individuals with MR/DD. Some studies showed the successful use of biofeedback to help individuals recognize the differences in their emotional states via an objective external measure. In situations where such advanced technology is not available, trained care providers can act as feedback sources relying on observable changes in mood and behavior.

Collaboration with Care Providers

Utilizing family, staff, and other care providers as collegial partners in clinical intervention has been a preferred treatment practice for individuals with dual diagnoses who reside in the community, especially for those individuals with more severe cognitive and adaptive deficits (Petronko, Harris, & Kormann, 1994). The care providers must receive parallel psychoeducation to take on the task of being a treatment partner—prompting the individual in specific situations, helping to identify apparent emotions, triggers, and behaviors for the person to promote and reinforce learning, to help the person practice skills at home, to begin to verbally direct the person to relax and other methods at first sign of marked anxiety, and to communicate regarding these experiences with the therapist.

CBT APPLICATIONS: SPECIFIC APPLICATIONS

Depression

Nezu, Nezu, Rothenburg, DelliCarpini, and Groag (1995) found that cognitive models can account for depression in individuals with MR. Their results revealed higher rates of automatic negative thoughts and feelings of hopelessness, and lower rates of self-reinforcement and social support in the dually diagnosed patients they studied. Studies have also shown similarities in the social interaction patterns in depressed adults both with and without DD. Hurley and Sovner (1991) suggest that patients with social skills deficits as part of their depression are good candidates for CBT. The treatment package that Hurley and Sovner recommend includes the reinforcement of behaviors incompatible with depression (e.g., making eye contact), improvement of social skills, and the challenging of negative interpretations.

Anxiety Disorders

Anxiety has been demonstrated to be a very common mental health problem in people with DD. The complete spectrum of anxiety disorders is represented in this population as opposed to their noncognitively challenged counterparts.

Relaxation training is a common component in a CBT approach to treating anxiety. Individuals with MR/DD are reported to have better results learning relaxation training when modeling and physical guidance were used to teach the difference between tense and relaxed states. It is essential to include methods of physical relief in anxiety management with dually diagnosed individuals as it may be more difficult to teach and convince these individuals that some physical sensations can be psychological in nature, i.e., that there is nothing physically wrong and that they are not sick. Without this acknowledgment, cognitive methods to relabel and address the physical sensations may be ineffective.

Simple phobias in individuals with DD often resemble typical fears of children of similar developmental level/mental age. In vivo desensitization has been reported to be the treatment technique of choice for this problem. In individuals with MR/DD, external reinforcement is typically needed to motivate the individual to remain in the phobic situation, and exposure to these situations may always need to be therapist- or other-assisted, rather than a progression to self-exposure.

Participant modeling has been reported to be successful in treatment of dually diagnosed individuals. In this approach, the subject observes the "model" approach to the feared object or situation without the experience of the feared negative consequences, which then facilitates the person's own approach. Again, individuals can be reinforced with praise or tangible rewards for their attempts to approach the feared stimulus.

Self-instruction training has much potential for use with people with dual diagnosis. With the initial aid of a therapist and the eventual goal of internalization, this technique seeks to change maladaptive self-statements or insert positive ones into performance or social anxiety-provoking situations.

In contrast to the better representation of phobias in the professional literature, other anxiety disorders have rarely been investigated. For example, there are few reports of Posttraumatic Stress Disorder (PTSD) in persons with DD. In reality, individuals with DD are more likely to be abused physically, emotionally, and sexually and because of their cognitive deficits, may be more vulnerable to the emotional sequelae of traumatic experiences. Some reported biases specific to this disorder revealed that mental health professionals again claimed their belief that persons with MR do not experience trauma. Many persons with MR/DD who have suffered abuse have never been asked about this experience in mental health or other evaluations. Screening measures developed for use with the dually diagnosed typically do not include PTSD as a diagnostic category. Recommended treatment in the literature for PTSD in persons with MR/DD involves the judicious use of medication, habilitative modifications to monitor and contain traumatic stimuli, and psychotherapy to work through grief and learn to feel safe.

Research on the treatment of Obsessive–Compulsive Disorder (OCD) in persons with MR/DD has demonstrated an overreliance on behavioral approaches, e.g., utilizing overcorrection to accomplish response prevention. An assessment obstacle for this population is the need to distinguish compulsive stereotypic behaviors from compulsive behaviors performed to alleviate obsessional anxiety. This may be difficult to ascertain in individuals whose self-report is nonexistent or unreliable. Another challenge to treating the mentally retarded individual with OCD is the potential lack of insight into the irrationality and excessiveness of the obsessions. This insight is typically helpful in enlisting the patient to challenge these fears and beliefs through cognitive techniques and exposure exercises.

Anger Management

A widely used treatment package developed by Benson (1986) is the Anger Management Training (AMT) Program, which focuses on identification of feelings; recognition of connections between events and feelings, and feelings and behavior; relaxation training; self-instruction training utilizing coping statements; and problem-solving training. Reported results of participation in AMT revealed improvements in other areas as well (even when the actual utilization of anger management techniques was not necessarily successful), including increase in self-confidence, increase in personal responsibility, and willingness to address other problem areas.

SOCIAL SKILLS TRAINING

As a predominantly behavioral approach, Social Skills Training (SST) has been one of the major approaches to working with individuals with dual diagnosis. This is an important area of focus because a range of social skill deficits is typically observed in individuals with DD. These individuals may be reacted to with fear and avoidance; they are often treated as children; and they are not always held responsible for inappropriate behaviors. Although SST has evidenced some success in improving social skills, a high degree of success is unlikely because of the complex nature and unpredictability of interpersonal interactions.

The goal of SST is to increase interpersonal functioning in areas of communication, including expressive elements such as content of message, intended recipient, and delivery of message (voice volume, nonverbal factors); and receptive elements, such as attending and listening, and physical factors such as interpersonal distance. A typical CBT "package" for SST includes defining the target behavior, providing psychoeducation including a rationale for change, modeling of the skills, practice of the skills with reinforcement, and plans for generalization of the skills in other settings.

SST has also been used to treat the behavioral aspects of depression. One specific form of SST is assertiveness training, the goal of which is to teach the skill of defending one's own rights in a way that does not violate others' rights. The typical passivity and apathy observed in persons with DD justifies the need to consider assertiveness training; however, without system reform in the course of social role valorization, trained skills may not be functional if they are not reinforced. It is hoped that the assertive efforts of the self-advocacy movement have effected some progress in this area.

FUTURE DIRECTIONS FOR RESEARCH AND TREATMENT

Unfortunately, despite increasing awareness and professional interest in dual diagnosis, the research inquiry into therapeutic effectiveness for this population peaked in the 1980s, rather than demonstrating more linear growth.

Maintenance and generalization are always key areas to consider when measuring treatment outcomes; however, these phenomena are especially important for results regarding people with DD, as cognitive deficiencies may well impact memory and judgment over time.

Reversing attributional biases on the part of CBT researchers/clinicians represents the most pressing area for future research. Without this, CBT and/or evidence-based therapy with this population will continue to be an oxymoron.

See also: Anxiety/anger management training (AMT), Developmental disabilities in community settings, Mental retardation—adult, Social skills training

REFERENCES

American Association on Mental Retardation. (2000). Expert consensus guidelines. *American Journal on Mental Retardation, 105*(3), entire issue.

Benson, B. A. (1986). Anger management training. *Psychiatric Aspects of Mental Retardation Reviews, 5*, 51–55.

Dagnan, D., Chadwick, P., & Proudlove, J. (2000). Toward an assessment of suitability of people with mental retardation for cognitive therapy. *Cognitive Therapy and Research, 24*, 627–636.

Hatton, C. (2002). Psychosocial interventions for adults with intellectual disabilities and mental health problems: A review. *Journal of Mental Health, 11*, 357–374.

Hurley, A. D., & Sovner, R. (1991). Cognitive behavioral therapy for depression in individuals with developmental disabilities. *The Habilitative Mental Healthcare Newsletter, 10*, 41–47.

Nezu, C. M., Nezu, A. M., & Gill-Weiss, M. J. (1992). *Psychopathology in persons with mental retardation: Clinical guidelines for assessment and treatment*. Champaign, IL: Research Press.

Nezu, C. M., Nezu, A. M., Rothenburg, J. L., DelliCarpini, L., & Groag, I. (1995). Depression in adults with mild mental retardation: Are cognitive variables involved? *Cognitive Therapy and Research, 19*, 227–239.

Petronko, M. R., Harris, S. L., & Kormann, R. J. (1994). Community-based behavioral training approaches for people with mental retardation and mental illness. *Journal of Consulting and Clinical Psychology, 62*, 49–54.

Reiss, S., Levitan, G. W., & Szyszko, J. (1982). Emotional disturbance and mental retardation: Diagnostic overshadowing. *American Journal of Mental Deficiency, 86*, 567–574.

E

Exposure Therapy

Victoria M. Follette and
Alethea A. A. Smith

Keywords: exposure, cognitive processing therapy, PTSD, stress inoculation training

Exposure therapy has increasingly been found efficacious with a variety of anxiety-related disorders including phobias, generalized anxiety disorder, and posttraumatic stress disorder. Originally developed using concepts from basic learning theory, concerns about enhancing the efficacy of exposure therapy have led to the enhancement of this technique with additional components. The primary augmentation has been the integration of cognitive techniques. As cognitive conceptualizations of various forms of psychopathology, particularly anxiety and depressive disorders, became dominant, the integration of cognitive and exposure strategies grew to be routine practice.

Based in learning theory, exposure techniques have been conceptualized to function as a form of counterconditioning or extinction. In an early form of exposure therapy based on counterconditioning, Wolpe (1958) used systematic desensitization, the pairing of relaxation with confronting anxiety-producing situations, to weaken anxiety responses. Mowrer's two-factor theory (1960) represents yet another early conceptualization of behavior problems. In Mowrer's model, fears are acquired through classical conditioning processes and maintained by means of operant conditioning. Specifically, the conditioned stimulus (CS) is paired with an unconditioned stimulus (UCS), which elicits a fear response. Through avoidance of the CS, the fear is maintained by negative reinforcement. Several significant therapeutic advances were generated from this seminal work. One of the most notable of these was the development of implosive therapy, which used exposure to interrupt the fear process through extinction (Stampfl & Levis, 1967).

Exposure therapy for anxiety disorders has continued to be elaborated and comprises a set of techniques designed to help patients confront their feared objects, situations, memories, and images in a therapeutic manner. Commonly, the core components of exposure programs are imaginal exposure (i.e., repeated visualization of images or action or repeated recounting of memories) and in vivo exposure (i.e., repeated confrontation with the feared objects or situations). Programs may also include psychoeducation, relaxation training, processing of the exposure sessions, or combinations of each of these elements.

While exposure alone does have strong empirical support across a variety of anxiety-related disorders, there have been several consistent concerns regarding this approach. First, studies using exposure often report high attrition rates in the exposure treatment group which is sometimes interpreted as a sign that it is difficult for clients to accept exposure as a treatment modality. Second, the use of exposure with victims of traumatic events has been criticized as unnecessarily increasing patient suffering and even exacerbating PTSD and anxiety symptoms. Third, some clients, particularly those with a trauma history, have difficulty with basic skills including emotion regulation, distress tolerance, and interpersonal relationships and are thus seen as not having the capacity to complete an exposure program. Finally, it has been suggested that exposure should be enhanced in order to address additional problems, such as negative appraisals including guilt and shame. Client concerns such as anger and dissociation may also require adjunctive treatments.

Cognitive–behavioral therapy has incorporated basic learning theory along with cognitive strategies to address some of the above concerns. One early integrative example is stress inoculation training (SIT) which uses modified forms of exposure and cognitive techniques (Meichenbaum, 1974). In addition to exposure, SIT provides patients with management skills to help them reduce anxiety (e.g., relaxation training, controlled breathing, positive imagery, cognitive restructuring, and distraction). Cognitive processing therapy (CPT; Resick & Schnicke, 1992) takes a different perspective, using information processing theory as its theoretical foundation. While somewhat modified in form, it does merge features of cognitive and exposure therapies. Clients spend time writing about trauma experiences and working to restructure core schemas such as safety and trust.

In some cases, therapies are developed that can be conceptualized as incorporating cognitive and exposure strategies, although they do not explicitly address these constructs. A prototypical example of this is acceptance and commitment therapy (ACT; Hayes, Strosahl, & Wilson, 1999). In this approach, efforts are made to reduce experiential avoidance which generally involves changing the client's relationship to language as well as exposure to feared experiences by engaging in behaviors consistent with valued life goals. Eye movement desensitization and reprocessing (EMDR) is another example of a treatment that includes cognitive and exposure components, while espousing a different theoretical foundation. This therapy consists of a form of exposure therapy that involves processing the traumatic event while engaging in saccadic eye movements (Shapiro, 1995). Patients are also asked to replace negative thoughts with more positive or adaptive ones. While the treatment remains somewhat controversial, particularly with respect to the mechanism of change, some data suggest there is utility in the approach.

EMPIRICAL FINDINGS

There are several studies that support the combination of exposure therapy with other cognitive–behavioral therapies. Resick, Nishith, Weaver, Astin, and Feuer (2002) compared CPT with prolonged exposure (PE) and a wait-list control for the treatment of PTSD in female rape victims. Analysis indicated that both 12 sessions of CPT and 9 sessions of PE were effective in reducing PTSD symptoms in comparison to a minimal-attention wait-list control group. At posttreatment, CPT and PE patients showed an average reduction in PTSD symptoms of 72 and 67%, respectively, and these results were maintained at a 9-month follow-up. One difference between the two treatments was that CPT produced better scores on two of four guilt subscales.

Foa et al. (1999) compared the efficacy of PE alone, SIT alone, and a combination of PE and SIT. After nine twice-weekly sessions, PTSD symptom severity decreased an average of 55–60% for both the PE and PE/SIT groups. Results for both groups were maintained at a 12-month follow-up. Blanchard, Hickling, and Devineni (2003) also used a combined PE/SIT protocol and compared it to supportive counseling for patients with PTSD following motor vehicle accidents. At posttreatment, individuals in the PE/SIT group showed an average reduction in PTSD symptoms of 65% compared to 38% for those in the supportive counseling group and 18% in a wait-list control. Results were maintained at follow-up.

Several studies have been conducted to evaluate the efficacy of EMDR and the role of the eye movements; several reviews suggest that compared to no treatment or nonspecific therapies for PTSD, EMDR is successful. However, a meta-analytic review found EMDR less effective than other exposure therapy programs (Davidson & Parker, 2001). In addition, Devilly and Spence (1999) compared EMDR to a modified version of combined PE and SIT. At posttreatment, PE/SIT reduced symptom severity by 63% versus 46% in the EMDR condition and 3-month follow-up showed an average symptom reduction of 61% for PE/SIT and only 12% for the EMDR condition.

A different approach has been to introduce another CBT component separate from the exposure intervention. Cloitre, Koenen, Cohen, and Han (2002) randomly assigned women with PTSD related to childhood abuse to either a two-phase cognitive–behavioral treatment or a wait-list control. The first phase of the treatment consisted of 8 weeks of skills training in affective and interpersonal regulation. The second phase consisted of 8 weeks of modified PE. Compared to those on the wait list, participants in the skills/PE condition showed significant gains in affect regulation, interpersonal skills deficits, and PTSD symptoms. Gains were maintained at both 3- and 9-month follow-ups. Furthermore, Cloitre et al. showed that Phase 1 negative mood regulation skills and therapeutic alliance measures were predictive of success in reducing PTSD symptoms during Phase 2.

Finally, several studies have examined the effect of augmenting exposure therapy with other CBT techniques. Most of these studies show very little augmenting effect. The Foa et al. (1999) study discussed above showed no significant differences between the PE condition and a condition combining PE and SIT. Foa (Foa, Rothbaum, & Furr, 2003) reports on a study comparing PE to a combination of PE and cognitive restructuring (CR) and a wait-list control. In this study the PE condition showed an average symptom reduction of 78% while the combined PE/CR condition showed an average symptom reduction of 62%. In both of the above studies, Foa and her colleagues suggest that the CBT therapies may not be augmenting the exposure therapy due to increased demands on the patients. The PE condition alone is more efficient and more time may be needed to successfully implement a combined approach.

Marks, Lovell, and Noshirvani (1998) also conducted a study comparing exposure and CR. In this study they had an exposure alone condition, a CR alone condition, a combination exposure/CR condition, and a relaxation control. The exposure used in this study consisted of five sessions of imaginal exposure followed by five sessions of in vivo exposure. Results of the study are mixed. At follow-up, there were no significant differences in PTSD severity between any of the groups including the relaxation control condition with an average severity reduction between 35 and 50%. At 6-month follow-up, the conditions that received exposure alone or CR in combination with exposure seemed to show further improvement while the CR alone condition did not. Reductions in symptom severity were 81, 53, and 74% for the exposure alone, CR alone, and combined exposure/CR conditions, respectively. These findings do not support the hypothesis that CR augmented exposure. However, exposure did seem to augment CR at least for the follow-up assessment.

Paunovic and Ost (2001) were also unable to find support for augmenting PE with CR in a population of Swedish refugees with PTSD. Comparing PE alone to a combined PE/CR condition, PTSD symptoms were reduced by 53% and 48%, respectively. Similar patterns were maintained at 6-month follow-up and across measures of depression and anxiety.

One study that did find an augmentation effect (Bryant, Moulds, Guthrie, Dang, & Nixon, in press) compared conditions of imaginal exposure, imaginal exposure with a cognitive component, and supportive counseling. Symptom reduction at treatment end was 48%, 67%, and 22%, respectively, and this pattern of results was maintained through follow-up. While this does give support for an augmentation effect, it is also important to note that this study did not incorporate an *in vivo* exposure component, which is found in all of the previous studies.

SUMMARY

Exposure therapy has increasingly been used in conjunction with other cognitive–behavioral therapies in a variety of formats and techniques, particularly in the treatment of anxiety disorders. Reasons for the addition of cognitive enhancements to exposure therapy include concerns for client well-being and/or an interest in increasing client willingness to engage the treatment. Other newer therapies such as CPT, ACT, and EMDR, while based in differing theoretical paradigms, incorporate cognitive and behavioral strategies that are consistent with exposure and cognitive change.

Several empirical studies support combinations of exposure and other cognitive–behavioral therapies. However, studies evaluating a possible augmenting effect of other CBT components have generally shown equally promising effects with exposure alone and exposure combined conditions. Further research is needed to more fully understand which components of other cognitive–behavioral therapies are most helpful in addressing concerns of using exposure therapy alone, and the manner in which exposure therapy can be most effectively integrated.

See also: Panic disorder, PTSD, Severe OCD

REFERENCES

Blanchard, E. B., Hickling, E. J., & Devineni, T. (2003). A controlled evaluation of cognitive behavioral therapy for posttraumatic stress in motor vehicle accident survivors. *Behavioral Research and Therapy, 41*, 79–96.

Bryant, R. A., Moulds, M. L., Guthrie, R. M., Dang, S. T., & Nixon, R. D. V. (2004). Imaginal exposure alone and imaginal exposure with cognitive restructuring in treatment of posttraumatic stress disorder. *Journal of Consulting and Clinical Psychology, 71*, 706–712.

Cloitre, M., Koenen, K. C., Cohen, L. R., & Han, H. (2002). Skills training in affective and interpersonal regulation followed by exposure: A phase based treatment for PTSD related to childhood abuse. *Journal of Consulting and Clinical Psychology, 70*, 1067–1074.

Davidson, P. R., & Parker, K. C. H. (2001). Eye movement desensitization and reprocessing (EMDR): A meta-analysis. *Journal of Consulting and Clinical Psychology, 69*, 305–319.

Devilly, G. J., & Spence, S. H. (1999). The relative efficacy and treatment distress of EMDR and a cognitive–behavioral trauma protocol in the amelioration of posttraumatic stress disorder. *Journal of Anxiety Disorders, 13*, 131–157.

Foa, E. B., Dancu, C. V., Hembree, E. A., Jaycox, L. H., Meadows, E. A., & Street, G. P. (1999). A comparison of exposure therapy, stress inoculation training, and their combination for reducing posttraumatic stress disorder in female assault victims. *Journal of Consulting and Clinical Psychology, 67*, 194–200.

Foa, E. B., & Rothbaum, B. O. (1998). *Treating the trauma of rape*. New York: Guilford Press.

Foa, E. B., Rothbaum, B. O., & Furr, J. M. (2003). Augmenting exposure therapy with other CBT procedures. *Psychiatric Annals, 33*, 47–53.

Hayes, S. C., Strosahl, K., & Wilson, K. G. (1999). *Acceptance and commitment therapy: An experiential approach to behavior change*. New York: Guilford Press.

Marks, I., Lovell, K., & Noshirvani, H. (1998). Treatment of posttraumatic stress disorder by exposure and/or cognitive restructuring: A controlled study. *Archives of General Psychiatry, 55*, 317–325.

Meichenbaum, D. (1974). *Cognitive behavior modification*. Morristown, NJ: General Learning Press.

Mowrer, O. A. (1960). *Learning theory and practice*. New York: Wiley.

Paunovic, N., & Ost, L. (2001). Cognitive–behavior therapy vs. exposure therapy in treatment of PTSD in refugees. *Behavior Research and Therapy, 39*, 1183–1197.

Resick, P. A., Nishith, P., Weaver, T. L., Astin, M. C., & Feuer, C. A. (2002). A comparison of cognitive processing therapy with prolonged exposure and a waiting condition for the treatment of chronic posttraumatic stress disorder in female rape victims. *Journal of Consulting and Clinical Psychology, 70*, 867–879.

Resick, P. A., & Schnicke, M. K. (1992). Cognitive processing therapy for sexual assault victims. *Journal of Consulting and Clinical Psychology, 60*, 748–756.

Shapiro, F. (1995). *Eye movement desensitization and reprocessing: Basic principles, protocols, and procedures*. New York: Guilford Press.

Stampfl, T. G., & Levis, D. J. (1967). Essentials of implosive therapy: A learning based psychodynamic behavioral therapy. *Journal of Abnormal Psychology, 72*, 496–503.

Wolpe, J. (1958). *Psychotherapy by reciprocal inhibition*. Stanford, CA: Stanford University Press.

F

Family Caregivers

Ann M. Steffen and Kristin R. Mangum

Keywords: formal caregivers, informal caregivers, activities of daily living, older adults

TYPES OF CAREGIVING RESPONSIBILITIES

The focus of this article is on informal, family caregivers who are providing assistance with both ADLS and IADLS in older adults with a dementia. Concern about the mental health needs of such family caregivers of impaired older adults continues to be high. This interest exists for good reasons; most older adults live in noninstitutional settings, and families remain the most common source of assistance for community-dwelling older adults who have some functional impairment. Ory, Yee, Tennstedt, and Schulz (1999) provide a review of definitions and prevalence of family caregiving, caregiver characteristics, and health effects. According to their review, family caregivers provide assistance with a wide variety of tasks, ranging from light assistance with independent activities of daily living (e.g., accompanying on medical visits, shopping, transportation) to intensive in-home care. The majority of caregivers are either spouses or adult children of the impaired individual. Although women more commonly assume the caregiving role, approximately 30% of all caregivers are men. These male caregivers remain an understudied population in terms of their needs and responsiveness to psychosocial interventions.

PREVALENCE OF PSYCHOSOCIAL DISTRESS

Although there is a great deal of variability in individuals' responses to the challenges of providing care, family caregiving is associated with higher rates of psychosocial distress and mental health problems. This is especially true for family caregivers of individuals with dementia. Studies of dementia family caregivers have found elevated rates of depressed, irritated, and anxious mood, clinical depression, and generalized anxiety disorder among this population. In addition, dementia family caregivers tend to report poorer perceived sleep and general health, and an increased use of psychotropic medications (Ory et al., 2000). These declines in psychosocial functioning not only affect the caregivers' general well-being and quality of life, they also can affect their ability to provide care. Thus, interventions that aim to reduce caregiver psychosocial distress are extremely important. Before we begin our review of such interventions, however, we want to highlight that levels of emotional distress and psychiatric impairment in caregivers are quite variable, and are only indirectly related to the degree of physical and cognitive impairment in the family member receiving care.

COGNITIVE AND BEHAVIORAL INTERVENTIONS FOR DEMENTIA FAMILY CAREGIVERS

Most community-based interventions for family caregivers, whether they involve educational programs, support groups, respite services, or case management, share an interest in multiple outcomes. That is, many programs aim to improve caregivers' problem-solving abilities, reduce their emotional distress, and improve their management of patient care. Some programs also seek to improve interpersonal family relationships or to delay institutionalization of the patient. Behavioral and cognitive treatments are distinguished from others, not necessarily by the expected outcomes, but by the conceptualization of the problem(s) and proposed mechanisms of the intervention. The following limited summary is by no means an exhaustive review of cognitive–behavioral interventions for family caregivers of cognitively impaired older adults. Rather, this section describes several exemplars that demonstrate the usefulness of individual and group-based cognitive and behavioral interventions for this population.

Individual-Based Approaches

Individual cognitive–behavioral approaches have been used to reduce depression and other forms of psychosocial distress in caregivers of impaired and disabled older family members. For example, in a randomized clinical trial, Gallagher-Thompson and Steffen (1994) assigned depressed family caregivers of physically and cognitively impaired older adults ($N = 66$) to time-limited (i.e., 16–20 sessions) cognitive–behavioral or brief psychodynamic individual psychotherapy. They found that participants with longer caregiving careers (i.e., 4.5 years or more) benefited more from and showed clinically significant benefits from the cognitive–behavioral intervention. Notably, these longer-term caregivers are also the group most likely to seek help for emotional distress, perhaps due to the depletion of social and personal resources that occurs over time.

In addition to the psychosocial distress of family caregivers, both physically and cognitively impaired older adults have increased rates of clinical depression, relative to healthy controls. In impaired older adults, this depression results in additional ("secondary") disability and tends to exacerbate their cognitive and/or physical impairment. Thus, with good reason, patient depression is very concerning to family caregivers. Additionally, because improved management of depressive symptoms and other patient problem behaviors reduces the number and severity of caregiving stressors, it logically follows that interventions aimed at reducing patient depression may also positively impact caregiver mental health. For example, Teri and her colleagues have demonstrated the efficacy of training family caregivers in the use of behavioral strategies to reduce patient depression, with a resulting decrease in caregiver depressive symptoms as well (Teri, Logsdon, Uomoto, & McCurry, 1997). Two active behavioral interventions (i.e., behavioral activation, problem solving) were shown to be superior to control conditions (wait-list, treatment as usual) in reducing depression for dementia patients and their family caregivers. This study is notable in that its target was both the caregiver and the dementia patient. It is only one of a number of studies conducted by Teri and colleagues that have successfully demonstrated the efficacy of behavioral interventions for both dementia patients and their caregivers.

Individual cognitive and behavioral interventions for family caregivers of older adults are also firmly rooted in the nursing intervention literature. An 8-week cognitive–behavioral nursing intervention focused on training dementia family caregivers ($N = 65$) to handle dressing and eating deficits of persons with dementia (Chang, 1999). Female caregivers, primarily spouses, were randomly assigned to either attention-only telephone calls, or video- and telephone-based training in behavior management of specific deficits. Compared to control participants, caregivers in the cognitive–behavioral intervention showed a reduction in their level of depression over the course of the intervention (Chang, 1999). In a different nursing intervention utilizing a larger sample of caregivers ($N = 237$), dementia caregivers were taught how to manage behavioral problems of dementia patients using a conceptual model based on behavioral principles (Gerdner, Buckwalter, & Reed, 2002). Relative to control participants, caregivers receiving the behavioral intervention evidenced lower rates of emotional distress (i.e., lower depression, anxiety, anger, and fatigue) and reported less upset following memory and behavior problems in the patient. Interestingly, psychoimmunology study from this research group examined a subset of these participants and found that intervention participants showed stronger T-cell proliferative responses to both PHA and Con A challenges at follow-ups than did control participants. This suggests that the behavioral intervention not only changed the caregivers' emotional state, it also appeared to have had a positive effect on their physical health as well.

Unfortunately, until recently, well-constructed and large-scale clinical trials of interventions for emotionally distressed family caregivers have been quite rare (Schulz et al., 2002). In 1995, the National Institute on Aging (NIA) and National Institute on Nursing Research (NINR) sponsored a multisite intervention research program called Resources for Enhancing Alzheimer's Caregiver Health (REACH). The REACH program was designed to test the effectiveness of multiple different interventions, as well as to evaluate the overall pooled effect of REACH interventions. The interventions varied across sites, and site-specific outcomes for the REACH studies are currently in press (Schulz et al., 2003). Because of the focus of this article, we will describe the two intervention sites that are notable for their use of cognitive–behavioral conceptualizations and strategies and their success in involving an ethically diverse pool of research participants. At one site, Gallagher-Thompson and colleagues (in press) used a cognitive–behavioral group format with Latina and European American female caregivers;

their study and findings will be reviewed in the following section on group-based interventions.

At another site, Burgio, Stevens, Guy, Roth, and Haley (2003) used cognitive–behavioral skills training implemented primarily in the homes of African American and European American family caregivers.

In their study, African American (n = 48) and European American (n = 70) dementia caregivers were randomly assigned to either the active intervention or a minimal support condition. After attending a 3-hour group workshop that introduced behavioral management, problem solving, and cognitive restructuring skills, caregivers in the active intervention participated in 16 in-home treatment sessions (focused on skills training) over a 12-month period. Skill development was also supported through the use of therapeutic phone calls. Of particular interest was their finding that African American caregivers in the skills training condition showed the greatest reduction in bother and upset following patient behavior problems (Burgio et al., 2003).

In summary, there are at least several individual-oriented approaches to cognitive and behavioral interventions that have been demonstrated to be effective in reducing emotional distress in family caregivers. The majority of studies using randomized clinical trial designs with family caregivers (e.g., REACH study) have been in the area of dementia and cognitive impairment, rather than physical impairment. We believe, however, that a number of these interventions could be applied to work with family caregivers of physically impaired older adults (e.g., Teri and colleagues' (1991) behavioral intervention for depression, because depression can cause secondary disability in physically impaired older adults as well as in dementia patients).

Group-Based Approaches

In general, group interventions for caregivers have many functions, including the provision of respite for caregivers, an opportunity for caregivers to receive and give peer support, and an increase in caregivers' self-efficacy. Unlike support groups, psychoeducational interventions teach caregivers practical skills for caregiving and specific coping strategies in addition to providing support through a group format. Psychoeducational interventions also tend to be more intensive and time-limited than traditional support groups. Although not all psychoeducational group interventions use a behavioral or cognitive–behavioral orientation, most are grounded in cognitive and behavioral principles. Caregivers participating in cognitive–behavioral psychoeducational groups may learn how to (a) challenge negative thoughts, (b) be more assertive, and (c) control their frustration level, as well as learn specific caregiving skills derived from behavioral principles (e.g., managing difficult behaviors in someone with dementia).

Gallagher-Thompson and colleagues have developed several efficacious cognitive–behavioral group interventions. A number of these have been tested specifically with dementia caregivers; others have targeted caregivers of either physically or cognitively impaired older adults. Their research is notable for the random assignment of participants to clearly defined, manualized interventions that have specifically targeted depression (e.g., "Coping with the Blues" class) and anger and irritation (e.g., "Coping with Frustration" class). In their most recent study that was part of the REACH research program, they randomly assigned Latina (n = 110) and Anglo (n = 147) female dementia family caregivers to either 10 weeks of an enhanced support group or a cognitive–behavioral psychoeducational "Coping with Caregiving" group. The psychoeducational group included relaxation training, assertion training, behavioral activation, and cognitive reframing. Both programs were delivered in either English or Spanish, depending on the needs of caregivers in specific classes/groups. Compared to those in the Enhanced Support control group, caregivers in the cognitive–behavioral group intervention showed a significant reduction in depressive symptoms and an increased use of adaptive coping strategies; results were similar for both ethnic groups (Gallagher-Thompson et al., 2003). The work of this research group has helped us to better understand Latina caregivers, as well as been at the forefront of demonstrating that Latina caregivers respond well to culturally sensitive cognitive and behavioral interventions.

CHALLENGES TO MENTAL HEALTH PROFESSIONALS

The literature on caregiving suggests that family caregivers often place their own mental and physical health needs secondary to those of their impaired family member. When they recognize that emotional distress is adversely impacting their functioning, family caregivers are more likely to select pharmacologic (i.e., antidepressants and/or anxiolytics prescribed by their general practitioner) and community-based programs (e.g., support groups and educational programs) for themselves, compared to traditional mental health services. This tendency has important implications for how interventions are packaged and delivered, which has led many cognitive and behavioral interventionists to appropriately label their programs as educational classes, or coping workshops, rather than individual or group therapy (i.e., use of the terms *therapy* and *psychotherapy* is not common in these interventions).

In addition, clinicians should note that the majority of the interventions described in this article were delivered away from university, hospital, clinic, or office settings.

Most of the individual-based approaches cited were either entirely home-based, or included a combination of home- and community-based sessions. For interventions delivered via a group format, most were located in an accessible part of the community (e.g., libraries, churches, senior centers), and in places other than traditional mental health settings. These community- and home-based approaches to intervention may be challenging for mental health practitioners who are used to office and/or hospital-based work. This strategy, however, is important to providing accessible and generalizable cognitive and behavioral interventions to family caregivers. Thus, mental health practitioners who are interested in working with this population may want to consider adapting to this trend.

FUTURE DIRECTIONS

Development and Evaluation of Mechanisms to Individualize Treatment

Behavioral and cognitive treatments generally include close attention to initial and ongoing assessments of target problems. Interventions using these theoretical orientations also emphasize a strong collaborative relationship between service recipient and clinician, as well as careful selection of which problem areas to begin to work on. Even highly structured and manualized treatments involve a focus on helping the caregiver apply the intervention strategies to his or her specific life situation. For that reason, one of our first recommen-dations fits well with the majority of these treatment approaches: Interventions for family caregivers should include mechanisms for tailoring the intervention to the specific needs of the participants. This recommendation is based on the heterogeneity of caregiving situations and the dynamic nature of providing care. We have not identified any research that directly compares more versus less flexible treatments. However, the tremendous variability in caregiving situations, coupled with the fact that caregiving needs change over time, suggests that caregivers would benefit from approaches that individualize some aspects of the treatment.

Use of Behavioral and Cognitive Strategies to Assess and Intervene with Barriers to Treatment

There is a general recognition in the caregiving literature that most family caregivers either underutilize available services, or delay utilization until a specific service is no longer appropriate. Examples of this include enrolling an older adult in a home-delivered meals program when the family member actually needs daily supervision, or considering use of an adult day care center when the level of need is for residential care. These behaviors are often labeled as "denial" by service providers and are hypothesized to represent an emotionally driven failure by the family to recognize the older adult's true level of chronic impairment. Such occasions of "denial," however, have not been studied in detail using cognitive and/or behavioral perspectives. Consequently, it is not always clear exactly what "denial" means, how it functions throughout the caregiving career, and what might be appropriate intervention strategies. This area is ripe for assessment and interventions targeting the behaviors and beliefs of family caregivers.

SUMMARY

Despite the widespread acknowledgment that family caregiving can adversely impact mental health and psychosocial functioning, the provision of empirically supported interventions for this population has been quite variable. For the most part, research with distressed family caregivers has lagged somewhat behind the progress made in behavioral treatments for other mental health problems. Only recently has there been a significant expansion of the development and testing of effective cognitive and behavioral interventions for family caregivers.

The behavioral and cognitive interventions that do exist offer support for the usefulness of these strategies with caregivers of impaired older adults. However, as we consider the ongoing professional interest in the topic of family caregiving, along with the growing popularity of behavioral and cognitive–behavioral treatments for mental disorder in general, *we are primarily struck by the limited number of such studies examining cognitive–behavioral interventions with family caregivers*. Dementia caregivers have been the population of most interest, and few researchers have focused on intervening with other types of caregivers (e.g., for stroke, cancer, heart disease, chronic physical impairments). The most important conclusion of the literature to date is that there is considerable room for growth in behavioral and cognitive treatments for family caregivers. On the other hand, we have little new content to add to existing critiques of the general caregiver intervention literature (e.g., small number of randomized studies, small sample sizes, limited outcome investigations, limited long-term follow-up). The REACH intervention studies have helped to address many of the concerns in the dementia caregiving literature, and we believe treatment studies involving other populations of caregivers merit similar attention and research sophistication. The other articles in this volume speak to the breadth and depth of cognitive and behavioral interventions when applied to many different populations and problems of living. We are optimistic that future investigators will adapt and evaluate a variety of these interventions for use by family caregivers.

See also: Aging and dementia, Depression and personality disorders—older adults

REFERENCES

Burgio, L., Stevens, A., Guy, D., Roth, D. L., & Haley, W. E. (2003). Impact of two psychosocial interventions on white and African American family caregivers of individuals with dementia. *The Gerontologist, 43*, 568–579.

Chang, B. (1999). Cognitive–behavioral intervention for homebound caregivers of persons with dementia. *Nursing Research, 48*, 173–182.

Gallagher-Thompson, D., Coon, D. W., Solano, N., Ambler, C., Rabinowitz, Y., & Thompson, L. W. (2003). Change in indices of distress among Latina and Anglo female caregivers of elderly relatives with dementia: Site specific results from the REACH National Collaborative Study. *The Gerontologist, 43*, 580–591.

Gallagher-Thompson, D., & Steffen, A. M. (1994). Comparative effects of cognitive/behavioral and brief psychodynamic psychotherapies for depressed family caregivers. *Journal of Consulting and Clinical Psychology, 62*, 543–549.

Gerdner, L. A., Buckwalter, K. C., & Reed, D. (2002). Impact of a psychoeducational intervention on caregiver response to behavioral problems. *Nursing Research, 51*, 363–374.

Ory, M. G., Yee, J. L., Tennstedt, S. L., & Schulz, R. (1999). The extent and impact of dementia care: Unique challenges experienced by family caregivers. In R. Schulz (Ed.), *Handbook on dementia caregiving: Evidence-based interventions for family caregivers*. (pp. 1–32). New York: Springer.

Schulz, R., Burgio, L., Burns, R., Eisdorfer, C., Gallagher-Thompson, D., Gitlin, L. N. et al. (2003). Resources for Enhancing Alzheimer's Caregiver Health (REACH): Overview, site specific outcomes and future directions. *The Gerontologist, 43*, 514–520.

Schulz, R., O'Brien, A., Czaja, S., Ory, M., Norris, R., Martire, L. M. et al. (2002). Dementia caregiver intervention research: In search of clinical significance. *The Gerontologist, 42*, 589–602.

Teri, L., Logsdon, R. G., Uomoto, J., & McCurry, S. M. (1997). Behavioral treatment of depression in dementia patients: A controlled clinical trial. *Journal of Gerontology: Psychological Sciences, 52B*, P159–P166.

RECOMMENDED READINGS

Coon, D. W., Gallagher-Thompson, D., & Thompson, L. W. (2002). *Interventions for family caregivers*. New York: Springer.

Coon, D. W., & Thompson, L. W. (2002). Family caregiving for older adults: Ongoing and emergent themes for the behavior therapist. *Behavior Therapist, 25*, 17–20.

Olshevski, J. L., Katz, A. D., & Knight, B. G. (1999). *Stress reduction for caregivers*. Philadelphia: Taylor & Francis.

Yeo, G., & Gallagher-Thompson, D. (2000). *Ethnicity and the dementias*. Washington, DC:

DEFINITIONS

Activities of daily living skills (ADLS) involve the ability to perform basic personal care tasks required on a daily basis; these skills are necessary for an individual to live without close monitoring and supervision. The number of tasks included in this category is typically small (e.g., bathing, dressing, toileting, eating, getting out of bed, moving unassisted). Those who are unable to perform these tasks are usually not able to live independently. These limitations can be temporary or chronic, and can be due to physical, cognitive, or mental health problems.

Formal caregivers are individuals who provide "hands-on" assistance as part of their professional role or through a formal agreement with the care recipient. Most formal caregivers fall in the categories of home-care assistants, nursing assistants, or other nursing professionals. Sometimes occupational therapists, physical therapists, social workers, or other care managers are included in this definition, but usually they are not. Unpaid volunteers are often included in this group when they represent the services of an organization or agency (i.e., a service agency provides the volunteer who has no previous relationship with the care recipient).

Independent activities of daily living skills (IADLS) involve the ability to perform a much broader range of tasks than ADLS, not all of which are required on a daily basis or linked to personal safety. Some of these tasks are more easily supported without close daily monitoring (e.g., housework, shopping, meal preparation, transportation, managing finances), at least in concept, than others (e.g., use of telephone, ability to correctly take medications). Limitations in IADLS can be either temporary or chronic, and due to physical, cognitive, or emotional problems.

Informal caregivers are nonpaid acquaintances who provide some form of assistance with daily living tasks, beyond what is typical or usual in the history of that relationship prior to the onset of impairment. The majority of such individuals are family members of the individual requiring assistance; however, this category also typically includes friends, neighbors, church members, and others whose assistance is based on a previous acquaintance with the care recipient.

G

Generalized Anxiety Disorder

Adrian Wells

Keywords: generalized anxiety disorder, worry, metacognition, beliefs

Generalized Anxiety Disorder (GAD) is characterized by excessive and uncontrollable worrying and the presence of specific symptoms that include muscle tension, irritability, sleep disturbance, and feeling keyed up or on edge. Worrying has become the predominant cognitive feature of GAD since the advent of DSM-III-R (APA, 1987) and the criterion of uncontrollability of worrying was added with the introduction of DSM-IV (APA, 1994). Worrying has been defined as a chain of thoughts that are negatively affect-laden and aimed at problem solving (Borkovec, Robinson, Pruzinsky, & DuPree, 1983). It is predominantly a verbal rather than imaginal process and can be distinguished from other types of intrusive thoughts such as obsessions. Worry in GAD should concern at least two different topics and not be confined to any coexisting emotional disorder. GAD is a chronic disorder that can have a relatively early onset.

NATURE AND EFFECTIVENESS OF CBT

Cognitive–behavioral treatments of GAD have differed in their nature and emphasis. Early approaches consisted of biofeedback, relaxation therapies, and anxiety management training with later combinations of cognitive and behavioral strategies. The cognitive therapy component has been based around self-instructional training or the cognitive methods of Beck and Emery (1985). Controlled trials with DSM-III-R- or DSM-IV-diagnosed GAD patients demonstrate that cognitive–behavioral treatments are associated with significant clinical improvement. Moreover, these studies show that treatment gains are maintained at 6 and 12 months following the end of therapy. In one study there was evidence of maintenance of gains at 2 years (Borkovec, Newman, Pincus, & Lytle, 2002). Cognitive–behavioral therapy (CBT) appears to be associated with the largest treatment effect when compared with anxiety management, nondirective psychotherapy, or psychoanalytic psychotherapy (Durham et al., 1994). Fisher and Durham (1999) examined recovery rates in GAD in six randomized controlled trials published since 1990. Each of these studies used the trait version of the Speilberger State–Trait Anxiety Inventory as one of the outcome measures allowing direct comparisons of the clinical significance of change on this measure. The treatments included CBT, behavior therapy, applied relaxation, cognitive therapy plus relaxation, nondirective therapy, analytic psychotherapy, anxiety management training, combinations of applied relaxation plus self-controlled desensitization, and cognitive therapy plus applied relaxation plus self-controlled desensitization. In the sample as a whole, a recovery rate of 40% was found. Twelve out of 20 treatment conditions maintained only modest recovery rates of 30% or less. Two treatment approaches—individual CBT and applied relaxation—did particularly well with overall recovery rates at 6-month follow-up of 50–60%. Examination of individual studies shows considerable variation in the percentage of patients showing no change, improvement, or recovery across studies. This variation may be due to sample characteristics, such as sample size and comorbidity, differential rates of attrition, and/or the influence of the group classification of treatments which leads to a heterogeneous set of approaches being classified as cognitive therapy or CBT. Other factors such as additional psychotherapy or pharmacotherapy administered during the follow-up period need to be controlled in cross-study evaluations. Moreover, measures such as trait anxiety provide only a restricted index of symptoms, and few early studies actually include a measure of excessive and uncontrollable worrying.

Borkovec et al. (2002) attempted to identify the critical ingredients in CBT by comparing their CBT package with two other treatments consisting of individual components of (a) cognitive therapy alone and (b) applied relaxation training combined with self-controlled desensitization. The authors also attempted to increase the effectiveness of CBT by increasing therapy time by 50% over that in their previous trial to allow for more thorough cognitive therapy. The authors predicted that their CBT would generate superior outcomes relative to the two component conditions. Cognitive therapy was conducted according to Beck and Emery (1985) and began with a presentation of the cognitive model of anxiety, training in self-monitoring, and identification of cues that trigger interpretations of threat. Patients receiving self-controlled desensitization were told that therapy would involve learning new coping techniques for reducing anxiety and worry, and would involve monitoring of internal reactions, learning to catch the spiral of anxiety early and to intervene with a variety of relaxation responses to anxious thoughts, feelings, and images. The treatment also consisted of instructions to create new coping habits such as learning to focus attention on present moment experience rather than on mentally created past events or future possibilities. The CBT treatment condition contained all of these elements. Analysis of pre- to posttreatment effects showed significant improvements on all outcome measures. Between-group analysis revealed no significant differences between therapeutic conditions. No significant between-group differences were obtained at 6-, 12-, or 24-month follow-up. Trait-anxiety scores at pre- and posttreatment in the cognitive therapy condition reveal that patients improved 39.29% at posttreatment; in the CBT condition using all treatment techniques, the degree of improvement was 42.53% at posttreatment. Overall the data showed that increasing the duration of treatment, and including multiple strategies, is not superior to cognitive techniques or self-control desensitization alone. The percentage improvement in trait anxiety suggests that the treatments fall within the typical range obtained for outcome effects in CBT. Borkovec et al. (2002) conclude that they were unable to support their prediction that CBT would be superior to its components and furthermore their efforts to increase therapeutic effectiveness of CBT were not successful.

In summary, CBT is an effective treatment for GAD. However, a significant proportion of patients fail to respond, and the degree of improvement in specific measures such as trait anxiety is disappointing. Only a limited number of studies have assessed the impact of treatment on worry measures and CBT, applied relaxation, and cognitive therapy appear to impact on worrying to a similar degree. Increasing therapist contact or increasing the focus on a range of cognitive, somatic, and affective subsystems in GAD does not seem to significantly improve treatment effectiveness. A limitation of existing treatment trials is that they have been based on evaluating the effectiveness of treatment techniques or methods, without an understanding of the factors that maintain or contribute to the development of GAD. More effective treatments are needed and progress in this area is likely to emerge from developments in theory.

THEORETICAL APPROACHES

Advances in treating pathological worry in GAD should emerge from a specification of cognitive factors involved in the escalation and persistence of worrying. Initial theoretical attempts and hypotheses concerning the function and origin of worry emphasized concepts of blocked emotional processing (Borkovec & Inz, 1990). Borkovec and colleagues suggest that worry is an attempt to avoid future aversive events. It may also divert attention away from negative thought intrusions in the form of imagery. Worrying itself can be negatively reinforced by its suppressing effects on aspects of somatic anxiety experience. The long-term consequences of this process include inhibition of emotional processing and the maintenance of anxious meanings.

A detailed cognitive model of pathological worry and GAD was subsequently advanced by Wells (1995, 1997). The model emphasizes the role of metacognitive beliefs and metacognitive appraisals in the development and persistence of excessive and out-of-control worrying. In this model, worry in GAD is not merely a symptomatic consequence of anxiety but is seen as an active and motivated style of appraisal and coping driven by the individual's beliefs. The person with GAD uses worry in order to cope with anticipated dangers and threats. The model is depicted diagrammatically in Figure 1.

Worry is often triggered by an intrusive thought that occurs in the form of a "what if" question such as "what if my partner is involved in a traffic accident" or as a negative image of catastrophe. This initial thought activates positive metacognitive beliefs about the usefulness of worrying as a coping strategy. Examples of positive beliefs include "worrying helps me cope; worrying keeps me safe; if I worry I'll

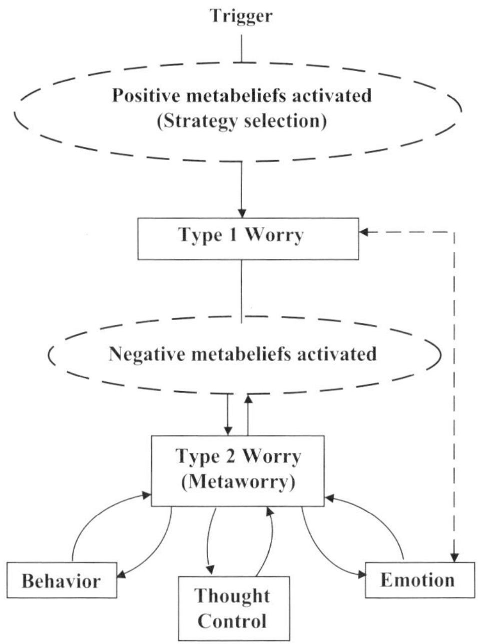

Figure 1. The metacognitive model of GAD. (Reproduced from Wells, 1997, with permission.)

be prepared." The person with GAD executes Type 1 worry sequences in which a range of "what if" questions are contemplated and potential strategies for dealing with these scenarios are generated. The content of Type 1 worrying focuses on external events and noncognitive internal events such as physical symptoms. Type 1 worrying leads to emotional responses as depicted by the bidirectional dotted line in Figure 1. The contemplation of dangerous scenarios leads to an escalation of anxiety and the somatic symptoms of arousal. However, when the Type 1 worry process meets its goal of generating acceptable coping responses, anxiety diminishes. The duration of anxiety responses linked to Type 1 worry is associated with the length of time taken to meet goals for coping. The person with GAD continues with worry until he assesses that he will be able to effectively cope with danger. This assessment is often based on internal cues such as a "felt sense" that he will be able to cope, the belief that all-important outcomes have been considered or a superstitious reasoning process. Although worrying stops when these internal goals are met, worrying may also be replaced by distracting or competing activities. Positive beliefs about worry are not unique to GAD, since most people have them. However, GAD patients tend to overuse worry as a strategy.

In the course of the development and persistence of GAD, negative beliefs about worrying develop. This is a crucial aspect in the development of the disorder. Once negative beliefs develop, the propensity for anxious responses increases. Negative beliefs include the following: "worrying is uncontrollable; worrying could make me go crazy; worrying will damage my body." During worry episodes, negative beliefs become activated and this leads to negative appraisal of the worry process. This negative appraisal or Type 2 worry intensifies anxiety and if emotional symptoms or worry itself is interpreted as imminently dangerous, rapid escalations of anxiety in the form of panic can result. Two further mechanisms lead to a persistence of Type 2 worry and negative beliefs. These are depicted by the behavioral responses and thought control boxes in Figure 1.

To prevent the feared consequences of worrying, the person with GAD engages in a number of behaviors. These are typically subtle forms of avoidance such as avoiding media material or news articles, which may trigger worrying thoughts, and seeking reassurance in order to terminate worry sequences or to avoid the need to worry in the first instance. The problem with these behaviors is that the person rarely attempts to interrupt worry, which deprives the person of information that can challenge negative beliefs about uncontrollability. By avoiding situations that trigger worrying, individuals also avoid an opportunity to discover that worrying is harmless. Furthermore, the individual who avoids worry triggers is unable to practice alternative strategies for appraisal and coping when exposed to stress or negative thoughts.

The other process in problem maintenance is thought control. As the person with GAD believes that worrying is beneficial, few attempts are made to interrupt worry sequences before the goal of worrying is achieved. In fact, the person may oscillate in their attempts to actively control thoughts. Because a state of cognitive dissonance exists in which both positive and negative beliefs about worry occur, the individual attempts to escape from this position by trying not to activate worry in the first place. This often consists of attempts to suppress thoughts about worry topics. For example, a person currently worrying about accidents may attempt not to think about accidents. The problem with thought suppression is that it is rarely entirely successful, which further reinforces beliefs about loss of mental control. Once worrying is activated, few attempts are made to actively interrupt the process in a consistent and highly motivated way. As a result, individuals have few experiences of successfully interrupting the worry process, which would provide evidence challenging negative beliefs concerning uncontrollability. However, even if individuals did successfully interrupt worrying, this would not provide evidence that worrying is not dangerous. Thus, a number of vicious cycles and conflicts emerging from positive and negative metacognitive beliefs about worrying underlie the development and persistence of GAD.

EMPIRICAL STATUS OF METACOGNITIVE THEORY

Research on patients with GAD and worry-prone nonpatients support several central aspects of this model. Individuals meeting criteria for GAD give positive reasons for worrying such that it contributes to motivation, preparation, and avoidance. Proneness to pathological worrying is positively associated with metacognitive factors including positive and negative beliefs about worrying. Patients with DSM-III-R-diagnosed GAD, compared to patients suffering from social phobia, panic disorder, or nonpatient controls, report significantly greater scores on negative beliefs about worrying and Type 2 worry. In discriminant analysis, patients with GAD were characterized by high levels of negative metacognitions while other patients were better characterized by the content of their Type 1 worries (Wells & Carter, 2001). Type 2 worry is a better predictor of pathological worry than Type 1 worry frequency and negative metacognitions predict the subsequent development of GAD 12–14 weeks later in prospective analyses.

In summary, experimental data from several sources are supportive of central aspects of the metacognitive model. This model has several implications for developing effective treatments of GAD. The model helps to explain the modest response rate for existing CBT interventions, suggesting that previous approaches have not focused on underlying metacognitive beliefs. A metacognitive treatment based on this model has been developed and is currently undergoing evaluation. This treatment develops a case conceptualization based on the model in Figure 1, and initially focuses on challenging negative beliefs about the uncontrollability of worrying through verbal reattribution and behavioral experiments. This is followed by challenging negative beliefs concerning the dangers of worrying, and finally modifying positive beliefs that lead to the inflexible use of worrying as a predominant means of coping. Specific techniques have been developed for these purposes and the interested reader should consult an appropriate treatment manual (Wells, 1997, 2000).

SUMMARY

Cognitive–behavioral treatment for GAD is an effective intervention. However, treatment effects are only modest and a significant proportion of patients fail to meet criteria for recovery. Advances in understanding and treating GAD are likely to result from theoretical conceptualizations of the cognitive processes involved in the maintenance and development of excessive and out-of-control worrying. Theoretical developments such as those offered by the metacognitive model direct treatment to specific cognitive mechanisms with the possibility of improving treatment effectiveness.

See also: Anxiety—adult, Anxiety—children, Anxiety in children—FRIENDS program, Social anxiety disorder 1, Social anxiety disorder 2

REFERENCES

Beck, A. T., & Emery, G. (1985). *Anxiety disorders and phobias: A cognitive perspective*. New York: Basic Books.

Borkovec, T. D., & Inz, J. (1990). The nature of worry in generalized anxiety disorder: A predominance of thought activity. *Behavior Research and Therapy*, *28*, 153–158.

Borkovec, T. D., Newman, M. G., Pincus, A. L., & Lytle, R. (2002). A component analysis of cognitive–behavioral therapy for generalized anxiety disorder and the role of interpersonal problems. *Journal of Consulting and Clinical Psychology*, *70*, 288–298.

Borkovec, T. D., Robinson, E., Pruzinsky, T., & DePree, J. A. (1983). Preliminary exploration of worry: Some characteristics and processes. *Behavior Research and Therapy*, *21*, 9–16.

Durham, R. C., Murphy, T., Allan, T., Richard, K., Treliving, L. R., & Genton, G. (1994). Cognitive therapy, analytic psychotherapy and anxiety management training for generalized anxiety disorder. *British Journal of Psychiatry*, *165*, 315–323.

Fisher, P. L., & Durham, R. C. (1999). Recovery rates in generalized anxiety disorder following psychological therapy: An analysis of clinically significant change in the STAI-T across outcome studies since 1990. *Psychological Medicine*, *29*, 1425–1434.

Wells, A. (1995). Meta-cognition and worry: A cognitive model of generalised anxiety disorder. *Behavioral and Cognitive Psychotherapy*, *23*, 301–320.

Wells, A. (1997). *Cognitive therapy of anxiety disorders: A practice manual and conceptual guide*. New York: Wiley.

Wells, A. (2000). *Emotional disorders and metacognition: Innovative cognitive therapy*. New York: Wiley.

Wells, A., & Carter, K. (2001). Further tests of a cognitive model of generalized anxiety disorder: Metacognitions and worry in GAD, panic disorder, social phobia, depression, and nonpatients. *Behavior Therapy*, *32*, 85–102.

RECOMMENDED READINGS

Davey, G., & Tallis, F. (1994). *Worrying: Perspectives on theory, assessment and treatment*. New York: Wiley.

Wells, A. (1997). *Cognitive therapy of anxiety disorders: A practice manual and conceptual guide*. New York: Wiley.

Wells, A. (1999). A metacognitive model and therapy of generalized anxiety disorder. *Clinical Psychology and Psychotherapy*, *6*, 86–95.

Wells, A. (2000). *Emotional disorders and metacognition: Innovative cognitive therapy*. New York: Wiley.

Group Therapy

Arthur Freeman and Sharon Morgillo-Freeman

Keywords: group therapy, groups

The history of group psychotherapy, beginning with Freud, has spanned the twentieth century. The early group models paralleled the then-current models of the psychodynamic individual therapy work. The therapeutic focus was on explicating underlying conflicts and exploring the issues of transference and resistance, but within the group context. Groups have become, for any of a number of reasons, a major therapeutic modality in clinical practice. They are used with inpatients, in partial hospital settings, as an outpatient modality, and as an aftercare modality. Groups are used with various patient populations, and can be modified for just about any population or diagnostic group.

OVERVIEW OF GROUP THERAPY MODELS

Historically, the three most commonly practiced group therapy models involved (1) individual therapy within a group context focusing on intrapsychic issues, (2) group dynamics approaches focused on interpersonal issues, and (3) group approaches targeting broad common symptom problems. Early work focused on the psychodynamic treatment models. In one of the first models, the therapist worked with each participant individually in the group, dividing the time and effort until all participants were reached. The best known example of this type of model was the Gestalt technique requiring one person on the "hot seat." The therapist would, at times, invite group members to respond to, and be involved with, the person currently on the "hot seat." It was, however, the therapist who did the majority of the therapy work. In the dynamic group work model, interpersonal issues of group membership, the relationship of members to others in the group, and how one comes across to others were targeted for discussion and clarification. These were, in many cases, issues more of concern to social psychologists than to clinical psychologists.

The third approach placed individuals into the group who, ideally, had similar problems, e.g., depression or anxiety disorders. In some cases, the "shared" problem might be that all of the members were in the same treatment unit. The "shared problem" groups were generally held in hospitals or community mental health centers and combined both the intrapersonal and interpersonal foci with the group work specific to some area of mutual concern, e.g., reducing anxiety. In inpatient hospital-based units, for example, patients are automatically entered into a psychoeducational group, even if formal group therapy is not prescribed.

THERAPEUTIC ASPECTS OF GROUP THERAPY

Group therapy is an economical way to deliver treatment. The rationale for including group cognitive therapy (GCT) in current treatment programs rests in part on nonspecific operational principles such as universality, support, and peer feedback that are shared with other group therapies (Yalom, 1985). However, GCT has the advantage of being a short-term, problem-oriented approach, consistent with individually administered CBT. Several of the more important reasons for utilizing GCT are described below.

Therapeutic Engagement

When people are experiencing depression or any of the range of psychological disorders, they may feel overwhelmed, helpless, and/or hopeless. These types of individuals may develop the belief that something will be done "for" or "to" them. GCT offers an opportunity to challenge this assumption. The group leaders (and, one hopes, group members) endorse the premise that self-control of thoughts, feelings, and behavior not only is possible, but is important. The group setting promotes collaboration through a number of procedures, including agenda setting, role-playing, and self-help exercises.

Diagnostic Functions

By directly observing the participant's behavioral, verbal, and emotional interactions with peers on a social level, clinicians are given a glimpse into the participant's repertoire or deficits of interpersonal skills. Participants who can appear quite intact in a one-to-one interview may have more trouble maintaining their stability when they are faced with the added stimuli generated in a group setting. Conversely, personal strengths, such as empathy skills, that are not readily apparent in individual therapy may be drawn out in the environment of group therapy.

Universality

"Normalizing" behavior is what Yalom (1985) observed as a sense of universality as one of the most helpful features of group therapy. Sharing perceptions and reactions in the group allows participants to see that they are not alone in their suffering and that other people have problems of a similar nature.

Relatedness and Support

The group can help to foster relatedness for the chronically isolated participant, can offer support for an individual who may be going through a personal loss or trauma, and also for the individual who needs "shoring up" either in decision making or in carrying through on a decision.

Psychoeducational Format

Special psychoeducational group programs can be designed for groups of participants who have shared life issues. Many GCT programs develop written materials, often combined in a folder or notebook that is presented on admission to the unit/program to help participants learn skills in an orderly sequence. Perhaps one of the best models for this is *Mind Over Mood* (Greenberger & Padesky, 1995) and *Treating Borderline Personality Disorder* (Freeman & Fusco, 2004). Social skills practice, assertiveness training, and other behavioral skills can be introduced, practiced, and assigned as homework.

Laboratory for Experimentation

A group can serve as a laboratory where participants can test out automatic thoughts and experiment with behaviors in a relatively safe environment.

Modeling and Social Skill Practice

Participants often model the behaviors of other group members or the therapists. In the process, the individual can learn effective coping strategies (e.g., assertiveness, empathic responding, goal setting, and problem solving).

Awareness

Awareness is another interesting facet of group therapy. This involves monitoring both internal and external data.

Rehearse New Behaviors

Prior to trying a new behavior in the world, the behavior can be role-played and practiced in the group before taking the leap to try it out "in real life." The group can offer a vehicle for reality testing and increasing participant responsibility.

Resource Management

Groups offer cost effectiveness at a time of shortages of staff, money, and resources.

GROUP SELECTION

Often, the participant population of the particular setting largely identifies group selection. In general, the optimum number of group members is 6 to 10 (although some psychoeducational family and community meetings have many more participants). There are advantages and disadvantages to group homogeneity in terms of age, sex, diagnosis, and problem focus. Homogeneous groups that focus on problems such as depression or eating disorders can enhance identification and empathy of group members.

Participants with organic brain syndromes, acute psychosis, or mania are generally not suitable for GCT; however, they will often benefit from an activity group that focuses on reality testing and social interaction. Participants with severely disruptive personality disorders may need to be excluded from any type of group inasmuch as they take up the time and may squander the resources of the group with little returned to the group in terms of more altruistic participation.

Length and Frequency of Sessions

Generally, we recommend that core groups meet for a minimum of $1\frac{1}{2}$ hours. This allows the group to have time to set an agenda, do meaningful therapeutic work, and close the session with review and homework. Groups with limited goals (e.g., orientation meetings for new participants, psychoeducational sessions for family members, assertiveness training) may be able to function effectively in an hour or less.

Location and Setting

The group should be held in a room that has adequate and comfortable seating and is well lighted and ventilated. Sufficient room for the group members to get up and move around for role-playing is another requirement. A chalkboard or easel, pads of paper, pens and markers, and any other materials and equipment should also be readily available.

Therapist Variables

The group can serve as an excellent educational opportunity for therapists-in-training. By working as a cotherapist, the novice can learn the therapy process in vivo. The cotherapist can also assist with role-playing or behavioral modeling in the session. The professional training of the group leader is of lesser import, as long as their training satisfies the criteria above.

Here-and-Now Focus

When therapy is short-term, it is extremely difficult for the group to obtain a historical perspective by reviewing the childhood experiences of each of the members. Some patient schemas are very obvious and will be recognized quickly by the therapist and the group members. Other schemas are not so clearly delineated and will be inferred from the participant's cognitive style, verbalizations, and/or behavior within the group. There are some participants, especially abused individuals or those with severe personality disorders, who have such firmly held maladaptive beliefs that historical reconstructive work may be required (Beck et al., 2004).

Cognitive Approaches

Ideally, each individual in the group assists with identifying and testing the thoughts of the other participants. The participant thus gains experience in thought monitoring while helping other group members. The group therapist and the participant's individual therapist work to clarify and modify schemas. Many of the basic techniques of cognitive therapy can be applied in the group setting.

Behavioral Procedures

GCT can be used to practice adaptive behaviors, such as dealing directly with a significant other, a boss, or a friend. The group and the therapist can give feedback on the participant's performance and coach the participant on more effective response styles. With some participants, the other group members or the therapist may need to demonstrate or to model different behaviors. For example, participants can role-play phone calls, family visits, or components of graded task hierarchies. The role-play can be supervised by the therapist or performed as a homework assignment and reported back at the next therapy session.

Nonadherence to Therapy Work

It is rare to have a group in which all members are highly motivated for substantive growth. Most groups contain individuals who are there grudgingly, or ambivalent about a commitment to therapy. These types of participants present special challenges to the group therapist. A significant number (3 or more in an 8- to 10-participant group) of poorly motivated participants can derail the group process. Thus, the therapist needs either to stimulate a more collaborative effort by using GCT to modify the negative cognitions about treatment, or, when this is not possible, to alter the composition of the group by "selecting out" individuals who cannot apply themselves to the work of the group. Some may see this exclusion from the group as punishing to the patient. It is important to stress that the excluded member is welcome when and if they can use the group to their advantage and the advantage of others. One member cannot hold the group hostage to their pathology. There must be the greatest good for the greatest number.

GCT FORMATS

We can identify several formats for GCT. These include open-ended group therapy, the rotating theme model, and programmed group therapy.

Open-Ended GCT

All of the basic procedures for GCT described earlier are utilized in the open-ended group. Participants are screened carefully in order to select group members who can enter rapidly into the therapy process and profit from the experience. Advance preparation is important. At a minimum, the participant is exposed to the cognitive model before attending GCT through one or more of the following: individual therapy, readings and other homework assignments, or instructional sessions with a nurse or auxiliary therapist. At least two therapists are recommended for any of the core GCT groups. The therapist and cotherapist adopt a very active therapy style for an open-ended group. As the only permanent members of the group, they have the primary responsibility for transmission of the group culture (i.e., basic theories, rules, responsibilities, parameters of therapeutic relationships). The therapists must also structure the group process effectively and keep the pace of the session at a level that maximizes the chances for learning and minimizes the possibilities of confusion or overload. Yalom (1983) recommends that each group session be viewed as a self-contained therapeutic experience, so that even if individuals can attend only one session, they are able to understand and respond to it. The following are suggestions for using GCT procedures to make each open-ended group session a "therapy within a therapy."

1. Emphasize the psychoeducational aspects of treatment.
2. Set a meaningful agenda.
3. Maintain the agenda.
4. Use homework to link GCT with the rest of the participant's life.

Rotating Theme Groups

The rotating theme group was developed specifically for use in hospital settings (Bowers, 1989). In this type of GCT, an external structure for the therapy agenda is used in an attempt to circumvent some of the problems that are encountered with rapid participant turnover. By focusing a set number of sessions on a particular theme (e.g., the stigma of depression, dealing with children, coping with parents, problems with school or work, or other common areas of difficulty), the therapist can structure a comprehensive GCT experience. Initially, the topics for the sessions can be developed by the group therapists based on their experiences with the range of participants typically encountered in the treatment setting. The topic list should be matched to the population mix. For example, themes for GCT on a program that specializes in depression might include building self-esteem, choosing pleasurable activities, or coping with loss. On the other hand, themes for group therapy for an eating disorders program might include body image, meal planning, or thoughts about eating. The topic list evolves as the group therapists have the opportunity to experiment with various group themes. A shift in the composition of the participant group would suggest that the session themes be altered. The topics for each session would be listed in advance of the session, and participants are asked to prepare in advance for each of the group meetings. Participants are instructed to write out two questions, problems, or thoughts relative to the selected theme of that group and to bring the card to the next group session. Index cards are supplied for writing down ideas. Nurses and other staff members help prepare the participants by reviewing the material on the cards before the group meeting. The staff can help to generate ideas, write down ideas when the patient has difficulty, and remind them to bring the card to the group.

Although not every theme is fully relevant to every participant, the topic areas should be of broad interest so as to capture the attention of most group members. Some participants, however, may have to wait for a future session before dealing with their primary problem. Writing down questions or ideas allows participants who have difficulty being spontaneous in the group or who have problems in identifying problems to have a mechanism for expressing themselves.

As the agenda is set, the group therapist or cotherapist reads the cards and a group "scribe" writes the items on a board. The therapist can then put two or more items of similar meaning together. Alternatively, group members are then asked to read what they have written on their index cards. Usually, 10 members do not generate 20 distinct issues; a good deal of overlap almost always occurs. A hierarchy of agenda items is established, and the group begins to work.

The therapist prepares psychoeducational materials that are relevant to each theme and may outline the general content and procedure for the session in advance. However, it is also important to involve the group members in setting the agenda and providing input on the direction for therapy. The rotating theme group is more structured than the open-ended group, but spontaneity and vigorous group interaction are still encouraged.

Programmed Groups

The third type of cognitive therapy group provides a series of sessions that are designed to convey a defined body of knowledge about cognitive therapy. These groups are a hybrid between open-ended, rotating theme, and more circumscribed psychoeducational groups. Compared to other groups, the programmed group relies the most on structure and didactic techniques and the least on spontaneous processes of group interaction. Covi & Primakoff (1988) have described the successful use of programmed content groups for depressed outpatients. In the outpatient setting, all of the participants go through the sequence of sessions in the same order and at the same time. This allows the leaders to develop a package of treatment sessions that is arranged like an educational course. Each session is a building block for the next. The basic cognitive model is described at the beginning of every meeting, so that new members will have an overview of the cognitive approach before launching into the session. After reviewing homework, the therapist briefly presents the topic for the day, such as identifying automatic thoughts or using graded-task assignments. This didactic material is designed to be understandable even if the participant has not had the benefit of earlier sessions in the sequence. Diagrams and handouts are used to accelerate the learning process. When programmed groups are used, it is advisable to have concurrent individual sessions to allow processing of each participant's particular agenda for therapy.

SUMMARY

GCT helps participants to engage rapidly in the overall treatment process, assists the treatment team in obtaining a multifaceted picture of the participant's disorder, and provides accurate peer feedback to group members. This form of cognitive therapy also promotes a sense of universality that helps to ease the participant's isolation and burden of shame and guilt. However, the main contribution of GCT is a resolution of symptoms through the identification and modification of cognitive–behavioral pathology.

See also: Social skills training

REFERENCES

Beck, A. T., Freeman, A., Davis, D. D., & Associates. (2004). *Cognitive therapy of personality disorders* (2nd ed.). New York: Guilford Press.

Beck, A. T., Rush, A. J., Shaw, B. F., & Emery, G. (1979). *Cognitive therapy of depression*. New York: Guilford Press.

Bowers, W. A. (1989). Cognitive therapy with inpatients. In A. Freeman, K. M. Simon, L. E. Beutler, & H. Arkowitz (Eds.), *Comprehensive handbook of cognitive therapy* (pp. 583–596). New York: Plenum Press.

Covi, L., & Primakoff, L. (1988). Cognitive group therapy. In A. J. Frances & R. E. Hales (Eds.), *American Psychiatric Press Review of psychiatry* (pp. 608–626). Washington, DC: American Psychiatric Press.

Covi, L., Roth, D., & Lipman, R. S. (1982). Cognitive group psychotherapy of depression: The close-ended group. *American Journal of Psychotherapy*, *36*(4), 459–469.

Free, M. L., Oei, T. P. S., & Sanders, M. R. (1991). Treatment outcome of a group cognitive therapy program for depression. *International Journal of Group Psychotherapy*, *41*, 533–547.

Freeman, A., & Fusco, G. M. (2004). *Treating Borderline Personality Disorder. Therapist's manual*. New York: Norton.

Fusco, G. M., & Freeman, A. (2004). *Treating Borderline Personality Disorder. Patient's workbook*. New York: Norton.

Linehan, M. M. (1987). Dialectical behavior therapy in groups: Treating borderline personality disorders and suicidal behavior. In C. M. Brody (Ed.), *Working in groups* (pp. 145–162). New York: Springer.

Shaffer, C. S., Shapiro, J., Sank, L. I., & Coghlan, D. J. (I 981). Positive changes in depression, anxiety, and assertion following individual and group cognitive behavior therapy intervention. *Cognitive Therapy and Research*, *5*, 149–157.

Shaw, B. F. (1977). A comparison of cognitive therapy and behavior therapy in the treatment of depression. *Journal of Consulting and Clinical Psychology*, *45*, 543–551.

Yalom, I. D. (1983). *Inpatient group psychotherapy*. New York: Basic Books.

Yalom, I. D. (1985). *The theory and practice of group psychotherapy* (3rd ed.). New York: Basic Books.

H

Health Anxiety

Mark A. Reinecke and Joseph B. Dilley

Keywords: health anxiety, hypochondriasis, cognitive–behavioral therapy

"Anxiety is not fear, being afraid of this or that definite object, but the uncanny feeling of being afraid of nothing at all." The irony implied in William Barrett's (1958) observation of pronounced, but unnecessary apprehension is perhaps nowhere more salient than in the experience of health anxiety. Health anxiety is the relatively new term for the phenomenon conventionally referred to as *hypochondriasis*. Hypochondriasis is defined by the *Diagnostic and Statistical Manual of Mental Disorders—Fourth Edition, Text Revision* (DSM-IV-TR) as a misinterpretation of bodily symptoms that results in preoccupation with fears of having, or the idea that one has, a serious disease, despite medical evaluation and reassurance (American Psychiatric Association, 2000). In short, hypochondriasis is severe health anxiety (Salkovskis, 1989). Hypochondriasis is bound by explicit definitional parameters not common to the more general notion of health anxiety. Thus, hypochondriasis can be more readily measured and most research in this area has employed hypochondriasis as a yardstick of health anxiety.

Epidemiological studies indicate that hypochondriasis affects 1–5% of the general public, and 2–7% of outpatient populations (American Psychiatric Association, 2000; Comer, 2001). Males and females are at equal risk for hypochondriasis, and although onset can occur at any age, the disorder is most commonly diagnosed during early adulthood, with the peak age of incidence falling between 30 and 39 (American Psychiatric Association, 2000; Comer, 2001; see Iezzi, Duckworth, & Adams, 2001). As they tend to report more aging- and death-related fears, hypochondriacal patients generally seek more medical treatment than persons not meeting criteria for the disorder, but ironically, place less confidence in their primary care physicians and take no better physical care of themselves (see Iezzi et al., 2001).

Health anxiety of many types and levels of severity plays a role in maintaining most somatic problems, including hypertension, dizziness, irritable bowel syndrome, asthma, psychogenic vomiting, and body dysmorphic disorder (Salkovskis, 1989). As such, health anxiety is experienced more pervasively than is reflected by the prevalence rates of hypochondriasis per se. Indeed, over 90% of the general population will experience common somatic problems like headaches or insomnia (Salkovskis, 1989), and above-average nervousness with regard to illness or injury is reported by nearly one-quarter of adults in randomly selected community studies (Noyes et al., 2000).

Health anxiety shares features and is often comorbid with several other psychological conditions, most commonly those falling within the affective spectrum, but also including obsessive–compulsive disorder (OCD), panic disorder, and agoraphobia, as well as personality and psychotic-spectrum disorders (see Iezzi et al., 2001; Margarinos, Zafar, Nissenson, & Blanco, 2002; Warwick, 1995). The considerable symptom overlap between health anxiety and other psychological conditions necessitates comprehensive assessment—both to determine differential psychiatric diagnoses, and to sufficiently rule out the presence of a primary physical illness, so that appropriate interventions can be determined (Kaplan, 2002; Warwick, 1995).

Certain factors make differential diagnosis a complex endeavor. For example, patients experiencing hypochondriasis report the intrusive and recurrent thoughts also reported by patients who experience OCD, so clinicians must rely on their assessment of preoccupational *content* in order to distinguish these disorders. Specifically, the content of concerns in hypochondriasis is confined to health issues, but may span a variety of contexts in OCD (Foa & Franklin, 1999).

The inherent complexity of differential diagnosis also can be observed in assessing for hypochondriasis versus illness phobia, as both of these disorders share the element of fear-provoking stimuli, and thus clinicians must rely on their ascertainment of the *source* of the stimuli in order to distinguish these disorders. Specifically, illness fears are elicited directly by external stimuli, while hypochondriacal fears are elicited and maintained directly by internal stimuli (Salkovskis, 1989).

A final example of diagnostic complication is that hypochondriasis has been posited as one stage in the occurrence of panic disorder (Buffone, 1994), warranting the thorough evaluation of symptoms to ascertain whether a patient presently experiencing symptoms of hypochondriasis is actually suffering from a more primary panic disorder. Certainly, the problem of differential diagnosis is central to diagnostic formulations of hypochondriasis and other disorders that share health anxiety as a perpetuator (see Iezzi et al., 2001), but whether diagnostic reformulations will be offered is a question to be answered by DSM-V.

COGNITIVE FORMULATION

Health anxiety is part of the anxiety spectrum of disorders. As such, cognitive behavioral formulations of this condition emphasize elements that are central to other experiences of anxiety. Specifically, perceptual and memory biases give rise to the cognitive distortion or magnification of problems, engagement in affective reasoning (e.g., "If I feel it, it must be true"), and underestimation of coping ability. Feelings of apprehension and worry are experienced as a result, which exacerbate existing cognitive distortions and the cycle repeats itself.

Salkovskis and Warwick (1986; see also: Salkovskis, 1989; Warwick, 1995; Warwick & Salkovskis, 1991) offer an explicit cognitive formulation of health anxiety. A description of this formulation follows. The formulation is comprised of six core features:

1. Preoccupation with health.
2. Insufficient organic pathology to account for the concerns expressed.
3. Selective attention to bodily changes or features.
4. Negative interpretation of bodily signs and symptoms.
5. Selective attention to and disbelief of medical and nonmedical communications.
6. Persistent seeking of reassurance/checking bodily status/information.

Conceptualizing health anxiety as a condition maintained by these features provides a framework for both understanding and treating the patient's distress. Integral to understanding the patient's distress is an emphasis on the development of dysfunctional assumptions about health that usually occurs during childhood. This notion is consistent with findings that hypochondriacal patients report a higher rate of traumatic experiences during childhood (Barsky, Wool, Barnett, & Clary, 1994).

Although dysfunctional assumptions can be amended throughout the life course, they cause the health anxiety patient to pay *selective attention* to evidence of threats to personal health. Over time, events that are consistent with dysfunctional assumptions, or *critical incidents*, occur and bodily signs and symptoms are misinterpreted as evidence of serious illness. Misinterpretation of bodily signs and symptoms is a hallmark feature of health anxiety, and is the key element necessary for the formation of cognitive *confirmation biases*, which perpetuate the process: further engagement in selective attention and misinterpretation, which in turn elicit *negative automatic thoughts* about danger or threat.

For the health anxiety patient, this process reifies the belief that a serious physical illness has befallen him, making it extremely difficult for the patient to believe otherwise. In addition, this process catalyzes change in four areas of functioning: physiological, cognitive, behavioral, and affective. Of particular import is the notion that responses within each of these areas interact to perpetuate each other and thereby maintain or increase what physical symptoms are present, as well as the emotional reactions accompanying them.

Physiological

Normal and transient indicators of increased physiological arousal are interpreted as indicators of illness by the health anxiety patient. Such misinterpretation autonomically intensifies the current experience of physiological arousal and/or induces physiological arousal in other parts of the body. For example, the patient who becomes anxious on misinterpreting a (normal) drop in body temperature as a sign of hypothermia subsequently may experience shortness of breath.

Cognitive

The health anxiety patient believes that he has, to this point, failed to perceive bodily signs and symptoms for what they really "must" be: indications of a serious illness. Bodily states that previously went unrecognized or were considered normal the patient now automatically considers unprecedented and threatening, and remains extra vigilant to them in order to compensate for having "missed" them in the past. Concomitantly, the patient tends to ruminate, dismiss positive information, and further increase his monitoring of bodily states, despite the belief that doing so will ultimately prove futile. For example, the patient who believes he has hypothermia will discount observable signs that his hands are warming up, such as reddening of the skin that occurs with increased bloodflow, and instead remain focused on the fact that his hands unexpectedly had become cold.

An increased awareness of bodily states may cause the patient to present with pressured and long speeches recounting many complaints, problems, and concerns (see Iezzi et al., 2001). Other, more common behavioral indicators of this hypervigilance to bodily states are reviewed in the following section.

Behavioral

Unlike the disease phobic patient, who responds by avoiding external stimuli associated with the feared condition, the health anxiety patient cannot escape from his own bodily sensations. Thus, the patient with health anxiety responds similarly to the obsessional patient: by trying to ameliorate the anxiety itself. Two common means of pursuing this goal are bodily checking and reassurance seeking, often manifested in the posing of subtle but excessive inquiries to family, friends, and medical personnel. These behaviors have the potential to exacerbate physiological and emotional symptoms. For example, the patient who believes he has hypothermia and compulsively asks his spouse to take his temperature with an under-the-tongue thermometer will likely agitate oral tissue and experience subsequent discomfort in his mouth, as well as put off his spouse. However, the potential for physical and emotional discomfort introduced by these behaviors is far outweighed by the temporary relief of anxiety they assuredly yield. As such, these behaviors are positively reinforced. Unfortunately, the relief these behaviors offer is temporary, because the patient was already and remains convinced that he has or will acquire a serious illness. Thus, instead of leading to long-term reductions in anxiety, these behaviors are practiced again and thereby ultimately lead to increases in anxiety and mental preoccupation.

Another common behavior constitutes a more direct response to the need to avoid fear-provoking stimuli. Specifically, the patient with health anxiety avoids engaging in threat reappraisal. Under normal circumstances, reappraising threat would serve to render a person's fears unrealistic, and thus unworthy of attention. However, for patients who are convinced of their grave health status, threat reappraisal causes further distress and forces the patient to remain hypervigilant. This, in turn, increases the frequency of negative thoughts and the extent of cognitive preoccupation.

Affective

As implied in the above discussion of comorbidity, anger, depression and malaise, and other emotional states are common correlates of health anxiety. These states, in turn, may give rise to other psychological conditions, such as chronic fatigue (see Iezzi et al., 2001). Thus, it is easy to observe the self-perpetuating manner in which the affective conditions associated with health anxiety interact. For example, the patient who believes he is about to die from hypothermia is likely to experience sadness and hopelessness, anger toward healthy others, and (once he believes he has successfully avoided death for the time being) apprehension with regard to other life situations. Repeated exposure to these feelings increases their duration and places the patient at increased risk for subsequent cognitive distortion. Negative moods, such as anxiety and depression, may contribute to the activation of memories of similar experiences in the past through the process of state-dependent learning.

TREATMENT

Health anxiety can be difficult to treat (Warwick & Salkovskis, 1991), frequently taking a chronic course that waxes and wanes over time (Comer, 2001). Because patients with health anxiety frequently present with attitudes mirroring those experiencing OCD, cognitive–behavioral methods of treatment parallel those employed in treating OCD. Salkovskis (1989) proposes a cognitive–behavioral therapy (CBT) approach for the treatment of health anxiety; this approach is consistent with and makes direct use of the elements of the cognitive formulation. Eight general principles for treating the health anxiety that accompanies somatic conditions serve to guide therapy.

1. Identify what the problem *is*, not what the problem is not.
2. Acknowledge the authentic presence of the symptoms (the treatment is designed to accurately explain their presence).
3. Relevant information may help the patient, while irrelevant or repetitive information is likely to exacerbate the patient's distress.
4. Treatment is to be collaborative, not confrontational.

5. Instead of discounting the patient's unrealistic beliefs, help him identify the observations that serve as evidence of illness and what is maintaining the problem and the distress.
6. Establish a short-term contract to test alternative (i.e., more realistic) explanations for the symptoms.
7. Educate the patient about the interaction among the four functional contexts affected by health anxiety; conduct demonstrations that exemplify how easy it can be for innocuous stimuli to prompt anxiety.
8. Consistently elicit feedback from the patient to ensure his understanding and prevent the potential for intervention to result in increased anxiety.

Using these guiding principles enables the therapist to accurately ascertain the factors that maintain the patient's physical and emotional symptoms and subsequently break the cycle operating among them. However, means to this end are complicated by factors unique to therapy with the health anxiety patient.

As discussed earlier, patients with health anxiety often are skeptical of positive information. Thus, a convincing argument that might ordinarily nullify unrealistic fears does little to loosen the health anxiety patient's tight grip on dysfunctional beliefs of illness. Indeed, attempts to reassure the patient of his well-being ultimately are likely to fail. Although reassurance will temporarily alleviate the patient's anxiety, precisely the fact that it does will reinforce the patient to seek it again when the anxiety returns. Further, attempts to convince the patient that his beliefs are simply false may invalidate the patient's distress.

These factors make the therapist's efforts to engage these patients in treatment a critical component of the change process. Indeed, it is considered necessary to explicitly involve the patient in behavioral experiments and follow-up assessments so that they may appraise for themselves the plausibility of other, less morose explanations for their distress.

Treatment Efficacy

A favorable prognosis for recovery from health anxiety is indicated by the following characteristics: acute onset, brief duration, mild or a low number of symptoms, low reliance on the health care system, the presence of a veritable general medical condition, and the absence of a comorbid mental illness and the potential for secondary gain (Comer, 2001; Hiller, Leibbrand, Rief, & Fichter, 2002). However, given mediating factors such as the chronicity of health anxiety, the overlap of its symptoms with those of other psychological conditions, and the reinforcement of maladaptive behavioral responses, it is unlikely that more than one or two positive prognostic indicators will be present. Indeed, prognosis for recovery from health anxiety is generally poor (Warwick & Salkovskis, 1991). However, the implementation of CBT interventions for health anxiety has risen over the past decade, and relatively recent empirical measurement of outcomes has yielded encouraging results.

Recent reviews of randomized controlled studies using CBT to treat the health anxiety associated with a range of somatic conditions, including body dysmorphic disorder, chronic fatigue syndrome, and noncardiac chest pain, suggest that CBT is efficacious for this purpose (Looper & Kirmayer, 2002; Margarinos et al., 2002). In addition, there is evidence for the preeminent efficacy of CBT relative to family and dynamic therapies in treating the health anxiety of international populations (Rodriguez & Martinez, 2001). Relative to medication treatment for health anxiety, it appears that patients would both prefer CBT and expect it to yield higher rates of improvement (Walker, Vincent, Furer, Cox, & Kjernisted, 1999). Evidence for the efficacy of intense doses of CBT to treat inpatient hypochondriasis has also emerged (Hiller et al., 2002).

With regard to the maintenance of positive outcomes, there is evidence to suggest that hypochondriacal patients treated with CBT demonstrate significantly greater improvements than controls on self-report, therapist, and assessor measures and maintain improvement 3 months later (Warwick, Clark, Cobb, & Salkovskis, 1996). Other studies document improvements lasting from 7 months to 1 year, but these also suggest that cognitive therapy may only be as efficacious in the maintenance of improvement as are certain other interventions, such as exposure plus response prevention and behavioral stress management (Clark et al., 1998).

Finally, evidence for the efficacy of group CBT to treat health anxiety is also amassing (Lidbeck, 1997; Looper & Kirmayer, 2002; Margarinos et al., 2002). Evidence that CBT can be efficacious in treating the health anxiety experienced by members of circumscribed populations, such as survivors of traumatic brain injury, has recently emerged and constitutes a direction for future research (Williams, Evans, & Fleminger, 2003).

CONCLUSION

In sum, the cognitive formulation of health anxiety appears to account sufficiently for the experiences of health anxiety patients, and the efficacy of CBT for health anxiety is gradually gaining empirical support. Should more support follow, the continued implementation of this intervention will be warranted and should reduce the incidence of the distressing and ironic phenomenon known as health anxiety.

REFERENCES

American Psychiatric Association. (2000). *Diagnostic and statistical manual of mental disorders* (4th ed.). Washington, DC: Author.

Barrett, W. (1958). *Irrational man: A study in existential philosophy*. New York: Anchor Books.

Barsky, A. J. (2002). Hypochondriasis [correspondence]. *The New England Journal of Medicine, 346*, 783–784.

Barsky, A. J., Wool, C., Barnett, M. C., & Cleary, P. D. (1994). Histories of childhood trauma in adult hypochondrial patients. *American Journal of Psychiatry, 151*, 397–401.

Buffone, G. W. (1994). Treatment of panic disorder: An overview. *Medical Psychotherapy: An International Journal, 4*, 131–144.

Clark, D. M., Salkovskis, P. M., Hackman, A., Wells, A., Fennell, M., Ludgate, J., Ahmad, S., Richards, H. C., & Gelder, M. (1998). Two psychological treatments for hypochondriasis: A randomized controlled trial. *British Journal of Psychiatry, 173*, 218–225.

Comer, R. J. (2001). *Abnormal psychology* (4th ed.). New York: Worth Publishers.

Foa, E. B., & Franklin, M. E. (1999). Cognitive behavior therapy. In M. Hersen & A. Bellack (Eds.), *Handbook of comparative interventions for adult disorders* (2nd ed., pp. 359–377). New York: Wiley.

Hiller, W., Leibbrand, R., Rief, W., & Fichter, M. M. (2002). Predictors of course and outcome in hypochondriasis after cognitive–behavioral treatment. *Psychotherapy and Psychosomatics, 71*, 318–325.

Iezzi, T., Duckworth, M. P., & Adams, H. E. (2001). In H. Adams & P. Sutker (Eds.), *Comprehensive handbook of psychopathology* (3rd ed., pp. 211–258). New York: Kluwer Academic/Plenum.

Kaplan, N. M. (2002). Hypochondriasis [correspondence]. *The New England Journal of Medicine, 346*, 783–784.

Lidbeck, J. (1997). Group therapy for somatization disorders in general practice: Effectiveness of a short cognitive–behavioural treatment model. *Acta Psychiatriaca Scandinavica, 96*, 14–24.

Looper, K. J., & Kirmayer, L. J. (2002). Behavioral medicine approaches to somatoform disorders. *Journal of Consulting and Clinical Psychology, 70*, 810–827.

Margarinos, M., Zafar, U., Nissenson, K., & Blanco, C. (2002). Epidemiology and treatment of hypochondriasis. *CNS Drugs, 16*, 9–22.

Noyes, R., Hartz, A. J., Doebbeling, C. C., Malis, R. W., Happel, R. L., Werner, L. A., & Yagla, S. J. (2000). Illness fears in the general population. *Psychosomatic Medicine, 62*, 318–325.

Rodriguez, C. F., & Martinez, R. F. (2001). Efficacious psychological treatments for hypochondriasis [Spanish]. *Psicothema, 13*, 407–418.

Salkovskis, P. M. (1989). Somatic problems. In K. Hawton, P. Salkovskis, J. Kirk, & D. Clark (Eds.), *Cognitive behaviour therapy for psychiatric problems: A practical guide* (pp. 235–276). New York: Oxford University Press.

Salkovskis, P. M., & Warwick, H. M. C. (1986). Morbid preoccupations, health anxiety and reassurance: A cognitive behavioural approach to hypochondriasis. *Behaviour Research and Therapy, 24*, 597–602.

Walker, J., Vincent, N., Furer, P., Cox, B., & Kjernisted, K. (1999). Treatment preference in hypochondriasis. *Journal of Behavior Therapy and Experimental Psychiatry, 30*, 251–258.

Warwick, H. M. C. (1995). Assessment of hypochondriasis. *Behaviour Research and Therapy, 33*, 845–853.

Warwick, H. M. C., Clark, D. M., Cobb, A. M., & Salkovskis, P. M. (1996). A controlled trial of cognitive–behavioral treatment of hypochondriasis. *British Journal of Psychiatry, 169*, 189–195.

Warwick, H. M. C., & Salkovskis, P. M. (1991) Hypochondriasis. In J. Scott, J. Williams, & A. Beck (Eds.), *Cognitive therapy in clinical practice: An illustrative casebook* (pp. 78–102). New York: Routledge.

Williams, W. H., Evans, J. J., & Fleminger, S. (2003). Neuro-rehabilitation and cognitive–behaviour therapy of anxiety disorders after brain injury: An overview and case illustration of obsessive–compulsive disorder. *Neuropsychological Rehabilitation, 13*, 133–148.

History of Behavioral Medicine

Stephanie H. Felgoise

Keywords: behavioral medicine, history

The historical routes of behavioral medicine are often attributed to "psychosomatic medicine" and Sigmund Freud. However, the innovation of studying psychological principles applied to physical illness and health actually predates the formal discipline of psychology. In fact, the history of behavioral medicine can be traced to Hippocrates, with continued development to the present day. Following each era in the development of behavioral medicine it is fascinating to note that ideas and "innovations" in the twenty-first century may really represent technological advancements and better science rather than new concepts or practice.

TERMS AND DEFINITIONS

Semantics and terminology have had a tremendous impact on the historical documentation of behavioral medicine. For example, Lee Birk first used the term "behavioral medicine," which appeared in the title of his book, *Biofeedback: Behavioral Medicine* (1973). Based on this publication, "behavioral medicine" was mistakenly understood to mean "biofeedback" (Gentry, 1984).

In 1977, the first official definition of "behavioral medicine" was created at the Yale Conference of Behavioral Medicine. This definition was then revised in 1978 by the United States National Academy of Science's Institute of Medicine. The final definition, which remains today, is as follows: "Behavioral medicine is the *interdisciplinary* field concerned with the development and integration of behavioral and biomedical science, knowledge and techniques relevant to health and illness and the application of this knowledge and these techniques to prevention, diagnosis, treatment, and rehabilitation" (Schwartz & Weiss, 1978, p. 250). Distinctly, the interdisciplinary approach of this field differentiates it from related fields that are unidisciplinary, such as "health psychology" or "medical psychology."

HISTORICAL REVIEW

Medicine Prior to the 1800s

Hippocrates (500 B.C.) is best known for his theory that health was a state of harmonic mixture of the humors. Disease was a state of disharmony among the humors (Stone, 1979). This theory explained both physical and mental disorders. The representation of a disorder, such as any odd thoughts, behavior, or symptomatology, dictated treatment. Although mental processes had been recognized, treatment meant intervening to restore balance between the humors either by, for example, an invasive procedure (bleeding individuals) or causing the release of bile (forced vomiting) (Engel, 1977). Galen (second century, A.D.) strayed from Hippocrates' theory of illness and health. He believed and promulgated that impairment in functioning must be the result of physical malady in the originating organ or system (Stone, 1979). Based on this assumption, Galen's philosophy was disease oriented. One could argue that he initiated the reductionist view of medicine.

Prior to the 1800s, "the disease model" dominated the approach to health and medical care. Essentially, the disease model was a reductionist view of physical and psychological illnesses. Physicians focused exclusively on biological factors in the understanding and treatment of illness. This view is still maintained by many practitioners today.

Despite the emphasis on biological processes, several people are noted for introducing psychological techniques and theory into the understanding and practice of medicine. In the 1600s, Thomas Sydenham used clinical observation to gain a better understanding of his patients and the manifestations of their diseases. He believed that external emotional events could affect the "animal spirits" of the body, which, in turn, caused "hysteria" (Shorter, 1991). In 1770, John Gregory wrote about chronic pain in nervous patients. The connection between "nervous patients" and "chronic pain" indicates recognition of a correlation between disturbed "mental states" (as it was referred to at that time) and somatic complaints. Yet, the formal acknowledgment of "psychosomatics" does not appear for another century.

Psychology in Medicine in the 1800s

Stone (1990) reflects on his review of the historical literature: "as long as there have been psychologists there have been efforts to apply psychology to phenomena of health, illness, and health care" (p. 7). It is well known that the efforts of Wilhelm Wundt and Emil Kraepelin (1800s) demonstrated and shaped the integration of psychology in the medical setting. Briefly, Wundt was the founder of experimental psychology. He had the first lab, wrote the first book, started the first journal, taught the first course, and provided the first outline describing the essence of experimental psychology. Although Wundt was opposed to applied psychology, his ability to spread his ideas and concepts through his students was a springboard for experimental research on self-reported thoughts, feelings, and attention. Emil Kraepelin, influenced by Wundt, is considered the father of modern psychiatry. His notoriety is due, in part, to his classification of mental disorders, and systematic work in psychopharmacology.

Edward B. Titchener, a psychologist in the late 1800s was also greatly influenced by Wundt. He studied the relationship between somatic symptoms and mental processes. Specifically, he studied quantitative and qualitative sensations of defecation, vomiting, and other physical responses to thoughts and feelings. Thus, the impact of Wundt's research laboratory, combined with applied psychological principles as they related to mental disorders in the medical setting, represented the idea of psychology in medicine (Hergenhahn, 1992).

Shorter (1991) makes the argument that behavioral medicine could not exist prior to being able to distinguish between physical origins and psychological origins of maladaptive symptoms, which became possible in the 1860s. Once this occurred, terminology was created to describe a variety of "mental symptoms." By 1869, all disorders with symptoms that were thought to arise in the mind were called "psychogenic." In the late nineteenth century, the term "psychoneurosis" was coined to describe people with psychological disorders who were not psychotic. During this era, physicians often diagnosed what was considered "neurasthenia" or nervous exhaustion. Moreover, practitioners began to recognize "hysteria," which was the term to describe highly emotional people who exhibited signs of organic diseases, yet, biologically, no organic disease could be found. This term was most often applied to females.

Concrete examples of perhaps some of the earliest markers of the need for the emerging field of behavioral medicine arose in the study of digestive dysfunctions. Walter Cannon, a Harvard physiologist, postulated, based on his research, that digestive dysfunctions were largely due to persons' nervous character (Shorter, 1991, p. 143). Other developments in the 1880s and 1890s occurred in Germany. German internists recognized that stomach pain or vomiting could result from either physical irritation or "nervous" symptoms. The term "neurasthenic dyspepsia" or "emotional dyspepsia" was labeled by a Berlin internist to describe digestive problems of psychological origin. Recognizing the brevity of this review, and the attempt only to highlight historical routes of behavioral medicine, it follows that the early 1900s was a particularly progressive point in the telling of this history.

The Early 1900s Prior to 1950

During the early 1900s the "medical model" prevailed. The medical model held the view that medical professionals superseded all nonphysicians in social status, and the practice of health care. The elitist status afforded to physicians enabled nonmedical treatments to be efficacious. The predominant interventions for physical disorders of psychological origins included suggestion, "the rest cure," and persuasive consultation.

Suggestion was a powerful tool that "cured" many physical ailments. Part of the efficacy of the treatment was due to patients' unquestionable faith in medical doctors. Suggestive procedures included surgery, massage, or sugar pills (placebos). Weir Mitchell and Paul Dubois had noted considerable success with such treatment regimens. Paul Dubois instituted the "rest cure" in 1904, which entailed isolation in a nursing home, overfeeding of milk products, massage, and electrotherapy. He spoke with his patients at length, persuading them that indeed their medical status was improving. Moral persuasion continued to develop, which can be followed to Norman Vincent Peale's (1952) book *The Power of Positive Thinking*.

Watson's Attempt to Introduce Psychology into Medical Schools

The Zeitgeist was that medical doctors remained the most competent to respond to the psychological problems of their patients. Perhaps this is why the work of John B. Watson, in 1912, did not result in the immediate changes he recommended for medical school curriculums. Watson advocated for the integration of psychologists in medical schools to provide a more "holistic" approach to treatment of medical patients (Millon, 1982; Stone, 1979). He emphasized the importance of recognizing the *person* who presented with a disease, rather than just the disease itself. Watson and a physiological psychologist, Shepherd Ivory Franz, approached a panel of physicians to suggest that psychological research and theory should be included in medical student training. Also, they proclaimed that training and appreciation of mental states and memory would better prepare physicians to practice psychiatry. When none of these suggestions matriculated, Watson, Franz, and Southard began a quest for members of the American Psychological Association to facilitate the integration of psychology in medical schools. They conducted a series of surveys of medical schools to assess nationwide interest. During the 1930s, minimal change in the presentation of psychological concepts occurred in medical school training. In fact, clinical psychologists only began actually working in medical settings in the late 1940s. Agras (1982) suggests that Watson's (and colleagues') attempt to interest physicians in behavioral training as a mechanism for change may have failed due to the responsibility he placed on the physicians. Had he not introduced the physician as the primary agent for change he may have been more successful.

Psychosomatic Medicine

The increase in recognition of the mind–body connection, and the physical manifestations of psychological processes led to the study of "psychosomatic medicine" in the early 1900s. The contributions of Freud and Pavlov to this field were first recognized during this time. "Psychosomatic medicine" is a term that evolved from psychodynamic theory and the biomedical sciences. The focus of psychosomatic medicine was on the mind–body relationship as it pertained to illness (rather than health), and physiological disorders that were thought to be activated by intrapsychic repressions (Millon, 1982). In keeping with the medical and illness models, psychosomatic medicine emphasized the pathogenesis of physical disease. Shorter (1991) documented that in the 1940s in a clinic in Boston, 400 out of 1000 patients were documented as having "neuropsychiatric problems," of which the great majority were a mixture of "nervous exhaustion, nervous digestive problems, and tension headaches" (p. 149). Thus, psychological influences on physical well-being had gained increased attention.

The impact of this era on behavioral medicine is apparent in that physicians attended to the relationship between psychological disorders and their physical manifestations. The meaning of the term "psychosomatic medicine" later expanded to refer more generally to "psychological factors affecting physical disorders" (Shorter, 1991, p. 148). The integration of nonphysician, behavioral approaches to treatment and prevention of physical disease appears several decades later, and the term "psychosomatic medicine" is replaced with "behavioral medicine."

The Emergence of "Behavioral Medicine": 1950s–1970s

Despite physicians' resistance to incorporate behavioral training into medical school curriculums in the early 1900s, the importance of the role of psychology in medicine had becomes evident in the 1950s (Stone, 1979). For example, a lecture series was presented at the University of Pittsburgh on "The Relationship of Psychology to Medicine" (Dennis, 1950; as cited in Stone, 1979). During this time, physicians began to acquire behavioral training and psychologists increasingly became employed by medical facilities (Miller, 1992).

Psychologists' roles expanded from just conducting research to also providing clinical and teaching services in health settings. However, this happened only when they began to emulate the physicians' practice in the late 1950s through the 1970s. Specifically, in the 1960s, psychologists began to generate income from private practice, which enabled them to engage in voluntary teaching activities.

Initially, nonpsychiatric medical professionals considered psychologists and psychiatrists interchangeable. By the mid-1970s, psychologists gradually developed an independent reputation for their unique contributions to health care. Psychologists' expertise included biofeedback training, preventive education, family therapy, and research (Millon, 1982). Yet their status was below that of their psychiatry colleagues (Stone, 1990). The psychologist's job was primarily to focus on "emotional and behavioral disturbances that perplexed health care providers" (Stone, 1979).

Later, in the 1960s and early 1970s, the conflict between psychology and psychiatry heightened (Gentry, 1984). Psychiatrists disallowed psychologists the same access to patients and monopolized treatment of mental disorders in hospitals. The American Psychological Association (APA) sought representation on the Joint Council on Accreditation of Hospitals in order to increase the awareness of psychologists' skills, and have a voice in hospital legislation. However, the APA's request was not well-received. The APA then complained to the Federal Trade Commission because it appeared that disallowing psychologists to obtain hospital privileges constituted a restraint on trade. Likewise, psychologists challenged the imposed difficulties and obstacles to receiving third-party reimbursement. A class-action suit was filed against insurance companies for depriving their clients from seeking services from psychologists. These efforts resulted in political legislation mandating the right of patients to choose to see psychologists from among the mental health professionals in a hospital setting or private practice. The acceptance of psychologists in the medical setting denotes the beginning of formal opportunities for interdisciplinary communication and collaboration related to health care and the treatment of illness. The development of behavioral medicine can be considered an emergence from this increase in communication and interaction.

Several other factors likely have contributed to the emergence of behavioral medicine. In the 1960s and 1970s the incidence of chronic illnesses such as cancer and heart disease increased. Medical technology improved considerably which arguably further depersonalized medical care (Miller, 1992). Technology diminished the amount of time doctors spent with their patients because there was more ability to mechanically evaluate patients and, therefore, less need to talk extensively with them to obtain information for diagnosis and treatment. Patients had less opportunity to seek emotional support or advice from their physicians. Meanwhile, the empirical research of psychologists made substantial contributions to the understanding of health, illness, and behavior. The development of new theories and applications of psychological principles redirected the emphasis from *teaching* physicians to incorporate behavioral techniques into their practice to *increasing their awareness* of such techniques, enabling them to make appropriate referrals. Thus, a shift in health and mental health care occurred.

Agras (1982) and Miller (1992) suggested three core reasons believed to lead the movement toward behavioral medicine. First, biomedical and behavioral researchers have been unable to independently explain the differences between persons who become ill and those who do not. Thus, prevention was beyond the control of medicine, and etiologies of many illnesses remain unknown. Meanwhile, behaviorally oriented clinicians began to apply their therapy to medically related problems. The technology of biofeedback and the ability to empirically assess physiological responses may have increased the interest of psychologists to apply their techniques to medical populations (Blanchard, 1982). Likewise, physicians may have recognized the potential to gain answers to their medical queries. Thus, behavioral medicine developed from interdisciplinary collaboration and the *behavioral* sciences, rather than *biomedical* sciences (Gentry, 1984).

The increase in medical interventions to prolong life, and the resulting increase in chronic illnesses perhaps also contributed to the development of the behavioral medicine field. Health professionals faced the challenge of helping people manage diseases that could not be cured, but that may not be as imminently fatal as in the past. Commensurate with need, psychologists increased their focus on behavioral or emotional problems associated with physical illness or the prevention or reduction of risk for certain diseases.

A third major influence on the field of behavioral medicine was the growing body of psychological and physiological research highlighting the relationships among behavior, stress, and illness. Clinical psychologists and other professionals in the medical setting demonstrated their ability to intervene between the relationship of stress and illness with a variety of techniques (Stone, 1979). Relaxation and desensitization training was used to reduce psychologically induced stress. Analysis of antecedents and consequences guided the implementation of behavior modification to modify semivolitional behavior such as vomiting. Biofeedback was also used extensively to bring physiological functions under control (e.g., heart rate, blood pressure).

In the 1970s, the medical and illness models fell out of favor and were challenged by Engel's (1977) "biopsychosocial" model. Engel's model perhaps represents the most influential formulation of how interdependent processes explain health and illness, and methods to prevent illness and improve overall functioning. Concurrently, there was a move away from Skinner's operant conditioning theory to

Bandura's (1977) social learning theory. Professionals began to recognize the effectiveness of psychological and learning-theory-based approaches to pain management and some physical illnesses. There was an increase in understanding that faulty habits, behaviors, and lifestyles may be important causal components of many physical disorders. Furthermore, correcting these faulty behaviors reduced the risk associated with these disorders. Psychoeducation also became more popular. Perhaps, psychoeducation was acceptable because it represented a developed form of "suggestion" as used by physicians in the early 1900s.

The Creation of Formal Organizations of Behavioral Medicine: The Late 1970s–Present

The Yale Conference on Behavioral Medicine in 1977 was the first conference held to discuss the new field of behavioral medicine, its defining characteristics, research, and application of its principles. Ten of the seventeen participants were psychologists. Several other advancements took place in 1978. The Institute of Medicine's National Academy of Sciences revised and adapted the definition of behavioral medicine. The *Journal of Behavioral Medicine* was established to facilitate interdisciplinary research and communication. Also in 1978, the National Institutes of Health established a Study Section on behavioral medicine for peer review of research and training grants. The National Cancer Institute and National Heart, Lung and Blood Institute followed the NIH in establishing branches of behavioral medicine for similar purposes.

In 1979, two behavioral psychologists, Ovide Pomerleau and Paul Brady, established one of the two earliest centers for behavioral medicine at the University of Pennsylvania in Philadelphia. The second lab, the Lab for the Study of Behavioral Medicine, was located at Stanford University in California (Agras, 1982). Pomerleau and Brady advanced and redefined the definition of behavioral medicine to go beyond "treatment and development of knowledge related to physical health and illness." They included the emphasis of *research* as the basis for the development of assessment and intervention techniques and the development of knowledge. The clinical application of basic research became a strength of the discipline. Thus, the defining characteristics of the field of behavioral medicine are (1) the multidisciplinary composition of participants, (2) the contributions that science has made to the field, and (3) the contribution the discipline makes to science (Agras, 1982).

Brady and Pomerleau established the Society of Behavioral Medicine in 1979 (Gentry, 1984). This professional organization originated out of a Special Interest Group of the Association of the Advancement of Behavior Therapy. When this organization was first established, behavioral medicine was criticized for its narrow focus. Members tended to focus on research and limited their services to helping patients modify habits associated with stress, obesity, and smoking. Restricting their interests to these fields, practitioners relied primarily on biofeedback, relaxation training, or simple operant conditioning (Millon, 1982). Millon further suggested that practitioners overlooked other efficacious clinical and therapeutic techniques that could have benefited a greater variety of individuals. Millon reviewed suggestions that this narrow focus was due to the predominance of physiologists and behavioral psychologists involved in the field. Again, arguing the terminology, "behavioral" in "behavioral medicine" is also thought to have deterred involvement by professionals from other theoretical orientations. The Society of Behavioral Medicine began two publications, *Behavioral Medicine Update* and *Behavioral Medicine Abstracts*, which helped promulgate the aims and efforts of this new discipline.

CONCLUSION

Over the years, whereas the collaboration between psychiatry and psychology has decreased, the interaction and reliance between psychologists and other medical specialists has increased. Specifically, psychologists often serve core roles in the treatment of patients under the care of cardiology, gastroenterology, obstetrics and gynecology, rehabilitation and physical medicine, oncology, surgery, pain clinics, and others. Each period in history made significant contributions to the development of behavioral medicine. Today, "75% of all patient visits in primary care practices can be attributed to psychological problems that present through physical complaints" (Roberts, 1994; cited in Wickramasekera, Davies, & Davies, 1996). Furthermore, behavioral factors seem to be the bases of at least half of deaths seen or medical problems treated by physicians (McGinnis & Foege, 1993). These statistics do not differ greatly from 1977, when a study of U.S. family physicians showed that onehalf to two-thirds of their patients sought relief from depression, "neuroses," or psychologically related physical disorders (Shorter, 1991, p. 249). Similarly, in 1917 the second most common complaint presented to physicians was of "nervous" problems (after coughs and colds; Shorter, 1991, p. 149).

Physical manifestations of psychological disorders have been evident throughout the history of medicine. Continuous efforts have improved on and advanced the assessment, diagnosis, treatment, and prevention of psychological problems or difficulties as they relate to medical illness. Yet, it is only within the last 30 years that the formal collaboration of professionals from the biomedical, behavioral, social sciences, and the medical specialties has culminated in the establishment of the field of behavioral medicine.

See also: Clinical health psychology

REFERENCES

Agras, W. S. (1982). Behavioral medicine in the 1980s: Nonrandom connections. *Journal of Consulting and Clinical Psychology, 50*(6), 797–803.

Bandura, A. (1977). *Social learning theory*. Englewood Cliffs, NJ: Prentice-Hall.

Birk, L. (Ed.). (1973). *Biofeedback: Behavioral medicine*. New York: Grune & Stratton.

Blanchard, E. B. (1982). Behavioral medicine: Past, present, and future. *Journal of Consulting and Clinical Psychology, 50*(6), 795–796.

Davidson, P. O., & Davidson, S. M. (Eds.). (1980). *Behavioral medicine: Changing health lifestyles*. New York: Brunner/Mazel.

Engel, G. L. (1977). The need for a new medical model: A challenge for biomedicine. *Science, 196*, 129–136.

Gentry, W. D. (Ed.). (1984). *Handbook of behavioral medicine*. New York: Guilford Press.

Hergenhahn, B. R. (1992). *An introduction to the history of psychology* (2nd ed.). Belmont, CA: Wadsworth.

McGinnis, J. M., & Foege, W. (1993). Actual causes of death in the United States. *Journal of the American Medical Association, 270*, 2207–2212.

Miller, N. E. (1992). Some trends from the history to the future of behavioral medicine. *Annals of Behavioral Medicine, 14*(4), 307–309.

Millon, T. (1982). On the nature of clinical health psychology. In T. Millon, C. Green, & R. Meagher (Eds.), *Handbook of clinical health psychology* (pp. 1–27). New York: Plenum Press.

Schwartz, G. E., & Weiss, S. M. (1978). Behavioral medicine revisited: An amended definition. *Journal of Behavioral Medicine, 1*, 249–251.

Shorter, E. (1991). *Doctors and their patients: A social history*. New Brunswick, NJ: Transaction Publishers.

Stone, G. C. (1979). Health and the health system: A historical overview and conceptual framework. In G. C. Stone, F. Cohen, N. E. Adler, & Associates (Eds.), *Health psychology—A handbook: Theories, applications, and challenges of a psychological approach to the health care system* (pp. 1–17). San Francisco: Jossey-Bass.

Stone, G. C. (1990). An international review of the emergence and development of health psychology. *Psychology and Health, 4*, 3–17.

Wickramasekera, I., Davies, T. E., Davies, S. M. (1996). Applied psyphysiology: A bridge between the biomedical model and the biopsychosocial model in family medicine, *Professional Psychology: Research and Practice, 27*, 221–233.

Homework

Arthur A. Freeman and Bradley Rosenfield

Keywords: self-help, therapeutic collaboration, coping activities

> homework. *n.* **1**: an assignment given a student to be completed outside the classroom **2**: preparatory reading or research
>
> *The Merriam-Webster Dictionary* (1995). Springfield, MA: Merriam-Webster, Inc.

Homework or self-help work is an essential part of cognitive behavioral work. Simply, when therapy ends, regardless of the number of sessions, focus of the sessions, or goals of the therapy, everything that the patient does must be viewed as homework. If what the patient learns in therapy is that he or she must depend on the therapist and the therapy sessions for more effective coping without acquiring new and specific skills, then the therapy must continue ad infinitum. If, however, the patient has acquired the basic and necessary skills required for effective coping, then he or she will, ideally, be able to cope more effectively. Homework he or she is a key ingredient in therapeutic change.

Homework has several salutary effects on psychotherapy. First, it extends the therapy contact. Rather than therapy being one or two hours per week, out-of-session activity (homework) allows the patient to be involved in therapeutic activities for as many hours of a day or of the week as he or she chooses.

Second, homework offers the therapist an opportunity to gauge the patient's level of motivation for therapy. If the patient is motivated for change, then the homework provides an arena for action.

Third, self-help work offers the patient an opportunity for practicing the skills learned in the sessions. The session may be viewed as the "lecture" in a college course. The homework provides the "laboratory" to test out new ideas, behaviors, or emotions.

Fourth, the homework can be used to set up experiences that would allow the patient to test many of the assumptions identified in the therapy sessions. Homework offers an opportunity to collect data relevant to insights gained in the session.

Fifth, the homework offers a continuity between the sessions so that therapy is not a series of discrete moments in time but a contiguous set of experiences. By reviewing the homework in the succeeding session, the therapist demonstrates the importance of the homework and how it provides value to the ongoing therapy.

Sixth, homework can allow the involvement of significant others in the therapy. Some homework may involve how others respond to the patient. The accumulation of these views can be useful.

Finally, homework is essential for preventing relapse. After all, when therapy ends, everything the patient does is homework or self-help.

Homework needs to be introduced very early in the therapeutic collaboration. It is raised not so much as one additional tribulation to endure, but rather the course of action that will make the therapy work faster and better, even to the point of having the patient come to therapy for a shorter time. Paradoxically, the problematic affect and behaviors that distress and impair the patients in daily life and impel his or her to seek treatment often become the very obstacles to complying with the treatment interventions that might relieve the patient's suffering. Homework noncompliance correlates with premature treatment termination (Burns & Nolen-Hoeksema, 1992).

The key issue in therapy involves motivating the patient to collaborate with the therapist, to engage in a therapeutic dialogue, to establish and maintain a therapeutic alliance, and to use that framework to make changes. This is seen to be a Herculean task, and most patients are acutely aware of limited treatment duration due to the pressures of managed care and to their own limited financial resources. The therapist may use these constraints to motivate patients to make best use of the valuable time between sessions by performing self-help homework assignments.

Patient willingness to try various new coping activities has correlated with treatment success in ameliorating depression, whereas the frequency of actively engaging in coping activities and the expected efficacy of treatment appear unrelated to positive treatment outcome (Burns & Nolen-Hoeksema, 1992). Patients who are the most willing to attempt new strategies for coping with personal problems before beginning treatment engage more actively in the treatment process, carry the therapy outside of the treatment room, and experience relatively greater clinical improvement. Surprisingly, although willingness was only marginally correlated with actual homework compliance between sessions, both willingness and homework compliance made separate and additive contributions in mitigating depression (Burns & Nolen-Hoeksema, 1991; Persons, Burns, & Perloff, 1988). Burns and Nolen-Hoeksema (1991) hypothesize that high willingness may reflect increased motivation and a general cooperative response set, indicating that these patients would be more willing to express their feelings openly, take medications consistently, or engage in introspection.

Therapists may capitalize on this knowledge by alerting patients to the research indicating that those most willing to experiment with various techniques experience the greatest improvement. The homework compliance is a means for the therapist and patient to collaboratively acheive the patient's most desired treatment goals and increase patient motivation to actively participate in the process. Thus, it becomes vital to assess task-interfering beliefs when patients fail to complete homework assignments or express low willingness to try new skills.

From the outset, therapists and patients should collaboratively set specific, reasonable, desirable, and measurable treatment goals and identify clear rationale for each homework assignment (Beck, Freeman, Davis et al., 2004). Thus, in the very first session, the therapist and patient can collaboratively generate goals in the behavioral, emotional, cognitive, and physiological domains. Furthermore, having the patient endorse, prioritize, and keep a copy of the goals for reference serves to increase commitment, cue consistent behavior, and illustrate how each homework activity brings patients closer to their own most desired goals in a way that patients may construe as being more volitional than as an imposition.

By presenting a cogent rationale for how each homework activity is relevant to the patient's treatment goals, the therapist can increase both the salience of the goals and the probability of homework adherence (Beck, Rush, Shaw, & Emery, 1979). It is vital to reframe each collaboratively generated homework assignment as a positive incremental step on the road to increasing social skills, mood elevation, anxiety reduction, and other desirable goals. Simultaneously, the therapist and patient collaboratively test problematic thoughts, beliefs, assumptions, and schemas. The therapist must socialize the patient to the cognitive model (Addis & Carpenter, 2000). In this way, new skills replace lifelong deficits increasing self-efficacy, reinforcing treatment attendance, and gradually challenge maladaptive core beliefs.

It is imperative for the patient to recognize the relationship between the homework task, the patient's core beliefs and automatic thoughts, and his or her emotional and behavioral response (Beck, 1996). Consequently, it would be appropriate for the therapist to focus on a collaborative examination and resolution of specific task-interfering beliefs, which prevent the patient from performing specific homework assignments. It is also beneficial for the therapist to predict an increase in anxiety and to orient the patient to the crucial nature of anxiety in producing enduring change. Consequently, teaching patients how to deal with anxiety and tolerate frustration (McMullin, 2000) should reduce discomfort, provide generalizable skills, and prevent premature termination (e.g., Beck & Emery, 1985).

This model promotes the acquisition of generalizable communication and problem-solving strategies. Therapy in general, and homework in particular, may be modified to optimize motivation. For instance, highly autonomous individuals may prefer and benefit more from a task-oriented approach, while highly sociotropic individuals may prefer and benefit from a more interpersonal focus.

To further subvert homework nonadherence, the therapist must identify the patient's cognitions regarding the homework assignment and the consequences of change (Beck Freeman, & Associates, 1990). Cognitive restructuring and graded task assignments can help to reduce distorted task-interfering cognitions. Homework nonadherence may reflect perfectionism, shame, or simply a failure to understand instructions. Collaborative exploration of patients' idiosyncratic cognitions should elicit task-interfering beliefs. Increasing emotional tolerance and social skills training can further reduce avoidance (Beck et al., 1990, 2004; Linehan, 1993).

Using a homework diary can further help to prompt patient compliance and increase commitment. Cost–benefit analysis of change is an adroit way to put oppositional and autonomous patients in the position to convince the therapist of the desirability of change (Burns, 1989). Because unexpected outcomes lead to greater emotional distress than expected outcomes (McAuley & Duncan, 1989), another way to inculcate and maintain motivation is to predict occasional setbacks in the very first session.

In selecting homework activities we must consider the patient's current abilities and readiness to change. For example, the patient's perception of the problem, motivation, distress tolerance, communication skills, and even reading or writing ability need to be considered (Prochaska & DiClemente, 1983). Allowing patients to select among homework activities that are equivalent to their own abilities can further increase commitment, responsibility, and homework adherence. Merely offering the patient a choice of ways and times to complete the assignments can have the similar effect (Beck et al., 1979; Kazantsis & Deanne, 1999).

Once a homework assignment is selected, in-session cognitive or behavioral rehearsal can help to shape adaptive skills, increase the probability of homework adherence, and illuminate any potential obstacles to completing the task (Beck et al., 1979). In addition, the therapist may ask patients how confident they are that they will be able to complete the homework assignment on a 0–100 scale. If the patient indicates low levels of confidence, the therapist can solicit expected obstacles, which can then be directly addressed (Kazantsis & Deanne, 1999). These obstacles may include distressing beliefs, cognitive and emotional avoidance, as well as real-world problems like scheduling, inclement weather, and lack of transportation, among others. Solving each obstacle can be the most valuable grist for the therapeutic mill.

To increase motivation and reduce perfectionism, each task may be framed as an experiment to test beliefs, practice skills, and/or find cognitive and other obstacles to goal attainment. It is a no-lose, win-win proposition. Patients either return to the next session having completed their homework or they have identified the obstacles that impede their progress (Beck et al., 1979; Freeman et al., 1990, 2004).

However, many patients will find it difficult to communicate these obstacles; this may be because the obstacles are schema related and thus generate high levels of affect and are difficult to verbalize. By reframing the exercise as a valuable opportunity to identify, explore, and modify the obstacles that plague patients in daily life and prevent them from reaching their most desired goals, one can increase patient motivation to pursue these fundamental issues.

Regardless of the task, homework assignments should be concrete teaching hypothesis-testing skills. The essence of homework is to have patients examine specific beliefs, conduct direct tests of these beliefs, and practice hypothesis-testing skills in specific in-session and between-session exercises (Beck et al., 1979; DeRubeis & Feeley, 1990. Belief testing also produced more improvement in depressive symptoms posttreatment than less cognitive tasks.

Homework assignments should be written, concretely specifying time, place, activity, duration, the beliefs, which are to be tested, and the patient's predictions. Motivation and adherence may be enhanced by allowing the patient to make a choice, providing mild counterarguments, and then asking the patient to make a public commitment (Mahrer, Gagnon, Fairweather, Boulet, & Herring, 1994; Meichenbaum & Turk, 1987). Several patient workbooks with accompanying therapist manuals exist that offer the therapist and the patient structure and guidance in assigning homework (Greenberg, Padesky, 1995; Linehan, 1993).

For instance, if the goal is to confront an avoided situation to test catastrophic beliefs and practice new coping skills, the therapist may Socratically draw out from the patient an appropriate situation, time, and duration of the activity. Even if an assignment is prescribed by the therapist, merely providing the patient with a choice about when to record the results can increase his or her autonomy and involvement and subsequent compliance (Kazantsis & Deanne, 1999; Meichenbaum & Turk, 1987; Shelton & Levy, 1981).

The therapist can also provide corrective feedback to shape more adaptive behavior and cognitions (Meichenbaum & Turk, 1987; Walters, 1996). Before attempting any intervention, the therapist must explain or Socratically elicit the rationale, objective, and potential benefits to be gained. Homework must be framed as a win-win situation (Linehan, 1993). The patient either learns adaptive new skills or solves vexing problems, or discovers the obstacles that then become the focus of the next session (Beck et al., 1979).

It is wise to recruit social support from significant others in the patient's own environment (Meichenbaum & Turk, 1987). This support should increase public commitment, promote between-session practice, assist in contingency management/positive reinforcement regimes, and prevent inadvertent sabotage of patients' efforts. Patients also may be encouraged to use positive labels to produce similarly salubrious expectations and consonant behavior.

For example, after a successful impulse control homework assignment, a BPD patient may label himself as "thoughtful."

Modeling by the therapist, videotape, bibliotherapy, and competent people in the patient's environment can be used to promote skills training, reduce inhibitions, and provide vicarious reinforcement for new adaptive behavior (Linehan, 1993). To further increase motivation, overt or covert behavioral rehearsal procedures can be employed to shape and reinforce adaptive behavior and identify possible obstacles, such as cognitive distortions and cultural myths, fear, shame, and helplessness, which become valuable grist for the therapeutic mill. Nonadherence may represent the patient's attempt to gain some control over the illness and the treatment, as well as pessimism about treatment efficacy (Meichenbaum & Turk, 1987, p. 48).

Optimum behavioral rehearsal and skills training occur in situations similar to those in which the skills will be used. Both Behavioral Rehearsal and Covert Rehearsal are elegant means of increasing motivation in that it they illuminate and reduce obstacles to change and provide an opportunity for the therapist to shape desired behavior. Therapist reinforcement can be particularly powerful in teaching, shaping, and strengthening adaptive behavior for individuals who have been nurtured in punishing, negative environments, such as BPD patients (Linehan, 1993). Patient perceptions of therapist empathy correlate with patient motivation and homework compliance (Burns & Nolen-Hoeksema, 1992).

The Dysfunctional Thought Record (Beck et al., 1979) and downward arrow technique (Beck et al., 1985; Burns, 1989) are also useful homework assignments that can be used in identifying and modifying activated schemas that generate negative cognitions, high levels of affect, and blame. With Axis II patients, it often becomes crucial for the therapist to revisit these overgeneralized and inflexible schemas utilizing a myriad of techniques in the context of specific real-life situations that distress the patient (Beck et al., 1979, 2004; Burns, 1989). This makes homework an ideal method to generate and test schema-related hypotheses. Actual skills deficits should be addressed with specific skills training (Beck et al., 2004; Burns, 1989; Linehan, 1993).

An elegant assignment targeting hypersensitivity to evaluation and decreasing grandiosity is to have patients seek feedback directly from others. The therapist may also use this exercise to target more adaptive interpretation of events, evaluate the importance of the evaluation, and develop frustration tolerance (Beck et al., 2004; McMullin, 2000). Therapists can further increase the efficacy of the procedure and ameliorate mind reading by having patients predict the type of feedback they will receive (Beck et al., 1985, 2004). For patients who demonstrate a pattern of abuse of others' rights and feelings, the problem may be conceptualized as a lack of empathy and social skills and a fascinating constellation of cognitive distortions. The most frequent cognitive distortions for individuals with exploitative and aggressive behavior are: euphemistically labeling their own injurious actions, favorably contrasting their own behavior with even worse behavior, rationalizing behavior as serving a higher purpose, and denigrating victims. These patients may also dwell on perceived grievances and ruminate on punitive retaliations (Bandura, Barbaranelli, Caprara, & Pastorelli, 1996). Role-play, progressing to role reversals, can help to identify these cognitive distortions and maladaptive schemas and increase awareness of appropriate anticipatory guilt and likely social sanctions. The therapist should alert the patient to actively attend to other people's feelings and to accurately label abuse and exploitation. Finally, didactic training for social skills, communications, and prosocial attitudes can teach valuable skills and beliefs that the patient may have never learned (Bandura et al., 1996; Beck et al., 2004; Burns, 1989; Linehan, 1993).

SUMMARY

Homework, or self-help, is a required part of cognitive–behavioral treatment. It offers several opportunities for the therapist to extend and increase therapy contact by having the patient "live" the therapy outside of the consulting room. It can also serve as a measure of the patient's motivation for therapy or for change. If patients are unwilling to work outside of the session, they are, in fact, decreasing their opportunities for change. Homework offers the patient an opportunity to practice what has been discussed in the session. By trying out new behaviors, new ideas, or new emotional responses, the patient can make "real" what has been an abstraction in the therapeutic dialogue. The homework becomes an opportunity for gathering data. Inasmuch as the homework grows "organically" from the session content, it is relevant and timely. Homework provides continuity between sessions. Rather than sessions being discrete moments in time, they are chained together by the homework from the previous session being included in the agenda for the subsequent session.

The homework can be structured to involve significant others. This is essential in many therapeutic situations, and having the significant others involved can substantially aid in relapse prevention. Finally, effective homework helps to build therapeutic collaboration.

REFERENCES

Addis, M. E., & Carpenter, K. M. (2000). Treatment rationale in cognitive therapy: Psychological mechanisms and clinical guidelines. *Cognitive and Behavioral Practice, 7*, 147–156.

Addis, M. E., & Jacobson, N. S. (1996). Reasons for depression and the process and outcome of cognitive–behavioral psychotherapies. *Journal of Consulting and Clinical Psychology, 64*, 1417–1424.
Andrus, B. C. (1969). *The infamous of Nuremberg*. London: Fravin.
Bandura, A., Barbaranelli, C., Caprara, G. V., & Pastorelli, C. (1996). Mechanisms of moral disengagement in the exercise of moral agency. *Journal of Personality and Social Psychology, 71*, 364–374.
Beck, A. T., Rush, A. J., Shaw, B. F. & Emery, G. (1979). *Cognitive therapy of depression*. New York: Guilford Press.
Beck, A. T., & Emery, G., with Greenberg, R. L. (1985). *Anxiety disorders and phobias*. New York: Basic Books.
Beck, A. T., Freeman, A., and Associates. (1990). *Cognitive therapy of personality disorders*. New York: Guilford Press.
Beck, A. T., Freeman, A., Davis, D. D., and Associates. (2004). *Cognitive therapy of personality disorders* (2nd ed.). New York: Guilford Press.
Beck, J. S. (1995). *Cognitive therapy: Basics and beyond*. New York: Guilford Press.
Beck, J. S. (1996). Cognitive therapy of personality disorders. In P. M. Salkovskis (Ed.), *Frontiers of cognitive therapy* (pp. 165–181). New York: Guilford Press.
Burns, D. D. (1989). *The feeling good handbook: Using the new mood therapy in everyday life*. New York: Morrow.
Burns, D. D., & Nolen-Hoeksema, S. (1991). Coping styles, homework compliance, and the effectiveness of cognitive–behavioral therapy. *Journal of Consulting and Clinical Psychology, 59*, 305–311.
Burns, D. D., & Nolen-Hoeksema, S. (1992). Therapeutic empathy and recovery from depression in cognitive–behavioral therapy: A structural equation model. *Journal of Consulting and Clinical Psychology, 60*, 441–449.
DeRubeis, R. J., & Feeley, M. (1990). Determinants of change in cognitive therapy for depression. *Cognitive Therapy and Research, 14*, 469–482.
Edwards, D. J. A. (1990). Cognitive therapy and the restructuring of early memories through guided imagery. *Journal of Cognitive Psychotherapy, 4*, 33–50.
Ellis, A. (1974). *How to stubbornly refuse to be ashamed of anything* (cassette recording). New York: Institute for Rational Living.
Ellis, A. (1977). Anger—*How to live with and without it*. New York: Carol Publishing Group.
Frank, E., Kupfer, D. J., Jacob, M., & Jarrett, D. (1987). Personality features and response to acute treatment in recurrent depression. *Journal of Personality Disorders, 1*, 14–26.
Freeman, A., Pretzer, J., Fleming, B., & Simon, K. (1990). *Clinical applications of cognitive therapy*. New York: Plenum Press.
Greenberg, L. S., & Safran, J. D. (1987). *Emotion in psychotherapy: Affect, cognition, and the process of change*. New York: Guilford Press.
Greenberg, L. S., & Safran, J. D. (1989). Emotion in psychotherapy. *American Psychologist, 44*, 19–29.
Heider, F. (1958). *The psychology of interpersonal relations*. New York: Wiley.
Kazantzis, N. & Deane, F. P. (1999). Psychologists' use of homework assignments in clinical practice. *Professional Psychology: Research and Practice, 30*, 581–585.
Linehan, M. M. (1993). *Skills training manual for treating borderline personality disorder*. New York: Guilford Press.
McAuley, E., & Duncan, T. E. (1989). Causal attributions and affective reactions to disconfirming outcomes in motor performance. *Journal of Sport and Exercise Psychology, 11*, 187–200.
McMullin, R. E. (2000). *The new handbook of cognitive therapy techniques*. New York: Norton.
Mahrer, A. R., Gagnon, R., Fairweather, D. R., Boulet, D. B., & Herring, C. B. (1994). Client commitment and resolve to carry out postsession behaviors. *Journal of Counseling Psychology, 41*, 407–414.
Meichenbaum, D., & Turk, D. (1987). *Facilitating treatment adherence: A practitioner's handbook*. New York: Plenum Press.
Newman, C. F. (1994). Understanding client resistance: Methods for enhancing motivation to change. *Cognitive and Behavioral Practice, 1*, 47–69.
Persons, J. B., Burns, D. D., & Perloff, J. M. (1988). Predictors of dropout and outcome in cognitive therapy for depression in a private practice setting. *Cognitive Therapy and Research, 12*, 557–575.
Prochaska, J. O., & DiClemente, C. C. (1983). Stages and processes of self-change of smoking: Toward an integrative model of change. *Journal of Consulting and Clinical Psychology, 51*, 390–395.
Rotter, J. B. (1966). Generalized expectancies for internal versus external control of reinforcement. *Psychological Monographs, 80*(1, Whole No. 609).
Rude, S. S., & Rehm, L. P. (1991). Response to treatments for depression: The role of initial status on targeted cognitive and behavioral skills. *Clinical Psychology Review, 11*, 493–514.
Safran, J., & Segal, Z. V. (1990). *Interpersonal process in cognitive therapy*. New York: Basic Books.
Schulthesis, G. M. (1998). *Brief therapy homework planner*. New York: Wiley.
Shea, M. T., Pilkonis, P. A., Beckham, E., Collins, J. F., Elkin, I., Sotsky, S. M., & Docherty, J. P. (1990). Personality disorders and treatment outcome in the NIMH Treatment of Depression Collaborative Research Program. *American Journal of Psychiatry, 147*, 711–718.
Shelton, J. L., & Levy, R. L. (1981). *Behavioral assignments and treatment compliance: A handbook of clinical strategies*. Champaign, IL: Research Press.

Hypnotherapy

E. Thomas Dowd

Keywords: hypnosis, hypnotherapy, imagery

In its relatively short history, cognitive therapy has proved to be not only an efficacious treatment for a wide variety of psychological and behavior problems, but also an integrating theory of tremendous heuristic power (Afford & A. T. Beck, 1997). It originally began, independently by A. T. Beck (1976) and Ellis (1962), as a system of therapy based on changing maladaptive cognitions (automatic assumptions, irrational thoughts) in the *here and now* in service of greater emotional health. Over time, it was further modified to treat personality disorders (A. T. Beck, Freeman, & Associates, 1990) as well as the more transitory problems of anxiety and depression. This process led to the consideration of the core cognitive schemas underlying different personality styles and disorders (J. S. Beck, 1995; Young, 1999). In the process, cognitive therapists of necessity began to examine the developmental history of their clients and how their early experiences had contributed in forming their later psychological states, which would have been considered highly inappropriate and unnecessary in earlier years.

In a sort of recycling phenomenon, earlier Freudian concepts such as unconscious processes began to infiltrate the cognitive therapy literature, although without the conceptual baggage and metaphorical language of earlier formulations. Meichenbaum and Gilmore (1984) developed a tripartite model of cognition consisting of cognitive contents (automatic self-statements), cognitive processes (cognitive distortions), and cognitive structures (cognitive schemas). Mahoney (1991), in his discussion of *Core Ordering Processes*, argued that tacit knowledge (or cognitive deep structure) is surrounded by a "protective belt" which quite appropriately and wisely protects the cognitive system itself from too-rapid changes in its core constructs of personal meaning. Rapid change can threaten the very sense of self on which our identity is built, a deeply frightening experience for all of us. Outside the protective belt is the surface structure activity which consists of our daily activities and thoughts. Dowd and Courchaine (1996) linked core cognitive schemas to the experimental psychology literature on tacit and implicit knowledge and drew implications for the practice of cognitive therapy.

Cognitive hypnotherapy uses the developmental themes present in latter-day cognitive therapy, the imagery work of J. S. Beck and Ellis, and hypnotherapeutic techniques, especially those of the indirect hypnotic approach developed by Milton Erickson. In developing the cognitive hypnotherapeutic model, I followed the tripartite model of cognition presented by Meichenbaum and Gilmore (1984), along with the Early Maladaptive Schemas (EMSs) of Young (1999). J. S. Beck (1995) devoted a chapter to imagery work in cognitive therapy. She identified several imagery techniques that are similar to hypnotic procedures, including *jumping ahead in time (age progression), distancing (telescope technique)*, and *changing the image (memory substitution)*. Ellis (1993) has also used imagery in rational emotive imagery (RET). It was after reviewing their work that I decided to write an extended treatise on cognitive hypnotherapy (Dowd, 2000).

COGNITIVE DEVELOPMENTAL HYPNOTHERAPY

The model is quite new on the therapeutic scene, having been presented explicitly in two book chapters (Dowd, 1993, 1997), one book (Dowd, 2000), and one article (Dowd, 2001). It retains the cognitive–developmental emphasis on modifying cognitive structures (or core cognitive schemas) which are laid down developmentally early in life and thereafter progressively elaborated on and differentiated but not substantially changed. As these schemas become more organized and differentiated, they increasingly constrain the interpretation of new sensory data in consonance with one's preexisting cognitive rules and categories, thus resulting in the truism that people tend to interpret new events in light of what they already know and believe. Indeed, they may not even notice schema-disconfirming events at all! Because these cognitive schemas are laid down at an early age, often before the elaborate use of language, they may be more amenable to change via nonverbal, imagery-based procedures, rather than verbal procedures.

The indirect hypnotherapeutic techniques developed by Milton Erickson may be especially useful for addressing maladaptive core cognitive schemas. The basic assumption is that hypnosis may be especially useful in assessing and modifying core cognitions around the important domains of personal identity, self-concept, and dysfunctional tacit rules, rather than by addressing explicitly more peripheral behaviors and attitudes (Dowd, 2000). Erickson considered the "unconscious" to be a vast storehouse of positive skills and tacit knowledge which serves as a fundamental regulator of human behavior. Because of its nonverbal nature, hypnotic imagery and related emotional processing may be useful in modifying tacit knowledge structures, which are often preverbal and implicitly learned. The nonverbal nature of these hypnotic techniques may allow them to access directly the preverbal tacit cognitions in core schemas. In addition, because of the very indirectness of these techniques (which makes them difficult to resist), resistance to change may be reduced. In reducing resistance, Erickson often made use of the "utilization technique," in which hypnotic suggestions are worded in such a permissive manner that anything clients do can be interpreted as a sign they are entering a trance.

CHANGING COGNITIVE CONTENTS

These (sometimes called cognitive events) are the automatic self-statements clients (as well as everyone else) say to themselves constantly, such as "I'll never complete this task!" or "What a dumb thing to do!" They might be considered the "what" of thinking. Self-statements such as these are considered by Araoz (1985) to be a form of ongoing negative self-hypnosis. These cognitive events are relatively easy to access with judicious therapist questioning (e.g., "What was going through your mind just now?"). Using standard cognitive therapy techniques, alternative, more adaptive self-statements can be developed jointly by the therapist and client.

Clients are then placed in a hypnotic trance and first instructed to say the maladaptive self-statements aloud (or to themselves), then say the more adaptive self-statements. This is repeated until they can easily say and focus on the adaptive self-statements. The repetition involved in this can become rather boring for therapists but the technique can be helpful with motivated clients. Essentially, these are direct hypnotic suggestions for change. Clients can also be taught self-hypnosis and instructed to practice this at home.

CHANGING COGNITIVE PROCESSES

Cognitive processes may be best described as ways of thinking, or the "how" of thinking. For example, the cognitive errors identified by A. T. Beck (1976), such as overgeneralizing, catastrophizing, and dichotomous thinking, as well as the irrational beliefs described by Ellis (1962), are examples of dysfunctional cognitive processes. Usually, these cognitive errors involve a selective attention to negative information and a filtering out of positive information, resulting in a dysphoric attitude. Cognitive errors can occur in a positive direction, however, resulting in an overly Pollyannish, overly optimistic attitude.

In changing cognitive processes, either direct or indirect hypnotic methods may be used. In the first, the therapist uses direct suggestions, such as "You can see yourself speaking more and more slowly, more and more clearly … feeling more and more confident," in the case of a client with speech anxiety. For a client with a work anxiety, the therapist might say, "As you look your boss in the eye, standing up straight, you can begin to feel your anxiety diminish … as you answer him calmly and clearly."

Indirect suggestions for changing cognitive processes are more difficult to describe. Essentially, they involve implanting suggestions for change or new ways of thinking about a problem via metaphor and allusion. These suggestions are often embedded in a natural flow of conversation and may refer to common experiences encountered by most people as a way of suggesting change. They may also make use of divided consciousness, where the suggestions are directed to the "unconscious mind" (a metaphor) while the "conscious mind" (also a metaphor) is instructed to occupy itself elsewhere. A truncated example (adapted from Dowd, 2000) for a depressed woman who overgeneralized and used selective abstraction is:

> All of us tend, if we're not careful, to look at one side of an issue, don't we?
>
> None of us can pay attention to everything, can we? But it's important to look at several sides of an issue, isn't it? All of us sometimes make mistakes and sometimes don't. We can't ever assume we will or won't, can we? One is a part of the other. And the more we pay attention to many things, the more attention we can pay to one or two things. As you think about that, let it roll around in your mind, you can begin to understand its meaning at a deeper level, as many levels as you wish.

CHANGING COGNITIVE STRUCTURES

As described earlier, cognitive structures (or core cognitive schemas) are the associational networks of tacit rules and assumptions about the nature of reality and the meaning of events that organize prior experience. While they can be very adaptive in that they enable people to process complex information rapidly, this same rapid processing can result in entrenched maladaptive schemas. Because they are laid down at an early age and are part of the implicit knowledge structure (Dowd & Courchaine, 1996), it is difficult to access them or accept them if accessed by others. These schemas are typically experienced as "That's just the way things are! That's just reality!" These maladaptive schemas are strongly implicated in the personality disorders, and attempts to change them or even discuss them are often met with considerable resistance. Young (1999) has provided a comprehensive taxonomy of Early Maladaptive Schemas (EMSs), which are stable and enduring cognitive themes that develop during childhood and are subsequently only elaborated on rather than significantly changed. They form our view of ourselves, our personal identity, the world, and our place in the world. They are unconditional beliefs; self-perpetuating and self-fulfilling.

Because of the resistance aroused by assaults on core cognitive schemas involving personal meaning structures (Mahoney, 1991), indirect hypnotherapeutic methods are recommended for changing cognitive structures. The metaphors, allusions, and stories contained in these routines are ideal for implanting ideas without actually having to relate them directly and explicitly to clients. Here is a truncated example of an indirect hypnotic routine (adapted from Dowd, 2000) for addressing a young man with an EMS of defectiveness/shame (Young, 1999) or a core schema of unlovability (J. S. Beck, 1995):

> Your unconscious mind can begin to look at new ways of thinking, new ways of acting. Your unconscious mind can begin to see new and desirable possibilities—not only what you desire but also what others desire in you, how others desire you. And the more you think of that, the more comfort you can feel, desiring even more comfort and seeing yourself as desirable. Opening up new and desirable possibilities for you …

In this short example, note the repetition of the embedded word "desirable" as a suggestion for new ways of the client thinking of himself in relation to women.

THE COGNITIVE HYPNOTHERAPEUTIC TREATMENT OF PSYCHOLOGICAL DISORDERS

Cognitive hypnotherapy has been applied to many problems, including anxiety and phobias, stress-related disorders, depression, and habit disorders, as well as general life-enhancing interventions (Dowd, 2000). More recently, it has been applied to pain reduction (Dowd, 2001) and obsessive–compulsive disorders (Dowd, 2003). In treating all these (and other) disorders, the model is the same. First the therapist must identify (in collaboration with the client as much as possible) the cognitive contents, cognitive processes, and cognitive structures. Then the therapist develops hypnotic routines, either direct or indirect, to address the cognitive dysfunctions. These are used while the client is in a trance. In the case of depression, the therapist may wish to use a form of "alert hypnosis" (Golden, Dowd, & Friedberg, 1987) in which hypnosis is used to energize, rather then relax, the client. Life-enhancing interventions also possess an energizing aspect.

Why should anyone use hypnosis at all in cognitive therapy? Although the literature is somewhat equivocal, there is evidence that hypnosis may result in clients suspending their usual critical, evaluating cognitive processes, enabling them to hold two somewhat contradictory ideas in their minds simultaneously (what has been called "trance logic"). It has also been argued that a hypnotic trance may lower resistance to considering new ideas by taking advantage of and fostering increased openness to experience. Finally, hypnosis often has the ability, perhaps because of its reputation and the social context in which it is used, of engaging clients' interest and thereby enhancing their motivation. Irving Kirsch and his colleagues (Kirsch, Montgomery, & Sapirstein, 1995), in a meta-analysis, found that hypnosis added significantly to the therapeutic effect size of cognitive–behavior therapy alone.

SUGGESTIONS FOR THE FUTURE

It is important that cognitive hypnotherapy be applied to a greater range of psychological problems, especially personality disorders. It has much in common with "Mindfulness Meditation" (Segal, Williams, & Teasdale, 2002) as well as other forms of meditation, even prayer (Dowd, in press). Many of these interventions are ancient and the similarities and differences among them should be more fully explored and tested. The research outcomc literature on these imagery/meditation-based interventions is sparse indeed and research should be conducted not only to test their efficacy but their differential efficacy relative to other forms of cognitive–behavior therapy and therapeutic approaches.

REFERENCES

Alford, B. A., & Beck, A. T. (1997). *The integrating power of cognitive therapy*. New York: Guilford Press.

Araoz, D. L. (1985). *The new hypnosis*. New York: Brunner/Mazel.

Beck, A. T. (1976). *Cognitive therapy and the emotional disorders*. New York: International Universities Press.

Beck, A. T., Freeman, A., & Associates. (1990). *Cognitive therapy of personality disorders*. New York: Guilford Press.

Beck, J. S. (1995). *Cognitive therapy: Basics and beyond*. New York: Guilford Press.

Dowd, E. T. (1993). Cognitive–developmental hypnotherapy. In J. W. Rhue, S. J. Lynn, & I. Kirsch (Eds.), *Handbook of clinical hypnosis* (pp. 215–232). Washington, DC: American Psychological Association.

Dowd, E. T. (1997). The use of hypnosis in cognitive–developmental therapy. In R. L. Leahy (Ed.), *Practicing cognitive therapy: A guide to interventions*. Livingston, NJ: Jason Aronson.

Dowd, E. T. (2000). *Cognitive hypnotherapy*. Livingston, NJ: Jason Aronson.

Dowd, E. T. (2001). Cognitive hypnotherapy in the management of pain. *Journal of Cognitive Psychotherapy: An International Quarterly, 15*, 87–97.

Dowd, E. T. (2003). *Hypnotherapy in obsessive–compulsive disorder*. Symposium presentation at the XXXIII Congress of the European Association for Behavioural and Cognitive Therapies, Prague, Czech Republic.

Dowd, E. T. (in press). Expanding the cognitive therapy model: Imagery, meditation, and hypnosis. *Journal of Cognitive Psychotherapy: An International Quarterly*.

Dowd, E. T., & Courchaine, K. (1996). Implicit learning, tacit knowledge, and implications for stasis and change in cognitive psychotherapy. *Journal of Cognitive Psychotherapy: An International Quarterly, 10*, 163–180.

Ellis, A. (1962). *Reason and emotion in psychotherapy*. Secaucus, NJ: Citadel.

Ellis, A. (1993). Rational–emotive imagery: RET version. In A. Ellis & R. Grieger (Eds.), *The RET book for practitioners* (pp. 11-8–11-10). New York: Institute for Rational–Emotive Therapy.

Golden, W. L., Dowd, E. T., & Friedberg, F. (1987). *Hypnotherapy: A modern approach*. New York: Pergamon Press.

Kirsch, I., Montgomery, G., & Sapirstein, G. (1995). Hypnosis as an adjunct to cognitive behavioral psychotherapy: A meta-analysis. *Journal of Consulting and Clinical Psychology, 63*, 214–220.

Mahoney, M. J. (1991). *Human change processes*. New York: Basic Books.

Meichenbaum, D., & Gilmore, J. B. (1984). The nature of unconscious processes: A cognitive–behavioral perspective. In K. S. Bowers & D. Meichenbaum (Eds.), *The unconscious reconsidered* (pp. 273–298). New York: Wiley.

Segal, Z. V., Williams, J. M. G., & Teasdale, J. D. (2002). *Mindfulness-based cognitive therapy and the prevention of relapse in depression*. New York: Guilford Press.

Young, J. E. (1999). *Cognitive therapy for personality disorders: A schema-focused approach*. Sarasota, FL: Professional Resource Press.

I

Imagery

Mervin Smucker, Jo M. Weis, and
Jane G. Dresser

Keywords: images, imagery rescripting, trauma, imaginal exposure

Images are a powerful and pervasive form of cognition. Long before we develop language, our memories are encoded in images. From its inception, psychotherapy has emphasized verbal communication, but concurrently has also explored the importance of imagery in understanding the human psyche. Contemporary psychotherapy continues to affirm the value of images in understanding and transforming human experience and to explore new applications of imagery within the therapeutic context.

HISTORICAL OVERVIEW

The therapeutic use of imagery has its roots in late nineteenth-century Europe. From his work with "hysterical" patients at the Salpêtrière in Paris, Pierre Janet (1898) noted that traumatic experiences left indelible memories, to which an individual repeatedly returned. These "idees fixes" often presented themselves in the form of frightening perceptions, intrusive images, obsessional preoccupations, and somatic sensations. Janet developed a procedure called "imagery substitution" to help patients reexperience and replace upsetting images with adaptive images, which is the earliest documentation of cognitive restructuring with distressing images. With its focus on having patients remember, relive, and rework their upsetting images, Janet's "symptom substitution" technique is strikingly similar to "imagery modification" and "imagery rescripting," both of which are imagery-based, CBT interventions developed a century later by Beck (Beck, Emery, & Greenberg, 1985) and Smucker (Smucker, 1997; Smucker & Dancu, 1999; Smucker, Dancu, Foa, & Niederee, 1995).

Subsequent European visionaries (e.g., Breuer, Charot, Freud, Jung) in the early twentieth century further developed a variety of therapeutic interventions that combined imagery with language as a means of helping patients to process dissociated and distressing images more meaningfully. Jung viewed mental imagery as a creative process of the psyche that could be employed for attaining heightened individual, interpersonal, and spiritual integration. Much of Jung's clinical work focused on helping patients progress from a state of mental passivity vis-à-vis their upsetting images to one of action and mastery using their "active imagination" (Jung, 1955).

IMAGERY IN CBT

In recent years, an increasing number of cognitive–behavioral oriented clinicians have elaborated on the clinical application of imagery as a means of modifying maladaptive cognitions/schemas and restructuring disturbing events and associated meanings. Within the CBT family, behaviorists were the first to report the clinical use of imagery in their work with phobias. As part of their systematic desensitization treatment, covert desensitization was employed as a means of deconditioning and extinguishing anxiety responses.

After learning progressive deep muscle relaxation in the presence of pleasant imagery, patients were assisted in going back and forth from a physiologically relaxed state to an anxiety state that was induced by imaginal exposure to a hierarchy of fear-evoking stimuli. Each imaginal exposure segment was followed by relaxation until no further anxiety was reported during exposure. Imaginal flooding was also employed by behaviorists with anxious patients, which involved repeated, prolonged imaginal exposure to the feared stimuli until the anxiety response was extinguished. Variations of covert desensitization and imaginal flooding continue to be employed by CBT clinicians today who work with anxious patients (e.g., specific phobias, GAD, OCD, and PTSD).

Beck et al. (1985) acknowledged the emotional and cognitive power of imagery in creating corrective experiences with anxious patients who have upsetting, catastrophic visual images of danger before and during bouts of anxiety. As with verbal cognitions, these visual cognitions often represent a distortion of reality whereby patients who visualize such upsetting scenes tend to react as though they were actually occurring. Beck and colleagues found it useful to have patients visually "relive" and "reexperience" their inaccurately constructed beliefs as a means of enhancing cognitive restructuring. They further observed that a patient's distressing visual images can be activated, challenged, and modified by an array of imagery modification interventions, e.g., induced imagery, modification of induced images, identifying cognitive distortions within the imagery, decatastrophizing imagery, substituting positive imagery, substituting contrasting imagery, imagery rehearsal, and a variety of other types of coping imagery.

Dowd (1997) asserted that adding a hypnotherapy component to treatment may enhance CBT interventions by minimizing avoidance and thereby increasing the patient's capacity to confront and habituate to the experienced or anticipated noxious events. An array of guided imagery techniques have been used as part of cognitive hypnotherapy as a means of modifying dysfunctional behaviors, as well as negative automatic images, maladaptive beliefs, and core schemas. Such imagery techniques may include evocative imagery, replacement and coping imagery, age regression imagery, desensitization and flooding imagery, visual cognitive rehearsal, imaginary dialogues with significant others, and modification of distorted images relating to past memories.

The use of imagery as a primary therapeutic agent in fostering emotional processing of traumatic events has been emphasized by a growing number of CBT theorists and clinicians in recent years. Since traumatic memories and their associated meanings tend to be encoded as vivid images and sensations, they are not likely to be accessible through linguistic retrieval alone. The notion that traumatic imagery is not likely to change in the absence of corrective imagery was articulated by Beck, Freeman, and Associates (1990) in the following passage:

> Simply talking about a traumatic event may give intellectual insight about why the patient has a negative self-image, but it does not actually change the image. In order to modify the image, it is necessary to go back in time, as it were, and re-create the situation. When the interactions are brought to life, the misconstruction is activated—along with the affect—and cognitive restructuring can occur. (p. 92)

It thus appears that directly identifying, challenging, and modifying the trauma victim's distressing imagery (e.g., recurring flashbacks, repetitive nightmares) can be a potent therapeutic means of providing "corrective" information and facilitating emotional processing with this population (Smucker & Dancu, 1999).

Although much attention has been given to the clinical application of imagery techniques within CBT circles, to date only two cognitive–behavioral treatments (with treatment manuals) have been developed that use imagery as a primary therapeutic agent: Prolonged Imaginal Exposure (PE; Foa, Rothbaum, Riggs, & Murdock, 1991) and Imagery Rescripting and Reprocessing Therapy (IRRT; Smucker & Dancu, 1999; Smucker et al., 1995). Both of these imagery-based treatments were designed to facilitate cognitive and emotional processing of traumatic events, and are especially geared to individuals suffering from symptoms of PTSD.

PE is a cognitive–behavioral treatment that relies predominantly on the processes of exposure, habituation, desensitization, and extinction to reduce trauma-related fear and anxiety. Essentially, patients are taught that their upsetting visual memories are tolerable and manageable and that the anxiety and fear associated with these memories will eventually subside during exposure. The PE sessions themselves involve the visual and sensory reliving of the distressing/traumatic material. Patients are asked to visualize and verbalize aloud, in detail, the entire upsetting experience using the first person and present tense, as though it were happening at the moment. Patients are asked to rate their discomfort level (SUDS: Subjective Units of Distress Scale) every 5–10 minutes as a means of conducting an ongoing assessment of their affective involvement and distress. The 60- to 90-minute imaginal exposure session is audiotaped and given to the patient for daily listening in order to enhance habituation and desensitization. Some discussion may take place before and after each PE session that addresses the patient's trauma-related emotions and beliefs (e.g., fear, guilt, shame), although this is not done in a structured or methodical manner. The standard PE treatment involves eight imaginal exposure sessions. In vivo exposure interventions may also be implemented during treatment to confront maladaptive avoidance outside the therapy sessions (Foa et al., 1991).

While there is considerable evidence supporting the use of PE with trauma victims (e.g., victims of rape) suffering from PTSD, preliminary outcome data from a study with over 800 occupation-related injuries (treated over a period of 20 years) indicated that PE was the treatment of choice with Type I victims when fear was the predominant trauma-related emotion and avoidance was the primary coping strategy, but that PE by itself was not a good treatment choice for trauma victims whose predominant emotions are other than fear, e.g., guilt, shame, anger, self-blame. In such instances, treatment effects were significantly enhanced when imaginal exposure was supplemented with an imagery-based cognitive restructuring intervention.

By contrast, IRRT (Smucker & Dancu, 1999) is a multifaceted, imagery-based, cognitive–behavioral treatment designed to help trauma victims cope more effectively with recurring trauma-related images (e.g., flashbacks, nightmares) and related beliefs and schemas (e.g., powerlessness, unlovability, abandonment). A primary goal of IRRT is to transform victimization imagery into adaptive imagery, thereby enabling trauma survivors to "see" themselves responding to the trauma as empowered individuals no longer paralyzed in a powerless state of victimization.

The IRRT treatment itself combines *imaginal exposure* (activating the upsetting imagery and its associated affect) with *imagery rescripting* (replacing distressing imagery with coping/mastery imagery), *self-calming/self-nurturing imagery* (visualizing one's ADULT SELF today, or another compassionate adult, entering into the imagery in order to calm, sooth, nurture, and reassure the "traumatized" or "distressed" self), and *emotional–linguistic processing* (transforming the distressing imagery and accompanying emotions into narrative language, while challenging and modifying the underlying traumagenic beliefs/schemas). SUDS ratings are used throughout each imagery session as a means of assessing the patient's emotional state and identifying "hot spots" that may require further attention. An audiotape of each imagery session is given to the patient for daily listening and processing. The patient's subjective reactions to the imagery tape are recorded in a journal. Three SUDS levels (beginning SUDS, ending SUDS, and peak SUDS) are also recorded on a homework sheet immediately following each audiotape listening. Patients are asked to bring the SUDS sheets to each treatment session for review and additional processing. The homework SUDS sheets are also useful for ascertaining homework compliance as well as progress. The standard IRRT treatment consists of eight sessions ranging from 60 to 90 minutes each, although the length of treatment may be adapted according to the specific needs of a given patient.

A distinguishing feature of IRRT is its use of *Socratic imagery*, which is essentially guided discovery applied in the context of imagery modification. Patients are thus challenged to develop their own coping/mastery imagery as well as their own self-calming/self-soothing imagery. Socratic imagery emanates from the Beckian notion that it is more empowering for patients to create their own solutions (e.g., developing their own mastery imagery) than to have the therapist suggest, direct, or dictate solutions to them (Smucker & Dancu, 1999).

Another component of IRRT that is viewed as critical in the processing of emotionally upsetting material is the interplay of primary and secondary cognitive processing. A "primary cognitive process" involves nonverbal, nonlinguistic mental activity that is essentially iconic and auditory in nature (e.g., visually reliving a traumatic event), whereas verbalizing (talking or writing) one's reactions to an event is viewed as a "secondary cognitive process." In IRRT, the cognitive processing of traumatic material occurs both at a primary level (reliving the traumatic imagery) and at a secondary level (talking about the imagery, putting the imagery into words). Periodically, during an IRRT session, the upsetting imagery is put "on pause"—especially during times of heightened affect—so that the patient's thoughts and feelings about the imagery and its symbolic meaning can be discussed and processed. While secondary cognitive processing involves the patient's immediate response to the imagery itself, it may also address core schemas that serve to reinforce and provide a cognitive template for the recurring, upsetting imagery. Immediately following an IRRT session, patients are asked to verbalize their reactions to the imagery session, which further promotes the processing of primary material at a secondary level of cognitive processing (Smucker, 1997).

While there is considerable empirical evidence supporting the efficacy of IRRT with both Type I and Type II trauma survivors (Smucker & Dancu, 1999), it appears to be especially effective with those whose predominant trauma-related emotions are other than fear, e.g., guilt, shame, anger, powerlessness, humiliation (Grunert, Smucker, Weis, & Rusch, 2003).

SUMMARY

Images, as a pervasive form of human cognition, will likely remain central to the treatment of emotional disorders, with their power to influence and transform thought and behavior. Psychotherapy and the psychotherapeutic healing process can be enhanced by the exploration of imagery, and in some cases is effective only when images are used concurrently with verbal processing. With its primary emphasis on cognitive processes and recent innovations in the use of imagery, CBT is at the forefront of research and clinical treatment with imagery applications.

See also: Imagery rescripting and reprocessing therapy

REFERENCES

Beck, A. T., Emery, G., & Greenberg, R. L. (1985). *Anxiety disorders and phobias: A cognitive perspective*. New York: Basic Books.

Beck, A. T., Freeman, A., & Associates. (1990). *Cognitive therapy of personality disorders*. New York: Guilford Press.

Dowd, E. T. (1997). The use of hypnosis in cognitive–developmental therapy. In R. L. Leahy (Ed.), *Practicing cognitive therapy* (pp. 21–36) Northvale, NJ: Jason Aronson.

Foa, E. B., Rothbaum, B. O., Riggs, D. S., & Murdock, T. B. (1991). Treatment of posttraumatic stress disorder in rape victims: A comparison between cognitive–behavioral procedures and counseling. *Journal of Consulting and Clinical Psychology, 59*, 715–723.

Grunert, B. K., Smucker, M. R., Weis, J. M., & Rusch, M. D. (2003). When prolonged exposure fails: Adding an imagery-based cognitive restructuring component in the treatment of industrial accident victims suffering from PTSD. *Cognitive and Behavioral Practice, 10*, 333–346.

Janet, P. (1898). *Nervoses et idees fixes*. Paris: Alcan.

Jung, C. G. (1955). *The collected works* (Bollingen Series XX), R. F. C. Hull (Trans.), H. Read, M. Fordham, & G. Adler (Eds.). Princeton, NJ: Princeton University Press.

Smucker, M. R. (1997). Posttraumatic stress disorder. In R. L. Leahy (Ed.), *Practicing cognitive therapy* (pp. 193–220). Northvale, NJ: Jason Aronson.

Smucker, M. R., & Dancu, C. V. (1999). *Cognitive–behavioral treatment for adult survivors of childhood trauma: Imagery rescripting and reprocessing*. Northvale, NJ: Jason Aronson.

Smucker, M. R., Dancu, C. V., Foa, E. B., & Niederee, J. L. (1995). Imagery rescripting: A new treatment for survivors of childhood sexual abuse suffering from posttraumatic stress. *Journal of Cognitive Psychotherapy: An International Quarterly, 9*(1), 3–17.

Smucker, M. R., Grunert, B., & Weis, J. (2003). Posttraumatic stress disorder: A new algorithm treatment model. In R. L. Leahy (Ed.), *Overcoming roadblocks in cognitive therapy practice* (pp. 175–194). New York: Guilford Press.

Imagery Rescripting and Reprocessing Therapy

Mervin R. Smucker

Keywords: child sexual abuse, imagery rescripting, schemata, CBT, PTSD

The alarming prevalence of childhood sexual abuse (CSA) and its long-term deleterious effects on the lives of victims is well documented. A history of sexual abuse in childhood is frequently associated with a range of psychological disturbances in adulthood, including chronic depression and anxiety, suicidality and self-injurious behaviors, relationship disturbances, sexual difficulties, and chronic PTSD symptoms (e.g., recurring flashbacks, nightmares, chronic sleep disturbance, dissociation). Feelings of guilt, shame, self-blame, self-hatred, self-disgust, low self-esteem, and fear of intimacy, along with schemas of powerlessness, incompetence, unlovability, abandonment, and mistrust of others are frequently cited as long-term psychological effects of CSA (Herman, 1992). These effects may be, in part, attributed to maladaptive beliefs about the self and interpersonal relationships that become part of the child's cognitive schemas when the traumas occur and continue to be reinforced by subsequent experience (Smucker & Dancu, 1999).

While the modification of abuse-related beliefs and pathogenic schemas appears to be an essential component of cognitive–behavioral therapy with this population, research findings also indicate that a large percentage of adult CSA survivors meet criteria for posttraumatic stress disorder (PTSD). As such, the concurrent presence of PTSD and pervasive maladaptive schemas with this population suggests the need for a multifaceted treatment approach that addresses both the acute PTSD symptoms as well as the abuse-related, traumagenic beliefs/schemas. The usefulness of such a multifaceted approach with this population was noted by Resick and Schnicke (1990):

> It may be most advantageous to implement a therapy that will activate memories of the event and also provide corrective information for faulty attributions or expectations that interfere with complete processing of the event or cause other symptoms (depression, low self-esteem, fear). A combination of exposure and cognitive techniques might prove to be a more effective approach than either type of therapy alone. (p. 500)

IMAGERY RESCRIPTING AND REPROCESSING THERAPY (IRRT)

Developed as an extension of Beck's cognitive therapy model of anxiety disorders (Beck, Emery, & Greenberg, 1985), IRRT is a multifaceted, imagery-based treatment designed to simultaneously alleviate PTSD symptoms and alter abuse-related beliefs and schemas of CSA victims who, as adults, suffer from chronic PTSD (Smucker & Dancu, 1999; Smucker, Dancu, Foa, & Niederee, 1995; Smucker & Niederee, 1995). IRRT is based on an expanded information-processing model that conceptualizes the recurring trauma memories of the abuse survivor both within a PTSD framework and as part of the patient's core schemata. The primary goals of IRRT are to alleviate PTSD symptomatology, alter abuse-related beliefs and schemas (e.g., powerless, inherent badness, unlovability), and increase one's capacity for self-nurturance. The IRRT treatment essentially consists of four major components: (1) *imaginal exposure*—activating the upsetting abuse-related imagery and its associated effect, (2) *mastery imagery*—replacing victimization imagery with coping/mastery imagery, (3) *self-soothing/self-nurturing imagery*—visualizing oneself as an ADULT today calming, nurturing, and reassuring the traumatized CHILD, and (4) *emotional–linguistic processing*—transforming distressing imagery and related affect into narrative language, while actively challenging/modifying the traumagenic beliefs and schemata.

Recommended Inclusion and Exclusion Criteria

Before treatment begins, a clinical interview is conducted that includes demographic information, current life situation, family history, history of traumatic experiences, current psychological adjustment, health status, alcohol and drug use, and severity of PTSD symptoms. Individuals who have been victims of childhood trauma, and who continue to experience recurring intrusive recollections (e.g., recurring flashbacks, repetitive nightmares) of their trauma(s) are likely to be good candidates for IRRT. Before proceeding with IRRT, however, it is important to review the following recommended exclusion criteria: (1) a diagnosis of schizophrenia, acute psychosis, or dissociative identity disorder (especially if the patient is dissociative during imagery sessions); (2) active involvement in substance or alcohol abuse; (3) current involvement in a highly abusive relationship; (4) the presence of overwhelming daily stressors; and (5) the presence of vague or incomplete traumatic memories.

Presenting the Treatment Rationale

Once the appropriateness of IRRT has been established, the therapist educates the patient about the nature of trauma and how PTSD develops from inadequate emotional processing of traumatic events. A brief treatment rationale is then offered to the patient (see standard treatment rationale in Smucker & Dancu, 1999, pp. 42–44). Patients are fully informed of the emotional distress and heightened state of arousal that they are likely to experience when their traumatic memories are activated in the sessions. It is also important to emphasize that the reliving of upsetting memories in a therapy session is quite different from experiencing them in one's everyday environment, that the abuse is not actually occurring at such times, and that the therapist's voice and supportive presence provides a "therapeutic anchor" throughout the imagery sessions. Any questions, concerns, or fears are best addressed in a succinct and candid manner. It is crucial that the patient feel listened to, understood, and validated, especially since the presence of a good therapeutic alliance is crucial to effective outcomes with this clinical population.

Imaginal Exposure Phase

If a patient reports the presence of a number of intrusive abuse-related memories, the therapist has two choices: (1) inquire if the patient is willing to begin with the most upsetting memory or (2) ask which memory the patient prefers to work on first. When the targeted memory has been determined and agreed on, the patient is asked to "relive" the upsetting memory by visualizing and verbalizing aloud the entire traumatic scene—in the first person, present tense—as though it were happening at the moment. The therapist's role is to provide a supportive, safe environment in which the patient can visualize and verbalize the traumatic imagery while accessing and processing the associated painful effect. It is imperative that the therapist remain facilitative rather than directive and not intervene other than to ask for more details of the abuse scene or to ask the patient for SUDS (Subjective Units of Distress Scale) levels. SUDS ratings are taken every 5–10 minutes throughout the imagery session as a means of ascertaining the patient's affective state and degree of emotional involvement. (Low SUDS may reflect affective avoidance, which, in turn, is likely to significantly diminish the therapeutic effects of the treatment.)

Mastery Imagery Phase: Rescripting the Abuse Scene

Following imaginal exposure to the abuse scene, the rescripting or mastery imagery phase begins. Initially, the rescripting phase closely resembles the exposure imagery. This time, however, when the abuse imagery appears to have reached its zenith (i.e., when the SUDS level is at its peak), the patient is asked to visualize her ADULT self today entering the abuse scene. (From this point on in the imagery, the ADULT is addressed in the second person as "you," and the CHILD is addressed in the third person as "she or "her.") The therapist may facilitate this prompted transformation through such questions as: "Can you now visualize yourself as an ADULT today entering the scene?" "Can you get a picture of that?" "Does the perpetrator see you?" "How does s/he respond to your presence?" "What would you, the ADULT, like to do at this point?"..."Can you see yourself doing that?" "How does the perpetrator respond?" The specific goal of the mastery imagery phase is to replace victimization imagery with coping imagery. As such, the task of the ADULT is to rescript the abuse imagery and produce a better outcome by visually confronting the perpetrator, rescuing the CHILD from the traumatic scene, and providing protection for the CHILD, using whatever means necessary to accomplish this. If the ADULT is unable to rescue the CHILD, additional support people (e.g., a spouse, a police officer) may be brought into the abuse scene to help accomplish the task. Throughout the mastery imagery phase, the therapist remains nondirective and is careful not to tell the patient what to do, or suggest what should be happening. It is critical that patients decide for themselves what coping strategies to employ in the mastery imagery.

Self-Nurturing Phase

Following successful completion of the mastery imagery (i.e., after the CHILD has been rescued from the abuse scene and the perpetrator is out of the picture), the therapist fosters "adult-nurturing-child" imagery, in which the ADULT is encouraged to interact directly with the traumatized CHILD. The therapist may facilitate this by asking such questions as: "What would you, the ADULT, like to do or say to the CHILD?" "Can you see yourself doing/saying that?" "How does the CHILD respond?" "What does the CHILD need at this point?" In many instances the ADULT will begin to hold or hug the CHILD, reassure the CHILD that the abuse will not happen again, and promise not to abandon the CHILD. If, however, the ADULT has difficulty nurturing the CHILD, or blames the CHILD for the abuse and wants to abandon or hurt the CHILD, it is sometimes useful to ask the patient: "How far away are you, the ADULT, from the CHILD?" "Might you be able to go up close to the CHILD and tell her why you feel she is to blame for the abuse?" "When you look directly into the CHILD's eyes from up close, what do you see?" Generally, as the ADULT moves closer to the CHILD in the imagery, the ADULT becomes more affected by the CHILD's pain and finds it more difficult to continue blaming, hurting, or abandoning the CHILD. Such intense ADULT–CHILD interactions tend to heighten the patient's overall level of affect and evoke strong feelings toward the CHILD that are empathic, apologetic, or conciliatory in nature.

With more severely disturbed patients, such intimate ADULT–CHILD exchanges may trigger an unlovable schema whereby strong negative emotions are evoked toward the CHILD, who may symbolize the perceived bad/unlovable parts of the patient in the imagery. When this occurs, it can provide a unique therapeutic opportunity to confront the patient's bad/unlovable schema directly via the ADULT–CHILD exchanges within the context of a supportive, therapeutic relationship (see case examples in Smucker & Dancu, 1999, pp. 161–218).

Once it appears that the CHILD has received sufficient nurturance and reassurance from the ADULT and the patient is ready to end the imagery, the therapist asks: "Is there anything more that you, the ADULT, would like to do or say to the CHILD before bringing the imagery to a close?" Once the patient indicates a readiness to terminate the imagery, the therapist concludes: "When you are ready, you may let the imagery fade away and open your eyes." After the patient has had several moments to adjust to the completion of the imagery phase, the therapist administers the Post-Imagery Questionnaire (PIQ: Smucker & Dancu, 1999, Appendix B), which consists of 10 items on which the patient is asked to rate on a 0–100 scale the vividness of the imagery, as well as the emotions felt toward the perpetrator (e.g., fear, anger, powerlessness, blame) and the CHILD (e.g., blame, anger, acceptance, nurturance).

Postimagery Processing and Debriefing

After the PIQ is administered, reactions to the imagery session are discussed and processed together with the patient. To facilitate such processing, the therapist may ask: "How was that for you?" "How are you feeling now?" "What are your reactions to the imagery session today?" Above all, the therapist avoids asking closed-ended or leading questions, such as "Are you feeling better now?"

Assessing Self-Calming/Self-Nurturing Abilities

Following debriefing, the therapist inquires about the patient's ability to self-calm and self-nurture, especially when feeling upset. It is critical to emphasize the difference between self-calming strategies that are self-abusive (e.g., cutting or other forms of self-injury) and adaptive self-calming strategies that are not abusive (e.g., writing in a journal, working out, engaging in a self-nurturing activity, calling a friend or other support person). The therapist and patient then collaboratively explore various self-calming strategies for the patient to experiment with between sessions.

Contracting for Safety

Whether or not any previous history of self-abuse or suicidality exists, the therapist and patient work out a safety contract, whereby the patient commits not to engage in any self-injurious, self-harming, or suicidal behavior during treatment. The patient agrees to call the therapist between sessions should strong urges to self-abuse or self-harm arise.

Homework

An audiotape of the entire imagery session is given to the patient for daily review. The patient is asked to record on a standardized sheet beginning SUDS, peak SUDS, and end SUDS immediately after listening to the imagery tape.

The patient also records personal, subjective reactions to the audiotape in a journal. Any involuntary abuse-related flashbacks, nightmares, or intrusive recollections experienced between sessions are recorded and reported at the next session. The patient also documents efforts to self-calm and self-nurture between sessions, the results of which are processed at the next session.

The above procedure is repeated for another three sessions or until no further intrusive images of the targeted abuse memory are reported. After session 4 the abuse imagery is no longer activated, and for sessions 5–8 only the "adult-nurturing-child" imaginal interactions are facilitated. If no further recurring flashbacks or other intrusive abuse memories are reported at the end of the eight sessions, two additional follow-up sessions are scheduled at 1- and 3-month follow-ups. If, however, the patient reports experiencing additional traumatic recollections, flashbacks, or nightmares, the most distressing memory is targeted for further processing. In such instances, three additional IRRT sessions are allocated for each trauma memory, followed by two additional "adult-nurturing-child" sessions.

Although this format is standard, adjustments should be made according to individual need. For example, if a patient continues to have difficulty developing self-nurturing imagery after the initial eight sessions, but experiences no further PTSD symptoms (e.g., recurring abuse flashbacks), additional "adult-nurturing-child" imagery sessions may be indicated until the patient's ability to self-calm and self-nurture is significantly enhanced. In contrast, if a patient reports a complete absence of intrusive imagery following one IRRT session, and self-nurturing does not appear to be a significant problem, the eight-session format may be shortened.

There is considerable empirical evidence supporting the efficacy of IRRT with adult survivors of CSA in reducing their PTSD symptoms as well as modifying their trauma-based schemas (Dancu, Foa, & Smucker, 1993; Smucker & Dancu, 1999). Recent studies have also found IRRT to be effective in reducing PTSD symptoms with victims of industrial accidents and occupational injuries (Grunert, Smucker, Weis, & Rusch, 2003; Smucker, Grunert, & Weis, 2003).

See also: Child abuse, Imagery

REFERENCES

Beck, A. T., Emery, G., & Greenberg, R. L. (1985). *Anxiety disorders and phobias: A cognitive perspective*. New York: Basic Books.

Dancu, C. V., Foa, E. B., & Smucker, M. R. (1993, November). *Treatment of chronic posttraumatic stress disorder in adult survivors of incest: Cognitive/behavioral interventions*. Paper presented at the annual meeting of the Association for the Advancement of Behavior Therapy, Atlanta, GA.

Grunert, B. K., Smucker, M. R., Weis, J. M., & Rusch, M. D. (2003). When prolonged exposure fails: Adding an imagery-based cognitive restructuring component in the treatment of industrial accident victims suffering from PTSD. *Cognitive and Behavioral Practice, 10*, 333–346.

Resick, P., & Schnicke, M. K. (1990). Treating symptoms in adult victims of sexual assault. *Journal of Interpersonal Violence, 5*, 488–506.

Smucker, M. R., & Dancu, C. V. (1999). *Cognitive–behavioral treatment for adult survivors of childhood trauma: Imagery rescripting and reprocessing*. Northvale, NJ: Jason Aronson.

Smucker, M. R., Dancu, C. V., Foa, E. B., & Niederee, J. L. (1995). Imagery rescripting: A new treatment for survivors of childhood sexual abuse suffering from posttraumatic stress. *Journal of Cognitive Psychotherapy: An International Quarterly, 9*(1), 3–17.

Smucker, M. R., Grunert, B. K., & Weis, J. M. (2003). Posttraumatic stress disorder: A new algorithm treatment model. In R. L. Leahy (Ed.), *Overcoming roadblocks in cognitive therapy practice* (pp. 175–194). New York: Guilford Press.

Smucker, M. R., & Niederee, J. L. (1995). Treating incest-related PTSD and pathogenic schemas through imaginal exposure and rescripting. *Cognitive and Behavioral Practice, 2*, 63–93.

Inpatient Treatment

Wayne A. Bower

Keywords: cognitive therapy, treatment, depression, inpatient, psychotherapy

Cognitive therapy (CT) has become one of the most prominent treatment models in mental health and has been adapted for use with a wide range of medical patients. Initially designed as an outpatient treatment, CT has been adapted and used in an extensive variety of settings such as crisis intervention, day-treatment, partial hospital programs, and inpatient settings. Various authors have described the adaptation of CT to inpatient settings (Wright, Thase, Beck, & Ludgate, 1993). Research on the use of CT to treat depressed inpatients found that this model improved response to antidepressants and suggested that the combination of CT and medications sustained inpatient improvement over a 1-year follow-up (Wright et al., 1993). Thase, Bowler, and Harden (1991) also looked at the use of CT with unmedicated inpatients. Their results indicated that intensive (five sessions a week) treatment contributed to significant improvement in depressive symptomatology.

The initial positive studies with CT on an inpatient unit contributed to more scholarly writing in this area. Wright et al. (1993) published a book that described various models of CT that could be integrated to an inpatient setting.

The Primary Therapist Model has been described as using a single therapist to implement the CT. In this model, there are other treatment modalities being delivered (biological, behavior therapy, interpersonal therapy) and the unit staff has a general knowledge of CT principles to support the primary therapist. However, the actual use of CT is the responsibility of the primary therapist. Integration of this CT model into a hospital unit is accomplished when the primary therapist is part of a multidisciplinary treatment team working on the overall planning of treatment. A Staff Model usually occurs when patients are admitted to a hospital unit where the psychiatrist (who may have little knowledge of CT) treats the patient with pharmacotherapy. Existing unit staff (psychologists, social workers, or psychiatric nurses), having been trained in CT, implement the CT to the patient either in a group format or on an individual basis. The easiest type of CT inpatient unit to develop is called an Add-On Model. This approach consists of one or more individuals who have had training in CT working on the unit primarily to administer the therapy. This model differs from the Primary Therapist Model in that the unit personnel and medical staff may or may not have a working knowledge of CT. The therapist will be on the unit to administer the CT (group or individual format) but have only minimal contact with the remainder for the inpatient staff. The most complex use of inpatient CT is called the Comprehensive Model. In this type of inpatient milieu, all therapeutic activities are steeped in CT and all staff have been trained in the theory and interventions of CT. The comprehensive model requires an extensive commitment to the training and supervision of hospital unit staff.

At the time of the publication of their book, Wright et al. (1993) listed 26 inpatient programs (23 in the United States and 3 in Europe) that were based on one of these CT models. Their book detailed the use of inpatient CT in a wide variety of medical settings and with many different patient populations (psychiatric and medical). Along with this volume, there were continued publications describing the use of CT on inpatient units and discussing its implementation and clinical value for acute care psychiatric hospitals. Positive reports for CT with depression were shared when used in a group format as part of a larger milieu in a private hospital setting. More recently the use of CT during intensive inpatient treatment positively improves work, leisure, housing, social relations, psychological well-being, and global satisfaction with life. Additionally, 60% of those treated in this inpatient CT program displayed significant improvement in global depressive symptoms of depression (Lenz & Demal, 2000).

CT has been identified as an integral part for the treatment of various psychiatric disorders. CT and theory has been developed specifically for the inpatient treatment of anorexia and described as part of a stepped care approach in the treatment of anorexia nervosa. Across the country, inpatient programs using the Comprehensive Model have been designed and are running. These programs include adaptations of CT to this population. CT has also been used in several large-scale research projects working with the treatment of alcoholism. These studies found that CT had a positive effect on symptom severity, a decrease in conflict, and an overall improvement in well-being. Hoffart (1995) examined the use of inpatient CT on agoraphobia suggesting better endstate functioning compared to guided imagery. An intensive CT inpatient program for hypochondriasis has been reported by Hiller, Leibbrand, Rief, and Fechter (2002). At the end of inpatient treatment, 60% of the sample were seen as responders to the CT interventions and had shown substantial improvement in their symptoms.

CT has been used as part of a comprehensive approach to the treatment of PTSD (Humphreys, Westerink, Giarratano, & Brooks, 1999). Their study suggests that when CT is used as part of a comprehensive program, it can reduce symptoms of anxiety and depression as well as help to maintain these changes over a 2-year period. A more recent use of CT with inpatients has been with individuals suffering from psychosis. Haddock et al. (1999) report that when CT is used as an adjunct to standard inpatient treatment, it is found to be an acceptable treatment for recent-onset acutely psychotic individuals. And it has been suggested that CT can have a positive benefit when used in a comprehensive program in the treatment of schizophrenia.

CT has also been applied to medical problems on an inpatient basis. When used during inpatient treatment, CT was shown to have positive effects for individuals suffering from chronic pain and positive effects on musculoskeletal pain (Johansson, Dahl, Jannert, Melin, & Andersson, 1998). A 10-week cognitive–behavioral treatment program for obese individuals was studied to assess long-term outcome. At the 18-month follow-up, there was a general reduction in both eating and a broad spectrum of psychopathology (Leibbrand & Fechter, 2002).

Looking at the research on the use of CT with inpatients, a startling picture emerges. More of the inpatient research is coming from Europe and less from the United States. This mirrors a fundamental shift in psychiatric care in the Unites States from an inpatient model to an outpatient model. Early research on inpatient treatment of depression (and other disorders) suggested that individuals were hospitalized for a month or longer. With the introduction of managed care and health maintenance organizations (HMOs), the length of stay in a hospital had dramatically dropped. In the 1990s, long-term hospital stays dropped by as much as 50% for adults and 20% among children and adolescents. Also, in the United States, there was a greater emphasis on shifting care from an inpatient setting to day hospitals and partial hospital programs. Other data indicate the average length of stay in a psychiatric hospital decreased 25% between 1988 and 1992.

It would seem that inpatient CT for disorders such as depression or anxiety are no longer feasible when the length of stay on a hospital unit ranges from 3 to 7 days. With this dramatic shift in the length of time a patient can remain on an inpatient service, how or where do you find the use of CT in this environment? Also, what is the future for CT when considering inpatient work or research? Additionally, given the models described in the early 1990s for CT, what might be the most effective use of these models? The literature on inpatient treatment of psychiatric care gives some clues as to what the future may bring. Opportunities still remain to use CT with an inpatient population. Specialty units (either free-standing or within more general hospital units) that work with disorders such as obsessive–compulsive disorders, borderline personality disorder, or eating disorders (primarily anorexia nervosa) still maintain strong CT influences. Some specialty units are designed using the Comprehensive Model while others use a Primary Therapist Model. Units like these, although fewer in number, still offer opportunities to work effectively with CT principles and interventions and continue to report positive outcomes when treating individuals on an inpatient basis.

One newer environment for CT as a consequence of HMOs' push to reduce inpatient length of stay is the development of Day Hospitals and Partial Hospital Programs. Although these programs are influenced by their own health care climates, there are similarities in these programs to what was offered within a hospital setting. Among the common elements are use of multidisciplinary staff, group and individual therapy as primary treatments, and for some programs the use of a continuum of care. A day hospital or partial hospital program is often connected to an inpatient program and this forms one of the referral sources for these less intensive programs. Some programs, such as those for obsessive–compulsive disorder or anorexia nervosa, have a continuum of care that offers a "step up" or "step down" for individuals who shift in the need for more or less intensive treatment. These programs run from 3 to 5 days a week and either integrate some form of CT into their program or, as stated previously, function from a more standard CT Comprehensive Model. The scant literature on these programs suggests they are effective in continuing gains from an inpatient treatment program and can assist reduction in symptoms when patients "step up" from outpatient care.

The future of CT with inpatients is very uncertain. With changes in treatment philosophies and a continued drive to reduce inpatient length of stay, there will need to be a reanalysis of how to implement CT in a shorter-term framework. It may be more fruitful to design CT interventions for specific disorders based on what outpatient care will be offered when an individual is discharged from a hospital. Additionally, its use with depression and/or anxiety disorders may be more beneficial when CT is integrated into a day or partial hospital program. There is also a need to produce more research in this area. Specifically, in the United States there will be a need to draw on our current resources to assess if there remains a useful role for CT for depression and/or anxiety in a short hospital admission. More scholarship is also needed to understand the role of CT with inpatients and the expansion of CT into the newly created models for health care. CT will remain a force in health care but without an emphasis on its application with inpatient, day treatment, or partial hospital programs, there is a risk that CT's utility will be lost and that would truly be a sad legacy to the history of CT with an inpatient population.

See also: Depression—adult, Depression—general

REFERENCES

Haddock, G., Tarrier, N., Morrison, A. P., Hopkins, R., Drake, R., & Lewis, S. (1999). A pilot study evaluating effectiveness of individual inpatient cognitive–behavioural therapy in early psychosis. *Social Psychiatry and Psychiatric Epidemiology, 34*, 254–258.

Hiller, W., Leibbrand, R., Rief, W., & Fechter, M. M. (2002). Predictors of course and outcome in hypochondriasis after cognitive–behavioral treatment. *Psychotherapy and Psychosomatics, 71*, 318–325.

Hoffart, A. (1995). A comparison of cognitive and guided mastery therapy of agoraphobia. *Behavior Therapy and Research, 33*, 423–434.

Humphreys, L., Westerink, J., Giarratano, L., & Brooks, R. (1999). An intensive program for chronic posttraumatic stress disorder: 2-year outcome data. *Australian and New Zealand Journal of Psychiatry, 33*, 848–854.

Johansson, C., Dahl, J., Jannert, M., Melin, L., & Andersson, G. (1998). Effects of cognitive–behavioral pain-management program. *Behavior Therapy and Research, 36*, 915–930.

Leibbrand, R., & Fechter, M. M. (2002). Maintenance of weight loss after obesity treatment: Is continuous support necessary? *Behavior Therapy and Research, 40*, 1275–1289.

Lenz, G., & Demal, U. (2000). Quality of life in depression and anxiety disorders: An exploratory follow-up study after intensive inpatient cognitive behaviour therapy. *Psychopathology, 33*, 297–302.

Thase, M. E., Bowler, K., & Harden, T. (1991). Cognitive behavior therapy of endogenous depression: Part 2. Preliminary findings in 16 unmedicated patients. *Behavior Therapy, 22*, 469–477.

Wright, J. H., Thase, M. E., Beck, A. T., & Ludgate, J. W. (1993). *Cognitive therapy with inpatients: Developing a cognitive milieu*. New York: Guilford Press.

L

Linguistic Therapy of Evaluation

Isabel Caro

Keywords: language, evaluation, intensional orientation, extensional orientation, meaning

The linguistic therapy of evaluation (LTE) comes from the theory of general semantics (GS) developed by Alfred Korzybski. GS emphasizes the role that language plays in evaluating the world of "events," that is, what is going on (WIGO in the individual's world). GS is the science of both evaluation and values. "Evaluation" implies that a similar degree of importance is given to thinking and feeling. When evaluating an experience, we construe the world through language.

Korzybski (1933, p. 24) defined a semantic reaction as "the psychological reaction of a given individual to words, language, symbols, and events, in connection with their meanings, and the psychological reactions, which become meanings and relational configurations the moment the given individual begins to analyse them or somebody else does that for him." For Korzybski, living takes place in a world of "events" that the individal interprets and perceives as "facts." GS theory assumes that every "fact" is a personal or idiosyncratic construction, that is, an interpretation through language. But language has a completly different structure from the world of objective "facts" or of "realities." We use language to "fix" what is in process and may be unclear.

Korzybski (1933) asserted that human beings should recognize and be trained in the implications of the three non-Aristotelian premises. At the core of his theory, they exemplify language/"fact" relationships. The first premise is that the map is not the territory, or we should never identify language with "facts"; second, language is incomplete, or the map cannot cover all the territory; and third, language is self-reflexive, or we can always make a map of a map of a map, etc.

The *Zeitgeist* of his theory was a modernist philosophy. As with other scientists of his time, he believed that the proper use of science could be of great help for solving human problems. Based on the application of mathematics to daily living, he developed a non-Aristotelian system where subjects educated in GS principles learn how to use language for a better representation of "reality." In this sense, he developed a non-Aristotelian training, described as the application of GS principles through reason, with the aim of making subjects scientists. Language as "representational," "rationalism," and "human beings as scientists" are the three main modernist characteristics of GS. However, the *modernist flavor* of GS contained a rupture with modernity. In some sense, Korzybski anticipated some current concerns, closer to a postmodern philosophy, such as the relevance of language and its influence on such cognitive characteristics as "knowing," the role of values and evaluation, "relativism," the importance of "nonverbal levels" of "reality" seen in an ongoing change and as a "joint phenomenon" between the observed and the observer, and so forth. These assumptions are at the core of LTE. We could consider LTE as a midpoint between modernist and postmodern perspectives.

EARLY WORK

The development of LTE began in 1985 (Caro, 1987). After several years of practicing clinically general semantics,

Caro presented the *cognitive therapy of evaluation* in 1987 (Caro, 1987), describing it later on (Caro, 1990). The change into *linguistic* (in 1993) better emphasized and described therapeutic aims, techniques, and the conceptualization of patients' problems. LTE represents the "translation" of GS to the cognitive therapy field. Also, it has been influenced by previous works in the applications of GS to psychotherapy and related fields (see Caro & Read, 2002).

THE PRESENT STATUS OF LTE

LTE has theoretical, epistemological, ontological, and practical differences from the two main approaches to cognitive therapy as defined by the author: "classical," closer to a modernist epistemological, and "constructionist," closer to a postmodern point of view (Caro, 1990, 2002).

LTE has shown its effectiveness for "anxiety" and "depressive" problems, using a number of well-established techniques. LTE is now trying to show and describe linguistic changes that occur in therapy and the best ways to enhance therapeutic effectiveness.

THERAPEUTIC AIMS

LTE is as an "interpretative" therapy. Its aim is to help patients find the meaning they give to WIGO. This meaning reflects the use of language and the influence it has on our nonverbal and verbal evaluations. We could describe the use of language in terms of an intensional or an extensional orientation. Both reflect two different kinds of evaluations. An *intensional orientation* is related to "emotional problems." It implies evaluations that reflect an improper structural similarity between the world of words and the world of "facts." This similarity implies three kind of evaluations: *identifications*, that is, identifying words with "facts"; *anticipations*, that is, putting words before "facts"; and *intensionalizations*, as when patients use a higher level of abstraction language, reflected in the use of absolutistic terms, such as "never," "always," or "all."

For Korzybski (1933) the aim of therapy was to help patients to *extensionalize*. The goal of therapy would be to help patients to develop an *extensional orientation*. When the individual reaches an extensional attitude or orientation, they first recognize the differences in structure between the world of words (our world of fictions, in Vaihinger's sense) and the world of "facts" (always in process, partially known) and second, structurally adjust both worlds. An extensional orientation represents three main evaluations: *nonidentification*, i.e., recognizing the difference in structure between the world of "words" and the world of "facts," *nonanticipation*, or stopping putting words before "facts," and *extensionalization*, i.e., using a flexible, conditional kind of language.

An example will help to clarify these two orientations. A woman of 53 wanted "to change all of her life" (*intensionalization*). Thinking about her life, her linguistic evaluation was: "I have done nothing at all (*intensionalization*), I'm a failure (*identification*), life will not change but get worse (*anticipation*)." After working with her to change her intensional orientation, she extensionalized and made more conditional theories and evaluations and started to evaluate her life, after several linguistic debates and sessions as follows: "Well, I have had positive and negative things in my life, some that I could control and some that I couldn't (*extensionalization*), so I am not a failure but a human being with experiences, some of which I do not like (*nonidentification*), I will try to solve what I can and concentrate better on the present than on the future (*nonanticipation*)."

THERAPEUTIC TECHNIQUES

The LTE bases its therapeutic aims on three main techniques: the GS debate, the orders of abstraction, and the extensional devices. The GS debate is an unstructured debate that focuses on the applications of the three non-Aristotelian premises. In fact, it represents putting into practice GS's assumptions and philosophy about language and its consequences for human knowledge and sanity. For instance, we could do a GS debate to help patients to accept some "facts." In this case patients should recognize what is the "fact" and what are the words used to construe it and differentiate between both of them (the map *is not* the territory). Also, patients should recognize some other things not seen (the map *does not* cover the whole territory), see if they give more importance to words or to "facts," recognizing the level of their reactions (language is self-reflexive), and recognizing, finally, what they could have changed or other events and experiences that they should accept, instead.

The orders of abstraction have the following structure: patients choose a particular event they want to discuss or solve. First, we explore all the theories/meanings they attach to the situation, and evaluate them with a "thermometer" (from −5 to +5). Second, patients should focus on the here and now (WIGO). They can then move to the verbal levels. Patients attach a *label* to what they experience, then *describe* what is behind the label, reaching, then, the *inferential* level. At this point the therapist helps the patients to make deductions, coming back again to their evaluations, pointing to their intensional orientation, their theories, and looking for the conditions of things, that is, exploring all the implications of their constructions through language.

Next, patients learn (through different linguistic operations) how to solve their intensional orientation, with the aim of developing an extensional orientation. Finally, we encourage patients to reach a *conclusion*. This conclusion should reflect (if the event has been successfully resolved) an extensional orientation. Finally, the whole process should be evaluated again with the thermometer. It does not imply a simple passing throughout levels, but a circular process going back and forth, connecting all the levels and recognizing the nonverbal and verbal evaluations of patients. Also, we devised a homework assignment based on the orders and with the same levels explained above (Caro, 1996).

Patients who follow the orders of abstraction seem to learn:

1. How to stop jumping immediately to conclusions, reacting not to the world of words, but to the world of "facts" experienced on the unspeakable level.
2. How to give a new, different meaning to (relabel) any situation experienced as an insurmountable one in the past or at that moment. Patients learn evaluational self-control based on a strict control of the language world.
3. Finally, they learn how to avoid the unnatural order of evaluation: words first, then "facts," to accomplish a more proper evaluation.

The extensional devices are the third main technique. The devices, devised by Korzybski (1933) and Johnson (1946), represent the clearer example of how we could adjust the structure of language to the structure of reality. We encourage patients to use them to "destroy" intensionalizations and identifications. First, patient and therapist decide which intensionalization should be "destroyed," and this is evaluated with a thermometer (-5 to $+5$). The devices are: *indexes* (differentiating between situations, persons, things, and so on), *defining the action* (looking for actions for destroying identifications), (remembering that to know implies to abstract), *dates* (remembering that things change, that "reality" is in an ongoing process of change), *quantifying* (avoiding talking in "all-or-nothing" terms), *plurals* (avoiding personalizations), *conditional* (remembering that things do not come out of the blue but rather depend on circumstances), and finally, *consciousness of projection* (avoiding "giving" theories to others, and "getting" theories from others). Then, the idea is to reach an *extensional conclusion*, validating, again, the whole process.

As in the case of the orders, they represent a long and complex in-session linguistic debate and are then transformed into a homework assignment (Caro, 1996).

The extensional devices are useful:

1. To "destroy" a negative thought or belief, finding different and alternative explanations about a "fact." The devices help patients to look for an extensionalized language, for maps more similar in structure to the territory, avoiding improper evaluations based on a language structure that does not correspond to the structure of "reality."
2. To become aware of self-evaluations or negative self-concepts. This usually means patients are intensionally addressing themselves.
3. To recognize how different it is to experience a "fact" than to talk about it.
4. To learn to use a language more similar in structure to the nonverbal world, that is, to use a more specific and descriptive language, before reaching a conclusion, to change their "knowledge" based on different language when new "facts" advise it.

EMPIRICAL BASIS FOR LTE

The International Society for General Semantics (San Francisco) and The Institute of General Semantics (New York) funded research in LTE through several grants. The research done in LTE is of two types: outcome and process researches. From 1987 until 1997 the goal was to attempt to demonstrate the effectiveness of LTE. From the outcome studies (review in Caro, 1997) we could assume that: (1) LTE seems to be particularly useful for the treatment of generalized anxiety disorders, hypochondria, or depressive neurosis; (2) there are no differences in effectiveness in relation to the kind of "diagnosis"; (3) there are no differences in effectiveness between the two main techniques: the orders of abstraction and the extensional devices; (4) results are maintained at follow-up.

During these years all sessions were recorded so the researchers have a pool of therapeutic moments ready for the later process research. The process research began in 1991 and was and is presently dedicated to the process analysis of linguistic change, related to the LTE core assumptions. Using task analysis methodology (Caro, 1999), the researchers correlated an improper use of language with different kinds of evaluations, an intensional orientation with "emotional" problems and an extensional orientation with positive outcomes in therapy. They have analyzed the orders of abstraction for describing patients' change from an intensional toward an extensional orientation. In this sense, they have discovered several relevant operations that better connect evaluations with the resolution of significant events and also with the core GS assumptions about the role language plays in our knowing processes.

Another kind of process research has used the taxonomy of *verbal response modes* from Stiles (1992). The taxonomy helped to describe the kind of therapy that LTE seems to be (Caro, 1997): *directive* (therapies centered on the therapist's frame of reference), *nondirective* (therapies centered on the patient's frame of reference), *analytic* (therapies centered on the client's source of experience), and *exhortatory* (therapies centered on the therapist's source of experience).

SHORTCOMINGS AND FUTURE DEVELOPMENTS OF LTE

Due to space requirements, only two issues will be emphasized. First, the clinical work offered new experiences that, framed on process research, have highly relevant implications for improving LTE. Briefly, if we identify these operations that best enhance clinical linguistic change, we could improve techniques and devise some new ones. The three original techniques could be changed in many ways; their structure is flexible and could be adapted, always, to patients' needs and to improved therapeutic procedures.

However, present concerns, shortcomings, and future theoretical and clinical developments involve working with the specific GS concepts about language. This will imply, first of all, to integrate or update the GS theory with present theories about language and narratives, and, second, receive from other cognitive and constructivist therapies other influences. For instance, we could relate one of these influences with exploring and developing with patients the *historical* origin of their intensional orientation. Korzybski (1933) emphasized that symbols and their meanings are culturally transmitted and time-bound. So, if we are able to develop the "ontogeny" and "epistemology" of patients' intensional orientations, they will understand better *why* and *how* they are construing the world and attaching meanings. Perhaps, the clinical change will be different and the influence of the therapy enhanced and maintained along time.

From all of the above, LTE seems to be alive and promising significant developments.

REFERENCES

Caro, I. (1987, July). *A new therapeutic procedure based on general semantics*. Paper presented at the International Meeting on General Semantics, Yale, University, New Haven, CT.

Caro, I. (1990). Semántica general y psicoterapia [General semantics and psychotherapy]. In I. Caro (Ed.), *Psicología y Semántica General*. Valencia: Promolibro. (Collection of Theoretical Psychology)

Caro, I. (1996). The linguistic therapy of evaluation: A perspective on language in psychotherapy. *Journal of Cognitive Psychotherapy, 10*(2), 83–104.

Caro, I. (1997). El estado de la cuestión en la terapia linguística de evaluación [The state-of-the-art in the linguistic therapy of evaluation]. In I. Caro (Ed.), *Manual de psicoterapias cognitivas* (pp. 279–290). Barcelona: Paidós.

Caro, I. (1999). La investigación de procesos: Análisis de tareas y cambio terapéutico en la terapia lingüística de evaluación [Process research: Task analysis and therapeutic change in the linguistic therapy of evaluation]. *Psicologemas, 13*(25–26), 1–192.

Caro, I. (2002). General semantics–cognitive therapy–constructivism: A relational approach. In I. Caro & C. Read (Eds.), *General semantics in psychotherapy* (pp. 324–352). New York: Institute of General Semantics.

Caro, I., & Read, C. (Eds.). (2002). *General semantics in psychotherapy*. New York: Institute of General Semantics.

Johnson, W. (1946). *People in quandaries*. San Francisco: International Society for General Semantics.

Korzybski, A. (1933). *Science and sanity*. Lakeville, CT: International Non-Aristotelian Library.

Stiles, W. B. (1992). *Describing talk. A taxonomy of verbal response modes*. Newbury Park, CA: Sage.

Low Self-Esteem

Melanie J. V. Fennell

Keywords: low self-esteem, core beliefs, rules for living, anxious predictions, self-criticism

Low self-esteem, a reflection of central negative beliefs about the self, seems a prime candidate for CBT. Yet until relatively recently it was rarely identified as a therapeutic target in its own right, perhaps because it is a transdiagnostic cognitive theme, and thus does not fit readily within the traditional psychiatric classifications that have shaped key developments in CBT. A negative sense of self may be an aspect of, consequence of, or vulnerability factor for a wide range of presenting problems. For example, it is central to the experience of depression (aspect), but often vanishes once mood lifts. It may emerge only when a specific disorder has become chronic (consequence), and resolve once the main presenting problem is effectively tackled. Or it may predispose to a range of other difficulties (vulnerability factor), for example, depression, suicidality, eating disorders, and social phobia. In this case, it may hinder effective treatment of presenting problems and persist even after they have been resolved, unless addressed in its own right.

Low self-esteem can be helpfully understood within a cognitive–behavioral conceptual framework, and effectively treated with CBT. The ease of achieving change will vary from patient to patient (Fennell, 1998). In some cases, where the negative sense of self is relatively situation-specific and where the person has access to alternative, more benign self-perspectives, substantial change may be achieved through classical short-term cognitive therapy (12–20 sessions). In other cases, where low self-esteem is intense, pervasive, and accompanied by substantial disability, and where no more kindly perspective is available, treatment is likely to be more protracted.

A COGNITIVE MODEL OF LOW SELF-ESTEEM

The development and maintenance of low self-esteem can be understood in terms of a cognitive model (Fennell, 1997) closely based on A. T. Beck's original cognitive model of emotional disorder (Beck, 1976).

The model, together with an example, is illustrated in Figure 1. It suggests that the essence of low self-esteem resides in negative core beliefs about the self (the "Bottom Line"), which derive from an interaction between inborn factors (including temperament) and experience. Influential experiences often occur in early childhood, but events can also shape self-esteem in later life. For example, a person who had previously had a solid, positive sense of self might experience radical change in the wake of a trauma that caused them to question their competence, strength, or worth (Dunmore, Clark, & Ehlers, 1997). The Bottom Line interacts with beliefs about others and the world, leading to the development of "Rules for Living" (dysfunctional assumptions) which, so long as their terms are met, more or less allow the person to maintain self-esteem. However, if the terms of the rules either *might not be met* (outcome is uncertain) or *have not been met* (there is no doubt), the Bottom Line is activated and is then maintained by biases in processing and self-defeating behavioral responses.

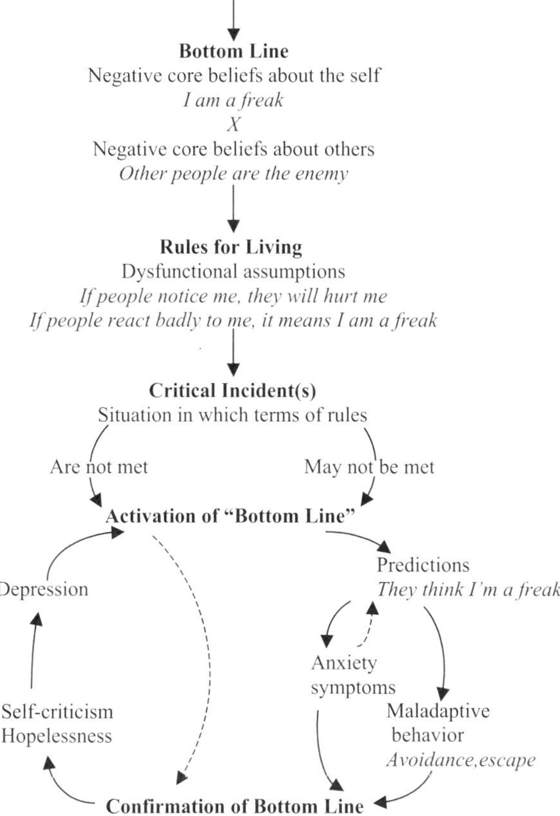

Figure 1. A cognitive model of low self-esteem (based on Fennell, 1997).

When outcome is uncertain (the terms of the rules *might not be met*), the response is an anxious one. Activation of the Bottom Line leads to negative predictions, which trigger anxiety (which may itself become a source of further predictions), and may lead to a range of maladaptive behaviors, e.g., avoidance, safety-seeking behaviors (Salkovskis, 1991), aggression, and self-medication (substance misuse). These prevent disconfirmation of the original anxious prediction, and may indeed make the situation worse. The combination of anxiety and maladaptive responses can genuinely disrupt or inhibit performance. However, even if anxious predictions are disconfirmed (outcome is in fact positive), this information is likely to be ignored or discounted, rather than accepted as a sign that the Bottom Line might be incorrect. The end result, subjectively, is confirmation of the Bottom Line. This leads to self-criticism and hopelessness, and thus to depressed mood, which may be transitory or become sufficiently severe and persistent to require treatment in its own right. So the circle closes: depression ensures that the Bottom Line remains active and continues to fuel the system. When the terms of the rules *have not been met* (there is no doubt about it), activation of the Bottom Line leads directly (perhaps simultaneously) to a sense of its truth (confirmation), with no intervening anxious uncertainty. In this case, depression is the predominant mood.

TREATING LOW SELF-ESTEEM

The model forms a basis for an individually tailored cognitive conceptualization of the difficulties for which the patient has sought therapy. It is the foundation for an integrated program of cognitive–behavioral interventions, which draws on established protocols for treating depression and anxiety, as well as the clinical literature on changing schemas and core beliefs (e.g., Beck, Freeman, &

Associates, 1990; Young, Klosko, & Weishaar, 2003). The program is briefly summarized in Table 1. It incorporates a range of treatment methods designed to counter the biases in perception and interpretation that, in interaction with self-defeating behavior, maintain the Bottom Line. Through these, data that are consistent with the prevailing view are readily noticed, accepted, and stored, whereas data that might disconfirm it are screened out, distorted, or forgotten.

Interventions are designed to target elements of the cognitive model in a systematic sequence. However, the exact order of events, and the relative emphasis given to different elements, will vary from patient to patient. The "rule of thumb" is to start with maintaining processes, relating specific day-to-day changes to background assumptions and beliefs, but waiting to work on these broader issues until the therapeutic relationship is firmly established and the patient has a sound grasp of the principles and practice of CBT and is able to work effectively with painful emotions. Specific, concrete changes are generally easier to achieve than transformation of longstanding cognitive structures, and so encourage engagement and hope. Equally, it may be the case that self-esteem is restored by working on presenting problems, especially if the implications of particular assignments are explicitly related back to assumptions and core beliefs (e.g., "What does that experiment tell us about how helpful it is to have perfectionist rules?" "What are the implications of this shift in your thinking for how you perceive yourself in general terms?"). However, if the Bottom Line (and associated beliefs about others and the world) are deeply entrenched, it may be necessary to introduce some flexibility into the system before being able to proceed with specific interventions (for example, by helping patients to entertain the idea that their beliefs, though powerful and understandable in terms of their experience, reflect opinions rather than facts).

Treatment first aims to undermine maintaining processes by teaching patients to become aware of, question, and test negative automatic thoughts (anxious predictions, self-criticism). Behavioral experiments encourage direct experiential learning and ensure that changes do not remain purely intellectual, but are accompanied by emotional transformation (Fennell & Jenkins, in press). At the same time, patients begin work on establishing and strengthening a more accepting perspective on the self, identifying and correcting the biases in perception and interpretation that lead them to focus on their faults and weaknesses at the expense of their qualities and strengths. Work on modifying negative thoughts and refocusing attention on positive aspects of the self forms a basis for questioning and reformulating Rules for Living, and for undermining negative core beliefs and constructing and reinforcing more benign alternatives. Just as day-to-day changes were linked back to wider issues at an earlier stage in therapy, so broad-brush changes in assumptions and beliefs are now linked back to day-to-day changes in thinking, emotion, and behavior (e.g., "What are the implications of this new view of yourself for how you will relate to people from now on? Can you think of a specific situation in the next week where you would have operated according to the old system? How exactly will you operate differently now? Shall we rehearse that?"). This phase of treatment may well incorporate a range of cognitive, behavioral, and imaginal interventions found in the literature on schema transformation.

The objective of therapy is not for patients' self-esteem to swing to the other end of the scale ("Every day, in every way, I'm getting better and better"), but rather to help them achieve a balanced, kindly sense of themselves, which acknowledges their human weaknesses and imperfections, but places these within the broader context of overall self-acceptance.

Table 1. CBT for Low Self-Esteem: Some Key Interventions

Assessment	Assess presenting problems Identify Bottom Line Assess severity of impact
Conceptualization	Develop a shared formulation Psychoeducation (introducing the cognitive model; a thought is not a fact)
Countering biases in perception	Direct attention to qualities; strengths; daily self-monitoring
Countering biases in interpretation	Question anxious predictions and self-critical thoughts; behavioral experiments; cost–benefit analysis of self-criticism
Reformulating assumptions	Identify more helpful rules for living and put them into practice
Undermining the Bottom Line	Reinterpret supporting "evidence"; continuum work; search for counter-evidence (including historical test); positive data log; formulate a more balanced view of the self and act in accordance with it; transform childhood memories

A CLINICAL EXAMPLE

Sam was a shy child, brought up on an isolated country farm. He was awkward with other children, and attracted bullying when he went to school. This became worse when he grew unusually tall, at an unusually early age. He developed an extreme, negative sense of himself: "I'm a freak" (the Bottom Line). He also learned to see others as hostile: "Other people are the enemy." His strategy, encapsulated in his Rules for Living, was one of avoidance: he said little, and kept his distance from other people as far as he could. Provided he was able to avoid contact, his sense of freakishness remained quiet. However, he was very lonely and as time went on became increasingly sad and bitter about how his life had turned out. He was referred by his family doctor for treatment of his social phobia. In addition, he met diagnostic criteria for avoidant personality disorder and for major depression, including suicidal thoughts. (Comorbidity is very frequent with low self-esteem—as indeed the model would imply. A combination of anxiety and depression is particularly common. A range of presenting problems may have a common root, and a cognitive formulation will help to make sense of this.)

Sam's treatment began by developing a cognitive formulation, focusing on his social anxiety as an initial point of leverage. He learned to test his predictions about the responses of others through a sequence of behavioral experiments, in which he dropped his usual self-protective maneuvers (safety-seeking behaviors) and closely observed others' reactions to him. During this time, he suffered a serious setback and became briefly acutely suicidal. A session of crisis management and then ongoing use of interventions for depression followed, interwoven with continuing work on social anxiety. Gradually Sam discovered that, when he allowed himself to approach people without precautions, most of them responded positively. There was no sign that anyone thought him a freak. A tentative new Bottom Line was formulated ("I am a human being"), together with a tentative new perspective on others ("Other people are mostly friendly and helpful"). Sam continued to test these ideas through further experiments, shifting focus from disconfirming his old predictions to collecting evidence to support the new views. At the same time, with his therapist, he made a list of his good qualities (for example, honesty and courage) and began to keep a record of these on a day-to-day basis. Over the weeks, his belief in his new ideas became stronger. Although he remained somewhat wary of people he did not know, and prone to self-doubt, he was able to approach others more freely and his confidence in himself increased.

SUMMARY

CBT has been shown to improve self-esteem, and is well established as a treatment for anxiety and depression (both proposed as key maintaining processes within low self-esteem). However, the cognitive model described here, and the treatment program derived from it, have not yet been subject to controlled test. The treatment package may prove difficult to evaluate, given the range of presenting problems among patients with low self-esteem. Nonetheless, it forms part of a cross-diagnostic trial of CBT for eating disorders currently under way (Fairburn, Cooper, & Shafran, 2003).

Research supports a number of elements hypothesized by the model, including:

- The relationship between early experience, subsequent low self-esteem, and a range of psychological difficulties (e.g., Abramson et al., 2002)
- The responsiveness of self-esteem to variations in circumstances (positive and negative life events)
- The degree to which events triggering psychopathology are central to people's sense of self-worth
- The biases in processing (selection and distortion of incoming information, memory biases) that maintain unhelpful perspectives
- The relationship between anxious predictions, physical symptoms, and maladaptive behavior evident in a range of anxiety disorders
- The reciprocal relationship between self-critical thinking, hopelessness, and depressed mood

See also: Social skills training

REFERENCES

Abramson, L. Y., Alloy, L. B., Hogan, M. E., Whitehouse, W. G., Donovan, P., Rose, D. T., Panzarella, C., & Raniere, D. (2002). Cognitive vulnerability to depression: Theory and evidence. In R. L. Leahy & E. T. Dowd (Eds.), *Clinical advances in cognitive psychotherapy: Theory and application* (pp. 75–92). New York: Springer.

Beck, A. T. (1976). *Cognitive therapy and the emotional disorders*. New York: International Universities Press.

Beck, A. T., Freeman, A., & Associates. (1990). *Cognitive therapy of personality disorders*. New York: Guilford Press.

Dunmore, E., Clark, D. M., & Ehlers, A. (1997). Cognitive factors in persistent versus recovered post-traumatic stress disorder after physical or sexual assault: A pilot study. *Behavioural & Cognitive Psychotherapy, 25*, 147–159.

Fairburn, C. G., Cooper, Z., & Shafran, R. (2003). Cognitive behavior therapy for eating disorders: A "transdiagnostic" theory and treatment. *Behavior Research & Therapy, 41*, 509–528.

Fennell, M. J. V. (1997). Low self-esteem: A cognitive perspective. *Behavioral & Cognitive Psychotherapy, 25*, 1–25.

Fennell, M. J. V. (1998). Low self-esteem. In N. Tarrier, A. Wells, & G. Haddock (Eds.), *Treating complex cases: The cognitive behaviour therapy approach* (pp. 217–240). New York: Wiley.

Fennell, M. J. V., & Jenkins, H. (in press). Low self-esteem. In J. Bennett-Levy, D. Westbrook, G. Butler, A. Hackmann, M. Mueller, & M. J. V. Fennell (Eds.), *The Oxford handbook of behavioural experiments*. Oxford: Oxford University Press.

Freeman, A., & Padesky, C. A. (1994). Schema change processes in cognitive therapy. *Clinical Psychology and Psychotherapy, 1*, 267–278.

Salkovskis, P. M. (1991). The importance of behaviour in the maintenance of anxiety and panic: A cognitive account. *Behavioural Psychotherapy, 19*, 16–19.

Young, J. E., Klosko, J. S., & Weishaar, M. E. (2003). *Schema therapy: A practitioners' guide*. New York: Guilford Press.

RECOMMENDED READINGS

Treatment for low self-esteem draws on established ideas and interventions widely described in the clinical literature. In addition to these classics, the following more specialized texts may be of use.

Fennell, M. J. V. (1997). Low self-esteem: A cognitive perspective. *Behavioral & Cognitive Psychotherapy, 25*, 1–25.

Fennell, M. J. V. (1998). Low self-esteem. In N. Tarrier, A. Wells, & G. Haddock (Eds.), *Treating complex cases: The cognitive behaviour therapy approach* (pp. 217–240). New York: Wiley.

Fennell, M. J. V. (1999). *Overcoming low self-esteem*. London: Constable Robinson.

Fennell, M. J. V., & Jenkins, H. (in press). Low self-esteem. In J. Bennett-Levy, D. Westbrook, G. Butler, A. Hackmann, M. Mueller, & M. J. V. Fennell (Eds.), *The Oxford handbook of behavioural experiments*. Oxford: Oxford University Press.

McKay, M., & Fanning, P. (1992). *Self-esteem* (2nd ed.). Oakland, CA: New Harbinger.

M

Medically Unexplained Symptoms

Elizabeth R. Lombardo and Arthur M. Nezu

Keywords: medically unexplained symptoms, chronic fatigue syndrome, fibromyalgia, noncardiac chest pain

Numerous studies have demonstrated that the majority of physical complaints presented to physicians are actually unexplained from a medical perspective (Nezu, Nezu, & Lombardo, 2001). Whereas eight common physical complaints (fatigue, backache, headache, dizziness, chest pain, dyspnea, abdominal pain, anxiety) account for more than 80 million physician visits annually in the United States, only 25% of these symptoms have a demonstrable organic cause (Lipsitt, 1996). "Medically unexplained symptoms" (MUS) refers to physical complaints for which there is no known medical, biological, or psychological etiology (i.e., not part of a psychiatric diagnosis). Such symptoms have similarities in that they are not caused by an identifiable pathology (e.g., disease), substance (e.g., toxins, drugs), or psychiatric disorder (e.g., heart palpitations in panic disorder). Furthermore, they are often chronic in nature with prolonged adverse effects on the individual's social, occupational, and physical functioning. Statistically, such symptoms are predominantly experienced by women. Individuals with MUS are often firmly committed to the belief that such physical symptoms are caused by biological factors.

Diagnostically, there is a diversity of labels for various MUS. In fact, the name applied can often depend on the specialty of the diagnosing physician. Because the criteria for somatization disorder are somewhat stringent, investigators have recently proposed additional diagnostic terms, such as "abridged somatization" (Escobar, Waitzkin, Silver, Gara, & Holman, 1998), which only requires experiencing 4 (for men) or 6 (for women) symptoms out of a list of 35. This is in contrast to having at least 8 physical symptoms of certain types (e.g., pain versus gastrointestinal), the requirement for the diagnosis of somatization disorder. Wessely, Nimnuan, and Sharpe (1999), using the term "functional somatic symptoms" as the umbrella for somatization, somatoform disorders, and unexplained medical symptoms, suggest that the similarities among these various disorders and phenomena actually outweigh the differences. As such, they recommend that a dimensional classification be adopted that focuses on the number of symptoms and their duration, associated mood disturbance, the patients' attributions for the symptoms, and identifiable physiological processes.

Regardless of the diagnostic label, and despite their high prevalence, conventional medical treatments for MUS are generally ineffective (Nezu et al., 2001). Such patients are high utilizers of medical care, often going from doctor to doctor, trying different medical or surgical procedures in an attempt to "be cured" with little success. This often leads to frustration by the patient, the patient's support system, and health care providers.

Coinciding with their high prevalence and health care usage, MUS are also quite costly. Health care costs for people with such physical complaints are almost 10 times greater than those of the average patient. Ten percent of primary care patients account for almost one-third of outpatient primary care visits, one-half of hospital days, one-half of specialty visits, and one-quarter of prescriptions (Katon et al., 1990). In addition, given the associated functional morbidity, work production is significantly decreased.

CBT CONCEPTUALIZATION OF MUS

MUS can be conceptualized from a biopsychosocial framework when considering the reciprocal interplay among the physical symptoms and various psychological and social variables (Nezu et al., 2001). *Physical symptoms* involve a wide variety of complaints including dizziness, pain, shortness of breath, muscle tension, fatigue, and gastrointestinal problems. The initial expression of these physical symptoms can be caused by a variety of factors including system breakdown, physical or psychological stress, fatigue, or injury.

Major psychological variables that serve to exacerbate and maintain such symptoms include cognitions, emotions, and behaviors. *Cognitive variables* that may be functionally related to such physical symptoms include negative appraisals (e.g., "there is nothing I can do") and catastrophic thinking (e.g., "because I can't work like I used to, I can't do anything"). For example, a sense of uncontrollability over one's pain and disability can lead to negative mood and maladaptive behaviors (e.g., avoidance), which perpetuates functional limitations, as well as emotional and physical distress. In addition, catastrophic thinking has been found to predict disability in persons with MUS. Medical attributions for the symptoms (e.g., "because I feel pain, there must be something wrong medically") and selective attention to the physical complaints can further exacerbate the physical symptoms. Individuals with MUS are more likely to express an external locus of control, holding the belief that medical professionals are the only people who can help them. Such maladaptive cognitions can further adversely influence emotions (e.g., negative affect), behaviors (e.g., more "doctor-shopping," avoiding activity), and physical symptoms (e.g., deconditioning secondary to inactivity).

Emotions such as anxiety, depression, hopelessness, and helplessness may prevail. Such negative affect may exacerbate maladaptive cognitions and behaviors, as well as physical symptoms. *Behaviors* that may influence MUS include attempts to decrease the symptoms (e.g., increased medical visits, inactivity) and avoidance of their impact (e.g., suppressing unpleasant thoughts, using illicit substances). Inactivity, by itself, can perpetuate physical symptoms by promoting deconditioning, resulting in greater physical symptoms (e.g., muscle tension or aches).

Additional relevant psychological variables include coping, personality, and history of abuse. For example, avoidant coping has been found to predict greater fatigue and functional impairment in patients with fibromyalgia. Research has also demonstrated that *thought suppression*, as a means of coping with painful thoughts, is related to chronic physical symptoms. Regarding personality, there is a higher rate of personality disorders and neuroticism, with lower incidence of extraversion, among persons with MUS as compared to the general public. Finally, it appears that people with a history of sexual abuse are at increased risk for developing MUS.

Finally, *social variables* may play an important role in maintaining MUS. Specifically, reactions from others about both the patients' symptoms (e.g., pampering the "sick" patient) and symptoms in general (e.g., perpetuating the belief that their etiology is medical, modeling how to cope with physical symptoms) can propagate maladaptive cognitions and behaviors, or even the symptoms themselves.

CBT INTERVENTIONS FOR MUS

The term "medically unexplained symptoms" is a catchall phrase that includes a wide variety of physical complaints. Certain constellations of symptoms have been grouped together and classified as functional syndromes (e.g., fibromyalgia). This article focuses on treatment studies of MUS and certain related functional syndromes, including chronic fatigue syndrome, fibromyalgia, and noncardiac chest pain.

CBT for MUS

CBT approaches have been applied to patients with MUS where the presenting complaints include dizziness, pain, fatigue, and gastrointestinal discomfort. In these investigations, CBT protocols have incorporated a range of techniques, including relaxation training, cognitive restructuring, coping skills training, assertiveness training, visualization, and the use of behavioral experiments (e.g., "testing assumptions" regarding various health beliefs). In most of these studies, patients are provided with a treatment rationale focusing on a biopsychosocial model (e.g., relationship between stress, physical symptoms, and coping skills).

Overall, with regard to patients experiencing MUS, CBT has been found to be effective in decreasing their physical and psychological complaints, as well as enhancing their overall social functioning. CBT-related financial benefits have also been identified: Kashner, Rost, Cohen, Anderson, and Smith (1995) found a 52% net savings in costs due to decreased health care utilization following treatment.

In reviewing this literature, two important findings should be highlighted: (a) frequency of therapy was significantly related to improvement rates and (b) adopting a biopsychosocial rationale regarding the etiopathogenesis of the MUS also corresponded with better outcomes.

CBT for Chronic Fatigue Syndrome

Chronic fatigue syndrome (CFS) involves disabling fatigue lasting greater than 6 months with ensuing reduction of daily activities to less than 50% below premorbid level. Rest does not significantly improve the fatigue. Other symptoms include muscle and joint pain, headache, low-grade fever, sore throat, muscle weakness, poor concentration, and sleep disturbance. The interpretation that such symptoms are medical in origin and unrelated to psychological factors is common in patients with CFS, as well as their family members.

CBT studies on CFS have assessed a wide variety of treatment components including relaxation training, cognitive restructuring, graded activity, and coping skills training. Results of these studies indicate significant improvement in CFS symptoms, psychological distress, activity level, and functional abilities following CBT. In a review of diverse treatments for CFS (e.g., pharmacological and nonpharmacological), CBT, in particular graded activity training, was identified as being the most effective (Whiting et al., 2001).

In evaluating the beneficial components of CBT for CFS, it appears that strategies concentrating on *changing* thoughts and behaviors (e.g., cognitive restructuring, graded activity, and problem-solving strategies) resulted in better outcomes than strategies "accommodating" to the physical symptoms (e.g., relaxation training) (Nezu et al., 2001). It may be that certain characteristics are associated with differential outcomes. For example, it has been hypothesized that there are two different types of individuals with CFS. One group entails low-functioning individuals who have an overwhelming fear of symptom exacerbation, while another group of patients is higher functioning and does not display such intense fears. Preliminary data demonstrate the former group benefits greatly from graded activity-oriented CBT, while the latter group benefits more from CBT strategies that focus on coping skills training. Similar to those investigations focused on patients with a range of MUS, the conviction that CFS symptoms are due to a biological cause served to hinder the benefits of CBT (e.g., Deale, Chalder, & Wessely, 1998).

CBT for Fibromyalgia

Fibromyalgia syndrome (FMS) is a musculoskeletal disorder characterized by widespread pain for at least 3 months, with muscle and connective tissue stiffness. There is increased pain sensitivity to palpation of at least 11 out of 18 tender points throughout the body (e.g., back, neck, shoulders). FMS is pervasive, with 3–6 million Americans suffering from this disorder. Furthermore, FMS symptoms tend to be chronic in nature and resistant to medical treatment.

CBT has been applied to this patient group in the form of a range of interventions including education, biofeedback, cognitive restructuring, and graded activity. Collectively, CBT appears to engender significant improvements in both psychological (e.g., emotional distress, self-efficacy beliefs) and physical (e.g., pain, tender points, physical condition) symptoms, as well as patients' overall quality of life. A recent meta-analysis found that CBT interventions are more efficacious than medications for FMS symptoms (Rossy et al., 1999).

CBT for Noncardiac Chest Pain

Noncardiac chest pain (NCCP) refers to persistent chest pain without an identifiable cardiac (e.g., ischemic disease) or psychiatric (e.g., chest pain related to panic disorder) etiology. Over 50% of patients referred to cardiology clinics have chest pain with no positive medical findings or known medical problems (e.g., mitrovalve prolapse). Symptoms often endure with about 75% of NCCP patients reporting continued chest pain at a 1-year follow-up.

Persons with NCCP are more likely to have psychiatric problems than either the general public or those with organic chest pain. Certain psychological factors appear to influence NCCP. For example, a psychiatric history and continually attributing the chest pain to cardiac problems generally sustain NCCP symptoms. Furthermore, patients with NCCP are more likely to be characterized by poor coping strategies (e.g., catastrophizing) when experiencing chest pain as compared to patients with other heart problems, such as coronary heart disease.

CBT interventions for this group have included education regarding noncardiac alternative explanations of chest pain, changing irrational beliefs, relaxation and breathing training, and graded activity. Positive treatment outcomes include reduced chest pain (up to 50% reporting no pain), activity limitation, and emotional distress (e.g., depressive symptoms and anxiety), as compared to control participants. Medication usage also appears to decrease following CBT.

Interestingly, treatment outcomes do not appear to be affected by the presence of an anxiety disorder. This finding is weighty because persons with NCCP and panic disorder are more disabled than those without panic disorder. However, certain cognitive variables do appear to influence treatment outcome. For example, developing appropriate beliefs about nonorganic causes of the chest pain is significantly related to reductions in chest pain (e.g., van Peski-Oosterbaan, Spinover, Van der Does, Bruschke, & Rooijmans, 1999). Conversely, patients who maintained the belief that they had organic heart disease had significantly fewer pain-free days per week and lower energy levels. In addition, even if cognitive changes did not result in reduced chest pain, anxiety and activity limitation demonstrated improvement. Overall, the research literature regarding CBT for NCCP suggests that providing credible nonorganic explanations for chest pain, assisting one's coping with the symptoms, and modifying attitudes toward symptoms are important treatment components for persons with NCCP.

CONCLUSIONS AND FUTURE DIRECTIONS

Overall, although only a limited number of well-controlled outcome studies are available (see Nezu et al., 2001), the available research does underscore the significant potential of CBT as an efficacious treatment approach for MUS and related functional disorders (i.e., chronic fatigue syndrome, fibromyalgia, and noncardiac chest pain). Specifically, CBT has demonstrated benefits in significantly improving the physical symptoms and psychological health of these patients.

While physical and psychological improvements have been supported, further research regarding CBT is needed. Given the vast personal, medical, and financial impact of MUS, additional empirical investigations are needed to gain a better understanding of what components of CBT are most effective. In addition, identifying the specific mechanism of action, as well as moderators and mediators of treatment, is important. Interventions should be geared not only for acute treatment, but also with regard to maintenance and prevention issues within different contexts (e.g., primary care office, bibliotherapy). Finally, given the ever-increasing rise in health care costs, economic effects of CBT should continue to be evaluated.

See also: Biopsychosocial treatment of pain, Chronic pain, Somatization

REFERENCES

Deale, A., Chalder, T., Marks, I., & Wessely, S. (1997). Cognitive behavior therapy for chronic fatigue syndrome: A randomized controlled trial. *American Journal of Psychiatry, 154*, 408–414.

Escobar, J. I., Waitzkin, H., Silver, R. C., Gara, M., & Holman, A. (1998). Abridged somatization: A study in primary care. *Psychosomatic Medicine, 60*, 466–472.

Kashner, T. M., Rost, K., Cohen, B., Anderson, M., & Smith, G. R. (1995). Enhancing the health of somatization disorder patients. *Psychosomatics, 36*, 462–470.

Katon, W., Von Korff, M., Lin, E. H. B., et al. (1990). Distressed high utilizers of medical care: DSM-III-R diagnoses and treatment needs. *General Hospital Psychiatry, 12*, 355–362.

Lipsitt, D. R. (1996). Primary care of the somatizing patient: A collaborative model. *Hospital Practice, 31*, 77–88.

Nezu, A. M., Nezu, C. M., & Lombardo, E. R. (2001). Cognitive–behavior therapy for medically unexplained symptoms: A critical review of the treatment literature. *Behavior Therapy, 32*, 537–583.

Rossy L. A., Buckelew, S. P., Dorr, N., Hagglund, K. J., Thayer, J. F., McIntosh, M. J. et al. (1999). A meta-analysis of fibromyalgia treatment interventions. *Annals of Behavioral Medicine, 21*, 180–191.

van Peski-Oosterbaan, A. S., Spinover, P., Van der Does, A. J., Bruschke, A. V. G., & Rooijmans, H. G. M. (1999). Cognitive change following cognitive behavioural therapy for noncardiac chest pain. *Psychotherapy and Psychosomatics, 68*, 214–220.

Wessely, S., Nimnuan, C., & Sharpe, M. (1999). Functional somatic syndromes: One or many? *Lancet, 354*, 936–939.

Whiting, P., Bagnall, A. M., Sowden, A. J., Cornell, J. E., Mulrow, C. D., & Ramirez, G. (2001). Interventions for the treatment and management of chronic fatigue syndrome: A systematic review. *JAMA, 286*, 1360–1368.

RECOMMENDED READINGS

Katon, W. J., & Walker, E. A. (1998). Medically unexplained symptoms in primary care. *Journal of Clinical Psychiatry, 59*, 15–21.

Looper, K. J., & Kirmayer, L. J. (2002). Behavioral medicine approaches to somatoform disorders. *Journal of Consulting and Clinical Psychology, 70*, 810–827.

Mayou, R., Bass, C., & Sharpe, M. (1995). *Treatment of functional somatic symptoms*. New York: Oxford University Press.

Mental Retardation—Adult

Christine Maguth Nezu and Michelle A. Peacock

Keywords: cognitive–behavior therapy, behavior therapy, mental retardation, developmental disabilities, dual diagnosis

Compared to the general population, individuals with mental retardation are at increased risk for developing behavioral, psychological, and emotional disorders. Characteristics associated with mental retardation such as deficits in social–cognitive processing ability and communication skills may negatively influence their ability to cope with stress and increase their vulnerability to developing psychopathology. Environmental factors often experienced by individuals with mental retardation that may also contribute to the development of psychopathology include poor learning opportunities, transient living situations, and staff turnover.

Until the nineteenth century, mental illness and mental retardation were treated as similar conditions, scientific interest being focused on mental illness with little attention directed toward patients with dual diagnosis (Nezu, Nezu, & Gill-Weiss, 1992). Despite the increased need for mental health services for this population during the normalization and integration movements in the 1970s, scientific recognition of co-occurring mental illness in persons with mental retardation did not occur until the 1980s. Despite this recognition, patients with mental retardation continue to be excluded from scientific studies that investigate the effectiveness of treatments for many psychological disorders (Nezu & Nezu, 1994).

People with mild to moderate mental retardation experience the same mental illnesses as the general population, although the manifestation of psychopathology may present somewhat differently as a function of the severity of the developmental disability (Nezu et al., 1992). Some mental disorders co-occur more frequently with mental retardation including personality disorders, severe behavior disorders, depression, and anxiety disorders (Nezu et al., 1992). Although a variety of cognitive–behavioral treatment strategies have been applied to address these disorders in nonhandicapped populations, methodologically rigorous studies designed to investigate the efficacy of psychotherapy in persons with mental retardation are lacking.

Diagnosing a mental disorder in a patient with mental retardation is frequently complicated by deficits associated with developmental disabilities (e.g., speech impediments). Mental health professionals often lack professional training in mental retardation and hold a common misperception that patients with mental retardation are immune to psychopathology (Nezu & Nezu, 1994). Studies have demonstrated that clinicians tend to make biased judgments about psychiatric symptoms in patients with mental retardation attributing the symptoms to the mental retardation rather than the mental illness (Jopp & Keys, 2001). When this phenomenon of *diagnostic overshadowing* occurs, patients with mental retardation do not receive the services and treatment they need to improve their symptoms. In addition, these biases and misconceptions have resulted in the lack of "scientific attention to discovering and verifying effective outpatient treatments for developmentally disabled populations" (Nezu & Nezu, 1994, p. 34).

Prout and Nowak-Drabik (2003) reviewed 92 outcome studies conducted over a 30-year period that examined psychotherapy applied to persons with mental retardation and found only nine studies that met standard criteria for a meta-analysis. The meta-analysis results of these nine studies indicated that a variety of psychotherapeutic interventions (e.g., group, individual, skills training) provided moderate benefits and produced moderate changes in patients with mental retardation. Exploratory analyses revealed that techniques demonstrating the greatest degree of change tended to be interventions provided in individual therapy, clinic-based treatment settings, and treatments with a behavioral orientation. Based on overall findings, the authors noted that clinicians should consider psychotherapy for patients with mental retardation more often than is currently the practice.

COGNITIVE-BEHAVIORAL THERAPY (CBT)

In 2000 (Rush & Frances, 2000), practical clinical guidelines based on expert consensus and relevant research for treating persons with mental retardation suffering from major mental disorders were developed to assist clinicians in treatment decision making. Applied behavior analysis, managing the environment, and client and family education were the most highly recommended psychosocial treatments for many disorders including autism, attention-deficit/hyperactivity disorder, conduct disorder, substance abuse and substance dependence, as well as target symptoms such as self-injurious behavior, aggression, and pica. CBT (e.g., anger management, assertiveness training, conflict resolution) was recommended as a first-line option for major depressive disorder, posttraumatic stress disorder, obsessive–compulsive disorder, and symptoms of anxiety. CBT was also recommended as a second-line option for bipolar disorder (manic phase), schizophrenia and other psychotic disorders, generalized anxiety disorder, conduct disorder, substance abuse or dependence, and adjustment disorder.

Operant Procedures

Treatment strategies based on the principles of operant conditioning include token economies, time out from reinforcements, differential reinforcement schedules, extinction, and overcorrection. These strategies have been effectively utilized to treat a wide range of disorders in patients with mental retardation such as eating disorders, anxiety disorders, depression, phobias, self-injurious behaviors, and aggression (Nezu & Nezu, 1994). For example, reinforcement (e.g., small prize) for attending weight loss meetings as well as losing weight was successfully used as one component of a self-monitoring behavioral weight loss program (Fox, Haniotes, & Rotatori, 1984).

Operant procedures are frequently used as part of multicomponent treatment strategies. For example, verbal reinforcement for socially appropriate statements was implemented as part of a social skills training protocol aimed at improving interpersonal functioning among mentally retarded adults (Matson & Senatore, 1981). Social reinforcement is often utilized as an additional learning strategy in conjunction with other treatment procedures such as assertiveness training (e.g., Nezu, Nezu, & Arean, 1991), relaxation training (e.g., Calamari, Geist, & Shahbazian, 1987), and social problem-solving training (Nezu et al., 1991).

Respondent-Based Procedures

Interventions based on respondent or classical conditioning procedures have also been found to be effective in the treatment of a variety of symptoms and disorders including decreasing avoidant behaviors, aggressive behaviors, and disruptive behaviors in persons with profound to mild mental retardation. For example, Calamari et al. (1987) investigated the efficacy of a progressive muscle relaxation training procedure combined with auditory electromyographic (EMG) feedback, modeling, and reinforcement procedures in comparison to a control group among developmentally disabled persons. Their results indicated that people with developmental disabilities learn to relax and benefit from a multicomponent relaxation training intervention, regardless of their level of intellectual and adaptive functioning (i.e., participants ranging from profound to mild range of mental retardation benefited).

Social Learning Approaches

Social learning strategies have been demonstrated as effective approaches for decreasing psychiatric symptoms and maladaptive behavior, as well as improving interpersonal skills and overall quality of life in persons with mental retardation (Nezu & Nezu, 1994). These interventions include social skills training, assertiveness training, problem-solving training, modeling, and self-reinforcement. Matson and Senatore (1981) compared the effects of social skills training, which involved techniques such as modeling and role-playing, to traditional psychotherapy and no treatment in outpatients with mild to moderate mental retardation. The results suggested that social skills training aimed at specific target behaviors was more effective than traditional psychotherapy or a no-treatment control condition for enhancing interpersonal functioning. Some reduction in performance was revealed at a 3-month follow-up, suggesting the need for maintenance therapy to sustain treatment gains.

Nezu et al. (1991) empirically investigated the effects of two cognitive–behavioral interventions, social problem-solving training and assertiveness skills training, in 28 adults with mild mental retardation and co-occurring mental illnesses. Diagnoses in addition to mental retardation consisted of anxiety disorder, schizophrenia, intermittent explosive disorder, adjustment disorder, and various personality disorders. Participants were randomly assigned to one of the following three conditions: (1) 5 weeks of problem-solving training followed by 5 weeks of assertiveness skills training, (2) 5 weeks of assertiveness skills training followed by 5 weeks of problem-solving training, or (3) a wait-list control condition. In comparison to the wait-list control group, at 5 weeks and posttreatment, participants in both treatment groups demonstrated significant reductions in aggressive behavior, psychiatric symptomatology, and feelings of distress. In addition, results revealed increases in assertiveness skills, problem-solving skills, and adaptive behavior.

Other studies have found positive results that focus on skills that enhance interpersonal functioning. For example, in comparison to a wait-list control group, participants with moderate to borderline mental retardation who received social skills training with an emphasis on dating skills demonstrated improvement in heterosocial interactions and social-sexual knowledge (Valenti-Hein, Yarnold, & Mueser, 1994). The results of this study, however, did not reveal reductions in social anxiety. Mildly mentally retarded adults have also benefited from assertiveness training provided in a group setting that consisting of focused instructions, modeling, behavioral rehearsal, and response feedback (Gentile & Jenkins, 1980). The results indicated increased use of appropriate verbal responses (i.e., making requests and refusing unreasonable requests).

Social learning treatment approaches have also been demonstrated to be effective in weight reduction programs for adults with mental retardation. For example, Fox et al. (1984) produced significant weight loss in adults with mental retardation through a behavioral weight loss program that included self-control strategies such as modeling, self-monitoring involving pictorial stimuli, self-reinforcement, increased physical activity, and reduction of food intake.

CBT FOR OFFENDERS WITH INTELLECTUAL DISABILITIES

Although empirical investigations are limited, cognitive–behavioral interventions for the treatment of offenders with intellectual disabilities are posited as potentially effective approaches in reducing recidivism rates. Barron, Hassiotis, and Banes (2002) in their review of the literature found evidence for the effectiveness of group cognitive therapy with social skills training in reducing anger and aggression, as well as reducing recidivism rates, in low-risk sex offenders with mild intellectual disabilities. Covert sensitization, a cognitive technique involving imagery based on operant and classical conditioning as well as observational learning, was successfully used as part of a multicomponent intervention strategy in the treatment of a fire setter (Clare, Murphy, Cox, & Chaplin as cited in Barron et al., 2002). Similar to other subgroups of persons with mental retardation, there is a dearth of empirical investigations that examine psychotherapeutic treatments for offenders with developmental disabilities

SUMMARY

Our review of the current literature indicates that cognitive–behavioral interventions are effective in the treatment of co-occurring mental disorders and several behavioral disorders, as well as improving the quality of life among persons with developmental disabilities. CBT for offenders with intellectual deficits is promising but in need of further investigation. In addition to improving emotional well-being and decreasing maladaptive behaviors, data suggest that individuals with mental retardation benefit from the acquisition of social skills and problem-solving skills as a means to cope with stress, thereby decreasing their vulnerability to psychopathology and ultimately enhancing quality of life.

Although treatment plans for patients with mental retardation typically employ behavioral techniques, the literature suggests that traditional psychotherapy techniques such as individual therapy and cognitive therapy can be effective as well (Prout & Nowak-Drabik, 2003). Prout and Nowak-Drabik note that the success of psychotherapeutic interventions with this population will likely require modification of traditional techniques to match the developmental level of the patient with mental retardation, such as providing information and instructions in a concrete manner (e.g., Nezu et al., 1991).

Despite the increased awareness of the need for quality research in this area, the current literature base continues to consist mostly of case studies. Future research examining the benefits of psychotherapeutic interventions for persons with developmental disabilities needs to employ empirical investigations with methodologically rigorous designs (e.g., control or comparison groups, random assignment).

See also: Developmental disabilities in community settings

REFERENCES

Barron, P., Hassiotis, A., & Banes, J. (2002). Offenders with intellectual disability: The size of the problem and the therapeutic outcomes. *Journal of Intellectual Disability Research, 46*(6), 454–463.

Calamari, J. E., Geist, G. O., & Shahbazian, M. J. (1987). Evaluation of multiple component relaxation training with developmentally disabled persons. *Research in Developmental Disabilities, 8*, 55–70.

Fox, R. A., Haniotes, H., & Rotatori, A. (1984). A streamlined weight loss program for moderately retarded adults in a sheltered workshop setting. *Applied Research in Mental Retardation, 5*, 69–79.

Gentile, C., & Jenkins, J. O. (1980). Assertiveness training with mildly mentally retarded persons. *Mental Retardation, 18*, 315–317.

Jopp, D. A., & Keys, C. B. (2001). Diagnostic overshadowing reviewed and reconsidered. *American Journal on Mental Retardation, 106*(5), 416–433.

Matson, J. L., & Senatore, V. (1981). A comparison of traditional psychotherapy and social skills training for improving interpersonal functioning of mentally retarded adults. *Behavior Therapy, 12*, 369–382.

Nezu, C. M., & Nezu, A. M. (1994). Outpatient psychotherapy for adults with mental retardation and concomitant psychopathology: Research and clinical imperatives. *Journal of Consulting and Clinical Psychology, 62*(1), 34–42.

Nezu, C. M., Nezu, A. M., & Arean, P. (1991). Assertiveness and problem-solving training for mildly mentally retarded persons with dual diagnosis. *Research in Developmental Disabilities, 12*, 371–386.

Nezu, C. M., Nezu, A. M., & Gill-Weiss, M. J. (1992). *Psychopathology in persons with mental retardation: Clinical guidelines for assessment and treatment*. Champaign, IL: Research Press.

Prout, H. T., & Nowak-Drabik, K. M. (2003). Psychotherapy with persons who have mental retardation: An evaluation of effectiveness. *American Journal of Mental Retardation, 108*(2), 82–93.

Rush, A. J., & Frances, A. (Eds.). (2000). Expert consensus guideline series: Treatment of psychiatric and behavioral problems in mental retardation. *American Journal on Mental Retardation, 105*(3), 168.

Valenti-Hein, D. C., Yarnold, P. R., & Mueser, K. T. (1994). Evaluation of the dating skills program for improving heterosocial interactions in people with mental retardation. *Behavior Modification, 18*(1), 32–46.

RECOMMENDED READINGS

Bregman, S. (1984). Assertiveness training for mentally retarded adults. *Mental Retardation, 22*, 12–16.

Fisher, E. (1986). Behavioral weight reduction program for mentally retarded adult females. *Perceptual and Motor Skills, 62*, 359–362.

LaGreca, A. M., Stone, W. L., & Bell, C. R. (1983). Facilitating the vocational–interpersonal skills of mentally retarded individuals. *American Journal of Mental Deficiency, 88*(3), 270–278.

Lindsay, W. R. (2002). Integration of recent reviews on offenders with intellectual disabilities. *Journal of Applied Research in Intellectual Disabilities, 15*, 111–119.

Models of Violent Behavior

George F. Ronan and Jennifer A. Slezak

Keywords: violence, models, assessment of risk factors

A variety of constructs can be subsumed under the heading of violence. For instance, emotional abuse, verbal aggression, and physical attacks are sometimes viewed as reflecting different types of violence. The use of an all-inclusive definition makes a brief review of the findings imprudent. For the purposes of this review, violence has been defined as an illegal act that entailed a deliberate attack on another. The expectation is that the attack resulted in, or could have resulted in, physical damage.

Attempts to predict violence have a relatively long history. Initial debates involved comparing the result of actuarial versus clinical predictions. These debates gave way to current findings of increased accuracy when predictions are derived from a combination of actuarial and clinical data. Nonetheless, estimating the risk of violent behavior remains a complex task and requires the relative weighting of a host of static and dynamic factors. Static factors include age at first episode of violence, comorbid psychiatric conditions, employment and relationship instability, evidence of early maladjustment, noncompliance with prior court-ordered conditions, past violent behavior, psychopathy, and other relatively stable factors. Dynamic factors include access to victims and weapons, behavioral and emotional instability, disordered personality states, lack of insight and/or realistic plans for the future, poor social support and poor supervision, and other relatively changeable factors. Some research has found that decisions based on a combination of static and dynamic factors result in a reasonable degree of accuracy when predicting violent behavior (see Douglas & Kropp, 2002).

MODELS OF VIOLENCE

One commonly accepted cognitive–behavioral model emphasizes the importance of distinguishing between affective and predatory aggression (see Sandoval & Edens, 1999). Affective aggression, which is preceded by intense emotional arousal, is described as reactive or hostile. Predatory aggression, also called proactive or instrumental aggression, is characterized by the use of aggression to achieve a goal. Violence is expected when the individual perceives a benefit, albeit short-term, from engaging in such behavior. Another commonly accepted cognitive–behavioral model conceptualizes anger as interacting with external events, cognitive processes, and behavioral reactions to increase the likelihood of violent responding (see Watt & Howells, 1999). Both of these popular models of violence require the identification of risk factors.

Cognitive–behavioral approaches for quantifying risk factors incorporate both actuarial and clinical information, which is subsequently organized into biological, personal, and environmental components. Relevant biological aspects often predispose individuals toward responding in a violent manner. For instance, some individuals evince a quick and intense emotional reaction to stressful situations. Other biological predispositions include being male, lower intelligence, and the abuse of psychoactive substances. Personal factors often include comorbid psychiatric conditions, poor impulse control, and distorted perceptions of motivations for behavior emitted by self and others (e.g., inflammatory thinking, hostile attributions). Skill deficits related to violent responding include poor communication, conflict management, and social problem-solving skills. Environmental factors include general psychosocial stressors and stimuli unique to the particular case (e.g., access to weapons, provocation). The identification and quantification of risk factors is essential for the accurate modeling of future violent behavior.

FORMATS FOR ASSESSING RISK FACTORS

Various formats exist for collecting information relevant to the assessment of risk for future violence. These methods include the use of self-report, collateral contacts, and the systematic direct observation of behavior under analogue and real-life situations. Self-report information may be collected using paper-and-pencil measures or interviews. Various paper-and-pencil measures exist to measure personal variables such as anger, self-control, and problem-solving skills. Structured or semistructured interviews can be utilized to collect demographic information, as well as to assess history of violence, present functioning, and the presence of destabilizing influences. An advantage to using interviews over paper-and-pencil measures is that interviews allow the examiner to immediately probe ambiguous answers and to follow up on responses that elicit concern. Several structured interviews have been developed to assess factors relevant to developing a model for predicting subsequent violent behavior (e.g., Douglas, Ogloff, Nicholls, & Grant, 1999).

Because violence is typically viewed as socially unacceptable, respondents can be motivated to present themselves in a less negative light by minimizing the frequency and intensity of past violent acts. Thus, the collection of collateral information is necessary to form a robust understanding of the client's propensity to use violence. A reasonable model for predicting future violence needs to account for situations where self-report information contradicts information gleaned from collateral contacts. Behavioral observations employing either analogue or real-life situations can help to gauge skills for dealing with high-risk situations. Commonly assessed processes include confrontation management skills, skills for managing level of arousal, and problem-solving skills that can be used to manage frustrating situations.

Developing an efficacious model for predicting violence requires considering a large number of variables across a variety of assessment formats, and this typically requires considerable time and effort. Partially for these reasons some have argued for a stepped approach (e.g., Miller, 2000). The first phase involves the identification and screening of critical biological, personal, and environmental factors related to an increased risk of harm. The second phase consists of conducting a detailed analysis of the identified high-risk areas. Results can subsequently be organized into static factors that are unlikely to change and dynamic factors that are likely to change. Following this process can lead to the development of a model of risk for future violence that remains sensitive to changing conditions. Steadman (2000) defined risk level as a statement indicating the likelihood that individual characteristics, history, and environmental factors will interact to produce violent behavior within a specific context. Regardless of the procedure followed, the final model should provide an indication of the probability of violence, as well as an indication of the likely type and severity of violence.

Questions remain with regard to how to weight the information collected. This question calls forth the debate between the use of clinical and actuarial methods. The clinical assessment of risk requires weighting variables using clinical judgment to specify level of risk. The actuarial approach assigns weights according to empirically established formulas for risk prediction. Difficulties with the use of both methods have been cited. Critics of the actuarial method argue that formulas for risk prediction contain methodological weaknesses, such as weak predictor and criterion variables (Wang & Diamond, 1999). Critics of the clinical method argue that clinicians often ignore base rates of violence, rely on salient cues, and engage in confirmatory and hindsight biases, which leads to an overestimation of the accuracy of a prediction (Elbogen, 2002).

The lack of available actuarial formulas for predicting violence is a major problem. Furthermore, effective actuarial methods should take into account base rates, suggesting that formulas for risk prediction need to be developed separately for specific populations in specific areas. Therefore, assessing risk for violence continues to require clinical judgment, using actuarial methods whenever possible to aid in the clinical decision-making process.

Violence continues to be a low-frequency, high-amplitude behavior. The relatively low frequency of within-individual occurrence makes model development difficult. Although research has uncovered both static and dynamic factors that predict future violent behavior, few studies have addressed how best to weight these factors. The major area in need of additional study is research on the optimal weighting of factors related to future violence. Both retrospective and prospective research are needed.

SUMMARY

Cognitive–behavioral researchers have identified a plethora of dynamic and static risk factors to consider when assessing violence risk potential. These factors may be assessed with self-report measures, interviews, collateral contacts, behavioral observations, and analogue procedures. Assessment for violence risk is a lengthy process, with some arguing for a two-step approach that involves screening questions followed by the collection of more detailed information in areas of identified risk. Integration of the information collected is essential and raises the difficulty of the optimal means of weighting and combining the information. Two general methods for combining information are available: clinical and actuarial methods. Use of either method contains drawbacks, and there is current support for supplementing clinical decision making with actuarial methods.

See also: Adolescent aggression and anger management, Anger—adult, Anger control problems

REFERENCES

Douglas, K. S., & Kropp, P. R. (2002). A prevention-based paradigm for violence risk assessment: Clinical and research applications. *Criminal Justice and Behavior, 29*, 617–658.

Douglas, K. S., Ogloff, J. R. P., Nicholls, T. L., & Grant, I. (1999). Assessing risk for violence among psychiatric patients: The HCR-20 violence risk assessment scheme and the Psychopathy Checklist: Screening Version. *Journal of Consulting and Clinical Psychology, 67*, 917–930.

Elbogen, E. B. (2002). The process of violence risk assessment: A review of descriptive research. *Aggression and Violent Behavior, 7*, 591–604.

Miller, M. C. (2000). A model for the assessment of violence. *Harvard Review of Psychiatry, 7*, 299–304.

Sandoval, A. R., & Edens, J. F. (1999). Assessment and treatment of violent offenders in criminal justice settings. In L. Vandecreek & T. L. Jackson (Eds.), *Innovations in clinical practice: A source book* (vol. 17, pp. 355–375). Sarasota, FL: Professional Resource Press/Professional Resource Exchange.

Steadman, H. J. (2000). From dangerousness to risk assessment of community violence: Taking stock at the turn of the century. *The Journal of the American Academy of Psychiatry and the Law, 28*(3), 265–271.

Wang, E. W., & Diamond, P. M. (1999). Empirically identifying factors related to violence risk in corrections. *Behavioral Sciences and the Law, 17*, 377–389.

Watt, B. D., & Howells, K. (1999). Skills training for aggression control: Evaluation of an anger management programme for violent offenders. *Legal and Criminological Psychology, 4*, 285–300.

RECOMMENDED READINGS

The following articles summarize considerations and criteria for conducting risk assessments or evaluating risk management.

VandeCreek, L., & Knapp, S. (2000). Risk management and life-threatening patient behaviors. *Journal of Clinical Psychology, 56*, 1335–1351.

Webster, C. D., Hucker, S. J., & Bloom, H. (2002). Transcending the actuarial versus clinical polemic in assessing risk for violence. *Criminal Justice and Behavior, 29*, 659–665.

Mood Disorders–Bipolar Disorder

Jan Scott

Keywords: cognitive therapy, bipolar disorders, manic depression

Until recently, bipolar disorders (BP) were widely regarded as a biological illness that should be treated with medication (Scott, 1995a). This view is gradually changing for two reasons. First, in the past three decades, there has been a greater emphasis on stress-vulnerability models. This has led to the development of new etiological theories of severe mental disorders that emphasize psychosocial and particularly cognitive aspects of vulnerability and risk and also increased the acceptance of cognitive therapy (CT) as an adjunct to medication for individuals with treatment-resistant schizophrenia and severe and chronic depressive disorders (Scott, 2003). Second, although medication is the mainstay of treatment in BP, there is a significant efficacy–effectiveness gap. Mood stabilizer prophylaxis protects about 60% of individuals against relapse in research settings, but protects only 25–40% of individuals against further episodes in clinical settings (Scott & Tacchi, 2002). The introduction of newer medications has not improved clinical or social outcomes for individuals with BP. This has also led to an increased interest in other treatment approaches.

This section gives an overview of CT for individuals with BP and reviews the randomized controlled treatment trials (RCTs) published to date.

BRIEF OVERVIEW OF COGNITIVE THERAPY

An optimal course of CT begins with a cognitive formulation of the individual's unique problems related to BP, particularly emphasizing the role of core maladaptive beliefs (such as excessive perfectionism, unrealistic expectations for social approval) that underpin and dictate the content of dysfunctional automatic thoughts and drive patterns of behavior. This formulation dictates which interventions are employed with a particular individual and at what stage of therapy that approach is used. Although each individual will define a specific set of problems, Basco and Rush (1995), Lam, Jones, Hayward, and Bright (1999), Newman, Leahy, Beck, Reilly-Harrington, and Gyulia (2001), and Scott (2000) have identified several common themes that arise in CT for patients with BP. These are summarized in Table 1.

At the first CT session, the parents are encouraged to tell their stories and to identify problem areas through the use of a life chart to map their own history of BP episodes and ongoing issues or events in their life related to such episodes. Current difficulties are then discussed and classified under three broad headings: intrapersonal (e.g., low self-esteem, cognitive processing biases), interpersonal (e.g., lack of social network), and basic problems (e.g., symptom severity, difficulties coping with work). These issues are explored in about 20–25 sessions of CT that are held weekly until about week 15 and then with gradually reducing frequency. The last two sessions are offered at about week 32 and week 40. These "booster sessions" are used to review the skills and techniques learned. The overall CT program comprises four stages.

A. Socialization into the CT model and development of an individualized formulation and treatment goals. Therapy begins with an exploration of the patient's understanding of BP and a detailed discussion of previous BP episodes focusing on identification of prodromal signs, events or stressors associated with onset of previous episodes, typical cognitive and behavioral concomitants of both manic and depressive episodes, and an exploration of interpersonal functioning (e.g., family interactions). Early sessions include development of an understanding of key issues identified in the life chart, education about BP, facilitation of adjustment to the disorder by identifying and challenging negative automatic thoughts, and developing behavioral experiments particularly focused on ideas about stigmatization and fragile self-esteem. Other sessions include collating accurate infor-

Table 1. Common Themes Arising in Cognitive Therapy of Bipolar Disorders

CT may be used to facilitate adjustment to the disorder and its treatment

1. Enhance medication adherence
2. Improve self-esteem and self-image
3. Reduce maladaptive or high-risk behaviors
4. Recognize and modify psychobiosocial factors that destabilize the individual's day-to-day functioning and mood state
5. Help the individual recognize and manage psychosocial stressors and interpersonal problems
6. Teach strategies to cope with the symptoms of depression, hypomania, and any cognitive and behavioral problems
7. Teach early recognition of relapse symptoms and develop effective coping techniques
8. Identify and modify dysfunctional automatic thoughts (negative or positive), and underlying maladaptive beliefs
9. Improve self-management through homework assignments

mation and enhancing the client's understanding of treatment approaches and prognosis of BP, and beginning to develop an individualized formulation of the patient's problems, which takes into account underlying maladaptive beliefs.

B. Cognitive and behavioral approaches to symptom management and dysfunctional automatic thoughts. Using information gathered previously, sessions are used to help people learn self-monitoring and self-regulation techniques, which enhance self-management of depressive and hypomanic symptoms, and to explore skills for coping with depression and mania. For example, this involves establishing regular activity patterns, daily routines, regular sleep patterns, developing coping skills, time management, use of support, and recognizing and tackling dysfunctional automatic thoughts about self, world, and future using thought diaries.

C. Dealing with cognitive and behavioral barriers to treatment adherence and modifying maladaptive beliefs. Problems with adherence to medication and other aspects of treatment are tackled, e.g., through exploration of barriers (challenging negative automatic thoughts about "drugs make me worse"; excessive self-reliance; or exploring attitudes to authority and control) and using behavioral and cognitive techniques to enhance treatment adherence (Scott & Tacchi, 2002). This and data from previous sessions are used to help the client identify maladaptive assumptions and underlying core beliefs and to commence work on modifying these beliefs.

D. Antirelapse techniques and belief modification. Further work is undertaken on recognition of early signs of relapse and coping techniques. For example, developing self-monitoring of symptoms, identifying characteristic prodromal features (the "relapse signature"), developing a list of "at-risk situations" (e.g., exposure to situations that activate specific personal beliefs), high-risk behaviors (e.g., increased alcohol intake), combined with a hierarchy of coping strategies for each; identifying strategies for managing medication intake and obtaining advice regarding it; and planning how to cope and self-manage problems after discharge from CT. Sessions also include typical CT approaches to the modification of maladaptive beliefs, which may otherwise increase vulnerability to relapse.

OUTCOME STUDIES OF CT FOR BP

Encouraging single case reports, case series, and open or nonrandomized studies (e.g., Scott, 1995b; Zaretsky, Segal, & Gemar, 1999) suggested benefits from the use of CT as an adjunct to standard treatments, with individuals reporting improvements in medication adherence, reductions in manic and depressive symptoms, and, where measured, improvements in psychosocial functioning. There are five published RCTs of CT for individuals with BP (Cochran, 1984; Lam et al., 2000, 2003; Perry, Tarrier, Morriss, McCarthy, & Limb, 1999; Scott, Garland, & Moorhead, 2001) and the data from the largest multicenter RCT (n = 250) are now completed (Scott, personal communication). The RCTs reviewed are divided into those that used cognitive and behavioral techniques and those that employed a more typical case formulation-based CT approach.

1. Studies Using Cognitive and Behavioral Techniques

The aim of Cochran's study was to add CT to standard clinical care in order to enhance adherence with prophylactic lithium treatment. It compared 28 clients who were randomly assigned to six sessions of group CT plus standard clinical care or to standard clinical care alone (Cochran, 1984). Following treatment, enhanced lithium adherence was reported in the intervention group with only three patients (21%) discontinuing medication as compared with eight patients (57%) in the standard clinical care group. There were also fewer hospitalizations in the group receiving CT.

Perry et al. (1999) used cognitive and behavioral techniques to help people identify and manage early warning signs of relapse in clients at high risk of further relapse of BP who were in regular contact with mental health services. The results demonstrated that, in comparison to the control group (n = 34), the intervention group (n = 35) had significantly fewer manic relapses (27% versus 57%), significantly fewer days in hospital, significantly longer time to first manic relapse, higher levels of social functioning, and better work performance. However, the most intriguing finding was that the intervention did not have a significant impact on depression. The possible reasons for this have been discussed elsewhere (Scott, 2003).

2. Studies Using Cognitive Therapy

Scott et al. (2001) examined the effect of 20 sessions of CT in clients with BP. Clients (n = 42) were initially randomly allocated to the intervention group or to a "waiting list" control group, the latter group receiving CT after a 6-month delay. The randomized phase (6 months) allowed assessment of the effects of CT plus usual treatment versus usual treatment alone. Individuals from both groups who received CT were then monitored for a further 12 months post-CT. At initial assessment, 30% (n = 17) of participants met criteria for a current BP episode; 12 subjects also met criteria for drug and/or alcohol problems or dependence, 2 met criteria for other Axis I disorders, and about 60% of the sample met criteria for personality disorder. The results of the randomized controlled phase demonstrated that, compared with subjects receiving treatment as usual, those who received additional CT experienced statistically significant improvements in symptom levels, global functioning, and work and social adjustment. Those receiving CT demonstrated a 60% reduction in relapse rates in the 18 months after commencing CT as compared with the 18 months prior to receiving CT. Hospitalization rates showed parallel reductions. Scott et al. concluded that CT plus treatment as usual may offer some benefit and is a highly acceptable treatment intervention for about 70% of clients with BP.

Lam and colleagues (Lam, Jones, Hayward & Bright, 1999). undertook a small randomized controlled study of 12–20 sessions of outpatient CT for BP. Twenty-five subjects were randomly allocated to individual CT as an adjunct to mood-stabilizing medication or to usual treatment alone (mood stabilizers plus outpatient support). Independent assessments demonstrated that, after controlling for gender and illness history, the intervention group had significantly fewer BP relapses than the control group and a number of improvements in health and social functioning. These findings have now been replicated in a large-scale RCT ($n = 103$). Lam et al. (2003) found that, in comparison to the control group, individuals who received CT survived longer until their first relapse (adjusted hazard ratio 0.4; $p < 0.02$), had significantly fewer episodes of BP overall, had lower mean levels and less variability in depressive symptoms, experienced fewer hospitalizations, demonstrated higher social functioning, and better adherence with medication. The proportion of patients experiencing a relapse over 1 year was 44% in the CBT group and 75% in the control group. The CBT group was also significantly better at coping with manic prodromes at 6- and 12-month follow-up.

SUMMARY

Research into CT for individuals with BP is at an early stage. There is preliminary evidence that cognitive factors may influence vulnerability to BP relapse. The events associated with the onset of BP depression have many similarities to those linked with unipolar depression. Mania may arise in association with negative life events such as bereavement, but also after events that disrupt an individual's day-to-day social rhythms, following the sudden cessation of mood-stabilizing medication, or subsequent to goal attainment life events (Johnson & Miller, 1995). These may disrupt circadian rhythms, which in turn destablize mood and may lead to shifts in cognition. However, it should be remembered that cognitive style will also directly influence why individuals stop taking their medication, how meaningful their loss is to them specifically, and the unique causal attributions they make about any prodromal symptoms they experience and how they react to or cope with the early warning signs of impending relapse. As such, even if there is at present no specific and unique cognitive model of BP, the use of CT plus medication may together be a more fruitful approach than either treatment alone.

A review of the available RCTs suggests that brief interventions that utilize a fixed set of cognitive and behavioral strategies can be used to enhance medication adherence or to improve self-management of early warning signs of relapse. As demonstrated by Lam's and Scott's groups, there is also a role for CT in BP to utilize an individualized cognitive case conceptualization approach that provides a coherent and integrated understanding of the individual, their cognitive style and general coping behaviors, their adjustment to BP, and the risk factors for relapse. Scott and colleagues particularly target beliefs about social desirability, perfectionism, and autonomy. The evidence so far suggests that this triad may be important in individuals with BP. Lam and co-workers targeted similar constructs, namely, dysfunctional beliefs that are characterized by a "hyperpositive" sense of self and an excessive desire for personal goal attainment. These RCTs suggest a more classical CT approach is highly beneficial to individuals with BP, but may work best for those who begin treatment when euthymic and who have less complex or fewer comorbid disorders. Scott et al. (2001) conclude that CT for individuals with BP is often more complex than for unipolar disorders, requiring more flexibility and greater expertise on the part of the therapist. Finally, it is noteworthy that CT may be particularly beneficial in treating BP depression. It is ironic that, despite few differences in cognitive style between unipolar and BP depression, individuals with BP have always been excluded from treatment studies of depression. While modification of the CT protocol may be needed for BP depression, it is possible that CT will become a crucial alternative to antidepressant medication for this difficult-to-treat clinical condition. Large-scale trials of BP depression are warranted. Such research also affords an opportunity to further explore cognitive models of depression and the similarities and differences between individuals with unipolar and BP disorders.

See also: Bipolar disorder, Depression—adult

REFERENCES

Basco, M., & Rush, J. (1995). *Cognitive behaviour therapy for bipolar disorder*. New York: Guilford Press.

Cochran, S. (1984). Preventing medical non-adherence in the outpatient treatment of bipolar affective disorder. *Journal of Consulting and Clinical Psychology*, *52*, 873–878.

Johnson, S., & Miller, I. (1995). Negative life events and time to recovery from episodes of bipolar disorder. *Journal of Abnormal Psychology*, *106*, 449–457.

Lam, D. H., Bright, J., Jones, S., Hayward, P., Schuck, N., Chisolm, D., & Sham, P. (2000). Cognitive therapy for bipolar illness—A pilot study of relapse prevention. *Cognitive Therapy and Research, 24*(5), 503–520.

Lam, D. H., Jones, S., Hayward, P., & Bright, J. (1999). *Cognitive therapy for bipolar disorder*. New York: Wiley.

Lam, D. H., Watkins, E. R., Hayward, P., Bright, J., Wright, K., Kerr, N., Parr-Davis, G., & Sham, P. (2003). A randomized controlled study of cognitive therapy for relapse prevention for bipolar affective disorder: Outcome of the first year. *Archives of General Psychiatry, 60*, 145–152.

Newman, C., Leahy, R., Beck, A. T., Reilly-Harrington, N., & Gyulia, L. (2001). *Bipolar disorders: A cognitive therapy approach*. Washington, DC: American Psychological Association.

Perry, A., Tarrier, N., Morriss, R., McCarthy, E., & Limb, K. (1999). Randomized controlled trial of efficacy of teaching patients with bipolar disorder to identify early symptoms of relapse and obtain treatment. *British Medical Journal, 318*, 149–153.

Scott, J. (1995a). Psychotherapy for dipolar disorder: an unmet need? *British Journal of Psychiatry, 167*, 581–588.

Scott, J. (1995b). Cognitive therapy for clients with bipolar disorder : A case example. *Cognitive & Behavioural Practice, 3*, 1–23.

Scott, J. (2000). *Overcoming mood swings*. London: Constable & Robinson.

Scott, J. (2003). Treatment outcome studies. In S. Johnson & R. Leahy (Eds.), *Psychological approaches to bipolar disorders*. New York: Guilford Press.

Scott, J., Garland, A., & Moorhead, S. (2001). A pilot study of cognitive therapy in bipolar disorder. *Psychological Medicine, 31*, 459–467.

Scott, J., & Tacchi, M. (2002). A pilot study of concordance therapy for individuals with bipolar disorders who are non-adherent with lithium prophylaxis. *Journal of Bipolar Disorders, 4*, 386–392.

Zaretsky, A. E., Segal, Z. V., & Gemar, M. (1999). Cognitive therapy for bipolar disorder: A pilot study. *Canadian Journal of Psychiatry—Revue Canadienne de Psychiatrie, 44*, 491–494.

Motivational Interviewing

Frederick Rotgers

Keywords: motivating change, addictions, alcoholism, drug abuse, treatment facilitation, stages of change

Motivational interviewing (MI) is an approach to working with clients to reduce resistance to behavior change. It was developed initially in the early 1980s by William R. Miller at the University of New Mexico. In its earliest form (Miller, 1983), MI was designed as part of a feedback and informational session with problem drinkers that aimed at stimulating natural processes of change and movement from early stages of change as described by Prochaska, DiClemente, and Norcross (1992) (i.e., precontemplation/contemplation) into active behavior change. Subsequently, Miller joined with South African psychologist Stephen Rollnick (now at the University of Wales) to produce what has become a seminal volume in the behavior change motivation literature: *Motivational Interviewing: Preparing People to Change Addictive Behavior* (1991). In a recently published second edition (Miller & Rollnick, 2002), MI's thrust has been broadened from addictions to a variety of behaviors and populations traditionally considered difficult to change. These include adolescents, couples, criminal justice clients, patients in health care settings, patients who are noncompliant with medication, and patients who are dually diagnosed with addictive and mental health problems.

THEORETICAL FOUNDATIONS AND CONCEPTS

MI is grounded in the work of Rogers (1951) on therapeutic alliance and relationship, in work on the social psychology of persuasive communication (Brehm & Brehm, 1981), and decision-making (Janis & Mann, 1977).

While sometimes linked with Prochaska and DiClemente's Transtheoretical or "Stages of Change" Model (Prochaska et al., 1992), MI developed separately from that model, despite being quite consistent with it.

Consistent with these theoretical foundations, MI, in its broadest sense, has several defining tenets: (1) Clients are the sole agents of their own change. Personal autonomy (Ryan & Deci, 2000) is not only recognized but explicitly fostered in MI. Clients are also viewed as being the ultimate determiners of their own actions. The MI therapist is seen as a partner in helping clients develop cognitive maps of their behavior and change that will facilitate a healthier, more satisfying lifestyle, as the client defines it. (2) Client resistance to change is best seen as ambivalence with regard to change, particularly behaviors that are inherently reinforcing (such as substance use). In order for change to occur, ambivalence must be resolved in the direction of new behaviors. (3) Therapists do not produce change directly. Rather the therapist creates a climate within which change is welcomed, facilitated, and in which clients can make the decisions necessary to produce change. (4) Change is recognized as usually being incremental, rather than precipitous, and the therapist in MI encourages even small movements in a healthier direction. (5) The way in which the therapist interacts with the client is crucial to stimulating this process of self-reflection, ambivalence resolution, and decision-making. Therapist behaviors that are confrontational, instructional in a didactic or pedantic fashion, or that are demanding of specific changes are all to be avoided. Effective therapist behavior is marked by empathetic reflection of client concerns and values, acceptance of the client as an autonomous person, a gentle direction to focus on the client's own ambivalence, and an invitation to the client to consider alternatives to current behavior. MI therapists avoid labeling clients, or defining problems for them. Rather, the client's views of his/her current life situation, values, and future goals are accepted as the basis for initiation of behavior change.

Within MI, change is presumed to be a result of a process of cognitive restructuring based in decision-making. MI also draws on the affective valence of possible behavior changes and their consequences, as well as on the affective valence for the client of remaining unchanged. The MI therapist attempts to create conditions that foster a client's full consideration of options, restructuring of cognitions with respect to the likelihood of reaching important personal goals without change, and a restructuring of the client's view of possible new, healthier behavior. Integrated into this process are attempts by the therapist to elicit from the client his/her own strongly held values, and to stimulate the natural change processes believed to be inherent in all individuals. In this sense, MI can be considered to fall within the family of cognitive–behavioral interventions, while still retaining a strong link to Rogerian therapy.

MI TECHNIQUE

According to MI theory, change promotion is best accomplished by systematic implementation of what Miller and Rollnick (2002) call the "four basic principles" of MI: (1) express empathy (through the use of a variety of reflective listening techniques), (2) develop discrepancy (between current status and desired outcomes in the context of the client's personal values), (3) roll with resistance (rather than confronting or attempting to break through it), and (4) support self-efficacy (by fostering the view that even small changes are good, and that there is hope of effecting even larger changes over time). In their writings, Miller and colleagues (Miller & Rollnick, 1991, 2002; Miller, 1999; Miller, Zweben, DiClemente, & Rychtarik, 1992) have provided detailed protocols for therapists built around these four basic principles. Central to the MI process, however, is the skill of empathetic reflective listening. It is this skill that is the focus of virtually all MI training and implementation protocols.

Beyond the four priniciples, Rollnick and colleagues (Rollnick, Mason, & Butler, 1999) have developed a tripartite model of enhancing motivation for change that focuses on (1) the *importance* to the client of changing the target behavior, (2) the *readiness* of the client to implement the change process, and (3) the *confidence* of the client that he/she can effectively implement changes in the desired fashion. Using cognitive scaling techniques, clients are asked to rate themselves on a subjective 10-point Likert scale, with 1 being Low (Importance, Readiness, or Confidence) and 10 being High (Importance, Readiness, or Confidence) on each of these dimensions, and then asked to generate ideas about what would need to happen in order for the subjective rating to move closer to the high end of the scale. This cognitive exercise serves to generate potential tactics and strategies for effecting the desired changes.

In all MI interventions, a heavy emphasis is placed on therapist feedback to the client about various aspects of the client's behavior and ambivalence with regard to change. Specific techniques of reflective listening are used to highlight the client's ambivalence in the belief that doing so enhances change. The use of these reflective listening techniques allows the therapist to be selective in what he/she reflects, and thereby become more directive than would be the case in more traditional Rogerian therapy. For example, by selectively reflecting client verbalizations pointing toward change (what Miller and Rollnick, 2002, call "change talk") the therapist socially reinforces the client for producing those verbalizations and focuses client attention on the possibility and desirability of change.

USES OF MI

MI or adaptations (Burke, Arkowitz, & Dunn, 2002) have been used both as a stand-alone intervention and as a means of preparing clients to effectively engage in treatments that are distinct from MI itself. Much of the original work on MI focused on brief interventions for problem drinkers in which a very short (often no more than 10–15 minutes) interaction, using the MI principles described above, was used to prompt change in alcohol use. MI has also been the core of stand-alone interventions such as the Motivational Enhancement Therapy developed to treat alcohol-dependent persons for the National Institute of Alcohol Abuse and Alcoholism's Project MATCH (Miller et al., 1992). As a generic approach, MI can be used as a precursor to a variety of more specific, and theoretically distinct, behavior change approaches. For example, with the substance abuse treatment arena, MI has been used as precursor to cognitive–behavioral, 12-step, and therapeutic community treatments, which often bear little or no resemblance to MI itself. Rollnick and colleagues (2002) have characterized these diverse uses of MI and MI adaptations as falling into three categories, proceeding from shorter and opportunistic brief advice, to more extensive behavior change counseling, and finally, extensive MI proper, which includes both brief advice and behavior change counseling. MI proper focuses much more on helping clients articulate deeply held values and integrating them into the behavior change process than do the two briefer categories of intervention.

RESEARCH ON MI

Despite its widespread use with clients who show a range of problem behaviors, as of this writing there have been no controlled studies of MI as originally set forth by Miller and Rollnick (Burke et al., 2002). Nonetheless, there have been many studies of both brief and extended interventions in which what Burke et al. have termed "Adapted MI" (AMI) have been studied. Almost uniformly, MI or AMI approaches have outperformed no-treatment controls, and often other specific interventions, in producing both statistically and clinically significant behavior changes (Burke et al., 2002). As a stand-alone treatment, a 4-session AMI (the Motivational Enhancement Therapy of Project MATCH) has been shown to be as effective as two 12-session manualized treatments (cognitive–behavioral treatment and 12-Step Facilitation) for alcohol dependence (Project MATCH Research Group, 1997).

CRITICISMS OF MI

Given its emergence primarily within the often contentious field of substance abuse treatment, there have been no substantive criticisms of the MI approach to date (W. R. Miller, personal communication, February 19, 2003). While research on MI as a stand-alone treatment is lacking, research on AMI approaches has been consistent in supporting the general MI approach as an effective means of promoting behavior change, particularly with resistant clients. Further, there has been little examination, beyond theoretical writings, of the actual processes that produce change in MI. Of course, this is a problem that is not specific to MI, but characterizes cognitive–behavioral and other behavior change methods as well. Finally, MI's theoretical base needs more systematic articulation. Miller and Rollnick's seminal writings are focused much more on technical aspects of MI than on the development of a theoretical superstructure with which to describe both the process and technique by which MI produces enhanced motivation for change.

FUTURE DIRECTIONS

The development of a consistent, coherent theoretical basis for MI is an important need. There are growing bodies of work on motivation and the causes of behavior (Gollwitzer & Bargh, 1996; Ryan & Deci, 2000) that could provide such a basis, but little work has appeared in this area as of this writing.

In addition to a more complete articulation of the theoretical mechanisms behind MI, research is needed that delineates the specific active ingredients necessary for MI to be effective. There is some suggestion in the research literature that therapist effects are highly prominent in producing change through MI, and this needs further investigation (Burke et al., 2002). The link between MI technique and specific changes in client affect, cognition, and behavior also needs to be more clearly articulated through research.

See also: Addictive behavior—nonsubstance abuse, Addictive behavior—substance abuse, Couples therapy—substance abuse, Pathological gambling, Relapse prevention, Stages of change

REFERENCES

Brehm, S. S., & Brehm, J. W. (1981). *Psychological reactance: A theory of freedom and control*. New York: Academic Press.

Burke, B. L., Arkowitz, H., & Dunn, C. (2002). The efficacy of motivational interviewing and its adaptations: What we know so far. In W. R. Miller & S. Rollnick (Eds.), *Motivational interviewing: Preparing people to change* (2nd ed., pp. 217–250). New York: Guilford Press.

Gollwitzer, P. M., & Bargh, J. A. (1996). *The psychology of action: Linking cognition and motivation to behavior*. New York: Guilford Press.

Janis, I. L., & Mann, L. (1977). *Decision-making: A psychological analysis of conflict, choice and commitment*. New York: Free Press.

Miller, W. R. (1983). Motivational interviewing with problem drinkers. *Behavioural Psychotherapy, 11*, 147–172.

Miller, W. R. (Ed.). (1999). *Enhancing motivation for change in substance abuse treatment* (Treatment Improvement Protocol [TIP] Series No. 35). Rockville, MD: Center for Substance Abuse Treatment.

Miller, W. R., & Rollnick, S. (1991). *Motivational interviewing: Preparing people to change addictive behavior*. New York: Guilford Press.

Miller, W. R., & Rollnick, S. (2002). *Motivational interviewing: Preparing people to change* (2nd ed.). New York: Guilford Press.

Miller, W. R., Zweben, A., DiClemente, C. C., & Rychtarik, R. (1992). *Motivational enhancement therapy manual: A clinical research guide for therapists treating individuals with alcohol abuse and dependence* (Project MATCH Monograph Series, Vol. 2). Rockville, MD: National Institute on Alcohol Abuse and Alcoholism.

Prochaska, J. O., DiClemente, C. C., & Norcross, J. C. (1992). In search of how people change: Applications to addictive behaviors. *American Psychologist, 47*, 1102–1114.

Project MATCH Research Group. (1997). Matching alcoholism treatments to client heterogeneity: Project MATCH posttreatment drinking outcomes. *Journal of Studies on Alcohol, 58*, 7–29.

Rogers, C. R. (1951). *Client-centered therapy*. Boston: Houghton-Mifflin.

Rollnick, S., Allison, J., Ballasiotes, S., Barth, T., Butler, C. C., Rose, G. S. et al. (2002). Variations on a theme: Motivational interviewing and its adaptations. In W. R. Miller & S. Rollnick (Eds.), *Motivational interviewing: Preparing people to change* (2nd ed., pp. 270–283). New York: Guilford Press.

Rollnick, S., Mason, P., & Butler, C. C. (1999). *Health behavior change: A guide for practitioners*. London: Churchill Livingstone.

Ryan, R. M., & Deci, E. L. (2000). Self-determination theory and the facilitation of intrinsic motivation, social development, and well-being. *American Psychologist, 55*, 68–78.

O

Obesity

Michael G. Perri and Lesley D. Fox

Keywords: obesity, weight loss, weight maintenance, lifestyle intervention, diet and exercise

The past three decades have witnessed a worldwide epidemic of obesity. The prevalence of obesity in the United States has more than doubled during this period, rising from 14.5% in the 1970s to 30.9% in 1999–2000 (Flegal, Carroll, Ogden, & Johnson, 2002). Evidence continues to grow documenting the deleterious impact of excess weight on health and longevity. Obesity has been directly linked to cardiovascular disease, diabetes mellitus, hypertension, dyslipidemia, gallbladder disease, respiratory disease, osteoarthritis, and certain forms of cancer. Body mass index (BMI) is positively associated with premature death, disability, and reduced quality of life (National Heart, Lung, and Blood Institute, 1998). The mortality rates for obese persons are increased by 50 to 100% compared to people with BMIs in the range of 20 to 25, and the number of annual deaths attributable to obesity in the United States has reached 325,000. The total economic costs related to obesity exceed $110 billion, and the direct costs represent about 5.7% of the total health care expenditures in the United States. Furthermore, profound psychological costs often accompany obesity, including social discrimination, personal distress, and decreased emotional well-being. Indeed, the mountain of evidence documenting the rising prevalence of obesity and its detrimental consequences underscores the need for effective treatments.

CBT FOR OBESITY: THE PAST

Cognitive–behavioral therapy (CBT) constitutes the foundation of current lifestyle interventions for weight loss. Early behavioral theorists (e.g., Ferster, Nurnberger, & Levitt, 1962) invoked the principles of operant and classical conditioning to explain how learned patterns of overeating and sedentary behavior produce a positive energy balance and result in an excess accumulation of adipose tissue. From an operant conditioning perspective, overeating is viewed as a behavior largely controlled by immediate positive consequences. The taste of food serves as a powerful positive reinforcer, and the removal of the unpleasant sensation of hunger acts as a negative reinforcer. This combination of reinforcing properties strengthens the eating habit. In terms of classical conditioning, an association develops between the environmental circumstances that precede eating (e.g., mealtimes, the sight of food) and internal stimuli that are perceived as hunger (e.g., predigestive response of stomach motility). The act of eating further strengthens the association between environmental stimuli and the sensation of hunger via operant conditioning, and a variety of noneating stimuli (e.g., negative emotional states) may elicit the perception of hunger and in turn may prompt eating. Thus, the combination of operant and classical conditioning can produce inappropriate stimulus control over eating, thereby resulting in faulty eating patterns, excessive food consumption, and eventually obesity.

The early behavioral formulation postulated that obese persons could be taught to modify their eating habits so as to produce a negative energy balance and to lose weight.

This formulation of obesity and its control represents an oversimplification of the complex biobehavioral processes that regulate body weight (Wadden & Stunkard, 2002). Nonetheless, many of the treatment procedures developed by the early behavioral researchers have become the foundation of modern treatments for obesity. In its earliest form, behavior therapy for obesity generally involved four sets of strategies: (1) self-monitoring of eating, (2) control of the stimuli that elicit eating, (3) modification of the topography of food consumption (e.g., slowing the pace of eating), and (4) reinforcement of appropriate changes in eating patterns.

Since the early 1980s, additional treatment strategies have become routine components of treatment, including cognitive therapy procedures, nutritional training, and exercise. Two key considerations motivated the inclusion of cognitive therapy (Foreyt & Poston, 1998). First, there was the recognition that many obese people engage in negative or self-defeating monologues related to their eating, their physical appearance, and their self-worth. These maladaptive cognitions often result in emotional distress and poor treatment adherence. Second, the problem of weight regain following behavioral treatment heightened the role that cognitive factors play in relapse and suggested the possibility that the inclusion of cognitive strategies could prevent relapse and improve long-term outcome. As a consequence, behavioral treatment of obesity evolved into a comprehensive lifestyle intervention with CBT as its core.

Early treatments were conducted in weekly group sessions over the course of 8 to 12 weeks, and follow-up contacts were limited. Treatment typically produced mean weight losses of 3.8 kg, and weight loss ceased with the conclusion of therapy. As the need for achieving larger weight losses became apparent, interventions became more comprehensive, and the length of initial treatment increased. Moreover, as follow-up studies documented the problem of posttreatment weight regain, CBT programs often included booster sessions or additional periods of follow-up care.

CBT FOR OBESITY: THE PRESENT

More than 150 studies have evaluated the effectiveness of CBT for obesity. Reviews of randomized trials show that comprehensive interventions, typically delivered in 15 to 24 weekly group sessions, produce average weight losses of approximately 8.5 kg (Wadden, Brownell, & Foster, 2002). This amount of weight loss commonly produces clinically significant improvements in selected risk factors for disease (e.g., blood pressure, blood glucose, blood lipids) and beneficial changes in mood and psychological well-being. Indeed, a recent large-scale, randomized controlled trial in overweight persons at risk for diabetes demonstrated that an intensive CBT weight-loss intervention reduced the incidence of diabetes by 58% when compared with a placebo control condition (Diabetes Prevention Program Research Group, 2002).

The clinical significance of weight reductions achieved in CBT is determined by whether or not the weight loss is maintained over the long run. In most studies, treatment is ended by 4–6 months, and participants are commonly followed for an additional 6 to 12 months. By 18 months following study entry, participants maintain only about 50% of their initial weight loss (Perri & Corsica, 2002). Moreover, longer-term follow-ups of 3 to 5 years generally show a gradual but reliable return to pretreatment weights (Kramer, Jeffery, Forster, & Snell, 1989).

The poor maintenance of weight loss stems from a complex interaction of physiological, environmental, and psychological factors (Perri & Corsica, 2002). Physiological factors, such as reduced metabolic rate as a result of dieting, combined with constant exposure to an environment replete with tasty, high-calorie foods, prime the individual for lapses in behavioral control of eating habits acquired in CBT. Most obese persons cannot *on their own* sustain the substantial degree of psychological control needed to cope effectively with this unfriendly combination of environment and biology. A variety of strategies have been implemented to address the maintenance problem, including extended clinical contact, skills training, social support, and increased physical activity. Empirical support is greatest for programs of extended clinical care.

Providing additional treatment following an initial period of CBT improves long-term outcome in weight management. Perri and Corsica (2002) recently reviewed 13 studies of CBT interventions that continued beyond the usual treatment period of 4–6 months. These interventions typically employed an "extended care" program that included continued therapist contacts via additional weekly or biweekly sessions. Collectively, these studies provided 681 participants with a total of 30 to 65 group sessions ($N = 41$ sessions) over the course of 12 to 18 months. The inclusion of a control group (i.e., CBT *without* extended care) in three of the studies allowed a rough comparison between groups receiving the same initial treatment with and without extended care. At the conclusion of the extended treatment period, those groups that received interventions *with* extended contact demonstrated mean net weight losses of 10.3 kg and on average maintained 96% of the weight that they had lost in the initial 4–6 months of treatment. Over approximately the same period of time, those groups that received interventions *without* extended treatment had a mean net loss of 6.6 kg and on average maintained 66% of their initial weight reduction. Ten of the 13 studies included additional follow-up periods without further care. The results of these additional follow-ups conducted on average 21 months after the start of treatment showed that the extended treatment groups demonstrated mean net loss of 8.4 kg (79% of their initial reduction) compared to 3.8 kg (38% of their initial reduction) for the groups without extended contact. Collectively, these findings provide strong evidence that the longer patients remain in CBT, the more likely they are to sustain weight loss.

CBT FOR OBESITY: THE FUTURE

Does the CBT model of obesity require reformulation? Cooper and Fairburn (2002) have agued for the need to reformulate the theory, aims, and procedures used in CBT for obesity. These authors maintain that the problem of poor long-term outcome following CBT for obesity may be attributed to two factors: (a) inattention to the cognitive factors that contribute to weight regain and (b) ambiguity over treatment goals in long-term interventions. They note that long-term failure may be directly related to unrealistic expectations about weight loss and its benefits. Indeed, while CBT commonly produces body weight reductions of 8–10%, obese persons typically enter treatment expecting weight losses of 25–32% (Foster, Wadden, Vogt, & Brewer, 1997). Furthermore, Cooper and Fairburn observe that obese persons also have "personal goals" that they hope weight loss will produce for them, such as dramatically improving physical appearance, enhancing social acceptability, and increasing self-confidence and self-respect. After expending considerable effort in CBT, most participants realize that they will never accomplish their unreasonably high goals for weight and personal change. As a consequence, they devalue the modest but clinically significant changes accomplished in CBT and they lose motivation to sustain their self-management effort.

Cooper and Fairburn (2002) have also noted that most follow-up interventions advocate the "maintenance of weight loss" rather than the "maintenance of weight lost." They argue that long-term success is more likely to occur with a focus on teaching the skills necessary to maintain a stable weight (i.e., "maintenance of lost weight") rather than advocating continuing with a negative energy balance (i.e., "maintenance of weight loss"). Empirical support for efficacy of the reformulated CBT intervention advocated by Cooper and Fairburn awaits the results of a randomized clinical trial currently in progress in the United Kingdom. Nonetheless, their thoughtful analysis reminds researchers that CBT will be most effective when cognitive and behavioral procedures are used to identify and modify the mechanisms directly responsible for maintaining the target problem.

A final challenge facing CBT for obesity entails the need to develop treatment protocols that can be used with underserved populations in real-world settings. Most studies of CBT for obesity have consisted of "efficacy" trials conducted in academic health care settings with highly motivated middle-class volunteers treated by specially trained staff using state-of-the-art protocols. Efficacy studies evaluate the benefits of an intervention under optimal conditions. In contrast, "effectiveness" studies examine the extent to which an intervention is beneficial under "real world" conditions. Research is sorely needed that addresses methods to improve the *effectiveness* of CBT for obesity. In coming years, we must improve our knowledge of ways to treat obesity in underserved populations, particularly economically disadvantaged individuals, persons from ethnic and racial minority groups with high rates of obesity, and individuals who reside in communities with minimal access to preventive health care services.

SUMMARY

Evidence documenting the rising prevalence of obesity and its detrimental health consequences has highlighted the need for effective treatments. CBT for obesity can produce weight reductions of sufficient magnitude to decrease the risk for many diseases. However, the regaining of lost weight remains a significant clinical problem. Providing extended care has shown some benefit in this regard, but more research is needed on methods to enhance the long-term efficacy of CBT for obesity and to improve its effectiveness with underserved populations.

REFERENCES

Cooper, Z., & Fairburn, C. G. (2002). Cognitive–behavioral treatment of obesity. In T. A. Wadden & A. J. Stunkard (Eds.), *Handbook of obesity treatment* (pp. 465–477). New York: Guilford Press.

Diabetes Prevention Program Research Group. (2002). Reduction in the incidence of type 2 diabetes with lifestyle intervention or metformin. *New England Journal of Medicine, 346*, 393–403.

Ferster, C. B., Nurnberger, J. I., & Levitt, E. B. (1962). The control of eating. *Journal of Mathematics, 1*, 87–109.

Flegal, K. M., Carroll, M. D., Ogden, C. L., & Johnson, C. L. (2002). Prevalence and trends in obesity among US adults, 1999–2000. *Journal of the American Medical Association, 288*, 1723–1727.

Foreyt, J. P., & Poston, W. S., II (1998). What is the role of cognitive–behavior therapy in patient management? *Obesity Research, 6*(Suppl. 1), 18–22.

Foster, G. D., Wadden, T. A., Vogt, R. A., & Brewer, G. (1997). What is a reasonable weight loss? Patients' expectations and evaluations of obesity treatment outcomes. *Journal of Consulting and Clinical Psychology, 65*, 79–85.

Kraemer, F. M., Jeffrey, R. W., Forster, J. L., & Snell, M. K. (1989). Long-term follow-up of behavioral treatment for obesity: Patterns of weight regain among men and women. *International Journal of Obesity, 13*, 123–136.

National Heart, Lung, and Blood Institute. (1998). Clinical guidelines on the identification, evaluation, and treatment of overweight and obesity in adults: The evidence report. *Obesity Research, 6*(Suppl.), 51–209.

Perri, M. G., & Corsica, J. A. (2002). Improving the maintenance of weight lost in behavioral treatment of obesity. In T. A. Wadden & A. J. Stunkard (Eds.), *Handbook of obesity treatment* (pp. 357–374). New York: Guilford Press.

Wadden, T. A., Brownell, K. D., & Foster, G. D. (2002). Obesity: Responding to the global epidemic. *Journal of Consulting and Clinical Psychology, 70*, 510–525.

Wadden, T. A., & Stunkard, A. J. (Eds.). (2002). *Handbook of obesity treatment*. New York: Guilford Press.

GLOSSARY

Body mass index (BMI): an indicator of weight-for-height that is commonly used to classify overweight and obesity in adults; it is calculated as weight in kilograms divided by the square of height in meters (kg/m^2)

Desirable or normal weight range: a BMI of 18.5–24.9 kg/m^2

Obesity: a BMI $\geqslant$ 30 kg/m^2

Overweight: a BMI $\geqslant$ 25 kg/m^2

RECOMMENDED READINGS

National Heart, Lung, and Blood Institute. (1998). Clinical guidelines on the identification, evaluation, and treatment of overweight and obesity in adults: The evidence report. *Obesity Research*, *6*(Suppl.), 51–209.

Wadden, T. A., & Stunkard, A. J. (Eds.). (2002). *Handbook of obesity treatment*. New York: Guilford Press.

P

Panic Disorder

Raphael D. Rose, Autumn E. Braddock, and Michelle G. Craske

Keywords: panic disorder, agoraphobia, cognitive–behavioral treatment

Panic disorder (PD) is characterized by recurrent unexpected panic attacks involving intense fear or discomfort peaking within 10 minutes. Symptoms include, but are not limited to, palpitations, sweating, trembling, sensations of shortness of breath, chest pain, nausea, dizziness, derealization, numbness, chills, hot flashes, fear of losing control, and fear of dying. The individual is apprehensive about experiencing another attack, worries about the consequences of the attack, or experiences a significant change in behavior specifically related to the attacks for the minimum duration of 1 month (American Psychiatric Association, 2000).

Panic disorder with agoraphobia (PDA) is characterized by anxiety in and avoidance of situations in which escape or receiving assistance is difficult in the event of a panic attack. Agoraphobic situations commonly include being alone, crowds, movie theaters, unfamiliar places, or traveling (American Psychiatric Association, 2000). Estimates of prevalence suggest that between 2 and 6% of the population experiences PD and/or PDA at some point during their lifetime, with women twice as likely to be afflicted as men (Kessler et al., 1994). Gender differences become more apparent with intensifying levels of agoraphobia (Craske & Barlow, 2001). Typical age of onset is between 15 and 24 years (Craske, 1999). The peak in the hazard rate curve occurs between 15 and 19 years, with the gender difference becoming more pronounced during this period (Burke, Burke, Regier, & Rae, 1990). Although panic attacks represent the acute-onset event for PD, around 50% of individuals diagnosed with PD/PDA report paniclike symptoms before their first panic attack (Craske, 1999). Despite its prevalence and early onset, treatment typically is not sought for several years after symptom onset.

PD/PDA commonly co-occurs with other disorders, namely, specific phobias, social phobia, dysthymic disorder, generalized anxiety disorder, major depressive disorder, and substance abuse (Craske & Barlow, 2001). In addition, it is estimated that between 25 and 60% of individuals diagnosed with PD/PDA meet criteria for a personality disorder, most often avoidant and dependent personality disorders (Chambless & Renneberg, 1988), although reliability of such diagnoses limits the value of these estimates.

Debate exists over the etiology of PD/PDA, but research supports the notion that a fear of bodily sensations is at the root of the disorder. Clark (1986) suggested that individuals with PD/PDA tend to misinterpret bodily sensations as harmful, a notion that is supported by self-report measures of beliefs including the Anxiety Sensitivity Index (ASI; Reiss, Peterson, Gursky, & McNally, 1986) and various other studies of enhanced emotional reactivity to bodily sensations (e.g., Zinbarg & Barlow, 1996). Longitudinal studies of the panic attacks have demonstrated ASI's predictive capabilities, as well (e.g., Ehlers, 1995; Schmidt, Lerew, & Jackson, 1997). Related is the evidence for enhanced attentional awareness to internal physical sensations in individuals with PD (Ehlers & Breuer, 1992), as well as those at risk by virtue of occasional panic attacks (Zoellner & Craske, 1999). Overconcern with bodily sensations is thought to be acquired through direct aversive experiences (e.g., history of significant illness), vicarious observations (e.g., family members who experience anxiety sensitivity), and/or information transmissions (e.g., parental warnings). Genetic contributions to the etiology of PD/PDA appear to be largely nonspecific, shared with the genetic contributions to other anxiety disorders and to neuroticism in general (Kendler, 1995). Thus, the genetic contribution may be tied with the underlying vulnerability of negative affectivity or neuroticism rather than specific symptom profiles of PD.

The first panic attack is often experienced during a period of life stress within an environment where the feared sensations are viewed as dangerous. Environmental exacerbators of the threat appraisal of panic attacks are ones that involve impairment (e.g., driving), entrapment (e.g., air travel), negative social evaluation (e.g., social events), and lack of safety (e.g., novel experiences) (Craske, 1999). Once initial panic attacks are experienced, "fear of fear" is hypothesized to maintain distress and contribute to the disorder where fear of panic-specific bodily sensations develops after the initial panic attack due to interoceptive conditioning (i.e., learned fear of internal sensations through negative associations with panic attacks) and misinterpretations of innocuous physical sensations (e.g., racing heart, dizziness) (Craske, 1999). Subsequent avoidance of bodily sensations and the associated contexts and reliance on safety signals (e.g., traveling with a familiar person, mobile phone, or medication) are assured to maintain distress in the long term (Bouton, Mineka, & Barlow, 2001).

TREATMENT OF PD/PDA

Cognitive behavior therapy (CBT) for PD/PDA usually follows a manualized approach covering 8–12 structured sessions. Typically, treatment involves (1) psychoeducation, (2) breathing retraining, (3) cognitive restructuring, (4) interoceptive exposure, and (5) in vivo (situational) exposures. These intervention strategies address the cognitive, behavioral, and physical components of PD/PDA and are designed to help the individual not fear the bodily sensations associated with PD/PDA. Therapists present information to clients, model techniques, and provide feedback and reinforcement throughout the treatment period. A brief summary of the intervention techniques follows.

Psychoeducation provides patients with information about anxiety, panic, and their physical, cognitive, and behavioral components. This initial information also stresses the adaptive value of anxiety to humans, describes sensations associated with autonomic arousal (fear response) and why those sensations are not indicative of harm. The roles of learned fear responding to bodily sensations, their catastrophic misappraisals, and avoidance in maintaining the disorder are presented and linked with the treatment rationale.

Cognitive restructuring addresses cognitive distortions or errors in thinking such as "catastrophic" misappraisals of somatic sensations (e.g., "I'm having a heart attack," "I'm going crazy"). Individuals are taught techniques to address/correct errors in overestimation of risk (e.g., "I'm lightheaded, therefore I will faint") or predictions of catastrophic outcomes ("I won't be able to face my friends ever again if they see me panicking"). By addressing misappraisals of sensations, individuals with PD/PDA develop new ways of coping and managing with feelings of anxiety. Disconfirmation of misappraisals is achieved through logical empiricism and hypothesis testing experiments that are designed to provide disconfirmatory evidence. Some data indicate that cognitive restructuring alone is an effective treatment for PD/PDA (Margraf, Barlow, Clark, & Telch, 1993).

Breathing retraining instruction helps clients to breathe from their diaphragm rather than from their chest. This technique requires regular practice and is often coupled with cognitive strategies to reinforce the idea that sensations produced during panic are innocuous and manageable. Additionally, applied relaxation techniques such as pleasant imagery, cue-controlled relaxation, and progressive muscle relaxation can be utilized within a CBT program. Since clients are encouraged to learn that symptoms are not harmful (see interoceptive exposure below), they are instructed to use breathing retraining and applied relaxation to address physical feelings of discomfort but *not* out of desperation to avoid or prevent symptoms of anxiety (Schmidt et al., 2000).

Interoceptive exposure helps clients lessen their fear of bodily sensations by repeated and systematic exposure to the sensations. This is accomplished via exercises that induce sensations similar to panic (e.g., hyperventilating, head-shaking, spinning). Typically, interoceptive exposure is conducted in a graduated format (Craske & Barlow, 2001), and proceeds from in-session inductions to more naturalistic activities such as coffee ingestion, exercise, and other naturally activating tasks. Interoceptive exposure alone has been shown to be an effective treatment for some individuals with PD (Griez & van den Hout, 1986); however, it is usually conducted in conjunction with cognitive therapy and represents another way of disconfirming misappraisals of bodily sensations.

In vivo exposures involve repeated systematic exposure in real-life situations (e.g., shopping mall, restaurant, driving). These exercises are conducted in a variety of ways (e.g., self-directed versus therapist directed, massed versus spaced exposure). Real-life exposure helps clients manage and overcome fear and avoidance of agoraphobic situations by deliberately inducing feared bodily sensations in their real-life agoraphobic situations. This experience often provides the individual with new information about his/her ability to tolerate uncomfortable physical sensations in real-life situations and helps disconfirm misappraisals about the danger of those sensations and the perceived inability to cope with them in public. To maximize gains, clients are encouraged to conduct in vivo exposures without relying on safety signals (i.e., anxiety-reducing items such as mobile phones and significant others).

Most often, CBT for PD/PDA takes place in an outpatient clinic-office, primary care suite, or the natural environment. In the former setting, the anxiety management techniques described above are modeled with therapist feedback and reinforcement for the client. To help facilitate generalization to situations where the therapist is not present, self-directed in vivo exposures are encouraged. Clients practice anxiety management skills in "real-life" situations associated with panic so they can learn new information about their ability to manage panic in various situations and to generalize their new learning to as many different contexts as possible and thereby reduce the risk of relapse (Craske & Barlow, 2001).

Research supports the efficacy of group and individual treatment formats for PD/PDA (e.g., Neron, Lacroix, & Chaput, 1995). Groups generally have between three and six participants. Due to therapist–client ratio, financial considerations may render group CBT for PD/PDA the more attractive format (Otto, Pollack, & Maki, 2000).

TREATMENT OUTCOME

Numerous controlled clinical trials have demonstrated both the short- and long-term effectiveness of CBT in treating PD/PDA (see White & Barlow, 2002). For example, a summary of treatment outcome data from several studies revealed that after 11 treatment sessions, 76% of treatment completers were panic-free at posttreatment, and 78% were panic-free at a 2-year follow-up with a 10% dropout rate (Craske & Barlow, 2001). CBT has been associated with larger effect sizes and the lowest levels of attrition compared to drug treatments or integrated interventions using both psychological and drug treatments. Of note, cognitive–behavioral interventions implementing interoceptive exposures yielded the largest reductions in panic symptoms (White & Barlow, 2002).

Interestingly, CBT for PD/PDA yields positive effects on comorbid anxiety and depression disorders. That is, co-occurring anxiety and depression symptoms tend to improve when treating only PD/PDA (Tsao, Mystkowski, Zucker, & Craske, 2002). These data suggest that CBT for PD/PDA teaches skills and techniques that are helpful in addressing other anxiety or mood problems, and/or that the success in managing panic and related anxiety lessens overall emotional reactivity. In addition, co-occurring disorders at baseline may have a limited impact on CBT for PD/PDA, suggesting that baseline depression is not a contraindication for such treatment (e.g., McLean, Woody, Taylor, & Koch, 1998).

FUTURE TRENDS

In sum, CBT for PD/PDA is highly effective for the targeted disorder and perhaps for additional co-occurring problems as well. It is unfortunate, given the impressive treatment outcome findings, that only 15% of patients receive CBT (Goisman et al., 1994). More effective dissemination of highly effective treatments for PD is needed. Technology may help achieve this, as well as training programs in mental health adhering to empirically supported interventions.

Given economic pressures to keep health costs down, different treatment delivery methods have been investigated. As noted, group treatment is an effective and cost-saving format. Research also supports briefer treatments, as well as self-directed treatment (Craske & Zucker, 2001). A potential future treatment delivery medium is the Internet. Due to CBT's cost-effectiveness and efficacy in treating PD/PDA and other anxiety and mood disorders, prevention programs utilizing its techniques could prove useful. Additional research is needed to identify those at risk for developing PD/PDA and make available brief, efficacious, cost-effective treatments to the community.

See also: Exposure therapy

REFERENCES

American Psychiatric Association. (2000). *Diagnostic and statistical manual of mental disorders* (4th ed., text rev.). Washington, DC: Author.

Bouton, M. E., Mineka, S., & Barlow, D. H. (2001). A modern learning theory perspective on the etiology of panic disorder. *Psychological Review, 108*(1), 4–32.

Burke, K., Burke, J. D., Regier, D.A., & Rae, D. S. (1990). Age at onset of selected mental disorders in five community populations. *Archives of General Psychiatry, 47*(6), 511–518.

Chambless, D. L., & Renneberg, B. (1988, September). *Personality disorders of agoraphobics*. Paper presented at the World Congress of Behavior Therapy, Edinburgh, Scotland.

Clark, D. M. (1986). A cognitive approach to panic. *Behavior Research and Therapy, 24*, 461–470.

Craske, M. G. (1999). *Anxiety disorder: Psychological approaches to theory and treatment.* Boulder, CO: Westview Press.

Craske, M. G., & Barlow, D. H. (2001). Panic disorder and agoraphobia. In D. H. Barlow (Ed.), *Clinical handbook of psychological disorders: A step-by-step treatment manual*. New York: Guilford Press.

Craske, M. G., & Zucker, B. G. (2001). Consideration of the APA practice guideline for the treatment of patients with panic disorder: Strengths and limitations for behavior therapy. *Behavior Therapy, 32*(2), 259–281.

Ehlers, A. (1995). A 1-year prospective study of panic attacks: Clinical course and factors associated with maintenance. *Journal of Abnormal Psychology, 104*, 164–172.

Ehlers, A., & Breuer, P. (1992). Increased cardiac awareness in panic disorder. *Journal of Abnormal Psychology, 101*(3), 371–382.

Goisman, R. M., Warshaw, M. G., Peterson, L. G., Rogers, M. P., Cuneo, P., Hunt, M. F., Tomlin-Albanese, J. M., Kazim, A., Gollan, J. K., Epstein-Kaye, T., Reich, J. H., & Keller, M. B. (1994). Panic, agoraphobia, and panic disorder with agoraphobia: Data from a multicenter anxiety disorders study. *Journal of Nervous and Mental Disease, 182*(2), 72–79.

Griez, E., & van den Hout, M. A. (1986). CO_2 inhalation in the treatment of panic attacks. *Behavior Research and Therapy, 24*, 145–150.

Kendler, K. S. (1995). Genetic epidemiology in psychiatry. *Archives of General Psychiatry, 52*, 895–899.

Kessler, R. C., McGonagle, K. A., Zhao, S., Nelson, C. B., Hughes, M., Eshkeman, S., Wittchen, H.U., & Kendler, K. S. (1994). Lifetime and 12 month prevalence of DSM-III-R psychiatric disorders in the United States: Results from the National Comorbidity Study. *Archives of General Psychiatry, 51*, 8–19.

Margrat, J., Barlow, D. H., Clark, D. M., & Telch, M. J., (1993). Psychological treatment of panic: Work in progress on outcome, active ingredients, and follow-up. *Behaviour Research & Therapy, 31*, 1–8.

McLean, P. D., Woody, S. R., Taylor, S., & Koch, W. J. (1998). Comorbid panic disorder and major depression: Implications for cognitive–behavioral therapy. *Journal of Consulting and Clinical Psychology, 66*, 240–247.

Neron, S., Lacroix, D., & Chaput, Y. (1995). Group vs individual cognitive behaviour therapy in panic disorder: An open clinical trial with a six month follow-up. *Canadian Journal of Behavioural Science, 27*, 379–392.

Otto, M. W., Pollack, M. H., & Maki, K. M. (2000). Empirically supported treatments for panic disorder: Costs, benefits, and stepped care. *Journal of Consulting and Clinical Psychology, 68*, 556–563.

Reiss, S., Peterson, R. A., Gursky, D. M., & McNally, R. J. (1986). Anxiety sensitivity, anxiety frequency and the predictions of fearfulness. *Behavior Research and Therapy, 24*, 1–8.

Schmidt, N. B., Lerew, D. R., & Jackson, R. J. (1997). The role of anxiety sensitivity in the pathogenesis of panic: Prospective evaluation of spontaneous panic attacks during acute stress. *Journal of Abnormal Psychology, 106*, 355–364.

Schmidt, N. B., Woolaway-Bickel, K., Trakowski, J., Santiago, H., Storey, J., Koselka, M., & Cook, J. (2000). Dismantling cognitive–behavioral treatment for panic disorder. *Journal of Consulting and Clinical Psychology, 68*, 417–424.

Tsao, J. C., Mystkowski, J., Zucker, B. G., & Craske, M. G. (2002). Effects of cognitive–behavioral therapy for panic disorder on comorbid conditions: Replication and extension. *Behavior Therapy, 33*(4), 493–510.

White, K.S., & Barlow, D. H. (2002). Panic disorder and agoraphobia. In D. H. Barlow (Ed.), *Anxiety and its disorders: The nature and treatment of anxiety and panic* (2nd ed.). New York: Guilford Press.

Zinbarg, R. E., & Barlow, D. H. (1996). Structure of anxiety and the anxiety disorders: A hierarchical model. *Journal of Abnormal Psychology, 105*(2), 181–193.

Zoellner, L. A., & Craske, M. G. (1999). Interoceptive accuracy and panic. *Behaviour Research and Therapy, 37*, 1141–1158.

Paradoxical Intention and Related Techniques

L. Michael Ascher

Keywords: paradoxical intention, Viktor Frankl

Paradoxical intention is one of a number of therapeutic techniques that are subsumed under the label *therapeutic paradox*. Although they are considered to be unconventional, they have been incorporated into some therapeutic programs as a primary method for the establishment of therapeutic change. These procedures are also employed in an ancillary capacity to assist in gaining client cooperation when working with more conventional techniques.

Paradox, in all its forms, is pervasive in literature, and particularly in the literature of psychotherapy. The first to incorporate paradox into a therapeutic system was Alfred Adler. Basing his conception of paradox largely on Hegel's writings on dialectics, he developed a number of more or less specific strategies (Mozdzierz, Macchitelli, & Lisiecki, 1976) that he recommended for therapists' use with power struggles generated by patients during the course of therapy.

In 1925, Viktor Frankl (1967, 1975) began to use the procedure that he subsequently labeled *paradoxical intention*; he employed it as an aid in logotherapy, his existential approach to psychotherapy. Logotherapy aims to assist individuals in their search for the significant meaning of their lives. The recognition and acceptance of the contribution of personal responsibility in the individual's present circumstances is one element in the quest for life's meaning. The technique of paradoxical intention is typically employed to assist individuals to gain a sense of control—particularly with respect to their attitude—under difficult, anxiety-provoking circumstances.

Frankl hypothesized that excessive anxiety, experienced in anticipation of one's performance in frightening situations, operates to increase considerably individuals' general level of anxiety; this serves as a substantial impediment to their behavioral goals. The self-maintaining circular process formed by anticipatory anxiety exacerbates the difficulty.

A simple illustration involves an experienced headwaiter who had successfully carried many trays full of glasses and platters without having thought about the process (and without having dropped a single object). One evening, just prior to opening, the owner conducted a meeting with the younger waiters and drew their attention to the headwaiter as an example of the impeccable behavior that was expected of them. As a result, this waiter began to focus on his tray-carrying performance. He feared making a mistake. He noticed a problem for the first time—slight tremors—that could result in a "disaster." Performance anxiety generated these tremors, which, in turn, intensified the anxiety. The increased anxiety exacerbated the tremors, forming a pernicious circular process.

Paradoxical intention is intended to break this insidious circle. It was suggested to the headwaiter that he practice his tremors, becoming such an expert that he would be invited to model them for clinical psychology students. When the waiter stops "trying" not to have tremors, and instead *intends* his tremors in a motivated fashion, it is assumed that the circular process will have been broken.

Frankl was particularly interested in the enhancing effects of humor as an important component of therapeutic paradox. He would have dramatically described for the waiter the effects of his exaggerated tremors on those who observed them. They might have eventually laughed about the behavior. This would have transformed the tremors from a serious concern to something of somewhat less importance. It was Frankl's understanding that when his patients could exercise the "uniquely human" capacity to experience humor and laugh at their problems, they would have made significant progress in their course of therapy.

Another early contribution to the field of psychotherapeutic paradox is credited to Knight Dunlop (1928, 1930). Initially he focused on simple muscle twitches and tics and utilized a paradoxical procedure that he labeled *negative practice*. Rather than instructing his patients to apply some form of relaxation in opposition to the muscular process, he had them practice the troublesome behavior until it was fatigued and they could no longer emit the tic or twitch.

More recently, strategies classified as therapeutic paradox have been most closely associated with a diverse group of professionals collectively called *communication theorists* (e.g., Bateson, Fisch, Haley, Jackson, Watzlawick, Weakland). They were particularly interested in an aspect of communication that they considered to be a contributing factor in the development of psychogenic schizophrenia. This pathological communication they labeled the *double bind*. In a double bind communication, conflicting requirements place the individual in an inescapable situation that cannot be resolved in a positive manner. A typical example involves a mother who encourages a child to approach her for an exchange of affection. When the child moves toward the mother, she signals—often nonverbally—that actual contact would be unpleasant for her. If the child fails to approach the mother, she expresses her consequent feelings of rejection, possibly with some rancor.

The alternative of the pathogenic double bind is the therapeutic double bind, a constructive form of this communication model. In the therapeutic context, this positive double bind is labeled a *pragmatic paradox*, and is the model for the most common form of paradox used in therapy; it is related to Frankl's paradoxical intention. A typical example of such a paradoxical directive is provided to certain individuals who complain of sleep onset insomnia. They are told, on retiring for the evening, to try to remain awake for as long as possible. This suggestion fulfills the two requirements of all paradoxical procedures. The first is that they are organized around a directive that is surprising.

A surprising suggestion, of course, is one that is contrary to that which is expected. It is this aspect that causes people to laugh at the "punch line" of a joke. Congruent with Frankl's position, this contradiction to expectancy, and to commonly received opinion, has led to the association of paradoxical techniques with humor.

In many cases, clients consult therapists in order to gain assistance in changing troublesome behavior; but they wish to do this in the manner that makes sense to them. Most have developed methods that seem reasonable and bring them, fully formed, to the therapist. Their commitment to their self-directed method of treatment seems both to blind them to its failure, and to motivate them to look for supplementary professional assistance that they are certain will result in success with their method. Thus, these individuals expect therapists to suggest procedures that are congruent with the clients' systems of sleep induction (e.g., one of the many relaxation procedures). It is this attempt at self-treatment to which Watzlawick, Weakland, and Fisch (1974) refer in suggesting that the treatment is the problem.

Thus, the second requirement of the pragmatic paradox incorporated into the directive to remain awake is that which places the individual in a conflict. However, in contrast to the pathogenic double bind that offers the individual only negative solutions, the therapeutic double bind fashions a conflict that must be resolved positively. This is the consequence of individuals being forced to violate the directive in their efforts to obey it, and in obeying it they are fulfilling the central condition of all paradoxical procedures, *to remain unchanged*. This constraint, incidentally, serves to obviate self-treatment and the impediments that it generates.

With some exceptions, each approach to therapeutic paradox incorporates speculation regarding its efficacy. In addition to the hypotheses of Viktor Frankl and the communication theorists, briefly mentioned above, Ascher and Schotte (1999) have employed Wegner's (1994) model of ironic processing to provide an alternative explanation.

Wegner (1994) focused on the process of cognitive control using a bimodal system. He postulated an active, effortful regulator, the "operating" system (OS) that organizes cognitive activity to produce the desired control. A complementary, effortless "monitoring" system (MS) is constantly searching for cognitions that are in conflict with the preferred cognitive state. When the MS detects a cognition that is incompatible with the desired cognitive orientation, it activates the OS to bring the cognition under control. Under most circumstances this process functions smoothly to maintain the desired cognitive condition. However, if the OS is overloaded, as can occur at times of stress or anxiety, the OS may not have the resources sufficient to maintain control, resulting in the unobstructed intrusion of errant thoughts and the breakdown of the desired cognitive state.

Ascher and Schotte (1999) used the example of people with public speaking phobia whose goal is to remain calm during their presentations and endeavor to maintain cognitions that are congruent with this aim (e.g., there is nothing to worry about, these are all my friends). If they experience considerable anxiety in the public speaking context, their OS will not be available to handle the incompatible thoughts that become the focus of the MS (e.g., I am scared to death, what if I lose control while I am presenting). These thoughts will increase in frequency and will serve to support increasing discomfort.

Such individuals, exposed to paradoxical intention, would be instructed to enter the public speaking situation and *try to become anxious* in the idiosyncratic ways that each fears (e.g., try to have tremors, or perspire, or flush). If individuals actually surrender to this directive and act accordingly, then the thoughts that are incompatible with the orientation, and that would become the focus of the MS, would be calming thoughts. These would serve to assist in reducing discomfort and maintaining control. Parallels between paradoxical procedures used in a therapeutic context and those employed in hypnosis have also been a focus of interest by the communication theorists, especially of Jay Haley. His initial observations of Milton Erickson led to several important contributions both to hypnosis and to therapeutic paradox (Erickson, 1977; Haley, 1973).

Although family or systems therapy is most identified with therapeutic paradox (e.g., Weeks & L'Abate, 1982), behavior therapists and cognitive behavior therapists have also been adding procedures to their repertoires that are basically paradoxical in nature. In addition to Dunlop's negative practice and various methods of exposure, the principles of therapeutic paradox can be seen in dialectical behavior therapy (e.g., Shearin & Linehan, 1989), mindfulness, and acceptance and commitment therapy (e.g., Hayes, Stosahl, & Wilson, 1999), among others.

RESEARCH

Until relatively recently, the literature associated with paradoxical intention consisted almost exclusively of uncontrolled case studies (DiTomasso & Greenberg, 1989). Ascher and Efran (1978) published the first controlled investigation of paradoxical intention. Clients whose sleep difficulties remained refractory to a standard 10-week behavior therapy program were included in a study that incorporated a controlled multiple case study design. Their treatment focused on the administration of a paradoxical intention directive to remain awake, under circumstances otherwise optimal for sleep, for as long as possible. After 2 weeks, all of the subjects indicated that they were falling asleep within a satisfactory period of time.

Following Ascher and Efran (1978), the character of the body of literature associated with paradoxical intention began to change; uncontrolled case studies diminished in frequency while controlled case studies and experiments with more sophisticated designs became more prevalent (Ascher, Bowers, & Schotte, 1985). Along with related meta-analyses, these studies generally suggested that paradoxical intention was an effective procedure with a variety of behavioral complaints. Turner and Ascher (1979) presented the first study utilizing the random assignment of subjects to groups in testing the efficacy of paradoxical intention. The design included five groups, two control groups (attention-placebo and waiting-list), and three treatments groups (paradoxical intention, stimulus control, relaxation). Significant differences were only found between the treatment groups when compared with the control groups, suggesting that the paradoxical intention procedure was at least as effective as conventional behavioral approaches in ameliorating sleep onset insomnia. Ascher and Turner (1979a) in a partial replication of Turner and Ascher (1979) confirmed the efficacy of paradoxical intention in reducing latency to sleep onset.

Ascher and Schotte (1999) tested the hypothesis that paradoxical intention was the treatment of choice for difficulties associated with fear-of-fear, or recursive anxiety (Ascher, 1989), but may not be appropriate for behavioral problems that did not incorporate this anxiety complex. The subjects were individuals who clearly did or did not experience recursive anxiety in association with public speaking anxiety; they were randomly assigned to one of four groups in a 2 × 2 design: subjects having simple public speaking phobia were exposed to a standard behavioral treatment program including or excluding paradoxical intention, and subjects with public speaking phobia complicated by recursive anxiety were provided with a standard behavioral treatment program including or excluding paradoxical intention. The results supported the hypothesis that paradoxical intention was an effective treatment for those exhibiting fear-of-fear or recursive anxiety. Those subjects who had a recursive component in their clinical profiles responded significantly better to the treatment program when it included a paradoxical directive than when it did not. In contrast, those with simple public speaking phobia showed significantly greater improvement when the standard behavioral treatment program did not include paradoxical intention. In fact, a paradoxical directive served to significantly impede the performance of subjects in this latter group.

Broomfield and Espie (2003) recently conducted another investigation of paradoxical intention as a treatment for sleep onset insomnia. This study differed in a significant way from previous similar studies in that the authors employed an objective measure of sleep performance. They found that paradoxical intention was effective in reducing two important components of sleep onset insomnia: sleep effort and sleep performance anxiety. Their results were significant when compared to a control group. They suggest, "Together, results help determine putative mechanisms underlying PI have important implications for the clinical application of PI."

FINAL CONSIDERATIONS

A major criticism of paradoxical intention and related procedures is focused on the apparent subterfuge that is sometimes employed in their administration. First, it should be noted that when administered like any conventional behavioral technique, all aspects of the paradoxical procedure and its goals are fully disclosed to the client. However, when used in other contexts (e.g., family therapy), this is not always the case. Then, paradoxical strategies, used to reduce resistance, are presented in a more obscured manner. Naturally, regardless of how the procedure is employed, the concern remains the welfare of the client or clients, and the objective is always the achievement of the therapeutic goal.

Ascher and Turner (1979b) investigated the relative efficacy of these two methods for administering paradoxical intention. They randomly assigned volunteers who complained of clinically significant levels of sleep onset insomnia to one of four groups. These conditions included two treatment groups (paradoxical intention with veridical or obfuscated instructions) and two control groups (attention-placebo and waiting-list). Clients receiving the veridical instructions showed significantly greater treatment effects than did the group from whom the purpose of the procedure was obscured.

Finally, paradoxical procedures are those that occur in systems that have no mechanism for their explanation. In the future, it may be assumed that this loosely organized body of procedures that are subsumed under the aegis of therapeutic paradox will be individually incorporated into more cohesive systems. In fact, as is the case with any effective technique, whether systematic desensitization or hypnosis, paradoxical procedures are best employed within an organized, effective psychotherapeutic system. When administered in isolation of such a context, a variety of potential difficulties become possible.

REFERENCES

Ascher, L. M. (1981). Employing paradoxical intention in the treatment of agoraphobia. *Behaviour Research and Therapy, 19*, 533–542.

Ascher, L. M. (1989). Paradoxical intention and recursive anxiety. In L. M. Ascher (Ed.), *Therapeutic paradox* (pp. 93–137). New York: Guilford Press.

Ascher, L. M., Bowers, M. R., & Schotte, D. E. (1985). A review of data from controlled case studies and experiments evaluating the clinical efficacy of paradoxical intention. In G. R. Weeks (Ed.), *Promoting change through paradoxical therapy* (pp. 216–251). Homewood, IL: Dow Jones-Irwin.

Ascher, L. M., & Efran, J. (1978). Use of paradoxical intention in a behavioral program for sleep onset insomnia. *Journal of Consulting and Clinical Psychology, 46*, 547–550.

Ascher, L. M., & Schotte, D. E. (1999). Paradoxical intention and recursive anxiety. *Journal of Behavior Therapy and Experimental Psychiatry, 30*, 71–79.

Ascher, L. M., & Turner, R. M. (1979a). Paradoxical intention and insomnia: An experimental investigation. *Behavior Research and Therapy, 17*, 408–411.

Ascher, L. M., & Turner, R. M. (1979b). A comparison of two methods for the administration of paradoxical intention. *Behavior Research and Therapy, 18*, 121–126.

Broomfield, N. M., & Espie, C. A. (2003). Initial insomnia and paradoxical intention: An experimental investigation of putative mechanisms using subjective and actigraphic measurement of sleep. *Behavioural and Cognitive Psychotherapy, 31*, 313–324.

DiTomasso, R. A., & Greenberg, R. L. (1989). Paradoxical intention: The case of the case study. In L. M. Ascher (Ed.), *Therapeutic paradox* (pp. 32–92). New York: Guilford Press.

Dunlap, K. (1928). A revision of the fundamental law of habit formation. *Science, 57*, 360–362.

Dunlap, K. (1930). Repetition in the breaking of habits. *Science Monthly, 30*, 66–70.

Erickson, M. (1977). Hypnotic approaches to therapy. *American Journal of Clinical Hypnosis, 20*, 20–35.

Frankl, V. (1967). *Psychotherapy and existentialism: Selected papers on logotherapy*. New York: Simon & Schuster.

Frankl, V. (1975). Paradoxical intention and dereflection. *Psychotherapy: Theory, Research, and Practice, 12*, 226–237.

Haley, J. (1973). *Uncommon therapy: The psychiatric techniques of Milton H. Erickson, M.D.* New York: Norton.

Hayes, S. C., Stosahl, K., & Wilson, K. G. (1999). *Acceptance and commitment therapy: An experiential approach to behavior change*. New York: Guilford Press.

Mozdzierz, G., Macchitelli, F., & Lisiecki, J. (1976). The paradox in psychotherapy: An Adlerian perspective. *Journal of Individual Psychology, 32*, 169–185.

Shearin, E. N., & Linehan, M. M. (1989). Dialectics and behavior therapy: A metaparadoxical approach to the treatment of borderline personality disorder. In L. M. Ascher (Ed.), *Therapeutic paradox* (pp. 255–288). New York: Guilford Press.

Turner, R. M., & Ascher, L. M. (1979). Controlled comparison of progressive relaxation, stimulus control, and paradoxical intention therapies

for insomnia. *Journal of Consulting and Clinical Psychology, 47*, 500–508.
Watzlawick, P., Weakland, J., & Fisch, R. (1974). *Change: Principles of problem formulation and problem resolution*. New York: Norton.
Weeks, G. R., & L'Abate, L. (1982). *Paradoxical psychotherapy*. New York: Brunner/Mazel.
Wegner, D. M. (1994). Ironic processes of mental control. *Psychological Review, 101*, 34–52.

Parents of Children with ADHD

Andrea M. Chronis

Keywords: ADHD, parent training, behavior problems, oppositional defiant disorder, conduct disorder

Behavioral parent training has been established as an empirically supported treatment for attention-deficit/hyperactivity disorder (ADHD), oppositional defiant disorder (ODD), and conduct disorder (CD). Parent training programs focus on teaching parents behavior modification techniques based on social learning principles. Parents are instructed to modify antecedents and consequences of child misbehavior by rewarding prosocial behavior through contingent praise, positive attention, and rewards, and extinguishing maladaptive behavior through ignoring, response cost, and discipline techniques such as time-out. For parent training to be maximally effective, parents must implement these techniques consistently.

Although there is some evidence to suggest that participation in parent training may improve parent stress, parenting self-esteem, and marital adjustment, parent functioning is typically not addressed in most parent training programs. This is concerning when one considers evidence suggesting that parents' personal and marital problems are associated with poorer compliance with and outcomes following parent training. These findings are not surprising given that distressed individuals often lack motivation to complete effortful tasks that require ongoing work. Therefore, it can be concluded that standard treatment for children with ADHD and behavior problems should include assessment and treatment of parental psychopathology and/or marital discord, as these problems may impact parents' ability to effectively implement behavior management techniques.

Some well-established parent training programs address parent issues. For example, Forehand and Long's book, *Parenting the Strong Willed Child*, includes chapters on improving communication skills within the family (in parent–child interactions and marital interactions) and developing patience. The chapters discuss how parents' emotional reactions depend on how the parent thinks about her child's behavior, and outline stress management strategies such as changing negative patterns of thinking, removing oneself from stressful situations rather than responding with anger, taking breaks from the parenting role, using problem solving strategies, developing support systems, and attending to one's physical health (e.g., exercising, getting enough sleep, eating healthy). Webster-Stratton's *Incredible Years* includes four chapters devoted to controlling upsetting thoughts, "taking time out" from stress and anger, using effective communication skills, and problem solving for adults. Likewise, the parent training manual developed for the Multimodal Treatment Study for ADHD includes two sessions that focus on parent stress, anger, and mood management. These sessions present the relationship between thoughts, feelings, and behaviors related to parenting, relaxation techniques, and building social support networks. Although these programs recognize the value of attending to parents' thoughts and emotional well-being in order to optimize their ability to use behavioral parenting strategies, in most cases, it is unlikely that one or two sessions or book chapters will be sufficient to bring about significant change in negative thinking and depressive symptomatology, particularly for individuals for whom these issues may be most relevant.

Relatively few studies have evaluated the incremental benefit of adding a parent enhancement component to standard behavioral parent training for noncompliant, aggressive, or conduct-disordered children, and only one has examined such interventions in a population selected for ADHD specifically. Some of these studies have targeted a specific parent problem area, such as depression, marital problems, or limited social support, while others have utilized more general interventions aimed at reducing distress in multiple areas.

Five studies have evaluated adjunctive components addressing specific parent problems, including maternal depression, marital problems, and lack of social support. Sanders and McFarland (2000) evaluated the relative effects of parent training and an integration of parent training and cognitive–behavioral treatment for depressed mothers of disruptive children derived from several well-established models. Dadds, Schwartz, and Sanders (1987) evaluated the additive effect of partner support training for maritally distressed and nondistressed parents. Results of both studies, including parents of children referred for ODD or CD, suggested that adjunctive parent interventions had a positive, incremental effect on outcome at follow-up for distressed families, but no incremental effect beyond parent training at posttreatment.

Pfiffner, Jouriles, Brown, Etscheidt, and Kelly (1990) and Dadds and McHugh (1992) specifically targeted single-parent families in their adjunctive interventions. Pfiffner et al. used a social problem-solving skills intervention adapted from the work of D'Zurilla and Goldfried. Dadds and McHugh used a modified form of a partner support training method developed to improve the parents' social support by placing a parent-appointed individual in an ally role. They did not find any incremental benefit of ally support training beyond the effects of parent training; however, Pfiffner and colleagues found greater improvements of the problem solving intervention on parent ratings of externalizing child behavior at follow-up. Again, no acute treatment effects were found beyond the effects of parent training alone.

Three studies looked at the incremental effect of more general parent interventions beyond parent training alone. In the first of these studies, the "parent enhancement therapy" addressed parents' perceptions of their children's behavior and parents' personal, marital, and extrafamilial adjustment (Griest et al., 1982). Results of this study suggested that parent training plus enhancement therapy was more effective in improving child behavior and parents' use of behavioral strategies during home observations and better maintenance at the 2-month follow-up assessment than parent training alone. In the second of these studies, the ADVANCE videotape skills component involved training parents to cope with interpersonal distress through improved communication, problem solving, and self-control skills (Webster-Stratton, 1994). The addition of this treatment component produced improvements in parent communication, problem-solving skills, and consumer satisfaction beyond the standard parent training group. Both treatment groups (parent training alone and parent training plus ADVANCE) showed comparable reductions in parenting stress, depressive symptoms on the BDI, and mother- and father-reported child adjustment. More recently, Sanders, Markie-Dadds, Tully, and Bor (2000) evaluated the impact of their "Triple P-Positive Parenting Program" in high-risk families with a preschool-aged child. Results of this study suggested that the enhanced behavioral family intervention (parent training plus partner support and coping skills to address stress, depression, anxiety, and other parent problems) resulted in few differences beyond standard parent training on most outcome measures; however, the enhanced intervention resulted in more reliable change in child behavior and a greater normalization rate at posttreatment than standard parent training.

Only one study selected mothers of children diagnosed with ADHD; however, the vast majority of these children were diagnosed with comorbid ODD or CD. In their randomized, controlled study, Chronis, Roberts, Pelham, and Gamble (2001) found that Lewinsohn's *Coping with Depression Course* resulted in improvements on measures of maternal depressive symptomatology, self-esteem, and attributions and expectations related to child behavior at posttreatment that were maintained at follow-up. The largest effect sizes on these measures were found for mothers who reported at least mild depressive symptoms at pretreatment evaluation. However, no effects of the intervention were found on maternal ratings of child behavior.

Taken together, the results of these studies provide mixed support for the incremental benefit of interventions addressing parents' interpersonal problems beyond standard behavioral parent training alone. Most often, combined interventions have resulted in beneficial effects at follow-up assessment but not at posttreatment for parents of children with ODD or CD, particularly in studies that selected families experiencing distress in the area being targeted (e.g., social support). The one study targeting parents of children with ADHD found that an adjunctive CBT intervention was effective in addressing maternal symptomatology; yet, no effects of the intervention were found on child behavior.

Future studies are needed to address the important issue of how to best intervene with distressed parents of children with attention and behavior problems in order to remove or minimize the deleterious effects that parent problems have on the effectiveness of parent training. Most existing studies of adjunctive treatments introduced parent-focused treatment components in the maintenance phase (i.e., following parent training). Instead, it may prove useful to *begin* treatment by addressing and treating existing parent psychopathology. In doing so, parents may be better prepared for the demands of learning and consistently implementing behavior management strategies. Alternatively, behavioral parent training and cognitive–behavioral therapy may best be integrated in a manner that promotes their concurrent use. Future studies may randomly assign parents to the parent-focused intervention prior to, concurrent with, and following a behavioral parent training program to evaluate the optimal ordering of treatments.

Further, many of these studies focused on mothers of children with attention and behavior problems, likely due to mothers' traditional role as primary caregiver and the large literature documenting the relationship between maternal psychopathology (e.g., depression) and child adjustment. However, both mothers and fathers of these children may be suffering from a host of psychological problems, including anxiety disorders, marital distress, anger management problems, adult ADHD, and substance abuse. Future studies may address the benefit of matching adjunctive parent treatments to the needs of individual families, based on a comprehensive assessment of child and family problems.

See also: Attention-deficit/hyperactivity disorder—child

REFERENCES

Chronis, A. M., Roberts, J. E., Pelham, W. E., & Gamble, S. A. (2001, November). *The addition of "The Coping with Depression Course" to behavioral parent training for mothers of children with ADHD.* Poster presented at the annual meeting of the Association for the Advancement of Behavior Therapy, Philadelphia.

Dadds, M. R., & McHugh, T. A. (1992). Social support and treatment outcome in behavioral family therapy for child conduct problems. *Journal of Consulting and Clinical Psychology, 60*, 252–259.

Dadds, M. R., Schwartz, S., & Sanders, M. R. (1987). Marital discord and treatment outcome in behavioral treatment of child conduct disorders. *Journal of Consulting and Clinical Psychology, 55*, 396–403.

Griest, D. L., Forehand, R., Rogers, T., Breiner, J., Furey, W., & Williams, C. A. (1982). Effects of parent enhancement therapy on the treatment outcome and generalization of a parent training program. *Behavior Research and Therapy, 20*, 429–436.

Pfiffner, L. J., Jouriles, E. N., Brown, M. M., Etscheidt, M. A., & Kelly, J. A. (1990). Effects of problem-solving therapy on outcomes of parent training for single-parent families. *Child and Family Behavior Therapy, 12*, 1–11.

Sanders, M. R., Markie-Dadds, C., Tully, L. A., & Bor, W. (2000). The triple-p positive parenting program: A comparison of enhanced, standard, and self-directed behavioral family intervention for parents of children with early-onset conduct problems. *Journal of Consulting and Clinical Psychology, 68*, 624–640.

Sanders, M. R., & McFarland, M. (2000). Treatment of depressed mothers with disruptive children: A controlled evaluation of cognitive behavioral family intervention. *Behavior Therapy, 31*, 89–112.

Webster-Stratton, C. (1994). Advancing videotape parent training: A comparison study. *Journal of Consulting and Clinical Psychology, 62*, 583–593.

Pathological Gambling

Deborah Slalom and E. Thomas Dowd

Keywords: gambling, pathological gambling, high-risk behavior

Gambling has always existed in one form or another; however, since 1980, it has taken on a life of its own. It can be found in almost every area of life ranging from charitable bingo games to state lotteries to casinos and, now, online gambling. In fact, gross gambling revenues have increased from $10.4 billion in 1982 to $47.6 billion in 1996. This is greater than the combined revenue from movies, recorded music, cruise ships, sports, and live entertainment (Bondolfi & Ladouceur, 2001; Christiansen, 1998). With the ease of accessibility to a wide variety of gambling techniques, this has led to an increasing health problem known as pathological gambling.

First recognized in the *Diagnostic and Statistical Manual of Mental Disorders* in 1980, pathological gambling is characterized by maladaptive cognitions and behaviors such as an overpreoccupation with gambling, using gambling as a way of escaping problems, lying to conceal involvement with gambling, and committing illegal acts to finance gambling (American Psychiatric Association, 2000). These individuals tend not to seek treatment until they have used up the last of their resources and are struggling with the negative consequences caused by the gambling. Their preoccupation with gambling can border on the obsessional with particular emphasis placed on regaining lost monies or repeating wins (Ladouceur, Sylvain, Boutin, & Doucet, 2002).

Pathological gamblers develop these erroneous cognitions believing that they can control and even predict random events while gambling. This illusion of control motivates the gambler to develop strategies that are designed to increase their probability of winning. Even when there is an expectation of loss, because of these erroneous cognitions, the gambler is still encouraged to continue this pursuit (Ladouceur et al., 2001, 2002; Sylvain, Ladouceur, & Boisvert, 1997). These cognitive errors are aided by the fact that most gambling games are disguised in such a way that it appears possible to predict a win. This encourages gamblers to play even more, believing they can ultimately master the game.

With the continuation of gambling being encouraged by the cognitive errors, poor impulse control could develop, leading to maladaptive behaviors affecting personal, social, and business relationships. Gamblers have been known to lie about the extent of their involvement with gambling to their family, friends, therapists, and others. Indeed, one of the most common behaviors found among gamblers is lying. They will hide money destined for gambling and then create reasons justifying their lack of money. They often make up excuses for lateness or absences. They will also lie during therapy sessions not wanting to admit to having gambled again either because of embarrassment or fear of the consequences (Ladouceur et al., 2002).

Another behavior problem presents in the illegal acts committed to finance their gambling habit such as forgery, fraud, theft, or embezzlement. Gamblers have reported utilizing company credit cards, stealing products from the workplace and selling them, emptying their children's bank accounts, and even prostituting themselves. Committing any of these acts is an indicator of the severity of the gambling problem.

Gamblers have been known to "chase" after their losses, often returning to gamble on a daily basis. They are tortured by the memory of these losses and dream of winning their monies back. This is usually when the cycle of excessive gambling begins, often leading to the need to gamble with increasing amounts of money in order to reach a certain level of excitement. This excitement is utilized as a distraction for gamblers so they can avoid dealing with a broad range of interpersonal and intrapersonal problems (Bujold, Ladouceur, Sylvain, & Boisvert, 1994).

A cognitive–behavioral approach to treatment can address these perceptual and behavioral problems by helping gamblers understand their maladaptive cognitions and behaviors and developing interventions to aid them in creating a more balanced lifestyle. Treatment consists of four stages: awareness training, cognitive interventions, behavioral interventions, and relapse prevention. However, the therapist must always be aware that the gambler may lie during treatment and therefore be cautious in dealing with inconsistencies in the client's discourse because alienation may occur. The therapist must walk the fine line between maintaining the therapeutic alliance and being aware of the client's propensity to protect his or her image and habit.

Awareness training helps the pathological gambler to understand what factors influence the gambling behavior, with emphasis placed on physiological and cognitive reactions to gambling situations (Sharpe & Tarrier, 1992). This is accomplished through the use of self-monitoring data which record autonomic arousal, as well as the vocalized cognitions of the gambler indicating possible situations that could influence gambling behavior (Ladouceur et al., 2002; Sharpe & Tarrier, 1992). Another technique suggested by Toneatto (2002) is the therapist becoming a "naive observer," inquiring about gambling techniques. Through this method gamblers account for how they develop their erroneous cognitions and beliefs.

Gamblers also need to understand the difference between games of chance versus games of skill. Pathological gamblers tend to forget the real meaning of the word "chance." They develop an erroneous understanding of chance, believing that chance can be controlled, thereby influencing the outcome of a particular game. They also believe that chance is contagious, spreading from one area of life to gambling. This cognitive error creates an illusion that fosters their need for gambling and also supports their belief that they can predict a win or possibly master the game.

Another part of awareness training is to understand the difference between social and pathological gamblers. Social gamblers consider gambling to be a relaxing activity with no negative consequences. They can choose to gamble or not to gamble without developing poor impulse control. Pathological gamblers, on the other hand, do develop poor impulse control. They appear driven to gamble, which leads to negative consequences in both their own life and the lives of those with whom they interact. Finally, all of the information gathered during awareness training is utilized by the therapist in developing appropriate cognitive interventions for the gambler (Bondolfi & Ladouceur, 2001).

The goal of cognitive interventions is to help make the gamblers more aware of their behavior by modifying their thinking processes. The first part of the modification process is done through the use of exercises designed to teach the gambler how to control thoughts that tend to incite gambling. One of these exercises takes place during awareness training when gamblers vocalize their thoughts at the moment they occur. These thoughts are recorded and later reviewed by the therapist for cognitive errors. Other exercises can include the use of self-observation forms, an examination of the extent to which gambling occupies the gambler's life, thoughts, fantasies, and motivation.

Through the use of self-observation forms gamblers can chart their progress and identify problem areas and issues as they occur or confront them. The therapist is then able to reinforce the positive areas while noting erroneous thoughts that may be triggering the difficulties. When gamblers examine how much gambling occupies their lives, they often find that at least half their time is occupied by this behavior. Ladouceur et al. (2002) use a technique whereby the gambler colors in a portion of an empty circle. This portion represents the amount of time gambling occupies the gambler's life. It was found that most gamblers color in between one-half and three-quarters of the circle. This exercise enables gamblers to recognize the negative effects gambling has on their personal, familial, business, and social life, thus dispelling the illusion that others are not affected by what they do. Through the motivation exercises, gamblers are able to chart the pros and cons of gambling and the positive effects that might occur if they eliminated gambling entirely. This exercise enables gamblers to bring more focus into achieving their ultimate goal of cessation of gambling.

Another part of cognitive interventions is the identification of risky situations. Situations such as lottery ads, outstanding bills, or something as simple as payday could trigger erroneous cognitions leading to the gambling behavior. Because all risky situations cannot be controlled, gamblers must learn to recognize them so that if they cannot avoid them, they can attempt to control their own thoughts and behaviors. This is done through the use of cognitive restructuring.

By using cognitive restructuring techniques, erroneous beliefs and cognitions are challenged in order to produce a corrected understanding of the effects of pathological gambling. Core beliefs are challenged producing doubt. This doubt allows gamblers to examine their cognitions and make other choices that could lead to nongambling behaviors. Indeed, the success of treatment is dependent on dispelling these cognitive errors (Sharpe & Tarrier, 1992; Toneatto, 2002).

As cognitive interventions produce doubt, thus weakening the strength of the erroneous beliefs, it becomes easier to introduce behavioral interventions. These interventions include reduction of gambling exposure, instruction on how to handle finances, social skills training, and problem-solving techniques and can support and strengthen the effects of the cognitive interventions, affording the pathological gambler the ability to change his or her behavior. But, as mentioned earlier, successful treatment is based primarily on the full cooperation of the client.

Because gambling can be found in numerous forms in various places, it is important that gamblers adopt new behaviors designed to reduce their exposure to gambling locales. These places can range from casinos to church halls to drugstores, so there is some difficulty in accomplishing this goal. However, pathological gamblers can systematically avoid going to places that offer gambling, change their route while driving home to avoid gambling establishments, and in the case of drugstores, avoid the lottery ticket counters. If exposure is inevitable, the pathological gambler can leave as quickly as possible (Ladouceur et al., 2002).

To assist in this endeavor, pathological gamblers can be retrained in how they handle financial situations. The more money that is available to the gambler, the more likely it is they will gamble. Therefore, it is important to reduce the amount of accessible monies. To accomplish this goal, gamblers could cancel credit and ATM cards, allow their spouse or a close relative to manage their finances, or use a financial consultant to set them on a budget. They can also use direct deposit and have a cosigner for cash withdrawals.

Since excessive gambling has such a detrimental effect on relationships, pathological gamblers often find they are isolated from others. Gamblers must work to regain trust from others and essentially prove they have changed. Not only is this difficult, but often gamblers are challenged by repeated invitations to gamble, particularly from past gambling partners and establishments. This is why social skills training is important. Gamblers are taught how to interact and communicate with their families and friends and are also taught assertiveness training to aid them in refusing gambling invitations (Ladouceur et al., 2002; Sylvain et al., 1997).

Through problem-solving training, pathological gamblers learn to define problems by breaking them into aspects to be examined, then listing and evaluating each possible solution in order to choose the best answer. Not only does this help them handle daily problems, it also helps in improving communication skills as they gain the ability to explain their choices (Bujold et al., 1994; Sylvain, Boutin & Doucet, 2002; Ladouceur, Sylvain, Boutin, & Doucet, 2002).

Once gambling has completely ceased, pathological gamblers are challenged by the possibility of relapse. As Ladouceur et al. (2002) pointed out, gambling is a source of gratification and a means of escape. Therefore, abstinence can lead to frustration and tension because these desired goals are now blocked. One way to reduce these frustrations is through relaxation training. In a study by Sharpe and Tarrier (1992), the subjects described their urges in terms of physiological arousal. By using relaxation techniques, it was found that the intensity of these urges was significantly reduced.

Imaginal exposure is a technique by which gamblers imagine that they are in a difficult gambling situation. The scene is repeated during several treatment sessions with coping skills being gradually introduced. As these skills are introduced, the scene is shortened in length giving the client a sense of mastery over the urges.

In vivo exposure aids the client in gaining mastery over urges and reactions by exposing the gambler to influential stimuli that gradually increase in intensity over time. Exposure occurs between therapy sessions, Sharpe and Tarrier (1992) found that after 4 weeks of exposure, gamblers were able to perform difficult tasks with a minimum of anxiety.

Because gambling is so pervasive throughout society, it is impossible to avoid all problematic situations; therefore, it is important to develop emergency measures to aid in counteracting urges. Ladouceur et al. (2002) suggest that if the urge to gamble is present or gambling has occurred, it is useful to stop and go to an area where there are no distractions. It is important to avoid negative self-recriminations because they can increase the possibility of relapse. It is important for gamblers to think about why they want to stop gambling and the commitments they have made to achieve this goal. Examining the situation that has created the urge is important to better understand the triggers and to develop ways to avoid or counterract the urges. It is most important to ask for help.

If, during treatment, there have been indications of other psychopathology, appropriate referral or actions need to be taken. Lesieur and Blume (1990) found primary diagnoses such as paranoid schizophrenia and major depression among 105 psychiatric patients who were admitted for the treatment of pathological gambling. More research needs to be done to determine if the diagnoses are interconnected or are separate problems manifesting themselves at the same time. Also, the collection of data from family members concerning behavioral changes of the pathological gambler has not been done. Such data would lend additional support to the self-report measures of gamblers.

Pathological gambling is triggered by a combination of core erroneous cognitions and poor impulse control. These problems can be treated through the use of cognitive–behavioral therapy. Once erroneous cognitions are challenged, thereby creating doubt, the behavioral areas can be addressed.

See also: Addictive behavior—nonsubstance abuse, Motivational interviewing

REFERENCES

American Psychiatric Association. (2000). Pathological gambling. *Diagnostic and statistical manual of mental disorders* (4th ed.). Washington, DC: Author.

Bondolfi, G., & Ladouceur, R. (2001). Pathological gambling: An increasing public health problem. *Acta Psychiatrica Scandinavica, 104*, 241–242.

Bujold, A., Ladouceur, R., Sylvain, C., & Boisvert, M. (1994). Treatment of pathological gamblers: An experimental study. *Journal of Behavior Therapy and Experimental Psychiatry, 25*, 275–282.

Christiansen, E. M. (1998). Gambling and the American economy. In F. H. Frey (Ed.), *Gambling: Socioeconomic impacts and public policy* (pp. 36–52). Thousand Oaks, CA: Sage.

Ladouceur, R., Sylvain, C., Boutin, C., & Doucet, C. (2002). *Understanding and treating the pathological gambler*. New York: Wiley.

Ladouceur, R., Sylvain, C., Boutin, C., LaChance, S., Doucet, C., LeBlond, J. & Jacques, C. (2001). Cognitive treatment of pathological gambling. *The Journal of Nervous and Mental Disease, 189*, 774–780.

Lesieur, H. R., & Blume, S. B. (1990). Characteristics of pathological gamblers identified among patients on a psychiatric admissions service. *Hospital and Community Psychiatry, 41*, 1000–1012.

Sharpe, L., & Tarrier, N. (1992). A cognitive–behavioral treatment approach for problem gambling. *Journal of Cognitive Psychotherapy: An International Quarterly, 6*, 193–203.

Sylvain, C. C., Ladouceur, R., & Boisvert, J. M. (1997). Cognitive and behavioral treatment of pathological gambling: A controlled study. *Journal of Consulting and Clinical, 65*, 727–732.

Toneatto, T. (2002). Cognitive therapy for problem gambling. *Cognitive and Behavioral Practice, 9*, 191–199.

Perfectionism

Martin M. Antony and Randi E. McCabe

Keywords: perfectionism, OCD

Perfectionism has been defined in a number of ways. Conceptualized as a personality style, perfectionism is a trait whereby one's standards for the self or others are higher than necessary for a given situation (Hollender, 1978). From a cognitive perspective, perfectionism has been defined as a set of attitudes, beliefs, expectations, interpretations, and evaluation relating to the self or others involving rigid adherence to unrealistically high standards, and a tendency for self-worth to be dependent on performance and accomplishment (Burns, 1980). Both of these definitions emphasize pathological aspects of perfectionism.

However, some authors have distinguished between adaptive and maladaptive manifestations of perfectionism (e.g., Biding, Israeli, & Antony, in press). For some people, perfectionism is viewed as motivating, healthy, and "normal" (Hamachek, 1978), involving a "functional pursuit of excellence" (Shafran, Cooper, & Fairburn, 2002). For others, perfectionism may be maladaptive, dysfunctional, and "neurotic" (Hamachek, 1978), involving the pursuit of impossible standards despite clinically significant consequences (Shafran et al., 2002).

COGNITIVE AND BEHAVIORAL FEATURES OF PERFECTIONISM

Cognitive Features

The cognitive features that are often associated with perfectionism include distorted attitudes, beliefs, and evaluations about the self and others, including:

- Excessively high standards and rigid rules for the self or others
- Selective attention toward negative information (e.g., focusing on the 10% of incorrect responses on an exam, after receiving a grade of 90%) to the exclusion of positive information (Hollender, 1978)
- All-or-nothing thinking patterns (e.g., if I can't do it perfectly, then I am a failure") (Burns, 1980)
- Excessive social comparison (e.g., "I am the dumbest person in the class")
- Self-evaluation based on performance and achievement of goals to the exclusion of personal acceptance (Burns, 1980)

Behavioral Features

Behavioral features that are often associated with perfectionism include the following:

- Completing tasks until a certain standard is met (e.g., not being able to clean one room unless there is time to clean the entire house) or until it is "just right"
- Completing tasks in a certain way (e.g., having to vacuum so that the vacuum lines are all in the proper direction, or folding laundry so that all the creases are perfect.

- Needing to arrange items in the home or at work in a precise manner (e.g., not being able to leave the room unless objects are in their "assigned" spot)
- Avoidance of situations because standards have not been met (e.g., not being able to leave the house until everything is neat and tidy; avoiding social situations for fear of making an imperfect impression on others)
- Procrastination—putting off activities because it is too overwhelming to do them perfectly (e.g., organizing the hills, completing an assignment)
- Self-control strategies focused on achieving goals and limiting pleasurable activities that are not goal-relevant (Shafran et al., 2002) (e.g., not taking a break from studying because that would take time away from being completely prepared)
- Excessive checking or reassurance seeking to ensure that perfectionistic standards are met (e.g., going over a work assignment many times to ensure that there is not one mistake)

PERFECTIONISM AND PSYCHOPATHOLOGY

Research shows that perfectionism plays a role in the development and maintenance of a number of psychological disorders (for review, see Shafran & Mansell, 2001).

Anxiety Disorders

Perfectionism has been posited to play a central role in cognitive models of social phobia (Heimberg, Juster, Hope, & Mattia, 1995) and the development of obsessive–compulsive disorder (Obsessive Compulsive Cognitions Working Group, 1997). Indeed, research supports the hypothesis that both social phobia and obsessive–compulsive disorder (as well as panic disorder) are associated with higher than normal levels of perfectionism (e.g., Antony, Liss, Summerfeldt, & Swinson, 1998).

Obsessive–Compulsive Personality Disorder (OCPD)

Perfectionism is so closely associated with OCPD that the latter may be seen as the clinical manifestation of maladaptive perfectionism—terms of a global personality style. The hallmark feature of OCPD is a "pervasive pattern of preoccupation with orderliness, perfectionism, and metal and interpersonal control" (American Psychiatric Association, 2000).

Depression

Numerous studies indicate a positive association between perfectionism and depression (Hewitt & Flett, 1991). This relationship may be mediated by a number of factors including perceived control and self-esteem. In addition, perfectionism has been associated with increased levels of hopelessness and suicidality (Shafran & Mansell, 2001). Moreover, elevated perfectionism has been found to interfere with therapeutic gain from brief psychological treatment for depression (Blatt, Zuroff, Bondi, Sanislow, & Pilkonis, 1998).

Eating Disorders

Perfectionism plays a central role in cognitive theories of the development of eating disorders; it is manifested in extreme preoccupation with weight and shape, and rigid and excessive dieting and weight control behaviors. Studies provide evidence to support this role. For example, perfectionism has been identified as a specific risk factor for the development of both anorexia nervosa (Fairburn, Cooper, Doll, & Welch, 1999) and bulimia nervosa (Lilenfeld et al., 2000).

ASSESSMENT OF PERFECTIONISM

Over the past 25 years, a number of scales have been developed to measure perfectionism. The earliest of these (e.g., the *Burns Perfectionism* Scale; Burns, 1980) considered perfectionism to be a u-dimensional construct. More recently, researchers have begun to conceptualize perfectionism as a multidimensional construct, consisting of several unique, though related, components.

For example, the 35-item Frost et al. *Multidimensional Perfectionism Scale* (FMPS; Frost, Marten, Lahart, & Rosenblatt, 1990) is designed to assess six dimensions believed to be important for understanding perfectionism: (1) high personal standards, (2) excessive concern over making mistakes, (3) doubting one's actions, (4) a perception of high expectations from one's parents, (5) perceived parental criticism, and (6) a tendency to focus on precision, order, and organization. The subscales and total score have adequate to excellent internal consistency, and there is also evidence of adequate convergent validity (Roemer, 2001). However, some studies (e.g., Purdon, Antony, & Swinson, 1999) have not supported the six-factor structure of the scale.

The 45-item Hewitt and Flett *Multidimensional Perfectionism Scale* (HMPS; Hewitt & Flett, 1991; Hewitt, Flett, Turnbull-Donovan, & Mikhail, 1991) is another popular scale for measuring perfectionism. It consists of three subscales: (1) self-oriented perfectionism (excessively high standards held for oneself), (2) other-oriented perfectionism (excessively high standards held for others), and (3) socially prescribed perfectionism (the belief that others have excessively high standards for oneself). Reliability and validity of this scale are well established (Emms & Cox, 2002).

There are a number of other scales that are useful for measuring perfectionism. The *Almost Perfect Scale-Revised* (APS-R; for a review, see Slaney, Rice, & Ashhy, 2002) was developed to examine adaptive and maladaptive aspects of perfectionism. The *Perfectionism Cognitions Inventory* (PCI; Flett, Hewitt, Blankstein, & Gray, 1998) is a 25-item scale for measuring beliefs associated with perfectionism. Finally, several scales designed to measure eating disorder symptoms include items or subscales that measure perfectionism (e.g., Garner, Olmsted, & Polivy, 1983; Slade & Dewey, 1986).

COGNITIVE–BEHAVIORAL TREATMENT OF PERFECTIONISM

Although there are hundreds of studies examining the efficacy of cognitive–behavioral therapy (CBT) for psychological problems that are known to be associated with perfectionism (e.g., social phobia, depression, obsessive–compulsive disorder, eating disorders; Nathan & Gorman, 2002), there are no controlled studies examining the use of CBT for treating perfectionism directly (Shafran & Mansell, 2001). Instead, there are a few case studies examining the effects of CBT on perfectionism, a few studies examining the impact of perfectionism on CBT outcome, and a few studies on the effects of CBT for anxiety on perfectionism. The results of these studies are summarized below.

Preliminary case studies (e.g., Ferguson & Rodway, 1994; Hirsch & Hayward, 1994) suggest that CBT may be useful for reducing symptoms of perfectionism. In addition, Di Bartolo, Frost, Dixon, and Almodovar (2001) found that cognitive restructuring is an effective intervention for reducing cognitions associated with public speaking anxiety in individuals who are excessively concerned about making mistakes. Studies examining the effect of CBT social phobia on perfectionism have yielded mixed results. Antony et al. (2000) found that although CBT for social phobia led to significant reductions in OCD, anxiety, depression, and functional impairment, changes on the FMPS total and subscale scores were generally nonsignificant. In contrast, Lundh and Ost (2002) found that CBT for social phobia did lead to significant reductions in associated perfectionism. Finally, Blatt, Quinlan, Pilkonis, and Shea (1995) found that elevated perfectionism is associated with a poorer treatment outcome for individuals receiving CBT for depression, as well as those receiving other forms of treatment (e.g., interpersonal psychotherapy, medication, placebo).

A CBT Protocol for Treating Perfectionism

This section describes an example of how CBT might be used to treat perfectionism. Although CBT has not been evaluated specifically for that purpose, these strategies are used extensively in empirically based psychological treatments for psychological disorders that are associated with perfectionism, including depression and various anxiety disorders.

Typically, the initial treatment session would begin with presenting the rationale for the therapy. This would include some discussion of the nature of perfectionism, including consideration of strategies for discriminating between high standards that are appropriate and healthy versus standards that are excessive and impairing. To facilitate this process, clients are encouraged to ask questions such as:

- Am I able to meet my standards? Do I get overly upset if I don't meet my own standards?
- Are other people able to meet my standards? Do I get overly upset if others don't meet my standards?
- Do my standards help me to achieve my goals or do they get in the way (e.g., by making me overly disappointed or angry when my standards are not met; by making me get less work done)?
- What would be the costs and benefits of relaxing a particular standard or ignoring one of my rules?

In addition, clients are encouraged to discuss the features of their perfectionism, including the triggers, content areas, underlying beliefs, and associated behavioral responses. Goals and priorities for treatment are set, and an overview of cognitive and behavioral strategies for dealing with perfectionism is provided. Finally, potential obstacles to treatment are identified and discussed. These may include such things as poor insight by the client into the excessiveness of his or her perfectionistic standards, extreme life stress, negative expectations regarding the effectiveness of treatment, and significant comorbidity.

In subsequent sessions, a variety of standard cognitive and behavioral methods are used. As with CBT for other problems, homework is an important component of treatment, and it may be important to include significant others or family members in homework practices. For example, family members may be encouraged to fold the laundry "incorrectly" as part of an exposure practice for a client who is excessively concerned about domestic chores being completed "just right."

Cognitive Strategies. Cognitive strategies for changing perfectionistic patterns of thinking are similar to those used for related problems such as anxiety disorders, depression, anger, and body image issues. Clients are initially taught to identify specific beliefs and predictions that are associated with their perfectionism and to examine the evidence regarding these beliefs. They are encouraged to use strategies such as perspective taking (e.g., asking "how might someone else think about this situation?"), and to look at the "big picture" instead of getting caught up in minor details.

They are also taught to tolerate uncertainty and ambiguity more easily, a strategy that has been used with some success in the treatment of generalized anxiety and chronic worry. Patterns of social comparison (e.g., the types of people to which clients choose to compare themselves) may also be explored and changed if necessary. Finally, behavioral experiments (i.e., hypothesis testing) are used to assess the validity of particular beliefs. For example, if a client is convinced that it would be a disaster to be even five minutes late for a movie, he or she might be encouraged to arrive a few minutes late to see what happens.

Behavioral Strategies. Strategies are selected to target specific behavioral excesses and deficits that are associated with perfectionism. Clients are encouraged to use exposure-based strategies to reduce anxiety and avoidance associated with concerns about not meeting particular standards. For example, they may be taught to purposely make mistakes (e.g., wash the dishes incorrectly; pronounce a word incorrectly; "forget" their wallet when standing in line to buy an item; show up for an appointment on the wrong day) or to confront situations that were previously avoided due to a fear of not being perfect (e.g., social situations). In addition, clients are encouraged to discontinue any unreasonable or excessive behaviors that are designed to prevent them from making mistakes (e.g., excessive checking for mistakes; extensive research before buying a product; repeated reassurance seeking; excessive correcting of others). Communication training may also be included in the treatment if the individual's perfectionism leads to problems in his or her relationships, and the problems appear to be associated with poor communication skills (e.g., a tendency to use aggressive language instead of being appropriately assertive). Finally, if putting off important tasks for fear of not doing them correctly is a problem, the client may be taught strategies for overcoming procrastination, including breaking down large projects into smaller, more manageable tasks.

SUMMARY

Perfectionism is a personality trait involving rigid adherence to unrealistically high standards for the self and others. Perfectionism is maladaptive when the pursuit of impossible standards leads to clinically significant distress and impairment. Cognitive features of perfectionism include distorted attitudes about the self or others, maladaptive social comparisons, and self-evaluation based on performance rather than self-acceptance. Behavioral features of perfectionism involve completing tasks according to precise standards, avoidance, procrastination, self-control strategies, and excessive checking for mistakes. Perfectionism has been found to play a role in the development and maintenance of a number of psychological disorders including anxiety disorders, OCPD, depression, and eating disorders. Current assessment measures view perfectionism as a multidimensional construct. Research on the effectiveness of CBT specifically for perfectionism is limited. A CBT protocol for treating maladaptive perfectionism is presented.

See also: Body dysmorphia 1, Body dysmorphia 2, Severe OCD

REFERENCES

American Psychiatric Association. (2000). *Diagnostic and statistical manual of mental disorders* (4th ed., text rev.). Washington, DC: Author.

Antony, M. M., Liss, A., Summerfeldt, L. J., & Swinson, R.P. (2000, November). *Changes in perfectionism following cognitive-behavioural treatment of social phobia.* Paper presented at the meeting of the Association for Advancement of Behavior Therapy, New Orleans.

Biding, P. J., Israeli, A., & Antony, M. M. (in press). Is perfectionism good, bad, or both? Examining models of the perfectionism construct. *Personality and Individual I.*

Blatt, S. J., Quinlan, D. M., Pilkonis, P. A., & Shea, M. T. (1995). Impact of perfectionism and need for approval on the brief treatment of depression: The National Institute of Mental Health Treatment of Depression Collaborative Research Program revisited. *Journal of Consulting and Clinical Psychology, 63*, 125–132.

Blatt, S. I., Zuroff, D.C., Bondi, C. M., Sanislow, C. A., & Pilkonis, P. A. (1998). When and how perfectionism impedes the brief treatment of depression: Further analyses of the National Institute of Mental Health Treatment of Depression Collaborative Research Program. *Journal of Consulting and Clinical Psychology, 66*, 423–428.

Burns, D. D. (1980, November). The perfectionist's script for self-defeat. *Psychology Today*, pp. 34–57

Di Bartolo. P. M., Frost, R. O., Dixon, A., & Almodovar, S. (2001). Can cognitive restructuring reduce the disruption associated with perfectionistic concerns? *Behavior Therapy, 32*, 67–184.

Emms, M. W., & Cox, B. J. (2002). The nature and assessment of perfectionism: A critical analysis. In G. L. Flett & P. L. Hewitt (Eds.), *Perfectionism. Theory, research, and treatment* (pp. 33–62). Washington, DC: American Psychological Association.

Fairhurn, C. G., Cooper, Z., Doll, H. A., & Welch, S. L. (1999). Risk factors for anorexia nervosa: Three integrated case control comparisons. *Archives of General Psychiatry, 56*, 468–476.

Ferguson, K. E., & Rodway, M. R. (1994). Cognitive behavioral treatment of perfectionism: Initial evaluation studies. *Research on Social Work Practice, 4*, 283–308.

Flett, G. L., Hewitt, P. L., Blankstein, K. R., & Gray, L. (1998). Psychological distress and frequency of perfectionistic thinking. *Journal of Personality and Social Psychology, 75*, 1363–1381.

Frost, R. O., Marten, P., Lahart, C., & Rosenblatt, R. (1990). The dimensions of perfectionism. *Cognitive Therapy and Research, 14*, 449–468.

Garner, D. M., Olmsted, M. P., & Polivy, L. (1983). Development and validation of a multidimensional eating disorder inventory for anorexia nervosa and hulimia. *International Journal of Eating Disorders, 2*, 15–34.

Hamachek, D. E. (1978). Psychodynamics of normal and neurotic perfectionism. *Psychology: The Journal of Human Behavior, 14*, 27–33.

Heimberg, R. G., Juster, H. R., Hope, D. A., & Mattia, J. I. (1995). Cognitive behavioral group treatment: Description, case presentation, and empirical support. In M. B. Stein (Ed.), *Social phobia: Clinical and research perspectives* (pp. 293–321). Washington, DC: American Psychiatric Press.

Hewitt, P. L., & Flett, G. L. (1991). Perfectionism in the self and social contexts: Conceptualization, assessment, and association with psychopathology. *Journal of Personality and Social Psychology, 60*, 456–470.

Hewitt, P. L., Flett, G. L., Turnbull-Donovan, & Mikhail, S. F. (1991). The Multidimensional Perfectionism Scale: Reliability, validity, and psychometric properties in psychiatric samples. *Psychological Assessment, 3*, 464–468.

Hirsch, C. R., & Hayward, P. (1998). The perfect patient: Cognitive–behavioural therapy for perfectionism. *Behavioural and Cognitive Psychotherapy, 26*, 359–364.

Hollender, M. H. (1978). Perfectionism, a neglected personality trait. *Journal of Clinical Psychiatry, 39*, 384.

Lilenfeld, E. R., Stein, D., Bulik, C. M., Strober, M., Plotnicov, K. H., Pollice, C., Rao, R.N. & Kaye, W.H. (2000). Personality traits among currently eating disordered, recovered, and never ill first-degree female relatives of bulimic and control women. *Psychological Medicine, 30*, 1399–1410.

Lundh, E.-G., & Ost, L.-G. (2001). Attentional bias, self-consciousness, and perfectionism in social phobia before and after cognitive behaviour therapy. *Scandinavian Journal of Behaviour Therapy, 30*, 4–16.

Nathan, P. E., & Gorman, J. M. (Eds.), (2002). *A guide to treatments that* New York: Oxford University Press.

Obsessive Compulsive Cognitions Working Group. (1997). Cognitive assessment of obsessive compulsive disorder. *Behaviour Research and Therapy, 35*, 667–681.

Purdon, C. L., Antony, M. M., & Swinson, R. P. (1999). Psychometric properties of the Frost Multidimensional Perfectionism Scale in a clinical anxiety disorders sample. *Journal of Clinical Psychology, 55*, 1271–1286.

Roemer, L. (2001). Measures for anxiety and related constructs. In M. M. Antony, S. M. Orsillo, & L. Roemer (Eds.), *Practitioner's guide to empirically-based measures 0/ any ic/v* pp. 4")-83). New York: Kluwer Academic/Plenum.

Shafran, R., Cooper, Z. P., & Fairburn, C. G. (2002). Clinical perfectionism: A congnitive–behavioural analysis. *Behaviour Research and Therapy, 40*, 773–791.

Shafran, R., & Mansell, W. (2001). Perfectionism and psychopathology: A review of research and treatment. *Clinical Psychology Review, 21*, 879–906.

Slade, P. D., & Dewey, M. E. (1986). Development and preliminary validation of SCANS: A screening instrument for identifying individuals at risk of developing anorexia and bulimia nervosa. *International Journal of Eating Disorders, 5*, 517–538.

Slaney, R. B., Rice, K. G., & Ashby, J. S. (2002). A programmatic approach to perfectionism: The Almost Perfect Scales. In G. L. Flett & P. L. Hewitt (Eds.), *Perfectionism: Theory, research, and treatment* (pp. 63–88). Washington, DC: American Psychological Association.

RECOMMENDED ADDITIONAL READINGS

Antony, M. M., & Swinson, R. P. (1998). *When perfect isn't good enough. Strategies for coping with perfectionism.* Oakland, CA: New Harbinger.

Flett, G. L., & Hewitt, P. L. (Eds.). (2002). *Perfectionism—Theory, research, and treatment.* Washington, DC: American Psychological Association.

Personal Construct Psychology

Sally N. Phillips

Keywords: constructivism, George Kelly, personal construct psychology, repertory grid

Personal Construct Psychology (PCP), devised by George Kelly, is a comprehensive theory of human experience and action. Kelly elaborated the theory in his two-volume work, *The Psychology of Personal Constructs* (1955). Table 1 summarizes PCP in terms of a fundamental postulate and eleven corollaries.

PCP THEORY

PCP is a critical constructivist theory grounded in the philosophy of constructive alternativism. The theory transcends the "realist versus idealist" debate by adopting the metatheoretical assumption that the known is inextricably linked to the knower. For Kelly, there is a real world that we can never directly or objectively apprehend. Instead, we personally know and experience "reality" through our active construction of it in interaction with the environment. Moreover, there are always alternative possibilities to choose from in dealing with the world, and these constructions are themselves open to constant revision. This personal, active approach to knowledge implies an epistemological responsibility—we are responsible for our knowledge of the world in which we live.

Kelly stated, "Whatever nature may be, or howsoever the quest for truth will turn out in the end, the events we face today are subject to as great a variety of constructions as our wits will enable us to contrive. This is not to say that one construction is as good as any other. … But it does remind us that all our present perceptions are open to question and reconsideration, and it does broadly suggest that even the most obvious occurrences of everyday life might appear utterly transformed if we are inventive enough to construe them differently" (1970, p. 15). For Kelly, there is both freedom and determinism. We are determined to the extent that we are governed by our own constructs, and we are free to the extent that we can choose to reconstrue.

Kelly offers the metaphor of person-as-scientist as an attempt to grasp the person as a meaning creator, constantly experimenting in order to understand and anticipate the world that he or she inhabits. Persons test the world and create meaning through the use of bipolar constructs organized by varying degrees of differentiation and integration into

Table 1. Kelly's Fundamental Postulate and Eleven Corollaries

Fundamental Postulate:	A person's processes are psychologically channelized by the ways in which he or she anticipates events.
Construction Corollary:	A person anticipates events by construing their replications.
Individuality Corollary:	A person anticipates events by construing their replications.
Organization Corollary:	Each person characteristically evolves, for his or her convenience in anticipating events, a construction system embracing ordinal relationships between constructs.
Dichotomy Corollary:	A person's construction system is composed of a finite number of dichotomous constructs.
Choice Corollary:	A person chooses for himself or herself that alternative in a dichotomized construct through which he or she anticipates the greater possibility for extension and definition of his or her system.
Range Corollary:	A construct is convenient for the anticipation of a finite range of events only.
Experience Corollary:	A person's construction system varies as he or she successively construes the replication of events.
Modulation Corollary:	The variation in a person's construction system is limited by the permeability of the constructs within whose range of convenience the variants lie.
Fragmentation Corollary:	A person may successively employ a variety of construction subsystems which are inferentially incompatible with each other.
Commonality Corollary:	To the extent that one person employs a construction of experience which is similar to that employed by another, his or her psychological processes are similar to those of the other person.
Sociality Corollary:	To the extent that one person construes the construction process of another, he or she plays a role in a social process involving the other person.

Reproduced from Kelly (1955).

a complex hierarchy of both superordinate and subordinate constructs. Constructs are bipolar in that our understandings of the world inextricably involve contrast; we must know what something is not in order to understand what it is. Constructs are tested and evaluated through interactions with the environment in which some prove to be more viable than others, leaving the invalidated constructs to possible abandonment, alteration, or hostile maintenance. Since an infinite number of meanings can be attached to any particular event, the validation of a construct is an indication of the temporal utility of that construct rather than any absolute truth about external reality. This hypothesis testing is a constant process that allows meanings, or construct systems, to evolve in the context of a constantly changing world.

DISPOSITIONAL ASSESSMENT AND TRANSITIVE DIAGNOSIS

The PCP therapist continuously assesses the client's personal construct system in a way that frees both for constructive alternatives. Dispositional assessment facilitates the process of transitive diagnosis, which entails identifying important ways the client can change rather than simply distinguishing this client from other clients with a diagnostic label. All diagnostic systems consist of created meanings professionals utilize to understand their clients. However, "The client does not ordinarily sit cooped up in a nosological pigeonhole; he proceeds along his way" (Kelly, 1955, p. 775). Therefore, transitive diagnosis looks for transitions or bridges between a client's present and future. Kelly (1955) elaborated six areas of transitive diagnosis: description of the client's constructs, evaluation of the client's construct system, analysis of the milieu in which adjustment is sought, normative formulations of the client's problems, determination of immediate procedural steps, and planning management and treatment. The idiographic, process-oriented nature of PCP assessment and diagnosis provides for a wider range of convenience than a static, categorical understanding of psychological problems. From this perspective, psychological problems are seen as disorders of construction.

Dispositional assessment and transitive diagnosis are essential to treatment in that the aim of therapy is to assist in the continuous shifting of the client's construct system. Moreover, assessment and diagnosis are ongoing processes, as professional understandings of the client are constantly changing as a result of validation or invalidation of the therapist's constructions of the client. Since the theory is reflexive, the way the client is explained can be used to explain the therapist as he or she creates this explanation. Thus, any explanation that can be applied to the client must be able to be applied to the person who offers the explanation.

Kelly (1955) devised the repertory grid to elicit a sample of a person's construct system that can be used to infer how a person understands and predicts significant people in his or her life. The technique is flexible, and investigators and therapists can tailor the process to elicit personal constructs across a wide range of content areas in both research and clinical settings. The client generates constructs by either comparing and contrasting certain persons in his or her life or describing these persons. The client rates each person on each construct to determine how his or her constructs are interrelated. Thus, the method can be used to elicit and describe certain constructs as well as to evaluate aspects of construct system organization (e.g., complexity and differentiation). While the repertory grid technique has proven extremely fruitful, there is some concern regarding the limitations of heavy reliance on one particular technique. For instance, due to the mathematical complexity of grid calculations, the grid can be utilized in a mechanical fashion that may become removed from the client's experience. Leitner (1995) describes several nongrid assessment techniques, including self-characterization sketch, pyramid procedure, laddering techniques, and interview techniques.

PCP THERAPY

Kelly (1955) defined "disorder" as "any personal construction which is used repeatedly in spite of consistent invalidation" (p. 831). Thus, therapy can be seen as helping a person to reorganize and reconstrue even the most superordinate constructs. Basic features of the PCP therapeutic stance include the credulous approach and an invitational mode. Kelly first devised fixed role therapy as one therapeutic mode, and PCP has been elaborated along a number of other therapeutic dimensions.

Credulous Approach. The PCP therapist is challenged to construe the client's construction process in order to discern the inner meanings so integral to the "being" of the client and, thus, to therapeutic change. The credulous approach entails understanding the client from the assumption that everything he or she says is "true." In other words, the therapist chooses to trust the subjective reality of the client's experience and attempts to understand the truth that even the most severely disturbed client is communicating. This approach is similar to Laing's (1969) "therapeutic suspension" and "disciplined naiveté." Mahoney (1995) discusses the psychological demands of being a constructivist therapist in that the emotional presence necessary for one to attempt to grasp the clients' subjectivity entails that the therapist cannot remain distant from and untouched by the clients' suffering.

Invitational Mode. The invitational mode is a process of inviting psychological intimacy while simultaneously respecting the client's needs for safety. PCP therapists continuously invite but do not force intimacy, as many clients have already experienced massive invasion and invalidation in the past. Therefore, clients may feel threatened that the personal constructs that form the core of their existence may be disconfirmed. This threat can be so severe that the very process of meaning making can be frozen (Leitner, Faidley, & Celentana, 2000). The therapist must forge a collaborative therapeutic effort based on empathic understanding and reverence for the client's experience. This includes understanding and respecting areas of "resistance," which can be seen as the client's attempt to protect core constructs from invalidation. On the other hand, the therapist assesses the safety of the relationship by the clients spontaneous elaboration of material.

Fixed Role Therapy. Fixed role therapy traditionally involves a 2-week invitation to a client to explore some alternative ways of being. The client first writes an open self-description as if he or she is a character in a play. The therapist and client then co-create an alternative character for the client to enact, first in the therapy session and then in the outside world. The client undertakes enactments with low-risk persons (e.g., cashier) and then more important others (e.g., spouse). At the end of the 2 weeks, the therapist and client assess which experiences were valuable and should be built on and which to disregard. This procedure is based on the premise that self-consistency may be stultifying, and a temporary fragmentation in the form of an alternative role enactment can spark the creative imagination of a client, opening new possibilities for being.

Further Elaborations. A PCP framework has been utilized to explore a variety of areas in psychology. Dorothy Rowe (1991) outlines the building blocks that go into constructing the prison of depression and describes the journey out of this prison. Bannister (1965) has elaborated a PCP approach to schizophrenia in which the person's constructions of the future are serially invalidated, leading to a progressive loosening of the construct system. Constructs cannot be tested when they are too vague, thereby protecting the schizophrenic from further invalidation. Robert Neimeyer (2001) has integrated constructivist and narrative themes in describing grieving as a process of meaning reconstruction in the wake of loss. Constructivist grief therapy prompts the articulation and elaboration of the client's narrative of loss to promote a new sense of coherence and continuity. Ravenette (1997) utilizes drawings to elicit children's personal constructs.

Experiential personal construct psychotherapy (EPCP; Leitner et al., 2000) elaborates Kelly's sociality corollary by focusing on ROLE relationships, defined as intimate, interpersonal relationships where a person allows another to understand his or her core constructs and construction processes. ROLE relationships involve allowing another access to the most central, core parts of oneself and allowing the other to affirm these most crucial aspects of one's identity. However, such intimate relating can be terrifying because it also carries the potential for devastating invalidations. Psychopathology can be defined as an excessive retreat from ROLE relationships resulting in emptiness, meaninglessness, and numbness. EPCP engages the client around these struggles over intimacy in the living therapy relationship.

FUTURE DIRECTIONS

It is clear that PCP continues to evolve and grow. Future areas for development may involve further exploration of commonalities and differences with postmodernism, narrative psychology, hermeneutics, and social constructionism.

REFERENCES

Bannister, D. (1965). The genesis of schizophrenic thought disorder: Retest of the serial invalidation hypothesis. *British Journal of Psychiatry, 111*, 377–382.

Kelly, G. A. (1955). *The psychology of personal constructs* (2 vols.). New York: Norton.

Kelly, G. A. (1970). A brief introduction to personal construct theory. In D. Bannister (Ed.), *Perspectives in personal construct theory* (pp. 1–29). London: Academic Press.

Laing, R. D. (1969). *The divided self.* London: Penguin.

Leitner, L. M. (1995). Dispositional assessment techniques in experiential personal construct psychotherapy. *Journal of Constructivist Psychology, 8*, 53–74.

Leitner, L. M., Faidley, A. J., & Celentana, M. A. (2000). Diagnosing human meaning making: An experiential constructivist approach. In R. A. Neimeyer & J. D. Raskin (Eds.), *Constructions of disorder: Meaning-making frameworks for psychotherapy* (pp. 175–203). Washington, DC: American Psychological Association.

Mahoney, M. J. (1995). The psychological demands of being a constructive psychotherapist. In R. A. Neimeyer & M. J. Mahoney (Eds.), *Constructivism in psychotherapy* (pp. 385–399). Washington, DC: American Psychological Association.

Neimeyer, R. A. (2001). The language of loss: Grief therapy as a process of meaning reconstruction. In R. A. Neimeyer (Ed.), *Meaning reconstruction and the experience of loss* (pp. 261–292). Washington, DC: American Psychological Association.

Ravenette, T. A. (1997). *Tom Ravenette: Selected papers—Personal construct psychology and the practice of an educational psychologist.* Farnborough, UK: EPCA.

Rowe, D. (1991). *The depression handbook.* London: Fontana/Collins.

Personality Disorders

Arthur Freeman and Ray W. Christner

Keywords: personality, therapy relationship, schemas, chronic disorders

Therapists generally agree that patients with personality disorders as part of their clinical picture are challenging, resistant, and often difficult to treat (Beck, Freeman, Davis, & Associates, 2004; Freeman, Pretzer, Fleming, & Simon, 2004; Merbaum & Butcher, 1982; Rosenbaum, Horowitz, & Wilner, 1986). These patients generally require more work within the session, increased energy from the therapist, and often require a longer duration for treatment than do other patients. By definition, personality disorders involve long-standing, pervasive, persistent, relatively rigid patterns of thinking and behaving that present in a wide range of social and personal situations (American Psychiatric Association, 2000). Maladaptive beliefs or schemas about the world in general are often the basis for these patterns, which many times result in distress or functional impairment (American Psychiatric Association, 2000; Beck, Freeman, & Associates, 1990; Freeman, Pretzer, Fleming, & Simon, 1990, 2004).

In recent years, a number of leading cognitive–behavioral therapists have contributed cognitive–behavioral approaches in the treatment of personality disorders (Beck, Freeman, & Associates, 1990; Beck, Freeman, Davis, & Associates, 2004; Freeman, 1987, 1988; Freeman & Leaf, 1989; Freeman, Pretzer, Fleming, & Simon, 1990, 2004; Linehan, 1993; Linehan, Cochran, & Kehr, 2001; Pretzer & Fleming, 1989; Young, 1988, 1990). Cognitive–behavioral therapists not only focus on symptom structures or manifest problems, but also address underlying schemas or core beliefs and issues that perpetuate or exacerbate the patient's problems. This formulation is consistent with the principal contemporary theories of cognitive structure and cognitive development, all of which stress the function of schemas as determinants of rule-guided behavior (Galambos, Abelson, & Black, 1986; Neisser, 1976; Piaget, 1970, 1974, 1976, 1978; Schank & Abelson, 1977).

REFERRAL

Patients with personality disorders usually do not present for treatment to address underlying personality problems; rather, they desire relief of symptomatic complaints including depression, anxiety, or other clinical (Axis I) disorders. In some cases, the reported symptoms are separate from the personality patterns, whereas at other times, the Axis I symptoms are derived and fueled by the underlying personality disorder. Patients with comorbid clinical (Axis I) and personality (Axis II) disorders present a far more complicated clinical picture than do patients without a co-occurring personality disorder. Accordingly, cognitive–behavioral treatment of patients with personality disorder involves modified treatment duration, frequency, goals, and expectations for both the patient and the therapist.

The typical pattern for patients with personality disorders is that they generally see the problems they encounter or experience as outside of them and independent of their behavior. Pressure from significant others in their lives or from the judicial system is often the enforcing agent to these patients seeking or pursuing therapy. They often hold little insight about how they became the way they are, how they contribute to their life problems, or how to change their actions, what they experience, and how they think. In some cases, however, patients may be aware of the self-defeating nature of their personality problems (e.g., overdependence, inhibition, excessive avoidance), but they are at a total loss as to how to change these patterns. Still other patients may be motivated to change but do not have the skills to do so.

THERAPEUTIC RELATIONSHIP

The therapy session serves as a microcosm of the patient's interactions with other people and situations in his or her environment (e.g., lack of interpersonal skills, fear of closeness, or belief that interactions are unimportant). Therapists who are watchful for these behaviors can, in turn, point them out to the patient and use them as "grist for the therapeutic mill." These patients are frequently very sensitive to the slightest nuance or suggestion within the relationship, and they respond quickly and intensely when they perceive a slight, a challenge, a disagreement, or a loss. The therapist must bear in mind that the individual with a personality disorder is particularly vulnerable to making questionable attributions of the intent, thoughts, actions, attitudes, and emotions of the therapist as a reflection of the patient's inflexible ways of thinking and relating.

While it is important to stress the collaborative nature of CBT, therapists must realize that collaboration is not always 50:50. Indeed, with many Axis II patients, the collaboration is more realistically 70:30 or even 90:10, with the therapist needing to carry the greater burden. This imbalance of effort is often difficult for therapists, and brings on higher levels of stress and burnout (Freeman, Pretzer, Fleming, & Simon, 1990, 2004). However, without the therapist's active support, these patients may experience higher levels of anxiety, fear, or disillusionment, and subsequently leave therapy. As with all patients, the therapeutic collaboration involves setting mutually acceptable goals for treatment that are reasonable, sequential, realistic, meaningful, proximal, time-limited, and, most importantly, within the patient's repertoire.

As part of the careful structuring of the therapy session, the therapist should collaboratively set an agenda at the start of each session, inquire as to whether there are any other important topics to be addressed, and tell the patient when 15 minutes remain in the session. This avoids interrupting the patient and allows him or her to gain closure on the therapy session.

During the therapy session, the therapist should take precise notes to avoid his or her own misstatement or exaggeration. Some patients will perceive approximate statements as uncaring or lacking understanding and they may take offense. If the therapist is comfortable doing so, it can be powerful to use the patient's language or metaphors as often as possible. Therapists should not force themselves to use language in a manner that is not consistent with the way they would normally speak.

Patient feedback is an essential component when building a therapeutic relationship. This should occur at multiple times throughout therapy sessions and most importantly at the end of each session. In concluding the session, the therapist should inquire about what the patient will be taking home from the session. This will provide an assessment of the patient's understanding of the session content and may enable the therapist to identify potential issues and address them proactively.

ASSESSMENT

Assessment and data collection lead to the therapist's conceptualization of the problem(s) and to an appropriate and collaborative treatment plan. Patients with Axis I disorders are often willing to provide detailed information with hopes of gaining relief from their symptoms. In contrast, the assessment of patients with Axis II disorders is oftentimes more difficult, as these patients find it difficult to recognize their difficulties or are unwilling to disclose detailed information beyond basic symptoms (e.g., depressed mood). The assessment of these patients can be a daunting task for therapists. Some personality disorders are prominent from the onset of therapy, whereas in other cases, the therapist may not recognize the characterological nature, chronicity, and severity of the patient's problems as easily (Fabrega, Mezzich, Mezzich, & Coffman, 1985; Karno et al., 1986; Koenigsberg, Kaplan, Gilmore, & Cooper, 1985). If the therapist's conceptualization is accurate, it will explain the patient's past behavior, make sense of the patient's present experience, and help the therapist predict future behavior (Freeman, 2001).

The assessment for personality disorders involves both formal and informal techniques. The information gathered will not only contribute to the therapist's conceptualization of the patient's problems, and ultimately become part of the treatment planning, but may also become the target of treatment itself.

Commonly used formal measures include the *Millon Clinical Multiaxial Inventory–Third Edition* (MCMI-III; Millon, 1994) or the *Minnesota Multiphasic Personality Inventory–Second Edition* (MMPI-2; National Computer Systems, 1989). Both of these self-report inventories provide information on personality traits, as well as clinical symptoms, that assist in identifying personality disorders.

In addition to formal procedures, a number of informal clinical markers exist that are not diagnostic in general, but can alert the therapist to investigate the potential for a personality disorder. These include:

1. *Chronicity*. Despite patients with personality disorders being in therapy for years, they continue to engage in the same dysfunctional pattern of behaviors over time. The patient or a significant other may report, "I've always been this way," or "Oh, he has done that as long as I can remember."

2. *Compulsivity*. The patient's actions or behaviors are "need driven" rather than "situation driven." That is, the patient feels compelled to engage in certain behaviors that are independent of situational factors alone.

3. *Inflexibility*. By definition, personality disorders involve a stable pattern of perceiving, relating to, and thinking about the environment and oneself that is "inflexible and pervasive across broad range of social and personal situations" (American Psychiatric Association, 2000, p. 686). These patients will have great difficulty doing things differently. There are a number of reasons for this, including possible skill deficits, beliefs that what he or she does is the best way, or lack of awareness to his or her responses to certain beliefs.

4. *Thoughtlessness*. The patient tends to lack basic problem-solving strategies or approaches situations with "tunnel vision." He or she typically sees solutions to problems dichotomously, and may not consider alternative solutions. The patient may lack hindsight and forethought when presented certain situations, that is, he or she may not learn from past mistakes nor will he or she consider future consequences of his or her behavior.

5. *Highly noticeable*. Although others frequently notice the behaviors of patients with personality disorders, the patient may be unaware of the effect his or her behavior has on others. Others may complain of the patient's behaviors, but he or she seems to avoid looking in the mirror or self-monitoring his or her behavior.

6. *Generally negative*. The therapy session may become a matter of treating the *crisis du jour* (Freeman & Fusco, 2000), as patients with personality disorders seem to have frequent "brushfires" in their life. The therapist who focuses all of his or her energy on crisis management may be helping in the moment, but by neglecting the opportunity to assist the patient develop skills and strategies to address these situations independently may never get to address "core" issues of the patient's problems.

7. *Generally maladaptive*. The behaviors of patients with a personality disorder are often poorly suited to the intended purpose or situation.

8. *Unusually extreme*. While various patients may present with actions or behaviors that are atypical, the patient with a personality disorder may take his or her behaviors to an extreme.

9. *At odds with general community*. While the patient's actions may be reasonable and acceptable to him or her or his or her subgroup, the larger community may identify his or her behaviors as problematic or pathological. This pattern is likely one learned early in life and reinforced continually.

10. *Self-consonant (ego syntonic)*. The patient's thoughts, feelings, and actions are internally consistent for the individual. Despite the frequent problems these patients experience, they may continue to be perplexed by why he or she has the difficulties he or she does. This often results in the patient blaming others for difficulties.

11. *Energy consuming*. The patient's behaviors and actions cause notable strain and energy loss. Much of the time, the patient expends more energy on maintaining his or her maladaptive behaviors than it would take to change his or her behaviors to more adaptive and positive levels.

12. *Interpersonally conflictual*. Because of the patient's lack of self-monitoring and the monitoring of others, he or she may experience frequent problems with family, friends, and colleagues. The patient often "avoids looking in the mirror," and he or she may seem entirely unaware of the effect his or her behaviors have on others. The patient is likely attentive to the responses of others, but fails to address any dysfunctional behavior that he or she may exhibit that elicits the negative reactions of others.

13. *Personally distressing*. The patient reports clinically significant distress or discomfort in a variety of settings including home, work, school, and social. The patient's perception that his or her needs are unmet may relate to this distress.

14. *The patient may appear to be resistant or noncompliant*. Therapists must assess other factors such as frequent resistance or noncompliance, immediate stops in therapy for no apparent reason, "lip service" offered by the patient without noticeable change, and extensive past therapeutic contacts. While these are not diagnostic criteria, these factors can serve as a heuristic for the therapist to examine the possibility of a personality disorder further.

Therapists may also use chaining techniques or cognitive maps as an assessment tool to help identify potential areas for intervention. When using the chain analysis, the therapist walks the patient through a sequence of experiences from start to finish. Once a situation is identified, the therapist simply asks, "Then what happened?" The purpose of using the chaining technique is to identify the "weakest link" in the chain in order to offer possible interventions for future use. Therapists can use a simple chain diagram for this. In addition to using this as an assessment tool, the therapist may use the chain diagram as homework, to have the patient begin thinking about the sequence and consequences of his or her actions.

When more than one disorder is present, the therapist must address the synergy or effect each disorder has on the others. For example, a patient with a dependent personality disorder who also has a history of major depressive disorder may be particularly prone to a depressive episode when he perceives others are not providing him the other assistance he needs.

Although many do not think of personality disorders as varying in severity, we encourage therapists to assess whether the patient's problems are mild, moderate, or severe. Some patient's may function fairly well across most domains of their lives with relatively few areas of difficulty, while others experience more global and sometimes immobilizing problems such as inconsistent employment, continual family conflict, or frequent incidents of self-harm. Therapists can use the DSM-IV-TR coding system for major depressive disorders as an adjunct in the assessment of personality disorders. The coding system involves the addition of a fifth digit indicating the following: "1 for Mild severity, 2 for Moderate severity, 3 for Severe without Psychotic Features, 4 for Severe with Psychotic Features, 5 for Partial Remission, 6 for Full Remission, and 0 if Unspecified" (American Psychiatric Association, 2000, p. 319). The final area of the assessment is the patient's readiness to change. Freeman and Dolan (2001) offered revised stages of change that are beneficial to the assessment of personality disorders. These include noncontemplation (the patient is not aware that they need to change), anticontemplation (they are against changing), precontemplation (they may think about the possibility that change may be important), contemplation (they are willing to make some changes), action planning (a treatment plan is organized), action (the treatment plan is implemented), prelapse (there is a cognitive return to the old behavior), lapse (there is a behavioral return to the old behavior), relapse (more frequent and ongoing lapses), and maintenance (the new behavior is being sustained). The therapist must consider the patient's stage of change from the initial session and plan treatment from this point.

A basic rule of therapy is that the behavioral strategies that comprise the disorder may be seen as necessary for the survival of the individual, no matter how dysfunctional the world may judge them. Therapists must be aware that almost any intervention will evoke anxiety in patients because they may view therapy as forcing them to give up who they are. Patients with personality disorders may limit themselves so that they can remain safe, though in some cases, they may experience increased anxiety just by getting close to the edge of what they perceive is their safety zone. Part of the case conceptualization and focus of treatment will be to address anxiety reduction and coping strategies in order for the patient to advance toward the edge of his or her safety area.

HOMEWORK

Therapy does not and cannot occur for only one hour a week in the confines of the therapist's office. The between-session work gives the "flow" to therapy. In essence, when therapy ends, everything becomes between-session work. It is crucial then that therapists be skilled in the use of homework and that they socialize the patient to the use of homework early in treatment. The homework should develop from the session material, be cast as a no failure experience, and the patient and the therapist should agree on it. Homework is not optional, and the therapist should explain it as the laboratory component of the therapy process. When the patient completes homework, the therapist must review and discuss it as part of the session. Otherwise, patients will view it as unimportant. Homework can be used to practice new skills, monitor moods and automatic thoughts, plan practice behaviors, and schedule activities. Rosenthal (2000) provides an excellent resource of an array of homework assignments.

THERAPY TECHNIQUES

As with other disorders, CBT for personality disorders progresses from identifying distorted thinking to testing the meaning, reality, or validity of the patient's thoughts or perceptions. Cognitive and behavioral techniques play complementary roles in treatment. Behavioral techniques serve to move the patient into a new position, and cognitive interventions assist to develop new schemas or to modify or reinterpret old ones. Both cognitive and behavioral interventions require more care and precision than usual when patients have personality disorders. Even when patients have improved their behavior, they continue to require a larger variety and longer duration of cognitive reworking. While the first principle of treatment for personality disorders is to emphasize behavioral methods, the final principle is to follow up with thorough cognitive ones.

A rule of thumb in treating personality disorders would be that the precise mix of cognitive and behavioral techniques depends on the patient's particular needs (Figure 1). Typically, the more severe the patient's pathology, the more behavioral the approach will be. Similarly, the less severe the patient's pathology, the more cognitive the approach will be.

SCHEMAS

From birth through middle childhood, schemas develop as a set of rules to live by; core beliefs are based on these

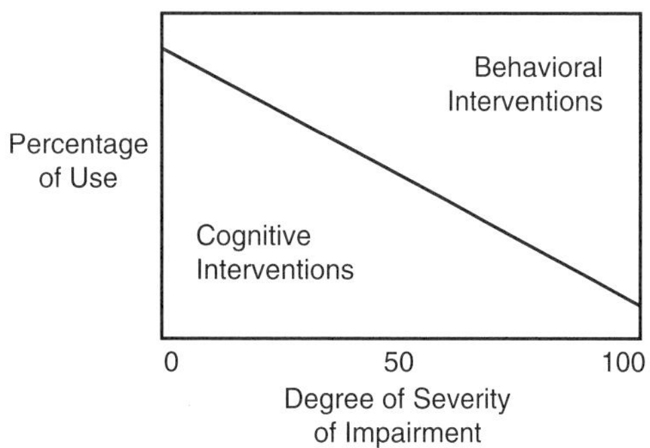

Figure 1. Determining relative use of cognitive and behavioral interventions.

templates that are set down over time and used as roadmaps for interpreting situations, people, images, and interactions. Schemas are in a constant stage of change as individuals continuously adapt to the demands of life situations through the processes of assimilation and accommodation. Individuals with personality disorders appear to have limited ability to assimilate or accommodate, that is, they have difficulty with emotional learning. For many reasons, some schemas do not mature and are maintained at an earlier level of development. Schemas that are functional in earlier life are applied during later, more demanding times. While most of these early schemas were at one time functional, they have long since lost their value. When a child at age 1 is demanding of attention and help, it is often thought of as cute. When that same schema is manifested at age 31, it is not cute, but may be quite dysfunctional. It is the individual's inability to unlearn or modify the belief in light of contradictory evidence and significant distress that fuels and maintains the personality disorder.

Schemas appear to become fixed when they are reinforced and/or modeled by significant others. In some cases they are reinforced by society, i.e., the teachers who encourage a budding obsessive–compulsive child who is "a real worker," "a kid who doesn't fool around," "a kid who really works hard and gets A's." Often compelling schemas that a patient "knows" are erroneous are hard to change. The degree to which schemas are on continua from active to inactive, compelling to noncompelling and from unchangeable to changeable are essential dimensions in conceptualizing the patient's problems (Beck, 1964, 1967; Beck, Freeman, & Associates, 1990; Beck, Freeman, Davis, & Associates, 2004; Freeman, 1988a,b; Freeman et al., 1990, 2004). The chronicity of the personality disorder results from the development of these schemas and the resultant cognitive distortions relatively early in life, and years of rehearsal and reinforcement have solidified their veracity.

There are several options when working with schemas. Identifying the level of schematic change that needs to occur is the first order of business. The change can include construction of new schemas, major reconstruction of existing schemas, schematic modification, schematic reinterpretation, or camouflaging the schemas.

Schemas that were once functionally used may, over time, lose their functionality. Take, for example, the hard-driving executive who was up at 5:00 a.m. and worked until 9:00 p.m. Having worked so hard, been successful, being financially secure, and a good provider for his family, he is at a loss to explain his difficulty at retirement. He feels himself to be a failure, based on his lack of productivity. The same schema "I am what I do, today," "I am judged by what I produce," and "I have no identity other than that coming from what I do," that have motivated him to be successful now drive him to despair.

SUMMARY

Personality disorders result from undeveloped schemas, and they exemplify Beck's idea of schemas being a central issue in the formation of dysfunction. A particular schema may be effective for the patient at one time but a source of distress or dysfunction at another. These schemas are neither good nor bad, adaptive nor maladaptive, but are best judged as the "goodness of fit." Schemas that are more active will have a greater effect on daily behavior. In addition, schemas acquired earlier in life will be more compelling and powerful, and thus more difficult to change.

Despite the chronicity of personality disorders, CBT is a successful form of treatment. The therapeutic relationship is a central component in this process. Because of the inherent difficulties working with patients with personality disorders, therapists must be aware of transference and countertransference issues. Additionally, therapists must identify and address various impediments to change that have the potential to mediate the positive effects of treatment and hinder progress. While patients with personality disorders require longer time in treatment and more energy from therapists, the rate of change and progress will not be the same as with patients whose problems are not complicated by characterological issues. While reconstructing the patient has been viewed as the goal of treatment for personality disorders in the past, we suggest that viewing changes on a continuum is more realistic and productive in therapy. Working with patients to modify or reinterpret their schemas will likely be the most efficient option. Homework is a necessary component to CBT that further helps patients make necessary changes to the environment and to maintain change over time.

Work with patients diagnosed with personality disorders is challenging, frustrating, and exhausting, though it can be exciting and rewarding as well. Therapists must recognize that the patient's frustrations may parallel theirs. Throughout treatment, challenging dysfunctional schemas through a myriad of interventions creates options and alternatives for the patient, and in the end, fosters a sense of hope for the patient.

See also: Depression and personality disorders—older adults

REFERENCES

American Psychiatric Association. (2000). *Diagnostic and statistical manual of mental disorders* (4th ed.). Washington, DC: Author.

Beck, A. T., Freeman, A., & Associates. (1990). *Cognitive therapy of personality disorders*. New York: Guilford Press.

Beck, A. T., Freeman, A., Davis, D. D. & Associates. (2003). *Cognitive therapy of personality disorders*. (2nd ed.). New York: Guilford Press.

Fabrega, H., Mezzich, J. E., Mezzich, A. C., & Coffman, G. A. (1986). Descriptive validity of DSM-III depressions. *Journal of Nervous and Mental Disease*, *174*(10), 573–584.

Freeman, A. (1998). Cognitive therapy of personality disorders. In C. Perris, I. Blackburn, & H. Perris (Eds.), *Cognitive psychotherapy: Theory and practice*. New York: Springer Verlag.

Freeman, A. (2001). Cognitive-behavioral therapy for severe personality disorders. In S. Hofmann & M. C. Tompson (Eds.), Treating chronic and severe mental disorders. New York: Guilford Press.

Freeman, A., & Dolan, M. (2001). Revisiting Prochaska and DiClemente's stages of change theory: An expansion and specification to aid in treatment planning and outcome evaluation. *Cognitive and Behavioral Practice*, *8*(3), 224–234.

Freeman, A., & Fusco, G. (2000). Treating high-arousal patients: Differentiating between patients in crisis and crisis-prone patients. In F. M. Dattilio & A. Freeman (Eds.), *Cognitive-behavioral strategies in crisis intervention* (2nd ed., pp. 27–58). New York: Guilford Press.

Freeman, A., & Leaf, R. (1989). Cognitive therapy applied to personality disorders. In A. Freeman, K. M. Simon, H. Arkowitz, & L. Beutler (Eds.), *Comprehensive handbook of cognitive therapy* (pp. 403–433). New York: Plenum Press.

Freeman, A., Pretzer, J., Fleming, B., & Simon, K. M. (1990). *Clinical applications of cognitive therapy*. New York: Plenum Press.

Freeman, A., Pretzer, J., Fleming, B., & Simon, K. M. (2004). *Clinical applications of cognitive therapy* (2nd ed.). New York: Kluwer Academic Publishers.

Hathaway, S. R., & McKinley, J. C. (1989). *Minnesota Multiphasic Personality Inventory – 2: Manual for administration and scoring*. Minneapolis: National Computer Services.

Karno, M., Hough, R. L., Burman, M. A., Escobar, J. I., Timbers, D. M., Santana, F., & Boyd, J. H. (1986). Lifetime prevalence of specific psychiatric disorders among Mexican Americans and non-Hispanic whites in Los Angeles. *Archives of General Psychiatry*, *44*(8), 695–701.

Koenigsberg, H., Kaplan, R., Gilmore, M., & Cooper, A. (1985). The relationship between syndrome and personality disorder in DSM-III: Experience with 2,462 patients. *American Journal of Psychiatry*, *142*, 207–212.

Linehan, M. M. (1993). *Cognitive-behavioral treatment of borderline personality disorder*. New York: Guilford Press.

Linehan, M. M., Cochran, B. N., & Kehrer, C. A. (2001). Dialectical behavior therapy for borderline personality disorder. In D. H. Barlow (Ed.), *Clinical handbook of psychological disorders* (3rd ed., pp. 470–522). New York: Guilford Press.

Merbaum, M., & Butcher, J. N. (1982). Therapists' liking of their psychotherapy patients: Some issues related to severity of disorder and treatability. *Psychotherapy: Theory, Research and Practice*, *19*(1), 6–76.

Millon, T., Davis, R., & Millon, C. (1997). *Millon Clinical Multiaxial Inventory – III Manual* (2nd ed.). Minneapolis: National Computer Services.

Neisser, U. (1976). *Cognition and reality*. San Francisco: W. H. Freeman & Co.

Piaget, J. (1970). *The child's conception of time*. New York: Basic Books.

Piaget, J. (1974). *Experiments in contradiction*. Chicago: University of Chicago Press.

Piaget, J. (1976). *The grasp of consciousness*. Cambridge, MA: Harvard University Press.

Piaget, J. (1978). *Success and understanding*. Cambridge, MA: Harvard University Press.

Pretzer, J. L., & Fleming, B. (1989). Cognitive-behavioral treatment of personality disorders. *The Behavior Therapist*, *12*, 105–109.

Rosenbaum, R. L., Horowitz, M. J., & Wilner, N. (1986). Clinician assessments of patient difficulty. *Psychotherapy*, *23*(3), 417–422.

Rosenthal, H. (2000). *Favorite counseling and therapy homework assignments: Leading therapists share their most creative strategies*. Philadelphia: Brunner/Routledge.

Young, J. E. (1990). *Cognitive therapy for personality disorders: A schema-focused approach* (3rd ed.). Sarasota, FL: Professional Resource Press.

Pharmacotherapy and Cognitive Therapy—Combined Treatment

Jesse H. Wright and David A. Casey

Keywords: pharmacotherapy, medication, combined treatment

Cognitive therapy and pharmacotherapy have common attributes of being structured, problem-oriented interventions with well-defined theories and strong empirical support for efficacy. Although these major treatment methods are derived from different theoretical perspectives, they are often used together to offer patients a full range of biological, cognitive, and behavioral therapies for psychiatric disorders. Research studies have typically implemented the two forms of therapy as separate entities, administered by different clinicians who may not share a unified model for treatment (Wright, 2004). The principal findings of research on combined treatment are discussed here, and methods are suggested for promoting integration of therapies in clinical practice.

The primary reason for combining cognitive behavior therapy (CBT) and pharmacotherapy is the prospect that using the two treatments together will lead to better results than either therapy alone. Several possible scenarios for interaction have been suggested: (1) *addition*—treatments given together produce results that are greater than the action of either component alone; (2) *synergism*—result of combined treatment is greater than the sum of the individual components; and (3) *inhibition*—treatment effects are impaired by the combination of approaches (Wright, 2004). Although the mechanism of potential interactions is still largely unknown, several possibilities exist. For example, CBT has been found to improve medication adherence (Wright, 2004). Also, pharmacotherapy can improve concentration, reduce painful affects and physiological arousal, and decrease distorted or irrational thinking. Positive changes in any of these areas could enhance participation in CBT.

Recent brain imaging studies suggest intriguing potential mechanisms for treatment interaction at the neurobiological level. PET scan research on CBT and pharmacotherapy for depression have found activation of different pathways. CBT appeared to act in the brain in a "top down" manner, activating cortical pathways before limbic structures. Pharmacotherapy had the opposite effects: subcortical processes were stimulated first (Goldapple et al., 2004). Earlier research on OCD demonstrated activation of similar pathways for both psychotherapy and pharmacotherapy (Baxter et al., 1992). Although these studies did not examine the effects of combined treatment, neuroimaging investigations could help elucidate central nervous system processes involved in both pharmacotherapy and cognitive therapy and in the interactions between these treatments.

Randomized, controlled trials of combined CBT and medication for depression have had varied results (Wright, 2004). The most recent, major investigation demonstrated a distinct advantage for combined CBT and medication over either therapy alone in the treatment of chronic depression (Keller et al., 2000). This very large and influential study involved random assignment of 662 patients to treatment with the cognitive–behavioral analysis system of psychotherapy (CBASP; a modified version of CBT for chronic depression), nefazadone, or both treatments. The response rates for treatment completers were 52% for CBASP, 55% for nefazadone, and 85% for combined therapy.

Two additional studies did not replicate these findings (Hollon et al., 1992; Murphy et al., 1984). However, there were trends for combined therapy to show better results. For example, Hollon et al. (1992) observed that mean ratings on the Hamilton, Raskin, and MMPI Depression scales were lowest at the end of treatment in patients who received both treatments. A clear advantage for combined treatment for *double depression* (major depression plus dysthymia) was reported by Miller, Norman, and Keitner (1999).

The overall results of studies of CBT and medication for depression suggest that for more severe or chronic disorders, a combined approach yields better results. For mild to moderate depression, controlled research indicates that similar effects can be achieved if treatments are used alone or together. However, there are several problems with investigations on combined treatment that raise questions about generalizing the results to clinical practice (Wright, 2004). Sample size may be particularly important in studies where all active treatments are known to exert substantial effects in reducing symptoms. Large sample sizes or meta-analyses of pooled data may be required to show differences between therapies with strong treatment effects.

Another difficulty with interpreting research on combined treatment for depression is that studies with mild to moderately ill patients utilized older, tricyclic antidepressants that have troublesome side effects and may interfere with concentration, learning, and memory (Wright, 2004). All of the more recent studies with newer antidepressants have found advantages for adding medication to CBT. The most important problem in extrapolating results of studies of combined therapy for depression to clinical populations is that constraints of the research design may have interfered with achieving optimal results. Typical research designs called for delivery of the treatment by separate clinicians in a tightly proscribed manner that lacked flexibility, cohesiveness, and integration.

Several studies of CBT for anxiety disorders have explored the interaction between pharmacotherapy and psychotherapy. A review of research on selective serotonin reuptake inhibitors (SSRI) combined with CBT concluded that combination therapy produced the greatest treatment gains (Bakker, van Balkom, & van Dyck, 2000). Because SSRIs may facilitate learning and memory, these medications may be useful in combination with CBT for anxiety disorders. However, benzodiazepines as well as tricyclic antidepressants have been found to have negative effects on learning and memory, and thus have a potential for interfering with CBT (Wright, 2004). There have been reports that short-acting, high-potency benzodiazepines, such as alprazolam, may reduce the effectiveness of cognitive–behavioral interventions for anxiety disorders (Wright, 2004). Despite these concerns, the overall results of investigations of combined treatment for anxiety disorders have demonstrated superiority for using pharmacotherapy plus CBT.

Investigations of combined therapy in bulimia nervosa have consistently shown an advantage for using CBT and pharmacotherapy together (Wright, 2004). The largest study (Walsh et al., 1997) involved 120 bulimic women who were randomly assigned to CBT plus medication, CBT plus placebo, psychodynamic therapy plus medication, psychodynamic therapy plus placebo, or medication alone. The pharmacotherapy in this study involved a trial of desipramine with a switch to fluoxetine after 8 weeks if the response was unsatisfactory or if there were significant side effects. The intent was to provide an optimal approach to pharmacotherapy. In this study, combined CBT and medication was found to be superior to CBT plus placebo. Also, CBT plus medication was superior to medication alone.

A superiority for combined treatment also has been noted for one of the newest applications of CBT, namely, psychotic disorders (Rector & Beck, 2001; Sensky et al., 2000; Wright, 2004). Although these studies have not examined the efficacy of CBT alone, CBT has been shown to augment medication treatment for both positive and negative symptoms (Sensky et al., 2000). A meta-analysis of studies in psychotic patients found that effect sizes were significantly higher for combined treatment (1.31) than medication plus routine care (0.04) or supportive therapy plus routine care (0.63) (Rector & Beck, 2001).

In order to maximize the potential of using CBT and medication together in clinical practice, it has been recommended that an integrative model be used to guide combined therapy (Wright, 2004). The theoretical background for a comprehensive approach involves several assumptions:

1. Cognitive processes modulate the effects of the external environment on the central nervous system for emotion and behavior.
2. Maladaptive cognitions can be influenced by both psychological and biological processes.
3. Pharmacotherapy and other biological treatments can alter cognitions.
4. Because cognitive and behavioral interventions can change biological processes, psychotherapy can thus be viewed as a biological treatment.
5. Environmental, cognitive, biological, emotional, and behavioral processes should be conceptualized as interacting with one another in a biopsychosocial system.
6. It is worthwhile to develop methods of combining and integrating cognitive and biological therapies with the goal of enhancing treatment outcome.

Combination therapy can be delivered by a psychiatrist trained in both CBT and pharmacotherapy. However, a more common arrangement involves a team approach with a physician and a nonmedical therapist. When treatment is delivered by such a team, several steps can help optimize its effectiveness. The clinicians should have a close working relationship and agree on a formulation for combined treatment. They also can discuss how the patient will be educated concerning the combined therapy. It is useful for the pharmacotherapist to have a working knowledge of CBT, and for the nonmedical therapist to be conversant about basic elements of medication treatment. Thus, the therapists can support and reinforce the work of one another. Basic CBT approaches such as agenda setting and problem-oriented interventions may be adapted to pharmacotherapy, while the psychotherapist may address issues such as automatic thoughts about taking medication and adherence. Both the cognitive therapist and pharmacotherapist can also utilize a psychoeducational approach to facilitate integrated treatment. A comprehensive and cohesive treatment program typically involves regular communication between therapists.

Whether the therapy is provided by a single clinician or a team, adherence can be a critical element of success. CBT methods for improving treatment adherence may readily be adapted to pharmacotherapy. For example, simple behavioral interventions (e.g., reminder systems, pairing medication taking with routine activities) or more detailed behavioral methods (e.g., reinforcement systems, analysis of barriers to adherence) may be used. Also, maladaptive cognitions about pharmacotherapy can be targeted for intervention. Some patients may see taking medication as a sign of personal weakness. Others may have difficulty trusting physicians. In addition, concerns about medication dependency or side effects can be addressed. The goal is to develop realistic cognitions about pharmacotherapy that will support treatment adherence.

In summary, a combined CBT and medication treatment approach may offer advantages for many clinical problems. Benefits of using treatments together may be greatest for patients who have more severe or chronic symptoms. The only clear evidence for a negative effect of medication on CBT is the reduced effectiveness associated with use of high-potency benzodiazepines for anxiety disorders. An integrated treatment method, in which the strengths of both treatments are used to enhance each other, is recommended for clinical practice of combined therapy.

REFERENCES

Bakker, A., van Balkolm, A. J., & van Dyck, R. (2000). Selective serotonin reuptake inhibitors in the treatment of panic disorder and agoraphobia. *International Clinical Psychopharmacology, 15*(Suppl. 2), 25–30.

Baxter, L. R., Jr., Schwartz, J. M., Bergman, K. S. et al. (1992). Caudate glucose metabolic rate changes with both drug and behavior therapy for obsessive–compulsive disorder. *Archives of General Psychiatry, 49*, 681–689.

Blackburn, I. M., & Bishop, S. (1983). Changes in cognition with pharmacotherapy and cognitive therapy. *British Journal of Psychiatry, 143*, 609–617.

Goldapple, K., Segal, Z., Garson, C. et al. (2004). Modulation of cortical–limbic pathways in major depression: Treatment specific effects of cognitive–behavior therapy. *Archives of General Psychiatry, 61*, 34–41.

Hollon, S. D., DeRubeis, R. J., Evans, M. D. et al. (1992). Cognitive therapy and pharmacotherapy for depression: Singly and in combination. *Archives of General Psychiatry, 49*, 774–781.

Keller, M. B., McCullough, J. P., Klein, D. N. et al. (2000). A comparison of nefazadone, the cognitive behavioral-analysis system of psychotherapy, and their combination for the treatment of chronic depression. *The New England Journal of Medicine, 342*, 1462–1470.

Miller, I. W., Norman, W. H., & Keitner, G. I. (1999). Combined treatment for patients with double depression. *Psychotherapy and Psychosomatics, 68*, 180–185.

Murphy, G. E., Simons, A. D., Wetzel, R. D. et al. (1984). Cognitive therapy and pharmacotherapy: Singly and together in the treatment of depression. *Archives of General Psychiatry, 41*, 33–41.

Rector, N. A., & Beck, A. T. (2001). Cognitive behavioral therapy for schizophrenia: An empirical review. *Journal of Nervous and Mental Disease, 189*, 278–287.

Sensky T., Turkington, D., Kingdon, D. et al. (2000). A randomized controlled trial of cognitive–behavioral therapy for persistent symptoms in schizophrenia resistant to medication. *Archives of General Psychiatry, 57*, 165–172.

Walsh, B. T., Wilson, G. T., Loeb, K. L. et al. (1997). Medication and psychotherapy in the treatment of bulimia nervosa. *American Journal of Psychiatry, 154*, 523–531.

Wright, J. H. (2004). Integrating cognitive therapy and pharmacotherapy. In R. L. Leahy (Ed.), *Contemporary cognitive therapy*. New York: Guilford Press.

Phobia

Katie M. Castille and Maurice F. Prout

Keywords: phobia, fear, phobic response, anxiety disorders

Anxiety disorders have been identified as the most prevalent mental health problem in the United States. According to the Epidemiologic Catchment Area (ECA) study sponsored by the National Institute of Mental Health, the 1-month prevalence rate for anxiety disorders is 7.3% (Regier et al., 1998). Among anxiety disorders, phobic disorders are the most common, with a prevalence rate of 6.2%. According to the *Diagnostic and Statistical Manual of Mental Disorders–IV–Text Revision* (DSM-IV-TR; American Psychiatric Association [APA], 2000), phobias are classified into three categories: agoraphobia with or without panic attacks, social phobia, and specific phobia.

An element common to phobias is the feeling of fear that individuals experience when they encounter the phobic situation or object. Fear is a basic emotion that acts as an alarm in response to present danger (Barlow, 2002). When in a feared situation, the natural tendency is to engage in the "fight-or-flight" response. There arises an overwhelming urge to escape the situation and to avoid any encounter in the future. If the situation cannot be avoided, it is endured with discomfort and dread (Dziegielewski & MacNeil, 1999). Clinically, fear is most evident in panic attacks, in which the individual experiences extreme feelings of fear and danger and an overwhelming urge to escape the situation. However, research has indicated that no important differences exist between panic attacks experienced by individuals with panic disorder and the reactions experienced by individuals with specific phobia when they encounter their feared object or situation (Craske, 1991). In fact, the DSM-IV-TR only discriminates these two responses by the presence or absence of an external cue, whereby an unexpected, or uncued, panic attack occurs in the context of panic disorders, while situationally bound or situationally predisposed panic attacks occur in the context of specific phobias and social phobias. Thus, fear and panic are beginning to be believed to be equivalent experiences.

Panic can manifest itself physically, somatically, and cognitively in the form of a full-blown panic attack or a limited-symptom panic attack. The DSM-IV-TR defines a panic attack as

> a discrete period of intense fear or discomfort, in which at least four (or more) of the following symptoms developed abruptly and reached a peak within 10 minutes: palpitations, pounding heart, or accelerated heart rate; sweating; trembling or shaking; sensations of shortness of breath or smothering; feeling of choking; chest pain or discomfort; nausea or abdominal distress; feeling dizzy, unsteady, lightheaded, or faint; derealization (feeling of unreality) or depersonalization (being detached from oneself); fear of dying; paresthesias (numbness or tingling sensations); and chills or hot flashes. Limited-symptom attacks require the same criteria, except that fewer than four symptoms of panic are required.

While panic attacks are most often thought of in regard to panic disorder, with and without agoraphobia, panic attacks can also be experienced in specific phobia and social phobia. One study examining specific phobias found that 47% of individuals with a phobia of heights, 20% of individuals with an animal phobia, 50% of individuals with a blood/injection phobia, and 36% of individuals with a driving phobia experienced a panic attack when encountering the phobic situation or object (Antony, Brown, & Barlow, 1997). Thus, the panic attacks or panic-like symptoms can exist among all of the phobias and may play an important role in the maintenance of the phobia. Zitrin, Klein, Woerner, and Ross (1983) found in their study that while individuals received treatment for agoraphobia and specific phobia, the occurrence of panic attacks would decrease, but avoidance behavior continued because anticipatory anxiety remained high. After continued treatment, in the absence of the panic attacks, the anticipatory anxiety decreased, followed by a decrease in phobic avoidance. Therefore, when the panic symptoms were no longer negatively reinforcing the avoidance behavior, the individual was able to face the phobic situation or object.

ETIOLOGY OF PHOBIAS

The development of phobias has been understood in various ways. It has been proposed that individuals who experience panic attacks or panic-like symptoms have high levels of anxiety sensitivity, or the tendency to perceive anxiety as harmful (Reiss, Peterson, Gursky, & McNally, 1986). Studies have found that individuals with panic disorder with agoraphobia have high scores on a measure of anxiety sensitivity, indicating their aversion to the experience of anxiety itself (Antony et al., 1997).

In addition to a higher level of anxiety sensitivity, there is enhanced attentional selectivity or interoception for physical cues (Barlow, 2001). Individuals with phobias tend to be more aware of body sensations related to arousal. Thus, these individuals have a vulnerability to be able to detect subtle bodily experiences, perceive these experiences as dangerous and aversive, and, as a consequence, are more prone to develop panic attacks or paniclike symptoms. These symptoms are maintained out of a "fear of fear" in which the experience of panic attacks or paniclike symptoms leads to a fear of experiencing these symptoms again. Because of the increased awareness of bodily sensations, any sensation resembling that of panic is perceived as panic. Phobia then develops as the individual begins to fear the occurrence of another panic attack or paniclike symptoms. They start to avoid situations or objects in which the panic may occur or in which the ability to escape such a situation would be difficult or impossible. Thus, a type of conditioning occurs in which the panic attacks or paniclike symptoms begin to be associated with particular situations or objects, especially those in which escape may not be possible. Studies have supported this idea, finding that the onset of agoraphobia and specific phobias occurred as a result of direct conditioning experiences (Ost, 1985, 1987). In one study, 81% of individuals with agoraphobia, 58% of individuals with social phobia, and between 45 and 68% of individuals with specific phobias ascribed the onset of their phobia to conditioning experiences (Ost, 1987).

Phobias can be understood from physiological, cognitive, and behavioral perspectives. Cognitive–behavioral therapy has been shown to be effective in treating agoraphobia, social phobia, and specific phobias by focusing on one or more of these three elements. The following sections will provide additional information about each phobia and its treatment.

AGORAPHOBIA

Agoraphobia refers to fear of being in situations or places from which escape may be difficult or embarrassing or in which help may be unavailable in the event of a panic attack or panic-like symptoms (APA, 2000; Dziegielewski & MacNeil, 1999; Pasnau & Bystritsky, 1990). Agoraphobia may occur with or without the presence of full-blown panic attacks. Panic attacks, or panic-like symptoms usually lead to anticipatory anxiety about experiencing the panic and, consequently, avoidance behavior (Zitrin et al., 1983). Panic disorder with agoraphobia has a lifetime prevalence rate of 3.5% while agoraphobia without a history of panic disorder has a lifetime prevalence rate of 5.3% (Kessler et al., 1994). The severity of the panic symptoms is what differentiates panic disorder with agoraphobia from agoraphobia with history of panic disorder. Individuals with panic disorder with agoraphobia experience full-blown panic attacks, while those with agoraphobia without history of panic disorder have never experienced a full-blown panic attack. However, 57% of individuals with agoraphobia without history of panic disorder report experiencing limited-symptoms attacks (Goisman et al., 1995). Agoraphobia typically has a later age of onset than the other phobias, with mean ages ranging from 25 to 29 years old (Ost, 1987; Zitrin et al., 1983). Between 70 and 75% of agoraphobics are women (Al-Kubaisy et al., 1992; Zitrin et al., 1983).

Initial treatments for agoraphobia conducted in the 1960s and 1970s consisted of systematic desensitization (Barlow, Raffa, & Cohen, 2002). This involved imaginal exposure to the feared situation coupled with muscle relaxation. Due to minimal success with this treatment, researchers and practitioners became interested in situational in vivo exposure. This required the patient to create a hierarchy of feared situations that they avoid and then entering these situations until the anxiety diminished. Some studies found that while initial improvements resulted from in vivo exposure, few patients were symptom-free at follow-up (McPherson, Brougham, & McLaren, 1980). Thus, researchers have focused on improving the effectiveness of situational in vivo exposure. Al-Kubaisy et al. (1992) compared three different treatment conditions: self-exposure plus clinician-accompanied exposure, self-exposure only, and self-relaxation with no exposure. Results indicate that both exposure groups showed significantly more improvement than the self-relaxation group. There was no difference in effectiveness between self-exposure alone and self-exposure with clinician-accompanied exposure. Thus, exposure is the therapeutic element, with no additional gains from clinician-accompanied exposure.

Researchers have also manipulated the pace in which exposure is administered in order to determine any difference in effectiveness. Chambless (1990) compared massed exposure (conducted daily) versus spaced exposure (conducted weekly). Results indicate that massed and spaced treatments were equally effective at posttest and 6-month follow-up. Further, there were no differences in the ratings of stress experienced during treatment for the two treatment conditions and no difference in dropout rates.

The way in which the agoraphobia was acquired was examined in the context of three different treatment approaches: behaviorally focused (in vivo exposure and social skills training), physiologically focused (systematic desensitization and applied relaxation), and cognitively focused (self-instruction and fading) (Ost, 1985). Results indicate that, for individuals who acquired their phobia through conditioning, the behaviorally and physiologically focused methods were more effective than the cognitively focused methods. For individuals who acquired their phobias through instruction or information (indirect acquisition), the behaviorally focused method was more effective than the physiologically and cognitively focused methods. Thus, the mode of acquisition of the phobia has some effect on the effectiveness of the treatment.

Pharmacological treatments for agoraphobia have also been examined. Zitrin et al. (1983) compared three conditions: behavior therapy (consisting of systematic desensitization and assertiveness training) and imipramine (a tricyclic antidepressant), behavior therapy and placebo, and supportive therapy and imipramine. Results indicate that behavior therapy plus imipramine was superior to behavior therapy plus placebo. When all drug-treated patients were compared with all placebo-treated patient irrespective of type of therapy treatment, imipramine was significantly superior to placebo in the treatment of agoraphobia.

As discussed previously, panic attacks or paniclike symptoms are common in patients with agoraphobia, which often results in avoidance of situations for fear of experiencing panic. Barlow, Raffa, and Cohen (2002) have proposed a treatment called *sensation-focused intensive therapy* that involves education, cognitive restructuring, and interoceptive exposure, followed by therapist-assisted exposure. Patients are educated on internal sensations and then are guided in ways to reinterpret these sensations. Interoceptive exposure involves inducing paniclike sensations by engaging in various exercises (e.g., spinning in a chair, inhaling carbon dioxide) in an attempt to lessen the fear of specific bodily cues. While comprehensive results of this proposed treatment have not been completed, they are likely to provide additional information about the mechanisms of change in treatment with agoraphobia.

SPECIFIC PHOBIA

Specific phobia refers to a persistent fear that is cued by the presence or anticipation of a specific object or situation (APA, 2000). When exposed to the situation or object, the individual experiences a panic attack or paniclike symptoms. As a result of anticipatory anxiety about experiencing further panic symptoms, the individual begins to avoid the phobic situation or endure it with great difficulty. The DSM-IV-TR (APA, 2000) identifies five subtypes that indicate the focus of fear in specific phobia: animal type (fear of animals or insects), natural environment type (fear of objects in the natural environment, such as storms, heights, or water), blood-injection-injury type (fear of seeing blood or injury or by receiving an injection), situational type (fear of specific situation such as public transportation, flying, driving, or enclosed spaces), and other type (fear of other stimuli).

Lifetime prevalence rates for specific phobia have been found to be 11% (Kessler et al., 1994). The age of onset of specific phobias varies based on the subtype, although the majority have their onset in childhood (Lipsitz, Barlow, Mannuzza, Hofmann, & Fyer, 2002; Ost, 1987). The average age of onset is 22 years for situational phobias, 9 years for animal phobias, 14 years for natural environment phobias, and 9 years for blood-injection-injury phobias. Overall, 63% of individuals with specific phobias had childhood onset (12 years of age or younger). In terms of each subtype, 18% of situational phobias, 90% of animal phobias, 84% of blood-injection-injury phobias, and 67% of natural environment phobias had childhood onset. Specific phobias are more common among women than men, with women comprising between 65 and 78% of individuals diagnosed with specific phobias (Al-Kubaisy et al., 1992; Ost, 1992). For specific fears, women are more likely to be diagnosed with snake, spider, lightning, darkness, and closed spaces phobias than men (Fredrickson, Annas, Fischer, & Wik, 1996).

As discussed previously, individuals with specific phobia reactions often experience panic attacks or paniclike symptoms when in the presence of the phobic object or situation. Individuals with a blood-injection-injury type of phobia, in addition to experiencing panic reactions when encountering the phobic situation, can at times have a reaction that is very different from that experienced by individuals with the other phobic types. Individuals with blood-injection-injury phobias experience a diphasic response, in which heart rate and blood pressure increase initially for a brief period of time, followed by a sudden decrease in arousal, often accompanied by fainting. This physiological reaction is known as a vasovagal syncope (Barlow, 2002; Schienle et al., 2003). In a study conducted by Ost (1992), 56% of injection phobics and 70% of blood phobics reported having fainted at least once in the phobic situation.

The treatment of choice for specific phobias is in vivo exposure. Al-Kubaisy et al. (1992) found that individuals with specific phobias showed more improvement to exposure-based treatment than to the use of self-relaxation with no exposure. Further, clinician-accompanied exposure was assessed to determine whether it was more effective than self-exposure. Results indicate that clinician-accompanied exposure was no more effective than self-exposure.

Another study assessed whether massed or spaced exposure was more effective in treating specific phobias (Chambless, 1990). From results at posttest, the massed treatment was more effective in reducing anxiety. However, no differences were found between massed and spaced exposure in terms of avoidance behavior. When assessed at the 6-month follow-up, there was no longer any significant difference in level of anxiety reported between the massed and the spaced condition. Thus, while individuals with specific phobias experience less anxiety initially when they are treated with massed exposure, no differences in level of anxiety exist after 6 months and no differences in avoidance behavior exist immediately after treatment or at 6-month follow-up.

The number of sessions required for exposure to be effective has been assessed in multiple studies (Hellstrom, Fellenius, & Ost, 1996; Ost, Alm, Brandberg, & Breitholtz, 2001). When comparing the effectiveness of one session of exposure treatment versus five sessions of exposure treatment for claustrophobia, no significant differences were noted (Ost et al., 2001). Both groups showed clinically significant improvements, as measured by increased time spent in a small room, increased time spent wearing a gas mask, and decreases in heart rate and blood pressure during exposure. When comparing one versus five sessions of exposure therapy for the treatment of blood phobias, both treatment groups showed equivalent levels of improvement, as measured by increased time watching a film with blood, decreases in reported anxiety, and decreases in fainting behavior. Thus, one session of exposure therapy was as effective as five sessions in the treatment of claustrophobia and blood phobia.

Exposure therapy for blood phobias involves an added element that is not present in the treatment for the other types of specific phobias. As discussed earlier, individuals with blood phobias experience a unique physiological reaction, a vasovagal syncope, in which there is an increase in heart rate in blood pressure, followed by a rapid decrease, which is then often accompanied by fainting. Treatment, therefore, for blood phobias addresses this physiological reaction that is characteristic of individuals with blood phobias. Hellstrom et al. (1996) discuss the use of applied tension to treat blood phobics. The purpose of applied tension is to teach the patient how to increase his or her blood pressure and to help the patient recognize the very early signs of a drop in blood pressure as a response to contact with blood/injury stimuli. By learning the tension techniques, the patient will be able to reverse the blood pressure drop and prevent fainting. Applied tension involves tensing the muscles in the arms, chest, and legs until a feeling of warmth rises in the face (usually 15–20 seconds). Then the patient lets go of the tension, without entering into a deeper state of relaxation than they were initially. After 20–30 seconds, the patient tenses his or her muscle again and then releases it. This procedure is repeated five times. After learning the tension technique, the patient is exposed to blood or injury stimuli and applies the tension technique at the earliest signs of a drop in blood pressure. Hellstrom et al. (1996) examined the effectiveness of applied tension by comparing three treatment conditions: one session of applied tension, five sessions of applied tension, and one session of tension only without exposure. Results indicate that all three groups showed equivalent levels of clinical improvement, as measured by increased blood pressure, increased time spent watching the film, and decreased fainting. One significant difference was noted in that individuals treated with five sessions of applied tension reported lower levels of anxiety at posttest than those treated with one session of applied tension or the tension-only group. However, no significant differences existed at 1-year follow-up. Thus, in the treatment for blood phobias, tension techniques are the essential ingredients, with or without the inclusion of exposure.

Pharmacological therapies are believed to have little benefit in the treatment of specific phobias (Barlow, 2002). In one study comparing the use of imipramine to that of placebo, no significant differences were found (Zitrin et al., 1983). Thus, the use of medications to treat specific phobias is not supported.

SOCIAL PHOBIA

Individuals with social phobia fear one or more social or performance situations because of a concern of being humiliated or embarrassed by performing poorly or displaying visible anxiety symptoms in front of others (APA, 2000). The social phobia may be generalized, in which the individual fears a multitude of social and performance situations, or it may be nongeneralized, in which only one or two social or performance situations are feared. The prevalence rate for social phobia has been found to be 13% (Kessler et al., 1994). The age of onset of social phobia is usually in the midteens, with a mean age of onset of approximately 16 (Barlow, 2002; Ost, 1987). Social phobia is typically more prevalent in women than in men, with the female-to-male ratio being approximately 3:2 (Den Boer, 2000; Kessler et al., 1994).

Several treatments for social phobia have been found to be effective, including exposure, cognitive restructuring, social skills training, and psychopharmacology. Al-Kubaisy et al. (1992) found clinician-accompanied exposure and self-exposure to be superior to self-relaxation with no exposure. In a comparison of cognitive therapy and social skills training to supportive therapy, cognitive therapy with social skills training was found to be superior to supportive therapy (Cottraux et al., 2000).

A combined treatment, cognitive behavior group therapy (CBGT), has shown promising results (Gelernter et al., 1991; Heimberg et al., 1990). CBGT has three primary components: exposure to feared social situations in session, cognitive restructuring, and homework assignments for in vivo exposure and associated cognitive resturcturing (Turk, Heimberg, & Hope, 2001). The group is designed to meet for 12 weekly $2\frac{1}{2}$-hour sessions. In a study conducted by Heimberg et al. (1990), CBGT was compared to an educational–supportive treatment. Results indicate that individuals receiving CBGT were less impaired, reported less anxiety, showed increases in positive cognitions, and showed decreases in negative cognitions. These improvements were also maintained at 6-month follow-up.

Several studies have also examined the effectiveness of medication for social phobia. Gelernter et al. (1991) compared CBGT, alprazolam, phenelzine, and placebo plus self-directed exposure. Results found no differences between groups on self-report measures of social avoidance, distress, fear of negative evaluation, and positive and negative self-statements, with all groups showing clinically significant improvements. When comparing the medication groups, the alprazolam- and phenelzine-treated patients were significantly less impaired, at posttest than the placebo-treated group. However, at the 2-month follow-up, after discontinuation of the medicine, only the phenelzine-treated group remained less impaired, while the alprazolam-treated group was no different than the placebo-treated group. In contrast, the CBGT-treated group showed clinically significant improvement at posttest and even greater improvement among the CBGT-treated group, while the alprazolam group showed initial improvement at follow-up. Thus, CBGT and phenelzine show maintenance of the therapeutic gains at follow-up, with even greater improvement among the CBGT-treated group, while the alprazolam shows initial improvement at posttest but demonstrates a relapse response at follow-up.

Another study compared the effectiveness of cognitive therapy with fluoxetine (Clark et al., 2003). There were three treatment conditions: cognitive therapy, fluoxetine plus self-exposure, and placebo plus self-exposure. The components of cognitive therapy included role-playing, addressing dysfunctional assumptions, video feedback, and in vivo exposure. Results indicate that all groups showed substantial improvement, but the cognitive therapy condition was superior to the fluoxetine plus self-exposure and to the placebo plus self-exposure conditions. The fluoxetine and placebo groups did not differ. Further, cognitive therapy remained superior to the fluoxetine plus self-exposure group at 12-month follow-up. Thus, cognitive therapy was shown to be effective in reducing fear and avoidance in social phobics at posttest and after 1 year. Fluoxetine itself was not found to be any more effective than placebo in the treatment of social phobia.

SUMMARY AND CONCLUSIONS

Phobias can be distressing and debilitating disorders. Individuals with agoraphobia, specific phobia, and social phobia experience fear in particular situations or around particular objects that often manifests itself in a panic attack or paniclike symptoms. The experience of panic leads to anticipatory anxiety about having future symptoms of panic, resulting in avoidance of the phobic situation. CBT has been found to be effective in treating these phobias through a combination of exposure, cognitive therapy, and psychopharmacology. Continued research on treatments for phobias will help to find the most cost-effective treatments that can be generalizable across various patients and settings.

REFERENCES

Al-Kubaisy, T., Marks, I. M., Logsdail, S., Marks, M. P., Lovell, K., Sungur, M., & Araya, R. (1992). Role of exposure homework in phobia reduction: A controlled study. *Behavior Therapy, 23*, 599–621.

American Psychiatric Association. (2000). *Diagnostic and statistical manual of mental disorders* (4th ed., text rev.). Washington, DC: Author.

Antony, M. M., Brown, T. A., & Barlow, D. H. (1997). Heterogeneity among specific phobia types in DSM-IV. *Behavior Research and Therapy, 35*, 1089–1100.

Barlow, D. H. (2001). *Clinical handbook of psychological disorders* (3rd ed.). New York: Guilford Press.

Barlow, D. H. (2002). *Anxiety and its disorders: The nature and treatment of anxiety and panic* (2nd ed.). New York: Guilford Press.

Barlow, D. H., Raffa, S. D., & Cohen, E. M. (2002). Psychological treatments for panic disorders, phobias, and generalized anxiety disorder. In P. E. Nathan & J. M. Gorman (Eds.), *A guide to treatments that work* (2nd ed., pp. 301–335). New York: Oxford University Press.

Chambless, D. L. (1990). Spacing of exposure sessions in treatment of agoraphobia and simple phobia. *Behavior Therapy, 21*, 217–229.

Clark, D. M., Ehlers, A., McManus, F., Hackmann, A., Fennell, M., Campbell, H. et al. (2003). Cognitive therapy versus fluoxetine in generalized social phobia: A randomized placebo-controlled trial. *Journal of Consulting and Clinical Psychology, 71*, 1058–1067.

Cottraux, J., Note, I., Albuisson, E., Yao, S. N., Note, B., Mollard, E. et al. (2000). Cognitive behavior therapy versus supportive therapy in social phobia: A randomized controlled trial. *Psychotherapy and Psychosomatics, 69*, 137–146.

Craske, M. G. (1991). Phobic fear and panic attacks: The same emotional states triggered by different cues? *Clinical Psychology Review, 11*, 599–620.

Den Boer, J. A. (2000). Social anxiety disorder/social phobia: Epidemiology, diagnosis, neurobiology, and treatment. *Comprehensive Psychiatry, 41*, 405–415.

Dziegielewski, S. F., & MacNeil, G. (1999). Time-limited treatment considerations and strategy for specific phobic conditions. *Crisis Intervention, 5*, 133–150.

Fredrickson, M., Annas, P., Fischer, H., & Wik, G. (1996). Gender and age differences in the prevalence of specific fears and phobias. *Behaviour Research and Therapy, 26*, 241–244.

Gelernter, C. S., Uhde, T. W., Cimbolic, P., Arnkoff, D. B., Vittone, B. J., Tancer, M. E., & Bartko, J. J. (1991). Cognitive–behavioral and pharmacological treatments of social phobia: A controlled study. *Archives of General Psychiatry, 48*, 938–945.

Goisman, R. M., Warshaw, M. G., Steketee, G. S., Fierman, E. J., Rogers, M. P., Goldenberg, I., Weinshenker, N. J., Vasile, R. G., & Keller, M. B. (1995). DSM-IV in the disappearance of agoraphobia without a history of panic disorder: New data on a controversial diagnosis. *American Journal of Psychiatry, 152*, 1438–1443.

Heimberg, R. G., Dodge, C. S., Hope, D. A., Kennedy, C. R., Zallo, L., & Becker, R. E. (1990). Cognitive–behavioral group treatment for social phobia: Comparison to a credible placebo control. *Cognitive Therapy and Research, 14*, 1–23.

Hellstrom, K., Fellenius, J., & Ost, L. G. (1996). One versus five sessions of applied tension in the treatment of blood phobia. *Behavior Research and Therapy, 34*, 101–112.

Kessler, R. C., McGonagle, K. A., Zhao, S., Nelson, C. B., Hughes, M., Eshleman, S., Wittchen, H. U., & Kendler, K. S. (1994). Lifetime and 12-month prevalence of DSM-III-R psychiatric disorders in the United States: Results from the National Comorbidity Survey. *Archives of General Psychiatry, 51*, 8–19.

Lipsitz, J. D., Barlow, D. H., Mannuzza, S., Hofmann, S. G., & Fyer, A. J. (2002). Clinical features of four DSM-IV-specific phobia subtypes. *Journal of Nervous and Mental Disease, 190*, 471–478.

McPherson, F. M., Brougham, L., & McLaren, S. (1980). Maintenance of improvement in agoraphobic patients treated by behavioral methods—Four-year follow-up. *Behavior Research and Therapy, 18*, 150–152.

Ost, L. G. (1985). Ways of acquiring phobias and outcome of behavioral treatments. *Behavior Research and Therapy, 23*, 683–689.

Ost, L. G. (1987). Age of onset of different phobias. *Journal of Abnormal Psychology, 96*, 223–229.

Ost, L. G. (1992). Blood and injection phobia. Background and cognitive, physiological, and behavioral variables. *Journal of Abnormal Psychology, 101*, 68–74.

Ost, L. G., Alm, T., Brandberg, M., & Breitholtz, E. (2001). One vs. five sessions of exposure and five sessions of cognitive therapy in the treatment of claustrophobia. *Behavior Research and Therapy, 39*, 167–183.

Pasnau, R. O., & Bystritsky, A. (1990). An overview of anxiety disorders. *Bulletin of the Menninger Clinic, 54*, 157–171.

Regier, D. A., Boyd, J. H., Burke, J. D., Jr., Rae, D. S., Myers, J. K., Kramer, M., Robins, L. N., George, L. K., Karno, M., & Locke, B. Z. (1998). One-month prevalence of mental disorders in the United States: Based on five Epidemiologic Catchment Area sites. *Archives of General Psychiatry, 45*, 977–986.

Reiss, S., Peterson, R., Gursky, D., & McNally, R. (1986). Anxiety sensitivity, anxiety frequency, and the prediction of fearfulness. *Behavior Research and Therapy, 24*, 1–8.

Schienle, A., Schafer, A., Stark, R., Walter, B., Kirsh, P., & Vaitl, D. (2003). Disgust processing in phobia of blood-injection-injury. *Journal of Psychophysiology, 17*, 87–93.

Turk, C. L., Heimberg, R. G., & Hope, D. A. (2001). Social anxiety disorder. In D. H. Barlow (Ed.), *Clinical handbook of psychological disorders: A step-by-step treatment manual* (3rd ed., pp. 114–153). New York: Guilford Press.

Zitrin, C. M., Klein, D. F., Woerner, M. G., & Ross, D. C. (1983). Treatment of phobias: Comparison of imipramine hydrochloride and placebo. *Archives of General Psychiatry, 40*, 125–138.

Play Therapy

Susan M. Knell

Keywords: play therapy, developmentally based psychotherapies, developmental issues in treatment, treating preschool-age children

Cognitive–behavioral play therapy (CBPT) is a unique adaptation of cognitive–behavioral therapy for very young children ($2\frac{1}{2}$–6 years old). As such, it incorporates traditional cognitive and behavioral interventions within a developmentally appropriate play therapy paradigm. Through the use of play, cognitive change is communicated indirectly, often using puppets, stuffed animals, and books to model strategies.

DEVELOPMENTAL ISSUES

Preschool and early school-age children present some unique challenges in psychotherapy. These challenges are compounded by the demands of cognitive therapy, which is verbally oriented, and typically demands a level of cognitive sophistication. Young children may have difficulty distinguishing between irrational, illogical thinking and more rational, logical thought. Although an adult may need some guidance in identifying and labeling irrational, illogical thoughts, the inconsistencies can be understood once identified. In order to help young children identify maladaptive thoughts, a more indirect approach, heavily focused on modeling, must be utilized.

CBPT VERSUS TRADITIONAL PLAY THERAPIES

Like all play therapies, CBPT is grounded in a positive therapeutic relationship, the use of play as a means of communication, and the notion that the play therapy setting is a safe place for the child to communicate his/her concerns. In contrast to more traditional play therapies, CBPT emphasized collaboration between the therapist and the child in the setting of goals and the selection of play materials and activities. Also, the play is psychoeducational in nature, with an emphasis on the transmission of adaptive coping skills.

PRINCIPLES OF COGNITIVE THERAPY RELATED TO WORK WITH CHILDREN

Many of the fundamental principles of CT as delineated by Beck and Emery (1985) are applicable to therapy with young children. For example, the cognitive model of emotional disorders as applied through brief treatment is applicable across the entire age span. Similarly, the importance of a sound therapeutic relationship as a necessary condition of CT applies to even the youngest patients. The focus on directive, structured, problem-oriented treatment applies to all individuals, as does the importance of CT as psychoeducational in nature.

With minor adjustments, other principles of CT are applicable. For example, CT with adults stresses a scientific approach, where the client's beliefs and cognitions are treated as hypotheses to be tested, and revised in light of new data. However, the inductive and Socratic methods stressed with adults, must be modified for use with young children. With preschoolers, such experiments can be conducted with and for the child, modeling through play materials, how new information can be used adaptively. Similarly, Socratic questions can be modified for children to include more open-ended queries (e.g., "I wonder what you think about that?" rather than "What do you think about that?"). This may allow the child to experience the therapist's interest and concern without applying undue pressure on the child to explain something beyond his or her ability. One principle of CT, collaborative effort, is changed with the young child. Although the team approach is still vitally important, the balance of initiative tips more toward the therapist, sometimes with help from the parents, with the very young child.

TREATMENT STAGES OF CBPT

CBPT is usually conducted weekly in individual sessions with the child. Parents are frequently involved in working with the therapist around child management issues, but do not typically participate in therapy sessions per se. Before CBPT begins, the parents are usually interviewed in order to obtain relevant history and background information.

CBPT can be conceptualized as having four stages. In the Introductory/Orientation stage, the child is prepared for therapy and the therapist often guides the parents in helping to prepare the child for treatment. This may involve teaching the parent how to tell the child about therapy in a developmentally appropriate way, and often includes the parents reading a book about play therapy to the child. Early sessions with the child serve as an introduction to treatment.

In the Assessment stage, the therapist conceptualizes a sense of the child's perceptions of his/her situation. This is done through the use of unstructured observations, structured play scenarios, and/or structured assessment tools, such as the Puppet Sentence Completion Task (Knell & Beck, 2000), in combination with information gathered from the parents.

During the Treatment stage, therapy focuses on the teaching of more adaptive responses to deal with specific situations faced by the child. A wide array of cognitive and behavioral interventions are utilized during the middle phase of CBPT. Reinforcing the gains and successes achieved by the child is vital to their sustainability over time, as well as to the child's achievement of additional successes.

Also during the Treatment stage, generalization and relapse prevention are integrated into the therapy. Generalization of adaptive behaviors to the natural environment is an important component of CBPT; the therapist must build in specific training that helps the child make connections to other settings and individuals. In particular, interventions that address self-control and teach new behaviors are critical. As a rule, all interventions should incorporate the issue of generalization by modeling real-life situations as much as possible.

Reinforcement of skills should come from the natural environment. Adaptive behaviors should be reinforced and emphasized beyond their initial acquisition in order to strengthen and support their continuation. In addition, relapse prevention is a critical focus of the middle stages of CBPT. The therapist prepares the child for setbacks by working on ways to handle future stressors and life situations. High-risk situations are identified, and the child is prepared for handling such situations, should they arise. As these skills are brought into CBPT, work is also being done with the parents around the same issues.

Finally, the Termination phase of CBPT takes place over several sessions. Preparation for the end of therapy deals with the concrete reality, as well as feelings that the child may have about the end of treatment. Some children benefit from very concrete representation of the ending of treatment (e.g., through calendars or construction chains representing each session).

SETTINGS/MATERIALS

Play materials used in CBPT are similar to those found in any type of play therapy. These include, but are not limited to, crayons/markers and paper, blocks, dolls, dollhouse, and puppets. Axline (1947) provided a list of toys that is still cited as a guideline for play therapy materials, despite the volumes of new toys created since the list was published. In general, the more directive techniques found in CBPT, compared especially with Axline's nondirective approach, require planning and forethought regarding choice of materials. There are certain clinical presentations (e.g., children with specific phobias) where specific play materials will be essential to the treatment. However, it is probably more important that options be available than that the therapy room be stocked with a wide array of toys.

TREATMENT INTERVENTIONS

Of necessity, CBPT emphasizes experiential, rather than verbal, approaches to interacting with the child. One extremely useful mechanism for the transmission of interventions is modeling through play. The therapist uses play materials to identify maladaptive beliefs, counter these beliefs, and provide positive coping statements and skills for the child.

A wide array of behavioral interventions may be used in CBPT. Among the most commonly used are systematic desensitization, contingency management, and activity scheduling. Many of these and other behavioral techniques can be adapted for children as young as 3–4 years old. Parent involvement may be critical to implement behavioral interventions that take place outside the therapy session.

Similarly, cognitive interventions can be adapted for use in CBPT. Cognitive change strategies and positive coping self-statements are two such cognitive interventions. Young children can be taught to modify thoughts and beliefs particularly if these efforts are incorporated into, and modeled through, play.

PRESENTING PROBLEMS AND POPULATIONS

CBPT has been used with a wide range of populations, with published reports of its use with children presenting with selective mutism, encopresis, fears and phobias, and separation anxiety. It has also been used to treat children who have experienced traumatic life events, such as sexual abuse and divorce (see Knell, 1999, for a description of CBPT with various populations). In general, CBPT would appear to be an appropriate approach for preschool and early school-age children, as these age groups are learning about cause–effect relationships but still lack the language skills for more verbally oriented therapeutic modalities. Virtually any presenting problem requiring the young child to learn more adaptive coping skills could be addressed through CBPT.

RESEARCH

CBPT is a model of psychotherapy that builds on the principles of two well-established and respected therapeutic treatments, cognitive and behavior therapy. It is a developmentally sensitive, integrated model of psychotherapy that uses proven techniques and has the flexibility of incorporating other empirically supported interventions, such as systematic desensitization. However, CBPT has yet to be subjected to rigorous empirical study.

See also: Aggressive and antisocial behavior in youth, Anxiety—children, Children—behavior therapy, Treatment of children

REFERENCES

Axline, V. (1947) *Play therapy*. Boston: Houghton-Mifflin.

Beck, A. T., & Emery, G. (1985). *Anxiety disorders and phobias: A cognitive perspective*. New York: Basic Books.

Knell, S. M. (1999). Cognitive–behavioral play therapy. In S.W. Russ & T. Ollendick (Eds.), *Handbook of psychotherapies with children and families* (pp. 385–404). New York: Plenum Press.

Knell, S. M., & Beck, K. W. (2000). Puppet sentence completion task. In K. Gitlin-Weiner, A. Sandgrund, & C. E. Schaefer (Eds.), *Play diagnosis and assessment* (2nd ed., pp. 704–721). New York: Wiley.

Primary Care Therapy

Robert A. DiTomasso and Christina Esposito

Keywords: primary care, behavioral medicine, clinical health psychology, behavior therapy, cognitive–behavioral therapy

Within the past several years there has been an increasing emphasis on the interface between primary care and psychotherapy. In large part this trend may be credited to the failure of the biomedical model and the developing impact of the biopsychosocial model. Physicians have begun to realize that a thorough understanding and treatment of the whole patient is critical in accurately conceptualizing patient problems and in developing effective interventions. Primary care patients present with a multitude of possible problems, many of which have central components that are behavioral in nature. Given the reciprocal and synergistic relationship that exists between mind and body phenomenon, there is little wonder why patients seeking care from primary care physicians may do so for a variety of mental and physical reasons. By offering empirically supported cognitive–behavioral interventions, clinicians may therefore provide a critical function in the effective and efficient delivery of health care in this setting.

ROLE OF COGNITIVE-BEHAVIORAL THERAPY IN PRIMARY CARE

Psychology's contribution, including advances in cognitive–behavioral therapy, to the prevention, assessment, treatment, and management of acute and chronic illnesses will undoubtedly play a major role in the future development of the profession (Levant et al., 2001). Major advances in assessment and treatment from a cognitive–behavioral perspective will likely lead the way. Health care delivery systems that acknowledge the behavioral and physical causes of disease are rapidly becoming the new framework for health care systems (American Psychological Association: Public Policy Office, 2000). The U.S. Department of Health and Human Services (2000) has noted that 8 of the top 10 leading health indicators are behavioral in nature: alcohol use, tobacco use, diet, physical activity, suicide, violence, unintentional injuries, and unsafe sex. Psychological problems often manifest themselves in the form of physical symptoms. Patients may therefore seek care for the physical manifestations of a psychological disorder, perhaps without even realizing the cause of the symptoms. Stress-related factors may precipitate physical symptoms and activate or exacerbate an existing psychophysiological disorder. Organic problems may present as psychological in nature to the physician, with the psychological manifestations resolving after medical management. Patients may also react psychologically to a current medical condition, requiring treatment of both conditions. While mental health difficulties are highly prevalent in primary care patients, a significant percentage of these problems are undetected and untreated by the primary care physician. For example, while about 6 to 10% of patients presenting to primary care physicians for any reason have a diagnosable major depression, about 30% have symptoms of depression (Zung, Broadhead, & Roth, 1993). A prevalence rate of 14.6% for any anxiety disorder has been reported for primary care patients (Nisenson, Pepper, Schwenk, & Coyne, 1998). Despite high rates of prevalence, primary care physicians appear to underdiagnose mental disorders (Schulberg & Burns, 1988). Between one-third and three-fourths of patients with major depression are not recognized or treated by primary care physicians. Evidence also suggests that mental disorders are misdiagnosed by generalists. Whatever the case, collaboration between primary care physicians and cognitive–behavioral therapists is essential in the effective delivery of health care today.

MEDICAL AND MENTAL PROBLEMS IN PRIMARY CARE

Cognitive–behaviorally oriented primary care clinicians play a unique role in the prevention or reduction of disease by helping patients to alter cognitive, emotional, and behavioral pathogenic risk factors. In addition, their knowledge in the assessment and treatment of mental health problems serves to contribute to the comprehensive, continuous care of patients across the life cycle. Over 25% of primary care patients have a diagnosable mental health disorder, most of which go undetected and untreated (Schulberg & Burns, 1998). Furthermore, undiagnosed psychological problems exert a tremendous impact on health care utilization, patient outcomes, and overall costs. There are considerable costs associated with untreated mental disorders such as depression and anxiety (Campbell et al., 2000). For example, depressed patients have higher rates of office visits, unexplained physical symptoms, and non-mental-health-related hospitalizations (Unutzer et al., 1997). In a meta-analysis of 91 studies conducted over a 30-year period on the impact of psychological interventions on health care costs, decreases in medical utilization following psychological intervention were evident in 90% of the studies (Chiles, Lambert, & Hatch, 1999).

FIT BETWEEN COGNITIVE-BEHAVIORAL THERAPY AND PRIMARY CARE

There are many reasons that cognitive–behavioral approaches fit well within the primary care model. First, cognitive–behavioral approaches are evidence-based, an approach that fits current thinking in primary care. Given the recent emphasis on evidence-based treatments in primary care, the climate is quite receptive to approaches that are empirically supported. Second, many of the problems seen in primary care are those for which cognitive–behavioral approaches have already been shown to be effective. These problems include mental and physical problems commonly seen by primary care physicians. Third, in the current age of accountability, increased emphasis has been placed on evidence-based therapies. The standard of care in the primary care setting is moving toward the use of these types of therapies. Fourth, the cognitive–behavioral model of conceptualization is comprehensive and attends to a variety of critical factors related to onset, development, and maintenance of problems. Patient problems are then more likely to be better understood and addressed as a result. Fifth, the cognitive–behavioral model is a short-term therapy approach that is quite amenable to patients in the primary care setting. Sixth, this model is easy for patients and physicians to understand and apply. Finally, patients may present significant challenges to primary care physicians who lack adequate training in this area and are often the sole providers of treatment for mental health problems. In this sense the cognitive–behavioral model has a great likelihood of becoming an accepted primary care therapy by the medical community.

Primary care therapy is generally concerned with improving patients' quality of life. Cognitive–behavioral clinicians in primary care settings are armed with a multitude of empirically based strategies that are likely to promote patient welfare and increase the potency of interventions. Cognitive interventions are used in primary care settings to modify thoughts, beliefs, and underlying assumptions negatively affecting the patient's health. Cognitive–behavioral factors may negatively influence health in many ways. First, irrational beliefs may contribute to health-risk behaviors and the avoidance of health-promoting behaviors (Masters, Burish, Hollon, & Rimm, 1987). For example, a patient who does not perceive a behavior as a risk to health, fails to see the behavior as personally threatening to health, and does not see that an alternative behavior will reduce the risk is less likely to change the behavior. Second, motivation to change a behavior appears to exert a powerful influence on the probability that a patient will change a health-risk behavior. Much of what primary care physicians do in their practices is prescribe changes in behavior to patients. Patients may be asked to do one or more of a variety of things including: quit smoking, lose weight, restrict salt intake, control carbohydrates, practice stress management, eat less fatty foods, reduce excessive alcohol use, sleep eight hours a night, practice safe sex, take a prescribed medication, and obtain a medical test. Physicians are traditionally taught to provide such recommendations to patients without considering the patient's level or stage of motivation to engage in behavior change. Patients may be given behavioral prescriptions when they have not even begun to contemplate the prospect of changing.

Third, even for those patients who do make a lifestyle change, little is offered in the way of facilitating maintenance and preventing relapse. Physicians often fail to address critical factors that are likely to promote long-term, stable changes in behavior including factors such as identifying high-risk situations, cognitive–behavioral coping strategies, self-efficacy, and the like.

Fourth, primary care clinicians possess extensive knowledge about facilitating adherence to treatment. Nonadherence to medical advice is a problem of monumental proportion in primary care, oftentimes undermining effective treatment, exposing patients to long-term consequences from disease states, and necessitating the use of stronger and more potent medications with negative side effects. Factors associated with treatment regimens, the physician–patient relationship, treatment settings, and the patient are important variables to consider in designing effective interventions.

Fifth, psychological distress has significant potential for contributing to the onset and exacerbation of medical problems. Cognitive–behavioral treatments may help to alleviate the psychologically based predisposing and precipitating risk factors.

FUTURE DIRECTIONS IN PRIMARY CARE THERAPY

As a primary care therapy, cognitive–behavioral approaches have much to offer patients. Examples of the application of cognitive–behavioral principles abound and include, but are not limited to, the following: promoting weight reduction, smoking cessation, increasing exercise, decreasing substance abuse, controlling sodium intake, promoting adherence to medical regimens, coping with chronic illness, preparing patients for stressful medical procedures, and enhancing self-care behaviors. As the field of cognitive–behavioral therapy and primary care continue to interface, the development and application of more effective treatments is likely to continue to grow.

See also: Clinical health psychology

REFERENCES

American Psychological Association: Public Policy Office. (2000, August). Psychology is a behavioral and mental health profession. Retrieved June 18, 2002, from http://www.apa.org/ppo/issues/ebsprofession.htm.

Campbell, T. L., Franks, P., Fiscella, K., McDaniel, S.H., Zwanzinger, J., Mooney, C. et al. (2000). Do physicians who diagnose more mental health disorders generate lower health costs? *The Journal of Family Practice, 49*(4), 305–310.

Chiles, J. A., Lambert, M. L., & Hatch, A. L. (1999). The impact of psychological intervention on medical cost offset: A meta-analytic review. *Clinical Psychology: Science and Practice, 6*(2), 204–220.

Levant, R. F., Ragusea, S., Reed, G. M., DiCowden, M., Sullivan, F., Stout, C. E. et al. (2001). Envisioning and accessing new roles for professional psychology. *Professional Psychology: Research and Practice, 32*(1), 79–87.

Masters, J. C., Burish, T. G., Hollon, S. D., & Rimm, D. C. (1987). *Behavior therapy*. Orlando, FL: Harcourt, Brace, Jovanovich.

Nisenson, L. G., Pepper, C. M., Schwenk, T. L., & Coyne, J. C. (1998). The nature and prevalence of anxiety disorders in primary care. *General Hospital Psychiatry, 20*, 21–28.

Schulberg, H. C., & Burns, B. J. (1998). Mental disorders in primary care: Epidemiologic, diagnostic, and treatment research directions. *Archives of Internal Medicine, 10*, 79–87.

Unutzer, J., Patrick, D. L., Simon, G., Greg, M. D., Grembowski, D., & Walker, E. (1997). Depressive symptoms and the cost of health services in HMO patients aged 65 years and older: A 4 year prospective study. *Journal of the American Medical Association, 277*, 1618–1623.

U.S. Department of Health and Human Services. (2000, November). Healthy people 2010: Leading health indicators. Retrieved June 15, 2002, from http://www.healthypeople.gov/LHI.

Zung, W. W., Broadhead, E., & Roth, M. E. (1993). Prevalence of depressive symptoms in primary care. *The Journal of Family Practice, 37*, 337–344.

Problem Solving–Depression

Arthur M. Nezu and Victoria M. Wilkins

Keywords: problem-solving therapy, depression, social problem solving, stress

According to a problem-solving formulation of depression, various problem-solving coping deficits can serve as vulnerability factors regarding the emergence and maintenance of depression in reaction to experiencing negative stressful events (Nezu, 1987). More specifically, when individuals are confronted with stressful life circumstances (e.g., loss of a spouse, being fired from a job, getting a divorce), the likelihood that they will also experience depression, in part, is a function of the degree to which they can effectively cope with such negative events.

SOCIAL PROBLEM SOLVING

Problem solving (often referred to as "social problem solving" to emphasize that such activities occur in social or interpersonal contexts) is the cognitive–behavioral process by which a person attempts to identify or discover effective or adaptive solutions for stressful problems encountered during the course of everyday living (D'Zurilla & Nezu, 1999; Nezu, in press). Problem-solving therapy (PST) provides for systematic training to help individuals cope more effectively with such stressful events by teaching them to apply a variety of skills geared to help them either (a) alter the nature of the problem (e.g., overcoming obstacles to a goal), (b) change their distressing reactions to the problem (e.g., acceptance that a problem cannot be changed), or (c) both.

THE SOCIAL PROBLEM-SOLVING PROCESS

Within a cognitive–behavioral framework, problem-solving outcomes are viewed as being largely determined by two general, but partially independent, dimensions: (a) problem orientation and (b) problem-solving style (D'Zurilla, Nezu, & Maydeu-Olivares, in press). *Problem orientation* is the set of relatively stable cognitive–affective schemas that represent a person's generalized beliefs, attitudes, and emotional reactions about problems in living and one's ability to successfully cope with such problems. This orientation can be either positive or negative in nature. A positive orientation is the constructive, problem-solving cognitive set that involves the general disposition to (a) appraise a problem as a "challenge" (i.e., opportunity for benefit or gain), (b) believe that problems are solvable ("optimism"), (c) believe in one's personal ability to solve problems successfully ("self-efficacy"), (d) believe that successful problem solving takes time, effort, and persistence, and (e) commit oneself to solving problems with dispatch rather than avoidance. In contrast, *negative problem orientation* is a dysfunctional or inhibitive cognitive–emotional set that involves the general tendency to (a) view problems as significant threats to one's well-being (psychological, social, economic), (b) doubt one's personal ability to solve problems successfully ("low self-efficacy"), and (c) easily become frustrated and upset when confronted with problems in living ("low frustration tolerance").

Problem-solving style refers to those core cognitive–behavioral activities that people engage in when attempting to cope with problems in living. Three differing problem-solving styles have been identified—one being an adaptive style, whereas the remaining two reflect maladaptive ways of coping.

Rational problem solving is the constructive problem-solving style that involves the systematic and planful application of certain skills, each of which makes a distinct contribution toward the discovery of an adaptive solution or coping response in a problem-solving situation. Specifically, the rational problem-solver carefully and systematically gathers facts and information about a problem, identifies demands and obstacles, sets realistic problem-solving goals, generates a variety of possible solutions, anticipates the consequences of the different solutions, judges and compares the alternatives, and then chooses and implements a solution while carefully monitoring and evaluating the outcome.

Impulsivity/carelessness represents one ineffective problem-solving style that involves a generalized response pattern characterized by impulsive, hurried, or careless attempts at problem resolution. An impulsive/careless style is often associated with individuals who have a low tolerance for uncertainty, distress, or negative emotions. *Avoidance style*, a second maladaptive coping pattern, is characterized by procrastination, passivity, and dependency. The individual with a strong avoidant style prefers to avoid problems rather than confront them, puts off solving problems for as long as possible, waits for problems to resolve themselves, and attempts to shift the responsibility for solving his or her problems to others.

A PROBLEM-SOLVING FORMULATION OF DEPRESSION

A problem-solving model of depression is based, in part, on the relational/problem-solving model of stress delineated by Nezu and D'Zurilla (1989). Within this model, stress is viewed as a function of the reciprocal relations among three major variables: (1) stressful life events, (2) emotional stress responses, and (3) problem-solving coping.

Stressful life events are life experiences that present a person with strong demands for personal, social, or biological readjustment. Two important types of stressful life events include major negative events and daily problems. A *major negative event* is a broad life experience or occurrence, such as a major negative life change, which often demands sweeping readjustments in a person's life (e.g., divorce, death of a loved one, job loss, major illness or injury). A *daily problem* (or problematic situation) is a more narrow and specific life experience characterized by a perceived discrepancy between adaptive demands and coping response availability (e.g., being late for work while caught in a traffic jam). In the stress literature, these specific stressful events are also referred to as "minor life events" or "daily hassles." Although daily problems or hassles are less dramatic than major negative events, research has demonstrated that the accumulation of these minor stressors over time has a greater impact on psychological and physical well-being than the number of major negative events one experiences.

The concept of *emotional stress* refers to the immediate emotional responses of a person to a stressful life event, as modified or transformed by appraisal and coping processes. Although emotional stress responses are often negative (e.g., depression), they can also be positive in nature (e.g., hope, relief, exhilaration). Negative emotions are likely to predominate when the person (a) appraises a problem as harmful or threatening to well-being, (b) doubts his or her ability to cope with the situation effectively, and/or (c) makes ineffective or maladaptive coping responses. On the other hand, positive emotions may emerge and compete with negative emotionality when the person (a) appraises the problem as a challenge or opportunity for benefit, (b) believes that he or she is capable of coping with the situation effectively, and (c) makes coping responses that are effective in reducing harmful or threatening conditions and/or the negative emotions that are generated by them.

The most important concept in the relational/problem-solving model is *problem-solving coping*, which integrates all cognitive appraisal and coping activities within a general social problem-solving framework. Specifically, when an individual is faced with a negative life event, various problems can occur, resulting in an increase in the likelihood of experiencing emotional stress. If the individual's ability to cope with such events is effective, then the stressful nature of this situation is reduced and little to no depressive symptoms are likely to emerge. However, if the person is not an effective problem-solver, he or she will have difficulty coping with the stress engendered by the negative life events and related set of problems. He or she will then have an increased likelihood of suffering from greater levels of depression. In this latter case, depression arises from actual or perceived negative consequences emanating from the problem situation. In general, such negative consequences can worsen current problems, engender future problems, decrease actual and perceived positive reinforcement, and discourage individuals from attempting to resolve problems in the future.

This model also focuses on the relation between depression and several of the major problem-solving components. More specifically, depression can result as a function of deficiencies, or decreased effectiveness, in problem orientation or rational problem-solving skills. For example, depressed individuals are often characterized by a strong negative orientation, having little faith in their ability to cope with stressful problems, believing that most problems are catastrophes, often blaming themselves for causing the problem, and becoming distressed when problems occur. Awareness and adaptive use of negative emotions are key aspects of problem orientation. Collectively, such beliefs decrease one's desire or motivation to engage in any meaningful coping attempts. One's ability to effectively define and formulate problems and to set realistic goals are also decreased when depressed, thus making it very difficult to identify effective solutions. Often depressed individuals set unrealistically high goals—when not achieved, self-blame occurs. Depressed individuals also tend to generate both fewer and less effective alternatives to problem situations. A negative problem orientation and lack of alternatives biases the depressed person to selectively attend to negative versus positive events and to immediate versus long-term consequences. The depressed individual may also have difficulty actually carrying out his or her plan due to specific behavioral and social skill deficits. Further, a negative problem orientation may impact on an individual's ability to be objective about the outcome of solution implementation. Thus, the depressed individual is unsatisfied with the coping attempt and may feel that the goals have not been achieved.

RELEVANT SUPPORTIVE RESEARCH

In support of a problem-solving model of depression, research has (a) established a strong correlation between various problem-solving deficits and depression (Nezu, Wilkins, & Nezu, in press), (b) supported the hypothesis that effective problem-solving ability serves to attenuate the likelihood that people will experience depression as a result of the occurrence of stressful events (Nezu, Wilkins, & Nezu, in press), and (c) underscored the efficacy of training depressed individuals to be more effective problem-solvers as a method to significantly reduce their depression (Nezu, D'Zurilla, Zwick, & Nezu, in press).

PROBLEM SOLVING AND DEPRESSION

A recent review of the available literature indicates that across several different samples of both clinical (e.g., adult outpatients reliably diagnosed with major depressive disorder, adult and adolescent inpatient groups, adult cancer patients) and nonclinical (e.g., high school students, college students, community residents) groups, strong associations exist between various problem-solving variables and depression (Nezu, Wilkins, & Nezu, in press). This appears to be true as well across various cultures (e.g., American, Chinese, and South African undergraduate students, French adolescents) and using various types of measures to assess problem solving (e.g., self-report and behavioral performance tests). For example, a negative problem orientation has been found to be an especially strong predictor of depression. Further, depressed adults, compared to matched nondepressed controls, evidence deficits in various problem-solving tasks related to real-life problems, such as identifying why a situation is a problem, generating possible solutions, making effective decisions, and delineating realistic personal goals.

PROBLEM SOLVING AS A BUFFER OF STRESS-RELATED DEPRESSION

Although the above research suggests a strong relationship between depression and various problem-solving deficits, the more important question involves whether problem solving serves to moderate the stress–depression relationship. In other words, does effective problem solving attenuate the likelihood that a person will experience depression that might be engendered by the experience of negative life events? Researchers have directly asked this question across differing patient populations, using varying measures of problem solving, and incorporating both cross-sectional and prospective experimental designs. In general, this body of research suggests strongly that effective problem solving is a significant moderator of the relationship between stressful events and consequent depression. More specifically, under *similar* levels of high stress, individuals with poor problem-solving skills have been found to experience significantly *higher* levels of depression than individuals characterized by effective problem solving.

PROBLEM-SOLVING THERAPY FOR DEPRESSION

Studies evaluating the efficacy of PST to treat adults with major depressive disorder (MDD), older adults with MDD, and adult cancer patients experiencing clinically high levels of depression have found it to be particularly effective (see Nezu, D'Zurilla et al., in press, for a review of this literature). Of conceptual importance is a study by Nezu and Perri (1989) that involved a dismantling study whereby adults with MDD were randomly assigned to one of three conditions: PST, PST minus training in the problem-orientation (PO) component, and a wait-list control. Their results underscore the importance of training in the full model, in that whereas patients who received training in rational problem-solving skills (but without PO training) fared significantly better than wait-list control participants, patients who received the full PST package experienced the greatest reduction in depression compared to the other two conditions.

PST has also been evaluated as a treatment for minor depression and dysthymia among primary care patients, although the research supporting this is not as strong (Barrett et al., 2001). However, this may be due to the fact that such treatment protocols did not include PO training, as would be suggested by the Nezu and Perri (1989) results. Consistent with this view is a study by Lynch, Tamburrino, and Nagel (1997) that did apply the full PST model to treat minor depression in a family practice setting and found it to be more efficacious than control conditions.

See also: Bipolar disorder, Depression—adult, Depression—youth, Mood disorders—bipolar disorder, Problem-solving therapy—general

REFERENCES

Barrett, J. E., Williams, J. W., Oxman, T. E., Frank, E., Katon, W., Sullivan, M., Hegel, M. T., Cornell, J. E., & Sengupta, A. S. (2001). Treatment of dysthymia and minor depression in primary care: A randomized trial in patients aged 18 to 59 years. *The Journal of Family Practice, 50*, 405–412.

D'Zurilla, T. J., & Nezu, A. M. (1999). *Problem-solving therapy: A social competence approach to clinical intervention* (2nd ed.). New York: Springer.

D'Zurilla, T. J., Nezu, A. M., & Maydeu-Olivares, A. (in press). What is social problem solving? Meaning, measures, and models. In E. C. Chang, T. J. D'Zurilla, & L. J. Sanna (Eds.), *Social problem solving: Theory, research, and training*. Washington, DC: American Psychological Association.

Lynch, D. J., Tamburrino, M. B., & Nagel, R. (1997). Telephone counseling for patients with minor depression: Preliminary findings in a family practice setting. *Journal of Family Practice, 44*, 293–298.

Nezu, A. M. (1987). A problem-solving formulation of depression: A literature review and proposal of a pluralistic model. *Clinical Psychology Review, 7*, 122–144.

Nezu, A. M. (in press). Problem solving and behavior therapy revisited. *Behavior Therapy*.

Nezu, A. M., & D'Zurilla, T. J. (1989). Social problem solving and negative affective states. In P. C. Kendall & D. Watson (Eds.), *Anxiety and depression: Distinctive and overlapping features* (pp. 285–315). New York: Academic Press.

Nezu, A. M., D'Zurilla, T. J., Zwick, M. L., & Nezu, C. M. (in press). Social problem solving therapy for adults. In E. C. Chang, T. J. D'Zurilla, &

L. J. Sanna (Eds.), *Social problem solving: Theory, research, and training*. Washington, DC: American Psychological Association.

Nezu, A. M., & Perri, M. G. (1989). Problem-solving therapy for unipolar depression: An initial dismantling investigation. *Journal of Consulting and Clinical Psychology, 57*, 408–413.

Nezu, A. M., Wilkins, V. M., & Nezu, C. M. (in press). Social problem solving, stress, and negative affective conditions. In E. C. Chang, T. J. D'Zurilla, & L. J. Sanna (Eds.), *Social problem solving: Theory, research, and training*. Washington, DC: American Psychological Association.

RECOMMENDED READINGS

Nezu, A. M. (1986). Efficacy of a social problem-solving therapy approach for unipolar depression. *Journal of Consulting and Clinical Psychology, 54*, 196–202.

Nezu, A. M., & Nezu, C. M. (2001). Problem-solving therapy. *Journal of Psychotherapy Integration, 11*, 187–205.

Nezu, A. M., Nezu, C. M., & Perri, M. G. (1989). *Problem-solving therapy for depression: Theory, research, and clinical guidelines*. New York: Wiley.

Nezu, A. M., Nezu, C. M., & Perri, M. G. (1990). Psychotherapy for adults within a problem-solving framework: Focus on depression. *Journal of Cognitive Psychotherapy, 4*, 247–256.

Nezu, A. M., & Ronan, G. F. (1985). Life stress, current problems, problem solving, and depressive symptoms: An integrative model. *Journal of Consulting and Clinical Psychology, 53*, 693–697.

Problem-Solving Therapy—General

Arthur M. Nezu and Thomas J. D'Zurilla

Keywords: problem-solving therapy, social problem solving

Social problem solving is the cognitive–behavioral process by which a person attempts to identify adaptive solutions for stressful problems. Problem-solving therapy (PST) helps individuals cope more effectively with such problems by teaching them to apply a variety of skills geared to help them either (a) alter the nature of the problem (e.g., overcoming obstacles to a goal), (b) change their distressing reactions to the problem (e.g., acceptance that a goal cannot be reached), or (c) both.

Problems can be single events (e.g., obtaining a loan from a bank), a series of related problems (e.g., continuous arguments with a spouse), or chronic situations (e.g., major chronic illness, such as cancer). Situations become problems when effective responses are required in order for the person to cope adaptively, but where such responses are not immediately available or identifiable due to the presence of various obstacles, such as ambiguity, unpredictability, conflicting demands, deficient skills, or lack of resources.

THE SOCIAL PROBLEM-SOLVING PROCESS

According to D'Zurilla and Nezu (1999), problem-solving outcomes in the real world are hypothesized to be largely determined by two general, but partially independent processes: (a) problem orientation and (b) problem-solving style. *Problem orientation* involves a set of generalized thoughts and feelings concerning problems in living, as well as one's ability to successfully resolve them. It can either be *positive* (e.g., viewing problems as opportunities to benefit in some way; perceiving oneself as able to solve problems effectively), which serves to enhance subsequent problem-solving efforts, or *negative* (e.g., viewing problems as a major threat to one's well-being; becoming immobilized when problems occur), which functions to inhibit attempts to solve problems.

Problem-solving style refers to various cognitive–behavioral activities aimed at coping with stressful problems. They can be either adaptive, leading to successful problem resolution, or dysfunctional, leading to negative consequences, such as psychological distress. *Rational problem solving* is the constructive style geared to identify an effective solution to the problem and involves the systematic application of specific problem-solving tasks (e.g., gathering information, generating alternative solutions, monitoring the consequences of an implemented solution). Dysfunctional problem-solving styles include (a) *impulsivity/carelessness* (i.e., impulsive, hurried, and incomplete attempts to solve a problem) and (b) *avoidance* (i.e., avoiding problems, procrastinating, and depending on others to solve one's problems).

EFFECTIVE VERSUS INEFFECTIVE PROBLEM SOLVERS

Important differences have been identified between individuals characterized as "effective" versus "ineffective" problem-solvers. In general, when compared to effective problem solvers, ineffective problem solvers report a greater number of life problems, more health and physical symptoms, more anxiety, more depression, and more psychological maladjustment. In addition, a negative problem orientation has been found to be associated with negative moods under routine and stressful conditions in general, as well as pessimism, negative emotional experiences, and clinical depression. Further, persons with a negative orientation tend to worry and complain more about their health (see Nezu, Wilkins, & Nezu, in press, for a review of this literature).

PROBLEM SOLVING AS A MODERATOR OF THE STRESS-DISTRESS RELATIONSHIP

How people cope with stressful experiences, including major events (e.g., undergoing a divorce, dealing with the death of a spouse) and daily problems (e.g., continued arguments with a co-worker, limited financial resources), can, in part, determine the degree to which they will experience long-lasting distress, particularly depression (Nezu, 1987; Nezu & D'Zurilla, 1989). Continued successful attempts at problem resolution will lead to a reduction or minimization of immediate emotional distress and a reduced likelihood of long-term negative affective states. Alternatively, if one's problem-solving coping skills are ineffective, or if extreme emotional distress impacts negatively on one's coping efforts, resulting in either reduced motivation, inhibition of problem-solving performance, or both, then the likelihood of long-term negative affective states will be increased. Further, such negative outcomes can lead to the exacerbation of existing problems and the creation of new ones, which in turn can lead to another major life event, and so forth. As such, how one copes with these problems can lead to either an escalation or an attenuation of the stress process. For example, research has demonstrated that under *similar* levels of high stress, individuals with poor problem-solving skills report significantly higher levels of depressive and anxiety symptoms than individuals characterized by more effective problem-solving skills, indicating that problem-solving skills serve to attenuate the negative effects of stress (see Nezu & D'Zurilla, 1989).

EFFICACY OF PROBLEM-SOLVING THERAPY (PST)

If effective problem-solving skills serve as an important buffering factor regarding the stress process, training individuals in such skills should lead to a decrease in emotional distress and improvement in psychological functioning. In fact, PST has been shown to be effective regarding a wide range of clinical populations, psychological problems, and the distress associated with chronic medical disorders. These include unipolar depression, geriatric depression, distressed primary care patients, social phobia, agoraphobia, obesity, coronary heart disease, adult cancer patients, schizophrenia, mentally retarded adults with concomitant psychiatric problems, HIV risk behaviors, drug abuse, suicide, childhood aggression, and conduct disorder (see Nezu, D'Zurilla, Zwick, & Nezu, in press, for a review of this literature).

PST also appears to be flexible with regard to treatment goals and methods of implementation (Nezu, in press). For example, it can be conducted in a group format (e.g., Nezu & Perri, 1989), on an individual and couples basis (e.g., Nezu, Nezu, Felgoise, McClure, & Houts, in press), as part of a larger cognitive–behavioral treatment package (e.g., García-Vera, Labrador, & Sanz, 1997), and over the phone (e.g., Allen et al., 2002). It can also be applied as a means of helping patients to overcome barriers associated with successful adherence to other medical or psychosocial treatment protocols (e.g., Perri et al., 2001).

TRAINING GUIDELINES

Specific PST objectives include (a) enhancing a person's positive orientation and application of specific rational problem-solving tasks (i.e., defining problems, generating possible solution ideas, making decisions in order to develop a solution plan, carrying out the plan, monitoring its effects, and evaluating the outcome) and (b) minimizing his or her negative orientation and tendency to engage in dysfunctional problem-solving style activities (i.e., impulsive or careless attempts to cope with problems; avoidance of problems). PST interventions include didactic explanations, training exercises, practice opportunities, and homework assignments geared to foster practice between training sessions.

Problem Orientation. Training in this problem-solving component is geared to facilitate: (a) positive self-efficacy beliefs (the perception that people can improve their quality of life through effective coping and problem solving); (b) beliefs that problems are inevitable (accepting the notion that it is common and "normal" to experience a wide range of problems); (c) the ability to identify problems accurately when they occur by using feelings as cues; and (d) the ability to inhibit emotional reactions that can lead to impulsive reactions or avoidance.

A variety of training approaches can be used to foster a positive problem orientation. One technique is the *reverse advocacy role-play strategy*. According to this strategy, the problem-solving therapist pretends to adopt a particular belief about problems and asks the patient to provide reasons why that belief is irrational, illogical, incorrect, and/or maladaptive. Such beliefs might include the following statements: "Problems are not common to everyone, if I have a problem, that means I'm crazy," "There must be a perfect solution to this problem," "I'll never be the same again." At times when the patient has difficulty generating arguments against the therapist's position, the counselor then adopts a more extreme form of the belief, such as "no matter how long it takes, I will continue to try to find the perfect solution to my problem." This procedure is intended to help patients identify alternative ways of thinking and then to dispute or contradict previously held negative beliefs with more adaptive perspectives.

Other related cognitive restructuring and cognitive therapy-based techniques are also useful in helping the patient to overcome specific distortions or deficiencies in information processing that may underlie a negative problem orientation, such as negative attributional style, negative appraisals, cognitive distortions, and irrational beliefs.

Patients are also taught to use feelings or emotions as *cues* that a problem exists by using visual images of a red traffic stop sign as a signal to *STOP and THINK*. In essence, patients are taught to recognize various situations as problems and to label them as such. Accurately labeling a problem *as* a problem serves to inhibit the tendency to act impulsively or automatically in reaction to such situations. It also facilitates the tendency to approach or confront problems, rather than to avoid them.

Problem Definition and Formulation. Problem definition can be likened to "mapping" a guide for the remainder of the problem-solving process. The major focus of this task is to better understand the nature of the problem and to set clearly defined and reasonable goals. In other words, locating a specific destination on a map makes it easier to find the best route to get there. Training in problem definition and formulation focuses on the following five specific tasks: (a) gathering all available information about the problem; (b) using clear and unambiguous language; (c) separating facts from assumptions; (d) identifying the factors that make the situation a problem; and (e) setting realistic problem-solving goals.

Generation of Alternatives. When generating alternative solutions to a problem, PST encourages broad-based, creative, and flexible thinking. In essence, patients are taught various brainstorming strategies (e.g., "the more the better," "defer judgment of ideas until a comprehensive list is created"). This helps to increase the likelihood that the best or most effective solution ideas will be discovered.

Decision Making. Once a list of alternative options has been generated, the problem solver begins to systematically and thoroughly evaluate the potential for each solution to meet the defined goal(s). Training in this component helps the patient to use the following criteria to conduct a cost–benefit analysis based on the utility of each alternative solution: (a) the likelihood that the solution will meet the defined goal; (b) the likelihood that the person responsible for solving the problem can actually carry out the solution plan optimally; (c) the personal (i.e., effects on oneself) and social (i.e., effects on others) consequences; and (d) the short- and long-term effects.

Solution Implementation and Verification. This last rational problem-solving task involves first carrying out the solution plan and then monitoring and evaluating the consequences of the actual outcome. PST encourages the patient to practice the performance aspect of solution implementation as a means of enhancing the probability that it will be carried out in its optimal form. Once the plan is under way, the patient is encouraged to monitor the actual results. Using this information allows the problem-solver to evaluate the results by comparing the actual outcome with his or her expectations or predictions about the outcome.

If this match is satisfactory, the patient is encouraged to administer some form of self-reinforcement, self-statements of congratulations, tangible gifts, or rewards. However, if the match is unsatisfactory, then he/she is encouraged to recycle through various aspects of the problem-solving process once again. In this troubleshooting process, particular care needs to be exercised in differentiating between difficulties with the performance of the solution plan and the problem-solving process itself.

Supervised Practice. After the majority of training has occurred, the remainder of PST should be devoted to practicing the newly acquired skills and applying them to a variety of stressful problems. Beyond actually solving stressful problems, continuous in-session practice serves three additional purposes: (a) the patient can receive "professional" feedback from the therapist; (b) increased facility with the overall PST model can decrease the amount of time and effort necessary to apply the various problem-solving tasks with each new problem; and (c) practice fosters maintenance and generalization of the skills.

The number of "practice" sessions required after formal PST training often is dependent on the competency level a patient achieves, as well as the actual improvement in his or her overall quality of life. Of the research protocols that have found PST to be an effective CBT intervention, the number of included sessions have ranged from 8 to 12 sessions.

See also: Problem solving—depression

REFERENCES

Allen, S. M., Shah, A. C., Nezu, A. M., Nezu, C. M., Ciambrone, D., Hogan, J., & Mor, V. (2002). A problem-solving approach to stress reduction among younger women with breast carcinoma: A randomized controlled trial. *Cancer, 94*, 3089–3100.

D'Zurilla, T. J., & Nezu, A. M. (1999). *Problem-solving therapy: A social competence approach to clinical intervention* (2nd ed.). New York: Springer.

García-Vera, M. P., Labrador, F. J., & Sanz, J. (1997). Stress-management training for essential hypertension: A controlled study. *Applied Psychophysiology and Biofeedback, 22*, 261–283.

Nezu, A. M. (1987). A problem-solving formulation of depression: A literature review and proposal of a pluralistic model. *Clinical Psychology Review, 7*, 122–144.

Nezu, A. M. (in press). Problem solving and behavior therapy revisited. *Behavior Therapy*.

Nezu, A. M., & D'Zurilla, T. J. (1989). Social problem solving and negative affective states. In P. C. Kendall & D. Watson (Eds.), *Anxiety and depression: Distinctive and overlapping features* (pp. 285–315). New York: Academic Press.

Nezu, A. M., D'Zurilla, T. J., Zwick, M. L., & Nezu, C. M. (in press). Social problem solving therapy for adults. In E. C. Chang, T. J. D'Zurilla, & L. J. Sanna (Eds.), *Social problem solving: Theory, research, and training*. Washington, DC: American Psychological Association.

Nezu, A. M., Nezu, C. M., Felgoise, S. H., McClure, K. S., & Houts, P. S. (in press). Project Genesis: Assessing the efficacy of problem-solving therapy for distressed adult cancer patients. *Journal of Consulting and Clinical Psychology*.

Nezu, A. M., & Perri, M. G. (1989). Problem-solving therapy for unipolar depression: An initial dismantling investigation. *Journal of Consulting and Clinical Psychology, 57*, 408–413.

Perri, M. G., Nezu, A. M., McKelvey, W. F., Schein, R. L., Renjilian, D. A., & Viegener, B. J. (2001). Relapse prevention training and problem-solving therapy in the long-term management of obesity. *Journal of Consulting and Clinical Psychology, 69*, 722–726.

RECOMMENDED READINGS

Chang, E. C., D'Zurilla, T. J., & Sanna, L. J. (Eds.). (in press). *Social problem solving: Theory, research, and training*. Washington, DC: American Psychological Association.

Nezu, A. M., Nezu, C. M., Friedman, S. H., Faddis, S., & Houts, P. S. (1998). *Helping cancer patients cope: A problem-solving approach*. Washington, DC: American Psychological Association.

Nezu, A. M., Nezu, C. M., & Perri, M. G. (1989). *Problem-solving therapy for depression: Theory, research, and clinical guidelines*. New York: Wiley.

PTSD

Sheila A.M. Rauch and Edna B. Foa

Keywords: PTSD, assault, trauma

In the past 15 years we have witnessed a proliferation of publications on the efficacy of a variety of cognitive–behavioral treatments in reducing PTSD and related symptoms. Given the vast research on CBT for PTSD, a comprehensive account of studies is beyond the scope of this article. The current review will focus on presentation of (1) descriptions of the different CBT programs; (2) studies demonstrating the basic efficacy of CBT for PTSD by comparing an active CBT with some control condition such as wait-list, supportive counseling, or relaxation; and (3) studies comparing the outcomes of the different CBT programs with proven efficacy.

EXPOSURE THERAPY

Exposure therapy is a general term used to describe a variety of treatments that focus on confrontation of anxiety-provoking stimuli until anxiety decreases. For PTSD, these programs include confrontation of trauma-related stimuli that may include the trauma memory and/or trauma-related people, place, or situations. One type of exposure therapy that has received significant empirical attention is prolonged exposure, which includes four components: psychoeducation, breathing retraining, imaginal exposure, and in vivo exposure. Psychoeducation focuses on common reactions to trauma and the rationale for exposure therapy. Breathing retraining teaches clients a specific technique to deescalate anxiety. During imaginal exposure, the client relives the trauma memory in imagination for a prolonged period of time (30 to 60 minutes per session). Imaginal exposure is repeated for maximum effectiveness. In vivo exposure involves repeated, prolonged exposure to objectively safe situations that are avoided due to trauma-related fear. In vivo exposure is usually conducted hierarchically starting with moderately difficult items and working up to the most difficult items. Foa and Kozak (1986) proposed that exposure therapy is effective due to the modification of cognitive fear structures. These fear structures contain pathological associations between stimulus, response, and meaning elements that maintain anxiety and the symptoms of PTSD. Through activation of the structure in the presence of corrective information during exposure, these pathological associations can be modified and a new structure containing more realistic associations is formed. For instance, for a client who completes in vivo exposures of going to a supermarket that she avoided because it reminds her of her rape, successful completion provides her with the information that the supermarket is not dangerous and that she can handle the anxiety that occurs when she is reminded of the rape. These modifications lead to reduction in PTSD symptoms, including escape and avoidance behaviors.

Other exposure therapy programs have included different variations of imaginal and in vivo exposure. For instance, Marks, Lovell, Noshirvani, Livanou, and Thrasher (1998) included both imaginal and in vivo exposure, but segregated the first few sessions for imaginal exposure and the last few sessions for in vivo exposure rather than simultaneously doing both. Other exposure therapy programs for PTSD have focused exclusively on imaginal exposure (i.e., Tarrier et al., 1999).

Exposure therapy, including prolonged exposure and several other exposure therapy programs, has been proven highly effective and superior to control conditions (i.e., wait list, supportive counseling, and relaxation) in reducing PTSD following a variety of traumas in several randomized controlled trials (e.g., Foa, Rothbaum, Riggs, & Murdock,

1991; Foa et al., 1999; Marks et al., 1998; Resick, Nishith, Weaver, Astin, & Feuer, 2002; Taylor et al., 2003). Further, exposure therapy has demonstrated reduction of depressive symptoms, general anxiety, guilt, and anger (e.g., Cahill, Rauch, Hembree, & Foa, in press; Foa et al., 1999; Resick et al., 2002; Tarrier et al., 1999). These changes are maintained at follow-up assessments up to 1 year after the end of treatment. Given the evidence supporting the efficacy of exposure therapy for PTSD, Rothbaum, Meadows, Resick, and Foy (2000) recommended exposure therapy as a first-line therapy for PTSD due to its demonstrated efficacy across a wide variety of studies and some evidence from comparative trials to suggest it may be more efficient and/or effective than alternate CBT approaches.

STRESS INOCULATION TRAINING (SIT)

Developed by Meichenbaum (1974), SIT is an anxiety management program that was modified for use with sexual assault survivors. SIT is made up of training in general anxiety management techniques to address the three channels of fear and anxiety (i.e., physical, behavioral, and cognitive). These techniques can then be applied in response to specific PTSD symptoms and in general. The rationale for SIT asserts that as clients are better able to use these techniques to manage their anxiety, their PTSD symptoms will be reduced. SIT programs vary somewhat in the exact techniques that are used, but are always made up of several components. The first component, psychoeducation, focuses on the nature of fear and anxiety, the three channels of fear and anxiety, the rationale for treatment, and common reactions to sexual assault. Following psychoeducation, SIT may include several of the remaining components: relaxation training, breathing retraining, role-playing, covert modeling, guided self-dialogue, and thought stopping (for a detailed description of these techniques see Calhoun & Resick, 1993).

SIT has demonstrated greater reductions in PTSD severity than wait-list and supportive counseling controls (Foa et al., 1991, 1999). SIT has also demonstrated reductions in depressive symptoms, anger, and general anxiety (Cahill et al., in press; Foa et al., 1999). These gains are maintained at follow-up assessments conducted up to 1 year after the end of treatment. However, all of the controlled trials of SIT have been conducted with female assault survivors so generalization to other trauma survivors has not been demonstrated.

COGNITIVE THERAPY (CT)

In CT, sessions focus on the interpretation of events rather than the events themselves as the source of emotional reactions (Beck & Emery, 1985). As such, the rationale for CT asserts that PTSD and other anxiety symptoms result from negative and unhelpful thoughts that may fall into common dysfunctional patterns. For instance, overgeneralization occurs when a person reacts to a new situation based on a previous experience that does not fit. For example, a rape survivor whose assailant had a beard may believe that all men with beards are dangerous and, thus, experience anxiety and fear whenever she sees a bearded man. In CT, these unhelpful thought patterns are identified, challenged (e.g., collecting evidence, looking for alternative interpretations), and replaced by more helpful alternative thoughts.

Controlled trials of CT in survivors of various types of trauma have demonstrated that CT reduced the rates of PTSD at posttreatment more than wait list and relaxation (Frank et al., 1988; Marks et al., 1998). In addition, CT has demonstrated reductions in general anxiety and depressive symptoms (Marks et al., 1998; Tarrier et al., 1999). Marks et al. (1998) also found that reductions in PTSD and associated symptoms were maintained at a 6-month follow-up.

COGNITIVE PROCESSING THERAPY (CPT)

Emphasizing CT techniques, CPT (Resick et al., 2002) includes both exposure and cognitive therapy. For exposure, the client writes a detailed account of the trauma that is read to the therapist. Stuck points, or points in the narrative that hold significant meaning and anxiety for the client, are identified and cognitive techniques are used to closely examine these points. In addition, trauma-related beliefs about safety, trust, power/control, esteem, and intimacy are examined in sessions that focus on each specific type of cognition.

Resick et al. (2002) found that CPT reduced PTSD severity more than a minimal attention control condition. In addition, CPT resulted in significant reduction in depressive symptoms and trauma-related guilt. These reductions were maintained at 9-month follow-up.

COMPARISONS AMONG TREATMENTS

Key studies comparing the previously discussed efficacious treatments for PTSD have found few differences in outcome between CBTs. For instance, in a study comparing SIT, exposure therapy, and their combination in a female assault sample with PTSD, only general anxiety was significantly lower in exposure therapy compared to exposure therapy/SIT (Foa et al., 1999). However, there was a trend for more clients in exposure therapy (52%) to obtain good end-state functioning (a composite of PTSD, depressive, and general anxiety symptoms) than SIT (31%) or exposure therapy/SIT (27%). Importantly, the combination treatment did not add to the benefit of the components alone.

Similarly, Marks et al. (1998) found few differences between exposure therapy, CT, and exposure therapy/CT while all were superior to relaxation. All resulted in significant reductions in anxiety, PTSD symptoms, and depression compared to relaxation. However, no treatment demonstrated significantly greater reduction compared to the other treatments, including no benefit for the combined treatment compared to either CT or exposure therapy. Similarly, when Paunovic and Ost (2001) compared a variation of exposure therapy and exposure therapy/CT in a sample of refugees with PTSD, both treatments were efficacious but the combined treatment did not offer more benefit than exposure therapy alone.

Finally, when comparing CPT, exposure therapy, and minimal attention control in sexual assault survivors, Resick et al. (2002) found both treatments were superior to control, but no differences between treatments were found in depression or PTSD severity.

SUMMARY AND FUTURE DIRECTIONS

Several CBTs have proven efficacy for the treatment of chronic PTSD, including exposure therapy, stress inoculation training, cognitive therapy, and cognitive processing therapy. Studies that have compared these efficacious treatments have not consistently demonstrated the superiority of one of these treatments over another. In addition, cognitive–behavioral treatment packages that combine elements of exposure therapy with stress inoculation training or cognitive therapy have also demonstrated efficacy, but have not demonstrated superior outcome compared to the component treatments alone.

While several efficacious psychotherapy treatment choices are available for chronic PTSD, in all of the studies presented, it is also apparent that there remains a significant minority of clients who continue to have PTSD even after completing these efficacious treatment programs. One direction for future research may include efforts to improve treatment outcome for this group. Such an effort may include augmentation of CBT strategies with other treatment modalities, identification of these clients prior to treatment and alterations to the program to meet their needs, or even the development of new treatment programs to address these clients' needs. Finally, although many of these CBTs have been available for years, difficulty in disseminating these programs to therapists has led to problems in consumer accessibility. Finding ways to effectively and efficiently disseminate these programs to mental health service providers is critical to the utility of CBT.

See also: Child abuse, Exposure therapy, PTSD—childhood, PTSD—older adults, PTSD—war related

REFERENCES

Beck, A. T., & Emery, G. (1985). *Anxiety disorders and phobias: A cognitive perspective*. New York: Basic Books.

Cahill, S. P., Rauch, S. A. M., Hembree, E. A., & Foa, E. B. (in press). Effect of cognitive–behavioral treatments for PTSD on anger. *Journal of Cognitive Psychotherapy*.

Calhoun, K. S., & Resick, P. A. (1993). Posttraumatic stress disorder. In D. H. Barlow (Ed.), *Clinical handbook of psychological disorders* (pp. 48–98). New York: Guilford Press.

Foa, E. B., Dancu, C. V., Hembree, E. A., Jaycox, L. H., Meadows, E. A., & Street, G. P. (1999). A comparison of exposure therapy, stress inoculation training, and their combination for reducing posttraumatic stress disorder in female assault victims. *Journal of Consulting and Clinical Psychology, 67*, 194–200.

Foa, E. B., Kozak, M. J. (1986). Emotional processing of fear: Exposure to corrective information. *Psychological Bulletin, 99*, 20–35.

Foa, E. B., Rothbaum, B. O., Riggs, D., & Murdock, T. (1991). Treatment of posttraumatic stress disorder in rape victims: A comparison between cognitive–behavioral procedures and counseling. *Journal of Consulting and Clinical Psychology, 59*, 715–723.

Frank, E., Anderson, B., Stewart, B. D., Dancu, C., Hughes, C., & West, D. (1988). Efficacy of cognitive behavior therapy and systematic desensitization in the treatment of rape trauma. *Behavior Therapy, 19*, 403–420.

Marks, I., Lovell, K., Noshirvani, H., Livanou, M., & Thrasher, S. (1998). Treatment of post-traumatic stress disorder by exposure and/or cognitive restructuring: A controlled study. *Archives of General Psychiatry, 55*, 317–325.

Meichenbaum, D. (1974). Self instructional methods. In F. H. Kanfer & A. P. Goldstein (Eds.), *Helping people change* (pp. 357–391). New York: Pergamon Press.

Paunovic, N., & Ost, L. G. (2001). Cognitive–behaviour therapy vs exposure therapy in the treatment of PTSD in refugees. *Behaviour Therapy and Research, 39*, 1183–1197.

Resick, P. A., Nishith, P., Weaver, T. L., Astin, M. C., & Feuer, C. A. (2002). A comparison of cognitive–processing therapy with prolonged exposure and a waiting condition for the treatment of chronic posttraumatic stress disorder in female rape victims. *Journal of Consulting and Clinical Psychology, 70*, 867–879.

Rothbaum, B. O., Meadows, E. A., Resick, P. A., & Foy, D. W. (2000). Cognitive–behavioral therapy. In E. B. Foa, T. M. Keane, & M. J. Friedman (Eds.), *Effective treatments for PTSD* (pp. 60–83). New York: Guilford Press.

Tarrier, N., Pilgrim, H., Sommerfield, C., Faragher, B., Reynolds, M., Graham, E., & Barrowclough, C. (1999). A randomized trial of cognitive therapy and imaginal exposure in the treatment of chronic posttraumatic stress disorder. *Journal of Consulting and Clinical Psychology, 67*, 13–18.

Taylor, S., Thordarson, D. S., Maxfield, L., Federoff, I. C., Lovell, K., & Ogrodniczuk, J. (2003). Efficacy, speed, and adverse effects of three PTSD treatments: Exposure therapy, relaxation training, and EMDR. *Journal of Consulting and Clinical Psychology, 71*, 330–338.

RECOMMENDED READINGS

Foa, E. B., Keane, T. M., & Friedman, M. J. (2000). *Effective treatments for PTSD*. New York: Guilford Press.

Foa, E. B., & Rothbaum, B. O. (1998). *Treating the trauma of rape*. New York: Guilford Press.

PTSD—Childhood

Wanda Grant-Knight, Helen MacDonald, Stephanie Clarke, and Karestan Koenen

Keywords: PTSD, childhood disorders, trauma

Although researchers have long been interested in children's responses to natural disasters, domestic violence, abuse, and loss associated with war (Pelcovitz & Kaplan, 1996), they have only recently explored posttraumatic stress disorder (PTSD) as an outcome of these experiences. While adult PTSD, which was officially recognized in the *Diagnostic and Statistical Manual of Mental Disorders—Third Edition* (DSM-III; American Psychiatric Association, 1980), shares some symptoms with child PTSD, researchers have discovered a unique set of age-specific responses to trauma that characterize this disorder in children. Thus, age-sensitive symptoms are included in both the DSM-III and DSM-IV (APA, 1994) diagnostic criteria for PTSD (Pelcovitz & Kaplan, 1996).

According to the DSM-IV, PTSD comprises three categories of symptoms that are associated with a traumatic event that is either experienced directly or witnessed. First, reexperiencing of the traumatic event occurs by way of flashbacks, nightmares, or feeling distress when encountering situations reminiscent of the original trauma. In children, this reexperiencing may occur by way of repetitive play and frightening dreams absent of coherent content. Second, one avoids situations or reminders of situations relating to the traumatic event. Finally, increased arousal occurs, which may include sleep irregularity, difficulty concentrating, hypervigilance, and exaggerated startle response. In addition to these core features of PTSD, there are numerous associated features that may cause impairment, including relationship difficulties, dissociation, and emotional numbing.

The effects of trauma differ by stage of development, therefore studying PTSD in children of different ages is imperative (Schwarz, McNally, & Yeh, 1998). Developmental biology underscores the need for age-sensitive research on PTSD in youth as growing evidence suggests that PTSD is a complex disorder that has lasting adverse impacts on children's neurocognitive and physiological development (DeBellis, 2002). The result of such changes in response to trauma is that PTSD symptoms, such as dissociative and somatic symptoms, exaggerated startle response, anxiety, motor hyperactivity, and sleep disturbance, may become enduring behaviors.

EPIDEMIOLOGY OF PTSD IN CHILDREN AND ADOLESCENTS

Data indicate that trauma exposure is highly prevalent among children. One study found that 25% of children aged 9–18 had experienced at least one potentially traumatic event in their lifetimes such as the death of a loved one, witnessing a traumatic event, or sexual abuse (Costello, Erkanli, Fairbank, & Angold, 2002). More specifically, as of 1995, epidemiological data indicate that 1.8 million adolescents from 12 to 18 had been sexually abused, 3.9 million had been severely assaulted, 2.1 million had been punished by physical abuse, and 8.8 million had witnessed someone being stabbed or shot, sexually assaulted, physically assaulted, or threatened with a weapon (Kilpatrick, Saunders, & Smith, 2003).

The high prevalence of traumatic exposures in children puts them at risk of developing traumatic responses such as PTSD, as indicated by several studies. For instance, Kilpatrick et al. (2003) found that a PTSD diagnosis, according to DSM-IV criteria, was present in 15.2% of boys and 27.4% of girls who were physically abused; 28.2% of boys and 29.8% of girls who had been sexually assaulted; and 11.2% of boys and 20.2% of girls who had witnessed violence.

FACTORS INFLUENCING THE EMERGENCE AND EXPRESSION OF PTSD IN CHILDREN AND ADOLESCENTS

Research shows that characteristics of traumatic experiences, such as severity, duration, and proximity, impact the emergence and expression of PTSD symptoms. For example, there is evidence of a dose–response relationship between traumatic events and the development of PTSD such that events that are life-threatening are associated with greater and more severe symptoms than traumatic events that are less threatening or are experienced less directly (Davis & Siegel, 2000; Green et al., 1991).

While trauma characteristics impact the emergence of PTSD, not all youth who experience traumatic events develop PTSD. There are many risk factors that influence the emergence of PTSD, such as the premorbid functioning of children and their families. Pretrauma etiological factors in children, such as age, developmental experience, intellectual ability, and psychiatric comorbidity, are associated with the development of PTSD. Studies of these factors generally indicate that children who are younger, have had negative developmental experiences (such as insecure/disorganized attachment), have lower IQ, and exhibit comorbid psychopathology are at increased risk of developing PTSD (Breslau, Davis, Andreski, Peterson, & Schultz, 1997; Davis & Siegel, 2000; Goenjian et al., 1995; Hubbard, Realmuto, Northwood, & Masten, 1995; Silva et al., 2000).

Familial characteristics, such as marital status, education, stability, reactivity, supportiveness, and psychopathology, have been associated with the emergence of PTSD in youth. Studies show that youth from supportive families are less likely than those in nonsupportive and/or dysfunctional families to develop PTSD. Further, parents' reactions to traumatic events are associated with PTSD symptomatology: when parents over- or underreact, youth tend to exhibit PTSD symptoms that are greater in number and severity than parents who react with an appropriate amount of emotion. Also, if parents experience the trauma with the child, the traumatization of the parent is significantly correlated with the child's PTSD. This suggests that the more traumatized parents are, the less able they are to deal with their children's response to the trauma, thus predicting greater likelihood of PTSD (Davis & Siegel, 2000).

TREATMENT FOR CHILDHOOD PTSD

Cognitive–behavioral therapy (CBT) is among the most widely investigated treatment for childhood PTSD. The theoretical model of CBT for treating PTSD draws on Mowrer's (1939) two-factor learning model, which integrates classical and operant conditioning approaches. In the classical conditioning model, neutral stimuli occur in close proximity to a traumatic event (unconditioned stimulus), which results in a series of involuntary responses, including fight-or-flight reactions (unconditioned responses). The neutral stimuli (conditioned stimuli) independently come to elicit the same involuntary responses (conditioned responses) as the traumatic event. Thus, when confronted with the conditioned stimuli, the child will experience the same fear response as during the traumatic event. Internal states, such as thoughts, memories, or feelings associated with the traumatic event, can also serve as conditioned stimuli. For example, a child hit by a car while riding his bicycle may experience intense fear (conditioned response) whenever he sees a car or a bicycle, passes the stretch of road where he was hit, or merely remembers the event (all are examples of conditioned stimuli). In addition, stimulus generalization and higher-order conditioning may occur, in which other previously neutral stimuli associated with the conditioned stimuli come to elicit the conditioned response. For example, the child may develop a fear response any time he hears an engine running or a horn honking, even though these events were not present during the initial traumatic event.

Operant conditioning explains the maintenance of the classically conditioned fear response. The traumatized child works to avoid the conditioned stimuli, thereby strengthening the relationship between the conditioned stimuli and the conditioned response through negative reinforcement, thus preventing extinction. Drawing on the above example, the child may avoid riding his bicycle because thoughts of riding it invoke feelings of fear, and he feels less anxious when he is not riding his bicycle. Avoidance of bicycle riding is reinforced by the reduction in his anxiety. These models of conditioning interact, such that the child is confronted with environmental reminders of the traumatic event that elicit a fear response. He responds with avoidance of these stimuli and therefore never has the opportunity to learn that these stimuli are not threatening in and of themselves. Avoidance can involve conscious behavior or unconscious internal responses to traumatic reminders.

Cognitive–behavioral treatments aim to disrupt the connection between the stimuli and the response, such that the traumatized child ceases to avoid the conditioned stimuli and habituates to the conditioned response until it becomes less anxiety provoking. This occurs through the use of imaginal flooding and gradual exposure techniques, which help children to process traumatic experiences in the context of a safe therapeutic relationship (Keane, Fairbank, Caddell, Zimering, & Bender, 1985).

Information processing theory represents another important element of conceptualizing cognitive–behavioral treatments for PTSD in children (Foa & Kozak, 1986). Information processing theory contends that stressors are not experienced objectively; they affect children differentially, based on children's individual beliefs about the world, such that not all traumatized children go on to develop PTSD. Cognitive models explain individual differences in terms of threat appraisal, attributions, and meaning-making associated with the trauma.

DEVELOPMENTAL ISSUES

Children manifest their traumatic histories differentially, based in part on their developmental stage. Thus, interventions should be fundamentally informed by developmental level. Preschool children are concrete and literal in their thinking. They express themselves most effectively through play and understand basic reward and punishment relations. As such, these approaches should be integrated into treatment, such as through communication of CBT techniques (such as relaxation) through doll play and use of star charts to enhance the child's implementation of these techniques. Additionally, parents should be taught to understand developmental differences in the expression of trauma-related symptoms as well as methods of improving young children's functioning. School-age children, who are developing enhanced abstraction and reasoning abilities, view the world as orderly and lawful. They are likely to respond best to treatments that foster their sense of mastery and exploration of cause-and-effect relations through structured exercises, such as thought stopping, generation of alternative responses to events, and role-plays. Interventions with adolescents, who have solidly developed abstraction and reasoning abilities, may focus more on anxiety reduction through exposure-based techniques to decrease avoidance and enhance independence, emotional processing, cognitive restructuring, and social skills training. Maintaining a developmental emphasis leads one to consider relevant tasks and milestones for children and adolescents and to use this knowledge to inform the implementation of the most appropriate treatments.

APPROACHES

1. *Individual* CBT for childhood PTSD is characterized by distinct modules, which are fairly uniform across treatments. These components include coping, skills training, psychoeducation, cognitive restructuring, exposure to trauma-related anxiety, and relapse prevention (Cohen & Mannarino, 1993; Saigh, Yule, & Inamdar, 1996). Treatments often begin with psychoeducation, stress management, and skills training in order to equip children with techniques to cope with the initial anxiety of the behavioral exposures, which comprise an important component of cognitive–behavioral approaches. The individual treatment modality provides the most intensive intervention, which can be catered specifically to index the child's relevant traumatic event and posttraumatic symptoms, in addition to being able to work closely with the particular issues the child's parent may be experiencing in the home.

2. Cognitive–behavioral *group* treatments for traumatized children can operate similarly to the individual treatments described above. These treatments focus on cognitive and behavioral exercises, components of which traditionally include psychoeducation, cognitive therapy, exposure-based behavior therapy, and relapse prevention (March, Amaya-Jackson, Murray, & Schulte, 1998). The aim of group cognitive–behavioral trauma-focused treatments is for children to integrate the traumatic memory within their broader conception of self through group-based exposures and cognitive exercises. School-based group interventions, such as March and colleagues' (1998), are uniquely beneficial in their potential to provide treatments to greater numbers of children in underserved populations. While other group treatments for traumatized children have been employed, such as *postdisaster interventions* incorporating problem-solving training, information clarification and consolidation, cognitive restructuring, and exposure-based exercises (Yule, 1992), and *psychological debriefing*, comprised of ventilation, normalization, and psychoeducation, the empirical literature on their efficacy is equivocal (Chemtob, Tomas, Law, & Cremniter, 1997).

3. *Parent training* (PT) is a vital component of psychotherapeutic treatment with younger traumatized children and a secondary element of treatment for older children and adolescents. PT is typically composed of three components: psychoeducation, behavior modification, and exposure-based cognitive interventions. In psychoeducation, parents learn the effects of trauma on children of different ages, as well as the symptoms children display following a traumatic event. In behavior modification, parents are taught skills and techniques to better manage their child (such as methods of discipline, reinforcement, and problem solving) that they can use at home to reinforce lessons the child learns in therapy and to ensure safety. This information allows parents to develop appropriate expectations of and responses to children so they can provide support and reinforcement for their children to facilitate their recovery from PTSD symptoms. In addition to a specific focus on the child, PT, through exposure-based cognitive interventions, allows parents the opportunity to express their own feelings regarding their child's traumatic experience. They work with a therapist to correct their own trauma-related cognitive errors, and learn stress management strategies designed to help them as well as their children cope with feelings of anxiety (Cohen, Mannarino, Berliner, & Deblinger, 2000). Because parents can provide important observational information about their child's home functioning that cannot be gleaned from conversations with the child, their involvement in treatment can enhance traditional interventions and facilitate recovery outside of the traditional treatment milieu.

TECHNIQUES

1. *Exposure therapy* techniques have been empirically supported for the treatment of PTSD in adults (e.g., Keane, Fairbank, Caddell, & Zimering, 1989) and have recently been extended to treat children with trauma histories (Deblinger & Heflin, 1996). These techniques "expose" the child to memories or reminders of the traumatic event in a safe and structured environment. Different models of

exposure have been implemented in work with traumatized children. In imaginal flooding, children imagine the specific details of the traumatic experience while therapists use prompts to determine children's concomitant subjective rating of emotional distress (Saigh et al., 1996). In gradual exposure, children describe aspects of their trauma and work with the therapist to process general or minor features of the traumatic experience (e.g., Cohen & Mannarino, 1993; Deblinger & Heflin, 1996). Ongoing sessions of gradual exposure therapy involve decreasing the child's distress around provoking aspects of the trauma through various media, including writing stories, drawing pictures, talking into tape recorders, and playing out aspects of the traumatic experience. Through these processes, children access, discuss, and process increasingly anxiety-provoking traumatic memories with the therapist. Both flooding and gradual exposure therapy operate under the theoretical premise that through controlled and safe reexperiencing of a traumatic event an individual will begin to disconnect the conditioned stimuli from the conditioned response, leading to increased habituation and decreased avoidance symptoms.

2. *Cognitive interventions* have proven efficacious in treating cognitive distortions in adult trauma survivors, particularly those with sexual assault histories (Foa, Rothbaum, Riggs, & Murdock, 1991). Such distortions are common in traumatized children as well and typically manifest themselves in thoughts of a foreshortened future, self-blame, survivor guilt, overgeneralization, and meaning-making of the traumatic event. The different types of cognitive therapies developed or adapted for children seek to correct cognitive errors and simultaneously hone children's coping skills. Two such interventions are cognitive processing therapy and cognitive coping.

Cognitive processing therapy, initially designed for treating adult sexual abuse survivors (Resick & Schnicke, 1992), has been adapted for use with traumatized children to examine and challenge their maladaptive cognitions. Children work with a therapist to identify current cognitions, assess the reasoning behind cognitive distortions, and supplant these distortions with more adaptive cognitions.

Deblinger and Heflin (1996) have modified *cognitive coping*, which maps closely onto Beck's (1976) cognitive treatment for depression, for use with traumatized children. This therapy teaches children with abuse histories to understand the relation between maladaptive automatic thoughts, negative emotional states, and dysfunctional behavior. Children learn skills to regulate their affect by shifting negative cognitions while concurrently assessing the impact of these changes on their behavior.

3. *Stress management* therapy teaches traumatized children muscle relaxation and diaphragmatic breathing techniques. This has been demonstrated to decrease symptoms of PTSD, anxiety, and depression in adult sexual assault victims (Foa et al., 1991) and teaching relaxation techniques alone has proven effective in decreasing anxiety symptoms in children without trauma histories (Ollendick & Cerny, 1981). Stress management techniques are often used in conjunction with other treatment modalities, such as exposure therapy, given their ability to enhance other interventions.

LITERATURE REVIEW

Empirical Support for CBT for Childhood PTSD

Several important treatment outcome studies have examined the efficacy of CBT for PTSD in children. In the late 1980s, following the introduction of PTSD into DSM-III (APA, 1980), Saigh (1987a,b; 1989) carried out a series of single-case trials of imaginal flooding therapy for traumatized children and adolescents in Lebanon. This treatment involved children identifying and describing their traumatic experiences over a multiple baseline with outcome, measured through self-reported ratings of anxiety and depression. This and other similar treatments have been associated with a reduction in trauma-related symptoms, including exaggerated startle response, nightmares, intrusive thoughts, avoidance, impaired concentration and memory, self-reported anxiety, depression, and guilt (Saigh et al., 1996).

Three research teams have empirically evaluated trauma-focused CBT, specifically developed for treating sexually abused children and their nonoffending caretakers (Cohen & Mannarino, 1996, 1997; Deblinger, McLeer, & Henry, 1990; Deblinger, McLeer, & Lippmann, 1999; King et al., 2000).

Deblinger et al. (1990, 1999) treated 19 children and their nonoffending caretakers individually across 12 sessions using cognitive–behavioral techniques including gradual exposure, modeling, education, coping, and prevention skills training. The therapists' specific aim in working with caretakers was to help them to respond more effectively and supportively to their child's trauma-related difficulties. Children demonstrated significant improvement in all PTSD symptom clusters, as well as externalizing and internalizing behaviors, and self-reported depression and anxiety scores from pre- to posttreatment. Treatment improvements were maintained at a 2-year follow-up (Deblinger et al., 1999).

In another model, Cohen and Mannarino (1996, 1997) randomly assigned a sample of 67 sexually abused preschoolers and their nonoffending parents either to a cognitive–behavioral treatment specifically targeting sexual abuse or to a nondirective supportive therapy. The CBT included modules of cognitive restructuring, thought-stopping, positive imagery, contingency reinforcement, parent training, and problem-solving (Cohen & Mannarino, 1996, 1997). Children in the cognitive–behavioral treatment modality demonstrated decreased symptoms at posttreatment on measures tapping general and sexual behavior problems, as well as internalizing symptoms when compared with the children in the nondirective supportive therapy. Further, children in the cognitive–behavioral treatment maintained these improvements over time, while the control group did not evidence improvement at the 1-year follow-up (Cohen & Mannarino, 1997).

In a third intervention, King et al. (2000) randomly assigned sexually abused children with posttraumatic stress symptoms to either a child CBT condition, a family CBT condition, or a wait-list condition. The child CBT condition included psychoeducation, coping skills training, relaxation training, cognitive therapy, behavioral rehearsal, graded exposures, and relapse prevention. The family CBT involved individual psychotherapy sessions with the child in addition to individual psychotherapy with the nonoffending mother. Developing communication skills, reducing avoidance, increasing behavioral management skills, and self-monitoring were key elements of these interventions. Results demonstrated significant differences between the child cognitive–behavioral treatment condition and the wait-list condition for all PTSD symptom clusters at posttreatment and follow-up but findings did not support the hypothesis that parent treatment positively impacts outcome.

March et al. (1998) introduced a manual-based trauma-focused cognitive–behavioral group treatment for children with PTSD following a single-incident stressor, Multi-Modality Trauma Treatment (MMTT). The 18-week protocol was delivered in a peer group format in the school setting, with individual "pullout" sessions dealing with issues particular to each participant's traumatic experience. March et al. (1998) implemented a single case across setting experimental design to examine the efficacy of this treatment, controlling for extraneous variables including the passage of time, history effects, effects specific to setting, or measurement error. Results demonstrated significant improvement across all symptom categories in children treated with MMTT.

Indications for and Limitations of CBT for Treating Childhood PTSD

Results from studies implementing cognitive–behavioral interventions for childhood PTSD demonstrate reduced symptomatology in all PTSD symptom clusters and suggest that intensive, short-term individual, parent, and group treatments are efficacious and safe in treating traumatized children across a range of developmental levels. In addition, while significantly reducing PTSD symptomatology in children, some trauma-focused CBTs also have proven equally effective at diminishing peripheral psychopathology, including depression and anxiety (March et al., 1998). This is an important finding as many children with PTSD may have comorbid conditions, commonly including depression, anxiety, and attention-deficit/hyperactivity disorder.

While the literature examining CBT for children with PTSD has resulted in impressive findings, further empirical research is needed to better understand the differential effects of CBT as compared with other treatment modalities in order to rule out common factors, as well as to enhance treatment effects. Specifically, controlled trials should be initiated, utilizing randomized assignment and manualized treatments in order to compare CBT with other psychotherapeutic and pharmacological therapies. Additionally, further research is needed to improve our understanding of the utility of CBT interventions with broader classes of traumatized children. For instance, researchers and clinicians have developed CBT targeting single-incident traumas (e.g., March et al., 1998) or specific types of trauma in children (e.g., Deblinger, Lippmann, & Steer, 1996; Yule, 1992). Given that many mental health practices serve children who have been exposed to a range of traumatic experiences with variable durations between trauma and treatment, further research must adapt and validate treatments for multiply and variably traumatized children. Additionally, it would be important to thoroughly evaluate the delivery of CBT in other settings, such as schools, to assess any benefits to incorporating other systems in treatment, as well as implications of this for generalizability and maintenance of treatment gains.

SUMMARY AND FUTURE DIRECTIONS

Overall, trauma-focused CBT should be considered the first line of treatment for childhood PTSD (AACAP, 1998). The combination of exposure-based behavioral techniques, including imaginal flooding and gradual exposures, with cognitive exercises, including relaxation, cognitive restructuring, emotional processing, and parental training, increases the therapeutic alliance to significantly reduce trauma-related symptoms in children. Further, cognitive–behavioral treatments work quickly, demonstrating change in 8 to 15 sessions, which bears important implications in this managed-care era. Despite the efficacy of this treatment modality for childhood PTSD, further research is needed to better understand the components of CBT that contribute to symptom improvement as well as to clarify which types of trauma, which populations, and which symptoms are most effectively targeted and improved by trauma-focused CBT. By doing this we can further develop and refine alternative interventions and assess which individual difference factors, such as developmental level, and which socioenvironmental factors, such as family involvement and culture, interact with treatment effects.

See also: Children—behavior therapy, Exposure therapy, PTSD, Treatment of children

REFERENCES

American Academy of Child and Adolescent Psychiatry. (1998). Practice parameters for the diagnosis and treatment of posttraumatic stress. *Journal of the American Academy of Child and Adolescent Psychiatry, 37*(10), 4S–26S.

American Psychiatric Association. (1980). *Diagnostic and statistical manual of mental disorders* (3rd ed.). Washington, DC: Author.

American Psychiatric Association. (1994). *Diagnostic and statistical manual of mental disorders* (4th ed.). Washington, DC: Author.

Beck, A. T. (1976). *Cognitive therapy and the emotional disorders.* New York: International Universities Press.

Breslau, N., Davis, G. C., Andreski, P. M., Peterson, E. L., & Schultz, L. R. (1997). Sex differences in posttraumatic stress disorder. *Archives of General Psychiatry, 54,* 1044–1048.

Chemtob, C. M., Tomas, S., Law, W., & Cremniter, D. (1997). Postdisaster psychosocial intervention: A field study of the impact of debriefing on psychological distress. *The American Journal of Psychiatry, 154*(3), 415–417.

Cohen, J. A., & Mannarino, A. P. (1993). A treatment model for sexually abused preschoolers. *Journal of Interpersonal Violence, 8*(1), 115–131.

Cohen, J. A., & Mannarino, A. P. (1996). A treatment outcome study for sexually abused preschool children: Initial findings. *Journal of the American Academy of Child and Adolescent Psychiatry, 35*(1), 42–50.

Cohen, J. A., & Mannarino, A. P. (1997). A treatment study for sexually abused preschool children: Outcome during a one-year follow-up. *Journal of the American Academy of Child and Adolescent Psychiatry, 36*(9), 1228–1235.

Cohen, J. A., Mannarino, A. P., Berliner, L., & Deblinger, E. (2000). Trauma-focused cognitive behavioral therapy for children and adolescents: An empirical update. *Journal of Interpersonal Violence, 15*(11), 1020–1223.

Costello, J. E., Erkanli, A., Fairbank, J. A., & Angold, A. (2002). The prevalence of potentially traumatic events in childhood and adolescence. *Journal of Traumatic Stress, 15,* 99–112.

Davis, L., & Siegel, L. J. (2000). Posttraumatic stress disorder in children and adolescents: A review and analysis. *Clinical Child and Family Psychology Review, 3,* 135–154.

DeBellis, M. D. (2002). Developmental traumatology: A contributory mechanism for alcohol and substance use disorders. *Psychoneuroendocrinology, 27,* 155–170.

Deblinger, E., & Heflin, A. H. (1996). *Treating sexually abused children and their nonoffending parents: A cognitive behavioral approach.* Thousand Oaks, CA: Sage.

Deblinger, E., Lippmann, J., & Steer, R. (1996). Sexually abused children suffering posttraumatic stress symptoms: Initial treatment findings. *Child Maltreatment, 1,* 310–321.

Deblinger, E., McLeer, S. V., & Henry, D. (1990). Cognitive behavioral treatment for sexually abused children suffering post-traumatic stress: Preliminary findings. *Journal of the American Academy of Child and Adolescent Psychiatry, 29*(5), 747–752.

Deblinger, E., McLeer, S. V., & Lippmann, J. (1999). Two-year follow-up study of cognitive behavioral therapy for sexually abused children suffering post-traumatic stress symptoms. *Child Abuse and Neglect, 12,* 1371–1378.

Foa, E. B., Kozak, M. J. (1986). Emotional processing of fear: Exposure to corrective information. *Psychological Bulletin, 99,* 20–35.

Foa, E. B., Rothbaum, D. S., Riggs, B. O., & Murdock, T. (1991). Treatment of PTSD in rape victims: A comparison between cognitive–behavioral procedures and counseling. *Journal of Consulting and Clinical Psychology, 59,* 715–723.

Goenjian, A. K., Pynoos, R. S., Steinberg, A. M., Najarian, L. M., Asarnow, J. R., Karayan, I., Ghurabi, M.B., & Fairbanks, L. (1995). Psychiatric comorbidity in children after the 1988 earthquake in Armenia. *Journal of the American Academy of Child & Adolescent Psychiatry, 34,* 1174–1184.

Green, B. L., Korol, M., Grace, M. C., Vary, M. G., Leonard, A. C., Gleser, G., & Smitson-Cohen, S. (1991). Children and disaster: Age, gender, and parental effects on PTSD symptoms. *Journal of the American Academy of Child and Adolescent Psychiatry, 30,* 945–951.

Hubbard, J., Realmuto, G. M., Northwood, A. K., & Masten, A. S. (1995). Comorbidity of psychiatric diagnoses with posttraumatic stress disorder in survivors of childhood trauma. *Journal of the American Academy of Child and Adolescent Psychiatry, 34,* 1167–1173.

Keane, T. M., Fairbank, J. A., Caddell, J. M., & Zimering, R. T. (1989). Implosive therapy reduces symptoms of PTSD in Vietnam combat veterans. *Behavior Therapy, 20,* 245–260.

Keane, T. M., Fairbank, J. A., Caddell, J. M., Zimering, R. T., & Bender, M. E. (1985). A behavioral approach to assessing and treating post-traumatic stress disorder in Vietnam veterans. In C. R. Figley (Ed.), *Trauma and its wake* (pp. 257–294). New York: Brunner/Mazel.

Kilpatrick, D. G., Saunders, B. E., & Smith, D. (2003, April). *Youth victimization: Prevalence and intervention: Bureau of Justice Statistics special report.* Washington, DC: U.S. Department of Justice.

King, N. J., Tonge, B. J., Mullen, P., Myerson, N., Heyne, D., Rollings, S., Martin, R. et al. (2000). Treating sexually abused children with post-traumatic stress symptoms: A randomized clinical trial. *Journal of the American Academy of Child and Adolescent Psychiatry, 39*(11), 1347–1355.

March, J. S., Amaya-Jackson, L., Murray, M. C., & Schulte, A. (1998). Cognitive–behavioral psychotherapy for children and adolescents with posttraumatic stress disorder after a single-incident stressor. *Journal of the American Academy of Child and Adolescent Psychiatry, 37*(6), 585–593.

Mowrer, O. H. (1939). Stimulus response theory of anxiety. *Psychological Review, 46,* 553–565.

Ollendick, T. H., & Cerny, J. A. (1981). *Clinical behavior therapy with children.* New York: Plenum Press.

Pelcovitz, D., & Kaplan, S. (1996). Post-traumatic stress disorder in children and adolescents. *Child and Adolescent Psychiatric Clinics of North America, 5,* 449–469.

Resick, P. A., & Schnicke, M. K. (1992). Cognitive processing therapy for sexual assault victims. *Journal of Consulting and Clinical Psychology, 60,* 748–756.

Saigh, P. A. (1987a). *In vitro* flooding of an adolescent's posttraumatic stress disorder. *Journal of Clinical Child Psychology, 16,* 147–150.

Saigh, P. A. (1987b). *In vitro* flooding of a childhood posttraumatic stress disorder. *School Psychology Review, 16,* 203–211.

Saigh, P. A. (1989). The use of *in vitro* flooding in the treatment of traumatized adolescents. *Journal of Behavioral and Developmental Pediatrics, 10,* 17–21.

Saigh, P. A., Yule, W., & Inamdar, S. C. (1996). Imaginal flooding of traumatized children and adolescents. *Journal of School Psychology, 34*(2), 163–183.

Schwarz, E. D., McNally, R. J., & Yeh, L. C. (1998). The trauma response of children and adolescents. *Child and Adolescent Psychiatric Clinics of North America, 7,* 229–239.

Silva, R. R., Alpert, M., Munoz, D. M., Singh, S., Matzner, F., & Dummit, S. (2000). Stress and vulnerability to posttraumatic stress disorder in children and adolescents. *American Journal of Psychiatry, 157,* 1229–1235.

Yule, W. (1992). Post-traumatic stress disorder in child survivors of shipping disasters: The sinking of the "Jupiter." *Psychotherapy and Psychosomatics, 57,* 200–205.

PTSD—Older Adults

Lee Hyer and Steve Sohnle

Keywords: posttraumatic stress, older adults

Posttraumatic stress disorder (PTSD) is a stress reaction characterized by symptoms of reexperiencing, avoidance/numbing, and hyperarousal following exposure of 1 month or more to an extreme trauma. In recent years there has been a spate of studies and meta-analyses on the treatment of this disorder, involving the key curative components of exposure and assimilative techniques, as well as secondary factors of relaxation and rescripting. Generally, these studies have involved CBT, cognitive reprocessing, or eye movement desensitization and reprocessing (EMDR). Unfortunately, there have been no studies on the application of any of these methods to older people with PTSD. Additionally, there are few data with this group regarding the assessment of the client's mediating and moderating influences, implicit models of cause and treatment, the importance of education on change, the importance of the therapist, and a host of other client-treatment factors (Hyer & Sohnle, 2001).

OVERVIEW

Hundreds of studies on stress have been performed during the past decade. About a quarter of the individuals who are exposed to serious trauma go on to develop PTSD (lifetime). Current rates of PTSD in people exposed to traumatic events range from about 5 to 11% (Kessler, Sonnega, Bromet, Hughes, & Nelson, 1995). Norris (1992) found the lifetime exposure rate to at least one major stressor event to be 69%. Ensel (1991) showed that most older community-dwelling adults (74%) had at least one major life event during the past 6 months that produced a negative impact.

In general, older victims are no worse off than younger ones despite increasing stress. Stressful events such as retirement, children leaving the home, death or separation from relatives and friends, physical illness and hospitalization, as well as other precipitating factors, such as war or prison camps or other retraumatizing events, do not potentiate underlying potential PTSD residual problems. The interference of aging with a sudden or brief traumatic experience, such as an accident or robbery, has yet to be corroborated.

Following the DSM categories of acute and chronic stress, there are two pathways to PTSD that apply to older people. One is a reaction to acute trauma, involving both Acute Stress Disorder and early PTSD. The Blanchard group at Albany has addressed this issue. Blanchard et al. (2003) assessed 78 motor vehicle accident survivors with chronic (greater than 6 months) PTSD, or severe subsyndromal PTSD who completed a randomized controlled comparison of CBT, supportive psychotherapy, or a wait-list control condition. Scores on the Clinician Administered PTSD Scale (CAPS) showed significantly greater improvement for those in CBT in comparison to the wait-list and support conditions. The support condition in turn was superior to the wait list. Categorical diagnostic data showed the same results. An analysis of CAPS scores, including 98 dropouts, also showed CBT to be superior to the wait-list. The CBT condition led to significantly greater reductions in comorbid major depression and GAD than the other two conditions. Results held up well at a 3-month follow-up on the two active treatment conditions. This same group applied CBT to acutely stressed people. Results showed that early provision of CBT in the initial month after trauma has long-term benefits for people who are at risk of developing PTSD. Blanchard and Hickling (1997) propose a 10-session CBT protocol for Acute Stress Disorder and highlight core features of exposure (reading the trauma), education, and coping as well as relaxation and pleasurable activity. These results and treatment model apply to older people.

The other pathway involves chronic or delayed PTSD. Often, a subclinical state may have been present. Often too, the symptom expression of trauma alters and mellows in later life, as aging-related variables assert a greater influence. In regard to combat trauma, roughly 20% are continuously troubled, 20% are symptom free totally, and the remainder experience intermittent symptoms (Hyer & Summers, 1995). The typical pattern of decline involves a continuation of lifelong problems, not a sudden development of a new disorder. Specific adaptations consider the particular client and the expression of trauma more than any adaptation for age.

In general, the study of trauma in older people, especially the diagnostic syndrome PTSD, is fraught with problems related to developmental issues and life span patterns. The interaction of aging and trauma involves many interacting factors including effects on development and personhood. Hyer and Sohnle (2001) discussed six variables especially important in the treatment of trauma in late life: (1) the presence of other stressors, (2) health status, (3) social support, (4) comorbidity, (5) cognitive decline, and (6) personality. Age, gender, socioeconomic status, and marital status also mediate the effects of trauma. Often PTSD does not emerge immediately after a trauma but involves an acute and then chronic reaction(s), the latter being reactions to the initial symptoms of the disorder: The longer PTSD lasts, the less central the actual trauma. Most anxiety disorders in the elderly begin much earlier in life. Additionally, patients who are over 85 may be substantially different from patients who are between 65 and 80. Arguably, subpopulations within the elderly (e.g., young old, middle old, and very old) should be treated differently. Finally, PTSD is not the only disorder specific to a poor trauma response. Depression, other anxiety disorders, as well as substance abuse are common. In fact, factors that initiate psychopathology are often not the same as those that maintain it into older age.

CBT AND THE TRAUMA MEMORY

There does not appear to be any superiority between cognitive therapy and exposure or between exposure and stress inoculation. There also does not appear to be any advantage of combining treatments so that exposure plus cognitive therapy or exposure plus stress inoculation are not superior to each intervention alone. There may be a slight advantage of individual therapy over group. That said, the exact components of care applied to older victims should be broadly considered and multiple in scope at least at the treatment planning stage. In effect, it is likely that all methods discussed have efficacy but the exact proportion for which older client is unknown.

Reviews have indicated that two forms of CBT are effective in the treatment of PTSD. In 1992 in a paper on treatment studies of PTSD, Solomon, Gerrity, and Muff (1992) identified only 11 outcome studies that utilized random assignment to treatment and control groups. While none involved older people, the active therapeutic ingredients for the treatment of PTSD remain striking to this day. They include systematic desensitization and CBT, exposure therapy, and cognitive reprocessing, as well as (but less so) general factors, including support and skills training. More recently, Solomon and Johnson (2002) reviewed the treatment research and found that several forms of therapy appear to be useful in reducing the symptoms of PTSD.

Strongest support is found for the treatments that combine cognitive and behavioral techniques. Imaginal exposure to trauma memories and hypnosis are techniques most likely to affect the intrusive symptoms of PTSD, while cognitive and psychodynamic approaches may better address numbing and avoidance symptoms. In general, treatment should be tailored to the severity and type of presenting PTSD symptoms, to the type of trauma experience, and to the many likely comorbid diagnoses and adjustment problems.

Trauma-related exposure therapy is an empirically supported treatment of PTSD (Chambless & Ollendick, 2001). Exposure involves both imaginal and in vivo exercises related to the traumatic memory. It appears that exposure-related therapies also maintain treatment gains for at least 12–15 months (Foa et al., 1999). Exposure therapy has the most empirical support because it was found to be effective across different populations of trauma victims with PTSD.

In one of the few studies (a case study) on an older patient, Russo, Hersen, and Van Hasselt (2001) carried out a single-case analysis to assess the effects of imaginal exposure in a 57-year-old woman suffering from current and reactivated PTSD following a transient ischemic attack. The client's responses to self-reported depression, anxiety, and PTSD symptoms were repeatedly recorded during four phases: (1) initial psychotherapy, (2) imaginal exposure, (3) skill generalization, and (4) fading of treatment. In addition to dramatic reduction in levels of depression and anxiety, results showed a significant improvement in PTSD symptoms relating to recent and remote traumatic experiences. Improvements were maintained approximately 16 months after imaginal exposure ended, despite ongoing external stressors.

Cognitive therapy is also effective. It addresses the internal representations of the trauma and its residual effects. Foa, Rothbaum, and Furr (2003) also noted empirically supported personal efficacy skills are built within the broad category of CBT. Again, they include exposure therapy, anxiety management programs, and cognitive therapy. These modalities have been developed to modify conditioned fear and erroneous cognitions that each thought to underlie PTSD. Resick (2003) reviewed seven studies that applied this method and concluded that each cognitive restructuring, involving varied methods of redressing the trauma, was effective and equal to exposure, either as part of exposure or independent of it. Combinations of therapies have also been used, and the value of these can be seen in groups (Foy, Ruzek, Glynn, Riney, & Gusman, 2002).

Finally, since EMDR was introduced 12 years ago, it has become one of the most utilized research treatments for PTSD and its efficacy has been widely recognized. EMDR is a comprehensive treatment protocol in which the client attends to emotionally disturbing material in short sequential doses while simultaneously focusing on an external stimulus. Taylor (2003) assessed the comparative efficacy, speed, and adverse effects of three treatments—exposure therapy, EMDR, and relaxation training—on 60 PTSD victims. Treatments did not differ in attrition, in the incidence of symptom worsening, or in their effects on numbing and hyperarousal symptoms. Compared with EMDR and relaxation training, exposure therapy (a) produced significantly larger reductions in avoidance and reexperiencing symptoms, (b) tended to be faster at reducing avoidance, and (c) tended to yield a greater proportion of participants who no longer met criteria for PTSD after treatment. EMDR and relaxation did not differ from one another in speed or efficacy.

APPLICATION TO OLDER VICTIMS

These studies apply to older trauma victims with several caveats. Chiefly older victims find the modal exposure treatments distressing to tolerate. Intensive exposure methods with older adults may be counterproductive. It increases the level of autonomic arousal, with adverse effects on cognitive performance. There are many benefits to the use of prolonged exposure, but older patients do best with dosed exposure and coping techniques. The primary therapeutic task in PTSD treatment becomes the activation of the traumatic memories while keeping autonomic nervous system arousal in the moderate range so that the secondary process program can effectively rewrite the original codes created by the automatic thinking program to classify the traumatic memories and/or the secondary process program can be used to revise the meta-cognitions that the traumatic material contradict.

Four therapies perform this task well. Anxiety management training, applied prior to exposure, reduces treatment dropout rates—patients are equipped to deal with the trauma memory. Stress inoculation therapy represents a more direct application on self-schema than on story renarration. EMDR provides a dosed exposure that targets state-specific information related to the trauma and has applicability with older victims. Unlike these other methods, EMDR is more active and guides the client when information is blocked (Hyer & Brandsma, 1997). Finally, cognitive processing therapy (noted above) applies gradual and multiple exposure to the trauma, consisting largely of rescripting and altering distortions. In all, it is probable that CBT strategies are effective because of their impact on cognitions, not because of their supposed impact on classically conditioned anxiety. Once the danger codes have been corrected, the recoded data must still be appropriately filed by conscious secondary process-dominated storytelling.

Increased socialization is also important as it improves credibility and enhances health belief models in compliant directions. These involve: (1) assessing the patient's implicit model of the causes and treatment of the disorder, (2) educating the client about the disorder and introducing the therapist's model, and (3) attempting to resolve any discrepancies between models.

Another alteration in this treatment involves the therapeutic consideration of multimodal components. Older victims share symptom expression of PTSD with volunteer groups. While untested, it is likely that older victims also suffer from excess anxiety sensitivity as a result of worry patterns in late life. As such, they may require pretreatment addressing anxiety sensitivity. Because of this and the provability of global symptoms, the model of Falseti, Erwin, Resnick, Davis, and Combs-Lane (2003) has special appeal to older victims. The MCET (Multiple Channel Exposure Therapy) presents patients with a cognitive–behavioral core in varied ways. Physiological reactivity is targeted with interoceptive exposure, cognitive components with writings about the trauma, and behavioral components with in vivo exposure to conditioned cues of anxiety. Cognitive restructuring skills (identifying maladaptive thoughts, disputing cognitive errors, and developing rational responses) are employed during exposures. Breathing retraining is also applied. Finally, social support is important. It is especially relevant in light of a robust literature on its benefits for this population. This includes behavioral activation principles, self-help, education, and supportive organizations of all types.

Hyer and Sohnle (2001) addressed most of these treatment components. They provided a six-step model of treatment: (1) stabilize symptoms; (2) relationship building; (3) attend to necessary developmental, treatment, and education factors and assure social supports, daily coping, and social skills and treatment compliance; (4) if avoidance/ other symptoms: use tactics of personality style; (5) build on self-defining memories (SDM); (6) if intrusions: decondition trauma memories by anxiety management techniques. First, the task is to stabilize symptoms, including the treatment of comorbid disorders and current stressors (including health). Second is the relationship itself. No other component of therapy is more accepted than this second treatment factor, the working alliance between client and therapist. The third task is to attend to necessary developmental and treatment factors, assure social supports, daily coping, and social skills and treatment compliance. Fourth, if resistance or avoidance predominate, use tactics of personality style. An analysis of personality (entrenched patterns of coping) improves the outcome of psychotherapy. The fifth involves the self-representational stories. The last (and complement of the fifth) component involves the trauma memory. The therapeutic task is to bring this implicit memory (easily triggered by emotional states, interpersonal contexts, external stimuli, and language cues) to be experienced as self-as-past, i.e., into language in the form of a narrative. The more the trauma memory is organized, narrativized, and placed into explicit memory, elaborated, disclosed, validated, and can be retrieved as less summary and more positive, the more general improvement occurs (Foa et al., 1999; Pennebacker, 1989). These efforts at explanation of the personal meaning of the trauma are critical since patients cannot undo their past grieving.

In effect, the therapist's role is as a "therapy manager," initially and foremost with schemas (the scaffold of the trauma) and then symptoms (the trauma). The integrated therapist influences healing, behavior change, and skill enhancement. Often operative tasks are basic: keeping the trauma victim in treatment, being supportive during difficult periods, maintaining appropriate arousal levels, and in general assuring commitment to the goals of therapy. The more pathological the victim is, the more influenced by trauma symptoms, the more the therapeutic tasks relate to the beginning parts of the model. The less the victim is impacted by the trauma, the less the therapist acts as a manager and the more the therapist can address the latter parts of the model and achieve lasting change.

CONCLUSION

In general, the data of the past two decades do not suggest that older adults are at greater risk than younger adults for negative psychosocial outcome following exposure to natural disasters. There is simply insufficient evidence to conclude that disaster causes more negative psychosocial consequences in older adults. Empirically supported therapies that apply to younger groups have applicability to older groups as well. These involve exposure and assimilation techniques within the context of a supportive and collaborative therapeutic relationship. In this way memories are modified or transformed. Often, factors related specifically to aging, mourning for losses, giving meaning to experiences, reestablishing self-coherence and self-continuity, achieve ego integration, and culture and social support are integrated also.

See also: Aging and dementia, Family caregivers, PTSD

REFERENCES

Blanchard, L. B., & Hickling, E. J. (1997). *After the crash: Assessment and treatment of motor vehicle accident survivors.* Washington, DC: American Psychological Association.

Blanchard, E. B., Hickling, E. J., Devineni, T., Veazey, C. H., Galouski, T. E. et al. (2003). A controlled evaluation of cognitive behavioral therapy for post-traumatic stress disorder in motor vehicle accident survivors. *Behaviour Therapy, 43*, 417–426.

Chambless, D. L., & Ollendick, T. H. (2001). Empirically supported psychological interventions: Controversies and evidence. *Annual Review of Psychology, 52*, 685–716.

Ensel, W. M. (1991). "Important" life events and depression among older adults: The role of psychological and social resources. *Journal of Aging and Health, 3*, 546–566.

Falseti, S. A., Erwin, B. A., Resnick, L. S., Davis, J., & Combs-Lane, A. M. (2003). *Multiple channel exposure therapy of PTSD: Impact of treatment on functioning and resources.* New York: Springer.

Foa, F. B., Dancu, C. N., Hembree, F. A., Jaycox, L. H., Meadows, F. A., & Street, G. P. (1999). A comparison of exposure therapy, stress inoculation training, and their combination for reducing posttraumatic stress disorder in female assault victims. *Journal of Consulting and Clinical Psychology, 67*, 194–200.

Foa, E., Rothbaum, B., & Furr, J. (2003). Augmenting exposure therapy with other CBT procedures. *Psychiatric Annals, 33*(1), 47–53.

Foy, D., Ruzek, J., Glynn, S., Riney, S., & Gusman, F. (2002). Trauma focus group therapy for combat-related PTSD: An update. *Journal of Clinical Psychology, 58*(8), 907–918.

Hyer, L., & Brandsma, J. (1997). EMDR minus eye movements equals good psychotherapy. *Journal of Traumatic Stress, 10*(3), 515–523.

Hyer, L., & Sohnle, S. (2001). *Trauma among older people: Issues and treatment.* Philadelphia: Brunner–Routledge.

Hyer, L., & Summers, M. (1995). *An understanding of combat trauma at later life.* VA Merit Review. Augusta, GA.

Kessler, R., Sonnega, A., Bromet, E., Hughes, M., & Nelson, C. (1995). Posttraumatic stress disorder in the National Comorbidity Survey. *Archives of General Psychiatry, 52*, 1048–1060.

Norris, F. (1992). Epidemiology of trauma: Frequency and impact of different potentially traumatic events on different demographic groups. *Journal of Consulting and Clinical Psychology, 60*, 409–418.

Pennebaker, J. W. (1989). Confession, inhibition, and disease. In L. Berkowitz (Ed.), *Advances in experimental social psychology* (Vol. 22). Orlando, FL: Academic Press.

Resick, P. A. (2003). Cognitive therapy for posttraumatic stress disorder. *Journal of Cognitive Psychotherapy, 15*(4), 321–330.

Russo, S. A., Hersen, M., & Van Hasselt, V. B. (2001). Treatment of reactivated post-traumatic stress disorder: Imaginal exposure in an older adult with multiple traumas. *Behavior Modification, 25*(1), 94–115.

Solomon, S., Gerrity, F. T., & Muff, A. M. (1992). Efficacy of treatments for posttraumatic stress disorder. *Journal of the American Medical Association, 268*, 633–638.

Solomon, S., & Johnson, D. (2002). Psychosocial treatment of posttraumatic stress disorder: A practice friendly review of outcome research. *Journal of Clinical Psychology, 58*(8), 947–959.

Taylor, S. (2003). Outcome predictors for three PTSD treatments: Exposure therapy, EMDR, and relaxation training. *Journal of Cognitive Psychotherapy, 17*(2), 149.

PTSD—War Related

Terence M. Keane and Meredith Charney

Keywords: PTSD, zone stressors, combat stressors, war veterans, military, refugees, internally displaced persons

Posttraumatic stress disorder (PTSD) is a disorder characterized by intrusive thoughts about, preoccupation with, and nightmares of an extremely stressful life event. Typically these events are life threatening either to the individuals themselves or their loved ones. Initially included in the diagnostic nomenclature in the third edition of the American

Psychiatric Association's *Diagnostic and Statistical Manual* (DSM-III; APA, 1980), PTSD is often a disabling condition associated with emotional avoidance and numbing, and a range of symptoms of hyperarousal including: insomnia, irritability, difficulty concentrating, hypervigilance, and exaggerated startle responses. This collection of symptoms must be present for a full month; if the duration of the symptoms is 3 months or less, it is referred to as *acute PTSD*. If the duration of symptoms exceeds 3 months, it is termed *chronic PTSD*. Occasionally, symptoms emerge no more than 6 months following the traumatic event and this is called *PTSD with delayed onset*.

The National Comorbidity Survey (NCS; Kessler, Sonnega, Bromet, Hushe, & Nelson, 1995) estimated the lifetime prevalence of PTSD in the United States to be 7.8% overall. Gender differences emerged in the prevalence of exposure to traumatic events and in the subsequent development of PTSD. Men are more likely to be exposed to traumatic events during their lives (60.7%), but the prevalence among women is also quite high (51.2%). Lifetime prevalence of PTSD in men was 5.0% and for women it was 10.4%. Women appear more likely to develop PTSD as a function of exposure; once exposed to a traumatic event, 20.4% of women ultimately develop PTSD as compared to 8.2% of men who, when exposed to a traumatic event, develop PTSD. Factors accounting for this significant gender difference in the development of PTSD may include the types of events to which men and women are differentially exposed and have socioeconomic differences, social support differences, and even biological/physiological variables. More research is required to understand why this, and other psychiatric conditions, appears to occur in one gender more frequently than the other.

Events that are observed to yield high rates of PTSD and related adverse outcomes include war, combat, sexual assault, physical assault, childhood neglect, and being threatened with a weapon. Unfortunately, these events were commonly observed in this nationally representative survey. PTSD is also frequently comorbid with other psychiatric conditions. For example, in the NCS more than 88% of the men with PTSD also met lifetime criteria for another disorder; among women 79% of those with PTSD also reached lifetime criteria for at least one other condition. While popular conceptions are that the impact of a traumatic event will be short term in its effects, the data suggest otherwise. Recovery typically occurs in the first 12 months following symptom onset. After this, the recovery curves become more gradual over the course of time that this function was measured. More than one-third of those who develop PTSD appear to still manifest symptoms 6 years postonset. For many of these people, this level of disorder is associated with chronic interpersonal problems, substance abuse, depression, vocational impairment, and marital and family problems (Keane & Barlow, 2002).

Among war veterans the prevalence of PTSD is best estimated by the National Vietnam Veterans Readjustment Study (NVVRS; Kulka et al., 1988). This study found that 30% of all Vietnam theater veterans developed war-related PTSD at some point following service in the war zone. Conducted in 1986–88, it was learned that 159 of these veterans still had PTSD some 15 years following conclusion of the war. Given the 3.1 million Americans who served there, these figures represent nearly 1 million cases of lifetime PTSD and nearly half a million cases of current PTSD in this cohort alone. Comparable figures for all of the wars and military actions are not available, yet the large number of veterans seeking care for war-related PTSD nationwide indicates that these problems exist across conflicts, gender, race, and ethnicity.

Increasingly, war affects more civilians than military combatants. The United Nations High Commission for Refugees (UNHCR) estimates that in 2002 nearly 20 million people fell under the mandate of the commission. This included 12 million refugees, nearly a half million returnees, about 1 million asylees, and over 6 million internally displaced people (IDPs). The United States is by far the largest recipient of refugees in the developed world, taking some 69,000 refugees in the year 2001. In that same year, 86,000 people sought asylum in the United States. Refugees and asylees represent an at-risk group for trauma exposure and PTSD. Many have survived war and observed the devastation of their homes and families, and been exposed to torture and related violence. Fleeing their country of origin results in the reduction of the stressors overall, but also yields additional stressors. Linguistic, financial, cultural, and vocational stressors are accompanied by resettlement stressors; the strain of losing known community and social supports adds to the burden of an already deeply trauma-exposed group. They are in need of mental health services that will address the presence of PTSD among the group as well as treatments developed to address their specific psychosocial problems secondary to acculturative stress.

CBT is designed to develop interventions specifically geared to the needs of this population. As a problem-oriented approach, CBT provides idiographic approaches to diagnosing the problems and assessing the needs of vulnerable at-risk populations. This is clearly the case for those people who have developed PTSD as a result of war zone stressors. For veterans and refugees alike, a problem-focused approach led to the successful development of CBT interventions that are addressing the needs of the large cohort of people currently living in Western countries who have been exposed to the traumas of war whether they are civilians or military-prepared combatants.

ORIGINS OF CBT FOR WAR-RELATED PTSD: THEORETICAL MODELS

Keane and Kaloupek (1982) treated a Vietnam theater veteran who presented with war-related PTSD, depression, and substance abuse problems. They offered a theoretical model that focused on two-factor learning theory to explain the development and maintenance of PTSD symptoms. Viewing PTSD as consisting of classical conditioning and instrumental avoidance, this model resulted in the use of treatments previously demonstrated as successful in other forms of anxiety disorders such as agoraphobia, panic, and obsessive–compulsive disorder. Implicit in the treatment developed was consideration of the traumatic memories and nightmares as the motivating factors in many of the symptoms of PTSD. Exposure therapy using imagery of the content of nightmares, flashbacks, images, and memories was effective in reducing symptoms of PTSD in a wide range of patient populations (Foa, Keane, & Friedman, 2000).

More recently, Keane and Barlow (2002) expanded the model to include a wider variety of variables considered key to the development of PTSD among trauma-exposed individuals. Their etiological model hypothesizes the equal importance of psychological and biological vulnerabilities. These can be inherited or acquired vulnerabilities: biological characteristics can influence psychological features and psychological characteristics can influence biological features of the individual. At the time of trauma exposure, there results a "true alarm" that involves the manifestation of extreme emotional and physiological responding. Here occurs the potential for conditioning external and internal cues to the emotional and physiological characteristics of the alarm. Thus, these cues acquire the potential to elicit aspects of the alarm reaction in the absence of the real threat. This is the notion of a "false alarm." So distressing is the occurrence of false alarms that they create aversive anticipatory cognitions that set in motion a wide range of cognitive and behavioral avoidance strategies by the individual. These avoidance strategies serve to maintain the strength of the fear conditioning. Only the presence of social support systems and coping skills can mitigate the development of PTSD, but the model requires that these support systems and coping skills are accessed and utilized fully by the exposed individual in order to mitigate the impact of the traumatic event.

LITERATURE REVIEW OF CBT FOR PTSD

These theoretical models led to the development of the three most widely used treatments for war-related PTSD today: cognitive therapy, anxiety management therapy, and exposure therapy. Depending on individual differences and the ways in which people emotionally process traumatic experiences, a patient may respond differently to each type of treatment modality. However, new treatment alternatives are constantly being developed and their efficacy tested: for example, eye movement desensitization and reprocessing (EMDR) and testimonial psychotherapy are treatments that have received recent attention in the literature.

Cognitive Therapy

PTSD develops into a chronic disorder when individuals cognitively process the trauma in a manner that leads them to feel constant threat. This feeling of threat exists due to consistent negative appraisal of the traumatic event and to the manner in which the event is encoded and established in the memory. These cognitive distortions prevent individuals from leading productive, normal lives because they are plagued by their past. As well, these aversive cognitions produce maladaptive behaviors such as substance abuse in an attempt to control their emotions. Cognitive restructuring is one type of cognitive therapy used in the treatment of PTSD. It involves recalling the experience and verbalizing what happened and what emotions they felt at the time and subsequently. This sampling of cognitions permits the therapist and the patient to identify faulty cognitions, beliefs, or appraisals. Using Socratic methods, the goal of treatment is to challenge the faulty cognitions that create distress for the individual. Cognitive restructuring allows the traumatized individual to perceive his or her trauma differently and more dispassionately, appraise appropriate beliefs about his or her role in the event, and acquire different and more accurate beliefs about the traumatic event and its effects on his or her.

Exposure Therapy

Exposure therapy is a generic term that incorporates a wide range of cognitive–behavioral strategies including: systematic desensitization, flooding, prolonged exposure, or implosive therapy. Exposure therapy can be accomplished using either in vivo or imaginal (in vitro) approaches. In vivo exposure includes returning to the scene of the traumatic experience, which will encourage the reduction of escape and avoidance behaviors while exposing the individual to the maximum number of conditioning cues possible. Imaginal exposure is used in place of in vivo exposure when returning to the scene of the trauma is not possible. For example, when treating a refugee from a war-torn country who has relocated to the United States, it becomes unfeasible to take the individual back to his or her home country. In the first clinical case of PTSD in the scientific literature, Keane and Kaloupek (1982) employed exposure therapy to treat a Vietnam veteran with PTSD. When the imagination of the scene was invoking noticeable distress, the subject was encouraged to remain in this state until his anxiety decreased. Following 18 sessions of treatment, there was significant reduction in PTSD symptoms. Keane, Fairbank, Caddell, and Zimering (1989) in a randomized clinical trial found that exposure therapy led to significant improvement in PTSD symptoms when compared to an anxiety management condition where there were multiple treatment dropouts and a wait-list comparison group.

Anxiety Management Training (AMT)

AMT teaches the patient the cognitive and behavioral skills to more effectively manage the aversive emotions experienced in PTSD. Typically, the specific skills taught are relaxation training, breathing retraining, trauma education, guided self-dialogue, cognitive restructuring, and communication skills. Although frequently considered a palliative approach to treating PTSD, AMT appears to possess the capacity to influence the frequency and intensity of PTSD symptoms across different types of traumatic events (e.g., Foa et al., 1999; Resick et al., 2002). In a large-scale trial of CBT among Australian Vietnam veterans with PTSD, Creamer, Morris, Biddle, and Elliot (1999) found striking changes in PTSD among this cohort of war-traumatized veterans. This multisite effort, while not randomly controlled, suggests great promise for treating war-related PTSD among military veterans (Frueh et al., 1996).

Eye Movement Desensitization and Reprocessing (EMDR)

EMDR is a new treatment technique that has received a modest amount of empirical attention. The basic approach includes recognition of images and memories related to the traumatic experience, the psychological problems associated with these images and memories, the development of an alternative mode of interpreting these images and memories, observing the physiological effects of these images and memories on the individual, remaining focused on a corrective appraisal of these images and memories, and the repetition of lateral eye movements as the patient concentrates on aspects of the traumatic experience (Keane & Barlow, 2002). In a clinical trial involving Vietnam theater veterans that compared EMDR to relaxation training, biofeedback, and a comparison group, EMDR subjects did better across all variables measured (Silver, Brooks, & Obenchain, 1995). The components of EMDR include exposure and cognitive interventions, yet research has yet to support the inclusion of the eye movements as factors influencing efficacy (Davidson & Parker, 2001).

Testimonial Psychotherapy

The refugee population is gaining increased recognition as a population that is susceptible to the development of PTSD. Testimonial psychotherapy has been developed as a symptom-based treatment for war-related PTSD (Weine, Kulenovic, Pavkovic, & Gibbons, 1998). Employed in small groups of people who have experienced this treatment, it accesses individuals' traumatic experiences and integrates their own story into a collection of stories including all of the refugees who shared their experiences. Among refugees it encompasses an effort to piece together the history of their culture as it has survived efforts at destruction. The goal is to review in great detail the elements of the trauma history while focusing on keeping important aspects of history and culture alive. Clearly there is a strong component of exposure therapy included in testimonial therapy, but it also incorporates meaning and highlights purpose in the refugees' lives. In a clinical trial, testimonial therapy significantly reduced PTSD diagnoses and symptom severity at posttreatment assessment in a group of refugees from Bosnia–Herzegovina (Weine et al., 1998).

SUMMARY AND FUTURE DIRECTIONS

Cognitive–behavioral treatments show great promise for the treatment of PTSD secondary to war experiences. Clinical interventions that involve combinations of CBT techniques such as exposure therapy, AMT, and cognitive therapy need to be examined in randomized clinical trials both alone and in conjunction with pharmacological approaches. No such trials currently exist for PTSD secondary to any type of traumatic event. There is a clear need and a demand for these clinical trials.

Perhaps most important, and especially so in light of the terrorist attacks on New York and Washington on September 11, 2001, is the need for understanding how to prevent PTSD. Efforts by mental health professionals and public health professionals to deliver psychological interventions in the aftermath of trauma exposures are in their nascent stage of development. Needed now are creative efforts to intervene when mass disaster or tragedy occurs. At this point there are preliminary data available to suggest that CBT can prevent PTSD. The questions remaining are who can deliver the interventions, who in particular needs these interventions, when after the traumatic event is the best time to intervene, and how do we provide the interventions. Given the enormity of the tragedy of 9/11 and the enormity of most war-related traumatic events, the use of the Internet and large-group formats may well be the future of preventive efforts for PTSD.

See also: Exposure therapy, PTSD

REFERENCES

American Psychiatric Association. (1980). *Diagnostic and statistical manual of mental disorders* (3rd ed.). Washington, DC: Author.

Davidson, P. R., & Parker, K. C. H. (2001). Eye movement desensitization and reprocessing (EMDR): A meta-analysis. *Journal of Consulting and Clinical Psychology, 69*(2), 305–316.

Foa, E. B., Dancu, C. V., Hembree, E. A., Jaycox, L. H., Meadows, E. A., & Street, G. P. (1999). A comparison of exposure therapy, stress inoculation training, and their combination for reducing posttraumatic stress disorder in female assault victims. *Journal of Consulting and Clinical Psychology, 67*, 194–200.

Foa, E. B., Keane, T. M., & Friedman, M. J. (Eds.). (2000). *Effective treatments for PTSD: Practice guidelines from the International Society for traumatic stress studies*. New York: Guilford Press.

Frueh, B. C., Turner, S. M., Beidel, D. C., Mirabella, R. F., & Jones, W. J. (1996). Trauma management therapy: A preliminary evaluation of a multicomponent behavioral treatment for chronic combat related PTSD. *Behavior Research and Therapy, 34*, 533–543.

Keane, T. M., & Barlow, D. H. (2002). Posttraumatic stress disorder. In D. H. Barlow (Ed.), *Anxiety and its disorders*. New York: Guilford Press.

Keane, T. M., Fairbank, J. A., Caddell, J. M., & Zimering, R. T. (1989). Implosive (flooding) therapy reduces symptoms of PTSD in Vietnam combat veterans. *Behavior Therapy, 20*, 245–260.

Keane, T. M., & Kaloupek, D. G. (1982). Imaginal flooding in the treatment of posttraumatic stress disorder. *Journal of Consulting and Clinical Psychology, 50*, 138–140.

Kessler, R. C., Sonnega, A., Bromet, E., Hughes, M., & Nelson, C. B. (1995).Posttraumatic stress disorder in the National Comorbidity Survey. *Archives of General Psychiatry, 52*, 1048–1060.

Kulka, R. A., Schlenger, W. E., Fairbank, J. A., Hough, R. L., Jordan, B. K., Maimai, C. R., & Weiss, D. S. (1990). *Trauma and the Vietnam war generation: Report of findings from the national Vietnam veterans readjustment study*. New York: Brunner/Mazel.

Resick, P. A., Nishith, P., Weaver, T. L., Astin, M. C., & Fever, C. A. (2002). A comparison of cognitive processing therapy with prolonged exposure and a waiting condition for the treatment of chronic posttraumatic stress disorder in female rape victims. *Journal of Consulting and Clinical Psychology, 70*(4), 867–879.

Silver, S. M., Brooks, A., & Obenchein, J. (1995). Treatment of Vietnam war veterans with PTSD: A comparison of eye movement desensitization and reprocessing, biofeedback, and relaxation training. *Journal of Traumatic Stress, 8*, 307–312.

Weine, S. M., Kulenovic, A. D., Pavkovic, I., & Gibbons, R. (1998). Testimonial psychotherapy in Bosnian refugees: A pilot study. *American Journal of Psychiatry, 155*, 1720–1725.

R

Rational Emotive Behavior Therapy

Windy Dryden

Keywords: rational emotive behavior therapy, rationality and irrationality, psychological interactionism, active-directive treatment

Rational Emotive Behavior Therapy (REBT) was founded in 1955 by Albert Ellis, a U.S. clinical psychologist. Originally trained as a psychoanalyst, Ellis was disappointed at the results he obtained from this form of therapy and after a period of experimentation in various therapeutic methods of the time, he brought together his early interests in a number of fields to form REBT. These fields included the practical application of philosophers such as Epictetus, Marcus Aurelius, and Bertrand Russell who all stressed the importance of cognition in understanding human affairs and the work of the early behavior therapists such as John B. Watson and Mary Cover Jones whose ideas helped Ellis to overcome public speaking anxiety and fears of approaching women. Originally, Ellis called his approach Rational Therapy (RT) because he wanted to emphasize its rational and cognitive features, but in 1961, he changed its name to Rational-Emotive Therapy to show critics that it did not neglect emotions. Over 30 years later (in 1993), Ellis renamed the approach Rational Emotive Behavior Therapy (REBT) to show critics that it did not neglect behavior.

In 1962, Ellis published *Reason and Emotion in Psychotherapy*, a collection of largely previously printed papers or previously delivered lectures, but which became a seminal work in the history of psychotherapy. Most of REBT's major, present-day features are described in Ellis's book, albeit some in embryonic form: the pivotal role of cognition in psychological disturbance, the principle of psychological interactionism where cognition, emotion, and behavior are seen as interacting, not separate systems, the advantages of self-acceptance over self-esteem in helping clients with their disturbed views of their self, the role that low frustration tolerance has in perpetuating psychological disturbance, and the importance of an active-directive therapeutic style to name but a few. Present-day features of REBT not found in this seminal book include its constructivistic and postmodern aspects.

BASIC ASSUMPTIONS

In REBT, rationality is a concept that is applied to a person's beliefs. Rational beliefs, which are deemed to be at the core of psychological health in REBT, are flexible, consistent with reality, logical, and self- and relationship-enhancing. Irrational beliefs, which are deemed to be at the core of psychological disturbance, are rigid, inconsistent with reality, illogical, and self- and relationship-defeating.

In REBT theory (Ellis, 1962, 1994), there are four types of rational beliefs: flexible preferences ("I want to be approved, *but* I don't have to be"), non-awfulizing beliefs ("It's bad to be disapproved, *but* it isn't the end of the world"), high-frustration-tolerance beliefs ("It is difficult to face being disapproved, *but* I can tolerate it and it is worth tolerating"), and acceptance beliefs (e.g., unconditional self-acceptance [USA]: "I failed to be approved, *but* I am not worthless. I am a fallible human being capable of being approved, disapproved, and treated neutrally," unconditional other-acceptance [UOA]: "You disapproved of me, *but* you are not a bad person for doing so. Rather, you are a fallible human being capable of good, bad, and neutral deeds," and unconditional life acceptance [ULA]: "Life conditions are really hard for me because of your disapproval, *but* life is not all bad. It is a tremendously complex mixture of good, bad, and neutral events").

Similarly, there are four types of rational beliefs: rigid demands ("I must be approved"), awfulizing beliefs ("If I'm disapproved, it's the end of the world"), low-frustration-tolerance beliefs ("I can't tolerate being disapproved"), and depreciation beliefs (e.g., self-depreciation: "I am worthless if I am disapproved," other-depreciation: "You are a horrible person if you disapprove of me" and life-depreciation: "Life is all bad because I have been disapproved").

REBT advocates an ABC model of psychological disturbance and health. "A" stands for activating event which can be actual or inferred, "B" stands for belief (rational or irrational), and "C" stands for consequences of holding a belief about A and can be emotional, behavioral, and cognitive. Thus, A's do not cause C's but contribute to them. B's are seen as the prime but not only determiner of C's.

REBT theory states that holding a rational belief about an A leads to healthy emotions, functional behavior, and realistic subsequent thinking, whereas holding an irrational belief about the same A leads to unhealthy emotions, dysfunctional behavior, and unrealistic subsequent thinking.

REBT theory holds that human beings are capable of thinking rationally and irrationally. The ease with which we transform our strong desires into rigid demands, for example, suggests that the tendency toward irrational thinking is biologically based, but can be buffered or encouraged by environmental contexts (Ellis, 1976). Clients often have the unfortunate experience of inheriting tendencies toward disturbance and being exposed to their parents' disturbed behavior. REBT is optimistic and realistic here. It argues that if such clients work persistently and forcefully to counter their irrational beliefs and act in ways that are consistent with their rational beliefs, then they can help themselves significantly. However, REBT also acknowledges that most clients will not put in this degree of effort over a long period of time and will therefore fall far short of achieving their potential for psychological health.

ORIGIN AND MAINTENANCE OF PROBLEMS

Paraphrasing the famous dictum of Epictetus, we say in REBT that people are not disturbed by events but by the rigid and extreme view they take of them. This means that while negative events contribute to the development of disturbance, particularly when these events are highly aversive, disturbance occurs when people bring their tendencies to think irrationally to these events.

REBT does not have an elaborate view of the origin of disturbance. Having said this, it does acknowledge that it is very easy for humans when they are young to disturb themselves about highly aversive events. However, it argues that even under these conditions people react differently to the same event, and thus we need to understand what a person brings to and takes from a negative activating event.

People learn their standards and goals from their culture, but disturbance occurs when they bring their irrational beliefs to circumstances where their standards are not met and their pursuit toward achieving their goals is blocked. In contrast, REBT has a more elaborate view of how disturbance is maintained. It argues that people perpetuate their disturbance for a number of reasons including the following: (1) They lack the insight that their disturbance is underpinned by their irrational beliefs and think instead that it is caused by events; (2) they think that once they understand that their problems are underpinned by irrational beliefs, this understanding alone will lead to change; (3) they do not work persistently to change their irrational beliefs and to integrate the rational alternatives to these beliefs into their belief system; (4) they continue to act in ways that are consistent with their irrational beliefs; (5) they lack or are deficient in important social skills, communication skills, problem-solving skills, and other life skills; (6) they think that their disturbance has payoffs that outweigh the advantages of the healthy alternatives to their disturbed feelings and/or behavior; and (7) they live in environments that support the irrational beliefs that underpin their problems.

CHANGE

REBT therapists consider that the core facilitative conditions of empathy, unconditional positive regard, and genuineness are often desirable, but neither necessary nor sufficient for constructive therapeutic change. For such change to take place, REBT therapists need to help their clients to do the following:

- Realize that they largely create their own psychological problems and that while situations contribute to these problems, they are in general of lesser importance in the change process
- Fully recognize that they are able to address and overcome these problems
- Understand that their problems stem largely from irrational beliefs
- Detect their irrational beliefs and discriminate between them and their rational beliefs
- Question their irrational beliefs and their rational beliefs until they see clearly that their irrational beliefs are false, illogical, and unconstructive while their rational beliefs are true, sensible, and constructive

- Work toward the internalization of their new rational beliefs by using a variety of cognitive (including imaginal), emotive, and behavioral change methods while refraining from acting in ways that are consistent with their old irrational beliefs
- Extend this process of challenging beliefs and using multimodal methods of change into other areas of their lives and to commit to doing so for as long as necessary

SKILLS AND STRATEGIES

REBT therapists see themselves as good psychological educators and therefore seek to teach their clients the ABC model of understanding and dealing with their psychological problems. They stress that there are alternative ways of addressing these problems and strive to elicit their client's informed consent at the outset and throughout the therapeutic process. If they think that a client is better suited to a different approach to therapy, they do not hesitate to effect a suitable referral.

REBT therapists frequently employ an active-directive therapeutic style and use both Socratic and didactic teaching methods. However, they vary their style from client to client (Dryden, 2002). They often begin by working with specific examples of identified client problems and help their clients to set healthy goals. They employ a sequence of steps in working on these examples that involves using the ABC framework, challenging beliefs, and negotiating suitable homework assignments with their clients. Helping clients to generalize their learning from situation to situation is explicitly built into the therapeutic process as is helping clients to identify, challenge, and change core irrational beliefs which are seen as accounting for disturbance across a broad range of relevant situations.

A major therapeutic strategy involves helping clients to become their own therapists. In doing this, REBT therapists teach their clients how to use a particular skill such as challenging irrational beliefs, model the use of this skill, and sometimes give the clients written instructions on how to use the skill on their own (Dryden, 2001). Constructive feedback is given to encourage the refinement of the skill. As clients learn how to use the skills of REBT for themselves, their therapists adopt a less active-directive, more prompting therapeutic style in order to encourage them to take increasing responsibility for their own therapeutic change.

REBT may be seen as an example of theoretically consistent eclecticism in that its practitioners draw on procedures that originate from other therapeutic approaches, but do so for purposes that are consistent with REBT theory (Dryden, 1995). REBT therapists are selective in their eclecticism and avoid the use of methods that are inefficient, mystical, or of dubious validity. REBT therapists have their preferred therapeutic goals for their clients, i.e., to help them to change their core irrational beliefs and to develop and internalize a set of core rational beliefs. However, they are ready to compromise these objectives when it becomes clear that their clients are unable or unwilling to change their core irrational beliefs. In such cases, REBT therapists help their clients by encouraging them to change their distorted inferences, to effect behavioral changes without necessarily changing their irrational beliefs or to remove themselves from negative activating events (Dryden, 1995).

The fact that REBT therapists are theoretically consistent in their eclecticism and are prepared to make compromises with their preferred therapeutic strategy shows that they are informed by REBT theory, but are flexible in their implementation of it in the consulting room. Since flexibility is a key concept in REBT, good REBT therapists in being therapeutically flexible demonstrate that they practice what they preach.

RESEARCH EVIDENCE

There is quite a lot of research indicating that psychological disturbance is correlated with irrational beliefs, but studies indicating that these beliefs are at the core of disturbance have yet to be carried out. Most scales that measure irrational and rational beliefs are deficient in one respect or another and there is a need to develop a scale with excellent psychometric properties.

Numerous studies on the effectiveness of REBT have been carried out and various meta-analyses of REBT outcome studies have been conducted which have come to different conclusions about the effectiveness of REBT. Well-controlled trials of REBT need to be done with clinical populations, employing well-trained REBT therapists who can be shown to adhere to a properly designed REBT adherence scale. Work is currently in progress to design such an adherence scale.

FUTURE DIRECTIONS

The future of REBT was considered a number of years ago in a survey of the then membership of the International Training Standards and Review Committee of the Albert Ellis Institute (Weinrach et al., 1995). Of the nine members of this committee, seven were basically optimistic about REBT's future and two were relatively pessimistic. Since I was one of the most pessimistic, I would like to explain the major source of my pessimism. My prediction is that in the future there will be increasing emphasis on empirically supported therapies (ESTs) in our field and REBT in its specific form will fail to meet the criteria of an EST. Indeed, REBT is not even mentioned in Lyddon and Jones's (2001) edited text on the empirically supported cognitive therapies. There are no academic centers of excellence where the empirical study of REBT is being conducted and as I noted in a previous section there is no well-validated therapist adherence or competency scale to determine that REBT will be correctly and competently delivered in any future efficacy studies.

Having said that, I do think that REBT's ideas will continue to be incorporated into generic CBT and will have their impact in future psychological education programs to which they are particularly suited. As such, REBT concepts will be alive and well but perhaps not under the rubric of REBT. Whether future authors acknowledge REBT as their source is debatable. But as Ellis reminds us, if this does not happen, it would be bad, but it would not be awful.

REFERENCES

Dryden, W. (Ed.). (1995). *A rational emotive behaviour therapy reader.* London: Sage.

Dryden, W. (2001). *Reason to change: A rational emotive behaviour therapy (REBT) workbook.* Hove: Brunner-Routledge.

Dryden, W. (Ed.). (2002). *Idiosyncratic rational emotive behaviour therapy.* Ross-on-Wye: PCCS Books.

Ellis, A. (1962). *Reason and emotion in psychotherapy.* Secaucus, NJ: Lyle Stuart.

Ellis, A. (1976). The biological basis of human irrationality. *Journal of Individual Psychology, 32,* 145–168.

Ellis, A. (1994). *Reason and emotion in psychotherapy.* Revised and updated edition. New York: Birch Lane Press.

Lyddon, W. J., & Jones, J. V., Jr. (Eds.). (2001). *Empirically supported cognitive therapies: Current and future applications.* New York: Springer.

Weinrach, S. G., Ellis, A., DiGiuseppe, R., Bernard, M., Dryden, W., Kassinove, H., Morris, G. B., Vernon, A., & Wolfe, J. (1995). Rational emotive behavior therapy after Ellis: Predictions for the future. *Journal of Mental Health Counseling, 17,* 413–427.

Rehabilitation Psychology

Timothy R. Elliott and Warren T. Jackson

Keywords: physical disability, rehabilitation, counseling, cognitive–behavioral therapy

The rate of permanent disability has increased steadily over the years, accompanying the aging of our population, increasing rates of survival from severe physical trauma, and the precipitous rise of debilitating, incurable chronic disease. Considerable evidence attests that people who possess adaptive social–cognitive characteristics typically experience a more optimal adjustment following disability than persons who have deficits in these characteristics (for a comprehensive overview on this field, see Frank & Elliott, 2000). These characteristics are essential in adhering to self-care regimens, preventing further complications and enhancing quality of life. CBT has great potential in promoting adjustment, well-being, and personal health among persons with disabling conditions. Cognitive–behavioral interventions are the most promising and widely accepted treatments in rehabilitation psychology.

Thus, the great variety of patient and family needs in rehabilitation and community settings provides a wonderful opportunity for application of virtually all CBT approaches: behavior management, learning theory as it applies to didactics and patient education, cognitive techniques that inform psychoeducational interventions, and empirically supported CBT protocols for specific disorders and adjustment difficulties. In rehabilitation settings, CBT may be conceptualized in its broadest form.

VARIED APPLICATIONS

Types of Injury/Illness

The successful practitioner of CBT must have familiarity with all of the different disorders that are commonly encountered in various rehabilitation settings. Disorders may be classified as central neurologic (stroke, head trauma), peripheral neurologic (spinal cord injury, Guillian–Barré syndrome), orthopedic (fractures, joint replacements), medical (major surgery, chronic metabolic illness), psychiatric (schizophrenia, mental retardation), and combined. Substance use disorders are considered elsewhere in this volume; however, they are certainly prevalent in rehabilitation settings (alcohol abuse, therapeutic dependence on pain medication) and often these disorders contribute to the onset of a disability and to the development of preventable secondary complications following disability (e.g., ER visits, infections, skin ulcers).

Treatment Settings

There has been a definite trend over the past 15 years for rehabilitation resources to be reallocated from the traditional inpatient postacute setting to outpatient and home-based programs. In addition, new initiatives such as telehealth approaches are being developed to augment ongoing treatment after discharge from acute and postacute treatment facilities and return to the community. Individuals may qualify for educational and/or vocational assistance from state or private agencies that will then participate in the rehabilitation process. CBT is applicable in inpatient settings when there are numerous treating professionals present and after their return to the community, when individuals may live independently or receive assistance from family members or home health therapists.

INTERDISCIPLINARY TREATMENT CONTEXT

In hospitals and other rehabilitation settings, practitioners of CBT will almost always be working with an interdisciplinary team. Depending on the particular setting, teams will generally include some combination of the following disciplines: physiatrists (physicians specializing in rehabilitation medicine) and psychiatrists; consulting physicians such as neurologists, orthopedists, internists, and others; nurses; physical therapists (PT); occupational therapists (OT); speech therapists; social workers; and vocational rehabilitation specialists. CBT is most potent in such practice environments when the practitioner formally communicates to other team members about the specific behaviors targeted for intervention during team meetings and is available for informal consultation with other staff members during the therapy week. Often, the practitioner will work very closely with nursing staff, PT, OT, and speech therapy when implementing behavioral management plans. A good working relationship with these disciplines is necessary for proper implementation of interventions.

CAVEATS FOR MODIFYING CBT PROTOCOLS

A major challenge to applying CBT in rehabilitation settings relates to the cognitive and physical difficulties experienced by patients. Modifying protocolized CBT is a skill that must be developed so that the unique capabilities of the patient are accounted for without sacrificing the empirical foundation of CBT. When dealing with patients with cognitive impairment or physical discomforts, it is generally recommended that the practitioner focus intervention on a limited domain of material and use repetition and written aids to promote learning and generalization. Hibbard, Grober, Gordon and Aletta (1990) offer a set of practical adaptations of CBT to compensate for cognitive deficits. In a recent volume edited by Radnitz (2000), the specifics of CBT as it applies to a variety of disabilities are presented: spinal cord injury, amputation, pain-related musculoskeletal disorders, chronic illness, cognitive impairment, visual and hearing impairment, autism, mental retardation, learning disabilities, and communication disorders.

ROLE OF COGNITIVE-BEHAVIORAL ASSESSMENT

Effective CBT begins with sound assessment of well-operationalized target behaviors, a definition of environmental antecedents, and determination of consequences that maintain the behavior as well as discovery of patient cognitions about self, others, and the world that moderate behavior. The data-based approach of CBT is quite compatible with the workings of the interdisciplinary treatment team as assessment information can be used for diagnosis, treatment planning, and outcome evaluation.

ACUTE CARE AND REHABILITATION SETTINGS

It is generally accepted that what defines a treatment setting as "acute" is the medical status of the patients in it rather than some characteristic of the facility. Thus, patients in an acute care setting are medically unstable and likely to experience rapid changes in status. The NICU and medical stabilization floors are good examples of acute care settings. Patients at this level are not able to tolerate several hours of therapy. Rather, the patient takes part in bedside rehabilitative therapy in an effort to minimize the effects of physical deconditioning so that the transition to formal rehabilitation is as smooth as possible. Upon medical stabilization, patients are transferred to a rehabilitation setting. Such environs take many forms, ranging from highly medicalized centers attached to large tertiary care hospitals to freestanding outpatient clinics that may provide a broad range of services to a general patient population (e.g., PT clinic) or specialty services to a particular patient population (e.g., chronic pain treatment).

It is essential that the practitioner conduct sensitive and thorough assessment of patient characteristics as soon as possible in the medical setting. A variety of behavioral disturbances may be observed soon after admission; yet these should be interpreted within the context of the admitting diagnosis and the behavioral patterns and level of personal adjustment that predate the admission. It is crucial to identify behavioral patterns that can complicate adjustment and compromise rehabilitation efforts and find areas that should be targeted in subsequent CBT.

Many individuals who acquire disabilities in high-impact incidents, for example, often have alcohol abuse problems that contributed to the accident. Others may have demonstrable problems with impulsivity and poor social judgment. Individuals who require surgical repairs for skin-related breakdowns accompanying diabetes or paralysis may have avoidant tendencies. Some individuals may have experienced trauma that placed them at risk for anxiety problems. For example, Koch and Taylor (1995) provide an excellent review of the psychological sequelae associated with motor vehicle crashes: posttraumatic stress disorder, depression, pain-related conditions, and phobic avoidance of stimuli associated with the accident. The authors emphasize the importance of assessing the nature and subjective meaning of the accident and examining the functional relationships between physical injuries and emotional disorders. Treatment issues include selecting the appropriate CBT interventions, determining the proper sequence of application, and managing complications such as litigation and medication adherence.

In the rehabilitation setting one of the most important functions of CBT is to help the patient optimize his or her therapy participation by increasing the frequency of behaviors that are therapeutically on-task and decreasing the frequency of therapy-competing behaviors. Contemporary behavioral strategies eschew use of aversive stimuli and punishment. Rather, focus is now on differential reinforcement of other (DRO) behavior whereby reinforcement is provided when the patient fails to perform a problem behavior during a specific time interval. The Premack principle is also applicable. Herein, a naturally occurring high-frequency response (e.g., resting quietly on exercise mat) reinforces a lower-frequency target response (e.g., participating in uncomfortable passive range-of-motion exercises). McGlynn (1990) offers an excellent critical review of behavioral approaches to neuropsychological rehabilitation pertaining to six categories of target behavior: inappropriate social behavior, attention and motivation, unawareness of deficits, memory, language and speech, and motor disturbance.

Inpatient rehabilitation programs often offer some form of patient and family education, but participants' educational needs persist long after their return to the community. Problems with attention, motivation, pain, and subjective stress may hinder education. Team members often refer patients with problems that disrupt therapeutic agendas (e.g., inappropriate interpersonal behaviors, pronounced mood disturbance) for psychological interventions. Individualized CBT may be employed to address these issues; brief, strategic interventions are more likely to be useful and valued by patient and staff (e.g., motivational interviewing, relaxation training, problem-solving skills training). Interventions that compete with required treatment hours in PT and OT may conflict with team goals, and patients may have difficulty appreciating these interventions at the expense of prescribed rehabilitation therapies. CBT groups in the inpatient setting may be more time-efficient in delivering a manualized protocol (e.g., assertiveness training, coping skills training), but participants might not share a sense of cohesion and individual needs may be neglected. Groups may be particularly helpful in normalizing individual experiences and fostering recognition and interest in CBT as a treatment option following discharge.

COMMUNITY-RESIDING INDIVIDUALS

Individuals and families who live with chronic disease and disability have more influence on their health status than any single health service provider. In most conditions, secondary complications and declines in health and personal adjustment are mediated by behavioral and social pathways. Therefore, psychological and social issues must be successfully navigated in some fashion—with or without professional assistance—to attain optimal adjustment following disability.

Vocational Rehabilitation

Traditionally, many persons with disability have received support from state vocational rehabilitation (VR) agencies, mandated by the federal government to assist qualified persons to return to gainful employment or other meaningful activity (for an overview, see Elliott & Leung, in press). Work and other related activity is associated with greater well-being and personal health among persons with disability. CBT is often integrated in VR programs to promote work adjustment. Although many technologies are relevant to this enterprise, supported employment strategies utilize low-cost counselors to teach clients relevant work skills and behaviors, and then maximize generalizability by shadowing clients following job placement to provide feedback and supervision on-site. This support slowly tapered off over time. Several clinical trials document the efficacy of supported employment in successfully increasing the employability of persons with a variety of disabilities including traumatic brain injury, mental retardation, and psychiatric disorders (Elliott & Leung, in press).

Other effective VR programs have been developed in multidisciplinary chronic pain rehabilitation programs that feature rigorous work hardening exercises complemented by CBT in individual and group formats. Although VR has often been synonymous with state agencies, recent legislation (e.g., the Ticket to Work and the Work Incentive programs) provides greater incentive and opportunities for CBT practitioners to participate in helping persons with disabilities return to work (Elliott & Leung, in press).

Individual Adjustment and Well-Being

In outpatient clinics and mental health centers, practically any CBT can be modified and applied for use in individual and group formats with community-residing persons with disability. There are situations in which individual CBT may be preferred over group interventions. For example, individualized CBT for depressed persons with multiple sclerosis may be more effective than group interventions because the practitioner can tailor strategies to the unique needs of the progressively degenerative symptoms experienced by the individual (Mohr, Boudewyn, Goodkin, Bostrom, & Epstein, 2001). However, assertion and other interpersonal skills may be best taught in group formats (Glueckauf & Quittner, 1992). These skills have long been recognized as essential in navigating tense interpersonal encounters and in managing the debilitating social stigma associated with visible disability. Social skills training is associated with greater well-being, mobility, and acceptance of disability among clients (Glueckauf & Quittner, 1992). In all of these circumstances, CBT is more likely to be successful when it is designed to meet the needs and problems as perceived and experienced by the client.

Similarly, practitioners of CBT should be familiar with overarching social issues that impede personal adjustment. Advocates have developed disability-affirmative therapy to help individuals find meaning in their circumstances, develop personal goals in the face of stigma and discrimination, and facilitate rewarding significant relationships with others based on acceptance and understanding (Olkin, 1999). Although clinical trials of this approach have yet to be conducted, disability-affirmative therapy clearly embraces the basic tenets of CBT and may be applicable to persons with considerable capacity for insight and learning.

Family Adjustment

Many persons with severe disability return to communities that lack resources for independent living, or their needs are such that a family member must assist daily in their self-care, health promotion, and activities of living. This can be a protracted career for some family members. Individuals who incur a severe disability in young adulthood may have a normal life expectancy and require the assistance of an unpaid family caregiver. Social problem-solving training has been successfully adapted and provided to family caregivers of stroke survivors in telephone sessions (Grant, Elliott, Weaver, Bartolucci, & Giger, 2002). In this study the only clinical trial to date in this area—family caregivers receiving CBT reported less depression and greater satisfaction with services over time than persons assigned to the control groups. CBT can be delivered in the home with long-distance technologies, circumventing problems with transportation and mobility, and increasing generalizability of the intervention.

See also: Clinical health psychology

REFERENCES

Elliott, T., & Leung, P. (in press). Vocational rehabilitation: History and practice. In W. B. Walsh, & M. Savickas (Eds.), *Handbook of vocational psychology* (3rd ed.). New York: Erlbaum.

Frank, R. G., & Elliott, T. (Eds.). (2000). *Handbook of rehabilitation psychology*. Washington, DC: American Psychological Association.

Glueckauf, R. L., & Quittner, A. L. (1992). Assertiveness training for disabled adults in wheelchairs: Self-report, role-play, and activity pattern outcomes. *Journal of Consulting and Clinical Psychology, 60*, 419–425.

Grant, J., Elliott, T., Weaver, M., Bartolucci, A., & Giger, J. (2002). A telephone intervention with family caregivers of stroke survivors after hospital discharge. *Stroke, 33*, 2060–2065.

Hibbard, M. R., Grober, S. E., Gordon, W. A., & Aletta, E. G. (1990). Modification of cognitive psychotherapy for the treatment of post-stroke depression. *The Behavior Therapist, 13*(1), 15–17.

Koch, W. J., & Taylor, S. (1995). Assessment and treatment of motor vehicle accident victims. *Cognitive and Behavioral Practice, 2*, 327–342.

McGlynn, S. M. (1990). Behavioral approaches to neuropsychological rehabilitation. *Psychological Bulletin, 108*, 420–441.

Mohr, D. C., Boudewyn, A., Goodkin, D., Bostrom, A., & Epstein, L. (2001). Comparative outcomes for individual cognitive–behavioral therapy, supportive–expressive group psychotherapy, and sertraline for the treatment of depression in multiple sclerosis. *Journal of Consulting and Clinical Psychology, 69*, 942–949.

Olkin, R. (1999). *What psychotherapists should know about disability*. New York: Guilford Press.

Radnitz, C. L. (Ed.). (2000). *Cognitive–behavioral therapy for persons with disabilities*. Northvale, NJ: Jason Aronson.

Relapse Prevention

Frederick Rotgers

Keywords: addiction, relapse, relapse prevention, substance abuse

Mark Twain, the smoker, was a chronic relapser who quipped, with no little irony, "to cease smoking is the easiest thing I ever did. I ought to know because I've done it a thousand times." The maintenance of behavior change following treatment of substance use disorders has been one of the major conundrums in the addictions treatment field.

Although methods to support changes in substance use or other so-called appetitive behavioral problems (problems such as compulsive sexual behavior, gambling, excessive shopping, or Internet usage, which are often lumped together with addictions in clinical thinking[1]) have been available for many years (i.e., attendance at support groups specifically for persons with these sorts of disorders), until the mid-1980s there was no systematic, theory-based psychological approach to maintaining change and preventing relapse.

In 1985 this situation changed with the publication of *Relapse Prevention: Maintenance Strategies in the Treatment of Addictive Behaviors* by G. Alan Marlatt & Judith Gordon (Marlatt and Gordon, 1985). Marlatt and Gordon presented the first cognitive–behavioral approach to maintaining behavior change. While the book focused primarily on substance use disorders, the applicability of relapse prevention (RP) strategies to other behavioral problems was readily apparent. Within the next 10 years RP approaches had been developed to sustain change following treatment of a variety of behavioral problems, including a variety of nonaddictive disorders, such as depression and agoraphobia, marital distress, stuttering, and chronic pain (Wilson, 1992). RP also stimulated a substantial body of research into its efficacy and the processes that both contributed to the persistence of addictive behaviors and made it so apparently difficult for treated individuals to maintain those changes.

THEORY OF RP

RP was solidly grounded in social learning theory and research on the factors that appeared to trigger a return to addictive behavior following treatment or self-change. Using this foundation, Marlatt and Gordon, and their successors, developed a model that incorporates aspects of classical and operant learning, cognition, and affect into a model of relapse. Before discussing this model, an important digression is in order to outline and define the most important term in this article, "relapse."

Defining "Relapse"

Although the definition of "relapse" may seem transparently obvious to many people, in the addictive behaviors field, with its almost obsessive emphasis on abstinence or the total cessation of the addictive behavior as the main clinical criterion for recovery, and the contrast between these clinical conceptions and those of the DSM models (in DSM-III, and all later editions, American Psychiatric Association, 1979) of substance use disorders, the definition of relapse becomes much more complicated.

Is relapse any use of the person's preferred substance, or even a single recurrence of the addictive behavior following treatment? Is it any use of any psychoactive substance, even if the target addictive behavior was a nonsubstance addiction? Abstinence-focused clinicians would answer in the affirmative to both of these questions.

In contrast, the DSM model of substance use disorders, while including the use of the substance (or the presence of the addictive behavior) as the foundational criterion for there being a "substance-related" disorder, in no other sense does substance use enter into the diagnosis of this class of disorder. Diagnosis of the disorder is based solely on the consequences resulting from substance use or the addictive behavior.[2] So, for a clinician who follows the DSM model, the answer to the two questions above would be "no."

Clearly a more articulated definition of "relapse" was needed. In order to meet this need, Marlatt and Gordon, and subsequent writers, have broken the term "relapse" down into several different components. A "slip" refers to a single recurrence of the target addictive behavior. A "lapse" refers to a group of slips, which may or may not occur in close temporal contiguity with each. Finally, "relapse" refers to not only a return to the target addictive behavior, but to the reemergence of the cluster of negative consequences sufficient to rediagnose the disorder using the DSM criteria. This distinction among "slips," "lapses," and "relapse" is critically important to Marlatt and Gordon's model of RP (see below).

Components of Relapse

According to Marlatt and Gordon's model (this description applies to all subsequent derivative models of relapse and RP, as well), relapse occurs when several circumstances obtain: (1) The person encounters a high-risk situation (i.e., one in which the addictive behavior has been highly likely to occur in the past); (2) ineffective coping with the high-risk situation; (3) the person engages in the addictive behavior to cope with behavioral, emotional, and cognitive consequences of coping failure; and (4) a set of cognitive processes that are grouped under the term "abstinence violation effect" (more recently "limit violation effect") and which include global negative self-statements

[1] Although controversy abounds as to whether all of these behaviors—substance use disorders and the other appetitive behavioral disorders—should be subsumed under the term "addictive behaviors", I will not address that issue. However, in the interest of brevity I will use the term "addictive behaviors" to refer to all of the behaviors in this class of behavioral disorders.

[2] It should be noted that the DSM model has been extensively validated by studies, too numerous to cite here, of both disordered and nondisordered substance users.

and attributions focused on the meaning of the return of the previously changed behavior. Preceding the encountering of high-risk situations, Marlatt and Gordon also postulate a series of "seemingly irrelevant decisions" that lead the person into the high-risk situation. These "seemingly irrelevant decisions" may be quasi-intentional in that they may be quite under the person's voluntary control (for example, taking a route home from work that passes one's favorite bar when one is attempting to abstain from alcohol), but often they simply reflect inadequate self- and contextual monitoring and vigilance.

High-risk situations are conceived of as either Intrapersonal (i.e., negative emotions, distorted thinking) or Interpersonal (i.e., conflicts with others, inability to cope with offers to engage in the addictive behavior, and so on). Early on in their work, Marlatt and Gordon and their colleagues identified a range of Intra- and Interpersonal factors that were most highly associated with relapse to substance use among treated addicts (Marlatt & Gordon, 1985).

Once the addictive behavior has occurred in response to a high-risk situation, whether or not that instance of the behavior is terminated as a slip, becomes a lapse, or develops into a full-blown relapse depends on the person's attributions about him- or herself and the meaning of the recurrence of the addictive behavior.

RP is conceived of as a self-management approach (Wilson, 1992). That is, the therapist's role becomes one of guiding the patient into identifying the potential components of a personal relapse, and developing a series of coping strategies that might be implemented to cope with those components. The goal is to provide the person with a set of behavioral and cognitive skills that can be molded by the patient and therapist collaboratively into a highly individualized set of strategies for RP. It is then up to the patient to monitor high-risk situations and implement the agreed upon coping strategies when those situations occur.

TECHNICAL ASPECTS OF RP

Based on the formulation outlined above, Marlatt and Gordon suggest a group of techniques that can be implemented to interrupt the process of relapse development. From a technical perspective, RP is a treatment goal, rather than a "technique" in itself (Miller, Wilbourne, & Hettema, 2003). The techniques proposed by Marlatt and Gordon to address RP are generally standard cognitive–behavioral techniques that are assembled in an individualized fashion based on an assessment of the patient's previous relapses (if any) and identification of current and past high-risk situations. While many of these techniques are discussed elsewhere in this volume (i.e., coping skills training, cognitive restructuring, rational thinking, urge management techniques, motivational enhancement, self-monitoring of seemingly irrelevant decisions and potential to encounter high-risk situations), several bear specific mention here.

True to their behavioral theory roots, Marlatt and Gordon proposed that, in addition to learning techniques for coping with high-risk situations, effective long-term maintenance of behavior change would be enhanced by several additional techniques: slip recovery and relapse crisis debriefing, lifestyle-focused interventions, and programmed relapse and relapse rehearsal.

Slip recovery and relapse crisis debriefing consists of a detailed functional analysis of recent slips, reassessment of the person's coping strategies for the particular high-risk situations associated with the slip, and a refinement of the person's plan for coping with similar situations in the future. If the person has experienced a relapse crisis (near relapse) or a relapse itself, an additional focus on defusing negative cognitions and self-attributions associated with the limit violation effect is added.

Marlatt and Gordon suggest that, in order for maintenance to be successful, and RP to be consistently achieved, the person must make lifestyle changes that support both new coping strategies and reduce the likelihood of encountering high-risk situations. For example, a person whose drinking is largely driven by the goal of relaxation and stress reduction associated with work might be encouraged either to change jobs, or to develop systematic stress-reducing activities that can be incorporated into the person's life outside of work.

The final nontraditional component of Marlatt and Gordon's original model, programmed relapse and relapse rehearsal, has been controversial almost from the beginning. This approach consists of having the person test the adequacy of his or her coping strategies plan by actually planning and executing a slip (i.e., a use of the person's substance of choice, or in the case of an appetitive behavior such as gambling, actually placing a small bet) followed by immediate execution of the coping plan. The outcome of this planned return to the problem behavior is then discussed with the therapist, and refinements to the plan are made. From a behavior theory perspective, this approach makes good sense. Behaviors are most effectively implemented if the person has the opportunity to practice them in the situations in which they must ultimately be performed. However, at least in part due to the clinical lore surrounding substance use disorders and their treatment (much of which has been found by systematic research to be incorrect), this aspect of Marlatt and Gordon's model has been downplayed or neglected by practitioners. Ethical concerns have also prevented research on this aspect of the Marlatt and Gordon RP model.

Other technical concerns in the implementation of RP include helping the person to maintain motivation to be continually vigilant for high-risk situations and to practice the coping skills plans on a regular basis when those situations are encountered. This is generally accomplished using such motivation techniques as the Decisional Balance Exercise. Helping the person cope with failure in a productive, problem-solving-focused manner is also a major clinical concern, one typically addressed through relapse debriefing and cognitive restructuring focused on the patient's beliefs about the meaning of the target behavior. Finally, helping the person to make use of support systems in the environment and develop a positive alternative lifestyle that tends to counter the desire or urge to return to old behaviors becomes a major focus once skills have been developed and coping plans implemented (Larimer, Palmer, & Marlatt, 1999).

RESEARCH ON RP

Because RP is a treatment goal, rather than a treatment per se, much of the research on RP has focused on the effects of implementing the various RP techniques on subsequent maintenance of behavior change (Miller et al., 2003). Nonetheless, Carroll (1996) reviewed 24 controlled clinical trials that tested cognitive–behavioral approaches to RP. Her review found that while RP was clearly effective compared to no-treatment controls, when compared to other treatments, the cognitive–behavioral approaches were less clearly superior.

In studies where RP produced positive outcomes, these fell into several categories including reduction in severity of relapses when they occurred, enhancing the durability of the effects of acute treatment, and patient treatment matching (Carroll, 1996).

Research has also focused on assessing the reliability and validity of the RP model. The Relapse Replication and Extension Project (RREP)(Lowman, Allen, Stout, & The Relapse Research Group, 1996) examined the reliability of Marlatt and Gordon's original typology of relapse situations. This study found only modest levels of interrater reliability for rater assessment of the specific triggers of relapse episodes, but good support was provided for other aspects of the RP model, specifically that exposure to high-risk situations alone does not predict relapse. Rather, the effectiveness of coping with those situations predicts relapse or maintenance most effectively. A second finding validated the theoretical importance that Marlatt and Gordon attach to negative emotional states and the limit (or abstinence) violation effect in predicting whether a slip or lapse would escalate to a full-blown relapse. Specifically, the extent to which patients experienced and failed to cope with negative emotional states, or endorsed strong beliefs in an "all or nothing" disease model view of substance use (i.e., if you use you've failed versus use is not necessarily an indication of failure) were more likely to escalate a slip or lapse into a full-blown relapse.

FUTURE DIRECTIONS

As noted previously, the RP model developed by Marlatt and Gordon is now being applied to a variety of psychological and behavioral disorders. In addition, there is promising research in the use of mindfulness-based enhancements based on Buddhist meditation techniques to enhance patients' ability to remain focused on negative thoughts and emotions triggered by high-risk situations and engage previously planned coping strategies (Breslin, Zack, & McMain, 2002). Researchers have already demonstrated the efficacy of adding this component to RP in the prevention of recurrence of major depressive episodes (Segal, Williams, & Teasdale, 2002).

CONCLUSION

Marlatt and Gordon's seminal model of RP has assumed a central role in the cognitive–behavioral treatment of a variety of psychological and behavioral disorders. Research has consistently supported the broad aspects of the model, and it is being increasingly applied to disorders other than addictive behaviors.

See also: Addictive behavior—nonsubstance abuse, Addictive behavior—substance abuse, Couples therapy—substance abuse

REFERENCES

American Psychiatric Association. (1979). *Diagnostic and statistical manual of mental disorders* (3rd ed.). Washington, DC: Author.

Breslin, F. C., Zack, M., & McMain, S. (2002). An information-processing analysis of mindfulness: Implications for relapse prevention in the treatment of substance abuse. *Clinical Psychology: Science and Practice, 9*, 275–299.

Carroll, K. M. (1996). Relapse prevention as a psychosocial treatment: A review of controlled clinical trials. *Experimental and Clinical Psychopharmacology, 4*, 46–54.

Larimer, M. E., Palmer, R. S., & Marlatt, G. A. (1999). Relapse prevention: An overview of Marlatt's cognitive–behavioral model. *Alcohol Research and Health, 23*, 151–160.

Lowman, C., Allen, J., Stout, R. L., & The Relapse Research Group (1996). Replication and extension of Marlatt's taxonomy of relapse precipitants: Overview of procedures and results. *Addiction, 91*(Suppl.), 89–98.

Marlatt, G. A., & Gordon, J. R. (Eds.) (1985). *Relapse prevention: Maintenance strategies in the treatment of addictive behaviors*. New York: Guilford Press.

Miller, W. R., Wilbourne, P. L., & Hettema, J. E. (2003). What works? A summary of alcohol treatment outcome research. In R. K. Hester & W. R. Miller (Eds.), *Handbook of alcoholism treatment approaches: Effective alternatives* (3rd ed., pp. 13–64). Needham Heights, MA: Allyn & Bacon.

Segal, Z. V., Williams, J. M. G., & Teasdale, J. D. (2002). *Mindfulness-based cognitive therapy for depression: A new approach to preventing relapse*. New York: Guilford Press.

Wilson, P. H. (1992). Relapse prevention: Conceptual and methodological issues. In P. H. Wilson (Ed.), *Principles and practice of relapse prevention* (pp. 1–22). New York: Guilford Press.

Religious Beliefs and Practices

Hank Robb

Keywords: religion, religious beliefs, spirituality

Albert Ellis officially announced the end of his psychoanalytic and psychoanalytically oriented psychotherapy practice in 1956 when he described what was then called "Rational Therapy" at the annual meeting of the American Psychological Association. However, like Freud, he continued taking a dim view of religion. Even so, within 15 years, Ellis's *Journal of Rational Living* was publishing papers showing compatibility between what was by then known as "Rational-Emotive Therapy" and Christian beliefs and practices (Hauck & Grau, 1968).

As a practicing psychologist, Ellis saw neurosis as a main impediment to the good life. As an ardent student of philosophy from late adolescence, he viewed the good life as one based on long-term hedonism with a clear bow to the Stoic philosophers, especially Epictetus (1890) and his dictum, "Men are not disturbed by events but by the view they take of them."

The "cognitive revolution" was in full swing by the late 1970's. Many behaviorally oriented theoreticians and practitioners who previously viewed themselves as more strictly behavioral began taking "private speech" as just one more type of behavior. Methodological behaviorism was largely abandoned. Under that doctrine, what a person said about their thoughts, images, or bodily sensations was admissible to scientific investigation but not the thoughts, images, and sensations themselves. Whatever "cognition" was, it was no longer regarded as existing in the spaceless, weightless, timeless mind-stuff suggested by René Descartes. It was more and more regarded as just more empirical or theoretical material of the same ontological type as overt behavior.

RELIGIOUS VALUES IN PSYCHOLOGICAL TREATMENT

The notion that counseling and psychotherapy could be "value free," which Carl Rogers had most eloquently expounded, was also under serious attack. By the early 1980s, Allen Bergin, among others, noted that clients often adopted the values of practitioners who provided them treatment. In addition, far fewer psychologists were, and are, nonreligious as compared to the general U.S. population. Bergin (1980) proposed linking psychotherapy and religious values. Ellis (1980) responded with an article connecting psychotherapy and atheistic values setting the stage for the conflict to be addressed empirically. Bergin (1991) marshaled evidence showing that religious beliefs and practices not only did not do harm, but could also make a positive contribution on a number of health indexes.

Two knotty theoretical problems have largely gone unresolved. First, how could any form of The Supernatural, including "The One True God," be subjected to empirical test since, by definition, The Supernatural is not empirical? Second, attempting to subordinate The Supernatural to the empirical does violence to the full majesty of The Supernatural, at least in the view of traditional believers. While quite a few cautions and apologetics have been offered regarding these issues, the difficulties have not stopped a substantial effort to empirically demonstrate that, just as life in all other aspects is made better when it is founded on religious beliefs and practices, so too is psychological treatment. Most often, though not exclusively, those making this effort have been researchers and practitioners who were deeply committed to religious beliefs and practices.

EMPIRICAL WORK BEGINS

Rebecca Propst and colleagues (Propst, Ostrom, Watkins, Dean, & Mashburn, 1992) succeeded in reducing depression by combining the principles of Cognitive Therapy with Christian beliefs and practices. Alone and with colleagues, Brad Johnson (1993; Johnson, Devries, Ridley, Pettorini, & Peterson, 1994) showed that the principles of Rational Emotive Behavior Therapy also could be combined with Christian beliefs and practices to reduce psychological disturbances such as depression. Quite importantly, Propst found that nonbelieving therapists were in no way less effective in using the combined approaches to reduce depression in Christian clients when compared to believing therapists, and that they were more effective in the short run. There has yet to be any evidence showing that nonbelieving therapists who are willing to deliver religiously oriented cognitive–behavioral treatment will be less capable of doing so when compared to believing therapists offering similar treatment.

There also has yet to be evidence that religiously oriented cognitive–behavioral treatments are more effective than nonreligiously based ones. However, it is also certain that some individuals will be more willing to participate in treatment that is consistent with, and related to, their religious beliefs and will do so with greater zeal. To date, virtually all the empirical research on CBT treatments has been done using Christian doctrines and practices with Christian clients.

A number of books on the inclusion of religious beliefs and practices with psychological interventions were published in the 1990s, including several by the American Psychological Association. Recanting his earlier views, Ellis (1992, 2000) publicly acknowledged that religious beliefs and practices were not, necessarily, a source of disturbance. Putting an exclamation point on this change in view, he is the third author of a book describing how to combine the principles of REBT with religious beliefs and practices when treating believing clients (Nielsen, Johnson & Ellis, 2001). Those asserting the positive value of religious beliefs and practices with regard to health-related issues as well as the inclusion of them in psychological treatments are now clearly in ascendancy (also see the Health and Religious Beliefs section of the *American Psychologist*, January 2003).

COMBINING CBT WITH RELIGIOUS BELIEFS AND PRACTICES

Cognitive–behavioral approaches are based on the notion that reduction in emotional and behavioral dysfunction can be accomplished if clients relinquish certain beliefs and adopt others. Most religious traditions with a large number of adherents have an articulated set of beliefs and practices. Thus, it is a relatively straightforward process to identify those religious beliefs and practices that are consistent with, or are otherwise supportive of, a change from disturbance-associated beliefs to those associated with more functional emoting and behaving.

At the outset, Scriptures can be used to orient clients to the therapeutic approach. For those with a Christian orientation, such scriptures as "For as he thinketh in his heart so is he" (Prov. 23:7), "I thought on my ways and turned my feet" (Ps. 119:59), "Be transformed by the renewing of your mind" (Rom. 12:2)," or "For I have learned to find resources in myself whatever my circumstances" (Phil. 4:11), all religiously ground the basic cognitive–behavioral principle that dysfunctional emotions and behaviors can be changed by focusing on changing beliefs about ourselves and the world in which we live. In actual practice, most religiously oriented clients can be readily brought to acknowledge that, in principle, they could be helped by sticking firmly with certain beliefs while refusing to be guided by other beliefs.

Once an individual is oriented, three questions remain: which beliefs are to be retained, which beliefs are to be discarded, and which alternative beliefs are to be adopted? Certain controversies will appear at this point in the area of means and ends. For example, if a person adheres to a religious tradition that prescribes both monogamy and sexual relations only between married individuals, then a psychological treatment goal of avoiding sorrow, guilt, or depression while having out-of-wedlock sexual relations may be seen as inappropriate and even immoral. Sorrow, guilt, or depression may be seen as the natural outcomes of such behavior. They may also be seen as providing motivation to turn toward the way of life prescribed by the religious tradition as well as motivation to avoid proscribed ways of living.

Practitioners, in principle, could point out to clients that they could change their religious beliefs. For example, clients might adopt the view that there is nothing, necessarily, wrong with sex outside of marriage or nonmonogamous sexual relations. Almost no authors, however, have taken this view. Instead, they have argued that even offering clients the possibility of changing religious beliefs is unethical because it is beyond the scope of psychological practice to suggest to clients that they might change their religious beliefs.

Once the client and practitioner agree, either tacitly or explicitly, that the client is to follow the way of living prescribed by his or her religious tradition, the issue of what to do about the sorrow, guilt, and depression will be addressed. Typically, the CBT practitioner will take the view that, while sorrow is helpful when one acts wrongly, depression and guilt are not. The practitioner next begins the standard cognitive–behavioral intervention and buttresses it with religious doctrine or Scripture. For example, if a Christian client is self-condemning for wrong behavior, the practitioner might point out that it is Christian doctrine that individuals are saved by the Grace of God rather than through good behavior. The practitioner might go on to note New Testament verses such as "Judge not, that ye be not judged" (Matt. 7:1), "For all have sinned and come short of the glory of God" (Rom. 3:23), or "God commended his love for us in that while we were sinners, Christ died for us" (Rom. 5:8).

If the practitioner recommends standard cognitive–behavioral homework assignments, then religious doctrine or Scripture might be used to underline that change is often only available to those who work and practice to bring it about. The practitioner might also take advantage of religious practices such as prayer or meditation as a means of enhancing homework assignments. For example, clients can be asked if they believe it is appropriate to pray for the forgiveness of their misdeeds and for the courage and determination to resist doing similar misdeeds in the future. If clients agree, such activities might be offered as the main form of homework or as additional homework. When practitioners and clients share the same religious practices, then those practices, such as prayer, might even be performed in the treatment session.

This general approach can be taken with any problem. Consider anxiety disorders and the specific problem of panic. From a CBT perspective, panic is generally agreed to be a function of responding to bodily sensations as if they were not only unpleasant and undesired, but also catastrophic and unbearable. In the standard CBT approach to panic, clients perform activities that are designed to produce bodily sensations similar to those experienced during panic. Once both the sensations and the client are psychologically present, the client can notice two facts. First, the sensations may indeed be quite unpleasant. However, that is all they are. The sensations are neither horrible nor unbearable. Second, despite the sensations being unpleasant, even quite unpleasant, nothing catastrophic actually happens either during or following an experience with these sensations. The practitioner can identify religious doctrine or Scriptures that underline these points and bring them to the attention of the client. Depending on their belief system, many believers can be reminded they are never alone in their trial because their Deity is always with them, even in their suffering. Prayer, meditation, or other religiously prescribed practices can help clients become willing to expose themselves to unpleasant bodily sensations long enough to learn the two points noted above. While clients may not come to like, or look forward to, such sensations, they also will find they no longer fear them either.

ETHICAL PRACTICE

The main therapeutic intervention rests on the practitioner finding scriptural or other doctrinal authority, and/or religious practices to support the cognitive–behavioral procedures that otherwise have been shown to be helpful with whatever problem is to be addressed. At the same time, the practitioner must find ways to avoid, or neutralize, the same type of material that would exacerbate or otherwise contribute to the problem. Many authors have argued that no, properly understood, religious tradition will be iatrogenic. The rub may come in the "proper understanding." Practitioners are commonly encouraged to consult with clergy or other authoritative sources. Almost without exception (Robb, 2001, 2002), authors writing in this area insist it is unethical for practitioners to cross the boundary between providing psychological service, for which they are trained, and providing religious guidance and interpretation, if they are not specifically trained to do the latter. In sum, the psychological practitioner may make use of the religious beliefs and practices the client brings to the session but may not alter or abolish them.

Examples of conflicts include depressed clients who have broken a prescribed standard, such as having had sex outside marriage, an abortion, or being sexually active with members of their same sex, and who also think themselves utterly worthless and not redeemable because of these actions. There is no conflict when religious doctrines and practices are available to refute the belief that the client is utterly worthless and unredeemable. However, significant problems arise when religious authorities are cited to show that they are. It should be emphasized that the problem is not about whether these activities are wrong, bad, or mistaken from the perspective of the religion in question. It is assumed that the religious stance is correct because the client has adopted that religious stance. Rather, to use religious language, the problem is to help the client condemn the sin but not him- or herself as the sinner when the client is maintaining the opposite view on religious grounds. To date, the field has not developed criteria that would both discriminate when practitioners are authorized to attack religious practices and doctrines that encourage individuals to condemn themselves or others, as well as other disturbance-associated "cognitive errors" that are asserted to have a religious base. Consulting religious authorities with the aim of obtaining authoritative refutation of the client's view that their disturbance-associated views are supported by their religious traditions and practices is the only agreed-upon approach at this time.

REFERENCES

Bergin, A. E. (1980). Psychotherapy and religious values. *Journal of Consulting and Clinical Psychology, 48*, 95–105.

Bergin, A. E. (1991). Values and religious issues in psychotherapy and mental health. *American Psychologist, 46*, 394–403.

Ellis, A. (1980). Psychotherapy and atheistic values: A response to A. E. Bergin's "Psychotherapy and religious values." *Journal of Consulting and Clinical Psychology, 48*, 635–639.

Ellis, A. (1992). My current views on rational-emotive therapy (RET) and religiousness. *Journal of Rational-Emotive & Cognitive-Behavior Therapy, 10*(1), 37–40.

Ellis, A. (2000). Can rational emotive behavior therapy (REBT) be effectively used with people who have devout beliefs in God and religion? *Professional Psychology: Research and Practice, 31*(1), 29–33.

Epictetus. (1890). *The collected works of Epictetus*. Boston: Little, Brown.

Hauck, P., & Grau, A. (1968). Comparisons: Christianity and rationality. *Rational Living, 3*(2), 36–37.

Johnson, W. (1993). Christian rational-emotive therapy: A treatment protocol. *Journal of Psychology and Christianity, 12*(13), 254–261.

Johnson, W. B., Devries, R., Ridley, C., Pettorini, D., & Peterson, D. (1994). The comparative efficacy of Christian and secular rational-emotive therapy with Christian clients. *Journal of Psychology and Theology, 22*(2), 130–140.

Nielsen, S. L., Johnson, W. B., & Ellis, A. (2001). *Counseling and psychotherapy with religious persons: A rational emotive behavioral therapy approach.* Mahwah, NJ: Erlbaum.

Propst, R., Ostrom, R., Watkins, P., Dean, T., & Mashburn, D. (1992). Comparative efficacy of religious and nonreligious cognitive–behavioral therapy for the treatment of clinical depression in religious individuals. *Journal of Consulting and Clinical Psychology, 60*(1), 94–103.

Robb, H. (2001). Facilitating rational emotive behavior therapy by including religious beliefs. *Cognitive and Behavioral Practice, 8*, 29–34.

Robb, H. B., III. (2002). Rational emotive behavior therapy and religious clients. *Journal of Rational-Emotive & Cognitive-Behavior Therapy, 20*(3/4), 169–200.

RECOMMENDED READINGS

Miller, W. R. (Ed.). (1999). *Integrating spirituality into treatment: Resources for practitioners.* Washington, DC: American Psychological Association.

Richards, P. S., &Bergin, A. E. (Eds.) (1997). *A spiritual strategy for counseling and psychotherapy.* Washington, DC: American Psychological Association.

Richards, P. S., & Bergin, A. E. (Eds.). (2000). *Handbook of psychotherapy and religious diversity.* Washington, DC: American Psychological Association.

Shafranske, E. P. (Ed.). (1996). *Religion and the clinical practice of psychology.* Washington, DC: American Psychological Association.

Resistance: Impediments to Effective Psychotherapy

Arthur Freeman and Roya McCluskey

Keywords: control, impediments, lack of motivation

The concept of resistance was first introduced to the psychological literature in the classic volume *Studies in Hysteria* in the 1890s (Breuer & Freud, 1893–1895/1955). Resistance was conceptualized as the patient's avoidance of thoughts, ideas, verbalizations, and behaviors as a way of coping against unbearable ideas that created anxiety which, by definition, signaled danger. The resistance manifested itself in the therapy by the patient's avoidance of interpretations, therapy sessions, or the ideas. The psychoanalytic focus was the interpretation of the resistance which thereby allowed patients access to the unacceptable core that they hid from themselves. Consequently, resistance was seen as a negative patient variable, and a form of pathology embedded in a narcissistic, false, and pathological character that strove to maintain the status quo at any cost (Menninger, 1958; Stark, 1994).

Over time, the therapeutic view of resistance has changed. Several authors (Adelman & Taylor, 1986; Gerber & Nehemkis, 1986; Deaton, 1985; Ellis, 1985; Freeman & McClosky, 2003; Leahy, 2001; Meichenbaum & Gilmore, 1982) have considered the adaptive nature of resistance. A patient may resist treatment as an attempt to gain control over a part of his or her life (Adelman & Taylor, 1986) by not complying with the role that the therapist defines for him or her (Leahy, 2001). Other examples of healthy resistance are to resist the therapist's authority when the therapist has a poor conceptualization of the patient's problem (Ellis, 1985), or when the therapist with an illusion of competence throws a series of techniques at the patient, and the patient does not feel emotionally validated (Leahy, 2001).

Lazarus and Fay (1982) take a position generally opposed to the psychoanalytic one wherein they dispute the concept of resistance. They believe that what the therapists label as resistance may in fact be a rationalization for their treatment failures. They recommend that rather than overgeneralizing and labeling every negative therapeutic outcome as resistance, the therapist must separate resistance of the patient, resistance of the problem, and the situational factors within which the resistance is maintained. Patient variables are only one of several major variables that impact therapeutic resistance.

Several theorists and clinicians have considered other factors such as therapist variables, relationship variables, and environmental variables as contributing to the therapeutic resistance. Relationship variables have continued to receive considerable research attention over the years, and the importance of therapeutic bond and its impact on therapeutic progress has been emphasized (Bordin, 1971; Ciechanowski, Katon, Russo, & Walker, 2001; Greenberg & Paivio, 1997; Keisler & Watkins, 1989; Luborsky, McLellan, Woody, O'Brien, & Auerbach, 1985; Persons & Burns, 1985; Safran, 1998; Safran & Segal, 1990). Ellis (1985) has taken the causes of therapeutic resistance beyond the patient and therapist variables. While he acknowledges therapist–patient relationship variables and patient variables such as severe disturbance, fear of discomfort, shame of disclosure, and fear of success impacting therapeutic resistance, he also has identified environmental factors such as significant others, disability, and addiction as contributing sources to therapeutic resistance.

A COGNITIVE-BEHAVIORAL PERSPECTIVE ON RESISTANCE

The causes of what may be termed resistance or noncompliance are manifold. Resistance can be cognitive (avoidance of ideas, thoughts, or beliefs that are uncomfortable). Resistance can be behavioral (missing therapy sessions, avoiding behaviors that create anxiety, or not doing homework) or situational (avoiding people, opportunities, or places that create anxiety). The resistance can be overt and clearly recognizable or covert and not seen for what it is or the effect it has on the individual. Perhaps more salutary terms for this cognitive or behavioral avoidance to change can be termed "roadblocks" (Leahy, 2003) or "impediments" (Freeman & McClosky, 2003).

We can, in fact, identify 50 specific sources of impediments or roadblocks to change in therapy. These impediments can stem almost equally from the patient, the therapist, the environment, and the patient's problem/pathology. The essential issue for the therapist is to identify the source(s) of impediment, make the impediment(s) manifest for the patient, and include in the treatment plan an organized approach for reducing the impediments so that therapy can proceed more smoothly and the patient can be helped toward greater adaptability.

PATIENT FACTORS

1. *Lack of patient skill to comply with therapeutic regimen and expectations.* Often, the assumption that is made by therapists and patients is that all patients have the basic skills to comply with therapeutic expectations. We assume that the depressed patient knows how to self-pleasure, or that the anxious patient has the skills and understanding to self-soothe.

2. *Patient has negative cognitions regarding previous treatment failure(s).* For the patient who is familiar to the mental health system, the negative experiences with agencies and therapists, the money spent on therapy, services not delivered as promised, medication not working as expected to, or maintenance of the problems over time can equal a negative set regarding therapy. Even when there have been gains in therapy or problems ameliorated, the patient may still perceive him- or herself having failed in therapy or therapy having failed him or her or he or she would not now be seated in the current therapist's office.

3. *Negative cognitions regarding the consequences to others of the patient changing.* Any change on the part of the patient to reduce his or her pathology is feared by the patient to create significant problems for others in the patient's system. The patient is concerned that if he or she changes, there will be some castastrophic consequence to significant others or, in cases of severe obsessive–compulsive disorder, to the world at large.

4. *The patient has secondary gain from his or her symptoms.* Many individuals learn that being impaired, despite the price they pay for that impairment and consequent decrease in adaptive function, brings about certain reward or advantage. The secondary gain may be a perception of power over others, a perception of security, or a perception of being loved. The gain may come from significant others, institutions, or a more simple relief of anxiety for the individual.

5. *Fear of changing one's actions, thoughts, or feelings.* This is best expressed as, "The devil that you know is better than the devil that you don't know." Some individuals are unhappy, disappointed, or depressed about their circumstance, but see any other approach as a black void that might swallow them up. They wonder what it would be like to be different, how different would feel, how others would view their being different, and what would happen if they did not like the difference.

6. *Lack of patient motivation to change.* In some cases there are forces that are "demotivating" to the patient. In other cases, there is simply no motivation to do things differently. The individual has reached a point of homeostasis and continues in what appears to be the most comfortable situation. Freeman and Dolan (2001) describe a clinical revision of the stages of change. They identify 10 stages: noncontemplation, anticontemplation, precontemplation, contemplation, action planning, action, prelapse, lapse, relapse, and maintenance. The patient must be assessed as to his or her present stage of motivation and then moved to the next stage(s).

7. *Negative set.* The patient demonstrates a readiness or even propensity to respond to almost any therapeutic strategy, intervention, or direction with an overt "no," or a covert "yes ... BUT." There is no one reason or rationale that can explain the negative set. It may be protective, it may be challenging, it may be habituated, or it may be stylistic of the individual's pathology. The set may, over time, become generalized so that an initial negative reaction to a therapist can become generalized to all therapists, and then to all therapy.

8. *Limited or poor self-monitoring or monitoring of others.* These patients seem to go through life with blinders on. Their tunnel vision causes them to respond to situations with partial data. They miss the environmental cues that will alert them to potential danger. These patients have poor or limited ability to assess sometimes gross and obvious situations.

9. *Patient frustrated with lack of treatment progress over time and perceived lower status by being in therapy.* The frustration may not all be in the past. Patients may also be frustrated with what they perceive as a lack of progress in the present therapy. They may have expected that they would have been able to change or to do things that they are still not able to act on. This could lead to anger and frustration.

A part of the picture may also be the idea that if one is in therapy there is something wrong with that person. Conversely, not being in therapy or resisting therapy can become a way of viewing oneself as being mentally healthy.

10. *Lack of personal resources (physical, cognitive, or intellectual).* As with the skills deficit described above, patients come into therapy with different physical, cognitive, or intellectual equipment. The individual who is physically challenged is not necessarily limited. He or she can compensate for challenges and use the challenge as a motive to excel. The same is true of any individual, whether the challenge is physical, cognitive, or intellectual. On the other hand, these life challenges can also become real and imagined impediments to success in any realm, including therapy.

Summary. The patient brings a number of factors to the therapeutic collaboration. Understanding that the collaboration will rarely be 50–50, the above-noted impediments are only part of the total picture.

PRACTITIONER/THERAPIST FACTORS

1. *Lack of therapist skill or experience.* Skill and experience are quite different. A novice therapist may have acquired the basic necessary skills for effective therapy, but lack of experience may encourage patient resistance. The unskilled therapist clearly needs skill building. Either situation may interfere with adequate treatment. What is necessary is the ability to collaboratively design a treatment plan that has a synergistic quality and then implement it. A good treatment plan is not just a mechanical introduction of a series of skills but also requires collaboration.

2. *Patient and practitioner distortions are congruent.* Although we do not expect the practitioners to be totally free of cognitive distortions, it is essential that therapists build the self-knowledge that will allow them to label their personal distortions. When these distortions are congruent with the distortions of the patient, a significant impediment emerges. There is also the potential that the patient's pathology may in fact be reinforced by the congruence.

3. *Poor socialization of patient to treatment and a specific treatment model.* Patients' socialization to psychotherapy comes from several sources, e.g., their previous experience, TV and films, friends and family, what is expected of them in therapy, other patients on an inpatient unit, and the therapist.

It is this latter source that is often not well utilized. For example, patients may not be aware of what the therapy entails, how it works, what is expected of them, what agreements are expected of them, or what is the length of the therapy.

4. *Lack of collaboration and a working alliance.* The working alliance is a central feature of all therapies. The therapist and patient work together as a team. The collaboration is not always 50–50, but may be 30–70, 90–10, or 95–5. In this latter case, the therapist will be providing most of the energy or work within the session or in the therapy more generally.

5. *Lack of data.* Sometimes practitioners focus on a label, and once they identify a "disorder," they proceed full force with treatment without any further data. The organized collection of data will give the therapist valuable information about the severity, situational variability, and individual uniqueness of the problem for the given patient. Without the necessary data, practitioners may implement general treatment guidelines that lack specificity, or the goals may be reached after much detour, and delay.

6. *Therapeutic narcissism.* Therapeutic narcissism takes many forms. Some practitioners pride themselves in their loyalty and dedication to their patients, because they consider how poorly their patients may do in their absence. They overestimate their importance in their patients' lives, and assume that the patients may not be able to survive without their help. Other variants are that therapists believe they are smarter than they are, or that they are more skilled than they are. Often they believe that charisma is an adequate substitute for skill and that theoretical grounding in any psychotherapy model is unnecessary.

7. *Poor timing of interventions.* Problems of timing can be rooted in the therapist's anxiety, therapeutic narcissism, lack of therapist skill, or the therapist's lack of understanding of the patient. Rather than allowing the intervention to "develop" and ripen, therapists may feel compelled to launch an intervention as soon as they think of it. If, by chance, the moment is appropriate, the intervention might work quite well. If, however, the patient is not ready, the intervention may be ignored, refused, or become a source of breach in the therapeutic relationship. Alternatively, an intervention that is withheld may rot on the vine or be poorly timed and thereby ineffective.

8. *Therapy goals are unstated, unrealistic, or vague, or there is a lack of patient agreement with therapy goals.* One of the most important steps in providing good treatment is clarification of the goals of therapy. Without such clarification, the therapist and the patient may be working on different goals. As a result, the patient and the therapist will not feel connected as each of them marches to an entirely different drummer. The therapist must be clear when working with the patient about setting goals for therapy. The goals must be reasonable, proximal, realistic, and possible. The patient must clearly state his or her agreement with the goals of therapy.

9. *Limited understanding of the developmental process.* DSM-IV-TR (APA, 2001) specifically enjoins the

diagnostician from making a diagnosis when the behaviors that have been identified can be better explained by developmental factors. For example, the term *rebellious adolescent* is as redundant as *dependent toddler*. In fact, behavior contrary to these developmental processes would be questionable. By taking a developmental perspective the therapist can easily craft interventions that will have a higher likelihood of working.

10. *Generalized negative beliefs about mental illness or unrealistic expectations of patient.* The therapist's negative beliefs about mental illness can directly impact on the conceptualization of the patient, as well as the formulation of his or her treatment. For example, if a practitioner believes that depression or anxiety is untreatable, and that it takes over the person, and makes the person useless in day-to-day functioning, not to mention in their relationships, then treatment will be limited.

11. *Lack of flexibility and creativity in treatment planning.* Many practitioners may find themselves stuck in rigidly using the same protocols without deviations with different patients who share a common condition. What these practitioners seem to focus on is treating the condition alone rather than the condition within a unique patient. They fail to use the "manual" as a base and make alterations as needed. What motivates one patient with a certain problem may be quite different from another patient with the same problem. Similarly, some patients find certain treatment plans easier to process and to incorporate into their lives than others.

Summary. Inasmuch as a CBT approach is, by definition, collaborative, the therapist contributes a substantial portion of the interaction. If the therapy is not going well, the therapist must be willing to evaluate what he or she is doing (or not doing) to facilitate the therapy.

ENVIRONMENTAL FACTORS

1. *Environmental stressors preclude changing.* Maslow's hierarchy of needs posits that when one's basic biological or physiological needs are in question, it is difficult for the individual to consider issues of self-actualization and may even choose to compromise safety and security to meet these needs. Often, patients have difficulty in therapy in that they need to cope with a high level of environmental stress. When DSM-III (APA, 1980) was published, it included for the first time a multiaxial system of diagnosis that included Axis IV, an assessment of the individual's psychosocial stressors.

2. *Significant others actively or passively sabotage therapy.* The boundaries between individuals and their significant others may range from poor to nonexistent. Patients may be living or working with significant others who will enable the negative behavior in any number of ways. They may serve to actively discourage change, passively discourage the patient changing, covertly interfere with change, or directly fight any different thoughts, feelings, and actions on the patient's part.

3. *Agency reinforcement of pathology and illness via compensation or benefits.* Individuals who receive benefits through Social Security Supplementary Income (SSI), veteran's benefits, or workmen's compensation often have their payments based on their degree of injury, dysfunction, or impairment. They may receive their pension until they no longer qualify. That might mean that if an individual is no longer impaired, they stand to lose their financial support. This is in no way a description of all benefit recipients. Many would prefer to be rid of their disability so that they could function more effectively.

4. *Cultural or family issues regarding help-seeking.* In some cultures and in some families, help-seeking is encouraged and even rewarded. In other cultures or families, seeking help is an admission of weakness or aberration. There may be issues of the therapist learning family secrets, or of family activities that the family would prefer not to expose.

In many cases the cultural issue may be reflective of the patient feeling uncomfortable with a therapist of a different cultural group just as a therapist may be equally uncomfortable with a patient of a different group.

5. *Significant family pathology.* Individuals coming from chaotic, dysfunctional, and pathological families can be said to come by their problems honestly. In other cases, the family pathology results in a physically, mentally, or psychologically abusive environment which requires that the therapist report the abusive setting or behaviors to social welfare or legal offices. This can become an impediment to therapy when the chaos or pathology of the family makes it difficult or impossible for the patient to change. The family pathology may also cause missed appointments, problems in doing homework, difficulty in maintaining gains, or the maintenance of a negative set concerning therapy.

6. *Unrealistic or conflicting demands made on the patient by family members.* Patients can be confused or even paralyzed by their internal demands. The demands may be accompanied by additional ideas of hopelessness related to inability to challenge their internal dialogue. In this case the patient may end up in a downward spiral. When the external voices of family, friends, and significant others is added to the mix, the patient may be frozen in place or may even take a contrary position and do whatever is opposed to the demands of others. The therapist may be placed in the same role as these demanding "others."

7. *Unrealistic or conflicting demands on patient by institutions.* The major demands on patients from

institutions and agencies are a two-edged sword. The message is that change is desired but that change must occur within a limited time frame due to reimbursement policies. Insurers and therapists voice the goal that there be services for patients in need. At the same time the patients know that if they do not or cannot change within the limits of reimbursed services, the therapy that they will receive may be insufficient.

8. *Financial factors limit change.* Financial factors can impede therapy in several ways. Related to the above-mentioned point, once reimbursed services run out, therapy will end unless the patient has the financial resources to continue (or if the therapist is willing to see the patient for a substantially reduced or no fee). The financial issue can also be a factor in abusive relationships in which a partner is frightened of leaving because she fears that she will not have the financial resources to support herself and her family.

9. *System homeostasis.* The system perspective posits that family systems, like physical systems, reach a balance or state of homeostasis. This implies that when there is any action that in any way disrupts or unbalances the system, the system will act to restore the balance. If, for example, the issue for patients is being in a position of power, any event or interaction that places them in a position that they see as less than powerful will cause them to take immediate action to restore their perception of power.

10. *Inefficient or limited support network.* Patients may come to see the therapist as their principal support person. The patient may experience few people in the world as accepting, understanding, caring, and thoughtful as the therapist. Patients may then place all of their eggs in the therapist's basket. One of the goals of therapy with all patients is to help them build a broader, more useful, more accepting, more available, more generous, and more appropriate support network. Sometimes this can be done through the use of recognized support groups, such as Alcoholics Anonymous, parenting groups, or disability-oriented groups.

Summary. Since no one lives in a vacuum, the effect of family, culture, friends, institutions, and the "system" cannot be ignored or downplayed.

PATHOLOGY FACTORS

1. *Patient rigidity foils treatment compliance.* Most individuals work hard to maintain control and to keep a certain level of stability in their daily lives. Most patients are, at best, ambivalent about the treatment process and the changes to come. Cognitive and emotional rigidity prevents patients from alternative thinking and more diverse problem-solving patterns. Therefore, these patients resist learning in therapy, and, regardless of what kind of therapy is offered, they may not develop healthier coping styles.

2. *Significant medical/physiological problems.* Medical/physiological problems present several variables that may impede treatment progress. First, even though the patient's emotional difficulties are a greater obstacle to successful coping, he or she may perceive medical problems as more "real" in comparison with emotional difficulties. If psychotherapy is introduced too early or at a time when the patient is preoccupied with medical complications, he or she may resist full participation in treatment.

Patients may receive far more support and sympathy from their significant others for their medical problems than for their emotional issues. Therefore, it is not surprising that some patients with physiological and medical problems may resist psychological treatment and recovery.

3. *Difficulty in establishing trust.* Trust is one of the most important ingredients in the therapeutic relationship. There are several reasons that patients may have difficulty trusting their therapists. First, the quality of the patient's relationship with his or her primary caregiver often serves as a blueprint for future relationships, and the therapeutic relationship is no exception. Previously established core beliefs about self and others will activate related negative thoughts that can prevent the patient from experiencing the therapist accurately.

4. *Autonomy press.* Some patients have a difficult time accepting help. They portray themselves as having an autonomous style, and they have difficulty allowing others into their emotional inner circle. Further, they often fear failure if they rely on someone else, whether family members or the therapist, to help them feel better. They fear loss of self-esteem if they allow themselves to engage in a therapeutic relationship. This need for autonomy will play itself out in problems in collaboration and difficulties in establishing a working alliance and cooperation with therapeutic planning and interventions.

5. *Impulsivity.* Impulsivity is characterized by poor decision making and by *reacting* to rather than acting in given situations. In their daily lives, they are often unable or unwilling to delay immediate gratification long enough to access the learned therapeutic tools. This is the reason impulsive patients resist treatment and often do not learn from their experiences.

Furthermore, their impulsivity and lack of therapeutic progress often activates the therapist's own negative cognitions, creating frustration for the therapist, which in turn affects the therapeutic relationship and progress.

6. *Confusion or limited cognitive ability.* The treatment plan has a greater chance of being effective after the patient fully understands the plan and agrees to actively participate in his or her treatment. When the patient has limited cognitive ability and does not understand what the therapist is presenting, the collaboration will be impeded. The plan may not be presented in the simple terms and procedures

that the patient can understand. In such cases, the patient not only does not feel relieved by the help that he or she is receiving but also feels further frustrated and may be angered by the complicated, difficult material presented. Therefore, minimal progress is made in treatment, and the patient may feel frustrated and resist further treatment.

7. *Symptom profusion.* It is rare that patients come to therapy with a single problem. They are often hesitant about presenting all of their problems to the therapist, either because they find the list of problems overwhelming or because they are embarrassed by it. When encountering patients with multiple serious problems, it is likely that even an experienced clinician may feel overwhelmed, not knowing where to begin. As progress is not happening fast enough, the patient may give up or passively resist treatment.

8. *Dependence.* Dependent patients seek solutions to their problems from others. Unlike autonomous individuals, they adopt a submissive position in relationships with the hope of gaining approval and nurturance. Dependent individuals are very sensitive to criticisms and disapproval, and the therapist may spend considerable time and effort addressing patients' responses to the feedback given to him or her in therapy. They avoid self-determination, downgrade their own accomplishments, and do not comfort themselves by what they do for themselves. Therefore, these patients may seek treatment year after year but avoid learning and practicing the essential therapeutic elements that are required in order to recover and to cope.

9. *Self-devaluation.* The patient's negative view of him- or herself can be a contributing factor to therapeutic resistance. These patients attribute negative outcomes to themselves rather than to a variety of potential factors. Such negative self-attributions affect the patient's self-esteem, leaving the patient questioning whether he or she is good enough, is healthy enough, or has achieved enough. In turn, the self-devaluation will impair the patient's performance, reinforcing that he or she is not good enough and is not capable of change. This in turn creates a sense of despair and hopelessness, which then fuels the ongoing pattern of self-defeating behaviors and ultimately self-punishment. He or she apologizes for his or her needs, and any discussions about needs lead to negative outcomes of depression and anxiety (Leahy, 2001).

10. *Limited energy.* After identifying the patient's problems or destructive beliefs, the therapist needs to assess the cognitive strength of the patient's beliefs and the force and energy that maintain them (Ellis, 1985). The patient must gain both intellectual and emotional insight into his or her problems, because intellectual insight alone does not lead to major powerful changes for the patient (Ellis, 1985). The goal in this case is to help the patient to develop a plan to get the ball rolling, not simply wait for the return of energy. Once the patient has an action plan, the therapist can guide him or her by providing the necessary steps toward change.

SUMMARY

When therapy is not going well, therapists must look to four areas to assess what might be impeding the therapy process and progress. To assist in doing this, we have developed a checklist survey. The therapist or supervisor can review the therapy work and evaluate where the sticking points are in therapy with this patient, at this point in time, at this point in therapy, and related to the goals of the therapy.

The patient must be included in addressing the impediments, as he or she is the one most affected by the therapy or change difficulties As the impediments are identified, the treatment plan can be revised to cope with the impediments. The interventions are then tailored to encourage overcoming the roadblocks to therapy.

REFERENCES

Adelman, H. S., & Taylor, L. (1986). Children's reluctance regarding treatment. Incompetence, resistance, or an appropriate response? *School Psychology Review, 15*, 91–99.

American Psychiatric Association. (1980). *Diagnostic and statistical manual of mental disorders* (3rd ed.). Washington, DC: Author.

Bordin, E. S. (1979). The generalizability of the psychoanalytic concept of the working alliance. *Psychotherapy: Theory, Research, and Practice, 16*, 252–260.

Breuer, J., & Freud, S. (1955). Studies on hysteria. In J. Strachey (Ed. and Trans.), *Standard edition of the complete psychological works of Sigmund Freud* (Vol. 2, pp. 1–311). London: Hogarth Press. (Original work published 1893–1895).

Burns, D. D. (1989). *The feeling good handbook: Using the new mood therapy in everyday life*. New York: Morrow.

Ciechanowski, P. S., Katon, W. J., Russo, J. E., & Walker, E. A. (2001). The patient–provider relationship: Attachment theory and adherence to treatment in diabetes. *American Journal of Psychiatry, 158*(1), 29–35.

Deaton, A. V. (1985). Adaptive non-compliance in pediatric asthma: The parent as expert. *Journal of Pediatric Psychology, 10*(1), 1–14.

Ellis, A. (1985). *Overcoming resistance: Rational-emotive therapy with difficult clients*. New York: Springer.

Freeman, A., & Dolan, M. (2001). Revisiting Prochaska and Diclemente's stages of change theory: An expansion and specification to aid in treatment planning and outcome evaluation. *Cognitive and Behavioral Practice, 8*(3), 224–234.

Freeman, A., & McClosky, R. D. (2003). Impediments to effective psychotherapy. In R. L. Leahy (Ed.), *Roadblocks in cognitive behavior therapy* (pp. 24–48). New York: Guilford Press.

Gerber, K. E., & Nehemkis, A. M. (Eds.). (1986). *Compliance: The dilemma of the chronically ill*. New York: Springer.

Greenberg, L., & Paivio, S. (1997). *Working with emotions in psychotherapy*. New York: Guilford Press.

Keisler, D. J., & Watkins, L. M. (1989). Interpersonal complementarity and the therapeutic alliance: A study of relationship in psychotherapy. *Psychotherapy: Theory, Research and Practice*, *26*, 183–194.

Lazarus, A. A., & Fay, A. (1982). Resistance or rationalization?: A cognitive–behavioral perspective. In P. L. Wachtel (Ed.), *Resistance: Psychodynamic and behavioral approaches* (pp. 115–132). New York: Plenum Press.

Leahy, R. L. (2001). *Overcoming resistance in cognitive therapy*. New York: Guilford Press.

Leahy, R. L. (Ed.). (2003). *Roadblocks in cognitive behavioral therapy*. New York: Guilford Press.

Luborsky, L., & Crits-Christoph, P. (1990). *Understanding transference: The core conflictual relationship theme method*. New York: Basic Books.

Luborsky, L., McLellan, A. T., Woody, G. E., O'Brien, C. P., & Auerbach, A. (1985). Therapist success and its determinants. *Archives of General Psychiatry*, *42*(6), 602–611.

Meichenbaum, D., & Gilmore, J. B. (1982). Resistance from a cognitive–behavioral perspective. In P. L. Wachtel (Ed.), *Resistance: Psychodynamic and behavioral approaches* (pp. 133–156). New York: Plenum Press.

Menninger, K. (1958). *Theory of psychoanalytic technique*. New York: Basic Books.

Persons, J. B., & Burns, D. D. (1985). Mechanisms of action of cognitive therapy: The relative contributions of technical and interpersonal interventions. *Cognitive Therapy and Research, 9*, 539–551.

Safran, J. D. (1998). *Widening the scope of cognitive therapy: The therapeutic relationship, emotion and the process of change*. Northvale, NJ: Jason Aronson.

Safran, J. D., & Segal, Z. V. (1990). *Interpersonal process in cognitive therapy*. New York: Basic Books.

Stark, M. (1994). *Working with resistance*. Northvale, NJ: Jason Aronson.

S

Schizophrenia

Alan S. Bellack and Wendy N. Tenhula

Keywords: schizophrenia, cognitive–behavior therapy, psychosis, hallucinations, delusions

Although antipsychotic medications are generally effective at reducing the positive symptoms of schizophrenia (e.g., hallucinations, delusions), moderate to high levels of symptoms continue to persist among a large number of schizophrenia patients. As many as 20% of patients may not be responsive to medication, and many others are only partially responsive. Residual symptoms are a source of considerable stress and depression, and may occasionally stimulate self-harm or aggression directed to others. Moreover, people with the disorder are often maintained on multiple antipsychotic medications or on high doses in an effort to control residual symptoms, which increase the probability of iatrogenic complications. Psychotic symptomatology has generally been viewed as the domain of psychopharmacology, and there has not been great interest in psychosocial treatments for this aspect of illness. However, since the early 1990s there has been a growing body of literature on the application of the principles of cognitive–behavioral therapy (CBT) to address residual symptoms.

Associated primarily with Aaron T. Beck, CBT has become the foremost approach for treating anxiety disorders and depression, and it has been used with positive effects for other nonpsychotic disorders. CBT is based in large measure on the hypothesis that psychological dysfunction (anxiety, depression, interpersonal difficulties) is characterized by illogical assumptions about the self and the world (e.g., *everyone must love me; I must be perfect*). Distress results when experience is incompatible with these illogical beliefs (e.g., the individual who believes he must be perfect makes a small error and interprets it as a catastrophic event). In contrast to thought disturbance in psychosis, in which there is a fundamental breakdown in the ability to perceive the world accurately and/or think logically, CBT posits that the cognitive problems in less severe disorders involve *normal* perception and reasoning processes that are distorted by illogical assumptions. Treatment involves a Socratic dialogue, or *collaborative empiricism*, in which the therapist tries to teach the client to challenge illogical beliefs and faulty thinking.

The application of CBT for schizophrenia is consistent with a biopsychosocial, stress vulnerability model of the illness. It is built on the assumption that there is a continuity between normal and abnormal cognitive processes, and that the inferential errors and faulty logic associated with hallucinations and delusions are similar to those experienced with other disorders (Dickerson, 2000; Rector & Beck, 2001). If this assumption is correct, CBT strategies should be equally valid for use with psychotic patients as for nonpsychotic populations.

Most of the work on CBT for psychosis has been conducted in the United Kingdom, where several research groups have developed cognitive–behavioral approaches. Each of these approaches has a slightly different emphasis and employs somewhat different techniques, but there are several commonalities, including: (a) the establishment of a strong therapeutic alliance characterized by acceptance, support, and mutual goals *before* introduction of behavior change techniques; (b) education about the nature of psychosis with the goal of reducing stigma; (c) reduction of stress, anxiety, and depression; (d) use of cognitive–behavioral techniques to help the person cope with psychotic symptoms; and (e) a focus on relapse prevention (Dickerson, 2000; Rector & Beck, 2001).

Like most psychosocial treatments for schizophrenia, CBT is intended to supplement other services, including pharmacotherapy and case management. As with CBT for less impaired patients, CBT for psychosis is a verbal therapy in which patients are taught to question faulty assumptions about themselves and the world, to accept psychotic symptoms as logical attempts to cope with stress rather than being *crazy* or signs of weakness, and to use coping strategies to control the distress produced by hallucinations and delusions. In most programs an effort is often made to reinforce coping strategies already used by patients, and to help them apply the techniques more effectively. Strategies range from simple use of physical or mental distraction (e.g., listening to music on headphones), to calling a friend for support, to the logical self-talk common to CBT with less impaired populations (e.g., *This is not a real voice, it is just my imagination. I can control this*). Patients generally receive homework assignments to practice coping strategies and more adaptive ways of thinking between sessions, in order to foster generalization. Though some recent trials have used a group therapy format, CBT is typically administered as an individual outpatient treatment. Therapists in most trials have been doctoral-level clinicians, but several recent trials have reported positive results with graduate students (Bach & Hayes, 2002), psychiatric nurses (Sensky et al., 2000), and community mental health workers (Turkington, Kingdom, & Turner, 2002). Treatment duration has varied from 6 to 10 sessions conducted over a few weeks to more than 20 sessions over 9 months, with the longer trials generally producing better results (Pilling et al., 2002).

EMPIRICAL EVIDENCE

Five literature reviews of CBT have appeared in peer-reviewed journals to date. Three were meta-analyses of seven studies (Gould, Mueser, Bolton, Mays, & Goff, 2001; Pilling et al., 2002; Rector & Beck, 2001), and two provided narrative reviews of 15 and 4 studies, respectively (Dickerson, 2000; Garety, Fowler, & Kuipers, 2000). The literature is difficult to integrate due to variations in treatment format and duration, control groups, and outcome measures. For example, in various trials, CBT has been compared to "standard care," supportive counseling, and *befriending*. CBT appears to be most effective for reducing belief in the veracity of delusions, distress associated with delusions, and overall levels of symptoms. There is limited evidence for its effectiveness in reducing frequency of and distress over hallucinations, which is disappointing given that most programs are intended to help patients cope with these symptoms. Similarly, there is some suggestion that CBT is helpful in reducing depression and negative symptoms, but here too the results are mixed and mood symptoms have not typically been the focus of treatment. Conversely, there is replicated evidence that it does not reduce relapse. CBT does not appear to confer any specific advantage to patients with recent-onset psychosis who are experiencing acute symptoms or who are in the post-acute illness phase. Follow-up data are also inconsistent, suggesting that longer term, more intensive interventions produce durable effects on some, but not all, domains (e.g., Kuipers et al., 1998; Tarrier et al., 1999). Most studies have focused on patients with schizophrenia, but CBT may be applicable to other patients who are bothered by residual psychotic symptoms as well.

CRITICISMS OF CBT FOR SCHIZOPHRENIA AND DIRECTIONS FOR FUTURE RESEARCH

The key assumption that the faulty logic associated with hallucinations and delusions is similar to that seen in other disorders has not been subjected to empirical evaluation, and runs counter to a large body of literature on the neurobiological basis of thought disorder in psychosis. While the validity of this assumption is an important issue for future research to address, CBT treatment strategies may nevertheless be effective in helping patients cope with symptoms.

Results for acute inpatients have been less impressive than for stabilized (chronic) outpatients with residual symptoms (Bach & Hayes, 2002; Lewis et al., 2002). Most trials have not recruited patients randomly. Rather, subjects have generally been selected so as to be appropriate for a verbal psychotherapy. Patients with significant cognitive impairment or with substance abuse problems have not been well-represented in these trials. It is questionable if the more abstract, cognitively demanding CBT techniques can work with highly impaired patients, or with dually diagnosed patients for whom attendance at treatment sessions is often more of a problem. As most trials have been conducted in the United Kingdom, CBT has been superimposed on a backdrop of the socialized care provided to SMI patients in the United Kingdom, rather than the more disjointed approach characteristic of mental health care in the United States. The only U.S. study to date compared a brief (four-session) trial of Acceptance and Commitment Therapy (ACT) to a treatment-as-usual control in acutely ill inpatients with psychosis. ACT had significant effects on self-reported believability of symptoms and rehospitalization rates over a 4-month follow-up, but these differences had begun to subside by the end of the follow-up period and may not have been sustained if patients had been followed longer. Controlled trials of CBT need to be conducted in the United States with outpatients in order to determine its effectiveness in typical U.S. public health systems.

The term "CBT" has been used very loosely in this literature to refer to a wide variety of different treatment techniques. As indicated above, they all have some common values and assumptions about the illness and how to relate to patients, but few, if any, would be immediately recognizable as CBT practiced with depressed and anxious patients. In appraising the literature as a whole, it is safer to conclude that there is good evidence for these values and the general style of interacting with patients, including the use of psychoeducation to decrease stigma, developing shared goals, and teaching patients how to cope, than for any specific or unique CBT techniques.

In addition to research on the applicability of the cognitive model to schizophrenia (noted above), future research on CBT for schizophrenia should focus on identifying characteristics of patients who are most likely to benefit from CBT, key elements of treatment, and optimal duration of therapy. In addition, it will be important to better understand factors associated with the implementation of CBT treatment programs into various mental health care settings and the successful training of competent therapists.

See also: Social skills training

REFERENCES

Bach, P., & Hayes, S. C. (2002). The use of acceptance and commitment therapy to prevent the rehospitalization of psychotic patients: A randomized controlled trial. *Journal of Consulting and Clinical Psychology, 70*, 1129–1139.

Dickerson, F. B. (2000). Cognitive behavioral psychotherapy for schizophrenia: A review of recent empirical studies. *Schizophrenia Research, 43*, 71–90.

Garety, P. A., Fowler, D., & Kuipers, E. (2000). Cognitive–behavioral therapy for medication-resistant symptoms. *Schizophrenia Bulletin, 26*, 73–86.

Gould, R. A., Mueser, K. T., Bolton, E., Mays, V., & Goff, D. (2001). Cognitive therapy for psychosis in schizophrenia: An effect size analysis. *Schizophrenia Research, 48*, 335–342.

Kuipers, E., Fowler, D., Garety, P., Chisholm, D., Freeman, D., Dunn, G., Bebbington, P., & Hadley, C. (1998). London—East Anglia randomized controlled trial of cognitive–behavioural therapy for psychosis III: Follow-up and economic evaluation at 18 months. *British Journal of Psychiatry, 173*, 61–68.

Lewis, S., Tarrier, N., Haddock, G., Bentall, R., Kinderman, P., Kingdon, D., Siddle, R., Drake, R., Everitt, J., Leadley, K., Benn, A., Grazebrook, K., Haley, C., Akhtar, S., Davies, L., Palmer, S., Faragher, B., & Dunn, G. (2002). Randomised controlled trial of cognitive–behavioral therapy in early schizophrenia: Acute-phase outcomes. *The British Journal of Psychiatry, 181*, 91–97.

Pilling, S., Bebbington, P., Kuipers, E., Garety, P., Geddes, J., Orbach, G., & Morgan, C. (2002). Psychological treatments in schizophrenia: I. Meta-analysis of family intervention and cognitive behaviour therapy. *Psychological Medicine, 32*, 763–782.

Rector, N. A., & Beck, A. T. (2001). Cognitive behavioral therapy for schizophrenia: An empirical review. *Journal of Nervous and Mental Disease, 189*, 278–287.

Sensky, T., Turkington, D., Kingdon, D., Scott, J. L., Scott, J., Siddle, R., O'Carroll, M., & Barnes, T. R. E. (2000). A randomized controlled trial of cognitive–behavioral therapy for persistent symptoms in schizophrenia resistant to medication. *Archives of General Psychiatry, 57*, 165–172.

Tarrier, N., Wittkowski, A., Kinney, C., McCarthy, E., Morris, J., & Humphreys, L. (1999). Durability of the effects of cognitive–behavioural therapy in the treatment of chronic schizophrenia: 12-month follow-up. *The British Journal of Psychiatry, 174*, 500–504.

Turkington, D., Kingdom, D., & Turner, T. (2002). Effectiveness of a brief cognitive–behavioural therapy intervention in the treatment of schizophrenia. *British Journal of Psychiatry, 180*, 523–527.

School-Based Therapy

Rosemary Mennuti and Ray W. Christner

Keywords: school-based interventions, CBT in schools

The provision of school-based psychological services dates back to the turn of the twentieth century when all states enacted compulsory attendance laws, the average number of school days increased, and public school enrollment was on the rise (Fagan, 2000). School-based clinicians received referrals to address academic problems, behavioral concerns, as well as issues complicated by health problems. While the types of referrals have remained the same, the need for comprehensive school-based psychological services has never been greater. Recently, a *Report of the Surgeon General's Conference on Children's Mental Health* noted that the country is now facing a crisis in mental health care. In the United States alone, 1 in 10 children and adolescents have a diagnosed mental illness severe enough to cause some level of impairment. Yet, in any given year, it is estimated that fewer than 1 in 5 of these children receive needed treatment (U.S. Public Health Service, 2001)

Education plays a dominant role in the lives of youth, and we believe it is a natural entry point for addressing the mental health needs of children and families. As emotional and behavioral problems arise with students, it is more likely that school-based clinicians will have an obligation to design and provide effective and efficacious interventions for various presenting problems and populations. Considering the needs of students and the legal dictum for the provision of psychological counseling in schools, we believe cognitive–behavioral therapy (CBT) represents a promising option for school-based clinicians as a well-founded, effective treatment model for a wide range of problems experienced by children.

USING CBT WITH CHILDREN AND ADOLESCENTS

CBT's initial momentum occurred as an innovative treatment for various adult disorders; however, it has moved to the forefront of treatment for a number of difficulties affecting children and adolescents (Friedberg & McClure, 2002; Reinecke, Dattilio, & Freeman, 2003). Research on the use of CBT with children and adolescents has grown in recent years, although the literature on the use of CBT within a school setting remains minimal.

When applying the CBT framework in the conceptualization and treatment of school-age children with problems, professionals must possess an understanding of the fundamentals of child and adolescent development. Those clinicians grounded in the "nuts and bolts" of development will avoid implementing interventions that are incompatible with a child's functional level. To benefit from a number of cognitive-based strategies, a child must have the capacity to attend to information, comprehend language, use working memory, and verbally express him- or herself. School-based practitioners should use and focus on these individual factors when designing a specific program for a student. In case conceptualization and treatment design, school-based clinicians should determine the precise mix of cognitive and behavioral techniques based on the student's developmental level. For instance, the more immature a student's cognitive or language development, the greater is the proportion of behavioral to cognitive interventions the clinician will use. This is not to say that cognitive techniques are inappropriate for use with young children, but instead that the use of cognitive interventions will be less relied on for those students at a lower developmental level. We note further that school-based clinicians should be aware that developmental level is not always consistent with chronological age.

In addition to cognitive and language development, school-based clinicians should also have awareness of other prominent research in the developmental psychopathology literature including risk factors (Coie et al., 1993) and protective factors (Rutter, 1985). Coie et al. (1993) grouped empirically derived risk factors into seven domains: (1) constitutional handicaps, (2) skills development delays, (3) emotional difficulties, (4) family circumstances, (5) interpersonal problems, (6) school problems, and (7) ecological risks. Similarly, Rutter (1985) identified three broad domains of protective factors including individual characteristics, interaction with the environment, and broader societal influences (e.g., quality schools). Coie et al. (1993) indicated that protective factors work in one of the following ways: (1) directly decreasing risk, (2) serving as a buffer through interaction with risk factors, (3) disrupting the chain reaction from risk factors to disorder, or (4) preventing the initial occurrence of the risk factor.

Clinicians can use this knowledge to help conceptualize and design interventions for students. When working with children and adolescents, the treatment may initially focus on building social skills and problem solving through psychoeducation. It is essential that the psychoeducational components facilitate skill building and the correction of maladaptive practices in order to promote protective factors while minimizing risk factors (e.g., strengthening peer relationships, increasing self-monitoring skills, improving parent–child interactions, and increasing school success). For instance, building social–cognitive skills in angry and aggressive children has been identified as an effective mediator in the reduction of angry or aggressive outburst (Kazdin & Weisz, 1998). Furthermore, CBT strategies such as cognitive restructuring have the potential to raise a child's protective mechanisms (e.g., cognitive skills) while lessening risk such as emotional dysregulation and low self-esteem.

A final key component regarding the use of CBT with children and adolescents in school settings is the collaborative relationship. Interestingly, professionals who are critical of CBT claim it ignores the relevance of the "therapeutic relationship." This assertion, however, is far from traditional practice, and in fact, it is contrary to work and writings of prominent figures in CBT such as Aaron Beck. Beck, Rush, Shaw, and Emery (1979) emphasize the need of active interaction between a therapist and a patient, and they refer to "slighting the therapeutic relationship" (p. 27) as a common drawback in therapy.

The idea of a connected, collaborative relationship when treating children is imperative to the child's process of healthy growth and development, as a positive authentic relationship facilitates the therapy process and the outcome. In a meta-analytic review, Shirk and Karver (2003) found that therapeutic relationship has a modest, but consistent, correlation with therapeutic outcome for youth. While collaboration generally suggests an "equal" involvement between the school-based clinician and child, this is not the case in actual treatment. In fact, a school-based clinician will need to meet a specific student at his or her level (based on age, motivation, and so on).

In addition to previously mentioned factors, a student's motivation and attitude have an impact on the collaborative relationship and subsequent treatment outcomes. A student referred by his teacher for losing his temper and displaying anger outbursts is not likely to be receptive of a directive approach that mimics existing interactions with others. However, using his motivation (e.g., getting his teacher off his back) may increase his adherence to interventions as well as foster a stronger partnership. Simple tasks such as frequent and brief summations throughout the session may further assist in keeping focus while establishing and maintaining the collaborative relationship. Summations communicate to the student that the clinician follows and understands what he or she is saying, though also obtaining feedback to clarify information or misunderstandings. This type of interaction empowers the student to confront the clinician appropriately, which is atypical with most school-based interactions.

RATIONALE FOR CBT IN SCHOOLS

While psychological counseling services may be difficult to "fit" into the educational culture, the structure and framework of CBT parallels other educational services making it more easily accepted among educators. The time-limited, present-oriented, and solution-focused aspects of CBT (Reinecke et al., 2003) are consistent with the educational environment, where both time and resources are often limited. The solution-focused and present-oriented approach of CBT is also appealing in education, as it addresses the student's issues without overly relying on diagnosing a specific pathology. Basic CBT components such as psychoeducation, skill building, between-session work (i.e., "homework"), agenda setting, and progress monitoring are activities congruent with most activities already existing in school settings. Thus, while these components assist in providing effective counseling services, they also strengthen the link between psychological counseling and other services provided in schools.

The combination of teacher interaction, peer influence, and personal performance efforts and outcomes provides school-based clinicians a unique environment to gain insight into a student's perceptions, to which many outside clinicians do not have access. The school setting is essentially a "natural laboratory" to observe interpersonal dynamics and to gather data about the problems facing students. Additionally, it provides a natural and "safe" setting for students to "experiment" with applying the new skills learned through CBT.

In addition to the parallels between CBT and other school activities, the provision of school-based CBT interventions further affords opportunities to students and families who may otherwise not have the resources to receive services outside of school. Despite the number of children and adolescents in need of psychological services, many youngsters never obtain the services needed while others frequently cancel and eventually drop out of counseling services (Kazdin, Holland, & Crowley, 1997). Kazdin et al. (1997) identified several characteristics that predict treatment dropout including socioeconomic status, high levels of stress and discord, and difficult life circumstances (e.g., single-parent families). Rendering school-based counseling services, such as CBT, may minimize the impact some of these barriers (e.g., transportation, time) have on children and families receiving effective services.

EMPIRICAL SUPPORT FOR CBT WITH CHILDREN

"Evidence-based practice" has become a common catchphrase within the educational and mental health professions. However, most of the literature on the use of CBT with children and adolescents has involved clinical populations rather than addressing the use of CBT in schools. The literature has shown CBT to be effective in the treatment of a number of childhood difficulties including depression, anxiety, and disruptive behaviors (see reviews in Kazdin & Weisz, 1998; Weisz & Jensen, 1999). There continues, however, to be a need for further investigation into a number of childhood difficulties including eating disorders, posttraumatic stress disorder, bipolar disorder, substance abuse, school-related problems, and other health conditions (e.g., pain management, obesity). Additionally, further investigation is necessary regarding the provision of CBT in alternative settings such as a school system.

CAUTIONS OF CBT WITH CHILDREN

Notwithstanding the positives of providing psychological counseling services in school, school-based clinicians must also consider a number of challenges and barriers. In the view of many educators, the primary purpose of school for children is to receive *academic* instruction. As teachers and other staff members provide valuable services to meet this goal, school-based clinicians must be mindful of the time constraints already facing these individuals. The presence of educational legislation (e.g., No Child Left Behind) has restricted the views of some educators and minimized the focus on students' emotional and behavioral needs. However, given the overwhelming and lasting effects that can accompany emotional and behavioral difficulties in children, including academic problems, there is a need for school-based clinicians to educate school systems regarding the necessity to meet the psychosocial needs of children and to enhance positive academic and behavioral outcomes for student success. School-based professionals must accomplish this, however, while respecting the challenges already facing educators. For children whose emotional and behavioral issues are interfering with academic functioning, psychological counseling services may assume a prominent role in the child's educational program. Scheduling weekly appointments is another challenge facing school-based clinicians. Coordination with various members of the student's educational team is essential in providing efficient and effective services.

The collaborative relationship between clinicians and students presents another obstacle. In the school environment, there are numerous occasions for casual interactions with the student (e.g., passing "hellos" in the hallway). While this may help facilitate the collaborative relationship with the child, it may also test the school-based clinician's ability to maintain appropriate boundaries.

The protection of the child's confidentiality further poses a conflict when providing psychological counseling services in schools. The issues of scheduling session times, the referral process itself, and the request for communication between referring teachers, parents, and school-based clinicians regarding the student's needs and progress may compromise traditional confidentiality standards.

School-based clinicians providing CBT services within the school system should consider and address each of the aforementioned issues from the onset of treatment. Having a structure and plan on handling such situations will prevent undue concerns over time. Those providing services in a school system must fully understand the state laws and ethics of their own profession and those of the educational system.

FUTURE DIRECTIONS FOR CBT IN SCHOOLS

The CBT model is ideal for delivering effective, short-term, and flexible psychological counseling services within the school environment. It complements the already existing structure and framework in the school environment while focusing on the cognitive, behavioral, affective, and social factors inherent in many difficulties seen in youth. Despite the already existing work in CBT with children and youth, several areas must be addressed before full advancements in the use of CBT in school will occur.

First, as noted above, research is needed to evaluate the efficacy and effectiveness of CBT with a wider variety of child and adolescent problems. Additionally, its application within the school setting may be contingent on studies focusing on nonpathological problems seen in educational settings such as academic motivation, test anxiety, student underachievement, home–school collaboration, and crisis intervention, to name a few.

Second, while there is definitely a need for school-based psychological counseling services in schools, there is a question whether school-based professionals have the training and education necessary to provide such services in a competent manner. This is a challenge facing university training facilities as well as those organizations providing continuing professional development for school-based practitioners. Effectively using CBT with children and adolescents, as well as any other populations, requires appropriate training and supervision beyond attending a workshop or reading an article.

Finally, providing CBT within a school setting will require an understanding of the school culture. Traditionally, psychological counseling services in many schools have involved primarily behavioral interventions. The move toward a model integrating cognitive and behavioral principles will require, to some extent, a paradigm shift in educators' views of these services. This may involve not only a change in the orientation of services but also an expanded view of the continuum of psychological counseling services that could be available to students including consultation, individual and group counseling, classwide interventions, and schoolwide mental health programs.

See also: Children—behavior therapy, Treatment of children

REFERENCES

Beck, A. T., Rush, A. J., Shaw, B. F., & Emery, G. (1979). *Cognitive therapy for depression*. New York: Guilford Press.

Coie, J. D., Watt, J. F., West, S. G., Hawkins, J. D., Asarnow, J. R., Markman, H. J., Ramey, S. L., Shure, M. B., & Long, B. (1993). The science of prevention: A conceptual framework and some direction for a national research program. *American Psychologist, 48*, 1013–1022.

Fagan, T. K. (2000). Practicing school psychology: A turn-of-the century perspective. *American Psychologist, 55*, 754–757.

Friedberg, R. D., & McClure, J. M. (2002). *Clinical practice of cognitive therapy with children and adolescents: The nuts and bolts*. New York: Guilford Press.

Kazdin, A. E., Holland, L. H., & Crowley, M. (1997). Family experiences of barriers to treatment and premature termination from child therapy. *Journal of Consulting and Clinical Psychology, 65*, 453–463.

Kazdin, A. E., & Weisz, J. R. (1998). Identifying and developing empirically supported child and adolescent treatments. *Journal of Consulting and Clinical Psychology, 66*, 19–36.

Reinecke, M. A., Dattilio, F. M., & Freeman, A. (Eds.). (2003). *Cognitive therapy with children and adolescents: A casebook for clinical practice* (2nd ed.). New York: Guilford Press.

Rutter, M. (1985). Resilience in the face of adversity: Protective factors and resistance to psychiatric disorders. *British Journal of Psychiatry, 147*, 598–611.

Shirk, S. R., & Karver, M. (2003). Prediction of treatment outcome from relationship variable in child and adolescent therapy: A meta-analytic review. *Journal of Consulting and Clinical Psychology, 71*, 452–464.

U.S. Public Health Service. (2000). *Report of the Surgeon General's Conference on Children's Mental Health: A National Action Agenda.* Washington, DC: U.S. Department of Health and Human Services.

Weisz, J. R., & Jensen, P. S. (1999). Efficacy and effectiveness of child and adolescent psychotherapy and pharmacotherapy. *Mental Health Services Research, 1*, 125–157.

Severe OCD

Jonathan D. Huppert and Edna B. Foa

Keywords: OCD, obsessions, compulsions, exposure, insight

Obsessive–compulsive disorder (OCD) is an anxiety disorder characterized by both obsessions and compulsions. Obsessions are intrusive thoughts, images, or impulses that come into one's mind for no apparent reason, are unwanted, and are distressing. Compulsions are characterized by repeated behaviors or thoughts that serve to decrease the obsessional distress. To meet criteria for OCD, obsessions and/or compulsions must take up at least 1 hour a day and be distressing or interfere with the patient's functioning in life. Severe OCD is characterized by substantial frequency of obsessions and compulsions (from 4 hours a day to every minute of the patient's waking hours), substantial impairment from the OCD (usually in all domains of life including social, work, and family), poor insight into the symptoms (or how realistic the patient thinks their fears are), and/or substantial comorbidity which complicates the presentation of the symptoms (e.g., posttraumatic stress disorder or schizophrenia).

Severity of symptoms, as characterized by high frequency of symptoms or significant distress, is often measured by the Yale–Brown Obsessive Compulsive Scale (Y-BOCS; Goodman et al., 1989), and can also be measured through self-report measures such as the Obsessive–Compulsive Inventory-Revised (OCI-R; Foa et al., 2002). Either of these scales may not capture all severe cases; however, administered together, the large majority of severe cases should be detected.

Poor insight, also known as overvalued ideation (OVI; Kozak & Foa, 1994), is also a predictor of worse outcome for CBT. OVI is assessed through the Y-BOCS, but also can be assessed using a number of measures including the Brown Assessment of Beliefs Scale (BABS; Eisen et al., 1998). The main characteristic of OVI is that the patient is convinced that his or her obsessional fears are realistic. A classic example is a patient who believes that touching doorknobs really can lead to contracting AIDS. Such a patient will often state that he or she is just extremely careful. For patients with extreme OVI of this type, most people in the world are viewed as careless, and they are either lucky that they have not contracted AIDS or may have it and not be aware because they have not had an AIDS test. Most patients with OVI will acknowledge that other people think differently, but attribute this difference to the idea that others are wrong. Patients with severe OVI may appear delusional, but they present differently than patients who have a co-occurring psychotic disorder such as schizophrenia.

Comorbid disorders may exacerbate OCD symptoms and make it harder to treat. There are few data on the treatment of OCD and comorbid schizophrenia with CBT, but our clinical experience suggests that most patients with schizophrenia who have co-occurring OCD do not benefit from exposure and ritual prevention. Recent studies have suggested that patients with severe depression (i.e., the top 10% of depressed patients; Abramowitz, Franklin, Foa, Gordon, & Kozak, 2000) or PTSD (Gershuny, Baer, Jenike, Minichiello, & Wilhelm, 2002) may respond less well to CBT. Depression has been found to interfere with habituation in patients with OCD, and may also interfere with cognitive changes. In such cases, treatment of the comorbid disorder either prior to conducting CBT for OCD or simultaneously may be indicated.

Standard CBT for OCD involves the use of exposure and response (ritual) prevention with cognitive processing (Foa & Wilson, 2001). The basic concept underlying the treatment is that patients with OCD attempt to avoid or escape their obsessional fears through a number of strategies including thought suppression, mental and behavioral compulsions, safety behaviors, and avoidance. All of the avoidance behaviors function to decrease or avoid anxiety in the short run, but perpetuate the vicious cycle of anxiety in the long run. Exposure encourages the patient to confront the fears, and ritual prevention serves to prevent the patient from engaging in behaviors that are intended to decrease anxiety and/or to prevent feared consequences. Through this treatment the patients learn that the feared consequences do not occur and their anxiety decreases even when confronting fears and not ritualizing. This new information creates new associations in the fear structure of the patient which become predominant through repeated exposure, rendering the pretreatment fear structure less likely to be activated (Foa & McNally, 1996), and thereby decreasing symptoms.

There are two types of exposure: in vivo and imaginal. In vivo exposure is direct confrontation with feared stimuli (turning on your stove and leaving the room on purpose or touching a doorknob, toilet, etc. without washing hands). In vivo exercises are usually conducted in a hierarchical fashion, beginning with less distressing situations and gradually moving on to the most distressing situation. The rate of progress up the hierarchy is dictated by the patient's ability to tolerate distress, the frequency of symptoms, how impaired the patient is, and the extent of OVI.

Imaginal exposure is conducted mainly with patients who are afraid that terrible consequences will occur in the future or if the intrusive thoughts are not fully activated through in vivo exposure. For example, the fear of going to hell after death cannot be confronted in real life and therefore cannot be disconfirmed via in vivo exposure. To habituate these kinds of fears, an individualized scenario about 15 minutes long is created for the patient in which the feared consequence occurs because the patient chose not to engage in rituals or avoidance (e.g., a patient chooses to use a steak knife with dinner and does not pray when she thinks about harming her family and therefore she ends up killing the whole family and serving a life sentence all because she lost control when eating steak). Imaginal exposures are usually introduced relatively early on in treatment and are further developed for the patient as necessary throughout the course of treatment.

For both types of exposure, it is essential that the patient refrain from ritualizing in response to the obsessional fears that are evoked by exposure either during or after the exposure. Frequently, all ritualizing is banned from the outset of treatment. Many patients with severe OCD symptoms are unable to cease ritualizing, but they may be able to decrease their compulsions significantly. In these cases, the therapist uses the hierarchy of exposures conducted in session to determine what rituals to ban between sessions as the patient engages in homework and naturalistic exposures. Thus, by the time the patient has reached the top of the hierarchy, he or she is actively trying to cease all rituals as well.

A significant amount of cognitive processing is conducted when treating patients with OCD with exposure and response prevention. Severe cases often require even more emphasis on cognitive processing. Most cognitive processing is conducted during in vivo exposures or after imaginal exposures. The main purpose of cognitive processing is to help the patient to process his/her cognitive and emotional reactions to the exposure. There are two main judgment biases that patients with anxiety disorders, including OCD, have: probability and cost. Patients overestimate the likelihood that negative outcomes will occur ("There is a 99% chance that I will get AIDS if I touch a public bathroom doorknob and do not wash my hands immediately"), and they overestimate the cost of negative outcomes ("If my handwriting is not perfect, then it will be illegible to the professor, and I will fail the exam"). In vivo exposures are particularly useful at decreasing immediate overestimated probability of a fear, while imaginal exposures help to gain perspective and thus reevaluate long-term probability of feared outcomes and to differentiate between thoughts and actions. It is important that the patient conducts assigned exposures daily during treatment.

Originally, most forms of CBT for OCD were conducted with daily exposure sessions with a therapist (e.g., Meyer, 1966). However, recent studies have suggested similar efficacy for patients who are treated twice weekly (Abramowitz et al., 2003). However, patients with severe OCD symptoms seem to benefit more from intensive daily treatment, as it allows the therapist to troubleshoot any problems on a daily basis and it promotes the patient's motivation for improvement. Patients whose OCD is so severe that it prevents them from participating in outpatient treatment may benefit from treatment delivered in an inpatient unit that specializes in the treatment of OCD. Such units usually have aides who assist the patient with their treatment plan 24 hours a day, and help the patient to fully engage in treatment. Most severe cases of OCD require intensive therapist involvement in the treatment, and weekly sessions or self-help regimens are likely insufficient. If a patient is willing to tolerate distress, highly motivated to change, not depressed, and has a healthy family environment that will be supportive of change, then less intensive treatment may be sufficient.

In most cases, it is useful to involve the patient's family in the treatment. In more severe cases, it is typical that the family is involved in ritualizing for the patient either through reassurance, assisting in avoidance, or by explicitly conducting rituals for the patient. The therapist needs to use clinical judgment about the degree of family involvement in the treatment. In most cases, family members should be encouraged to give emotional support to the patients. In some cases, however, the relationship between the patient and family members is so strained that it is more advisable for them to not get involved in the treatment and homework exercises. For most families, at least a single session of psychoeducation about the CBT model of OCD is advisable.

A substantial proportion of patients with severe OCD benefits from CBT. However, patients who are unable to tolerate distress, have severe OVI, are not motivated to change, or have severe OCD of the hoarding subtype seem to respond less well to treatment. Some suggestions have been made to include motivational interviewing to help to address all of these problems.

See also: Body dysmorphia 1, Body dysmorphia 2, Exposure therapy, Perfectionism

REFERENCES

Abramowitz, J. S., Franklin, M. E., Foa, E. B., Gordon, P. S., & Kozak, M. J. (2000). Effects of comorbid depression on response to treatment for OCD. *Behavior Therapy, 31*, 517–528.

Abramowitz, J. S., Franklin, M. E., & Foa, E. B. (2003). Exposure and ritual prevention for obsessive–compulsive disorder: Effects of intensive versus twice-weekly sessions. *Journal of Consulting and Clinical Psychology, 71*, 394–398.

Eisen, J. L., Phillips, K. A., Baer, L., Beer, D. A., Atala, K. D., & Rasmussen, S. A. (1998). The Brown Assessment of Beliefs Scale: Reliability and validity. *American Journal of Psychiatry, 155*, 102–108.

Foa, E. B., Huppert, J. D., Leiberg, S., Langner, R., Kitchik, R., Hajcak, G., & Salkovskis, P. M. (2002). The Obsessive–Compulsive Inventory: Development and validation of a short version. *Psychological Assessment, 14*, 485–496.

Foa, E. B., & McNally, R. J. (1996). Mechanisms of change in exposure therapy. In R. M. Rappe (Ed.), *Current controversies in the anxiety disorders* (pp. 329–343). New York: Guilford Press.

Foa, E. B., & Wilson, R. (2001). *Stop obsessing! How to overcome your obsessions and compulsions* (2nd ed.). New York: Bantam Doubleday Dell.

Gershuny, B. S., Baer, L., Jenike, M. A., Minichiello, W. E., & Wilhelm, S. (2002). Comorbid posttraumatic stress disorder: Impact on treatment outcome for obsessive–compulsive disorder. *American Journal of Psychiatry, 159*, 852–854.

Goodman, W. K., Price, L. H., Rasmussen, S. A., Mazure, C., Delgado, P., Heninger, G. R., & Charney, D. S. (1989). The Yale–Brown Obsessive Compulsive Scale: II. Validity. *Archives of General Psychiatry, 46*, 1012–1016.

Kozak, M. J., & Foa, E. B. (1994). Obsessions, overvalued ideas, and delusions in obsessive compulsive disorder. *Behavior Research and Therapy, 3*, 343–353.

Meyer, V. (1966). Modification of expectations in cases with obsessional rituals. *Behaviour Research and Therapy, 4*, 273–280.

RECOMMENDED READINGS

Abramowitz, J. S., Franklin, M. E., & Cahill, S. P. (2003). Approaches to common obstacles in the exposure-based treatment of obsessive–compulsive disorder. *Cognitive and Behavioral Practice, 10*, 14–22.

Foa, E. B., & Wilson, R. (2001). *Stop obsessing! How to overcome your obsessions and compulsions* (2nd ed.). New York: Bantam Doubleday Dell.

Kozak, M. J., & Foa, E. B. (1997). *Mastery of obsessive–compulsive disorder: A cognitive–behavioral approach (therapist guide)*. San Antonio, TX: Psychological Corporation.

Sex Offending

Christine Maguth Nezu and Jeffrey G. Stoll

Keywords: sex offending, rape, child molestation

Sex offending behavior is a serious and widespread public health problem that has a lasting and profound impact on its victims. At any given time, the majority of convicted offenders are not in prison but are currently under the supervision of law enforcement and living in the community. This situation has led to a growing demand for effective sex offender treatment and a challenge to cognitive–behavioral researchers to attempt to better understand why men rape women or molest children, from both a functional and a causal perspective.

EXPLANATORY BEHAVIORAL MODELS

Over the years several behavioral explanatory models of sexual aggression have been proposed. Early models were based on theories of conditioning and deviant arousal. This "sexual motivational conditioning" model proposed that deviant sexual behavior occurs because the offender's early deviant sexual fantasies are paired with masturbation (Maguire, Carlisle, & Young, 1965). Although many sex offenders may be diagnosed or identified as exhibiting deviant sexual interests, the presence of such interests does not always equal engagement in sex offending behavior. For example, some individuals with paraphilias, defined as recurrent, intense, sexually arousing fantasies, urges, or behaviors that are consensually specified as deviant and result in distress, do not actually engage in behaviors consistent with their urges (Lanyon, 2001). It is also possible for a person to legally offend but not express specific paraphilic interests. Therefore, sexual conditioning does not fully account for the range of sex offending behavior.

Other models that attempt to explain sex offending focus on the aggressive aspect of the behavior, listing emotional dyscontrol and poor coping skills as problems related to offending. Some of these models have focused on the offender's lack of social competency or the role of learning through aggressive models (Marshall, Anderson, & Fernandez, 1999). Through these social cognitive processing theories, the sex offender is seen as a person who lacks social and interpersonal skills, such as social problem solving, and uses sexual aggression to solve their personal problems. Additional models that may help to explain sex offending focus more on interpersonal vulnerabilities that result from the offender's developmental antecedents (history), such as the offender's own history of physical or sexual abuse or unpredictable and neglectful family backgrounds. These developmental theories suggest that offenders have a poor ability to form interpersonal attachments to other people (Hall, 1996). For example, with regard to how a given offender may learn to cope with his own history of physical or sexual abuse, he may see himself as alone in the world, where he must fight and control others, before he is hurt or victimized. He may have no desire to change.

Finally, if this type of coping style exists, any additional factors that may decrease behavioral self-control, such as alcohol or drug abuse, may be important contributing factors (Nezu, Nezu, & Dudek, 1998). As such, theories that focus on impulse control may also partially explain the problem.

At present, there is no clear consensus as to what "causes" sex offending. However, a concept on which most cognitive–behavioral theorists agree is that many of these possible causes may be combined, to form a general "vulnerability" to commit a sex offense. The term "vulnerability" refers to the idea that the different cognitive and behavioral theories provide us with an understanding of the different pathways or factors of vulnerability that lead to sexual aggression or offending behavior. Therefore, vulnerability can be conceptualized as the combination of an offender's attitudes, beliefs, cognitive and behavioral skill deficits, behavior patterns, and emotions—all of which are tied to learning (Marshal et al., 1999). When deficits are present in some combination of these areas, it can lead to an increased risk for sex offending behavior.

Many vulnerability factors have been identified through studies that focus on prediction of sex offending risk, that is, whether or not someone is likely to commit a sex offense in the future. Risk prediction studies provide scientific support that specific vulnerability factors are significantly correlated to the risk of committing a later offense. These include deviant sexual preferences, a past behavior pattern of sex offending with a range of victims, single marital status, negative characteristics of an early home environment, social incompetence, poor stress or emotional management, cognitive distortions such as use of minimization and denial, avoidance, impulsivity, poor relationships, empathy deficits, psychopathic characteristics, lack of motivation to change, and nonadherence to treatment (Hanson & Bussiere, 1998; Marshall et al., 1999).

These factors can be broken down into two types (Proulx et al., 1997). The first type comprises those factors that are not capable of modification—these are referred to as "static" factors and include factors such as past behavior patterns (for example, a history of drug and alcohol use or past criminal behavior), or a history of a negative (abusive) early home environment. The second type of vulnerability factors is referred to as "dynamic"—factors that are potentially changeable, such as poor stress management skills, deviant arousal, treatment adherence, lack of social and coping skills such as problem solving or anger management, and cognitive distortions. It should be noted that the type of cognitive distortions that are frequently observed in sex offenders are thoughts that tend to place the blame on the victim, or minimize the destructive consequences of the sex offending behavior.

Much of the research conducted with regard to these two types of vulnerability factors (static and dynamic) has focused on increasing accuracy of prediction; in other words, what factors predict who is likely to reoffend? This information is often helpful to law enforcement and treatment programs to make decisions about parole release or whether or not to require a person to attend treatment. However, such information is less helpful to individual clinicians who know that their patient is at risk for offense but face the challenge of designing treatment that will result in a meaningful reduction of risk for both the patient and the community. In this case it would be useful for the therapist to know which dynamic factors or combination of factors can be improved through treatment, specifically for a given patient, and thus result in lowered risk.

THE STATUS OF CBT TREATMENT RESEARCH

The significant problem that exists in the current treatment literature is that although the research has given us a strong technology to predict who is likely to offend, specific information is lacking concerning when or how it will happen, or how to reduce vulnerability or risk effectively. In other words, although significant vulnerability factors that contribute to risk are identified, we do not know how they interact or which ones are the most critical targets of treatment.

Recent treatment models have focused on applying cognitive–behavioral principles to some or all areas of vulnerability, with specific attention to the aggressive aspect of offending behavior, emotional dyscontrol, and poor coping skills (Marshall & Barbaree, 1988). Although CBT strategies show promise for helping sex offenders reduce their risk, the literature regarding these treatment approaches is mixed, with no clear consensus of treatment efficacy. This may be partially due to the unique characteristics of a sex offender population such as low motivation or forensic involvement, such that techniques that have been useful for the same targets in other populations may not be as effective with offenders.

Despite these problems, the reports from two meta-analyses have concluded that cognitive–behavioral treatments do appear somewhat effective (Hall, 1995; Hanson et al., 2002) although the treatment outcome studies are few in number and most are marked by serious methodological problems. These include a lack of randomized assignment to treatment and control conditions, involvement of comparison groups that at times are comprised of men who drop out or refuse treatment, failure to assess or measure dynamic risk factors as mechanisms of action, and exclusion of participants with low motivation or those who deny their offense. This may present unrealistic population parameters because some authors have estimated the presence of denial in offenders to be quite high (Marshall et al., 1999). Other methodological problems include poor treatment descriptions, inadequate report of treatment integrity, and different definitions of treatment outcome.

There are a number of other practical matters that make conducting outcome studies with this population difficult. For example, randomization is often not possible due to ethical considerations, and the use of self-report measures as dependent variables may be limited because offender self-report can be unreliable. For example, there is a tendency among the population to present themselves with a positive, self-serving bias. Moreover, many participants are mandated by the justice system to attend treatment. This often creates an initial approach to treatment that is marked by poor motivation and resistance. As an example of the difficulties in conducting research with this population, even the most methodologically sophisticated outcome studies and programs to date have reported very high dropout rates (Marques, 1999).

Overall, the problems with the current studies, most of which use CBT to change dynamic factors of vulnerability, are that they are both few in number and methodologically poor.

AN INDIVIDUAL CASE APPROACH TO ASSESSMENT AND TREATMENT

At present, there is no clear consensus as to what "causes" sex offending. However, a concept on which most cognitive–behavioral researchers agree is that multiple factors are likely to conglomerate and form a general vulnerability to commit a sex offense. As such, all vulnerability factors that have been empirically identified need to be assessed for each individual. This would include, but not be limited to, the following assessment methods: structured interviews; cognitive–behavioral self-report measures of affect (e.g., depression, anxiety, anger); measures of coping and social skills; assessment of motivation; information concerning static historic factors; criminal records; role-play measure of social competency, problem-solving, and empathy skills; phallometric and other assessment of deviant interests; measures of drug and alcohol abuse; and behavioral descriptions from collateral sources. An individual case approach to assessment and treatment can highlight what particular vulnerability factors are operating that may increase risk of offense in each case. As a result of such an assessment, a treatment approach focused on changing the various specific vulnerability factors can be designed in a prescriptive, cognitive–behavioral, multicomponent treatment package.

Once assessment across areas of possible sex offending vulnerability is complete, a behavioral case formulation approach can provide a clinical map with which to guide treatment as well as specific recommendations for determining an individual's level of risk for reoffense and required level of supervised community risk management (for a complete description, see Nezu, Nezu, Peacock, & Girdwood, 2004).

Treatment design flows directly from an individual's unique case formulation. Because the literature concerning treatment outcome for sex offenders is nonconclusive, any interventions that have received empirical support in the literature that address specific identified targets of vulnerability relevant for an individual patient should be considered. Examples of such interventions include techniques that have been shown to be effective with regard to changing cognitive distortions, increasing anger management, decreasing deviant sexual arousal, or increasing social problem-solving ability. Because the clinician is unable to rely on any one of the empirically supported cognitive–behavioral treatment programs specifically designed for sex offending behavior, there are many studies supporting the use of various CBT techniques that address the various vulnerability factors.

SUMMARY

Cognitive–behavioral approaches designed to reduce risk of reoffense for sex offenders show promise. Future clinical research is being directed toward ways in which CBT therapists can improve their effectiveness in the treatment of sex offenders. These include identification of the dynamic risk factors that are associated with risk for offense, documenting the effectiveness of well-defined CBT treatments that are aimed at changing these factors, and how information about effective treatment can be disseminated to clinical practitioners.

See also: Child abuse, Sexual offenders and paraphilias

REFERENCES

Hall, G. C. N. (1995). Sexual offender recidivism revisited: A meta-analysis of recent treatment studies. *Journal of Consulting and Clinical Psychology, 63*, 802–809.

Hall, G. C. N. (1996). *Theory-based assessment, treatment, and prevention of sexual aggression*. New York: Oxford University Press.

Hanson, R. K., & Bussiere, M. T. (1998). Predicting relapse: A meta-analysis of sexual offender recidivism studies. *Journal of Consulting and Clinical Psychology, 66*, 348–362.

Hanson, R. K., Gordon, A., Harris, A. J. R., Marques, J. K., Murphy, W., Quinsey, V. L., & Seto, M. C. (2002). First report of the collaborative outcome data project on the effectiveness of psychological treatment for sex offenders. *Sexual Abuse: A Journal of Research and Treatment, 14*(2), 169–193.

Lanyon, R. I. (2001). Psychological assessment procedures in sex offending. *Professional Psychology: Research and Practice, 32*, 253–260.

Maguire, R. J., Carlisle, J. M., & Young, B. G. (1965). Sexual deviations as conditioned behaviour: A hypothesis. *Behavior Research and Therapy, 2*, 185–190.

Marques, J. K. (1999). How to answer the question, "Does sex offender treatment work?" *Journal of Interpersonal Violence, 14*, 437–451.

Marshall, W. L., Anderson, D., & Fernandez, Y. (1999). *Cognitive behavioural treatment of sexual offenders* (pp. 93–110). New York: Wiley.

Marshall, W. L., & Barbaree, H. E. (1988). The long-term evaluation of a behavioral treatment program for child molesters. *Behaviour Research and Therapy, 26*(6), 499–511.

Nezu, A. M., Nezu, C. M., Peacock, M. A., & Girdwood, C. P. (2004). Case formulation in cognitive–behavior therapy. In S. N. Haynes & E. Heiby (Eds.), *Behavioral assessment*. New York: Wiley.

Nezu, C. M., Nezu, A. M., & Dudek, J. A. (1998). A cognitive–behavioral model of assessment and treatment for intellectually disabled sexual offenders. *Cognitive and Behavioral Practice, 5*, 25–64.

Proulx, J., Pellerin, B., Paradis, Y., McKibben, A., Aubut, J., & Oiumet, M. (1997). Static and dynamic predictors of recidivism in sexual aggressors. *Sexual Abuse: A Journal of Research and Treatment, 9*, 7–27.

RECOMMENDED READINGS

Heilbrun, K., Nezu, C. M., Keeney, M., Chung, S., & Wasserman, A. L. (1998). Sexual offending: Linking assessment, intervention, and decision-making. *Journal of Psychology, Public Policy and Law, 4*, 138–174.

Hudson, S. M., Wales, D. S., Bakker, L., & Ward, T. (2002). Dynamic risk factors: The Kia Marama evaluation. *Sexual Abuse: A Journal of Research and Treatment, 14*(2), 103–119.

Quinsey, V. L., Khanna, A., & Malcolm, P. B. (1998). A retrospective evaluation of the regional treatment centre sex offender treatment program. *Journal of Interpersonal Violence, 13*, 621–644.

Sexual Dysfunction

Barry McCarthy and L. Elizabeth Bodnar

Keywords: sexual dysfunction, impairment in desire, arousal, orgasm, or level of satisfaction, couple sex therapy, assessment of sexual problems, sexual exercises, sexual trauma, relapse prevention

The operational definition of healthy sexuality is the ability to experience desire, arousal, orgasm, and satisfaction. The prescription for healthy sexuality is that both the man and woman value intimacy, nondemand pleasuring, and erotic scenarios and techniques. Sexuality has a number of functions including being a shared pleasure, a means to deepen and reinforce intimacy, and a tension-reducer to deal with the stresses of life and marriage. A planned, wanted child is an optional function of sexuality. A crucial clinical adage is that when sexuality functions well in a relationship, it serves a small but integral role, contributing 15–20% to the marriage's vitality and satisfaction. However, when sexuality is dysfunctional, conflictual, or nonexistent, it is inordinately powerful, robbing the marriage of vitality and threatening its viability. Paradoxically, bad sex plays a more powerful role than the enhancing role of healthy sexuality (McCarthy, in press). While the sexual saturation of modern culture may suggest that rates of sexual dysfunction are low, in actuality rates of sexual dysfunction, dissatisfaction, and trauma are strikingly high (Laumann, Gagnon, Michael, & Michaels, 1994). The most commonly cited reasons for divorce within the first 2 years of marriage are a sexual conflict, extramarital affair, or sexual dysfunction (McCarthy & McCarthy, 2003).

THE HISTORY OF SEX THERAPY

Modern sex therapy was founded by Masters and Johnson (1970) using the model of a 2-week intensive therapy, the couple treated by a male–female co-therapy team, and sexual exercises done between therapy sessions. The core concepts adopted by the cognitive–behavioral sex therapy model are: (1) sexual dysfunction is best conceptualized, assessed, and treated as a couple issue; (2) sexual comfort, skill, and functioning can be learned utilizing a series of sexual exercises; (3) the couple develops a sexual style that is comfortable and functional for both partners; and (4) a relapse prevention program is integral for successful sex therapy (McCarthy, 2002). For a more thorough understanding of the growth of cognitive–behavioral sex therapy, the contributions of Barlow (1986) and LoPiccolo and Friedman (1988) are essential.

TYPES OF SEXUAL DYSFUNCTION

The best data sample (Laumann et al., 1994) indicates that rates of sexual dysfunction and problems have remained relatively constant or have increased in the past 30 years. However, the types and causes of sexual dysfunction have changed. Traditionally, sexual dysfunction had been caused by lack of information, repressive attitudes and values, a rigid male–female double standard, and prevalence of primary dysfunction (i.e., the person has never been sexually functional). Now, causes of sexual dysfunction and problems include new sexual performance myths, high rates of negative or traumatic sexual experiences, disappointment in the partner or relationship, and a predominance of secondary dysfunction, especially inhibited sexual desire (i.e., the person has experienced sexual desire but it is now low or nonexistent).

The most common female sexual dysfunctions are:

1. Inhibited sexual desire (about half primary and half secondary)
2. Secondary nonorgasmic response during partner sex
3. Dyspareunia (painful intercourse)
4. Primary nonorgasmic response during partner sex
5. Female arousal dysfunction (usually secondary)
6. Primary nonorgasmic response
7. Vaginismus

The most common male sexual dysfunctions are:

1. Premature ejaculation (usually primary)
2. Secondary erectile dysfunction
3. Secondary inhibited sexual desire
4. Ejaculatory inhibition (primary for young males, secondary for males over 50).

ASSESSMENT IN COGNITIVE-BEHAVIORAL COUPLE SEX THERAPY

The four-session assessment phase includes an initial couple session (to reinforce the concept of sexuality as a couple issue and to explore the sexual problem in the context of the relationship), an individual sexual history session for each person, and the couple feedback session.

The prime assessment procedure is the semistructured sexual history. Sexual histories are conducted individually so the person is able to give an uncensored report of his or her sexual strengths and weaknesses, both before the marriage and during the marriage. Although secrets are complex clinical issues for the couple and therapist, a greater danger is not knowing about crucial issues that may impact the therapeutic process. Sexuality, especially sensitive and secret issues, needs to be assessed individually so that the clinician has a clear understanding of the attitudes, behaviors, and emotions, which impact the individuals and couple. If the history is conducted with the partner present, the clinician is less likely fail to obtain a true picture since at least 75% of individuals report sensitive or secret material (McCarthy, 2003). During these sessions, the clinician must utilize open-ended questions, as well as be supportive and nonjudgmental. The history-taking interview should move from general, less anxiety provoking material to more sensitive and specific issues.

The feedback session is the core intervention in sex therapy and has three focuses: (1) present a way of understanding the sexual problem which motivates the couple and provides hope for change and resolution; (2) propose a therapeutic plan which focuses on specific individual and couple changes, as well as potential traps to monitor; and (3) give a sexual homework exercise and the assignment to process and clarify material from the feedback session. The couple leaves the feedback session with a clear understanding of the individual responsibility/intimate team model of change (each partner is responsible for his/her desire, arousal, and orgasm and the couple works together as an intimate team to develop a comfortable, functional sexual style), motivation to address the sexual problem, and willingness to explore personal and couple vulnerabilities in a nonblaming manner.

SEX THERAPY PROCESS

A core strategy in sex therapy is the use of semistructured sexual exercises to facilitate changing attitudes, behaviors, and emotions. A critical skill for the therapist is to describe, process, refine, and individualize sexual exercises. Exercises provide a continuous assessment to identify anxieties, inhibitions, and lack of skills. Behavioral exercises help the couple build sexual comfort and skill. Reading, discussing, and processing the exercises helps change cognitions, perceptions, and feelings (McCarthy & McCarthy, 2002).

Therapy sessions are structured, especially at the beginning. The first agenda item is to discuss experiences and exercises of the previous week. The therapist does a fine-grain analysis of the positive and negative attitudes, behaviors, and emotions elicited by the exercises. Initiation patterns, comfort level, receptivity, and responsivity to specific pleasuring techniques, interfering anxieties or inhibitions, and subjective and objective arousal are carefully explored. The model of personal responsibility for sexuality and being an intimate team is reinforced. The therapist is active, especially in the early stages of therapy, serving as a permission giver, sex educator, and advocate for intimate sexuality. As therapy progresses, the couple takes increasing responsibility for processing experiences and feelings, creating their own agenda, moving to individualized and free-form sexual experiences, exploring personal and relational anxieties and vulnerabilities, and acknowledging strengths and valued characteristics. Therapy becomes less sexually focused and more intimacy focused. The meanings of intimacy and sexuality are explored as well as setting positive, realistic expectations for couple sexuality.

An individualized relapse prevention plan is an integral component of sex therapy. Learning to be sexually functional is easier than integrating sexual expression into the couple's life. Researchers have reported high levels of relapse among couples, so it is crucial to have a program to maintain and generalize sexual gains and prevent relapse. Key to maintaining therapeutic gains are positive, realistic (nonperfectionistic) expectations. Partners who accept a variable, flexible sexual style and who realize it is normal to have occasional mediocre, unsatisfying, or dysfunctional experiences will be inoculated against sexual problems associated with physical and relational aging. Common relapse prevention techniques are to keep the session time, but rather than go to therapy session, have an intimacy date at home; to have a pleasuring session with a ban on intercourse (and perhaps a ban on orgasm) every 4 to 8 weeks so you reinforce the importance of sensuality; to develop and play out a new erotic scenario every 6 to 12 months, and, when there is an unsatisfying or dysfunctional encounter, to initiate a sensual or erotic date within 1 to 3 days. If the couple has not had a sexual encounter for 2 weeks, the partner with higher desire initiates a sexual date; if that does not occur, the other partner initiates a pleasuring date during the next week; if that does not occur and the couple has gone a month without a sexual connection, they schedule a "booster" therapy session. The couple is committed to not fall into the cycle of anticipatory anxiety, tense and performance-oriented sex, and avoidance. They maintain a cycle of positive anticipation and feeling they deserve sexuality to enhance their relationship, broad-based, pleasure-oriented sexual experiences, and maintain a regular rhythm of sexual connection.

The two worst mistakes therapists make are diverting the sexual focus and prematurely terminating treatment as soon as sex becomes functional. The therapist and couple may collude in avoidance because sexual dysfunction can be a sensitive and anxiety-provoking area, especially discussing erotic scenarios and techniques. It is crucial to deal with inhibitions and avoidance; for example, the man's fear of the "wax and wane" erection exercise or the woman's intimidation by exercises to guide a partner's hand or mouth to increase eroticism. The therapist stays with the therapeutic strategy and processes and refines the sexual exercises. Unless the clinician is willing and able to structure therapy so that sexual problems are confronted directly and anxieties, inhibitions, and skill deficits are dealt with, the goal of developing a vital, resilient sexual style will not be achieved.

SEX THERAPY WITH DIVERSE POPULATIONS

Sex therapy strategies and techniques can be modified for use with people without partners, nonmarried couples, and gay and lesbian couples. Sexual interventions and exercises must be altered and individualized in a sensitive manner, but the basic format is transferable. For people without partners, use of masturbation and fantasy exercises, bibliotherapy, guided imagery, modeling using psychoeducational videotapes, and discussing how to choose an appropriate partner and disclose the sexual dysfunction are possible interventions.

SEX THERAPY AND SEXUAL TRAUMA

Another significant group consists of couples where one or both partners have a history of sexual trauma. The major forms of sexual trauma are childhood sexual abuse, incest, and rape. Negative sexual experiences can be broadly defined to include dealing with an unwanted pregnancy, contracting a sexually transmitted disease, experiencing a sexual dysfunction, being sexually humiliated or rejected, guilt over masturbation, shame about sexual fantasies, being exhibited to or peeped on, receiving obscene phone calls, or being sexually harassed. Negative, confusing, guilt-inducing, or traumatic sexual experiences are almost universal phenomena for both men and women, whether in childhood, adolescence, adulthood, or old age.

The cognitive–behavioral approach to sexual trauma centers around two concepts. The first is that when the traumatized person is able to experience desire, arousal, orgasm, and feel intimately bonded, he/she has taken back control of sexuality. The person has become a proud survivor, not an angry or passive victim. The second concept is the challenge to the partner and couple to be "partners in healing" (Maltz, 2001). If the traumatized person vetoes a sexual behavior, the veto is respected and honored, which is the opposite of what occurred with sexual abuse. Couple sexuality is voluntary, mutual, and pleasure-oriented.

FUTURE DIRECTIONS

The major needs in the field are threefold. First, empirical research is needed on both the process and outcome of sex therapy, especially with minority, gay, and nonmarried populations, as well as multiproblem couples. Second, research on a model to integrate medical interventions (especially Viagra and testosterone) into a couple's intimacy, pleasuring, and eroticism style is imperative. Third, how to prevent relapse and generalize sexual gains to the couple's greater relationship should be explored.

SUMMARY

Cognitive–behavioral sex therapy is a subspecialty field requiring the therapist to be comfortable and competent with individual therapy, couple therapy, assessing sexual function and dysfunction, and designing interventions and exercises to confront sexual problems and develop a comfortable, functional couple sexual style. Couple sex therapy enhances desire, arousal, orgasm, and satisfaction. The prescription for healthy, integrated sexuality is intimacy, nondemand pleasuring, and erotic scenarios and techniques. Each person is responsible for his/her own sexuality, and the couple is an intimate team. These are core concepts in the assessment, treatment, and relapse prevention of sexual problems.

See also: Couples therapy

REFERENCES

Barlow, D. (1986). Causes of sexual dysfunction: The role of anxiety and cognitive interference. *Journal of Consulting and Clinical Psychology, 54*, 140–148.

Laumann, E., Gagnon, J., Michael, R., & Michaels, S. (1994). *The social organization of sexuality*. Chicago: University of Chicago Press.

Leiblum, S., & Rosen, R. (Eds.). (2000). *Principles and practice of sex therapy* (3rd ed.). New York: Guilford Press.

LoPiccolo, J., & Friedman, J. (1988). Broad-based treatment of low sexual desire. In S. Leiblum & R. Rosen (Eds.), *Sexual desire disorders* (pp. 107–144). New York: Guilford Press.

McCarthy, B. (2002). Sexuality, sexual dysfunction, and couple therapy. In A. Gurman & N. Jacobson (Eds.), *Clinical handbook of couple therapy* (3rd ed., pp. 629–652). New York: Guilford Press.

McCarthy, B. (2003). Marital sex as it ought to be. *Journal of Family Psychotherapy, 14*(2), 1–12.

McCarthy, B., & McCarthy, E. (2002). *Sexual awareness: Couple sexuality for the twenty-first century*. New York: Carroll & Graf.

McCarthy, B., & McCarthy, E. (2003). *Rekindling desire: A step-by-step program to help low-sex and no-sex marriages*. New York: Brunner–Routledge.

Maltz, W. (2001). *The sexual healing journey*. New York: HarperCollins.

Masters, W., & Johnson, V. (1970). *Human sexual inadequacy*. Boston: Little, Brown.

Sexual Offenders and Paraphilias

W. L. Marshall

Keywords: sexual offenders, paraphilia

In the early development of current behavioral (now cognitive–behavioral) approaches to the treatment of sexual offenders and paraphilics, almost all programs involved individual contacts between a single therapist and a single client. Since the late 1970s, programs for these clients have moved to progressively greater use of group therapy (still cognitive–behavioral in approach) with individual therapy being used either to facilitate or consolidate the benefits from group therapy, or to address those targets (e.g., deviant sexual arousal) that seem more suited to individual work. At least one current program (Marshall, Anderson, & Fernandez, 1999) conducts all treatment (including instructions for, and monitoring procedures aimed at, deviant arousal) in a group context.

The first modern interventions for paraphilics within a behavioral approach appeared in the late 1950s. However, there were far earlier examples of what today would be called behavioral treatments for these problems (Laws & Marshall, 2003). In keeping with the principle of parsimony, the problem behaviors of both sexual offenders and paraphilics were originally construed in the simplest terms. It was claimed that these individuals had developed through experience a sexual preference for unusual or deviant sexual acts. This notion was captured in the belief that eliminating a desire for sexually deviant behaviors would automatically lead to the development of normal sexual outlets. While this notion seems rather naive today, it served the field well in focusing attention on the need to develop procedures to reduce deviant responding.

From the late 1950s through the early 1970s a variety of procedures were utilized to reduce deviant sexual interests. The majority of these treatments involved aversive therapy which associated deviant stimuli with distressing agents such as nausea-inducing drugs, electric shocks, foul odors, or unpleasant covert images. The early British pioneers included Isaac Marks, John Bancroft, Stanley Rachman, Phil Feldman, and Malcolm McCulloch. Foremost among the early North American pioneers was Gene Abel but he was supported by Barry Maletzky, Richard Laws, Nicholas Groth, Vernon Quinsey, and others.

These early treatment approaches focusing on sexual preferences fortunately had available an assessment procedure that could identify problematic preferences in need of change and then evaluate whether or not changes were induced by treatment. This assessment procedure has been called "plethysmography" or "phallometry" and a large number of studies have examined its use. While there are still some psychometric problems with phallometry, it remains an important tool in the pre- and posttreatment assessment of both deviant and unusual sexual interests.

As the field progressed, it became obvious that additional components needed to be added for treatment to be effective. A variety of procedures were developed to enhance sexual arousal to normative sexual acts and partners, and procedures were added to broaden sexual knowledge, develop social skills, reduce cognitive distortions, and increase empathy (Marshall & Laws, 2003). At present, treatment programs for sexual offenders are quite comprehensive in the issues they address but by contrast the other paraphilias have received less attention, particularly in recent years (Laws & O'Donohue, 1997).

As we have seen from the mid-1970s on, treatment programs based on CBT for sexual offenders became progressively more comprehensive in the range of targets that were addressed. Current views of the treatment needs of sexual offenders and other paraphilics, derive essentially from a social learning view of human behavior. In this view, which integrates conditioning and social learning, sexual deviance is said to be acquired by the same processes that govern the acquisition of normative sexual interests (see Laws & Marshall, 1990, for illustrations). Since social learning analyses include not just the acquisition of overt behaviors but also schemas, attitudes, perceptions, and feelings, comprehensive CBT programs cover a broad range of issues. Current programs address the topics described below.

OVERCOMING RESISTANCE

Many sexual offenders, and to some degree all nonoffending paraphilics, offer some resistance to treatment. Some men convicted of sexual offenses deny having committed any crime despite in most cases clear evidence to the contrary. Even if they admit having offended, some are still resistant to treatment. Similarly, nonoffending paraphilics may be reluctant to give up their desired activity. Many fetishists or transvestites come to treatment only after pressure from spouses or other family members. Under these circumstances it is clear that the clients are at best, equivocal about abandoning their unusual sexual interests.

The most common responses to resistance in these clients are either to adopt a motivational interviewing approach or to develop a specific pretreatment program aimed at overcoming resistance. Not all clients, however, respond to these efforts. At least one program has been developed specifically for those who categorically deny having offended and who are unresponsive to attempts to overcome their resistance to entering standard treatment.

ACCEPTANCE OF RESPONSIBILITY

Accepting responsibility is thought to be critical in the treatment of sexual offenders but may also be relevant to nonoffending paraphilics. Sexual offenders characteristically attribute responsibility for their crimes to factors (abuse as a child) or people (their victims) external to themselves or to features of themselves that they claim disrupt their control (e.g., brain injury or intoxication). These offenders also tend to minimize aspects of their crimes. These issues are seen as obstacles to progress in treatment.

Once clients are comfortable in the treatment setting, therapists begin a process of firmly, but supportively, challenging the variety of client features that reflect a failure to accept responsibility. Independent information from other sources (spouse, family, friends, police, prosecutors) facilitates these challenges. Some therapists use polygraphy to access information that my help overcome resistance to accepting responsibility, although critics have challenged the scientific bases of polygraphy.

COGNITIVE DISTORTIONS

This descriptor is used here to refer to cognitive processes (i.e., structures, propositions, operations, and products) that mediate or translate incoming stimuli within the context of stored memories of past experience and motivational states that may be enduring or transient. Included here are schemas, attitudes, and beliefs, as well as current feeling states, that bias the interpretation of information in a self-serving way. Cognitive restructuring approaches are typically employed to challenge the client's views, identify the bases for and costs of such views, and offer alternative views that are more likely to serve the long-term needs of the client. Since these views are often dependent on the client's current desires and feelings, it is helpful when challenging these views to have the client role-play a scene that re-creates, to some degree, these influential desires and feelings. The relevant desires are related to the particular client's problematic behaviors, while the relevant feeling states are often idiosyncratic. Anger, for example, may be relevant to some rapists, whereas depressed mood or feelings of low self-worth may be more relevant to some child molesters.

EMPATHY

Sexual offender programs typically target the enhancement of empathy as a feature separate from cognitive distortions. This is based on the idea that sexual offenders lack empathy either toward all people or at the least toward all victims of sexual abuse. Recent research (see Fernandez, 2002), however, suggests that the majority of sexual offenders primarily lack empathy toward their own victims and that these empathy deficits are simply another manifestation of their cognitive distortions; in this case minimizations about the harm done to their victims. Approaching empathy problems with these clients, then, is best done using cognitive restructuring to address inappropriate views about the damage to victims.

SELF-ESTEEM

Enhancing the self-esteem of sexual offenders and other paraphilics is seen as essential to facilitating a commitment to the treatment process as well as bolstering the client's confidence that he can manage a problem-free life. Although currently available evidence indicates that these clients are lacking in a sense of self-worth, the enhancement of their self-esteem is both possible and facilitates changes in various other treatment targets. It is best to initiate procedures to enhance self-esteem as early as possible in treatment (or even in pretreatment programs) as it is difficult, for example, to challenge distortions effectively unless the client has the confidence to accept that there are other ways of construing his world.

SOCIAL FUNCTIONING

While some of these clients have broad-based social difficulties, the majority seem able to function reasonably effectively in most social situations. For those who are poorly equipped socially, programs have been developed to increase appropriate assertiveness, improve control over the expression of anger, and enhance the accuracy of social perceptions.

The most consistent social deficits displayed by sexual offenders concern intimate relationships. Intimacy deficits and emotional loneliness characterize most sexual offenders, and their style of attaching to others is typically inadequate. Programs have been developed to train sexual offenders to become more effective in intimate relationships and these have been shown to decrease loneliness and to enhance feelings of intimacy with their partners and friends. To date, similar approaches have not been reported for nonoffending paraphilics.

MOOD AND STRESS MANAGEMENT

Anger management is essential to the treatment of many sexual offenders. Jealousy is also a common problem but this is typically addressed within the component targeting intimacy skills. Other emotional problems have also been identified. For example, Ward (1999) described general problems in self-regulatory processes that included problematic emotional regulation. He suggested a variety of approaches to address this issue including impulse control techniques and mood management training.

When sexual offenders fail to cope effectively with issues, they respond with one or more negative emotions which trigger processes that unfold over time and, too frequently, end in offending behavior. A combination of stress management, training in an appropriate coping style, and enhancing specific coping skills is aimed at producing more adaptive responses to stress.

Recently CBT programs for sexual offenders have introduced procedures aimed at shifting clients' responses to their offending behaviors from shame to guilt. Evidence from the general psychological literature indicates that whereas guilt motivates people to change, shame encourages people to believe they are incapable of change. Distinguishing behaviors from the person reflects a traditional behavioral approach and shame is reflected in statements such as "I am a bad person" whereas guilt might impel the same person to say, "I did a bad thing."

SEXUAL PREFERENCES

As noted earlier, sexual preferences have been the focus of behavioral treatment for the paraphilias since its inception. Procedures have been developed for both the reduction of deviant sexual desires and an enhancement of desire for appropriate sexual activities. While aversive conditioning procedures utilizing electric shocks or nausea-inducing agents to reduce deviant interests have lost popularity, similar procedures using foul odors or aversive imagery remain part of many CBT programs, although the evidence supporting their effectiveness is limited. Alternative procedures such as satiation therapy have somewhat stronger support and appear to produce a more enduring loss of interest in deviant acts. Many programs also employ pharmacological agents (e.g., antiandrogens or SSRIs) to dampen sexual drive, or provide greater control over sexual impulses, for those clients who have highly repetitive and strong deviant urges.

Procedures for enhancing sexual interest in normative practices have primarily been restricted to one or another variation on masturbatory reconditioning. These procedures essentially require the client to deliberately replace deviant thoughts with appropriate sexual images during masturbation. Again the evidence is not strongly supportive but these procedures remain popular.

RELAPSE PREVENTION

Adopted in the early 1980s from the addiction field, RP procedures assist the client in identifying the factors (both background factors, such as poor coping styles, mood management problems, and substance abuse, as well as problem situations and thoughts) that put him at risk to sexually reoffend or reengage his paraphilia. These procedures are meant to reveal to the client the behaviors, thoughts, feelings, and situations that will make self-control more difficult. He is to avoid these factors as far as possible, or cope with them effectively should they unexpectedly occur. Recent reformulations of RP applied to sexual offenders have shifted the focus to more positive, enjoyable behaviors and thoughts that are exclusive of offending.

It is only in recent years that it has been possible to examine the long-term effects of CBT treatment for sexual offenders. Researchers have had to wait until a sufficient number of treated offenders had been released for a sufficient amount of time (at least 5 years) to examine relative rates of relapse. To date, there are no satisfactory studies of the long-term outcome of these programs with other paraphilias.

Early evaluations simply focused on determining the immediate effects of attempts to change sexual preferences. While this was important, the primary interest is whether or not the changes induced by treatment reduced subsequent relapses.

Early evaluations of the literature on long-term outcome for treatment with sexual offenders presented a seemingly dismal picture. These reviews, however, included numerous non-CBT programs. In an attempt to more carefully evaluate CBT programs, the Association for the Treatment of Sexual Abusers (ATSA) formed a committee of experts whose task was to search the literature, identify methodologically sound studies, and evaluate overall outcome. Forty-two studies involving over 9000 subjects were identified as meeting criteria. The evaluation demonstrated clear advantages for the treated subjects (Hanson et al., 2002). Further analyses revealed that it was only CBT programs operating since 1980 that produced effective reductions in reoffending.

CRITICISMS OF CBT

Given that CBT programs for sexual offenders are effective, it is difficult to think of many criticisms. Perhaps the most significant criticism has to do with the way in which many of these programs are delivered. The typical, and for the most part admirable, behavioral concern about specifying all aspects of treatment, has, unfortunately, led in some cases to the production of highly detailed and extensive treatment manuals. These meticulous manuals have, in turn, resulted in treatment being presented in a psychoeducational format as if therapy was an educational process. In this approach it is assumed that the influence of the therapist is minimal. Contrary to these ideas, recent research has shown that the behavior of the therapist in CBT with sexual offenders has a marked effect on the changes induced by treatment (Marshall et al., 2002). In addition, this and similar research demonstrated that adopting a confrontational approach when challenging sexual offenders produces no benefits and yet some therapists continue to employ a confrontative style.

Perhaps the most telling criticism is the neglect in recent years of attention to the development of comprehensive treatment programs for the nonoffending paraphilics. A recent thorough appraisal of the field of sexual deviance (Laws & O'Donohue, 1997) revealed that the programs suggested for fetishisms, transvestisms, masochisms, and various other nonoffending paraphilias, were simply adaptations of those developed for sexual offenders. No doubt there are aspects that these two sets of sexual problems have in common but there are also clear differences, not the least of which is the presence or absence of victims. Programs for the nonoffending paraphilias need to be based on evidence derived from these disorders; not simply the transfer of programs from other sexual problems.

DIRECTIONS FOR THE FUTURE

The most important future directions concern the need to: more fully develop training programs for therapists; more fully emphasize the role of the therapist in treatment; and generate problem-specific treatment programs for the nonoffending paraphilias. On this latter point, it seems that research interest in these clients has significantly waned in the past 20 years as attention has shifted to the more socially disruptive sexual offenders. While this makes some sense, it has led to the relative neglect of many of the paraphilias except among medical treatment providers who have shown the value of the SSRIs with these clients.

Continued research on the features of sexually problematic clients should inevitably lead to an increase in the targets addressed in treatment. Recent research has led to many changes in treatment programs and hopefully programs will continue to evolve in response to research findings.

Finally, modifications to current treatment approaches to emphasize the development of prosocial behaviors that increase life satisfaction among sexual offenders should prove beneficial. For example, attainment of a "good life" (Ward, 2002) by these offenders can be expected to represent a lifestyle that is exclusive of offending.

See also: Child abuse, Sex offending

REFERENCES

Fernandez, Y. M. (Ed.). (2002). *In their shoes: Examining the issue of empathy and its place in the treatment of offenders*. Oklahoma City, OK: Wood N' Barnes Publishing.

Hanson, R. K., Gordon, A., Harris, A. J. R., Marques, J. K., Murphy, W. D., Quinsey, V. L., & Seto, M. C. (2002). First report of the collaborative outcome data project on the effectiveness of psychological treatment for sex offenders. *Sexual Abuse: A Journal of Research and Treatment, 14*, 169–194.

Laws, D. R., & Marshall, W. L. (1990). A conditioning theory of the etiology and maintenance of deviant sexual preference and behavior. In W. L. Marshall, D. R. Laws, & H. E. Barbaree (Eds.), *Handbook of sexual assault: Issues, theories, and treatment of the offender* (pp. 209–229). New York: Plenum Press.

Laws, D. R., & Marshall, W. L. (2003). A brief history of behavioral and cognitive–behavioral approaches to sexual offenders: Part 1. Early developments. *Sexual Abuse: A Journals of Research and Treatment, 15*(2), 75–92.

Laws, D. R., & O'Donohue, W. (Eds.). (1997). *Sexual deviance: Theory, assessment, and treatment*. New York: Guilford Press.

Marshall, W. L., Anderson, D., & Fernandez, Y. M. (1999). *Cognitive behavioural treatment of sexual offenders*. New York: Wiley.

Marshall, W. L., & Laws, D. R. (2003). A brief history of behavioral and cognitive–behavioral approaches to sexual offenders: Part 2. The modern era. *Sexual Abuse: A Journal of Research and Treatment, 15*(2), 98–120.

Marshall, W. L., Serran, G., Moulden, H., Mulloy, R., Fernandez, Y. M., Mann, R. E., & Thornton, D. (2002). Therapist features in sexual offender treatment: Their reliable identification and influence on behavior change. *Clinical Psychology and Psychotherapy, 9*, 395–405.

Ward, T. (1999). A self-regulation model of the relapse process in sexual offenders. In B. K. Schwartz (Ed.), *The sex offender: Theoretical advances, treating special populations and legal developments* (pp. 6.1–6.8). Kingston, NJ: Civic Research Institute.

Ward, T. (2002). Good lives and the rehabilitation of offenders: Promises and problems. *Aggression and Violent Behavior: A Review Journal, 7*, 513–528.

RECOMMENDED READINGS

Marshall, W. L., Fernandez, Y. M., Hudson, S. M., & Ward, T. (Eds.). (1998). *Sourcebook of treatment programs for sexual offenders*. New York: Plenum Press.

Schwartz, B. K. (Ed.). (2002). *The sex offender: Current treatment modalities and systems issues* (Vol. IV). Kingston, NJ: Civic Research Institute.

Sleep Disorders

Kelly L. Gilrain and Jacqueline D. Kloss

Keywords: sleep disorders, sleep apnea, insomnia, jet lag, narcolepsy

Millions of Americans suffer from sleep disorders including, but not limited to, sleep apnea, insomnia, narcolepsy, restless legs syndrome, and circadian rhythm disorders. While the quality, extent, and severity of these symptoms depend on the nature and course of each particular condition, sleep disorders pose a serious personal and public health concern. Individuals with sleep problems may encounter a myriad of adverse nighttime and daytime sequelae ranging from frustration due to difficulty in falling or staying asleep at night, to excessive daytime sleepiness. Impaired concentration, fatigue, irritability, anxiety, depression, substance abuse (caffeine or alcohol), general physical malaise, compromised occupational performance, and interpersonal or marital distress are also among the most commonly reported symptoms. With some conditions, such as untreated narcolepsy or apnea, symptoms may even evolve into safety concerns, such as impaired driving due to the effects of sleep deprivation.

Independent of the nature of the dysfunction, sleep disorders are increasingly recognized as a growing public health concern that affects not only individuals' sleep, but also their psychological, social, and physical health. Because of underlying neuroendocrine, respiratory, and neurological etiologies, most sleep disorders are generally considered in the medical arena, and warrant appropriate medical or pharmacologic therapies. Nonetheless, behavioral, cognitive, and affective factors often serve as either contributors or consequences of sleep disorders and warrant attention to mitigate or prevent the impact of these conditions. The emerging area of behavioral sleep medicine incorporates the complex interactions between these psychological factors and physiological symptoms. Specifically, cognitive–behavioral strategies are ideally suited to help individuals manage sleep disorders and enhance quality of life for those who suffer from them.

APPLICATION OF COGNITIVE–BEHAVIORAL THERAPY

Most notably, psychophysiologic insomnia is recognized for its complex multifaceted etiology and manifestation, and is effectively conceptualized and treated through a CBT model. Treatment for primary insomnia with cognitive–behavioral strategies is well-documented and continues to be a rapidly growing area of research (Morin et al., 1999). Therapies such as stimulus control, progressive muscle relaxation, paradoxical intention, and cognitive therapy for insomnia (i.e., challenging dysfunctional beliefs and attitudes specifically about sleep) employ a variety of cognitive–behavioral principles aimed at improving sleep quality. For example, rumination about needing to get a full 8 hours of sleep every night or fear that insomnia will be fatal are common irrational beliefs that are likely to lead to cognitive or physiological arousal—states incompatible with sleep. In turn, the inability to sleep is likely to lead to further rumination, creating a vicious cycle. Employment of paradoxical intention (requesting that the patient *try to stay awake*) or challenging maladaptive cognitions, such as "I *need* to get 8 hours of sleep to function tomorrow," are shown to help break that cycle and therefore lead to greater sleep ability. In doing so, these therapies address the interplay between mind (e.g., cognitions) and body (e.g., levels of arousal or tension), and thereby enhance sleep quality.

While many other sleep disorders (e.g., sleep apnea, narcolepsy) have underlying physiological or neurological bases, strategies derived from cognitive–behavioral principles may be particularly useful in helping individuals prevent the exacerbation of symptoms, cope with the sequelae of such disorders, or increase compliance with medical treatment regimens. However, research on the application of cognitive–behavioral strategies for sleep disorders other than insomnia is relatively unexplored. Although very few cognitive–behavioral strategies have been empirically evaluated for disorders other than primary insomnia, the purpose of this article, therefore, is to target the psychological factors that contribute to these disorders and introduce how we can apply cognitive–behavioral models, principles, or techniques to a variety of common sleep disorders. Following is a synopsis of a select group of sleep disorders that are chosen to exemplify how cognitive and behavioral approaches are effectively or may potentially be applied.

DELAYED SLEEP PHASE SYNDROME AND ADVANCED SLEEP PHASE SYNDROME

The circadian rhythm disorders are characterized by chronophysiologic dysfunction—a desynchrony between environmental sleep/wake cycles and the actual timing of an individual's internal circadian sleep/wake rhythm. Examples of the circadian rhythm dyssomnias are shift work sleep disorder, delayed sleep phase syndrome (DSPS), advanced sleep phase syndrome (ASPS), and jet lag. DSPS produces sleep-onset insomnia and difficulty in awakening at a desired time when sleep is delayed in relation to the desired clock time. For example, an individual plans to go to bed at 10 p.m. but cannot fall asleep until 2 a.m., this then leads to a much later awakening than anticipated since sleep onset was disrupted. In contrast, ASPS is thought of as compelling evening sleepiness, or earlier onset sleep than an anticipated sleep time resulting in an awakening that is earlier than desired.

To illustrate CBT management, take, for example, a 21-year-old college student who presents with DSPS and complains of daytime symptoms of tiredness, inconsistent academic performance, and difficulty concentrating and attending class in the early morning hours. She tends to function better during later hours of the day and evening, and struggles with getting out of bed to attend her morning classes. Her late-night social activities, erratic sleep schedules, excessive daytime caffeine use, and frequent napping (2–3 hours in the late afternoon on most days)—all behavioral aspects—exacerbate and contribute to the problem.

From a physiological perspective, tools and therapies to buffer shifting of the circadian rhythm such as chronotherapy or bright light in the morning have met with some success (Bromley & Rajput, 1999) and may be tried with her. In addition, lifestyle changes, such as improved sleep hygiene, are often indicated to maintain regular sleep patterns and optimal daytime functioning (Carskadon, 2002). For example, keeping a regular wake-up time is critical so that the drive for sleep at night is sufficient enough to induce sleepiness at the desired bedtime. Psychoeducation to explain the adverse effects of her sleep-affecting behaviors and lifestyle, is often necessary for better sleep, but may not be sufficient in these circumstances. Cognitive and underlying beliefs also become increasingly relevant. Although she may "know the rules" and understand how behaviors affect her sleep, she may have difficulty implementing them when confronted with enticing late-night social activities or the drive to stay asleep when her alarm is buzzing at 8 a.m. For example, she may believe that "in order for me to be accepted by my peers I must party all night—no matter what cost to my sleep" or "pulling an 'all-nighter' will ensure I get an A." In these circumstances, evaluation of maladaptive cognitions and unrealistic beliefs and attitudes about college life, sleep, and performance may be undertaken. For example, her report of "I *can't* get out of bed until noon" might be reexamined and altered to "Although it's difficult to get out of bed, I can gradually work on trying to get up by 9 a.m. every day."

In addition, decision-making strategies that employ cost–benefit analyses may be employed to help her accommodate lifestyle changes without extensive cost to social activities or academic performance. While it may be unrealistic to keep her (or any adult) on a regimented schedule, helping her to understand the importance of sleep, her own sleep predisposition, and how it fits in with social, recreational, and academic activities would be beneficial. In a similar way, elderly individuals who are more prone to ASPS may benefit from decision-making, evaluation of dysfunctional beliefs and attitudes about sleep and performance, and cost–benefit analyses in extending bedtime and delaying wake-up time.

JET LAG

According to the ICSD (1997), jet lag is characterized by degrees of difficulty in initiating or maintaining sleep, the existence of excessive sleepiness, decrements in subjective daytime alertness and performance, and somatic symptoms (e.g., gastrointestinal function) following rapid travel across multiple time zones. This disturbance is closely related to shift work sleep disorder which is characterized by insomnia or excessive sleepiness that occurs as a transient phenomenon in relation to work schedules that are inconsistent with one's circadian rhythm.

From a pharmacological perspective, many individuals have found relief by utilizing medications (i.e., benzodiazepines) to assist with jet lag. Unfortunately, these drugs tend to simply promote sleep rather than adjust circadian rhythms, thus leading to continued difficulties with initiation and maintenance of sleep. Although the research on melatonin is equivocal, it may be effective in increasing sleep quality and reducing subjective ratings of jet lag. Further research is needed to determine the appropriate amount and timing of administration of this substance. Light exposure therapy for jet lag has also been found to be a potential treatment for individuals attempting to readapt their circadian rhythm after a flight. Alternatively, several behavioral strategies have been recommended to reduce the impact of jet lag: select specific flights that will allow early evening arrival, anticipate the time change for trips by getting up and going to bed earlier several days prior to an eastward trip and later for a westward trip, change your watch to the destination time zone, avoid alcohol or caffeine at least 3 to 4 hours before bedtime (since both act as "stimulants" and prevent sleep), avoid heavy meals, avoid heavy exercise close to bedtime.

SHIFT WORK

Boivin and James (2003) have also examined the usefulness of melatonin in the area of shift work. While melatonin has brought about modest improvement in increasing alertness and sleep quality for those working night shifts, it has had much lower efficacy in treatment protocols compared to bright light exposure. Research has demonstrated that light exposure has been an effective means of promoting circadian adaptation to night-shift work. This light should be administered at the beginning of the shift period in short or intermittent segments. Additionally, shielding these individuals from morning light and timing the sleep/dark periods produces phase shifts, which allow the individual to engage in more appropriate sleep cycles. Behavioral strategies have also been recommended for shift work difficulties including strategic napping. While short naps during specific times of the day have been found to decrease sleepiness and increase vigilance levels, these naps are to be timed so as not to interfere with appropriate sleep adaptation. For instance, if naps are utilized too frequently, they may ultimately shorten one's sleep drive (hence creating insomnia at bedtime) or create the desire for more frequent napping during work hours. One other precaution is that naps can also produce a transient period of sleep inertia—a groggy feeling on awakening that often leads to reduced levels of neurobehavioral functioning and performance.

NARCOLEPSY

Narcolepsy is a disorder characterized by four hallmark symptoms: (1) excessive daytime sleepiness which is most prominent, (2) cataplexy, (3) sleep paralysis, and (4) hypnagogic hallucinations. At times, the urge to sleep can be so irresistible that the individual experiences a sleep attack. It is primarily treated through the use of stimulants and antidepressants. Stimulants are the treatment of choice and are useful in keeping the individual awake but are not effective in relieving other symptoms and signs associated with the disorder (e.g., cataplexy, REM onset sleep). Antidepressants have been helpful in the regulation of REM sleep and cataplexy (Mahowald, 2002) and may even be helpful in managing depression that is often comorbid with narcolepsy.

Behavioral strategies that focus on psychoeducation, specifically the symptoms and risks associated with narcolepsy, may prove beneficial. As noted by Krahn, Black, and Silver (2001), behavioral management should focus on the prevention of sleep deprivation, by maintenance of regular sleep and wake times, engagement in a stimulating environment, and avoidance of shift work. Periodic naps throughout the day may also assist with some of the symptoms associated with narcolepsy. To minimize sleep inertia, shorter naps and sufficient wake-up times are recommended.

In addition, individuals with narcolepsy often confront interpersonal or occupational challenges that range from excessive sleepiness, yawning, or sleep attack, which can be quite socially embarrassing, to a lack of energy or motivation for social or occupational activity. As with any medical condition that leads to significant impact on quality of life, coping effectively with adverse sequelae is often paramount to therapeutic intervention. For example, because of social withdrawal or the inability to fully meet work expectations, negative self-evaluations or negative evaluations from others, and concomitant feelings of depression are not uncommon. Cognitive therapy targeted at these negative self-evaluations or catastrophic thinking, such as "I can't function at all when I am so sleepy," may be indicated as well as CBT for depression, if needed.

Sleep Apnea

Sleep apnea is a disordered breathing condition that is characterized by the constriction of the airway during sleep. Due to disrupted sleep throughout the night, individuals report tiredness, fatigue, sleepiness, memory and judgment problems, irritability, difficulty concentrating, and personality changes. Medical treatments involve nasal continuous positive airway pressure (CPAP), oral/dental devices, and surgical procedures to eliminate sleep fragmentation, apneas, and oxygen desaturation. CPAP, one of the most effective and widely used therapies, requires the patient to wear a mask. This mask fits over the apneic's face during sleep to assist with breathing. Despite the effectiveness of CPAP, the discomfort associated with wearing the mask, its cumbersome nature, and, for some, the sensation or fear of suffocation, often deters patients from its use. Therefore, compliance with utilization of the CPAP device is low and is an obstacle to effective management of sleep apnea (Sage, Southcott, & Brown, 2001). Cognitive–behavioral strategies can play a significant role by improving adherence and helping patients overcome their fears of suffocation.

Prochaska and colleagues' Stages of Change Model is a useful framework to increase motivation or readiness to change with a variety of behaviors (smoking cessation, weight loss, use of sunscreen), and may be well suited to conceptualize how to increase compliance to CPAP. The goal would be to use stage-appropriate strategies to motivate CPAP candidates from a precontemplative stage to contemplative stage, and eventually to the action and maintenance stage. To illustrate, consistent with the health belief model, if the symptoms are not perceived as distressful or if the treatment is worse than the problem itself, the patient may not readily engage in the recommended regimen, despite the adverse consequences to his or her mental and physical health. Motivational interviewing strategies, such as raising cognitive dissonance and evaluating use of CPAP through a cost–benefit analysis, may enhance readiness to adopt the therapy. Consequently, this may allow one to move someone from a precontemplative to contemplative stage, and furthermore to action and maintenance stages of change.

Alternatively, therapists might consider exposure-based models or systematic desensitization strategies to help patients overcome any anticipatory anxiety and fears of suffocation with regard to wearing the mask. Modeling may also be employed to demonstrate how fellow apnea patients successfully cope with the cumbersome treatment. Other treatment has focused on the reduction of snoring, sleepiness, and improvement in quality of life through the reduction of symptoms. More recently, researchers have begun to explore behavioral strategies that will assist apneics through the promotion of weight loss, avoidance of alcohol and other sedatives before sleep, and avoidance of the supine sleep position, each of which exacerbates apnea.

RESTLESS LEGS SYNDROME/PERIODIC LIMB MOVEMENT SYNDROME

Diagnostic features of restless legs syndrome (RLS) include an uncomfortable sensation in the legs accompanied by the urge to move one's legs. This sensation begins or worsens during periods of inactivity and relief is brought about through movement of the limbs. Periodic limb movements in sleep (PLMS) are repetitive movements, most commonly seen in the lower limbs, that occur every 20–40 seconds and are typically brief muscle twitches, jerking movements, or an upward flexing of the feet. These movements can also be comprised of involuntary flexing of the hips, knees, and ankles that affect sleep in the initiation and maintenance stages and cause fatigue, exhaustion, and excessive daytime somnolence. Approximately 80% of patients with RLS also have PLMS.

While walking or stretching may temporarily alleviate the sensations, current treatment of these disorders has leaned toward medications such as benzodiazepines, opioids, and dopaminergic agents. From a behavioral perspective, some symptom relief may be derived from practice of good sleep hygiene (Hening, 2002). For individuals with a mild case of RLS, psychoeducation on sleep, wake, and activity regulation, sleep setting and influences, can assist the individual to regulate behaviors that may be contributing to or exacerbating the dysfunctional movements. These behaviors include regular and adequate sleep hours, as sleep deprivation tends to aggravate RLS. Exercise has been found to assist with the modification of RLS, yet only a moderate amount of exercise has been found to be beneficial since excessive exercise may cause increased exacerbation of symptoms (Hening, 2002). Although behavioral therapies show promise in the decrease of symptoms, empirical support for these findings is not yet available and it is unlikely that these will sufficiently alleviate suffering. For example, while massage and cold compresses may provide temporary relief of symptoms, their effects are not long-lasting. Overall behavioral changes need to be determined on an individual basis, by targeting which activities may worsen or improve the symptoms of RLS. Behavioral changes that have been reported to be helpful for individuals with this disorder include a healthy balanced diet, walking, stretching, hot or cold bath, massage, acupressure, and practicing relaxation techniques (such as biofeedback, meditation, or yoga). Additionally, some individuals report that keeping their minds engaged in other activities (discussion, needlework, video games) assists with problematic symptoms while traveling.

BRUXISM

Bruxism, a movement disorder characterized by the grinding or clenching of the teeth during sleep, is related to the level of stress experienced by an individual (Long & Miltenberg, 1998). If we are able to reduce one's level of stress, we thereby may be able to decrease bruxism. The severity of bruxism may even be an index of their level of stress. CBT has been found to be effective in the reduction of stress and anxiety (Chambless & Ollendick, 2000). Future treatment for this disorder should examine the contributions of anxiety, stress, and underlying cognition as this information could lead to the development of beneficial cognitive and behavioral interventions.

NIGHTMARES

According to the ICSD (1997), nightmares are frightening dreams that usually awaken an individual from REM sleep. The DSM-IV indicates that nightmares are characterized by repeated awakenings from a sleep period with comprehensive recall of extremely frightening dreams. Themes usually involve threats to survival, security, or self-esteem. Estimates are that 10–50% of children between 3 and 5 years old have nightmares that may disturb their parents and approximately 75% of individuals can remember one or more nightmares in the course of their childhood. While 50% of adults report having at least an occasional nightmare, the condition of frequent nightmares (1+ per week) occurs in only 1% of the population. The most common causes of nightmares are anxiety or stress, the death of a loved one, adverse reaction or withdrawal from drugs and/or alcohol, or other sleep disorders. When assessing nightmares, it is important to distinguish between night terror disorder, delirium, posttraumatic stress disorder, the physiological effects of substance use, or the presence of other sleep disorders since the etiology and treatment of each may vary. Therapies predominantly used for nightmares include psychoeducation about problematic sleep, sleep hygiene, and therapeutic groups where trauma-related nightmares are processed (Daniels & McGuire, 1998). Most recently, imagery rehearsal has been found to be helpful for those experiencing nightmares associated with PTSD as well (Krakow et al., 2001).

In children, simple behavioral strategies can be used to alleviate distress associated with the dark and bedtime. As indicated by Mindell (2003), many parents will enter a child's room and turn on the light if he or she is having a nightmare; this may reinforce the idea that the light equals security and the dark is something to fear. Thus, it may be helpful to comfort the child in the dark or in a semilit room. Performing a functional analysis and determining what triggers, maintains, and reinforces nightmares may be of value to best understand these phenomena, particularly because nightmares are not caused by circadian changes per se; rather they coincide or can disrupt sleep/wake cycles.

SUMMARY AND FUTURE CONSIDERATIONS

Behavioral strategies and lifestyle modifications are paramount to managing sleep disorders and their sequelae. In addition to sleep hygiene, utilizing a cognitive–behavioral approach and conceptualization may produce additive benefit. Similar to helping patients with medical conditions, such as chronic pain or cardiovascular disease, examining the beliefs, attitudes, thoughts, and emotional responses of patients with sleep disorders is likely to provide an even greater understanding and treatment development compared to solely taking a medical-model approach. Charles Morin and colleagues address these factors in patients with insomnia and have achieved considerable success. Extending and combining these principles for patients with other sleep disorders may similarly provide a more comprehensive management compared to medical recommendations alone. While some strategies, such as systematic desensitization or exposure therapy, for CPAP users await further empirical validation, multifaceted approaches that address not only the physiology of sleep and their respective therapies, but also the cognitive aspects are likely to lead to the most holistic and successful responses. Cognitive–behavioral paradigms and techniques may provide new avenues for advancing the treatment of sleep disorders and for enhancing the quality of life among those who are challenged by these conditions.

REFERENCES

Boivin, D. B., & James, F. O. (2003). Insomnia due to circadian rhythm disturbances. In M. P. Szuba, J. D. Kloss, & D. F. Dinges (Eds.), *Principles and management of insomnia* (pp. 155–191). New York: Cambridge University Press.

Bromley, S. M., & Rajput, V. (1999). Chronic insomnia: A practical review. *American Family Physician, 60*(5), 1431–1438.

Carskadon, M. A. (Ed.). (2002). *Adolescent sleep patterns: Biological, social, and psychological influences*. New York: Cambridge University Press.

Chambless, D., & Ollendick, T. (2000). Empirically supported psychological interventions: Controversies and evidence. *Annual Review of Psychology, 52*, 685–716.

Daniels, L., & McGuire, T. (1998). Dreamcatchers. Healing traumatic nightmares using group dreamwork, sand play and other techniques of intervention. *Group, 22*(4), 205–226.

Hening, W. A. (2002). Restless legs syndrome. *Continuum: Lifelong Learning in Neurology, 8*(6), 63–88.

International classification of sleep disorders, revised: Diagnostic and coding manual. (1997). Rochester, MN: American Sleep Disorders Association.

Krahn, L. E., Black, J. L., & Silver, M. H. (2001). Narcolepsy: New understanding of irresistible sleep. *Mayo Clinical Proceedings, 76*, 185–194.

Krakow, B., Hollifield, M., Johnston, L., Koss, M., Schrader, R., Warner, T. D., Tandberg, D., Lauriello, J., McBride, L., Cutchen, L., Cheng, D., Emmons, S., Germain, A., Melendrez, D., Sandoval, D., & Prince, H. (2001). Imagery rehearsal therapy for chronic nightmares in sexual assault survivors with posttraumatic stress disorder: A randomized controlled trial. *Journal of the American Medical Association, 286*(5), 537–545.

Long, E. S., & Miltenberg, R. G. (1998). A review of behavioral and pharmacological treatments for habit disorders in individuals with mental retardation. *Journal of Behavior Therapy and Experimental Psychiatry, 29*, 143–156.

Mahowald, M. W. (2002). Narcolepsy and others causes of hypersomnia. *Continuum: Lifelong Learning in Neurology, 8*(6), 51–62.

Mindell, J. A. (2003). Insomnia in children and adolescents. In M. P. Szuba, J. D. Kloss, & D. F. Dinges (Eds.), *Principles and management of insomnia* (pp. 125–135). New York: Cambridge University Press.

Morin, C. M., Hauri, P. J., Espie, C. A., Spielman, A. J., Buysse, D. J., & Bootzin, R. R. (1999). Nonpharmacologic treatment of chronic insomnia. *Sleep, 22*(8), 1134–1156.

Sage, C. E., Southcott, A., & Brown, S. (2001). The health belief model and compliance with CPAP treatment for obstructive sleep apnea. *Behaviour Change, 18*(3), 177–185.

RECOMMENDED READINGS

Kryger, M. H., Roth, T., & Dement, W. C. (Eds.) (2000). *Principles and practice of sleep medicine*. Philadelphia: Saunders.

Szuba, M. P., Kloss, J. D., & Dinges, D. F. (Eds.). (2003). *Principles and management of insomnia*. New York: Cambridge University Press.

Social Anxiety Disorder 1

Talia I. Zaider and Richard G. Heimberg

Keywords: social anxiety disorder, social phobia, anxiety disorders, adults, children

Social Anxiety Disorder (SAD), also known as social phobia, is characterized by an excessive and persistent fear of one or more social or performance situations. Individuals suffering from SAD endure these situations with acute discomfort, and a great many avoid them altogether. The anxiety and associated avoidance behavior can be crippling, making it difficult for those affected to sustain relationships or function adequately at work, school, or in daily activities. The unrelenting and disruptive nature of SAD symptoms often leads to feelings of depression and hopelessness. Indeed, SAD is often accompanied by additional mood, anxiety, and substance use disorders (Schneier, Johnson, Hornig, Liebowitz, & Weissman, 1992).

SAD has garnered a great deal of research and clinical interest over the past two decades, due in part to a growing recognition of the prevalence of this disorder. Epidemiological data indicate that the lifetime prevalence rate of SAD among adults in the general population may be as high as 13% (Kessler et al., 1994). In the National Comorbidity Survey, SAD was the third most common mental disorder and the most prevalent of the anxiety disorders (Kessler et al., 1994). However, SAD is by no means restricted to adults. Approximately 5.5% of females and 2.7% of males between the ages of 14 and 17 years are afflicted with SAD (Wittchen, Stein, & Kessler, 1999). As with adults, children and adolescents who meet criteria for SAD are beset by numerous adverse outcomes including having few or no friends, deficits in social skills, loneliness, and dysphoria (Beidel, Turner, & Morris, 1999).

TREATMENT FOR ADULTS

The most widely investigated treatment approach for SAD is cognitive–behavioral therapy (CBT). The various treatment strategies that fall under this rubric differ with respect to technique but share certain key characteristics. All are time-limited and empirically guided interventions that, to varying degrees, aim to modify the cognitive, physiological, and behavioral components that contribute to, or maintain, social anxiety symptoms. These therapies include relaxation and social skills training, but most often involve guided, systematic exposure to feared situations and cognitive restructuring techniques. More detailed descriptions of these treatment strategies are provided by several comprehensive reviews (e.g., Turk, Fresco, & Heimberg, 1999).

One particular form of CBT that has earned substantial empirical support is Heimberg's cognitive–behavioral group therapy (CBGT). CBGT is a multicomponent treatment program that integrates cognitive restructuring with therapist-guided exposure exercises that are practiced both in and out of session (Heimberg & Becker, 2002). CBGT was included in a list of empirically supported treatments by the Society of Clinical Psychology's Task Force on Promotion and Dissemination of Psychological Procedures (Chambless et al., 1996). Additionally, CBGT has been associated with enduring benefits; patients who received CBGT maintained treatment gains as long as 4 to 6 years after treatment had ended (Heimberg, Salzman, Holt, & Blendell, 1993).

There is little evidence that the group modality has a clear advantage over individual CBT (Federoff & Taylor, 2001). Nevertheless, there have been recent attempts to provide practitioners in the community with the option of conducting CBT in either format. For example, Heimberg's CBGT for SAD was adapted for use with individual clients, and preliminary findings revealed effect sizes that compare favorably to the group treatment (Zaider, Heimberg, Roth, Hope, & Turk, 2003). A somewhat different picture is presented by a study comparing individual and group cognitive therapy based on Clark and Wells's (1995) model of SAD. Although both treatments yielded significant reductions in SAD symptoms, individual treatment was associated with greater reduction in symptoms both immediately after and at 6-month follow-up (Stangier, Heidenreich, Peitz, Lauterbach, & Clark, 2003).

The efficacy of CBT for individuals with SAD has been supported by an abundance of clinical research that spans the past two decades. Several meta-analyses attest to the efficacy of this treatment approach (e.g., Federoff & Taylor, 2001; Taylor, 1996). For example, Taylor (1996) reported that cognitive restructuring, social skills training, exposure alone, and exposure combined with cognitive restructuring each performed better than wait-list control groups in reducing self-reported social anxiety symptoms. Although there were no significant differences among these treatments, only combined exposure and cognitive restructuring yielded an effect size significantly larger than placebo treatment.

TREATMENT FOR CHILDREN AND ADOLESCENTS

Few treatments have been designed to specifically target SAD among children and adolescents. However, the use of CBT to treat anxiety disorders in this age group has substantial empirical support. Research in this area has typically examined mixed diagnostic samples, including children with SAD or avoidant disorder (a diagnosis subsumed under SAD in the most recent diagnostic manual).

One of the more widely investigated interventions for children with anxiety disorders is Kendall's (1992) Coping Cat program. In this 16-week program, children learn to recognize feelings of anxiety, identify negative and unrealistic thoughts, apply coping self-talk, and use self-reward as they undergo therapist-guided exposure exercises. Relaxation training is also utilized to enhance coping skills in feared situations. In the first controlled trial of this program, 64% of treated children (ages 9 to 13) were diagnosis-free at posttreatment by child and parent report. This was the case for only one child in the wait-list condition (Kendall, 1994). In a study replicating these findings, no differences were found in treatment outcome between diagnostic groups, suggesting that the Coping Cat program may be as effective for children with SAD as for children with other anxiety disorders (Kendall et al., 1997).

Attempts to augment treatment response among children receiving CBT have led investigators to include the family in the treatment process. Barrett, Dadds, and Rapee (1996) added a family anxiety management component to the Coping Cat program and found that compared to CBT only, CBT with the family component was associated with significantly higher remission rates at posttreatment (57% versus 84%, respectively).

One of the few interventions that was designed specifically for children with social fears is Social Effectiveness Therapy for Children (SET-C), a multifaceted behavioral treatment comprised of basic social skills training as well as individual and group exposure sessions (Beidel, Turner, & Morris, 2000). Compared to those who received a nonspecific intervention, children (ages 8 to 12) who received SET-C improved significantly more on child and parent ratings of anxiety, as well as on ratings of skill and anxiety in simulated social situations (Beidel et al., 2000). Approximately 67% of treated children no longer met criteria for SAD after treatment, compared with only 5% of those who received the nonspecific intervention. Furthermore, treatment gains were maintained 6 months after treatment ended. There is also evidence that the benefits of social skills-based CBT for children with SAD can be significantly enhanced when parents are systematically involved in treatment. Spence, Donovan, and Brechman-Toussaint (2000) found that when parents were involved in treatment, 87.5% of socially anxious children who received social skills-based CBT were diagnosis-free immediately after treatment, compared to 58% of children who received CBT only. A group therapy based on Heimberg's CBGT for adults has also demonstrated efficacy in the treatment of SAD in adolescents (Albano, Marten, Holt, Heimberg, & Barlow, 1995; Hayward et al., 2000).

FACTORS THAT AFFECT TREATMENT OUTCOME

Although CBT has yielded impressive response rates in controlled studies, many patients who receive treatment still remain symptomatic afterward and/or relapse after treatment is discontinued. Heterogeneity in the clinical presentation of the disorder itself may account for some of the variation in treatment response. Indeed, few patients present with a diagnostically pure form of SAD, and more often than not, their social fears are accompanied by various manifestations of anxiety and depression. Much research has been devoted to identifying prognostic factors in the treatment of SAD.

One of the clinical features that has received considerable attention is diagnostic subtype. The DSM-IV distinguishes between individuals who experience anxiety in most domains of social interaction or performance situations (generalized subtype) and those whose anxiety is more circumscribed (nongeneralized subtype) (American Psychiatric Association, 1994). Individuals with the generalized subtype of SAD are more impaired before treatment and remain so after treatment. Although generalized patients benefit from treatment at the same rate as nongeneralized patients, they are less likely to experience full symptom remission or achieve clinically significant change (Hope, Herbert, & White, 1995).

The presence of concurrent psychopathology is also known to affect treatment outcome for individuals with SAD. In one study, patients whose SAD was accompanied by a mood disorder were compared to patients with either uncomplicated SAD or a comorbid anxiety disorder. Those with comorbid mood disorders had more severe SAD symptoms and were more impaired before and after receiving CBGT (Erwin, Heimberg, Juster, & Mindlin, 2002). As was the case with subtype, patients with comorbid depression benefited from CBT to the same degree as those without comorbid depression. However, they remained relatively worse off following treatment. In an earlier study, patients who presented with high levels of depression at pretreatment were less likely to improve on measures of social anxiety and social skill following treatment with CBT (Chambless, Tran, & Glass, 1997). These findings highlight the importance of conducting a careful assessment of depressive symptoms among individuals seeking treatment for SAD. Moreover, those with concurrent depression may require a more extended course of treatment in order to achieve meaningful results. Other factors have been identified that may also relate to treatment response, including expectancy for positive treatment outcome (Safren, Heimberg, & Juster, 1997), homework compliance (Leung & Heimberg, 1996), and anger (Erwin, Heimberg, Schneier, & Liebowitz, 2003).

To date, we have a limited understanding of what factors predict outcome of CBT among children and adolescents with SAD. In part, this is due to the fact that few interventions for this age group are specific to SAD. Treatment response does not appear to be related to ethnicity, gender, age, or the presence of comorbid diagnoses (Kendall et al., 1997). Further research is needed to better understand and address potential treatment obstacles among children and adolescents with this disorder. This may include familial factors, parental characteristics, and therapy process variables that potentially facilitate or interfere with treatment gains.

SUMMARY AND FUTURE DIRECTIONS

Research consistently tells us that individuals with SAD who receive CBT enjoy significant reductions in their social and performance fears, and even enhancement in overall life satisfaction and subjective well-being (Eng, Coles, Heimberg, & Safren, 2001). Furthermore, there is evidence that patients maintain these improvements well past the acute phases of treatment.

Although challenges lie ahead for researchers in this area, recent trends promise an exciting future. One such trend is the growing interest in the role of CBT vis-à-vis medication treatments. Pharmacotherapy has proven to be a viable and well-tolerated treatment option for SAD. How does a practitioner decide which treatment to prescribe? Direct comparisons of CBT with medication do not clearly favor one or the other form of treatment (Heimberg et al., 1998). Medication may be associated with more efficient response than CBT, the success of which relies on more gradual skill development. Yet we know little about the long-term efficacy of medications, and CBT has been shown to yield enduring results. Recently, investigators have been exploring the use of CBT to facilitate discontinuation from medication, or prevent relapse.

Although empirical support exists for the use of CBT with children and adolescents with SAD, further research is needed to examine long-term outcome. As well, the question of how to involve parents in treatment (e.g., as co-clients versus co-therapists) is of great interest, as findings thus far suggest that parental involvement is a powerful way to enhance treatment response.

If one examines the kind of therapies typically received by individuals with SAD, CBT is not as well represented as would be suggested by its dominance in the empirical literature. In their review of treatment histories of adults with SAD, Rowa, Antony, Brar, Summerfeldt, and Swinson (2000) found that fewer than half had ever tried CBT for their social anxiety, with the majority having tried nonspecific supportive or psychodynamic therapies. There is a need to better disseminate and evaluate the utility of CBT among practitioners in the community. Advances in technology and use of the Internet offer exciting ways to enhance the transportability of treatments for this condition.

See also: Anxiety—adult, Anxiety—children, Anxiety in children—FRIENDS program, Generalized anxiety disorder, Social anxiety disorder 2, Social skills training

REFERENCES

Albano, A. M., Marten, P. A., Holt, C. S., Heimberg, R. G., & Barlow, D. H. (1995). Cognitive–behavioral group treatment for social phobia in adolescents: A preliminary study. *Journal of Nervous and Mental Disease, 183*, 649–656.

American Psychiatric Association. (1994). *Diagnostic and statistical manual of mental disorders* (4th ed.). Washington, DC: Author.

Barrett, P. M., Dadds, M. R., & Rapee, R. M. (1996). Family treatment of childhood anxiety: A controlled trial. *Journal of Consulting and Clinical Psychology, 64*, 333–342.

Beidel, D. C., Turner, S. M., & Morris, T. L. (1999). Psychopathology of childhood social phobia. *Journal of the American Academy of Child and Adolescent Psychiatry, 38*, 643–650.

Beidel, D. C., Turner, S. M., & Morris, T. L. (2000). Behavioral treatment of childhood social phobia. *Journal of Consulting and Clinical Psychology, 68*, 1072–1080.

Chambless, D. L., Sanderson, W. C., Shoham, V., Johnson, S. B., Pope, K. S., Crits-Christoph, P., Baker, M., Johnson, B., Woody, S., Sue, S., Beutler, L., Williams, D. A., & McCurry, S. (1996). An update on empirically validated treatments. *The Clinical Psychologist, 49*, 5–18.

Chambless, D. L., Tran, G. Q., & Glass, C. R. (1997). Predictors of response to cognitive–behavioral group therapy for social phobia. *Journal of Anxiety Disorders, 11*, 221–240.

Clark, D. M., & Wells, A. (1995). A cognitive model of social phobia. In R. G. Heimberg, M. R. Liebowitz, D. A. Hope, & F. R. Schneier (Eds.), *Social phobia: Diagnosis, assessment and treatment* (pp. 69–93). New York: Guilford Press.

Eng, W., Coles, M. E., Heimberg, R. G., & Safren, S. A. (2001). Quality of life in social anxiety disorder: Response to cognitive behavioral treatment. *Depression and Anxiety, 13*, 192–193.

Erwin, B. A., Heimberg, R. G., Juster, H. R., & Mindlin, M. (2002). Comorbid anxiety and mood disorders among persons with social anxiety disorder. *Behaviour Research and Therapy, 40*, 19–25.

Erwin, B. A., Heimberg, R. G., Schneier, F. R., & Liebowitz, M. R. (2003). Anger experience and anger expression in social anxiety disorder: Pretreatment profile and predictors of attrition and response to cognitive–behavioral treatment. *Behavior Therapy, 34*, 331–350.

Federoff, I. C., & Taylor, S. (2001). Psychological and pharmacological treatments of social phobia: A meta-anlaysis. *Journal of Clinical Psychopharmacology, 3*, 311–324.

Hayward, C., Varady, S., Albano, A. M., Thienemann, M., Henderson, L., & Schatzberg, A. F. (2000). Cognitive–behavioral group therapy for social phobia in female adolescents: Results of a pilot study. *Journal of the American Academy of Child and Adolescent Psychiatry, 39*, 721–726.

Heimberg, R. G., & Becker, R. E. (2002). *Cognitive–behavioral group therapy of social phobia: Basic mechanisms and clinical applications.* New York: Guilford Press.

Heimberg, R. G., Liebowitz, M. R., Hope, D. A., Schneier, F. R., Holt, C. S., Welkowitz, L. A., Juster, H. R., Campeas, R., Bruch, M. A., Cloitre, M., Fallon, B., & Klein, D. F. (1998). Cognitive behavioral group therapy versus phenelzine therapy in social phobia: 12-week outcome. *Archives of General Psychiatry, 55*, 1133–1141.

Heimberg, R. G., Salzman, D., Holt, C. S., & Blendell, K. (1993). Cognitive behavioral group treatment of social phobia: Effectiveness at 5-year follow-up. *Cognitive Therapy and Research, 17*, 325–339.

Hope, D. A., Herbert, J. D., & White, C. (1995). Diagnostic subtype, avoidant personality disorder, and efficacy of cognitive–behavioral group therapy for social phobia. *Cognitive Therapy and Research, 19*, 399–417.

Kendall, P. C. (1992). *Coping cat workbook.* Ardmore, PA: Workbook Publishing.

Kendall, P. C. (1994). Treating anxiety disorders in children: Results of a randomized clinical trial. *Journal of Consulting and Clinical Psychology, 62*, 100–110.

Kendall, P. C., Flannery-Schroeder, E., Panichelli-Mindel, S. M., Southam-Gerow, M., Henin, A., & Warman, M. (1997). Therapy for youths with anxiety disorders: A second randomized clinical trial. *Journal of Consulting and Clinical Psychology, 65*, 366–380.

Kessler, R. C., McGonagle, K. A., Zhao, S., Nelson, C. B., Hughs, M., Eshleman, S., Wittchen, H. U., & Kendler, K. S. (1994). Lifetime and 12 month prevalence of DSM III-R psychiatric disorders in the United States. *Archives of General Psychiatry, 51*, 8–19.

Leung, A. W., & Heimberg, R. G. (1996). Homework compliance, perceptions of control, and outcome of cognitive–behavioral treatment of social phobia. *Behaviour Research and Therapy, 34*, 423–432.

Rowa, K., Antony, M. M., Brar, S., Summerfeldt, L. J., & Swinson, R. P. (2000). Treatment histories of patients with three anxiety disorders. *Depression and Anxiety, 12*, 92–98.

Safren, S. A., Heimberg, R. G., & Juster, H. R. (1997). Client expectancies and their relationship to pretreatment symptomatology and outcome of cognitive–behavioral group treatment for social phobia. *Journal of Consulting and Clinical Psychology, 65*, 694–698.

Schneier, F. R., Johnson, J., Hornig, C. D., Liebowitz, M. R., & Weissman, M. M. (1992). Social phobia: Comorbidity and morbidity in an epidemiologic sample. *Archives of General Psychiatry, 49*, 282–288.

Spence, S. H., Donovan, C., & Brechman-Toussaint, M. (2000). The treatment of childhood social phobia: The effectiveness of a social skills training-based cognitive–behavioural intervention with and without parental involvement. *Journal of Child Psychology and Psychiatry, 41*, 713–726.

Stangier, U., Heidenreich, T., Peitz, M., Lauterbach, W., & Clark, D. M. (2003). Cognitive therapy for social phobia: Individual versus group treatment. *Behaviour Research and Therapy, 41*, 991–1007.

Taylor, S. (1996). Meta-analysis of cognitive–behavioral treatments for social phobia. *Journal of Behavior Therapy and Experimental Psychiatry, 27*, 1–9.

Turk, C. L., Fresco, D. M., & Heimberg, R. G. (1999). Social phobia: Cognitive behavior therapy. In M. Hersen & A. S. Bellack (Eds.), *Handbook of comparative treatments of adult disorders* (2nd ed., pp. 287–316). New York: Wiley.

Wittchen, H.-U., Stein, M. B., & Kessler, R. C. (1999). Social fears and social phobia in a community sample of adolescents and young adults: Prevalence, risk factors, and co-morbidity. *Psychological Medicine, 29*, 309–323.

Zaider, T. I., Heimberg, R. G., Roth, D. A., Hope, D., & Turk, C. (2003, November). *Individual cognitive–behavioral therapy for social anxiety disorder: Preliminary findings.* Paper presented at the 37th annual convention of the Association for the Advancement of Behavior Therapy, Boston.

RECOMMENDED READINGS

Crozier, W. R., & Alden, L. E. (Eds.). (2001). *International handbook of social anxiety: Concepts, research and interventions relating to the self and shyness.* New York: Wiley.

Heimberg, R. G., & Becker, R. E. (2002). *Cognitive–behavioral group therapy for social phobia: Basic mechanisms and clinical strategies.* New York: Guilford Press.

Hofmann, S. G., & DiBartolo, P. M. (Eds.). (2001). *From social anxiety to social phobia: Multiple perspectives.* Needham Heights, MA: Allyn & Bacon.

Social Anxiety Disorder 2

James D. Herbert and Kristy Dalrymple

Keywords: social anxiety, social phobia, cognitive–behavior therapy, social skills, group therapy

Social Anxiety Disorder (SAD; also known as Social Phobia) is defined by the fourth edition of the *Diagnostic and Statistical Manual of Mental Disorders* (DSM-IV) as "a marked and persistent fear of social or performance situations in which embarrassment may occur." These situations may include public speaking, eating in public, writing in public, speaking with authority figures, conversations, dating, as well as many others. The fear must be excessive or unreasonable, lead to avoidance and/or significant distress, and must interfere with occupational, academic, or social functioning. A cardinal feature of the disorder is fear of negative evaluation by others. Persons with SAD tend to hold negative beliefs about themselves (e.g., thoughts of inadequacy), and engage in excessive self-focus during social interactions.

Descriptions of social anxiety date back to antiquity, but the first modern theorist to describe the syndrome was Isaac Marks in the 1970s. The disorder only became part of the official diagnostic nomenclature with publication of the third edition of the DSM in 1980. The DSM-III described the prototypical case of SAD as limited to a single social situation. Research during the 1980s, however, revealed that the more common clinical presentation consisted of a pattern of fear and avoidance across a wide range of situations. In the revised third edition of the DSM published in 1987, a generalized subtype of SAD was introduced to describe this pattern. In contrast, a discrete subtype described situations in which fear is limited to one or two specific situations (e.g., public speaking). Studies comparing the generalized and discrete subtypes have found that those with the former were more frequently shy as children, more functionally impaired, and more likely to have problems with alcohol abuse (e.g., Stemberger, Turner, Beidel, & Calhoun, 1995).

Although inclusion as a diagnostic entity in the DSM has helped raise awareness of severe social anxiety among both clinicians and researchers, there remain several problems with the current diagnostic nomenclature. These include the lack of clear boundaries between normal and pathological social anxiety, the lack of clear criteria defining the generalized subtype, and the high degree of overlap with Avoidant Personality Disorder. With respect to the latter, several studies have found that the majority of persons with the generalized subtype of SAD also meet diagnostic criteria for Avoidant Personality Disorder, and it appears that the two labels actually describe the same fundamental type of psychopathology.

EPIDEMIOLOGY

The National Comorbidity Survey (NCS; Kessler et al., 1994) found a lifetime prevalence rate of 13.3% for SAD. Results from the NCS showed that SAD was the most common anxiety disorder among the U.S. population, and the third most common psychiatric disorder, following Major Depression and Alcohol Dependence. Gender differences in lifetime prevalence of SAD have also been reported; Kessler et al. (1994) reported a lifetime prevalence of 11.1% in males and 15.5% in females. However, treatment-seeking samples generally show an equal distribution across genders.

The mean age of onset of SAD has frequently been reported to be in early to mid-adolescence. However, closer examination of the data from the NIMH Epidemiological Catchment Area Study indicates a bimodal distribution of age of onset, with the first peak occurring before 5 years of age, and the second peak occurring around age 13. Many people diagnosed with SAD report shyness and social anxiety throughout their life span. Left untreated, the disorder follows a chronic and unremitting course.

SAD is often comorbid with many of the anxiety disorders, including specific phobias, generalized anxiety disorder, agoraphobia, and panic disorder. According to the NCS, 56.7% of people diagnosed with SAD also met criteria for another anxiety disorder (Kessler et al., 1994). SAD is also highly comorbid with depression, with 37.2% of those diagnosed with SAD also meeting criteria for major depressive disorder in the NCS. Finally, SAD often co-occurs with alcoholism, with 34.8% of those diagnosed with SAD meeting criteria for either alcohol abuse or dependence in the NCS study.

ETIOLOGY

Biological Factors

Heredity. Many studies have established a familial component to the development of SAD. For example, Fyer, Mannuzza, Chapman, Liebowitz, and Klein (1993) found that first-degree relatives of persons with SAD had a 16% risk for SAD, compared to only a 5% rate for the relatives of a normal control group. In addition, 33% of the SAD families in the study had at least one first-degree relative with social phobia, as compared to only 16% of the families of the normal controls.

Temperament. Temperament refers to the relatively stable mood and behavioral profiles that are observed in childhood and believed to be at least partially genetically based (Schwartz, Snidman, & Kagan, 1999). Behavioral inhibition is a temperamental style described by Kagan and colleagues as a shy demeanor and tendency to approach novel situations with restraint, avoidance, and distress. Some research has found that behaviorally inhibited children have an increased risk of anxiety disorders, especially SAD. In addition, Schwartz et al. (1999) found that 61% of adolescents who were inhibited as toddlers had current social anxiety, compared to 27% of those who were uninhibited as toddlers.

Environmental Factors

Child-Rearing Practices, Family Sociability, and Attachment Styles. Research has examined the association of various child-rearing practices with the development of SAD. Two types of parenting styles that have been associated with SAD include low levels of warmth and high levels of control and overprotection. Some studies have found that adults with SAD rated their parents as less warm and more controlling than nonclinical controls. Similarly, some studies have reported that insecure attachment styles are related to increased risk of anxiety disorders. Family sociability is another environmental factor that may be related to the development of SAD. Research indicates that individuals with social anxiety recall their parents as being socially isolated and encouraging family isolation and limiting contact with others. Parents may also model fear responses when in social situations by providing and reinforcing avoidant responses, highlighting information about risk, and expressing doubt about their own social competence. The findings on these environmental factors must be interpreted with caution, however, as this work is based primarily on retrospective self-reports of adults currently diagnosed with SAD. The causal role of any relationship cannot be determined on the basis of such data.

Traumatic Conditioning. Many persons with SAD recall a history of one or more traumatic social events, such as freezing while presenting a book report in school or doing something highly embarrassing with adolescent friends. A study by Stemberger et al. (1995) found that 56% of those diagnosed with the discrete subtype of SAD and 40% of those diagnosed with the generalized subtype reported the presence of a traumatic event. Like the data on other environmental factors, however, these data are based on retrospective reports, and are therefore at best suggestive of a causative role of trauma. Moreover, the fact that many persons with SAD do not recall a specific traumatic event suggests that such events are likely neither necessary nor sufficient for the development of the disorder.

Cognitive Biases

A core feature of SAD is negative interpretation of ambiguous events. A number of studies have documented various cognitive biases in SAD, including negatively interpreting others' emotions or judgments, anticipating that others will negatively interpret one's anxiety symptoms, and overly attending to perceived errors in social behavior or performance. Contemporary cognitive theories of SAD highlight these biases as critical to the development and maintenance of the disorder. Although research demonstrates a strong association between the presence of these cognitive biases and SAD, their causal status remains uncertain.

Social Skills Deficits

Several studies have found that SAD is associated with impairments in social behavior, although the degree to which this impairment reflects actual skills deficits, the disruptive effects of anxiety, or both remains unclear, as does the etiological status of disrupted social behavior. It appears likely that socially anxious persons are heterogeneous in this regard, with some having excellent social skills, some having acceptable skills but difficulty enacting those skills due to the disruptive effects of high anxiety, and others having poor skills (Herbert et al., in press).

ASSESSMENT

Diagnostic Interviews

Several structured diagnostic interviews have been developed for assessing SAD and related mood and anxiety syndromes. A particularly useful clinical interview is the Anxiety Disorders Interview Schedule for DSM-IV (ADIS-IV; Brown, Di Nardo, & Barlow, 1994). The ADIS-IV is a semistructured clinical interview designed primarily for the assessment of anxiety disorders, and possesses good reliability for a variety of Axis I disorders, and for SAD in particular.

Clinician-Administered Measures

One of the most frequently used clinician-administered measures is the Liebowitz Social Anxiety Scale (LSAS). This scale measures the severity of fear and avoidance separately for several interaction and performance situations, and has been shown to possess good psychometric properties.

Another common measure is the Brief Social Phobia Scale (BSPS), which assesses fear and avoidance of seven common social situations, as well as the severity of four physiological symptoms. The BSPS has good psychometric properties as well, including adequate test–retest reliability and interrater reliability.

Self-Report Questionnaires

Many self-report questionnaires have been created and used in assessing social anxiety symptoms. One of the most empirically validated measures is the Social Phobia and Anxiety Inventory (SPAI). The SPAI measures somatic, cognitive, and behavioral responses to several social situations. The SPAI has excellent psychometric properties, such as high test–retest and internal reliability and good convergent and discriminant validity. There is also a children's version of the SPAI (the SPAI-C). Other commonly used self-report measures include the Fear of Negative Evaluation Scale (FNE), Social Avoidance and Distress Scale (SADS), Social Phobia Scale (SPS), and Social Interaction Anxiety Scale (SIAS).

Behavioral Assessment

Behavioral assessment tests (BATs) comprise a systematic way of evaluating behavior in social situations. As applied to SAD, BATs frequently take the form of role-play tasks, and are helpful in observing social skills and anxiety responses (e.g., physiological responses, avoidance behaviors). Ratings of anxiety and thoughts can be recorded to augment information that is provided in self-report questionnaires. Typical situations used in BATs for SAD include conversations with same- or opposite-gender strangers and impromptu speeches. BATs can be standardized to compare performance across individuals or can be individually tailored. There is sufficient evidence for the reliability and validity of social skills ratings obtained from BATs.

Cognitive Assessment

Thought listing and self-monitoring records are two typical ways to measure cognitions that may occur before, during, or after social interactions. For thought listing forms, individuals are asked to list thoughts related to a simulated social situation, such as a BAT or an in vivo exposure assignment. Self-monitoring forms can provide helpful information about the typical situations encountered by individuals and associated thoughts throughout a typical week, which also can be used to measure progress in treatment (Hofmann & Barlow, 2002).

TREATMENT

Psychotherapy

There is little evidence to support the effectiveness of traditional psychotherapies such as psychoanalysis or psychodynamic psychotherapy for SAD. Cognitive–behavioral interventions are the most extensively studied approaches in the treatment of SAD. Cognitive–behavioral therapy (CBT) is based on the premise that fear and avoidance in social situations are associated with exaggerated negative beliefs about one's social performance and/or the threat of social situations. The goal of CBT is to modify these beliefs via interventions such as cognitive restructuring. The behavioral component of CBT emphasizes the role of avoidance in the maintenance of SAD. Behavioral avoidance limits opportunities to test the veracity of negative cognitions and to obtain corrective feedback from the social environment. Behavioral interventions such as simulated or in vivo exposure to feared social situations are used to decrease avoidance and to test dysfunctional beliefs.

Cognitive–behavioral group therapy (CBGT; Heimberg & Becker, 2002) has been widely used in the treatment of SAD. The treatment is conducted in groups of 6 to 8 participants, and includes cognitive restructuring, simulated exposures to feared situations, and in vivo exposure homework assignments. The efficacy of CBGT for adults has been demonstrated in several studies, and it is included on the list of empirically supported treatments developed by the American Psychological Association's Society of Clinical Psychology. Although little research has examined the efficacy of CBT with children and adolescents with SAD, preliminary results are promising.

There are several issues in the cognitive–behavioral treatment of SAD that remain unresolved. As noted above, the role of social skills deficits in SAD remains controversial. Likewise, although social skills training (SST) has been demonstrated to be an effective treatment for SAD in several studies, it is unclear how SST compares to cognitively oriented interventions. Although most CBT programs such as CBGT deemphasize SST, one recent study suggests that the addition of SST to the standard CBGT program significantly increased its effects (Herbert et al., 2003). Second, few dismantling studies of multicomponent intervention protocols like CBGT have been conducted. The results of component analysis studies, as well as meta-analytic reviews comparing studies utilizing various CBT components, have yielded mixed results. For example, the data are mixed as to whether cognitive restructuring has incremental benefits beyond exposure alone (Hofmann & Barlow, 2002). Third, the optimal format for delivering CBT requires further investigation. Although group therapy has been the standard for the past decade, structured group programs like CBGT pose inherent problems in scheduling a cohort of sufficiently homogeneous patients, thereby limiting their utility in front-line clinical settings. Clinical researchers are increasingly turning to individual therapy as a more practical alternative. Although preliminary research suggests that individual CBT is generally as effective as group interventions, further work is needed in this area.

Pharmacotherapy and Combined CBT Plus Drug Therapy

Several studies have demonstrated the efficacy of various pharmacologic agents in the treatment of SAD. Four clinical trials have shown the antidepressant monoamine oxidase inhibitor (MAOI) phenelzine to be efficacious in the treatment of SAD. One study compared phenelzine to CBGT and placebo; results showed that both drug treatment and CBGT were efficacious, but those receiving drug treatment were more likely to relapse than those who received CBGT (Heimberg et al., 1998). The adverse effects and dietary restrictions associated with MAOIs have led to the study of other medications that are better tolerated, such as the selective serotonin reuptake inhibitors (SSRIs). Various SSRIs have been shown to be more effective than pill placebo for SAD, including paroxetine, fluvoxamine, sertraline, and fluoxetine. Older tricyclic antidepressants have generally shown disappointing results. Preliminary support has been demonstrated for benzodiazepine anxiolytics, especially clonazepam. However, the risk of physical dependence with benzodiazepines raises concerns about their long-term use. Finally, some evidence supports the use of beta blockers such as propranolol and atenolol on an as-needed basis for the treatment of performance-related discrete SAD (e.g., public speaking anxiety). In general, a strength of pharmacotherapy for SAD is the relatively rapid onset of treatment effects.

Although pharmacotherapy is a viable treatment option for many patients, a critical limitation of the research in this area is the tendency not to include follow-up assessments after drug therapy is terminated. Those studies that have included such assessments reveal high relapse rates following medication discontinuation. In contrast, long-term follow-up of CBT programs reveals strong durability of treatment gains, even up to 5 years posttreatment. This raises the question of whether combined psychotherapy and pharmacotherapy might confer the best effects of both treatments, i.e., the relatively rapid effects of medication and the maintenance of gains associated with CBT. Although research in this area is only beginning, the results thus far have been disappointing. Two recent studies found little incremental benefit to the addition of either fluoxetine or phenelzine to CBGT over CBGT alone. Another study found that combined treatment may actually fare *worse* than exposure therapy alone in the long term. Haug et al. (2003) evaluated the effects of exposure alone, sertraline alone, and combined treatment at 28 weeks posttreatment. Patients who received exposure alone continued to improve over the course of the follow-up period, whereas deterioration was noted for those who received either sertraline alone or sertraline plus exposure.

Little research has been conducted on pharmacotherapy for children and adolescents with SAD. Preliminary reports have found promising effects for fluoxetine, citalopram, and buspirone. However, most of these studies are single-case reports, and/or are not specific to SAD and include samples of mixed-anxiety disordered patients.

SUMMARY AND CONCLUSIONS

Despite its relatively recent recognition as a distinct clinical entity, SAD has emerged as a common disorder associated with significant impairment in psychosocial functioning that follows a chronic and unremitting course. Relatively little is known about the etiology of SAD, although research points to the importance of both biological and environmental factors. Several useful assessment instruments with reasonably good psychometric properties have been developed. In addition, several effective treatments have emerged, including CBT programs and several medications. Unfortunately, the majority of persons diagnosed with SAD do not obtain treatment of any kind, and even among those who seek treatment, many do not receive an empirically supported intervention. Future clinical innovation and research is needed to target treatment-resistant patients, including those who benefit only partially from current treatments. In addition, dissemination efforts are needed to make effective treatment available to all those who suffer from this potentially debilitating condition. Finally, the majority of the research to date has focused on adults with SAD, with work with children and adolescents lagging far behind. Research targeting pediatric populations is especially critical to the goal of prevention and early intervention of SAD.

See also: Anxiety—adult, Anxiety—children, Anxiety in children—FRIENDS program, Generalized anxiety disorder, Social anxiety disorder 1, Social skills training

REFERENCES

Brown, T. A., Di Nardo, P. A., & Barlow, D. H. (1994). *Anxiety Disorders Interview Schedule for DSM-IV (ADIS-IV)*. San Antonio, TX: Psychological Corporation/Graywind Publications.

Fyer, A. J., Mannuzza, S., Chapman, T. F., Liebowitz, M. R., & Klein, D. F. (1993). A direct interview family study of social phobia. *Archives of General Psychiatry, 50*, 286–293.

Haug, T. T., Blomhoff, S., Hellstrøm, K., Holme, I., Humble, M., Madsbu, H. P., & Wold, J. E. (2003). Exposure therapy and sertraline in social phobia: 1-year follow-up of a randomized controlled trial. *British Journal of Psychiatry, 182*, 312–318.

Heimberg, R. G., & Becker, R. E. (2002). *Cognitive–behavioral group therapy for social phobia: Basic mechanisms and clinical strategies*. New York: Guilford Press.

Heimberg, R. G., Liebowitz, M. R., Hope, D. A., Schneier, F. R., Hold, C. S., Welkowitz, L., Juster, H. R., Campeas, R., Bruch, M. A., Cloitre, M., Fallon, B., & Klein, D. F. (1998). Cognitive–behavioral group therapy versus phenelzine in social phobia: 12-week outcome. *Archives of General Psychiatry, 55*, 1133–1141.

Herbert, J. D., Gaudiano, B. A., Rheingold, A. A., Harwell, V., Dalrymple, K., & Nolan, E. M. (in press). *Social skills training augments the effectiveness of cognitive behavioral group therapy for social anxiety disorder*.

Hofmann, S. G., & Barlow, D. H. (2002). Social phobia (social anxiety disorder). In D. H. Barlow (Ed.), *Anxiety and its disorders: The nature and treatment of anxiety and panic* (pp. 454–476). New York: Guilford Press.

Kessler, R. C., McGonagle, K. A., Zhao, S., Nelson, C. B., Hughes, M., Eshleman, S., Wittchen, H.-U., & Kendler, K. S. (1994). Lifetime and 12-month prevalence of DSM-III-R psychiatric disorders in the United States: Results from the National Comorbidity Survey. *Archives of General Psychiatry, 51*, 8–19.

Schwartz, C. E., Snidman, N., & Kagan, J. (1999). Adolescent social anxiety as an outcome of inhibited behavior in childhood. *Journal of the American Academy of Child and Adolescent Psychiatry, 38*, 1008–1015.

Stemberger, R. T., Turner, S. M., Beidel, D. C., & Calhoun, K. S. (1995). Social phobia: An analysis of possible developmental factors. *Journal of Abnormal Psychology, 104*, 526–531.

RECOMMENDED READINGS

Barlow, D. H. (2002). *Anxiety and its disorders: The nature and treatment of anxiety and panic* (2nd ed.). New York: Guilford Press.

Heimberg, R. G., & Becker, R. E. (2002). *Cognitive–behavioral group therapy for social phobia: Basic mechanisms and clinical strategies*. New York: Guilford Press.

Hofmann, S. G., & DiBartolo, P. M. (2001). From *social anxiety to social phobia: Multiple perspectives*. Needham Heights, MA: Allyn & Bacon.

Social Cognition in Children and Youth

Pier J. M. Prins and Teun G. van Manen

Keywords: cognition, aggression, conduct problems, children, youth

Aggressive and antisocial behaviors in children and adolescents represent a major public health problem. Prevalence rates range from 2 to 16%. Children with high levels of aggressive behavior comprise a heterogeneous group covering a variety of rule violations and hostile acts, ranging in intensity from swearing to criminal assault. Moreover, they experience psychopathology and impairment in multiple areas. Various terms have been used to describe this group of youths. The DSM-IV, for example, distinguishes between the diagnostic categories of conduct disorder (CD) and oppositional defiant disorder (ODD), the former referring to a pattern of behaviors that violate the rights of others, while the latter refers to a pattern of negativistic, hostile, defiant behaviors toward authority figures. Other distinctions are made based on the topography of the aggressive behavior, such as overt and covert aggression, or based on the age of onset such as childhood-onset and adolescent-onset conduct disorders. Another important distinction is made between an instrumental, proactive form of aggression and a hostile, reactive form of aggression (Dodge, Lachman, Harnish, Bates, & Pettit, 1997). The terms aggressive behavior and conduct problems will be used interchangeably throughout this article.

COGNITIVE–BEHAVIORAL ASSUMPTIONS AND AGGRESSION

The cognitive–behavioral framework assumes that aggression is not merely triggered by environmental events, but rather through the way in which these events are perceived and processed by the individual. This processing refers to the child's appraisal of the situation, anticipated reactions of others, and self-statements in response to particular events. A variety of cognitive and attributional processes have been found in aggressive youths. Deficits and distortions in cognitive problem-solving skills, attributions of hostile intent to others, and resentment and suspiciousness illustrate a few cognitive features associated with conduct problems. Individuals who engage in aggressive behaviors show distortions and deficiencies in various cognitive processes. These deficiencies are not merely reflections of intellectual functioning. A variety of cognitive processes have been studied, such as generating alternative solutions to interpersonal problems (e.g., different ways of handling social situations), identifying the means to obtain particular ends (e.g., making friends) or consequences of one's actions (e.g., what could happen after a particular behavior), making attributions to others of the motivation of their actions; perceiving how others feel; and expectations of the effects of one's own actions and others. Deficits and distortions among these processes relate to teacher ratings of disruptive behavior, peer evaluations, and direct assessment of overt behavior (Kazdin, 1997).

Attribution of intent to others represents a salient cognitive disposition critically important to understanding aggressive behavior. Aggressive youths tend to attribute hostile intent to others, especially in social situations where the cues of actual intent are ambiguous. Some researchers relate the attributional bias to particular physiological processes, while others assume that the hostile attributional bias may be caused by the intense anger experienced by some aggressive individuals (see Lochman, Whidby, & FitzGerald, 2000). Next to this attributional bias, aggressive children are characterized by cognitive deficits such as heightened sensitivity to hostile cues and by positive expectancies for aggressive behavior. Further, they have been found to value dominance and revenge over cooperation and affiliation, prefer aggressive solutions, have a restrictive repertoire of problem-solving strategies, and prefer action over thought and reflection (Durlak, Rubin, & Kahng, 2001).

A major model emphasizing the cognitive problems demonstrated by children with aggressive problems is the social information processing model developed by Crick and Dodge (1994). Briefly, this model identifies problems that aggressive children have in accurately judging social situations, selecting a strategy to deal with potential conflicts or challenges, and then implementing and evaluating that strategy. The model postulates that socially competent behavior is dependent on (a) accurate encoding of social cues and interpretation of others' intent, (b) generation and selection of appropriate responses, and (c) skillful enactment of the chosen course of behavior.

Problems at one or more points in the information processing model may characterize aggressive youths. For example, reactively aggressive and proactively aggressive types of antisocial youth not only differ in developmental histories but also in social information processing patterns. Reactively aggressive youth tend to display poorer scores on measures of social cognition at early stages of cue-oriented processing (e.g., encoding and interpretation of social situations), whereas proactively aggressive youth tend to demonstrate deficits at later stages of outcome-oriented processing (e.g., evaluation of selected response strategy) (Dodge et al., 1997).

TREATMENT PROCEDURES AND FORMATS

Child-based CBT interventions have been increasingly used to try to decrease children's aggressive, antisocial behavior and assume that children engage in aggressive behavior as a result of (a) learned cognitive distortions, such as biased attention to aggressive cues and the attribution of hostile intent to the action of others; (b) cognitive deficiencies, such as poor problem-solving and verbal mediation skills; and (c) a related tendency to respond impulsively to both external and internal stimuli, which has also been described as an inability to regulate emotion and behavior (Lochman et al., 2000). Accordingly, the child-focused CBT approach to treating child conduct problems targets the disturbed cognitive processes and behavioral deficits thought to produce aggressive and disruptive behaviors. They help the child identify stimuli that typically precede aggressive and antisocial behaviors and perceive ambiguous social situations in a nonhostile manner, challenge cognitive distortions, generate more assertive (versus aggressive) responses to possible social problems and develop more effective problem-solving skills, and tolerate feelings of anger and frustration without responding impulsively or aggressively (Nock, 2003).

Several CBT approaches have been developed to address these goals, such as problem-solving skills training, anger-coping training, assertiveness training, and rational–emotive therapy (Brestan & Eyberg, 1998). These CBT procedures use techniques such as cognitive restructuring and social skills training to remediate the cognitive and behavioral deficits of aggressive youths. Several of these programs also place a great deal of emphasis on teaching youths how to solve problems rationally and respond nonaggressively when they are actually aroused and angry.

Most of the treatment approaches occur within a short-term model of 10–15 weekly, hour-long sessions. No systematic reports on continued care studies are yet available. The format in which treatment is delivered is individual or group. Group format has been favored over individual treatments because of time and cost advantages. There are several advantages to the use of group therapy. Peer and group reinforcement are frequently more effective with children than reinforcement provided in a dyadic context, or by adults. This may be especially true for children with disruptive behavior disorders, who are relatively resistant to social reinforcement. Additionally, the group context provides in vivo opportunities for interpersonal learning and development of social skills (Lochman et al., 2000).

TWO EXAMPLES

Problem Solving Skills Training (PSST) consists of developing interpersonal cognitive problem-solving skills. Although many variations of PSST have been applied to conduct-problem children, several characteristics are usually shared. First, the emphasis is on how children approach situations, i.e., the thought processes in which the child engages to guide responses to interpersonal situations. The children are taught to engage in a step-by-step approach to solve interpersonal problems. They make statements to themselves that direct attention to certain aspects of the problem or tasks that lead to effective solutions. Second, behaviors that are selected (solutions) to the interpersonal situations are important as well. Prosocial behaviors are fostered (through modeling and direct reinforcement) as part of the problem-solving process. Third, treatment utilizes structured tasks involving games, academic activities, and stories. Over the course of treatment, the cognitive problem-solving skills are increasingly applied to real-life situations. Fourth, therapists usually play an active role in treatment. They model the cognitive processes by making verbal self-statements, apply the sequence of statements to particular problems, and provide cues to prompt use of the skills. Finally, treatment usually combines several different procedures, including modeling and practice, role-playing, and reinforcement and mild punishment (loss of points or tokens). These are deployed in systematic ways to develop increasingly complex response repertoires of the child (Kazdin, 1997).

The Anger Coping Program addresses both cognitive and affective processes, and is designed to remediate skills deficits in conflictual situations involving affective arousal. Specific goals are to increase children's awareness of internal cognitive, affective, and physiological phenomena related to anger arousal; enhance self-reflection and self-management skills; facilitate alternative, consequential, and means-end thinking in approaching social problems; and increase children's behavioral repertoire when faced with social conflict. To do so, sessions are organized around teaching specific social–cognitive skills. The major components of the program consist of self-management/monitoring skills, perspective-taking skills, and social problem-solving skills (Lochman et al., 2000).

EFFICACY OF CBT WITH AGGRESSIVE YOUTH

Meta-analytic reviews have yielded medium to large effect sizes (ESs = 0.47 to 0.90) for this treatment approach for child conduct problems. Five child-centered CBT treatments have been identified that met criteria for probably efficacious status, including anger-control training, anger-coping training, assertiveness training, problem-solving skills training, and rational–emotive therapy. These treatments await systematic replication by a second research team before advancing to well-established status (Bennett & Gibbons, 2000; Brestan & Eyberg, 1998).

CBT treatment packages have proven more efficacious than credible comparison groups, and children receiving CBT are more likely to be in the normal range of functioning after treatment than children in comparison conditions; however, it is notable that many children receiving CBT fail to reach such levels of improved functioning. Furthermore, most studies have relied exclusively on parent and teacher report of child functioning and have not employed observational or performance-based measures in the laboratory, or more socially valid measures of functioning, such as records of actual offending from school or police sources. Thus, the actual impact of such interventions on subsequent child functioning has not been sufficiently established (Kazdin, 1997; Nock, 2003). Further, it is unknown at this point in time which of the many components involved in CBT treatment packages for child conduct problems are necessary and sufficient for therapeutic change (Nock, 2003).

Several studies have demonstrated the improved efficacy associated with combining CBT with parent management training (PMT) approaches. Children who participated in child-based CBT and whose parents participated in parent training had greater decreases in antisocial behavior than children assigned to a problem-solving-only or to a parent-training-only condition (Bennett & Gibbons, 2000).

The efficacy of CBT interventions may vary depending on factors such as the specific components addressed (presence or absence of self-monitoring), number of therapy sessions, and child age. Children of older age (11–13 years), for example, and with greater cognitive ability have been shown to benefit more from CBT than younger (5–7 years), less cognitively developed children. In addition, a greater degree of dysfunction present in the child (e.g., higher number of conduct disorder symptoms), in the parent (higher parenting stress and depression scores, or adverse child-rearing practices), and in the family (more dysfunctional family environment) have all been associated with a poorer response to treatment (Nock, 2003).

In a meta-analysis by Bennet & Gibbons (2000), none of the studies included, examined the subtype of children's aggressive behavior. Given the greater peer problems, inadequate attention to relevant social cues, and more aggressive problem-solving of children who exhibit reactive (versus proactive) aggression, it is possible that child-based CBT interventions such as social problem-solving and anger-control training may be most effective for children who exhibit high rates of reactive aggression.

In summary, cognitive–behavioral interventions for antisocial youth represent a promising approach by effectively addressing the youth's cognitive and social problems and by reducing conduct problem behaviors and building prosocial skills (Burke, Loeber, & Birmaher, 2002). However, the evidence has not been entirely supportive. Although child-focused CBT appears to foster some change in the problems of these youth, such short-term, child-focused interventions do not appear to be the ideal solution. Only parent-focused interventions have thus far met criteria for well-established status. By only focusing on the child, CBT may lack sufficient attention to the familial variables that have been implicated in the development and maintenance of antisocial behavior in children. Adopting a broader-based treatment strategy—integrating social–cognitive training interventions within a family or societal framework—may result in greater generalization or maintenance of treatment effects.

FUTURE DIRECTIONS

It thus appears that child-based CBT interventions can be an effective part of a multimodal treatment for children, particularly older children, who exhibit high levels of aggressive behavior. Future research will be concerned with the following four issues. First, although many studies have shown that conduct-disordered youths experience various cognitive distortions and deficiencies, the specificity of these cognitive deficits among diagnostic groups and youths of different ages (Do cognitive distortions characterize youths with conduct problems rather than adjustment problems more generally?) needs to be established, as well as whether some of the cognitive processes are more central than others, and how these processes unfold developmentally (Kazdin, 1997). Second, intervention studies will have to be conducted with samples that are more similar to clinically referred subjects, that is, for those with high levels of comorbidity and living in disturbed families. Treatment trials will have to be extended to the clinical setting (real-world tests). Third, further work is needed to evaluate factors (child, family, and parent characteristics) that contribute to responsiveness to treatment, such as age, comorbidity, families with high levels of impairment, and lower reading achievement. Finally, more research will target the question of mechanisms of change in CBT for aggressive youths. Several studies have demonstrated that CBT affects the proposed mechanisms of change in the hypothesized directions (e.g., increases in problem-solving skills and self-control, and decreases in cognitive distortions and hostile attributions) and that changes in these proposed mediators are correlated with child behavior change at posttreatment. However, no studies have demonstrated that changes in the proposed mechanisms temporally precede the changes in therapeutic outcome and that changes in the proposed mechanisms account for the effect of treatment condition on therapeutic outcome. Until these criteria are met, researchers cannot be sure the therapeutic change associated with CBT for child conduct problems is the result of cognitive and behavioral changes in the child, rather than some other, related factor. Knowledge about why and how CBT with aggressive youths works eventually will serve as a basis for maximizing its efficacy in clinical practice (Weersing & Weisz, 2002).

See also: Treatment of children

REFERENCES

Bennett, D. S., & Gibbons, T. A. (2000). Efficacy of child cognitive–behavioral interventions for antisocial behavior: A meta-analysis. *Child & Family Behavior Therapy, 22*, 1–27.

Brestan, E. V., & Eyberg, S. M. (1998). Effective psychosocial treatments of conduct-disordered children and adolescents : 29 years, 82 studies, and 5,272 kids. *Journal of Clinical Child Psychology, 27*, 180–189.

Burke, J. D., Loeber, R., & Birmaher, B. (2002). Oppositional defiant disorder and conduct disorder: A review of the past 10 years, part II. *Journal of the American Academy of Child and Adolescent Psychiatry, 41*, 1275–1293.

Crick, N. R., & Dodge, K. A. (1994). A review and reformulation of social information-processing mechanisms in children's social adjustment. *Psychological Bulletin, 115*, 74–101.

Dodge, K. A., Lochman, J. E., Harnish, J. D., Bates, J. E., & Pettit, G. S. (1997). Reactive and proactive aggression in school children and psychiatrically impaired chronically assaultive youth. *Journal of Abnormal Psychology, 106*, 37–51.

Durlak, J. A., Rubin, L. A., & Kahng, R. D. (2001). Cognitive behavioural therapy for children and adolescents with externalising problems. *Journal of Cognitive Psychotherapy: An International Quarterly, 15*, 183–194.

Kazdin, A. E. (1997). Practitioner review: Psychosocial treatments for conduct disorder in children. *Journal of Child Psychology and Psychiatry, 38*, 161–178.

Lochman, J. E., Whidby, J. M., & FitzGerald, D. P. (2000). Cognitive–behavioral assessment and treatment with aggressive children. In P. C. Kendall (Ed.), *Child and adolescent therapy: Cognitive–behavioral procedures* (2nd ed., pp. 31–88). New York: Guilford Press.

Nock, M. K. (2003). Progress review of the psychosocial treatment of child conduct problems. *Clinical Psychology: Science and Practice, 10*, 1–28.

Weersing, V. R., & Weisz, J. R. (2002). Mechanisms of action in youth psychotherapy. *Journal of Child Psychology and Psychiatry, 43*, 3–29.

Social Skills Training

Irene Henriette Oestrich

Keywords: social skills, self-esteem, schizophrenia, group therapy

Feeling good about oneself, often called self-esteem, is not a static structure, but rather a continuous process. Personal development has its basis in change and requires both basic and complex cognitive and emotional processes. The vulnerability related to effective social functioning often causes pain and prevents the development of a constructive social repertoire and consequently impacts the ongoing process of developing self-esteem.

Humans are not born with an intact social repertoire. The more we learn to effectively cope, with a broad range of social situations, the less incompetent and anxious we feel in those and related social situations. The development of coping strategies is influenced by both behavioral and thinking processes. Avoidance and safety-seeking behaviors are a hindrance to the development of social skills, problem solving, and competence inasmuch as the lack of social engagement leads to a deficit in social skills.

Social competence is also connected to cognitions. In relationships with others, the personal meaning attached to those relationships and to the process of relating is especially important. Relationships are often influenced by strong emotional factors. The nuances in relationships are almost limitless and the meaning we connect to what happens in these relationships is important for the concept of self, how we interact in life, and to our self-esteem. The "healthy" mind develops an open, reflective, and experimental approach to life, which leads to and supports sound curiosity and an intact social repertoire.

BACKGROUND AND RESEARCH

Social skills training has been shown to be effective for a variety of mental health problems. It has been used in different forms throughout the past 20 years in the treatment of social anxiety, panic, depression, shyness, and low self-esteem as well as schizophrenia. The more severe the psychopathology is, the more structured and behavioral the interventions would be.

Social skills deficit seems to foster psychopathology, and also contribute to the development of psychological dysfunction. Social skills deficit has been linked to a number of psychiatric diagnoses and with all of them, in particular to low self-esteem. Skills acquisition was significant in hospitalized patients with schizophrenia, and group therapy for schizophrenia may reduce the number of inpatient days, when the aim is to balance education with emotional support for chronic patient groups and there have been promising aims to teach psychiatric patients to cope in the community using group treatment.

In depressive patients the psychotherapeutic part of the treatment involving cognitive restructuring is central especially since low self-esteem is a painful part of the psychopathological problem area. Enhancement of self-esteem and social skills works as an antidote to the depressive symptoms.

Likewise in anxiety disorders, social skills training is highlighted when working with personality disturbance, where the training is focused on relationships and communication. Social anxiety in schizophrenia is often treated in groups, leading to improvement on anxiety, social interaction, and quality of life. It is important to consider the potential value of group treatments when treating people with social difficulties.

SOCIAL SKILLS TRAINING AS A DYNAMIC PROCESS

In nonpsychotic states a more complex, open, and creative model is adopted. Patients decide which problems to deal with and how they will construct and carry out homework exercises. The process follows the model outlined, but is also supplemented by experimentation, overcoming limitations, and use of creative activities (e.g., games, fairy tales, metaphors, social activities).

In the psychotic patient a more structured and carefully planned approach is recommended. The patient needs a level of protection where exposure exercises are less demanding. The provision of structure within sessions is anxiety reducing in itself and every session is designed without surprises; an emphasis on socialization is used throughout the session to both motivate and create a supportive and calm atmosphere.

ASSESSMENT

A questionnaire measuring social skills, covering six areas of social competence, can be used to assess individual areas of competence or as an overall measure. Other measures include the Robsons Self Concept Questionnaire (SCQ) possibly supplemented by the Beck Depression Inventory (BDI) and Beck Anxiety Inventory (BAI).

The assessment phase includes a combination of interviewing scales, self-report inventories, and observations based around cognitive–behavioral principles. Assessment is continued during treatment and we often measure deterioration in the social skills repertoire first, as patients before the treatment starts often have avoided using the skills and thus are unaware of their true repertoire.

Social skills training (SST) is concerned with

- Improvement of the social repertoire
- Development of skills, being absent or defect
- Enhancement of self-esteem
- Enhancement of problem-solving skills
- Regulation of emotions
- Improving tolerance to stress and frustration
- Improving self-respect and self-esteem
- Changing negative thought processes
- Maintaining personal rights and defining important personal goals in life

THE SOCIAL REPERTOIRE

Social skills consist of a range of abilities built on each other:

- Nonverbal skills consisting of skills where language is less important and communication depends on bodily signals (e.g., eye contact, facial expression, gesticulation and movement, body posture, and voice level and modulation)
- Basic verbal skills, conversation
- Emotional skills
- Self-protective skills, complex communication and integration of skills
- Problem-solving skills—including identification of problems and goal setting
- Intimate skills—approach–avoidance in relationships and in relation to important goals in life, fulfillment of intimate needs

Most models build on problem-solving strategies.

A DYNAMIC SST MODEL

SST training can be carried out with individuals or as a group process. Working in carefully referred groups is often more powerful as it allows social exposure, although patients with chronic symptoms may have difficulties in tolerating group work. A degree of exposure is crucial in SST and the therapy room can act as a protected forum allowing the patients to practice before dealing with homework assignments often involving in vivo exposure.

The following procedure is followed in SST:

- Assessment
- Socialization
- Identification of problems and goal setting; specific cognitive criteria are followed and at the same time taught to the patients
- Identification of dysfunctional thinking and avoidance patterns
- Enhancing motivation
- Intervention, construction of a new reaction pattern
- Homework assignment
- Evaluation

This process is dynamic, not static. It implies experimentation and the creation of new possibilities rather than being rigid and excessively structured.

The process consists of a number of phases. The therapist approaches each phase using a variety of therapeutic tools. The imagination of the therapist is the only limit in the strategies employed in conjunction with the level of functioning. The core principles of exposure, response prevention, and cognitive restructuring are incorporated into each of the strategies used.

During the brainstorming process, all of the participants offer suggestions and different alternatives are tried. The evaluation and selection of alternatives to be tested needs to be carefully managed, as many patients still feel uncomfortable after the first attempts to change, although discomfort usually disappears with repetition. The patient, of course, actively participates in the evaluation:

1. Find alternative constructive thoughts and new behavior
2. Measure the belief (0–100%) and the emotion (0–10)
3. Compare the reactions of the new alternative with the first. How is your goal best achieved?

When the anxiety or other negative emotion and the negative belief is reduced, the new pattern needs to be enacted and reinforced through active learning. Homework is designed and the person is prepared for difficulties, possible unsympathetic environment, and the like.

The details of what to do the next time a critical situation occurs must be crystal clear and evaluation implies the question, *How convinced are you that you can carry this through?* A golden rule is that the patient needs to be more than 50% convinced or smaller steps are necessary. Potential hindrances need to be addressed during the session to help maximize the probability of success outside.

The skills that need most improvement are prioritized based on what is appropriate for the patient. Sometimes it is advisable to work with least demanding skills first. The patient needs strong conviction that it makes a difference and also needs to experience success to overcome the tendency of avoidance.

The open and creative model is preferred by most patients. However, certain psychiatric diagnoses require a more systematic and structured intervention than others. The skills training should be built around patient needs and paced to ensure that patients reach their goals in a step-by-step process.

FRAMEWORK

It is recommended to run the group sessions for a maximum of 2 hours. The first part of the session is used to review participants' homework and design the next homework assignments. Homework tasks are reviewed briefly as each patient in the group is addressed. Typically there are four to eight participants in each group. It is advantageous to use video analysis during presentation of the problem in the

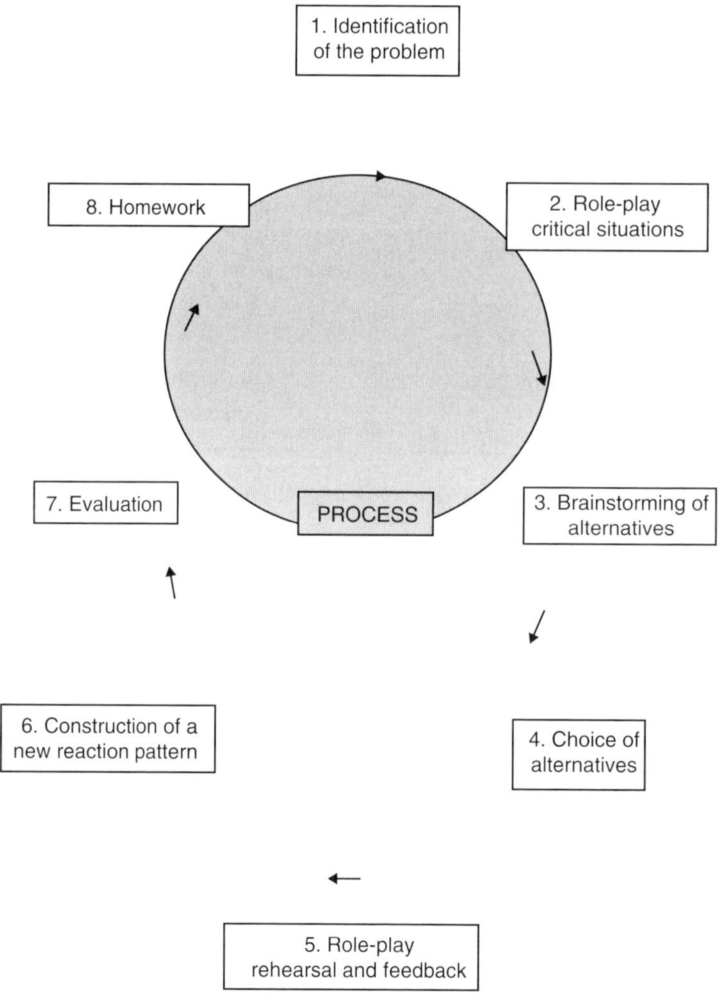

Figure 1. Model for social skills training.

role-playing phase. The video functions as a mirror that remembers, and the ability to pause the tape and explore the cognitive and emotional processes results in better problem formulations.

The person in focus is helped to set clear, realistic, and practical goals through cognitive analysis and to enhance motivation and probability for carrying through the training through cognitive coping and coaching.

During the whole process the person in focus is working on developing a better understanding of his or her own problems and the others in the group have an opportunity to provide support, generate alternative explanations, and offer empathy.

SELF-ESTEEM

Across different diagnostic groups there are common factors in psychological suffering. Low self-esteem is one of them. In many patients the stigmatization of suffering from a severe psychiatric disease creates typical self-esteem-destructive ideas and low self-esteem. Because schizophrenia was primarily considered a brain disease, such factors as low self-esteem and low social skills along with traumatic stress may have been understated in this group. There is, however, evidence to show it is significantly related to a number of clinical variables such as symptom severity, anxiety, hopelessness, and depression, and there is evidence that increasing self-esteem decreases those symptoms and improves quality of life.

DANISH RESEARCH PROJECT IN CLINICAL SETTING

One of the key research projects conducted at the Centre for Cognitive Therapy, Saint Hans Hospital in Denmark, has investigated the relationship between self-esteem and psychopathology in dual diagnosis patients. This project is taking place in collaboration with Nicholas Tarrier from the University of Manchester and is aimed at using cognitive–behavioral techniques to increase self-esteem and coping strategies in patients suffering from psychosis.

The patient group participating in the Danish part of the study suffers from chronic schizophrenia and regular drug abuse, and participants display significantly higher levels of psychopathology and poorer social skills than other patient groups. Patients with dual diagnoses also often experience a multitude of comorbid difficulties including anxiety, depression, and disturbances in personality.

The treatment is based on cognitive–behavioral principles that are used in the treatment of low self-esteem as outlined by Melanie Fennell (1999). The specific procedure used in the study is as follows:

- The patient is asked to identify 10 (or as many as possible) positive personal characteristics.
- The patient is then helped to measure how convinced he or she is that he or she owns this characteristic. The conviction is measured on a scale from 0 to 100%.
- Each characteristic is then reinforced, by asking the patient to describe as many situations as possible in vivid details, remembering actual situations, when he or she used the actual characteristic.
- The conviction is then measured again and is often increased.
- Each characteristic is given as a homework assignment, following cognitive principles and at the same time teaching the patient to focus on the good characteristic and overcome hindrances.

In the following session the conviction is measured again and the patient receives psychoeducation reinforcement in order to strengthen his or her ability to keep using the principle of enhancing self-esteem: *When you focus on and practice your good characteristics, you feel good.*

The preliminary findings from the Danish study are promising:

- Ninety percent of the patients displaying low or very low self-esteem showed a significant improvement in levels of self-esteem postintervention and at the 3-month follow-up.
- Eighty percent of the patients suffering from low or very low depression showed a significant improvement in levels of depression postintervention and at the 3-month follow-up.
- The majority of patients showed reduction approaching statistical significance in the levels of psychopathology experienced.

As these are only preliminary results, further longitudinal studies with larger numbers of patients are been conducted to fully determine the effectiveness of this brief cognitive intervention within the dual diagnosis patient group.

A second focus of research conducted at the center is addressing the challenges faced when attempting to conduct empirical studies within an actual life psychiatric setting. The center hopes to develop a set of guidelines that can be used by other psychiatric hospitals to promote the active empirical evaluation of treatment programs used within clinical settings.

SUMMARY

A large body of research over the past 20 years has confirmed the value and benefits of SST for people with schizophrenia. The concepts of self-esteem and SST are closely linked, and a number of recent studies demonstrate the benefit of focusing on self-esteem within different diagnostic areas, including the schizophrenic population, as a way to reduce psychopathology and promote coping strategies and social skills within the schizophrenic population.

A comprehensive model of SST training is described in phases as a method aimed to improve self-efficacy and quality of life, and the procedure of self-esteem training is suggested as a supplement to SST.

FUTURE DIRECTIONS

Models containing the effective elements of CBT as well as more creative and developmental-oriented ingredients can make a real difference to different groups of people suffering from social skills deficits and low self-esteem. We have valid assessment measures and research designs for continuing testing the effectiveness of these treatments, but it is necessary to use the same measures and the same model for comparison in future research studies.

It is known that SST needs to be integrated into an individualized treatment plan to maximize benefits; however, using a more creative and comprehensive SST model included self-esteem training still needs to be examined in valid studies. This treatment belongs to the recent concept of positive psychology, focusing less on warfare against psychopathology and more on positive emotions, building of skills, and the global healing factor of self-esteem.

See also: Low self-esteem, Schizophrenia

REFERENCES

Fennell, M. (1999). *Overcoming low self-esteem. A self-help guide using cognitive behavioural techniques*. London: Robinson.

Oestrich, I. (2003). *Self-esteem and new skills*. Copenhagen: Psychological Publishing.

Socratic Dialogue

Arthur Freeman

Keywords: Socratic dialogue, Socratic questioning, Socratic method, psychotherapy

The Socratic dialogue (SD) has become a basic part of cognitive–behavioral therapy (Beck, Rush, Shaw, & Emery, 1979; Ellis, 1962, 1989; Overholser, 1993a,b, 1994, 1995, 1996; Padesky, 1996). Leahy (2001) describes SD as a "mutual discovery ... where the therapist guides the patient through a series of questions and answers to elicit automatic thoughts, and assumptions and examine the logic and evidence that relate to them" (p. 38). SD is a radical departure from the interpretive style of the psychodynamic schools and from the nondirective style of client-centered work. The former essentially synthesizes the patient's ideas and feeds back to the patient a statement or idea that encapsulates the patient's intentions, motivations, and deep-seated conflicts. This will, ideally, lead to insight, integration, and eventually change(s). The latter enjoins the therapist from asking questions but rather specifies the use of restatement as the major technique in the therapeutic encounter, leading to insight and subsequent change(s).

It is important to differentiate between a discussion and a dialogue (Bolten, 2001). The difference lies in the goal of the interaction. In a therapeutic discussion or debate, the goal of each of the discussants is to convince one another of basic points and ideas or the thesis held by each. Participants in a discussion are focused on proving each other wrong so that their line of reasoning will be accepted as better, smarter, more important, or even as the "truth." In a therapeutic dialogue, knowledge and insight are gained from the patient which helps the therapist guide the therapy process. The interaction must be open with the therapist learning from the patient, not just being the "teacher." A therapeutic discussion and a therapeutic dialogue differ in the following ways (based on Bolten, 2001):

Socratic dialogue	Therapeutic discussion or debate
Mutually investigate an idea	Convince another of the "rightness" of one's position
Give patient time to speak	Demand "equal time" or take lion's share of the time
Pose questions to gain understanding	Look upon the patient's speaking as lost time
Work to understand what the patient means	Undermine the patient's position
Develop a mutually accepted position	Make the patient's position untenable
Make the position clear and explicit	Strive for approval of the therapist's viewpoint
Willingness to share data that support	Propose that the patient is ignorant of their true goals
Investigate differences in position and direction	Propose resistance as the reason that the therapist's position is not accepted
Strive for consensus and understanding	Strive for winning
Focus on investigating	Focus on convincing
Shared vision	Either therapist's vision or patient's vision

The "dialogue" component of SD uses a questioning format to facilitate the patient's movement toward greater recognition of areas, issues, and situations that cause difficulty.

The history, background, and elements of SD have been reviewed in detail by Overholser 1993a,b, 1994, 1995, 1996). SD, also referred to as Socratic facilitation, has been described as containing four distinct features. First, SD must be linked to the individual's personal experience, thereby making the process idiosyncratic. Second, the meanings must be validated by the patient, thereby making the dialogue relevant to the individual's experience. Third, when there is resistance, the therapist must be able to choose an alternate route and then later return to the initial focus of the questioning. Finally, there must be honesty on the part of both the "teacher" and the "student."

The basic elements of the model require that the teacher/therapist ask a number of questions of the "student." The growth or increase in knowledge on the part of the patient/student would come from the guidance offered by the "teacher." The questioning is not random or directionless as one might conclude from a brief exposure to the method. It is, in fact, a highly focused and directive method that leads the "student" in a predetermined and desired direction, even to a specific point. The technique involves formatting the questions, the content of the questions, the sequencing of the questions, and a summary of the questions. This systematic focus would occur within the process of the collaborative discussed by Beck et al. (1979). As summarized by

Overholser, Socratic questioning can be used to facilitate discovery, overcome resistance, produce autonomy, and develop the skill to use the dialogue independent of the therapy session.

A question often asked by students is, "How do I know what questions to ask?" or "Is there a book on what questions would be useful?" For many, the ideal of the SD is seen as the Holy Grail of CBT. As Overholser also points out, "few authors have delineated the structural and procedural components of the Socratic method in adequate detail" (1993a, p. 67). He identifies seven "types" of questions arranged from the simplest to the most complex: memory, translation, interpretation, application, analysis, synthesis, and evaluation. To this we would add an even more basic question, that of facts relating to background and personal history.

History questions are usually part of the basic intake data. While possibly influenced by memory, these questions relate to age, family constellation, educational history, or health issues. Questions can include: "How far did you go in school?" "What branch of service were you in?" Or "How many children do you have with your present husband?"

Memory questions involve the recall of internal or external experience. It must be remembered that the patient's recollection is influenced by interference, recency, and the "fact" not being of sufficient interest or value to warrant easy recall. The patient may easily project or be inaccurate in his or her recall. The "fact" is less important than how the patient constructs the memory. Memory questions might include: "When did you first experience the panic?" "What increased your energy before?" "How often was your mother hospitalized for her depression?"

Translation questions require that patients understand how the data refer to them. They take the data and reflect on the purpose and value of those data to their present experience. Ideally, they can serve to fill gaps in the patient's understanding on the relevance of the data (Overholser, 1993a). Questions include: "What does being depressed mean to you?" "How can we relate this to what you experience with your wife?" Or "How is this relevant to your not completing your work?"

Interpretation questions help the patient to identify relationships between facts and experience. These questions are essential in helping patients to make sense of their experiences. The connections are far better discovered by the patient rather than explicated by the therapist through interpretation. Questions might include: "How do your problems at work play themselves out at home?" " How are these two situations alike?" Or "How are these experiences different?"

Application questions ask the patient to apply previously mastered skills to a new situation. This requires that the skills or data be specified and highlighted. Questions might include: "How could you go about solving this problem?" "How have you dealt with these people before?" Or "Can you make a list of what has worked before?"

Analysis questions require breaking a problem into a number of parts. This is dependent on the patient having developed a problem-solving matrix that they can use in the present circumstance. Sanders (1966) makes the point that the problem-solving must be based on the patient having adequate data. In addition, the patient must have learned the basics of a problem-solving approach (D'Zurilla, 1988). Questions might include: "What evidence are you using to support your thinking?" "How might you tell if you are on the right track?" Or "What happens to make it worse?"

Synthesis questions require that the patient is led to use a more creative approach to problem solving. The issue here is that the patient look to alternate solutions. This type of questioning asks the patient to connect what might be viewed as disparate elements into a meaningful pattern. Questions might include: "Can you think of three other possible ways of dealing with your boss?" "What would it mean to you if you could not get into that graduate program?" Or "How could you go about letting your girlfriend know how you feel?"

Evaluation questions ask the patient to make decisions and judgments based on the accepted data. Overholser (1993a) states that, "This decision-making process involves first identifying appropriate standards, and then determining how closely the idea or behavior meets these standards" (p. 69). Questions might include: "What do you look for in a job?" "On a scale of 1–10, how would you rate your marriage?" Or "How would you say you are as a father?"

The choice of any of these questioning formats is determined on an "as-needed" basis in the therapy. The choice would be based on the specific goals at a particular point in therapy and what is appropriate at that moment in the therapy situation.

USING THE SOCRATIC DIALOGUE

The following basic "rules" or instructions for implementing and using SD are recommended.

1. The techniques must be embedded in the therapeutic collaboration. The collaboration involves an acceptance of the therapist as having a goal and direction for the therapy. The therapeutic goal is the roadway on which the therapist and patient will travel, the SD is the means of conveyance. As the road dips and curves, the SD will need to be adjusted in its speed, direction, and content. Rather

than the SD being a single technique, it is more the basis, manner, and style of the entire therapeutic encounter.

2. Using the problem list and the conceptualization that derives from that, the therapist must have an idea of where they hope to go. The SD is not a drifting technique that goes wherever the winds of chance or "crisis du jour" take it. If the conceptualization is reasonable, the therapist will not only have a direction, but also a speed limit. The direction is what Beck et al. (1979) referred to as "guided discovery." The key in this construct is that the discovery process is guided by the therapist, by the conceptualization, and by the goals of the therapy. This is in direct opposition to the psychodynamic focus on free association wherein the hope is that the patient will eventually and ultimately discover the insight that will bring about his or her relief by the unstructured associating and chaining of one thought/idea to another.

3. The questions must be short, focused, and targeted. Long, multipart, complex, and/or convoluted questions are confusing and distracting for both patient and therapist. The use of focused questioning allows the therapist greater control in moving the patient along the "road" in a series of small sequential steps. For example, the question, "Do you have trouble agreeing with your wife, or is this another example of how you get along with people based on how you were raised?" involves several questions. Each question would have value in helping the patient to move toward understanding. The complex question might, however, be answered as "yes" or "no." This would give the therapist and the patient little direction or insight. By asking three major questions and the appropriate subquestions, the therapy is advanced, the patient gains insight, and problem solving can occur. For example, "Do you have trouble agreeing with your wife?" "How does that play itself out?" "What are the consequences of the disagreement?" "Is this similar to how you interact with others?" "How has that affected you?" "What are the pros and cons of doing that?" "Where did you learn to respond that way?" "Was that typical of your home?" "How did it play itself out when you were a child?" "Is this way of responding worth keeping?" "Can you think of another way to respond that will get less conflict?" "Would that be something that you would be willing to do?"

The problem in asking short, focused questions is that therapists have often been taught that there is an economy to be sought in asking a single question that will have the necessary effect. Therapists then keep searching for this "magic" question.

4. A subset of the previous point is that the direct and focused questions serve to keep the patient's anxiety to a minimum. This is an essential part of the therapy process. Even apparently simple history questions can evoke great anxiety. For example, a patient was admitted to the emergency room on a Saturday evening. He was brought in by his wife who stated that he was just sitting in the living room silent and unresponsive to anything said to him. He came into the examining room quietly and without reluctance. In an attempt to make him comfortable, the interviewer (a graduate student) decided to ask simple questions. "What is your name?" she asked. The patient sat without verbally responding though he appeared to be thinking. This was noted by his facial grimaces. After a short time the interviewer asked, "Do you know where you are?" Again, no verbal response. She then asked, "What is today?" No question was answered. She excused herself and left to speak with her supervisor. She had concluded that the patient was psychotically mute and that he should be admitted and referred for medication.

The supervisor came into the examining room and took over the examination. He asked, "Do you know your name, just shake your head?" The patient slowly nodded in the affirmative. "Can you tell me your name?" This question got silence. The supervisor then asked, "Is it difficult for you to come up with a single name?" Again the head nod. "Are there several possible names that you might use?" Again the head nod.

The scene was repeated for the place and time. What came out of the careful questioning was that the patient's name was George Peter Smith. Friends called him "G. P." or "Pete." He did not use his first name and signed documents as G. Peter Smith. He could not decide whether to use his legal name, the names by which he was known, or his nicknames.

He similarly could not decide whether to state that he was in the county hospital, the emergency room of the county hospital, the psychiatric room of the emergency room of the county hospital, or simply in triage (the sign over the door). Finally, he could not decide whether the interviewer wanted the day, date, day and date, or day, date, and time. The lack of certainty as to the interviewer's goals led to him becoming anxious. Creating greater avoidance by promoting anxiety is counterproductive and contraindicated. He was admitted and responded well to both short-term medication and ongoing therapy.

5. Many patients enter therapy with a negative mindset. This negative set may be the result of being forced, required, or coerced into seeking therapy. Or, it may be a result of the individual feeling badly that he or she could not solve his or her problems and now needed a helper. In an effort to promote collaboration, the SD should be framed in the use of questions that will (ideally) elicit an affirmative response. For example:

Therapist: "Do you think that it would be helpful to confront your husband about his drinking?"

Patient: "No. He'll just get angry and leave the house. Then he'll come home drunk."

This question elicits a negative response that may reinforce that negative reaction already in place because of her husband's drinking.

A more effective framing of the questions would be the following:

Therapist: "I would guess that you are reluctant to address your husband's drinking. Is that accurate?"
Patient: "Yes. Exactly."
Therapist: "Does what he does get you angry?"
Patient: "Of course. It has been going on for so long."
Therapist: "Does his drinking always end up with him being drunk?"
Patient: "Yeah, pretty much all of the time."

Using this approach gives the patient the clear sense that the therapist understands her, is supportive for her, and can move the therapy along. She may even leave the session believing the therapist was in agreement with her long-suffering position. In fact, it was the careful questioning that has the patient agreeing with the therapist. The use of the affirmative response builds rapport.

6. The corollary of the above is that if a negative response is given, the question can be rephrased to elicit an affirmative response. For example:

Therapist: "How do you feel about coming to therapy?"
Patient: "I think that this stinks. I don't want to be here."
Therapist: "I can well imagine that there are lots of other things that you would rather be doing."
Patient: "Yeah! Better believe it!"
Therapist: "So you would like to get out of therapy as soon as possible, is that right?"
Patient: "Yes."
Therapist: "Shall we discuss the ways that you can get out ASAP?"

7. As the therapist is using the SD, it would be essential to monitor the patient's mood(s) and reactions on an ongoing basis. If a question or a direction increases a reaction, or stimulates a reaction, the therapist needs to address it immediately by inquiring what had just happened. Rather than try to interpret the patient's reaction, the therapist can ask, "I just noticed a reaction. What was it?"

8. The therapist must pace the questions to suit the patient's mood, style, and the content. Certain content may create a greater latency for response, some issues are responded to immediately.

9. The questions must be planned and offered in a logical sequence. The technique requires that the session is proactively planned rather than a reaction to what the patient offers. By setting out an explicit agenda and then having an internal map for the session, the therapist can ask the questions that move the session in the planned direction and toward the desired goals.

10. While the temptation may be strong to jump in and offer interpretations, the therapist must back away from this manner of response. The "interpretation" can best be framed through the SD. For example, the interpretation, "You seem angry" can best be framed as, "You seem to be having a strong reaction. What is it?" This is not only more respectful to the patient, but allows for greater clarity. For example, if the patient was not angry, but rather, annoyed, pissed off, or "really ticked," the question about the patient's reaction allows for the various shades of response rather than trying to capsule it as anger.

11. Self-disclosure should be limited. Comparing what the patient does with what the therapist does or did in similar situations, moves away from the SD and more to a discussion.

12. Everyday experiences can be used as therapeutic metaphors. These can then be referred to in the course of the therapy. Aesop's Fables are one example of the kind of metaphor that can be used to make therapeutic points. For example, the notion of "sour grapes" is a powerful image that can elicit both content and affect. The question then might be, "Is this an example of sour grapes?"

SUMMARY

The use of SD is a time-affirmed model of learning. Employed in education, business, and philosophy, it is an ideal fit in therapy. Beck, Ellis, and others use SD as the vehicle for therapy, asking a series of focused questions that include information about the patient's history, memory, translation of events, interpretation, application, analysis, synthesis, and evaluation.

SD has the effect of moving the therapy along in a clear direction that has been termed guided discovery or collaborative empiricism. SD requires a great deal of work in that the therapist is not simply responding to the patient's verbalizations but responding while at the same time using the patient's verbalizations and the direction offered by SD to achieve knowledge, insight, and ultimate change.

REFERENCES

Beck, A. T., Rush, A. J., Shaw, B. F., & Emery, G. (1979). *Cognitive therapy of depression*. New York: Guilford Press.

Bolten, H. (2001). Reason in practice. *Journal of Philosophy of Management*, *3*(1), 21–34.

D'Zurilla, T. (1986). *Problem-solving therapy: A social competence approach to clinical intervention*. New York: Springer.
D'Zurilla, T. (1988). Problem solving therapies. In K. Dobson (Ed.), *Handbook of cognitive behavioral therapies* (pp. 85–135). New York: Guilford Press.
Ellis, A. (1962). *Reason and emotion in psychotherapy*. Secaucus, NJ: Citadel.
Ellis, A. (1989). The ABCs of RET. In A. Freeman, K. M. Simon, L. E. Beutler, & H. Arkowitz (Eds.), *Comprehensive handbook of cognitive therapy* (pp. 5–20). New York: Plenum Press.
Leahy, R. L. (2001). *Overcoming resistance in cognitive therapy*. New York: Guilford Press.
Overholser, J. C. (1993a). Elements of the Socratic method: I. Systematic questioning. *Psychotherapy, 30*, 67–74.
Overholser, J. C. (1993b). Elements of the Socratic method: II. Inductive reasoning. *Psychotherapy, 30*, 75–85.
Overholser, J. C. (1994). Elements of the Socratic method: III. Universal definitions. *Psychotherapy, 31*, 286–293.
Overholser, J. C. (1995). Elements of the Socratic method: IV. Disavowal of knowledge. *Psychotherapy, 32*, 283–292.
Overholser, J. C. (1996). Elements of the Socratic method: V. Self-improvement. *Psychotherapy, 33*(4), 549–559.
Padesky, C. (1996). Developing cognitive therapist competency: Teaching and supervision models. In P. M. Salkovskis (Ed.), *Frontiers of cognitive therapy* (pp. 226–292). New York: Guilford Press.
Sanders, N. (1966). *Classroom questions: What kinds?* New York: Harper & Row.

Somatization

Lesley A. Allen and Robert L. WoolfolK

Keywords: somatization, somatoform disorders, stress management

Patients presenting with somatization provide significant challenges to health care providers. These patients tend to overuse health care services, derive little benefit from treatment, and experience protracted impairment, often lasting many years (Smith, Monson, & Ray, 1986). In addition, somatization patients present a theoretical challenge, in that the sources of their discomfort and their pathophysiology remain unclear. Because standard medical care has been relatively unsuccessful in treating somatization, alternative treatments have been developed. Cognitive–behavioral therapy (CBT) is the treatment most often studied with this population. This article reviews the rationale and empirical evidence for treating somatization with CBT.

DEFINITIONS

According to the *Diagnostic and Statistical Manual of Mental Disorders* (DSM-IV), somatization disorder is characterized by a lifetime history of at least four unexplained pain complaints (e.g., in the back, chest, joints), two unexplained nonpain gastrointestinal complaints (e.g., nausea, bloating), one unexplained sexual symptom (e.g., sexual dysfunction, irregular menstruation), and one pseudoneurological symptom (e.g., seizures, paralysis, numbness). The prevalence of somatization disorder has been estimated to be 0.1–0.4 in the general population and 1.0–5.0% in primary care clinics (Kirmayer & Robbins, 1991).

Although somatization disorder is classified as a distinct disorder in DSM-IV, it has been argued that somatization disorder represents the extreme end of a somatization continuum (Escobar, Burnam, Karno, Forsythe, & Golding, 1987; Kroenke et al., 1997). A broadening of the somatization construct has been encouraged to underscore the many patients encumbered by unexplained symptoms that are not numerous enough to meet criteria for full somatization disorder. Escobar and colleagues proposed the label *abridged somatization* for men experiencing four or more unexplained physical symptoms and women experiencing six or more unexplained physical symptoms (Escobar et al., 1987). Kroenke and colleagues suggested an alternative subthreshold somatization category, termed *multisomatoform disorder*, for all patients currently experiencing at least three unexplained physical symptoms and a 2-year history of somatization (Kroenke et al., 1997). The prevalence of these subthreshold somatization syndromes may be as high as 20% of primary care patients, substantially higher than that of full somatization disorder (Kirmayer & Robbins, 1991; Kroenke et al., 1997).

CLINICAL CHARACTERISTICS

Much attention has focused on somatization patients' illness behavior and the resulting impact of that behavior on the health care system. These patients disproportionately use and misuse health care services. When standard diagnostic evaluations fail to uncover organic pathology, somatization patients tend to seek additional medical procedures, including unnecessary hospitalizations and surgeries. One study found that somatization disorder patients incurred nine times the U.S. per capita health care cost (Smith et al., 1986). Abridged somatization and multisomatoform disorder have also been associated with significant health care utilization (Escobar et al., 1987; Kroenke et al., 1997).

The abnormal illness behavior of somatizing patients extends beyond medical clinics and hospitals to patients' jobs and households. Most patients withdraw from both productive and pleasurable activities because of physical discomfort and/or fears of exacerbating their symptoms. High levels of functional impairment have been associated with moderate and severe levels of somatization (Kroenke et al., 1997; Smith et al., 1986).

In addition to their physical complaints, many somatization patients complain of psychiatric distress. Anxiety and mood disorders are especially common in this population (Kroenke et al., 1997; Smith et al., 1986). In fact, severity of psychological distress seems to correlate positively with the number of functional somatic symptoms reported (Katon et al., 1991).

RATIONALE FOR CBT FOR SOMATIZATION

A cognitive–behavioral conceptualization of somatization provides a rationale for treating this disorder with CBT. The model emphasizes the interaction of physiology, cognition, emotion, behavior, and environment. Patients presenting with somatization may have higher levels of physiological arousal and be less likely to habituate to a stressful task than control subjects. This physiological arousal is compounded by a tendency to amplify somatosensory information; that is, these patients are hypersensitive to bodily sensations, which are experienced as intense, noxious, and disturbing. Further, somatization patients have negative cognitions about their physical sensations. For example, they may believe that pain, fatigue, and/or discomfort of any sort are signs of disease. In addition to misinterpreting somatic sensations, some patients may think catastrophically about their physical sensations, imagining these sensations to be signs of a fatal disease, such as cancer or AIDS. Thus, somatizers' excessive physiological arousal produces physical sensations that are not only disturbing, but also frightening.

These cognitive distortions elicit negative emotions and maladaptive behaviors. Thoughts of possible illness give rise to feelings of anxiety, dysphoria, and frustration, which are likely to maintain physiological arousal and physical symptoms. Intending to prevent injury or exacerbation of symptoms, somatization patients typically cope by withdrawing from activities. Such time away from activities provides opportunities for additional attention to be focused on one's physical health. Further, patients suffering from these physical symptoms, distorted cognitions, and negative affect may seek repeated physician visits and diagnostic assessments. Physicians, in turn, attempting to conduct thorough evaluations and avoid malpractice suits, may encourage somatizing behavior by ordering unnecessary diagnostic procedures. These tests, even if negative, reinforce somatizers' maladaptive belief that a physical symptom indicates organic pathology. Also, unnecessary medical procedures may result in iatrogenic illness.

EMPIRICAL BASIS FOR CBT FOR SOMATIZATION

The treatment of somatization with CBT is still in its infancy. Only one group of investigators has reported findings from a controlled trial of CBT for somatization disorder (Allen, Woolfolk, & Gara, 2001). Five other studies have examined the efficacy of cognitive–behavioral interventions for subthreshold somatization (Hellman, Budd, Borysenko, McClelland, & Benson, 1990; Lidbeck, 1997; McLeod, Budd, & McClelland, 1997; Speckens et al., 1995; Sumathipala, Hewege, Hanwella, & Mann, 2000). All six studies found that patients treated with CBT experienced greater improvement in their somatic complaints than did a control group of patients. Further, patients who received CBT reported greater reductions in functional impairment (Allen et al., 2001; Speckens et al., 1995) and physician visits (Hellman et al., 1990; Sumathipala et al., 2000) than did control patients.

While the aforementioned treatments have been categorized as CBT, a few variations in their content and format should be noted. All interventions were brief, lasting 6 to 16 sessions, and trained patients to alter dysfunctional cognitions and behaviors. One intervention emphasized relaxation training (Lidbeck, 1997); two others encouraged spousal participation in treatment (Allen et al., 2001; Sumathipala et al., 2000). Three studies examined the efficacy of group CBT (Hellman et al., 1990; Lidbeck, 1997; McLeod et al., 1997), whereas the other three investigated the efficacy of individual CBT (Allen et al., 2001; Speckens et al., 1995; Sumathipala et al., 2000). The setting in which treatment was implemented was either a psychiatry department (Allen et al., 2001) or a primary care clinic (Hellman et al., 1990; Lidbeck, 1997; McLeod et al., 1997; Speckens et al., 1995; Sumathipala et al., 2000).

OVERCOMING OBSTACLES IN TREATING SOMATIZATION

Engaging somatization patients in CBT is often challenging. These patients may harbor doubts about the relevance of a psychological intervention for their physical symptoms. Such doubts are likely to interfere with treatment compliance. Specific strategies are recommended to increase patients' commitment to treatment. First, therapists should work closely with patients' physicians. Those patients who observe their trusted physician collaborating with their new therapist, may be more open to therapy. Ideally, treatment would be conducted in primary care offices. Even when treatment occurs outside the primary care clinic, the link between the physician and therapist may help convey a biopsychosocial conceptualization of somatization symptoms. Second, therapists should communicate acceptance of patients' physical discomfort, while providing education about the mind–body connection. Physical symptoms should not be minimized. Instead, therapists respond empathically to patients' distress without reinforcing dysfunctional beliefs or behaviors related to the symptoms. Although irrational beliefs are eventually challenged, treatment is never combative. Instead, a biopsychosocial explanation of physical symptoms is presented as a theory for patients to test empirically.

Some somatization patients have difficulty describing their thoughts and feelings. Such difficulties not only make the task of self-monitoring frustrating but also obstruct the cognitive restructuring component of CBT. Therapists should respond to deficits in self-awareness by slowing down treatment to teach patients to attend to their cognitive and affective experiences. Cognitive restructuring cannot be undertaken until patients can identify their thoughts and feelings.

A third obstacle may arise when nonphysicians treat patients whose symptoms suggest the presence of a medical condition. Unable to rule out medical pathology, therapists may be uncertain how to respond to the presentation of new symptoms. Should the patient be encouraged to seek additional physician visits, even if the patient has a history of overusing health care services? Alternatively, should the patient be encouraged to challenge his/her beliefs about the symptoms and need for treatment, even if such interventions might discourage appropriate seeking of medical care? These decisions are easier to make when therapists collaborate closely with patients' physicians. In addition, frequent contact between the therapist and physician may enable each to support the other's treatment recommendations.

SUMMARY

The extraordinary costs of somatization make it a public health concern. Initial findings on characteristics of somatizing patients support a cognitive–behavioral rationale for treatment. Six controlled clinical trials suggest CBT may reduce physical discomfort, functional limitations, and physician visits. Additional research is required to replicate these findings.

Because somatization patients are often skeptical of psychological interventions and may withdraw prematurely from treatment, a few strategies for working with these patients have been suggested: (1) Therapists are encouraged to collaborate with patients' physicians throughout the treatment. (2) To engage patients in treatment, therapists should respond empathically to patients' distress without reinforcing "sick role" behavior. (3) Supplementary sessions in the early phase of treatment may be required to teach patients to describe their thoughts and feelings.

See also: Biopsychosocial treatment of pain, Chronic pain, Medically unexplained symptoms

REFERENCES

Allen, L. A., Woolfolk, R. L., & Gara, M. A. (2001). Cognitive behavior therapy for somatization disorder: A controlled study. *Psychosomatic Medicine, 63*, 93–94.

Escobar, J. I., Burnam, A., Karno, M., Forsythe, A., & Golding, J. M. (1987). Somatization in the community. *Archives of General Psychiatry, 44*, 713–718.

Hellman, C. J. C., Budd, M., Borysenko, J., McClelland, D. C., & Benson, H. (1990). A study of the effectiveness of two group behavioral medicine interventions for patients with psychosomatic complaints. *Behavioral Medicine, 16*(4), 165–173.

Katon, W., Lin, E., Von Korff, M., Russo, J., Lipscomb, P., & Bush, T. (1991). Somatization: A spectrum of severity. *American Journal of Psychiatry, 148*, 34–40.

Kirmayer, L. J., & Robbins, J. M. (1991). Three forms of somatization in primary care: Prevalence, co-occurrence, and sociodemographic characteristics. *Journal of Nervous and Mental Disease, 179*, 647–655.

Kroenke, K., Spitzer, R. L., deGruy, F. V., Hahn, S. R., Linzer, M., Williams, J. B., Brody, D., & Davies, M. (1997). Multisomatoform disorder: An alternative to undifferentiated somatoform disorder for the somatizing patient in primary care. *Archives of General Psychiatry, 54*, 352–358.

Lidbeck, J. (1997). Group therapy for somatization disorders in general practice: Effectiveness of a short cognitive–behavioural treatment model. *Acta Psychiatrica Scandinavica, 96*, 14–24.

McLeod, C. C., Budd, M. A., & McClelland, D. C. (1997). Treatment of somatization in primary care. *General Hospital Psychiatry, 19*, 251–258.

Smith, G. R., Monson, R. A., & Ray, D. C. (1986). Patients with multiple unexplained symptoms: Their characteristics, functional health, and health care utilization. *Archives of Internal Medicine, 146*, 69–72.

Speckens, A. E. M., van Hemert, A. M., Spinhoven, P., Hawton, K. E., Bolk, J. H., & Rooijmans, G. M. (1995). Cognitive behavioural therapy for medically unexplained physical symptoms: A randomised controlled trial. *British Medical Journal, 311*, 1328–1332.

Sumathipala, A., Hewege, S., Hanwella, R., & Mann, A. H. (2000). Randomized controlled trial of cognitive behaviour therapy for repeated consultations for medically unexplained complaints: A feasibility study in Sri Lanka. *Psychological Medicine, 30*, 747–757.

RECOMMENDED READINGS

Allen, L. A. (2000). Short-term therapy for somatization disorder: A cognitive behavioral approach. *Journal of Cognitive Psychotherapy, 14*, 373–380.

Allen, L. A., Escobar, J. I., Lehrer, P. M., Gara, M. A., & Woolfolk, R. L. (2002). Psychosocial treatments for multiple unexplained physical symptoms: A review of the literature. *Psychosomatic Medicine, 64*, 939–950.

Salkovskis, P. M. (1989). Somatic problems. In K. Hawton, P. M. Salkovskis, J. Kirk, & D. M. Clark (Eds.), *Cognitive behaviour therapy for psychiatric problems*. New York: Oxford University Press.

Stages of Change

Michael J. Dolan

Keywords: stages of change, readiness for change

Psychotherapy is often seen as an inconvenient and/or uncomfortable process by many clients. The reasons vary from the drug addict forced into treatment by the courts to the client who has been abused and must deal with painful trauma. The human condition is largely based on maintaining physical, emotional, cognitive, and environmental homeostasis. If one's "systems" are in balance, one can know what to expect. Change is an irritant to homeostasis and many times the first instinct is to reject this irritant. It is because of the potential for rejection that therapists must understand the process of change. The medical community has at its disposal a plethora of antirejection drugs, which serve to maintain change and prevent a return to the premorbid condition. Therapists have no such wonder drugs available to them. The revised stage of change model developed by Freeman and Dolan (2001) is designed to address these very issues and to provide the therapist with the necessary tools to be successful.

Understanding therapy begins with the theory to explain the change process and there are rarely studies in which the internal mechanism that causes change can be inferred (Kazdin, 2000). However, the focus of how we change has been relegated to the theoretical discussions of people in academia.

The process of change is the foundation of any psychotherapeutic endeavor. Stage theories have been a central part of many models including Freud's psychosexual stages (Freud, 1910), Erikson's psychosocial stages (Erikson, 1963), Kohlberg's stages of moral development (Kohlberg, 1963), Piaget's stages of cognitive development (Piaget, 1966), Prochaska and DiClemente's stages of change (Prochaska & DiClemente, 1982; Prochaska, DiClemente, & Norcross, 1992), and Maslow's hierarchy of needs (Maslow, 1968).

Why people change and why they do not is a question that therapists have asked for many years. We believe that people change in order to relieve emotional or psychological pain or to make improvements in themselves. Why people do not change has challenged clinicians and the answer has too often been the ubiquitous term *resistance*. The implication in the term and concept of resistance is that (1) the patient chooses to not change, (2) the individual has too much to gain from not changing what they do, or (3) unconscious forces or conflicts mitigate against the individual changing. These formulations of resistance are at best unsatisfactory and at worst are blaming of the patient for not doing what the therapist expects of them. A far more satisfying view is expressed in the stages of change literature.

Hayes and Strauss (1998) present a dynamic system, where stabilizing forces maintain the coherence or integrity of a system, and variability provides the flexibility necessary for growth and change. Change is viewed as movement through a series of states of stability, variability, and shifts in attractor states (Thelen & Smith, 1994).

Several authors have reconceptualized the process of change in individual psychotherapy from the perspective of dynamic systems theory (Caspar, Rothenfluh, & Segal, 1992; Greenberg, Rice, & Elliott, 1993; Mahoney, 1991; Schiepek, Fricke, & Kaimer, 1992). The components of these theories are not new; they have been presented in different literatures with a variety of labels and associated theories of change. Mahoney's (1991) theory is very comprehensive, demonstrating a convergence on a number of important points. According to dynamic systems theorists in individual psychotherapy (Caspar et al., 1992; Mahoney, 1991; Schiepek et al., 1992), psychological growth is a lifelong process that is characterized by periods of stability and instability. Psychopathology is viewed as a state of dynamic equilibrium, where the predominant state consists of well-organized patterns of cognitive/affective/behavioral and somatic functioning that interfere with the individual's well-being and everyday functioning (Mahoney, 1991). These patterns can become so well established that they are considered lifestyles (Schiepek et al., 1992). Because they provide structure to the individual's life, stabilizing forces maintain these patterns, even if the existing system does not function optimally.

Self-protective mechanisms (Mahoney, 1991), such as avoidance for the agoraphobic, must be overcome before change can occur, and thus they influence the pacing and direction of change (Mahoney, 1991). It is perhaps for this reason that client self-protection (often called resistance) is a well-documented predictor of negative outcomes in psychotherapy (Hanna, 1996; Orlinsky, Grawe, & Parks, 1994). To decrease this potentially self-destructive self-protection, the therapist must provide a secure, safe environment that can augment the client's strengths and self-esteem while developing more effective and efficient coping resources and social support leading to a greater sense of hope (Hanna, 1996). As in other dynamic systems, destabilization is viewed as a necessary and natural process that allows for growth and change. It would be through this "shaking up" process that change can occur. Mahoney (1991) described destabilization as a period of systemwide disorder marked by increased variability in such domains as thought patterns, affect, behavior, intimacy, sleep, appetite, and somatic functioning. Given the organism's natural movement toward stability and balance, the system in disorder will attempt to move toward order or adaptation as defined by Piaget (1966). According to Mahoney (1991), the therapist needs to assess and then enhance the client's readiness for change. Providing a secure, supportive therapeutic environment and strengthening internal and external resources can prepare the client to undergo destabilization or a movement from one stage of change to another (Caspar et al., 1992; Greenberg et al., 1993; Schiepek et al., 1992).

The new and experienced therapist must determine both the appropriate intervention and the timing of that intervention in order to elicit a change response. The stages of change model developed by Prochaska and DiClemente (1982) has been applied to determine a client's readiness for change. Some of these stages occur prior to any actual change. These stages are part of a dynamic process and are therefore open to revisions as experience or research provides more specificity. It is due to this very process that Freeman and Dolan (2001) undertook a revision of the Prochaska and DiClemente model. This revision involved the addition of new stages to increase the specificity of the stages and for them to more appropriately reflect the actual therapeutic process.

The stage model represents an orderly, often-cyclical progression that has not been demonstrated empirically. As Sutton (1996) observed, "Motivation or intention to change may be more realistically thought of as a continuum with no necessary assumption that people move along this continuum in one direction or through a sequence of discrete stages" (p. 203). As with cognitive–behavioral therapy, the order of the stages indicates that cognitive change precedes behavioral change.

From the beginning, the transtheoretical model has been used in both the health science and psychotherapy fields. It is regarded as both a scientific revolution and an "everyman" theory, derived from lessons learned from "thousands of ordinary people" (Prochaska & Velicer, 1997, p. 11). The model "seems to have caught the current mood and makes some of us feel more optimistic" (Davidson, 1992, p. 822). The stage model appeals to certain modern intellectual conceptualizations of human behavior. This view fits with the cognitive theory assumption that change is often the result of careful (cognitive) evaluation of alternatives and their consequences. The cognitive–behavioral therapies hold the belief that our thoughts and behavior are connected in a logical, orderly fashion and that if we understand these connections, then we might be better able to explain and possibly even predict behavior.

Carey, Purnine, Maisto, and Carey (1999) noted that it is important to distinguish readiness for change from readiness to participate in a particular treatment; some stage assessments appear to tap both constructs. Feelings connected with behavioral problems and with the prospect and processes of change are likely to influence readiness for change and the change process.

In Sutton's (1996) view, the stage of changes

> should be thought of not as a descriptive model but as a prescriptive model—a model of ideal change. It prescribes how, from the viewpoint of a therapist or health educator, people should change and suggests how they might be encouraged or helped to change. (p. 204)

Most scientists/practitioners agree that the model has heuristic value (Davidson, 1992; Pierce, Farkas, & Gilpin, 1998; Stockwell, 1996; Sutton, 1996). By suggesting that addictions and other behavioral problems are not easily remedied, the model may encourage greater patience and persistence in change efforts. It also underscores the importance of measuring progress toward realistic objectives (Prochaska & DiClemente, 1998). The Freeman and Dolan model enhances and refines the Prochaska and DiClemente model by an expansion of the stages as well as the inclusion of a process that is consistent with treatment experience. In this model, the authors take into account that some people may be unaware of the existence of a problem or their need to change. The noncontemplation stage was added to take into account this reality. As a therapist, you may have encountered clients who are forced or required to enter treatment for a number of reasons (i.e., courts, schools, family). These individuals are placed in a situation where they must decide between therapy and some threat (i.e., jail, suspension, or divorce). They are not at the present time willing to engage in the change process and may, in fact, be violently opposed to the process. The anticontemplation stage was developed to identify this process on the change continuum. The next two stages (precontemplation and contemplation), although named similarly to the Prochaska and DiClemente model, are not tied to commitment as described in Prochaska and DiClemente. They are the metacognitive and cognitive functions of the change process. The preparation stage of Prochaska and DiClemente is timed (within the next month) and requires an unsuccessful attempt at change within the past year. In the Freeman–Dolan model, action planning replaces the preparation stage and is designed as an interactive collaborative process between the therapist and the client. This is the stage at which treatment focus and active treatment planning begin. The action stage is the same for both models and is described as going from neutral to drive. The next three stages are new and reflect the complex cognitive process of upsetting the homeostasis of a person through the change process. The first of these stages is prelapse, in which a person is evaluating if the change made in the action stage is beneficial or needed. This is a cognitive process with no behavioral components. The lapse stage is the behavioral manifestation of the unsuccessful resolution of the prelapse stage. This is usually characterized by a single behavioral event, and if therapeutic redirection occurs, there is a return to the change state. If the resolution of the prelapse stage is unsuccessful or if redirection is ineffective, then the process will move to relapse, which is a return to old behaviors (prior to the change). Relapse includes a reemergence of not only the behavioral problems, but also the cognitive patterns that induce or reinforce the problem behavior. The lack of these stages in the Prochaska–DiClemente model prevented accurate identification and interventions necessary for the resolution of problems unique to these stages. The maintenance stage in both models is conceptually similar; however, the focus in Freeman and Dolan is to continually assess and fine-tune the changes, as well as to generalize these changes to other problem areas throughout a person's lifetime. The Freeman–Dolan model, through this expansion, seeks to provide the therapist with a tool that is more efficient and clinically relevant. This is accomplished by including stages that reflect scenarios common in most clinical practices.

Comparison of the Two Models

Prochaska–DiClemente	Freeman–Dolan
1. Precontemplation	1. Noncontemplation
2. Contemplation	2. Anticontemplation
3. Preparation	3. Precontemplation
4. Action	4. Contemplation
5. Maintenance	5. Action Planning
	6. Action
	7. Prelapse
	8. Lapse
	9. Relapse
	10. Maintenance

DISCUSSION

A model to assist therapists in conceptualizing and understanding complex and even abstract human behavior and processes has been used since the dawn of our profession. The Freeman–Dolan model has merely been an attempt to refine the work of Prochaska and DiClemente in the very complex area of understanding change and to retool it to reflect the experience of today's therapist. The inclusion of the five new stages and the redefining of the existing stages allow the therapist to more accurately determine where his/her client is on the continuum of change. The revisions open the door to a new way of conceptualizing clients, by seeing issues like resistance as merely a part of the process of change and not an obstacle to it. The revised model permits therapists to view clients within a model of change that is dynamic and flexible, instead of static, and defined by a set timeline. As therapists find themselves more and more accountable to third parties who require justification and empirical support for our treatment methods, it is important for our profession to explain the actual process of our clients' experience in therapy. For many years the work of the therapist was defined as assisting the client through the action planning and action stages. Yet, this is only a small and usually easy part of the therapeutic process. The ability to accurately identify the clients' problems and obstacles to change and then motivate them through the process requires far more time and work. For far too long, therapists in addictions failed to prepare their clients for working through the problems and obstacles of sobriety in cognitive, affective, and behavioral terms. The goal of achieving sobriety was sufficient for most insurance companies and for a lot of our clients, but without long-term recovery, sobriety is a short-term behavioral event. As the old saying goes, "If you give a man fish, he eats for a day, but if you teach him to fish, he will eat for a lifetime." The goals of therapy must look toward these long-term solutions as goals. The maintenance of change is necessary for this long-term process to occur. Identifying cognitive distortions (prelapse) that will lead back to drinking is more effective and humane than waiting for the client to return to drinking (lapse or relapse).

In a recent study (Dolan, 2003) to determine if the revisions proposed by Freeman and Dolan would fulfill the goal of the revised model to be of greater use than the Prochaska and DiClemente model, the study found that 87.4% of the participants agreed or strongly agreed with Freeman and Dolan in its ability to accurately identify stages versus 22.9% for the old model. The study also found that in a direct competition, 75.7% of participants agreed or strongly agreed that they preferred the Freeman–Dolan model, while only 27.2% agreed or strongly agreed that they preferred the Prochaska–DiClemente model.

The majority of our skill as clinicians are not only in the facilitation of behavioral change, but also motivating and assisting people in movement toward change. These skills and change processes have been difficult to identify in the past and were thrown into the vague category of rapport.

We now have the opportunity to explore this process by identifying it and expanding on the stages to deal with true clinical experience.

The concept of prelapse is needed to explain that as soon as we make a change, the person or organism initially goes through a process of rejection of these new behaviors similar to a body going through rejection of transplanted parts. As therapists, we do not have powerful antirejection drugs that prevent or delay this process. We need to include this rejection or a return to the previous homeostasis in our treatment process until we have incorporated a new homeostasis with the new behaviors.

Redirection is a process by which the therapist intervenes to put the change process back on track. Redirection can include a variety of therapeutic interventions such as cognitive restructuring, disputing beliefs, developing more coping skills, increasing support systems, and so on. Skills and techniques in this process are flexible to fit the needs of the client, the stage of change, and the theoretical orientation of the therapist.

This model will provide the clinician, the researcher, the third-party payer, and ultimately the patient with a more experience-centered focus from which to make decisions.

REFERENCES

Carey, K. B., Purnine, D. M., Maisto, S. A., & Carey, M. P. (1999). Assessing readiness to change substance abuse: A critical review of instruments. *Clinical Psychology: Science and Practice, 6*, 245–266.

Caspar, F., Rothenfluh, T., & Segal, Z. V. (1992). The appeal of connectionism for clinical psychology. *Clinical Psychology Review, 12*, 719–762.

Davidson, R. (1992). Prochaska and DiClemente's model of change: A case study? *British Journal of Addiction, 87*, 821–822.

Dolan, M. J. (2003). *Assessment of the revised stage of change model*. Unpublished doctoral dissertation, Philadelphia College of Osteopathic Medicine.

Erikson, E. (1963). *Childhood and society*. New York: Norton.

Freeman, A., & Dolan, M. (2001). Revisiting Prochaska and DiClemente's stages of change theory: An expansion and specification to aid in treatment planning and outcome evaluation. *Cognitive and Behavioral Practice, 8*, 224–234.

Freud, S. (1910). The origin and development of psychoanalysis. *American Journal of Psychology, 21*(2), 181–218.

Greenberg, L. S., Rice, L. N., & Elliott, R. (1993). *Facilitating emotional change. The moment-by-moment process*. New York: Guilford Press.

Hanna, F. J. (1996). Precursors of change: Pivotal points of involvement and resistance in psychotherapy. *Journal of Psychotherapy Integration, 6*, 227–264.

Hayes, A. M., & Strauss, J. S. (1998). Dynamic systems theory as a paradigm for the study of change in psychotherapy: An application to cognitive therapy for depression. *Journal of Consulting and Clinical Psychology, 66*(6), 939–947.

Kazdin, A. E. (2000). *Psychotherapy for children and adolescents: Directions for research and practice*. New York: Oxford University Press.

Kohlberg, L. (1963). Moral development and identification. In H. W. Stevenson (Ed.), *Child psychology* (pp. 277–332). Chicago: University of Chicago Press.

Mahoney, M. J. (1991). *Human change processes: The scientific foundations of psychotherapy*. New York: Basic Books.

Maslow, A. (1968). *Toward a psychology of being* (2nd ed.). New York: Van Nostrand Reinhold.

Nathan, P. E., & Gorman, J. M. (Eds.). (1998). *Treatments that work*. New York: Oxford University Press.

Orlinsky, D. E., Grawe, K., & Parks, B. K. (1994). Process and outcome in psychotherapy—Noch einmal. In A. E. Bergin & L. S. Garfield (Eds.), *Handbook of psychotherapy and behavior change* (pp. 270–376). New York: Wiley.

Piaget, J. (1966). *Psychology of intelligence*. Totowa, NJ: Littlefield, Adams.

Pierce, J. P., Farkas, A. J., & Gilpin, E. A. (1998). Beyond stages of change: The quitting continuum measures progress towards successful smoking cessation. *Addiction, 93*, 277–286.

Prochaska, J. O., & DiClemente, C. C. (1982). Transtheoretical therapy: Toward a more integrative model of change. *Psychotherapy: Theory Research and Practice, 20*, 161–173.

Prochaska, J. O., & DiClemente, C. C. (1998). Comments, criteria, and creating better models: In response to Davidson. In W. R. Miller & N. Heather (Eds.), *Treating addictive behaviors* (2nd ed., pp. 39–45). New York: Plenum Press.

Prochaska, J. O., DiClemente, C. C., & Norcross, J. C. (1992). In search of how people change. Applications to addictive behaviors. *American Psychologist, 47*, 1102–1114.

Prochaska, J. O., & Velicer, W. F. (1997). Misinterpretations and misapplications of the transtheoretical model. *American Journal of Health Promotion, 12*, 11–12.

Schiepek, G., Fricke, B., & Kaimer, P. (1992). Synergistics of psychotherapy. In G. Schiepek, W. Tschacher, & E. J. Brunner (Eds.), *Self organization and clinical psychology* (pp. 239–267). Berlin: Author.

Stockwell, T. (1996). Interventions cannot ignore intentions. *Addiction, 91*, 1283–1284.

Sutton, S. (1996). Can "stages of change" provide guidance in the treatment of addictions? A critical examination of Prochaska and DiClemente's model. In G. Edwards & C. Dare (Eds.), *Psychotherapy, psychological treatments and the addictions* (pp. 189–205). New York: Cambridge University Press.

Thelen, E., & Smith, L. B. (1994). *A dynamic systems approach to the development of cognition and action*. Cambridge, MA: MIT Press.

Suicide–Adult

Thomas E. Joiner, Jr. and Foluso M. Williams

Keywords: cognitive–behavioral therapy, suicide, parasuicide, dialectical behavioral therapy

Suicidality is undoubtedly a pressing clinical issue. Effective treatment of suicidal behavior can potentially save an individual's life. Therefore, it is imperative that the treatment of suicidality be grounded in empirical research. Cognitive–behavioral therapy (CBT) for suicidal behavior provides scientifically supported treatment for this serious condition. A recent review of the literature assessed treatments for suicidality (see Rudd, 2000, for a detailed summary of all studies). Treatments were divided into short-term (i.e., treatments lasting less than 6 months, $n = 14$) and long-term (i.e., treatments lasting 6 months or greater, $n = 2$). Among the short-term treatments, the majority ($n = 10$) provided some form of CBT, which integrated a component of problem solving as the core intervention. The cognitive–behavioral approach, by nature, is well-suited for short-term treatment. The cognitive–behavioral approach to be discussed is also advantageous in its ability to specifically identify treatment components, as well as clearly describe the implications for treatment outcome and relapse.

The review of the literature demonstrates the substantial efficacy of CBT in treating suicidal behavior. The combination of short-term CBT and problem-solving therapy effectively reduced symptoms of suicidal ideation, depression, and hopelessness up to 1 year after treatment (Rudd, Joiner, & Rajab, 2001). CBT lends itself well to the direct clinical applications of empirical findings in the specific areas of cognitive, emotional, behavioral, and interpersonal functioning. It is adaptable for integration and application in clinical practice, yet its clear structural framework allows for empirical investigation. These aspects of CBT are advantageous in the treatment of suicidal behavior.

An accurate conceptualization of suicidality is key to an appropriate, effective treatment. The cognitive–behavioral model of suicidal behavior provides such a conceptualization. The primary component of this model is the suicidal mode. According to Beck (1996), a mode is a "specific suborganization within the personality organization [that] incorporates the relevant components of the basic systems of personality: cognitive (information processing), affective, behavioral, and motivational" (p. 4). The affective, behavioral, and physiological components are all interrelated and are affected by cognitive change. The suicidal belief system (suicidal thoughts and ideations) and the cognitive triad (thoughts about the self, others, and the future) are two areas within the suicidal mode that are primary areas targeted in a cognitive–behavioral intervention. The core beliefs that permeate the cognitive triad fall within three domains. The first two, helplessness and unlovability, were specified by Beck (1996). The third is the domain of distress tolerance (e.g., "I can't stand feeling this way"), proposed by Linehan (1993).

There are certain variables that raise the risk for activating the suicidal mode. These variables, known as predisposing vulnerabilities, can increase the probability of future suicidal episodes, or heighten the risk for activation of the suicidal mode. For this reason, they are regarded as facilitating modes. Such predisposing vulnerabilities include Axis I and Axis II diagnoses, previous suicide attempts, developmental trauma, and a family history of suicidal behavior. The suicidal mode can be activated by the interaction of various predisposing vulnerabilities and identifiable triggers. Identifiable triggers consist of internal stressors, such as thoughts, feelings, images, and physical sensations. External stressors include situations, circumstances, and interpersonal encounters. All components of the suicidal mode interact with each other in a dynamic as opposed to a linear fashion. Since many parts of this mode can be simultaneously activated, suicidal behavior is manifested in a variety of ways.

In Rudd and colleagues' (2001) approach to the cognitive treatment of suicidal behavior, two distinct short-term foci are delineated. The first is the domain of symptoms, consisting of depression, hopelessness, guilt, suicidal ideation, anger, anxiety, and other related symptoms. The second domain consists of clear, identifiable skill deficits. These deficits involve problem solving, emotion regulation, distress tolerance, interpersonal skills, anger management, and self-monitoring. Problems in these domains are viewed as products of the suicidal mode, whether it is an active mode that triggers suicidal behavior, or a facilitating mode that increases the risk of suicidal behavior. An additional domain that is addressed during treatment is that of maladaptive personality traits. These traits are consistent with personality disorders, as defined in the DSM-IV-TR.

The first domain of symptoms includes the array of thoughts and behaviors experienced by an individual during a suicidal crisis. Symptoms include suicidal ideations, anger, sadness, and despair. This domain also includes preparatory behaviors, such as counting pills. The goal of symptom management is to focus on reducing these associated thoughts and behaviors and replacing them with more adaptive ones, as well as instilling hopefulness about the future.

The skills deficits comprising the second domain are identifiable areas that contribute to triggering or maintaining a suicidal crisis, as well as decrease the patient's level of functioning. In order for CBT of suicidal behavior to be effective, it must target three specific areas within the area of skills deficits: self-monitoring, distress tolerance, and emotion regulation. These are critical skills that are targeted as core interventions, regardless of the specific clinical presentation. This is specifically a function of the previously described theoretical model that serves as the basis of the CBT approach; each skill is necessary for an accurate conceptualization of the suicidal mode, effective crisis intervention, and specification of the suicidal cycle. The suicidal cycle is the detailed translation of the suicidal mode into an episode-specific example. This process is necessary to help identify areas that will be the target of intervention. Each of the previously mentioned skills, therefore, is inherent to the processes of case conceptualization and crisis intervention that are within the CBT framework.

Within the domain of personality development, there are three identifiable levels targeted by the CBT approach: personality stabilization, personality modification, and personality refinement. Stabilization is defined by the acquisition of behavioral skills involving elimination of suicidal, self-injurious, and self-destructive behaviors, as well as a general improvement of overall functioning. Modification is achieved by the targeting of maladaptive traits. Personality refinement is characterized by generalization of learned skills as well as fundamental and enduring changes in personality.

Skill building is a critical part of CBT for suicide, and specific methods used to promote this aspect of suicidal treatment will be described. Past research has shown that individuals with chronic suicidal behavior possess deficits in the areas of self-monitoring, distress tolerance, and emotional regulation (Linehan, 1993; Rudd, Joiner, & Rajab, 1996). These three constructs are interrelated; therefore, it is posited that as one's levels of emotional awareness increase, the effectiveness in regulating mood increases; as a result, the tolerance for distress increases and the manifestations of impulsivity decrease.

One way to achieve self-monitoring is through the use of a suicidal thought record. The suicidal thought record provides a means to connect thoughts, feelings, and behaviors in a concrete and identifiable manner, consistent with a CBT conceptualization. The suicidal thought record is an elaboration of the Dysfunctional Thought Record developed by Beck, Rush, Shaw, and Emery (1979). The suicidal thought record provides the patient with a structured way of analyzing the suicidal mode. Through use of the suicidal thought record, the client can identify various aspects of the suicidal mode, such as triggers and various thoughts comprising the suicidal belief system. In addition, the suicidal thought record provides the patient with a method to rate the severity and duration of their suicidal thoughts, as well as an organized response to these thoughts and the change associated with these responses over time. The suicidal thought record is particularly beneficial to individuals who lack insight into the nature of their suicidal thoughts, and to individuals who are especially reactive to internal triggers and become chronically suicidal as a result. Additional benefits include improvement of emotional awareness, emotional regulation, distress tolerance, and reduction of impulsivity.

It is evident that skill building is a critical component of the cognitive–behavioral approach to treating suicidal behavior. Cognitive restructuring is another important component of this therapeutic intervention. Skill building and cognitive restructuring are complementary processes within this cognitive–behavioral framework. Skill building provides behavioral experiments yielding conclusions for the patient to use in restructuring aspects of the suicidal belief system. There are various methods to achieve cognitive restructuring.

One approach to cognitive change is the ICARE intervention method. ICARE is an acronym outlining the steps used to identify and change faulty cognitions. "I" stands for *identification* of the specific automatic thought and the core underlying core belief. "C" stands for *connection* of the automatic thought to the distortion inherent to the belief. "A" stands for *assessment* of the thought. Assessment includes reviewing evidence that supports or contradicts the belief, as well as alternative explanations for the distressful circumstance. "R" stands for *restructuring* the belief in light of its evaluation. More reasonable alternatives to the dysfunctional beliefs are constructed. "E" stands for *execution*, that is, responding and acting as if the new belief were true. Part of this step involves the formulation of behaviors that are consistent with the new belief. This forms evidence for a behavioral experiment, which can be used to disconfirm existing erroneous beliefs.

Emotion regulation is another important component within the CBT framework. It can be defined as the "ability to identify, understand, express, and respond effectively to the full range of human emotions" (Rudd et al., 2001, p. 237). There are three steps in the process of emotion regulation. The first step is that of identification of the particular feeling. The next step is expression of the feeling in a method that is appropriate and desirable to the patient, such as journaling. The final step is responding to the feeling in a way that is congruent with facilitating recovery. Part of this process will involve changing destructive behaviors and dysfunctional thoughts.

Completing a suicidal thought record can be incorporated into emotion regulation. It aids in promoting control in an area that seems out of control by providing a structured and organized outlet for dysphoric emotions. Most importantly, the suicidal thought record provides the client with evidence demonstrating that suicidal feelings do not last forever. This is a difficult concept for the suicidal client to grasp in the midst of experiencing intense emotional distress. However, demonstrating that suicidal feelings are limited in their duration helps the client in tolerating distress and taking steps to facilitate his or her own recovery.

Dialectical behavioral therapy (DBT) also focuses on emotion regulation. According to the theory that forms the basis of this therapy, behavior patterns that comprise suicidality, such as self-injurious behavior, parasuicidal behavior, and actual suicide attempts, have developed, in part, to regulate emotions that the person has not learned to regulate in a more adaptive way (Linehan, 1993). Part of the processes in DBT acknowledge the regulatory functions that these behaviors present to the client, while using other techniques, such as problem solving, to construct more effective and adaptive ways to regulate emotions. The expectation that self-injurious behavior will reduce the intensity of negative moods is addressed. DBT explicitly targets dysfunctional ways of mood regulation by enhancing mood regulation expectancies and skills. Various studies have found that DBT is effective in reducing parasuicidal behavior in clients with borderline personality disorder (Barley et al., 1993; Linehan, Armstrong, Suarez, Allmon, & Heard, 1991; Linehan, Heard, & Armstrong, 1993).

According to the cognitive–behavioral model, suicidality is reduced when the components of the model are changed. According to CBT, a necessary condition for change is the management of *hot cognitions*, an "actively, emotionally charged, accessible, and accordingly modifiable belief system" (Rudd et al., 2001, p. 162). Based on this framework, the suicidal mode and the suicidal belief system are the most receptive to change during periods of crises in which they are activated. However, recent research has shown that periods of crises are not the only times in which suicidal behavior becomes more easily modified. A study by Joiner et al. (2001) found that clients more prone to positive moods displayed more positive problem-solving attitudes and, in turn, demonstrated an enhanced response following treatment for suicidal behavior. This finding supports the broaden and build model of positive emotions, by Fredrickson (1998), which proposes that positive emotions have the effect of "broadening" cognition and behavior, increasing the likelihood of exploration, experimentation, and the long-term effect of building up physical, social, and intellectual resources. These findings suggest that times when a client is experiencing positive mood can be capitalized on to broaden the repertoire of adaptive behaviors and skills that serve to decrease suicidal behavior.

In summary, the general mechanism of CBT for suicidal behavior is to decrease suicidality by transforming the suicidal mode. As the client makes progress in treatment, the suicidal mode is activated less easily and, in the long run, is replaced by adaptive modes. As a result, nonsuicidal behavior responses are formed in response to events, thoughts, and feelings that formerly triggered suicidal behavior.

See also: Suicide—child and adolescent, Suicide—children

REFERENCES

Alford, B. A., & Beck, A. T. (1997). *The integrative power of cognitive therapy*. New York: Guilford Press.

Barley, W. D., Buie, S. E., Peterson, E. W., Hollingsworth, A. S., Griva, M., Hickerson, D. C., Lawson, J. E., & Bailey, B. J. (1993). Development of an inpatient cognitive–behavioral treatment program for borderline personality disorder. *Journal of Personality Disorders, 7*, 232–240.

Beck, A. T. (1996). Beyond belief: A theory of modes, personality, and psychopathology. In P. Salkovskis (Ed.), *Frontiers of cognitive therapy* (pp. 1–25). New York: Guilford Press.

Beck, A. T., Rush, A. J., Shaw, B. F., & Emery, G. (1979). *Cognitive therapy of depression*. New York: Guilford Press.

Fredrickson, B. L. (1998). What good are positive emotions? *Review of General Psychology*, *2*, 300–319.

Joiner, T. E., Jr., Petit, J. W., Perez, M., Burns, A. B., Gencoz, T., Gencoz, F., & Rudd, M. D. (2001). Can positive emotion influence problem-solving attitudes among suicidal adults? *Professional Psychology, Research and Practice, 32*, 507–512.

Lerner, M., & Clum, G. (1990). Treatment of suicide ideators: A problem-solving approach. *Behavior Therapy*, *21*, 403–411.

Linehan, M. (1993). *Cognitive–behavioral treatment of borderline personality disorder*. New York: Guilford Press.

Linehan, M. M., Armstrong, H. E., Suarez, A., Allmon, D., & Heard, H. L. (1991). Cognitive–behavioral treatment of chronically parasuicidal borderline clients. *Archives of General Psychiatry*, *48*, 1060–1064.

Linehan, M. M., Heard, H. L., & Armstrong, H. E. (1993). Naturalistic follow-up of a behavioral treatment for chronically parasuicidal borderline patients. *Archives of General Psychiatry*, *51*(5), 971–974.

Rudd, M. D. (2000). Integrating science into the practice of clinical suicidology: A review of the psychotherapy literature and a research agenda for the future. In R.W. Maris, S.S. Canetto, J. L. McIntosh, & M. M. Silverman (Eds.), *Review of suicidology, 2000* (pp. 47–83). New York: Guilford Press.

Rudd, M. D., Joiner, T. E., & Rajab, M. H. (1996). Relationships among suicide ideators, attempters, and multiple attempters in a young adult sample. *Journal of Abnormal Psychology, 105*, 541–550.

Rudd, M., Joiner, T., & Rajab, M. (2001). *Treating suicidal behavior: An effective, time-limited approach*. New York: Guilford Press.

RECOMMENDED READINGS

Freeman, A., & Reinecke, M.A. (1993) *Cognitive therapy of suicidal behavior: A manual for treatment*. Philadelphia: La Salle.

Linehan, M. (1993). *Cognitive–behavioral treatment of borderline personality disorder*. (pp. 97–120). New York: Guilford Press.
Rudd, M., Joiner, T., & Rajab, M. (2001). *Treating suicidal behavior: An effective, time limited approach*. New York: Guilford Press.

Suicide–Child and Adolescent

Matthew K. Nock

Keywords: suicide, self-injurious behavior, child and adolescent

Suicide is the primary cause of mortality associated with psychiatric disorders among children and adolescents. It is the sixth leading cause of death of those 5–14 years old and the third leading cause of death among those 15–24 years old. Perhaps greater cause for concern is the increasing rate of completed suicide among children and adolescents. Since 1950, the suicide rate for European American males aged 15–24 has tripled, while it has more than doubled for European American females in this age group. More recently, suicide rates have increased markedly in younger children and African Americans in particular. For instance, from 1980 to 1996 the rate of suicide among all children aged 10–14 increased by 100% and the rate among African American males aged 15–19 increased by 105% (Centers for Disease Control and Prevention, 2002). Despite these alarming statistics, research in this area, and thus our knowledge of the causes of suicide and these increasing rates, remains limited.

ETIOLOGIES OF CHILD AND ADOLESCENT SUICIDE

Early scholarly considerations of suicide, such as work in this area by Durkheim and Freud, were theoretically strong but lacking in empirical support. In contrast, recent work has been empirically robust and has identified multiple correlates and risk factors for suicidal thoughts, suicide attempts, and completed suicide among children and adolescents. For instance, recent research has revealed that although adolescent girls contemplate and attempt suicide approximately twice as often as boys, boys completed suicide more than girls at a ratio of over 4 : 1. Moreover, the presence of certain psychiatric disorders increases the risk for suicide, as over 90% of children and adolescents who die by suicide meet DSM criteria for a psychiatric disorder, most often a mood disorder, conduct disorder, and/or a substance use disorder (Brent, 2001; Shaffer et al., 1996). Although knowledge of such correlates increases the probability of identifying those at risk for completed suicide, such research by itself does not necessarily inform our understanding of *why* individuals contemplate and attempt suicide.

Cognitive–behavioral models of child and adolescent suicide build on the aforementioned research and are aimed at understanding the mechanisms through which suicidal thoughts and behaviors develop, and ultimately at modifying such thoughts and behaviors through effective psychosocial treatments. This work has focused primarily on the confluence of affective, cognitive, and behavioral factors associated with suicidal thoughts and behaviors. Affectively, depressed mood and anhedonia, a diminished capacity to experience pleasure, are correlates of suicidal thoughts and behaviors (Nock & Kazdin, 2002). Cognitively, it has been proposed that suicidal thoughts and behaviors are the result of cognitive distortions, through which an individual systematically misconstrues the environment in a negative way. Research has supported this theory by demonstrating that suicidal ideation is associated with a higher frequency of negative automatic thoughts, and more impressively by showing that thoughts of hopelessness about the future are reliably associated with future episodes of suicidal ideation, suicide attempts, and completed suicide. Behaviorally, engagement in impulsive, risky, and aggressive behaviors, as well as the presence of a previous suicide attempt, are all associated with an increased risk of suicidal behavior (Brent, 2001; Lewinsohn, Rohde, & Seeley, 1994). In addition, factors that cut across these domains have been associated with suicidal behavior, such as poor problem-solving or decision-making skills, poor emotion regulation and distress tolerance skills, and problems in the family environment (Brent, 2001; King et al., 2001).

Most cognitive–behavioral models of suicide have adopted a vulnerability–stress model, which suggests that individuals possess some psychological vulnerability that predisposes them to develop suicidal thoughts and behaviors when exposed to stressful events. There is significant variability regarding theories of the proposed vulnerability and these models have developed over time from simple linear models of suicide risk to more complex, integrative models proposing multiple pathways to suicidal thoughts and behaviors.

ASSESSMENT OF CHILD AND ADOLESCENT SUICIDE

Research and clinical advances in the assessment of child and adolescent suicide have been facilitated by attempts to more clearly and consistently operationalize key constructs. For example, rather than continuing to use vague terminology, such as stating a child is "suicidal" without specifying whether the child has endorsed thoughts of suicide, engaged in self-harm behavior with no intent to die, or made an attempt to end his or her life, leading researchers (i.e., O'Carroll et al., 1996) have recommended a specific nomenclature to clarify such issues. As such, *suicide* refers to death from a self-inflicted injury in which the individual *intended* to die. *Suicide attempt* refers to potentially self-injurious, but currently nonfatal, behavior in which the individual *intended* to die. *Suicidal ideation* refers to self-reported thoughts of making a suicide attempt. In addition, a distinction is made between suicidal behavior and *self-mutilative behavior*, which refers to intentional destruction of one's own body tissue in which there is *no intent* to die. Clinical assessment of self-injurious thoughts and behaviors should include the collection of data related to each of these constructs.

Assessment should also examine the presence, frequency, and severity of the correlates and risk factors mentioned above. These include demographic factors that place the individual at risk such as age, gender, and ethnicity, as well as the presence of a mood disorder, particularly with hopelessness and anhedonia; a substance use disorder; anxiety and agitation; difficulties with problem solving and impulsiveness; and a previous history of a suicide attempt. The evaluation should assess the degree of planning of and preparation for self-injurious behavior, and the individual's ability to implement any identified plan should be taken into consideration (e.g., Does the individual have access to a firearm, pills, sharp object, or other means of self-injury?).

Children and adolescents often underreport psychological symptoms to parents or clinicians, and may be motivated to distort or omit facts related to their self-injurious thoughts and behaviors. For these reasons it is important the evaluation draw on multiple assessment methods (i.e., rating scales, clinical interviews, and direct observation) and informants (i.e., child/adolescent, parent/family, teacher, and clinician) and consider behavior across multiple contexts (Prinstein, Nock, Spirito, & Grapentine, 2001). There are currently a wide range of reliable and valid assessment measures available for the assessment of child and adolescent self-injury that the interested reader is strongly encouraged to obtain (see Goldston, 2001).

TREATMENT OF CHILD AND ADOLESCENT SUICIDE

Efforts to develop and evaluate cognitive–behavioral treatments (CBT) for self-injurious thoughts and behaviors have increased greatly in recent years. As a result, there is a growing database of studies evaluating the efficacy of relatively short-term CBT for self-injurious thoughts and behaviors. The good news is several brief CBT packages have demonstrated some success at decreasing suicidal ideation and attempts as well as depressed mood and negative cognitions. The bad news is, to date, the results of these studies have not been strong enough to satisfy the criteria for empirically supported treatment status for reducing suicidal ideation, suicide attempts, or self-mutilative behaviors. In addition, this research has focused almost exclusively on adult populations. Few treatment studies have used child and adolescent samples, and there are currently no empirically supported treatments for these age groups.

Overall, CBT approaches in this area center directly on reducing the frequency of self-injurious thoughts and behaviors, as well as on modifying correlates or risk factors that are present that might play a role in the generation or maintenance of self-injurious thoughts and behaviors. Perhaps the most common component in CBT for self-injurious thoughts and behaviors is the improvement of interpersonal problem-solving skills. This typically consists of teaching the individual a series of steps for identifying problems, generating solutions, evaluating the consequences of each solution, choosing and implementing a solution, and engaging in self-evaluation.

CBT for self-injurious thoughts and behaviors also typically emphasizes developing emotion regulation and distress tolerance skills. Self-injury often functions as a method of increasing or decreasing an individual's affective experience, and sometimes occurs in the context of an inability to inhibit impulsive responding to provocative events. Therefore, more adaptive skills for generating or relieving one's affective experience or for tolerating distress and inhibiting impulsive responding are taught and practiced. These skills include identifying and labeling positive and negative emotions, expressing emotions verbally and nonverbally, engaging in pleasurable activities, and engaging in distraction and relaxation exercises. Consistent with the CBT approach, there is also a consistent emphasis on self-monitoring of thoughts, behaviors, and emotions. Similarly, attention is devoted to evaluating the antecedents and consequences of self-injurious thoughts and behaviors.

In addition to direct attempts at ameliorating suicide-related phenomena, several other treatment foci are common to CBT approaches in this area. Most treatments aim at relieving the psychiatric symptoms that may be maintaining self-injurious thoughts and behaviors, such as depressed mood, negative cognitions, anxiety, and substance use. CBT approaches also stress the importance of careful and continuous evaluation of self-injurious thoughts and behaviors, as well as an emphasis on the importance of facilitating treatment attendance and adherence. Both of these goals are often attained by incorporating the child's or adolescent's family in the treatment process in some form. This can range from enlisting a family member to aid with homework completion and treatment attendance to including all family members in each treatment session.

DIRECTIONS FOR FUTURE RESEARCH

Research on child and adolescent suicide and self-injury has made impressive advances over the past several decades. However, there are still many questions in need of answers in order to improve our ability to accurately identify and assess, and effectively treat, self-injurious children and adolescents. All future research in this area should give great consideration to the terminology and assessment methods and measures used. Researchers and clinicians should also take great care in selecting constructs for examination and methods of assessment, particularly given the dangerousness of the dependent variables involved. Studies examining the etiologies of self-injurious thoughts and behaviors must use longitudinal designs and large samples spanning developmental periods if we are to understand the multiple pathways that lead to (i.e., rather than that are associated with) self-injurious thoughts and behaviors. Researchers working in the area of assessment must deviate from simple self-report measures and develop and evaluate more performance-based measures aimed at revealing the cognitive, affective, and behavioral processes involved in the maintenance and development of self-injurious thoughts and behaviors, particularly given the potential motivation of self-injurious individuals to conceal their thoughts or intentions as well as the difficulties in child and adolescent self-report due to developmental level and limited verbal abilities. Finally, research on the treatment of child and adolescent self-injury must continue to develop and evaluate treatment models that are theoretically derived. Studies are sorely needed in virtually all areas of suicide treatment research, including basic studies of treatment efficacy and effectiveness, and ultimately studies delineating the mechanisms and moderators of clinical change. Although there is much work to be done, it is strongly encouraged, as the benefits of advancing our knowledge in these areas will undoubtedly result in the reduction of suffering and mortality for many of our children and adolescents.

See also: Suicide—adult, Suicide—children

REFERENCES

Brent, D. A. (2001). Assessment and treatment of the youthful suicidal patient. *Annals of the New York Academy of Sciences, 932*, 106–131.

Centers for Disease Control and Prevention. (2002). Web-based Injury Statistics Query and Reporting System (WISQARS) [Online]. National Center for Injury Prevention and Control, Centers for Disease Control and Prevention (producer). Retrieved August 23, 2003. www.cdc.gov/ncipc/wisqars.

Goldston, D. (2001). *Review of measures of suicidal behavior: Assessment of suicidal behaviors and risk among children and adolescents.* National Institute of Mental Health. Retrieved from: http://www.nimh.nih.gov/research/measures.pdf

King, R. A., Schwab-Stone, M., Flisher, A. J., Greenwald, S., Kramer, R. A., Goodman, S. H., Lahey, B. B., Shaffer, D., & Gould, M. S. (2001). Psychosocial and risk behavior correlates of youth suicide attempts and suicidal ideation. *Journal of the American Academy of Child and Adolescent Psychiatry, 40*, 837–846.

Lewinsohn, P. M., Rohde, P., & Seeley, J. R. (1994). Psychosocial risk factors for future adolescent suicide attempts. *Journal of Consulting and Clinical Psychology, 62*, 297–305.

Nock, M. K., & Kazdin, A. E. (2002). Examination of cognitive, affective, and behavioral factors and suicide-related outcomes in children and young adolescents. *Journal of Clinical Child and Adolescent Psychology, 31*, 48–58.

O'Carroll, P. W., Berman, A. L., Maris, R. W., Moscicki, E. K., Tanney, B. L., & Silverman, M. M. (1996). Beyond the Tower of Babel: A nomenclature for suicidology. *Suicide & Life Threatening Behavior, 26*, 237–252.

Prinstein, M. J., Nock, M. K., Spirito, A., & Grapentine, W. L. (2001). Multi-method assessment of suicidality in adolescent psychiatric inpatients: Preliminary results. *Journal of the American Academy of Child and Adolescent Psychiatry, 40*, 1053–1061.

Shaffer, D., Goudl, M. S., Fisher, P., Trautman, P., Moreau, D., Kleinman, M., & Flory, M. (1996). Psychiatric diagnosis in child and adolescent suicide. *Archives of General Psychiatry, 53*, 339–348.

RECOMMENDED READINGS

Brent, D. A., & Poling, K. (1997). *Cognitive therapy treatment manual for depressed and suicidal youth*. Pittsburgh, PA: University of Pittsburgh, Services for Teens at Risk.

Lewinsohn, P. M., Rohde, P., & Seeley, J. R. (1996). Adolescent suicidal ideation and attempts: Prevalence, risk factors, clinical implications. *Clinical Psychology: Science and Practice, 3*, 25–46.

Miller, A. L., & Glinski, J. (2000). Youth suicidal behavior: Asessment and intervention. *Journal of Clinical Psychology, 56*, 1131–1152.

Rudd, M. D., Joiner, T., & Rajab, M. H. (2001). *Treating suicidal behavior: An effective, time-limited approach*. New York: Guilford Press.

Shaffer, D., & Pfeffer, C. R. (2001). Work group on quality issues. Practice parameters for the assessment and treatment of children and adolescents with suicidal behavior. *Journal of the American Academy of Child and Adolescent Psychiatry, 40*(Suppl.), 245–515.

Suicide–Children

Theresa M. Schultz and Erin B. Marek

Keywords: suicide, depression, children, cognitive, behavioral, affective

Suicide in children (approximately 5–14 years of age)[1] has thus far received little research attention within the psychological literature. This is despite the reported dramatic 109% rise in completed suicides for 10- to 14-year-olds in the United States during approximately the past two decades, and the apparent high rates of suicidal ideation (i.e., thoughts of suicide) and attempts for this entire age group (Centers for Disease Control and Prevention, 2003). This article attempts to provide an overview of the most current psychological literature on suicide in children; because of the limited information available on this topic, the article includes other theoretical and empirical conceptualizations of suicide that may enhance our thinking about suicide in children.

Several factors may have contributed to the limited research on suicide in children. First, it is critical to acknowledge the inherent complexities in suicide research—no matter what age group is being considered. It is widely acknowledged by researchers and clinical practitioners alike that the study and treatment of suicide is intrinsically challenging. Suicidality is a multidimensional phenomenon whose expression is dependent on the interactions among a host of psychological, social, and environmental factors, which may vary dramatically from individual to individual. Second, most suicide research has historically focused on adults, with more recent attention to adolescents, but much less attention to children, likely because the base rates for children relative to other age groups are quite low. Third, predictors of suicide other than depressed mood (including other psychological and personality characteristics, as well as stresses) have not yet been fully explored. Finally, there are inconsistencies in operational definitions for suicide-related outcomes, such as suicidal ideation and suicide attempts (Nock & Kazdin, 2002).

The relationship between suicidal ideation and suicide attempts appears to be complex. Some researchers have noted, for example, that suicidal ideation is common in children and adolescents; in fact, it appears to be much more common than suicide attempts among children, and is not always associated with suicide attempts or psychopathology (Shaffer & Pfeffer, 2001). Furthermore, while suicidal ideation may be a common referral reason for psychiatric emergency room visits for children, suicidal ideation in this age group may often be misinterpreted by clinicians conducting risk assessments (e.g., in an emergency room setting) as an attempt by a child to manipulate his/her environment or to engage in an extreme form of attention-seeking behavior, although these assumptions are not supported by current research (e.g., Stewart, Manion, & Davidson, 2001).

Rates of suicide attempts and completed suicides for children vary by gender and within cultural groups (e.g., Nock & Kazdin, 2002; Shaffer & Pfeffer, 2001). For example, the ratio of suicide attempts for females and males within this age group is approximately 1.6 : 1. Hispanic youths have a higher number of attempts than Caucasian or African American youths. Suicide rates (i.e., completed suicides) are significantly higher for males than females—approximately 3 : 1 for prepubertal children and 5.5 : 1 for children who have reached puberty. Yet, suicide rates for children are currently greatest for Caucasian males, with high rates of suicide also occurring within other groups (e.g., Native Americans and Alaskan Natives). Of all groups, suicide rates continue to accelerate most dramatically among African American males.

While suicide rates differ for male and female children, most risk factors tend to be similar for both genders. There is a significant relationship between increased likelihood of suicidal ideation and attempts and the presence of such psychosocial risk factors as: depression or anxiety, stressful life events; family history of psychopathology; limited parental monitoring, low levels of family support, family discord, and poor family communications; and low social competence (e.g., King, Schwab-Stone, & Flisher, 2001; Shaffer et al., 1996). Previous suicide attempts represent another significant risk factor, and one that differs for males and females; that is, previous suicide attempts are more predictive of suicide in males than in females (Shaffer & Pfeffer, 2001).

Mood disorders, particularly early onset major depressive episodes, are often associated with increased risk of suicide attempts in children and adolescents (Shaffer & Pfeffer, 2001). A cognitive–behavioral theoretical perspective seems particularly useful in further examining the relationship between depressed mood and suicide-related outcomes. This approach is principally based on Beck's original assumptions, as well as more recent refinements related to Beck's cognitive theory, cognitive therapy model for depression, and cognitive framework for suicide (e.g., Beck, 1996).

Beck defines several key theoretical constructs and features related to his cognitive conceptualizations of personality and psychological functioning. In general, Beck suggests that psychological well-being or distress are products of

[1] "Children" herein refers to 5–14-year-olds, unless otherwise noted.

complex interactions among biological, environmental, and social factors, as well as an individual's thoughts and beliefs about the self, others, and important life events. Beck uses the term *cognitive schema* to specifically represent the core thoughts, assumptions, and beliefs that reflect an individual's view of the world. Schemas can be either positive (adaptive) or negative (maladaptive), depending on the situation. Beck believes that schemas emerge early in life (at a time when there may likely be errors in reasoning and logic); when these errors occur, *cognitive distortions* (as a result of inaccurate or ineffective information processing) are formed. These distortions are thus a part of negative schemas, and make one more vulnerable to maladaptive ways of thinking about oneself, others, and life experiences; in turn, this vulnerability makes one more predisposed to psychological distress.

Schemas and beliefs are activated in response to any life event one perceives as notable. Beck uses the term *automatic thoughts* to describe those thoughts that seem to occur spontaneously (i.e., without effort or planning) in response to these events. Automatic thoughts, while not inherently negative, are often inaccurate, unrealistic, or otherwise distorted in the presence of psychological distress or dysfunction. Further, these automatic thoughts directly impact our emotions and behaviors, acting to precipitate or perpetuate maladaptive responses.

Beck's fundamental assumption is that our emotions and behaviors are determined largely by our interpretation (i.e., thoughts and beliefs) about circumstances and events, rather than by the events themselves. Depression is thus viewed as a function of a distorted, maladaptive system of thoughts and beliefs. Specifically, Beck suggests that maladaptive or dysfunctional beliefs are the product of cognitive distortions, often conceptualized in the context of Beck's *cognitive triad*, in which one holds negative views of the self, the world (others), and the future. These negative views (i.e., faulty cognitions) direct one's behavior in a negative way. Cognitive conceptualizations of suicide strongly support that suicidal individuals tend to hold negative views of themselves, attribute their shortcomings to themselves (i.e., to internal, stable attributions) rather than to situations or events (i.e., to external circumstances), and hold pessimistic and hopeless views of the world and future (Freeman & Reinecke, 1993).

There are currently no specific cognitive–behavioral models for suicidal risk or behavior in children. Yet, the work of Beck (e.g., 1996) and Rudd (2000) offer a promising theoretical cognitive–behavioral conceptualization of suicidality that may be useful in understanding the cognitive and emotional vulnerability to suicidal risk and likelihood of suicidal behavior in children (and adolescents).

Rudd's (2000) cognitive–behavioral model of suicidality attempts to define and elaborate on Beck's concept of *the suicidal mode*, found in Beck's (1996) expanded theoretical model of cognitive therapy. Herein, Beck introduces the concept of *mode* in relationship to personality organization and psychological functioning. Mode is defined by Beck as an organizational unit that houses schemas. One's personality structure is consequently characterized as being composed of multiple modes, each containing a specific subset of schemas—"cognitive (information processing), affective, behavioral, and motivational," and can thus be viewed as an "integrated cognitive–affective–behavioral network" (p. 4).

Rudd (2000) attempts to define "suicidal mode" within his proposed cognitive–behavioral model of suicidality, wherein he identifies aspects of each of Beck's (1996) modes (i.e., the cognitive, affective, behavioral, and emotional) that represent relevant characteristics of the "suicidal mode." First, suicidal beliefs are linked to Beck's cognitive mode, which includes Beck's notion of the cognitive triad. A suicidal belief system is therefore viewed as rooted in the maladaptive ways in which information is processed and interpreted, as well as in the ineffective cognitive strategies used to manage this information. Second, in Rudd's "suicidal mode," the cognitive mode is integrally linked to the affective mode. One's distorted beliefs and/or negative interpretation of an event may increase the likelihood of a negative affective experience related to that event. This may, in turn, heighten an individual's affective sensitivity and emotionality, which are sustained, in part, by the individual's increased attention and focus on negative affective experiences. Rudd also emphasizes that the suicidal individual's negative affective experiences are not limited to symptoms of depressed mood, but are instead "dysphoric," in that the experiences represent a mix of negative emotions (e.g., sadness, anxiety, guilt). Finally, Rudd notes that when the "suicidal mode" is activated, the behavioral and motivational modes (and coincident physiological arousal) are also engaged to permit the individual to respond to a given event. The behavioral and motivational modes are, of course, strongly influenced by the cognitive and affective modes (i.e., the cognitive misinterpretation of an event, the likelihood of negative affective experiences and heightened emotional arousal and sensitivity). Risk for suicide is elevated when the "suicidal mode" is active, but suicidal behavior is not solely dependent on this mode; it is also dependent on the complex interactions and convergence of many different factors, including "situational distress, emotional dysphoria, psychiatric disturbance, impaired cognitive functioning, and deficient problem-solving" (p. 25).

While Beck's cognitive–behavioral conceptualization of suicide (e.g., 1996) and Rudd's (2000) cognitive–behavioral model of suicidality (i.e., "the suicidal mode") focus primarily on adults, Nock and Kazdin's (2002) cognitive–behavioral research specifically examines factors related to suicidal outcomes in children (6.8–13.9 years of age, in a psychiatric inpatient setting). Moreover, Nock and Kazdin consider factors that reflect the primary *modes* identified by Beck: cognitive, affective, and behavioral.

Nock and Kazdin (2002) distinguish among several possible suicidal outcomes for children in this study: suicidal ideation, current suicide attempts (an attempt immediately preceding the psychiatric hospitalization), and suicidal intent (i.e., a conscious intention to die). Overall findings of this research suggest that specific cognitive factors (i.e., negative automatic thoughts, hopelessness), affective factors (i.e., self-reported depressed mood and anhedonia—a diminished ability to derive pleasure from enjoyable activities or experiences), and behavioral factors (i.e., past suicide attempts) may be associated with suicide in children.

While depressed mood is critically important in the consideration of suicide risk, researchers (e.g., Nock & Kazdin, 2002; Stewart et al., 2001) note that depressed mood alone may not always predict suicidal outcomes (i.e., suicidal ideation, suicidal intent, suicide attempts, or completed suicides). The picture is, not surprisingly, much more complex. Nock and Kazdin (2002) note that "negative automatic thoughts, hopelessness, and anhedonia provide unique information regarding the severity of suicidal ideation, the presence of an attempt, and the severity of the intent" (p. 55) in children. Nock and Kazdin's research strongly supports the need for cognitive–behavioral assessment of suicide risk (i.e., the likelihood of suicidal ideation and attempts) that includes close examination of negative cognitions and anhedonia. This is essential, as suicidal ideation may be present in children who report or exhibit depressed mood, hopelessness, and negative automatic thoughts. Assessing past suicide attempts is also important because they are positively related to anhedonia and current attempts in children. Further, Nock and Kazdin report that a history of past suicide attempts and current anhedonia strongly indicate the need to identify the extent of suicidal intent in children.

Thus, cognitive–behavioral assessment of suicide risk in children must consider many factors in addition to depressed mood. Ideally, any assessment should be comprehensive in scope, and at the very least should evaluate a child's motivations and intent to die, as well as such factors as depression, hopelessness, isolation, and history of previous attempts (e.g., Carney & Hazler, 1998; Nock & Kazdin, 2002). The assessment should also incorporate empirically derived measures and other available sources of information, particularly developmental, historical, and observational data regarding a child's cognitive, affective, and behavioral functioning from parents, other caretakers, and family members.

Empirically based measures of depression in children include Beck's Children's Depression Inventory (CDI) and the Children's Depression Scale (CDS), which assesses both depression and anhedonia (Lang & Tisher, 1978). The Automatic Thoughts Questionnaire (ATQ; Hollon & Kendall, 1980), adapted by Kazdin (1990) for use with children, along with Kazdin's Hopelessness Scale for Children (HSC; Kazdin, Rodgers, & Colbus, 1986) are useful in assessing relevant aspects of cognitive functioning. Nock and Kazdin's (2002) modified versions of the Scale for Suicidal Ideation (SSI; Beck, Kovacs, & Weissman, 1979) and the Suicidal Intent Scale (SIS; Beck, Schuyler, & Herman, 1974) for use with children can provide some additional objective data regarding suicide risk.

In addition to these important assessment components, an effective cognitive–behavioral assessment of suicide in children must also consider the methodological approach to the evaluation. That is, in the ideal, the assessment should be an ongoing process, beginning with the gathering of baseline data (using the aforementioned forms of assessment). This should be followed by continued objective, clinical reassessment of suicide risk (Carney & Hazler, 1998) until the clinician determines that the child is no longer at risk.

Once a cognitive–behavioral assessment of suicide risk is completed and a child has been identified as suicidal, appropriate interventions must then be considered. The efficacy of CBT techniques in the treatment of depression in adults (and adolescents) has been widely documented (e.g., Carney & Hazler, 1998); the successful use of CBT for suicidal behavior has also been reported (e.g., Freeman & Reinecke, 1993). In fact, Freeman and Reinecke note that cognitive–behavioral techniques are particularly valuable when addressing negative automatic thoughts and maladaptive behaviors in suicidal patients.

The success of cognitive–behavioral techniques is critically dependent on the collaborative nature of the therapist–client relationship. Within this therapeutic partnership, the client's automatic, maladaptive thoughts and dysfunctional beliefs are challenged via a thorough examination of the evidence (e.g., hypothesis testing) supporting the client's thoughts and beliefs. For suicidal clients, it is especially important to question perceptions that may be rigid or limited in scope and to examine inaccurate or ineffective information processing that may yield cognitive distortions (e.g., catastrophizing).

CBT interventions also provide opportunities for the client to learn and rehearse more effective coping strategies, in order to redirect one's thinking and provide a more adaptive way to address suicidal impulses, including the use of cognitive dissonance as a deterrent to suicide (Carney & Hazler, 1998). Typical interventions in this therapeutic approach include: the use of a no-suicide behavioral contract; the practice and application of new coping strategies through self-instruction, via such techniques as thought stopping, positive self-talk (to replace negative thoughts with positive ones), self-monitoring of thoughts, emotions, and behaviors (e.g., recording in a log or diary), and role-playing adaptive behavioral responses.

These CBT techniques require further evaluation as effective interventions for suicidal children. One critical consideration in such an evaluative process is careful examination of developmental issues. For example, a child's understanding of the finality and irreversibility of death (vis-à-vis a completed suicide) varies based on level of cognitive maturity (e.g., Koocher, 1973), which likely impacts the value and reliability of no-suicide behavioral contracts with children (see Davidson & Range, 2000, for a review of professionals' ratings of the appropriateness and effectiveness of such contracts). This example clearly reveals the importance of considering developmental issues in clinical research on the application of CBT models (originally developed for adults and adolescents) for suicidal children. It further highlights the broader complexities and challenges of developing cognitive–behavioral theory and practice that is appropriate and effective for suicidal children.

See also: Suicide—adult, Suicide—child and adolescent

REFERENCES

Beck, A. T. (1996). Beyond belief: A theory of modes, personality, and psychopathology. In P. Salkovkis (Ed.), *Frontiers of cognitive therapy* (pp. 1–25). New York: Guilford Press.

Beck, A. T., Kovacs, M., & Weissman, A. (1979). Assessment of suicidal intention: The scale for suicidal ideation. *Journal of Clinical and Consulting Psychology*, *47*, 343–352.

Beck, A. T., Schuyler, D., & Herman, I. (1974). Development of the suicidal intent scales. In A. T. Beck, H. L. Resnik, & D. J. Lettieri (Eds.), *The prediction of suicide* (pp. 45–56). Bowie, MD: Charles Press.

Carney, J. V., & Hazler, R. J. (1998). Suicide and cognitive–behavioral counseling: Implications for mental health counselors. *Journal of Mental Health Counseling*, *20*(1), 28–42.

Centers for Disease Control and Prevention. (2003). Web-based Injury Statistics Query and Reporting System (WISQARS). National Center for Injury Prevention and Control [2003 March 27]. Retrieved August 17, 2003, from the World Wide Web: http://www.cdc.gov/ncipc/wisqars

Davidson, M., & Range, L. M. (2000). Age appropriate no-suicide agreements: Professionals' ratings of appropriateness and effectiveness. *Education and Treatment of Children*, *23*(2), 143–155.

Freeman, A., & Reinecke, M. A. (1993). *Cognitive therapy of suicidal behavior*. New York: Springer.

Hollon, S. D., & Kendall, P. C. (1980). Cognitive self-statements in depression: Development of an automatic thoughts questionnaire. *Cognitive Therapy and Research*, *4*, 383–395.

Kazdin, A. E., (1990). Evaluation of the Automatic Thoughts Questionnaire: Negative cognitive processes and depression among children. *Psychological Assessment*, *2*, 73–79.

Kazdin, A. E., Rodgers, A., & Colbus, D. (1986). The Hopelessness Scale for Children: Psychometric characteristics and concurrent validity. *Journal of Consulting and Clinical Psychology*, *54*, 241–245.

King, R. A., Schwab-Stone, M., & Flisher, A. J. (2001). Psychological and risk behavior correlates of youth suicide attempts and suicidal ideation. *Journal of the American Academy of Child and Adolescent Psychiatry*, *40*(7), 837–846.

Koocher, G. P. (1973). Childhood, death, and cognitive development. *Developmental Psychology*, *9*, 369–375.

Lang, M., & Tisher, M. (1978). *Children's Depression Scale*. Victoria: Australian Council for Educational Research.

Nock, M. K., & Kazdin, A. E. (2002). Examination of affective, cognitive, and behavioral factors and suicide-related outcomes in children and young adolescents. *Journal of Clinical Child and Adolescent Psychology*, *31*(1), 48–58.

Rudd, M. D. (2000). The suicidal mode: A cognitive–behavioral model of suicidality. *Suicide and Life-Threatening Behavior*, *30*(1), 18–32.

Shaffer, D., Gould, M. S., Fisher, P., Trautman, P., Moreau, D., Kleinman, M., & Flory, M. (1996). Psychiatric diagnosis in child and adolescent suicide. *Archives of General Psychiatry, 53*, 339–348.

Shaffer, D., & Pfeffer, C. R. (2001). Practice parameter for the assessment and treatment of children and adolescents with suicidal behavior. *Journal of the American Academy of Child and Adolescent Psychiatry*, *40*(7), 24S–51S.

Stewart, S. E., Manion, I. G., & Davidson, S. (2001). Suicidal children and adolescents with first emergency room presentations: Predictors of six-month outcome. *Journal of the American Academy of Child and Adolescent Psychiatry*, *40*(5), 580–587.

T

Terminal Illness

Stephanie H. Felgoise and Holly Kricher

Keywords: terminal illness, grief, coping, loss, quality of life

The psychological sequelae to a terminal illness diagnosis, also termed life-threatening illness, are complex and ideographic. Terminal illness or life-threatening illness is operationally defined as any condition that shortens normative life expectancy, a condition that is not due to normative causes. Some examples of these types of illnesses include AIDS, COPD, cardiac conditions, and some forms of cancer. Individuals often struggle with medical treatment, end-of-life planning, cognitive and behavioral changes, grief issues, and more. Although empirical data specific to psychological interventions for persons with life-threatening illnesses are sparse, cognitive–behavioral treatments seem appropriate and promising to facilitate coping and adjustment for such patients.

The diagnosis of a life-threatening illness and subsequent treatment invariably means addressing loss in some form, coping and adjusting to altered life circumstances, modified life plans and/or goals, and facing the possibility of one's death. The immediacy of expected death will likely determine the rate at which individuals grieve losses, adjust to the reality of a life-threatening illness, and confront existential issues. Also, the type and severity of illness affects the course of the illness, society's support for or reaction to the ill person, and the skills needed for adjustment and coping.

As death becomes imminent, improving *quality of life* versus quantity of life becomes the focus and goal of treatment for medical and mental health professionals alike. Research and clinical attention has shifted to focus on quality of life moreso in the past 20 years. As such, cognitive–behavioral therapy interventions for persons with life-threatening illnesses focus on grief, loss, acceptance, quality of life, coping, adjustment, psychosocial and spiritual peace, and problem solving surrounding these issues.

GRIEF AND LOSS

Unfortunately, there remains an inconsistent use of terms and definitions in the grief literature, leading to sometimes confusing conclusions. For the sake of clarity, grief is defined here as representing the particular reactions one experiences while in a state of bereavement. These reactions to the perception of loss can be psychological, social, and physical. Bereavement has been conceptualized as the experiential state one endures after realizing a loss. It refers to the emotions, experiences, changes, and conditions that take place as a result of the loss.

Using these definitions, patients who are diagnosed with a life-threatening illness are undoubtedly in a state of bereavement as they navigate the changing landscape the illness brings. It might be said that they are in a state of mourning. Mourning can be conceptualized as involving both intrapsychic processes and cultural responses to a loss. Intrapsychic processes, according to the cognitive–behavioral literature, might include affective components as well as cognitive components such as information processing, decision making, perception, judgment, and schema organization. Cultural responses may include behavioral manifestations of grief.

The early literature surrounding grief and bereavement was based on stage theories, beginning with the pioneering work of Elizabeth Kubler-Ross (1969). It was proposed that an individual moved through predictable stages to a final state of acceptance and resolution. Significant contributors to stage theories included John Bowlby, who integrated attachment theory and information processing models, postulating that the closer one is attached to another individual or object, the greater the potential for loss and the more intense the behavioral response to the loss. Others have detailed the course of grief as comprised of components, tasks, and phases.

Sanders's (1999) integrative theory of bereavement proposes physiological, behavioral, and psychological manifestations of each of five phases of bereavement: shock, awareness of loss, conservation-withdrawal, healing, and renewal. She postulates that the psychological forces that operate during the process of grief are linked to biological forces involved in the physical well-being of the person. This theory is based on a biopsychosocial model and is particularly relevant to cognitive–behavioral interventions.

While grief has traditionally been viewed as a "letting go" process that is aimed at detaching oneself from the deceased or lost object, more recent theorists propose the grief process as an accommodation to the reality of life without the lost object. Instead of detaching completely, the idea of building "continuing bonds" is proposed (Klass, Silverman, & Nickman, 1996). This entails maintaining a connection with the lost object, which may be a lost role or identity, even though the connection takes on a different form.

Cognitive–behavioral interventions that focus on helping individuals maintain a sense of connectedness to their previous roles or other lost objects may be important to individuals as life-threatening illnesses progress. For example, a person who is no longer able to work outside the home may take on a consultant role, offering advice to former co-workers, thereby maintaining a connection to his/her work identity.

Furthermore, individuals and families may desire to maintain a sense of continuing bonds with each other even after the death of the ill person. Treatment may involve helping individuals review their life stories, identifying themes that are important and meaningful, and developing strategies that their families can use to continue these themes. For example, an individual who may have devoted a significant amount of energy into gardening with the family may wish to plant a tree or develop an area of the yard that will be a memorial to this part of their life. In this way, the family or significant others will be able to maintain a sense of connectedness or a continuing bond with the deceased whenever they gaze at the tree or tend the garden. This thought may be comforting to both the individual with the life-threatening illness as well as the family involved.

COPING AND ADJUSTMENT

In addition to dealing with the losses associated with the illness process, coping with the day-to-day problems that arise is important to individuals faced with this stressor. Many problems can present as a result of changing roles, financial status, medical treatment, and decreasing physical health. Lazurus and Folkman (1984) have proposed that there are two primary forms of coping: emotion-focused and problem-focused coping. Although it may be tempting to view these forms of coping as separate and distinct, the line between them is blurred and there exists a reciprocal relationship between the two. Coping has been found to be associated with four types of emotions: disgust and anger, pleasure and happiness, confidence, and, to a lesser extent, worry and fear (Folkman & Lazurus, 1988). Cognitive–behavioral interventions are aimed at improving both problem-focused coping and emotion-focused coping.

Assessment

A comprehensive assessment is necessary to individualize treatment and is the starting point for any cognitive–behavioral intervention. The assessment should be multimodal, multimethodological, and collaborative in nature, and should gather information in all realms of biopsychosocial functioning, including an assessment of spiritual/religious orientation and importance. Furthermore, death and dying impacts persons' families, significant others, and the community to a greater or lesser extent, depending on the culture.

Sulmasy (2002) advances a comprehensive model of care for patients at the end of life, termed a biopsychosocial–spiritual model. The author defines spirituality as an individual's relationship with the transcendent, however that may be construed. He notes that it is important to consider how an individual searches for ultimate meaning and the nature of the individual's relationship with the transcendent when doing assessments. From a cognitive–behavioral perspective, this may mean assessing cognitions and affective states related to the purpose of life, God or a higher power, and how the individual fits into a larger, universal picture. Also important is assessing how an individual's behaviors relate to these schemas and what behaviors are most helpful to promote a sense of "connectedness" with the transcendent.

Treatment

General Strategies. Cognitive–behavioral therapy for individuals with a life-threatening illness addresses functioning in cognitive, affective, and behavioral domains to promote both emotion-focused and problem-focused coping. Modalities include psychoeducation, individual, group, and family therapies. Because many of the difficulties of living with a life-threatening illness and the emotional reactions that accompany these difficulties can be anticipated, cognitive–behavioral skills can be taught early in the treatment process when the patient and the family may be most receptive. This ensures that coping strategies are in place when they are needed by the patient and the family.

In the cognitive domain, patients may experience significant difficulty adjusting core beliefs about themselves (self-schemas), others, and the world as a disease progressively alters their functioning. Cognitive restructuring, developing coping statements, thought-stopping, and evaluating and adjusting expectations can be useful for helping individuals who are struggling in this area. Increasing a sense of self-efficacy in the face of changing demands or increasing the individual's perceived control over demands may be the focus of treatment. Assessing and changing problematic automatic thoughts that interfere with a patient's adjustment and coping behaviors may also be important for therapy. Other cognitive targets for treatment include enhancing capabilities related to perception and judgment, using distraction techniques, improving decision-making skills, and utilizing and sharing aspects of wisdom.

Affective components of treatment include identifying, labeling, and expressing affective states as well as regulating and modulating emotions. For example, a client may have difficulty recognizing and managing anger relating to one's life-threatening illness. Education about the normative affective components that comprise a grief reaction and the physiological correlates of anger may be necessary to help the client identify and accept this emotion in him- or herself. Furthermore, teaching and rehearsing necessary skills for modulating anger may be helpful.

Behavioral aspects of treatment for those with a life-threatening illness are varied and can be used to facilitate the grieving process, promote coping, and/or increase quality of life. Some interventions targeting behavior change or skill acquisition might include learning relaxation and other anxiety reducing techniques, scheduling activities to build structure into daily functioning and create opportunities for pleasant activities, self-monitoring targeted behaviors or pain, and learning how to deliver self-reinforcement for accomplishing goals. Homework assignments are typically given between sessions to effect progress toward goals and maintenance of therapeutic gains. A rather unique behavioral intervention may include prescribing the use of family rituals to promote the sense of continuing bonds and a connection to the transcendent, as mentioned earlier. Patients and families connect with meaning and each other through the use of rituals or predictable acts used to transmit information about physiologic, psychological, or sociological states.

Communication skills training may be indicated to help clients and families express and communicate affective states to each other, friends, family members, or members, of the health care team. Assertiveness training using role-playing may be particularly helpful for rehearsing the effective communication skills that are needed to ensure one's needs are being met, to modulate affect. Using the previous example, a patient who determines she is angry because of lost vocational roles may need to communicate a desire for increased responsibility in the day-to-day functioning of the family as a means of promoting feelings of usefulness, thereby reducing anger.

Stress inoculation training can be used to help individuals cope with a variety of affective states related to a life-threatening illness. For example, an individual who must undergo painful medical procedures, and therefore experiences a significant amount of anxiety around these procedures, could be led through visualization exercises that detail the necessary aspects of coping with the procedure. Exposure to the imagined stimuli reduces the anxiety and promotes the use of more effective coping skills.

Problem-Solving Therapy. One model of treatment that includes cognitive, affective, and behavioral dimensions to promote coping and adjustment and has garnered much attention in the coping literature is problem-solving therapy (PST; D'Zurilla & Nezu, 1999). This therapy can be used to promote emotion-focused or problem-focused coping or a combination of the two, and offers a coherent treatment approach to increase coping with a life-threatening illness. PST is a flexible, yet structured, cognitive–behavioral treatment that incorporates many of the techniques previously described. It aims at increasing individuals' coping with major life events and, even more importantly, the daily problems that arise from such events. This therapy is tailored to individual patients and therefore may address spirituality, family systems, or unique concerns of a person with a life-threatening illness.

PST focuses on problem orientation variables, or the cognitive and affective components of how one views problems and thinks about themselves and the world, behavioral response styles (approachful versus avoidant), and problem solving proper (defining problems and goals, generating alternative solutions, decision making, solution implementation, and verification). PST focuses on helping individuals or couples change the nature of problematic situations, one's reaction to problems, or both.

Enhancing an individual's ability to find "solutions" to the myriad problems that present during a terminal illness would naturally seem to promote an improved quality of life. In fact, studies have shown that PST for persons with cancer is effective in improving quality of life, decreasing distress, and improving problem-solving skills, while fostering an increased sense of control (Nezu, Nezu, Friedman, Houts, & Faddis, 1998). Thus, even when faced with a problem as immutable as impending death, patients and their families have options that increase their sense of control over the dying process.

EMPIRICAL BASIS

The empirical support for cognitive–behavioral therapy with terminally ill individuals is limited but growing. In a review of the grief literature, Malkinson (2001) found that the few studies that exist and have been cited as effective have utilized desensitization to avoided stimuli, cognitive restructuring, visualization, stress inoculation training, thought-stopping, relaxation exercises, and skill acquisition to assist individuals in coping with grief reactions. While these studies focused on individuals who lost loved ones, it makes intuitive sense that these interventions could be used to help an individual with a terminal illness cope with the reactions to a number of losses that may occur during the illness (e.g., occupational roles, future opportunities, autonomy).

In a review of studies conducted to evaluate the effectiveness of interventions with cancer patients, Andersen (1992) found that therapy components across studies included an emotionally supportive context to address fears and anxieties about the disease, information about the disease and treatment, behavioral coping strategies, cognitive coping strategies, and relaxation training. These interventions were generally found to be effective, especially with patients who were considered low to moderate risk. For those patients who were considered high risk, those whose disease had progressed and death was imminent, interventions tended to shift content to specific death or quality-of-life issues. At this point, therapy tasks might include coping with one's own death or making decisions about no treatment versus a toxic regimen.

Bucher et al. (2001) evaluated the effectiveness of a 90-minute problem-solving education session for persons with advanced cancer and their families. They found that participants reported low confidence about their ability to provide cancer care and felt uninformed about community resources before treatment began. Two months after receiving the treatment sessions, participants reported feeling more informed about community resources and achieved higher scores for problem-solving ability. The authors point out that sessions focused on building skills and teaching problem-solving skills rather than simply providing information, can be successfully delivered; family caregivers are especially likely to benefit from this type of program.

CRITICISMS OF CBT

Literature specifically focusing on persons with AIDS, COPD, cardiac conditions, cancer, and others may offer support to cognitive–behavioral interventions for terminally ill persons. However, caution is warranted in generalizing across populations due to the inherent differences in disease processes, length of time from diagnosis to death, societal reactions to such illnesses, and medical technology and knowledge addressing such conditions. Cognitive–behavioral therapies have traditionally been characterized as cold, methodological, and promoting a logical analysis rather than emotional expression. It has often been characterized as technique focused rather than process focused. Although various techniques have been cited in the previous sections, it is equally important to develop the therapeutic relationship in which the context of therapy takes place. Working with this population requires sensitivity, creativity, and attention to one's own beliefs about grief, loss, pain, and existential issues.

Other criticisms state that cognitive–behavioral therapies have their roots in European culture and may not be applicable to other cultures and ethnic groups, making knowledge of and sensitivity to other cultures and practices surrounding illness and death especially important when working with this population. Another criticism might be that cognitive–behavioral approaches tend to utilize an individual therapy mode. However, as the COPE model points out, it is especially important to involve family members as much as possible and cognitive–behavioral interventions may be delivered across a variety of treatment modalities including couples, group, and family sessions. A final criticism involves the lack of empirical evidence linking cognitive–behavioral interventions with theories of grief and loss in individuals with life-threatening illnesses; this has yet to be directly addressed in the literature.

FUTURE DIRECTIONS

A myriad of possibilities exist for theoretical development and research. Learning which components of cognitive–behavioral therapies are most powerful to use for which individuals with specific illnesses and how nonnormative groups respond will lead to more effective interventions.

Although the scope of this article does not permit a discussion of treatment issues with nonnormative populations, it should be noted that many of the previously mentioned techniques can be adapted for use with special populations.

As previously stated, there remains a need for clear operational definitions of some of the concepts surrounding coping with a life-threatening illness. Concepts such as grief, bereavement, and mourning are often used interchangeably, contributing to confusion in understanding these processes. There is also a need for operational definitions of spiritual aspects of coping. For example, what does it mean to have a sense of connectedness or maintain continuing bonds?

There needs to be a more integrative approach to theories surrounding coping with grief and loss and coping with the problems that arise as a result of life changes due to a life-threatening illness. It may be somewhat artificial to view these as separate areas of coping. In order to promote a better understanding of the coping process and test specific theories, there must be improved assessment instruments and intervention methods consistent with theories. Furthermore, attention should be focused on unique characteristics of various conditions with regard to assessment and treatment mechanisms. Outcome research from a holistic, multidisciplinary, biopsychosocial–spiritual perspective with application of cognitive–behavioral techniques is needed to illuminate what interventions are most effective with specific populations.

Finally, there remains a need to develop an understanding of therapist issues involved in working with this population. In what ways are therapists affected by working with this population and what kinds of cognitive–behavioral techniques do therapists use on themselves to maintain adequate self-care? Working with individuals who are facing daily pain and the possibility of death is a demanding enterprise. It is not uncommon for these individuals to express a desire to end their suffering, which may raise ethical issues for mental health professionals who are trained to respond to suicidal ideation with crisis intervention. These issues require sensitivity and an ability to communicate effectively around difficult issues, raising questions about therapist characteristics and training programs for professionals.

Clearly we have just begun to understand the relevance of cognitive–behavioral therapy for individuals facing terminal or life-threatening illness. If we were to conceptualize it as a journey, we have just embarked. The landscape ahead is unknown, but it is rich with possibilities and opportunities.

REFERENCES

Andersen, B. L. (1992). Psychological interventions for cancer patients to enhance quality of life. *Journal of Counseling and Clinical Psychology, 60*, 552–568.

Bucher, J. A., Loscalzo, M., Zabora, J., Houts, P.S., Hooker, C., & BrintzenhofeSzoc, K. (2001). Problem-solving cancer care education for patients and caregivers. *Cancer Practice, 9*, 66–70.

D'Zurilla, T. J., & Nezu, A. M. (1999). *Problem-solving therapy: A social competence approach to clinical intervention* (2nd ed.). New York: Springer.

Folkman, S., & Lazarus, R. S. (1988). Coping as a mediator of emotion. *Journal of Personality and Social Psychology, 54*, 466–475.

Klass, D., Silverman, P., & Nickman, S. (1996). *Continuing bonds: New understandings of grief.* London: Taylor & Francis.

Kubler-Ross, E. (1969). *On death and dying.* New York: Scribner's.

Lazarus, R. S., & Folkman, S. (1984). *Stress, appraisal, and coping.* New York: Springer.

Malkinson, R. (2001). Cognitive–behavioral therapy of grief: A review and application. *Research on Social Work Practice, 11*, 671–698.

Nezu, A. M., Nezu, C. M., Friedman, S. H., Houts, P. S., & Faddis, S. (1998). *Helping cancer patients cope: A problem solving perspective.* Washington, DC: American Psychological Association.

Nezu, A. M., Nezu, C. M., Houts, P. S., Friedman, S. H., & Faddis, S. (1999). Relevance of problem-solving therapy to psychosocial oncology. *Journal of Psychosocial Oncology, 16*, 5–26.

Sanders, C. M. (1999). *Grief: The mourning after.* New York: Wiley.

Sulmasy, D. P. (2002). A biopsychosocial–spiritual model for the care of patients at the end of life. *The Gerontologist, 42*, 24–33.

RECOMMENDED READINGS

Nezu, A. M., Nezu, C. M., Friedman, S. H., Houts, P. S., & Faddis, S. (1998). *Helping cancer patients cope: A problem solving perspective.* Washington, DC: American Psychological Association.

Sanders, C. M. (1999). *Grief: The mourning after.* New York: Wiley.

Sulmasy, D. P. (2002). A biopsychosocial–spiritual model for the care of patients at the end of life. *The Gerontologist, 42*, 24–33.

Therapeutic Alliance

Lesia M. Ruglass and Jeremy D. Safran

Keywords: therapeutic relationship, alliance, collaborative empiricism, alliance ruptures, nonspecific factors

The therapeutic relationship was not initially recognized by cognitive–behavioral theorists as a highly significant factor, due to their emphasis on the technical aspects of treatment. The principles and techniques of behavior therapy were assumed to be more important than the relational aspects of treatment. However, as social learning theory infiltrated the behavior tradition, the therapeutic relationship was awarded a more important role. Alongside this new interest was a growing body of literature which revealed that, though behavior therapists neglected the relationship, patients viewed the therapeutic relationship as significant to their treatment (Safran & Segal, 1990).

Early theories from the cognitive tradition examined the therapeutic relationship only insofar as it facilitated the implementation of cognitive therapy techniques (e.g., Beck, Rush, Shaw, & Emery, 1979). The therapeutic relationship was not viewed as a change mechanism in and of itself but rather as a prerequisite for the successful employment of certain cognitive–behavioral strategies. Therapists were encouraged to display positive characteristics such as warmth, accurate empathy, and genuineness. These qualities were viewed as essential to the development and maintenance of the therapeutic relationship, which would presumably be one of trust, rapport, and collaboration. Beck et al. (1979) emphasized the process of *collaborative empiricism* that developed between patient and therapist in the service of the treatment goals. The idea here is that the therapist and patient form an alliance around the task of examining the validity of the patient's thoughts and beliefs in a scientific fashion. For instance, the patient and therapist work together to examine and test the inferences and underlying assumptions inherent in the patient's maladaptive thought patterns and to help the patient discover and experiment with new problem-solving strategies. The therapeutic relationship itself was considered secondary to the actual techniques. It remained a necessary but insufficient component of success in treatment.

Safran and Segal (1990), in a comprehensive review of the existing literature on the therapeutic relationship in cognitive–behavioral therapy (CBT), highlighted several ways in which the relationship between patient and client can effect change. One way is through a *social influence process*. The therapists' personal characteristics such as empathy, warmth, and genuineness impact the therapeutic process in a positive manner by increasing the likelihood that the patient will adhere to the treatment protocol and develop *positive therapeutic expectancies*. The therapist uses certain techniques to instill in the patient the expectation that treatment will ultimately be successful. Further, the therapist uses him- or herself as a *role model* by actually modeling possible strategies for dealing with certain problems.

Safran and Segal (1990) also argued that is important to go beyond conceptualizing the therapeutic relationship as a necessary but not sufficient component of change. They suggested that it is critical to conceptualize the therapeutic relationship as a potential mechanism of change in and of itself. From their perspective the therapeutic relationship can provide an important vehicle for challenging patients' interpersonal schemas. For example, the patient who anticipates that others will abandon him if he expresses dependency needs may begin to change this belief if the therapist responds to him in a manner that challenges these expectations (see also Safran, 1998). This emphasis on the importance of the therapeutic relationship has emerged as increasingly prominent in the literature as cognitive therapists have turned their attention to personality disordered patients who do not benefit as readily from straightforward cognitive intervention of a more traditional type (e.g., Beck, Freeman, & Associates, 1990).

ORIGIN AND EVOLUTION OF THE CONCEPT OF THERAPEUTIC ALLIANCE

The concept of the therapeutic alliance can be traced back to the writing of Sigmund Freud. Freud spoke about the importance of using various means to make the patient a "collaborator" in the therapeutic process. Ralph Greenson's (1967) conceptualization of the alliance was also central to the evolution of the concept. He argued that this relationship consists of both *transferential* (i.e., distorted) and *real* dimensions. Greenson suggested that the *real relationship* consists of the rapport that develops between the patient and therapist, including mutual liking, respect, trust, and undistorted perceptions. The *real relationship* forms the core of the *working alliance*, which permits the patient and therapist to collaborate on the task of examining and challenging the transferential or distorted aspects of the relationship. While cognitive therapists have recently become more interested in the psychoanalytic concept of transference, traditionally it was eschewed. This may have had something to do with their reluctance to embrace Greenson's conceptualization of the alliance, which is grounded in the distinction between transferential and real aspects of the relationship. A second factor is that the traditional conceptualization of the alliance assumes that the primary vehicle of change consists of the analysis of the transference.

Despite these obstacles, cognitive therapists have become increasingly interested in the concept of the alliance in the past decade or so. One reason for this has been the vast amount of empirical evidence supporting the importance of the alliance across a range of different treatment modalities including cognitive therapy (see Horvath, 2001). Bordin's (1979) reformulation of the alliance as a transtheoretical construct played a central role in stimulating interest by psychotherapy researchers and in making the construct more meaningful to cognitive therapists. Bordin posited that change in all forms of psychotherapy has to be predicated on a good alliance. His conception of the alliance included three interdependent components: *tasks*, *goals*, and the *bond*. Bordin maintained that the degree of agreement between patient and therapist about the tasks and goals of therapy, in addition to the quality of the relational bond between them, determines the strength of the alliance. The three components thereby mutually influence and continually inform one another by providing a working framework for achieving lasting benefit from treatment. The tasks of the therapy are the specifics on which the patient and therapist must attempt to attain agreement in order to achieve the long-term goals of the therapy. The bond component of the alliance consists of the affective quality of the relationship between patient and therapist. The relational bond that develops between therapist and patient influences the extent to which they are able to agree on the tasks and goals of therapy. In turn, the process of negotiation about tasks and goals affects the quality of the relational bond. Bordin's (1979) conceptualization offers a multidimensional view of the alliance that reflects the dynamic, mutual influence that the patient and therapist have on each other and that extends its applicability beyond the psychoanalytic tradition.

THERAPEUTIC ALLIANCE AND OUTCOME IN CBT

Studies conducted to assess the quality of the alliance in CBT and outcome tend to be comparative clinical trials examining the difference between CBT and other treatment modalities. For example, Raue, Goldfried, and Barkham (1997) compared the ratings of alliance in CBT and psychodynamic–interpersonal therapy of 57 depressed clients. They selected two sessions from each client's treatment (1 high-impact and 1 low-impact) within each treatment condition and had observers rate the alliance using the Working Alliance Inventory (see Raue et al. for further information on this measure). They found that, overall, CBT sessions had significantly better alliance scores than psychodynamic–interpersonal sessions. They hypothesized that the differences between the two treatments in overall alliance ratings may be related to CBT's adherence to instilling hope and positive expectancies as well as encouraging the use of adaptive problem-solving strategies. Conversely, the psychodynamic–interpersonal therapists may have had difficulty providing the patients with the necessary "corrective experiences" within the therapeutic relationship.

Gaston, Thompson, Gallagher, Cournoyer, and Gagnon (1998) conducted a comparative study examining the impact of alliance on psychotherapy outcome across three different modalities (behavioral [BT] cognitive [CT], and brief dynamic therapy [BDT]) with 120 elderly depressed women. Using the California Psychotherapy Alliance Scales (CALPAS), participants and clinical judges assessed the alliance throughout the span of treatment (beginning, middle, and late sessions). In general, they found greater alliance scores for BDT and CT compared to BT. Better alliance was in turn related to improved depression symptomatology at the end of treatment across treatment modalities. However, when they conducted analyses separately by treatment condition, the relationship between alliance and outcome was maintained only for CT. They theorized that the effectiveness of CT may be related to the therapists' ability to maintain agreement about the tasks and goals of the treatment, benefit from the patient's commitment to the treatment objectives, and the careful use of exploratory strategies when needed, especially during alliance ruptures.

Horvath (2001) in a comprehensive review of the empirical research conducted over the past 20 years, found that the quality of the therapeutic alliance was repeatedly related to psychotherapy outcome regardless of type of treatment modality (e.g., cognitive–behavioral or dynamic), source of information (patient versus observer), or outcome measures employed. Thus, the therapeutic alliance appears to be an important component of success in therapy and therefore needs to be taken into consideration by all treatment providers.

REPAIRING ALLIANCE RUPTURES IN CBT

Since the alliance is an essential ingredient in the treatment process outcome, it is important to determine when ruptures in the alliance occur and how best to resolve these breakdowns in the collaborative process (Safran, 1998). Unresolved alliance ruptures can lead to treatment failure. Safran and Muran (2000) conceptualize ruptures according to Bordin's formulation of the alliance. Ruptures may include disagreements about the *tasks* or *goals* of therapy or *problems* with the relational *bond* and the interplay thereof. Safran and Muran (2000) identify several intervention strategies that can be used to repair a ruptured therapeutic alliance. Interventions targeted at disagreements on tasks and goals may include providing a therapeutic rationale, reframing the meaning of certain tasks and goals, or simply changing the tasks and goals. Interventions designed to resolve problems associated with the relational bond may include the clarification of misunderstandings, allying with the patient's resistance, or acting in a way that disconfirms the patient's dysfunctional interpersonal schema (see Safran & Muran, 2000, for a detailed discussion).

SUMMARY AND FUTURE DIRECTIONS

While the therapeutic relationship has always been viewed as important within cognitive therapy, there has been an evolution in the direction of emphasizing its centrality and of viewing it as a vehicle of change in and of itself. One reason for this has been the vast body of psychotherapy research literature documenting the critical role that the alliance plays across therapeutic modalities. Another has been the emerging interest in the application of cognitive–behavioral interventions to personality disordered patients who do not readily benefit from straightforward cognitive interventions. A focus of growing interest by cognitive therapists as well as therapists from other treatment modalities revolves around the topics of delineating different types of ruptures in the therapeutic alliance and developing intervention strategies for resolving them when they emerge.

In the future it will be increasingly important to conduct research that empirically maps out the different types of ruptures in the alliance that occur as well as the processes through which they are resolved. It will also be important to manualize treatment interventions for dealing with alliance ruptures and to test the effectiveness of these interventions for purposes of working with difficult-to-treat patients.

See also: Behavioral assessment

REFERENCES

Beck, A. T., Freeman, A., & Associates. (1990). *Cognitive therapy of personality disorders*. New York: Guilford Press.

Beck, A. T., Rush, A. J., Shaw, B. F., & Emery, G. (1979). *Cognitive therapy of depression*. New York: Guilford Press.

Bordin, E. (1979). The generalizability of the psychoanalytic concept of the working alliance. *Psychotherapy: Theory, Research and Practice, 16*, 252–260.

Gaston, L., Thompson, L., Gallagher, D., Cournoyer, L., & Gagnon, R. (1998). Alliance, technique, and their interactions in predicting outcome of behavioral, cognitive, and brief dynamic therapy. *Psychotherapy Research, 8*, 2, 190–209.

Greenson, R. R. (1967). *The technique and practice of psychoanalysis*. New York: International Universities Press.

Horvath, A. O. (2001). The alliance. *Psychotherapy, 38*, 365–372.

Raue, P. J., Goldfried, M. R., & Barkham, M. (1997). The therapeutic alliance in psychodynamic–interpersonal and cognitive–behavioral therapy. *Journal of Consulting and Clinical Psychology, 65*, 582–587.

Safran, J. D. (1998). *Widening the scope of cognitive therapy: The therapeutic relationship, emotion and the process of change*. Northvale, NJ: Jason Aronson.

Safran, J. D., & Muran, J. C. (2000). *Negotiating the therapeutic alliance: A relational treatment guide*. New York: Guilford Press.

Safran, J. D., & Segal, Z. V. (1990/1996). *Interpersonal process in cognitive therapy*. New York: Basic Books. (2nd ed. Northvale, NJ: Jason Aronson).

RECOMMENDED READINGS

Leahy, R. L. (2001). *Overcoming resistance in cognitive therapy*. New York: Guilford Press.

Safran, J. D., Muran, J. C., Samstag, L. W., & Stevens, C. (2002). Repairing alliance ruptures. In J. C. Norcross (Ed.), *Psychotherapy relationships that work* (pp. 235–254). Oxford: Oxford University Press.

Young, J. E. (1990). *Cognitive therapy for personality disorders: A schema-focused approach*. Sarasota, FL: Professional Resource Exchange.

Therapeutic Assessment: The Rorschach in Cognitive–Behavioral Practice

Stephanie Yoder and Maurice Prout

This article will examine therapeutic assessment (TA; Finn, 1996b) with the Rorschach from a cognitive–behavioral perspective. TA is a testing paradigm that more closely resembles a therapy session and stresses the importance of collaboration that distinguishes it from typical assessment. Many of the principles espoused by the TA paradigm clearly mimic many of the principles of CBT. TA, like CBT, is a collaboration between the therapist and the client that works to uncover, evaluate, and change the cognitive patterns that clients may have which are problematic. Through the collaborative nature of CBT and TA, and through cognitive restructuring, a client is able to identify his or her own problems and maladaptive behaviors (Newman & Greenway, 1997). While the assessor (or therapist) may aid the person in uncovering the origins of his or her distress, the client collaborates in determining the goals for treatment. Much like CBT, the client is engaged in defining the questions for the assessment, weighs whether the question is relevant or not, and then works collaboratively within the session to begin finding alternatives to dysfunctional behaviors. TA can also provide information about the relationship of maladaptive behaviors and the origins of the problem behaviors (schemas), both of which are critical in providing CBT. In essence, the collaborative feedback regarding this information is the vehicle for correcting behaviors in TA.

TA can be used with a variety of assessment tools, including the Rorschach inkblot method (RIM). Additionally, as Exner (1991) and Weiner (1996) note, RIM data can be viewed from any theoretical perspective. Moreover, many of the components of the Rorschach can provide valuable information in helping to devise cognitive–behavioral treatment plans, as well as supplying information about the "cognitive workings" of individuals, including their core schemas. According to Finn (1996a), the Rorschach is a superior method for exposing difficulties with cognition, perception, and emotions that develop in unstructured, interpersonal, and emotionally provocative circumstances. Therefore, the information gleaned from the Rorschach can be used in CBT by providing therapists with a picture of the underlying schemas of individuals. The remainder of this article will look at various components of the RIM together with the Comprehensive System of interpretation, and how these components can be applied to CBT and TA.

SIX DIMENSIONS OF INTERPRETATION

Interpretation of the Rorschach from a CBT perspective is best done by looking at the structural characteristics of the RIM. According to Weiner (1998), this structural approach is based on the belief that the Rorschach measures perception, and that the subject's test responses are a representative sample of his or her behavior. In this way, the RIM is seen as a problem-solving task. How the client responds to this perceptual–cognitive task provides therapists with information about how he or she is likely to deal with other perceptual–cognitive tasks in his or her life. Overall, therapists are provided with knowledge about character traits, as well as current emotional and attitudinal states. Essentially, structural interpretation of the Rorschach allows therapists to describe personality styles and strengths and weaknesses of each individual. A general level of adjustment is measured across six dimensions: how people attend to experience, how they use ideation, how they modulate affect, how they manage stress, how they view themselves, and how they relate to others. The core experiences involved with these six dimensions are presented in Table 1. These six arenas coincide with the five clusters described in the Comprehensive System: the cognitive triad (consisting of information processing, cognitive mediation, and ideation), affect, controls and stress, self-perception, and interpersonal perception (Exner, 1991).

Attending to Experience

The dimension of attending to experience describes ways in which people focus their attention and perceive events and objects in their environment (Weiner, 1998). Attending to experience is broken down into: being open to experience (Lambda), the ability to organize information efficiently (Zd), and the ability to perceive events in a realistic and conventional manner (X−%, W:D:Dd, Xu%, and P).

When the RIM indicates someone is closed off to experiences and has a tendency to view the world and oneself with a very narrow lens, such people may act in socially inappropriate or insensitive ways (Exner, 1991; Weiner, 1998). In contrast, others' profiles may show an oversensitivity to experiences and a heavy focus on the events of their lives, which can lead to becoming scattered, distracted, and too concerned about situations over which they may have no control. People with either of these scenarios may require social skills training, which could be role-played in therapy or in the feedback session with TA. Clients could also fill out a Mood Log, or a Dysfunctional Thought Record to help them unearth different ways of viewing things and to help change their maladaptive thoughts.

In treating clients who have difficulty organizing information because they are taking in more information than they can efficiently process, several CBT techniques may be beneficial including breaking tasks down into component parts, time management techniques, and homework addressing distorted cognitions about what it means to be perfect, what it means if other people are not perfect, and so on. These cognitions could easily be challenged within the TA feedback session as well. For people who tend to not take in enough information and thereby make hasty decisions, similar techniques could be utilized, including cognitive training exercises that have proven beneficial with people with ADHD.

Perceiving events in a realistic and conventional manner is measured by several variables on the Rorschach including X−%, W:D:Dd, Xu%, and P. The X−% demonstrates whether clients are seeing things in a realistic fashion (Exner, 1991; Weiner, 1998). The more distorted these perceptions are, the more likely the client is experiencing some sort of psychosis. As such, the client should be treated appropriately with pharmaceuticals. CBT has also been shown to be effective with patients with psychosis and these

Table 1. Six Dimensions of Adjustment with the RIM

Dimension	Core experiences
Attending to experience	How open one is to new experiences; ability to process information and perceive things in an ordinary and realistic manner
Using ideation	How one thinks about his or her own experiences (logically, flexibly, and constructively)
Modulating affect	How one deals with emotions and emotions of others sufficiently, pleasurably, and moderately
Managing stress	What resources one has for dealing with stress, minimizing distress, and consistently dealing with stress
Viewing oneself	How realistically and positively one views the self, including self-esteem, self-regard, and self-awareness
Relating interpersonally	How one anticipates intimacy in relationships, maintains relationships, and is empathetic

principles can be applied to treatment for those with a high X−%. When performing a TA with such individuals, it is wise to respect the level of disturbance of the client, avoiding being too challenging in the feedback until the client has achieved some level of mental stability. With the *Economy Index* (W:D:Dd), the therapist gains an understanding of whether clients attend to situations in a conventional manner. It indicates an ability to deal with aspects of everyday life, while understanding the bigger picture of things, including what is normal and what is unusual. Working with such individuals may require similar interventions used in working with high-Lambda clients. Looking at things in a conventional or conformist manner is also measured by the Xu% and the number of P responses. Such levels of conventionality may not be problematic for clients, and they may in fact enjoy a livelihood based on their individualism (e.g., artists, musicians, actors). However, collaboration with the client will help to determine if this is a factor in their dysfunctional behaviors and thoughts and should be explored in both TA and traditional cognitive therapy. If it is problematic, clients should be guided in unearthing different cognitions and behaviors within the assessment, and should be given assignments to help them externalize their core beliefs, analyze and weigh them, and come up with alternatives in order to change their maladaptive patterns.

Using Ideation

How people cogitate about their personal experiences and how they devise their thoughts about these situations characterize the dimension of using ideation (Weiner, 1998). Ideation consists of thinking logically and coherently, thinking flexibly, thinking constructively, and thinking in moderation.

Thinking in a logical and coherent fashion is measured by the *Wsum6* variable of the Rorschach (Exner, 1991; Weiner, 1998). Problem solving, making decisions, and communicating clearly to others are all dependent on thinking in a coherent fashion. When the *Wsum6* is highly elevated, the more likely it is that the client is suffering from a thought disorder such as the kind associated with schizophrenia or other disorders involving psychotic thinking. As such, feedback in TA should pay specific attention to not overwhelming the client or by being too challenging, and by not showing surprise or distaste for a client's delusions. Eventually, once stabilized, these clients could be treated with CBT techniques that challenge the delusional beliefs in a collaborative fashion (Alford & Beck, 1997). Clients are helped to understand that their beliefs are not reality per se, but constructions of reality.

Flexible thinking is measured by the *Active/Passive Ratio (a:p)* on the Rorschach (Exner, 1991; Weiner, 1998). Thinking flexibly affords people ease in seeing alternative perspectives and the ability to change their own point of view. People who are very rigid in their ways of thinking may have difficulty in therapy, especially with TA and CBT techniques. As searching for alternatives to their behaviors and ways of thinking is the cornerstone of these techniques, inflexible thinkers may greatly resist attempts at change.

Ma:Mp measures constructive thinking, or the ability to use ideation in a realistic and task-oriented manner to problem solve and concoct specific action plans (Exner, 1991; Weiner, 1996). Instead of thinking about how they can resolve problems, clients with a higher passive score may fantasize about how other people or extraneous circumstances can save them from a problem. In working with such individuals, a useful technique may be to role-play with this individual so that the therapist is the client, or the client may role-play someone who they feel is an effective decision maker. During the role-plays, the client may gain insight into how to do things in a more effective way, without eroding his or her defensive fantasy life. Over time, the role-plays may become "closer to home" and ask specific questions about how the client will deal with various problems with decision-making tasks once a change in the client's maladaptive beliefs has already begun.

Thinking in moderation is evaluated by *EBPer, INTELL, and FM+m* variables on the Rorschach (Exner, 1991; Weiner, 1998). Being able to balance thinking and feeling provides one with effective coping skills, and the ability to avoid becoming overwhelmed with disturbing thoughts. *EBPer* measures the capacity people have in flexibly using their thoughts and feelings in decision-making and problem-solving activities. For those who are better at thinking than doing and become overwhelmed by emotional situations, CBT and TA would most likely begin with learning to identify emotions and what they mean, as opposed to just looking at what they "think" about a situation. Following this labeling process, clients may begin to connect their emotions, thoughts, and actions through the use of a Mood Log.

Another indicator of a tendency to distance from affect is an elevated *INTELL* score, which demonstrates an attempt to deal with feelings through an intellectual mind-set that minimizes the impact of the emotions and can negatively impact interpersonal relations. Such intellectualizing may also signify underlying negative affect that may be indicative of depressive symptoms. In addition, high *FM+m* scores denote intrusive thoughts that are beyond conscious control and cannot be easily removed from awareness. Difficulties with concentration due to uncontrolled worries may be found in people suffering from insomnia, PTSD, or severe concentration problems. In treating such individuals, progressive relaxation, imagery, and other techniques for dealing with anxiety may be used. Through TA or CBT, the dysfunctional worrisome beliefs can be examined and then scrutinized for alternative explanations to help create more adaptive and functional belief systems within clients.

Modulating Affect

The way in which people process emotions, as well as their comfort level in doing so, comprises the dimension of modulating affect (Exner, 1991; Weiner, 1998). This includes not only how people deal with their emotions, but how they deal with the feelings of others, including involvement in emotion-laden situations. This element is broken down into modulating affect sufficiently, pleasurably, and in moderation.

Dealing with affect sufficiently suggests being able to effectively interact in emotional situations as well as exchange feelings with others. Using the RIM, *Afr, WsumC,* and *SumC* all indicate different ways people process, express, and experience emotions. People with difficulties modulating their affect sufficiently would benefit from treatments that focus on learning to understand their emotions and connect them to their thoughts and behaviors in a manner described above. Once this occurs, it is likely that any somatic complaints that exist due to inability to properly modulate affect will dissipate as well.

Another component of modulating affect is doing so pleasurably, which means the capacity to maintain a positive emotional tone, as well as feeling happy and enjoying oneself. On the RIM, *Sum C', Color-Shading Blends, SumShading, Fm+m,* and *S* are all indicators for this aspect of affect. Difficulties in experiencing affect in a pleasurable manner can contribute to cognitive distortions associated with depression. As a result, CBT and TA techniques aimed at challenging and restructuring the global negative beliefs about the self and world associated with depression would help allay these symptoms.

Finally, an ability to modulate affect in moderation indicates the capacity to balance effectively between emotions and ideations when expressing oneself, to express emotions in an acceptable manner, and to easily process emotions in a positive fashion. These components are indicated on the RIM through *EBPer, FC:CF+C,* and *CP*. Disturbances in this balance may be exhibited by unstable moods and intense emotional outbursts, which may imply bipolar or cyclothymic disorder, or perhaps some characterological disorder. On the other hand, such an imbalance may result in emotional reserved behaviors and difficulty expressing feelings adequately. People with difficulty modulating their affects will likely need to learn techniques such as anger management skills to control their emotional displays. In addition, situations may be broken down into segments (such as What happened just prior to the incident? What happened during the outburst? What was the end result?) so that clients can analyze the cognitive and affective reactions they are experiencing throughout each phase of the emotion-provoking incident. From these insights, clients can reevaluate their reactions and devise alternative ways of thinking and acting.

Stress Management

How people deal with stress and the resources they bring to bear in coping with stress are factors involved in a positive mental life. On the Rorschach, stress management is comprised of resources people have available for dealing with stress *(EA* and *CDI)*, how capable people are at minimizing the distress they may feel *(Adj D* and *D Scores)*, and maintaining consistency in dealing with stress *(EbPer Style)*.

When working with those who appear to have less resources for dealing with daily stresses, and are less likely to deal with demands in an effective and gratifying manner, one should work on bolstering effective coping skills. This includes exploring various coping techniques through CBT and during the feedback portion of TA. When a pattern on the RIM indicates possible problems handling interpersonal relationships in a gratifying and relaxed manner, CBT techniques should focus on reducing social anxiety and bolstering social skills.

For those people who exhibit a pattern on the RIM indicating they are unable to minimize the amount of anxiety they are feeling, treatment should focus on stress reduction techniques such as relaxation techniques, or on cognitive restructuring to change their perceptions about events in their lives. When a patient is currently feeling a great deal of distress, there is typically more motivation to change and seek therapy, and such individuals will be ripe for CBT methods that tend to concentrate on the present context. When treating people who are indicating chronic distress on the RIM, it may be useful to carefully unearth the nature and origin of the anxiety and the core beliefs and schemas that accompany it, and then work to change these maladaptive beliefs. This may also require that the patient learn better coping mechanisms for dealing with a consistently hostile environment, for example. In such a scenario, role-playing alternative behaviors may be particularly useful.

Viewing the Self

Another determinant of psychological wellness is the degree to which one views him- or herself in a positive yet realistic light. With regard to the Rorschach, viewing oneself is broken down into a client's ability to maintain positive self-esteem, to promote positive self-regard, to enhance self-awareness, and to form a consistent sense of identity.

The ability to maintain an adequate level of self-esteem is depicted on the Rorschach through *reflection responses* and the *egocentricity index* (Exner, 1991; Weiner, 1998). In treating individuals who may be showing a "superiority complex," therapists need to be careful not to deflate the overvalued sense of self or severe depression could ensue. However, TA is a wonderful tool to use with such clients because the nature of the method itself does, in fact, increase self-esteem levels of clients (Finn & Tonsager, 1992; Newman & Greenway, 1997). Once self-esteem and symptomatology have decreased following administration of the TA, cognitive restructuring can begin to help change the maladaptive beliefs that these clients have about themselves. Cognitive therapy will also benefit any reactive depressions that may arise by working with such sensitive core beliefs.

On the Rorschach, the capacity to promote positive self-regard is measured by *V* and *MOR (morbid)* responses (Exner, 1991; Weiner, 1998). Changing dysfunctional beliefs about vulnerability and control are key issues in working with individuals exhibiting *V* and *MOR* responses. These variables are very cognitive in nature because they entail self-talk, which reinforces the negative affirmations about the self. Such self-talk should be monitored, externalized (such as through homework or logs), analyzed, and eventually challenged.

The ability to have a healthy level of personal insight is important to psychological health and is reflected on the RIM through the *FD* variable. People who tend to lack personal insight are probably best treated with CBT because they cannot understand more insight-oriented therapies. The focus of therapy could be to first help the client understand concrete aspects of his or her behavior, and then help the client to understand the reactions of other people by externalizing the client's thoughts and beliefs. This could be done through various homework exercises such as Mood Logs that carefully dissect the connections between thoughts, behaviors, and feelings. Alternative behaviors can then be processed, but work will need to be concrete, structured, and carefully broken down.

Finally, a stable identity and identification with other people is demarcated on the Rorschach through *Human (H) responses* and *H: Hd, (H), + (Hd)*. Treating people with an unstable identity may entail careful unraveling of core beliefs and helping people construct clear and achievable goals for themselves. This task could be accomplished by carefully scrutinizing the characteristics they appreciate in others, and then devising behavioral contracts for developing similar characteristics in themselves.

Interpersonal Relationships

Adaptive and functional relationships are imperative to achieving or maintaining good psychological fortitude. Characteristics of healthy relationships include the ability to retain interest, involvement, and comfort in interpersonal relations, the ability to anticipate intimacy and security in relationships, the capacity to balance cooperativeness and compliance with assertion and competition, and the competence to remain interpersonally empathic.

The ability to maintain interpersonal interest, involvement, and comfort is measured on the Rorschach through *H:Hd+(H)+(Hd)* and the *Isolation Index* (Exner, 1991; Weiner, 1998). People who do not indicate much interest in interpersonal relationships may exhibit patterns of social withdrawal and avoidant behaviors. When helping people become more integrated into the realm of social relationships, CBT techniques used with social anxiety may be useful. This would include determining idiosyncratic beliefs about relationships and reconstructing maladaptive convictions.

Determining how people view forming intimate relationships and enjoy the experiences of doing so can be indicated on the Rorschach through the sum of all *T* responses, as well as through the *Hypervigilance Index (HVI)* (Exner, 1991; Weiner, 1998). People may exhibit a reactive depression with regard to their capacity for forming and enjoying intimate relationships, and CBT techniques could be used to help deal with maladaptive depressive cognitions. In addition, the RIM may indicate that some people view interpersonal relationships with alarm and mistrust, and typically avoid them to maintain privacy. CBT techniques generally used with those suffering from PTSD may be carefully applied to such people to help alleviate some of their anxiety around dealing with interpersonal and social contexts, and to decrease some of the paranoid flavor they are likely to manifest.

The capacity to balance interpersonal collaboration and acquiescence with competitiveness and assertiveness is shown on the Rorschach by the *COP, AG*, and *a:p* variables (Exner, 1991; Weiner, 1998). CBT focusing on assertiveness training can be helpful for people who are too aggressive or those who are too passive.

A final component of maintaining healthy interpersonal relations with others is the ability to remain empathic, which is depicted by human movement *(M)* responses (Exner, 1991; Weiner, 1998). Again, when treating people with difficulties in social perception, social skills training can supplement other therapeutic interventions such as searching for alternative strategies for maladaptive behaviors that may manifest during the course of a TA. After exploring options for alternative behaviors during the feedback session of TA, further work can be done through CBT. Alternative explanations for the behavior (or reactions to the behavior) can be sought, scrutinized, and weighed in order to foster insight into maladaptive behaviors.

In conclusion, each of the six dimensions used in determining psychological adjustment can be viewed as broad core experience. Within each of the six dimensions, more specific information about core experiences and thoughts of each client can be determined by viewing the various components and codes that make up each dimension. By looking at the idiosyncratic components of each client's core experiences, specific treatment plans and pertinent techniques for therapy can be ascertained. With each component listed above, suggestions for CBT interventions are provided. In addition, although it may not be explicitly noted, these techniques may be utilized or modified to fit in with the feedback session of TA. In this way, using these techniques in TA will help emphasize the issues that are poignant for therapy, as well as begin the process of change within the assessment process.

See also: Behavioral assessment

REFERENCES

Alford, B. A., & Beck, A. T. (1997). *The integrative power of cognitive therapy*. New York: Guilford Press.

Exner, J. E., Jr. (1991). *The Rorschach: A comprehensive system: Vol. 2. Interpretation* (2nd ed.). New York: Wiley.

Finn, S. E. (1996a). Assessment feedback integrating MMPI-2 and Rorschach findings. *Journal of Personality Assessment, 67*(3), 543–557.

Finn, S. E. (1996b). *Manual for using the MMPI-2 as a therapeutic intervention*. Minneapolis: University of Minnesota Press.

Finn, S. E., & Tonsager, M. E. (1992). Therapeutic effects of providing MMPI-2 test feedback to college students awaiting therapy. *Psychological Assessment, 4*(3), 278–287.

Newman, M. L., & Greenway, P. (1997). Therapeutic effects of providing MMPI-2 test feedback to clients at a university counseling service: A collaborative approach. *Psychological Assessment, 9*(2), 122–131.

Weiner, I. B. (1996). Some observations on the validity of the Rorschach Inkblot Method. *Psychological Assessment, 8*(2), 206–213.

Weiner, I. B. (1998). *Principles of Rorschach interpretation*. Mahwah, NJ: Erlbaum.

Treatment Integrity Issues

Keith S. Dobson and Alisa R. Mintz

Keywords: integrity, adherence, competence

Treatment integrity is a general term that encompasses the two components of treatment delivery of adherence (how much a particular therapy is or is not provided) and competence (how skillfully or poorly the treatment techniques are used, how timely they are, the ability of the therapist to modify the work that they do to meet a particular client's clinical needs). With the development of cognitive–behavioral therapy (CBT) as a set of treatment methods, the need for reasonable standards of control of the treatment(s) in psychotherapy research, and the recent push for the delivery of competent psychotherapy, issues of treatment integrity have surfaced as important matters in both the research and practice of CBT.

REVIEW OF RELEVANT LITERATURE

Luborsky and DeRubeis (1984) referred to the development of treatment manuals as a "small revolution" in the field of psychotherapy research. Treatment manuals, however, were a direct reflection of the need to control the "independent variable" in randomized clinical trials that involved various therapy approaches, and to concomitantly reduce the "error variance" associated with inconsistencies in the delivery of therapies that might suppress the effects of these various treatments. Knowing precisely what therapists do in psychotherapy research also contributes to the establishment of internal and construct validity of treatment outcome research. From a clinical perspective, knowing that certain clinical procedures can be identified and manualized also provides some direction to the psychotherapy field, in that effective treatments can be replicated in the context of clinical practice.

Early efforts to delineate those aspects of treatment that were manualized and could be measured focused on the concept of competence. Quickly, though, it also became clear that as a prerequisite for the competent administration of a given therapy, it first had to be specifically delivered (Waltz, Addis, Koerner, & Jacobson, 1993). That is, being adherent to a given therapy is a precondition for competence; it does not, however, ensure that simply because a treatment is being used, it is being used in a skillful or competent manner (McGlinchey & Dobson, 2003). Early efforts in the field included the development of the Cognitive Therapy Scale (CTS; Young & Beck, 1980), as a measure of competence, and the Minnesota Therapy Rating Scale (DeRubeis, Hollon, Evans, & Bemis, 1982; later revised to be the Collaborative Study Psychotherapy Scale; Hollon et al., 1988), as a measure of the relative adherence to cognitive therapy, interpersonal therapy, and pharmacotherapy.

Generally, measures of adherence consist of a series of items that reflect the inclusive range of possible techniques within that treatment. As such, treatment adherence measures may be quite short and focused for well-defined treatments, but may also be quite broad and inclusive for treatments that reflect systems of techniques. It can be argued that comprehensive adherence measures should also include the assessment of proscribed interventions, to ensure that the therapist not only is doing what she or he is supposed to be doing, but also is not "contaminating" the therapy with theoretically inconsistent techniques. Measures of adherence are sometimes in the form of checklists, which simply indicate whether or not a specific behavior was observed; others are in the form of rating scales, which reflect how much the therapy behavior occurred in a given therapy session (McGlinchey & Dobson, 2003). Trained university students have been used as raters of adherence, with considerable reliability being observed (Hollon et al., 1992).

In contrast to measures of adherence, measures of therapy competence reflect the overall or global sense of expertise that therapists demonstrate in the work that they do. Typically, these rating measures involve a series of items that contribute to an overall score, which theoretically reflects treatment competence. In order to make competence ratings, the rater must try to discern not only what the therapist attempted to do in the session, but also what the optimal set of interventions would have been. Such ratings necessarily involve the use of expert raters, as only an expert can make the critical decision about what the optimal strategy, or timing of different techniques, might have been.

THE MEASUREMENT OF TREATMENT FIDELITY

Treatment adherence and competence scales have been devised in recent years, typically for use in the evaluation of a clinical trial. The Collaborative Study Psychotherapy Rating Scale (CSPRS; Hollon et al., 1988) is a 48-item measure that rates therapists on whether or not they provided a number of treatment methods in a given session, including CBT techniques, general therapeutic skills, therapist directiveness, IPT techniques, and clinical management. The CSPRS has demonstrated adequate discriminability of these various therapy behaviors. It has also been adapted for other research; notably the component analysis of cognitive therapy for depression conducted by Jacobson et al. (1996; Gortner, Gollan, Dobson, & Jacobson, 1998). In the latter study, the adapted CSPRS was able to discriminate between behavioral, automatic thought, and core belief interventions in cognitive therapy.

The principal alternative measure of adherence in CBT is the Cognitive Therapy Adherence and Competence Scale (CTACS; Liese, Barber, & Beck, 1995), which was developed in the context of a randomized clinical trial for cocaine users. The CTACS uses Likert-type scales, which are used to first rate the extent to which various behaviors are conducted, and then to rerate each item as to how competently it was practiced. Psychometric evaluation of the CTACS in the context of a drug addiction study has been generally positive (Liese et al., 1995), and this measure warrants broader evaluation.

The Cognitive Therapy Scale (CTS; Young & Beck, 1980) is the principal measure of CBT competence. The CTS consists of 11 items, each of which is rated on a 7-point Likert (each scored from 0 to 6) scale reflecting increasing competence. Six items measure general interpersonal and relationship factors, while five items measure cognitive therapy techniques. Overall total scores of 40 or above are considered as evidence of "competent" CT (Shaw & Dobson, 1988). The CTS has demonstrated strong internal consistency (coefficient alpha = 0.95) and high interrater reliability (0.54–0.87) (Dobson, Shaw, & Vallis, 1985). The CTS has been widely accepted as a measure of overall CT competence, and has even been adopted by the Academy of Cognitive Therapy as the major index of competent practice in cognitive therapy (*www.academyofct.org*). The CTS has also been adapted for measuring competence in the delivery of cognitive therapy for psychosis (Haddock et al., 2001).

THE RELATIONSHIP OF FIDELITY TO OUTCOME

Research has suggested that specific and structuring behavioral aspects of therapy are associated with more symptom change than more abstract or theoretical aspects of treatment (Feeley, DeRubeis, & Gelfand, 1999). Feeley et al. (1999), for example, measured treatment adherence using the CSPRS and alliance in predicting therapeutic change in depressed patients treated by one of four CBT therapists. They found that the CT concrete scale was a significant positive predictor of change in depressive symptoms, in that the more the therapists delivered concrete skills early on in the therapy sessions, the greater the symptom relief. The CT abstract subscale had no relation to symptom change.

Shaw et al. (1999) investigated the relationship between treatment competence and outcome in 37 individuals with major depression. The competence of eight cognitive–behavioral therapists was evaluated using the CTS. Results indicated limited support for the relationship between therapist competence and reduction of depressive symptoms. The component of competence that was highly related to outcome was the therapist's ability to structure treatment. A major problem with the CTS is that because there is a great deal of overlap between items, the specific areas of CB therapists' performance may not adequately be measured by the CTS (Shaw et al., 1999).

ISSUES AND DIRECTIONS FOR FUTURE RESEARCH

The measurement of competence has been problematic. As Elkin (1999) has argued, competency may be an amalgamation of several variables. Some researchers have included therapist variables that are independent of working with the client (i.e., demographics, personality variables, discipline, level of didactic training) (Strupp, Butler, & Rosser, 1988), while other researchers have included the importance of variables that are directly relevant to the specific clinical case (Dobson & Shaw, 1988). It has been argued that an optimal competency evaluation should include explicit standards of CBT techniques combined with standards of other nonspecific therapeutic factors (Shaw & Dobson, 1988). An agreed-upon set of guidelines for measuring competence would enhance the consistency and generalization across studies, as well as improve methodology in order to address issues, such as the predictors of treatment competence and how it relates to treatment outcome.

The issue of whether competency should be conceptualized as a stable traitlike construct, or more as a state, in which therapist skillfulness varies across sessions, cases, and time, has arisen (Shaw & Dobson, 1988). Training models often act as if competency is a trait, in that once it is acquired it "stays with" the therapist. It is also possible, however, that competence is variable; longitudinal analysis of therapist competence across cases and over the course of treatment is recommended for understanding the stability of the construct. The state position also implies that for professional training, competency should be viewed as a state that is consistent across cases with a minimal standard exemplified over the course of several months or years (Shaw & Dobson, 1988).

It is hoped that the future of CBT research will also include the development of more finely tuned measurement scales of treatment fidelity, for specific disorders or CBT techniques. With the exceptions of treatment for psychosis and for cocaine use, there has been a lack of research targeting the issues of treatment integrity in the context of specific disorders. What is needed is the development of integrity measures that evaluate the delivery of CBT techniques in the context of specific disorders. Further research is also needed to evaluate issues of competency in the administration of specific CBT techniques that target cognitive content and processes.

The question of how to train and evaluate therapists in adherence and competence also remains uncertain. What is needed is the development of well-designed cognitive–behavioral training programs that evaluate trainees for the development of their adherence and competency skills. Allowing one's clinical behavior to be assessed by more senior experts can be anxiety provoking. Therefore, it is important that such evaluations be conducted in an environment that fosters willingness and openness for learning about one's skillfulness. Periodic evaluations of treatment integrity could then be conducted prior to, during, and following the training program. Such evaluations could then be used to modify the training program in order to maximize the development of therapists' skills.

SUMMARY

Treatment integrity is a general term that includes treatment adherence (how much a particular therapy is or is not provided) and competence (how skillfully or poorly the treatment techniques are used). A number of measures have been developed for measuring treatment adherence and competence. The few studies that have investigated the impact of treatment integrity on therapeutic outcome have generally yielded inconclusive results. A number of conceptual and methodological issues have been identified, which include the lack of consensus regarding the nature and definition of treatment competency, the need for more finely tuned measurement scales, and the generalizability of treatment integrity to the clinical setting. Future research needs to address these issues in order to improve the evaluation and delivery of cognitive–behavioral techniques for the treatment of a wide range of disorders in both research and clinical settings.

REFERENCES

DeRubeis, R. J., Hollon, S. D., Evans, M. D., & Bemis, K. M. (1982). Can psychotherapies for depression be discriminated? A systematic investigation of cognitive and interpersonal therapy. *Journal of Consulting and Clinical Psychology, 50*, 744–756.

Dobson, K. S., & Shaw, B. F. (1988). The use of treatment manuals in cognitive therapy: Experience and issues. *Journal of Consulting and Clinical Psychology, 56*, 673–680.

Dobson, K. S., Shaw, B. F., & Vallis, T. M. (1985). Reliability of a measure of the quality of cognitive therapy. *British Journal of Clinical Psychology, 24*, 295–300.

Elkin, I. (1999). A major dilemma in psychotherapy outcome research: Disentangling therapists from therapies. *Clinical Psychology: Science and Practice, 6*, 3–10.

Feeley, M., DeRubeis, R. J., & Gelfand, L. A. (1999). The temporal relation of adherence and alliance to symptom change in cognitive therapy for depression. *Journal of Consulting and Clinical Psychology, 67*, 578–582.

Gortner, F. T., Gollan, J. K., Dobson, K. S., & Jacobson, N. S. (1998). Cognitive–behavioral treatment for depression: Relapse prevention. *Journal of Consulting and Clinical Psychology, 66*, 377–384.

Haddock, G., Devane, S., Bradshaw, T., McGovern, J., Tarrier, N., Kinderman, P. et al. (2001). An investigation into the psychometric properties of the Cognitive Therapy Scale for Psychosis (CTS-Psy). *Behavioural & Cognitive Psychotherapy, 29*, 221–233.

Hollon, S. D., DeRubeis, R. J., Evans, M. D., Wiemer, M. J., Garvey, M. J., Grove, W. M. et al. (1992). Cognitive therapy and pharmacotherapy for depression. *Archives of General Psychiatry, 49*, 774–781.

Hollon, S. D., Evans, M. D., Auerbach, A., DeRubeis, R. J., Elkin, I., Lowery, H. A. et al. (1988). *Development of a system for rating therapies of depression: Differentiating cognitive therapy, interpersonal psychotherapy and clinical management pharmacotherapy.* Unpublished manuscript, University of Minnesota, Minneapolis.

Jacobson, N. S., Dobson, K. S., Truax, P. A., Addis, M. E., Koerner, K., Gollan, J. K. et al. (1996). A component analysis of cognitive behavioural treatment for depression. *Journal of Consulting and Clinical Psychology, 64*, 295–304.

Liese, B. S., Barber, J., & Beck, A. T. (1995). *The Cognitive Therapy Adherence and Competence Scale.* Unpublished manuscript, University of Kansas Medical Center.

Luborsky, L., & DeRubeis, R. J. (1984). The use of psychotherapy treatment manuals: A small revolution in psychotherapy research style. *Clinical Psychology Review, 4*, 5–14.

McGlinchey, J. B., & Dobson, K. S. (2003). Treatment integrity concerns in cognitive therapy for depression. *Journal of Cognitive Psychotherapy: An International Quarterly, 17*(4), 299–318.

Shaw, B. F., & Dobson, K. S. (1988). Competency judgments in the training and evaluation of psychotherapists. *Journal of Consulting and Clinical Psychology, 56*, 666–672.

Shaw, B. F., Elkin, I. F., Yamaguchi, J., Olmsted, M., Vallis, T. M., Dobson, K. S., et al. (1999). Therapist competence ratings in relation to clinical outcome in cognitive therapy for depression. *Journal of Consulting and Clinical Psychology, 67*, 837–846.

Strupp, H. H., Butler, S. F., & Rosser, C. L. (1988). Training in psychodynamic therapy. *Journal of Consulting and Clinical Psychology, 56*, 689–695.

Waltz, J., Addis, M. E., Koerner, K., & Jacobson, N. (1993). Testing the integrity of a psychotherapy protocol: Assessment of adherence and competence. *Journal of Consulting and Clinical Psychology, 61*, 620–630.

Young, J., & Beck, A. T. (1980). *Cognitive Therapy Scale: Rating manual.* Unpublished manuscript, University of Pennsylvania, Philadelphia.

Treatment of Children

Joanna A. Robin and Philip C. Kendall

Keywords: cognitive behavioral therapy, childhood therapy, cognitive distortions, cognitive deficiencies, randomized clinical trial, empirically supported treatment, coping, anxiety disorders, aggression, depression

Cognitive–behavioral therapy (CBT) adheres to a model that emphasizes the role of the child's internal and external environments in the development, maintenance, and remediation of psychological distress. For example, CBT addresses the child's social information processing, the role of contingencies, and the contribution of models in the environment (Kendall, 2000). Accordingly, CB therapists use demonstrations, role-plays, and performance-based strategies, with rewards, along with cognitive interventions to facilitate changes in feelings, thinking, and behavior. It should be noted that affect is not ignored within the CB perspective. Instead, CBT helps the child identify and regulate emotions and connect them with their thoughts and behavior. Within the CB framework, social context plays a crucial role, particularly important when working with children. Contextual forces, such as parents and peers, are examined, considered, and incorporated into treatment. Often, the parent(s) is considered to be a collaborator, consultant, or even co-therapist within this framework.

THE THERAPIST'S ATTITUDE (MENTAL "POSTURE")

In CBT, the therapist's "posture" involves being a diagnostician, a consultant, and an educator. As a diagnostician, the therapist combines his or her knowledge of normal development and psychopathology with information from parents, schools, and the child to determine the nature of the child's problem and the most appropriate strategy. Knowledge of normal development is crucial to meaningful intervention. As a consultant, the therapist does not have all the answers, but instead helps the child design ways to test dysfunctional beliefs (e.g., through behavioral experiments). The therapist and child work together to problem-solve about coping with difficult situations, and the child's perspective is valued. The therapist offers support through praise and encourages independence. As an educator, the therapist uses the child's strengths when teaching information on emotions, cognitive skills, and problem solving. The therapist teaches these skills in a flexible manner that is individualized for each child based on his or her interests, gender, and developmental level.

DEVELOPMENTAL LEVEL

It is a myth to see uniformity in the term "children" (Kendall, 1984). Indeed, youth of different ages with the same problems and youth of the same age with varied problems are not alike and their problems have differential effects on their social and interpersonal worlds. The CB therapist uses information regarding the child's developmental level to arrange a treatment plan. For example, younger children may not have the cognitive ability necessary for certain didactic sessions focusing on cognitive restructuring (changing thinking styles). Therefore, the therapist working with younger children would create brief, active sessions with role-plays to address the cognitive content. Younger children may also benefit from parental participation in features of the treatment, to help transfer the skills the child learns in therapy to real-world situations. Peer and achievement-related issues are also typical themes for treatment that vary with the age of the child.

ROLE FOR PARENTS

As mentioned, CBT considers the social context when formulating and implementing treatment. Given that parents play an important role in the socialization of their children, attending to and addressing parental roles can be useful (e.g., Barrett, Dadds, & Rapee, 1996). Parent training sessions may involve recognizing contingencies: adding rewards in some instances and changing contingencies to encourage adaptive behavior in others. In addition, parents can be shown how their thinking, emotional expression, and behavior can contribute to their child's distress. Parents also benefit from learning problem-solving and conflict resolution skills that complement skills their child learns in treatment.

CONSIDERING COGNITION

Not surprisingly, CBT emphasizes children's cognitive functioning. CBT seeks to educate children about their cognitive processes and help reduce maladaptive and dysfunctional beliefs. Cognitive functioning is complex, and children vary in the nature of their cognitive dysfunction. For example, it is important to recognize the distinction between cognitive *deficiency* (lacking of information processing) and cognitive *distortion* (biased, flawed thinking). Distorted thinking has been implicated in internalizing disorders such as depression and anxiety, where the child misperceives, misinterprets, or misconstrues some aspect of his or her environment. In contrast, impulsive or hyperactive children suffer more from cognitive deficiencies—in a variety of situations they may act without thinking about consequences. CBT is tailored for the child so that cognitive distortions can be identified, tested-out/challenged, and replaced. Additional problem solving (putting thinking between stimulus and response) can help the child reduce cognitive deficiencies.

A GOAL OF CBT: DEVELOPING A COPING TEMPLATE

One of the goals of CBT is to help a child develop a new cognitive structure or new way of looking at experiences in the world. A cognitive structure or schema (Beck, 1976) refers to the template through which an individual views and makes sense of the world. Through identifying and modifying a child's self-talk and shaping new ways to view his/her environment, CBT aims to help the child develop a "coping" template—a way to approach future events with a less detrimental mental set. CBT uses behavioral interventions that arouse affect, while attending to the child's thinking before and after these behavioral events. The therapist explores the child's expectations about upcoming events and discusses attributions about past events—all to help modify the child's dysfunctional schema.

CBT PRACTICE

The following skill-building procedures and strategies are typically used in CBT for children: affective education, relaxation, cognitive restructuring, problem solving, coping modeling, homework assignments, role-plays, and exposures. Affective education focuses on helping the child learn about his or her emotional responses to situations and emphasizes the adaptive value of emotions. Relaxation training helps children become aware of and in control of their physical responses to emotions. This commonly used procedure requires that major muscles in the body are systemically tensed and relaxed, so that the child understands that the tenseness in his or her body is a trigger to relax. The therapist teaches the child relaxation training in session and gives him or her assignments to practice these techniques at home.

Cognitive restructuring is used to correct maladaptive self-talk. This can be done by teaching the child to label distorted thoughts. The therapist guides the child in generating alternative thoughts that promote more adaptive behavioral responses. The child develops coping statements he or she can use when confronted with anger-provoking, self-blaming, anxious, or other detrimental self-talk.

Problem solving is used to help children become confident in their ability to face challenging situations. The first step of the five-step procedure outlined by D'Zurilla and Goldfried (1971) involves a discussion of the prevalence of problems in everyday life. Second, the therapist helps the child articulate the problem in concrete and workable terms. Third, the therapist and child generate solutions to the problem without critiquing them. Fourth, the child and the therapist evaluate the solution they have posited, based on the expected outcome, and put a solution into effect. In the fifth stage, the child verifies the merit of the chosen solution. Through practice, the child begins to see the many choices that he or she has in difficult situations. For example, when working with aggressive children, helping them to see the pros and cons of aggressive and nonaggressive responses helps them cope in situations where they feel threatened.

Coping modeling is used to help children see how nondistorted thinking and problem solving can lead to adaptive responses to difficult situations. The therapist models responses to situations that are specific to the child's needs. Coping modeling means that the therapist does *not* model error-free behavior, but rather that the therapist models problematic situations like those for the child (e.g., where cognitive misperceptions or deficiencies may lead to problematic situations) and then models how certain strategies can be used to correct these problems.

Role-plays are very helpful when working with children of all ages because they allow them to experience some of the effect involved in a situation, as well as getting them to use problem solving and coping self-talk in the situation. Role-plays give the child opportunities to practice managing affectively arousing experiences within a therapy session. The therapist provides structure and reinforces the child's adaptive responses. Exposure tasks involve placing the child in an emotion-provoking experience either imaginally or in vivo so that the child can experience the distress while practicing the newly acquired coping skills (e.g., relaxation, coping self-talk, problem solving). Exposure tasks are usually conducted in a hierarchical fashion: beginning with less difficult situations and gradually moving to more difficult situations. Exposure tasks are typically used with children with anxiety disorders to help them learn that their feared response may not be accurate and that they can in fact face anxiety-provoking experiences. However, programs for depressed youth, angry and aggressive youth, and impulsive youth also provide real-world opportunities for practice and mastery.

Homework tasks, which usually relate to material covered in the therapy session, are an important part of CBT for youth. A homework task can be either writing in a journal or participating in a behavioral experiment or observational task. Homework assignments allow the therapist to check the child's grasp of the session material and allow the child to practice new skills.

EMPIRICAL SUPPORT FOR CBT WITH CHILDREN

Studies of treatment outcomes of CBT for youth, with both internalizing (e.g., anxiety disorders, depression) and externalizing difficulties (e.g., aggression), have provided some empirical support (i.e., the data document beneficial gains associated with CBT treatment). For example, randomized clinical trials of CBT for anxious youth (e.g., Kendall et al., 1997) have been reviewed and deemed as evidence that CBT is probably efficacious in treating anxiety disorders in youth (Kazdin & Weisz, 1998; Ollendick & King, 2000). Follow-up studies suggest that the reductions in anxiety symptomatology are maintained posttreatment (e.g., Barrett, Duffy, Dadds, & Rapee, 2001; Kendall et al., 2004). A review of school-based programs for treating depression in youth revealed that in five out of the six studies, CBT was more effective than no treatment or to wait-list control (Curry, 2001).

CBT for externalizing disorders have resulted in less consistent results. For example, CBT for ADHD has been found to be less effective than medication (e.g., MTA, 1999). However, CBT for aggression and conduct-related problems (e.g., Kazdin, 2002; Lochman, 1990; Lochman, Whidby, & FitzGerald, 2000) may be effective in reducing aggressive behavior and increasing prosocial behavior. Unfortunately, it is not clear that gains can be maintained over time and generalized to other situations.

CBT emphasizes the important interplay among cognitive, behavioral, affective, contextual, and socioemotional variables in the etiology and maintenance of problems in children. CBT strategies are used to address the specific needs of the child within his or her real and perceived environment. Empirical support suggests that CBT can be an efficacious treatment for youth. Although it is reasonable to suggest that CBT for children can be helpful in treating childhood psychopathology, research is needed (a) to better understand the role of "in-session" process variables (e.g., child involvement) that may predict outcome and (b) on the forces that influence the transportability of CBT from research clinics to community service clinics.

See also: Aggressive and antisocial behavior in youth, Anxiety—children, Children—behavior therapy, Play therapy

REFERENCES

Barrett, P., Dadds, M., & Rapee, R. (1996). Family treatment of childhood anxiety: A controlled trial. *Journal of Consulting and Clinical Psychology, 64*, 333–342.

Barrett, P. M., Duffy, A. L., Dadds, M. R., & Rapee, R. M. (2001). Cognitive–behavioral treatment of anxiety disorders in children: Long-term (6-year) follow-up. *Journal of Consulting and Clinical Psychology, 69*, 135–141.

Beck, A. T. (1976). *Cognitive therapy and emotional disorders*. New York: International Universities Press.

Curry, J. F. (2001). Specific psychotherapies for childhood and adolescent depression. *Biological Psychiatry, 49*, 1091–1100.

D'Zurilla, T. J., & Goldfried, M. R. (1971). Problem-solving and behavior modification. *Journal of Abnormal Psychology, 78*, 107–126.

Kazdin, A. E. (2002). Psychosocial treatments for conduct disorder in children and adolescents. In P. E. Nathan & J. M. Gorman (Eds.), *A guide to treatments that work* (2nd ed., pp. 57–85). New York: Oxford University Press.

Kazdin, A. E., & Weisz, J. R. (1998). Identifying and developing empirically supported child and adolescent treatments. *Journal of Consulting and Clinical Psychology, 66*, 19–36.

Kendall, P. C. (1984). Cognitive processes and procedures in behavior therapy. In G. T. Wilson, C. M. Franks, K. D. Brownell et al. (Eds.), *Annual review of behavior therapy, Vol. 9*. New York: Guilford Press, *59*, 132–179.

Kendall, P. C. (2000). Guiding theory for therapy with children and adolescents. In P. C. Kendall (Ed.), *Child and adolescent therapy: Cognitive–behavioral procedures* (2nd ed.). New York: Guilford Press.

Kendall, P. C., Flannery-Schroeder, E., Panicelli-Mindel, S. M., Southam-Gerow, M., Henin, A., & Warman, M. (1997). Therapy for youths with anxiety disorders: A second randomized clinical trial. *Journal of Consulting and Clinical Psychology, 65*, 366–380.

Kendall, P. C., Safford, S., Flannery-Schroeder, E., & Webb, A. (in revision). Child anxiety treatment: Maintenance of outcomes in adolescence and impact on substance use and depression at 7.4 year follow-up. *Journal of Consulting and Clinical Psychology*, *72*, 276–288.

Lochman, J. E. (1990). Modification of childhood aggression. In M. Hersen, R. M. Eisler et al. (Eds.), *Progress in behavior modification, Vol. 25* (pp.3–22). New York: Guilford Press.

Lochman, J. E., Whidby, J. M., & FitzGerald, D. P. (2000). Cognitive–behavioral assessment and treatment with aggressive children. In P. C. Kendall (Ed.), *Child and adolescent therapy: Cognitive–behavioral procedures* (2nd ed., pp. 31–87). New York: Guilford Press.

MTA Cooperative Group. (1999). A randomized clinical trial of treatment strategies for attention deficit hyperactivity disorder (ADHD). *Archives of General Psychiatry*, *56*, 1073–1086.

Ollendick, T. H., & King, N. J. (2000). Empirically supported treatments for children and adolescents. In P.C. Kendall (Ed.), *Child and adolescent therapy: Cognitive–behavioral procedures* (2nd ed., pp. 386–425). New York: Guilford Press.

RECOMMENDED READINGS

Kazdin, A.E. (2002). Psychosocial treatments for conduct disorder in children and adolescents. In P.E. Nathan & J.M. Gorman (Eds.), *A guide to treatments that work* (2nd ed., pp. 57–85). New York: Oxford University Press.

Kendall, P.C. (2000). Guiding theory for therapy with children and adolescents. In P.C. Kendall (Ed.), *Child and adolescent therapy: Cognitive–behavioral procedures* (2nd ed.). New York: Guilford Press.

Russ, S.W., & Ollendick, T. (Eds.). (1999). *Handbook of psychotherapies with children and families*. New York: Plenum Press.

U

Understanding Schemas

Arthur Freeman and Sharon Freeman

Keywords: schema, schema change, belief systems

In every human action, reaction, and interaction, we are guided by the template of the personal, cultural, family, religious, gender, and age-related schemas that we have developed over the years (Beck, Freeman, & Associates, 1990; Beck, Freeman, Davis, & Associates, 2003; Beck, Rush, Shaw, & Emery, 1979; Freeman & Leaf, 1989; Freeman, Pretzer, Fleming, & Simon, 1990, 2004). Schemas both direct our behavior and affect in particular directions and help to give meaning to our world. The schemas are involved in memory (what is selected for recall or what is "suppressed"), cognition (the abstraction and interpretation of information), affect (the generation of feelings), motivation (wishes and desires), action and control (self-monitoring, inhibition, or direction of action) (Beck, Freeman et al., 1990). By this selectivity, the schemas allow for more efficient information processing (Taylor & Crocker, 1978).

Bartlett (1995) reports that the term *schema* "was first used in relation to changes that occur in recall and recognition following stimulation with complex material" (pp. 60–61). Individuals tend to use schemas to simplify and make understandable events and situations that are too complex for understanding. Schemas are defined as "dynamically flexible organizations of past events, their characteristics, contexts, and implications, with a large capacity for further modification by new events" (Bartlett, 1983, 1995, pp. 60–61).

There have been a number of attempts to typify schemas. Hastie (1984) organized schemas into three broad categories: prototypes (central tendency schemas which are representations of knowledge and understanding), frames (template schemas for organizing knowledge), and scripts (procedural schemas which provide rules and procedures for activating schemas). We might also view schemas as basic rules, with the combination of those rules being scripts. The script is a recognizable sequence of schemas. The combination of schemas and scripts might be termed the lifestyle inasmuch as it becomes emblematic of the individual's behavior and self-definition. The schemas serve as a "filter" for expressive and receptive data. If, for example, the individual holds a depressive bias, they will view the world through dark lenses. Similarly, a bias regarding the danger abundant in the world would result in the individual seeing danger everywhere and would then avoid those experiences and situations that are seen by the individual as dangerous. This filtering effect is especially obvious in individuals with personality disorders (Beck, Freeman, Davis & Associates, 2004).

Understanding schemas, belief systems, or underlying attitudes is, then, the essential ingredient in understanding the behavior of individuals, families, or groups. It will influence individuals in their role as a member of a family or group, and will then impact on the behaviors of entire cultures. These societal influences generate both stereotyping and what are objectively acknowledged to be cultural descriptives of a group or subgroup.

The schemas are the wellspring of attributions and perceptions that generate the idiosyncratic behavior of the individual. These schemas and the resultant behaviors begin to be established from the moment of birth. Some schemas are strongly and vigorously held, while others are more transient and easily surrendered, disputed, or modified by the individual. The schemas that are strongly held often appear immutable (to both therapist and patient) and become the ways in which the patient is defined by self and others. A particular pattern of schemas about the need for perfection in thought and deed would likely result in the individual perceiving the world in dichotomous terms. This would result in the individual experiencing a constant demand on self and others for perfect performance with consequent feelings of failure if performance is only 98%. Schemas are not isolated, but are interlocking and appear in various constellations. For example, while most people would subscribe to the basic personal/religious/cultural schema "Thou shall not steal," they might not return money to the phone company that was returned in a pay phone after they completed a call. Their rationale for this would probably be based on other parallel "rules" such as "getting even is okay/important," which may serve to generate the idea that "since the phone company has taken our money for so many years we can rightfully take theirs." If, however, one applies the rule that "getting even is okay/important" more broadly, it would allow someone to take money from someone else (be they stranger or friend) if their money had been taken by someone else. While it may be "okay" to "get even" with a large corporation, one would probably not deem it appropriate to get even with an individual.

Schemas may be active or inactive. Active schemas govern day-to-day behavior while inactive schemas are dormant until they are stimulated into activity by internal or external stressors. For example, a dormant schema may be triggered by a stressor but will return to its dormant state when the stressor is reduced or removed. Of course, one would expect that when and if the patient is stressed in the future, these same dormant schemas will emerge once again. If this were the case for an individual, an important focus of therapy would be on stress reduction or techniques to allow the patient to keep dormant schemas inactive (Freeman & Simon, 1989), modifying the schemas when possible (Beck, Freeman et al., 1990; Freeman et al., 1990), and identifying any of a number of "vulnerability factors" that increase the likelihood of dormant schemas being activated (Freeman & DeWolfe, 1992; Freeman & Simon, 1989). These vulnerability factors decrease the active threshold of response to stressors, and make the individual more likely to interpret stimuli as stressful, and to respond to stimuli that they were previously able to ignore.

UNDERSTANDING SCHEMAS

An understanding of the schemas will explain past behavior, make sense of present behavior, and help to predict future behavior. The first major therapeutic task is discerning and making manifest specific schemas which will then allow the therapist to work with the patient to examine a schema, the advantages and disadvantages of maintaining it, and various ways of modifying it.

The situational nature of schemas has been examined by Schank and Abelson (1977) who found that many of an individual's governing schemas appear to shift, depending on their construction of a particular situation. Accordingly, a single schema may be responsible for generating a broad range of dysfunctional thoughts, feelings, and behaviors. For example, the schema "To be loved (approved of, accepted, cherished) I must be perfect" might generate a number of cognitions and behaviors in both work and interpersonal areas. On the other hand, the schema might be specific to either work OR interpersonal issues. When more vulnerable, for example, the individual may be far more responsive to the schema, place greater weight on the consequent cognitions, and find the schema far more believable than might be expected at other, higher threshold times. Inasmuch as the schemas are the basis for our construction and understanding of the world, they are also the source of the everyday internal dialogue. When the schemas serve to generate negative and self-depreciating thoughts about self, world, or the future, the major ingredients for depression are in place. If the schemas generate fear or concerns about personal safety, the result would by anxiety. The self-deprecating life view may have been learned by an individual (e.g., "I'm no good") or be part of a broader cultural belief (e.g., "We're no good").

Systemically, significant others not only help to form the schemas, but also help to maintain them regardless of whether the effect is negative or positive. McGoldrick (1982) stresses that families view the world through their own cultural filters so that the particular belief systems may be familial or more broadly cultural. Family schemas based on cultural beliefs might be basic rules regarding sexual behavior, food, education, reaction to other racial, ethnic, or religious groups, or particular religious beliefs. Family-based schemas may be rooted in a particular culture, or be present in many apparently diverse cultures. For example, many people learned to eat everything on their plate because of the parental injunction, "Children are starving in _____." The rule, "Eat everything on your plate" may persist long after the parent is gone, such as when one is at a fine restaurant having a meal and despite being satiated, has the thought that everything on the plate must be eaten. Rules about eating can be easily traced to parents and their direct instructions or modeling.

The essential therapeutic question is not WHERE the behavior comes from, but what maintains the schemas as active over many years despite disconfirming data, negative experiences, negative reactions from others, and personal discomfort. The careers and avocational pursuits that we choose are similarly governed by our schemas. For example, the famous open ocean racer, Sir Francis Chichester, was known for his single-handled transoceanic crossings. He was quoted as saying, "Somehow, I never seemed to enjoy so much doing things with other people. I know I don't do a thing nearly so well when with someone. It makes me think I was cut out for solo jobs, and any attempt to diverge from that lot only makes me half a person." In the preceding quote, Chichester describes schemas typical of Schizoid Personality Disorder (Beck, Freeman, Davis, & Associates, 2004). As Chichester's life was governed by these schemas, he sought a career that allowed him the maximum expression of these schemas. He sailed alone for months at a time.

SCHEMATIC DEVELOPMENT

Schemas are in a constant state of change and evolution. From the child's earliest years, previously formed schemas are altered and new schemas are being developed to meet the increasingly complex demands of the world. Infants' perceptions of reality are governed by their limited interaction with their world; thus, the infant may initially perceive the world as crib and the few caretakers who care for him or her. As infants develop additional skills of mobility and interaction, they perceive their world as significantly broader, both in size and in complexity. During the exploratory period, the child develops mobility, and begins to examine their world more extensively. The child can see that their "world" is indeed huge. With increased interaction with the world, the child begins to incorporate family and cultural schemas.

One way of conceptualizing the change process is to utilize the Piagetian concept of adaptation with its two interrelated processes, assimilation and accommodation (Rosen, 1989). Assimilation involves the way in which individuals utilize their environment in terms of how they conceive the world. Environmental data and experience are only "taken in" by the individual as they can be utilized in terms of the individual's subjective experiences. The self-related schemas then become selective as the individual may ignore environmental stimuli that they were not able to integrate or synthesize.

The process of accommodation involves the ability to modify a schema based on the subjective judgment that the schema no longer serves to organize and explain experiences adequately. The assimilative and accommodative processes are interactive and stand in opposition to each other. We then have an active and evolutionary process whereby all perceptions and cognitive structures are applied to new functions (assimilation) while new cognitive structures are developed to serve old functions in new situations (accommodation). Individuals who exhibit the greatest dysfunction persist in utilizing old structures without fitting them to the new circumstances in which they are involved, but using them *in toto* without measuring for fit or appropriateness (schematic shift potential).

They may further fail to accommodate or build new structures. Schemas are often difficult to alter because they are comprised of five factors in differing proportions. First is a strong affective component. A particular belief or belief system may engender a great deal of emotion and is emotionally bound to the individual's past experience. Second is the amount of time that the schemas have been held. Schemas the are "old," having been part of the personal history for many years, will be more powerful. Third involves the individuals from whom the schemas were acquired. The more important (and credible) the source, the more powerfully held will be the schema. Fourth, the cognitive element of the schema accounts for the manner in which it pervades the individual's thoughts and images. The schemas can be described in great detail, and can also be deduced from behavior. Finally, there is the behavioral component of the schema that involves the way the belief system governs the individual's component of the schema that involves the way the belief system governs the individual's responses to a particular stimulus or set of stimuli.

In seeking to alter particular schemas that have endured for a long period of time, are strongly believed, and were learned from a significant and credible source, it would be necessary to help the patient examine the belief from as many different perspectives as possible. The goal of psychotherapy, according to Adler (1927), is "essentially to get the patient to recognize the mistake in his lifestyle [schemas], … as the therapist has understood it, and thereby to increase the patient's ability to cooperate [in the change process]. This is a process of a cognitive reorganization, of belated maturation."

For some individuals a particular set of core schemas are well-established in early to middle childhood. What then differentiates the child who develops a schema that is held with moderate strength and amenable to change later on from the individual who develops a core belief that is powerful and apparently immutable? We would posit several possibilities: (1) In addition to the core belief, the child maintains an associated belief that they cannot change; (2) the belief system is powerfully reinforced by parents or significant others; (3) while the dysfunctional belief system is not especially reinforced, any attempt to believe the contrary may not be reinforced or may even be punished, e.g., if it were implied to a child that "You may be able to change, but we are not sure we would love you if you did change"; (4) the child is not explicitly told he or she lacks worth, but any attempt to assert worth would be ignored: (5) the parents or significant others may offer direct instruction contrary to developing a positive image, e.g., "It's not nice to brag" or "It's not nice to toot your own horn because people will think less of you." The structure of schemas that comprise what we see as "self" may, at times, hinder performance or life satisfaction. Despite the negative impact, the rules are not easily shaken, much less given up. When the rules are challenged, the individual often experiences great anxiety. Although the schematic structure may be quite limiting, it provides a structure and protection against the world, against the unknown. By sticking to the rules, anxiety can be minimized. When stepping outside the rules, the individual becomes vulnerable, with anxiety accompanying the feelings of vulnerability.

EARLY MALADAPTIVE SCHEMAS

Young (1990) proposes the notion of Early Maladaptive Schemas (EMS) (p. 9). He identifies them as having several defining characteristics:

1. The EMS are unconditional as opposed to more conditional underlying assumption that "hold out the possibility of success."
2. EMS are self-perpetuating and therefore more resistant to change.
3. EMS, by definition, are dysfunctional in some significant and recurring manner.
4. EMS are activated by events relevant to that schema.
5. EMS are tied to high levels of affect.
6. EMS are the result of early life experiences within the family constellation and with peers.

Young goes on to identify 15 EMS divided into four categories. We would suggest that schemas in and of themselves are not necessarily "good" or "bad," "adaptive" or "maladaptive." It is instead the individual's interpretation or expression of their schemas rather than the schemas themselves that determines whether one behaves adaptively or not. If we look at the first of Young's EMS which he labels Dependence ("Belief that one is unable to function on one's own" p. 13), we can question whether dependence, in and of itself, is maladaptive. It might be the motive for seeking a supportive and nurturant partner, or choosing a bureaucratic job wherein all eventualities are proscribed. The shift from adaptive to maladaptive can be seen when individuals who had been quite functional when guided by particular schemas experience a life change. The schemas may, at that point, very quickly become maladaptive.

SCHEMATIC CHANGE POTENTIAL

Some schemas are more easily changed than others. For individuals who see a particular schema as an integral part of who they are, how they see themselves, or how they define themselves, that schema will be far more difficult to modify. Schemas that are less a part of "self" are more easily changed. We would identify a continuum consisting of five states of schematic change potential. At one end of the continuum is schematic paralysis. The keyword that we would associate with that state is "ossified." The rules are literally encased in stone. Nothing will make the individual modify the basic rule, for example, parents whose religious schemas are so powerful that they would not seek medical attention for their child who is dying. Their belief in divine intervention is unshakeable. The death of the child, no matter how painful that prospect, is not enough to give up their religious schemas.

The next point on the continuum is schematic rigidity. The keyword is "dogmatic." The schemas are powerfully believed but under extreme pressure the rules can be modified, if even slightly, and only for a short time. For example, Orthodox Jews can break the rules of the Sabbath if a life is at stake. This is not done lightly, and not seen as precedent for other allowances. This is done only in that situation and at that moment.

The midpoint of the continuum is schematic stability. The keyword is "stable." The schemas are clearly and strongly in place. The individual's behavior is clearly governed by the schemas. However, if needed, the rules can be modified or even broken. For example, an individual who believes in obeying the law may speed when driving in a new car, just to try it out.

The next point is schematic flexibility. The keyword is "creativity." The individual who has greater flexibility will tend to stretch the rules, though not necessarily to break them. For example, they will be able to see many alternative solutions to a problem because they are not so "rule-bound."

The anchor point at the extreme of the continuum is schematic instability. The keyword is "chaotic." These individuals are driven by rules that may vacillate or alternate. The rule shifts will often come unbidden and often unexpectedly. They are often baffled and appear at the mercy of their rapidly shifting rules. The only person more confused than the therapist is the patient. For example, during a therapy session with a patient with a Borderline Personality Disorder, the therapist may observe that at one point in the session the patient's verbalizations and behavior are governed by the rule, "I must protect myself at all times." The patient may physically and emotionally pull back from the therapist, become combative, and retreat into a protective shell. At another moment the patient's behavior and verbalizations may be governed by the schema, "I am weak and helpless and need a strong person to assist me." At that point they will become dependent and seek the therapist's affection by being complimentary to the point of being obsequious. The therapist may find their head spinning by these apparent disconnected fluctuations in the patient's mood, behavior, verbal content, and body language.

By compensating particular EMS, Young states that the individual can overcome the EMS and replace it or them with healthier schemas (reconstruction). We would argue that the manner in which the schemas are addressed is what makes them maladaptive. For example, a child in grade school may be in constant trouble for demanding attention. The difficulty would be subsumed under what Young labels "insufficient limits." The student might call out in class, fool around, and generally make a nuisance of him- or herself. The schemas, "It is important to be noticed," "Public recognition helps me to build self-esteem," or "To be noticed is to be liked/loved/respected," all may contribute to a less than successful school career. The same schemas may later contribute to a successful professional career as a teacher or writer wherein the schemas have been used adaptively. The maladaptive expression of those same schemas would be for the individual to be the world's greatest failure, or a front-page criminal.

EMERGENCE OF SCHEMA IN THERAPY

By listening to and understanding the nature of the patient's words and thoughts, the therapist can begin to identify the schemas by general thematic areas of concern. The patient's verbalizations are the signposts that point to the schemas. Specifically, the particular crisis that the schemas may represent becomes clear, allowing the therapist to begin to develop affective, cognitive, or behavioral interventions to help the patient test not only the automatic thoughts but also the underlying schemas. In order to promote long-term therapeutic gain, it is important for the therapist and patient to focus on the schemas rather than merely having the patient challenge or dispute his or her automatic thoughts. The initial therapeutic focus for the therapy and likely the most fruitful areas for change and adaptation, involve dealing with the automatic thoughts, the spontaneously generated ideas, perceptions, and biases. The patient can be helped to verbalize his or her thoughts not simply because the verbalization in and of itself is cathartic and curative, but also because by identifying the automatic thoughts the patient can gain the skills to confront his or her problems and to challenge the thoughts. The thoughts will then direct our attention to the schemas that serve as a substrate for the thoughts. For example, the dependent patient may indicate that they keep agreeing with others whether or not they believe the "others" to be correct. The underlying schema may be, "If I challenge anyone on any topic they may not be available to me when I need them and I always need someone to help me."

By asking patients to challenge or directly dispute their dysfunctional beliefs, we are then asking them to directly challenge their very being. When the challenge to self is perceived, the individual usually responds with anxiety. The individual is then placed in conflict as to whether he or she would prefer to maintain his or her particular symptoms or to experience anxiety. Particular schemas become powerful underlying core schemas and are pervasive in the individual's cognitions and behavior. The core schemas are those that are continuously reinforced by others, utilized by the individual, and have self-reinforcing and maintenance mechanisms within the schemas. For example, patients who are perfectionists generally maintain the belief that if they are not perfect, they are less lovable or acceptable. This schema is difficult to challenge because it is usually reinforced by the family and society.

SUMMARY

An understanding of the individual, family, and cultural schemas is essential for patients to understand why and how they respond. An understanding of the schemas will explain patients' past behavior, make sense of their present behavior, and help them to anticipate their future behavior. The major therapeutic task is help them identify the schemas, where they came from, what effect they have on their life, and how likely they are to change them.

The therapeutic steps are (1) the explication of the schemas based on the patient's verbalizations, (2) exploration of the schemas to ascertain the value and power they have for the individual, (3) assessment of the thoughts and ideas that maintain particular schemas, (4) identifying and focusing on the attendant feelings and behaviors that derive from the schemas, (5) structuring specific interventions based on the patient's idiosyncratic personal, family, and cultural schemas, and (6) structuring relapse prevention strategies to assist the patient in generalizing the therapeutic gain to other situations and occurrences. By confronting, disputing, or responding more adaptively to powerful, long-held schemas and to the emotional, affective, and cognitive sequelae of the schemas, we can begin to help the patient to move in more productive and coping directions.

These templates for understanding how people learn to understand their world are the essential ingredients in cognition, affect, and behavior. Schemas then become the main focus for all CBT.

REFERENCES

Adler, A. (1927). *Understanding Human Nature*. New York: Greenberg.

Beck, A.T., Freeman, A., and Associates, (1990). *Cognitive Therapy of Personality Disorders*. New York: Guilford.

Beck, A.T., Freeman, A., Davis, D.D., and Associates (2003). *Cognitive Therapy of Personality Disorders* (2nd ed.). New York: Guilford.

Beck, A.T., Rush, A.J., Shaw, B.F., and Emery, G. (1979). *Cognitive Therapy of Depression*. New York: Guilford.

Freeman, A., and DeWolfe, R. (1992). *The Ten Dumbest Mistakes Smart People Make*. New York: HarperCollins.

Freeman, A. and Leaf, R. (1989). *Cognitive therapy of personality disorders*. In A. Freeman, K. M. Simon, L.E. Beutler, and H. Arkowitz, *Handbook of Cognitive Therapy of Personality Disorders*. New York: Plenum.

Freeman, A., Pretzer, J., Fleming, B., and Simon, K.M. (1990). *Clinical Applications of Cognitive Therapy*. New York: Plenum.

Freeman, A., Pretzer, J., Fleming, B., and Simon, K.M. (2004). *Clinical Applications of Cognitive Therapy*, (2nd ed.). New York: Kluwer Academic/Plenum Publishers.

Hastie, R. (1984). Causes and effects of causal attributions. *Journal of Personality and Social Psychology*, 46(1), 44–56.

McGoldrich, M. (1982). *Normal Family Process*. New York: Guilford.

Rosen, H., (1989). Piagetian dimensions of clinical relevance, in A. Freeman, K.M. Simon, L.E. Beutler and H. Arkowitz, *Comprehensive Handbook of Cognitive Therapy*. New York: Plenum.

Schank, R.C., and Abelson, R.P. (1977). *Scripts, plans, goals, and understanding*. Hinsdale, NJ: Erlbaum.

Taylor, S., Crocker, J., and D'Agotino, J. (1978). Schematic bases of social problem-solving, *Personality & Social Psychology Bulletin, 4*(3) 447–451.

Young, J. (1991). *Cognitive Therapy for Personality Disorders: A Schematic Focused Approach*. Sarasota. FL: Professional Resource Press.

Contributors

Lyn Y. Abramson, Department of Psychology, University of Wisconsin-Madison, Madison, WI

Lesley A. Allen, **Robert Wood Johnson**, Medical School, University of Medicine and Dentistry of New Jersey, Piscataway, NJ

Lauren B. Alloy, Department of Psychology, Temple University, Philadelphia, PA

Martin M. Antony, St. Joseph's Healthcare, Hamilton, Ontario, Canada

L. Michael Ascher, Department of Psychology, Philadelphia College of Osteopathic Medicine, Philadelphia, PA

Tony Attwood, Asperger's Syndrome Clinic, Queensland, Australia

L. Stuart Barbera, Department of Psychology, Philadelphia College of Osteopathic Medicine, Philadelphia, PA

Paula M. Barrett, Mt. Gravatt Campus, Griffith University, Queensland, Australia

Brian Baucom, Department of Psychology, University of California-Los Angeles, Los Angeles, CA

Aaron T. Beck, Department of Psychiatry, University of Pennsylvania, Beck Institute, Philadelphia, PA

Alan S. Bellack, VA Capitol Health Care Network, MIRECC, University of Maryland, Baltimore, MD

David Black, Department of Psychology, George Mason University, Fairfax, VA

L. Elizabeth Bodnar, Department of Psychology, American University, Washington, D.C.

Wayne A. Bower, Department of Psychology, University of Iowa, Iowa City, IA

Christine Bowman, Department of Psychology, California State University, Fresno, Fresno, CA

Autumn E. Braddock, Department of Psychology, University of California at Los Angeles, Los Angeles, CA

Jennifer Butcher, Department of Psychology, Central Michigan University, Kalamazoo, MI

Daniel Joseph Cahill, Department of Psychology, California State University, Fresno, Fresno, California

Isabel Caro, Department of Psychology, University of Valencia, Valencia, Spain

David A. Casey, University of Louisville, School of Medicine, Louisville, KY

Katie M. Castille, Institute for Clinical Psychology, Widener University, Chester, PA

Meredith Charney, Department of Veterans Affairs, National center for PTSD, School of Medicine, Boston University, Boston, MA

Eunice Y. Chen, Department of Psychology, University of Washington, Seattle, WA

Ray W. Christner, Department of Psychology, Philadelphia College of Osteopathic Medicine, Philadelphia, PA

Andrea M. Chronis, University of Maryland, College Park, MD

Stephanie Clarke, School of Medicine, Boston University, Boston, MA

Michelle G. Craske, Department of Psychology, University of California at Los Angeles, Los Angeles, CA

Kristy Dalyrimple, Department of Psychology, Drexel University, Philadelphia, PA

Frank M. Dattilio, Department of Psychiatry, Harvard University, Boston, MA

Beth Arburn Davis, Department of Psychology, Philadelphia College of Osteopathic Medicine, Philadelphia, PA

Esther Deblinger, Center for Children's Support, School of Osteopathic Medicine, University of Medicine and Dentistry of New Jersey, Stratford, NJ

Jerry L. Deffenbacher, Department of Psychology, Colorado State University, Fort Collins, CO

Doreen M. DiDomenico, Rutgers University, Piscataway, NJ

Robert J. DeRubeis, Department of Psychology, University of Pennsylvania, Philadelphia, PA

Joseph B. Dilley, Department of Psychiatry, Feinberg School of Medicine, Northwestern University, Chicago, IL

Robert A. DiTomasso, Department of Psychology, Philadelphia College of Osteopathic Medicine, Philadelphia, PA

Keith S. Dobson, Department of Psychology, University of Calgary, Calgary, Alberta, Canada

Michael J. Dolan, Department of Psychology, Philadelphia College of Osteopathic Medicine, Philadelphia, PA

Deidre Donaldson, The May Institute, Boston, MA

E. Thomas Dowd, Department of Psychology, Kent State University, Kent, OH

Jane G Dresser, The Medical-Psychiatric Nursing Consultation Service, Bristol, TN

Windy Dryden, Department of Psychology, Goldsmiths College, London, United Kingdom

Thomas J. D'Zurilla, Department of Psychology, State University of New York at Stony Brook, Stony Brook, NY

Ricardo Eiraldi, The Children's Hospital of Philadelphia, University of Pennsylvania, Philadelphia, PA

Timothy R. Elliot, Department of Psychology, University of Alabama at Birmingham, Birmingham, AL

Christina Esposito, Department of Psychology, Philadelphia College of Osteopathic Medicine, Philadelphia, PA

William Fals-Stewart, University of Buffalo, State University of New York, Buffalo, NY

Eva L. Feindler, Department of Psychology, C. W. Post Campus, Long Island University, Brookville, New York

Stephanie H. Felgoise, Department of Psychology, Philadelphia College of Osteopathic Medicine, Philadelphia, PA

Melanie J. V. Fennell, Department of Psychiatry, Oxford University, Oxford, United Kingdom

Edna B. Foa, Center for the Treatment and Study of Anxiety, University of Pennsylvania, Philadelphia, PA

Victoria M. Follette, Department of Psychology, University of Nevada, Reno, Reno, NV

Lesley D. Fox, Department of Psychology, University of Florida, Gainesville, FL

Arthur Freeman, Department of Psychology, University of Saint Francis, Fort Wayne, IN

Brian M. Gale, Cedars-Sinai Medical Center, Los Angeles, CA

Robert Gilman, Department of Psychology, Philadelphia College of Osteopathic Medicine, Philadelphia, PA

Jennifer M. Gillis, Institute for Child Development, State University of New York-Binghamton, Binghamton, NY

Kelly L. Gilrain, Department of Psychology, Drexel University, Philadelphia, PA

Barbara A. Golden, Department of Psychology, Philadelphia College of Osteopathic Medicine, Philadelphia, PA

Elizabeth A. Gosch, Department of Psychology, Philadelphia College of Osteopathic Medicine, Philadelphia, PA

Wanda Grant-Knight, School of Medicine, Boston University, Boston, MA

Dan Gruener, Department of Psychiatry, Jefferson Medical College, Philadelphia, PA

W. Rodney Hammond, National Center for Injury Prevention and Control, Centers for Disease Control and Prevention, Atlanta, GA

Steven C. Hayes, Department of Psychology, University of Nevada, Reno, Reno, NV

Heather D. Hoyal, Department of Psychology, Brigham Young University, Provo, UT

Richard G. Heimberg, Adult Anxiety Clinic, Temple University, Philadelphia, PA

James D. Herbert, Department of Psychology, Drexel University, Philadelphia, PA

Arthur MacNeill Horton, Jr., Psych Associates, Bethesda, MD

Jonathon D. Huppert, Center for the Treatment and Study of Anxiety, University of Pennsylvania, Philadelphia, PA

Lee Hyer, University Behavioral Healthcare, The University of Medicine and Dentistry of New Jersey, Piscataway, NJ

Warren T. Jackson, Department of Psychology, University of Alabama at Birmingham, Birmingham, AL

John W. Jacobson, Center for Applied Behavior Analysis, Sage Colleges, Troy, NY

Robin B. Jarrett, Psychosocial Research and Depression Clinic, The University of Texas, Southwestern Medical Center at Dallas, Dallas, TX

Thomas E. Joiner, Jr., Department of Psychology, Florida State University, Tallahassee, FL

Terence M. Keane, Department of Veterans Affairs, National Center for PTSD, School of Medicine Boston University, Boston, MA

Phillip C. Kendall, Department of Psychology, Temple University, Philadelphia, PA

Howard Kassinove, Department of Psychology, Hofstra University, Hempstead, NY

Jacqueline D. Kloss, Department of Psychology, Drexel University, Philadelphia, PA

Susan M. Knell, Hillcrest Hospital, Case Western Reserve University, Cleveland, OH

Karestan Koenen, School of Medicine, Boston University, Boston, MA

Russell J. Kormann, Department of Psychology, Rutgers University, Piscataway, NJ

Holly Kricher, Department of Psychology, Philadelphia College of Osteopathic Medicine, Philadelphia, PA

Marsha M. Linehan, Department of Psychology, University of Washington, Seattle, WA

Elizabeth R. Lombardo, The University of Texas, Southwestern Medical Center at Dallas, Dallas, TX

Thomas R. Lynch, Department of Psychology, Duke University, Durham, NC

Hellen MacDonald, School of Medicine, Boston University, Boston, MA

Kristin R. Magnum, Department of Psychology, University of Missouri-St. Louis, St. Louis, MO

Erin B. Marek, Chicago School of Professional Psychology, Chicago, IL

W. L. Marshall, Rockwood Psychological Services, Kingston, Ontario, Canada

Elizabeth A. Meadows, Department of Psychology, Central Michigan University, Kalamazoo, MI

Donald Meichenbaum, University of Waterloo and, The Melissa Foundation, Waterloo, Ontario, Canada

Rosemary Mennuti, Department of Psychology, Philadelphia College of Osteopathic Medicine, Philadelphia, PA

Sharon Morgillo-Freeman, Department of Nursing, Indiana University-Purdue University, Fort Wayne, IN

Randi E. McCabe, Department of Psychology, McMaster University, Hamilton, Ontario, Canada

Barry McCarthy, Department of Psychology, American University, Washington, DC

Roya D. McCluskey, Department of Psychology, Philadelphia College of Osteopathic Medicine, Philadelphia, PA

Lawrence Needleman, Ohio State University, Department of Psychiatry, Columbus, OH

Alisa R. Mintz, Department of Psychology, University of Calgary, Calgary, Alberta, Canada

Cory F. Newman, Center for Cognitive Therapy, Department of Psychiatry, University of Pennsylvania, Philadelphia, PA

Arthur M. Nezu, Department of Psychology, Center for Behavioral Medicine and Mind/Body Studies, Drexel University, Philadelphia, PA

Christine M. Nezu, Department of Psychology, Center for Behavioral Medicine and Mind/Body Studies, Drexel University, Philadelphia, PA Philadelphia, PA

Matthew K. Nock, Department of Psychology, Harvard University, Boston, MA

Irene Henriette Oestrich, Center for Cognitive Therapy, Copenhagen, Denmark

Timothy J. O'Farrell, Department of Psychiatry, Harvard Medical School, Boston, MA

Krista Olex, Department of Psychology, Philadelphia College of Osteopathic Medicine, Philadelphia, PA

Thomas H. Ollendick, Department of Psychology, Virginia Polytechnic Institute and State University, Blacksburg, VA

Melanie L. O'Neill, Department of Psychology, University of British Columbia, Vancouver, British Columbia, Canada

Michelle A. Peacock, Drexel University, Philadelphia, PA

Michael G. Perri, Department of Psychology, University of Florida, Gainesville, FL

Michael R. Petronko, Rutgers University, Piscataway, NJ

Sally N. Phillips, Northwestern Memorial Hospital, Northwestern University, Chicago, IL

Heather Pierson, Department of Psychology, University of Nevada, Reno, Reno, NV

Aaron Pollock, Department of Psychology, Philadelphia College of Osteopathic Medicine, Philadelphia, PA

Pier J. M. Prins, Department of Clinical Psychology, University of Amsterdam, Amsterdam, Netherlands

Maurice Prout, Institute for Clinical Psychology, Widener University, Chester, PA

J. Russell Ramsey, Department of Psychiatry, University of Pennsylvania, Philadelphia, PA

Sheila A. M. Rauch, Department of Psychiatry, University of Pennsylvania, Philadelphia, PA

Mark A. Reinecke, Department of Psychiatry, Feinberg School of Medicine, Northwestern University, Chicago, IL

John H. Riskind, Department of Psychology, George Mason University, Fairfax, VA

Hank Robb, Jr., Private Practice, Lake Oswego, OR

Joanna A. Robin, Department of Psychology, Temple University, Philadelphia, PA

Raymond R. Romanczyk, Institute for Child Development, State University of New York-Binghamton, Binghamton, NY

George F. Ronan, Department of Psychology, Central Michigan University, Kalamazoo, MI

Raphael D. Rose, Department of Psychology, University of California at Los Angeles, Los Angeles, CA

Bradley Rosenfield, Department of Psychology, Philadelphia College of Osteopathic Medicine, Philadelphia, PA

Anthony L. Rostain, Department of Psychiatry, University of Pennsylvania, Philadelphia, PA

Frederick Rotgers, Department of Psychology, Philadelphia College of Osteopathic Medicine, Philadelphia, PA

Lesia M. Ruglass, Department of Psychology, New School University, New York, NY

Melissa K. Runyon, Center for Children's Support, School of Osteopathic Medicine, University of Medicine and Dentistry of New Jersey, Stratford, NJ

Dennis Russo, The May Institute, Boston, MA

Jeremy D. Safran, Department of Psychology, New School University, New York, NY

Theresa M. Schultz, Department of Psychology, Dominican University, River Forest, IL

Jan Scott, Institute of Psychiatry, University of London, London, United Kingdom

Laura D. Seligman, Department of Psychology, University of Toledo, Toledo, OH

Deborah Slalom, Department of Psychology, Kent State University, Kent, OH

Jennifer A. Slezak, Department of Psychology, Central Michigan University, Kalamazoo, MI

D. Kristen Small, Department of Psychiatry, School of Medicine, University of Louisville, Louisville, KY

Alethea A. A. Smith, Department of Psychology, University of Nevada, Reno, Reno, NV

Mervin Smucker, Department of Psychiatry, Medical College of Wisconsin, Milwaukee, WI

Steven Sohnle, University Behavioral Healthcare, The University of Medicine and Dentistry of New Jersey, Piscataway, NJ

Robi Sonderegger, Mt. Gravatt Campus, Griffith University, Queensland, Australia

Diane L. Spangler, Department of Psychology, Brigham Young University, Provo, UT

Ann M. Steffen, Department of Psychology, University of Missouri-St. Louis, St. Louis, MO

Daniel R. Strunk, Department of Psychology, University of Pennsylvania, Philadelphia, PA

Jeffrey G. Stoll, Department of Psychology, Drexel University, Philadelphia, PA

Richard M. Suinn, Department of Psychology, Colorado State University, Fort Collins, CO

Raymond Chip Tafrate, Department of Psychology, Central Connecticut State University, New Britain, CT

Wendy Tenhula, School of Medicine, University of Maryland, Baltimore, MD.

Steven R. Thorp, Duke University Medical Center, Durham, NC

Teun G. van Manen, Zaans Medical Center, Zaandam, Netherlands

David Veale, Royal Free and University College Medical School, University of London, London, United Kingdom

Kimberly Villarin, School of Education, Temple University, Philadelphia, PA

Adrian Wells, Department of Psychology, University of Manchester, Manchester, United Kingdom

Jo M. Weis, Department of Psychiatry, Medical College of Wisconsin, Milwaukee, WI

Beverly White, Department of Psychology, Philadelphia College of Osteopathic Medicine, Philadelphia, PA

Maureen L. Whittal, University of British Columbia, Vancouver, British Columbia, Canada

Victoria M. Wilkens, Department of Psychology, Drexel University, Philadelphia, PA

Foluso M. Williams, Florida State University, Department of Psychology, Tallahassee, FL

Mark J. Williams, Psychosocial Research and Depression Clinic, The University of Texas, Southwestern Medical Center at Dallas, Dallas, TX

Carrie Winterowd, Department of Psychology, Oklahoma State University, Stillwater, OK

Robert L. Woolfolk, Robert Wood Johnson medical School, University of Medicine and Dentistry of New Jersey, Piscataway, NJ

Jesse H. Wright, Department of Psychiatry, School of Medicine, University of Louisville, Louisville, KY

Jennifer M. Wyatt, National Center for Injury Prevention and Control, Centers for Disease Control and Prevention, Atlanta, GA

Stephanie Yoder, Institute for Clinical psychology, Widener University, Chester, PA

Carrie L. Yurica, Department of Psychology, Philadelphia College of Osteopathic Medicine, Philadelphia, PA

Talia I. Zaider, Adult Anxiety Clinic, Temple University, Philadelphia, PA

Steven H. Zarit, Department of Psychology, Pennsylvania State University, State College, PA

Index

A

B

C

D

E

F

L

M

Q

R

S

W

Y